Less managing. More teaching. Greater learning.

 INSTRUCTORS...

Would you like your **students** to show up for class more **prepared**? *(Let's face it, class is much more fun if everyone is engaged and prepared...)*

Want ready-made application-level **interactive assignments,** student progress reporting, and auto-assignment grading? *(Less time grading means more time teaching...)*

Want an **instant view of student or class performance** relative to learning objectives? *(No more wondering if students understand...)*

Need to **collect data and generate reports** required for administration or accreditation? *(Say goodbye to manually tracking student learning outcomes...)*

Want to **record and post your lectures** for students to view online?

 With McGraw-Hill's *Connect Management,*

INSTRUCTORS GET:

- Interactive Applications – **book-specific interactive assignments** that require students to APPLY what they've learned.

- Simple **assignment management,** allowing you to spend more time teaching.

- **Auto-graded** assignments, quizzes, and tests.

- **Detailed Visual Reporting** where student and section results can be viewed and analyzed.

- Sophisticated **online testing** capability.

- A **filtering and reporting** function that allows you to easily assign and report on materials that are correlated to accreditation standards, learning outcomes, and Bloom's taxonomy.

- An easy-to-use **lecture capture** tool.

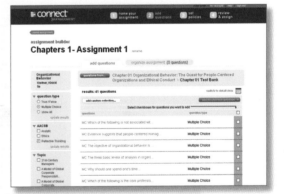

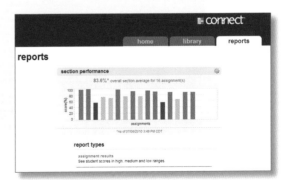

STUDENTS...

Want an online, **searchable version** of your textbook?

Wish your textbook could be **available online** while you're doing your assignments?

Connect Plus Management eBook

If you choose to use *Connect® Plus Management*, you have an affordable and searchable online version of your book integrated with your other online tools.

Connect Plus Management eBook offers features like:

- Topic search
- Direct links from assignments
- Adjustable text size
- Jump to page number
- Print by section

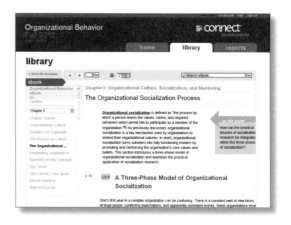

STUDENTS...

Want to get more **value** from your textbook purchase?

Think learning management should be a bit more **interesting**?

Check out the STUDENT RESOURCES section under the *Connect®* Library tab.

Here you'll find a wealth of resources designed to help you achieve your goals in the course. You'll find things like **quizzes, PowerPoints, and Internet activities** to help you study. Every student has different needs, so explore the STUDENT RESOURCES to find the materials best suited to you.

organizational behavior

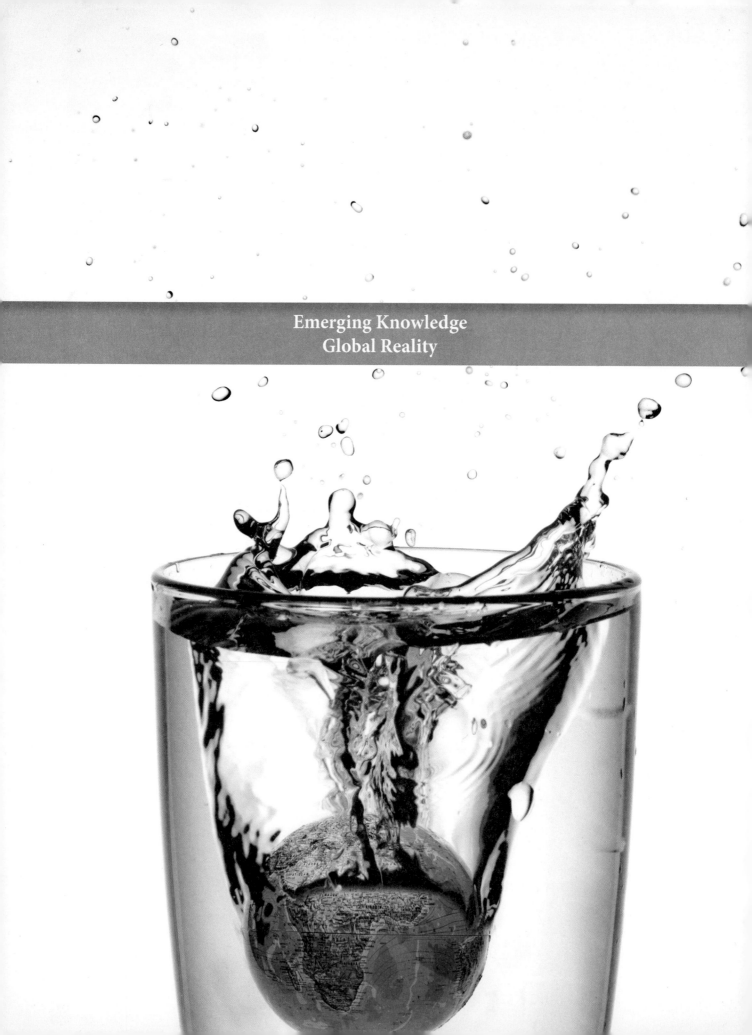

Emerging Knowledge
Global Reality

organizational behavior

6TH EDITION

Steven L. McShane
The University of Western Australia

Mary Ann Von Glinow
Florida International University

McGraw-Hill Irwin

The McGraw·Hill Companies

**McGraw-Hill
Irwin**

ORGANIZATIONAL BEHAVIOR:
EMERGING KNOWLEDGE, GLOBAL REALITY

Published by McGraw-Hill/Irwin, a business unit of The McGraw-Hill Companies, Inc., 1221 Avenue of the Americas, New York, NY, 10020. Copyright © 2013, 2010, 2008, 2005, 2003, 2000 by The McGraw-Hill Companies, Inc. All rights reserved. Printed in the United States of America. No part of this publication may be reproduced or distributed in any form or by any means, or stored in a database or retrieval system, without the prior written consent of The McGraw-Hill Companies, Inc., including, but not limited to, in any network or other electronic storage or transmission, or broadcast for distance learning.

Some ancillaries, including electronic and print components, may not be available to customers outside the United States.

This book is printed on acid-free paper.

1 2 3 4 5 6 7 8 9 0 QDB/QDB 1 0 9 8 7 6 5 4 3 2

ISBN 978-0-07-811264-5
MHID 0-07-811264-8

Vice president and editor-in-chief: *Brent Gordon*
Editorial director: *Paul Ducham*
Executive editor: *Michael Ablassmeir*
Executive director of development: *Ann Torbert*
Development editor II: *Kelly I. Pekelder*
Editorial coordinator: *Andrea Heirendt*
Vice president and director of marketing: *Robin J. Zwettler*
Marketing director: *Amee Mosley*
Senior marketing manager: *Michelle Heaster*
Vice president of editing, design, and production: *Sesha Bolisetty*
Lead project manager: *Christine A. Vaughan*
Buyer II: *Debra R. Sylvester*
Cover and interior design: *Pam Verros*
Senior photo research coordinator: *Keri Johnson*
Photo researcher: *Jen Blankenship*
Senior media project manager: *Susan Lombardi*
Media project manager: *Joyce J. Chappetto*
Typeface: *10/12 Minion Pro Regular*
Cover Image: © *Getty Images*
Compositor: *Aptara®, Inc.*
Printer: *Quad/Graphics*

Library of Congress Cataloging-in-Publication Data

McShane, Steven Lattimore.
    Organizational behavior : emerging knowledge, global reality / Steven L. McShane,
Mary Ann Von Glinow.—6th ed.
      p. cm.
    Includes index.
    ISBN-13: 978-0-07-811264-5 (alk. paper)
    ISBN-10: 0-07-811264-8 (alk. paper)
    1. Organizational behavior. I. Von Glinow, Mary Ann Young, 1949- II. Title.
HD58.7.M42 2013
658—dc23

                              2011043121

www.mhhe.com

{ about the authors }

Steven L. McShane

Steven L. McShane is Winthrop Professor of Management at the University of Western Australia (UWA) Business School, where he receives high teaching ratings from students in Perth, Singapore, Manila, and other cities where UWA offers its programs. He previously taught in the business faculties at Simon Fraser University and Queen's University in Canada. Steve has conducted executive programs with Nokia, TÜV-SÜD, Wesfarmers Group, Main Roads WA, McGraw-Hill, ALCOA World Alumina Australia, and many other organizations. He is also a popular visiting speaker, having given numerous invited presentations over the past four years to faculty and students in the United States, China, India, Canada, the Philippines, Malaysia, and other countries.

Steve earned his Ph.D. from Michigan State University in organizational behavior, human resource management, and labor relations. He also holds a Master of Industrial Relations from the University of Toronto, and an undergraduate degree from Queen's University in Canada. Steve is a past President of the Administrative Sciences Association of Canada (the Canadian equivalent of the Academy of Management) and Director of Graduate Programs in the business faculty at Simon Fraser University.

Along with coauthoring *Organizational Behavior,* Sixth Edition, Steve is coauthor of *M: Organizational Behavior* (2012) with Mary Ann Von Glinow; *Organisational Behaviour on the Pacific Rim,* Third Edition (2010) with Mara Olekahns (University of Melbourne) and Tony Travaglione (Curtin University); and *Canadian Organizational Behaviour,* Eighth Edition (2013) with Sandra Steen (University of Regina). Steve is also coauthor of editions or translations of his organizational behavior book in China, India, Quebec, Taiwan, and Brazil. Steve has published several dozen articles and conference papers on workplace values, training transfer, organizational learning, exit-voice-loyalty, employee socialization, wrongful dismissal, media bias in business magazines, and other diverse topics.

Steve enjoys spending his leisure time swimming, body board surfing, canoeing, skiing, and traveling with his wife and two daughters.

Mary Ann Von Glinow

Dr. Von Glinow is Knight Ridder Eminent Scholar Chair in International Mangement, and Director of the Center for International Business Education and Research at Florida International University for the past 17 years. She is the 2010–2012 President of the Academy of International Business (AIB) and an editor of JIBS. Previously on the Marshall School faculty of the University of Southern California, she has an MBA and Ph.D. in Management Science from The Ohio State University. Dr. Von Glinow was the 1994–95 President of the Academy of Management, the world's largest association of academicians in management, and is a Fellow of the Academy and the Pan-Pacific Business Association. She sits on eleven editorial review boards and numerous international panels. She teaches in executive programs in Latin America, Central America, the Caribbean region, Asia, and the U.S.

Dr. Von Glinow has authored over 100 journal articles and 13 books. Her most recent books include *Managing Multinational Teams* (Elsevier, 2005) and *Organizational Learning Capability* (Oxford University Press, 1999; in Chinese and Spanish translation), which won a Gold Book Award from the Ministry of Economic Affairs in Taiwan in 2002. She has also coauthored the popular *Organizational Behavior,* Sixth Edition, textbook and *M: Organizational Behavior,* First Edition (McGraw-Hill/Irwin, 2012). She heads an international consortium of researchers delving into "Best International Human Resource Management Practices," and her research in this arena won an award from the American Society for Competitiveness' Board of Trustees. She also received an NSF grant to study globally distributed work. Dr. Von Glinow is the 2005 Academy of Management recipient of the Distinguished Service Award, one of the Academy's three highest honors bestowed.

Mary Ann consults to a number of domestic and multinational enterprises, and serves as a mayoral appointee to the Shanghai Institute of Human Resources in China. Since 1989, she has been a consultant in General Electric's "Workout" and "Change Acceleration Program" including "Coaching to Management." Her clients have included Asia Development Bank, American Express, Diageo, Knight Ridder, Burger King, Pillsbury, Westinghouse, Southern California Edison, The Aetna, State of Florida, Kaiser Permanente, TRW, Rockwell Int'l, Motorola, N.Y. Life, Amoco, Lucent, and Joe's Stone Crabs, to name a few. She is on the Board of Friends of WLRN, Fielding University, Friends of Bay Oaks, Pan-Pacific Business Association, and Animal Alliance in Los Angeles. She is actively involved in several animal welfare organizations and received the 1996 Humanitarian Award of the Year from Miami's Adopt-a-Pet.

brief contents

(contents)

Chapter 3 Perceiving Ourselves and Others in Organizations 66

Chapter 4 Workplace Emotions, Attitudes, and Stress 96

Part 3
Team Processes 224

Chapter 10 Power and Influence in the Workplace 288

Chapter 11 Conflict and Negotiation in the Workplace 316

Part 4
Organizational Processes 374

Appendix A

Appendix B

(preface)

Welcome to the dynamic world of organizational behavior! Knowledge is replacing infrastructure. Social media and virtual teams are transforming the way employees interact and accomplish organizational objectives. Values and self-leadership are replacing command-and-control management. Companies are looking for employees with emotional intelligence and team competencies, not just technical smarts.

Organizational Behavior, Sixth Edition is written in the context of these emerging workplace realities. This edition explains how emotions are the foundation of employee motivation, attitudes, and decisions; how social networks generate power and shape communication patterns; how self-concept influences individual behavior, team cohesion, and leadership; and how adopting a global mindset has become an important employee characteristic in this increasingly interconnected world. This book also presents the reality that organizational behavior is not just for managers; it is relevant and valuable to anyone who works in and around organizations.

Linking Theory with Reality

Every chapter of *Organizational Behavior,* Sixth Edition, is filled with examples to make OB knowledge more meaningful and reflect the relevance and excitement of this field. These stories about real people and organizations translate academic theories into relevant knowledge and real-life applications. For example, we describe how employees at Zappos, the online retailer, extensively use social media communication; how L'Oreal Canada minimizes cross-generational conflict among staff through special training sessions; how OhioHealth improves employee performance through innovative rewards and performance guidelines; how employee involvement saved Queensland Nickel's Yabulu refinery from almost certain shutdown; and how emotional intelligence helps USAF Pararescue recruits complete their grueling training program.

These real-life stories appear in many forms. Every chapter of *Organizational Behavior,* Sixth Edition, is filled with photo captions and in-text anecdotes about work life. Lengthier examples are distinguished in a feature we call *Connections,* which "connects" OB concepts with real organizational incidents and situations. Case studies in each chapter also connect OB concepts to the emerging workplace realities. These stories provide representation across the United States and around the planet. They also cover a wide range of industries—from software to government, and from small businesses to the largest global organizations.

Global Focus

From its first edition, this book has been crafted around the notion that we live in a world of increasing globalization. *Organizational Behavior,* Sixth Edition, continues this global focus by introducing the theme in the first chapter and by discussing global and cross-cultural issues in many other chapters. Furthermore, every chapter includes truly global examples, not just how American companies operate in other parts of the world. For example, this book describes how KenGen, Kenya's electricity generation company, has created a flatter organizational structure; how French automaker PSA Peugeot Citroen introduced an obeya room to improve team dynamics; how employees at Brasilata in Sao Paulo, Brazil, are continuously innovating; and how Malaysia Airlines trains employees to display desired emotions.

Contemporary Theory Foundation

Organizational Behavior has a solid foundation of contemporary and classic research and writing. You can see this in the references. Each chapter is based on dozens of articles, books, and other sources. The most recent literature receives thorough coverage, resulting in what we believe is the most up-to-date organizational behavior textbook available. These references also reveal that we reach out to marketing, information management, human resource management, and other disciplines for new ideas. Our approach is also to focus on information that readers value, namely, OB knowledge and practices. Consequently, with a few classic exceptions, we avoid writing a "who's-who" book; most scholars are named in the references, not in the main text.

One of the driving forces for writing *Organizational Behavior* was to provide a faster conduit for emerging OB knowledge to reach students, practitioners, and fellow scholars. To its credit, this is apparently the first textbook to discuss the self-concept model (not just core self-evaluation), workplace emotions, social identity theory, four-drive theory, appreciative inquiry, affective events theory (but without the jargon), somatic marker theory (also without the jargon), virtual teams, future search events, Schwartz's values model, employee engagement, learning orientation, workaholism, and several other groundbreaking topics. This edition continues this leadership by introducing the latest knowledge on global mindset, the elements of social networks (e.g., weak ties, centrality, and structural holes), communication strategies for social media, decision overload, and mindfulness in ethical behavior.

Organizational Behavior Knowledge for Everyone

Another distinctive feature of *Organizational Behavior,* Sixth Edition, is that it is written for everyone in organizations, not just "managers." The philosophy of this book is that everyone who works in and around organizations needs to understand and make use of organizational behavior knowledge. The contemporary reality is that people throughout the organization—systems analysts, production employees, accounting professionals—are taking on more responsibilities as companies remove layers of management and give the rest of us more autonomy and accountability for our work outcomes. This book helps everyone to make sense of organizational behavior, and provides the conceptual tools to work more effectively in the workplace.

Active Learning and Critical Thinking Support

We teach organizational behavior, so we understand how important it is to use a textbook that offers deep support for active learning and critical thinking. Business school accreditation associations also emphasize the importance of the learning experience, which further reinforces our attention on classroom activities. *Organizational Behavior,* Sixth Edition, includes almost three dozen case studies in various forms and levels of complexity. It offers four dozen self-assessments, most of which have been empirically tested and validated. This book is also a rich resource for in-class activities, some of which are not available in other organizational behavior books, such as Deciphering the (Social) Network, Test Your Knowledge of Personality, Mist Ridge, and the Cross-Cultural Communication Game. Furthermore, this edition introduces the "Debating Point" feature in every chapter—a valuable resource for critical thinking and class discussion about relevant OB issues.

Changes to the Sixth Edition

Organizational Behavior, Sixth Edition, has benefited from reviews since the previous edition by dozens of organizational behavior instructors and researchers in several countries. The most significant structural change is that we have shifted some content across the first few chapters to improve the fit and flow of various topics. This edition also substantially updates the section on negotiation (Chapter 11) and has developed a full section on social networks (Chapter 10). This edition also introduces "Debating Point," a valuable feature in every chapter that helps students think critically about seemingly obvious ideas. In addition, we have introduced factoids, which present interesting survey and statistical information related to the topic discussed on those pages. More generally, this edition updates topics in every chapter and provides fresh real-world examples to illustrate theories and concepts. The most notable improvements to this edition are as follows:

- *Chapter 1: Introduction to the Field of Organizational Behavior*—The most significant change in this chapter is that the topic on the types of individual behavior has been moved to Chapter 2, where it has a more logical link to other topics. This edition further develops the four perspectives of organizational effectiveness, which instructors recognize as the cornerstone of organizational behavior. This chapter updates discussion on contemporary challenges in OB, adds more details about evidence-based management, and supplements information about the historical foundations of OB.

- *Chapter 2: Individual Behavior, Personality, and Values*—This edition inserts the types of individual behavior after the MARS model of individual behavior. We have also moved self-concept to Chapter 3. This edition has several small, yet meaningful changes, including new content on presenteeism, role perceptions, situational factors, mindfulness in ethics, the MBTI model, ways that companies support ethical behavior, the relationship between Big 5 and performance, problems with cross-cultural knowledge, and problems with personality testing.

- *Chapter 3: Perceiving Ourselves and Others in Organizations*—The previous edition was apparently the first to introduce the full model of self-concept and connect that model to various organizational behavior topics. This edition further refines and clarifies the three self-concept characteristics as well as the four self-concept processes. We moved the topic to this chapter because of the logical flow from self-perception (self-concept) to social perception (perceiving others). Another change in this chapter is that behavior modification and social learning (social cognitive) theories have been moved to the motivation chapter (Chapter 5). Another development in this chapter is the section on global mindset—an important emerging topic that crosses cross-cultural thinking with the perceptual process.

- *Chapter 4: Workplace Emotions, Attitudes, and Stress*—This chapter has minor changes, particularly on cognitive dissonance, emotional labor across cultures, the relationship between job satisfaction and performance and customer service, and individual differences in stress.

- *Chapter 5: Foundations of Employee Motivation*—This chapter further refines discussion of drives, needs, and behavior, which we believe is fundamental to understanding employee motivation. We also update our coverage of employee engagement, which continues to gain attention in the world of work. This chapter incorporates and condenses the topics of behavior modification and social cognitive theory in the context of learning expectancies in expectancy theory. This edition also updates the topics of balanced scorecard (previously in Chapter 6) and strengths-based feedback.

- *Chapter 6: Applied Performance Practices*—This edition has relatively minor updating to the topics on applied performance practices.

- *Chapter 7: Decision Making and Creativity*—This edition updates information about the levels and contingencies of employee involvement, stakeholder framing, and the characteristics of creative people.

- *Chapter 8: Team Dynamics*—This edition has minor changes to a few team dynamics topics, including informal groups, team diversity, the effect of cohesion on performance (and vice versa), and brainstorming.

- *Chapter 9: Communicating in Teams and Organizations*—The previous edition introduced social media (Web 2.0); this edition further updates this important communication development, including a model on the functions of social media. Furthermore, this edition updates the topics of communication barriers, the importance of communication, persuasive communication, and the encoding-decoding process.

- *Chapter 10: Power and Influence in the Workplace*—You will find several new developments in this chapter. Most important is discussion of social networks, including strong ties, weak ties, centrality, and structural holes. We have also folded the two forms of information power into their respective sources of power (legitimate and expert). This edition also revises and updates writing on the meaning of power and the dependency model of power, legitimate power and the norm of reciprocity, the consequences of power, and exchange as an influence tactic.

- *Chapter 11: Conflict and Negotiation in the Workplace*—The most noticeable change in this chapter is that the negotiation section has been completely rewritten and updated. It is now organized around claiming value and creating value, and adds key negotiation concepts such as BATNA. The section on the benefits and problems with conflict has been improved, and the section on structural approaches to conflict management has been rewritten with more examples and clarification. This chapter also has some minor re-organization of topics.

- *Chapter 12: Leadership in Organizational Settings*—Two editions ago, we introduced the topic of shared leadership; this edition gives more attention to this important topic. The previous edition introduced the emerging topic of authentic leadership, which also receives more emphasis in this edition. This chapter also devotes more attention to servant leadership. Other topics have been revised and updated, including managerial leadership, charismatic leadership, and romance of leadership.

- *Chapter 13: Designing Organizational Structures*—This chapter has relatively minor updates and revisions, particularly on concurrent engineering and network structures.

- *Chapter 14: Organizational Culture*—This chapter introduces psychological contracts, provides fuller coverage of organizational socialization (e.g., information exchange conflicts, improving the socialization process), and has minor updates of a few topics (e.g. espoused versus enacted values).

- *Chapter 15: Organizational Change*—*Organizational Behavior* was apparently the first OB book to discuss appreciative inquiry. Subsequent editions refined the topic, and this edition adds new information about the five principles on which appreciative inquiry is based. This edition also introduces the role of social networks and viral change in organizational transformations. Various topics also receive minor updates and rewriting, including ways to minimize resistance to change and strategies to diffuse change from a pilot project.

acknowledgments

Organizational behavior is a fascinating subject. It is also incredibly relevant and valuable, which is apparent while developing a world-class book such as *Organizational Behavior, Sixth Edition*. Throughout this project, we witnessed the power of teamwork, the excitement of creative thinking, and the motivational force of the vision that we collectively held as our aspiration. The tight coordination and innovative synergy was evident throughout this venture. Our teamwork is even more amazing when you consider that most people on this project are located across the United States, and the lead coauthor (Steve) spends most of his time on the other side of the planet.

Executive editor Mike Ablassmeir led the development of *Organizational Behavior, Sixth Edition*, with unwavering enthusiasm and foresight. Developmental editor Kelly Pekelder orchestrated the daily process with superhuman skill and determination, which is particularly important given the magnitude of this revision, the pressing deadlines, and the 24-hour time zones in which we operated. Jennifer Blankenship, our photo researcher, continues to amaze us. She tracked down photos that we sought from every corner of the globe. Pam Verros created a refreshing book design that elegantly incorporated the writing, exhibits, anecdotes, photos, and many other resources that we pack into this volume. We also extend our thanks to Elisabeth Nevins Caswell for superb copy editing, Christine Vaughan and Jill Eccher for leading the production process like a precision timepiece, and Anke Weekes for her excellent marketing and sales development work. Thanks to you all. This has been a truly wonderful journey!

Several dozen instructors around the world reviewed parts or all of *Organizational Behavior, Sixth Edition*, or related editions in Canada, the Pacific Rim, and elsewhere over the past two years. Their compliments were energizing, and their suggestions significantly improved the final product. The following people from U.S. colleges and universities provided the most recent feedback for improvements specifically for *Organizational Behavior, Sixth Edition*:

Richard Blackburn
Kenan-Flagler Business School

David C. Brower
SUNY Delhi

Constance Campbell
Georgia Southern University

Sarah Carroll
University of Vermont

Elizabeth Cooper
University of Rhode Island

Debi Griggs
Bellevue College

Dr. David J. Hill
Mount Olive College, Mount Olive, NC 28365

Kanata A. Jackson
Hampton University

Dr. Sean Jasso
University of California, Riverside

Stacey Kessler
Montclair State University

Chris P. Long
Georgetown University

Mary Sue Love, Ph.D.
Southern Illinois University Edwardsville

Dr. Randy McCamey
Tarleton State University

Ben Rosen
University of North Carolina

Holly A. Schroth
University of California, Berkeley

Marguerite Teubner
Nassau Community College, Garden City, NY 11530

Beth Zuech Schneider
Winston-Salem State University

We also extend our sincere thanks to the many instructors in the United States and abroad who contributed cases and exercises to this edition of *Organizational Behavior*.

Steve would also like to extend special thanks to his students in Perth, Manila, and Singapore for sharing their learning experiences and assisting with the development of the three organizational behavior textbooks in the United States, Canada, and the Pacific Rim. Along with working with Mary Ann, Steve is honored to work with his other coauthors, including Professor Mara Olekalns at the University of Melbourne and Professor Tony Travaglione at Curtin University for the Pacific Rim edition, and Sandra Steen at the University of Regina for the Canadian edition. He also thanks his coauthors of other translations and adaptations. Steve is also grateful to his colleagues at the University of Western Australia for their support during these changing times. But more than anything else, Steve is forever indebted to his wife Donna McClement and to their wonderful daughters, Bryton and Madison. Their love and support give special meaning to Steve's life.

Mary Ann would also like to acknowledge the many professionals at McGraw-Hill/Irwin who have worked to make the sixth edition a reality. In addition, she would like to thank the many, many students who have used and hopefully enjoyed this book. Student appreciation of this book is apparent by the number of times Mary Ann has been stopped on various campuses all over the world by students who say that they recognize her picture and want to thank her! There are a few who have actually asked for Mary Ann's autograph, and that did not happen when she was president of the Academy of Management! Thus, it is to the students that Mary Ann says thank you, particularly for making this learning venture fun and exciting. She would also like to thank the faculty and staff at Florida International University, as well as her CIBER staff: Sonia, Robert, and Alex. By far and away, Mary Ann thanks coauthor Steve McShane for his tireless efforts. Finally, Mary Ann would like to thank her family, starting with the immediate ones—Emma, Zack, and Googun, Coco-Blue, Lucky, Bette Davis, and Blue—but also John, Rhoda, Lauren, Lindsay, and Christy, and a few critters they own: Gabby and Bossman. She also wants to acknowledge the critical role that some very special people play in her life: Janet, Peter M, Bill, Karen, Alan, Danny, Peter W, Letty D, John D, CEK & Jeff, Damian, Debra, Mary T, Lorraine, Marjorie, Sam P, Alan R, Tunga K, and Linda C. I thank you all!

supporting the learning process

AUTHOR'S GLOBAL TEAM: INTERNATIONAL AUTHOR BACKGROUND FOR THE GLOBAL EMPLOYEE.

Highly regarded for its global focus, **Organizational Behavior**, Sixth Edition, is written by global authors. Steve McShane teaches in Australia and Singapore and gives talks each year to schools throughout Asia and North America. Mary Ann Von Glinow is president of the Academy of International Business (AIB). She also regularly visits and conducts research in South America and China and elsewhere around the planet.

DEBATING POINTS

Debating Point boxes help students to think critically and to recognize that even seemingly obvious ideas have logical counterarguments. Debating Points also raise the bar by focusing on topics that are central to the world of work.

Debating Point
ARE VIRTUAL TEAMS MORE TROUBLE THAN THEY'RE WORTH?

Virtual teams were rare before the Internet was born. Two decades later, they are almost as commonplace as face-to-face teams. Virtual teams are increasingly possible because more of us are employed in knowledge work rather than physical production. Furthermore, information technologies make it easier to communicate instantaneously with coworkers around the globe. To some extent, virtual teams have even become "cool." It is almost a badge of honor to say that you are a member of a far-flung team of people from several continents.

But whether they are stylish or commonplace, virtual teams seem to be increasingly necessary for an organization's competitive advantage. This chapter points out that we need virtual teams to effectively engage in organizational learning. Knowledge has become the currency of organizational success, and globalization has ensured that such knowledge is scattered around the world. In short, organizations are at a disadvantage unless they use lots of virtual teams.

How could anyone claim that virtual teams aren't worth the effort, particularly when organizational learning is one of the four pillars of organizational effectiveness (see Chapter 1)? Well, actually, there are a few arguments against them. For the most part, critics don't deny the potential value of sharing knowledge through virtual teams. Rather, they have added up the negative features and concluded that they outweigh the benefits. In fact, when chief information officers were asked to identify the top challenges of globalization, 70 percent listed managing virtual teams as the top concern.[86]

One persistent problem with virtual teams is that they lack the richness of face-to-face communication. We'll provide more detail about this important matter in Chapter 9, but no information technology to date equals the volume and variety of information transmitted among people located in the same room. This is one reason Toyota, PSA Peugeot Citroën, and other companies arrange for teams to meet in the same physical space. They can exchange information in larger volumes, much faster, and more accurately compared with the clumsy methods currently available to virtual teams. Multiperson video chat is getting closer to face-to-face, but it requires considerable bandwidth and still falls short on communication richness.

Another problem with virtual teams is that people trust others more easily when they are nearby.[87] Various studies have reported that virtual team members either have lower trust compared with co-located team members, or their trust is much more fragile. In fact, experts offer one main recommendation to increase trust among virtual team members—have them spend time together as co-located teams. "When you're starting a company, everybody needs to be on the same page about what is important," warns Leonard Speiser, a serial Internet entrepreneur who has also worked at Yahoo and eBay. "You have to be able to get together and talk, get to know each other. It takes great effort to do that virtually."[88]

A third drawback with virtual teams is that the farther away people are located, the more they differ in experiences, beliefs, culture, and expectations. These differences can be advantageous for some decisions, of course, but they can also be a curse for team development and performance. "Everyone must have the same picture of what success looks like," advises Rick Maurer, a leadership consultant in Arlington, Virginia. "Without that laser-like focus, it is too easy for people in Bangalore to develop a different picture of success than the picture held by their colleagues in Brussels. Now multiply that by a couple more locations and you've got a mess."[89]

Here's one more reason why companies should think twice before relying on virtual teams: People seem to have less influence or control over distant than over co-located coworkers. A team member who stops by your cubicle to ask how your part of the report is coming along has much more effect than an impersonal—or even a flaming—e-mail from afar.

Perhaps that is why surveys reveal less satisfaction with virtual team members than co-located team members.[90] One study reported that distant colleagues received two to three times as many complaints as co-located colleagues about working half-heartedly (or not at all) on shared projects, falling behind on projects, not making deadlines, failing to warn about missing deadlines, making changes without warning, and providing misleading information. When asked how long it takes to resolve these problems, more than half of the respondents indicated a few days for co-located team members, whereas most estimated a few weeks or longer for distant team members.

> *In a market filled with books trying to do the same thing, McShane/Von Glinow does it better than most.*

–Richard Blackburn,
University of North Carolina Kenan-Flagler Business School

CURRENCY AND RESEARCH

Strongly anchored in contemporary research, *Organizational Behavior* has introduced several emerging OB concepts and practices, such as workplace emotions, appreciative inquiry, Schwartz's values model, strengths-based coaching, and employee engagement. This edition continues that leadership with new knowledge on self-concept, social networks, social media, and global mindset.

> *This [text] provides excellent coverage of key organizational behavior topics and is grounded in current research. It does an excellent job of clarifying learning objectives and linking the course material to actual organizations, including ones in other countries/cultures.*
>
> –Sarah Carroll,
> University of Vermont

SELF-ASSESSMENTS

Self-assessments are an important and engaging part of the active learning process. This edition features more than four dozen self-assessments, including new scales such as proactive personality, romance of leadership, work centrality, sensing-intuitive type, and learning goal orientation. All self-assessments are available online in Connect, and each chapter presents one fully in text.

> *Very popular and useful part of the package.*
>
> –Ben Rosen,
> University of North Carolina

SELF-ASSESSMENT 12.4 DO LEADERS MAKE A DIFFERENCE?

PURPOSE This assessment is designed to help you assess your beliefs about the influence of leaders.

INSTRUCTIONS Read each of the statements below and circle the response that best indicates your personal belief about that statement. Then use the scoring key in Appendix B to calculate the results for each leadership dimension. After completing this assessment, be prepared to discuss in class the relevance and level of implicit leadership theory.

Romance of Leadership Scale

TO WHAT EXTENT DO YOU AGREE OR DISAGREE THAT …	STRONGLY AGREE	AGREE	NEUTRAL	DISAGREE	STRONGLY DISAGREE
1. Even in an economic recession, a good leader can prevent a company from doing poorly.	☐	☐	☐	☐	☐
2. The quality of leadership is the single most important influence on how well the organization functions.	☐	☐	☐	☐	☐
3. The CEO and executive team have relatively little effect on the company's success or failure.	☐	☐	☐	☐	☐
4. Sooner or later, bad leadership at the top will result in declining organizational performance.	☐	☐	☐	☐	☐
5. The effect of a company's leaders on organizational performance is fairly weak.	☐	☐	☐	☐	☐
6. A company is only as good or as bad as its leaders.	☐	☐	☐	☐	☐
7. Even the best leaders can't help an organization very much when the economy is bad or competition is tough.	☐	☐	☐	☐	☐
8. It is impossible for an organization to do well when its leaders are average.	☐	☐	☐	☐	☐
9. Compared with the economy, competition, and other external forces, leaders have only a small influence on a firm's performance.	☐	☐	☐	☐	☐
10. The company's top executives have the power to make or break the organization.	☐	☐	☐	☐	☐

Source: This instrument is adapted and condensed from B. Schyns, J.R. Meindl, and M.A. Croon, "The Romance of Leadership Scale: Cross-Cultural Testing and Refinement," *Leadership* 3, no. 1 (2007), pp. 29–46.

> *It provides a means of self-reflection and a chance for students to make a connection between themselves and the course content. It also allows them to evaluate their learning—and formulate a plan to improve understanding of the main content of the chapter.*
>
> –David Brower, SUNY Delhi

FACTOIDS AND WRITING STYLE

Organizational Behavior engages students with a writing style that appeals to their learning process. It suppresses the jargon, sprinkles the writing with interesting real-world incidents, and cuts out theories that have outlived their usefulness. This edition also adds enticing "factoids"—interesting surveys or data related to specific topics.

> *Readable—the narrative flows and its voice does connect with the undergraduate.*
>
> —Sean Jasso, University of California Riverside

> *Students like it—and they actually read it!*
>
> —David Brower, SUNY Delhi

REAL-WORLD EXAMPLES FOR THE GLOBAL WORKPLACE

A signature feature of this book is its vivid, real-world, global stories and examples in every chapter. The opening vignettes set the stage for the chapter. Captioned photos visualize OB concepts in the emerging global workplace. The Connections feature presents more detailed vignettes.

connections 2.1

Infosys Bridges the Cross-Cultural Divide[89]

Infosys Technologies, a technology outsourcing firm in India, was prepared for cross-cultural differences when it acquired an Australian company. Sean Fernando, Infosys general manager of human resources in Australia, provides a vivid example of one of these cultural differences: When asked to travel on business, Infosys employees in India would pack their bags without hesitation and be ready to go even though they lacked details about the trip. Australian staff, on the other hand, wanted to know about the accommodation, allowances, and project specifics before they felt at ease. In other words, employees from India had noticeably lower levels of uncertainty avoidance.

Another difference was that staff in India expect the boss to give them instructions on what to do, whereas Australian employees expect to be consulted. In other words, Australian employees have much lower power distance. Fernando recalls an incident where an Australian project manager met with a project team from India. He described the project and then suggested that they share ideas about how to successfully complete the project. "They didn't know what he meant," says Fernando. "Then one of the people just said: 'We were wondering when you are going to tell us what the plan was.'"

To minimize cross-cultural conflict, Infosys Australia holds three-hour sessions in which employees from both countries learn about their cultures and discuss how they can manage employees with these different values.

Infosys is training its managers to be aware of cross-cultural differences when working with employees from other countries.

> *MV is a very readable and often compelling text directed at the practical aspects of OB. The authors cover theory as it applies to the current workplace, not simply because it is 'required history.'*
>
> —Debi Griggs, Bellevue College

instructor support materials

Organizational Behavior, Sixth Edition, includes a variety of supplemental materials to help instructors prepare and present the material in this textbook more effectively.

Instructor's Manual

This is one of the few textbooks for which the authors write the *Instructor's Manual*. This ensures that the instructor materials represent the textbook's content and support instructor needs. Each chapter includes the learning objectives, glossary of key terms, a chapter synopsis, complete lecture outline with thumbnail images of corresponding PowerPoint slides, and suggested answers to the end-of-chapter discussion questions. Also included are teaching notes for the chapter case(s), team exercises, and self-assessments. The *Instructor's Manual* also provides complete teaching notes for the additional cases.

Test Bank and EZ Test

Updated for this edition, the Test Bank includes more than 2,000 multiple-choice, true/false, and essay questions. Each question identifies the relevant page reference and difficulty level.

ASSURANCE OF LEARNING READY

Educational institutions are often focused on the notion of assurance of learning, an important element of many accreditation standards. *Organizational Behavior* is designed specifically to support your assurance-of-learning initiatives with a simple, yet powerful, solution. We've aligned our Test Bank questions with Bloom's Taxonomy and AACSB guidelines, tagging each question according to its knowledge and skill areas. Each Test Bank question for *Organizational Behavior* also maps to a specific chapter learning objective listed in the text. You can use our Test Bank software, EZ Test, to easily query for learning objectives that directly relate to the learning objectives for your course. You can use the reporting features of EZ Test to aggregate student results in a similar fashion, making the collection and presentation of assurance-of-learning data quick and easy.

EZ TEST ONLINE

McGraw-Hill's *EZ Test Online* is a flexible and easy-to-use electronic testing program. The program allows instructors to create tests from book-specific items, accommodates a wide range of question types, and enables instructors to even add their own questions. Multiple versions of a test can be created, and any test can be exported for use with course management systems such as WebCT and Blackboard or with any other course management system. EZ Test

Online is accessible to busy instructors virtually anywhere via the Web, and the program eliminates the need for them to install test software. For more information about EZ Test Online, please see the Web site at www.eztestonline.com.

PowerPoint Presentation Slides

Organizational Behavior has received considerable praise for its professional-looking PowerPoint slides. Each PowerPoint file has more than two dozen slides relating to the chapter, including two or more photographs from the textbook and notes offering tips for using the slides. The PowerPoint slides have been prepared by the authors, allowing seamless integration between the slides and the *Instructor's Manual*.

McGraw-Hill *Connect Management*

connect | MANAGEMENT **LESS MANAGING. MORE TEACHING. GREATER LEARNING.**

McGraw-Hill *Connect Management* is an online assignment and assessment solution that connects students with the tools and resources they'll need to achieve success. McGraw-Hill *Connect Management* helps prepare students for their future by enabling faster learning, more efficient studying, and higher retention of knowledge.

MCGRAW-HILL *CONNECT MANAGEMENT* FEATURES

Connect Management offers a number of powerful tools and features to make managing assignments easier, so faculty can spend more time teaching. With *Connect Management,* students can engage with their coursework anytime and anywhere, making the learning process more accessible and efficient. *Connect Management* offers you the features described below.

ONLINE INTERACTIVES

Online Interactives are engaging tools that teach students to apply key concepts in practice. These Interactives provide them with immersive, experiential learning opportunities. Students will engage in a variety of interactive scenarios to deepen critical knowledge on key course topics. They receive immediate feedback at intermediate steps throughout each exercise, as well as comprehensive feedback at the end of the assignment. All Interactives are automatically scored and entered into the instructor gradebook.

STUDENT PROGRESS TRACKING

Connect Management keeps instructors informed about how each student, section, and class is performing, allowing for more productive use of lecture and office hours. The progress-tracking function enables you to:

- View scored work immediately and track individual or group performance with assignment and grade reports.

- Access an instant view of student or class performance relative to learning objectives.
- Collect data and generate reports required by many accreditation organizations, such as AACSB.

SMART GRADING

When it comes to studying, time is precious. *Connect Management* helps students learn more efficiently by providing feedback and practice material when they need it, where they need it. When it comes to teaching, your time also is precious. The grading function enables you to:

- Have assignments scored automatically, giving students immediate feedback on their work and side-by-side comparisons with correct answers.
- Access and review each response; manually change grades or leave comments for students to review.
- Reinforce classroom concepts with practice tests and instant quizzes.

SIMPLE ASSIGNMENT MANAGEMENT

With *Connect Management,* creating assignments is easier than ever, so you can spend more time teaching and less time managing. The assignment management function enables you to:

- Create and deliver assignments easily with selectable end-of-chapter questions and Test Bank items.
- Streamline lesson planning, student progress reporting, and assignment grading to make classroom management more efficient than ever.
- Go paperless with the eBook and online submission and grading of student assignments.

INSTRUCTOR LIBRARY

The *Connect Management* Instructor Library is your repository for additional resources to improve student engagement in and out of class. You can select and use any asset that enhances your lecture. The *Connect Management* Instructor Library includes:

- Instructor Manual
- PowerPoint files
- Test Bank
- Management Asset Gallery
- eBook

STUDENT STUDY CENTER

The *Connect Management* Student Study Center is the place for students to access additional resources. The Student Study Center:

- Offers students quick access to lectures, practice materials, eBooks, and more.
- Provides instant practice material and study questions, easily accessible on the go.
- Gives students access to the Personalized Learning Plan.

LECTURE CAPTURE VIA TEGRITY CAMPUS

Increase the attention paid to lecture discussion by decreasing the attention paid to note taking. For an additional charge Lecture Capture offers new ways for students to focus on the in-class discussion, knowing they can revisit important topics later. See below for further information.

MCGRAW-HILL *CONNECT PLUS MANAGEMENT*

McGraw-Hill reinvents the textbook learning experience for the modern student with *Connect Plus Management*. A seamless integration of an eBook and *Connect Management*, *Connect Plus Management* provides all of the *Connect Management* features plus the following:

- An integrated eBook, allowing for anytime, anywhere access to the text-book.
- Dynamic links between the problems or questions you assign to your students and the location in the eBook where that problem or question is covered.
- A powerful search function to pinpoint and connect key concepts in a snap.

In short, *Connect Management* offers you and your students powerful tools and features that optimize your time and energies, enabling you to focus on course content, teaching, and student learning. *Connect Management* also offers a wealth of content resources for both instructors and students. This state-of-the-art, thoroughly tested system supports you in preparing students for the world that awaits.

For more information about Connect, go to **www.mcgrawhillconnect.com**, or contact your local McGraw-Hill sales representative.

Tegrity Campus: Lectures 24/7

Tegrity Campus is a service that makes class time available 24/7 by automatically capturing every lecture in a searchable format for students to review when they study and complete assignments. With a simple one-click start-and-stop process, you capture all computer screens and corresponding audio. Students can replay any part of any class with easy-to-use browser-based viewing on a PC or Mac.

Educators know that the more students can see, hear, and experience class resources, the better they learn. In fact, studies prove it. With Tegrity Campus, students quickly recall key moments by using Tegrity Campus's unique search feature. This search helps students efficiently find what they need, when they need it, across an entire semester of class recordings. Help turn all your students' study time into learning moments immediately supported by your lecture.

Lecture Capture enables you to:

- Record and distribute your lecture with a click of a button.
- Record and index PowerPoint presentations and anything shown on your computer so it is easily searchable, frame by frame.
- Offer access to lectures anytime and anywhere by computer, iPod, or mobile device.
- Increase intent listening and class participation by easing students' concerns about note taking. Lecture Capture will make it more likely you will see students' faces, not the tops of their heads.

To learn more about Tegrity, watch a 2-minute Flash demo at **http://tegritycampus.mhhe.com.**

Assurance of Learning Ready

Many educational institutions today are focused on the notion of *assurance of learning*, an important element of some accreditation standards. *Organizational Behavior* is designed specifically to support your assurance-of-learning initiatives with a simple, yet powerful, solution.

Each Test Bank question for *Organizational Behavior* maps to a specific chapter learning outcome/objective listed in the text. You can use our Test Bank software, EZ Test and EZ Test Online, or *Connect Management* to easily query for learning outcomes/objectives that directly relate to the learning objectives for your course. You can then use the reporting features of EZ Test to aggregate student results in similar fashion, making the collection and presentation of assurance-of-learning data simple and easy.

AACSB Statement

The McGraw-Hill Companies is a proud corporate member of AACSB International. Understanding the importance and value of AACSB accreditation, the authors of *Organizational Behavior, Sixth Edition*, recognize the curricula guidelines detailed in the AACSB standards for business accreditation by connecting selected questions in the text and/or the Test Bank to the six general knowledge and skill guidelines in the AACSB standards.

The statements contained in *Organizational Behavior, Sixth Edition* are provided only as a guide for the users of this textbook. The AACSB leaves content coverage and assessment within the purview of individual schools, the mission of the school, and the faculty. While *Organizational Behavior* and the teaching package make no claim of any specific AACSB qualification or evaluation, we have within *Organizational Behavior* labeled selected questions according to the six general knowledge and skill areas.

McGraw-Hill and Blackboard

McGraw-Hill Higher Education and Blackboard have teamed up. What does this mean for you?

1. **Your life, simplified.** Now you and your students can access McGraw-Hill's *Connect* and Create right from within your Blackboard course—all with one single sign-on. Say goodbye to the days of logging in to multiple applications.

2. **Deep integration of content and tools.** Not only do you get single sign-on with *Connect* and Create, but you also get deep integration of McGraw-Hill content and content engines right in Blackboard. Whether you're choosing a book for your course or building *Connect* assignments, all the tools you need are right where you want them—inside Blackboard.

3. **Seamless gradebooks.** Are you tired of keeping multiple gradebooks and manually synchronizing grades into Blackboard? We thought so. When a student completes an integrated *Connect* assignment, the grade for that assignment automatically (and instantly) feeds into your Blackboard grade center.

4. **A solution for everyone.** Whether your institution is already using Blackboard or you just want to try Blackboard on your own, we have a solution for you. McGraw-Hill and Blackboard can now offer you easy access to industry—leading technology and content, whether your campus hosts it or we do. Be sure to ask your local McGraw-Hill representative for details.

McGraw-Hill Customer Care Contact Information

At McGraw-Hill, we understand that getting the most from new technology can be challenging. That's why our services don't stop after you purchase our products. You can e-mail our Product Specialists 24 hours a day to get product-training online. Or you can search our knowledge bank of Frequently Asked Questions on our support website. For Customer Support, call **800-331-5094**, e-mail **hmsupport@mcgraw-hill.com**, or visit **www.mhhe.com/support**. One of our Technical Support Analysts will be able to assist you in a timely fashion.

McGraw-Hill's Expanded Management Asset Gallery!

McGraw-Hill/Irwin Management is excited to now provide a one-stop shop for our wealth of assets, making it quick and easy for instructors to locate specific materials to enhance their courses.

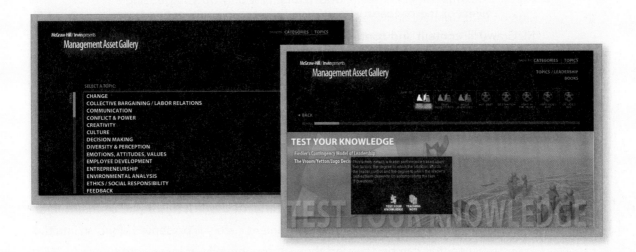

All of the following can be accessed within the Management Asset Gallery.

MANAGER'S HOT SEAT This interactive, video-based application puts students in the manager's hot seat, builds critical thinking and decision-making skills, and allows students to apply concepts to real managerial challenges. Students watch as 15 real managers apply their years of experience when confronting unscripted issues such as bullying in the workplace, cyber loafing, globalization, intergenerational work conflicts, workplace violence, and leadership versus management.

SELF-ASSESSMENT GALLERY Unique among publisher-provided self-assessments, our 23 self-assessments give students background information to ensure that they understand the purpose of the assessment. Students test their values, beliefs, skills, and interests in a wide variety of areas, allowing them to personally apply chapter content to their own lives and careers.

Every self-assessment is supported with PowerPoints and an instructor manual in the Management Asset Gallery, making it easy for the instructor to create an engaging classroom discussion surrounding the assessments.

TEST YOUR KNOWLEDGE To help reinforce students' understanding of key management concepts, Test Your Knowledge activities give students a review of the conceptual materials followed by application-based questions to work through. Students can choose practice mode, which gives them detailed feedback after each question, or test mode, which provides feedback after the entire test has been completed. Every Test Your Knowledge activity is supported by instructor notes in the Management Asset Gallery to make it easy for the instructor to create engaging classroom discussions surrounding the materials that students have completed.

MANAGEMENT HISTORY TIMELINE This web application allows instructors to present and students to learn the history of management in an engaging and interactive way. Management history is presented along an intuitive timeline that can be traveled through sequentially or by selected decade. With the click of a mouse, students learn the important dates, see the people who influenced the field, and understand the general management theories that have molded and shaped management as we know it today.

VIDEO LIBRARY DVDS McGraw-Hill/Irwin offers the most comprehensive video support for the *Organizational Behavior* classroom through a course library video DVD. This discipline has a library volume DVD tailored to integrate and visually reinforce chapter concepts. The library volume DVD contains more than 40 clips! The rich video material, organized by topic, comes from sources such as PBS, NBC, BBC, SHRM, and McGraw-Hill. Video cases and video guides are provided for some clips.

Online Learning Center (OLC)

www.mhhe.com/mcshane6e

Find a variety of online teaching and learning tools that are designed to reinforce and build on the text content. Students will have direct access to the learning tools, while instructor materials are password-protected.

eBook Options

eBooks are an innovative way for students to save money and to "go green." McGraw-Hill's eBooks are typically 40% off the bookstore price. Students have the choice between an online and a downloadable CourseSmart eBook.

Through CourseSmart, students have the flexibility to access an exact replica of their textbook from any computer that has Internet service, without plug-ins or special software, via the online version or to create a library of books on their hard drive via the downloadable version. Access to the CourseSmart eBooks lasts for one year.

FEATURES CourseSmart eBooks allow students to highlight, take notes, organize notes, and share the notes with other CourseSmart users. Students can also search for terms across all eBooks in their purchased CourseSmart library. CourseSmart eBooks can be printed (five pages at a time).

MORE INFO AND PURCHASE Please visit **www.coursesmart.com** for more information and to purchase access to our eBooks. CourseSmart allows students to try one chapter of the eBook, free of charge, before purchase.

McGraw Hill create

Create

Craft your teaching resources to match the way you teach! With McGraw-Hill Create, **www.mcgrawhillcreate.com**, you can easily rearrange chapters, combine material from other content sources, and quickly upload content you have written, like your course syllabus or teaching notes. Find the content you need in Create by searching through thousands of leading McGraw-Hill textbooks. Arrange your book to fit your teaching style. Create even allows you to personalize your book's appearance by selecting the cover and adding your name, school, and course information. Order a Create book and you'll receive a complimentary print review copy in three to five business days or a complimentary electronic review copy (eComp) via e-mail in about one hour. Go to **www.mcgrawhillcreate.com** today and register. Experience how McGraw-Hill Create empowers you to teach *your* students *your* way.

organizational behavior

(1)

Introduction to the Field of Organizational Behavior

learning objectives

After studying Chapter 1, you should be able to:

LO1 Define *organizational behavior* and *organizations,* and discuss the importance of this field of inquiry.

LO2 Compare and contrast the four current perspectives of organizational effectiveness, as well as the early goal attainment perspective.

LO3 Debate the organizational opportunities and challenges of globalization, workforce diversity, and emerging employment relationships.

LO4 Discuss the anchors on which organizational behavior knowledge is based.

Brasilata don't see it that way. The Brazilian company has figured out how to tap into employee knowledge and motivation to fuel its extraordinary productivity and innovation. It has won top industry and supplier awards almost every year, including the coveted Sherwin-Williams "Best Packaging Supplier" award. It has also been ranked among the 20 most innovative companies in Brazil, as well as one of the best places to work in that country.

At the heart of Brasilata's business model is the Simplification Project (*Projeto Simplificação*), which encourages all 900 employees across the company's four production facilities to think up as many suggestions as possible. "The Simplification Project is like panning for ideas (incremental innovations), thereby stimulating the internal innovative environment and entrepreneurial spirit," explains Brasilata's CEO Antonio Carlos Álvares Teixeira, who is also a business professor.

Ideas are so important that Brasilata employees are called "inventors," and everyone signs an "innovation contract" that reinforces their commitment to continuous improvement. After a slow start two decades ago (with only one idea per person each year), the company now receives more than 200,000 ideas each year—an average of more than 220 ideas per employee. Brasilata holds a party every six months, at which all employees celebrate teams and individuals with the best ideas. Employees are also rewarded with bonuses representing 15 percent of net annual profits.

Some employee suggestions have sown the seeds of innovative products, such as an award-winning paint can that withstands heavy impact when dropped. Other ideas have dramatically improved productivity. Some changes have made jobs redundant, but employees aren't worried. Brasilata has been able to maintain a no-layoff policy even during the worst downturns.

Brasilata's success is also built on teamwork. The company compares its workforce with a soccer team, in which winning goals depends on everyone. "Teamwork is one of the leading forces of the company," says the company's website. The company also emphasizes employee initiative and open communication. "In our opinion, innovative action is stimulated by a corporate environment where the communications channels are always open, new ideas are respected and errors tolerated," explains Brasilata's CEO Teixeira.[1]

Brasilata has become one of the most innovative and productive manufacturing businesses in Brazil by applying organizational behavior practices.

Welcome to the Field of Organizational Behavior!

The opening story about Brasilata reveals some important truths about organizations that succeed in today's turbulent environment. In every sector of the economy, organizations need to be innovative, employ skilled and motivated people who can work in teams, have leaders with foresight and vision, and make decisions that consider the interests of multiple stakeholders. In other words, the best companies succeed through the concepts and practices that we discuss in this book on organizational behavior.

The purpose of this book is to help you understand what goes on in organizations, including the thoughts and behavior of employees and teams. We examine the factors that make companies effective, improve employee well-being, and drive successful collaboration among coworkers. We look at organizations from numerous and diverse perspectives, from the deepest foundations of employee thoughts and behavior (personality, self-concept, commitment, etc.) to the complex interplay between the organization's structure and culture and its external environment. Along this journey, we emphasize why things happen and what you can do to predict and manage organizational events.

We begin in this chapter by introducing you to the field of organizational behavior (OB) and why it is important to your career and to organizations. Next, this chapter describes the "ultimate dependent variable" in OB by presenting the four main perspectives of organizational effectiveness. This is followed by an overview of three challenges facing organizations: globalization, increasing workforce diversity, and emerging employment relationships. We complete this opening chapter by describing four anchors that guide the development of organizational behavior knowledge.

The Field of Organizational Behavior

LO1

Organizational behavior (OB) is the study of what people think, feel, and do in and around organizations. It looks at employee behavior, decisions, perceptions, and emotional responses. It examines how individuals and teams in organizations relate to one another and to their counterparts in other organizations. OB also encompasses the study of how organizations interact with their external environments, particularly in the context of employee behavior and decisions. OB researchers systematically study these topics at multiple levels of analysis, namely, the individual, team (including interpersonal), and organization.[2]

The definition of organizational behavior begs the question: What are organizations? **Organizations** are groups of people who work interdependently toward some purpose.[3] Notice that organizations are not buildings or government-registered entities. In fact, many organizations exist without either physical walls or government documentation to confer their legal status. Organizations have existed for as long as people have worked together. Massive temples dating back to 3500 BC were constructed through the organized actions of multitudes of people. Craftspeople and merchants in ancient Rome formed guilds, complete with elected managers. More than 1,000 years ago, Chinese factories were producing 125,000 tons of iron each year.[4]

Throughout history, these and other organizations have consisted of people who communicate, coordinate, and collaborate with one another to achieve common objectives. One key feature of organizations is that they are collective entities. They consist of human beings (typically, but not necessarily, employees), and these people interact with one another in an *organized* way. This organized relationship requires some minimal level of communication, coordination, and collaboration to achieve organizational objectives. As such, all organizational members have degrees of interdependence with one another; they accomplish goals by sharing materials, information, or expertise with coworkers.

A second key feature of organizations is that their members have a collective sense of purpose. This collective purpose isn't always well defined or agreed on. Furthermore, though most companies have vision and mission statements, these documents are

Until the 1930s, most organizational research and practice tried to improve work efficiency by changing working conditions and job duties. Employee thoughts and feelings were ignored and usually considered irrelevant. Elton Mayo (left in photo); his research assistant, and later professor in his own right, Fritz Roethlisberger (right); and others at Harvard University adopted a completely different view. Their "human relations" studies at Western Electric Hawthorne Works near Chicago found that employee attitudes, formal team dynamics, informal groups, and supervisor leadership style strongly influenced employee performance and well-being. Historians suggest that this human relations view laid the foundation for the field of organizational behavior as we know it today.[7]

sometimes out of date or don't describe what employees and leaders try to achieve in reality. Still, imagine an organization without a collective sense of purpose. It would be a collection of people without direction or unifying force. So, whether it's manufacturing steel cans at Brasilata or designing better aircraft at Boeing, people working in organizations do have some sense of collective purpose. "A company is one of humanity's most amazing inventions," said the late Steve Jobs, cofounder of Apple Inc. and Pixar Animation Studios. "It's totally abstract. Sure, you have to build something with bricks and mortar to put the people in, but basically a company is this abstract construct we've invented, and it's incredibly powerful."[5]

HISTORICAL FOUNDATIONS OF ORGANIZATIONAL BEHAVIOR

Organizational behavior emerged as a distinct field around the early 1940s, but organizations have been studied by experts in other fields for many centuries. The Greek philosopher Plato wrote about the essence of leadership. Around the same time, the Chinese philosopher Confucius discussed the virtues of ethics and leadership. In 1776, Adam Smith discussed the benefits of job specialization and division of labor. One hundred years later, the German sociologist Max Weber wrote about rational organizations, the work ethic, and charismatic leadership. Soon after, industrial engineer Frederick Winslow Taylor proposed systematic ways to organize work processes and motivate employees through goal setting and rewards.[6]

From the 1920s to the 1940s, Elton Mayo, Fritz Roethlisberger, and their Harvard University colleagues introduced the "human relations" school of management, which emphasized the study of employee attitudes and informal group dynamics in the workplace. Also during that time, political philosopher and social worker Mary Parker Follett advocated new ways of thinking about several OB topics, including constructive conflict, team dynamics, organizational democracy, power, and leadership. In the late 1930s, Chester Barnard wrote insightful reviews of organizational communication, coordination, leadership and

organizational behavior (OB)
The study of what people think, feel, and do in and around organizations.

organizations
Groups of people who work interdependently toward some purpose.

authority, organizations as open systems, and team dynamics.[8] This brief historical tour indicates that OB has been around for a long time; it just wasn't organized into a unified discipline until the 1940s.

WHY STUDY ORGANIZATIONAL BEHAVIOR?

Organizational behavior instructors face a challenge: Students who have not yet begun their careers tend to value courses related to specific jobs, such as accounting and marketing.[9] However, OB doesn't have a specific career path—there is no "vice president of OB"—so students sometimes have difficulty recognizing the value that OB knowledge can offer to their future. Meanwhile, students with several years of work experience identify OB as one of the most important courses. Why? Because they have learned through experience that OB *does make a difference* to one's career success. OB helps us make sense of and predict the world in which we live.[10] We use OB theories to question our personal beliefs and assumptions and to adopt more accurate models of workplace behavior. Some experts suggest that OB knowledge even helps us make sense of the broader world, not just what goes on inside organizations.[11]

But probably the greatest value of OB knowledge is that it helps people get things done in organizations.[12] Everyone in business, government, and not-for-profit firms works with other people, and OB provides the knowledge and tools to interact with others more effectively. Building a high-performance team, motivating coworkers, handling workplace conflicts, influencing your boss, and changing employee behavior are just a few of the areas of knowledge and skills offered in organizational behavior. No matter what career path you choose, you'll find that OB concepts play an important role in how you perform your job and work more effectively within organizations.

Organizational Behavior Is for Everyone   Organizational behavior is important for anyone who works in organizations, not just for managers. In fact, this book pioneered the notion that OB knowledge is for everyone. Whether you are a geologist, financial analyst, customer service representative, or chief executive officer, you need to understand and apply the many organizational behavior topics that are discussed in this book. Yes, organizations will continue to have managers, and this book recognizes the relevance of OB knowledge in these vital roles. But this book also recognizes the reality that all employees are increasingly expected to manage themselves and work effectively with one another in the workplace. In the words of one forward-thinking OB writer more than four decades ago: Everyone is a manager.[13]

OB and the Bottom Line   Up to this point, our answer to the question "Why study OB?" has focused on how organizational behavior knowledge benefits you as an individual. However, OB knowledge is just as important for the organization's financial health. Brasilata has flourished because it leverages human capital, employee engagement, creativity, and teamwork. Numerous studies have reported that these and other OB practices discussed in this book tend to improve the organization's survival and success.[14]

For example, one investigation found that hospitals with higher levels of specific OB activities (e.g., training, staff involvement, reward and recognition) have lower patient mortality rates. Another study found that companies receiving "best place to work" awards have significantly higher financial and long-term stock market performance. And as we will learn in Chapter 5, employee engagement is associated with significantly higher sales and profitability. The bottom-line value of organizational behavior is also supported by human capital and investment portfolio studies. These investigations suggest that specific OB characteristics (employee attitudes, work–life balance, performance-based rewards, leadership, employee training and development, etc.) are important "positive screens" for selecting companies with the best long-term stock appreciation.[15]

organizational effectiveness
A broad concept represented by several perspectives, including the organization's fit with the external environment, internal subsystems configuration for high performance, emphasis on organizational learning, and ability to satisfy the needs of key stakeholders.

Perspectives of Organizational Effectiveness

LO2

connect

To assist your learning and test your knowledge about perspectives of organizational effectiveness, go to **www.mcgrawhillconnect.com**, which has activities and test questions on this topic.

Apple, Inc., and Google, Inc., are the two most admired companies in the world, according to *Fortune* magazine's annual list.[16] Yet, neither of these companies was on anyone's radar screen a dozen years ago. Apple was on life support in the late 1990s, barely clinging on to a few percentage points of market share in the computer industry. Google wasn't even registered as a company. It was little more than a computer project by two Stanford PhD students that was quickly outgrowing the dorm room where their equipment was housed.

How did Apple and Google achieve their incredible success? They relied on innovation as their engine for growth, invested in and supported their employees, were led by visionary leaders, and applied many other practices that we will discuss throughout this book. More generally, Apple and Google have consistently applied the four perspectives of organizational effectiveness that we discuss over the next few pages.

Almost all organizational behavior theories have the implicit or explicit objective of making organizations more effective.[17] In fact, **organizational effectiveness** is considered the "ultimate dependent variable" in organizational behavior.[18] This means that organizational effectiveness is the outcome that most OB theories are ultimately trying to achieve. Many theories use different labels—organizational performance, success, goodness, health, competitiveness, excellence—but they are basically presenting models and recommendations that help organizations be more effective.

Over the next several pages, we will describe a coherent model of organizational effectiveness that incorporates four complementary perspectives. But first, we need to mention the now discredited "goal attainment" definition of organizational effectiveness. This view, which was popular for many years, states that companies are effective when they achieve their stated organizational objectives.[20] According to this definition, Home Depot, the world's largest retailer of home improvement products, would be an effective organization if it meets or exceeds its annual sales and profit targets. Today, we know this isn't necessarily so. Any leadership team could set corporate goals that are easy to achieve yet would put the organization out of business. These goals could also be left in the dust by competitors' more aggressive objectives.

Worse still, some goals might aim the organization in the wrong direction. Consider the following true story: The board of directors of a major airline gave the incoming CEO

Apple, Inc., is rated as one of the world's most admired companies, yet a dozen years ago it was on life support with a dwindling computer market share. Apple's incredible turnaround illustrates how companies achieve success by paying attention to all four perspectives of organizational effectiveness. Apple deftly anticipated and fluidly adapted to rapidly changing consumer needs (such as by introducing the iPod, iPhone, and iPad). It became a learning organization by hiring key people and acquiring small firms. It nurtured high-performance teams for hardware design, software development, and marketing. And except for a few trip-ups, it has generally met stakeholder expectations and improved its corporate social responsibility.[19]

a mandate to reduce costs and dramatically improve profitability. The CEO accomplished these organizational goals by reducing the training budget and canceling the purchase of new aircraft. Within a few years (after the CEO had taken a job with another airline), the company was suffering from higher maintenance costs to keep the old planes flying safely and was losing customers to airlines with better-trained staff and more modern fleets. This airline never recovered; it was eventually acquired by a larger competitor. The CEO achieved the company's goals, but the result was a less effective organization in the long run.

This book takes the view that the best yardstick of organizational effectiveness is a composite of four perspectives: open systems, organizational learning, high-performance work practices, and stakeholders.[21] Organizations are effective when they have a good fit with their external environment, are learning organizations, have efficient and adaptive internal subsystems (i.e., high-performance work practices), and satisfy the needs of key stakeholders. Let's examine each of these perspectives in detail.

OPEN SYSTEMS PERSPECTIVE

The **open systems** perspective of organizational effectiveness is one of the earliest and most well-entrenched ways of thinking about organizations.[22] Indeed, the other major organizational effectiveness perspectives might be considered detailed extensions of the open systems model. The open systems perspective views organizations as complex organisms that "live" within an external environment, rather like the illustration in Exhibit 1.1. The word *open* describes this permeable relationship, whereas *closed systems* operate without dependence on or interaction with an external environment.

As open systems, organizations depend on the external environment for resources, including raw materials, job applicants, financial resources, information, and equipment. The external environment also consists of rules and expectations, such as laws and cultural norms, that place demands on how organizations should operate. Some environmental resources (e.g., raw materials) are transformed into outputs that are exported to the external environment, whereas other resources (e.g., job applicants, equipment) become subsystems in the transformation process.

EXHIBIT 1.1   Open Systems Perspective of Organizations

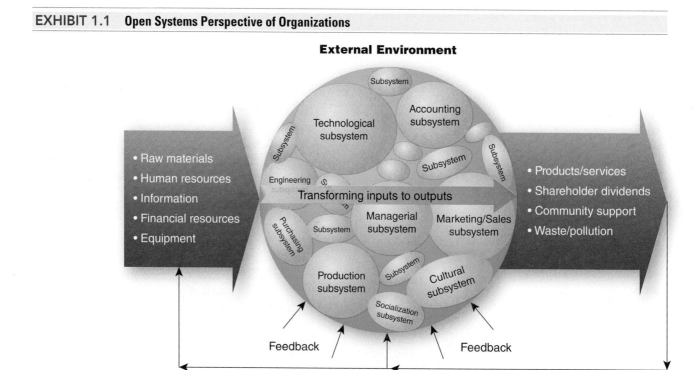

Inside the organization are numerous subsystems, such as departments, teams, informal groups, work processes, technological configurations, and other elements. Rather like the Russian matryoshka dolls nested within each other, organizational subsystems are also systems with their own subsystems.[23] For example, the Nordstrom department store in Spokane, Washington, is a subsystem of the Nordstrom chain, but the Spokane store is also a system with its own subsystems of departments, teams, and work processes. An organization's subsystems are interconnected so they interact to transform inputs into various outputs. Some outputs (e.g., products, services, community support) may be valued by the external environment, whereas other outputs (e.g., employee layoffs, pollution) are by-products that may have adverse effects on the environment and the organization's relationship with that environment. Throughout this process, organizations receive feedback from the external environment regarding the value of their outputs and the availability of future inputs.

Organization–Environment Fit   According to the open systems perspective, organizations are effective when they maintain a good "fit" with their external environment.[24] Good fit exists when the organization puts resources where they are most useful, so it can adapt to and align with the needs of the external environment. For instance, Apple, Inc., has a good fit with its many external environments—just look at the lines for new iPads and the skyrocketing market share of Apple laptops and iPhones. In contrast, companies with a poor fit with the environment offer the wrong products and operate inappropriately in their environments.

Successful organizations maintain a good fit by anticipating changes in the environment and fluidly reconfiguring their subsystems to become more consistent with that environment. To illustrate, food manufacturers have changed their ingredients and production processes to satisfy more health- and environment-conscious consumers. Companies also maintain a good fit by actively managing their external environment. For example, they might try to limit competitor access to critical resources (e.g., gaining exclusive rights), change consumer perceptions and needs (e.g., through marketing), or support legislation that strengthens their position in the marketplace.

The third fit strategy is to move into different environments if the current environment is too challenging. For instance, Nokia started in 1865 as a pulp and paper company. The Finnish company entered the rubber and cable business in the 1920s, moved into electronics in the 1960s, and began producing cell phones a decade later. These strategic choices moved the company decisively into new external environments that seemed more appealing for Nokia's long-term survival and success.[25]

Internal Subsystems Effectiveness   The open systems perspective considers more than an organization's fit with the external environment. It also defines effectiveness by how well the company operates internally, that is, how well it transforms inputs into outputs. The most common indicator of this internal transformation process is **organizational efficiency** (also called *productivity*), which is the ratio of inputs to outcomes.[26] Companies that produce more goods or services with less labor, materials, and energy are more efficient.

Successful organizations require more than efficient transformation processes, however. They also need to have more *adaptive* and *innovative* transformation processes.[27] Brasilata illustrates both efficiency and innovation in the transformation process. As we described in the opening story to this chapter, a continuous flow of employee suggestions has made the Brazilian steel can manufacturer highly efficient, which allows it to compete

open systems
A perspective which holds that organizations depend on the external environment for resources, affect that environment through their output, and consist of internal subsystems that transform inputs to outputs.

organizational efficiency
The amount of outputs relative to inputs in the organization's transformation process.

better than less efficient companies. Many of these suggestions are also innovative, because they identify new ways to manufacture cans, manage inventory, and market Brasilata's products to businesses that buy these products.

One last observation about the open systems perspective is that coordination is vital in the relationship among organizational subsystems, but this coordination is usually far from ideal.[28] Information gets lost, ideas are not shared, materials are hoarded, communication messages are misinterpreted, resources and rewards are distributed unfairly, and so forth. These coordination challenges are amplified as organizations grow, such as when employees are clustered into several departments and when departments are clustered into several organizational divisions. A slight change in work practices in one subsystem may ripple through the organization and undermine the effectiveness of other subsystems. For example, a new accounting procedure in the financial subsystem might unintentionally reduce the sales staff's motivation to sell products with higher profit margins.

ORGANIZATIONAL LEARNING PERSPECTIVE

The open systems perspective has traditionally focused on physical resources that enter the organization and are processed into physical goods (outputs). This was representative of the industrial economy but not the "new economy," where the most valued input is knowledge. The **organizational learning** perspective (also called *knowledge management*) views knowledge as the main driver of competitive advantage. Specifically, organizational learning is founded on the idea that organizational effectiveness depends on the organization's capacity to acquire, share, use, and store valuable knowledge.

Intellectual Capital: The Stock of Organizational Knowledge   The organizational learning perspective views knowledge as a resource, and this stock of knowledge exists in three forms, collectively known as **intellectual capital.**[29] The most commonly mentioned form of intellectual capital is **human capital**—the knowledge, skills, and abilities that employees carry around in their heads. Human capital has been described as valuable, rare, difficult to imitate, and nonsubstitutable.[30] It is valuable because employees help the organization discover opportunities and minimize threats in the external environment. Human capital is rare and difficult to imitate, meaning that talented people are difficult to find, and they cannot be cloned like sheep. Finally, human capital is nonsubstitutable because it cannot be easily replaced by technology.

Because of these characteristics, human capital is a competitive advantage as well as a huge risk for most organizations. When key people leave, they take with them some of the most valuable knowledge that makes the company effective. "Innovation is the key to success in this business, and creativity fuels innovation," explains Jim Goodnight, CEO of SAS Institute, Inc., a leading statistical software developer in Cary, North Carolina. "As such, 95 percent of my assets drive out the gate every evening. It's my job to maintain a work environment that keeps those people coming back every morning. The creativity they bring to SAS is a competitive advantage for us."[31]

Fortunately, some intellectual capital remains even if every employee did leave the organization. **Structural capital** (also called *organizational capital*) includes the knowledge captured and retained in an organization's systems and structures, such as the documentation of work procedures and the physical layout of the production line.[32] Structural capital also includes the organization's finished products, because knowledge can be extracted by taking them apart to discover how they work and are constructed (i.e., reverse engineering).

The third form of intellectual capital is **relationship capital,** which is the value derived from an organization's relationships with customers, suppliers, and others who provide added mutual value for the organization. It includes the organization's goodwill, brand image, and combination of relationships that organizational members have with people outside the organization.[33]

connect

To assist your learning and test your knowledge about organizational learning, go to **www.mcgrawhillconnect.com,** which has activities and test questions on this topic.

organizational learning
A perspective which holds that organizational effectiveness depends on the organization's capacity to acquire, share, use, and store valuable knowledge.

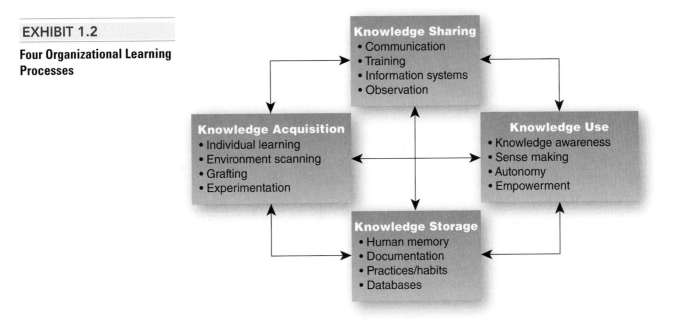

EXHIBIT 1.2

Four Organizational Learning Processes

Organizational Learning Processes Organizations nurture their intellectual capital through four organizational learning processes: knowledge acquisition, sharing, use, and storage (see Exhibit 1.2).[34]

- *Knowledge acquisition.* This includes extracting information and ideas from the external environment, as well as through insight. One of the fastest and most powerful ways to acquire knowledge is by hiring individuals or acquiring entire companies (called grafting). Knowledge also enters the organization when employees learn from external sources. As Connections 1.1 describes, the Duha Group in Winnipeg, Canada, acquires knowledge by sending staff on training programs and by touring other companies to learn about their best practices. A third knowledge acquisition strategy is experimentation. Companies receive knowledge through insight as a result of research and other creative processes.

- *Knowledge sharing.* This aspect of organizational learning involves distributing knowledge to others across the organization. Knowledge sharing is often equated with computer intranets and digital repositories of knowledge. These systems are relevant, but knowledge sharing mainly occurs through structured and informal communication, as well as various forms of learning (e.g., observation, experience, training, practice). For example, Pixar Animation Studios deliberately centralized its cafeteria, mailroom, and restroom facilities so employees would "bump into" and coincidentally share knowledge with people from other areas of the organization rather than just with their own team members.[35]

- *Knowledge use.* The competitive advantage of knowledge comes from applying it in ways that add value to the organization and its stakeholders. To do this, employees must realize that the knowledge is available and that they have enough autonomy to apply it. This requires the type of culture found at Brasilata, which supports the

intellectual capital
A company's stock of knowledge, including human capital, structural capital, and relationship capital.

human capital
The stock of knowledge, skills, and abilities among employees that provide economic value to the organization.

structural capital
Knowledge embedded in an organization's systems and structures.

relationship capital
The value derived from an organization's relationships with customers, suppliers, and other.

connections 1.1

Duha Group's Learning Organization Strategies[36]

Nestled away in an industrial section of Winnipeg, Canada, is Duha Group, a role model for the learning organization. The global manufacturer, marketer, and supplier of paint fandecks (color cards) and color samples depends on lean manufacturing for its quality and efficiency, and organizational learning practices enable it to continuously raise these standards. Duha's 290 Winnipeg employees (the company also has plants in New York, Mexico, Europe, Asia, and Australia) acquire external knowledge by touring other companies to learn about their best practices. Knowledge is also brought in through company-supported formal off-site training (such as health and safety officer training at a nearby college). In addition, Duha employees are encouraged to discover new knowledge through experimentation within their work area and through Kaizen Blitzes (where teams identify more effective ways to operate entire work areas). "We are encouraged to give our ideas a try even if they fail," says a Duha employee. "It's rewarding to apply new concepts that add value or improvement."

Duha Group employees engage in knowledge sharing through formal in-house training programs, mentoring arrangements, and informal hands-on training sessions. Also, detailed company operating manuals and other documents are centrally located with access to all staff. A popular form of knowledge sharing is Duha Group's lunch-and-learn sessions, where employees teach coworkers about lean management, specific production practices, health and safety, environmental, quality, and human resources while enjoying a hot, company-supplied meal. Knowledge sharing also occurs through departmental

Duha Group applies organizational learning through Kaizen Blitzes, off-site training, lunch-and-learn sessions, and daily huddles.

huddles, held every day for five minutes. Employees congregate around a huddle board where they post suggestions for improvement, describe work process changes in their area, and hear about company news. "The huddles are a great idea," says a Duha employee. "I think that's one of our best outlets for communication."

Finally, Duha Group encourages employees to put knowledge to use by giving them plenty of autonomy and support. Indeed, every employee has a learning plan they review with management as well as a learning journal to maintain their focus on continuous learning. Knowledge use also occurs more readily because the huddle boards in each department show, who has specific knowledge they might require.

learning process by encouraging experimentation and open communications and recognizing that mistakes are part of that process.

- *Knowledge storage.* Knowledge storage includes any means by which knowledge is held for later retrieval. It is the process that creates organizational memory. Human memory plays a critical role here, as do the many forms of documentation and database systems that exist in organizations. Individual practices and habits hold less explicit (more tacit) knowledge.

Absorptive Capacity   An important prerequisite for acquiring, sharing, and using new knowledge is the amount and quality of knowledge already held within the organization. Just as students need to learn knowledge in core courses before they can understand content in more advanced courses, companies need to have employees with a sufficient foundation of expertise to receive and apply new knowledge. This knowledge prerequisite is known as the organization's **absorptive capacity.**[37] For example, many companies were slow to develop online marketing practices because no one in the organization had enough knowledge about the Internet to fathom its potential or apply that knowledge to the company's business. In some cases, companies had to acquire entire teams of people with the requisite knowledge to realize the potential of this marketing channel.

Organizational Memory and Unlearning   Corporate leaders need to recognize that they are the keepers of *organizational memory.*[38] This unusual metaphor refers to the storage and preservation of intellectual capital. It includes knowledge that employees possess, as well as knowledge embedded in the organization's systems and structures. It includes documents, objects, and anything else that provides meaningful information about how the organization should operate.

How do organizations retain intellectual capital? One way is by keeping knowledgeable employees. Progressive companies achieve this by adapting their employment practices to become more compatible with emerging workforce expectations. A second organizational memory strategy is to systematically transfer knowledge to other employees. This occurs when newcomers apprentice with skilled employees, thereby acquiring knowledge that is not documented. A third strategy is to transfer knowledge into structural capital. This includes bringing out hidden knowledge, organizing it, and putting it in a form that can be available to others. Reliance Industries, India's largest business enterprise, applies this strategy by encouraging employees to document their successes and failures through a special intranet knowledge portal. One of these reports provided information that later prevented a costly plant shutdown.[39]

The organizational learning perspective states not only that effective organizations learn but also that they unlearn routines and patterns of behavior that are no longer appropriate.[40] Unlearning removes knowledge that no longer adds value and, in fact, may undermine the organization's effectiveness. Some forms of unlearning involve replacing dysfunctional policies, procedures, and routines. Other forms of unlearning erase attitudes, beliefs, and assumptions. For instance, employees rethink the "best way" to perform a task and how to serve clients. Organizational unlearning is particularly important for organizational change, which we discuss in Chapter 15.

HIGH-PERFORMANCE WORK PRACTICES (HPWP) PERSPECTIVE

The open systems perspective states that successful companies are good at transforming inputs into outputs. However, it does not identify the subsystem characteristics that distinguish effective organizations from others. Consequently, an entire field of research has blossomed around the objective of discovering the best 'bundle' of organizational practices that offers competitive advantage. This research has had various labels over the years, but it is now most commonly known as **high-performance work practices (HPWP)**.[41]

Similar to organizational learning, the HPWP perspective is founded on the belief that human capital—the knowledge, skills, and abilities that employees carry around in their heads—is an important source of competitive advantage for organizations.[42] The distinctive feature of the HPWP perspective is that it tries to identify a specific bundle of systems and structures that generate the most value from this human capital.

Researchers have investigated numerous potential high-performance work practices, but we will focus on four that are recognized in most studies.[43] Two of these are employee involvement and job autonomy. Both activities tend to strengthen employee motivation as well as improve decision making, organizational responsiveness, and commitment to change. In high-performance workplaces, employee involvement and job autonomy often take the form of self-directed teams (see Chapter 8).

Another key variable in the HPWP model is employee competence. Specifically, organizations are more effective when they recruit and select people with relevant skills, knowledge, values, and other personal characteristics. Furthermore, successful companies invest in employee development through training and development. A fourth characteristic of high-performance organizations is that they link performance and skill development to various forms of financial and nonfinancial rewards valued by employees. Each of these four work practices—involvement, autonomy, employee competence, and performance/skill-based rewards—individually improves

absorptive capacity
The ability to recognize the value of new information, assimilate it, and use it for value-added activities.

high-performance work practices (HPWP)
A perspective which holds that effective organizations incorporate several workplace practices that leverage the potential of human capital.

American Express has taken a page from the high-performance work practices playbook. The financial services company encourages employees to go "off script," meaning that they have the autonomy to customize their conversations rather than rely on memorized statements. Employees also have the discretion to solve problems on the spot, such as setting up a conference call to settle a dispute with a vendor. "We are getting more and more power to make the decisions at our level," says Teresa Tate, an American Express customer service employee in Phoenix.[45]

organizational performance, but recent evidence suggests that they have a stronger effect when bundled together.[44]

Why are HPWP associated with organizational effectiveness? Early studies were criticized for ignoring this question,[46] but OB experts are now building and testing more theoretical explanations.[47] The first reason is that HPWP build human capital, which improves performance as employees develop the skills and knowledge to perform the work. A second explanation is that superior human capital may improve the organization's adaptability to rapidly changing environments. Employees respond better when they have a wide skill set to handle diverse tasks as well as the confidence to handle unfamiliar situations. A third explanation for why HPWP improve organizational effectiveness is that these activities strengthen employees' motivation and attitudes toward the employer. For instance, HPWP represent the company's investment in and recognition of its workforce, which motivates employees to reciprocate through greater effort in their jobs and assistance to coworkers.

The HPWP perspective is still developing, but it already reveals important information about specific organizational practices that improve the input–output transformation process. Still, this perspective has been criticized for focusing on shareholder and customer needs at the expense of employee well-being.[48] This concern illustrates that the HPWP perspective offers an incomplete picture of organizational effectiveness. The remaining gaps are mostly filled by the stakeholder perspective of organizational effectiveness.

STAKEHOLDER PERSPECTIVE

The three organizational effectiveness perspectives described so far mainly pay attention to processes and resources, yet they only minimally recognize the importance of relations with **stakeholders.** Stakeholders include anyone with a stake in the company—employees, stockholders, suppliers, labor unions, government, communities, consumer and environmental interest groups, and so on (see Exhibit 1.3). In other words, organizations are more effective when they consider the needs and expectations of any individual group or other entity that affects, or is affected by, the organization's objectives and actions. This approach requires organizational leaders and employees to understand, manage, and satisfy the interests of their stakeholders.[49] The stakeholder perspective personalizes the open systems perspective; it identifies specific people and social entities in the external environment as well as within the organization (the internal environment). It also recognizes that stakeholder relations are dynamic; they can be negotiated and managed, not just taken as a fixed condition.[50]

Consider the troubles that Walmart has faced in recent years.[51] For decades, the world's largest retailer concentrated on customers by providing the lowest possible prices and on stockholders by generating healthy financial returns. Yet emphasizing these two stakeholders exposed the company to increasing hostility from other groups in society. Some accused Walmart of destroying America's manufacturing base and

Learning how to use chopsticks might not be the most important item in cross-cultural training. But it is one of the skills that Millennium: The Takeda Oncology Co. is teaching its managers in Cambridge, Mass., as part of a class on Japanese customs. The Japanese-owned biotechnology firm, which employs 1,300 people in the United States, encourages its employees to develop global knowledge and skills.[70]

Globalization offers numerous benefits to organizations in terms of larger markets, lower costs, and greater access to knowledge and innovation. At the same time, there is considerable debate about whether globalization benefits developing nations, and whether it is primarily responsible for increasing work intensification, as well as reducing job security and work–life balance in developed countries.[68] Globalization is now well entrenched, so the most important issue in organizational behavior is how corporate leaders and employees alike can lead and work effectively in this emerging reality.[69]

Throughout this book, we will refer to the effects of globalization on teamwork, diversity, cultural values, organizational structure, leadership, and other themes. Each topic highlights that globalization has brought more complexity to the workplace, but also more opportunities and potential benefits for individuals and organizations. Globalization requires additional knowledge and skills that we will also discuss in this book, such as emotional intelligence, a global mindset, nonverbal communication, and conflict handling.

INCREASING WORKFORCE DIVERSITY

Walk into the offices of Verizon Communications, and you can quickly see that the telecommunications giant values workforce diversity. Women and people of color constitute nearly 60 percent of the company's 195,000-person workforce and nearly half of the company's board of directors. African Americans represent 20 percent of Verizon's workforce (compared with 11 percent of the U.S. labor force). More than one-quarter of senior management (vice president and above) positions are held by women. The company also actively supports diversity among its many suppliers. Verizon's inclusive culture has won awards from numerous organizations and publications representing Hispanic, African American, gay/lesbian, people with disabilities, and other groups. "Verizon incorporates diversity in all that we do," says CEO Ivan Seidenberg. "It's part of our credo to encourage each other to embrace diversity and personal development, not only because it's the right thing to do but also because it's smart business."[71]

Verizon Communications is a model employer and a reflection of the increasing diversity of people living in the United States and in many other countries. The description of Verizon's diversity refers to **surface-level diversity**—the observable demographic and other overt differences in people, such as their race, ethnicity, gender,

globalization
Economic, social, and cultural connectivity with people in other parts of the world.

surface-level diversity
The observable demographic or physiological differences in people, such as their race, ethnicity, gender, age, and physical disabilities.

EXHIBIT 1.4

America's Multigenerational Workforce[75]

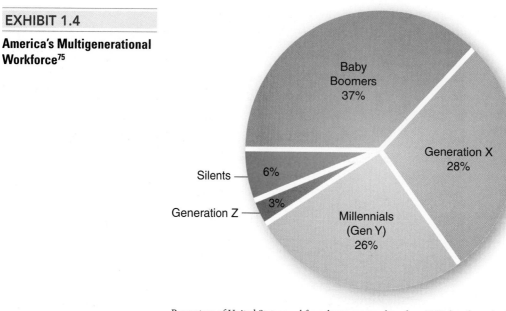

Percentage of United States workforce by age group, based on 2009 data from the U.S. Bureau of Labor Statistics. "Silents" represent the generation of employees born before 1946. Generation-Z employees were born after 1990, though some sources consider this group part of Millennials.

age, and physical capabilities. Surface-level diversity has changed considerably in the United States over the past few decades. People of non-Caucasian or Hispanic origins represent one-third of the American population, and this is projected to increase substantially over the next few decades. Within the next 50 years, one in four Americans will be Hispanic, 14 percent will be African American, and 8 percent will be of Asian descent. By 2060, people with European non-Hispanic ethnicity will be a minority.[72] Many other countries are also experiencing increasing levels of racial and ethnic diversification.

Diversity also includes differences in the psychological characteristics of employees, including personalities, beliefs, values, and attitudes.[73] We can't directly see this **deep-level diversity,** but it is evident in a person's decisions, statements, and actions. A popular example is the apparent deep-level diversity across generations.[74] Exhibit 1.4 illustrates the distribution of the American workforce by major generational cohort: 37 percent *Baby Boomers* (born between 1946 and 1964), 28 percent *Generation X* (born from 1965 to 1980), and 26 percent *Millennials* (also called *Generation Y,* born after 1980).

Do these generational cohorts have different attitudes and expectations, particularly regarding work? The answer is a qualified "yes." Differences exist, but some are smaller than depicted in the popular press, and some of these differences are due to age, not cohort (i.e., Boomers had many of the same attitudes as Millennials when they were that age).[76] One recent investigation of 23,000 undergraduate college students reported that Millennials expect rapid career advancement regarding promotions and pay increases.[77] These observations are consistent with other studies, which have found that Millennials are more self-confident and more narcissistic (self-centered) and have less work centrality (i.e., work is less of a central life interest) when compared with Boomers. Generation-X employees typically average somewhere between these two cohorts.[78]

One high-quality study, which compared attitudes of senior U.S. high school students in 1976 (Boomers), 1991 (Gen-Xers), and 2006 (Millennials), reported that Gen-Xers prefer leisure significantly more than do Boomers, and Millennials prefer leisure significantly more than do Gen-Xers.[79] This longitudinal cohort study also revealed that Millennials and Gen-Xers value extrinsic rewards significantly more than do Boomers, Millennials value intrinsic motivation significantly less than do Boomers, and Millennials value social interaction significantly less than do Boomers or Gen-Xers.

Of course, these results don't apply to everyone in each cohort, but they do suggest that deep-level diversity exists across generations.

Consequences of Diversity   Diversity presents both opportunities and challenges in organizations.[80] Diversity is an advantage because it provides a broader spectrum of knowledge. Furthermore, teams with some forms of diversity (particularly occupational diversity) make better decisions on complex problems than do teams whose members have similar backgrounds. There is also some evidence that companies that have won diversity awards have higher financial returns, at least in the short run.[81] This is consistent with anecdotal evidence from many corporate leaders, namely, that having a diverse workforce improves customer service and creativity. "As a company serving customers around the globe, we greatly value the diverse opinions and experiences that an inclusive and diverse workforce brings to the table," says Magda Yrizarry, Verizon's chief diversity officer and vice president for talent management.[82]

This information supports the popular refrain that workforce diversity is a sound business proposition. Unfortunately, it's not that simple. Most forms of diversity offer both advantages and disadvantages.[83] Teams with diverse employees usually take longer to perform effectively. Diversity brings numerous communication problems as well as "fault lines" in informal group dynamics. Diversity is also a source of conflict, which can lead to lack of information sharing and, in extreme cases, morale problems and higher turnover.

Whether or not workforce diversity is a business advantage, companies need to make it a priority because surface-level diversity is a moral and legal imperative. Ethically, companies that offer an inclusive workplace are, in essence, making fair and just decisions regarding employment, promotions, rewards, and so on. Fairness is a well-established influence on employee loyalty and satisfaction. "Diversity is about fairness; we use the term inclusive meritocracy," says a Bank of America New Jersey executive. "What it does for our workforce is build trust and assures that individual differences are valued."[84] In summary, workforce diversity is the new reality and organizations need to adjust to this reality both to survive and to experience its potential benefits for organizational success.

EMERGING EMPLOYMENT RELATIONSHIPS

Combine globalization with emerging workforce diversity; then add in recent developments in information technology. The resulting concoction has created incredible changes in employment relationships. A few decades ago, most (although not all) employees in the United States and similar cultures would finish their workday after eight or nine hours and could separate their personal time from the workday. There were no iPhones, Blackberrys, or Internet connections to keep them tethered to work on a 24/7 schedule. Even business travel was more of an exception due to its high cost. Most competitors were located in the same country, so they had similar work practices and labor costs. Today, work hours are longer (although arguably less than 100 years ago), employees experience more work-related stress, and there is growing evidence that family and personal relations are suffering.

Little wonder that one of the most important employment issues over the past decade has been **work–life balance.** Work–life balance occurs when people are able to minimize conflict between their work and nonwork demands.[85] Most employees lack this balance because they spend too many hours each week performing or thinking about their job, whether at the workplace, at home, or on vacation. This focus on work leaves too little time to fulfill nonwork needs and obligations. Our discussion of work-related stress (Chapter 4) will examine work–life balance issues in more detail.

Another employment relationship trend is **virtual work,** whereby employees use information technology to perform their jobs away

deep-level diversity
Differences in the psychological characteristics of employees, including personalities, beliefs, values, and attitudes.

work–life balance
The degree to which a person minimizes conflict between work and nonwork demands.

virtual work
Work performed away from the traditional physical workplace by using information technology.

A few years ago, Chris Keehn had a three-hour round trip commute between his home and office at Deloitte LLC in downtown Chicago. Most days, his young daughter would be asleep when he left in the morning and when he returned home at night. The senior tax accountant got his life back by becoming a teleworker four days each week. Working from home now gives Keehn more time to take his daughter to school and attend her evening basketball games. Keehn even found that he communicates more often with his team. "I actually talk to them more now," he says.[87]

evidence-based management The practice of making decisions and taking actions based on research evidence.

from the traditional physical workplace. Some virtual work occurs when employees are connected to the office while traveling or at clients' offices. However, the most common form involves working at home rather than commuting to the office (often called *telecommuting* or *teleworking*). Estimates of the number of teleworkers vary from one survey to the next. One estimate is that the number of American employees who work from home at least one day per month has increased from 7.6 million in 2004 to well above 17 million today. This figure will increase substantially over the next few years because the U.S. federal government's new telework legislation requires departments to establish policies and practices that encourage more government employees to work from home one or more days per week.[86]

Telework is already well established in several companies. More than two-thirds of the employees at Agilent Technologies work from home or off-site some or all of the time. Employees at Cisco Systems, the Internet technology company, work from home an average of two days per week. Deloitte LLP has had a telework program for the past 15 years. More than 80 percent of the professional services and accounting firm's 45,000 American employees currently work remotely for at least 20 percent of the workweek.[88]

The benefits and risks of virtual work, particularly working from home, have received much study and debate. The evidence suggests that telework attracts job applicants as well as improves the employee's work–life balance (which reduces stress) and productivity.[89] One recent study of 25,000 IBM employees found that employees who worked at home most of the time could perform 50 hours of work per week before experiencing work–life conflict compared to 46 hours per week for those who worked only at the office. Female telecommuters with children were able to work 40 hours per week, whereas non-telecommuters could only manage 30 hours before feeling work–life balance tension.

Telework also offers environmental benefits. Cisco Systems estimates that telecommuting among its employees worldwide avoids almost 50,000 metric tons of greenhouse gas emission and saves employees $10 million in fuel costs each year. Deloitte saved $30 million in one year due to the reduced office space requirements as more employees worked part of the week from home. Productivity also usually improves with telework in place. One study found that employees allocate 60 percent of the time they would have been commuting to work and use the other 40 percent of that time for personal activities. When a major blizzard shut federal government offices in Washington, DC, 30 percent of employees teleworked, saving the government $30 million per day.[90]

Against these potential benefits, work-at-home employees face a number of real or potential challenges. Family relations may suffer rather than improve if employees lack sufficient space and resources for a home office. Some employees complain of social isolation and reduced promotion opportunities when they work away from the office most of the time. Telework is clearly better suited to people who are self-motivated and organized, can work effectively with broadband and other technology, and have sufficient fulfillment of social needs elsewhere in their life. "They tend to be the kind of people who would stay late and do the job at the office, people who know what they're responsible for and want to get it done," says Michelle van Schouwen, president of van Schouwen Associates, an advertising and marketing firm in Longmeadow, Mass.[91] Virtual work arrangements are also more successful in organizations that evaluate employees by their performance outcomes rather than face time.[92]

Anchors of Organizational Behavior Knowledge

LO4

Globalization, increasing workforce diversity, and emerging employment relationships are just a few of the trends that challenge organizations and make the field of organizational behavior more relevant than ever before. To understand these and other topics, the field of organizational behavior relies on a set of basic beliefs or knowledge structures (see Exhibit 1.5). These conceptual anchors represent the principles on which OB knowledge is developed and refined.[93]

THE SYSTEMATIC RESEARCH ANCHOR

A key feature of OB knowledge is that it should be based on systematic research, which typically involves forming research questions, systematically collecting data, and testing hypotheses against those data.[94] Appendix A at the end of this book provides a brief overview of these research methods. Systematic research investigation produces **evidence-based management,** which involves making decisions and taking actions based on this research evidence. It makes perfect sense, doesn't it, that management practice should be founded on the best available systematic knowledge? Yet many of us who study organizations using systematic methods are amazed at how often corporate leaders embrace fads, consulting models, and their own pet beliefs without bothering to find out if they actually work![95]

There are many reasons people have difficulty applying evidence-based management. Leaders and other decision makers are bombarded with so many ideas from newspapers,

EXHIBIT 1.5

Anchors of Organizational Behavior Knowledge

Systematic research anchor	OB should study organizations using systematic research methods
Multidisciplinary anchor	OB should import knowledge from other disciplines, not just create its own knowledge
Contingency anchor	OB theory should recognize that the effects of actions often vary with the situation
Multiple levels of analysis anchor	OB events should be understood from three levels of analysis: individual, team, and organization

Debating Point

IS THERE ENOUGH EVIDENCE TO SUPPORT EVIDENCE-BASED MANAGEMENT?

One of the core anchors of organizational behavior is that knowledge must be built on a solid foundation of scientifically based research. This evidence-based management (EBM) approach particularly embraces scientific methods—relevant measures, appropriate sampling, systematic experimental design, and the like—because they produce more valid theories to guide management decisions. Scholars also advise that managers need to become more aware of these well-studied cause-and-effect principles, be sensitive to the conditions when applying these EBM principles, and use diagnostic tools (e.g., surveys, checklists) to guide their application to the workplace. Invariably, supporters of the evidence-based management movement contrast this systematic approach with reliance on management fads, hyped consulting, and untested personal mental models.

It seems obvious that we should rely on good evidence rather than bad evidence (or no evidence at all) to make sound decisions in the workplace. Yet, there is another side to this debate.[96] The question isn't whether good evidence is valuable; it is about the meaning of "good evidence." One concern is that scholars might be advocating an interpretation of good evidence that is far too narrow. They typically limit evidence to empirical research and consider qualitative information "anecdotal." Albert Einstein tried to avoid this questionable view by keeping the following message framed on his wall: "Not everything that can be counted counts, and not everything that counts can be counted."

Another concern is that managers seldom view organizational research as sufficiently relevant to the issues they face.[97] This bias partly occurs because scholarly journal reviewers usually accept only studies with uncontaminated, quantifiable measures in environments that control for other factors. But managers do not operate in these pristine conditions. Their world is much more complex, with vague estimates of key variables. One indicator of this research–practice gap is that managers typically require knowledge of specific interventions, yet only about 2 percent of organizational studies conduct real-world interventions.[98] Most published studies analyze data from self-reported questionnaires.

A third critique of the EBM movement is that the systematic elements of organizational research studies (e.g., sample size, measurement reliability, advanced data analysis methods) sometimes mask other potentially serious faults. Cross-cultural studies, for instance, often use college student samples to represent an entire culture. Lab studies with students assume they replicate workplace conditions without recognizing that the sample (students versus employees), setting (lab versus workplace), and activity studied are considerably different. Indeed, some meta-analyses report substantially different results from studies using students versus employees. Finally, even if the published research is valid, it is usually biased because research with nonsignificant results is much less likely to be published.

---

books, consultant reports, and other sources that it is a challenge to figure out which ones are based on good evidence. Another problem is that good OB research is necessarily generic; it is rarely described in the context of a specific problem in a specific organization. Managers therefore have the difficult task of figuring out which theories are relevant to their unique situation.

A third reason organizational leaders accept fads and other knowledge that lacks sufficient evidence is that consultants and popular book writers are rewarded for marketing their concepts and theories, not for testing to see if they actually work. Indeed, some management concepts have become popular—they are even found in some OB textbooks!—because of heavy marketing, not because of any evidence that they are valid. Finally, as we will learn in Chapter 3, people form perceptions and beliefs quickly and tend to ignore evidence that their beliefs are inaccurate. To counter these opposing forces, OB experts have proposed a few simple suggestions to create a more evidence-based organization (see Exhibit 1.6).

THE MULTIDISCIPLINARY ANCHOR

Organizational behavior is anchored around the idea that the field should welcome theories and knowledge in other disciplines, not just from its own isolated research base. For instance, psychological research has aided our understanding of individual and interpersonal behavior. Sociologists have contributed to our knowledge of team dynamics, organizational

EXHIBIT 1.6

Creating an Evidence-Based Management Organization

1. Stop treating old ideas as if they were brand new.
2. Be suspicious of "breakthrough" ideas and studies.
3. Celebrate and develop collective brilliance.
4. Emphasize drawbacks as well as virtues.
5. Use success (and failure) stories to illustrate sound practices, but not in place of a valid research method.
6. Adopt a neutral stance toward ideologies and theories.

Source: J. Pfeffer and R. I. Sutton, "Evidence-Based Management," *Harvard Business Review* 84, no. 1 (2006), pp. 62–74.

socialization, organizational power, and other aspects of the social system. OB knowledge has also benefited from knowledge in emerging fields such as communications, marketing, and information systems. Borrowing from other disciplines is inevitable. Organizations have central roles in society, so they are the subject of many social sciences. Furthermore, organizations consist of people who interact with one another, so there is an inherent intersection between OB and most disciplines that study human beings.

Borrowing theories from other disciplines has helped the field of OB nurture a diversity of knowledge and perspectives about organizations, but there are a few concerns.[99] One issue is whether OB suffers from a "trade deficit"—importing far more knowledge from other disciplines than it exports to other disciplines. By relying on theories developed in other fields, OB knowledge necessarily lags rather than leads in knowledge production. In contrast, OB-bred theories allow researchers to concentrate on the quality and usefulness of the theory.

Heavy reliance on theories borrowed from other disciplines may also leave OB vulnerable to a lack of common identity. The field could potentially become a place for researchers who are raised in and mainly identify with the other disciplines (psychology, sociology, and so on) rather than with organizational behavior. The lack of identification as an "OB scholar" might further challenge the field's ability to develop its own theory and weaken its focus on practical relevance.

THE CONTINGENCY ANCHOR

People and their work environments are complex, and the field of organizational behavior recognizes this by stating that a particular action may have different consequences in different situations. In other words, no single solution is best all of the time.[100] Of course, it would be so much simpler if we could rely on "one best way" theories, in which a particular concept or practice has the same results in every situation. OB experts do search for simpler theories, but they also remain skeptical about surefire recommendations; an exception is usually somewhere around the corner. Thus, when faced with a particular problem or opportunity, we need to understand and diagnose the situation and select the strategy most appropriate *under those conditions*.[101]

THE MULTIPLE LEVELS OF ANALYSIS ANCHOR

This textbook divides organizational behavior topics into three levels of analysis: individual, team (including interpersonal), and organization. The individual level includes the characteristics and behaviors of employees as well as the thought processes that are attributed to them, such as motivation, perceptions, personalities, attitudes, and values. The team level of analysis looks at the way people interact. This includes team dynamics, team decisions, communication, influence, social networks, conflict, and leadership. At the organizational level, we focus on how people structure their working relationships and on how organizations interact with their environments.

Although an OB topic is typically pegged into one level of analysis, it usually relates to multiple levels.[102] For instance, communication is located in this book as a team (interpersonal) process, but we also recognize that it includes individual and organizational processes. Therefore, you should try to think about each OB topic at the individual, team, and organizational levels, not just at one of these levels.

The Journey Begins

This chapter gives you some background about the field of organizational behavior. But it's only the beginning of our journey. Throughout this book, we will challenge you to learn new ways of thinking about how people work in and around organizations. We begin this process in Chapter 2 by presenting a basic model of individual behavior; then we introduce over the next few chapters various stable and mercurial characteristics of individuals that relate to elements of the individual behavior model. Next, this book moves to the team level of analysis. We examine a model of team effectiveness and specific features of high-performance teams. We also look at team decision making communication, power and influence, conflict, and leadership. Finally, we shift our focus to the organizational level of analysis, where the topics of organizational structure, organizational culture, and organizational change are examined in detail.

[chapter summary]

LO1 Define *organizational behavior* and *organizations*, and discuss the importance of this field of inquiry.

Organizational behavior is the study of what people think, feel, and do in and around organizations. Organizations are groups of people who work interdependently toward some purpose. OB theories help people (a) make sense of the workplace, (b) question and rebuild their personal mental models, and (c) get things done in organizations. OB knowledge is for everyone, not just managers. OB knowledge is just as important for the organization's financial health.

LO2 Compare and contrast the four current perspectives of organizational effectiveness as well as the early goal attainment perspective.

The goal attainment perspective, which states that organizations are effective if they achieve their stated objectives, is no longer accepted because (a) the goals set may be too easy, (b) goals may be too abstract to determine their accomplishment, and (c) achievement of some goals may threaten the company's survival.

The open systems perspective views organizations as complex organisms that "live" within an external environment. They depend on the external environment for resources and then use organizational subsystems to transform those resources into outputs, which are returned to the environment. Organizations receive feedback from the external environment to maintain a good "fit" with that environment. Fit occurs by adapting to the environment, managing the environment, or moving to another environment.

According to the organizational learning perspective, organizational effectiveness depends on the organization's capacity to acquire, share, use, and store valuable knowledge.

The ability to acquire and use knowledge depends on the firm's absorptive capacity. Intellectual capital consists of human capital, structural capital, and relationship capital. Knowledge is retained in the organizational memory; companies also selectively unlearn.

The high-performance work practices (HPWP) perspective identifies a bundle of systems and structures to leverage workforce potential. The most widely identified HPWP are employee involvement, job autonomy, developing employee competencies, and performance-skill-based rewards. HPWP improve organizational effectiveness by building human capital, increasing adaptability, and strengthening employee motivation and attitudes.

The stakeholder perspective states that leaders manage the interests of diverse stakeholders by relying on their personal and organizational values for guidance. Ethics and corporate social responsibility (CSR) are natural extensions of values-based organizations because they rely on values to guide the most appropriate decisions involving stakeholders. CSR consists of organizational activities intended to benefit society and the environment beyond the firm's immediate financial interests or legal obligations.

LO3 Debate the organizational opportunities and challenges of globalization, workforce diversity, and emerging employment relationships.

Globalization, which refers to various forms of connectivity with people in other parts of the world, has several economic and social benefits, but it may also be responsible for work intensification and reduced job security and work–life balance. Workforce diversity is apparent at both the surface level (observable demographic and other overt differences in people) and the deep level (differences in personalities, beliefs, values, and attitudes). There is some evidence of deep-level diversity across generational cohorts. Diversity may offer a competitive advantage by improving decision making and team performance on complex tasks, yet it also brings numerous challenges such as team "fault lines," slower team performance, and interpersonal conflict. One emerging employment relationship trend is the call for more work–life balance (minimizing conflict between work and nonwork demands). Another employment trend is virtual work, particularly working from home. Working from home potentially increases employee productivity and reduces employee stress, but it may also lead to social isolation, reduced promotion opportunities, and tension in family relations.

LO4 Discuss the anchors on which organizational behavior knowledge is based.

The multidisciplinary anchor states that the field should develop from knowledge in other disciplines (e.g., psychology, sociology, economics), not just from its own isolated research base. The systematic research anchor states that OB knowledge should be based on systematic research, which is consistent with evidence-based management. The contingency anchor states that OB theories generally need to consider that there will be different consequences in different situations. The multiple levels of analysis anchor states that OB topics may be viewed from the individual, team, and organization levels of analysis.

[key terms]

absorptive capacity, p. 13
corporate social responsibility (CSR), p. 17
deep-level diversity, p. 21
ethics, p. 17
evidence-based management, p. 22
globalization, p. 19
high-performance work practices (HPWP), p. 13

human capital, p. 11
intellectual capital, p. 11
open systems, p. 9
organizational behavior (OB), p. 5
organizational effectiveness, p. 6
organizational efficiency, p. 9
organizational learning, p. 10
organizations, p. 5

relationship capital, p. 11
stakeholders, p. 15
structural capital, p. 11
surface-level diversity, p. 19
values, p. 15
virtual work, p. 21
work–life balance, p. 21

[critical thinking questions]

1. A friend suggests that organizational behavior courses are useful only to people who will enter management careers. Discuss the accuracy of your friend's statement.

2. Name some of the practices that Brasilata does differently that seem innovative to you. How does this square with how you think OK works? Is Brasilata different from Apple or Google in its innovative strategies?

3. A number of years ago, employees in a city water distribution department were put into teams and encouraged to find ways to improve efficiency. The teams boldly crossed departmental boundaries and areas of management discretion in search of problems. Employees working in other parts of the city began to complain about these intrusions. Furthermore, when some team ideas were implemented, managers discovered that a dollar saved in the water distribution unit may have cost the organization two dollars in higher costs elsewhere. Use the open systems perspective to explain what happened here.

4. After hearing a seminar on organizational learning, a mining company executive argues that this perspective ignores the fact that mining companies cannot rely on knowledge alone to stay in business. They also need physical capital (such as extracting and ore-processing equipment) and land (where the minerals are located). In fact, these two may be more important than what employees carry around in their heads. Evaluate the mining executive's comments.

5. It is said that the CEO and other corporate leaders are keepers of the organization's memory. Please discuss this.

6. A common refrain among executives is "People are our most important asset." Relate this statement to any two of the four perspectives of organizational effectiveness presented in this chapter. Does this statement apply better to some perspectives than to others? Why or why not?

7. Corporate social responsibility is one of the hottest issues in corporate boardrooms these days, partly because it is becoming increasingly important to employees and other stakeholders. In your opinion, why have stakeholders given CSR more attention recently? Does abiding by CSR standards potentially cause companies to have conflicting objectives with some stakeholders in some situations?

8. Look through the list of chapters in this textbook, and discuss how globalization could influence each organizational behavior topic.

9. "Organizational theories should follow the contingency approach." Comment on the accuracy of this statement.

10. What does *evidence-based management* mean? Describe situations you have heard about in which companies have practiced evidence-based management, as well as situations in which companies have relied on fads that lacked sufficient evidence of their worth.

CASE STUDY 1.1 HOSPITALS ARE DRIVING TOWARD A LEANER ORGANIZATION

Steven L. McShane, University of Western Australia

How is serving surgical patients similar to manufacturing a car? The answer is clear to staff at Sunderland Royal Hospital. The health facility in northern England borrowed several ideas from the nearby Nissan factory, one of the most efficient car plants in Europe, to improve its day surgery unit. "We took [Sunderland hospital staff] on a tour of our plant, showing them a variety of lean processes in action, and let them decide which ones could be applied back at the hospital," says a training manager at Nissan's factory in Sunderland.

Lean management involves seeking ways to reduce and remove waste from work processes. Employees are typically involved, where they map out the work process and identify ways to reduce steps, time, spaces, and other resources without threatening the work objectives. Sunderland's day surgery staff were actively involved in applying lean management to their work unit. After attending Nissan's two-day workshop, they mapped out the work processes, questioned assumptions about the value or relevance of some activities, and discovered ways to reduce the lengthy patient wait times (which were up to three hours). There was some initial resistance and skepticism, but the hospital's day surgery staff soon realized significant improvements in efficiency and service quality.

"By working with Nissan's staff, we have streamlined the patient pathway from 29 to 11 discrete stages," says Anne Fleming, who oversees Sunderland's 32-bed day case unit and its 54 staff members. "We have done this by reducing duplication, halving the time that patients spend in the unit to three hours by giving them individual appointment times, and introducing the just-in-time approach to the patient pathway." Fleming also reports that Sunderland's operating theaters are now much more efficient.

Sunderland Royal Hospital is one of many health care centers around the world that are improving efficiency through lean thinking. After receiving training in Japan on lean practices, several teams of doctors, nurses, and other staff from Virginia Mason Medical Center in Seattle, Washington, redesigned their work flows to eliminate 34 miles of unnecessary walking each day. Park Nicollet Health Services in Minneapolis, Minnesota, improved efficiency at its ambulatory clinic to such an extent that the unit does not require a patient waiting area. One Park Nicollet team worked with orthopedic surgeons to reduce by 60 percent the variety of instruments and supplies they ordered for hip and knee surgeries.

Flinders Medical Center also adopted lean management practices after the South Australian medical facility experienced severe congestion of patients in its emergency department. After mapping out the steps in patients' journey through the department, the staff realized that the process was inefficient and stressful for everyone, particularly as lower-priority patients got "bumped" down the queue when more serious cases arrived. Now, incoming emergency patients are immediately streamed to one of two emergency teams: those who will be treated and sent home, and those who will be treated and admitted. This change immediately improved efficiency and the quality of patient care.

Bolton Hospitals NHS Trust in the United Kingdom is yet another illustration of how lean management practices can improve organizational efficiency and effectiveness. By involving employees in an analysis of procedures, the hospital reduced average wait times for patients with fractured hips by 38 percent (from 2.4 to 1.7 days), which also resulted in a lower mortality rate for these patients. By smoothing out the inflow of work orders and rearranging the work process, Bolton's pathology department cut the time to process samples from 24–30 hours to just 2–3 hours and reduced the space used by 50 percent.

"We know that our case for extra funding will fall on deaf ears unless we cut out waste in the system," explains Dr. Gill Morgan, chief executive of the UK NHS Confederation. "Lean works because it is based on doctors, nurses, and other staff leading the process and telling us what adds value and what doesn't. They are the ones who know."[103]

Discussion Questions

1. What perspective(s) of organizational effectiveness best describe(s) the application of lean management practices? Describe how specific elements of that perspective relate to the interventions described in this case study.

2. Does lean management ignore some perspectives of organizational effectiveness? If so, what are the unintended consequences of these practices that might undermine, rather than improve, an organization's effectiveness?

3. In what situations, if any, would it be difficult or risky to apply lean management practices? What conditions make these practices challenging in these situations?

CASE STUDY 1.2 PIXAR MAGIC

Steven L. McShane, University of Western Australia

One of Robert Iger's first tasks as Walt Disney Co.'s new CEO was to acquire Pixar Animation Studios and put its leaders, Ed Catmull and John Lassiter, in charge of Disney's own animation unit, Walt Disney Animation Studios. The studio that brought us Mickey Mouse and *The Lion King* had become moribund over the past decade, eclipsed by

Pixar's award-winning productions. Disney already had lucrative distribution rights to Pixar's first five films, including any sequels, but Iger wanted something much more valuable: He wanted the practices that have made Pixar a powerhouse filmmaker, from *Toy Story* to *Up*.

Pixar's success is founded on the notion that companies depend on the quality of their employees and how well they collaborate with one another. "From the very beginning, we recognized we had to get the best people, technically, from the computer science world, and from the artistic filmmaking animation world, and get them working together," explains John Lasseter, who is now chief creative officer of both Pixar and Disney Animation Studios. "That, right there, is probably the secret to Pixar."

Pixar enables people to work together in several ways. First, the company relies on long-term employment relationships rather than short-term project contracts. These long-term relationships improve team development and social networks. "The problem with the Hollywood model is that it's generally the day you wrap production that you realize you've finally figured out how to work together," says Randy Nelson, head of Pixar University. "We've made the leap from an idea-centered business to a people-centered business." Second, Pixar's campus in Emeryville, California, enables employees to work well together. The buildings were designed to cluster people into teams yet also encourage chance encounters with people from other projects. "When people run into each other and make eye contact, innovative things happen," says Pixar director Brad Bird.

Third, Pixar's egalitarian, no-nonsense, perfectionist culture is another reason the animation studio's staff work effectively. The company gives power to its production teams rather than to senior executives, but these teams are also ruthless at writing and rendering scenes several times until they look right. All employees, from entry-level newcomer to the CEO, are encouraged to be creative and offer candid feedback about work in progress. Production teams have regular "sweatbox" sessions to discuss problems openly. Even the most successful films undergo a "postmortem" to discover how they could have been improved. "Our job is to address problems even when we're successful," explains Pixar/Disney Animation president Ed Catmull, whose leadership has been identified as the foundation of Pixar's unique culture.[104]

Discussion Questions

1. Explain Pixar's effectiveness as an organization using any two perspectives of organizational effectiveness.

2. Scanning through the chapter titles of this book, which topics seem to dominate Pixar's organizational practices? Why would these practices be emphasized in this type of organization?

WEB EXERCISE 1.3 DIAGNOSING ORGANIZATIONAL STAKEHOLDERS

PURPOSE This exercise is designed to help you understand how stakeholders influence organizations as part of the open systems anchor.

MATERIALS Select a company and, prior to class, retrieve and analyze publicly available information over the past year or two about that company. This information may include annual reports, which are usually found on the websites of publicly traded companies. Where possible, you should also scan full-text newspaper and magazine databases for articles published over the previous year about the company.

INSTRUCTIONS The instructor may have you work alone or in groups for this activity. Students will select a company and investigate the relevance and influence of various stakeholder groups on the organization. Stakeholders can be identified from annual reports, newspaper articles, website statements, and other available sources. Stakeholders should be rank-ordered in terms of their perceived importance to the organization.

Students should be prepared to present or discuss their rank ordering of the organization's stakeholders, including evidence for this ordering.

Discussion Questions

1. What are the main reasons certain stakeholders are more important than others for this organization?

2. On the basis of your knowledge of the organization's environmental situation, is this rank order of stakeholders in the organization's best interest, or should other specific stakeholders be given higher priority?

3. What societal groups, if any, are not mentioned as stakeholders by the organization? Does this lack of reference to these unmentioned groups make sense?

SELF-ASSESSMENT 1.4 IT ALL MAKES SENSE?

PURPOSE This exercise is designed to help you comprehend how organizational behavior knowledge can help you understand life in organizations.

INSTRUCTIONS (*Note:* Your instructor might conduct this activity as a self-assessment or as a team activity.) Read each of the statements below and circle whether each statement is true or false, in your opinion. The class will consider the answers to each question and discuss the implications for studying organizational behavior.

Due to the nature of this activity, the instructor will provide the answers to these questions. There is no scoring key in Appendix B.

1. True False A happy worker is a productive worker.
2. True False A decision maker's effectiveness increases with the number of choices or alternatives available to her or him.
3. True False Organizations are more effective when they minimize conflict among employees.
4. True False Employees have more power with many close friends than with many acquaintances.

5. True False Companies are more successful when they have strong corporate cultures.
6. True False Employees perform better without stress.
7. True False The best way to change people and organizations is by pinpointing the source of their current problems.
8. True False Female leaders involve employees in decisions to a greater degree than do male leaders.
9. True False The best decisions are made without emotion.
10. True False If employees feel they are paid unfairly, nothing other than changing their pay will reduce their feelings of injustice.

 After reading this chapter go to www.mhhe.com/mcshane6e for more in-depth information and interactivities that correspond to the chapter.

Individual Behavior, Personality, and Values

learning objectives

After studying Chapter 2, you should be able to:

LO1 Describe the four factors that directly influence individual behavior and performance.

LO2 Summarize the five types of individual behavior in organizations.

LO3 Describe personality, the "Big Five" personality dimensions, and four MBTI types, and explain how personality relates to individual behavior in organizations.

LO4 Summarize Schwartz's model of individual values and discuss the conditions under which values influence behavior.

LO5 Describe three ethical principles and discuss four factors that influence ethical behavior.

LO6 Review five values commonly studied across cultures and discuss cultural diversity within the United States.

literally gives them the red carpet treatment. After 20 years of employment, and every 5 years after that, employees at Ohio's largest health care provider are chauffeured to a local shopping mall for a company-paid shopping spree and cheered on by coworkers as they walk along a red carpet at a conference center. Some employees postpone their retirement just to participate in this special event. Little wonder that OhioHealth is one of the best places to work in America and has a turnover rate far below the industry average.

"We want engaged, happy, well-compensated workers," says OhioHealth CEO David Blom. "This reward and recognition [the long-service shopping spree] stirs the emotions and passions of people."

Along with retaining staff, OhioHealth is equally successful at attracting applicants in nursing and other difficult-to-fill occupations. Several OhioHealth hospitals are Magnet facilities accredited by the American Nursing Association. Magnet hospitals have collegial and nonhierarchical work environments that focus on quality care and give nurses autonomy, respect, and representation in decisions. "In nursing we have shared governance and many of our facilities are designated as Magnet facilities," explains Paul Patton, OhioHealth's Senior VP of Human Resources. "We use the strong communication process developed in that atmosphere in our decision making."

OhioHealth keeps absenteeism low through an incentive program that motivates employees to keep fit and eat well. It also strengthens employee performance through high-quality training programs, structured goal setting, and plenty of feedback. One initiative, called GOFAR ("gotta own functional areas of responsibility"), encourages employees "to take initiative, proactively make reports, relentlessly pursue results, overcome obstacles and meet deadlines," says Pam Carlisle, OhioHealth's corporate director of patient access services. Jane Berkebile, another OhioHealth executive, adds: "The strongest and most consistent message we receive from our staff is that they know exactly what they're supposed to do, what their objectives are, and their level of performance at any given time."[1]

OhioHealth coworkers cheer on Jody Porter and other employees with 20 or more years of service, one of many ways that Ohio's largest health care provider supports employee performance and well-being.

OhioHealth has weathered the economic recession and thrived when economic growth left other health care providers short-staffed. It has done so by being an employer of choice for job applicants, minimizing absenteeism and turnover, encouraging extra-role behavior, and supporting high performance. This chapter examines these forms of individual behavior as well as the factors that influence those behaviors.

The chapter begins with the MARS model, which outlines the four direct drivers of individual behavior and results. It then reviews the five types of individual behavior that represent the individual-level dependent variables found in most organizational behavior research. The second half of this chapter looks closely at two of the most stable characteristics of individuals: personality and values. The section on personality specifically looks at personality development, personality traits, and how personality relates to behavior in organizational settings. The final section of this chapter turns our attention to values, including the various types of personal values, how values relate to individual behavior, the dynamics of values congruence, ethical values and practices, and cross-cultural values.

MARS Model of Individual Behavior and Performance

LO1

For most of the past century, experts have investigated the direct predictors of individual behavior and performance.[2] One of the earliest formulas was *performance = person × situation,* where *person* includes individual characteristics, and *situation* represents external influences on the individual's behavior. Another frequently mentioned formula is *performance = ability × motivation.*[3] Sometimes known as the "skill-and-will" model, this formula elaborates two specific characteristics within the person that influence individual performance. Ability, motivation, and situation are by far the most commonly mentioned direct predictors of individual behavior and performance, but in the 1960s researchers identified a fourth key factor: role perceptions (the individual's expected role obligations).[4]

Exhibit 2.1 illustrates these four variables—motivation, ability, role perceptions, and situational factors—which are represented by the acronym *MARS.*[5] All four factors are critical influences on an individual's voluntary behavior and performance; if any one of them is low in a given situation, the employee would perform the task poorly. For example,

EXHIBIT 2.1   MARS Model of Individual Behavior and Results

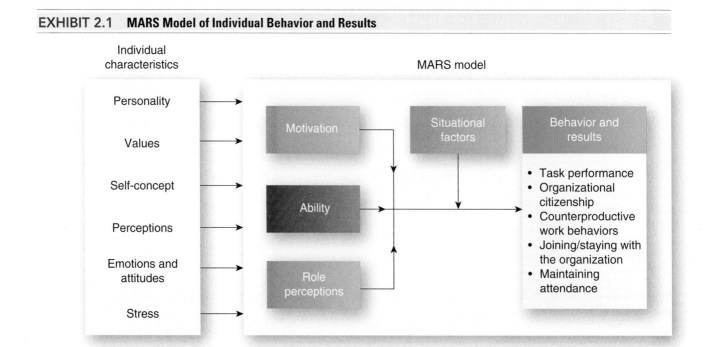

motivated salespeople with clear role perceptions and sufficient resources (situational factors) will not perform their jobs as well if they lack sales skills and related knowledge (ability). Motivation, ability, and role perceptions are clustered together in the model because they are located within the person. Situational factors are external to the individual but still affect his or her behavior and performance.[6] Let's look at each of these four factors in more detail.

EMPLOYEE MOTIVATION

Motivation represents the forces within a person that affect his or her direction, intensity, and persistence of voluntary behavior.[8] *Direction* refers to the path along which people engage their effort. People have choices about where they put their effort; they have a sense of what they are trying to achieve and at what level of quality, quantity, and so forth. In other words, motivation is goal-directed, not random. People are motivated to arrive at work on time, finish a project a few hours early, or aim for many other targets. The second element of motivation, called *intensity,* is the amount of effort allocated to the goal. Intensity is all about how much people push themselves to complete a task. For example, two employees might be motivated to finish their project a few hours early (direction), but only one of them puts forth enough effort (intensity) to achieve this goal.

Finally, motivation involves varying levels of *persistence,* that is, continuing the effort for a certain amount of time. Employees sustain their effort until they reach their goal or give up beforehand. To help remember these three elements of motivation, consider the metaphor of driving a car in which the thrust of the engine is your effort. Direction refers to where you steer the car, intensity is how much you put your foot down on the gas pedal, and persistence is for how long you drive toward that destination. Remember that motivation is a force that exists within individuals; it is not their actual behavior. Thus, direction, intensity, and persistence are cognitive (thoughts) and emotional conditions that directly cause us to move.

ABILITY

Employee abilities also make a difference in behavior and task performance. **Ability** includes both the natural aptitudes and the learned capabilities required to successfully complete a task. *Aptitudes* are the natural talents that help employees learn specific tasks more quickly and perform them better. There are many physical and mental aptitudes, and our ability to acquire skills is affected by these aptitudes. For example, finger dexterity is an aptitude by which individuals learn more quickly and potentially achieve higher performance at picking up and handling small objects with their fingers. Employees with high finger dexterity are not necessarily better than others at first; rather, their learning tends to be faster and performance potential tends to be higher. *Learned capabilities* are the skills and knowledge that you currently possess. These capabilities include the physical and mental skills and knowledge you have acquired. Learned capabilities tend to wane over time when not in use.

Aptitudes and learned capabilities are closely related to *competencies,* which has become a frequently used term in business. **Competencies** are characteristics of a person that result in superior performance.[7] These characteristics include knowledge, skills, aptitudes, and behaviors. Some experts extend the meaning of competencies to include personality and values, while others suggest that competencies are action-oriented results of these characteristics, such as serving customers, coping with heavy workloads, and providing creative ideas. Some studies have

connect

To assist your learning and test your knowledge about the MARS model and its four elements, go to **www.mcgrawhillconnect.com,** which has activities and test questions on this topic.

motivation
The forces within a person that affect his or her direction, intensity, and persistence of voluntary behavior.

ability
The natural aptitudes and learned capabilities required to successfully complete a task.

competencies
Skills, knowledge, aptitudes, and other personal characteristics that lead to superior performance.

attempted to identify a list of core competencies for performance in all jobs. For example, one stream of research has identified competencies that are most important in all jobs, such as leading/deciding, supporting/cooperating, creating/conceptualizing, adapting/coping, and four others.[9]

The challenge is to match a person's competencies with the job's competency requirements. A good person–job match produces higher performance; it also tends to increase the employee's well-being. One way to match a person's competencies with the job's task requirements is to select applicants who already demonstrate the required competencies. For example, companies ask applicants to perform sample work, provide references to check their past performance, and complete various selection tests. A second strategy is to provide training, which has a strong influence on individual performance and organizational effectiveness.[10] The third person–job matching strategy is to redesign the job so that employees are given only tasks that reflect their current learned capabilities. For example, a complex task might be simplified—with some aspects of the work transferred to others—so that a new employee performs only those tasks that he or she is currently able to perform. As the employee becomes more competent at these tasks, other tasks are added back into the job.

ROLE PERCEPTIONS

Motivation and ability are important influences on individual behavior and performance, but employees also require accurate **role perceptions** to perform their jobs well. Role perceptions refer to how clearly people understand the job duties (roles) assigned to them or expected of them. For instance, OhioHealth employees perform their jobs well partly because "they know exactly what they're supposed to do." These perceptions are critical because they guide the employee's direction of effort and improve coordination with coworkers, suppliers, and other stakeholders. Employees with clearer role perceptions also tend to have higher motivation.

Unfortunately, many employees do not have clear role perceptions. One survey reported that although 76 percent of employees understand the organization's business goals, only 39 percent said they understood how to achieve those goals in their own job. Similarly, when a recent global survey asked what would most improve their performance, employees in most countries identified "greater clarity about what the organization needs from me" as the first or second most important factor.[12]

Black Friday—the day after Thanksgiving—is the busiest shopping day of the year, so Best Buy holds special rehearsals to ensure that every employee has crystal-clear role perceptions. This photo shows customer assistance supervisor Aaron Sanford orchestrating a Black Friday practice run at a Best Buy store in Denver. These events help employees to understand their specific duties and responsibilities, the priority of those tasks, and the correct way to complete them.[11]

Role clarity exists in three forms. First, employees have clear role perceptions when they understand the specific tasks assigned to them, that is, when they know the specific duties or consequences for which they are accountable. This may seem obvious, but employees are occasionally evaluated on job duties they were never told were within their zone of responsibility. For example, the Metro transit system in Washington, DC, experienced a serious train derailment a few years ago because the track department did not lubricate the tracks. An investigation revealed that the department had lubricated tracks several years earlier, but this work activity stopped after the previous department managers had transferred or retired. The incoming managers did not know about the department's track lubrication duties, so they didn't inform employees that lubricating tracks was part of their job.[13]

The second form of role clarity refers to how well employees understand the *priority* of their various tasks and performance expectations. This is illustrated in the classic dilemma of prioritizing quantity versus quality, such as how many customers to serve in an hour (quantity) versus how well the employee should serve each customer (quality). It also refers to properly allocating time and resources to various tasks, such as how much time a manager should spend coaching employees each week versus spending time with suppliers and clients. The third form of role clarity involves understanding the *preferred behaviors* or procedures for accomplishing the assigned tasks. This refers to situations in which employees have the knowledge and skills to perform a particular task in more than one way. Employees with clear role perceptions know which of these methods is preferred or required by the organization.

SITUATIONAL FACTORS

Employees' behavior and performance also depend on the situation.[14] The situation mainly refers to conditions beyond the employee's immediate control that constrain or facilitate behavior and performance.[15] For example, employees who are motivated, are skilled, and know their role obligations will nevertheless perform poorly if they lack time, budget, physical work facilities, and other situational conditions. Some situational constraints—such as consumer preferences and economic conditions—originate from the external environment and, consequently, are beyond the employee's and organization's control.

Along with situational constraints, situational factors also refer to the clarity and consistency of cues provided by the environment to employees regarding their role obligations and opportunities.[16] The importance of situational clarity and consistency is illustrated in workplace accidents. Let's say that you are motivated, are able, and have a clear role obligation to act safely in your job. Even so, you are more likely to have an accident if the work setting does not clearly and consistently communicate a nearby electrical hazard or other safety risk. Your unsafe behavior and accident likelihood are affected by the situation, namely, the lack of signs and other indicators of the safety risk or inconsistent placement of these warnings across the workplace.

Types of Individual Behavior

The four elements of the MARS model—motivation, ability, role perceptions, and situational factors—affect all voluntary workplace behaviors and their performance outcomes. There are many varieties of individual behavior, but most can be organized into the five categories described over the next few pages: task performance, organizational citizenship, counterproductive work behaviors, joining and staying with the organization, and maintaining work attendance (Exhibit 2.2).

TASK PERFORMANCE

Task performance refers to goal-directed behaviors under the individual's control that support organizational objectives.[17] Task performance behaviors transform raw materials

role perceptions
The extent to which a person accurately understands the job duties (roles) assigned to or expected of him or her.

EXHIBIT 2.2

Five Types of Individual Behavior in the Workplace

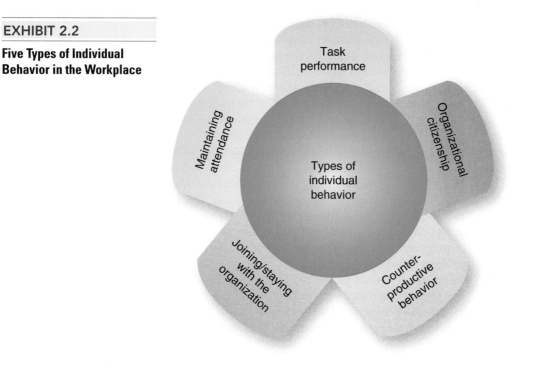

into goods and services or support and maintain these technical activities. For example, foreign exchange traders at BGC Partners, Inc., make decisions and perform various tasks to buy and sell currencies. Most jobs consist of several tasks. For instance, foreign exchange traders at BGC must be able to quickly identify profitable trades, analyze economic data, keep track of and complete account information, assist in training new staff, and use specialized computer software and equipment without error. More generally, tasks might involve working with data, people, or things; working alone or with other people; and degrees of influencing others.[18]

ORGANIZATIONAL CITIZENSHIP

Few companies would survive if employees performed only their formal job duties. They also need to engage in **organizational citizenship behaviors (OCBs)**—various forms of cooperation and helpfulness to others that support the organization's social and psychological context.[19] In other words, companies excel when employees go the "extra mile" beyond the required job duties. Organizational citizenship behaviors take many forms. Some are directed toward individuals, such as assisting coworkers with their work problems, adjusting work schedules to accommodate coworkers, showing genuine courtesy toward coworkers, and sharing work resources (supplies, technology, staff) with coworkers. Other OCBs represent cooperation and helpfulness toward the organization, such as supporting the company's public image, taking discretionary action to help the organization avoid potential problems, offering ideas beyond those required for the job, attending voluntary functions that support the organization, and keeping up with new developments in the organization.[20]

COUNTERPRODUCTIVE WORK BEHAVIORS

Organizational behavior is interested in all workplace behaviors, including dysfunctional activities collectively known as **counterproductive work behaviors (CWBs)**. These voluntary behaviors have the potential to directly or indirectly harm the organization.[22] Some of the many types of CWBs include harassing coworkers, creating unnecessary conflict, deviating from preferred work methods (e.g., shortcuts that risk work quality), being untruthful,

An important shipment of materials had arrived at customs for Procter & Gamble (P&G) India, but the government shut down all its offices (including customs) due to heavy rains. Undeterred by the weather, a P&G plant engineer arranged to transport a customs official from his home to the customs office and back so the clearance paperwork could be completed. The engineer then arranged for the materials to be delivered to the plant the same day. The P&G India engineer engaged in organizational citizenship behaviors (and encouraged similar behaviors by the customs officer), which kept the production lines running.[21]

stealing, sabotaging work, avoiding work obligations (tardiness), and wasting resources. And CWBs are not minor concerns; research suggests that they can substantially undermine the organization's effectiveness.

JOINING AND STAYING WITH THE ORGANIZATION

Task performance, organizational citizenship, and the lack of counterproductive work behaviors are obviously important, but if qualified people don't join and stay with the organization, none of these performance-related behaviors would occur. Consider the shortage of nurses. Although the recent recession temporarily eased matters, the long-term trend is for the number of nursing positions to far outstrip the number of nurses available. There are already many examples in the United States and other countries where beds had to be closed or hospital services deteriorated because of a lack of nursing staff.[23] OhioHealth has proactively reduced this risk. As the opening vignette to this chapter described, the health care provider has become an employer of choice by achieving the nursing association's "Magnet" designation and being rated as one of the best places to work in America.

Even when companies are able to hire qualified staff in the face of shortages, they need to ensure that these employees stay with the company. Companies with high turnover suffer because of the high cost of replacing people who leave. More important, as was mentioned in the previous chapter, much of an organization's intellectual capital is the knowledge carried around in employees' heads. When people leave, some of this vital knowledge is lost, often resulting in lower productivity, poorer customer service, and so forth. Some employers attract job applicants and minimize turnover by nurturing an enjoyable work environment. For example, the opening vignette described how OhioHealth celebrates employees with long service and provides a high-involvement environment where staff are regularly consulted about organizational issues.

organizational citizenship behaviors (OCBs)
Various forms of cooperation and helpfulness to others that support the organization's social and psychological context.

counterproductive work behaviors (CWBs)
Voluntary behaviors that have the potential to directly or indirectly harm the organization.

MAINTAINING WORK ATTENDANCE

Along with attracting and retaining employees, organizations need everyone to show up for work at scheduled times. American employees miss an average of five days of scheduled work each year, which is lower than in most other countries. For example, one study reported that more than 25 percent of primary and secondary school teachers in India, Uganda, and Indonesia are absent from work on any given work day. The report warned that this chronic level of absenteeism undermined the quality of children's education to such an extent that it threatened the economic development of those countries.[24]

Most employees blame the situation for their absenteeism, such as bad weather, a transit strike, or family demands (e.g., children or parents require care). However, some people show up for work under these conditions because of their strong motivation to attend work, whereas others take sick leave even when they are not genuinely unwell. Employees who experience job dissatisfaction or work-related stress are more likely to be absent or late for work because taking time off is a way of temporarily withdrawing from stressful or dissatisfying conditions. Absenteeism is also higher in organizations with generous sick leave because this benefit minimizes the financial loss of taking time away from work. Another factor in absenteeism is the person's values and personality.[25] Finally, studies report that absenteeism is higher in teams with strong absence norms, meaning that team members tolerate and even expect coworkers to take time off.[26]

Presenteeism   Along with attending work when expected, maintaining work attendance requires staying away from scheduled work when attendance would be dysfunctional for the individual and organization. In fact, OB experts warn that **presenteeism**—attending work when one's capacity to work is significantly diminished by illness, fatigue, personal problems, or other factors—may be more serious than being absent when capable of working.[27] Employees who attend work when they are unwell or unfit may worsen their own condition and increase the health risks for coworkers. These employees are also usually less productive and may reduce the productivity of coworkers.

Presenteeism is more common among employees with low job security (such as new and temporary staff), who lack sick leave pay or similar financial buffers, and whose absence would immediately affect many people (i.e., high centrality). Company or team norms about absenteeism also account for presenteeism. Personality also plays a role; some people possess traits that motivate them to show up for work when others would gladly recover at home. Personality is a widely cited predictor of most forms of individual behavior. It is also the most stable personal characteristic, so we introduce this topic next.

Personality in Organizations

LO3

While applying for several jobs in the publishing industry, Christina was surprised that three of the positions required applicants to complete a personality test. "One page is a list of characteristics—sentimental, adventurous, attractive, compelling, helpful, etc.—and you check off the ones that best describe what others expect of you," Christina recalls of one personality test. "The second page is the same list, but you check off the ones that you think truly describe you." Christina didn't hear back from the first company after completing its personality test, so for the second company she completed the personality test "according to a sales personality," because that job was in sales. When writing the personality test at the third firm, she answered questions the way she thought someone would who was "a good person, but honest" about what he or she thought. None of the applications resulted in a job offer, leaving Christina wondering what personality profile these companies were seeking and whether her strategy of guessing the best answer on these personality tests was a good idea.[28]

Personality is an important individual characteristic, which explains why several companies try to estimate the personality traits of job applicants and employees. Most of us also think about personality every day in our dealings with others. We use these traits (talkative, risk-oriented, thoughtful, etc.) to simplify our perception of each person and to predict their future behavior. **Personality** is the relatively enduring pattern of thoughts, emotions, and behaviors that characterize a person, along with the psychological processes behind those characteristics.[29] It is, in essence, the bundle of characteristics that make us similar to or different from other people. We estimate an individual's personality by what he or she says and does, and we infer the person's internal states—including thoughts and emotions—from these observable behaviors.

A basic premise of personality theory is that people have inherent characteristics or traits that can be identified by the consistency or stability of their behavior across time and situations.[30] For example, you probably have some friends who are more talkative than others. You might know some people who like to take risks and others who are risk averse. This behavioral tendency is a key feature of personality theory, because it attributes a person's behavior to something within that person—the individual's personality—rather than to purely environmental influences.

Of course, people do not act the same way in all situations; in fact, such consistency would be considered abnormal because it indicates a person's insensitivity to social norms, reward systems, and other external conditions.[31] People vary their behavior to suit the situation, even if the behavior is at odds with their personality. For example, talkative people remain relatively quiet in a library where "no talking" rules are explicit and strictly enforced. However, personality differences are still apparent in these situations, because talkative people tend to do more talking in libraries relative to how much other people talk in libraries.

People typically exhibit a wide range of behaviors, yet within that variety are discernible patterns that we refer to as *personality traits*. Traits are broad concepts that allow us to label and understand individual differences. Furthermore, traits predict an individual's behavior far into the future. For example, studies report that an individual's personality in childhood predicts various behaviors and outcomes in adulthood, including educational attainment, employment success, marital relationships, illegal activities, and health-risk behaviors.[32]

PERSONALITY DETERMINANTS: NATURE VERSUS NURTURE

What determines an individual's personality? Most experts now agree that personality is shaped by both nature and nurture, although the relative importance of each continues to be debated and studied. *Nature* refers to our genetic or hereditary origins—the genes that we inherit from our parents. Studies of identical twins, particularly those separated at birth, reveal that heredity has a very large effect on personality; up to 50 percent of variation in behavior and 30 percent of temperament preferences can be attributed to a person's genetic characteristics.[33] In other words, genetic code not only determines our eye color, skin tone, and physical shape; it also significantly affects our attitudes, decisions, and behavior.

Some similarities of twins raised apart are surreal. Consider Jim Springer and Jim Lewis, twins who were separated when only four weeks old and didn't meet each other until age 39. In spite of being raised in different families and communities in Ohio, the "Jim twins" held similar jobs, smoked the same type of cigarettes, drove the same make and color of car, spent their vacations on the same Florida beach, had the same woodworking hobby, gave their first sons almost identical names, and had been married twice. Both their first and second wives also had the same first names![34]

Although personality is heavily influenced by heredity, it is also affected by *nurture*—the person's socialization, life experiences, and other forms of interaction with the environment. Personality development and change occurs mainly until young adulthood; personality stabilizes by the time people reach 30 years of age, although some personality changes may continue to age 50.[35]

The main explanation for why personality becomes more stable over time is that we form a clearer and more rigid self-concept as we get older.[36] This increasing clarity

presenteeism
Attending scheduled work when one's capacity to perform is significantly diminished by illness or other factors.

personality
The relatively enduring pattern of thoughts, emotions, and behaviors that characterize a person, along with the psychological processes behind those characteristics.

of "who we are" serves as an anchor for our behavior because the executive function—the part of the brain that manages goal-directed behavior—tries to keep our behavior consistent with our self-concept. Because our self-concept becomes clearer and more stable with age, our behavior and personality therefore also become more stable and consistent. We discuss self-concept in more detail in the next chapter. The main point here is that personality is not completely determined by heredity; life experiences, particularly early in life, also shape each individual's personality traits.

FIVE-FACTOR MODEL OF PERSONALITY

One of the most important ideas of personality theory is that people possess specific personality traits. Traits such as sociable, depressed, cautious, and talkative represent clusters of thoughts, feelings, and behaviors that allow us to identify, differentiate, and understand people.[37] Hundreds of personality traits have been described over the years, so personality experts have tried to organize them into smaller clusters. The most widely respected clustering of personality traits is the **five-factor model (FFM),** also known as the "Big Five" personality dimensions. Several decades ago, personality experts identified more than 17,000 words that describe an individual's personality. These words were distilled down to five abstract personality dimensions. Similar results were found in studies of different languages, suggesting that the five-factor model is fairly robust across cultures.[38] These "Big Five" dimensions, represented by the handy acronym *CANOE*, are outlined in Exhibit 2.3 and described next:

- *Conscientiousness.* **Conscientiousness** characterizes people who are organized, dependable, goal-focused, thorough, disciplined, methodical, and industrious. People with low conscientiousness tend to be careless, less thorough, disorganized, and irresponsible.
- *Agreeableness.* This dimension includes the traits of being trusting, helpful, good-natured, considerate, tolerant, selfless, generous, and flexible. Some scholars prefer the label "friendly compliance" for this dimension, with its opposite being "hostile noncompliance." People with low agreeableness tend to be uncooperative and intolerant of others' needs, as well as more suspicious and self-focused.
- *Neuroticism.* **Neuroticism** characterizes people who tend to be anxious, insecure, self-conscious, depressed, and temperamental. In contrast, people with low neuroticism (high emotional stability) are poised, secure, positive, and calm.
- *Openness to experience.* This dimension is the most complex and has the least agreement among scholars. It generally refers to the extent to which people are imaginative,

EXHIBIT 2.3

Five-Factor Model's Big Five Personality Dimensions

Personality dimension	People with higher scores on this dimension tend to be more:
Conscientiousness	Organized, dependable, goal-focused, thorough, disciplined, methodical, industrious
Agreeableness	Trusting, helpful, good-natured, considerate, tolerant, selfless, generous, flexible
Neuroticism	Anxious, insecure, self-conscious, depressed, temperamental
Openness to experience	Imaginative, creative, unconventional, curious, nonconforming, autonomous, perceptive
Extraversion	Outgoing, talkative, energetic, sociable, assertive

creative, unconventional, curious, nonconforming, autonomous, and aesthetically perceptive. Those who score low on this dimension tend to be more resistant to change, less open to new ideas, and more conventional and fixed in their ways.

- *Extraversion.* **Extraversion** characterizes people who are outgoing, talkative, energetic, sociable, and assertive. The opposite is *introversion,* which characterizes those who are quiet, cautious, and less interactive with others. Extraverts get their energy from the outer world (people and things around them), whereas introverts get their energy from the internal world, such as personal reflection on concepts and ideas. Introverts do not necessarily lack social skills. Rather, they are more inclined to direct their interests to ideas than to social events. Introverts feel quite comfortable being alone, whereas extraverts do not.

Big Five Personality Dimensions and Workplace Behavior   The personality dimensions in the five-factor model influence employee motivation and role clarity in various ways.[39] Some experts suggest that agreeableness, conscientiousness, and emotional stability (low neuroticism) cluster around the broad characteristic of "getting along." People with high agreeableness are more sensitive to others (more considerate and selfless), those with high conscientiousness are more dependable, and those with high emotional stability are more upbeat. Some writers suggest that extraversion also relates to getting along because extraverts are more sociable. Openness to experience, extraversion, conscientiousness, and emotional stability cluster around the broad characteristic of "getting ahead." Those with high openness to experience are more eager to try out new ideas, extraverts are more assertive, those with high conscientiousness are more goal-oriented, and those with high emotional stability are more confident in their ability to perform well.

Personality traits reflect an individual's behavioral tendencies, so they are fairly good at predicting a number of workplace behaviors and outcomes, even after controlling for employee ability and other factors. Personality traits are even apparent in the content of our Facebook profiles and other website information. Conscientiousness and emotional stability (low neuroticism) stand out as the personality traits that best predict individual performance in almost every job group.[40] Both are motivational components of personality, because they energize a willingness to fulfill work obligations within established rules (conscientiousness) and to allocate resources to accomplish those tasks (emotional stability). Various studies have reported that conscientious employees set higher personal goals for themselves, are more motivated, and have higher performance expectations than do employees with low levels of conscientiousness. They also tend to have higher levels of organizational citizenship and work better in organizations that give employees more freedom than in traditional command-and-control workplaces.[41]

The other three personality dimensions predict more specific types of employee behavior and performance.[43] Extraversion is associated with performance in sales and management jobs, where employees must interact with and influence people. Agreeableness is associated with performance in jobs where employees are expected to be cooperative and helpful, such as working in teams, customer relations, and other conflict-handling situations. People high on the openness-to-experience personality dimension tend to be more creative and adaptable to change. Finally, personality influences employee well-being

five-factor model (FFM)	**conscientiousness**	**neuroticism**	**extraversion**
The five abstract dimensions representing most personality traits: conscientiousness, emotional stability, openness to experience, agreeableness, and extroversion.	A personality dimension describing people who are careful, dependable, and self-disciplined.	A personality dimension describing people with high levels of anxiety, hostility, depression, and self-consciousness.	A personality dimension describing people who are outgoing, talkative, sociable, and assertive.

Companies spend big dollars on personality tests, yet recent studies have found that job applicants already reveal some of their personality traits through the content of their Facebook pages, blogs, or other personal websites. Even the act of blogging or participating in social network sites can indicate specific personality traits. Extraversion, openness to experience, and agreeableness are usually the easiest traits to estimate from the content of online sources, whereas neuroticism is the most difficult.[42]

connect

Can you identify an individual's personality from the words he or she uses when blogging? Go to **www.mcgrawhillconnect.com** to assess how well you can estimate personality traits from blogging words.

connect

Are you a sensing or intuitive type? Go to **www.mcgrawhillconnect.com** to assess how you score on this Jungian personality type.

in various ways.[44] Overall, personality influences a person's typical emotional reactions to the job, how well he or she copes with stress, and what career path would make that person happier.

JUNGIAN PERSONALITY THEORY AND THE MYERS-BRIGGS TYPE INDICATOR

The five-factor model of personality is the most respected and supported in research, but it is not the most popular in practice. That distinction goes to Jungian personality theory, which is measured through the **Myers-Briggs Type Indicator (MBTI)** (see Exhibit 2.4). Nearly a century ago, Swiss psychiatrist Carl Jung proposed that personality is primarily represented by the individual's preferences regarding perceiving and judging information.[45] Jung explained that perceiving, which involves how people prefer to gather information or perceive the world around them, occurs through two competing orientations: *sensing (S)* and *intuition (N)*. Sensing involves perceiving information directly through the five senses; it relies on an organized structure to acquire factual and preferably quantitative details. Intuition, on the other hand, relies more on insight and subjective experience to see relationships among variables. Sensing types focus on the here and now, whereas intuitive types focus more on future possibilities.

Jung also proposed that judging—how people process information or make decisions based on what they have perceived—consists of two competing processes: *thinking (T)* and *feeling (F)*. People with a thinking orientation rely on rational cause-and-effect logic and systematic data collection to make decisions. Those with a strong feeling orientation, on the other hand, rely on their emotional responses to the options presented, as well as to how those choices affect others. Jung noted that along with differing in the four core processes of sensing, intuition, thinking, and feeling, people also differ in their degrees of extraversion–introversion, which was introduced previously as one of the Big Five personality traits.

Along with measuring the personality traits identified by Jung, the MBTI measures Jung's broader categories of *perceiving* and *judging,* which represent a person's attitude toward the external world. People with a perceiving orientation are open, curious, and flexible; prefer to adapt spontaneously to events as they unfold; and prefer to keep their options open. Judging types prefer order and structure and want to resolve problems quickly.

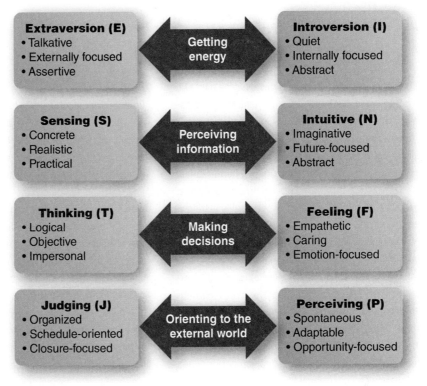

The MBTI is one of the most widely used personality tests in work settings as well as in career counseling and executive coaching.[47] Even so, the MBTI and Jung's psychological types model have received uneven support.[48] On the one hand, MBTI seems to improve self-awareness for career development and mutual understanding. It also does a reasonably good job of representing Jung's psychological types. On the other hand, the MBTI poorly predicts job performance and is generally not recommended for employment selection or promotion decisions. For example, although one study found that intuitive types are more common in higher-level than lower-level management, other research has found no relationship between any MBTI types and effective leadership. One recent large-scale study also reported that team member MBTI scores do not predict the team's effective development. Finally, the MBTI overlaps with four of the five dimensions of the five-factor personality model, yet it does not measure these four dimensions as well as existing Big Five scales.[49]

PERSONALITY TESTING IN ORGANIZATIONS

Personality has become one of the "hot" topics in organizational behavior and gained considerable attention in the workplace. Most often, these tests are applied for personal development, such as career development and team dynamics. For example, many staff at Southwest Airlines post their Myers-Briggs Type Indicator (MBTI) results in their offices. "You can walk by and see someone's four-letter [MBTI type] posted up in their cube," says Southwest's director of leadership development. Southwest began using the MBTI a decade ago to help staff understand and respect coworkers' different personalities and thinking styles. "Behaviors that might have once caused misunderstanding and frustration now are viewed through a different filter," suggests the Southwest Airlines manager.[50]

As Christina discovered while job hunting in the publishing industry (see the opening story to this section), personality tests are also being incorporated into the employment selection and promotion decision process. When Amtrak won the contract to operate the Metrolink commuter service in Southern California, for example, it

Myers-Briggs Type Indicator (MBTI)
An instrument designed to measure the elements of Jungian personality theory, particularly preferences regarding perceiving and judging information.

Debating Point

SHOULD COMPANIES USE PERSONALITY TESTS TO SELECT JOB APPLICANTS?

Personality theory has made significant strides over the past two decades, particularly in demonstrating that specific traits are associated with specific workplace behaviors and outcomes. Various studies have reported that specific Big Five dimensions predict overall job performance, organizational citizenship, leadership, counterproductive work behaviors, training performance, team performance, and a host of other important outcomes. These findings cast a strong vote in favor of personality testing in the workplace.

A few prominent personality experts urge caution, however.[52] They point out that although traits are associated with workplace behavior to some extent, there are better predictors of work performance, such as work samples and past performance. Furthermore, selection procedures typically assume that more of a personality trait is better, whereas several (although not all) studies indicate that the best candidates might be closer to the middle than the extremes of the range.[53] For instance, job performance apparently increases with conscientiousness, yet employees with high conscientiousness might be so thorough that they become perfectionists, which can stifle rather than enhance job performance.[54] A third concern is that, depending on how the selection decision applies the test results, personality instruments may unfairly discriminate against specific groups of people.[55]

A fourth worry is that most personality tests are self-reported scales, so applicants might try to fake their answers. Worse, the test scores might not represent the individual's personality or anything else meaningful because test takers often don't know what personality traits the company is looking for. Studies show that candidates who try to fake "good" personality scores change the selection results. Supporters of personality testing offer the counterargument that few job applicants try to fake their scores (i.e., Christina was an exception).[56] One major study recently found that most personality dimensions are estimated better by observers than by self-ratings, but few companies rely on ratings from other people.[57]

Finally, personality testing might not convey a favorable image of the company. Amtrak's use of personality testing at Metrolink resulted in conflict with the railway worker unions. The British operations of PricewaterhouseCoopers (PwC) discovered that its personality test discouraged female applicants from applying because of concerns that the test was too impersonal and could be faked. "Our personality test was seen to alienate women and so we had to respond to that," says PwC's head of diversity.[58]

required the previous contractor's train engineers and conductors to complete a Big Five personality inventory as a condition of future employment. Amtrak apparently prefers train crew members with a "focused introverted" personality, because employees with these traits are not distracted while operating the train or performing repetitive tasks. Amtrak cites a horrendous Metrolink accident before Amtrak's takeover to justify the personality test. Two dozen people lost their lives when a train engineer ran a red light while text messaging (apparently an indicator of extraversion).[51]

Personality testing wasn't always this popular in organizations. Less than two decades ago, companies shunned these instruments due to concerns that they do not predict job-related behavior and might unfairly discriminate against visible minorities and other identifiable groups. Personality testing slowly regained acceptance as studies reported that specific traits correlated with specific indicators of job performance (as we described previously). Today, personality testing flourishes to such an extent that some experts warn we may be relying too much on personality testing in organizational settings.

Values in the Workplace

LO4

Colleen Abdoulah developed a strong set of personal values from her parents while she was growing up. For example, her father emphasized that "no matter how much you earn, you're no better than anyone and they are no better than you," recalls Abdoulah. She also learned the importance of having the courage to do the right thing and of forming relationships with people so they feel a sense of ownership. Abdoulah not only practices these personal values every day but has instilled them at Wide Open West, the Denver-based Internet, cable, and phone provider where she is CEO to 1,300 employees. "[Our employees] display the courage to do the right thing, serve each other and our customers with humility, and celebrate our learnings and success with grace," says Abdoulah. "Anyone can set values, but we have operationalized our values so that they affect everything we do every day."[59]

Colleen Abdoulah and other successful people often refer to their personal values and the critical events that formed those values earlier in life. *Values,* a concept that we introduced in Chapter 1, are stable, evaluative beliefs that guide our preferences for outcomes or courses of action in a variety of situations.[60] They are perceptions about what is good or bad, right or wrong. Values tell us what we "ought" to do. They serve as a moral compass that directs our motivation and, potentially, our decisions and actions.

People arrange values into a hierarchy of preferences, called a *value system.* Some individuals value new challenges more than they value conformity. Others value generosity more than frugality. Each person's unique value system is developed and reinforced through socialization from parents, religious institutions, friends, personal experiences, and the society in which he or she lives. As such, a person's hierarchy of values is stable and long-lasting. For example, one study found that value systems of a sample of adolescents were remarkably similar 20 years later when they were adults.[61]

Notice that our description of values has focused on individuals, whereas executives often describe values as though they belong to the organization. In reality, values exist only within individuals—we call them *personal values.* However, groups of people might hold the same or similar values, so we tend to ascribe these *shared values* to the team, department, organization, profession, or entire society. The values shared by people throughout an organization (*organizational values*) receive fuller discussion in Chapter 14 because they are a core component of corporate culture. The values shared across a society (*cultural values*) receive attention later in this chapter.

Values and personality traits are related to each other, but the two concepts differ in a few ways.[62] The most noticeable distinction is that values are evaluative—they tell us what we *ought* to do—whereas personality traits describe what we naturally *tend* to do. A second distinction is that personality traits have fairly low conflict with each other (e.g., you can have high agreeableness and high introversion), whereas some values are opposed to other values. For example, someone who values excitement and challenge would have difficulty also valuing stability and moderation. Third, although personality and values are partly determined by heredity, values are influenced much more by socialization, whereas personality traits are influenced as much by heredity.

TYPES OF VALUES

Values come in many forms, and experts on this topic have devoted considerable attention to organizing them into clusters. Several decades ago, social psychologist Milton Rokeach developed two lists of values, distinguishing means (instrumental values) from end goals (terminal values). Although Rokeach's lists are still mentioned in some organizational behavior sources, they were replaced by another model almost two decades ago. The instrumental–terminal values distinction was neither accurate nor useful, and Rokeach's model overlooked values that are now included in the current dominant model.

Today, the most widely accepted model of personal values is Schwartz's Values Circumplex.[63] Developed and tested by social psychologist Shalom Schwartz and his colleagues, this model organizes 57 values into 10 clusters in the circular model (circumplex) shown in Exhibit 2.5.[64] Studies around the world have consistently found that the 57 values cluster into these 10 categories. For example, conformity includes the specific values of politeness, honoring parents, self-discipline, and obedience. Furthermore, the 10 clusters of values are associated with one another in similar or opposing ways. For instance, the value cluster of benevolence is similar to (positively correlated with) universalism but is opposite to (negatively correlated with) hedonism.

EXHIBIT 2.5   Schwartz's Values Circumplex

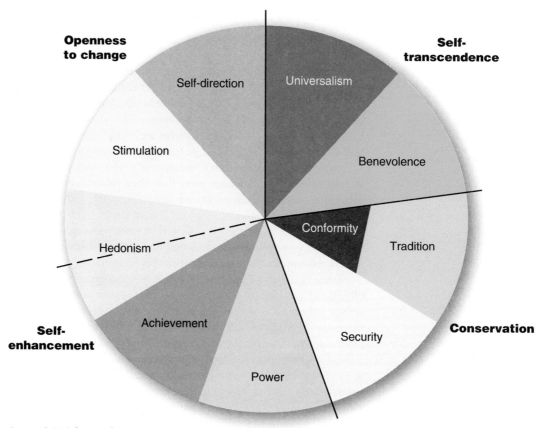

Sources: S. H. Schwartz, "Universals in the Content and Structure of Values: Theoretical Advances and Empirical Tests in 20 Countries," *Advances in Experimental Social Psychology* 25 (1992), pp. 1–65; S. H. Schwartz and G. Sagie, "Value Consensus and Importance: A Cross-National Study," *Journal of Cross-Cultural Psychology* 31 (July 2000), pp. 465–97.

The circumplex model further organizes the 10 broad values categories into four quadrants.

- *Openness to change.* This quadrant refers to a person's motivation to pursue innovative ways. It includes the value categories of self-direction (creativity, independent thought), stimulation (excitement and challenge), and hedonism (pursuit of pleasure, enjoyment, gratification of desires).
- *Conservation.* This quadrant, which is opposite to openness to change, represents a person's motivation to preserve the status quo. It includes the value categories of conformity (adherence to social norms and expectations), security (safety and stability), and tradition (moderation and preservation of the status quo).
- *Self-enhancement.* This quadrant refers to how much a person is motivated by self-interest. It includes the value categories of achievement (pursuit of personal success), power (dominance over others), and hedonism (a value category shared with openness to change).
- *Self-transcendence.* This quadrant, which is opposite self-enhancement, represents a person's motivation to promote the welfare of others and nature. It includes the value categories of benevolence (concern for others in one's life) and universalism (concern for the welfare of all people and nature).

VALUES AND INDIVIDUAL BEHAVIOR

Personal values guide our decisions and actions to some extent, but this connection isn't always as strong as most people believe. Habitual behavior tends to be consistent with our values, but our everyday conscious decisions and actions apply our values much less consistently. The main reason for the "disconnect" between personal values and individual behavior is that values are abstract concepts, so their relevance to specific situations is not obvious much of the time.

Three conditions strengthen the linkage between personal values and behavior.[65] First, we tend to apply our values only when we can think of specific reasons for doing so. In other words, we need logical reasons for applying a specific value in a specific situation. Second, we tend to apply our values when the situation allows or encourages us to do so. Work environments influence our behavior, at least in the short term, so they necessarily encourage or discourage values-consistent behavior. Third, we are more likely to apply values when we actively think about them. This occurs naturally when confronted with situations that obviously violate our values. For example, you become aware that you value security when asked to perform a risky task.

People also become more mindful of their values—and consequently act consistently with those values—when they are literally reminded of them by others. This effect was apparent in a recent study:[66] Students were given a math test and paid for each correct answer. One group submitted their results to the experimenter for scoring, so they couldn't lie about their results. A second group could lie because they scored the test themselves and told the experimenter their test score. A third group was similar to the second (they scored their own test), but they were required to sign their name to the following statement: "I understand that this short survey falls under (the university's) honor system." (The university had no such honor system.) The researchers estimated that some students cheated when they scored their own test without the "honor system" statement, whereas no one given the "honor system" form lied about their results. Similar results occurred when, instead of an honor statement, the third group was first asked to recall the Ten Commandments. The message here is that people are more likely to apply their values (honesty, in this case) when explicitly reminded of those values.

VALUES CONGRUENCE

Values tell us what is right or wrong and what we ought to do. This evaluative characteristic affects how comfortable we are with specific organizations and individuals. The key concept here is *values congruence,* which refers to how similar a person's values hierarchy is to the values hierarchy of the organization, a coworker, or another source of comparison. *Person–organization values congruence* occurs when a person's values are similar to the organization's dominant values. This form of values congruence increases (to some extent) the chance that employees will make decisions and act in ways consistent with organizational expectations. It also leads to higher job satisfaction, loyalty, and organizational citizenship, as well as lower stress and turnover.[67] "The most difficult but rewarding accomplishment in any career is 'living true' to your values and finding companies where you can contribute at the highest level while being your authentic self," says Cynthia Schwalm, a senior executive at Optimer Pharmaceuticals in New York City.[68]

Do the most successful organizations employ people whose personal values are identical to the company's desired values? Not at all! While a comfortable degree of values congruence is necessary for the reasons just noted, organizations also benefit from some level of incongruence. Employees with diverse values offer different perspectives, which potentially lead to better decision making. Also, too much congruence can create a "corporate cult" that potentially undermines creativity, organizational flexibility, and business ethics.

A second type of values congruence involves how consistent the values apparent in our actions (enacted values) are with what we say we believe in (espoused values). This *espoused–enacted values congruence* is especially important for people in leadership positions, because any obvious gap between espoused and enacted values undermines their perceived integrity, a critical feature of effective leaders. One global survey reported that 55 percent of employees believe senior management behaves consistently with the company's core values.[70] Some companies try to maintain high levels of

Soon after joining Chick-fil-A while in high school, Scott Reed (far right) discovered that the restaurant chain's strong family values were similar to his personal values. "Chick-fil-A's core values line up well with mine," says Reed, who opened a Chick-fil-A franchise in Marietta, Georgia, after completing university two decades ago. Reed's two brothers have also worked at the company for several years. His sister, Lauren McGuire, recently joined Chick-fil-A as a franchisee. Values congruence also attracted her to the company: "This is a company that embodies the principles of my heart and soul," says McGuire.[69]

espoused–enacted values congruence by surveying subordinates and peers about whether the manager's decisions and actions are consistent with the company's espoused values.

A third category, *organization–community values congruence,* refers to the similarity of an organization's dominant values with the prevailing values of the community or society in which it conducts business.[71] An organization headquartered in one country that tries to impose its value system on employees and other stakeholders located in another culture may experience higher employee turnover and have more difficult relations with the communities in which the company operates. Thus, globalization calls for a delicate balancing act: Companies depend on shared values to maintain consistent standards and behaviors, yet they need to operate within the values of different cultures around the world.

Ethical Values and Behavior

To assist your learning and test your knowledge about business ethics, go to **www.mcgrawhillconnect.com,** which has activities and test questions on this topic.

When asked to identify the most important attribute of a leader, employees often mention intelligence, decisiveness, or compassion, but these characteristics don't top the list. Instead, across numerous surveys, employees typically choose honesty/ethics as the most important characteristic of effective corporate leaders.[72] Ethics refers to the study of moral principles or values that determine whether actions are right or wrong and outcomes are good or bad (see Chapter 1). People rely on their ethical values to determine "the right thing to do." The importance of ethical corporate conduct is embedded in business programs and appears regularly in the news, yet there doesn't seem to be any noticeable decline in wrongdoing. Almost half of the American employees in a recent survey said they had witnessed misconduct on the job, such as abuse of company resources, abusive behavior, lying to employees, e-mail or Internet abuse, conflicts of interest, discrimination, and lying to outside stakeholders.[73] Exhibit 2.6 lists the least corrupt countries in the world.

THREE ETHICAL PRINCIPLES

To better understand business ethics, we need to consider three distinct types of ethical principles: utilitarianism, individual rights, and distributive justice.[75] While your personal

EXHIBIT 2.6   Factors Influencing Perceived Moral Intensity*

MORAL INTENSITY FACTOR	MORAL INTENSITY QUESTION	MORAL INTENSITY IS HIGHER WHEN:
Magnitude of consequences	How much harm or benefit will occur to others as a result of this action?	The harm or benefit is larger.
Social consensus	How many other people agree that this action is ethically good or bad?	Many people agree.
Probability of effect	(a) What is the chance that this action will occur? (b) What is the chance that this action will cause good or bad consequences?	The probability is higher.
Temporal immediacy	How long after the action will the consequences occur?	The time delay is shorter.
Proximity	How socially, culturally, psychologically, and/or physically close to me are the people affected by this decision?	Those affected are close rather than distant.
Concentration of effect	(a) How many people are affected by this action? (b) Are the people affected by this action easily identifiable as a group?	Many people are affected. Those affected are easily identifiable as a group.

*These are factors that people tend to ask themselves about when determining the moral intensity of an issue. Whether some of these questions should be relevant is itself an ethical question.

Source: Based on information in T. J. Jones, "Ethical Decision Making by Individuals in Organizations: An Issue Contingent Model," *Academy of Management Review* 16 (1991), pp. 366–95.

values might sway you more toward one principle than the others, all three should be actively considered to put important ethical issues to the test.

- *Utilitarianism.* This principle advises us to seek the greatest good for the greatest number of people. In other words, we should choose the option that provides the highest degree of satisfaction to those affected. This is sometimes known as a *consequential principle,* because it focuses on the consequences of our actions, not on how we achieve those consequences. One problem with utilitarianism is that it is almost impossible to evaluate the benefits or costs of many decisions, particularly when many stakeholders have wide-ranging needs and values. Another problem is that most of us are uncomfortable engaging in behaviors that seem unethical even though they attain results that are ethical.

- *Individual rights.* This principle reflects the belief that everyone has entitlements that let her or him act in a certain way. Some of the most widely cited rights are freedom of movement, physical security, freedom of speech, fair trial, and freedom from torture. The individual rights principle includes more than legal rights; it also includes human rights that everyone is granted as a moral norm of society. One problem with individual rights is that certain individual rights may conflict with others. The shareholders' right to be informed about corporate activities may ultimately conflict with an executive's right to privacy, for example.

- *Distributive justice.* This principle suggests that people who are similar to one another should receive similar benefits and burdens; those who are dissimilar should receive different benefits and burdens in proportion to their dissimilarity. For example, we expect that two employees who contribute equally in their work should receive similar rewards, whereas those who make a lesser contribution should receive less. A variation of the distributive justice principle says that inequalities are acceptable when they benefit the least well off in society. Thus, employees in risky jobs should be paid more if their work benefits others who are less well off. One problem with the distributive justice principle is that it is difficult to agree on who is "similar" and what factors are "relevant."

Twenty Least Corrupt Countries in the World[74]

RANK	COUNTRY	SCORE	RANK	COUNTRY	SCORE
1	Denmark	9.3	11	Iceland	8.5
1	New Zealand	9.3	11	Luxembourg	8.5
1	Singapore	9.3	13	Hong Kong	8.4
4	Finland	9.2	14	Ireland	8.0
4	Sweden	9.2	15	Austria	7.9
6	Canada	8.9	15	Germany	7.9
7	Netherlands	8.8	17	Barbados	7.8
8	Australia	8.7	17	Japan	7.8
8	Switzerland	8.7	19	Qatar	7.7
10	Norway	8.6	20	United Kingdom	7.6

Source: 2010 results from the Corruption Perceptions Index published by Transparency International. The index score is calculated on the basis of up to 13 reports. Reprinted from Corruption Perceptions Index. Copyright © 2010 Transparency International: the global coalition against corruption. Used with permission. For more information, visit http://www.transparency.org.

MORAL INTENSITY, ETHICAL SENSITIVITY, AND SITUATIONAL INFLUENCES

Along with ethical principles and their underlying values, four other factors influence ethical conduct in the workplace: the moral intensity of the issue, the individual's ethical sensitivity, situational factors, and mindfulness.[76] **Moral intensity** is the degree to which an issue demands the application of ethical principles. Decisions with high moral intensity have greater importance, so the decision maker needs to apply ethical principles more carefully to resolve it. Several factors influence the moral intensity of an issue, including those listed in Exhibit 2.6. Keep in mind that this list represents the factors people tend to think about; some of them might not be considered morally acceptable when people are formally making ethical decisions.[77]

Even if an issue has high moral intensity, some employees might not recognize its ethical importance because they have low **ethical sensitivity.** Ethical sensitivity is a personal characteristic that enables people to recognize the presence of an ethical issue and determine its relative importance.[78] Ethically sensitive people are not necessarily more ethical. Rather, they are more likely to sense whether an issue requires ethical consideration; that is, they can more accurately estimate the moral intensity of the issue. Ethically sensitive people tend to have higher empathy. They also have more information about the specific situation. For example, accountants would be more ethically sensitive regarding the appropriateness of specific accounting procedures than would someone who has not received training in this profession.

The third important factor explaining why good people engage in unethical decisions and behavior is the situation in which the conduct occurs. Employees say they regularly experience pressure from top management that motivates them to lie to customers, breach regulations, or otherwise act unethically. According to a global survey of managers and human resource managers, the leading cause of unethical corporate behavior is pressure from top management or corporate boards to meet unrealistic deadlines and business objectives.[79] Situational factors do not justify unethical conduct. Rather, we need to be aware of these factors so that organizations can reduce their influence in the future.

moral intensity
The degree to which an issue demands the application of ethical principles.

ethical sensitivity
A personal characteristic that enables people to recognize the presence of an ethical issue and determine its relative importance.

A final reason people engage in unethical conduct is that they engage in mindless behavior. In other words, they don't consciously think about whether their actions might be unethical.[80] As we explained previously in this chapter, people abide by their values only when they think about them. Research suggests that many behaviors are on automatic pilot, so employees seldom evaluate whether their actions violate personal values or ethical principles. This mindless behavior is particularly true when (as often happens) employees are located away from the situation where their decisions have an impact (i.e., low moral intensity).

Mindless behavior is further supported by assumptions that key decision makers have high moral standards. Employees quickly dismiss any ethical concerns about their work when they believe their boss who assigned that work is inherently ethical. For instance, one of the largest cases of accounting fraud occurred because the company's chief financial officer was highly respected in the industry, so employees assumed he was introducing innovative—and legal—accounting procedures. In reality, these activities were extreme forms of accounting fraud.[81]

SUPPORTING ETHICAL BEHAVIOR

Most large and medium-sized organizations apply one or more strategies to improve ethical conduct. One of the most basic steps in this direction is a code of ethical conduct—a statement about desired practices, rules of conduct, and philosophy about the organization's relationship to its stakeholders and the environment. Almost all *Fortune* 500 companies in the United States and the majority of the 500 largest companies in the United Kingdom have ethics codes.[82] These codes are supposed to motivate and guide employee behavior, signal the importance of ethical conduct, and build the firm's trustworthiness to stakeholders. However, critics suggest that they do little to reduce unethical conduct. A glaring illustration is that Enron had a well-developed ethics code, yet Enron's senior executives engaged in wholesale wrongdoing, resulting in the energy company's bankruptcy.[83]

Many firms supplement ethics codes with ethics training. At Texas Instruments, employees receive a business-card-sized

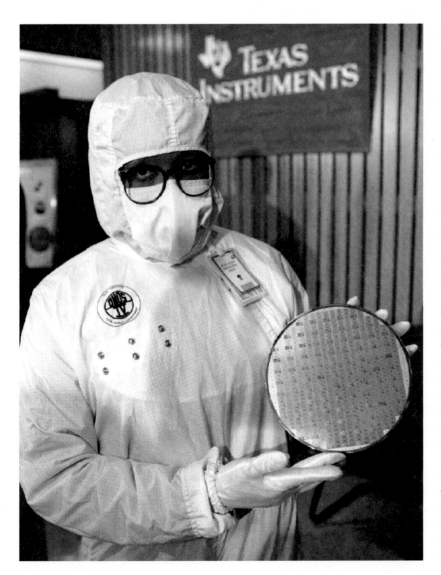

Texas Instruments (TI) is rated as one of the world's most ethical and reputable companies. TI gives every employee the "TI Ethics Booklet" (available in 10 languages), which includes the electronics company's ethics codes as well as seven questions to guide employees through ethical dilemmas. TI's ethics office has a confidential hotline. Employees must complete a series of short, computer-based ethics and compliance training modules for every business unit. "We want employees to have the tools and training they need to do their jobs within the law and TI standards, and to help maintain our reputation as a company that operates with integrity," says David Reid, TI's vice president and director of ethics and compliance.[85]

pamphlet that has the following questions as their moral compass: "Is the action legal? Does it comply with our values? If you do it, will you feel bad? How would it look in the newspaper? If you know it's wrong, don't do it! If you're not sure, ask. Keep asking until you get an answer." Molson Coors developed an award-winning online training program set up as an expedition: Employees must resolve ethics violations at each "camp" as they ascend a mountain. The first few camps present real scenarios with fairly clear ethical violations of the company's ethics code; later camps present much fuzzier dilemmas requiring more careful thought about the company's underlying values.[84]

Some companies also have ways to confidentially communicate wrongdoing, such as an anonymous hotline or a web link that employees can use to raise ethical issues or concerns about ethical conduct. A few companies employ ethics ombudspersons who receive information confidentially from employees and proactively investigate possible wrongdoing. Ethics audits are also conducted in some organizations but are more common for evaluations of corporate social responsibility practices.[86]

These additional measures support ethical conduct to some extent, but the most powerful foundation is a set of shared values that reinforce ethical conduct. "If you don't have a culture of ethical decision making to begin with, all the controls and compliance regulations you care to deploy won't necessarily prevent ethical misconduct," warns a senior executive at British communications giant Vodafone. This culture is supported by the ethical conduct and vigilance of corporate leaders. By acting with the highest standards of moral conduct, leaders not only gain support and trust from followers; they role-model the ethical standards that employees are more likely to follow.[87]

Values Across Cultures

Sean Billing had been working as director of rooms at Fairmont Hotels in Chicago when he casually asked his boss whether the luxury hotel chain could use his skills and knowledge elsewhere. Soon after, Fairmont transferred Billing to a management position in Kenya, assigned to bring the new properties in the African country up to world-class standards through training and technology without losing their distinctive Kenyan character. Billing jumped at the opportunity, but he also soon discovered the challenge of infusing Fairmont's deep values of customer service, environmentalism, and empowerment into another culture. "It's a little bit of hotel culture shock . . . things are quite different here," admits Billing.[88]

Fairmont Hotels & Resorts operates world-class hotels in several countries and is eager to help Sean Billing and other employees develop and strengthen their cross-cultural competence. As Connections 2.1 describes, people think and act differently across cultures, and these differences are due to unique norms of behavior, as well as emphases on different values.

INDIVIDUALISM AND COLLECTIVISM

Of the many values studied across cultures, the five summarized in Exhibit 2.7 are by far the most popular. This exhibit also lists countries that have high, medium, or low emphasis on these values. Two seemingly inseparable cross-cultural values are individualism and collectivism. **Individualism** is the extent to which we value independence and personal uniqueness. Highly individualist people value personal freedom, self-sufficiency, control over their own lives, and appreciation of the unique qualities that distinguish them from others. Americans, Chileans, Canadians, and South Africans generally exhibit high individualism, whereas Taiwan and Venezuela are countries with low individualism.[90] **Collectivism** is the extent to which we value our duty to groups to which we belong and to group harmony. Highly collectivist people define themselves by their group memberships, emphasize their personal connection to others in their in-groups, and value the goals

connections 2.1

Infosys Bridges the Cross-Cultural Divide[89]

Infosys Technologies, a technology outsourcing firm in India, was prepared for cross-cultural differences when it acquired an Australian company. Sean Fernando, Infosys general manager of human resources in Australia, provides a vivid example of one of these cultural differences: When asked to travel on business, Infosys employees in India would pack their bags without hesitation and be ready to go even though they lacked details about the trip. Australian staff, on the other hand, wanted to know about the accommodation, allowances, and project specifics before they felt at ease. In other words, employees from India had noticeably lower levels of uncertainty avoidance.

Another difference was that staff in India expect the boss to give them instructions on what to do, whereas Australian employees expect to be consulted. In other words, Australian employees have much lower power distance. Fernando recalls an incident where an Australian project manager met with a project team from India. He described the project and then suggested that they share ideas about how to successfully complete the project. "They didn't know what he meant," says Fernando. "Then one of the people just said: 'We were wondering when you are going to tell us what the plan was.'"

To minimize cross-cultural conflict, Infosys Australia holds three-hour sessions in which employees from both countries learn about their cultures and discuss how they can manage employees with these different values.

Infosys is training its managers to be aware of cross-cultural differences when working with employees from other countries.

---

and well-being of people within those groups.[91] Low collectivism countries include the United States, Japan, and Germany, whereas Israelis and Taiwanese have relatively high collectivism.

Contrary to popular belief, individualism is not the opposite of collectivism. In fact, an analysis of most previous studies reported that the two concepts are unrelated.[92] For example, cultures that highly value duty to one's group do not necessarily give a low priority to personal freedom and uniqueness. Generally, people across all cultures define themselves by both their uniqueness and their relationship to others. It is an inherent characteristic of everyone's self-concept, which we discuss in the next chapter. Some cultures clearly emphasize uniqueness or group obligations more than the other, but both have a place in a person's values and self-concept.

Also note that people in Japan have relatively low collectivism. This is contrary to many cross-cultural books, which claim that Japan is one of the most collectivist countries on the planet! There are several explanations for the historical misinterpretation, ranging from problems defining and measuring collectivism to erroneous reporting of early cross-cultural research. Whatever the reasons, studies consistently report that people in Japan tend to have relatively low collectivism and moderate individualism (as indicated in Exhibit 2.7).[93]

individualism
A cross-cultural value describing the degree to which people in a culture emphasize independence and personal uniqueness.

collectivism
A cross-cultural value describing the degree to which people in a culture emphasize duty to groups to which they belong and to group harmony.

EXHIBIT 2.7   Five Cross-Cultural Values

VALUE	SAMPLE COUNTRIES	REPRESENTATIVE BELIEFS/BEHAVIORS IN "HIGH" CULTURES
Individualism	High: United States, Chile, Canada, South Africa Medium: Japan, Denmark Low: Taiwan, Venezuela	Defines self more by one's uniqueness; personal goals have priority; decisions have low consideration of effect on others; relationships are viewed as more instrumental and fluid.
Collectivism	High: Israel, Taiwan Medium: India, Denmark Low: United States, Germany, Japan	Defines self more by one's in-group membership; goals of self-sacrifice and harmony have priority; behavior regulated by in-group norms; in-group memberships are viewed as stable with a strong differentiation with out-groups.
Power Distance	High: India, Malaysia Medium: United States, Japan Low: Denmark, Israel	Reluctant to disagree with or contradict the boss; managers are expected and preferred decision makers; perception of dependence (versus interdependence) with the boss.
Uncertainty Avoidance	High: Belgium, Greece Medium: United States, Norway Low: Denmark, Singapore	Prefer predictable situations; value stable employment, strict laws, and low conflict; dislike deviations from normal behavior.
Achievement Orientation	High: Austria, Japan Medium: United States, Brazil Low: Sweden, Netherlands	Focus on outcomes (versus relationships); decisions based on contribution (equity versus equality); low empathy or showing emotions (versus strong empathy and caring).

Sources: Individualism and collectivism descriptions and results are from the meta-analysis reported by D. Oyserman, H. M. Coon, and M. Kemmelmeier, "Rethinking Individualism and Collectivism: Evaluation of Theoretical Assumptions and Meta-Analyses," *Psychological Bulletin* 128 (2002), pp. 3–72. The other information is from G. Hofstede, *Culture's Consequences*, 2d ed. (Thousand Oaks, CA: Sage, 2001).

POWER DISTANCE

Power distance refers to the extent to which people accept an unequal distribution of power in a society.[94] Those with high power distance accept and value unequal power. They value obedience to authority and are comfortable receiving commands from their superiors without consultation or debate, and they prefer to resolve differences through formal procedures rather than directly. In contrast, people with low power distance expect relatively equal power sharing. They view the relationship with their boss as one of interdependence, not dependence; that is, they believe their boss is also dependent on them, so they expect power sharing and consultation before decisions affecting them are made. People in India and Malaysia tend to have high power distance, whereas people in Denmark and Israel generally have low power distance. Americans collectively have medium-low power distance.

To understand the effect of power distance, consider the experience of a Southeast Asian engineer who immigrated to Canada not long ago. In his home country, the engineer generated data analysis reports and submitted them to his supervisor without recommendations. His boss would look at the factual information and make a decision. Including recommendations in those reports would have shown disrespect for the supervisor's higher position, which may have resulted in dismissal. But when the engineer moved to Canada, he

power distance
A cross-cultural value describing the degree to which people in a culture accept unequal distribution of power in a society.

uncertainty avoidance
A cross-cultural value describing the degree to which people in a culture tolerate ambiguity (low uncertainty avoidance) or feel threatened by ambiguity and uncertainty (high uncertainty avoidance).

achievement–nurturing orientation
A cross-cultural value describing the degree to which people in a culture emphasize competitive versus cooperative relations with other people.

was expected to propose recommendations along with the technical data. Excluding recommendations from an engineering report in Canada would be evidence of incompetence, which may result in dismissal. To remain employed, the engineer had to overcome a huge shift in power distance values and expectations.[95]

UNCERTAINTY AVOIDANCE

Uncertainty avoidance is the degree to which people tolerate ambiguity (low uncertainty avoidance) or feel threatened by ambiguity and uncertainty (high uncertainty avoidance). Employees with high uncertainty avoidance favor structured situations in which rules of conduct and decision making are clearly documented. They usually prefer direct rather than indirect or ambiguous communications. Uncertainty avoidance tends to be high in Belgium and Greece and very high in Japan. It is generally low in Denmark and Singapore. Americans collectively have medium-low uncertainty avoidance.

ACHIEVEMENT–NURTURING ORIENTATION

Achievement–nurturing orientation reflects a competitive versus cooperative view of relations with other people.[96] People with a high achievement orientation value assertiveness, competitiveness, and materialism. They appreciate people who are tough, and they favor the acquisition of money and material goods. In contrast, people in nurturing-oriented cultures emphasize relationships and the well-being of others. They focus on human interaction and caring rather than competition and personal success. Sweden, Norway, and the Netherlands have very low scores on achievement orientation (i.e., they have a high nurturing orientation). In contrast, very high achievement orientation scores have been reported in Japan and Austria. The United States places a little above the middle of the range on achievement–nurturing orientation.

CAVEATS ABOUT CROSS-CULTURAL KNOWLEDGE

Cross-cultural organizational research has gained considerable attention over the past two decades, likely due to increased globalization and cultural diversity within organizations. Our knowledge of cross-cultural dynamics has blossomed, and many of these findings will be discussed throughout this book, particularly regarding leadership, conflict handling, and influence tactics. However, we also need to raise a few warning flags about cross-cultural knowledge. One problem is that too many studies have relied on small, convenient samples (such as students) to represent an entire culture.[97] The result is that many cross-cultural studies draw conclusions that might not generalize to the cultures they intended to represent.

A second problem is that cross-cultural studies often assume that each country has one culture.[98] In reality, many countries (including the United States) have become culturally diverse. As more countries embrace globalization and multiculturalism, it becomes even less appropriate to assume that an entire country has one unified culture.

A third concern is that cross-cultural research and writing continue to rely on a major study conducted almost four decades ago of 116,000 IBM employees across dozens of countries. That study helped ignite subsequent cross-cultural research, but its findings are becoming out of date as values in some cultures have shifted over the years. For example, value systems seem to be converging across Asia as people in these countries interact more frequently with one another and adopt standardized business practices.[99] Several recent reviews have recommended that future studies should no longer rely on the IBM study to benchmark values of a particular culture.[100]

CULTURAL DIVERSITY WITHIN THE UNITED STATES

You might think from reading some cross-cultural studies that the United States is a homogenous country where people hold identical or very similar values and beliefs. Of course, anyone who lives or visits here long enough knows otherwise. But even Americans may be surprised at how much cultural diversity exists within this country, even when excluding the incredible variety of new citizens who grew up elsewhere in the world.[101]

In Chapter 1, we described the high degree of workplace diversity in the United States. Surface-level diversity characteristics are continuously evolving, such as the increasing percentage of non-white Americans, and particularly of the Hispanic population as the country's largest non-white ethnic group. But most workplace diversity experts now recognize that deep-level diversity has greater importance and impact in the workplace. These differences in beliefs, values, and expectations are often clustered around demographic factors such as age, gender, and ethnicity.

Previously in this chapter, we cited research evidence that the United States has high individualism and low collectivism. That broad-brush statement masks significant variations within the country. A meta-analysis of past studies finds that, on average, African Americans have significantly higher individualism than European and Hispanic Americans, whereas Asian Americans have the lowest individualism among these demographic groups. European Americans have somewhat lower degrees of collectivism compared with Asian and Hispanic Americans.[102]

Regional Diversity Across the United States   The United States also has a rich history of cultural variations across regions. One recent study revealed that typical personality profiles vary across regions. Neuroticism scores are highest in the Northeast and Southeast United States and lowest in the Midwest and West. The New England, Middle Atlantic, and Pacific regions have high openness to experience, whereas people living in the Great Plains, Midwest, and Southeastern states have the lowest scores. Regional differences are less distinctive for the other Big Five personality dimensions. Other studies have found regional clusters of Schwartz's values and similar belief systems.[103] Furthermore, a few studies report that Americans hold distinct stereotypes of people across regions, and these stereotypes are similar to actual personality profiles in these regions.[104] Collectivism also seems to vary across America. Using social indicators (percentage living alone, self-employed, households inhabited with grandchildren, etc.) rather than surveys, one study found that collectivism is highest across the Southern states, California, and Hawaii; it is lowest among residents in the Mountain, Northwest, and Great Plains states.[105]

There are a few possible reasons regional variations occur.[106] One explanation is that local rather than national institutions—such as local governments, educational systems, and dominant religious groups—influence socialization practices, which reinforce personal values. A related argument is that the natural environment shapes culture to some extent. People might emphasize different values depending on the physical environment (flat versus mountainous), climatic conditions (temperate versus tropical), and socioeconomic conditions (low income versus relatively wealthy). A third explanation is that people migrate to places that they believe are more consistent with their values and self-views. Someone raised in the Midwest, for example, might be more motivated to move to California if his or her values emphasize discovery and change rather than tradition and dedication.

This brief overview of culture within the United States highlights two important points. First, we need to remember that the United States—as well as many other nations—has diverse forms of surface-level and deep-level diversity. Describing Americans as though they have a homogeneous culture distorts reality. Second, cultural diversity extends beyond demographic differences. As we noted, the United States has a rich history of cultural diversity across regions, and these clusters are less visible than are demographic differences. In Chapter 1, we also noted that some differences in values exist across generational cohorts. Overall, organizational leaders and employees need to be aware of these complex forms of diversity and be sensitive to how they produce variations in self-concepts, social perceptions, and attitudes. These three topics are examined more closely over the next two chapters.

(chapter summary)

LO1 Describe the four factors that directly influence individual behavior and performance.

Four variables—motivation, ability, role perceptions, and situational factors, which are represented by the acronym MARS—directly influence individual behavior and performance. Motivation represents the forces within a person that affect his or her direction, intensity, and persistence of voluntary behavior; ability includes both the natural aptitudes and the learned capabilities required to complete a task successfully; role perceptions are the extent to which people understand the job duties (roles) assigned to them or expected of them; situational factors include conditions beyond the employee's immediate control that constrain or facilitate behavior and performance.

LO2 Summarize the five types of individual behavior in organizations.

There are five main types of workplace behavior. Task performance refers to goal-directed behaviors under the individual's control that support organizational objectives. Organizational citizenship behaviors consist of various forms of cooperation and helpfulness to others that support the organization's social and psychological context. Counterproductive work behaviors are voluntary behaviors that have the potential to harm the organization directly or indirectly. Joining and staying with the organization refers to agreeing to become an organizational member and remaining with the organization. Maintaining work attendance includes minimizing absenteeism when capable of working and avoiding scheduled work when not fit (i.e., low presenteeism).

LO3 Describe personality, the "Big Five" personality dimensions, and four MBTI types, and explain how personality relates to individual behavior in organizations.

Personality is the relatively enduring pattern of thoughts, emotions, and behaviors that characterize a person, along with the psychological processes behind those characteristics. Personality traits are broad concepts about people that allow us to label and understand individual differences. Personality is developed through hereditary origins (nature) and socialization (nurture). The "Big Five" personality dimensions include conscientiousness, agreeableness, neuroticism, openness to experience, and extraversion. Conscientiousness and emotional stability (low neuroticism) predict individual performance in most job groups. Extraversion is associated with performance in sales and management jobs, whereas agreeableness is associated with performance in jobs requiring cooperation, and openness to experience is associated with performance in creative jobs.

Based on Jungian personality theory, the Myers-Briggs Type Indicator (MBTI) identifies competing orientations for getting energy (extraversion vs. introversion), perceiving information (sensing versus intuiting), processing information and making decisions (thinking vs. feeling), and orienting to the external world (judging vs. perceiving). The MBTI improves self-awareness for career development and mutual understanding but is more popular than valid. Overall, it is useful to understand an individual's personality, but testing for personality in organizations raises a few concerns.

LO4 Summarize Schwartz's model of individual values and discuss the conditions under which values influence behavior.

Values are stable, evaluative beliefs that guide our preferences for outcomes or courses of action in a variety of situations. Compared with personality traits, values are evaluative (rather than descriptive), more likely to conflict, and formed more from socialization than heredity. Schwartz's model organizes 57 values into a circumplex of 10 dimensions along 2 bipolar dimensions: openness to change to conservation and self-enhancement to self-transcendence. Values influence behavior in three conditions: (1) when we can think of specific reasons for doing so, (2) when the situation supports those values, and (3) when we actively think about them. Values congruence refers to how similar a person's values hierarchy is to the values hierarchy of another source (organization, person, etc.).

LO5 Describe three ethical principles and discuss four factors that influence ethical behavior.

Ethics refers to the study of moral principles or values that determine whether actions are right or wrong and outcomes are good or bad. Three ethical principles are utilitarianism, individual rights, and distributive justice. Ethical behavior is influenced by the degree to which an issue demands the application of ethical principles (moral intensity), the individual's ability to recognize the presence and relative importance of an ethical issue (ethical sensitivity), situational forces, and the extent to which people actively evaluate their decisions and actions in comparison with ethical and personal values (i.e., mindfulness). Ethical conduct at work is supported by codes of ethical conduct, ethics training, mechanisms for communicating ethical violations, the organization's culture, and the leader's behavior.

LO6 Review five values commonly studied across cultures and discuss cultural diversity within the United States.

Five values that are often studied across cultures are individualism (valuing independence and personal uniqueness); collectivism (valuing duty to in-groups and to group harmony); power distance (valuing unequal distribution of power); uncertainty avoidance (tolerating or feeling threatened by ambiguity and uncertainty); and achievement–nurturing orientation (valuing competition versus cooperation). Although cross-cultural knowledge is valuable, we need to be concerned that some of this knowledge is based on non-representative samples, old information, and lack of sensitivity to cultural differences within countries.

Rather than being a homogeneous culture, the United States has diverse forms of surface-level and deep-level diversity. This cultural diversity also reflects some differences across regions. Regional diversity might exist because socialization practices are shaped by local institutions, the natural environment shapes culture to some extent, or people migrate to places that they believe are more consistent with their values and self-views.

ability, p. 35

achievement–nurturing orientation, p. 57

collectivism, p. 54

competencies, p. 35

conscientiousness, p. 42

counterproductive work behaviors (CWBs), p. 38

ethical sensitivity, p. 52

extraversion, p. 43

five-factor model (FFM), p. 42

individualism, p. 54

moral intensity, p. 52

motivation, p. 35

Myers-Briggs Type Indicator (MBTI), p. 44

neuroticism, p. 42

organizational citizenship behaviors (OCBs), p. 38

personality, p. 40

power distance, p. 56

presenteeism, p. 40

role perceptions, p. 36

uncertainty avoidance, p. 57

(critical thinking questions)

1. An insurance company has high levels of absenteeism among the office staff. The head of office administration argues that employees are misusing the company's sick leave benefits. However, some of the mostly female staff members have explained that family responsibilities interfere with work. Using the MARS model, as well as your knowledge of absenteeism behavior, discuss some of the possible reasons for absenteeism here and how it might be reduced.

2. It has been said that all employees are motivated. Do you agree with this statement?

3. You notice that the sales representative for one region made 20 percent fewer sales to new clients over the past quarter than salespeople located elsewhere across the country. Use the model of individual behavior to explain why his or her performance was lower than the performance of other salespeople.

4. Studies report that heredity has a strong influence on an individual's personality. What are the implications of this in organizational settings?

5. Suppose that you give all candidates applying for a management trainee position a personality test that measures the five dimensions in the five-factor model. Which personality traits would you consider to be the most important for this type of job? Explain your answer.

6. Compare and contrast personality with personal values, and identify values categories in Schwartz's values circumplex that likely relate to one or more personality dimensions in the five-factor personality model.

7. This chapter discussed values congruence mostly in the context of an employee's personal values versus the organization's values. But values congruence also relates to the juxtaposition of other pairs of value systems. Explain how values congruence is relevant with respect to organizational versus professional values (i.e., values of a professional occupation, such as physician, accountant, pharmacist).

8. "All decisions are ethical decisions." Comment on this statement, particularly by referring to the concepts of moral intensity and ethical sensitivity.

9. People in a particular South American country have high power distance and high collectivism. What does this mean, and what are the implications of this information when you (a senior executive) visit employees working for your company in that country?

CASE STUDY 2.1 SK TELECOM GOES EGALITARIAN

Until recently, Hur Jae-hoon could end debate with junior staff members just by declaring that the discussion was over. Employed at the fourth tier in SK Telecom Co.'s five-tier management/professional hierarchy, the 33-year-old strategist held the corresponding title of "Hur Daeri" and received plenty of respect from people in lower positions. No one below Hur was allowed to question his decisions, and Hur was expected to silently comply with requests from above. South Korea's culture of deferring to people in higher positions was deeply ingrained in the telecommunications company. In some South Korean companies, such as Samsung, junior staff members aren't even allowed to initiate conversations with anyone above their boss.

Now, in spite of South Korea's strong hierarchical culture, SK Telecom wants to support more egalitarian values. It has already removed its five management ranks and their differentiated titles and status. The English word "Manager" is now used to address anyone employed throughout the five former ranks. (Hur Jae-hoon's title has changed from Hur Daeri to "Hur Manager.") Only vice presidents and above retain their previous status titles. People in charge of projects or people are also called "Team Leader." Furthermore, the company is assigning project leadership responsibilities to employees in their 20s, whereas these roles were previously held only by people with much more seniority. As an added change, the company is allowing a more casual dress code at work.

Through this dramatic shift in values and practices, SK Telecom's senior executives hope that junior staff will speak up more freely, thereby improving creativity and decision making. They particularly want to avoid incidents such as one that occurred several years ago in which an excellent idea from younger employees was initially shot down by their bosses. The junior staff suggested that allowing customers to change their cell phone ringtones to music chosen by the friend they've phoned would generate revenue through music licensing. Fortunately, the idea was introduced several months later, after a few persistent employees proposed the idea again.

SK Telecom's initiative is not completely new to South Korea. Small high-tech companies already embrace egalitarian values and flatter corporate structures. But SK Telecom is among the first large firms in the country to attempt this culture shift, and it has met with resistance along the way. SK Telecom executives were initially divided over how quickly and to what extent the company should distance itself from South Korea's traditional hierarchical culture. "There were ideas for gradual versus all-out reforms," recalls chief executive Kim Shin-bae. "But the word 'gradually' means 'not now' to some people. So we decided to go all-out."

According to a company survey, 80 percent of employees support the changes. However, even with the changes in titles, many still look for subtle evidence of who has higher status and, therefore, should receive more deference. Some also rely on what positions managers held under the old five-tier hierarchy. "I know what the old titles were," says an LG Electronics Co. manager who supplies cell phones to SK Telecom. "So unconsciously, I keep that in mind."

Hur Jae-hoon admits there are times when he prefers a more hierarchical culture, but he believes that SK Telecom's more egalitarian values and practices are already showing favorable results. In one recent meeting, a younger colleague sparred with Hur over the better way to complete a strategy project. "For a moment, I wished it was back in the old days when I could have shut that guy down," Hur recalls. "But I had to admit his opinion was better than mine, and I adjusted. So the system worked."

Discussion Questions

1. Which South Korean cultural value is SK Telecom attempting to distance itself from? What indicators of this value are identified in this case study? What other artifacts of this cultural value would you notice while visiting a South Korean company that upheld this national culture?

2. In your opinion, why is this particular value so strong in South Korea? What are the advantages and disadvantages of this value in societies?

3. Do you think SK Telecom will be successful in integrating a more egalitarian culture, even though it contrasts with South Korea's culture? What are some of the issues that may complicate or support this transition?

Source: Adapted from E. Ramstad, "Pulling Rank Gets Harder at One Korean Company," *Wall Street Journal*, August 20, 2007, p. B1.

CASE STUDY 2.2 PUSHING PAPERS CAN BE FUN

A large city government was putting on a number of seminars for managers of various departments throughout the city. At one of these sessions, the topic discussed was motivation—how to get public servants motivated to do a good job. The plight of a police captain became the central focus of the discussion:

I've got a real problem with my officers. They come on the force as young, inexperienced rookies, and we send them out on the street, either in cars or on a beat. They seem to like the contact they have with the public, the action involved in crime prevention, and the apprehension of criminals. They also like helping people out at fires, accidents, and other emergencies.

The problem occurs when they get back to the station. They hate to do the paperwork, and because they dislike it, the job is frequently put off or done inadequately. This lack of attention hurts us later on when we get to court. We need clear, factual reports. They must be highly detailed and unambiguous. As soon as one part of a report is shown to be inadequate or incorrect, the rest of the report is suspect. Poor reporting probably causes us to lose more cases than any other factor.

I just don't know how to motivate them to do a better job. We're in a budget crunch and I have absolutely no financial rewards at my disposal. In fact, we'll probably have to lay some people off in the near future. It's hard for me to make the job interesting and challenging because it isn't—it's boring, routine paperwork, and there isn't much you can do about it.

Finally, I can't say to them that their promotions will hinge on the excellence of their paperwork. First of all, they know it's

not true. If their performance is adequate, most are more likely to get promoted just by staying on the force a certain number of years than for some specific outstanding act. Second, they were trained to do the job they do out in the streets, not to fill out forms. All through their career it is the arrests and interventions that get noticed.

Some people have suggested a number of things, like using conviction records as a performance criterion. However, we know that's not fair—too many other things are involved. Bad paperwork increases the chance that you lose in court, but good paperwork doesn't necessarily mean you'll win. We tried setting up team competitions based upon the excellence of the reports, but the officers caught on to that pretty quickly. No one was getting any type of reward for winning the competition, and they figured why should they bust a gut when there was no payoff.

I just don't know what to do.

Discussion Questions

1. What performance problems is the captain trying to correct?

2. Use the MARS model of individual behavior and performance to diagnose possible causes of the unacceptable behavior.

3. Has the captain considered all possible solutions to the problem? If not, what else might be done?

Source: T. R. Mitchell and J. R. Larson, Jr., *People in Organizations*, 3d ed. (New York: McGraw-Hill, 1987), p. 184. Used with permission.

CLASS EXERCISE 2.3 TEST YOUR KNOWLEDGE OF PERSONALITY

PURPOSE This exercise is designed to help you think about and understand the effects of the Big Five personality dimensions on individual preferences and outcomes.

INSTRUCTIONS (LARGE CLASS) Below are several questions relating to the Big Five personality dimensions and various preferences or outcomes. Answer each of these questions relying on your personal experience or best guess. Later, the instructor will show you the answers based on scholarly results. You will *not* be graded on this exercise, but it may help you to better understand the effect of personality on human behavior and preferences.

INSTRUCTIONS (SMALL CLASS)

1. The instructor will organize students into teams. Members of each team work together to answer

each of the questions below relating to the Big Five personality dimensions and various preferences or outcomes.

2. The instructor will reveal the answers based on scholarly results. (*Note:* The instructor might create a competition to see which team has the most answers correct.)

PERSONALITY AND PREFERENCES QUESTIONS

1. You have been asked to select job applicants for a nine-month over-winter assignment working in an Antarctic research station with a dozen other people. Assuming that all candidates have equal skills, experience, and health, identify the preferred level of each personality dimension for people working in these remote, confined, and isolated conditions.

PERSONALITY DIMENSION	LOW	BELOW AVERAGE	AVERAGE	ABOVE AVERAGE	HIGH
Conscientiousness	☐	☐	☐	☐	☐
Agreeableness	☐	☐	☐	☐	☐
Neuroticism	☐	☐	☐	☐	☐
Openness to experience	☐	☐	☐	☐	☐
Extraversion	☐	☐	☐	☐	☐

2. Listed below are several jobs. Please check no more than two personality dimensions that you believe are positively associated with preferences for each occupation.

	PERSONALITY DIMENSION				
JOB	EXTRAVERSION	CONSCIENTIOUSNESS	AGREEABLENESS	NEUROTICISM	OPENNESS TO EXPERIENCE
Budget analyst	☐	☐	☐	☐	☐
Corporate executive	☐	☐	☐	☐	☐
Engineer	☐	☐	☐	☐	☐
Journalist	☐	☐	☐	☐	☐
Life insurance agent	☐	☐	☐	☐	☐
Nurse	☐	☐	☐	☐	☐
Physician	☐	☐	☐	☐	☐
Production supervisor	☐	☐	☐	☐	☐
Public relations director	☐	☐	☐	☐	☐
Research analyst	☐	☐	☐	☐	☐
Schoolteacher	☐	☐	☐	☐	☐
Sculptor	☐	☐	☐	☐	☐

3. On which two personality dimensions should team members have the highest scores, on average, to produce the best team performance?

☐ Conscientiousness

☐ Agreeableness

☐ Neuroticism

☐ Openness to experience

☐ Extraversion

4. Rank order (1 = highest, 5 = lowest) the Big Five personality dimensions in terms of how much you think they predict a person's degree of life satisfaction. (*Note:* Personality dimensions are ranked by their absolute effect, so ignore the negative or positive direction of association.)

_____ Conscientiousness

_____ Agreeableness

_____ Neuroticism

_____ Openness to experience

_____ Extraversion

5. Which two Big Five personality dimensions are positively associated with enjoyment of workplace humor?

☐ Conscientiousness

☐ Agreeableness

☐ Neuroticism

☐ Openness to experience

☐ Extraversion

TEAM EXERCISE 2.4 COMPARING CULTURAL VALUES

PURPOSE This exercise is designed to help you determine the extent to which students hold similar assumptions about the values that dominate in other countries.

INSTRUCTIONS (SMALL CLASS) The terms in the left column represent labels that a major consulting project identified with businesspeople in a particular country, based on its national culture and values. These terms appear in alphabetical order. In the right column are the names of countries, also in alphabetical order, corresponding to the labels in the left column.

1. Working alone, connect the labels with the countries by relying on your perceptions of these countries. Each label is associated with only one country, so each label should be connected to only one country, and vice versa. Draw a line to connect the pairs, or put the label number beside the country name.

2. The instructor will form teams of four or five members. Members of each team will compare their results and try to reach consensus on a common set of connecting pairs.

3. Teams will post the results so that all can see the extent to which students hold common opinions about businesspeople in other cultures. Class discussion can then consider the reasons why the results are so similar or different, as well as the implications of these results for working in a global work environment.

INSTRUCTIONS (LARGE CLASS)

1. Working alone, connect the labels with the countries by relying on your perceptions of these countries. Each label is associated with only one country, so each label should be connected to only one country, and vice versa. Draw a line to connect the pairs, or put the label number beside the country name.

2. Asking for a show of hands, the instructor will find out which country is identified by most students with each label. The instructor will then post the correct answers.

Value Labels and Country Names

VALUES LABEL (ALPHABETICAL)	COUNTRY NAME (ALPHABETICAL)
1. Affable humanists	Australia
2. Ancient modernizers	Brazil
3. Commercial catalysts	Canada
4. Conceptual strategists	China
5. Efficient manufacturers	France
6. Ethical statesmen	Germany
7. Informal egalitarians	India
8. Modernizing traditionalists	Netherlands
9. Optimistic entrepreneurs	New Zealand
10. Quality perfectionists	Singapore
11. Rugged individualists	Taiwan
12. Serving merchants	United Kingdom
13. Tolerant traders	United States

Source: Based on R. Rosen, P. Digh, M. Singer, and C. Phillips, *Global Literacies* (New York: Simon & Schuster, 2000).

TEAM EXERCISE 2.5 ETHICS DILEMMA VIGNETTES

PURPOSE This exercise is designed to make you aware of the ethical dilemmas people face in various business situations, as well as the competing principles and values that operate in these situations.

INSTRUCTIONS (SMALL CLASS) The instructor will form teams of four or five students. Team members will read each case and discuss the extent to which the company's action in each case was ethical. Teams should be prepared to justify their evaluation using ethics principles and the perceived moral intensity of each incident.

INSTRUCTIONS (LARGE CLASS) Working alone, read each case and determine the extent to which the company's action in each case was ethical. The instructor will use a show of hands to determine the extent to which students believe the case represents an ethical dilemma (high or low moral intensity) and the extent to which the main people or company in each incident acted ethically.

Case One A large European bank requires all employees to open a bank account with that bank. The bank deposits employee paychecks to those accounts. The bank explains that this is a formal policy which all employees agree to at the time of hire. Furthermore, failure to have an account with the bank shows disloyalty, which could limit the employee's career advancement opportunities with the bank. Until recently, the bank has reluctantly agreed to deposit paychecks to accounts at other banks for a small percentage of employees. Now, bank executives want to reinforce the policy. They announced that employees have three months to open an account with the bank or face disciplinary action.

Case Two A 16-year-old hired as an office administrator at a small import services company started posting her thoughts about the job on her Facebook site. After her first day, she wrote: "first day at work. omg!! So dull!!" Two days later, she complained "all i do is shred holepunch n scan paper!!! omg!" Two weeks later she added "im so totally bord!!!" These comments were intermixed with the other usual banter about her life. Her Facebook site did not mention the name of the company where she worked. Three weeks after being hired, the employee was called into the owner's office, where he fired her for the comments on Facebook and then had her escorted from the building. The owner argues that these comments put the company in a bad light, and her "display of disrespect and dissatisfaction undermined the relationship and made it untenable."

Case Three Computer printer manufacturers usually sell printers at a low margin over cost and generate much more income from subsequent sales of the high-margin ink cartridges required for each printer. One global printer manufacturer now designs its printers so that they work only with ink cartridges sold in the same region. Ink cartridges purchased in the United States will not work with the same printer model sold in Europe, for example. This "region coding" of ink cartridges does not improve performance. Rather, it prevents consumers and grey marketers from buying the product at a lower price in another region. The company says this policy allows it to maintain stable prices within a region rather than continually changing prices due to currency fluctuations.

Case Four Judy Price is a popular talk show radio personality and opinionated commentator on the morning phone-in show of a popular radio station in a large U.S. city. Price is married to John Tremble, an attorney who was recently elected mayor of the city even though he had no previous experience in public office. The radio station's board of directors is very concerned that the station's perceived objectivity will be compromised if Price remains on air as a commentator and talk show host while her husband holds such a public position. For example, the radio station manager believes that Price gave minimal attention to an incident in which environmental groups criticized the city for its slow progress on recycling. Price denied that her views are biased and that the incident didn't merit as much attention as other issues that particular week. To ease the board's concerns, the station manager has transferred Price from a talk show host and commentator to the hourly news reporting position, where most of the script is written by others. Although technically a lower position, Price's total salary package remains the same. Price is now seeking professional advice to determine whether the radio station's action represents a form of discrimination on the basis of marital status.

Case Five For the past few years, the design department of a small (40-employee) company has been using a particular software program, but the three employees who use the software have been complaining for more than a year that the software is out of date and is slowing down their performance. The department agreed to switch to a competing software program, costing several thousand dollars. However, the next version won't be released for six months and buying the current version will not allow much discount on the next version. The company has put in advance orders for the next version. Meanwhile, one employee was able to get a copy of the current version of the software from a friend in the industry. The company has allowed the three employees to use this current version of the software even though they did not pay for it.

SELF-ASSESSMENT 2.6 ARE YOU INTROVERTED OR EXTRAVERTED?

PURPOSE This self-assessment is designed to help you estimate the extent to which you are introverted or extraverted.

INSTRUCTIONS The statements in the scale below refer to personal characteristics that might or might not be characteristic of you. Mark the box indicating the extent to which the statement accurately or inaccurately describes you. Then use the scoring key in Appendix B at the end of this book to calculate your results. This exercise should be completed alone so that you can assess yourself honestly without concerns of social comparison. Class discussion will focus on the meaning and implications of extraversion and introversion in organizations.

IPIP Introversion-Extraversion Scale

HOW ACCURATELY DOES EACH OF THE STATEMENTS LISTED BELOW DESCRIBE YOU?	VERY ACCURATE DESCRIPTION OF ME	MODERATELY ACCURATE	NEITHER ACCURATE NOR INACCURATE	MODERATELY INACCURATE	VERY INACCURATE DESCRIPTION OF ME
1. I feel comfortable around people.	☐	☐	☐	☐	☐
2. I make friends easily.	☐	☐	☐	☐	☐
3. I keep in the background.	☐	☐	☐	☐	☐
4. I don't talk a lot.	☐	☐	☐	☐	☐
5. I would describe my experiences as somewhat dull.	☐	☐	☐	☐	☐
6. I know how to captivate people.	☐	☐	☐	☐	☐
7. I don't like to draw attention to myself.	☐	☐	☐	☐	☐
8. I am the life of the party.	☐	☐	☐	☐	☐
9. I am skilled in handling social situations.	☐	☐	☐	☐	☐
10. I have little to say.	☐	☐	☐	☐	☐

Source: Adapted from instruments described and/or presented in L. R. Goldberg, J. A. Johnson, H. W. Eber, R. Hogan, M. C. Ashton, C. R. Cloninger, and H. C. Gough, "The International Personality Item Pool and the Future of Public-Domain Personality Measures," *Journal of Research in Personality* 40 (2006), pp. 84–96.

After reading this chapter go to www.mhhe.com/mcshane6e for more in-depth information and interactivities that correspond to the chapter.

Perceiving Ourselves and Others in Organizations

learning objectives

After reading this chapter, you should be able to:

LO1 Describe the elements of self-concept and explain how they affect an individual's behavior and well-being.

LO2 Outline the perceptual process and discuss the effects of categorical thinking and mental models in that process.

LO3 Discuss how stereotyping, attribution, self-fulfilling prophecy, halo, false-consensus, primacy, and recency effects influence the perceptual process.

LO4 Discuss three ways to improve perceptions, with specific applications to organizational situations.

LO5 Outline the main features of a global mindset and justify its usefulness to employees and organizations.

student has been reluctant to let anyone know. "I was afraid to tell anybody when I was younger because I thought it was a guy thing," admits Parziale. Fortunately, she and more than a dozen other teenage girls were able to experience firefighting skills firsthand at Camp Fully Involved, a six-day intensive course in Nashua, New Hampshire. Participants learned how to climb 100-foot ladders, cut ventilation holes in a roof with an axe, fight fires in the woods, rappel off a building, and conduct search-and-rescue missions.

Women represent only 3.4 percent of firefighters in the United States. Camp Fully Involved aims to increase this number by helping young women perceive firefighting as an exciting occupation compatible with their self-concepts. The camp also helps build their self-confidence for any career. "You see all these girls walk a little taller when they leave," says Nashua Fire Department Lieutenant Jess Wyman, who organized the camp. "They're more willing to be outgoing and to try things they've never done before."

The Houston Fire Department offers one of the few other firefighting camps for teenage girls. It also hopes this direct experience will get more women interested in firefighting by breaking stereotypes and building a "can-do" attitude in participants. "We wanted to show the girls they can do it," says one of Houston's female firefighters about the training camp.

But even as these programs encourage more women to define themselves as firefighters, the occupation's macho stereotype remains a problem. "We don't have a lot of parents telling their daughters 'hey honey, when you grow up, you can be a firefighter,'" admits Houston Fire Department Assistant Chief Karen DuPont. Stereotyping also causes problems in fire stations. For example, the Equal Employment Opportunities Commission recently concluded that two female Houston Fire Department firefighters were harassed and discriminated against because male firefighters rejected women in these roles.[1]

Camp Fully Involved, a six-day intensive firefighter course for teenage girls, builds self-confidence and dissolves the stereotype that firefighting is only for men.

Firefighting services around the United States and globally face two challenges in attracting and keeping women in this occupation: (1) the self-concept women have about themselves versus their image of firefighters and (2) perceptions that others have about firefighters and of women in these roles. We discuss both of these related topics in this chapter. First, we examine how people perceive themselves—their self-concepts—and how that self-perception affects their decisions and behavior. Next, we focus on perceptions in organizational settings, beginning with how people select, organize, and interpret information, followed by several specific perceptual processes such as stereotyping, attribution, and self-fulfilling prophecies. We then identify potentially effective ways to improve perceptions, such as corporate volunteering. The final section of this chapter reviews the main elements of global mindset, a largely perceptual process valued in this increasingly globalized world.

Self-Concept: How We Perceive Ourselves

LO1

How much does work define your self-concept? Go to **www. mcgrawhillconnect.com** to assess how you score the work centrality scale.

Why are there so few female firefighters in the United States and most other countries? The opening vignette to this chapter offers a few reasons, one of which is that women do not see themselves as firefighters and have doubts about doing that job. "I don't think women automatically think they can be a firefighter," admits Kate Bailey, who entered this line of work a few years ago in southeastern England. This self-concept incompatibility is further reinforced by gendered perceptions of firefighters held by family, friends, and the media. "My family told me they thought I'd be an interior designer or something," recalls Maria Dominguez, a firefighter in Odessa, Texas. "They would say, 'Why's she doing that [becoming a firefighter]? It's a man's job.'"[2]

We begin this chapter by looking at how people perceive themselves, that is, their self-concept. **Self-concept** refers to an individual's self-beliefs and self-evaluations. It is the "Who am I?" and "How do I feel about myself?" that people ask themselves and that guide their decisions and actions. Whether contemplating a career as a firefighter or a financial analyst, we compare our images of that job with our current (perceived self) and desired (ideal self) images of ourselves. We also evaluate our current and desired competencies to determine whether there is a good fit with that job. A growing number of OB writers are discovering that how people perceive themselves helps explain their attitudes, motivation, decisions, and behavior in the workplace.

SELF-CONCEPT COMPLEXITY, CONSISTENCY, AND CLARITY

Self-concepts vary in their complexity, consistency, and clarity (see Exhibit 3.1).[3] First, self-concepts have varying degrees of *complexity*, that is, the number of distinct and important roles or identities that people perceive about themselves. Everyone has some degree of complexity because they see themselves in more than one role (student, friend, daughter, sports enthusiast, etc.). Complexity is determined not only by the number of selves but also by the separation of those selves.[4] A self-concept has low complexity when the individual's most

EXHIBIT 3.1

Self-Concept Dimensions

SELF-CONCEPT DIMENSION	DESCRIPTION
Complexity	How many distinct and important roles or identities does a person think about to define him- or herself?
Consistency	How compatible are the person's self-concept identities with one another and with the person's personality, values, and other attributes?
Clarity	To what extent does the person define him- or herself clearly, confidently, and consistently over time?

important identities are highly interconnected, such as when they are all work-related (manager, engineer, family income-earner).

A second characteristic of self-concept is its internal *consistency.* People have high internal consistency when most of their self-perceived roles require similar personality traits, values, and other attributes. Low consistency occurs when some self-perceptions require personal characteristics that conflict with characteristics required for other aspects of self. Low self-concept consistency would exist if you saw yourself as a very exacting engineer yet also a cavalier and risk-oriented skier. *Clarity,* the third characteristic of self-concept, is the degree to which you have a clear, confidently defined, and stable self-concept. Clarity occurs when we are confident about who we are, can describe our important identities to others, and provide the same description of ourselves across time. Self-concept clarity increases with age, as well as with the consistency of a person's multiple selves.[5]

Self-concept complexity, consistency, and clarity are important because they influence a person's well-being, behavior, and performance. People tend to have psychological well-being when they have multiple selves (complexity) that are well established (clarity) and are similar and compatible with personal traits (consistency). Complexity is important because it protects our self-evaluations when some roles are threatened or damaged.[6] A complex self-concept is rather like a ship with several compartments that can be sealed off from one another. If one compartment is damaged, it can be isolated so most of the ship remains intact. People with low complexity, on the other hand, suffer severe loss when they experience failure because these events affect a large part of themselves.

A person's well-being also increases to some extent when his or her multiple selves are in harmony (consistency).[7] Some self-concept diversity helps people adapt, but too much variation causes internal tension and conflict. Finally, well-being tends to increase with self-concept clarity. When we lack confidence in ourselves, we are more easily influenced by others, experience more stress when making decisions, and feel more threatened by social forces that undermine our self-confidence and self-esteem.[8]

Self-concept complexity, consistency, and clarity have more varied effects on behavior and performance.[9] On the one hand, people who define themselves mainly by their work (i.e., low complexity) tend to have lower absenteeism and turnover. They also potentially perform better due to their greater investment in skill development, longer hours, more concentration on work, and so forth. On the other hand, low complexity commonly results in higher stress and depression when the main self aspect is damaged or threatened, which further undermines individual performance. Self-concept clarity tends to improve performance and is considered vital for leadership roles.[10] However, people with very high clarity may have role inflexibility; they have more difficulty adapting to emerging work roles.

Complexity, consistency, and clarity describe characteristics of a person's self-concept. In addition to these characteristics, four processes shape self-concept and influence a person's decisions and behavior. Let's look at each of these four "selves": self-enhancement, self-verification, self-evaluation, and social self (social identity).

SELF-ENHANCEMENT

People across most (and likely all) cultures are inherently motivated to perceive themselves (and to be perceived by others) as competent, attractive, lucky, ethical, and important.[11] This **self-enhancement** is observed in many ways. Individuals tend to rate themselves as above average, believe that they have a better-than-average probability of success, and attribute their successes to personal motivation or ability while blaming the situation for their mistakes. For instance, a recent U.S. government survey reported that 69 percent of government workers rated their performance above average compared with that of other coworkers in their unit; only 1 percent rated their performance below average. Even more extreme is that 94 percent of university professors

self-concept
An individual's self-beliefs and self-evaluations.

self-enhancement
A person's inherent motivation to have a positive self-concept (and to have others perceive him/her favorably), such as being competent, attractive, lucky, ethical, and important.

Most executives say they want their employees to feel appreciated, but few translate this desire into practice as well as Donna Gadient. "The most important part of my job is to make sure people feel valued," says the global human resources vice president at Indianapolis, Indiana–based R.W. Armstrong. Gadient recognizes that the engineering company's 550 employees want to have a positive self-concept, and organizations can tap into that motivation by appreciating their contribution. Employees are "hungry for [employers] to recognize who they are and what they can bring to the world," Gadient explains.[15]

in one study rated themselves as above-average teachers compared with others at their university; two-thirds rated themselves in the top quartile![12] People don't see themselves as above average in all circumstances, but this bias is apparent for conditions that are common rather than rare and that are important to them.[13]

Self-enhancement has both positive and negative consequences in organizational settings.[14] On the positive side, individuals tend to experience better mental and physical health and adjustment when they view their self-concept in a positive light. On the negative side, self-enhancement can result in bad decisions. For example, some studies report that self-enhancement causes managers to overestimate the probability of success in investment decisions. Other research suggests that self-enhancement is a factor in high accident rates among novice drivers. Generally though, successful companies strive to help employees feel that they are valued and integral members of the organization.

SELF-VERIFICATION

Along with being motivated by self-enhancement, people try to confirm and maintain their existing self-concept.[16] This process, called **self-verification,** stabilizes an individual's self-concept, which in turn provides an important anchor that guides his or her thoughts and actions. Employees actively communicate their self-concepts so coworkers can provide feedback that reinforces those self-concepts. For example, you might let coworkers know that you are a very organized person; later, they point out situations where you have indeed been very organized. Unlike self-enhancement, self-verification occurs when we seek out feedback that supports our self-view, even when it isn't flattering (e.g., "I'm a numbers person, not a people person"). Social scientists continue to debate whether and under what conditions people prefer information that supports self-enhancement or self-verification.[17] In other words, do we prefer compliments rather than accurate critiques about our known weaknesses?

Self-verification has several implications for organizational behavior.[18] First, it affects the perceptual process because employees are more likely to remember information that is consistent with their self-concept and screen out information that seems inconsistent with it. Second, the clearer the individual's self-concept, the less he or she will accept feedback that contradicts that self-concept. Third, employees are motivated to interact with others who affirm their self-concept, which affects how well they get along with their bosses and other team members.

SELF-EVALUATION

Almost everyone strives to have a positive self-concept, but some people have a more positive evaluation of themselves than do others. This *self-evaluation* is mostly defined by three elements: self-esteem, self-efficacy, and locus of control.[19]

Self-Esteem   *Self-esteem*—the extent to which people like, respect, and are satisfied with themselves—represents a global self-evaluation. Some experts also believe that self-esteem is a person's rating of his or her success at social inclusion. In other words, people have higher self-esteem when they believe they are connected to and accepted by others. People with high self-esteem are less influenced by others, tend to persist in spite of failure, and think more rationally. Self-esteem regarding specific aspects of self (e.g., a good student, a good driver, a good parent) predicts specific thoughts and behaviors, whereas a person's overall self-esteem predicts only large bundles of thoughts and behaviors.[20]

Self-Efficacy   **Self-efficacy** refers to a person's belief that he or she can successfully complete a task.[21] Those with high self-efficacy have a "can-do" attitude. They believe they possess the energy (motivation), resources (situational factors), understanding of the correct course of action (role perceptions), and competencies (ability) to perform the task. In other words, self-efficacy is an individual's perception regarding the MARS model in a specific situation. Although originally defined in terms of specific tasks, self-efficacy is also a general trait related to self-concept.[22] General self-efficacy is a perception of one's competence to perform across a variety of situations. The higher the person's general self-efficacy, the higher is his or her overall self-evaluation.

Locus of Control   **Locus of control** is defined as a person's general beliefs about the amount of control he or she has over personal life events.[23] Individuals with an internal locus of control believe that their personal characteristics (i.e., motivation and competencies) mainly influence life's outcomes. Those with more of an external locus of control believe that events in their life are due mainly to fate, luck, or conditions in the external environment. Locus of control is a generalized belief, so people with an external locus can feel in control in familiar situations (such as performing common tasks). However, their underlying locus of control would be apparent in new situations in which their control over events is uncertain.

People with a more internal locus of control have a more positive self-evaluation. They also tend to perform better in most employment situations, are more successful in their careers, earn more money, and are better suited for leadership positions. Internals are also more satisfied with their jobs, cope better in stressful situations, and are more motivated by performance-based reward systems.[24] One worrisome observation is that young people have significantly shifted from an internal to more of an external locus of control over the four decades since the early 1960s.[25]

THE SOCIAL SELF

Everyone has a self-concept that includes at least a few identities (manager, parent, golfer, etc.), and each identity is defined by a set of attributes. These attributes highlight both the person's uniqueness (personal identity) and his or her association with others (social identity).[26] *Personal identity* (also known as internal self-concept) consists of attributes that make us unique and distinct from people in the social groups to which we have a connection. For instance, an unusual achievement that distinguishes you from other people typically becomes a personal

self-verification
A person's inherent motivation to confirm and maintain his/her existing self-concept.

self-efficacy
A person's belief that he or she has the ability, motivation, correct role perceptions, and favorable situation to complete a task successfully.

locus of control
A person's general belief about the amount of control he or she has over personal life events.

EXHIBIT 3.2

Social Identity Theory Example

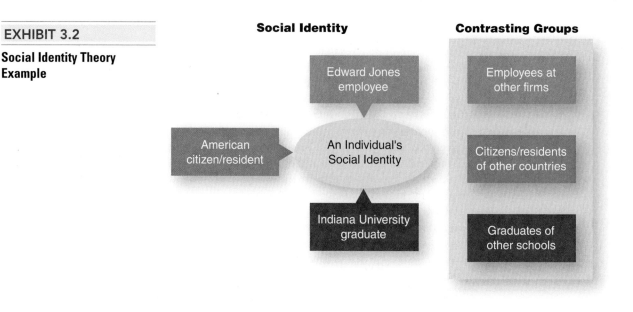

Social Identity

Contrasting Groups

Edward Jones employee

American citizen/resident

An Individual's Social Identity

Indiana University graduate

Employees at other firms

Citizens/residents of other countries

Graduates of other schools

identity characteristic. Personal identity refers to something about you as an individual, without reference to a larger group.

At the same time, human beings are social animals; they have an inherent drive to be associated with others and recognized as part of social communities. This drive to belong is reflected in self-concept by the fact that all individuals define themselves to some degree by their relationships.[27] This *social identity* (also called external self-concept) is the central theme of **social identity theory,** which says that people define themselves by the groups to which they belong or have an emotional attachment. For instance, someone might have a social identity as an American, a graduate of Indiana University, and an employee at Edward Jones (see Exhibit 3.2).

Social identity is a complex combination of many memberships arranged in a hierarchy of importance. One factor determining importance is how easily we are identified as a member of the reference group, such as by our gender, age, and ethnicity. A second factor is our minority status in a group. It is difficult to ignore your gender in a class where most other students are the opposite gender, for example. In that context, gender tends to become a stronger defining feature of your social identity than it is in social settings where there are many people of the same gender.

Along with demographic characteristics, the group's status is an important factor in determining whether we include it in our social identity, because this association makes us feel better about ourselves (i.e., self-enhancement). Medical doctors usually define themselves by their profession because of its high status. Some people describe themselves by where they work ("I work at Mayo Clinic") because their employer has a good reputation. Others never mention where they work because their employer is noted for poor relations with employees or has a poor reputation in the community.[28]

Everyone tries to balance his or her personal and social identities, but the priority for uniqueness (personal identities) versus relatedness (social identities) differs from one person to the next. People whose self-concepts are heavily defined by social rather than personal identities are more motivated to abide by team norms and more easily influenced by peer pressure. Those who place more emphasis on personal identities, on the other hand, speak out more frequently against the majority and are less motivated to follow the team's wishes. Furthermore, expressing disagreement with others is a sign of distinctiveness and can help employees form a clearer self-concept, particularly when that disagreement is based on differences in personal values.[29]

social identity theory
A theory stating that people define themselves by the groups to which they belong or have an emotional attachment.

perception
The process of receiving information about and making sense of the world around us.

SELF-CONCEPT AND ORGANIZATIONAL BEHAVIOR

Self-concept has become a hot topic in several disciplines and is now gaining attention in organizational behavior as a cluster of theories to explain employee attitudes and behavior. According to recent studies, self-concept helps explain leadership, team dynamics, employee motivation, decision making, influence, organizational commitment, and other topics that we will discuss in this book.[30] Consequently, self-concept and its specific elements will be mentioned in relation to several topics throughout this book, including later parts of this chapter.

Many organizational leaders are already well aware that supporting employee self-views can significantly improve their performance and well-being. For more than 50 years, Johnson & Johnson managers have lived by the health products company's credo that every employee "must be considered as an individual" and that the company "must respect their dignity and recognize their merit." Executives at Intercontinental Hotels Group (IHG) point out that the quality of service that employees give their guests depends on how well those employees feel valued by management. As one IHG executive recently explained: "Everything you do in the business must make [employees] feel like heroes and heroines and you must acknowledge the huge contribution they make. Everyone says they do this, but very few companies do. That's how you galvanize an organization—by making people feel that they belong to something special."[31]

Perceiving the World Around Us

LO2

We spend more time perceiving ourselves (thinking about our self-concept) than any other person. Nevertheless, our perceptual energy is directed toward the outer world most of the time. Whether as a structural engineer, forensic accountant, or senior executive, you need to pay attention to how to make sense of the world around you, including the conditions that challenge the accuracy of those perceptions. **Perception** is the process of receiving information about and making sense of the world around us. It entails determining which information to notice, how to categorize this information, and how to interpret it within the framework of our existing knowledge. This perceptual process generally follows the steps shown in Exhibit 3.3. Perception begins when environmental stimuli are received through our senses. Most stimuli that bombard our senses are screened out; the rest are organized and interpreted.

EXHIBIT 3.3

Model of the Perceptual Process

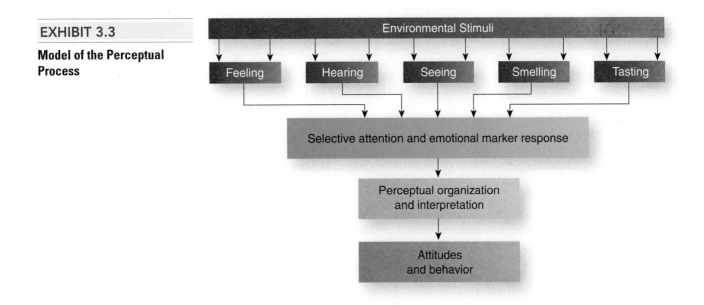

The process of attending to some information received by our senses and ignoring other information is called **selective attention.** Selective attention is influenced by characteristics of the person or object being perceived, particularly size, intensity, motion, repetition, and novelty. For example, a small, flashing red light on a nurse station console is immediately noticed because it is bright (intensity), flashing (motion), and a rare event (novelty), and it has symbolic meaning that a patient's vital signs are failing. Notice that selective attention is also influenced by the context in which the target is perceived. The selective attention process is triggered by things or people who might be out of context, such as those with a foreign accent in a setting where most people have American accents.

Characteristics of the perceiver also influence selection attention, usually without the perceiver's awareness.[32] When information is received through the senses, our brain quickly and nonconsciously assesses whether it is relevant or irrelevant to us and then attaches emotional markers (worry, happiness, boredom) to that information. These emotional markers help us store information in memory; they also reproduce the same emotions when we are subsequently thinking about this information.[33] The selective attention process is far from perfect however. The Greek philosopher Plato acknowledged this imperfection long ago when he wrote that we see reality only as shadows reflecting against the rough wall of a cave.[34]

One perceptual bias in selective attention is the effect of our assumptions and conscious anticipation of future events. You are more likely to notice a coworker's e-mail among the daily bombardment of messages when you expect to receive that e-mail (particularly when it is important to you). Unfortunately, expectations and assumptions also cause us to screen out potentially important information. In one study, students were asked to watch a 30-second video clip in which several people passed around two basketballs. Students who were instructed just to watch the video clip easily noticed someone dressed in a gorilla suit walking among the players for nine seconds and stopping to thump his or her chest. But only half of the students who were asked to count the number of times one basketball was passed around noticed the intruding gorilla.[35]

Another selective attention problem, called **confirmation bias,** is the tendency for people to screen out information that is contrary to their decisions, beliefs, values, and assumptions, whereas confirming information is more readily accepted through the perceptual process.[36] This bias occurs, for instance, when we form an opinion or theory about something, such as a consumer trend or an employee's potential. The preconception causes us to select information that is consistent with the theory and to ignore contrary or seemingly irrelevant information. Studies have reported that this faulty selective attention occurs when police detectives and other forensic experts quickly form theories about what happened.[37]

There are many examples of confirmation bias in scientific research, where scientists have ignored or removed evidence that contradicts their prized theories. One classic case occurred in the 1970s when nuclear particle researchers at CERN in Europe found an unusual dip in the pattern formed by a colliding particle. This was an exciting discovery, until a growing chorus of nuclear researchers elsewhere reported that they could not replicate that dip in their data. CERN vigorously defended the existence of the dip until the contrary evidence was overwhelming. What happened? CERN's researchers looked closely at batches of data that did not show any dip. They were convinced that the missing dip was due to bad data, so they invariably found enough justification to discard batches that didn't have any dip. Meanwhile, batches of confirming data were accepted without scrutiny. In effect, CERN discarded the evidence that opposed their exciting, but short-lived, discovery![39]

"It is a capital mistake to theorize before you have all the evidence," warned the mythical detective Sherlock Holmes in *A Study in Scarlet.* "It biases the judgment." Law enforcement agencies around the world try to follow Holmes's advice. To reduce the risk of wrongful conviction, detectives *avoid* embracing any theories too early in the investigation. "We can't succumb to tunnel vision or we could miss obvious signs in front of our face about what happened," says Lt. Sean Crosier about a missing person in West Virginia.[38]

PERCEPTUAL ORGANIZATION AND INTERPRETATION

People make sense of information even before they become aware of it. This sense making partly includes **categorical thinking**—the mostly nonconscious process of organizing people and objects into preconceived categories that are stored in our long-term memory.[40] Categorical thinking relies on a variety of automatic perceptual grouping principles. Things are often grouped together based on their similarity or proximity to others. If you notice that a group of similar-looking people includes several professors, for instance, you will likely assume that the others in that group are also professors. Another form of perceptual grouping is based on the need for cognitive closure, such as filling in missing information about what happened at a meeting that you didn't attend (e.g., who was there, where it was held). A third form of grouping occurs when we think we see trends in otherwise ambiguous information. Several studies have found that people have a natural tendency to see patterns that really are random events, such as presumed winning streaks among sports stars or in gambling.[41]

The process of making sense of the world around us also involves interpreting incoming information. This happens as quickly as selecting and organizing because the previously mentioned emotional markers are tagged to incoming stimuli, which are essentially quick judgments about whether that information is good or bad for us. How much time does it take to make these quick judgments? Recent studies estimate that we make reliable judgments about another individual's trustworthiness based on viewing a facial image for as little as 50 milliseconds (1/20th of a second) In fact, whether we see a face for a minute or for just 200 milliseconds, our opinion of whether we like or trust that person is about the same.[42] Collectively, these studies reveal that selective attention, perceptual organization, and interpretation operate very quickly and to a large extent without our awareness.

Mental Models   To achieve our goals with some degree of predictability and sanity, we need road maps of the environments in which we live. These road maps, called **mental models,** are internal representations of the external world.[43] They consist of visual or relational images in our mind, such as what the classroom looks like or what happens when we submit an assignment late. Mental models partly rely on the process of perceptual grouping to make sense of things; they fill in the missing pieces, including the causal connection among events. For example, you have a mental model about attending a class lecture or seminar, including assumptions or expectations about where the instructor and students arrange themselves in the room, how they ask and answer questions, and so forth. We can create a mental image of a class in progress.

Mental models play an important role in sense making, yet they also make it difficult to see the world in different ways. For example, accounting professionals tend to see corporate problems from an accounting perspective, whereas marketing professionals see the same problems from a marketing perspective. Mental models also block our recognition of new opportunities. How do we change mental models? That's a tough challenge. After all, we developed models from several years of experience and reinforcement. The most important way to minimize the perceptual problems with mental models is to constantly question them. We need to ask ourselves about the assumptions we make. Working with people from diverse backgrounds is another way to break out of existing mental models. Colleagues from different cultures and areas of expertise tend to have different mental models, so working with them makes our own assumptions more obvious.

connect

How much perceptual structure do you need? Go to **www. mcgrawhillconnect.com** to assess yourself on this aspect of social perception, as well as assist your learning on various perceptual errors.

selective attention
The process of attending to some information received by our senses and ignoring other information.

confirmation bias
The process of screening out information that is contrary to our values and assumptions and to more readily accept confirming information.

categorical thinking
Organizing people and objects into preconceived categories that are stored in our long-term memory.

mental models
Visual or relational images in our mind representing the external world.

Specific Perceptual Processes and Problems

LO3

Embedded within the general perceptual process are specific subprocesses and associated errors that have received considerable attention by social scientists. Over the next several pages, we will examine several of these perceptual processes and biases, as well as their implications for organizational behavior. We begin with the most widely known perceptual process and bias: stereotyping.

STEREOTYPING IN ORGANIZATIONS

One reason few women become firefighters is that they, along with their families and friends, usually depict firefighters as rugged, risk-oriented, physically strong, and male. Although this image has kernels of truth—firefighting requires above-average physical strength and has above-average risk—several important features of the occupation are seldom mentioned, such as helping others, teamwork, and a focus on safety. In other words, people have a stereotype of firefighters that is neither accurate nor desirable for most women.

Stereotyping is the perceptual process by which we assign characteristics to an identifiable group and then automatically transfer those features to anyone we believe is a member of that group.[44] The assigned characteristics tend to be difficult to observe, such as personality traits and abilities, but they can also include physical characteristics and a host of other qualities. For instance, most people hold the stereotype that professors are intelligent and absentminded. Stereotypes are formed to some extent from personal experience, but they are mainly provided to us through media images (e.g., movie characters) and other cultural prototypes. They are beliefs held across an entire society and sometimes across several cultures, rather than beliefs that differ from one person to the next.

Stereotyping involves assigning a group's perceived attributes to individuals known or believed to be members of that group. Consequently, everyone identified with the stereotyped group is assumed to possess these characteristics. If we learn that someone is a professor, for example, we implicitly assume the person is also intelligent and absentminded. Historically, researchers also defined stereotypes as exaggerations or falsehoods. This is often true, but stereotypes often have some degree of accuracy.

Why People Stereotype   One reason people engage in stereotyping is that, as a form of categorical thinking, it is a natural and mostly nonconscious "energy-saving" process that simplifies our understanding of the world. It is easier to remember features of a stereotype than the constellation of characteristics unique to everyone we meet.[45] A second reason is that we have an innate need to understand and anticipate how others will behave. We don't have much information when first meeting someone, so we rely heavily on stereotypes to fill in the missing pieces. The higher the perceiver's need for cognitive closure, the higher the reliance on stereotypes.

A third reason stereotyping occurs is because it enhances our self-concept. Earlier in this chapter we explained that people define themselves by the groups to which they belong or have an emotional attachment. They are also motivated to maintain a positive self-concept. This combination of social identity and self-enhancement leads to the processes of categorization, homogenization, and differentiation:[46]

Categorization   Social identity is a comparative process, and the comparison begins by categorizing people into distinct groups. By viewing someone (including yourself) as a Texan, for example, you remove that person's individuality and, instead, see him or her as a prototypical representative of the group called Texans. This categorization then allows you to distinguish Texans from people who live in, say, California or New Hampshire.

Homogenization   To simplify the comparison process, we tend to think that people within each group are very similar to one another. For instance, we think Texans

stereotyping
The process of assigning traits to people based on their membership in a social category.

collectively have similar attitudes and characteristics, whereas Californians collectively have their own set of characteristics. Of course, every individual is unique, but we tend to lose sight of this fact when thinking about our social identity and how we compare to people in other social groups.

Differentiation   Self-enhancement motivates us to have a positive self-concept. Thus, in addition to categorizing and homogenizing people, we differentiate them by assigning more favorable characteristics to people in our groups than to people in other groups. This differentiation is often subtle, but it can escalate into a "good guy–bad guy" contrast when groups are in conflict.[47] In other words, when out-group members threaten our self-concept, we are particularly motivated (often without our awareness) to assign negative stereotypes to them.

Problems with Stereotyping

Everyone engages in stereotyping, but this process distorts perceptions in various ways. Although stereotypes are not completely fictional, neither do they accurately describe every person in a social category. Consider how accountants are typically stereotyped in films and literature. According to various studies, they are usually depicted as boring, monotonous, cautious, unromantic, obtuse, antisocial, shy, dysfunctional, devious, calculating, and malicious.[48] Fortunately, recent studies also note a more positive trend; some accountant characters are loyal, conscientious, and everyday heroes. The traditional accountant stereotype may fit the description of a few accountants, but it is certainly not characteristic of all—or even most—people in this profession. Even so, once we categorize someone as an accountant, the stereotypic features of accountants (boring, antisocial, etc.) are transferred to that person, even though we have not attempted to verify those characteristics in that person.

Jason Blumer defies anyone's stereotype of an accountant. The president (he prefers Chief Innovation Officer) of a boutique CPA firm in Greenville, South Carolina, usually wears jeans, T-shirts, and flip-flops around the office. He writes a popular blog, is a Twitter maniac, Skypes with clients, and hams it up with distorted photos on his iPad. "There is a new day dawning, and this country better realize we CPAs are now cool, Mac-loving, flip-flop wearing, global-serving, math-hating innovators," says Blumer about his stereotype-busting ways.[49]

Another problem with stereotyping is that it lays the foundation for discriminatory attitudes and behavior. Most of this perceptual bias occurs as *unintentional (systemic) discrimination*, whereby decision makers rely on stereotypes to establish notions of the "ideal" person in specific roles. A person who doesn't fit the ideal tends to receive a less favorable evaluation. This subtle discrimination often shows up in age discrimination claims, such as the case in which Ryanair's recruitment advertising said it was looking for "young dynamic" employees. Recruiters at the Irish discount airline probably didn't intentionally discriminate against older people, but the tribunal concluded that systemic discrimination did occur because none of the job applicants was over 40 years old.[50]

The more serious form of stereotype bias is *intentional discrimination* or *prejudice,* in which people hold unfounded negative attitudes toward people belonging to a particular stereotyped group.[51] Is overt prejudice less common today? Perhaps, but there are plenty of examples to remind us that it still exists. As the opening story to this chapter mentioned, female firefighters in Houston complained that they were harassed by a few male colleagues who held prejudiced views of women in these jobs. Consistent with these incidents, an earlier study of female firefighters reported that sexual harassment is much more prevalent in fire stations where men hold strong sex stereotypes of women.[52]

Further evidence of prejudicial discrimination comes from a French study of 2,300 help-wanted ads. The study found that job applicants with French-sounding names were much more likely to get job interviews than were applicants with North African or sub-Saharan African names, even though employers received identical résumés for both names! Furthermore, when applicants personally visited human resource staff, those with foreign names were often told the job had been filled, whereas few of the applicants with French names received this message (even when visiting afterwards). Similar studies also found degrees of job applicant discrimination involving Turkish applicants in Germany, Albanians in Greece, and Arabs in Sweden.[53]

If stereotyping is such a problem, shouldn't we try to avoid this process altogether? Unfortunately, it's not that simple. Most experts agree that categorical thinking (including stereotyping) is an automatic and nonconscious process. Specialized training programs can minimize stereotype activation to some extent, but for the most part, the process is hardwired in our brain cells.[54] Also remember that stereotyping helps us in several valuable (though fallible) ways: minimizing mental effort, filling in missing information, and supporting our social identity. The good news is that while it is very difficult to prevent the *activation* of stereotypes, we can minimize the *application* of stereotypic information. In other words, though we automatically categorize people and assign stereotypic traits to them, we can consciously minimize the extent that we rely on that stereotypic information. Later in this chapter, we identify ways to minimize stereotyping and other perceptual biases.

ATTRIBUTION THEORY

Another widely discussed perceptual phenomenon in organizational settings is the **attribution process.** Attribution involves deciding whether an observed behavior or event is caused mainly by the person (internal factors) or by the environment (external factors).[55] Internal factors include the person's ability or motivation, whereas external factors include lack of resources, other people, or just luck. If a coworker doesn't show up for an important meeting, for instance, we infer either internal attributions (the coworker is forgetful, lacks motivation, etc.) or external attributions (traffic, a family emergency, or other circumstances prevented the coworker from attending).

People rely on the three attribution rules shown in Exhibit 3.4 to determine whether someone's behavior mainly has an internal or external attribution. Internal attributions are made when the observed individual behaved this way in the past (high consistency), he or she behaves like this toward other people or in different situations (low distinctiveness), and other people do not behave this way in similar situations (low consensus). On the other hand, an external attribution is made when there is low consistency, high distinctiveness, and high consensus.

EXHIBIT 3.4

Rules of Attribution

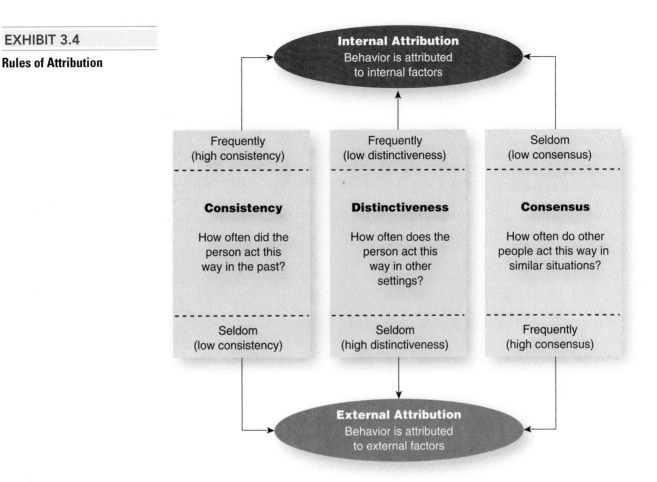

To illustrate how these three attribution rules operate, suppose that an employee is making poor-quality products one day on a particular machine. We would probably conclude that there is something wrong with the machine (an external attribution) if the employee has made good-quality products on this machine in the past (low consistency), the employee makes good-quality products on other machines (high distinctiveness), and other employees have recently had quality problems on this machine (high consensus). We would make an internal attribution, on the other hand, if the employee usually makes poor-quality products on this machine (high consistency), other employees produce good-quality products on this machine (low consensus), and the employee also makes poor-quality products on other machines (low distinctiveness).[56]

Attribution is a necessary process; we need to form cause-and-effect relationships to survive in our environment. How we react to a coworker's poor performance depends on our internal or external attribution of that performance. Students who make internal attributions about their poor performance are more likely to drop out of their programs.[57] As we see next, however, people distort their perceptions through various attribution errors.

Attribution Errors   Attribution is the source of a few perceptual errors, the two most common of which are fundamental attribution error and self-serving bias. **Fundamental attribution error** refers to our tendency to perceive another person's actions as caused mainly by internal attributions, whereas we recognize both internal and external causes of our own actions.[58] We tend to identify a coworker's motivation as the main reason

attribution process
The perceptual process of deciding whether an observed behavior or event is caused largely by internal or external factors.

fundamental attribution error
The tendency to see the person rather than the situation as the main cause of that person's behavior.

Too often, employees blame the situation for past mistakes and, over time, believe that good performance is beyond their control (an external attribution). Employee coaching reframes that perception to a stronger internal attribution. Through dialogue, employees can realize "that they have the ability and capacity to take responsibility for their situation and do something about it," says CJ Scarlet, who coaches employees through Roving Coach.[62]

why he or she is late for work (e.g., doesn't like the job), whereas we attribute our own lateness partly or mostly to external factors such as traffic jams, failed alarm clocks, or unexpected emergencies getting the kids ready for school. Fundamental attribution error occurs because observers can't easily see the external factors that constrain the person's behavior. We didn't see the traffic jam that caused the person to be late, for instance. Research suggests that fundamental attribution error is more common in Western countries than in Asian cultures, where people are taught from an early age to pay attention to the context in interpersonal relations and to see everything as being connected in a holistic way.[59]

Nearly a century ago, fictional New York crime investigator Philo Vance quipped, "Bad luck is merely a defensive and self-consoling synonym for inefficiency." Vance was referring to an attribution error known as the **self-serving bias,** which is the tendency to attribute our failures to external causes (e.g., bad luck) more than internal causes (e.g., inefficiency) while believing that successes are due more to internal than external factors.[60] Simply put, we take credit for our successes and blame others or the situation for our mistakes. In annual reports, for example, executives mainly refer to their personal qualities as reasons for the company's successes and to external factors as reasons for the company's failures. Similarly, entrepreneurs in one recent study overwhelmingly cited situational causes for their business failure (funding, economy), whereas they noticeably understated their lack of vision, social capital skills, and other personal causes.[61] Philo Vance's comment about bad luck points out that self-serving bias is associated with self-enhancement. By relying on external causes of failure and internal causes of success, people generate a more positive (and self-consoling) self-concept.

SELF-FULFILLING PROPHECY

A **self-fulfilling prophecy** occurs when our expectations about another person cause that person to act in a way that is consistent with those expectations. In other words, our perceptions can influence reality. Exhibit 3.5 illustrates the four steps in the self-fulfilling prophecy process, using the example of a supervisor and a subordinate.[63] The process begins when the supervisor forms expectations about the employee's future behavior and performance. These expectations are sometimes inaccurate, because first impressions are usually formed from limited information. The supervisor's expectations influence his or her treatment of employees. Specifically, high-expectancy employees

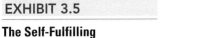

EXHIBIT 3.5

The Self-Fulfilling Prophecy Cycle

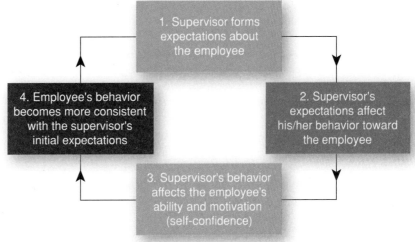

(those expected to do well) receive more emotional support through nonverbal cues (e.g., more smiling and eye contact), more frequent and valuable feedback and reinforcement, more challenging goals, better training, and more opportunities to demonstrate good performance.

The third step in a self-fulfilling prophecy includes two effects of the supervisor's behavior on the employee. First, through better training and more practice opportunities, a high-expectancy employee learns more skills and knowledge than a low-expectancy employee. Second, the employee becomes more self-confident, which results in higher motivation and willingness to set more challenging goals.[64] In the final step, high-expectancy employees have higher motivation and better skills, resulting in better performance, while the opposite is true of low-expectancy employees.

There are many examples of self-fulfilling prophecies in work and school settings.[65] Research has found that women perform less well on math tests after being informed that men tend to perform better on them. Women perform better on these tests when they are not exposed to this negative self-fulfilling prophecy. Similarly, people over 65 years of age receive lower results on memory tests after hearing that mental ability declines with age. Another study reported that the performance of Israeli Defense Force trainees was influenced by their instructor's expectations regarding the trainees' potential in the program. Self-fulfilling prophecy was at work here because the instructor's expectations were based on a list provided by researchers showing which recruits had high and low potential, even though the researchers had actually listed these trainees randomly.

Contingencies of Self-Fulfilling Prophecy   Self-fulfilling prophecies are more likely to occur at the beginning of a relationship, such as when employees are first hired. It is also stronger when several people (rather than just one person) hold the same expectations of the individual. In other words, we might be able to ignore one person's doubts about our potential but not the collective doubts of several people. The self-fulfilling prophecy effect is also stronger among people with a history of low achievement. High achievers can draw on their past successes to offset low expectations, whereas low achievers do not have past successes to support their self-confidence. Fortunately, the opposite is also true: Low achievers respond more favorably than high achievers to positive self-fulfilling prophecy. Low achievers don't receive this positive encouragement very often, so it probably has a stronger effect on their motivation to excel.[66]

The main lesson from self-fulfilling prophecy literature is that leaders need to develop and maintain a positive, yet realistic, expectation toward all employees. This

self-serving bias
The tendency to attribute our favorable outcomes to internal factors and our failures to external factors.

self-fulfilling prophecy
The perceptual process in which our expectations about another person cause that person to act more consistently with those expectations.

recommendation is consistent with the emerging philosophy of **positive organizational behavior,** which suggests that focusing on the positive rather than negative aspects of life will improve organizational success and individual well-being. Communicating hope and optimism is so important that it is identified as one of the critical success factors for physicians and surgeons. Training programs that make leaders aware of the power of positive expectations seem to have minimal effect, however. Instead, generating positive expectations and hope depends on a corporate culture of support and learning. Hiring supervisors who are inherently optimistic toward their staff is another way of increasing the incidence of positive self-fulfilling prophecies.

OTHER PERCEPTUAL EFFECTS

Self-fulfilling prophecy, attribution, and stereotyping are among the most common perceptual processes and biases in organizational settings, but there are many others. Four of them that have received attention in organizational settings are briefly described next.

Halo Effect
The **halo effect** occurs when our general impression of a person, usually based on one prominent characteristic, distorts our perception of other characteristics of that person.[67] If a supervisor who values punctuality notices that an employee is sometimes late for work, the supervisor might form a negative image of the employee and evaluate that person's other traits unfavorably as well. The halo effect is most likely to occur when concrete information about the perceived target is missing or we are not sufficiently motivated to search for it. Instead, we use our general impression of the person to fill in the missing information.

False-Consensus Effect
The **false-consensus effect** (also called *similar-to-me effect*) occurs when people overestimate the extent to which others have similar beliefs or behaviors to their own.[68] Employees who are thinking of quitting their jobs overestimate the percentage of coworkers who are also thinking about quitting, for example. There are several explanations for the false-consensus effect. One is that we are comforted by the belief that others are similar to us, particularly regarding less acceptable or divisive behavior. Put differently, we perceive "everyone does it" to reinforce our self-concept regarding behaviors that do not have a positive image (quitting, parking illegally, etc.). A second explanation is that we interact more with people who have similar views and behaviors, which causes us to overestimate how common those views/behaviors are in the entire organization or society. Third, as noted previously in this chapter, we are more likely to remember information that is consistent with our own views and selectively screen out communication that is contrary to our beliefs. Finally, our social identity process homogenizes people within groups, so we tend to think that everyone in that group has similar opinions and behavior, including the false-consensus topic.

Primacy Effect
The **primacy effect** is our tendency to quickly form an opinion of people on the basis of the first information we receive about them.[69] It is the notion that first impressions are lasting impressions. This rapid perceptual organization and interpretation occurs because we need to make sense of the world around us. The problem is that first impressions—particularly negative first impressions—are difficult to change. After categorizing someone, we tend to select subsequent information that supports our first impression and screen out information that opposes that impression.

Recency Effect
The **recency effect** occurs when the most recent information dominates our perceptions.[70] This perceptual bias is most common when people (especially those with limited experience) are making an evaluation involving complex information. For instance, auditors must digest large volumes of information in their judgments about financial documents, and the most recent information received prior to the decision tends to get weighted more heavily than information received at the beginning of the audit. Similarly, when supervisors evaluate the performance of employees over the previous year, the most recent performance information dominates the evaluation because it is the most easily recalled.

positive organizational behavior
A perspective of organizational behavior that focuses on building positive qualities and traits within individuals or institutions as opposed to focusing on what is wrong with them.

Improving Perceptions

LO4

We can't bypass the perceptual process, but we should try to minimize perceptual biases and distortions. Three potentially effective ways to improve perceptions include awareness of perceptual biases, self-awareness, and meaningful interaction.

AWARENESS OF PERCEPTUAL BIASES

One of the most obvious and widely practiced ways to reduce perceptual biases is by knowing that they exist. For example, diversity awareness training tries to minimize discrimination by making people aware of systemic discrimination as well as prejudices that occur through stereotyping. This training also attempts to dispel myths about people from various cultural and demographic groups. Awareness of perceptual biases can reduce these biases to some extent by making people more mindful of their thoughts and actions. However, awareness training has only a limited effect.[71] One problem is that teaching people to reject incorrect stereotypes has the unintended effect of reinforcing rather than reducing reliance on those stereotypes. Another problem is that diversity training is ineffective for people with deeply held prejudices against those groups.

Self-fulfilling-prophecy awareness training has also failed to live up to expectations.[72] This training approach informs managers about the existence of the self-fulfilling prophecy effect and encourages them to engage in more positive rather than negative self-fulfilling prophecies. Unfortunately, research has found that managers continue to engage in negative self-fulfilling prophecies after they complete the training program.

IMPROVING SELF-AWARENESS

A more successful way to minimize perceptual biases is by increasing self-awareness.[73] We need to become more aware of our beliefs, values, and attitudes and, from that insight, gain a better understanding of biases in our own decisions and behavior. This self-awareness

---

halo effect
A perceptual error whereby our general impression of a person, usually based on one prominent characteristic, colors our perception of other characteristics of that person.

false-consensus effect
A perceptual error in which we overestimate the extent to which others have beliefs and characteristics similar to our own.

primacy effect
A perceptual error in which we quickly form an opinion of people based on the first information we receive about them.

recency effect
A perceptual error in which the most recent information dominates our perception of others.

Debating Point

DO WE NEED DIVERSITY TRAINING PROGRAMS?[74]

In most large corporations, diversity training programs are well-entrenched bastions in the battle against workplace discrimination. In most programs, participants are reminded to respect cultural and gender differences. They also learn common assumptions and biases that people make about other demographic groups. When companies lose discrimination cases, one of their first requirements is to introduce diversity training.

In spite of its good intentions, diversity training might not be very useful. One concern is that most sessions are mandatory, so employees aren't really committed to their content. Furthermore, biases and prejudices are deeply anchored, so a half-day lecture and group chat on diversity won't change employee perceptions and behavior. Even if these programs motivate employees to be more tolerant of others and to avoid stereotypes, these good

intentions evaporate quickly in companies that lack a diversity culture.

It gets worse. One major review reported that the presence of diversity training increased the percentage of white women in management, but it decreased the percentage of black women in management by the same degree. There is some concern that discussing cultural differences increases rather than decreases stereotyping. For instance, students in one study showed more bias against the elderly after watching a video encouraging them to be less biased against older people! Diversity training programs might also produce ill-feelings among participants. One program for incoming freshmen at the University of Delaware was cancelled after white students complained it made them feel racist and gay students felt pressured to reveal their sexual orientation.

tends to reduce perceptual biases by making people more open-minded and nonjudgmental toward others. Self-awareness is equally important in other ways. The emerging concept of authentic leadership emphasizes self-awareness as the first step in a person's ability to effectively lead others (see Chapter 12). Essentially, we need to understand our own values, strengths, and biases as a foundation for building a vision and leading others toward that vision.[75]

But how do we become more self-aware? One approach is to complete formal tests that indicate any implicit biases you might have toward others. One such procedure is the Implicit Association Test (IAT). Although the accuracy of the IAT is being hotly debated by scholars, it attempts to detect subtle racial, age, and gender biases by associating positive and negative words with specific demographic groups.[76] Many people are much more cautious about their stereotypes and prejudices after discovering that their test results show a personal bias against older people or individuals from different ethnic backgrounds.[77]

Another way to increase self-awareness and thereby reduce perceptual biases is by applying the **Johari Window.**[78] Developed by Joseph Luft and Harry Ingram (whose first names combine to produce "Johari"), this model of self-awareness and mutual understanding divides information about you into four "windows"—open, blind, hidden, and unknown—based on whether your own values, beliefs, and experiences are known to you and to others (see Exhibit 3.6). The *open area* includes information about you that is known both to you and to others. The *blind area* refers to information that is known to others but not to you. For example, your colleagues might notice that you are self-conscious and awkward when meeting the company chief executive, but you are unaware of this fact. Information known to you but unknown to others is found in the *hidden area*. Finally, the *unknown area* includes values, beliefs, and experiences that aren't known to you or others.

The main objective of the Johari Window is to increase the size of the open area so that both you and colleagues are aware of your perceptual limitations. This is partly accomplished by reducing the hidden area through *disclosure*—informing others of your beliefs, feelings, and experiences that may influence the work relationship. The open area also increases through *feedback* from others about your behavior. This information helps you to reduce your blind area because, according to recent studies, people near you are good

EXHIBIT 3.6

Johari Window Model of Self-Awareness and Mutual Understanding

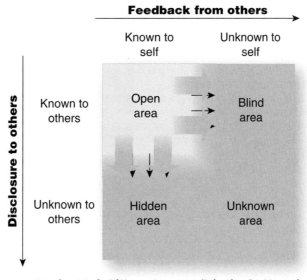

Source: Based on J. Luft, *Of Human Interaction* (Palo Alto, CA: National Press Books, 1969).

sources of information about many (but not all) of your traits and behaviors.[79] Finally, the combination of disclosure and feedback occasionally produces revelations about information in the unknown area.

MEANINGFUL INTERACTION

While the Johari Window relies on dialogue, self-awareness and mutual understanding can also improve through *meaningful interaction*.[80] Meaningful interaction is founded on the **contact hypothesis,** which states that under certain conditions, people who interact will be less prejudiced or perceptually biased toward one another.[81] Simply spending time with members of other groups can improve your understanding and opinion of those persons to some extent. However, meaningful interaction is strongest when people work closely and frequently on a shared goal that requires cooperation and reliance on one another. Furthermore, everyone should have equal status in that context and should be engaged in a meaningful task. Connections 3.1 describes several examples of meaningful interaction in which CEOs and other executives work beside frontline staff.

Meaningful interaction reduces dependence on stereotypes to understand others, because we gain better knowledge about that individual and experience the unique attributes of that person in action. Meaningful interaction also potentially improves empathy toward others. **Empathy** refers to understanding and being sensitive to the feelings, thoughts, and situations of others.[82] People empathize when they cognitively transpose themselves into the other person's place as if they were the other person. This perceptual experience is both cognitive and emotional, meaning that empathy is about understanding as well as feeling what the other person feels in that context. Empathizing with others improves our sensitivity to the external causes of another person's performance and behavior, thereby reducing fundamental attribution error. A supervisor who imagines what it is like to be a single parent, for example, would become more sensitive to the external causes of lateness and other events among such employees.

Johari Window
A model of mutual understanding that encourages disclosure and feedback to increase our own open area and reduce the blind, hidden, and unknown areas.

contact hypothesis
A theory stating that the more we interact with someone, the less prejudiced or perceptually biased we will be against that person.

empathy
A person's understanding of and sensitivity to the feelings, thoughts, and situations of others.

CEOs Gain Meaningful Interaction by Working on the Front Line

If the meal service seems a bit slower than usual on your next Air New Zealand flight, it might be because CEO Rob Fyfe is doing the serving while chatting with passengers. Fyfe and his top executive team often take time away from the firm's headquarters in Auckland to serve as flight attendants, check-in counter staff, or baggage handlers. (The executives had to pass tests to work as part of the cabin crew.) Helmut Wieser, an executive vice president at Alcoa, also works beside frontline staff on the shop floor of several plants four times a year. As part of a television series on CEOs in frontline jobs, Herschend Family Entertainment CEO Joel Manby worked incognito alongside employees at the entertainment company in jobs ranging from waiting tables to washing gigantic aquariums.

Working in these frontline jobs gives executives a reality check about the business and its employees. For example, along with getting to know staff, Joel Manby became aware that he had been too reclusive during the financial crisis. "Working with [these employees] helped me realize that during the recession, I had become withdrawn and detached, affected by difficult business decisions," Manby acknowledges. "They showed me the importance of getting back in touch with people."

Some companies have extended this frontline experience to professional and administrative staff. At WideOpenWest, the Denver-based telecommunication company, professional and management staff spend time every quarter working at the call center or traveling to work sites with technology staff. Every-

Herschend Family Entertainment CEO Joel Manby and other executives keep their perceptions in focus by working alongside frontline staff.

one at Domino's head office in Ann Arbor, Michigan, attends Pizza Prep School, where they learn how to make pizzas and run a pizza store. Every year, PortionPac Chemical, a Chicago-based manufacturer of cleaning fluids, holds a "Front-to-Back Day" to help front office employees gain a better understanding of work in the factory. On that day, everyone, from the receptionist to CEO, receives work assignments from plant supervisor Mary Jaramillo. "We want them to see how difficult the jobs are," says Jaramillo.[83]

Global Mindset: Developing Perceptions Across Borders

LO5

Anne Connelly had previously worked outside North America, but her current job at Médecins Sans Frontières (Doctors Without Borders) pushed her even further onto the global stage. Connelly was sent to the Central African Republic to help the government with some of its financial programs. The setting wasn't for the fainthearted. "There has been civil unrest in the country for a while, mainly caused by poor government and warring rebel tribes coming in from neighboring countries," Connelly explains. But the experience of working in other lands with people who have different perceptions and experiences is exactly what Connelly had been seeking. "DeGroote [MBA program] taught me to develop a global mindset of how businesses operate at the international level," she says. "By learning the culture, the languages, the people, the climate, everything, you can develop more holistic solutions to any given problem."[84]

Organizational leaders are paying much more attention these days to employees such as Anne Connelly who are developing a global mindset. A **global mindset** refers to an individual's ability to perceive, know about, and process information across cultures. It includes (1) an awareness of, openness to, and respect for other views and practices in the world; (2) the capacity to empathize and act effectively across cultures; (3) an ability to process complex information about novel environments; and (4) the ability to comprehend and reconcile intercultural matters with multiple levels of thinking.[85]

Let's look at each of these features. First, global mindset occurs as people develop more of a global than a local/parochial frame of reference about their business and its

global mindset
An individual's ability to perceive, appreciate, and empathize with people from other cultures, and to process complex cross-cultural information.

environment. They also have more knowledge and appreciation of many cultures and do not judge the competence of others by their national or ethnic origins. Second, global mindset includes understanding the mental models held by colleagues from other cultures, as well as their emotional experiences in a given situation. Furthermore, this empathy translates into the effective use of words and behaviors that are compatible with the local culture. Third, people with a strong global mindset are able to process and analyze large volumes of information in new and diverse situations. Fourth, a global mindset involves the capacity to quickly develop useful mental models of situations, at both local and global levels of analysis.

As you might imagine, employees offer tremendous value to organizations as they develop a global mindset.[86] They develop better relationships across cultures by understanding and showing respect to distant colleagues and partners. They can sift through huge volumes of ambiguous and novel information transmitted in multinational relationships. They have a capacity to form networks and exchange resources more rapidly across borders. They also develop greater sensitivity and respond more quickly to emerging global opportunities.

DEVELOPING A GLOBAL MINDSET

Developing a global mindset involves improving one's perceptions, so the practices of awareness, self-awareness, and meaningful interaction are relevant. As with most perceptual capabilities, a global mindset begins with self-awareness—understanding one's own beliefs, values, and attitudes. Through self-awareness, people grow more open-minded and nonjudgmental when receiving and processing complex information for decision making. In addition, employees develop a global mindset when they are given opportunities to compare their own mental models with those of coworkers or partners from other regions of the world. For example, employees might engage in virtual dialogues about how well the product's design or marketing strategy is received in the United States versus India or Chile. When companies engage in regular discussions about global competitors, suppliers, and other stakeholders, they eventually move the employee's sphere of awareness more toward that global stratum.

A global mindset develops through better knowledge of people and cultures. Some of that knowledge is acquired through formal programs, such as diversity training, but deeper absorption results from immersion in those cultures. Just as executives need to experience frontline jobs to better understand their customers and employees, so too do they and other employees need to have meaningful interaction with colleagues from other cultures in those settings. The more people embed themselves in the local environment (such as following local practices, eating local food, and using the local language), the more they tend to understand the perspectives and attitudes of their colleagues in those cultures.

For three months John Leiter was transplanted from his Ernst & Young office in Boston to Montevideo, assisting a young information technology company with its first real five-year strategic plan. Leiter (center in this photo with staff at the Uruguayan firm) was performing different work in a different country with a different culture and language. "We need people with a global mindset, and what better way to develop a global mindset, and what more realistic way, than for somebody to have an immersion experience with just enough safety net?" says Deborah Holmes, Ernst & Young global director of corporate responsibility.[87]

Developing a Global Mindset Through Immersion

Ernst & Young, IBM, Procter & Gamble, and a few other organizations have introduced special programs to accelerate global mindset development by sending teams of employees on social responsibility missions in developing countries for one or two months. IBM's Corporate Service Corps program is one of the leading examples. Each year about 500 IBMers from dozens of countries are organized into small teams and dispatched to developing countries. For one month, these diverse teams assist local people on an economic or social development project. "These people actually go out and work in emerging markets, to work in NGOs [nongovernment organizations], to work in these other kinds of environments, so they can get a perspective and learn . . . how to think about problems from another perspective, from another point of view," explains IBM CEO Sam Palmisano.[88]

Mike Goddard can attest that IBM's Corporate Service Corps program improved his global mindset.[89] The IBM information technology architect was teamed up with a dozen other IBMers from Italy, Japan, and other countries to assist local Tanzanian projects, such as more effectively distributing pumps to farmers. On arrival, Goddard quickly learned that his usual way of getting the job done wouldn't work in Tanzania. "We came in with these expectations of what we'd achieve if we were at home," admits Goddard, referring particularly to the extremely slow and intermittent Internet services. "We take it for granted, but in Tanzania you can't get to it. We had to think of other ways of working."

Goddard's second discovery was how two people interpret the same conversations differently: "Just hearing what the client was saying within the room, I'd interpret it one way, Sara [another IBM team member] from Italy would interpret it another way." Goddard's third insight from the Tanzania trip was that he and other Westerners focus too much on the work rather than the relationship. "Perhaps we do charge around too much and lose sight; the task becomes more important than the person," he suggests. "Over there [in Tanzania] it's very much the person and the interaction with the people is still more important than the job." Goddard explains that "rushing into a meeting—'Hi I want to know this, let's go, bang'—is very offensive" in Tanzania.

[chapter summary]

LO1 Describe the elements of self-concept and explain how they affect an individual's behavior and well-being.

Self-concept includes an individual's self-beliefs and self-evaluations. It has three structural dimensions, complexity, consistency, and clarity, all of which influence employee well-being, behavior, and performance. People are inherently motivated to promote and protect their self-concept (self-enhancement) and to verify and maintain their existing self-concept (self-verification). Self-evaluation consists of self-esteem, self-efficacy, and locus of control. Self-concept also consists of both personality identity and social identity. Social identity theory explains how people define themselves in terms of the groups to which they belong or have an emotional attachment.

LO2 Outline the perceptual process and discuss the effects of categorical thinking and mental models in that process.

Perception involves selecting, organizing, and interpreting information to make sense of the world around us. Perceptual organization applies categorical thinking—the mostly nonconscious process of organizing people and objects into preconceived categories that are stored in our long-term memory. Mental models—internal representations of the external world—also help us make sense of incoming stimuli.

LO3 Discuss how stereotyping, attribution, self-fulfilling prophecy, halo, false-consensus primacy, and recency effects influence the perceptual process.

Stereotyping occurs when people assign traits to others based on their membership in a social category. This assignment economizes mental effort, fills in missing information, and enhances our self-concept, but it also lays the foundation for prejudice and systemic discrimination. The attribution process involves deciding whether an observed behavior or event is caused mainly by the person (internal factors) or the environment (external factors). Attributions are decided by perceptions of the consistency, distinctiveness, and consensus of the behavior. This process is subject to fundamental attribution error and self-serving bias. A self-fulfilling prophecy occurs when our expectations about another person cause that person to act in a way that is consistent with those expectations. This effect is stronger when employees first join the work unit, when several people hold these expectations, and when the employee has a history of low achievement. Four other perceptual errors commonly noted in organizations are the halo effect, false-consensus effect, primacy effect, and recency effect.

LO4 Discuss three ways to improve perceptions, with specific applications to organizational situations.

One way to minimize perceptual biases is to become more aware of their existence. Awareness of these biases makes people more mindful of their thoughts and actions, but this training sometimes reinforces rather than reduces reliance on stereotypes and tends to be ineffective for people with deeply held prejudices. A second strategy is to become more aware of biases in our own decisions and behavior. Self-awareness increases through formal tests such as the IAT and by applying the Johari Window, which is a process in which others provide feedback to you about your behavior, and you offer disclosure to them about yourself. The third strategy is meaningful interaction, which applies the contact hypothesis that people who interact will be less prejudiced or perceptually biased toward one another. Meaningful interaction is strongest when people work closely and frequently with relatively equal status on a shared meaningful task that requires cooperation and reliance on one another. Meaningful interaction helps improve empathy, which is a person's understanding and sensitivity to the feelings, thoughts, and situations of others.

LO5 Outline the main features of a global mindset and justify its usefulness to employees and organizations.

A global mindset is a multidimensional competency that includes the individual's ability to perceive, know about, and process information across cultures. This includes (1) an awareness of, openness to, and respect for other views and practices in the world; (2) the capacity to empathize and act effectively across cultures; (3) an ability to process complex information about novel environments; and (4) the ability to comprehend and reconcile intercultural matters with multiple levels of thinking. A global mindset enables people to develop better cross-cultural relationships, to digest huge volumes of cross-cultural information, and to identify and respond more quickly to emerging global opportunities. Employees develop a global mindset through self-awareness, opportunities to compare their own mental models with people from other cultures, formal cross-cultural training, and immersion in other cultures.

{ key terms }

attribution process, p. 78
categorical thinking, p. 75
confirmation bias, p. 74
contact hypothesis, p. 85
empathy, p. 85
false-consensus effect, p. 82
fundamental attribution error, p. 79
global mindset, p. 86

halo effect, p. 82
Johari Window, p. 84
locus of control, p. 71
mental models, p. 75
perception, p. 73
positive organizational behavior, p. 82
primacy effect, p. 82
recency effect, p. 82

selective attention, p. 74
self-concept, p. 68
self-efficacy, p. 71
self-enhancement, p. 69
self-fulfilling prophecy, p. 80
self-serving bias, p. 80
self-verification, p. 70
social identity theory, p. 72
stereotyping, p. 76

{ critical thinking questions }

1. You are manager of a district that has just hired several recent university and college graduates. Most of these people are starting their first full-time job, although most or all have held part-time and summer positions in the past. They have general knowledge of their particular skill area (accounting, engineering, marketing, etc.) but know relatively little about specific business practices and developments. Explain how you would nurture the self-concepts in these new hires to strengthen their performance and maintain their psychological well-being. Also explain how you might reconcile the tendency for self-enhancement while preventing them from forming a negative self-evaluation.

2. Several years ago, senior executives at energy company CanOil wanted to acquire an exploration company (HBOG) that was owned by another energy company, AmOil. Rather than face a hostile takeover and unfavorable tax implications, CanOil's two top executives met with the CEO of AmOil to discuss a friendly exchange of stock to carry out the transaction. AmOil's chief executive was previously unaware of CanOil's plans, and as the meeting began, the AmOil executive warned that he was there merely to listen. The CanOil executives were confident that AmOil wanted to sell HBOG because energy legislation at the time made HBOG a poor investment for AmOil. AmOil's CEO remained silent for most of the meeting, which CanOil executives interpreted as an implied agreement to proceed to buy AmOil stock on the market. But when CanOil launched the stock purchase a month later, AmOil's CEO was both surprised and outraged. He thought he had given the CanOil executives the cold shoulder, remaining silent to show his disinterest in the deal. The misunderstanding nearly bankrupted CanOil because AmOil reacted by protecting its stock. What perceptual problem(s) likely occurred that led to this misunderstanding?

3. What mental models do you have about attending a college or university lecture? Are these mental models helpful? Could any of these mental models hold you back from achieving the full benefit of the lecture?

4. During a diversity management session, a manager suggests that stereotypes are a necessary part of working with

others. "I have to make assumptions about what's in the other person's head, and stereotypes help me do that," she explains. "It's better to rely on stereotypes than to enter a working relationship with someone from another culture without any idea of what they believe in!" Discuss the merits of and problems with the manager's statement.

5. You may have heard the expression: "If it is your perception, it is your reality." Please discuss this issue, and comment on how easy/difficult it may be to change one's perception.

6. Describe how a manager or coach could use the process of self-fulfilling prophecy to enhance an individual's performance.

7. Self-awareness is increasingly recognized as an important ingredient for effective leadership. Suppose that you are responsible for creating a leadership development program in a government organization. What activities or processes would you introduce to help participants in this program to constructively develop a better self-awareness of their personality, values, and personal biases?

8. Almost everyone in a college or university business program has developed some degree of global mindset. What events or activities in your life have helped to nurture the global mindset you have developed so far? What actions can you take now, while still attending school, to further develop your global mindset?

CASE STUDY 3.1 HY DAIRIES, INC.

Syd Gilman read the latest sales figures with a great deal of satisfaction. The vice president of marketing at Hy Dairies, Inc., a large Midwestern milk products manufacturer, was pleased to see that the marketing campaign to improve sagging sales of Hy's gourmet ice cream brand was working. Sales volume and market share of the product had increased significantly over the past two quarters compared with the previous year.

The improved sales of Hy's gourmet ice cream could be credited to Rochelle Beauport, who was assigned to the gourmet ice cream brand last year. Beauport had joined Hy less than two years ago as an assistant brand manager after leaving a similar job at a food products firm. She was one of the few women of color in marketing management at Hy Dairies and had a promising career with the company. Gilman was pleased with Beauport's work and tried to let her know this in annual performance reviews. He now had an excellent opportunity to reward her by offering her the recently vacated position of market research coordinator. Although technically only a lateral transfer with a modest salary increase, the marketing research coordinator job would give Beauport broader experience in some high-profile work, which would enhance her career with Hy Dairies. Few people were aware that Gilman's own career had been boosted by working as marketing research coordinator at Hy several years before.

Rochelle Beauport had also seen the latest sales figures on Hy's gourmet ice cream and was expecting Gilman's call to meet with her that morning. Gilman began the conversation by briefly mentioning the favorable sales figures, and then explained that he wanted Beauport to take the marketing research coordinator job. Beauport was shocked by the news. She enjoyed brand management and particularly the challenge involved with controlling a product that directly affected the company's profitability. Marketing research coordinator was a technical support position—a "backroom" job—far removed from the company's bottom-line activities. Marketing research was not the route to top management in most organizations, Beauport thought. She had been sidelined.

After a long silence, Beauport managed a weak, "Thank you, Mr. Gilman." She was too bewildered to protest. She wanted to collect her thoughts and reflect on what she had done wrong. Also, she did not know her boss well enough to be openly critical.

Gilman recognized Beauport's surprise, which he assumed was her positive response to hearing of this wonderful career opportunity. He, too, had been delighted several years earlier about his temporary transfer to marketing research to round out his marketing experience. "This move will be good for both you and Hy Dairies," said Gilman as he escorted Beauport from his office.

Beauport was preoccupied with several tasks that afternoon but was able to consider the day's events that evening. She was one of the top women and few minorities in brand management at Hy Dairies and feared that she was being sidelined because the company didn't want women or people of color in top management. Her previous employer had made it quite clear that women "couldn't take the heat" in marketing management and tended to place women in technical support positions after a brief term in lower brand management jobs. Obviously Syd Gilman and Hy Dairies were following the same game plan. Gilman's comments that the coordinator job would be good for her was just a nice way of saying that Beauport couldn't go any further in brand management at Hy Dairies.

Beauport now faced the difficult decision of whether to confront Gilman and try to change Hy Dairies' sexist and possibly racist practices or to leave the company.

Discussion Questions

1. Apply your knowledge of stereotyping and social identity theory to explain what went wrong here.

2. What other perceptual errors are apparent in this case study?

3. What can organizations do to minimize misperceptions in these types of situations?

CASE STUDY 3.2 FROM LIPPERT-JOHANSON INCORPORATED TO FENWAY WASTE MANAGEMENT

Lisa V. Williams, Jeewon Cho, and Alicia Boisnier, SUNY, Buffalo

Part 1 Catherine O'Neill was excited to finally graduate from Flagship University at the end of the semester. She had always been interested in accounting, following from her father's lifelong occupation, and she very much enjoyed the challenging major. She was involved in many highly regarded student clubs in the business school and worked diligently to earn good grades. Now her commitment to the profession would pay off, she hoped, as she turned her attention to her job search. In late fall, she had on-campus interviews with several firms, but her interview with the prestigious Lippert-Johanson Incorporated (LJI) stood out in her mind as the most attractive opportunity. That's why Catherine was thrilled to learn she made it to the next level of interviews, to be held at the firm's main office later that month.

When Catherine entered the elegant lobby of LJI's New York City offices, she was immediately impressed by all there was to take in. Catherine had always been one to pay attention to detail, and her acute observations of her environment had always been an asset. She was able to see how social and environmental cues told her what was expected of her, and she always set out to meet and exceed those expectations. On a tour of the office, she had already begun to size up her prospective workplace. She appreciated the quiet, focused work atmosphere. She liked how everyone was dressed: Most wore suits, and their conservative apparel supported the professional attitudes that seemed omnipresent. People spoke to her in a formal but friendly manner and seemed enthusiastic. Some of them even took the time to greet her as she was guided to the conference room for her individual interviews. "I like the way this place feels and I would love to come to work here every day," Catherine thought. "I hope I do well in my interview!"

Before she knew it, Catherine was sitting in a nicely appointed office with one of the eight managers in the firm. Sandra Jacobs was the picture of a professional woman, and Catherine naturally took her cue from her about how to conduct herself in the interview. It seemed to go very quickly, though the interview lasted an hour. As soon as Catherine left the office, she could not wait to phone her father about the interview. "I loved it there and I just know I'm a good fit!" she told her proud father. "Like them, I believe it is important to have the highest ethical standards and quality of work. Ms. Jacobs really emphasized the mission of the firm, as well as its policies. She did say that all the candidates have an excellent skill set and are well qualified for the job, so mostly, they are going to base their hiring decision on how well they think each of us will fit into the firm. Reputation is everything to an accounting firm. I learned that from you, Dad!"

After six weeks of apprehensive waiting, Catherine's efforts were rewarded when LJI and another firm contacted her with job offers. Catherine knew she would accept the offer from LJI. She saw the firm as very ethical, with the highest standards for work quality and an excellent reputation. Catherine was grateful to have been selected from such a competitive hiring process: "There couldn't be a better choice for me! I'm so proud to become a member of this company!"

Catherine's first few days at LJI were a whirlwind of a newcomer's experiences. She had meetings with her supervisor to discuss the firm mission statement, her role in the firm, and what was expected of her. She was also told to spend some time looking at the employee handbook that covers many important policies of the firm, such as dress code, sick time, grievances, the chain of command and job descriptions, and professional ethics. Everyone relied on the handbook to provide clear guidance about what is expected of each employee. Also, Catherine was informed that she would soon begin participating in continuing professional education, which would allow her to update her skills and knowledge in her field. "This is great," thought Catherine, "I'm so glad to know the firm doesn't just talk about its high standards; it actually follows through with action."

What Catherine enjoyed most about her new job were her warm and welcoming colleagues, who invited her to their group lunches beginning her first day. They talked about work and home; they seemed close, both professionally and personally. She could see that everyone had a similar attitude about work: They cared about their work and the firm, they took responsibility for their own tasks, but they also helped one another out. Catherine also got involved in LJI activities outside of work, like their baseball and soccer teams, happy hours, picnics, and parties, and she enjoyed the chance to mingle with her coworkers. In what seemed like no time at all, Catherine started to really see herself as a fully integrated member of LJI.

Before tax season started, Catherine attended some meetings of the AICPA and other professional accounting societies. There, she met many accountants from other firms who all seemed very impressed when she told them where she worked. Catherine's pride and appreciation for being a member of LJI grew as she realized how highly regarded the firm was among others in the accounting industry.

Part 2 Over the past seven years, Catherine's career in New York had flourished. Her reputation as one of the top tax accountants in her company was well established, recognized by colleagues outside the firm as well. However, Catherine entered a new chapter of her life when she married Ted Lewis, an oncology intern, who could not turn down an offer of residency at a top cancer center in upstate New York. Wanting to support Ted's once-in-a-lifetime career opportunity, Catherine decided it was time to follow the path of many of her colleagues and leave public accounting for a position that would be more conducive to starting a family. Still, her heart was in the profession, so she took an available position as a controller of a small recycling company located a few miles from Catherine and Ted's new upstate home. She knew that with this position she could both have children and maintain her career.

Fenway Waste Management is small—about 35 employees: 25 people in the warehouse, 3 administrative assistants, 2 supervisors, and 5 people in management. Catherine is finding she has to adjust to her new position and surroundings. Often she finds herself doing work that formally belongs to someone else; because it is a smaller company, managers seem to wear many hats. This was quite different from what she had experienced at LJI. In addition, the warehouse workers often have to work with greasy materials and sometimes track the grease into the offices. Catherine half-laughed and half-worried when she saw a piece of paper pinned to the wall that said, "Clean Up After Yourself!" She supposed that the nature of the business was why the offices were functional but furnished with old pieces. She couldn't imagine having a business meeting there! Also, for most employees, their casual dress matches the casual attitudes. But Catherine continues to wear a dressed-down version of her formal LJI attire, even though her new coworkers consider her overdressed.

With all the changes Catherine has experienced, she has maintained one familiar piece of her past. Although it is not required for her new position, Catherine still attends AICPA meetings and makes a point to continue updating her knowledge of current tax laws. At this year's conference, she told a former colleague, "Being here, I feel so much more like myself—I am so much more connected to these people and this environment than to those at my new job. It's too bad I don't feel this way at Fenway. I guess I'm just more comfortable with professionals who are similar to me."

Discussion Questions: Part 1

1. Discuss the social identity issues present in this case.

2. What indicated Catherine's positive evaluation of the groups described in Part 1? How did her evaluations foster her social identity?

3. What theory helps us understand how Catherine learned about appropriate behaviors at LJI?

Discussion Questions: Part 2

1. Compare and contrast LJI and Fenway.

2. What was Catherine's reaction after joining Fenway Waste Management, and why was her level of social identification different from that of LJI?

3. Is there evidence that Catherine experienced the categorization–homogenization–differentiation process? What details support your conclusion?

TEAM EXERCISE 3.3 WHO AM I?

PURPOSE This exercise is designed to help you understand the elements and implications of self-concept and social identity theory.

MATERIALS None.

INSTRUCTIONS

Step 1: Working alone (no discussion with other students), use the space provided below or a piece of paper to write down 12 words or phrases that answer the question "Who am I?" Write your words or phrases describing you as they come to mind; don't worry about their logical order here. Please be sure to fill in all 12 spaces.

Step 2: Print an "S" beside the items that define you in terms of your social identity, such as your demographics and formal or informal membership in a social group or institution (e.g., school, company, religious group). Print a "P" beside the items that define you in terms of your personal identity—that is, something unique about you, such as an accomplishment, trait, or skill that few around you possess. Next, underline one or more items that you believe will still be a strong characteristic of you 10 years from now.

Step 3: Form small groups. If you have a team project for this course, your project team would work well for this exercise. Compare your list with the lists that others in your group wrote about themselves. Discuss the following questions in your group and prepare notes for class discussion and possible presentation of these questions:

1. Among members of this team, what was the typical percentage of items representing the person's social versus personal identity? Did some team members have many more or less social identity items compared with other team members? Why do you think these large or small differences in emphasis on social or personal identity occurred?

	S/P		S/P
(a) I am _____ ___		(g) I am _____ ___	
(b) I am _____ ___		(h) I am _____ ___	
(c) I am _____ ___		(i) I am _____ ___	
(d) I am _____ ___		(j) I am _____ ___	
(e) I am _____ ___		(k) I am _____ ___	
(f) I am _____ ___		(l) I am _____ ___	

2. What characteristics did people in your group underline as being the most stable (i.e., remaining the same 10 years from now)? Were these underlined items mostly social or personal identity features? How similar or different were the underlined items among team members?

3. What do these lists say about the dynamics of your group as a team (whether or not your group for this activity is actually involved in a class project for this course)?

Sources: M. H. Kuhn and T. S. McPartland, "An Empirical Investigation of Self-Attitudes," *American Sociological Review* 19 (February 1954), pp. 68–76; C. Lay and M. Verkuyten, "Ethnic Identity and Its Relation to Personal Self-Esteem: A Comparison of Canadian-Born and Foreign-Born Chinese Adolescents," *Journal of Social Psychology* 139 (1999), pp. 288–99; S. L. Grace and K. L. Cramer, "The Elusive Nature of Self-Measurement: The Self-Construal Scale versus the Twenty Statements Test," *Journal of Social Psychology* 143 (2003), pp. 649–68.

WEB EXERCISE 3.4 DIVERSITY & STEREOTYPING ON DISPLAY IN CORPORATE WEBSITES

PURPOSE This exercise is designed to help you diagnose evidence of diversity and stereotyping in corporate websites.

MATERIALS Complete your research for this activity prior to class, including selecting one or more medium- to large-sized public or private organizations and retrieving sample images of people from the organization's website.

INSTRUCTIONS The instructor may have students work alone or in groups for this activity. Select one or more medium- to large-sized public or private organizations. Closely examine images in the selected company's website in terms of how women, visible minorities, people with disabilities, Aboriginal peoples, and older employees and clients are portrayed. Specifically, students

should be prepared to discuss and provide details in class regarding:

1. The percentage of images showing (i.e., visual representations of) women, visible minorities, people with disabilities, Aboriginal peoples, and older employees and clients. Students should also be sensitive to the size and placement of these images in the website or documents therein.

2. The roles in which women, visible minorities, people with disabilities, Aboriginal peoples, and older employees and clients are depicted. For example, are women shown more in traditional or nontraditional occupations and roles on these websites?

3. The best examples of diversity on display, as well as stereotypic images from websites to show in class, whether in printed form or as a web link that can be displayed in class.

TEAM EXERCISE 3.5 DO YOU HAVE A GLOBAL MINDSET?

PURPOSE This exercise is designed to help you examine and explore your global experiences and perspectives acquired while traveling, working, or studying in countries outside your home country.

MATERIALS The instructor will distribute a copy of a world map for each student.

INSTRUCTIONS
Step 1: Working alone, place a dot to mark locations (outside your home country) that you recall visiting or residing in at some point in your life. Did you spend one consecutive month or more at any of these locations? If yes, mark those locations with a triangle.

Step 2: Form teams with four or five members. Take another unmarked copy of the world map and compile your team's composite results. Within your team, discuss interactions and experiences you have had while traveling, studying, and/or working globally. Are you able to carry on a conversation in

more than one language? Did you routinely eat local foods? Did you have meaningful direct contact with locals? Did you ever feel outside your "comfort zone"?

Step 3: The instructor leads a class discussion, guided by the following questions.

CRITICAL THINKING QUESTIONS
1. How would you characterize your knowledge and appreciation of other cultures?

2. What kinds of things have you done while traveling, working, or studying in another country that have contributed to your knowledge and appreciation of other cultures?

3. How have your experiences traveling, working, or studying globally influenced your attitudes, beliefs, and/or perceptions?

4. How can employers benefit from employees with a global mindset?

SELF-ASSESSMENT 3.6   HOW MUCH DOES WORK DEFINE YOUR SELF-CONCEPT?

Work is an important part of our lives, but some people view it as secondary to other life interests, whereas others view work as central to their identity as individuals. The following scale estimates the extent to which you view work as a central or not-so-central life interest. Read each of the statements below and decide how accurate each one is in describing your focus in life. Then use the scoring key in Appendix B at the end of this book to calculate your results. Remember that there are no right or wrong answers to these questions. Also, this self-assessment should be completed alone so that you can rate yourself honestly without concerns of social comparison. Class discussion will focus on the meaning of this scale and its relevance to self-concept and perceptions.

WORK CENTRALITY SCALE

PLEASE INDICATE THE EXTENT TO WHICH YOU AGREE OR DISAGREE WITH EACH STATEMENT BELOW IN DESCRIBING *YOUR FOCUS IN LIFE*	STRONGLY DISAGREE	MODERATELY DISAGREE	SLIGHTLY DISAGREE	SLIGHTLY AGREE	MODERATELY AGREE	STRONGLY AGREE
1. The most important things that happen in life involve work.	☐	☐	☐	☐	☐	☐
2. Work is something people should get involved in most of the time.	☐	☐	☐	☐	☐	☐
3. Work should be only a small part of one's life.	☐	☐	☐	☐	☐	☐
4. Work should be considered central to life.	☐	☐	☐	☐	☐	☐
5. In my view, an individual's personal life goals should be work-oriented.	☐	☐	☐	☐	☐	☐
6. Life is worth living only when people get absorbed in work.	☐	☐	☐	☐	☐	☐

Source: R. N. Kanungo, *Work Alienation: an Integrative Approach* (New York: Praeger, 1982).

 After reading this chapter go to www.mhhe.com/mcshane6e for more in-depth information and interactivities that correspond to the chapter.

Workplace Emotions, Attitudes, and Stress

learning objectives

After reading this chapter, you should be able to:

LO1 Explain how emotions and cognition (logical thinking) influence attitudes and behavior.

LO2 Discuss the dynamics of emotional labor and the role of emotional intelligence in the workplace.

LO3 Summarize the consequences of job dissatisfaction, as well as strategies to increase organizational (affective) commitment.

LO4 Describe the stress experience and review three major stressors.

LO5 Identify five ways to manage workplace stress.

but one particular flight from Pittsburgh to New York City was more than he could handle. Even before the flight departed, Slater apparently received a bloody gash on his forehead from an overhead compartment while resolving a luggage space scuffle between two passengers. One of those passengers then cursed Slater when he sent her oversized luggage to be checked in. As the plane taxied after landing in New York, the same passenger stood up and demanded that Slater bring her the checked-in luggage. She then swore at him, after Slater ordered her to sit down until the plane had stopped.

That's when Slater snapped. Grabbing the intercom, he announced a few colorful words to the misbehaved passenger, then said to the rest: "Those of you who have shown dignity and respect these last 20 years, thanks for a great ride. That's it. I've had it." Slater then grabbed some beer from the trolley, activated the emergency escape chute, slid down to the tarmac, and calmly walked to his car.

Slater's actions were glorified, vilified, and dissected by the media and public over the next few weeks. Flight attendants and other airline insiders revealed their daily challenges with ill-behaved passengers, long hours, hurried service, and congested working conditions. Other commentators, including a couple of passengers on Slater's flight, suggest that Slater lacked the ability to work effectively with people. However, one of Slater's neighbors claims that Slater "is a very conscientious, engaging, compassionate type of guy. He is articulate, very sociable." One passenger noted that Slater was very pleasant on previous flights but was disturbed and agitated on that day. Slater personally claimed that his rash behavior was due to events on that flight, as well as stress about his mother's illness.

Whatever the cause of his behavior, Slater was charged with criminal mischief, trespassing, and reckless endangerment (deploying the emergency slide could have injured the ground crew). He was fired from his job and agreed to pay $10,000 to replace the emergency chute. The incident also produced a new phrase: To "hit the slide" means to quit your job in a stunning or spectacular way.[1]

JetBlue flight attendant Steven Slater had more emotional upset than he could handle on a flight from Pittsburgh to New York City, so he bailed out of the plane and his job through the emergency slide.

Steven Slater's outburst and final exit from a JetBlue flight illustrates several of the topics covered in this chapter. It dramatically shows the effects of strong emotions and job dissatisfaction on employee behavior and customer service. It shows how employees are expected to manage their emotions and to display specific types of emotions, even in difficult situations. This vignette also highlights the effects of work-related stress, which Steven Slater was experiencing due to work and nonwork challenges. This chapter begins by defining and describing emotions and explaining why researchers are so eager to discover how emotions influence attitudes and behavior. Next, we consider the dynamics of emotional labor, followed by the popular topic of emotional intelligence. The specific work attitudes of job satisfaction and organizational commitment are then discussed, including their association with various employee behaviors and work performance. The final section looks at work-related stress, including the stress experience, three prominent stressors, individual differences in stress, and ways to combat excessive stress.

Emotions in the Workplace

LO1

Emotions influence almost everything we do in the workplace. This is a strong statement, and one that you would rarely find a dozen years ago among organizational behavior experts. Most OB theories still assume that a person's thoughts and actions are governed primarily or exclusively by logical thinking (called *cognition*).[2] Yet groundbreaking neuroscience discoveries have revealed that our perceptions, attitudes, decisions, and behavior are influenced by emotions as well as cognitions.[3] In fact, emotions may have a greater influence because they often occur before cognitive processes and, consequently, influence the latter. By ignoring emotionality, many theories have overlooked a large piece of the puzzle about human behavior in the workplace.

Emotions are physiological, behavioral, and psychological episodes experienced toward an object, person, or event that create a state of readiness.[4] These "episodes" are very brief events that typically subside or occur in waves lasting from milliseconds to a few minutes. Emotions are directed toward someone or something. For example, we experience joy, fear, anger, and other emotional episodes toward tasks, customers, or a software program we are using. This differs from *moods,* which are not directed toward anything in particular and tend to be longer-term emotional states.[5]

Emotions are experiences. They represent changes in our physiological state (e.g., blood pressure, heart rate), psychological state (e.g., thought process), and behavior (e.g., facial expression). Most of these emotional reactions are subtle and occur without our awareness. This is an important point because the topic of emotions often conjures up images of people "getting emotional." In reality, most emotions are fleeting, low-intensity events that influence our behavior without our conscious awareness. Finally, emotions put us in a state of readiness. When we get worried, for example, our heart rate and blood pressure increase to make our body better prepared to engage in fight or flight. Strong emotions also trigger our conscious awareness of a threat or opportunity in the external environment.[6]

TYPES OF EMOTIONS

People experience many emotions, as well as various combinations of them, but all of them have two common features. First, emotions generate a global evaluation (called *core affect*) that something is good or bad, helpful or harmful, to be approached or to be avoided. In other words, all emotions communicate that the perceived object or event is either positive or negative. Second, all emotions produce some level of activation; that is, they generate some level of energy or motivational force within us. Some

© 1999 Ted Goff

"Biosensors. The whole company knows instantly when I'm displeased."

Credit: Copyright © Ted Goff.

EXHIBIT 4.1

Circumplex Model of Emotions

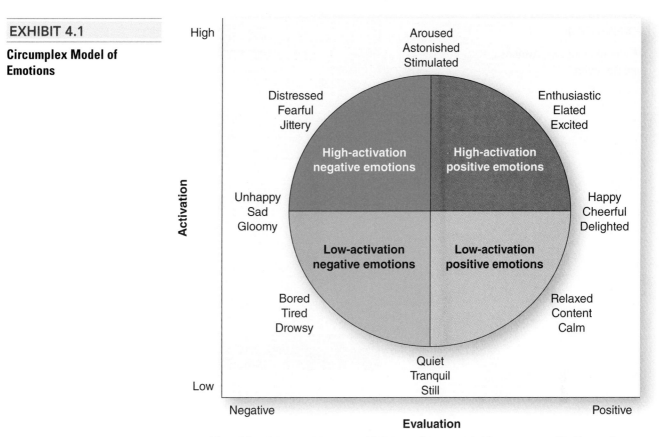

Source: Adapted from J. Larson, E. Diener, and R.E. Lucas, "Emotion: Models, Measures, and Differences," in *Emotions in the Workplace*, ed. R.G. Lord, R.J. Klimoski, and R. Kanfer (San Francisco: Jossey-Bass, 2002), pp. 64–113; J.A. Russell, "Core Affect and the Psychological Construction of Emotion," *Psychological Review* 110, no. 1 (2003), pp. 145–72.

emotional experiences, such as those experienced by JetBlue flight attendant Steve Slater (see the opening vignette), are strong enough that they consciously motivate employees to act. Most emotional experiences are subtle, but they still energize us enough to make us more aware of our environment. These two dimensions of emotions are the foundation of the circumplex model shown in Exhibit 4.1.[7] For instance, fearful is a negative emotion that generates a high level of activation, whereas relaxed is a pleasant emotion that has fairly low activation.

EMOTIONS, ATTITUDES, AND BEHAVIOR

To understand how emotions influence our thoughts and behavior in the workplace, we first need to know about attitudes. **Attitudes** represent the cluster of beliefs, assessed feelings, and behavioral intentions toward a person, object, or event (called an *attitude object*).[8] Attitudes are *judgments,* whereas emotions are *experiences.* In other words, attitudes involve conscious logical reasoning, whereas emotions operate as events, usually without our awareness. We also experience most emotions briefly, whereas our attitude toward someone or something is more stable over time.[9]

Until recently, experts believed that attitudes could be understood just by the three cognitive components illustrated on the left side of Exhibit 4.2: beliefs, feelings, and behavioral intentions. Now evidence suggests that a parallel emotional process is also at work, shown

emotions
Physiological, behavioral, and psychological episodes experienced toward an object, person, or event that create a state of readiness.

attitudes
The cluster of beliefs, assessed feelings, and behavioral intentions toward a person, object, or event (called an *attitude object*).

EXHIBIT 4.2

Model of Emotions, Attitudes, and Behavior

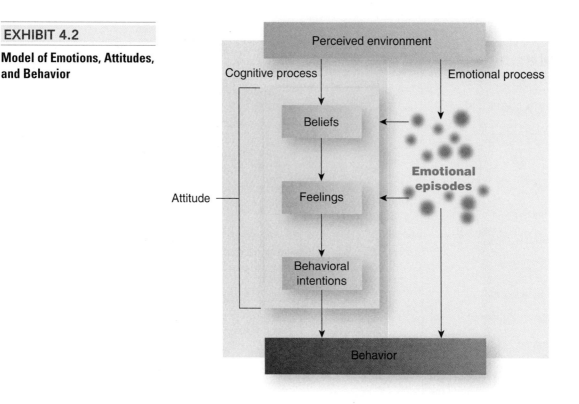

on the right side of the exhibit.[10] Using attitude toward mergers as an example, let's look more closely at this model, beginning with the traditional cognitive perspective of attitudes.

- *Beliefs.* These are your established perceptions about the attitude object—what you believe to be true. For example, you might believe that mergers reduce job security for employees in the merged firms, or that mergers increase the company's competitiveness in this era of globalization. These beliefs are perceived facts that you acquire from experience and other forms of learning.

- *Feelings.* Feelings represent your conscious positive or negative evaluations of the attitude object. Some people think mergers are good; others think they are bad. Your like or dislike of mergers represents your assessed feelings. According to the traditional cognitive perspective of attitudes (left side of the model), feelings are calculated from your beliefs about mergers. If you believe that mergers typically have negative consequences such as layoffs and organizational politics, you will form negative feelings toward mergers in general or about a specific planned merger in your organization.

- *Behavioral intentions.* Intentions represent your planned motivation to engage in a particular behavior regarding the attitude object.[11] Upon hearing that the company will merge with another organization, you might become motivated to look for a job elsewhere or possibly to complain to management about the merger decision. Your feelings toward mergers influence your behavioral intentions, and which actions you choose depends on your past experience, personality, and social norms of appropriate behavior.

Exhibit 4.2 illustrates that behavioral intentions directly predict behavior. However, whether your intentions translate into behavior depends on the situation and possibly other elements of the MARS model. For example, you might intend to quit after hearing about the merger but do not do so because of lack of better job opportunities (situation). Attitudes are also more likely to influence behavior when they are strong, meaning that they are anchored by strong emotions.

How Emotions Influence Attitudes and Behavior   As we mentioned, emotions play a central role in forming and changing employee attitudes.[12] The right side of Exhibit 4.2 illustrates this process, which (like the cognitive process) also begins with perceptions of the world around us. Our brain tags incoming sensory information with emotional markers based on a quick and imprecise evaluation of whether that information supports or threatens our innate drives. These markers are not calculated feelings; they are automatic and nonconscious emotional responses based on very thin slices of sensory information.[13]

Consider your attitude toward mergers. You might experience worry, nervousness, or relief upon learning that your company intends to merge with a competitor. The fuzzy dots on the right side of Exhibit 4.2 illustrate the numerous emotional episodes you will experience upon hearing the merger announcement, subsequently thinking about the merger, discussing the merger with coworkers, and so on. These emotions are transmitted to the reasoning process, where they are logically analyzed along with other information about the attitude object.[14] Thus, while you are consciously evaluating whether the merger is good or bad, your emotions are already sending normative (good/bad) signals, which then sway your conscious evaluation. In fact, we often deliberately "listen in" on our emotions to help us consciously decide whether to support or oppose something.[15]

The influence of both cognitive reasoning and emotions on attitudes is most apparent when they disagree with each other. People occasionally experience this mental tug-of-war, sensing that something isn't right even though they can't think of any logical reason to be concerned. This conflicting experience indicates that the person's logical analysis of the situation (left side of Exhibit 4.2) can't identify reasons to support the automatic emotional reaction (right side of Exhibit 4.2).[16] Should we pay attention to our emotional response or our logical analysis? This question is not easy to answer, but some studies indicate that while executives tend to make quick decisions based on their gut feelings (emotional response), the best decisions tend to occur when executives spend time logically evaluating the situation.[17] Thus, we should pay attention to both the cognitive and emotional sides of the attitude model, and hope they agree with each other most of the time!

Generating Positive Emotions at Work   Some companies seem to be well aware of the dual cognitive–emotional attitude process, because they try to inject more positive experiences in the workplace.[19] For instance, employees at Dixon Schwabl enjoy

LeasePlan USA boasts one of the highest job satisfaction ratings in its category in North America. There are several reasons for the high morale, including the extracurricular activities planned by the Atlanta-based vehicle fleet leasing company's "Fun at Work" committee. This photo shows LeasePlan's human resource director handing out Atlanta Braves baseball tickets to winners of the Patty's Ping-Pong Tournament held on St. Patrick's Day.[18]

Debating Point

IS HAVING FUN AT WORK REALLY A GOOD IDEA?

"Fun at work" has become such a hot business fad that companies without a "fun committee" are considered insensitive task masters. Having fun at work can improve employee attitudes in many situations, but are special fun events really necessary or beneficial?

Some critics vote "no!" They argue that contrived fun events at work can backfire.[20] Employees might be offended by the silliness of some activities. Others resent having fun forced on them. One expert recently warned: "Once the idea of fun is formally institutionalized from above, it can lead to employees becoming resentful. They feel patronized and condescended, and it breeds anger and frustration."

The meaning and value of fun at work might also vary across generations; what works for Millennials could backfire for Baby Boomers, and vice versa. Another concern is that fun-focused companies might take their eye off the bottom line. "At the end of the day, you have to make money to stay here," says Mike Pitcher, CEO of LeasePlan USA (which does have a fun committee). "If work was [all] fun, they'd call it fun."[21]

bocce tournaments, softball leagues, golf chipping contests, water balloon toss events, Halloween pumpkin-decorating contests, a padded primal scream room to release tension, and a spiral slide for those who want to descend more quickly to the main floor. "Fun is not just a word here, it is a way of life!" wrote one employee at the 75-person marketing and public relations firm in Rochester, New York.[22] Similarly, employees at Razer, the Singapore-based gaming peripherals company, zoom around on scooters and pit their gaming skills against one another on the state-of-the-art online gaming console. "Sometimes I can't believe that I have been here for seven months already," admits one Razer employee. "I guess you don't feel the time passing when you are having so much fun."[23]

Some critics might argue that the organization's main focus should be to create positive emotions through the job itself as well as everyday natural occurrences such as supportive coworkers and polite customers. Still, most people perform work that produces some negative emotions, and research has found that humor and fun at work—whether natural or contrived—can potentially offset some of the negative experiences.[24] Overall, corporate leaders need to keep in mind that emotions shape employee attitudes, and as we will discuss later, attitudes influence various forms of work-related behavior.

One last comment about Exhibit 4.2: Notice the arrow from the emotional episodes to behavior. It indicates that emotions directly (without conscious thinking) influence a person's behavior. This occurs when we jump suddenly if someone sneaks up on us. It also occurs in everyday situations because even low-intensity emotions automatically change our facial expressions. These actions are not carefully thought out. They are automatic emotional responses that are learned or hardwired by heredity for particular situations.[25]

Cognitive Dissonance   Emotions and attitudes usually lead to behavior, but the opposite sometimes occurs through the process of **cognitive dissonance.**[26] Cognitive dissonance occurs when we perceive an inconsistency in our beliefs, feelings, and behavior. This inconsistency generates emotions (such as feeling hypocritical) that motivate us to create more consistency by changing one or more of these elements. Suppose that you think of yourself as someone who supports environmentalism. You also work at an oil company that seemed to be environmentally friendly until news reports accuse the company and others in the industry of creating environmental damage. This internal tension occurs because your "green" self-concept (beliefs) and positive regard for environmentalism (feelings) are inconsistent with your employment at a company with a poor environmental record (behavior). People experience an internal tension because they want to see themselves as rational creatures, which requires some alignment between their thoughts and actions.[27] Working for a company that has a poor environmental reputation seems inconsistent with your beliefs and attitudes about environmentalism, so you would be motivated to reduce that discrepancy.

How do people reduce cognitive dissonance? Changing behavior is one option, but it is more difficult and often more costly than changing beliefs and feelings. You might be very reluctant to quit your job with the oil company, for instance. Changing behavior is particularly difficult when others know about the behavior, you performed the behavior voluntarily, and the consequence of the behavior can't be undone. Although you could quit your job, you can't hide the fact that you have worked for an oil company or claim someone forced you to work there.

When it is difficult to undo or change behavior, people instead reduce cognitive dissonance by changing their beliefs and feelings. As an employee at an oil company, you might convince yourself that problems with the company's environmental record have been exaggerated or that they fail to take into account the company's most recent environmental initiatives. Research suggests that people sometimes reduce cognitive dissonance by rebalancing their self-concept indirectly. So, rather than deny the company's environmental record, you might reduce the inconsistency by emphasizing your personal environmental behaviors (e.g., using public transport to get to work, composting food waste at home). Overall, these mental acrobatics maintain some degree of consistency between your behavior (working for the oil company) and your beliefs and attitudes toward environmentalism.

Emotions and Personality　Our coverage of the dynamics of workplace emotions wouldn't be complete unless we mentioned that emotions are also partly determined by a person's personality, not just workplace experiences.[28] Some people experience positive emotions as a natural trait. People with more positive emotions typically have higher emotional stability and are extroverted (see Chapter 2). Those who experience more negative emotions tend to have higher neuroticism (lower emotional stability) and are introverted. Positive and negative emotional traits affect a person's attendance, turnover, and long-term work attitudes.[29] While positive and negative personality traits have some effect, other research concludes that the actual situation in which people work has a noticeably stronger influence on their attitudes and behavior.[30]

MANAGING EMOTIONS AT WORK

LO2

The Elbow Room Café is packed and noisy on this Saturday morning. A customer at the restaurant in downtown Vancouver, Canada, half shouts across the room for more coffee. A passing waiter scoffs: "You want more coffee, get it yourself!" The customer laughs. Another diner complains loudly that he and his party are running late and need their food. This time, restaurant manager Patrick Savoie speaks up: "If you're in a hurry, you should have gone to McDonald's." The diner and his companions chuckle. To the uninitiated, the Elbow Room Café is an emotional basket case, where staff turn rudeness into a fine art. But it's all a performance—a place where guests can enjoy good food and play out their emotions about dreadful customer service. "It's almost like coming to a theatre," says Savoie, who spends much of his time inventing new ways to insult the clientele.[31]

Whether giving the most insulting service at Elbow Room Café in Vancouver or the superior treatment on a Singapore Airlines flight, people are expected to manage their emotions in the workplace. They must conceal their frustration when serving an irritating customer, display compassion to an ill patient, and hide their boredom in a long meeting with senior management. These are all forms of **emotional labor**—the effort, planning, and control needed to express organizationally desired emotions during interpersonal transactions.[32] Almost everyone is expected to abide by *display rules*—norms requiring us to display specific emotions and to hide other emotions. Emotional labor demands are higher in jobs requiring a variety of emotions (e.g., anger as well as joy) and more intense emotions (e.g., showing delight rather than smiling

■ connect

What is your emotional personality?
Go to **www.mcgrawhillconnect.com**
to assess your emotional trait tendencies.

cognitive dissonance
Condition that occurs when we perceive an inconsistency between our beliefs, feelings, and behavior.

emotional labor
The effort, planning, and control needed to express organizationally desired emotions during interpersonal transactions.

Managing emotions is an important part of flight attendant training at the Malaysia Airlines Academy in Petaling Jaya. Students learn how to smile, make eye contact, and keep their chin up at a level that displays confidence without arrogance. The academy even has large mirrors on some walls so students constantly see how their facial expressions appear to others.

weakly), as well as in jobs where interaction with clients is frequent and longer. Emotional labor also increases when employees must precisely rather than casually abide by the display rules.[33] This particularly occurs in service industries, where employees have frequent face-to-face interaction with clients.

For example, Malaysia Airlines flight attendants receive extensive training on how to remain composed and pleasant in difficult situations. "Are they presentable? Respectable? Do they make you feel comfortable? Do they seem approachable?" asks Madam Choong Lee Fong, Malaysia Airlines' cabin crew training and standards manager. Students at the Malaysia Airlines Academy in Petaling Jaya learn the fine art of smiling, making eye contact, and keeping their chin up at a level that displays confidence without arrogance. The academy even has large mirrors on some walls so students constantly see how their facial expressions appear to others. Students receive training in voice enrichment and public speaking. They also learn about personal grooming as well as different formalities of behavior in countries where the airline flies.[34]

Emotional Display Norms Across Cultures   Not long ago, the Paris-based magazine *L'Express* published a special series of articles about living in North America. Among other things, the Paris-based magazine commented that American and Canadian restaurant servers provide "hyper-friendly, always smiling" service, which can seem a bit too insincere to many Europeans. "It's too much. It's too friendly," explains Laurence Pivot, who edited the special edition of *L'Express*.[35] The French magazine's comment highlights cultural differences regarding emotional display norms.[36] In the United States and Canada, restaurant servers are expected to consistently show friendliness and other positive emotions toward customers. French customers also appreciate friendly service, but they expect servers to be more transparent than artificial in their duties. If a server is having a bad day, he or she should not completely hide the corresponding emotions.

One major study points to Ethiopia, Japan, and Austria (among others) as cultures that discourage emotional expression. Instead, people are expected to be subdued, have relatively monotonic voice intonation, and avoid physical movement and touching that display emotions. In contrast, cultures such as Kuwait, Egypt, Spain, and Russia allow or encourage more vivid display of emotions and expect people to act more consistently with their true emotions. In these cultures, people are expected to more honestly reveal their thoughts and feelings, be dramatic in their conversational tones, and be animated in their use of nonverbal behaviors. For example, 81 percent of Ethiopians and 74 percent of Japanese agreed that it is unprofessional to express emotions overtly in their culture, whereas 43 percent of Americans, 33 percent of Italians, and only 19 percent of Spaniards, Cubans, and Egyptians agreed with this statement.[37]

emotional intelligence (EI)
A set of abilities to perceive and express emotion, assimilate emotion in thought, understand and reason with emotion, and regulate emotion in oneself and others.

Emotional Dissonance   The comedian George Burns once said: "The secret to being a good actor is honesty. If you can fake *that*, you've got it made." Burns's humor highlights an important reality in emotional labor, namely, that it is very difficult to hide our true emotions in the workplace. Emotional labor can be challenging because it is difficult to conceal true emotions and to display the emotions required by the job. Joy, sadness, worry, and other emotions automatically activate a complex set of muscle movements (particularly facial) that are difficult to prevent and equally difficult to fake. Pretending to be cheerful or concerned requires the adjustment and coordination of several specific facial muscles and body positions. Meanwhile, our true emotions tend to reveal themselves as subtle gestures, usually without our awareness. More often than not, observers see when we are faking and sense that we feel a different emotion.[38]

Emotional labor also creates conflict between required and true emotions. The larger the gap, the more employees tend to experience stress, job burnout, and psychological separation from self.[39] This problem can be minimized through deep acting rather than surface acting.[40] *Surface acting* involves pretending to show the required emotions but continuing to hold different internal feelings. *Deep acting* involves changing true emotions to match the required emotions. In other words, you train yourself to actually feel the emotion you are supposed to express. Deep acting also requires considerable emotional intelligence, which we discuss next.

Emotional Intelligence

Buckman Laboratories International, Inc., pays close attention to the emotional intelligence of its job applicants and employees. The Memphis, Tennessee, chemical company has identified key emotional intelligence competencies of team players, which are then assessed in job interviews. "By defining the concrete behaviors that demonstrate emotional intelligence, we can better focus our behavioral interviewing questions," explains Buckman's head of human resources. The company also evaluates its leaders on 19 leadership competencies, "many of which are based on the ability of the leader to perceive, influence, and manage the emotions of themselves and others."[41]

Buckman Labs is among the growing flock of companies that recognize **emotional intelligence (EI)** as a key factor in the organization's effectiveness. Emotional intelligence includes a set of *abilities* to perceive and express emotion, assimilate emotion in thought, understand and reason with emotion, and regulate emotion in oneself and others.[42] Although several EI dimensions have been proposed over the past decade, the research findings seem to be converging around the four-quadrant model shown in Exhibit 4.3.[43] This model organizes EI into four dimensions representing the recognition of emotions in ourselves and in others, as well as the regulation of emotions in ourselves and in others.

Are you in touch with your emotions? Go to **www. mcgrawhillconnect.com** to assess how well you understand your emotional intelligence.

- *Awareness of own emotions.* This is the ability to perceive and understand the meaning of your own emotions. You are more sensitive to subtle emotional responses to events and understand their message. Self-aware people are better able to eavesdrop on their emotional responses to specific situations and to use this awareness as conscious information.[44]

- *Management of own emotions.* Emotional intelligence includes the ability to manage your own emotions, something that we all do to some extent. We keep disruptive impulses in check. We try not to feel angry or frustrated when events go against us. We try to feel and express joy and happiness toward others when the occasion calls for these emotional displays. We try to create a second wind of motivation later in

EXHIBIT 4.3

Dimensions of Emotional Intelligence

Abilities		Yourself	Others
	Recognition of emotions	**Awareness of own emotions**	**Awareness of others' emotions**
	Regulation of emotions	**Management of own emotions**	**Management of others' emotions**

Sources: D. Goleman, "An EI-Based Theory of Performance," in *The Emotionally Intelligent Workplace,* ed. C. Cherniss and D. Goleman (San Francisco: Jossey-Bass, 2001), p. 28; Peter J. Jordan and Sandra A. Lawrence, "Emotional Intelligence in Teams: Development and Initial Validation of the Short Version of the Workgroup Emotional Intelligence Profile (WEIP-S)," *Journal of Management & Organization* 15 (2009), pp. 452–69.

the workday. Notice that management of your own emotions goes beyond displaying behaviors that represent desired emotions in a particular situation. It includes generating or suppressing emotions. In other words, the deep acting described earlier requires high levels of the self-management component of emotional intelligence.

- *Awareness of others' emotions.* This dimension refers to the ability to perceive and understand the emotions of other people. To a large extent, awareness of other people's emotions is represented by *empathy*—having an understanding of and sensitivity to the feelings, thoughts, and situations of others (see Chapter 3). This ability includes understanding the other person's situation, experiencing his or her emotions, and knowing his or her needs even if they are unstated. Awareness of others' emotions extends beyond empathy to include being organizationally aware, such as sensing office politics and understanding social networks.

- *Management of others' emotions.* This dimension of EI involves managing other people's emotions. This includes consoling people who feel sad, emotionally inspiring your team members to complete a project on time, getting strangers to feel comfortable working with you, and managing dysfunctional emotions among staff who experience conflict with customers or other employees.

These four dimensions of emotional intelligence form a hierarchy.[45] Awareness of your own emotions is lowest because you need awareness to engage in the higher levels of EI. You can't manage your own emotions if you don't know what they are (i.e., low self-awareness). Managing other people's emotions is the highest level of EI because this ability requires awareness of our own and others' emotions. To diffuse an angry conflict between two employees, for example, you need to understand the emotions they are experiencing and manage your emotions (and display of emotions). To manage your own emotions, you also need to be aware of your current emotions.

Most jobs involve social interactions with coworkers or external stakeholders, so employees need EI to work effectively. Emotional intelligence is particularly important for managers because their work requires management of their own emotions and the emotions of others. Research indicates that people with high EI are better at interpersonal relations, perform better in jobs requiring emotional labor, are superior leaders, make better decisions involving social exchanges, are more successful in many aspects of job interviews, and are better at organizational learning activities. Teams whose members have high EI initially perform better than teams with low EI.[46] However, emotional intelligence does not improve some forms of performance, such as tasks that require minimal social interaction.[47]

ASSESSING AND DEVELOPING EMOTIONAL INTELLIGENCE AT WORK

Emotional intelligence is associated with some personality traits, as well as with the EI of one's parents. For this reason, many companies *try* to measure EI in job applicants. (We emphasize the word "try" because a high-quality test of EI remains elusive.) The U.S. Air Force (USAF) is one of the best-known examples of this practice. A decade or so ago, the USAF was hiring 400 recruiters each year, but approximately 100 of them failed to meet expectations. When the USAF discovered that the top recruiters had significantly higher EI scores, it began selecting recruiters partly on how well they score on an EI test. The failure rate of new USAF recruiters has apparently fallen by as much as 90 percent.[48]

Within the past few years, the USAF has been investigating how EI testing can improve trainee success in hard-to-fill, high-cost training programs with high attrition rates. One of those programs is pararescue jumper (PJ) training, which costs $250,000 per graduate and has an 80 percent failure rate. USAF research has found that trainees who score highly on several EI dimensions are two or more times as likely to successfully complete the PJ program.[49]

Emotional intelligence significantly predicts completion of the grueling U.S. Air Force pararescue jumper training program. Trainees who have better self-awareness of their emotions, can manage their emotions, and can maintain optimism and a positive outlook are more likely to successfully complete the 21-month program.

Emotional intelligence can also be learned. One recent study reported that a four-month training program resulted in a significant increase in EI among staff members working in two Dutch residential operations for people with intellectual disabilities, compared with staff members who did not receive the training. In early stages of the program, trainees learned about the meaning and value of EI, reviewed feedback on their initial EI test scores, applied EI dimensions to case studies, and developed two personal goals to improve their EI profile. Later stages of the program consisted of professional feedback to trainees based on videos showing trainees meeting with difficult clients.[50]

Sony Europe incorporates EI training in its executive development program, including an exercise in which leaders keep a journal of their emotional experiences throughout a week of work. At the orthopedic device manufacturer Exactech, Inc., two dozen leadership development participants learn how to improve their EI skills in self-awareness and interaction with other staff members.[51] Personal coaching, plenty of practice, and frequent feedback are particularly effective at developing EI. Emotional intelligence also increases with age; it is part of the process called maturity.[52]

Before leaving this topic, we should mention an ongoing debate about the usefulness of EI as a concept.[53] The concept has not been as clear as some would hope. Even the label "intelligence" is erroneous because EI is a skill, not a form of intelligence. Critics also suggest that general intelligence and personality traits overlap with most of EI's contribution to knowledge. These criticisms are serious, yet the meaning of EI is becoming clearer, and several studies (cited in the previous pages) suggest that EI is relevant to workplace behavior. Overall, emotional intelligence offers considerable potential, but we also have a lot to learn about its measurement and effects on people in the workplace.

So far, this chapter has introduced the model of emotions and attitudes, as well as EI as the means by which we manage emotions in the workplace. The next two sections look at two specific attitudes: job satisfaction and organizational commitment. These two attitudes are so important to our understanding of workplace behavior that some experts suggest the two combined should be called "overall job attitude."[54]

Job Satisfaction

LO3

Probably the most studied attitude in organizational behavior is **job satisfaction,** a person's evaluation of his or her job and work context.[55] It is an *appraisal* of perceived job characteristics, work environment, and emotional experiences at work. Satisfied employees have a favorable evaluation of their jobs, based on their observations and emotional experiences. Job satisfaction is best viewed as a collection of attitudes about different aspects of the job and work context. You might like your coworkers but be less satisfied with your workload, for instance.

job satisfaction
A person's evaluation of his or her job and work context.

How satisfied are employees at work? The answer depends on the person, the workplace, and the country. Global surveys indicate with some consistency that job satisfaction tends

EXHIBIT 4.4   Stability in Job Satisfaction in America

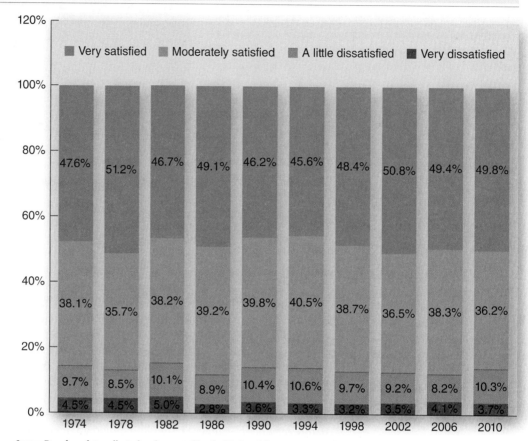

Source: Based on data collected and reported by the National Opinion Research Center/University of Chicago.

to be highest in the Nordic countries (Denmark, Sweden, Norway, and Finland), as well as in India and the United States. The lowest levels of overall job satisfaction are usually recorded in Hungary and several Asian countries (e.g., mainland China, Hong Kong, South Korea).[56] Furthermore, as Exhibit 4.4 illustrates, more than 85 percent of Americans are moderately or very satisfied with their jobs, a level that has been consistent for the past three decades.[57]

Can we conclude from these results that Americans are happy at work? Possibly, but not as much as these statistics suggest. One problem is that surveys often use a single direct question, such as "How satisfied are you with your job?" Many dissatisfied employees are reluctant to reveal their feelings in a direct question, because this is tantamount to admitting that they made a poor job choice and are not enjoying life. There is some evidence that overall job satisfaction scores are inflated. Surveys that report high overall job satisfaction also find that most employees are also dissatisfied with several aspects of their job, including how much they are paid, promotion opportunities, and recognition for work accomplishments. Furthermore, one recent study found that, if given the choice, only half of Americans would definitely remain with the same employer over the next year.[58] In summary, employees in the United States, Denmark, India, and other countries have fairly high job satisfaction, but probably not as much as they claim in the overall ratings.

A second problem is that cultural values make it difficult to compare job satisfaction across countries. People in China and Japan tend to subdue their emotions in public, and there is evidence that they also avoid extreme survey ratings such as "very satisfied." A third problem is that job satisfaction changes with economic conditions. Employees with the highest job satisfaction in current surveys tend to be in countries where the economies are chugging along quite well.[59]

JOB SATISFACTION AND WORK BEHAVIOR

Brad Bird pays a lot of attention to job satisfaction. "In my experience, the thing that has the most significant impact on a budget—but never shows up in a budget—is morale," advises Bird, who directed *Ratatouille* and other award-winning films at Pixar Animation Studios. "If you have low morale, for every dollar your spend, you get 25 cents of value. If you have high morale, for every dollar your spend, you get about $3 dollars of value."[60]

Brad Bird's opinion about the importance of job satisfaction is consistently reflected in the actions of leaders in many companies. Many companies carefully monitor job satisfaction and related employee attitudes, and they actively compete to win best workplace awards. In some firms, executive bonuses depend partly on employee satisfaction ratings. The reason for this attention is simple: Job satisfaction affects many of the individual behaviors introduced in Chapter 2 (task performance, organizational citizenship, quitting, absenteeism, etc.). A useful template for organizing and understanding the consequences of job dissatisfaction is the **exit-voice-loyalty-neglect (EVLN) model.** As the name suggests, the EVLN model identifies four ways that employees respond to dissatisfaction:[61]

connect

To assist your learning and test your knowledge about the EVLN model and other job satisfaction concepts, go to **www.mcgrawhillconnect.com,** which has activities and test questions on this topic.

- *Exit.* Exit includes leaving the organization, transferring to another work unit, or trying to get away from the dissatisfying situation. The traditional theory is that job dissatisfaction builds over time and is eventually strong enough to motivate employees to search for better work opportunities elsewhere. This is likely true to some extent, but the most recent opinion is that specific "shock events" quickly energize employees to think about and engage in exit behavior. For example, the emotional reaction you experience to an unfair management decision or a conflict episode with a coworker motivates you to look at job ads and speak to friends about job opportunities where they work. This begins the process of realigning your self-concept more with another company than with your current employer.[62]

- *Voice.* Voice is any attempt to change, rather than escape from, the dissatisfying situation. Voice can be a constructive response, such as recommending ways for management to improve the situation, or it can be more confrontational, such as filing formal grievances or forming a coalition to oppose a decision.[63] In the extreme, some employees might engage in counterproductive behaviors to get attention and force changes in the organization.

- *Loyalty.* In the original version of this model, loyalty was not an outcome of dissatisfaction. Rather, it determined whether people chose exit or voice (i.e., high loyalty resulted in voice; low loyalty produced exit).[64] More recent writers describe loyalty as an outcome, but in various and somewhat unclear ways. Generally, they suggest that "loyalists" are employees who respond to dissatisfaction by patiently waiting—some say they "suffer in silence"—for the problem to work itself out or be resolved by others.[65]

- *Neglect.* Neglect includes reducing work effort, paying less attention to quality, and increasing absenteeism and lateness. It is generally considered a passive activity that has negative consequences for the organization.

Which of the four EVLN alternatives do employees use? It depends on the person and situation.[66] The individual's personality, values, and self-concept are important factors. For example, people with a high-conscientiousness personality are less likely to engage in neglect and more likely to engage in voice. Past experience also influences which EVLN action is applied. Employees who were unsuccessful with voice in the past are more likely to engage in exit or neglect when experiencing job dissatisfaction in the future. Another factor is loyalty, as it was originally intended in the EVLN model. Specifically, employees are more likely to quit when they have low loyalty to the company, and they are more likely to engage in voice when they have high loyalty. Finally, the response to dissatisfaction depends on the situation. Employees are less likely to use the exit option when there are few alternative job prospects, for example. Employees who hold central positions in the work process such that other employees are dependent on them (see Chapter 10) are more likely to use voice when dissatisfied.[67]

exit-voice-loyalty-neglect (EVLN) model
The four ways, as indicated in the name, that employees respond to job dissatisfaction.

Job Satisfaction and Performance   Is a happy worker a more productive worker? Most corporate leaders likely think so. Yet for most of the past century, organizational behavior scholars have challenged this happy–productive employee belief, concluding that job satisfaction minimally affects job performance. Now OB experts believe that maybe the popular saying is correct after all; there is a *moderately* positive relationship between job satisfaction and performance. In other words, workers tend to be more productive *to some extent* when they have more positive attitudes toward their job and workplace.[68]

Why isn't the job satisfaction–performance relationship even stronger? One reason is that general attitudes (such as job satisfaction) don't predict specific behaviors very well. As the EVLN model explains, dissatisfaction might lead to turnover, complaining, or patient waiting rather than reduced performance (a form of neglect). A second reason is that dissatisfaction might affect performance only when employees have control over their job performance. People working in a chemical processing plant, for example, would produce about the same quantity and quality output no matter what they think about their job. A third consideration is that job performance might cause job satisfaction, rather than vice versa.[69] Higher performers receive more rewards (including recognition) and consequently are more satisfied than low-performing employees who receive fewer rewards. The connection between job satisfaction and performance isn't stronger because many organizations do not reward good performance very well.

Job Satisfaction and Customer Satisfaction   Wegmans Food Markets in Rochester, New York, and HCL Technologies in Noida, India, are on the opposite sides of the planet and in quite different industries, yet they both have the same unusual motto: *Employees first, customers second.* Why don't these companies put customers at the top of the stakeholder list? Their rationale is that customer satisfaction is a natural outcome of employee satisfaction. Put differently, it is difficult to keep customers happy if employee morale is low. "It just seems common sense to me that if you start with a happy, well-motivated workforce, you're much more likely to have happy customers," suggests Sir Richard Branson, who applies the same principle at Virgin Group.[70]

These companies are applying the **service profit chain model,** which proposes that job satisfaction has a positive effect on customer service, which flows on to shareholder financial returns. Exhibit 4.5 diagrams this process. Specifically, workplace practices affect job satisfaction, which influences employee retention, motivation, and behavior. These employee outcomes affect service quality, which then influences customer satisfaction and perceptions of value, customer referrals, and, ultimately, the company's profitability and growth.[71]

EXHIBIT 4.5   Service Profit Chain Model

Source: This model is based on J.I. Heskett, W.E. Sasser, and L.A. Schlesinger, *The Service Profit Chain* (New York: The Free Press, 1997); A.J. Rucci, S.P. Kirn, and R.T. Quinn, "The Employee-Customer-Profit Chain at Sears," *Harvard Business Review* 76 (1998), pp. 83–97; S.P. Brown and S.K. Lam, "A Meta-Analysis of Relationships Linking Employee Satisfaction to Customer Responses," *Journal of Retailing* 84, no. 3 (2008), pp. 243–55.

connections 4.1

Happy Employees, Happy Customers

A few years ago, contact center employees at Clydesdale Bank were not a happy group. Up to 12 percent of the 300-person staff at the major Scottish bank were absent each day. Employee turnover was around 65 percent annually—a level so high that managers spent much of their time hiring and inducting replacements. Kevin Page, head of Clydesdale's contact center at the time, quipped, "We were a professional recruitment and training company." Customer service suffered, operating costs were 25 percent above the industry average in Europe, and employee productivity was substantially below average.

Two years later, Clydesdale's contact center had become a global role model. Job satisfaction and commitment improved substantially. Absenteeism dropped to 4 percent each day; employee turnover was cut in half. Customers were much more satisfied with their contact center calls. Due to this dramatic improvement, Clydesdale Bank was awarded the best contact center in the region (including Europe, the Middle East, and Africa). A few months later, it was named the best large contact center in the world, beating 1,000 entrants across all industries.

How did Clydesdale Bank achieve this amazing turnaround? According to Kevin Page, now Clydesdale Bank's operations director, the answer is treating employees well so they treat customers well. Page and his management team listened to

Scotland's Clydesdale Bank has improved customer service by improving employee satisfaction.

and acted on employee concerns, spruced up the work environment, introduced career development programs, provided better coaching, and gave staff more freedom to decide how to serve clients. "Our staff started to treat their jobs more seriously," says Page. "They felt their role was important and felt better about themselves."[73]

Behind the service profit chain model are two key explanations for why satisfied employees tend to result in happier and more loyal customers.[72] First, employees are usually in a more positive mood when they feel satisfied with their jobs and working conditions. Employees in a good mood more naturally and frequently display friendliness and positive emotions. When employees have good feelings, their behavior "rubs off" on most (but not all) customers, so customers feel happier and consequently form a positive evaluation of the service experience (i.e., higher service quality).

Second, satisfied employees are less likely to quit their jobs, so they have better knowledge and skills to serve clients. Lower turnover also enables customers to have the same employees serve them, so there is more consistent service. Some evidence indicates that customers build their loyalty to specific employees, not to the organization, so keeping employee turnover low tends to build customer loyalty. Connections 4.1 presents a dramatic example of how the service profit chain model has helped the bottom line at Clydesdale Bank in Scotland.

JOB SATISFACTION AND BUSINESS ETHICS

Before leaving the topic of job satisfaction, we should mention that job satisfaction is also an ethical issue that influences the organization's reputation in the community. People spend a large portion of their time working in organizations, and many societies now expect companies to provide work environments that are safe and enjoyable. Indeed, employees in several countries closely monitor ratings of the best companies to work for, an indication that employee satisfaction is a virtue worth considerable goodwill for employers. This virtue is apparent when an organization has low job satisfaction. The company tries to hide this fact, and when morale problems become public, corporate leaders are usually quick to improve the situation.

service profit chain model
A theory explaining how employees' job satisfaction influences company profitability indirectly through service quality, customer loyalty, and related factors.

Organizational Commitment

Organizational commitment represents the other half (with job satisfaction) of what some experts call "overall job attitude." **Organizational commitment**—or more specifically, **affective commitment**—is the employee's emotional attachment to, identification with, and involvement in a particular organization.[74] Affective commitment is a person's feeling of loyalty to the place where he or she works.

Affective commitment is often distinguished from **continuance commitment,** which is a calculative attachment to the organization. Employees have high continuance commitment when they feel bound to remain with the organization because it would be too costly to quit. In other words, they choose to stay because the calculated (typically financial) value of staying is higher than the value of working somewhere else. You can tell an employee has high calculative commitment when he or she says: "I hate this place but can't afford to quit!" This reluctance to quit may exist because the employee would lose a large bonus by leaving early or is well established in the community where he or she works.[75]

CONSEQUENCES OF AFFECTIVE AND CONTINUANCE COMMITMENT

Affective commitment can be a significant competitive advantage.[76] Loyal employees are less likely to quit their jobs and be absent from work. They also have higher work motivation and organizational citizenship, as well as somewhat higher job performance. Organizational commitment improves customer satisfaction because long-tenure employees have better knowledge of work practices and because clients like to do business with the same employees. One warning is that employees with very high loyalty tend to have high conformity, which results in lower creativity. There are also cases of dedicated employees who violated laws to defend the organization. However, most companies suffer from too little rather than too much affective commitment.

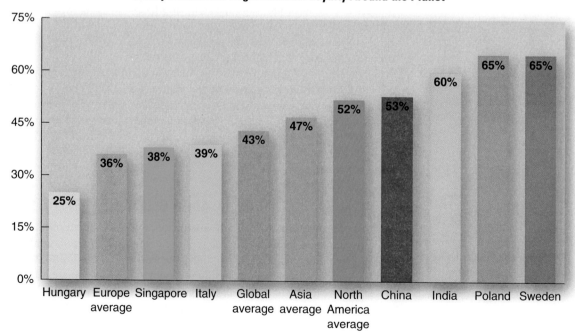

Totally Committed: Organizational Loyalty Around the Planet

Hungary	25%
Europe average	36%
Singapore	38%
Italy	39%
Global average	43%
Asia average	47%
North America average	52%
China	53%
India	60%
Poland	65%
Sweden	65%

Percentage of employees surveyed in selected countries who say they feel "totally committed" to their employer. More than 134,000 people in 29 countries were surveyed.

In contrast with the benefits of affective commitment, employees with high levels of continuance commitment are more likely to have *lower* performance and are *less* likely to engage in organizational citizenship behaviors. Furthermore, unionized employees with high continuance commitment are more likely to use formal grievances, whereas employees with high affective commitment engage in more constructive problem solving when employee–employer relations sour.[77] Although some level of financial connection may be necessary, employers should not confuse continuance commitment with employee loyalty. Employers still need to win employees' hearts (affective commitment) beyond tying them financially to the organization (continuance commitment).

BUILDING ORGANIZATIONAL COMMITMENT

There are almost as many ways to build organizational loyalty as there are topics in this textbook, but the following list is most prominent in the literature:

- *Justice and support.* Affective commitment is higher in organizations that fulfill their obligations to employees and abide by humanitarian values, such as fairness, courtesy, forgiveness, and moral integrity. These values relate to the concept of organizational justice, which we discuss in the next chapter. Similarly, organizations that support employee well-being tend to cultivate higher levels of loyalty in return.[78]

- *Shared values.* The definition of affective commitment refers to a person's identification with the organization, and that identification is highest when employees believe their values are congruent with the organization's dominant values. Also, employees experience more comfort and predictability when they agree with the values underlying corporate decisions. This comfort increases their motivation to stay with the organization.[79]

- *Trust.* **Trust** refers to positive expectations one person has toward another person in situations involving risk.[80] Trust means putting faith in the other person or group. It is also a reciprocal activity: To receive trust, you must demonstrate trust. Employees have stronger commitment to the organization when they trust its leaders. This explains why layoffs are one of the greatest blows to employee loyalty; when employees have less job security, they feel less trust in their employer and the employment relationship.[81]

- *Organizational comprehension.* Organizational comprehension refers to how well employees understand the organization, including its strategic direction, social dynamics, and physical layout.[82] This awareness is a necessary prerequisite to affective commitment because it is difficult to identify with or feel loyal to something that you don't know very well. Furthermore, lack of information produces uncertainty, and the resulting stress can distance employees from that source of uncertainty (i.e. the organization). The practical implication here is to ensure that employees develop a reasonably clear and complete mental model of the organization. This occurs by giving staff information and opportunities to keep up to date about organizational events, interact with coworkers, discover what goes on in different parts of the organization, and learn about the organization's history and future plans.[83]

- *Employee involvement.* Employee involvement increases affective commitment by strengthening the employee's psychological ownership and social identity with the organization.[84] Employees feel that they are part of the organization when they participate in decisions that guide the organization's future (see Chapter 7). Employee involvement also builds loyalty because giving this power is a demonstration of the company's trust in its employees.

organizational (affective) commitment
The employee's emotional attachment to, identification with, and involvement in a particular organization.

continuance commitment
An employee's calculative attachment to the organization, whereby an employee is motivated to stay only because leaving would be costly.

trust
Positive expectations one person has toward another person in situations involving risk.

Organizational commitment and job satisfaction represent two of the most often studied and discussed attitudes in the workplace. Each is linked to emotional episodes and cognitive judgments about the workplace and relationship with the company. Emotions also play an important role in another concept that is on everyone's mind these days: stress. The final section of this chapter provides an overview of work-related stress and how it can be managed.

Work-Related Stress and Its Management

LO4, LO5

connect

To assist your learning and test your knowledge about work-related stress and its management, go to **www.mcgrawhillconnect.com**, which has activities and test questions on this topic.

The past few years have been rough on many employees at France Telecom. The former state-owned company was privatized and restructured, resulting in 22,000 job cuts (about 20 percent of the company's workforce) through layoffs or attrition. Management developed a "time to move" doctrine of regularly shifting people around to new locations and different types of jobs. Several telephone engineers have been transferred to call centers, for example. The stress has been overwhelming for some staff. More than two dozen France Telecom employees took their own lives, and another dozen attempted to do so over the past two years. Several left notes saying they couldn't stand the pressure any longer or blamed management for terrorizing them. The CEO who led the transition resigned over this matter. Stephane Richard, France Telecom's current CEO, claims he will be more sensitive to employee stress. "The former management needed to change the nature of people's jobs due to technological change and increased competition, but the company underestimated the consequences," Richard acknowledges.[85]

Many employees at France Telecom were experiencing extreme levels of stress. Experts have trouble defining **stress,** but it is most often described as an adaptive response to a situation that is perceived as challenging or threatening to the person's well-being.[86] Stress is a physiological and psychological condition that prepares us to adapt to hostile or noxious environmental conditions. Our heart rate increases, muscles tighten, breathing speeds up, and perspiration increases. Our body also moves more blood to the brain, releases adrenaline and other hormones, fuels the system by releasing more glucose and fatty acids, activates systems that sharpen our senses, and conserves resources by shutting down our immune system. One school of thought suggests that stress is a negative evaluation of the external environment. However, critics of this cognitive appraisal perspective point out that stress is more accurately described as an emotional experience, which may occur before or after a conscious evaluation of the situation.[87]

Whether stress is a complex emotion or a cognitive evaluation of the environment, it has become a pervasive experience in the daily lives of most people. Three out of four Americans (and a similar percentage of people in Germany, Canada, Australia, and the United Kingdom) say they frequently or sometimes feel stress in their daily lives. Another recent survey reported that 77 percent of Americans are stressed by one or more issues at work; low pay, long commutes to work, high workload, and the risk of being fired or laid off top the list of stressors. In a recent survey of 115,000 employees in 33 countries, respondents in Japan reported the most stress-related health complaints, followed by Canada, the Ukraine, Finland, Hong Kong, and Hungary.[88]

Stress is typically described as a negative experience. This is known as *distress*—the degree of physiological, psychological, and behavioral deviation from healthy functioning. However, some level of stress—called *eustress*—is a necessary part of life because it activates and motivates people to achieve goals, change their environments, and succeed in life's challenges. For example, more than two-thirds of 42,000 American employees polled report that on-the-job stress either energizes them or has no effect.[89] Our focus is on the causes and management of distress, because it has become a chronic problem in many societies.

GENERAL ADAPTATION SYNDROME

More than 500 years ago, people began using the word *stress* to describe the human response to harsh environmental conditions. However, it wasn't until the 1930s that researcher Hans Selye (often described as the father of stress research) first documented the stress experience,

EXHIBIT 4.6

General Adaptation Syndrome

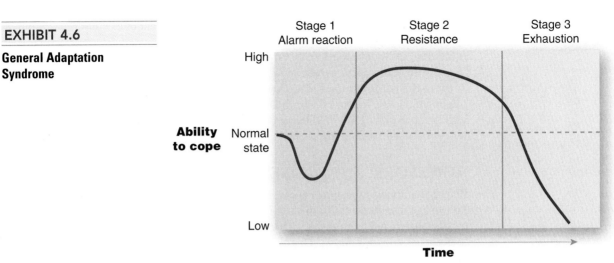

Source: Adapted from H. Selye, *The Stress of Life* (New York: McGraw-Hill, 1956).

called the **general adaptation syndrome.** Selye determined (initially by studying rats) that people have a fairly consistent and automatic physiological response to stressful situations, which helps them cope with environmental demands.[90]

The general adaptation syndrome consists of the three stages shown in Exhibit 4.6. The *alarm reaction* stage occurs when a threat or challenge activates physiological stress responses. The individual's energy level and coping effectiveness decrease in response to the initial shock. The second stage, *resistance,* activates various biochemical, psychological, and behavioral mechanisms that give the individual more energy and engage coping mechanisms to overcome or remove the source of stress. To focus energy on the source of the stress, the body reduces resources to the immune system during this stage. This explains why people are more likely to catch a cold or some other illness when they experience prolonged stress. People have a limited resistance capacity, and if the source of stress persists, the individual will eventually move into the third stage, *exhaustion.* Most of us are able to remove the source of stress or remove ourselves from that source before becoming exhausted. However, people who frequently reach exhaustion have increased risk of long-term physiological and psychological damage.[91]

CONSEQUENCES OF DISTRESS

Stress takes its toll on the human body.[92] Many people experience tension headaches, muscle pain, and related problems mainly due to muscle contractions from the stress response. Studies have found that high stress levels also contribute to cardiovascular disease, including heart attacks and strokes, and may be associated with some forms of cancer. Stress also produces various psychological consequences, such as job dissatisfaction, moodiness, depression, and lower organizational commitment. Furthermore, various behavioral outcomes have been linked to high or persistent stress, including lower job performance, poor decision making, and increased workplace accidents and aggressive behavior. Most people react to stress through "fight or flight," so increased absenteeism is another outcome, because it is a form of flight.[93]

Job Burnout **Job burnout** is a particular stress consequence that refers to the process of emotional exhaustion, cynicism, and reduced feelings of personal accomplishment.[94] *Emotional exhaustion,* the first stage, is

How stressed are you? Go to **www. mcgrawhillconnect.com** to assess your perceived general level of stress.

stress
An adaptive response to a situation that is perceived as challenging or threatening to the person's well-being.

general adaptation syndrome
A model of the stress experience, consisting of three stages: alarm reaction, resistance, and exhaustion.

job burnout
The process of emotional exhaustion, cynicism, and reduced personal accomplishment resulting from prolonged exposure to stressors.

characterized by a lack of energy, tiredness, and a feeling that one's emotional resources are depleted. This is followed by *cynicism* (also called *depersonalization*), which is an indifferent attitude toward work, emotional detachment from clients, a cynical view of the organization, and a tendency to strictly follow rules and regulations rather than adapt to the needs of others. The final stage of burnout, called *reduced personal accomplishment,* entails feelings of diminished confidence in one's ability to perform the job well. In such situations, employees develop a sense of learned helplessness, as they no longer believe that their efforts make a difference.

STRESSORS: THE CAUSES OF STRESS

Before identifying ways to manage work-related stress, we must first understand its causes, known as stressors. **Stressors** include any environmental conditions that place a physical or emotional demand on a person.[95] There are numerous stressors in the workplace and in life in general. In this section, we'll highlight three of the most common work-related stressors: harassment and incivility, work overload, and lack of task control.

Harassment and Incivility
One of the fastest-growing sources of workplace stress is **psychological harassment.** Psychological harassment includes repeated hostile or unwanted conduct, verbal comments, actions, and gestures that undermine an employee's dignity or psychological or physical integrity. This definition covers a broad landscape of behaviors, from threats and bullying to subtle yet persistent forms of incivility.[96]

Psychological harassment permeates the corporate landscape. Two-thirds of Americans think people are less civil today than 20 years ago; 10 percent say they witness incivility daily in their workplaces and are targets of that abuse at least once each week. The government of Quebec, Canada, which passed the first workplace anti-harassment legislation in North America, received more than 2,500 complaints in the first year alone! Labor bureaus in Japan received more than 32,000 complaints of harassment in a recent year, a fivefold increase from six years earlier. A survey of more than 100,000 employees in Asia reported that between 19 percent (China) and 46 percent (Korea) of employees experience incivility monthly or more often.[97]

Sexual harassment is a type of harassment in which a person's employment or job performance is conditional and depends on unwanted sexual relations (called *quid pro quo* harassment) and/or the person experiences sexual conduct from others (such as posting pornographic material) that unreasonably interferes with work performance or creates an intimidating, hostile, or offensive working environment (called *hostile work environment harassment*).[98]

Work Overload
University of Michigan professor Dave Ulrich recalls life at IBM's headquarters in Armonk, New York, three decades ago, when he delivered executive programs there. Almost everyone, including professional and management staff members, worked 35–45 hours per week. The offices were vacant by 5:30 p.m. IBM employees took sick leave whenever they experienced health problems. They also took real vacations of up to five weeks, with no cell phones, computers, or other electronics to keep them tethered to the job. Those days are long gone, says Ulrich. "Today, the employees in that same building work 60 to 80 hours per week, keep on working through most health problems, and take almost no real vacation."[99]

IBM isn't the only company where employees work long hours and seldom take vacations. Surveys by the Families and Work Institute report that 44 percent of Americans say they are overworked, up from 28 percent who felt this way a few years earlier. Almost 25 percent of Canadian employees work more than 50 hours per week, compared with only 10 percent a decade ago. More recently, Canadians identified work overload as the second highest stressor, after insufficient salary. In another recent study, 40 percent of Americans say they haven't had a real vacation within the previous two years (where vacation consists of leisure travel for a week or more to a destination at least 100 miles from home).[101]

An extreme example of workplace bullying was recently reported in the transportation department at the City of Mississauga, Canada. For almost five years, new hires received a punishing hazing ritual in which they were tied up with duct tape and pelted with water balloons. Permanent staff received birthday "spankings," which included kicks to the face and groin. A temporary employee fled one such initiation and never returned; a permanent employee is on long-term stress leave. After these incidents became public, the city decided to suspend two managers for the ongoing harassment.[100]

Why do employees work such long hours? One explanation is the combined effects of technology and globalization. "Everyone in this industry is working harder now because of e-mail, wireless access, and globalization," says marketing executive Christopher Lochhead. "You can't even get a rest on the weekend." A second factor is that many people are caught up in consumerism; they want to buy more goods and services, and doing so requires more income through longer work hours. A third reason, called the "ideal worker norm," is that professionals expect themselves and others to work longer hours. For many, toiling away far

stressors
Any environmental condition that places a physical or emotional demand on the person.

psychological harassment
Repeated and hostile or unwanted conduct, verbal comments, actions, or gestures that affect an employee's dignity or psychological or physical integrity and that result in a harmful work environment for the employee.

sexual harassment
Unwelcome conduct of a sexual nature that detrimentally affects the work environment or leads to adverse job-related consequences for its victims.

beyond the normal workweek is a badge of honor, a symbol of their superhuman capacity to perform above others.[102] This badge of honor is particularly serious in several (but not all) Asian countries, to the point where "death from overwork" is now part of the common language (*karoshi* in Japanese and *guolaosi* in Chinese).[103]

Low Task Control   One of the most important findings emerging from stress research is that employees are more stressed when they lack control over how and when they perform their tasks, as well as the pace of work activity. Work is potentially more stressful when it is paced by a machine, involves monitoring equipment, or follows a schedule controlled by someone else. Low task control increases the risk of job burnout because employees face high workloads without the ability to adjust the pace of the load to their own energy, attention span, and other resources. Furthermore, the degree to which low task control is a stressor increases with the burden of responsibility the employee must carry.[104] Assembly line workers have low task control, but their stress can be fairly low if their level of responsibility is also low. In contrast, sports coaches are under immense pressure to win games (high responsibility), yet they have little control over what happens on the playing field (low task control).

INDIVIDUAL DIFFERENCES IN STRESS

People experience different stress levels when exposed to the same stressor. One factor is the employee's physical health. Regular exercise and a healthy lifestyle produce a larger store of energy to cope with stress. A second individual difference is the coping strategies employees use to ward off a particular stressor.[105] People sometimes figure out ways to remove the stressor or to minimize its presence. Other coping mechanisms include seeking support from others, reframing the stressor in a more positive light, blaming others for the stressor, and denying the stressor's existence. Some coping strategies work better for specific stressors, and some work well for all stressors.[106] Thus, someone who uses a less effective coping mechanism in a particular situation would experience more stress in response to that situation. People have a tendency to rely on one or two coping strategies, and those who rely on generally poor coping strategies (such as denying the stressor exists) are going to experience more stress.

Personality is the third and possibly the most important reason people experience different levels of stress when faced with the same stressor.[107] Individuals with low neuroticism (high emotional stability) usually experience lower stress levels because, by definition, they are less prone to anxiety, depression, and other negative emotions. Extraverts also tend to experience lower stress than do introverts, likely because extraversion includes a degree of positive thinking, and extraverts interact with others, which helps buffer the effect of stressors. People with a positive self-concept—high self-esteem, self-efficacy, and an internal locus of control (see Chapter 3)—feel more confident and in control when faced with a stressor. In other words, they tend to have a stronger sense of optimism.[108]

While positive self-concept protects us from stress, workaholism attracts more stressors and weakens the capacity to cope with them. The classic **workaholic** (also called *work addict*) is highly involved in work, feels compelled or driven to work because of inner pressures, and has a low enjoyment of work. Workaholics are compulsive and preoccupied with work, often to the exclusion and detriment of personal health, intimate relationships, and family.[109]

MANAGING WORK-RELATED STRESS

Many people deny the existence of their stress until it has more serious outcomes. This avoidance strategy creates a vicious cycle, because the failure to cope with stress becomes another stressor on top of the one that created the stress in the first place. To prevent this vicious cycle, employers and employees need to apply one or more of the following stress management strategies: remove the stressor, withdraw from the stressor, change stress perceptions, control stress consequences, and receive social support.[110]

Are you a workaholic? Go to **www. mcgrawhillconnect.com** to assess yourself on this stress-related personal characteristic.

Remove the Stressor   There are many ways to remove the stressor, but some of the more common actions involve assigning employees to jobs that match their skills and preferences, reducing excessive workplace noise, having a complaint system and taking corrective action against harassment, and giving employees more control over the work process. Another important way that companies can remove stressors is by facilitating better work–life balance. Work–life balance initiatives minimize conflict between the employee's work and nonwork demands (see Chapter 1). Five of the most common work–life balance initiatives are flexible and limited work time, job sharing, telecommuting, personal leave, and child care support.[111]

- *Flexible and limited work time.* An important way to improve work–life balance is limiting the number of hours that employees are expected to work and giving them flexibility in scheduling those hours. For example, electronics retailer Best Buy has become a role model in work–life balance by giving employees very flexible work hours. The Minneapolis-based retailer's 3,000 head office employees are evaluated by their results, not their face time, through the results-only work environment (ROWE) initiative. San Jorge Children's Hospital offers a unique form of work flexibility that has dramatically reduced turnover and stress. The Puerto Rican medical center introduced a "ten-month work program," in which employees can take summer months off to care for their children while school is out.[112]

- *Job sharing.* Job sharing splits a career position between two people so that they experience less time-based stress between work and family. They typically work different parts of the week, with some overlapping work time in the weekly schedule to coordinate activities. This strategy gives employees the ability to work part-time in jobs that are naturally designed for full-time responsibilities.

- *Telecommuting.* Telecommuting (also called *teleworking*) involves working from home or a site close to home rather than commuting a longer distance to the office every day (see Chapter 1). By reducing or eliminating commuting time, employees can more easily fulfill family obligations, such as temporarily leaving the home office to pick the kids up from school. Consequently, telecommuters tend to experience better work–life balance.[113] However, teleworking may increase stress for those who crave social interaction and who lack the space and privacy necessary to work at home.

- *Personal leave.* Employers with strong work–life values offer extended maternity, paternity, and personal leave for employees to care for a new family or take advantage of a personal experience. Most countries provide 12 to 16 weeks of paid leave, with some offering one year or more of fully or partially paid maternity leave.[114]

- *Child care support.* According to one estimate, almost one-quarter of large U.S. employers provide on-site or subsidized child care facilities. Child care support reduces stress, because employees are less rushed to drop off children and less worried during the day about how well their children are doing.[115]

Withdraw from the Stressor   Removing the stressor may be the ideal solution, but it is often not feasible. An alternative strategy is to permanently or temporarily remove employees from the stressor. Permanent withdrawal occurs when employees are transferred to jobs that are a better fit for their competencies and values. Temporarily withdrawing from stressors is the most frequent way that employees manage stress. Vacations and holidays are important opportunities for employees to recover from stress and reenergize for future challenges. A small number of companies offer paid or unpaid sabbaticals. "Sabbaticals result in happier, healthier employees," says Mark Synnott, managing director of Colliers International New Zealand. "People recharge their batteries and come back clear-headed and motivated." Synott has taken four sabbaticals during his career.[116] Many firms also provide innovative ways for employees to withdraw from stressful work throughout the day, such as games rooms, karaoke rooms, ice cream cart breaks, nap rooms, and cafeterias that include live piano recitals.

workaholic
A person who is highly involved in work, feels compelled to work, and has a low enjoyment of work.

A few years ago, electronics retailer Best Buy realized that it made more sense to reward employees for their performance than for their face time. The company's emerging results-only work environment (ROWE) has produced significant improvements in work–life balance while maintaining productivity. "ROWE has helped me to find the right balance in my work and home life, and now I actually have a life," says Best Buy strength coach Christy Runningen. "I know my family would tell you that I am a lot less stressed out overall than I used to be."[117]

Change Stress Perceptions   Earlier, we learned that employees experience different stress levels because they have different levels of positive self-evaluations and optimism. Consequently, another way to manage stress is to help employees improve their self-concept so that job challenges are not perceived as threatening. Personal goal setting and self-reinforcement can also reduce the stress that people experience when they enter new work settings. Research also suggests that some (but not all) forms of humor can improve optimism and create positive emotions by taking some psychological weight off the situation.[118]

Control Stress Consequences   Regular exercise and maintaining a healthy life-style is an effective stress management strategy because it controls stress consequences. Research indicates that physical exercise reduces the physiological consequences of stress by helping employees moderate their breathing and heart rate, muscle tension, and stomach acidity.[119] Many companies offer pilates, yoga, and other exercise and meditation classes during the workday. Research indicates that various forms of meditation reduce anxiety, reduce blood pressure and muscle tension, and moderate breathing and heart rate.[120] Wellness programs can also help control the consequences of stress. These programs inform employees about better nutrition and fitness, regular sleep, and other good health habits. Many large employers offer *employee assistance programs (EAPs)*—counseling services that help employees resolve marital, financial, or work-related troubles. Some EAP counseling varies with the industry (e.g. support following bank robberies).

connect

How do you cope with stressful situations? Go to **www.mcgrawhillconnect.com** to identify the type of coping strategy you prefer to use in stressful situations.

Receive Social Support   Social support occurs when coworkers, supervisors, family members, friends, and others provide emotional and/or informational support to buffer an individual's stress experience. For instance, one recent study found that employees whose managers were good at empathizing experienced fewer stress symptoms than did employees whose managers were less empathetic. Social support potentially (but not always) improves a person's optimism and self-confidence, because support makes people feel valued and worthy. Social support also provides information to help the person interpret, comprehend, and possibly remove the stressor. For instance, to reduce a new employee's stress, coworkers could describe ways to handle difficult customers. Seeking social support is called a "tend and befriend" response to stress, and research suggests that women often follow this route rather than the "fight-or-flight" response mentioned previously.[121]

Employee emotions, attitudes, and stress influence employee behavior mainly through motivation. Recall, for instance, that behavioral intentions are judgments or expectations about the motivation to engage in a particular behavior. The next chapter introduces prominent theories of employee motivation.

{ chapter summary }

LO1 Explain how emotions and cognition (conscious reasoning) influence attitudes and behavior.

Emotions are physiological, behavioral, and psychological episodes experienced toward an object, person, or event that create a state of readiness. Emotions differ from attitudes, which represent a cluster of beliefs, feelings, and behavioral intentions toward a person, object, or event. Beliefs are a person's established perceptions about the attitude object. Feelings are positive or negative evaluations of the attitude object. Behavioral intentions represent a motivation to engage in a particular behavior toward the target.

Attitudes have traditionally been described as a purely rational process in which beliefs predict feelings, which predict behavioral intentions, which predict behavior. We now know that emotions have an influence on behavior that is equal to or greater than that of cognition. This dual process is apparent when we experience an internal conflict between what logically seems good or bad and what we emotionally feel is good or bad in a situation. Emotions also affect behavior directly. Behavior sometimes influences our subsequent attitudes through cognitive dissonance.

LO2 Discuss the dynamics of emotional labor and the role of emotional intelligence in the workplace.

Emotional labor consists of the effort, planning, and control needed to express organizationally desired emotions during interpersonal transactions. It is more common in jobs requiring a variety of emotions and more intense emotions, as well as in jobs where interaction with clients is frequent and has a long duration. Cultures also differ regarding the norms of displaying or concealing a person's true emotions. Emotional dissonance occurs when required and true emotions are incompatible with each other. Deep acting can minimize this dissonance, as can the practice of hiring people with a natural tendency to display desired emotions.

Emotional intelligence is the ability to perceive and express emotion, assimilate emotion in thought, understand and reason with emotion, and regulate emotion in oneself and others. This concept includes four components arranged in a hierarchy: self-awareness, self-management, social awareness, and management of others' emotions. Emotional intelligence can be learned to some extent, particularly through personal coaching.

LO3 Summarize the consequences of job dissatisfaction, as well as strategies to increase organizational (affective) commitment.

Job satisfaction represents a person's evaluation of his or her job and work context. Four types of job dissatisfaction consequences are quitting or otherwise getting away from the dissatisfying situation (exit), attempting to change the dissatisfying situation (voice), patiently waiting for the problem to sort itself out (loyalty), and reducing work effort and performance (neglect). Job satisfaction has a moderate relationship with job performance and with customer satisfaction. Affective organizational commitment (loyalty) is the employee's emotional attachment to, identification with, and involvement in a particular organization. This contrasts with continuance commitment, which is a calculative bond with the organization. Companies build loyalty through justice and support, shared values, trust, organizational comprehension, and employee involvement.

LO4 Describe the stress experience and review three major stressors.

Stress is an adaptive response to a situation that is perceived as challenging or threatening to a person's well-being. The stress experience, called the general adaptation syndrome, involves moving through three stages: alarm, resistance, and exhaustion. Stressors are the causes of stress and include any environmental conditions that place a physical or emotional demand on a person. Three stressors that have received considerable attention are harassment and incivility, work overload, and low task control.

LO5 Identify five ways to manage workplace stress.

Many interventions are available to manage work-related stress, including removing the stressor, withdrawing from the stressor, changing stress perceptions, controlling stress consequences, and receiving social support.

{ key terms }

affective commitment, p. 112

attitudes, p. 99

cognitive dissonance, p. 102

continuance commitment, p. 112

emotional intelligence (EI), p. 105

emotional labor, p. 103

emotions, p. 98

exit-voice-loyalty-neglect (EVLN) model, p. 109

general adaptation syndrome, p. 115

job burnout, p. 115

job satisfaction, p. 107

organizational commitment, p. 112

psychological harassment, p. 116

service profit chain model, p. 110

sexual harassment, p. 116

stress, p. 114

stressors, p. 116

trust, p. 113

workaholic, p. 118

critical thinking questions

1. A recent study reported that university instructors are frequently required to engage in emotional labor. Identify the situations in which emotional labor is required for this job. In your opinion, is emotional labor more troublesome for college instructors or for telephone operators working at an emergency service?

2. "Emotional intelligence is more important than cognitive intelligence in influencing an individual's success." Do you agree or disagree with this statement? Support your perspective.

3. Do you remember where you were when a disastrous event like the falling of the Twin Towers in NYC, or the bombing of several hotels and restaurants in Mumbai, or the killing of scores of innocent children in schoolrooms around the world occurred? Based on what you have learned in this chapter, discuss what has happened to you in terms of your cognitive reasoning, your emotional reactions, and your ability to logically deal with these stressful situations.

4. Job satisfaction leads to increased job performance. This statement has supplanted earlier thought on how job performance doesn't necessarily depend on job satisfaction.

What has caused the shift in thought over the years, and do you agree with this assessment?

5. What factors influence an employee's organizational loyalty?

6. In this chapter, we highlighted work-related stressors such as harassment and incivility, workload, and lack of task control. Of course, there are many non-work-related stressors that increasingly come into the discussion. Please discuss these and discuss their impact on the work environment.

7. Two college graduates recently joined the same major newspaper as journalists. Both work long hours and have tight deadlines for completing their stories. They are under constant pressure to scout out new leads and be the first to report new controversies. One journalist is increasingly fatigued and despondent and has taken several days of sick leave. The other is getting the work done and seems to enjoy the challenges. Use your knowledge of stress to explain why these two journalists are reacting differently to their jobs.

8. A senior official of a labor union stated: "All stress management does is help people cope with poor management. [Employers] should really be into stress reduction." Discuss the accuracy of this statement.

CASE STUDY 4.1 ROUGH SEAS ON THE LINK650

Professor Suzanne Baxter was preparing for her first class of the semester when Shaun O'Neill knocked lightly on the open door and announced himself: "Hi, Professor, I don't suppose you remember me?" Professor Baxter had large classes, but she did remember that Shaun was a student in her organizational behavior class a few years ago. Shaun had decided to work in the oil industry for a couple of years before returning to school to complete his diploma.

"Welcome back!" Baxter said as she beckoned him into the office. "I heard you were working on an oil rig in the United Kingdom. How was it?"

"Well, Professor," Shaun began, "I had worked two summers in the Texan oil fields and my family's from Ireland, so I hoped to get a job on the LINK650. It's that new WestOil drilling rig that arrived with so much fanfare in the North Sea fields a few years ago. The LINK650 was built by LINK, Inc., in Texas. A standard practice in this industry is for the rig manufacturer to manage its day-to-day operations, so employees on the LINK650 are managed completely by LINK managers with no involvement from WestOil. We all know that drilling rig jobs are dangerous, but they pay well and offer generous time off. A local newspaper there said that nearly 1,000 people lined up to complete job applications for the 50 nontechnical positions. I was lucky enough to get one of those jobs.

"Everyone hired on the LINK650 was enthusiastic and proud. We were one of the chosen few and were really

pumped up about working on a new rig that had received so much media attention. I was quite impressed with the recruiters—so were several other hires—because they really seemed to be concerned about our welfare out on the platform. I later discovered that the recruiters came from a consulting firm that specializes in hiring people. Come to think of it, we didn't meet a single LINK manager during that process. Maybe things would have been different if some of those LINK supervisors had interviewed us.

"Working on LINK650 was a real shock, even though most of us had some experience working in the oil fields. I'd say that none of the 50 nontechnical people hired was quite prepared for the brutal jobs on the oil rig. We did the dirtiest jobs in the biting cold winds of the North Sea. Still, during the first few months most of us wanted to show the company that we were dedicated to getting the job done. A couple of the new hires quit within a few weeks, but most of the people hired with me really got along well—you know, just like the ideas you mentioned in class. We formed a special bond that helped us through the bad weather and grueling work.

"The LINK650 supervisors were another matter. They were mean taskmasters who had worked for many years on oil rigs in the Gulf of Mexico or North Sea. They seemed to relish the idea of treating their employees the same way they had been treated before becoming managers. We put up with their abuse for the first few months, but things got worse when the LINK650 was shut down twice to correct mechanical problems. These setbacks embarrassed LINK's management and they put more pressure on the supervisors to get us back on schedule.

"The supervisors started to ignore equipment problems and pushed us to get jobs done more quickly without regard to safety procedures. They routinely shouted obscenities at employees in front of others. A couple of my work mates were fired, and a couple of others quit their jobs. I almost lost my job one day just because my boss thought I was deliberately working slowly. He didn't realize—or care—that the fittings I was connecting were damaged. Several people started finding ways to avoid the supervisors and get as little work done as possible. Many of my coworkers developed back problems. We jokingly called it the 'rigger's backache,' because some employees faked their ailment to leave the rig with paid sick leave.

"Along with having lousy supervisors, we were always kept in the dark about the problems on the rig. Supervisors said that they didn't know anything, which was partly true, but they said we shouldn't be so interested in things that didn't concern us. But the rig's problems, as well as its future contract work, were a major concern to crew members who weren't ready to quit. Their job security depended on the rig's production levels and whether WestOil would sign contracts to drill new holes. Given the rig's problems, most of us were concerned that we would be laid off at any time.

"Everything came to a head when Bob MacKenzie was killed because someone secured a hoist improperly. Not sure if it was mentioned in the papers here, but it was big news around this time last year. A government inquiry concluded that the person responsible wasn't properly trained and that employees were being pushed to finish jobs without safety precautions. Anyway, while the inquiry was going on, several employees decided to unionize the rig. It wasn't long before most employees on LINK650 had signed union cards. That really shocked LINK's management and the entire oil industry because it was, I think, just the second time that a rig had ever been unionized there.

"Since then, management has been doing everything in its power to get rid of the union. It sent a 'safety officer' to the rig, although we eventually realized that he was a consultant the company hired to undermine union support. Several managers were sent to special seminars on how to manage a unionized work force, although one of the topics was how to break the union.

"So you see, Professor, I joined LINK as an enthusiastic employee and quit last month with no desire to lift a finger for them. It really bothers me, because I was always told to do your best, no matter how tough the situation. It's been quite an experience."

Discussion Questions

1. Identify the various ways that employees expressed their job dissatisfaction on the LINK650.
2. Shaun O'Neill's commitment to the LINK organization dwindled over his two years of employment. Discuss the factors that affected his organizational commitment.

Source: © Copyright Steven L. McShane. This case is based on actual events, though names and some information have been changed.

CASE STUDY 4.2 RIDING THE EMOTIONAL ROLLER COASTER

Louise Damiani's work is an emotional roller coaster most days. The oncology nurse at CentraState Healthcare System in Freehold Township, New Jersey, soars with joy when patients beat their cancer into remission. Then there are the low points when her patients are given grim news about their cancer. She also battles with the frustration of office politics.

But even after a long shift, Damiani doesn't let her negative emotions surface until she gets into her car and heads home. "You have to learn how to pick and choose and not bring that emotion up," Damiani advises. "You say, 'OK, I can deal with this. I can focus on the priority, and the priority is the patient.'"

As well as managing her own emotions, Damiani has mastered the skill of creating positive emotions in others. She recently received an award in recognition of her extraordinary sensitivity to patients' needs and concerns. For example, one of Damiani's patients wanted to return to her native Mexico but, with an advanced stage of cancer, such a journey wasn't possible. Instead, Damiani brought "Mexico" to the hospital by transforming a visitors' lounge into a fiesta-type setting and inviting the patient's family, friends, and hospital staff to attend the special event.

Lisa Salvatore, a charge nurse at the recently built Leon S. Peters Burn Center in Fresno, California, also recognizes that her job involves supporting patients' emotional needs, not just their physical problems. "With burns, you don't just treat something on the outside," she says. "You treat something on the inside that you can't see." Salvatore also experiences the full range of emotions, including the urgency of getting burn patients out of emergency within an hour to improve their prospects of recovery. "I like high stress. I like trauma," she says. Still, she acknowledges the emotional challenges of treating children with burns. "I deal with it and then I cry all the way home. I just sob on my way driving home."

Anil Shandil, a medic from the 328th Combat Support Hospital in Fort Douglas, Utah, has witnessed more severe burns and injuries than most medical professionals. For two years at the Landstuhl Army Regional Medical Center in Germany, he aided soldiers who had been wounded in Iraq or Afghanistan. The tour of duty was extremely emotionally taxing. "You get a lot of severed limbs, a lot of traumatic brain injuries, a lot death and dying," says Shandil. "So the compassion fatigue is rather high." People who work closely with victims of trauma often suffer compassion fatigue, also known as secondary traumatic stress disorder. The main symptom is a decreasing ability to feel compassion for others.

In spite of the risk of compassion fatigue, Shandil has volunteered for an even more challenging assignment: He and 85 other soldiers in the 328th are now in Iraq providing medical care for Iraqi detainees being held there by the U.S. military. So, along with managing emotions from constant exposure to trauma cases, these medics must also show respectful compassion to those who fought against their American comrades. Shandil knows it will be hard. "Yes, these are people who were not kind to us. But as a medic, it's our job to care for them, no matter if that is your friend or your enemy."

Discussion Questions

1. To what extent do the three people featured in this case study manage their own emotions on the job? How would they accomplish this? To what extent do you think they effectively manage emotions under these circumstances?

2. This case study states that nurses and other medical staff need to manage the emotions of their patients. Why is this emotions management important in this job? In what ways do medical staff alter the emotions of their patients?

3. Stress is mentioned throughout this case study. How does this stress occur? What stress outcomes occur for people in these types of jobs? How can these people try to minimize high levels of stress?

Sources: "Providing Emotional Comfort," *Journeys: CentraState Medical Center Magazine* 4 (Winter 2008), p. 1; M. L. Diamond, "When Job Stress Bubbles Up, Keep a Lid on Your Emotions," *Seattle Times*, May 4, 2008, p. H2; B. Anderson, "First Stop on a Long Road," *Fresno Bee*, May 25, 2008, p. A1; M. D. LaPlante, "Medics' Compassion to Be Tested," *Salt Lake Tribune*, September 17, 2008.

CLASS EXERCISE 4.3 STRENGTHS-BASED COACHING

PURPOSE To help students practice a form of interpersonal development, built on the dynamics of positive emotions.

MATERIALS None.

BACKGROUND Several chapters in this book introduce and apply the emerging philosophy of *positive organizational behavior*, which suggests that focusing on the positive rather than negative aspects of life will improve organizational success and individual well-being. An application of positive OB is strengths-based or appreciative coaching, in which the coach focuses on the person's strengths rather than weaknesses to help the person realize his or her potential. As part of any coaching process, the coach listens to the employee's story and uses questions and suggestions to help that person redefine her or his self-concept and perceptions of the environment. Two important skills in effective coaching are active listening and probing for information (rather than telling the person a solution or direction). The instructions below identify specific information and issues that the coach and coachee will discuss.

INSTRUCTIONS

Step 1: Form teams of four people. One team can have six people if the class does not have multiples of four. For odd-numbered class sizes, one person may be an observer. Divide into pairs in which one person is coach and the other coachee. Ideally for this exercise, the coach and coachee should have little knowledge of each other.

Step 2: Coachees will describe something about themselves in which they excel and for which they like to be recognized. This competency might be work-related, but not necessarily. It would be a personal achievement or ability that is close to their self-concept (how they define themselves). The coach mostly listens, but also prompts more details from the coachee using "probe" questions ("Tell me more about that," "What did you do next?" "Could you explain that further, please?" or "What else can you remember about that event?"). As the coachee's story develops, the coach will guide the coachee to identify ways to leverage this strength. For example, the pair would explore situational barriers to practicing the coachee's strength as well as aspects of this strength that require further development. The strength may also be discussed as a foundation for the coachee to develop strengths in other, related ways. The session should end with some discussion of the coachee's goals and action plans. The first coaching session can be any length of time specified by the instructor, but 15 to 25 minutes is typical for each coaching session.

Step 3: After completing the first coaching session, regroup so that each pair consists of different partners than those in the first pair (i.e., if pairs were A–B and C–D in session 1, the pairs are A–C and B–D in session 2). The coaches become coachees to their new partners in session 2.

Step 4: The class will debrief regarding the emotional experience of discussing personal strengths, the role of self-concept in emotions and attitudes, the role of managers and coworkers in building positive emotions in people, and the value and limitations of strengths-based coaching.

Source: For further information about strengths-based coaching, see Sara L. Orem, Jacqueline Binkert, and Ann L. Clancy, *Appreciative Coaching* (San Francisco: Jossey-Bass, 2007); Marcus Buckingham and C. Coffman, *First, Break All the Rules* (New York: Simon & Schuster, 1999).

CLASS EXERCISE 4.4 RANKING JOBS ON THEIR EMOTIONAL LABOR

PURPOSE This exercise is designed to help you understand the jobs in which people tend to experience higher or lower degrees of emotional labor.

INSTRUCTIONS

Step 1: Individually rank-order the extent that the jobs listed below require emotional labor. In other words, assign a "1" to the job you believe requires the most effort, planning, and control to express organizationally desired emotions during interpersonal transactions. Assign a "10" to the job you believe requires the least amount of emotional labor. Mark your rankings in column 1.

Step 2: The instructor will form teams of four or five members, and each team will rank-order the items on the basis of consensus (not simply averaging the individual rankings). These results are placed in column 2.

Step 3: The instructor will provide expert ranking information. This information should be written in column 3. Then students calculate the differences in columns 4 and 5.

Step 4: The class will compare the results and discuss the features of jobs with high emotional labor.

Occupational Emotional Labor Scoring Sheet

OCCUPATION	(1) INDIVIDUAL RANKING	(2) TEAM RANKING	(3) EXPERT RANKING	(4) ABSOLUTE DIFFERENCE OF 1&3	(5) ABSOLUTE DIFFERENCE OF 2&3
Bartender					
Cashier					
Dental hygienist					
Insurance adjuster					
Lawyer					
Librarian					
Postal clerk					
Registered nurse					
Social worker					
Television announcer					
TOTAL					
				Your score	Team score

(The lower the score, the better.)

SELF-ASSESSMENT 4.5 ARE YOU IN TOUCH WITH YOUR EMOTIONS?

PURPOSE This self-assessment is designed to help you understand the meaning and dimensions of emotional intelligence and to estimate your perceptions of your emotional intelligence.

OVERVIEW Emotional intelligence has become an important concept and ability in the workplace. It is a skill that people develop throughout their lives to help them interact better with others, make better decisions, and manage the attitudes and behavior of other people. Although emotional intelligence is best measured as an ability test, this scale offers you an opportunity to

estimate your perceptions and self-awareness of this ability in yourself.

INSTRUCTIONS Read each of the statements below and select the response that best describes you. Then use the scoring key in Appendix B of this book to calculate your results. This self-assessment should be completed alone so that students rate themselves honestly without concerns of social comparison. However, class discussion will focus on the meaning and dimensions of emotional intelligence, its application in the workplace, and the best ways to measure emotional intelligence.

Emotional Intelligence Self-Assessment

TO WHAT EXTENT DO YOU AGREE OR DISAGREE WITH EACH OF THESE STATEMENTS?	STRONGLY AGREE	MODERATELY AGREE	SLIGHTLY AGREE	SLIGHTLY DISAGREE	MODERATELY DISAGREE	STRONGLY DISAGREE
1. I tend to describe my emotions accurately.	☐	☐	☐	☐	☐	☐
2. I show respect for others' opinions, even when I think those opinions are wrong.	☐	☐	☐	☐	☐	☐
3. I know how others are feeling, even when they try to hide their feelings.	☐	☐	☐	☐	☐	☐
4. I am good at getting people enthusiastic and motivated.	☐	☐	☐	☐	☐	☐
5. When I get worried or angry, I have difficulty suppressing those emotions such that others do not notice them.	☐	☐	☐	☐	☐	☐
6. I have a talent for gauging a person's true feelings from his or her body language.	☐	☐	☐	☐	☐	☐
7. I usually know when I am feeling frustrated.	☐	☐	☐	☐	☐	☐
8. I tend to have difficulty getting people in the right emotional frame of mind.	☐	☐	☐	☐	☐	☐
9. I am very much aware of my own emotions.	☐	☐	☐	☐	☐	☐
10. I am able to understand all sides of a disagreement before forming an opinion.	☐	☐	☐	☐	☐	☐
11. I can easily cheer people up when they are feeling discouraged or sad.	☐	☐	☐	☐	☐	☐
12. I am sometimes unaware when I get emotional about an issue.	☐	☐	☐	☐	☐	☐
13. I can tell when others do not mean what they say.	☐	☐	☐	☐	☐	☐

(continued)

TO WHAT EXTENT DO YOU AGREE OR DISAGREE WITH EACH OF THESE STATEMENTS?	STRONGLY AGREE	MODERATELY AGREE	SLIGHTLY AGREE	SLIGHTLY DISAGREE	MODERATELY DISAGREE	STRONGLY DISAGREE
14. I am good at controlling my own emotions when the situation requires such control.	☐	☐	☐	☐	☐	☐
15. I sometimes don't realize how others are feeling about an issue.	☐	☐	☐	☐	☐	☐
16. I have a talent for getting others to share my keenness for an idea.	☐	☐	☐	☐	☐	☐

Source: Copyright © 2011 Steven L. McShane. This self-assessment was inspired by similar instruments, particularly P.J. Jordan and S.A. Lawrence, "Emotional Intelligence in Teams: Development and Initial Validation of the Short Version of the Workgroup Emotional Intelligence Profile (WEIP-S)," *Journal of Management & Organization* 15 (2009), pp. 452–69; C.-S. Wong and K.S. Law, "The Effects of Leader and Follower Emotional Intelligence on Performance and Attitude: An Exploratory Study," *Leadership Quarterly* 13 (2002), pp. 243–74; N.S. Schutte, J.M. Malouff, L.E. Hall, D.J. Haggerty, J.T. Cooper, C.J. Golden, and L. Dornheim, "Development and Validation of a Measure of Emotional Intelligence," *Personality and Individual Differences* 25, no. 2 (1998), pp. 167–77.

 After reading this chapter go to www.mhhe.com/mcshane6e for more in-depth information and interactivities that correspond to the chapter.

Foundations of Employee Motivation

learning objectives

After reading this chapter, you should be able to:

LO1 Define *employee engagement*.

LO2 Explain the role of human drives and emotions in employee motivation and behavior.

LO3 Summarize Maslow's needs hierarchy, McClelland's learned needs theory, and four-drive theory, and discuss their implications for motivating employees.

LO4 Discuss the expectancy theory model, including its practical implications.

LO5 Outline organizational behavior modification (OB Mod) and social cognitive theory and explain their relevance to employee motivation.

LO6 Describe the characteristics of effective goal setting and feedback.

LO7 Summarize equity theory and describe ways to improve procedural justice.

better than most banks, partly because it created an environment that builds a highly engaged workforce. "If more firms were to positively tackle employee engagement, I think we would improve productivity and performance substantially," advises Standard Chartered senior executive Tim Miller. The London-based bank's Hong Kong business is a three-time winner of the Gallup Great Workplace Award. Its operations in Thailand, Uganda, India (Scope International-India), and Korea (First Bank Korea Ltd.) are also recognized as top-rated employers globally or in their countries.

More than half of Standard Chartered's employees are highly engaged, compared with only 25–30 percent in most organizations. The bank's employees weren't always so highly motivated, however. Standard Chartered's employee engagement scores have more than doubled over the past decade because the company introduced specific practices. First, it trained managers to more actively coach employees on clear key performance indicators (KPIs), constructive feedback, and building competencies. Second, Standard Chartered invested more in employee development, to the point that almost all the bank's staff say they understand their role and have confidence in performing those objectives.

Third, Standard Chartered rewards performance through career development opportunities and a stock ownership program. Fourth, the bank supports social interaction through team-based volunteering events and structured, fun activities in the workplace. Finally, Standard Chartered focuses on employee strengths rather than weaknesses. "Our culture is very much based on the positive psychology movement of playing to strengths," says Tim Miller. "We know that when people are doing what they like doing, they are going to be far more productive than if they are in roles where there is less interest."

Standard Chartered's focus on employee engagement is paying off in employee well-being as well as in the organization's bottom line. "Using this focus [employee engagement], we have seen spectacular results," says Miller. "Our most engaged bank branches [have] significantly higher deposit growth, better cost-income ratios, and lower employee attrition than less engaged branches."[1]

Standard Chartered Bank has significantly improved employee engagement and motivation through goal setting, strengths-based feedback, community involvement, and career development.

Goal setting, strengths-based feedback, rewards, and various social bonding events are designed to maintain and improve employee motivation at Standard Chartered Bank. This motivation has sustained the company's performance throughout the great financial crisis and has ranked it as one of the most admired or best places to work in several emerging market countries. Motivation refers to the forces within a person that affect the direction, intensity, and persistence of his or her voluntary behavior.[2] Motivated employees are willing to exert a particular level of effort (intensity), for a certain amount of time (persistence), toward a particular goal (direction). Motivation is one of the four essential drivers of individual behavior and performance (see Chapter 2).

This chapter introduces the core theories of employee motivation. We begin by discussing employee engagement, an increasingly popular concept associated with motivation. Next, we explain how drives and emotions are the prime movers of employee motivation. Three theories that focus on drives and needs—Maslow's needs hierarchy, McClelland's learned needs theory, and four-drive theory—are introduced and evaluated. Next, we turn our attention to the popular rational decision model of employee motivation: expectancy theory. Organizational behavior modification and social cognitive theory are then introduced, which relate to learning the expectancies that motivate employees through the expectancy theory model. Next, we look at goal setting and feedback, which are considered the most robust and useful motivational concepts and practices in organizations. This chapter closes with the topic of motivation through organizational justice, including the dimensions and dynamics of equity theory and procedural justice.

Employee Engagement

LO1

When executives discuss employee motivation these days, they are just as likely to use the phrase **employee engagement.** Although its definition is still being debated,[3] we cautiously define employee engagement as an individual's emotional and cognitive (rational) motivation, particularly a focused, intense, persistent, and purposive effort to achieve work-related goals. It is typically described as an emotional involvement in, commitment to, and satisfaction with the work. Employee engagement also includes a high level of absorption in the work—the experience of focusing intensely on the task with limited awareness of events beyond that work. Finally, employee engagement is often described in terms of self-efficacy—the belief that you have the ability, role clarity, and resources to get the job done (see Chapter 3).

Employee engagement is on the minds of many business leaders these days, because it seems to be a strong predictor of employee and work unit performance. Standard Chartered Bank finds that branches with higher employee engagement provide significantly higher customer service quality, have 46 percent lower employee turnover, and produce 16 percent higher profit margin growth than branches with lower employee engagement. At JCPenney, stores with the top 25 percent engagement scores generate 36 percent greater operating income than similar-size stores with the lowest 25 percent of scores. Electronics retailer Best Buy reports that a 0.1 increase (on a 5.0-point scale) in a store's employee engagement score is associated with a $100,000 increase in that store's profitability for the year. A recent U.K. government report concluded that employee engagement is so important to the country's international competitiveness that government should urgently raise awareness of and support for employee engagement practices throughout all sectors of the economy.[4] It isn't always clear from these studies whether employee engagement makes companies more successful,

employee engagement
Individual's emotional and cognitive motivation, particularly a focused, intense, persistent, and purposive effort toward work-related goals.

drives
Hardwired characteristics of the brain that correct deficiencies or maintain an internal equilibrium by producing emotions to energize individuals.

or whether company success makes employees more engaged. However, the interventions at Standard Chartered, Best Buy, and some other companies suggest that employee engagement causes the company outcomes more than vice versa.

The challenge facing organizational leaders is that most employees aren't very engaged.[5] The numbers vary, but generally only about 30 percent of U.S. employees are highly engaged, which is above the global average. Approximately half of all employees are somewhat or not engaged, and approximately one-fifth have low engagement or are actively disengaged. Actively disengaged employees don't just lack motivation to work; they are frustrated enough to actively disrupt the workplace and undermine the motivation of other employees. Employees in several Asian countries (notably, Japan, China, and South Korea) and a few European countries (notably, Italy, the Netherlands, and France) have the lowest levels of employee engagement, whereas the highest scores are usually found in the United States, Brazil, and India.

This leads to the question: What are the drivers of employee engagement? Goal setting, employee involvement, organizational justice, organizational comprehension (knowing what's going on in the company), employee development opportunities, sufficient resources, and an appealing company vision are some of the more commonly mentioned influences.[6] In other words, building an engaged workforce calls on most topics in this book, such as the MARS model (Chapter 2), building affective commitment (Chapter 4), motivation practices (Chapter 5), and leadership (Chapter 12).

Employee Drives and Needs

LO2, LO3

To figure out how to nurture a more engaged and motivated workforce, we first need to understand the motivational "forces" or prime movers of employee behavior.[7] Our starting point is **drives** (also called *primary needs*), which we define as hardwired characteristics of the brain that attempt to keep us in balance by correcting deficiencies. Drives accomplish this task by producing emotions that energize us to act on our environment.[8] Drives are receiving increasing attention because recent neuroscience (brain) research has highlighted the central role of emotions in human decisions and behavior. There is no agreed upon list of human drives, but several are consistently identified in research, such as the drive for

B&Q, the world's third largest home improvement retailer, has one of the most engaged workforces on the planet. The British company not only trains, involves, and rewards employees; it encourages fun activities where staff can fulfill their drive to bond. For example, employees at all 330 B&Q stores recently participated simultaneously in a five-minute dance routine during store hours. The charity event attempted to break a world record flash mob. "It puts a smile on the faces of our staff which hopefully transfers into great customer service," says one B&Q store manager about the flash mob event.[9]

EXHIBIT 5.1

Drives, Needs, and Behavior

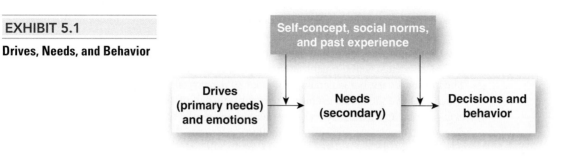

social interaction, for competence or status, to know what's going on around us, and to defend ourselves against physiological and psychological harm.[10]

Drives are innate and universal, which means that everyone has them, and they exist from birth. Furthermore, drives are the "prime movers" of behavior because they generate emotions, which put people in a state of readiness to act on their environment. Emotions play a central role in motivation.[11] In fact, both words (*emotion* and *motivation*) originate from the same Latin word, *movere,* which means "to move."

Exhibit 5.1 illustrates how drives and emotions translate into felt needs and behavior. Drives, and the emotions produced by these drives, produce human needs. We define **needs** as goal-directed forces that people experience. They are the motivational forces of emotions channeled toward particular goals to correct deficiencies or imbalances. As one leading neuroscientist explained, "Drives express themselves directly in background emotions and we eventually become aware of their existence by means of background feelings."[12]

Consider the following example: You arrive at work to discover a stranger sitting at your desk. Seeing this situation produces emotions (worry, curiosity) that motivate you to act. These emotions are generated from drives, such as the drive to defend and drive to know. When strong enough, they motivate you to do something about this situation, such as finding out who that person is and possibly seeking reassurance from coworkers that your job is still safe. In this case, you have a need to know what is going on, to feel secure, and possibly to correct a sense of personal violation. Notice that your emotional reactions to seeing the stranger sitting at your desk represent the forces that move you, but you channel those emotions toward specific goals.

INDIVIDUAL DIFFERENCES IN NEEDS

Everyone has the same drives; they are hardwired in us through evolution. However, people develop different intensities of needs in a particular situation. Exhibit 5.1 explains why this difference occurs. The left side of the model shows that the individual's self-concept (as well as personality and values), social norms, and past experience amplify or suppress drive-based emotions, thereby resulting in stronger or weaker needs.[13] People who define themselves as very sociable typically experience a stronger need for social interaction if alone for a while, whereas people who view themselves as less sociable would experience a less intense need to be with others over that time. These individual differences also explain why needs can be "learned" to some extent. Socialization and reinforcement may cause people to alter their self-concept somewhat, resulting in a stronger or weaker need for social interaction, achievement, and so on. We will discuss learned needs later in this chapter.

Self-concept, social norms, and past experience also regulate a person's motivated decisions and behavior, as the right side of Exhibit 5.1 illustrates. Consider the earlier example of the stranger sitting at your desk. You probably wouldn't walk up to the person and demand that he or she leave; such blunt behavior is contrary to social norms in most cultures. Employees who view themselves as forthright might approach the stranger directly, whereas those who have a different self-concept or have had negative experiences with direct confrontation are more likely to first gather information from coworkers before

EXHIBIT 5.2

Maslow's Needs Hierarchy

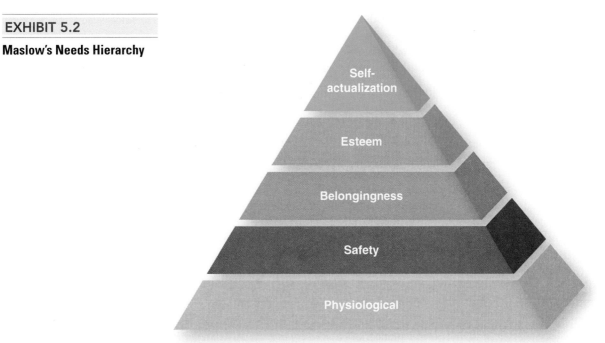

Source: Based on information in A.H. Maslow, "A Theory of Human Motivation," *Psychological Review* 50 (1943), pp. 370–96.

approaching the intruder. In short, your drives (to know, to defend, to bond, etc.) and resulting emotions energize you to act, and your self-concept, social norms, and past experience direct that energy into goal-directed behavior.

Exhibit 5.1 provides a useful template for understanding how drives and emotions are the prime sources of employee motivation and how individual characteristics (self-concept, experience, values) influence goal-directed behavior. You will see pieces of this theory when we discuss four-drive theory, expectancy theory, equity theory, and other concepts in this chapter. The remainder of this section describes theories that try to explain the dynamics of drives and needs.

MASLOW'S NEEDS HIERARCHY THEORY

By far, the most widely known theory of human motivation is **Maslow's needs hierarchy theory** (see Exhibit 5.2). Developed by psychologist Abraham Maslow in the 1940s, the model condenses and integrates the long list of drives and needs that had been previously studied into a hierarchy of five basic categories (from lowest to highest):[14] *physiological* (need for food, air, water, shelter, etc.), *safety* (need for security and stability), *belongingness/love* (need for interaction with and affection from others), *esteem* (need for self-esteem and social esteem/status), and *self-actualization* (need for self-fulfillment and the realization of one's potential). Along with developing these five categories, Maslow identified the desire to know and the desire for aesthetic beauty as two innate drives that do not fit within the hierarchy. Maslow suggested that we are motivated simultaneously by several primary needs (drives), but the strongest source of motivation is the lowest unsatisfied need at the time. As the person satisfies a lower-level need, the next higher need in the hierarchy becomes the primary motivator and remains so even if never satisfied.

Limitations and Contributions of Maslow's Work

In spite of its popularity, Maslow's needs hierarchy theory has been dismissed by most motivation experts.[15] Studies have concluded that people do not progress through the hierarchy as the theory predicts.

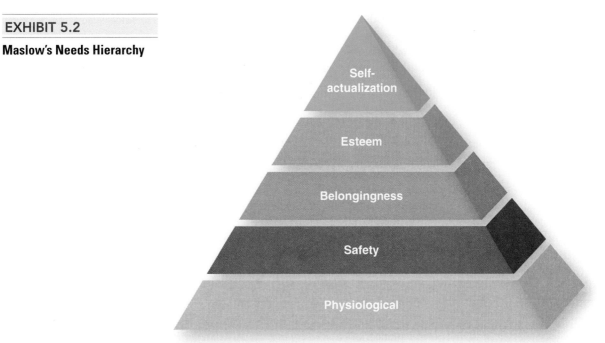

connect

Do you want a motivating job? Go to **www.mcgrawhillconnect.com** to assess your growth (self-actualization) need strength.

needs
Goal-directed forces that people experience.

Maslow's needs hierarchy theory
A motivation theory of needs arranged in a hierarchy, whereby people are motivated to fulfill a higher need as a lower one becomes gratified.

Needs hierarchy theory also suggests that needs are fulfilled for a long time, whereas evidence suggests that need fulfillment exists for a much shorter time period. Although needs hierarchy theory has failed the reality test, Maslow deserves credit for bringing a more holistic, humanistic, and positive approach to the study of human motivation.[16]

- *Holistic perspective.* Maslow explained that the various needs should be studied together (holistically) because human behavior is typically initiated by more than one need at the same time. Previously, motivation experts had splintered needs or drives into dozens of categories, each studied in isolation.[17]
- *Humanistic perspective.* Maslow introduced the then-novel idea that higher-order needs are influenced by personal and social influences, not just instincts.[18] In other words, he was among the first to recognize that human thoughts (including self-concept, social norms, past experience) play a role in motivation. Previous motivation experts had focused almost entirely on human instincts without considering that motivation could be shaped by human thought.
- *Positive perspective.* Maslow popularized the concept of *self-actualization,* suggesting that people are naturally motivated to reach their potential and that organizations and societies need to be structured to help people continue and develop this motivation.[19] This positive view of motivation contrasted with the dominant position that needs became activated by deficiencies such as hunger. Indeed, Maslow is considered a pioneer in *positive organizational behavior.* Positive OB says that focusing on the positive rather than negative aspects of life will improve organizational success and individual well-being (see Chapter 3). In other words, this approach advocates building positive qualities and perspectives within individuals or institutions as opposed to focusing on trying to fix what might be wrong with them.[20]

What's Wrong with Needs Hierarchy Models?   Maslow's theory ultimately failed to explain human motivation because people don't fit into a one-size-fits-all needs hierarchy. There is growing evidence that people have different hierarchies. Some place social status at the top of their personal hierarchy; others view personal development and growth above social relations or status. Employee needs are strongly influenced by self-concept, personal values, and personality.[21] If your most important values lean toward stimulation and self-direction, you probably pay more attention to self-actualization needs. If power and achievement are at the top of your value system, status needs will likely be at the top of your needs hierarchy. This connection between values and needs suggests that a needs hierarchy is unique to each person and can possibly change over time, just as values change over a lifetime.[22]

LEARNED NEEDS THEORY

Earlier in this chapter we stated that drives are innate, whereas needs are shaped, amplified, or suppressed through self-concept, social norms, and past experience. Maslow noted this when he wrote that individual characteristics influence the strength of higher-order needs, such as the need to belong. Psychologist David McClelland further investigated the idea that need strength can be altered through social influences. In particular, he recognized that a person's needs can be strengthened through reinforcement, learning, and social conditions. McClelland examined three "learned" needs: achievement, power, and affiliation.[23]

Need for Achievement   People with a strong **need for achievement (nAch)** want to accomplish reasonably challenging goals through their own effort. They prefer working alone rather than in teams, and they choose tasks with a moderate degree of risk (i.e., neither too easy nor impossible to complete). High-nAch people also desire unambiguous feedback and recognition for their success. Money is a weak motivator, except when it provides feedback and recognition.[24] In contrast, employees with a low nAch perform their work better when money is used as an incentive. Successful entrepreneurs tend to have a high nAch, possibly because they establish challenging goals for themselves and thrive on competition.[25]

Adriana Cisneros (right) demonstrated a strong need for achievement long before joining her family's Latin American media and entertainment empire. "She has immense drive. She's tireless. She has very good ideas and wants to carry them out," says Gustavo Cisneros (left), Adriana's father and CEO of Cisneros Group in Coral Gables, Florida. Adriana, who is the company's director of strategy and vice chair, claims her need for achievement was learned as well as genetic. "Nurture is a big part of it," she suggests. "My parents were extremely supportive of their kids coming up with crazy ideas."[26]

Need for Affiliation

Need for affiliation (nAff) refers to a desire to seek approval from others, conform to their wishes and expectations, and avoid conflict and confrontation. People with a strong nAff try to project a favorable image of themselves. They tend to actively support others and try to smooth out workplace conflicts. High-nAff employees generally work well in coordinating roles to mediate conflicts and in sales positions where the main task is cultivating long-term relations. However, they tend to be less effective at allocating scarce resources and making other decisions that potentially generate conflict. People in decision-making positions must have a relatively low need for affiliation so that their choices and actions are not biased by a personal need for approval.[27]

Need for Power

People with a high **need for power (nPow)** want to exercise control over others and are concerned about maintaining their leadership position. They frequently rely on persuasive communication, make more suggestions in meetings, and tend to publicly evaluate situations more frequently. McClelland pointed out that there are two types of nPow. Individuals who enjoy their power for its own sake, use it to advance personal interests, and wear their power as a status symbol have *personalized power*. Others mainly have a high need for *socialized power* because they desire power as a means to help others.[28] McClelland argues that effective leaders should

need for achievement (nAch)
A learned need in which people want to accomplish reasonably challenging goals and desire unambiguous feedback and recognition for their success.

need for affiliation (nAff)
A learned need in which people seek approval from others, conform to their wishes and expectations, and avoid conflict and confrontation.

need for power (nPow)
A learned need in which people want to control environment, including people and material resources, to benefit either themselves (personalized power) or others (socialized power).

have a high need for socialized rather than personalized power. They must have a high degree of altruism and social responsibility and be concerned about the consequences of their own actions on others.

Learning Needs   McClelland believed that needs can be learned (more accurately, strengthened or weakened), and the training programs he developed supported that proposition. In his achievement motivation program, trainees wrote achievement-oriented stories and practiced achievement-oriented behaviors in business games. They also completed a detailed achievement plan for the next two years and formed a reference group with other trainees to maintain their new-found achievement motivation.[29] Participants attending these achievement motivation programs subsequently started more new businesses, had greater community involvement, invested more in expanding their businesses, and employed twice as many people compared with a matched sample of non-participants. These training programs increased achievement motivation by altering participants' self-concepts and reinforced experiences, such that they amplified related emotions generated by innate drives. When writing an achievement plan, for example, participants were encouraged (and supported by other participants) to experience the anticipated thrill of succeeding.

FOUR-DRIVE THEORY

One of the central messages of this chapter is that emotions play a key role in employee motivation. This view is supported by a groundswell of research in neuroscience, but it has been slow to gain recognition in organizational behavior theories. Social scientists in several fields (psychology, anthropology, etc.) increasingly agree that human beings have several hardwired drives, including social interaction, learning, and getting ahead. One of the few motivation theories to apply this emerging knowledge is **four-drive theory**.[30] Developed by Harvard Business School professors Paul Lawrence and Nitin Nohria, four-drive theory states that everyone has the drive to acquire, bond, learn, and defend:

- *Drive to acquire.* This is the drive to seek, take, control, and retain objects and personal experiences. The drive to acquire extends beyond basic food and water; it includes enhancing one's self-concept through relative status and recognition in society.[31] Thus, it is the foundation of competition and the basis of our need for esteem. Four-drive theory states that the drive to acquire is insatiable because the purpose of human motivation is to achieve a higher position than others, not just to fulfill one's physiological needs.

- *Drive to bond.* This is the drive to form social relationships and develop mutual caring commitments with others. It explains why people form social identities by aligning their self-concept with various social groups (see Chapter 3). It may also explain why people who lack social contact are more prone to serious health problems.[32] The drive to bond motivates people to cooperate and, consequently, is a fundamental ingredient in the success of organizations and the development of societies.

- *Drive to comprehend.* This is the drive to satisfy our curiosity, to know and understand ourselves and the environment around us.[33] When observing something that is inconsistent with or beyond our current knowledge, we experience a tension that motivates us to close that information gap. In fact, studies have revealed that people who are removed from any novel information will crave even boring information; the drive to comprehend generated such strong emotions that the study participants eventually craved month-old stock reports![34] The drive to comprehend is related to the higher-order needs of growth and self-actualization described earlier.

- *Drive to defend.* This is the drive to protect ourselves physically and socially. Probably the first drive to develop, it creates a "fight-or-flight" response in the face of personal danger. The drive to defend goes beyond protecting our physical selves. It includes defending our relationships, our acquisitions, and our belief systems.

EXHIBIT 5.3   Four-Drive Theory of Motivation

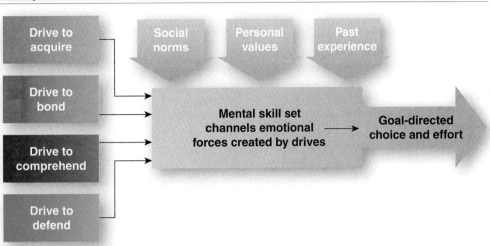

Source: Based on information in P.R. Lawrence and N. Nohria, *Driven: How Human Nature Shapes Our Choices* (San Francisco: Jossey-Bass, 2002).

These four drives are innate and universal, meaning that they are hardwired in our brains and are found in all human beings. They are also independent of one another. There is no hierarchy of drives, so one drive is neither dependent on nor inherently inferior or superior to another drive. Four-drive theory also states that these four drives are a complete set—there are no fundamental drives excluded from the model. Another key feature is that three of the four drives are proactive—we regularly try to fulfill them. Only the drive to defend is reactive—it is triggered by threat. Thus, any notion of fulfilling drives is temporary, at best.

How Drives Influence Employee Motivation

Four-drive theory is derived from recent neuroscience research regarding the emotional marker process and how emotions are channeled into decisions and behavior. As we described in previous chapters, our perceptions of the world around us are quickly and nonconsciously tagged with emotional markers.[35] According to four-drive theory, the four drives determine which emotions are tagged to incoming stimuli. Consider our earlier example: If you arrive at work one day to see a stranger sitting in your office chair, you might quickly experience worry, curiosity, or both. These emotions are automatically created by one or more of the four drives. In this example, the emotions produced are likely strong enough to demand your attention and motivate you to act on this observation.

Most of the time, we aren't aware of our emotional experiences because they are subtle and fleeting. However, emotions do become conscious experiences when they are sufficiently strong or when we experience conflicting emotions. Under these circumstances, our mental skill set relies on social norms, past experience, and personal values to direct the motivational force of our emotions to actions that deal with that situation (see Exhibit 5.3). In other words, our mental skill set chooses courses of action that are acceptable to society, are consistent with our own moral compass, and have a high probability of achieving the goal.[36] This is the process described at the beginning of this chapter, namely, that drives produce emotions; our self-concept, social norms, and past experience translate these emotions into goal-directed needs, and these individual characteristics also translate needs into decisions and behavior.

Evaluating Four-Drive Theory

Although four-drive theory was introduced very recently, it is based on a deep foundation of research that dates back more than three decades. The drives have been identified from psychological and anthropological studies. Furthermore, Shalom Schwartz recently reported that four-drive theory maps

four-drive theory
A motivation theory based on the innate drives to acquire, bond, learn, and defend that incorporates both emotions and rationality.

Radialpoint, one of the best-managed companies in Canada, develops cutting-edge technology for Verizon, Bell Canada, and other Internet giants. Cofounder and CEO Hamnett Hill believes that balancing the fulfillment of employee drives is a factor in this success. "People want to do interesting work that makes a difference and is rewarding," explains Hill. The Montreal-based company's 250 staff members fulfill their drive to acquire through personal development, challenging work, and performance rewards. But they also work in a supportive culture with team building and open-book communication. "You want to feel respected and valuable, like you're working on important things and have a great team of people around you," says Hill.[39]

well onto the 10 dimensions in his circumplex model of personal values (see Chapter 2).[37] The translation of drives into goal-directed behavior originates from considerable research on emotions and neural processes. The theory explains why needs vary from one person to the next, but it avoids the assumption that everyone has the same needs hierarchy. Notice, too, that four-drive theory satisfies two of Maslow's criteria for any motivation theory: It is holistic (it relates to all drives, not just one or two) and humanistic (it acknowledges the role of human thought and social influences, not just instinct). Four-drive theory also provides a much clearer understanding of the role of emotional intelligence in employee motivation and behavior. Employees with high emotional intelligence are more sensitive to competing demands from the four drives, are better able to avoid impulsive behavior from those drives, and can judge the best way to act to fulfill those drive demands in a social context.

Even with its well-researched foundations, four-drive theory is far from complete. Most experts would argue that one or two other drives exist that should be included. Furthermore, social norms, personal values, and past experience probably don't represent the full set of individual characteristics that translate emotions into goal-directed effort. For example, personality and self-concept likely also play a significant role in translating drives into needs and needs into decisions and behavior.

Practical Implications of Four-Drive Theory

The main recommendation from four-drive theory is that organizations should ensure that jobs and workplaces provide a balanced opportunity to fulfill the four drives.[38] There are really two recommendations here. The first is that the best workplaces for employee motivation and well-being offer conditions that help employees fulfill all four drives. Employees continually seek fulfillment of their innate drives, so successful companies provide sufficient rewards, information about organizational events, social interaction, and so forth for all employees.

The second recommendation is that fulfillment of the four drives must be kept in balance; that is, organizations should avoid too much or too little opportunity to fulfill each drive. The reason for this advice is that the four drives counterbalance one another. The drive to bond counterbalances the drive to acquire; the drive to defend counterbalances the drive to comprehend. An organization that fuels the drive to acquire

expectancy theory
A motivation theory based on the idea that work effort is directed toward behaviors that people believe will lead to desired outcomes.

without the drive to bond may eventually suffer from organizational politics and dysfunctional conflict. Change and novelty in the workplace will aid the drive to comprehend, but too much of it will trigger the drive to defend to such an extent that employees become territorial and resistant to change. Thus, the workplace should offer enough opportunity to keep all four drives in balance.

These recommendations help explain why Standard Chartered Bank, described at the beginning of this chapter, has a motivated workforce and is rated as one of the best places to work in the world. The company motivates employees to achieve challenging goals (drive to acquire), yet balances this motivation with social events and egalitarian rewards. The company encourages new ideas, yet also maintains a degree of stability in everyone's work lives and seeks ways to improve employee well-being.

Expectancy Theory of Motivation

LO4

connect

To assist your learning and test your knowledge about expectancy theory of motivation, go to **www.mcgrawhillconnect.com**, which has activities and test questions on this topic.

The theories described so far mainly explain the internal origins of employee motivation. But how do these drives and needs translate into specific effort and behavior? Four-drive theory recognizes that social norms, personal values, and past experience direct our effort, but it doesn't offer any more detail. **Expectancy theory,** in contrast, offers an elegant model based on rational logic to predict the chosen direction, level, and persistence of motivation. Essentially, the theory states that work effort is directed toward behaviors that people believe will lead to desired outcomes. In other words, we are motivated to achieve the goals with the highest expected payoff.[40] As illustrated in Exhibit 5.4, an individual's effort level depends on three factors: effort-to-performance (E-to-P) expectancy, performance-to-outcome (P-to-O) expectancy, and outcome valences. Employee motivation is influenced by all three components of the expectancy theory model. If any component weakens, motivation weakens.

- *E-to-P expectancy.* This is the individual's perceived probability that his or her effort will result in a particular level of performance. In some situations, employees may believe that they can unquestionably accomplish the task (a probability of 1.0). In other situations, they expect that even their highest level of effort will not result in the desired performance level (a probability of 0.0). In most cases, the E-to-P expectancy falls somewhere between these two extremes.

EXHIBIT 5.4

Expectancy Theory of Motivation

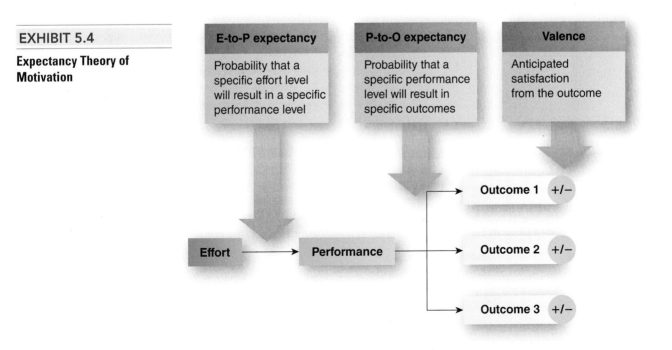

- *P-to-O expectancy.* This is the perceived probability that a specific behavior or performance level will lead to a particular outcome. In extreme cases, employees may believe that accomplishing a particular task (performance) will definitely result in a particular outcome (a probability of 1.0), or they may believe that successful performance will have no effect on this outcome (a probability of 0.0). More often, the P-to-O expectancy falls somewhere between these two extremes.
- *Outcome valences. Valence* is the anticipated satisfaction or dissatisfaction that an individual feels toward an outcome. It ranges from negative to positive. (The actual range doesn't matter; it may be from −1 to +1 or from −100 to +100.) An outcome valence represents a person's anticipated satisfaction with the outcome.[41] Outcomes have a positive valence when they are consistent with our values and satisfy our needs; they have a negative valence when they oppose our values and inhibit need fulfillment.

EXPECTANCY THEORY IN PRACTICE

One of the appealing characteristics of expectancy theory is that it provides clear guidelines for increasing employee motivation.[42] Several practical applications of expectancy theory are listed in Exhibit 5.5 and described in this section.

Increasing E-to-P Expectancies   E-to-P expectancies are influenced by the individual's belief that he or she can successfully complete the task. Some companies increase this can-do attitude by assuring employees that they have the necessary competencies, clear role perceptions, and necessary resources to reach the desired levels of performance. An important part of this process involves matching employees' competencies to job requirements and clearly communicating the tasks required for the job. Similarly, E-to-P expectancies are learned, so behavioral modeling and reinforcement (which we discuss next) typically strengthen the individual's belief that he or she is able to perform the task.

EXHIBIT 5.5   Practical Applications of Expectancy Theory

EXPECTANCY THEORY COMPONENT	OBJECTIVE	APPLICATIONS
E → P expectancies	To increase the belief that employees are capable of performing the job successfully	• Select people with the required skills and knowledge. • Provide required training and clarify job requirements. • Provide sufficient time and resources. • Assign simpler or fewer tasks until employees can master them. • Provide examples of similar employees who have successfully performed the task. • Provide coaching to employees who lack self-confidence.
P → O expectancies	To increase the belief that good performance will result in certain (valued) outcomes	• Measure job performance accurately. • Clearly explain the outcomes that will result from successful performance. • Describe how the employee's rewards are based on past performance. • Provide examples of other employees whose good performance has resulted in higher rewards.
Outcome valences	To increase the expected value of outcomes resulting from desired performance	• Distribute rewards that employees value. • Individualize rewards. • Minimize the presence of countervalent outcomes.

Increasing P-to-O Expectancies   The most obvious ways to improve P-to-O expectancies are to measure employee performance accurately and distribute more valued rewards to those with higher job performance. Because P-to-O expectancies are perceptions, employees also need to believe that higher performance will result in higher rewards. Furthermore, they need to know how that connection occurs, so leaders should use examples, anecdotes, and public ceremonies to illustrate when behavior has been rewarded.

Increasing Outcome Valences   One size does not fit all in the business of motivating and rewarding people. Organizational leaders need to find ways to individualize rewards or, where standard rewards are necessary, to identify rewards that do not have a negative valence for some staff. Consider the following story: Top-performing employees in one organization were rewarded with a one-week Caribbean cruise with the company's executive team. Many were likely delighted, but at least one top performer was aghast at the thought of going on a cruise with senior management. "I don't like schmoozing, I don't like feeling trapped. Why couldn't they just give me the money?" she complained. The employee went on the cruise but spent most of her time working in her stateroom.[43]

One more recommendtion for increasing outcome valences: Watch out for countervalent outcomes that might cancel any positive outcomes. For example, several employees in one work unit were individually motivated to perform well because this achievement gave them a feeling of accomplishment and rewarded them with higher pay. But their performance was considerably lower when they worked together with others because peer pressure discouraged performance above a fairly low standard. In this situation, the positively valent outcomes (feeling of accomplishment, higher pay) were offset by the negatively valent outcome of peer pressure.

Overall, expectancy theory is a useful model that explains how people rationally figure out the best direction, intensity, and persistence of effort. It has been tested in a variety of situations and predicts employee motivation in different cultures.[44] However, critics have a number of concerns about how the theory has been tested. Another concern is that expectancy theory ignores the central role of emotion in employee effort and behavior. The valence element of expectancy theory captures some of this emotional process, but only peripherally.[45] Finally, expectancy theory outlines how expectancies (probability of outcomes) affect motivation, but it doesn't explain how employees develop these expectancies. Two theories that provide this explanation are organizational behavior modification and social cognitive theory, which we describe next.

Organizational Behavior Modification and Social Cognitive Theory

LO5

Expectancy theory states that motivation is determined by employee beliefs about expected performance and outcomes. But how do employees learn these expectancies? The answer to this question directs us to two theories: organizational behavior modification (OB Mod) and social cognitive theory. Although these theories explain how people *learn* what to expect from their actions, they are also theories of motivation because, as in expectancy theory, learned expectancies affect a person's direction, intensity, and persistence of effort.

ORGANIZATIONAL BEHAVIOR MODIFICATION

organizational behavior modification
A theory that explains employee behavior in terms of the antecedent conditions and consequences of that behavior.

For most of the first half of the 1900s, the dominant paradigm about managing individual behavior was *behaviorism,* which argues that a good theory should rely exclusively on behavior and the environment and ignore nonobservable cognitions and emotions.[46] Although behaviorists don't deny the existence of human thoughts and attitudes, they would view them as unobservable and, therefore, irrelevant to scientific study. A variation of this paradigm, called **organizational behavior modification** or OB Mod, eventually entered organizational studies of motivation and learning.[47]

EXHIBIT 5.6   A-B-Cs of Organizational Behavior Modification

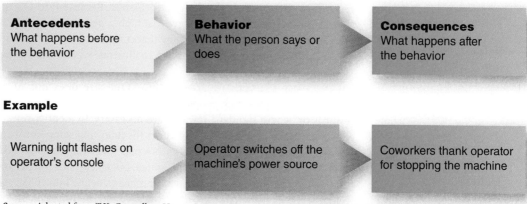

Antecedents
What happens before the behavior

Behavior
What the person says or does

Consequences
What happens after the behavior

Example

Warning light flashes on operator's console

Operator switches off the machine's power source

Coworkers thank operator for stopping the machine

Sources: Adapted from T.K. Connellan, *How to Improve Human Performance* (New York: Harper & Row, 1978), p. 50; F. Luthans and R. Kreitner, *Organizational Behavior Modification and Beyond* (Glenview, IL: Scott, Foresman, 1985), pp. 85–88.

The A-B-Cs of OB Mod   The A-B-C model shown in Exhibit 5.6 represents OB Mod's core elements. Essentially, OB Mod attempts to change behavior (B) by managing its antecedents (A) and consequences (C).[48] *Consequences* are events following a particular behavior that influence its future occurrence, such as the compliments or teasing received from coworkers when the employee wears safety goggles. Consequences also include no outcome at all, such as when no one says anything about how well you have been serving customers.

Antecedents are events preceding the behavior, informing employees that a particular action will produce specific consequences. An antecedent may be a sound from your computer signaling that an e-mail has arrived or a request from your supervisor asking you to complete a specific task by tomorrow. Notice that antecedents do not cause behavior. The computer sound doesn't cause us to open our e-mail. Rather, the sound (antecedent) is a cue telling us that if we check our e-mail (behavior), we are certain to find a new message (consequence). OB Mod identifies four types of consequences.[49]

- *Positive reinforcement.* This consequence occurs when its introduction increases or maintains the frequency or future probability of a specific behavior. This occurs, for example, when receiving praise after completing a project.

- *Punishment.* This occurs when a consequence decreases the frequency or future probability of a behavior. Most of us would consider being demoted or ostracized by our coworkers as forms of punishment.

- *Negative reinforcement.* This consequence is *not* punishment. Rather, it occurs when the removal or avoidance of a consequence increases or maintains the frequency or future probability of a specific behavior. Supervisors apply negative reinforcement when they *stop* criticizing employees whose substandard performance has improved.

- *Extinction.* This consequence occurs when the target behavior decreases because no consequence follows it. For instance, research suggests that performance tends to decline when managers stop congratulating employees for their good work.[50]

Which contingency of reinforcement works best? In most situations, positive reinforcement should follow desired behaviors, and extinction (do nothing) should follow undesirable behaviors. This approach is preferred because punishment and negative reinforcement generate negative emotions and attitudes toward the punisher (e.g., supervisor) and organization. However, some form of punishment (dismissal, suspension, demotion, etc.) may be necessary for extreme behaviors, such as deliberately hurting a coworker or stealing inventory. Indeed, research suggests that under certain conditions, punishment maintains a sense of fairness.[52]

Along with the types of reinforcement, the frequency and timing of the reinforcers also motivate employees in different ways.[53] The most effective reinforcement schedule for learning new tasks is *continuous reinforcement*—providing positive reinforcement after

Walking to work is starting to look much more appealing to city employees in Stoke-on-Trent, Staffordshire. The British municipality issued pedometers to its staff and encouraged them to develop a regimen of daily walking. The city wants to get sedentary employees walking at least 10,000 steps each day for five days a week. The pedometers provide instant feedback, thereby providing positive reinforcement for longer walks. Some organizations monetize these footsteps by rewarding employees with gift certificates and health insurance discounts.[51]

every occurrence of the desired behavior. The best schedule for motivating employees is a *variable ratio schedule* in which employee behavior is reinforced after a variable number of times. Salespeople experience variable ratio reinforcement because they make a successful sale (the reinforcer) after a varying number of client calls. The variable ratio schedule makes behavior highly resistant to extinction, because the reinforcer is never expected at a particular time or after a fixed number of accomplishments.

Evaluating OB Mod Everyone uses organizational behavior modification principles in one form or another to motivate others. We thank people for a job well done, are silent when displeased, and sometimes try to punish those who go against our wishes. OB Mod also occurs in various formal programs to reduce absenteeism, improve task performance, encourage safe work behaviors, and have a healthier lifestyle. Burger Boat Company, a luxury yacht builder in Wisconsin, has a safety incentive program that reinforces safe work behaviors. Ochsner Health System, which operates hospitals and clinics throughout Louisiana, has a wellness incentive program that provides positive reinforcement in the form of cash rewards (up to $300 in cash rewards and $2,000 in health insurance discounts each year) for engaging in healthy behaviors.[54]

Organizational behavior modification has a number of limitations, one of which is "reward inflation," in which the reinforcer is eventually considered an entitlement. For this reason, most OB Mod programs must run infrequently and for a short duration. Another concern is that the variable ratio schedule of reinforcement tends to create a lottery-style reward system, which might be viewed as too erratic for formal rewards and is unpopular to people who dislike gambling. Probably the most significant problem is OB Mod's radical view that behavior is learned only through personal interaction with the environment.[55] This view is no longer accepted; instead, experts recognize that people also learn and are motivated by observing others and inferring possible consequences of their actions. This learning process is explained by social cognitive theory.

SOCIAL COGNITIVE THEORY

social cognitive theory
A theory that explains how learning and motivation occur by observing and modelling others as well as by anticipating the consequences of our behavior.

Social cognitive theory states that much learning and motivation occurs by observing and modeling others, as well as by anticipating the consequences of our behavior.[56]

Although observation and modeling (imitation) have been studied for many years as sources of motivation and learning, social scientist Albert Bandura reframed these ideas within a cognitive (internal thoughts) perspective as an alternative to the behaviorist approach. There are several pieces to social cognitive theory, but the three most relevant to employee motivation are learning behavior consequences, behavioral modeling, and self-regulation.

Learning Behavioral Outcomes   People learn the consequences of behavior by observing or hearing about what happened to other people, not just by directly experiencing the consequences.[57] Hearing that a coworker was fired for being rude to a client increases your perception that rude behavior will result in being fired. In the language of expectancy theory, learning behavior consequences changes a person's perceived P-to-O probability. Furthermore, people logically anticipate consequences in related situations. For instance, the story about the fired employee might also strengthen your P-to-O expectancy about getting fired if you are rude toward coworkers and suppliers.

Behavior Modeling   People learn not only by observing others but also by imitating and practicing those behaviors.[58] Direct sensory experience helps a person acquire tacit knowledge and skills, such as the subtle person-machine interaction that is required while driving a vehicle. Behavioral modeling also increases self-efficacy (see Chapter 3), because people gain more self-confidence after observing others and performing the task successfully themselves. Self-efficacy particularly improves when observers identify with the model, such as someone who is similar in age, experience, gender, or related features.

Self-Regulation   An important feature of social cognitive theory is that human beings set goals and engage in other forms of intentional, purposive action. They establish their own short- and long-term objectives, choose their own standards of achievement, work out a plan of action, consider back-up alternatives, and have the forethought to anticipate the consequences of their goal-directed behavior. Furthermore, people self-regulate by engaging in **self-reinforcement;** that is, they reward and punish themselves for exceeding or falling short of their self-set standards of excellence.[59] For example, you might have a goal of completing the rest of this chapter, after which you reward yourself by having a snack. Raiding the refrigerator is a form of self-induced positive reinforcement for completing this reading assignment.

Self-regulation has become an important topic in the social sciences. It is also the cornerstone of motivation through goal setting and feedback, which we discuss next.

Goal Setting and Feedback

LO6

To assist your learning and test your knowledge about goal setting, go to **www.mcgrawhillconnect.com,** which has activities and test questions on this topic.

Walk into almost any customer contact center (i.e., call center)—whether Sitel's offices in Albuquerque, New Mexico, or Dell's contact center in Quezon City in the Philippines—and you will notice that work activities are dominated by goal setting and plenty of feedback.[60] Contact-center performance is judged on several *key performance indicators (KPIs),* such as average time to answer the call, average handle time, and abandon rates (customers who hang up before the call is handled by a customer service representative). Some contact centers have large electronic boards showing how many customers are waiting, the average time they have been waiting, and the average time before someone talks to them. A few even have "emotion detection" software, which translates words and voice intonation into a measure of the customer's level of happiness or anger during the telephone conversation.[61]

Goal setting is the process of motivating employees and clarifying their role perceptions by establishing performance objectives. It potentially improves employee performance in two ways: (1) by amplifying the intensity and persistence of effort and (2) by giving employees clearer role perceptions so that their effort is channeled toward behaviors that will improve work performance. Goal setting is more complex than simply telling someone to "do your best." It requires several specific characteristics.[62] One popular acronym, SMARTER, captures these characteristics fairly well:[63]

- *Specific.* Employees put more effort into a task when they work toward goals that state what needs to be accomplished; how it should be accomplished; and where,

Jeff Gross is a big fan of goal setting. "Setting goals is one of the most important aspects of building and maintaining a successful business," according to the president of GOH Lending in Anchorage, Alaska, and Costa Mesa, California. Gross explains that goals are the bridges between ideas and achievements. "It is the best way to tell whether a business is improving and can shed light on the areas that need improvement," he claims. Gross also believes that goals can stretch performance. His latest goal is to double business in the Anchorage office within one year without easing lending requirements.[64]

Mc Graw Hill connect

What is your goal orientation? Go to **www.mcgrawhillconnect.com** to assess how much you have a learning or avoidance goal orientation.

self-reinforcement
Reinforcement that occurs when an employee has control over a reinforcer but doesn't 'take' it until completing a self-set goal.

goal setting
The process of motivating employees and clarifying their role perceptions by establishing performance objectives.

when, and with whom it should be accomplished. Specific goals clarify performance expectations, so employees can direct their effort more efficiently and reliably.

- *Measurable.* Goals need to be measurable. Otherwise, we wouldn't know whether they have been achieved. This measurement ideally includes how much (quantity), how well (quality), and at what cost the goal was achieved. Measurement can be a problem however, because people focus on goals that are easily measured. As Albert Einstein once warned: "Not everything that can be counted counts, and not everything that counts can be counted."[65]

- *Achievable.* Ideally, goals should be challenging without being so difficult that employees lose their motivation to achieve them.[66] This idea reflects the E-to-P expectancy described earlier in this chapter. The lower the E-to-P expectancy that the goal can be accomplished, the less committed (motivated) the employee is to the goal.

- *Relevant.* Goals need to be relevant to the individual's job and within his or her control. For example, a goal to reduce waste materials would have little value if employees had no control over waste in the production process.

- *Time-framed.* Goals need a due date. They should specify when the objective should be completed or when it will be assessed for comparison against a standard.
- *Exciting.* Goals tend to be more effective when employees are committed to them, not just compliant. Challenging goals tend to be more exciting for most (but not all) employees because they are more likely to fulfill a person's achievement or growth needs when the goal is achieved. Goal commitment also increases when employees are involved in goal setting.[67]
- *Reviewed.* The motivational value of goal setting depends on employees receiving feedback about reaching those goals.[68] Measurement is part of that feedback, but so is the process of reviewing goal progress (during) and accomplishment (after). Reviewing goal progress and accomplishment helps employees redirect their effort. It is also a potential source of recognition that fulfills growth needs.

BALANCED SCORECARD

Balanced scorecard (BSC) offers an organization-level form of goal setting and feedback that attempts to represent objectives across various stakeholders and processes. It translates the organization's vision and mission into specific, measurable key performance indicators (KPIs) related to financial, customer, internal, and learning/growth (i.e., human capital) processes. These goals cascade down to departments and to employees within those departments. For example, an airline might include on-time performance as one of its customer process goals and number of hours of safety training per employee as a learning and growth process goal. These specific goals are linked to various work units and employees (such as department managers). BSC goals are often weighted and scored to create a composite measure of achievement across the organization each year.

Several organizations have introduced balanced scorecards, including Veolia Water, Volkswagen do Brasil, Royal Canadian Mounted Police, and the Richmond School Board in Virginia. The Richmond School Board BSC has six goals (e.g., improving student achievement, promoting a safe and nurturing environment), each of which has several outcome measures. For instance, the goal of improving student achievement includes a dozen measures, such as the percentage of students who meet the state-sanctioned completion rate, percentage of special education students moving to a higher reading level, and percentage of students enrolling in specific math and science courses. "Our BSC lays out a challenging set of process measures and targets for us, and it holds us accountable for reaching our goals," explains Yvonne Brandon, superintendent of Richmond Public Schools.[69]

In spite of their popularity, BSCs present a number of challenges. As with most goal setting and feedback systems, the quality of the process is only as good as the goals established and the feedback available. Some companies choose goals that are easily measured rather than valuable. Others go to great lengths to measure internal processes, but these measures create a paperwork bureaucracy that raises overhead costs and employee resentment for diverting resources from the company's main functions. One recent report from the Royal Canadian Mounted Police (RCMP), which has a highly regarded BSC, warned that people get caught up on the measures, whereas they need more discipline to focus on achieving BSC goals. The RCMP report also noted that BSC systems suffer when they become overburdened with too many indicators and when those indicators don't resonate with employees.[70]

CHARACTERISTICS OF EFFECTIVE FEEDBACK

Feedback—information that lets us know whether we have achieved the goal or are properly directing our effort toward it—is a critical partner in goal setting. Along with clarifying role perceptions and improving employee skills and knowledge, feedback motivates when it is constructive and when employees have strong self-efficacy.[71] Effective feedback has many of the same characteristics as effective goal setting. It should be *specific* and *relevant;* that is, the information should refer to specific metrics (e.g., sales increased by 5 percent last month) and to the individual's behavior or outcomes within his or her control. Feedback should also be *timely;* the information should be available soon after the behavior or results occur so that employees

Sony Europe focused on employee strengths rather than fight an uphill battle against their weaknesses. Each employee was asked to identify activities in which he or she excels, enjoys the work, and feels at ease. This information helped Sony Europe redesign jobs around these strengths. This strengths-based coaching "ensures that everybody in Sony is focusing on what they do best," says Ray White, Sony Europe's vice president of human resources.[74]

see a clear association between their actions and the consequences. Effective feedback is also *credible*. Employees are more likely to accept feedback from trustworthy and credible sources.

The final characteristic of effective feedback is that it should be *sufficiently frequent*. How frequent is "sufficiently"? The answer depends on at least two things. One consideration is the employee's knowledge and experience with the task. Feedback is a form of reinforcement, so employees working on new tasks should receive more frequent feedback because they require more behavior guidance and reinforcement. Employees who perform familiar tasks can receive less frequent feedback. The second factor is how long it takes to complete the task. Feedback is necessarily less frequent in jobs with a long cycle time (e.g., executives, scientists) than in jobs with a short cycle time (e.g., grocery store cashiers).

Feedback Through Strengths-Based Coaching   Forty years ago, Peter Drucker recognized that leaders are more effective when they focus on strengths rather than weaknesses. "The effective executive builds on strengths—their own strengths; the strengths of superiors, colleagues, subordinates; and on the strength of the situation," wrote the late management guru.[72] Standard Chartered Bank, described at the beginning of this chapter, has adopted this positive OB approach to improve employee engagement. It gives employees opportunities to develop their strengths rather than requiring them to focus on areas where they have limited interest or talent.

This is the essence of **strengths-based coaching** (also known as *appreciative coaching*): maximizing

balanced scorecard (BSC)
A goal-setting and reward system that translates the organization's vision and mission into specific, measurable performance goals related to financial, customer, internal, and learning/growth (i.e., human capital) processes.

strengths-based coaching
A positive organizational behavior approach to coaching and feedback that focuses on building and leveraging the employee's strengths rather than trying to correct his or her weaknesses.

employees' potential by focusing on their strengths rather than weaknesses.[73] In strengths-based coaching, employees describe areas of work where they excel or demonstrate potential. The coach guides this discussion by asking exploratory questions that help employees to discover ways of leveraging this strength. Situational barriers to leveraging the employee's potential are identified, along with strategies to overcome those barriers.

Strengths-based coaching can motivate employees because they inherently seek feedback about their strengths, not their flaws. Thus, strengths-based feedback is consistent with the process of self-enhancement (see Chapter 3). Strengths-based coaching also makes sense because personality usually has become quite stable by the time of a person's early career, which limits the flexibility of the person's interests, preferences, and competencies.[75] In spite of these research observations, most companies focus their goal setting and feedback on tasks that employees are performing poorly. After the initial polite compliments, many coaching or performance feedback sessions analyze the employee's weaknesses, including determining what went wrong and what the employee needs to do to improve. These inquisitions sometimes produce so much negative feedback that employees become defensive; they can also undermine self-efficacy, thereby making the employee's performance worse rather than better. By focusing on weaknesses, companies fail to realize the full potential of the employee's strengths.

SOURCES OF FEEDBACK

Feedback can originate from nonsocial or social sources. Nonsocial sources provide feedback without someone communicating that information. Employees at contact centers view electronic displays showing how many callers are waiting and the average time they have been waiting. Nova Chemicals operators receive feedback from a computer screen that monitors in real time the plant's operational capacity, depicted as a gently flowing green line, and actual production output, shown as a red squiggly line. Soon after Nova installed the feedback system, employees engaged in friendly bouts of rivalry to determine who could keep the actual production output as close as possible to the plant's maximum capacity.[76]

Corporate intranets allow many executives to receive feedback instantaneously on their computer, usually in the form of graphic output on an executive dashboard. Almost half of Microsoft's employees use a dashboard to monitor project deadlines, sales, and other metrics. Microsoft CEO Steve Ballmer regularly reviews dashboard results in one-on-one meetings with his division leaders. "Every time I go to see Ballmer, it's an expectation that I bring my dashboard with me," says the head of the Microsoft Office division.[77]

Multisource (360-Degree) Feedback   **Multisource (360-degree) feedback** is a social form of feedback that has been widely used in organizations. As the name implies, multisource feedback is information about an employee's performance, collected from a full circle of people, including subordinates, peers, supervisors, and customers. Multisource feedback tends to provide more complete and accurate information than feedback from a supervisor alone. It is particularly useful when the supervisor is unable to observe the employee's behavior or performance throughout the year. Lower-level employees also feel a greater sense of fairness and open communication when they are able to provide upward feedback about their boss's performance.[78]

However, multisource feedback creates challenges. Having several people review so many other people can be expensive and time-consuming. With multiple opinions, the 360-degree process can also produce ambiguous and conflicting feedback, so employees may require guidance to interpret the results. A third concern is that peers may provide inflated rather than accurate feedback to avoid conflicts during the forthcoming year. A final concern is that employees experience a stronger emotional reaction when they receive critical feedback from many people rather than from just one person (such as the boss). "Initially you do take it personally," admits a manager at software maker Autodesk. "[360-degree feedback] is meant to be constructive, but you have to internally battle that."[79]

Choosing Feedback Sources   With so many sources of feedback—multisource feedback, executive dashboards, customer surveys, equipment gauges, nonverbal communication from your boss—which one works best under which conditions? The preferred feedback source depends on the purpose of the information. To learn about their progress toward goal accomplishment, employees usually prefer nonsocial feedback sources, such as computer printouts or feedback directly from the job. This is because information from nonsocial sources is considered more accurate than information from social sources. Performance feedback from nonsocial sources is also less damaging to self-esteem. In contrast, social sources tend to delay negative information, leave some of it out, and distort the bad news in a positive way.[80] When employees want to improve their self-image, they seek out positive feedback from social sources. It feels better to have coworkers say that you are performing the job well than to discover this from a computer screen.

EVALUATING GOAL SETTING AND FEEDBACK

Goal setting represents one of the "tried-and-true" theories in organizational behavior, so much so that it is rated by experts as one of the top OB theories in terms of validity and usefulness.[81] In partnership with goal setting, feedback also has an excellent reputation for improving employee motivation and performance. At the same time, putting goal setting into practice can create problems.[82] One concern is that goal setting tends to direct employee focus to a narrow subset of measurable performance indicators while ignoring aspects of job performance that are difficult to measure. The saying, "What gets measured, gets done," applies here. A second problem is that when goal achievement is tied to financial rewards, many employees are motivated to set easy goals (while making the boss think they are difficult) so that they have a higher probability of attaining the bonus or pay increase. As a former CEO at Ford once quipped: "At Ford, we hire very smart people. They quickly learn how to make relatively easy goals look difficult!"[83] A third problem is that setting performance goals is effective in established jobs but seems to interfere with the learning process in new, complex jobs. Thus, we need to be careful not to apply goal setting where an intense learning process is occurring.

Organizational Justice

LO7

When Robert Meggy first introduced a profit-sharing plan at Great Little Box Company, he felt that the size of the profit-sharing bonus should correspond to the person's position and seniority in the organization. "It used to be a program based on seniority and a number of other variables but there were a number of complaints about that," Meggy recalls. "Now that it's equal across the board, we don't have that problem." In other words, employees felt that the original bonus distribution system lacked fairness, a condition that Meggy considers vital to a successful company. "I certainly believe in fair pay," he says. "You don't have to be the best paying, but you do have to be fair."[84]

Most organizational leaders know that treating employees fairly is both morally correct and good for employee motivation, loyalty, and well-being. Yet feelings of injustice and inequity are regular occurrences in the workplace. To minimize these incidents, we need to first understand that there are two forms of organizational justice: distributive justice and procedural justice.[85]

Distributive justice refers to perceived fairness in the outcomes we receive compared with our contributions and the outcomes and contributions of others. **Procedural justice** instead refers to fairness of the procedures used to decide the distribution of resources.

multisource (360-degree) feedback
Information about an employee's performance collected from a full circle of people, including subordinates, peers, supervisors, and customers.

distributive justice
Perceived fairness in the individual's ratio of outcomes to contributions compared with an other's ratio of outcomes to contributions.

procedural justice
Perceived fairness of the procedures used to decide the distribution of resources.

Debating Point

DOES EQUITY MOTIVATE MORE THAN EQUALITY?[86]

It seems obvious that employees with higher performance, skills, or other contributions to the organization should receive more generous pay and other rewards. Increasing the pay differential (wage dispersion) between high and low contributors should boost employee motivation to achieve a higher standard of performance. It should also increase company performance by motivating the top performers to stay and the bottom performers to leave. A large wage dispersion is also consistent with justice and fairness. Differentiating rewards based on employee performance, skills, and other forms of contribution is consistent with the principle of meritocracy. It is also consistent with the principle of justice, which states that those who contribute more should receive more in return (Chapter 2). Furthermore, performance-based pay is one of the pillars of high performance work practices (see Chapter 1).

But workplaces that have large wage dispersions might not be receiving the performance dividends they expect. Several (but not all) studies have found that sports teams with relatively small pay differences among team members perform better than sports teams with relatively high pay differences. Teams that pay huge salaries or bonuses to stars do not score more points or win more games. Also, turnover among players and managers tends to

increase with the size of the wage dispersion. One recent study extended these observations to all industries. Companies that have a higher dispersion of wage increases (larger increases to higher-paid staff) perform worse than companies with an equal dispersion of wage increases. Another study reported that information technology companies with larger salary differences among top management teams had worse shareholder returns and market-to-book value compared with IT companies with less pay inequality.

Why would larger pay ranges undermine rather than enhance employee and organizational performance? One reason is that pay differences produce status differences, which can undermine cooperation among employees. A second reason is that large pay differences might increase (rather than decrease) feelings of injustice. Most people think they are above average, so large pay differences clearly place many employees below their self-evaluations. Also, employees tend to underestimate the contribution of more highly paid coworkers and assume those higher-paid coworkers also receive other rewards (such as preferential treatment). In short, lower-paid employees often believe higher-paid employees are overpaid, which reduces the lower-paid workers' motivation and performance.

EQUITY THEORY

At its most basic level, the employment relationship is about exchanging an employee's time and services for pay, opportunities to develop skills and knowledge, fulfilling work, and so forth. What is considered "fair" in this exchange relationship varies with each person and situation. We apply an *equality principle* when we believe that everyone in the group should receive the same outcomes, such as when everyone gets subsidized meals in the company cafeteria. The *need principle* is applied when we believe that those with the greatest need should receive more outcomes than others with less need. The *equity principle* implies that people should be paid in proportion to their contribution. The equity principle is the most common distributive justice rule in organizational settings, so let's look at it in more detail.

Feelings of equity are explained by **equity theory,** which says that employees determine feelings of equity by comparing their own outcome/input ratio to the outcome/input ratio of some other person.[87] As Exhibit 5.7 illustrates, the *outcome/input ratio* is the value of the outcomes you receive divided by the value of the inputs you provide to the exchange relationship. Inputs include such things as skill, effort, reputation, performance, experience, and hours worked. Outcomes are what employees receive from the organization, such as pay, promotions, recognition, interesting jobs, and opportunities to improve their skills and knowledge.

> **equity theory**
> A theory explaining how people develop perceptions of fairness in the distribution and exchange of resources.

Equity theory states that we compare our outcome/input ratio with that of a comparison other.[88] The comparison other might be another person or group of people in other jobs (e.g., comparing your pay with the CEO's pay) or another organization. Some research suggests that employees frequently collect information on several referents to form a "generalized" comparison other.[89] For the most part, however, the comparison other varies from one person to the next and is not easily identifiable.

The comparison of our own outcome/input ratio with the ratio of someone else results in perceptions of equity, underreward inequity, or overreward inequity. In the equity

EXHIBIT 5.7

Equity Theory Model

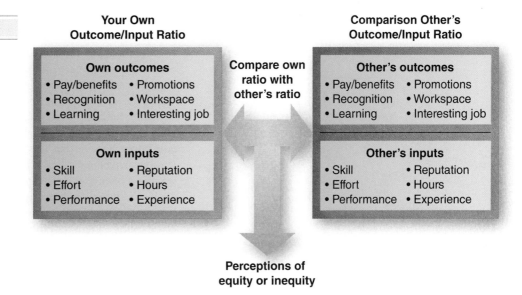

condition, people believe that their outcome/input ratio is similar to the ratio of the comparison other. In the underreward inequity situation, people believe their outcome/input ratio is lower than the comparison other's ratio. In the overreward inequity condition, people believe their ratio of outcomes/inputs is higher than the comparison other's ratio.

Inequity and Employee Motivation   How do perceptions of equity or inequity affect employee motivation? The answer is illustrated in Exhibit 5.8. When people believe they are under- or overrewarded, they experience negative emotions (called inequity tension). As we have pointed out throughout this chapter, emotions are the engines of motivation. In the case of inequity, people are motivated to reduce the emotional tension. Imagine the following: You discover that a coworker earns slightly more than you do, even though he or she began the job at the same time you did, has the same background, and doesn't seem to perform any better. Most people have a strong emotional response to this information, and this emotion nags them until they take some sort of action to correct the perceived inequity.

There are many ways that people might try to reduce the inequity tension.[90] Let's consider each of these in the context of underreward inequity. One action would be to reduce our inputs so the outcome/input ratio is similar to that of the higher-paid coworker. Some employees do this by working more slowly, offering fewer suggestions, and engaging in less organizational citizenship behavior. A second action might be to increase our outcomes. Some people who think they are underpaid ask for a pay raise. Others make unauthorized use of company resources. A third behavioral response is to increase the comparison other's inputs. You might subtly ask the better-paid coworker to do a larger

EXHIBIT 5.8   Motivational Effects of Inequity Perceptions

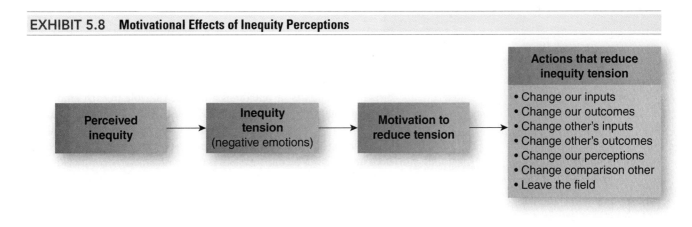

"O.K., if you can't see your way to giving me a pay raise, how about giving Parkerson a pay cut?"

share of the work, for instance. A fourth action would be to reduce the comparison other's outcomes. This might occur by ensuring that the coworker gets less desirable jobs or working conditions. Another action, though uncommon, would be asking the company to reduce the coworker's pay so it is the same as yours.

A fifth action is perceptual rather than behavioral. It involves changing our beliefs about the situation. For example, you might believe that the coworker really is doing more (e.g., working longer hours) for that higher pay. Alternatively, we might change our perceptions of the value of some outcomes. Although initially upset that a coworker gets more travel opportunities than you do, you eventually believe the travel is more a nuisance than a desirable feature of the job. A sixth action to reduce the inequity tension would be to change the comparison other. You might compare yourself more with a friend or neighbor who works in a similar job rather than use the higher-paid coworker as the comparison. Finally, if the inequity tension is strong enough and can't be reduced through other actions, you might leave the field. This occurs by moving to another department, joining another company, or keeping away from the work site where the overpaid coworker is located.

Although the seven responses to inequity remain the same, people who feel overreward inequity would, of course, act differently. Some overrewarded employees reduce their feelings of inequity by working harder. However, many overrewarded employees don't work harder. Some might encourage the underrewarded coworker to work at a more leisurely pace. A common reaction, however, is that the overrewarded employee changes his or her perceptions to justify the more favorable outcomes. As the late author Pierre Burton once said: "I was underpaid for the first half of my life. I don't mind being overpaid for the second half."[91]

Individual Differences: Equity Sensitivity   People vary in their *equity sensitivity,* that is, how strongly they feel about outcome/input ratios with others.[92] At one end of the equity sensitivity continuum are people who are tolerant of situations where they are underrewarded. They might still prefer equal outcome/input ratios, but they don't mind if others receive more than they do for the same inputs. In the middle are people who fit the standard equity theory model; they want their outcome/input ratio to be equal to the outcome/input ratio of the comparison other. At the other end of the equity sensitivity continuum are people who feel more comfortable when they receive proportionately more than others. They might accept having the same outcome/input ratio as others, but they would prefer receiving more than others performing the same work.

Evaluating Equity Theory   Equity theory is widely studied and quite successful at predicting various situations involving feelings of workplace injustice.[93] However, equity theory isn't so easy to put into practice, because it doesn't identify the comparison other and doesn't indicate which inputs or outcomes are most valuable to each employee. The best solution here is for leaders to know their employees well enough to minimize the risk of inequity feelings. Open communication is also a key, enabling employees to let decision makers know when they feel decisions are unfair. A second problem is that equity theory accounts for only some of our feelings of fairness or justice in the workplace. Experts now say that procedural justice is at least as important as distributive justice.

Not Paid What They Think They're Worth

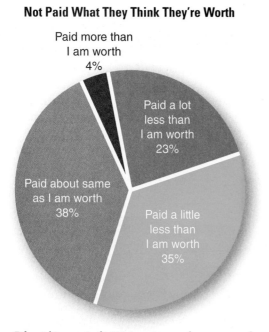

Fifty-eight percent of 1,000 American employees surveyed say they are paid a little or a lot less than they believe they are worth. Only 4 percent believe they are overpaid.

PROCEDURAL JUSTICE

Recall that *procedural justice* refers to the fairness of the procedures used to decide the distribution of resources. How do companies improve procedural justice?[94] A good way to start is by giving employees "voice" in the process; encourage them to present their facts and perspectives on the issue. Voice also provides a "value-expressive" function; employees tend to feel better after having an opportunity to speak their mind. Procedural justice is also higher when the decision maker is perceived as unbiased, relies on complete and accurate information, applies existing policies consistently, and has listened to all sides of the dispute. If employees still feel unfairness in the allocation of resources, those feelings tend to subside when they have the opportunity to appeal the decision to a higher authority.

Finally, people usually feel less injustice when they are given a full explanation of the decision and their concerns are treated with respect. If employees believe a decision is unfair, refusing to explain how the decision was made could fuel their feelings of inequity. For instance, one study found that nonwhite nurses who experienced racism tended to file grievances only after experiencing disrespectful treatment in their attempt to resolve the racist situation. Another study reported that employees with repetitive strain injuries were more likely to file workers' compensation claims after experiencing disrespectful behavior from management. A third recent study noted that employees have stronger feelings of injustice when the manager has a reputation of treating people unfairly most of the time.[95]

Consequences of Procedural Injustice   Procedural justice has a strong influence on a person's emotions and motivation. Employees tend to experience anger toward the source of the injustice, which generates various response behaviors that scholars categorize as either withdrawal or aggression.[96] Notice how these response behaviors are similar to the fight-or-flight responses described earlier in the chapter regarding situations that activate our drive to defend. Research suggests that being treated unfairly threatens our self-concept and social status, particularly when others see that we have been unjustly treated. Employees retaliate to restore their self-concept and reinstate their status and power in the relationship with the perpetrator of the injustice. Employees also engage in these counterproductive behaviors to educate the decision maker, thereby trying to minimize the likelihood of future injustices.[97]

[chapter summary]

LO1   Define *employee engagement*.

Employee engagement is defined as an individual's emotional and cognitive (rational) motivation, particularly a focused, intense, persistent, and purposive effort toward work-related goals. It is emotional involvement in, commitment to, and satisfaction with the work, as well as a high level of absorption in the work and sense of self-efficacy about performing the work.

LO2   Explain the role of human drives and emotions in employee motivation and behavior.

Motivation consists of the forces within a person that affect his or her direction, intensity, and persistence of voluntary behavior in the workplace. Drives (also called primary needs) are neural states that energize individuals to correct deficiencies or maintain an internal equilibrium. They are the "prime movers" of behavior, activating emotions that put us in a state of readiness to act. Needs—goal-directed forces that people experience—are

shaped by the individual's self-concept (including personality and values), social norms, and past experience.

LO3   Summarize Maslow's needs hierarchy, McClelland's learned needs theory, and four-drive theory and discuss their implications for motivating employees.

Maslow's needs hierarchy groups needs into a hierarchy of five levels and states that the lowest needs are initially most important, but higher needs become more important as the lower ones are satisfied. Although very popular, this theory lacks research support because it wrongly assumes that everyone has the same hierarchy. Emerging evidence suggests that needs hierarchies vary from one person to the next, according to their personal values.

McClelland's learned needs theory argues that needs can be strengthened through learning. The three needs studied in this respect are need for achievement, need for power, and need for affiliation. Four-drive theory states that everyone has four innate drives—the drives to acquire, bond, learn, and defend. These drives activate emotions that people regulate through a skill set that considers social norms, past experience, and personal values. The main recommendation from four-drive theory is to ensure that individual jobs and workplaces provide a balanced opportunity to fulfill the four drives.

LO4 Discuss the expectancy theory model, including its practical implications.

Expectancy theory states that work effort is determined by the perception that effort will result in a particular level of performance (E-to-P expectancy), the perception that a specific behavior or performance level will lead to specific outcomes (P-to-O expectancy), and the valences that the person feels for those outcomes. The E-to-P expectancy increases by improving the employee's ability and confidence to perform the job. The P-to-O expectancy increases by measuring performance accurately, distributing higher rewards to better performers, and showing employees that rewards are performance-based. Outcome valences increase by finding out what employees want and using these resources as rewards.

LO5 Outline organizational behavior modification (OB Mod) and social cognitive theory and explain their relevance to employee motivation.

Organizational behavior modification states that the environment teaches people to alter their behavior so that they maximize positive consequences and minimize adverse consequences. Antecedents are environmental stimuli that provoke (not necessarily cause) behavior. Consequences are events following behavior that influence its future occurrence. Consequences include positive reinforcement, punishment, negative reinforcement, and extinction. The schedules of reinforcement also influence behavior.

Social cognitive theory states that much learning and motivation occur by observing and modeling others, as well as by anticipating the consequences of our behavior. It suggests that people typically infer (rather than only directly experience) cause-and-effect relationships, anticipate the consequences of their actions, develop self-efficacy in performing behavior, exercise personal control over their behavior, and reflect on their direct experiences. The theory emphasizes self-regulation of individual behavior, including self-reinforcement, which is the tendency of people to reward and punish themselves as a consequence of their actions.

LO6 Describe the characteristics of effective goal setting and feedback.

Goal setting is the process of motivating employees and clarifying their role perceptions by establishing performance objectives. Goals are more effective when they are SMARTER (specific, measurable, achievable, relevant, time-framed, exciting, and reviewed). Effective feedback is specific, relevant, timely, credible, and sufficiently frequent. Strengths-based coaching (also known as appreciative coaching) maximizes employees' potential by focusing on their strengths rather than weaknesses. Employees usually prefer nonsocial feedback sources to learn about their progress toward goal accomplishment.

LO7 Summarize equity theory and describe ways to improve procedural justice.

Organizational justice consists of distributive justice (perceived fairness in the outcomes we receive relative to our contributions and the outcomes and contributions of others) and procedural justice (fairness of the procedures used to decide the distribution of resources). Equity theory has four elements: outcome/input ratio, comparison other, equity evaluation, and consequences of inequity. The theory also explains what people are motivated to do when they feel inequitably treated. Companies need to consider not only equity in the distribution of resources but also fairness in the process of making resource allocation decisions.

❴ key terms ❵

balanced scorecard (BSC), p. 146
distributive justice, p. 149
drives, p. 131
employee engagement, p. 130
equity theory, p. 150
expectancy theory, p. 139
four-drive theory, p. 136

goal setting, p. 144
Maslow's needs hierarchy theory, p. 133
multisource (360-degree) feedback, p. 148
need for achievement (nAch), p. 134
need for affiliation (nAff), p. 135
need for power (nPow), p. 135
needs, p. 133

organizational behavior modification, p. 141
procedural justice, p. 149
self-reinforcement, p. 144
social cognitive theory, p. 143
strengths-based coaching, p. 147

❴ critical thinking questions ❵

1. Four-drive theory is conceptually different from Maslow's needs hierarchy (as well as ERG theory) in several ways. Describe these differences. At the same time, needs are based on drives, so the four drives should parallel the seven needs that Maslow identified (five in the hierarchy and two additional needs). Map Maslow's needs onto the four drives in four-drive theory.

2. Learned needs theory states that needs can be strengthened or weakened. How might a company strengthen the achievement needs of its management team?

3. Two friends who have just completed an organizational behavior course at another college inform you that employees must fulfill their need for self-esteem and social esteem before they can reach their full potential through

self-actualization. What theory are these friends referring to? How does their statement differ from what you learned about that theory in this chapter?

4. Use all three components of expectancy theory to explain why some employees are motivated to show up for work during a severe storm whereas others make no effort to leave their home.

5. Describe a situation in which you used organizational behavior modification to motivate someone's behavior. What specifically did you do? What was the result?

6. Using your knowledge of the characteristics of effective goals, establish two meaningful goals related to your performance in this class.

7. Several service representatives are upset that the newly hired representative with no previous experience will be paid $3,000 a year above the usual starting salary in the pay range. The department manager explained that the new hire would not accept the entry-level rate, so the company raised the offer by $3,000. All five reps currently earn salaries near the top of the scale ($15,000 higher than the new recruit), although they all started at the minimum starting salary a few years earlier. Use equity theory to explain why the five service representatives feel inequity in this situation.

8. A large organization has hired you as a consultant to identify day-to-day activities for middle managers to minimize distributive and procedural injustice. The company explains that employees have complained about distributive injustice because they have different opinions about what is fair (equity, equality, need) and what outcomes and inputs have the greatest value. They also experience procedural injustice due to misperceptions and differing expectations. Given these ambiguities, what would you recommend to middle managers?

9. As we have discussed, most people think they are "worth more" than they are paid. Furthermore, most employees seem to feel that they exhibit better leadership skills and interpersonal skills than others. Please comment on this nonrational aspect of human behavior.

CASE STUDY 5.1 PREDICTING HARRY'S WORK EFFORT

Robert J. Oppenheimer, Concordia University

Interviewer: Hi, Harry. I have been asked to talk to you about your job. Do you mind if I ask you a few questions?

Harry: No, not at all.

Interviewer: Thanks, Harry. What are the things that you would anticipate getting satisfaction from as a result of your job?

Harry: What do you mean?

Interviewer: Well, what is important to you with regard to your job here?

Harry: I guess most important is job security. As a matter of fact, I can't think of anything that is more important to me. I think getting a raise would be nice, and a promotion would be even better.

Interviewer: Anything else that you think would be nice to get, or for that matter, that you would want to avoid?

Harry: I certainly would not want my buddies to make fun of me. We're pretty friendly, and this is really important to me.

Interviewer: Anything else?

Harry: No, not really. That seems to be it.

Interviewer: How satisfied do you think you would be with each of these?

Harry: What do you mean?

Interviewer: Well, assume that something that you would really like has a value of $+1.0$ and something you would really not like, that is, you would want to avoid, has a value of -1.0, and something you are indifferent about has a value of 0.

Harry: Okay. Getting a raise would have a value of .5; a promotion is more important, so I'd say .7; and having my buddies make fun of me, .9.

Interviewer: But I thought you didn't want your buddies to make fun of you.

Harry: I don't.

Interviewer: But you gave it a value of .9.

Harry: Oh, I guess it should be $-.9$.

Interviewer: Okay, I just want to be sure I understand what you're saying. Harry, what do you think the chances are of these things happening?

Harry: That depends.

Interviewer: On what?

Harry: On whether my performance is high or just acceptable.

Interviewer: What if it is high?

Harry: I figure I stand about a 50–50 chance of getting a raise and/or a promotion, but I also think that there is a 90 percent chance that my buddies will make fun of me.

Interviewer: What about job security?

Harry: I am certain my job is secure here, whether my performance is high or just

Harry:	With all the questions you asked me, you should be able to tell me.
Interviewer:	You may be right!
Harry:	Yeah? That's nice. Hey, if you don't have any other questions, I'd like to join the guys for coffee.
Interviewer:	Okay, thanks for your time.
Harry:	You're welcome.

acceptable. I can't remember the last guy who was doing his job and got fired. But if my performance is just acceptable, my chances of a raise or promotion are about 10 percent. However, then the guys will not make fun of me. That I am certain about.

Interviewer: What is the likelihood of your performance level being high?

Harry: That depends. If I work very hard and put out a high degree of effort, I'd say that my chance of my performance being high is about 90 percent. But if I put out a low level of effort—you know, if I just take it easy— then I figure that the chance of my doing an acceptable job is about 80 percent.

Interviewer: Well, which would you do: put out a low level or a high level of effort?

Discussion Question

1. Use the expectancy theory model to predict Harry's motivation to achieve high or acceptable performance in his job. Identify and discuss the factors that influence this motivation.

Source: By Robert J. Oppenheimer, Professor, Department of Management, John Molson School of Business, Concordia University, Montreal, Quebec, Canada. Reprinted with permission.

CASE STUDY 5.2 CINCINNATI SUPER SUBS

Steven L. McShane, University of Western Australia, based on an earlier case by J.E. Dittrich and R.A. Zawacki

Cincinnati Super Subs is one of the larger Super Subs outlets, a chain of 300 take-away restaurants in Indiana, Ohio, and Michigan. This outlet has a restaurant manager, an assistant manager, and several part-time team leaders. The restaurant manager rarely has time to serve customers, and frontline work by managers is discouraged by the head office. The assistant manager serves customers for a couple of hours during the busy lunchtime but otherwise assists the restaurant manager with purchasing, accounts, hiring, and other operations. Most team leaders are college students and serve customers alongside other employees, particularly from late afternoon to night closing. Most employees are also students who work part-time; a few are in high school. All regular staff earn minimum pay rates.

Cincinnati Super Subs has experienced below average profitability over the past 18 months, which has reduced the monthly bonus paid to the restaurant manager and assistant manager. This bonus is calculated by percentage of "wastage" (unsold, damaged, or unaccounted for food and drinks) relative to sales; the lower the percentage of wastage, the higher the bonus. Wastage occurs when employees drop or spill food, cut up more toppings than are sold, burn heated subs, prepare an order incorrectly, and eat or give away food without permission. When employees make mistakes, the expense is supposed to come out of their paycheck. Unauthorized eating and giving away food are grounds for immediate dismissal. However, team leaders are reluctant to report any accidental or deliberate wastage, even when confronted by the restaurant manager about the store's high wastage over the previous week and month. One team leader who reported several accidental wastage incidents eventually quit after being snubbed by coworkers who attended the same college classes.

Cincinnati Super Subs gives employees a food allowance if they work continuously for at least four and one-half hours. Staff complain that the allowance is meager and that they are often ineligible for the food allowance because many shifts are only three or four hours. Employees who work these shorter shifts sometimes help themselves to food and drinks when the managers aren't around, claiming that their hard work justifies the free meal. Some also claim the food is a low company expense and makes up for their small paycheck, relative to what many of their friends earn elsewhere. Several (but not most) employees give some of their friends generous helpings as well as occasional free soft drinks and chips. Employees say handing out free food to friends makes them more popular to their peers.

Five months ago, the Cincinnati restaurant's wastage (mainly deliberate wastage) had risen to the point where the two managers no longer received a bonus. The restaurant manager reacted by giving the food allowance only to those who work for six or more hours in a single shift. This action excluded even more staff from receiving the food allowance, but it did not discourage employees from eating or giving away food. However, almost 20 percent of the experienced college staff left for other jobs over the next two months. Many of those who stayed discouraged friends from considering jobs at Super Subs. Morale declined, which dampened the fun atmosphere that had been experienced to some extent in past times. Relations between employees and managers soured further.

With relatively low unemployment, the restaurant manager found it difficult to hire replacements, particularly people with previous work experience of any kind. Temporary staff shortages required the two managers to spend more time working in food preparation and training the new staff. Their increased presence in the restaurant significantly reduced deliberate wastage, but accidental wastage increased somewhat as the greater number of inexperienced staff made more mistakes.

After three months, Cincinnati Super Subs' manager and assistant manager were confident that the situation had improved, so they spent less time training staff and serving customers. Indeed, they received a moderate bonus after the third month in the store. However, wastage increased again soon after the managers withdrew from daily operations. The experienced employees started eating more food, and the new staff soon joined this practice. Exasperated, the restaurant manager took bolder steps. He completely removed the food allowance and threatened to fire any employee caught consuming or giving away food.

Wastage dropped somewhat over the next month but is now creeping upward again.

Discussion Questions

1. What symptom(s) in this case suggest that something has gone wrong?
2. What are the main causes of these symptoms?
3. What actions should Cincinnati Super Subs' managers take to correct these problems?

© 2011 Steven L. McShane.

CLASS EXERCISE 5.3 NEEDS PRIORITY EXERCISE

PURPOSE This class exercise is designed to help you understand employee needs in the workplace.

INSTRUCTIONS (SMALL CLASS)

Step 1: The table below lists, in alphabetical order, 16 characteristics of the job or work environment. Working alone, use the right column to rank-order the importance of these characteristics to you personally. Write in "1" beside the most important characteristic, "2" for the second most important, and so on through to "16" for the least important characteristic on this list.

Step 2: Identify any three of these work attributes that you believe have the largest score differences between Generation Y (Millennial) male and female college students in your country (i.e., those born in 1980 or after). Indicate which gender you think identifies that attribute as more important.

Step 3: In teams, assigned by your instructor, compare your rank-order results, as well as perceived gender differences in needs. Note reasons for the largest variations in rankings and be prepared to discuss these reasons with the entire class. You

should pay close attention to different needs, self-concepts, and various forms of diversity (culture, profession, age, etc.) within your class to identify possible explanations for any variation in the results across students.

Step 4: The instructor will provide results of a recent large-scale survey of Generation Y college students (i.e., born in 1980 or after). In these results, identify the reasons for any noticeable differences in the class. Relate the differences to your understanding of the emerging view of employee needs and drives in work settings. For gender differences, discuss reasons men and women might differ on these work-related attributes.

INSTRUCTIONS (LARGE CLASS)

Step 1 and Step 2: Same as above.

Step 3: The instructor will ask you, by a show of hands (or use of classroom technology), to identify your top-ranked attributes, as well as the attributes you believe have the greatest gender differences among Generation-Yers.

Step 4: Same as above.

Personal Ranking of Work-Related Attributes

ATTRIBUTES OF WORK (LISTED ALPHABETICALLY)	YOUR RANKING (1 = MOST IMPORTANT)
Challenging work	
Commitment to social responsibility	
Good health and benefits plan	
Good initial salary level	
Good people to report to	
Good people to work with	
Good training opportunities/developing new skills	
Good variety of work	
Job security	
Opportunities for advancement in position	
Opportunities to have a personal impact	
Opportunities to have a social impact	
Opportunity to travel	
Organization is a leader in its field	
Strong commitment to employee diversity	
Work–life balance	

CLASS EXERCISE 5.4 THE LEARNING EXERCISE

PURPOSE This exercise is designed to help you understand how learning and motivation are influenced by the contingencies of reinforcement in organizational behavior modification.

MATERIALS Any objects normally available in a classroom will be acceptable for this activity.

INSTRUCTIONS (SMALL OR LARGE CLASSES)
The instructor will ask for three volunteers, who will receive a briefing outside the classroom. The instructor will spend a few minutes describing the exercise to students in the class about their duties. Then, one of the three volunteers will enter the room to participate in the exercise. When completed, the second volunteer enters the room and participates in the exercise. When completed, the third volunteer enters the class and participates in the exercise.

For students to gain the full benefit of this exercise, no other information is provided here. However, the instructor will have more details at the beginning of this fun activity.

CLASS EXERCISE 5.5 BONUS DECISION EXERCISE

Steven L. McShane, University of Western Australia

PURPOSE This exercise is designed to help you understand the elements of equity theory and how people differ in their equity perceptions.

INSTRUCTIONS Four managers in a large national insurance company are described below. The national sales director of the company has given your consulting team (first individually, then together) the task of allocating $100,000 in bonus money to these four managers. It is entirely up to your team to decide how to divide the money among these people. The only requirements are that all of the money must be distributed and that no two branch managers can receive the same amount. The names and information are presented in no particular order. You should assume that economic conditions, client demographics, and other external factors are very similar for these managers.

Step 1: Working alone, read information about the four managers. Then fill in the amount you would allocate to each manager in the "Individual Decision" column.

Step 2: Still working alone, fill in the "Equity Inputs Form." First, in the "Input Factor" column, list in order of importance the factors you considered when allocating these bonus amounts (e.g., seniority, performance, age). The most important factor should be listed first and the least important last. Next, in the "Input Weight" column, estimate the percentage weight that you assigned to this factor. The total of this column must add up to 100 percent.

Step 3: Form teams (typically four to six people). Each team will compare their results and note any differences. Then, for each job, team members will reach a consensus on the bonus amount that each manager should receive. These amounts will be written in the "Team Decision" column.

Step 4: The instructor will call the class together to compare team results and note differences in inputs and input weights used by individual students. The class will then discuss these results using equity theory.

INSTRUCTIONS (LARGE CLASS)
Step 1 and *Step 2:* Same as above.

Step 3: The instructor will ask students, by a show of hands (or use of classroom technology), to identify which manager would receive the highest bonus and then how much should be allocated to that manager. Repeat with the manager receiving the lowest bonus. (Some classroom technology allows students to indicate their bonus amount allocated to that manager directly.) Discuss these results using equity theory.

MANAGER PROFILES
Bob B. Bob has been in the insurance business for over 27 years and has spent the past 21 years with this company. A few years ago, Bob's branch typically made the largest contribution to regional profits. More recently, however, it has brought in few new accounts and is now well below average in terms of its contribution to the company. Turnover in the branch has been high, and Bob doesn't have the same enthusiasm for the job as he once did. Bob is 56 years old and is married with five children. Three children are still living at home. Bob has a high school diploma as well as a certificate from a special course in insurance management.

Edward E. In the two years that Edward has been a branch manager, his unit has brought in several major accounts and now stands as one of the top units in the country. Edward is well respected by his employees. At 29, he is the youngest manager in the region and one of the youngest in the country. The regional director initially doubted the wisdom of giving Edward the position of branch manager because of his relatively young age and lack of experience in the insurance industry. Edward received an undergraduate business degree from a regional college and worked for five years as a sales representative before joining this company. Edward is single and has no children.

Lee L. Lee has been with this organization for seven years. The first two years were spent as a sales representative in the office that she now manages. According to the regional director, Lee rates about average as a branch manager. She earned an undergraduate degree in geography from a major university and worked as a sales representative for four years with another insurance company before joining this organization. Lee is 40 years old, divorced, and has no children. She is a very ambitious person but sometimes has problems working with her staff and other branch managers.

Sandy S. Sandy is 47 years old and has been a branch manager with this company for 17 years. Seven years ago, her branch made the lowest contribution to the region's profits, but this has steadily improved and is now slightly above average. Sandy seems to have a mediocre attitude toward her job but is well liked by her staff and other branch managers. Her experience in the insurance industry has been entirely with this organization. She previously worked in non-sales positions, and it is not clear how she became a branch manager without previous sales experience. Sandy is married and has three school-aged children. Several years ago, Sandy earned a diploma in business from a nearby community college by taking evening courses.

Bonus Allocation Form

NAME	INDIVIDUAL DECISION	TEAM DECISION
Bob B.	$ _____	$ _____
Edward E.	$ _____	$ _____
Lee L.	$ _____	$ _____
Sandy S.	$ _____	$ _____
TOTALS:	$100,000	$100,000

Equity Inputs Form

INPUT FACTOR*	INPUT WEIGHT**
_____	_____ %
_____	_____ %
_____	_____ %
_____	_____ %
_____	_____ %
TOTAL:	100%

*List factors in order of importance, with most important factor listed first.

**The weight of each factor is a percentage ranging from 1 to 100. All factor weights together must add up to 100 percent.

SELF-ASSESSMENT 5.6 NEED-STRENGTH QUESTIONNAIRE

Although everyone has the same innate drives, secondary or learned needs vary from one person to the next in the same situation. This self-assessment provides an estimate of your need strength on selected secondary needs. Read each of the statements below and check the response that you believe best reflects your position regarding each statement. Then use the scoring key in Appendix B at the end of the book to calculate your results. To receive a meaningful estimate of your need strength, you should answer each item honestly and by reflecting on your personal experiences. Class discussion will focus on the meaning of the needs measured in this self-assessment, as well as their relevance in the workplace.

Personal Needs Questionnaire

HOW ACCURATELY DO EACH OF THE FOLLOWING STATEMENTS DESCRIBE YOU?	VERY ACCURATE DESCRIPTION OF ME	MODERATELY ACCURATE	NEITHER ACCURATE NOR INACCURATE	MODERATELY INACCURATE	VERY INACCURATE DESCRIPTION OF ME
1. I would rather be myself than be well thought of.	☐	☐	☐	☐	☐
2. I'm the type of person who never gives up.	☐	☐	☐	☐	☐
3. When the opportunity occurs, I want to be in charge.	☐	☐	☐	☐	☐
4. I try not to say things that others don't like to hear.	☐	☐	☐	☐	☐

(continued)

Personal Needs Questionnaire   (*continued*)

HOW ACCURATELY DO EACH OF THE FOLLOWING STATEMENTS DESCRIBE YOU?	VERY ACCURATE DESCRIPTION OF ME	MODERATELY ACCURATE	NEITHER ACCURATE NOR INACCURATE	MODERATELY INACCURATE	VERY INACCURATE DESCRIPTION OF ME
5. I find it difficult to talk about my ideas if they are contrary to group opinion.	☐	☐	☐	☐	☐
6. I tend to take control of things.	☐	☐	☐	☐	☐
7. I am not highly motivated to succeed.	☐	☐	☐	☐	☐
8. I usually disagree with others only if I know my friends will back me up.	☐	☐	☐	☐	☐
9. I try to be the very best at what I do.	☐	☐	☐	☐	☐
10. I seldom make excuses or apologize for my behavior.	☐	☐	☐	☐	☐
11. If anyone criticizes me, I can take it.	☐	☐	☐	☐	☐
12. I try to outdo others.	☐	☐	☐	☐	☐
13. I seldom change my opinion when people disagree with me.	☐	☐	☐	☐	☐
14. I try to achieve more than what others have accomplished.	☐	☐	☐	☐	☐
15. To get along and be liked, I tend to be what people expect me to be.	☐	☐	☐	☐	☐

Sources: Adapted from instruments described and/or presented in L.R. Goldberg, J.A. Johnson, H.W. Eber, R. Hogan, M.C. Ashton, C.R. Cloninger, and H.C. Gough, "The International Personality Item Pool and the Future of Public-Domain Personality Measures," *Journal of Research in Personality* 40 (2006), pp. 84–96; H.J. Martin, "A Revised Measure of Approval Motivation and Its Relationship to Social Desirability," *Journal of Personality Assessment* 48 (1984), pp. 508–19.

After reading this chapter go to www.mhhe.com/mcshane6e for more in-depth information and interactivities that correspond to the chapter.

Applied Performance Practices

learning objectives

After reading this chapter, you should be able to:

LO1 Discuss the meaning of money and identify several individual, team, and organizational-level performance-based rewards.

LO2 Describe five ways to improve reward effectiveness.

LO3 List the advantages and disadvantages of job specialization.

LO4 Diagram the job characteristics model and describe three ways to improve employee motivation through job design.

LO5 Define *empowerment* and identify strategies that support empowerment.

LO6 Describe the five elements of self-leadership and identify specific personal and work environment influences on self-leadership.

manufacturing plants. Many factory employees in this sprawling area north of Hong Kong work by piece rate; the more they produce, the more they earn. Employees at Shenzhen Rishen Cashmere Textile factory earn (all figures in U.S. currency) 17 cents for each garment sewed—about $240 per month for the fastest employees and little more than $100 for the slowest. Other factories pay a flat amount for reaching the production quota and a bonus based on output beyond the quota. Most factories also use financial disincentives. Employees' pay is docked if they are late for work, lose their ID card, talk with coworkers, walk on the grass, or produce less than the production quota.

Many factories in the Pearl River Delta require employees to work overtime. Work shifts often violate China's regulations, but employees usually accept the long hours because of the pay-for-performance rewards. "I always wanted to work overtime because we got paid more if we exceeded our daily quota of pillows," says Wang, who works at a pillow factory. Unfortunately, the long hours also cause fatigue. Wang mangled his right hand on a machine while working overtime. "I'd been working 11 hours straight and was tired," he explains.

Most factory work is tedious. Li Mei's first job at a toy factory in the Pearl River Delta involved using four pens to paint the eyes on dolls. The 18-year-old was given exactly 7.2 seconds to paint each doll—about 4,000 every day. Eventually, the paint fumes made Li Mei too faint to work, so she was moved to another department that stamped out plastic doll parts. Again, the work was repetitive: Open the machine, insert the plastic, press the machine, remove the plastic. Li Mei repeated this cycle 3,000 times each day. After several months of this work, Li Mei has grown exhausted and disillusioned. "I'm tired to death and I don't earn much," she says despondently. "It makes everything meaningless."[1]

Most factory workers in China's Pearl River Delta are paid for the number of units they produce. The work is usually repetitive, cycling several thousand times each day.

This opening vignette is not a good news story about rewards and job design, but it does illustrate the importance of pay and job duties in motivating and demotivating employees. This chapter looks at both of these topics, as well as two other applied performance practices: empowerment and self-leadership. The chapter begins by examining the meaning of money. This is followed by an overview of financial reward practices, including the different types of rewards and how to implement rewards effectively. Next, we look at the dynamics of job design, including specific job design strategies for motivating employees. We then consider the elements of empowerment, as well as conditions that support empowerment. The final part of the chapter explains how employees manage their own performance through self-leadership.

The Meaning of Money in the Workplace

LO1, LO2

Rewarding people with money is one of the oldest and certainly the most widespread applied performance practices. At the most basic level, money and other financial rewards represent a form of exchange; employees provide their labor, skill, and knowledge in return for money and benefits from the organization. From this perspective, money and related rewards align employee goals with organizational goals. This concept of economic exchange can be found across cultures. The word for *pay* in Malaysian and Slovak means "to replace a loss"; in Hebrew and Swedish, it means "making equal."[2]

However, money is much more than an object of compensation for an employee's contribution to organizational objectives. Money relates to our needs, our emotions, and our self-concepts. It is a symbol of achievement and status, a reinforcer and motivator, and a source of enhanced or reduced anxiety.[3] According to one source, "Money is probably the most emotionally meaningful object in contemporary life: only food and sex are its close competitors as common carriers of such strong and diverse feelings, significance, and strivings."[4]

The meaning of money varies considerably from one person to the next.[5] Studies report that money is viewed as a symbol of status and prestige, as a source of security, as a source of evil, or as a source of anxiety or feelings of inadequacy. It is considered a taboo topic in many social settings. Recent studies also depict money both as a "tool" (i.e., money is valued because it is an instrument for acquiring other things of value) and as a "drug" (i.e., money is an object of addictive value in itself).

One large-scale study revealed that money generates a variety of emotions, most of which are negative, such as anxiety, depression, anger, and helplessness.[6] A widely studied model of money attitudes suggests that people have a strong "money ethic" when they believe that money is not evil; that it is a symbol of achievement, respect, and power; and that it should be budgeted carefully. These attitudes toward money influence an individual's ethical conduct, organizational citizenship, and many other behaviors and attitudes.[7]

The meaning of money seems to differ between men and women. One large-scale survey revealed that in almost all 43 countries studied, men attach more importance or value to money than do women. Men particularly tend to view money as a symbol of power and status.[8] Personal and cultural values influence the meaning of money. People in countries with high power distance (such as China and Japan) tend to have a high respect and priority for money, whereas people in countries with a strong egalitarian culture (such as Denmark, Austria, and Israel) are discouraged from openly talking about money or displaying their personal wealth. One study suggests that Swiss culture values saving money, whereas Italian culture places more value on spending it.[9]

Many experts now believe that the motivational effect of money is much greater than was previously believed, more because of its inherent and symbolic value than because of what it can buy.[10] Philosopher John Stuart Mill made this observation 150 years ago when he wrote: "The love of money is not only one of the strongest moving forces of human life, but money is, in many cases, desired in and for itself."[11] People who earn higher pay tend to have higher job performance because the higher paycheck makes them feel more valued in the organization (i.e., it enhances their self-concept). Others have noted that the symbolic value of money and other rewards is particularly motivational when few people receive this reward. In these situations, the reward gives beneficiaries a degree of social distinction, which is consistent with the drive to acquire (see Chapter 5).

Overall, current organizational behavior knowledge indicates that money is much more than a means of exchange between employer and employee. It fulfills a variety of needs, influences emotions, and shapes or represents a person's self-concept. This is important to remember when the employer is distributing financial rewards in the workplace. Over the next few pages, we look at various reward practices and how to improve the implementation of performance-based rewards.

Financial Reward Practices

Financial rewards come in many forms, which can be organized into the four specific objectives identified in Exhibit 6.1: membership and seniority, job status, competencies, and performance.

MEMBERSHIP AND SENIORITY-BASED REWARDS

Membership-based and seniority-based rewards (sometimes called "pay for pulse") represent the largest part of most paychecks. Some employee benefits, such as free or discounted meals in the company cafeteria, remain the same for everyone, whereas others increase with seniority. Some companies, such as the Paul Sherrer Institut near Zurich, Switzerland, have a loyalty bonus for long-service employees. Those with 10 or more years of service at the natural and engineering sciences research center receive an annual loyalty bonus equal to a half month's salary; those with 20 or more years of service receive a bonus equivalent to a full month's salary. Toyota Motor Company and many other Japanese firms have wage scales and increases determined by the employee's age.[12]

EXHIBIT 6.1 Reward Objectives, Advantages, and Disadvantages

REWARD OBJECTIVE	SAMPLE REWARDS	ADVANTAGES	DISADVANTAGES
Membership/seniority	• Fixed pay • Most employee benefits • Paid time off	• May attract applicants • Minimizes stress of insecurity • Reduces turnover	• Doesn't directly motivate performance • May discourage poor performers from leaving • "Golden handcuffs" may undermine performance
Job status	• Promotion-based pay increase • Status-based benefits	• Tries to maintain internal equity • Minimizes pay discrimination • Motivates employees to compete for promotions	• Encourages hierarchy, which may increase costs and reduce responsiveness • Reinforces status differences • Motivates job competition and exaggerated job worth
Competencies	• Pay increase based on competency • Skill-based pay	• Improves workforce flexibility • Tends to improve quality • Is consistent with employability	• Relies on subjective measurement of competencies • Skill-based pay plans are expensive
Task performance	• Commissions • Merit pay • Gainsharing • Profit sharing • Stock options	• Motivates task performance • Attracts performance-oriented applicants • Organizational rewards create an ownership culture • Pay variability may avoid layoffs during downturns	• May weaken job content motivation • May distance reward giver from receiver • May discourage creativity • Tends to address symptoms, not underlying causes of behavior

These membership and seniority-based rewards potentially attract job applicants (particularly those who desire predictable income) and reduce turnover. However, they do not directly motivate job performance; on the contrary, they discourage poor performers from seeking work better suited to their abilities. Instead, the good performers are lured to better-paying jobs. Some of these rewards are also "golden handcuffs"—they discourage employees from quitting because the deferred bonuses or generous benefits are not available elsewhere. However, golden handcuffs potentially weaken job performance because they generate continuance rather than affective commitment (see Chapter 4).

JOB STATUS–BASED REWARDS

Almost every organization rewards employees to some extent on the basis of the status or worth of the jobs they occupy. In some parts of the world, companies measure job worth through **job evaluation.** Most job evaluation methods give higher value to jobs that require more skill and effort, have more responsibility, and have more difficult working conditions.[13] The higher the worth assigned to a job, the higher the minimum and maximum pay for people in that job. Along with receiving higher pay, employees with more valued jobs sometimes receive larger offices, company-paid vehicles, and other perks.

Job status–based rewards try to improve feelings of fairness, such that people in higher-valued jobs should get higher pay. These rewards also motivate employees to compete for promotions. However, at a time when companies are trying to be more cost-efficient and responsive to the external environment, job status–based rewards potentially do the opposite by encouraging a bureaucratic hierarchy. These rewards also reinforce a status mentality, whereas Generation-X and Generation-Y employees expect a more egalitarian workplace. Furthermore, status-based pay potentially motivates employees to compete with one another for higher-status jobs and to raise the value of their own jobs by exaggerating job duties and hoarding resources.[14]

COMPETENCY-BASED REWARDS

Over the past two decades, many companies have shifted reward priorities from job status to skills, knowledge, and other competencies that lead to superior performance. The most common practices identify a list of competencies relevant across all job groups as well as competencies specific to each broad job group. Employees progress through the pay range within that job group, based on how well they demonstrate each of those competencies.[15]

Skill-based pay plans are a more specific variation of competency-based rewards in which people receive higher pay based on their mastery of measurable skills. For example, technicians who work for the City of Flagstaff, Arizona, are paid for the number of skill blocks they have mastered. New hires must complete the first skill block during probation and can eventually progress through the five other skill blocks to earn almost twice the base (designating a single skill block) salary. Technicians demonstrate proficiency in a skill block through in-house or formal certification assessments.[16]

Competency-based rewards motivate employees to learn new skills.[17] This tends to improve organizational effectiveness by creating a more flexible workforce; more employees are multiskilled and can perform a variety of jobs, and they are more adaptive to embracing new practices in a dynamic environment. Product or service quality also tends to improve because employees with multiple skills are more likely to understand the work process and know how to improve it. However, competency-based pay plans have not always worked out as well as promised by their advocates. They are often over-designed, making it difficult to communicate these plans to employees. Competency definitions are often vague, which raises questions about fairness when employers are relying on these definitions to award pay increases. Skill-based pay systems measure specific skills, so they are usually more objective. However, they are expensive because employees spend more time learning new tasks.[18]

PortionPac Chemical has built its reputation on helping customers use less product more efficiently and safely. For this reason, salespeople at the Chicago-based cleaning fluids manufacturer don't earn the usual sales commission based on how much they sell. "High-commission salespeople are going to sell the customer as much as they can. We want customers to use the right amount," explains PortionPac chairman and cofounder Marvin Klein. Instead, PortionPac rewards sales staff for achieving environmentally friendly targets, such as signing customers up for "shared savings" contracts (in which PortionPac delivers the right amount of product and educates the customer on how to use that product efficiently).[19]

PERFORMANCE-BASED REWARDS

Performance-based rewards have existed since Babylonian days, 4,000 years ago, but their popularity has increased dramatically over the past few decades. Here is an overview of some of the most popular individual, team, and organizational performance-based rewards.

Individual Rewards Many employees receive individual bonuses or other rewards for accomplishing a specific task or exceeding annual performance goals. Real estate agents and other salespeople typically earn *commissions,* in which their pay increases with sales volume. Housekeeping staff in many hotels are paid a piece rate—a specific amount earned for each room cleaned. Other hotels pay an hourly rate plus a per-room bonus. The opening vignette to this chapter described how most factory workers in China are also on a piece rate pay system in which they earn money for each product they complete.

Team Rewards Organizations have shifted their focus from individuals to teams over the past two decades, and accompanying this transition has been the introduction of more team-based rewards. At Forrest General Hospital in Hattiesburg, Mississippi, for example, all employees in patient accounts and registration receive a bonus if the team meets its time-of-service and self-pay collections targets. "[The team incentive] is set up so that either everyone gets the incentive, or no one gets it," explains a Forrest General Hospital executive.[20] Nucor Inc. also relies heavily on team-based rewards. The steelmaker's employees earn bonuses, which can exceed half their total pay, based on how much steel is produced by the team. This team-based bonus system also includes penalties. If employees catch a bad batch of steel before it leaves the mini-mill, they lose their bonus for that shipment. But if a bad batch makes its way to the customer, the team loses three times its usual bonus.[21]

job evaluation
Systematically rating the worth of jobs within an organization by measuring their required skill, effort, responsibility, and working conditions.

Another form of team-based performance reward, called a **gainsharing plan,** calculates bonuses from the work unit's cost savings and productivity improvement. Whole Foods Market uses gainsharing to motivate cost savings in its grocery stores. The food retailer assigns a monthly payroll budget to teams operating various departments within a store. If payroll money is unspent at the end of the month, the surplus is divided among members of that Whole Foods Market team.[22] Several hospitals have cautiously introduced a form of gainsharing, whereby physicians and medical staff in a particular medical unit (cardiology, orthopedics, etc.) are collectively rewarded for cost reductions in surgery and patient care. These cost reductions mainly occur through negotiating better prices of materials.[23] Gainsharing plans tend to improve team dynamics, knowledge sharing, and pay satisfaction. They also create a reasonably strong link between effort and performance, because much of the cost reduction and labor efficiency is within the team's control.[24]

Organizational Rewards

Along with individual and team-based rewards, many firms rely on organizational-level rewards to motivate employees. Some firms reward all staff members for achieving challenging sales goals or other indicators of organizational performance. An interesting organizational-level incentive is the promise to take the entire workforce on an all-expenses-paid vacation if they achieve challenging annual performance goals. For example, Spruceland Millworks has flown its employees (and family members of longer-service staff) to a Mexican resort every year that they exceeded a challenging annual objective. "I've always strongly believed my job is to recognize people and reward their efforts, and that they go home at night feeling significant," says Spruceland founder Ben Sawatzky.[25]

Employee stock ownership plans (ESOPs) encourage employees to buy company stock, usually at a discounted price or through a no-interest loan. The financial incentive occurs as dividends and market appreciation of the stock. Due to tax concessions in the United States and a few other countries, most ESOPs are designed as retirement plans. Today, more than 20 percent of Americans working in the private sector hold stock in their companies.[26] Publix Super Markets has one of the largest and oldest ESOPs in America. The Lakeland, Florida, grocery chain distributes a portion of company profits to employees in the form of company stock. Employees can also purchase additional stock from the privately held company.[27]

While ESOPs involve purchasing company shares, **stock options** give employees the right to purchase company stock at a predetermined price up to a fixed expiration date. For example, an employer might offer employees the right to purchase 100 shares at $50 at any time between two and six years from now. If the stock price is, say, $60 two years later, employees could earn $10 from these options, or they could wait up to six years for the share price to rise further. If the stock price never rises above $50 during that time, they are "out of the money," and employees would just let the options expire. The intention of stock options is to motivate employees to make the company more profitable, thereby raising the company's stock price and enabling them to reap the value above the exercise price of the stock options.

Profit-sharing plans represent another type of organizational-level reward in which employees receive a percentage of the previous year's company profits. An interesting application of this reward occurs at Svenska Handelsbanken AB. In years when the Swedish bank is more profitable than the average of competing banks, it transfers one-third of the difference in profits to an employee fund. Every employee receives one share in the fund for each year of service, which can be cashed out at 60 years of age (even if they continue working for the bank beyond that age).[28]

Evaluating Organizational-Level Rewards

How effective are organizational-level rewards? Research indicates that ESOPs and stock options tend to create an ownership culture in which employees feel aligned with the organization's success.[29] Profit sharing tends to create less ownership culture, but it has the advantage of automatically adjusting employee compensation with the firm's prosperity, thereby reducing the need for layoffs or negotiated pay reductions during recessions.

The main problem with ESOPs, stock options, and profit sharing is that employees often perceive a weak connection between their individual effort and corporate profits or the value of company shares. Even in small firms, the company's stock price or profitability is influenced by economic conditions, competition, and other factors beyond the employee's immediate control. This low individual performance-to-outcome expectancy weakens employee motivation. Another concern is that some companies (notably in the United States) use ESOPs as a replacement for employee pension plans. This is a risky strategy because these pension plans lack diversification. If the company goes bankrupt, employees lose both their jobs and a large portion of their retirement nest egg.[30]

IMPROVING REWARD EFFECTIVENESS

Performance-based rewards have come under attack over the years for discouraging creativity, distancing management from employees, distracting employees from the meaningfulness of the work itself, and being quick fixes that ignore the true causes of poor performance. Recent studies have even found that very large rewards (relative to the usual income) can result in lower, rather than higher, performance.[31] While these issues have kernels of truth in specific circumstances, they do not necessarily mean that we should abandon performance-based pay. On the contrary, top-performing companies are more likely to have performance-based rewards, which is consistent with evidence that these rewards are one of the high-performance work practices (see Chapter 1).[32] Reward systems do motivate most employees, but only under the right conditions. Here are some of the more important strategies for improving reward effectiveness.

Link Rewards to Performance   Organizational behavior modification theory and expectancy theory (Chapter 5) both recommend that employees with better performance should be rewarded more than those with poorer performance. Unfortunately, this simple principle seems to be unusually difficult to apply. Few employees see a relationship between job performance and the amount of pay they and coworkers receive. According to one survey, only 32 percent of U.S. employees believe that people who perform their jobs better at their company get better pay and benefits than those who do a poor job. This is consistent with another survey, which reported that only 27 percent of Canadian employees say there is a clear link between their job performance and pay.[33]

How can companies improve the pay–performance linkage? Inconsistencies and bias can be minimized through gainsharing, ESOPs, and other plans that use objective performance measures. Where subjective measures of performance are necessary, companies should rely on multiple sources of information. Companies also need to apply rewards soon after the performance occurs, and in a large-enough dose (such as a bonus rather than a pay increase), so that employees experience positive emotions when they receive the reward.[34]

Ensure That Rewards Are Relevant   Companies need to align rewards with performance within the employee's control. The more employees see a "line of sight" between their daily actions and the reward, the more they are motivated to improve performance. BHP Billiton applies this principle by rewarding bonuses to top executives based on the company's overall performance, whereas frontline mining staff earn bonuses based on the production output, safety performance, and other local indicators. Reward systems also need to correct for situational factors. Salespeople in one region may have higher sales because the economy is stronger there than elsewhere, so sales bonuses need to be adjusted for such economic factors.

gainsharing plan	**employee stock ownership plan (ESOP)**	**stock option**	**profit-sharing plan**
A team-based reward that calculates bonuses from the work unit's cost savings and productivity improvement.	A reward system that encourages employees to buy company stock.	A reward system that gives employees the right to purchase company stock at a future date at a predetermined price.	A reward system that pays bonuses to employees on the basis of the previous year's level of corporate profits.

Debating Point
IS IT TIME TO DITCH THE PERFORMANCE REVIEW?

More than 90 percent of *Fortune* 500 companies use performance reviews to link rewards to the performance of some or most employees. Advocates argue that these evaluations provide the critical documentation, communication, and decisions necessary to reward contributors and remove those who fail to reach the minimum standard. Indeed, it can be difficult to fire poor performers in some jurisdictions unless the company has systematically documented the employee's shortfalls. Evaluations provide clear feedback about job performance, so employees know where they stand and are motivated to improve. Performance reviews have their faults, but supporters say these problems can be overcome by using objective information (such as goal setting and 360° feedback) rather than subjective ratings, being supportive and constructive throughout the review, and providing informal performance feedback throughout the year.

Several experts—and most employees—disagree.[35] Despite mountains of advice over the years on how to improve performance reviews, this activity seems to inflict more damage than deliver benefits. Apple Inc. trashed its formal performance evaluation process a decade ago. Zappos and dozens of other companies have since followed Apple's lead. Most companies that have ditched their performance reviews never brought them back again.

According to various polls and studies, performance reviews are stressful, morale sapping, and dysfunctional events that typically descend into political arenas and paperwork bureaucracies. Even when managers actively coach employees throughout the year, the annual appraisal meeting places them in the awkward and incompatible role of being an all-powerful and all-knowing evaluator. Another issue is that rating employees, even on several factors, grossly distorts the complexity of performance in most jobs. A single score on customer service, for instance, would hide variations in knowledge, empathy, efficiency, and other elements of service. "Who am I to tell somebody they're a three out of five?" asks Don Quist, CEO of the Hood Group. Quist is so opposed to performance reviews that employees at the engineering firm were issued badges with a big "X" through the phrase "Employee Evaluation."[36]

Many perceptual biases—halo, recency, primacy, stereotyping, fundamental attribution error—are common in performance reviews and difficult to remove through training. Seemingly objective practices such as goal setting and 360° feedback are fraught with bias and subjectivity. Various studies have also found that managers across the organization use different criteria to rate employee performance. One study discovered that management's evaluations of 5,000 customer service employees were unrelated to ratings that customers gave those employees. "The managers might as well have been rating the employees' shoe sizes, for all the customers cared," quipped one investigator.[37]

Is there an alternative to the performance evaluation? One repeated suggestion is to conduct "performance previews" or "feedforward" events that focus on future goals and advice. Instead of a postmortem dissection of the employee's failings, managers use past performance as a foundation for development.[38] Also, substantial rewards should never be based on performance reviews or similar forms of evaluation. Instead, they should be linked to measurable team- and organizational-level outcomes, as well as judiciously to individual indicators (sales, project completion, etc.), where appropriate.

Use Team Rewards for Interdependent Jobs   Team rewards are better than individual rewards when employees work in highly interdependent jobs, because it is difficult to measure individual performance in these situations. Nucor Corp. relies on team-based bonuses for this reason; producing steel is a team effort, so employees earn bonuses based on team performance. Team rewards also encourage cooperation, which is more important when work is highly interdependent. A third benefit of team rewards is that they tend to support employee preferences for team-based work. One concern, however, is that employees (particularly the most productive employees) in the United States and many other low-collectivism cultures prefer rewards based on their individual performance rather than team performance.[39]

Ensure That Rewards Are Valued   It seems obvious that rewards work best when they are valued. Yet companies sometimes make false assumptions about what employees want, with unfortunate consequences. For instance, one manager honored an employee's 25th year of service by buying her a box of doughnuts to be shared with other staff. The employee was insulted. She privately complained later to coworkers that she would rather

connections 6.1

When Rewards Go Wrong

There is an old saying that "what gets rewarded gets done." But what companies reward isn't always what they had intended their employees to do. Here are a few dramatic examples of how performance-based rewards produce unintended consequences:

- Until recently, most public transit bus drivers in Santiago, Chile, were paid by the number of fare-paying passengers. This incentive system motivated drivers to begin their route on time, take shorter breaks, and drive efficiently, but it also had horrendous unintended consequences. To take on more passengers, bus drivers aggressively raced with competing buses to the next passenger waiting area, sometimes cutting off each other and risking the safety of people in nearby vehicles. Drivers reduced time at each stop by speeding off before passengers were safely on board. They also left the bus doors open, resulting in many passenger injuries and fatalities during the journey. Some drivers drove past waiting areas if there was only one person waiting. Studies reported that Santiago's transit buses caused one fatal accident every three days, and that drivers paid per passenger caused twice as many traffic accidents as drivers paid per hour. Santiago now pays drivers partly by the distance traveled. Unfortunately, drivers are no longer motivated to ensure that passengers pay the fare (about one-third are freeloaders), and they sometimes skip passenger stops altogether when they are behind schedule.[40]

- Several years ago, a food processing plant discovered that insect parts were somehow getting into the frozen peas during processing. To solve this serious problem, management decided to reward employees for any insect parts they found in the peas. The incentive worked! Employees found hundreds of insect parts that they dutifully turned in for the bonus. The problem was that many of these insect pieces came from the employees' backyards, not from the production line.

- UBS AG lost more than $37 billion (yes, *billion*) during the first year of the recent global financial meltdown because of its exposure to high-risk mortgage securities. The massive loss forced Switzerland's largest bank to lay off staff,

When transit bus drivers in Santiago, Chile, were paid per passenger, they engaged in dangerous driving to receive as many passengers as possible.

close down a hedge fund business, borrow from foreign governments, and suffer an exodus of clients. Many financial institutions suffered massive losses, and a few went bankrupt during the subprime mortgage crisis, but UBS openly acknowledged that a faulty reward system was partly responsible. Specifically, the bonus plan motivated its traders to generate short-term revenue without penalizing them for exposing the bank to high-risk investments. "Essentially, bonuses were measured against gross revenue with no formal account taken of the quality or sustainability of those earnings," says a UBS report submitted to the Swiss banking regulator.[41]

- Integrated steel companies often rewarded managers for increased labor efficiency. The lower the labor-hours required to produce a ton of steel, the larger the manager's bonus. Unfortunately, steel firms usually didn't count the work of outside contractors in the formula, so the reward system motivated managers to hire expensive contractors in the production process. By employing more contractors, the true cost of production increased, not decreased.[42]

receive nothing than "a piddling box of doughnuts."[43] The solution, of course, is to ask employees what they value. Campbell Soup did this a few years ago at one of its distribution centers. Executives thought the employees would ask for more money in a special team reward program. Instead, distribution staff said the most valued reward was a leather jacket with the Campbell Soup logo on the back. The leather jackets cost much less yet were worth much more than the financial bonus the company had intended to distribute.[44]

Watch Out for Unintended Consequences Performance-based reward systems sometimes have an unexpected—and undesirable—effect on employee behaviors. Consider the pizza company that decided to reward its drivers for on-time delivery. The plan got more hot pizzas to customers on time, but it also increased the accident rates of the company's drivers, because the incentive motivated them to drive recklessly.[45] Connections 6.1

describes a few other examples in which reward systems had unintended consequences. The solution here is to carefully think through the consequences of rewards and, where possible, test incentives in a pilot project before applying them across the organization.

Financial rewards come in many forms and, as was mentioned at the outset of this section, influence employees in complex ways. But money isn't the only thing that motivates people to join an organization and perform effectively. In one recent very large survey, 51 percent of North American employees polled said they were prepared to accept a lesser role or lower wage to perform work that is more meaningful to them or their organization. "High performers don't go for the money," warns an executive at Imation Corp. "Good people want to be in challenging jobs and see a future where they can get even more responsibilities and challenges."[46] In other words, companies motivate employees mainly by designing interesting and challenging jobs, which is the topic we discuss next.

Job Design Practices

LO3, LO4

How do you build a better job? That question has challenged organizational behavior experts as well as psychologists, engineers, and economists for a few centuries. Some jobs have very few tasks and usually require very little skill. Other jobs are immensely complex and require years of experience and learning to master them. From one extreme to the other, jobs have different effects on work efficiency and employee motivation. The challenge, at least from the organization's perspective, is to find the right combination so that work is performed efficiently but employees are engaged and satisfied.[47] This objective requires careful **job design**—the process of assigning tasks to a job, including the interdependency of those tasks with other jobs. A *job* is a set of tasks performed by one person. To understand this issue more fully, let's begin by describing early job design efforts aimed at increasing work efficiency through job specialization.

JOB DESIGN AND WORK EFFICIENCY

The opening vignette to this chapter not only described how factory workers in China are paid; it also highlighted how much of the work they produce is tedious and repetitive. For example, recall Li Mei, who painted the eyes on 4,000 dolls every day. White collar jobs (whether in China or elsewhere) can also be highly repetitive. For instance, Melody Zou earns close to $600 per month as an accountant for a media company in Shanghai, but the novelty of her work wore off after the first six months. "I do the same thing day by day, month by month, year by year," complains Zou.[48]

Li Mei and Melody Zhou perform jobs with a high degree of **job specialization.** Job specialization occurs when the work required to make a toy—or any other product or service—is subdivided into separate jobs assigned to different people. Each resulting job includes a narrow subset of tasks, usually completed in a short cycle time. *Cycle time* is the time required to complete the task before starting over with a new work unit. Li Mei had an average cycle time of 7.2 seconds, which means she repeats the same set of tasks at least 450 times each hour.

Why would companies divide work into such tiny bits? The simple answer is that job specialization potentially improves work efficiency. One reason for this higher efficiency is that employees spend less time changing activities because they have fewer tasks to juggle. Even when people can change tasks quickly, their mental attention lingers on the previous task, which slows down performance on the new task.[49] A second reason for increased work efficiency is that specialized jobs require fewer physical and mental skills to accomplish the assigned work, so less time and fewer resources are needed for training. A third reason is that shorter work cycles give employees more frequent practice with the task, so jobs are mastered more quickly. A fourth reason specialization tends to increase work efficiency is that employees with specific aptitudes or skills can be matched more precisely to the jobs for which they are best suited.[50]

The Arsenal of Venice introduced job specialization 200 years before Adam Smith famously praised this form of job design. Founded in 1104 AD, the state-owned shipbuilder eventually employed up to 4,000 people in specialized jobs (carpenters, iron workers, warehouse supervisors, etc.) to build ships and accessories (e.g., ropes). In 1570, the Arsenal had become so efficient through specialization that it built 100 ships in two months. The organization even had an assembly line along the waterway where workers apportioned food, ammunition, and other supplies from specially designed warehouses to the completed vessels.[51]

The benefits of job specialization were noted more than 2,300 years ago by the Chinese philosopher Mencius and the Greek philosopher Plato. Scottish economist Adam Smith wrote 250 years ago about the advantages of job specialization. Smith described a small factory where 10 pin makers collectively produced as many as 48,000 pins per day because they performed specialized tasks, such as straightening, cutting, sharpening, grinding, and whitening the pins. In contrast, Smith explained, if these 10 people worked alone producing complete pins, they would collectively manufacture no more than 200 pins per day.[52]

Scientific Management   One of the strongest advocates of job specialization was Frederick Winslow Taylor, an American industrial engineer who introduced the principles of **scientific management** in the early 1900s.[53] Scientific management consists of a toolkit of activities. Some of these interventions—employee selection, training, goal setting, and work incentives—are common today but were rare until Taylor popularized them. However, scientific management is mainly associated with high levels of job specialization and standardization of tasks to achieve maximum efficiency.

According to Taylor, the most effective companies have detailed procedures and work practices developed by engineers, enforced by supervisors, and executed by employees. Even the supervisor's tasks should

job design
The process of assigning tasks to a job, including the interdependency of those tasks with other jobs.

job specialization
The result of division of labor in which work is subdivided into separate jobs assigned to different people.

scientific management
The practice of systematically partitioning work into its smallest elements and standardizing tasks to achieve maximum efficiency.

be divided: One person manages operational efficiency, another manages inspection, and another is the disciplinarian. Taylor and other industrial engineers demonstrated that scientific management significantly improves work efficiency. No doubt, some of the increased productivity can be credited to the training, goal setting, and work incentives, but job specialization quickly became popular in its own right.

Problems with Job Specialization   Frederick Taylor and his contemporaries focused on how job specialization reduces labor "waste" by improving the mechanical efficiency of work (i.e., matching skills, faster learning, less switchover time). Yet they didn't seem to notice how this extreme job specialization adversely affects employee attitudes and motivation. Some jobs—such as painting eyes on dolls—are so specialized that they soon become tedious, trivial, and socially isolating. Employee turnover and absenteeism tend to be higher in specialized jobs with very short time cycles. Companies sometimes have to pay higher wages to attract job applicants to this dissatisfying, narrowly defined work.[54]

Job specialization often reduces work quality because employees see only a small part of the process. As one observer of an automobile assembly line reports: "Often [employees] did not know how their jobs related to the total picture. Not knowing, there was no incentive to strive for quality—what did quality even mean as it related to a bracket whose function you did not understand?"[55]

Equally important, job specialization can undermine the motivational potential of jobs. As work becomes specialized, it tends to become easier to perform but less interesting. Work motivation increases (to a point) as jobs become more complex, but complex jobs also take much longer to master. Maximum job performance occurs somewhere between these two extremes, where most people can eventually perform the job tasks efficiently yet the work is interesting.

JOB DESIGN AND WORK MOTIVATION

Industrial engineers may have overlooked the motivational effect of job characteristics, but it is now the central focus of many job design changes. Organizational behavior scholar Frederick Herzberg is credited with shifting the spotlight when he introduced **motivator-hygiene theory** in the 1950s.[56] Motivator-hygiene theory proposes that employees experience job satisfaction when they fulfill growth and esteem needs (called *motivators*), and they experience dissatisfaction when they have poor working conditions, job security, and other factors categorized as lower-order needs (called *hygienes*). Herzberg argued that only characteristics of the job itself motivate employees, whereas the hygiene factors merely prevent dissatisfaction. It might seem obvious to us today that the job itself is a source of motivation, but the concept was radical when Herzberg proposed the idea.

Motivator-hygiene theory has been soundly rejected by research studies, but Herzberg's ideas generated new thinking about the motivational potential of the job itself.[57] Out of subsequent research emerged the **job characteristics model,** as shown in Exhibit 6.2. The job characteristics model identifies five core job dimensions that produce three psychological states. Employees who experience these psychological states tend to have higher levels of internal work motivation (motivation from the work itself), job satisfaction (particularly satisfaction with the work itself), and work effectiveness.[58]

Core Job Characteristics   The job characteristics model identifies five core job characteristics. Under the right conditions, employees are more motivated and satisfied when jobs have higher levels of these characteristics:

- *Skill variety.* **Skill variety** refers to the use of different skills and talents to complete a variety of work activities. For example, salesclerks who normally only serve customers might be assigned the additional duties of stocking inventory and changing storefront displays.

motivator-hygiene theory
Herzberg's theory stating that employees are primarily motivated by growth and esteem needs, not by lower-level needs.

job characteristics model
A job design model that relates the motivational properties of jobs to specific personal and organizational consequences of those properties.

EXHIBIT 6.2

The Job Characteristics Model

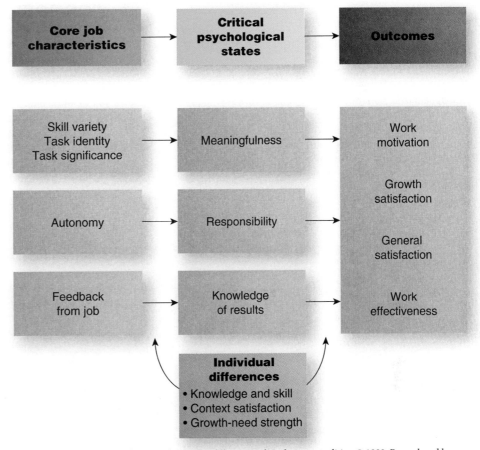

Source: From J. Richard Hackman and Greg R. Oldham, *Work Redesign*, 1st edition © 1980. Reproduced by permission of Pearson Education, Inc., Upper Saddle River, New Jersey.

- *Task identity.* **Task identity** is the degree to which a job requires completion of a whole or identifiable piece of work, such as assembling an entire broadband modem rather than just soldering in the circuitry.
- *Task significance.* **Task significance** is the degree to which the job affects the organization and/or larger society. It is an observable characteristic of the job (you can see how it benefits others), as well as a perceptual awareness, as Connections 6.2 illustrates. Rudy Magararu perceives high task significance because he sees how his work benefits others. This lab technician at Adnexus Therapeutics, Inc., in Waltham, Massachusetts, grows and harvests cells before the scientists arrive to conduct their experiments. "I start their jobs so that by the time they come in, half of their experiments are completed," Magararu explains. "That makes me feel good, because if they discover something in this experiment, I know I am part of that experiment."[59]
- *Autonomy.* Jobs with high levels of **autonomy** provide freedom, independence, and discretion in scheduling the work and determining the procedures to be used

skill variety
The extent to which employees must use different skills and talents to perform tasks within their jobs.

task identity
The degree to which a job requires completion of a whole or an identifiable piece of work.

task significance
The degree to which a job has a substantial impact on the organization and/or larger society.

autonomy
The degree to which a job gives employees the freedom, independence, and discretion to schedule their work and determine the procedures used in completing it.

connections 6.2

Customer Talks Raise Task Significance and Identity

Repairing aircraft engines is a complex business, involving the specialized work of dozens of people. However, people working in specialized jobs tend to have lower task identity and task significance. "We work on airplane engines, but individual employees work on different parts, and don't necessarily know what the customer uses it for," says Maurice Carter, a bearing technician lead hand at the Rolls Royce Engine Services facility in Oakland, California.

For this reason, Rolls Royce introduced "Voice of the Customer," an initiative in which customer representatives visit the facility and talk to production staff about how the quality of these engines is important to them. "[A customer's visit] allows you to know that your quality is key to the rescue of someone who may be stranded in a remote area, who relies on your ability to make sure that engine starts and continues to run in any adverse circumstance," says Carter.

"Voice of the customer isn't just a nicety," explains a Rolls Royce Engine Services executive. "It gives employees with relatively repetitive jobs the sense that they're not just working on a part but rather are key in keeping people safe."[60]

Rolls Royce Engine Services in California improved employees' task significance and task identity through its Voice of the Customer program.

to complete the work. In autonomous jobs, employees make their own decisions rather than relying on detailed instructions from supervisors or procedure manuals.

- *Job feedback.* Job feedback is the degree to which employees can tell how well they are doing on the basis of direct sensory information from the job itself. Airline pilots can tell how well they land their aircraft, and road crews can see how well they have prepared the roadbed and laid the asphalt.

Critical Psychological States   The five core job characteristics affect employee motivation and satisfaction through three critical psychological states in Exhibit 6.2. One of these psychological states is *experienced meaningfulness*—the belief that one's work is worthwhile or important. Skill variety, task identity, and task significance directly contribute to the job's meaningfulness. If the job has high levels of all three characteristics, employees are likely to feel that their jobs are highly meaningful. The meaningfulness of a job drops as one or more of these characteristics declines.

Work motivation and performance increase when employees feel personally accountable for the outcomes of their efforts. Autonomy directly contributes to this feeling of *experienced responsibility*. Employees must be assigned control of their work environment to feel responsible for their successes and failures. The third critical psychological state is *knowledge of results*. Employees want information about the consequences of their work effort. Knowledge of results can originate from coworkers, supervisors, or clients. However, job design focuses on knowledge of results from the work itself.

Individual Differences   Job design doesn't increase work motivation for everyone in every situation. Employees must have the required skills and knowledge to master the more challenging work. Otherwise, job design tends to increase stress and reduce job performance. The original model also suggests that increasing the motivational potential of jobs will not motivate employees who are dissatisfied with their work context (e.g., working conditions, job security) or who have a low growth-need strength. However, research findings have been mixed, suggesting that employees might be motivated by job

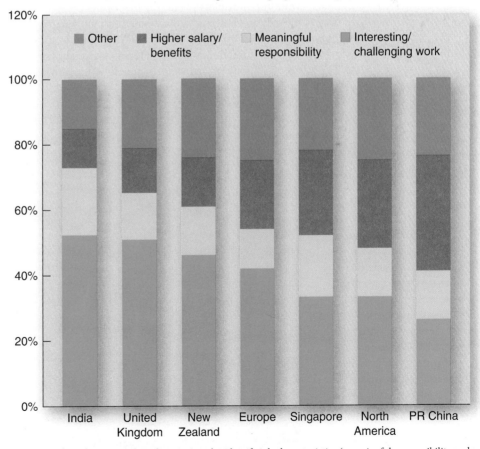

Preference for Interesting, Challenging, Meaningful Jobs[62]

Percentage of employees in selected countries who identify job characteristics (meaningful responsibility and interesting/challenging work), higher salary/benefits, or other job features as the aspect of the job that would make them most committed and engaged at work. Based on a sample of 134,000 people in 29 countries. The United Kingdom sample is included in the European results as well as separately in this exhibit.

design no matter how they feel about their job context or how high or low they score on growth needs.[61]

JOB DESIGN PRACTICES THAT MOTIVATE

Three main strategies can increase the motivational potential of jobs: job rotation, job enlargement, and job enrichment. This section also identifies several ways to implement job enrichment.

Job Rotation

Most Chrysler assembly-line employees in the United States have a high degree of job specialization. According to one estimate, these production workers have an average cycle time of about 65 seconds. Chrysler executives are aware of the motivational and physiological problems that this repetitive work can create, so they have introduced **job rotation,** whereby employees work in teams and rotate to a different workstation within that team every few hours. "The whole idea of job rotation makes a big difference," says one Chrysler executive. "The job naturally gets better, quality improves, throughput improves." Chrysler reported significant improvements in productivity and morale within the first year of its job rotation program. Job rotation offers "important ergonomic benefits to workers, improvements in product quality, and higher employee satisfaction," says a senior manager at Chrysler's plant in Toledo, Ohio.[63]

From the experience at Chrysler and many other companies, we can identify three potential benefits of job rotation. First, it minimizes health risks from repetitive strain and heavy lifting because employees use different muscles and physical positions in the various jobs. Second, it supports multi-skilling (employees learn several jobs), which increases workforce flexibility in staffing the production process and in finding replacements for employees on vacation. A third benefit of job rotation is that it potentially reduces the boredom of highly repetitive jobs. However, organizational behavior experts continue to debate whether job rotation really is a form of job redesign, because the jobs remain the same; they are still highly specialized. Critics argue that job redesign requires changes within the job, such as job enlargement.

Job Enlargement

Job enlargement adds tasks to an existing job. It might involve combining two or more complete jobs into one or just adding one or two more tasks to an existing job. Either way, skill variety increases because there are more tasks to

Bang & Olufsen has always had fairly complex jobs at its manufacturing plants. But when the Danish government established guidelines for employers to reduce monotonous and repetitive work, the audio and multimedia company took further steps by empowering production teams to schedule their work and include plenty of job rotation. Bang & Olufsen employees are trained on all assembly stations and change jobs so repetitive work on each shift occurs for less than three or four hours.[64]

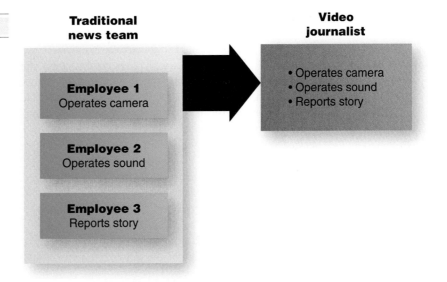

EXHIBIT 6.3

Job Enlargement of Video Journalists

perform. Video journalist is an example of an enlarged job. As Exhibit 6.3 illustrates, a traditional news team consists of a camera operator, a sound and lighting specialist, and the journalist who writes and presents or narrates the story. One video journalist performs all of these tasks.

Job enlargement significantly improves work efficiency and flexibility. However, research suggests that simply giving employees more tasks won't affect motivation, performance, or job satisfaction. These benefits result only when skill variety is combined with more autonomy and job knowledge.[65] In other words, employees are motivated when they perform a variety of tasks *and* have the freedom and knowledge to structure their work to achieve the highest satisfaction and performance. These job characteristics are at the heart of job enrichment.

Job Enrichment   **Job enrichment** occurs when employees are given more responsibility for scheduling, coordinating, and planning their own work.[66] For example, American Express and other companies are now allowing their customer service employees to go "off-script," meaning that they use their own discretion regarding how long they should spend with a client and what to say to him or her.[67] Previously, employees had to follow strict statements and take a fixed time for specific types of customer issues. Generally, people in enriched jobs experience higher job satisfaction and work motivation, along with lower absenteeism and turnover. Productivity is also higher when task identity and job feedback are improved. Product and service quality tend to improve because job enrichment increases the jobholder's felt responsibility and sense of ownership over the product or service.[68]

One way to increase job enrichment is by combining highly interdependent tasks into one job. This *natural grouping* approach is reflected in the video journalist job. Video journalist was earlier described as an enlarged job, but it is also an example of job enrichment because it naturally groups tasks together to complete an entire product (i.e., a news story). By forming natural work units, jobholders have stronger feelings of responsibility for an identifiable body of work. They feel a sense of ownership and therefore tend to increase job quality. Forming natural work units increases task identity and task significance because employees

job rotation
The practice of moving employees from one job to another.

job enlargement
The practice of adding more tasks to an existing job.

job enrichment
The practice of giving employees more responsibility for scheduling, coordinating, and planning their own work.

perform a complete product or service and can more readily see how their work affects others.

A second job enrichment strategy, called *establishing client relationships,* involves putting employees in direct contact with their clients rather than using the supervisor as a go-between. By being directly responsible for specific clients, employees have more information and can make decisions affecting those clients.[69] Establishing client relationships also increases task significance, because employees see a line-of-sight connection between their work and consequences for customers. City Telecom in Hong Kong redesigned customer service jobs around customers for this reason. "We introduced a one-stop service for our customers," explains Ellis Ng, City Telecom's head of learning and development. "Each of our staff in the special duty unit (SDU) can handle all inquiries including sales, customer service and simple troubleshooting. They are divided into small working units and serve a set number of customers so they have the chance to build a rapport and create a personalized service."[70]

Forming natural task groups and establishing client relationships are common ways to enrich jobs, but the heart of the job enrichment philosophy is to give employees more autonomy over their work. This basic idea is at the core of one of the most widely mentioned—and often misunderstood—practices, known as empowerment.

Empowerment Practices

LO5

One of Europe's most successful banks doesn't believe in budgets or centralized financial targets. Executives at Svenska Handelsbanken AB learned decades ago that these costly controls from the head office stifle rather than motivate employees. Instead, the Swedish bank gives its 10,000 employees and managers across 450 branches in 21 countries (mostly Nordic countries and the United Kingdom) considerable autonomy to run the local branches as their own businesses. Branches have the freedom to prepare their own action plans as well as decide how to advertise products, how much to pay for property

Svenska Handelsbanken gives employees and managers considerable autonomy to run the local branches as their own businesses. The Swedish bank's branches (which are located throughout northern Europe) have the freedom to prepare their own action plans as well as decide how to advertise products, how much to pay for property leases, how many staff to hire, and so forth. "Being empowered and having this trust leads to better decisions and higher satisfaction," explains a Handelsbanken's executive in northern Britain.

leases, how many staff to hire, and so forth. "The culture of our company is based on entrusting employees and allowing those who are closest to the customer and who know the customer best to take decisions," says a Handelsbanken's executive in northern Britain. "Being empowered and having this trust leads to better decisions and higher satisfaction."[71]

Svenska Handelsbanken is a role model for organizations that want to nurture employee **empowerment.** Empowerment is a term that has been loosely tossed around in corporate circles and the subject of considerable debate among academics. However, the most widely accepted definition is that empowerment is a psychological concept represented by four dimensions: self-determination, meaning, competence, and impact of the individual's role in the organization.[72]

- *Self-determination.* Empowered employees feel that they have freedom, independence, and discretion over their work activities.
- *Meaning.* Employees who feel empowered care about their work and believe that what they do is important.
- *Competence.* Empowered people are confident about their ability to perform the work well and have a capacity to grow with new challenges.
- *Impact.* Empowered employees view themselves as active participants in the organization; that is, their decisions and actions have an influence on the company's success.

SUPPORTING EMPOWERMENT

Chances are that you have heard leaders say they are "empowering" the workforce. Yet empowerment is a state of mind, so what these executives really mean is that they are changing the work environment to support the feeling of empowerment.[73] Numerous individual, job design, and organizational or work-context factors support empowerment. At the individual level, employees must possess the necessary competencies to be able to perform the work, as well as handle additional decision-making requirements.[74] Job characteristics clearly influence the degree to which people feel empowered.[75] Employees are much more likely to experience self-determination when working in jobs with a high degree of autonomy and minimal bureaucratic control. They experience more meaningfulness when working in jobs with high levels of task identity and task significance. They experience more self-confidence when working in jobs that allow them to receive feedback about their performance and accomplishments.

Several organizational and work-context factors also influence empowerment. Employees experience more empowerment in organizations where information and other resources are easily accessible. Empowerment also requires a learning orientation culture. In other words, empowerment flourishes in organizations that appreciate the value of employee learning and that accept reasonable mistakes as a natural part of the learning process. Furthermore, as mentioned in the description of Handelsbanken, empowerment requires corporate leaders who trust employees and are willing to take the risks that empowerment creates.[76]

empowerment
A psychological concept in which people experience more self-determination, meaning, competence, and impact regarding their role in the organization.

With the right individuals, job characteristics, and organizational environment, empowerment can substantially improve motivation and performance. For instance, a study of bank employees concluded that empowerment improved customer service and tended to reduce conflict between employees and their supervisors. A study of nurses reported that empowerment is associated with higher trust in management, which ultimately influences job satisfaction, belief and acceptance of organizational goals and values, and effective organizational commitment. Empowerment also tends to increase personal initiative because employees identify with and assume more psychological ownership of their work.[77]

Self-Leadership Practices

LO6

What is the most important characteristic that companies look for in their employees? Leadership potential, ability to work in a team, and good communication skills are important, but they don't top the list in a survey of 800 British employers. Instead, the most important employee characteristic is self-motivation. Frode Gronvold can identify with these survey results. The chairman of Linstow Management Center, which develops and manages major shopping centers in Latvia and Estonia, seeks out people who demonstrate self-leadership. "I really appreciate when I have colleagues who take initiative," says Gronvold. "I like people with a creative state of mind, who at the same time are autonomous, self-driven, self-motivated, with the ability to cooperate and get the best out of each other. These are the main skills that I am looking for in my employees."[78]

Most of the concepts introduced in this chapter and in Chapter 5 have assumed that leaders do things to motivate employees. Certainly, these theories and practices are valuable, but they overlook the fact that the most successful employees ultimately motivate and manage themselves. In other words, they engage in self-leadership. **Self-leadership** refers to the process of influencing oneself to establish the self-direction and self-motivation needed to perform a task.[79] This concept includes a toolkit of behavioral activities borrowed from social cognitive theory and goal setting. It also includes constructive thought processes that have been extensively studied in sports psychology. Overall, self-leadership suggests that individuals mostly regulate their own actions through these behavioral and cognitive (thought) activities.

SELF-LEADERSHIP STRATEGIES

Although self-leadership consists of several processes, the five main activities are identified in Exhibit 6.4. These elements, which generally follow one another in a sequence, are personal goal setting, constructive thought patterns, designing natural rewards, self-monitoring, and self-reinforcement.[80]

Mc Graw Hill connect

Do you have a proactive personality? Go to **www.mcgrawhillconnect.com** to assess the extent to which taking personal initiative is part of your disposition.

Personal Goal Setting   The first step in self-leadership is to set goals for your own work effort. This step applies the ideas learned in Chapter 5 on goal setting, such as identifying goals that are specific, relevant, and challenging. The main difference is that self-leadership involves setting goals alone, rather than having them assigned by or jointly decided with a supervisor. Research suggests that employees are more focused and perform better when they set their own goals, particularly in combination with other self-leadership practices.[81] Personal goal setting also requires a high degree of self-awareness, because people need to understand their current behavior and performance before establishing meaningful goals for personal development.

Constructive Thought Patterns   Before beginning a task and while performing it, employees should engage in positive (constructive) thoughts about that work and its accomplishment. In particular, employees are more motivated and better prepared to accomplish a task after they have engaged in positive self-talk and mental imagery.

Positive Self-Talk   Do you ever talk to yourself? Most of us do, according to a major study of college students.[82] **Self-talk** refers to any situation in which we talk to ourselves

---

EXHIBIT 6.4   Elements of Self-Leadership

Personal goal setting	→	Constructive thought patterns	→	Designing natural rewards	→	Self-monitoring	→	Self-reinforcement

Bayer CropScience's business in North Carolina is expanding, but it only wants job applicants with special characteristics. "It's difficult to fill [these jobs]," says site leader Nick Crosby. "We're not in the game these days of just getting people who can read, write and shovel stuff around." Instead, Bayer CropScience wants employees who practice self-leadership. "We need self-motivated people who work well with empowered teams—people who can think for themselves, do basic diagnosis, and keep the plants operating at an optimum," he says.[83]

about our own thoughts or actions. The problem is that most self-talk is negative; we criticize much more than encourage or congratulate ourselves. Negative self-talk undermines our confidence and potential to perform a particular task. In contrast, positive self-talk creates a "can-do" belief and thereby increases motivation by raising our self-efficacy and reducing anxiety about challenging tasks.[84] We often hear that professional athletes "psych" themselves up before an important event. They tell themselves that they can achieve their goal and that they have practiced enough to reach that goal. They are motivating themselves through self-talk.

Mental Imagery   You've probably heard the phrase, "I'll cross that bridge when I come to it!" Self-leadership takes the opposite view. It suggests that we need to mentally practice a task and imagine successfully performing it beforehand. This process, known as **mental imagery,** has two parts. One part involves mentally practicing the task, anticipating obstacles to goal accomplishment, and working out solutions to those obstacles before they occur. By mentally walking through the activities required to accomplish the task, we gain the advantage of anticipating problems that may occur. We can then imagine what responses would be best for each contingency.[85]

While one part of mental imagery helps us anticipate things that could go wrong, the other part involves visualizing successful completion of the task. You might imagine the experience of completing the task and the positive results that follow, such as being promoted, receiving a prestigious award, or taking time off work. This visualization increases goal commitment and motivates people to complete the task effectively. This is the strategy that Tony Wang applies to motivate himself. "Since I am in sales, I think about the reward I get for closing new business—the commission check—and the things it will allow me to do that I really enjoy," explains the sales employee from Washington, DC. "Or I think about the feeling I get when I am successful at something and how it makes me feel good, and use that to get me going."[86]

self-leadership
The process of influencing oneself to establish the self-direction and self-motivation needed to perform a task.

self-talk
The process of talking to ourselves about our own thoughts or actions.

mental imagery
The process of mentally practicing a task and visualizing its successful completion.

Designing Natural Rewards   Self-leadership recognizes that employees actively craft their jobs. To varying degrees, they can alter tasks and work relationships to make the work more motivating.[87] One way to build natural rewards into the job is to alter the way a task is accomplished. People often have enough discretion in their jobs to make slight changes to suit their needs and preferences. "In 28 years I do not think I have ever had a bad job—it is about the attitude that you bring to your work," says Steve Collier, National Australia Bank's general manager of sales and distribution services. "Self-motivation has meant that even in tough times I have changed the job or changed the way I did it." Collier's advice seems to work; he received top honors as the best contact center leader in the world.[88]

Self-Monitoring   Self-monitoring is the process of keeping track at regular intervals of one's progress toward a goal by using naturally occurring feedback. Some people can receive feedback from the job itself, such as members of a lawn maintenance crew who can see how they are improving the appearance of their client's property. But many of us are unable to observe our work output so readily. Instead, many people need to design feedback systems. Salespeople might arrange to receive monthly reports on sales levels in their territory. Production staff might have gauges or computer feedback systems installed so that they can see how many errors are made on the production line. Research suggests that people who have control over the timing of performance feedback perform their tasks better than do those with feedback assigned by others.[89]

Self-Reinforcement   Self-leadership includes engaging in *self-reinforcement,* which is part of social cognitive theory described in Chapter 5. Self-reinforcement occurs whenever an employee has control over a reinforcer but doesn't "take" the reinforcer until completing a self-set goal.[90] A common example is taking a break after reaching a predetermined stage of your work. The work break is a self-induced form of positive reinforcement. Self-reinforcement also occurs when you decide to do a more enjoyable task after completing a task that you dislike. For example, after slogging through a difficult report, you might decide to spend time doing a more pleasant task, such as catching up on industry news by scanning websites.

EFFECTIVENESS OF SELF-LEADERSHIP

Self-leadership is shaping up to be a valuable applied performance practice in organizational settings. A respectable body of research shows consistent support for most elements of self-leadership. Self-set goals and self-monitoring increased the frequency of wearing safety equipment among employees in a mining operation. Airline employees who received constructive thought training experienced better mental performance, enthusiasm, and job satisfaction than coworkers who did not receive this training. Mental imagery helped supervisors and process engineers in a pulp-and-paper mill transfer what they learned in an interpersonal communication skills class back to the job.[91] Studies also indicate that constructive thought processes improve individual performance in cycling, hockey goaltending, ice skating, soccer, and other sports. Indeed, studies show that almost all Olympic athletes rely on mental rehearsal and positive self-talk to achieve their performance goals.[92]

SELF-LEADERSHIP CONTINGENCIES

As with most other forms of organizational behavior, self-leadership is more or less likely to occur depending on the person and the situation. With respect to individual differences, preliminary research suggests that self-leadership behaviors are more frequently found in people with higher levels of conscientiousness and extroversion. Some writers also suggest that people with a positive self-concept evaluation (i.e., self-esteem, self-efficacy, and internal locus of control) are more likely to apply self-leadership strategies.[93]

Although the research is still sparse, the work environment also seems to influence the extent to which employees engage in self-leadership strategies. In particular, employees require some degree of autonomy to engage in some or most aspects of self-leadership. They probably also feel more confident with self-leadership when their boss is empowering rather than controlling and where there is a high degree of trust between them. Employees are also more likely to engage in self-monitoring in companies that emphasize continuous measurement of performance.[94] Overall, self-leadership promises to be an important concept and practice for improving employee motivation and performance.

[chapter summary]

LO1   Discuss the meaning of money and identify several individual, team, and organizational-level performance-based rewards.

Money (and other financial rewards) is a fundamental part of the employment relationship, but it also relates to our needs, our emotions, and our self-concepts. It is viewed as a symbol of status and prestige, as a source of security, as a source of evil, or as a source of anxiety or feelings of inadequacy.

Organizations reward employees for their membership and seniority, job status, competencies, and performance. Membership-based rewards may attract job applicants, and seniority-based rewards reduce turnover, but these reward objectives also tend to discourage turnover among those with the lowest performance. Rewards based on job status try to maintain internal equity and motivate employees to compete for promotions. However, they tend to encourage a bureaucratic hierarchy, support status differences, and motivate employees to compete and hoard resources. Competency-based rewards are becoming increasingly popular because they improve workforce flexibility and are consistent with the emerging idea of employability. However, they tend to be subjectively measured and can result in higher costs as employees spend more time learning new skills.

Awards and bonuses, commissions, and other individual performance-based rewards have existed for centuries and are widely used. Many companies are shifting to team-based rewards such as gainsharing plans and to organizational rewards such as employee stock ownership plans (ESOPs), stock options, and profit sharing. ESOPs and stock options create an ownership culture, but employees often perceive a weak connection between individual performance and the organizational reward.

LO2   Describe five ways to improve reward effectiveness.

Financial rewards have a number of limitations, but reward effectiveness can be improved in several ways. Organizational leaders should ensure that rewards are linked to work performance, rewards are aligned with performance within the employee's control, team rewards are used where jobs are interdependent, rewards are valued by employees, and rewards have no unintended consequences.

LO3 List the advantages and disadvantages of job specialization.

Job design is the process of assigning tasks to a job, including the interdependency of those tasks with other jobs. Job specialization subdivides work into separate jobs for different people. This increases work efficiency because employees master the tasks quickly, spend less time changing tasks, require less training, and can be matched more closely with the jobs best suited to their skills. However, job specialization may reduce work motivation, create mental health problems, lower product or service quality, and increase costs through discontentment, absenteeism, and turnover.

LO4   Diagram the job characteristics model and describe three ways to improve employee motivation through job design.

The job characteristics model is a template for job redesign that specifies core job dimensions, psychological states, and individual differences. The five core job dimensions are skill variety, task identity, task significance, autonomy, and job feedback. Contemporary job design strategies try to motivate employees through job rotation, job enlargement, and job enrichment. Organizations introduce job rotation to reduce job boredom, develop a more flexible workforce, and reduce the incidence of repetitive strain injuries. Job enlargement involves increasing the number of tasks within the job. Two ways to enrich jobs are clustering tasks into natural groups and establishing client relationships.

LO5   Define *empowerment* and identify strategies that support empowerment.

Empowerment is a psychological concept represented by four dimensions: self-determination, meaning, competence, and impact regarding the individual's role in the organization. Individual characteristics seem to have a minor influence on empowerment. Job design is a major influence, particularly autonomy, task identity, task significance, and job feedback. Empowerment is also supported at the organizational level through a learning orientation culture, sufficient information and resources, and corporate leaders who trust employees.

LO6   Describe the five elements of self-leadership and identify specific personal and work environment influences on self-leadership.

Self-leadership is the process of influencing oneself to establish the self-direction and self-motivation needed to perform a task. This includes personal goal setting, constructive thought patterns, designing natural rewards, self-monitoring, and self-reinforcement. Constructive thought patterns include self-talk and mental imagery. Self-talk occurs in any situation in which a person talks to himself or herself about his or her own thoughts or actions. Mental imagery involves mentally practicing a task and imagining successfully performing it beforehand. People with higher levels of conscientiousness, extroversion, and a positive self-concept are more likely to apply self-leadership strategies. It also increases in workplaces that support empowerment and have high trust between employees and management.

(key terms)

autonomy, p. 175

employee stock ownership plan (ESOP), p. 168

empowerment, p. 181

gainsharing plan, p. 168

job characteristics model, p. 174

job design, p. 172

job enlargement, p. 178

job enrichment, p. 179

job evaluation, p. 166

job rotation, p. 178

job specialization, p. 172

mental imagery, p. 183

motivator-hygiene theory, p. 174

profit-sharing plans, p. 168

scientific management, p. 173

self-leadership, p. 182

self-talk, p. 182

skill variety, p. 174

stock options, p. 168

task identity, p. 175

task significance, p. 175

(critical thinking questions)

1. As a consultant, you have been asked to recommend either a gainsharing plan or a profit-sharing plan for employees who work in the four regional distribution and warehousing facilities of a large retail organization. Which reward system would you recommend? Explain your answer.

2. You are a member of a team responsible for developing a reward system for your college or university faculty unit. Assume that the faculty is nonprofit, so profit sharing is not an option. What other team or organization-level rewards might work in this situation? Describe specific measures that could be used to calculate the amount of bonus.

3. Waco Tire Corporation redesigned its production facilities around a team-based system. However, the company president believes that employees will not be motivated unless they receive incentives based on their individual performance. Give three explanations why Waco Tire should introduce team-based rather than individual rewards in this setting.

4. What can organizations do to increase the effectiveness of financial rewards?

5. Most of us have watched pizzas being made while waiting in a pizzeria. What level of job specialization do you usually notice in these operations? Why does this high or low level of specialization exist? If some pizzerias have different levels of specialization than others, identify the contingencies that might explain these differences.

6. Can a manager or supervisor "empower" an employee? Discuss fully.

7. Describe a time when you practiced self-leadership to successfully perform a task. With reference to each step in the self-leadership process, describe what you did to achieve this success.

8. Can self-leadership replace formal leadership in an organizational setting?

CASE STUDY 6.1 YAKKATECH, INC.

Steven L. McShane, University of Western Australia

YakkaTech Inc. is an information technology services firm employing 1,500 people throughout Washington and Oregon. YakkaTech has a consulting division, which mainly installs and upgrades enterprise software systems and related hardware on the client's site. YakkaTech also has a customer service division that consists of four customer contact centers serving clients within each region.

Each customer service center consists of a half-dozen departments representing functional specializations (computer systems, intranet infrastructure, storage systems, enterprise software systems, customer billing, etc.). These centers typically have more than two dozen employees in each department. When a client submits a problem to the center by e-mail or telephone, the message or call is directed to the department where the issue best applies. The query is given a "ticket" number and assigned to the next available employee in that department. Individual employees are solely responsible for the tickets assigned to them.

The employee investigates and corrects the issue, and the ticket is "closed" when the problem has been resolved.

If the client experiences the same problem again, even a few days later, a new ticket is issued and sent to whichever employee is available to receive the ticket. A client's problems are almost always handled by different employees each time, even when the issue is sent to the same department. Furthermore, when a customer center department is heavily backlogged, clients are redirected to the same department at another regional center where their problem can be addressed more quickly.

At one time, YakkaTech operated more than a dozen small customer contact centers throughout the region because client problems had to be diagnosed and resolved on-site. Today, employees can investigate most software and hardware system faults from the center through remote monitoring systems, rather than personally visit the client. Consequently, eight years ago, YakkaTech amalgamated its customer service operations into four large regional centers. Customer service staff work entirely within the center. When a client visit is required, the ticket is transferred to an individual or team in the consulting business, who then visits the client.

YakkaTech's customer service business has nearly doubled over the past five years, but with this growth has come increasing customer complaints regarding poor quality service. Many say that employees seem indifferent to the client's problems. Others have commented on the slow response to their problems where the issue requires involvement of more than one department. Several clients have also complained that they are continually educating YakkaTech's customer service employees about details of their unique IT systems infrastructure.

Another concern is that until 18 months ago, YakkaTech's voluntary employee quit rates in the contact centers were above the industry average. This increased labor costs due to the cost of recruiting new technical staff, as well as the lower productivity of new employees. According to results of an employee survey two years ago (as well as informal comments since then), many employees felt that their work is monotonous. Some also said that they felt disconnected from the consequences of their work. A few also complained about ongoing conflicts with people in other departments and the stress of serving dissatisfied clients.

Eighteen months ago, YakkaTech's executive team decided to raise pay rates for its customer service staff to make them among the highest in the industry around the Pacific Northwest. The assumption was that the high pay rates would improve morale and reduce turnover, thereby reducing hiring costs and improving productivity. In addition, YakkaTech introduced a vested profit-sharing plan, in which employees received the profit-sharing bonus only if they remained with the company for two years after the bonus was awarded. Employees who quit or were fired for just cause before the vesting period forfeited the bonus.

Employee turnover rates dropped dramatically, leading the executive team to conclude that customer service quality and productivity would improve. Instead, customer complaints and productivity remain below expectations and, in some cases, have worsened. Experienced employees continue to complain about the work. There have been a few disturbing incidents in which employees were careless in solving client problems or did not bother to forward tickets that belong in another department. Employee referrals (in which staff members recommend friends to join the company) have become rare events, whereas at one time they represented a significant source of qualified job applicants. Furthermore, a few executives have recently overheard employees say that they would like to work elsewhere but can't afford to leave YakkaTech.

Discussion Questions

1. What symptom(s) in this case suggest that something has gone wrong?
2. What are the main causes of these symptoms?
3. What actions should YakkaTech executives take to correct these problems?

TEAM EXERCISE 6.2 IS STUDENT WORK ENRICHED?

PURPOSE This exercise is designed to help you learn how to measure the motivational potential of jobs and evaluate the extent that jobs should be further enriched.

INSTRUCTIONS (SMALL CLASS) Being a student is like a job in several ways. You have tasks to perform, and someone (such as your instructor) oversees your work. Although few people want to be students most of their lives (the pay rate is too low!), it may be interesting to determine how enriched your job is as a student.

1. Form teams (preferably four or five people).
2. Working alone, complete both sets of measures in this exercise. Then, using the guidelines below, individually calculate your score for the five core job characteristics, as well as the overall motivational potential score for the job.

3. Compare your individual results with members of your team. The group should identify differences of opinion for each core job characteristic. Also note which core job characteristics have the lowest scores, and recommend ways to increase these scores.

4. The entire class will then meet to discuss the results of the exercise. The instructor may ask some teams to present their comparisons and recommendations for a particular core job characteristic.

INSTRUCTIONS (LARGE CLASS)

1. Working alone, complete both sets of measures in this exercise. Then, using the guidelines below, calculate your score for the five core job characteristics, as well as the overall motivational potential score for the job.

2. Using a show of hands or classroom technology, indicate your results for each core job characteristic. The instructor will ask for results for several bands across the range of the scales. Alternatively, you might complete this activity prior to class and submit your results through online classroom technology. Later, the instructor will provide feedback to the class showing the collective results (i.e., distribution of results across the range of scores).

3. Where possible, the instructor should ask students with very high or very low results to discuss their views with the class.

Job Diagnostic Survey

CIRCLE THE NUMBER ON THE RIGHT THAT BEST DESCRIBES STUDENT WORK	VERY LITTLE			MODERATELY			VERY MUCH
1. To what extent does student work permit you to decide on your own how to go about doing the work?	1	2	3	4	5	6	7
2. To what extent does student work involve doing a whole or identifiable piece of work, rather than a small portion of the overall work process?	1	2	3	4	5	6	7
3. To what extent does student work require you to do many different things, using a variety of your skills and talents?	1	2	3	4	5	6	7
4. To what extent are the results of your work as a student likely to significantly affect the lives and well-being of other people (e.g., within your school, your family, society)?	1	2	3	4	5	6	7
5. To what extent does working on student activities provide information about your performance?	1	2	3	4	5	6	7

CIRCLE THE NUMBER ON THE RIGHT THAT BEST DESCRIBES STUDENT WORK	VERY INACCURATE			UNCERTAIN			VERY ACCURATE
6. Being a student requires me to use a number of complex and high-level skills.	1	2	3	4	5	6	7
7. Student work is arranged so that I do *not* have the chance to do an entire piece of work from beginning to end.	7	6	5	4	3	2	1
8. Doing the work required of students provides many chances for me to figure out how well I am doing.	1	2	3	4	5	6	7
9. The work students must do is quite simple and repetitive.	7	6	5	4	3	2	1
10. The work of a student is the type where a lot of other people can be affected by how well the work gets done.	1	2	3	4	5	6	7
11. Student work denies me any chance to use my personal initiative or judgment in carrying out the work.	7	6	5	4	3	2	1
12. Student work provides me the chance to completely finish the pieces of work I begin.	1	2	3	4	5	6	7
13. Doing student work by itself provides very few clues about whether I am performing well.	7	6	5	4	3	2	1
14. As a student, I have considerable opportunity for independence and freedom in how I do the work.	1	2	3	4	5	6	7
15. The work I perform as a student is *not* very significant or important in the broader scheme of things.	7	6	5	4	3	2	1

Source: Adapted from the Job Diagnostic Survey, developed by J.R. Hackman and G.R. Oldham. The authors have released any copyright ownership of this scale. See J.R. Hackman and G. Oldham, *Work Redesign* (Reading, MA: Addison-Wesley, 1980), p. 275.

Calculating the Motivational Potential Score

Scoring Core Job Characteristics: Use the following set of calculations to estimate the motivational potential score for the job of being a student. Use your answers from the Job Diagnostic Survey.

Skill variety (SV) $\dfrac{\text{Question } 3 + 6 + 9}{3} = \underline{\hspace{1cm}}$

Task identity (TI) $\dfrac{\text{Question } 2 + 7 + 12}{3} = \underline{\hspace{1cm}}$

Task significance (TS) $\dfrac{\text{Question } 4 + 10 + 15}{3} = \underline{\hspace{1cm}}$

Autonomy $\dfrac{\text{Question } 1 + 11 + 14}{3} = \underline{\hspace{1cm}}$

Job feedback $\dfrac{\text{Question } 5 + 8 + 13}{3} = \underline{\hspace{1cm}}$

Calculating Motivational Potential Score (MPS): Use the following formula and the results above to calculate the motivational potential score. Notice that skill variety, task identity, and task significance are averaged before being multiplied by the score for autonomy and job feedback.

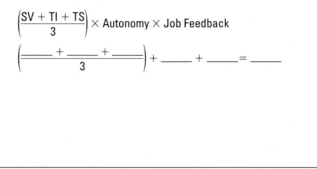

$$\left(\frac{SV + TI + TS}{3}\right) \times \text{Autonomy} \times \text{Job Feedback}$$

$$\left(\frac{\underline{\hspace{0.6cm}} + \underline{\hspace{0.6cm}} + \underline{\hspace{0.6cm}}}{3}\right) + \underline{\hspace{0.6cm}} + \underline{\hspace{0.6cm}} = \underline{\hspace{0.6cm}}$$

SELF-ASSESSMENT 6.3 WHAT IS YOUR ATTITUDE TOWARD MONEY?

PURPOSE This exercise is designed to help you understand the types of attitudes toward money and to assess your attitude toward money.

INSTRUCTIONS Read each of the statements below and circle the response that you believe best reflects your position regarding each statement. Then use the scoring key in Appendix B at the end of the book to calculate your results. This exercise should be completed alone so that you can assess yourself honestly without concerns of social comparison. Class discussion will focus on the meaning of money, including the dimensions measured here and other aspects of money that may have an influence on behavior in the workplace.

Money Attitude Scale

TO WHAT EXTENT DO YOU AGREE OR DISAGREE THAT . . .	STRONGLY AGREE	AGREE	NEUTRAL	DISAGREE	STRONGLY DISAGREE
1. I sometimes purchase things because I know they will impress other people.	5	4	3	2	1
2. I regularly put money aside for the future.	5	4	3	2	1
3. I tend to get worried about decisions involving money.	5	4	3	2	1
4. I believe that financial wealth is one of the most important signs of a person's success.	5	4	3	2	1
5. I keep a close watch on how much money I have.	5	4	3	2	1
6. I feel nervous when I don't have enough money.	5	4	3	2	1
7. I tend to show more respect to people who are wealthier than I am.	5	4	3	2	1
8. I follow a careful financial budget.	5	4	3	2	1
9. I worry about being financially secure.	5	4	3	2	1

(*continued*)

Money Attitude Scale *(continued)*

TO WHAT EXTENT DO YOU AGREE OR DISAGREE THAT...	STRONGLY AGREE	AGREE	NEUTRAL	DISAGREE	STRONGLY DISAGREE
10. I sometimes boast about my financial wealth or how much money I make.	5	4	3	2	1
11. I keep track of my investments and financial wealth.	5	4	3	2	1
12. I usually say "I can't afford it," even when I can afford something.	5	4	3	2	1

Sources: Adapted from J.A. Roberts and C.J. Sepulveda, "Demographics and Money Attitudes: A Test of Yamauchi and Templer's (1982) Money Attitude Scale in Mexico," *Personality and Individual Differences* 27 (July 1999), pp. 19–35; K. Yamauchi and D. Templer, "The Development of a Money Attitudes Scale," *Journal of Personality Assessment* 46 (1982), pp. 522–28.

 After reading this chapter go to www.mhhe.com/mcshane6e for more in-depth information and interactivities that correspond to the chapter.

Decision Making and Creativity

Learning Objectives

After reading this chapter, you should be able to:

LO1 Describe the rational choice paradigm.

LO2 Explain why people differ from the rational choice paradigm when identifying problems/opportunities, evaluating/choosing alternatives, and evaluating decision outcomes.

LO3 Discuss the roles of emotions and intuition in decision making.

LO4 Describe employee characteristics, workplace conditions, and specific activities that support creativity.

LO5 Describe the benefits of employee involvement and identify four contingencies that affect the optimal level of employee involvement.

managers to be leaders," says Sergio Marchionne. In reality, the CEO of Fiat S.p.A. and Chrysler Group LLC makes more critical decisions in a week than most of us would make in a year. He was one of four people who negotiated the final proposal for Fiat to acquire a controlling share of Chrysler. He sped up decision making by getting Fiat and Chrysler teams to work intensively on new projects rather than with other organizations. Marchionne is also a role model of business acumen. He currently leads three businesses (the third is Fiat's truck division) and carries three cell phones with him to make decisions for each of these organizations.

In "pushing managers to be leaders," Marchionne refers to developing their capacity to become better decision makers. At multiday weekend meetings, junior managers present their business plans to Marchionne and his 23 direct reports, who then vote on them using majority rule. Furthermore, he pushes decision making further down the hierarchy, such as having Fiat and Chrysler teams work together to develop and launch new vehicles in record time.

Marchionne has brought in several people to reinforce quick and creative decision making. One standout example is Olivier François, head of the Chrysler brand, as well as chief marketing officer of both Chrysler and Fiat. "Meetings [led by François] tend to run fast," notes one advertising executive. Another remarks that working with François is "like working with a creative director on the client side." To illustrate: At a time when the perceived quality of American cars was far below that of imports, François spearheaded Chrysler's risky "Imported From Detroit" brand revival, including an expensive two-minute Superbowl commercial featuring music by Eminem.

Reinvigorating creative thinking at Chrysler is part of Sergio Marchionne's strategy to revive Chrysler. "The creativity at Chrysler had been pushed very far underground [by its previous owners]," observes one auto industry expert. "Now Marchionne is bringing it out and he will put his mark on it." But Marchionne recognizes the challenges of reinvigorating creative decision making at Chrysler. "Any attempt to dominate (one culture over another) is going to stifle the creative element of that organization," says Marchionne, referring to relations between Fiat and Chrysler.[1]

Fiat and Chrysler CEO Sergio Marchionne encourages better decision making, involvement, and creativity to revitalize Chrysler Corp.

Decision making is a vital function of an organization's health, rather like breathing is to a human being. Indeed, turnaround experts such as Sergio Marchionne sometimes see themselves as physicians who resuscitate organizations by encouraging and teaching employees at all levels to make decisions more quickly and effectively. All businesses, governments, and not-for-profit agencies depend on employees to foresee and correctly identify problems, to survey alternatives and pick the best one based on a variety of stakeholder interests, and to execute those decisions effectively.

Decision making is the process of making choices among alternatives with the intention of moving toward some desired state of affairs.[2] The decision-making process can be viewed from three paradigms, and this chapter investigates all three of them. The chapter begins by outlining the rational choice paradigm of decision making. Next, the limitations of this paradigm are discussed, including the human limitation of rational choice. We also examine the emerging paradigm that decisions consist of a complex interaction of logic and emotion. The latter part of this chapter focuses on two activities that are found in most decisions: creativity and employee involvement. We present these topics separately rather than within any stage of decision making, because they deserve more detailed inspection and, in the case of creativity, because it occurs throughout the decision-making process.

Rational Choice Paradigm of Decision Making

LO1

How should people make decisions in organizations? Most business leaders would likely answer this question by saying that effective decision making involves identifying, selecting, and applying the best possible alternative. In other words, the best decisions use pure logic and all available information to choose the alternative with the highest value—such as highest expected profitability, customer satisfaction, employee well-being, or some combination of these outcomes. These decisions sometimes involve complex calculations of data to produce a formula that points to the best choice.

In its extreme form, this calculative view of decision making represents the **rational choice paradigm,** which has dominated decision-making philosophy in Western societies for most of written history.[3] It was established 2,500 years ago when Plato and his contemporaries in ancient Greece raised logical debate and reasoning to a fine art. A few centuries later, Greek and Roman Stoics insisted that one should always "follow where reason leads" rather than fall victim to passion and emotions. About 400 years ago, Descartes and other European philosophers emphasized that the ability to make logical decisions is one of the most important accomplishments of human beings.

In the 1700s, Scottish philosophers proposed that the best choice is the one that offers the "greatest good for the greatest number." This eventually evolved into the ethical principle of utilitarianism (described in Chapter 2), as well as maximization, which is at the heart of contemporary economics, as well as several organizational behavior theories (e.g., expectancy theory of motivation described in Chapter 5). By the 1900s, social scientists and mathematicians had developed elegant rational choice models and formulae that are now embedded in operations research, economics, and other decision sciences.

The ultimate principle of the rational choice paradigm is to choose the alternative with the highest **subjective expected utility.**[4] Subjective expected utility is the probability (expectancy) of satisfaction (utility) for each alternative. Rational choice assumes that decision makers naturally select the alternative that offers the greatest level of happiness (i.e., maximization), such as the highest returns for stockholders and highest satisfaction for customers, employees, government, and other stakeholders. The maximum subjective expected utility depends on the value (utility) of outcomes resulting from that choice and the probability of those outcomes occurring.

To understand subjective expected utility in practice, let's briefly look at decision making in the hiring process. An organization typically wants to hire the best people—those who will provide the greatest value. This choice involves determining what the company values in its employees, such as skills and knowledge, capacity to learn, flexibility, and social skills.

EXHIBIT 7.1

Rational Choice Decision Making Process

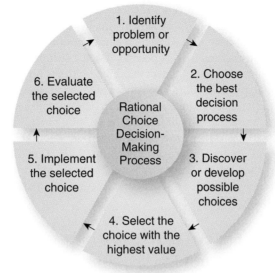

connect

To assist your learning and test your knowledge about the decision making process and its human limitations, go to **www.mcgrawhillconnect.com**, which has activities and test questions on this topic.

These features represent the "utility" or value employees bring to the organization. Next, the selection process gathers information about the probability that each applicant will provide each of these desired characteristics. According to the rational choice paradigm, the company chooses applicants with the highest probability of having each of the desired characteristics. In other words, it wants to choose applicants with the highest subjective expected utility. The key point from this example is that all decisions rely to some degree on (a) the expected value of the outcomes (utility) and (b) the probability of those good or bad outcomes occurring (expectancy).

RATIONAL CHOICE DECISION-MAKING PROCESS

Along with the principle of making decisions based on subjective expected utility, the rational choice paradigm assumes that decision makers follow the systematic process illustrated in Exhibit 7.1.[5] The first step is to identify the problem or recognize an opportunity. A *problem* is a deviation between the current and the desired situation—the gap between "what is" and "what ought to be." This deviation is a symptom of more fundamental causes that need to be corrected.[6] The "ought to be" in problem identification represents goals, and these goals later help evaluate the selected choice. An *opportunity* is a deviation between current expectations and a potentially better situation that was not previously expected. In other words, decision makers realize that some decisions may produce results beyond current goals or expectations.

The second step involves choosing the best decision process. This step is really a meta-decision—deciding how to decide—because it refers to choosing among the different approaches and processes to make the decision.[7] One meta-decision is whether to solve the problem alone or involve others in the process. Later in this chapter, we'll examine the contingencies of employee involvement in the decision. Another meta-decision is whether to assume the decision is programmed or nonprogrammed. *Programmed decisions* follow standard operating procedures; they have been resolved in the past, so the optimal solution has already been identified and documented. In contrast, *nonprogrammed decisions* require all steps in the decision model because the problems are new, complex, or ill-defined.

---

decision making
The conscious process of making choices among alternatives with the intention of moving toward some desired state of affairs.

rational choice paradigm
The view in decision making that people should—and typically do—use logic and all available information to choose the alternative with the highest value.

subjective expected utility
The probability (expectation) of satisfaction (utility) resulting from choosing a specific alternative in a decision.

The third step in the rational choice decision process is to identify and/or develop a list of possible choices. This usually begins by searching for ready-made solutions, such as practices that have worked well on similar problems. If an acceptable solution cannot be found, then decision makers need to design a custom-made solution or modify an existing one. The fourth step is to select the choice with the highest subjective expected utility. This calls for all possible information about all possible alternatives and their outcomes, but the rational choice paradigm assumes it can be accomplished with ease.

The fifth step in the rational choice decision process is to implement the selected alternative. Rational choice experts have little to say about this step because they assume implementation occurs without any problems. This is followed by the sixth step, evaluating whether the gap has narrowed between "what is" and "what ought to be." Ideally, this information should come from systematic benchmarks so that relevant feedback is objective and easily observed.

PROBLEMS WITH THE RATIONAL CHOICE PARADIGM

The rational choice paradigm seems so logical, yet it is impossible to apply in reality. One reason is that the model assumes people are efficient and logical information-processing machines. In reality, people have difficulty recognizing problems; they cannot (or will not) simultaneously process the huge volume of information needed to identify the best solution; and they have difficulty recognizing when their choices have failed. The second reason the rational model doesn't fit reality is that it focuses on logical thinking and completely ignores the fact that emotions also influence—perhaps even dominate—the decision-making process. As we shall discover in this chapter, emotions both support and interfere with our quest to make better decisions.[8] With these points in mind, let's look again at each step in the rational choice decision-making process, but with more detail about what really happens.

Identifying Problems and Opportunities

LO2, LO3

When Albert Einstein was asked how he would save the world in one hour, he replied that the first 55 minutes should be spent defining the problem and the last 5 minutes solving it.[9] Einstein's point is that problem identification is not just the first step in decision making; it is arguably the most important step. But problems and opportunities are not clearly labeled objects that magically appear on our desks or computer screens. Instead, they are conclusions that we form from ambiguous and conflicting information.[10]

PROBLEMS WITH PROBLEM IDENTIFICATION

The problem identification stage is itself filled with problems. Below are five of the most widely recognized concerns.[11]

Stakeholder Framing   Employees, suppliers, customers, and other stakeholders have vested interests when bringing good or bad news to corporate decision makers. Whether deliberately or unwittingly, stakeholders filter information to amplify or suppress the seriousness of the situation, which highlights or hides specific problems and opportunities. Employees point to external factors rather than their own faults as the cause of production delays. Suppliers warn that problems will occur (or opportunities be lost) if the decision maker does not buy their product or service. Stakeholder framing sometimes occurs by emphasizing or withholding information. Occasionally, stakeholders offer a concise statement of the problem in the hope the decision maker will accept their verdict without further analysis.

Decision makers easily fall prey to these constructed realities because they have a need to simplify the overwhelming volume of complex and often ambiguous information in the external environment. Consequently, as one popular management theory emphasizes, organizational

connections 7.1

Famous Missed Opportunities

Mental models create road maps that guide our decisions. Unfortunately, these maps also potentially block our ability to see emerging problems and opportunities. Here are a few famous examples:

- Even though *Harry Potter* books were becoming the world's best-sellers, Hollywood filmmakers were reluctant to produce film versions unless the Hogwarts School of Witchcraft was set in the United States or, at least, that Harry was an American at the British academy. Some filmmakers believed that to have any degree of success, the film needed most characters to be Americans. Fortunately, after considerable persuasion, Hollywood decision makers reluctantly agreed to keep the location and characters all British.[13]

- One of the most famous commercials in history, the Apple Macintosh "1984" ad, almost never got aired because the computer maker's external board members thought it was the worst commercial they had ever seen. They complained that the commercial mentioned the product and company only in the last few seconds. The company asked the creative agency that produced the commercials to sell the two Superbowl time slots where they would have been shown, but the agency's CEO claimed that he could not find a buyer for the 60-second slot. The single 60-second ad shown during the Superbowl became one of the top news stories over the following week and has since been rated as the best commercial in history. Apple's board members subsequently apologized for their misjudgment of the "1984" commercial and applauded the Macintosh team for a successful launch.[14]

- Graphical user interfaces, mice, windows, pull-down menus, laser printing, distributed computing, and Ethernet technologies weren't invented by Apple, Microsoft, or IBM. These essential elements of contemporary personal computing originated in the 1970s from researchers at Xerox PARC. Unfortunately, Xerox executives were focused on their photocopier business and didn't recognize the value of

Due to their preconceived mental models, Hollywood filmmakers believed the *Harry Potter* films would fail if they emphasized the British culture apparent in the books.

the Xerox PARC inventions, many of which never got patented. The lost value of Xerox PARC's discoveries is much larger than the entire photocopier industry today.[15]

decisions and actions are influenced mainly by what attracts management's attention, rather than by what is truly important.[12] This attention process is subject to a variety of cognitive biases, such as the decision maker's perceptual process, specific circumstances, and (as mentioned) the ways that stakeholders shape or filter incoming information.

Mental Models Even if stakeholders don't frame information, decision makers inherently create their own framing through preconceived mental models. Mental models are visual or relational images of the external world; they fill in information that we don't immediately see, which helps us understand and navigate in our surrounding environment (see Chapter 3). Many mental images are also prototypes—they represent models of how things should be. Unfortunately, these mental models also blind us from seeing unique problems or opportunities because they produce a negative evaluation of things that are dissimilar to the mental model. If an idea doesn't fit the existing mental model of how things should work, then it is quickly dismissed as unworkable or undesirable. Examples of missed opportunities and mistaken problems dot the corporate landscape, as Connections 7.1 illustrates.

Decisive Leadership   According to various studies, employees believe that decisiveness is a characteristic of effective leaders.[16] Being decisive includes quickly forming an opinion of whether an event signals a problem or opportunity. Consequently, eager to look effective, many leaders quickly announce problems or opportunities before having a chance to logically assess the situation. The result, according to research, is more often a poorer decision than would result if more time had been devoted to identifying the problem and evaluating the alternatives.

Solution-Focused Problems   Decision makers tend to define problems as veiled solutions.[17] For instance, someone might say: "The problem is that we need more control over our suppliers." This statement doesn't describe the problem; it is really a slightly rephrased presentation of a solution to an ill-defined problem. Decision makers engage in solution-focused problem identification because it provides comforting closure to the otherwise ambiguous and uncertain nature of problems. People with a strong need for cognitive closure (those who feel uncomfortable with ambiguity) are particularly prone to solution-focused problems. Some decision makers take this solution focus a step further by seeing all problems as solutions that have worked well for them in the past, even though they were applied under different circumstances. As Abraham Maslow once quipped, "When the only tool you have is a hammer, all problems begin to resemble nails."[18] Again, the familiarity of past solutions makes the current problem less ambiguous or uncertain.

Perceptual Defense   People sometimes block out bad news as a coping mechanism. Their brain refuses to see information that threatens their self-concept. This phenomenon is not true for everyone. Some people inherently overlook negative information, whereas others are more aware of it. Recent studies also report that people are more likely to disregard danger signals when they have limited control over the situation.[19]

For example, an investigation of the space shuttle *Columbia* disaster in 2003 revealed that NASA managers were in denial that the shuttle and its seven crew members were in trouble. NASA management almost immediately rejected a proposal by a team of engineers to have military satellites take photos of Columbia's exterior to determine if any damage was visible. Managers also criticized tests suggesting that damage could have occurred, yet quickly accepted a faulty test indicating that the shuttle was in trouble. In one meeting, *Columbia*'s lead flight director candidly admitted: "I don't think there is much we can do, so you know it's not really a factor during the flight because there isn't much we can do about it."[20]

IDENTIFYING PROBLEMS AND OPPORTUNITIES MORE EFFECTIVELY

Recognizing problems and opportunities will always be a challenge, but one way to improve the process is by becoming aware of the five problem identification biases described above. For example, by recognizing that mental models restrict a person's perspective of the world, decision makers are more motivated to consider other perspectives of reality. Along with increasing their awareness of problem identification flaws, leaders require considerable willpower to resist the temptation of looking decisive when a more thoughtful examination of the situation should occur.

A third way to improve problem identification is for leaders to create a norm of "divine discontent." They are never satisfied with the status quo, and this aversion to complacency creates a mindset that more actively searches for problems and opportunities.[21] Finally, employees can minimize problem identification errors by discussing the situation with colleagues. It is much easier to discover blind spots in problem identification when listening to how others perceive the situation. Opportunities also become apparent when outsiders explore this information from their different mental models.

bounded rationality
The view that people are bounded in their decision-making capabilities, including access to limited information, limited information processing, and tendency toward satisficing rather than maximizing when making choices.

Searching for, Evaluating, and Choosing Alternatives

According to the rational choice paradigm of decision making, people rely on logic to evaluate and choose alternatives. This paradigm assumes that decision makers have well-articulated and agreed-on organizational goals, efficiently and simultaneously process facts about all alternatives and the consequences of those alternatives, and choose the alternative with the highest payoff.

Nobel Prize–winning organizational scholar Herbert Simon questioned these assumptions a half century ago. He argued that people engage in **bounded rationality** because they process limited and imperfect information and rarely select the best choice.[22] Simon and other OB experts demonstrated how people evaluate and choose alternatives differently from the rational choice paradigm in several ways, as illustrated in Exhibit 7.2. These differences are so significant that many economists are now shifting from rational choice to bounded rationality assumptions in their theories. Let's look at these differences in terms of goals, information processing, and maximization.

PROBLEMS WITH GOALS

The rational choice paradigm assumes that organizational goals are clear and agreed on. In fact, these conditions are necessary to identify "what ought to be" and therefore provide a standard against which each alternative is evaluated. Unfortunately, organizational goals are often ambiguous or in conflict with one another.

EXHIBIT 7.2   Rational Choice Assumptions versus Organizational Behavior Findings about Choosing Alternatives

Rational Choice Paradigm Assumptions	Observations from Organizational Behavior
Goals are clear, compatible, and agreed upon	Goals are ambiguous, in conflict, and lack agreement
Decision makers can calculate all alternatives and their outcomes	Decision makers have limited information-processing abilities
Decision makers evaluate all alternatives simultaneously	Decision makers evaluate alternatives sequentially
Decision makers use absolute standards to evaluate alternatives	Decision makers evaluate alternatives against an implicit favorite
Decision makers use factual information to choose alternatives	Decision makers use perceptually distorted information
Decision makers choose the alternative with the highest payoff	Decision makers choose the alternative that is good enough (satisficing)

PROBLEMS WITH INFORMATION PROCESSING

The rational choice paradigm also makes several assumptions about the human capacity to process information. It assumes that decision makers can process information about all alternatives and their consequences, whereas this is not possible in reality. Instead, people evaluate only a few alternatives and only some of the main outcomes of those alternatives.[23] For example, there may be dozens of computer brands to choose from and dozens of features to consider, yet people typically evaluate only a few brands and a few features.

A related problem is that decision makers typically evaluate alternatives sequentially rather than all at the same time. This sequential evaluation occurs partly because all alternatives are not usually available to the decision maker at the same time.[24] Consequently, as a new alternative comes along, it is immediately compared with an **implicit favorite**—an alternative that the decision maker prefers and that is used as a comparison with other choices. When choosing a new computer system, for example, people typically have an implicit favorite brand or model in their heads that they use to compare with the others. This sequential process of comparing alternatives with an implicit favorite occurs even when decision makers aren't consciously aware that they are doing this.[25]

Although the implicit favorite comparison process seems to be hardwired in human decision making (i.e., we naturally compare things), it often undermines effective decision making because people distort information to favor their implicit favorite over the alternative choices. They tend to ignore problems with the implicit favorite and advantages of the alternative. Decision makers also overweight factors on which the implicit favorite is better and underweight areas in which the alternative is superior.[26]

Biased Decision Heuristics

Subjective expected utility is the cornerstone of rational choice decision making, yet psychologists Amos Tversky and Daniel Kahneman discovered that human beings have built-in *decision heuristics* that automatically distort either the probability of outcomes or the value of those outcomes. Three of the most widely studied heuristic biases are anchoring and adjustment, availability, and representativeness:[27]

- **Anchoring and adjustment heuristic.** This heuristic states that we are influenced by an initial anchor point and do not sufficiently move away from that point as new information is provided.[28] The anchor point might be an initial offer price, initial opinion of someone, or initial estimated probability that something will occur. This bias affects the value we assign to choices and their outcomes. For example, suppose you ask someone whether the population of Chile is above or below 50 million; then you ask that person to estimate Chile's population. Next, you ask a second person whether the population of Chile is above or below 10 million; then you ask him or her to estimate that country's actual population. If these two people don't actually know Chile's population, chances are that the first person will give a much higher population estimate than will the second person. The initial anchor point (50 million vs. 10 million) biases their estimate.

- **Availability heuristic.** The availability heuristic is the tendency to estimate the probability of something occurring by how easily we can recall those events. The problem is that how easily we recall something is due to more than just its frequency (probability).[29] For instance, we easily remember emotional events (such as earthquakes and shark attacks), so we overestimate how often these traumatic events occur. We also have an easier time recalling recent events. If the media report several incidents of air pollution, we likely give more pessimistic estimates of air quality generally than if there have been no recent reports.

- **Representativeness heuristic.** This heuristic states that we pay more attention to whether something resembles (is representative of) something else than on more precise statistics about its probability.[30] Suppose that one-fifth of the students in your class are in engineering and the others are business majors. Statistically, there

implicit favorite
A preferred alternative that the decision maker uses repeatedly as a comparison with other choices.

is a 20 percent chance that any individual in that class is an engineering student. Yet, if one student looks and acts like a stereotype of an engineer, we tend to believe the person is an engineer, even though there is much stronger and more reliable statistical evidence that he or she is a business major. Another form of the representativeness heuristic, known as the *clustering illusion,* is the tendency to see patterns from a small sample of events when those events are, in fact, random. For example, most players and coaches believe that players are more likely to have a successful shot on the net when their previous two or three shots have been successful. The representativeness heuristic is at work here because players and coaches believe these sequences are causally connected (representative) when, in reality, they are more likely random events.

PROBLEMS WITH MAXIMIZATION

One of the main assumptions of the rational choice paradigm is that people want to—and are able to—choose the alternative with the highest payoff (i.e., the highest "utility" in subjective expected utility). Yet rather than aiming for maximization, people engage in **satisficing**—they choose an alternative that is satisfactory or "good enough."[31] People satisfice when they select the first alternative that exceeds a standard of acceptance for their needs and preferences. Satisficing partly occurs because alternatives present themselves over time, not all at once. Consider the process of hiring new employees. It is impossible to choose the best possible job candidate because people apply over a period of time, and the best candidate might not apply until next month, after earlier candidates have found other jobs. Consequently, as we mentioned earlier, decision makers rely on sequential evaluation of new alternatives against an implicit favorite. This necessarily calls for a satisficing decision rule: Choose the first alternative that is "good enough."

A second reason people engage in satisficing rather than maximization is that they lack the capacity and motivation to process the huge volume of information required to identify the best choice. Studies report that people like to have choices, but making decisions when there are many alternatives can be cognitively and emotionally draining. Consequently, when exposed to many alternatives, decision makers become cognitive misers by engaging in satisficing.[32] They also respond to many choices by discarding many of them using easily identifiable factors (i.e., color, size) and by evaluating alternatives using only a handful of criteria.

When presented with a large number of choices, people often choose a decision strategy that is even less cognitively challenging than satisficing; they don't make any decision at all! One study reported that many employees put off registering for the company's pension plan when they face dozens of investment options, even though signing up would give them tax benefits, company contributions to that plan, and long-term financial security. The company pension plan registration rate increases dramatically when employees are given only two or three initial investment options, such as a growth fund, balanced fund, and capital stable investment. The dozens of other investment choices are then presented after the employee has signed up.[33] Four decades ago, futurist Alvin Toffler warned about the increasing

---

anchoring and adjustment heuristic
A natural tendency for people to be influenced by an initial anchor point such that they do not sufficiently move away from that point as new information is provided.

availability heuristic
A natural tendency to assign higher probabilities to objects or events that are easier to recall from memory, even though ease of recall is also affected by nonprobability factors (e.g., emotional response, recent events).

representativeness heuristic
A natural tendency to evaluate probabilities of events or objects by the degree to which they resemble (are representative of) other events or objects rather than on objective probability information.

satisficing
Selecting an alternative that is satisfactory or "good enough," rather than the alternative with the highest value (maximization).

People avoid making choices in decisions that have too many alternatives. In one study, grocery store customers saw one of two jam-tasting booths. Thirty percent of consumers who visited the booth displaying 6 types of jam purchased one of those products. In contrast, only 3 percent of customers who saw the booth displaying 24 types of jam made a purchase. The larger number of choices discouraged them from making any decision. Other studies of decisions about chocolates, term essays, and pension plan investment options have revealed similar results.[34]

risk of choice overload: "People of the future may suffer not from an absence of choice, but from a paralyzing surfeit of it. They may turn out to be victims of that peculiarly super-industrial dilemma: overchoice."[35]

EVALUATING OPPORTUNITIES

Opportunities are just as important as problems, but what happens when an opportunity is "discovered" is quite different from the process of problem solving. Research suggests that decision makers do not evaluate several alternatives when they find an opportunity; after all, the opportunity *is* the solution, so why look for others?! An opportunity is usually experienced as an exciting and rare revelation, so decision makers tend to have an emotional attachment to the opportunity. Unfortunately, this emotional preference motivates decision makers to apply the opportunity and short-circuit any detailed evaluation of it.[36]

EMOTIONS AND MAKING CHOICES

Herbert Simon and many other experts have found plenty of evidence that people do not evaluate alternatives nearly as well as is assumed by the rational choice paradigm. However, they neglected to mention another glaring weakness with rational choice: It completely ignores the effect of emotions in human decision making. Just as both the rational and emotional brain centers alert us to problems, they also influence our choice of alternatives.[37] Emotions affect the evaluation of alternatives in three ways.

Emotions Form Early Preferences   The emotional marker process described in previous chapters (Chapters 3–5) determines our preferences for each alternative before we consciously think about those alternatives. Our brains very quickly attach specific emotions to information about each alternative, and our preferred alternative is strongly influenced by those initial emotional markers.[38] Of course, logical analysis also influences which alternative we choose, but it requires strong logical evidence to change our initial preferences (initial emotional markers). Yet even logical analysis depends on emotions to sway our decision. Specifically, neuroscientific evidence says that information produced from logical analysis is tagged with emotional markers that then motivate us to choose or avoid a particular alternative. Ultimately, emotions, not rational logic, energize us to make the preferred choice. In fact, people with damaged emotional brain centers have difficulty making choices.

Emotions Change the Decision Evaluation Process   A considerable body of literature indicates that moods and specific emotions influence the *process* of evaluating alternatives.[39] For instance, we pay more attention to details when in a negative mood, possibly because a negative mood signals that there is something wrong that requires attention. When in a positive mood, on the other hand, we pay less attention to details and rely on a more programmed decision routine. This phenomenon explains why executive teams in successful companies are often less vigilant about competitors and other environmental threats.[40] Research also suggests that decision makers rely on stereotypes and other shortcuts to speed up the choice process when they experience anger. Anger also makes them more optimistic about the success of risky alternatives, whereas the emotion of fear tends to make them less optimistic. Overall, emotions shape *how* we evaluate information, not just which choice we select.

Emotions Serve as Information When We Evaluate Alternatives   The third way that emotions influence the evaluation of alternatives is through a process called "emotions as information." Marketing experts have found that we listen in on our emotions to gain guidance when making choices.[41] This process is similar to having a temporary improvement in emotional intelligence. Most emotional experiences remain below the level of conscious awareness, but people actively try to be more sensitive to these subtle emotions when making a decision.

When buying a new car, for example, you not only logically evaluate each vehicle's features; you also try to gauge your emotions when visualizing what it would be like to own each of the cars on your list of choices. Even if you have solid information about the quality of each vehicle on key features (purchase price, fuel efficiency, maintenance costs, resale value, etc.), you are swayed by your emotional reaction and actively try to sense that emotional response when thinking about it. Some people pay more attention to these gut feelings, and personality tests such as the Myers-Briggs Type Indicator (see Chapter 2) identify individuals who listen in on their emotions more than others.[42] But all of us use our emotions as information to some degree. This phenomenon ties directly into our next topic, intuition.

INTUITION AND MAKING CHOICES

Greg McDonald felt uneasy about a suspicious-looking crack in the rock face, so the veteran miner warned a coworker to stay away from the area. "There was no indication there was anything wrong—just a little crack," McDonald recalled. A few minutes later, the ceiling in the mine shaft 3,000 feet underground caved in. Fortunately, the coworker had heeded McDonald's advice. "If he had been there, he would be dead," McDonald said in an interview following a near-sleepless night after the incident.[43]

The gut instinct that helped Greg McDonald save his coworker's life is known as **intuition**—the ability to know when a problem or opportunity exists and to select the best course of action without conscious reasoning.[44] Intuition is both an emotional experience and a rapid nonconscious analytic process. As mentioned in the previous section, the gut feelings we experience are emotional signals that have enough intensity to make us consciously aware of them. These signals warn us of impending danger, such as a dangerous mine wall, or motivate us to take advantage of an opportunity. Some intuition also directs us to preferred choices relative to other alternatives in the situation.

All gut feelings are emotional signals, but not all emotional signals are intuition. The key distinction is that intuition involves rapidly comparing our observations with deeply held patterns learned through experience.[45] These templates represent tacit knowledge that has been implicitly acquired over time. They are mental models that help us understand whether the current situation is good or bad, depending on how well that situation fits our mental model. When a template fits or doesn't fit the current situation, emotions are produced that motivate us to act. Greg McDonald's years of experience produced mental templates of unsafe rock faces that matched what he saw on that fateful day. Studies have also found that chess masters receive emotional signals when they sense an opportunity through quick observation of a chessboard. When given the opportunity to think about the situation, chess masters can explain why they see a favorable move on the chessboard. However, their intuition signals the opportunity long before this rational analysis takes place.

As mentioned, some emotional signals are not intuition. As a result, some experts warn that we should not trust our gut feelings. The problem is that emotional responses are not always based on well-grounded mental models. Instead, they occur when we compare the current situation to more remote templates, which may or may not be relevant. A new employee might feel confident about relations with a supplier, whereas an experienced employee senses potential problems. The difference is that the new employee relies on templates from other experiences or industries that might not work well in this situation. Thus, whether the emotions we experience in a situation represent intuition or not depends largely on our level of experience in that situation.

So far, we have described intuition as an emotional experience (gut feeling) and a process in which we compare the current situation with well-established templates of the mind. Intuition also relies on *action scripts*—programmed decision routines that speed up our responses to pattern matches or mismatches.[46] Action scripts effectively shorten the decision-making process by jumping from problem identification to selection of a solution. In other words, action scripting is a form of programmed decision making. Action scripts are generic, so we need to consciously adapt them to the specific situation.

MAKING CHOICES MORE EFFECTIVELY

It is very difficult to get around the human limitations of making choices, but a few strategies help minimize these concerns. One important discovery is that decisions tend to have a higher failure rate when leaders are decisive rather than contemplative about the available options. Of course, decisions can also be ineffective when leaders take too long to make a choice, but research indicates that a lack of logical evaluation of alternatives is a greater concern. By systematically assessing alternatives against relevant factors, decision makers minimize the implicit favorite and satisficing problems that occur when they rely on general subjective judgments. This recommendation does not suggest that we ignore intuition; rather, it suggests that we use it in combination with careful analysis of relevant information.[47]

A second piece of advice is to remember that decisions are influenced by both rational and emotional processes. With this point in mind, some decision makers deliberately revisit important issues later so that they look at the information in different moods and have allowed their initial emotions to subside. For example, if you sense that your team is feeling somewhat too self-confident when making an important competitive decision, you might decide to have the team members revisit the decision a few days later when they are thinking

Scenario planning helps decision makers figure out the best solutions to crises before they occur. Dreyer Kompetense, a Norwegian company, has created "What If," a board game that applies scenario planning to shipping, IT security, and other industries. Participants first review several dozen scenarios and choose an event with the greatest risk. For example, one scenario in the shipping exercise is a situation where a fire knocks out all engines, resulting in a collision with another vessel. The team then identifies actions to prepare their company or ship for these high-risk scenarios.[49]

more critically. Another strategy is **scenario planning,** which is a disciplined method for imagining possible futures. It typically involves thinking about what would happen if a significant environmental condition changed and what the organization should do to anticipate and react to such an outcome.[48] Scenario planning is a useful vehicle for choosing the best solutions to possible scenarios long before they occur. Why? Because alternative courses of action are evaluated without the pressure and emotions that occur during real emergencies.

Implementing Decisions

Implementing decisions is often skipped over in writing about the decision-making process. Yet leading business writers emphasize that execution—translating decisions into action—is one of the most important and challenging tasks of leaders. "When assessing candidates, the first thing I looked for was energy and enthusiasm for execution," says Larry Bossidy, the former CEO of Honeywell and Allied Signal.[50]

Evaluating Decision Outcomes

Contrary to the rational choice paradigm, decision makers aren't completely honest with themselves when evaluating the effectiveness of their decisions. One problem is *confirmation bias* (also known as *post-decisional justification* in the context of decision evaluation), which is "unwitting selectivity in the acquisition and use of evidence."[51] When evaluating decisions, people with a confirmation bias ignore or downplay the negative outcomes of the selected alternative and overemphasize its positive outcomes. Confirmation bias gives people an excessively optimistic evaluation of their decisions, but only until they receive very clear and undeniable information to the contrary. Unfortunately, it also inflates the decision maker's initial evaluation of the decision, so reality often comes as a painful shock when objective feedback is finally received.

intuition
The ability to know when a problem or opportunity exists and to select the best course of action without conscious reasoning.

scenario planning
A systematic process of thinking about alternative futures and what the organization should do to anticipate and react to those environments.

ESCALATION OF COMMITMENT

Another reason decision makers don't evaluate their decisions very well is due to **escalation of commitment**—the tendency to repeat an apparently bad decision or allocate more resources to a failing course of action.[52] For example, executives at five health boards across Ireland decided to develop a common payroll system, called PPARS (payroll, payment, and related systems), which would cost (in U.S. dollars) $12 million and be completed in three years. Four years later, costs had doubled even though the system was still far from completion. A few years later, a major consulting firm concluded the PPARS project should continue, but the government needed to invest another $120 million. A dozen years after the project began, PPARS was officially canceled with a sunk cost exceeding $250 million.[53]

Causes of Escalating Commitment   Why are decision makers led deeper and deeper into failing projects? Several explanations have been identified and discussed over the years, but the four main influences are self-justification, prospect theory effect, perceptual blinders, and closing costs.

- *Self-justification.* Decision makers typically want to appear rational and effective. One such impression management tactic is to demonstrate the importance of a decision by continuing to invest in it, whereas pulling the plug symbolizes the project's failure and the decision maker's incompetence. This self-justification effect is particularly evident when decision makers are personally identified with the project, have staked their reputations to some extent on the project's success, and have low self-esteem.[54]

- *Prospect theory effect.* Escalation of commitment is partly fueled by the **prospect theory effect.** This is the tendency to experience stronger negative emotions when losing something of value than the positive emotions experienced when gaining something of equal value. This prospect theory effect motivates us to avoid losses, which typically occurs by taking the risk of investing more in that losing project. Stopping a project is a certain loss, which is more painful to most people than the uncertainty of success associated with continuing to fund the project. Given the choice, decision makers choose the less painful option.[55]

- *Perceptual blinders.* Escalation of commitment sometimes occurs because decision makers do not see the problems soon enough.[56] They nonconsciously screen out or explain away negative information to protect self-esteem. Serious problems initially look like random errors along the trend line to success. Even when decision makers see that something is wrong, the information is sufficiently ambiguous that it can be misinterpreted or justified.

- *Closing costs.* Another disincentive to axing a failing project is the cost of doing so. Terminating a project may have financial penalties and loss of goodwill with partner organizations. Closing costs are particularly important in political situations because closing the project is an acknowledgment that the decision makers made a grave mistake in their previous decisions.

Escalation of commitment is usually framed as poor decision making, but some experts argue that throwing more money into a failing project is sometimes a logical attempt to further understand an ambiguous situation. This strategy is essentially a variation of testing unknown waters. By adding more resources, the decision maker gains new information about the effectiveness of these funds, which provides more feedback about the project's future success. This strategy is particularly common where the project has high closing costs.[57]

EVALUATING DECISION OUTCOMES MORE EFFECTIVELY

One of the most effective ways to minimize escalation of commitment and confirmation bias is to ensure that the people who made the original decision are not the same people who later evaluate that decision. This separation of roles minimizes the self-justification effect because the person responsible for evaluating the decision is not connected to the original decision. However, the second person might continue to escalate the project if he or she empathizes with the decision maker, has a similar mindset, or has similar attributes such as age. A second strategy is to publicly establish a preset level at which the decision is abandoned or reevaluated. This is similar to a stop-loss order in the stock market, whereby the stock is sold if it falls below a certain price. The problem with this solution is that conditions are often so complex that it is difficult to identify an appropriate point to abandon a project.[58]

A third strategy is to find a source of systematic and clear feedback.[59] At some point, even the strongest escalation and confirmation bias effects deflate when the evidence highlights the project's failings. A fourth strategy to improve the decision evaluation process is to involve several people in the evaluation. Coworkers continuously monitor one another and might notice problems sooner than someone working alone on the project.

Creativity

LO4

The entire decision-making process described over the preceding pages depends on **creativity**—the development of original ideas that make a socially recognized contribution.[60] Creativity is at work when imagining opportunities, such as how a company's expertise might be redirected to untapped markets. Creativity is present when developing alternatives, such as figuring out new places to look for existing solutions or working out the design of a custom-made solution. Creativity also helps us choose alternatives because we need to visualize the future in different ways and to figure out how each choice might be useful or a liability in those scenarios. In short, creativity is an essential component of decision making as well as a powerful resource for corporate competitive advantage and individual career development.

The value of creativity in decision making is evident at Google, the Internet search engine company. Google's creative culture includes a natural practice of experimenting with ideas and seeking out different uses of technology. Perhaps most famous is the company's policy of giving engineers 20 percent of their time to develop projects of their choosing. "Almost everything that is interesting which Google does started out as a 20 percent time idea," explains a Google executive. Google News and the photos linked to Google Maps were two projects developed from the 20 percent time rule.[61]

THE CREATIVE PROCESS

How does creativity occur? This question has puzzled experts for hundreds of years and has been the fascination of Einstein, Poincaré, and many other scientists who have reflected on the creative experience that contributed to their own important discoveries. More than a century ago, German physicist Hermann von Helmholtz gave a public talk in which he described the process that led to his many discoveries (energy physics, instruments for examining eyes, and many others). A few decades later, London School of Economics professor Graham Wallas built on Helmholtz's ideas to construct the four-stage model

"It's a new financial world and this bank needs to think outside the box, so, anybody got any ideas...any ideas at all?"

US Banker, 2010. Reprinted with permission of Kevin Pope.

escalation of commitment
The tendency to repeat an apparently bad decision or allocate more resources to a failing course of action.

prospect theory effect
A natural tendency to feel more dissatisfaction from losing a particular amount than satisfaction from gaining an equal amount.

creativity
The development of original ideas that make a socially recognized contribution.

EXHIBIT 7.3   The Creative Process Model

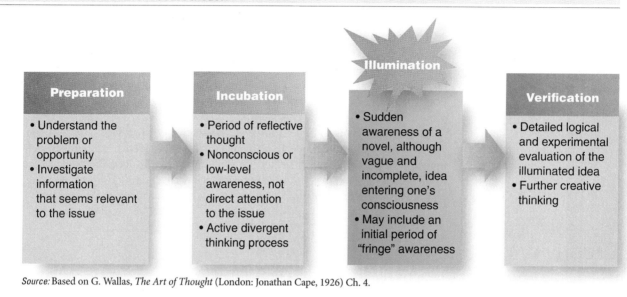

Source: Based on G. Wallas, *The Art of Thought* (London: Jonathan Cape, 1926) Ch. 4.

shown in Exhibit 7.3.[62] Although there are other ways of viewing the creative process, many of them overlap with Wallas's model, which remains the most reputable and influential.

The first stage is *preparation*—the process of investigating the problem or opportunity in many ways. Preparation involves developing a clear understanding of what you are trying to achieve through a novel solution and then actively studying information seemingly related to the topic. It is a process of developing knowledge and possibly skills about the issue or object of attention. The second stage, called *incubation,* is the period of reflective thought. We put the problem aside, but our mind is still working on it in the background.[63] The important condition here is to maintain a low-level awareness by frequently revisiting the problem. Incubation does not mean that you forget about the problem or issue.

Incubation assists **divergent thinking**—reframing the problem in a unique way and generating different approaches to the issue. This contrasts with *convergent thinking*—calculating the conventionally accepted "right answer" to a logical problem. Divergent thinking breaks us away from existing mental models so that we can apply concepts or processes from completely different areas of life. The discovery of Velcro is a case in point. In the 1940s, Swiss engineer Georges de Mestral had just returned home from a walk with his dog through the countryside when he noticed that his clothing and the dog's fur were covered in burrs. While struggling to remove the barbed seeds, de Mestral engaged in divergent thinking by developing the idea that the adhesion used by burrs could be used to attach other things together. It took another dozen years of hard work, but de Mestral eventually perfected the hook-and-loop fastener, which he trademarked as Velcro.[64]

Illumination (also called insight), the third stage of creativity, refers to the experience of suddenly becoming aware of a unique idea.[65] Wallas and others also suggest that this stage begins with a "fringe" awareness before the idea fully enters our consciousness. Illumination is often visually depicted as a lightbulb, but a better image would be a flash of light or perhaps a briefly flickering candle—these bits of inspiration are fleeting and can be quickly lost if not documented. For this reason, many creative people keep a journal or notebook nearby so that they can jot down their ideas before they disappear. Also, flickering ideas don't keep a particular schedule; they might come to you at any time of day or night.

Illumination presents ideas that are usually vague, roughly drawn, and untested. *Verification* therefore provides the essential final stage of creativity, whereby we flesh out the illuminated ideas and subject them to detailed logical evaluation and experimentation. This

EXHIBIT 7.4

Characteristics of Creative People

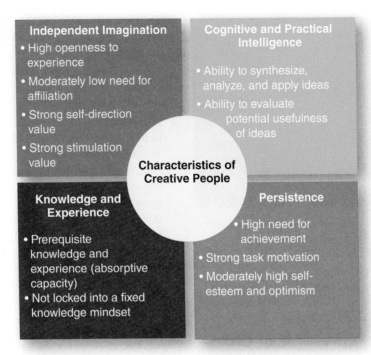

Independent Imagination
- High openness to experience
- Moderately low need for affiliation
- Strong self-direction value
- Strong stimulation value

Cognitive and Practical Intelligence
- Ability to synthesize, analyze, and apply ideas
- Ability to evaluate potential usefulness of ideas

Characteristics of Creative People

Knowledge and Experience
- Prerequisite knowledge and experience (absorptive capacity)
- Not locked into a fixed knowledge mindset

Persistence
- High need for achievement
- Strong task motivation
- Moderately high self-esteem and optimism

stage often calls for further creativity as the ideas evolve into finished products or services. Thus, though verification is labeled the final stage of creativity, it is really the beginning of a long process of creative decision making toward the development of an innovative product or service.

CHARACTERISTICS OF CREATIVE PEOPLE

Everyone is creative, but some people have a higher potential for creativity. Four of the main characteristics that give individuals more creative potential are intelligence, persistence, knowledge and experience, and a cluster of personality traits and values representing independent imagination (see Exhibit 7.4).

- *Cognitive and practical intelligence.* Creative people have above-average intelligence to synthesize information, analyze ideas, and apply their ideas.[66] Like the fictional sleuth Sherlock Holmes, creative people recognize the significance of small bits of information and are able to connect them in ways that few others can imagine. They also have *practical intelligence*—the capacity to evaluate the potential usefulness of their ideas.

- *Persistence.* Creative people have persistence, which is based on a higher need for achievement, a strong motivation from the task itself, and a moderate or high degree of self-esteem. In support of this, one study reported that inventors have higher levels of confidence and optimism than do people in the general population, and these traits motivate inventors to continue working on and investing in a project after receiving diagnostic advice to quit.[67]

- *Knowledge and experience.* Creative people require a foundation of knowledge and experience to discover or acquire new knowledge (the idea of *absorptive capacity* that was discussed in Chapter 1).[68] However, this expertise is a double-edged sword. As people acquire knowledge and experience about a specific topic, their mental models tend to become more rigid. They are less adaptable to new information or rules about that knowledge domain. Some writers suggest that expertise also increases "mindless behavior" because expertise reduces the tendency to question why things happen.[69] To overcome the limitations of expertise, some corporate leaders

connect

Do you have a creative personality? Go to **www.mcgrawhillconnect.com** to assess the extent to which you have a disposition for creative thinking.

divergent thinking
Reframing a problem in a unique way and generating different approaches to the issue.

When it comes to creative thinking, Alex Beim sees the light. The founder and chief creative technologist of Tangible Interaction Design in Vancouver, Canada, designed the digital graffiti walls at a Chanel outlet in New York City and Converse Shoes in Amsterdam, as well as the color-changing illuminated lightweight orbs (called zygotes) at the Vancouver Olympics. "I get ideas all the time for designs I want to create," says Beim, who now employs a team of people. "I love researching the idea, seeing it come to life and watching the happiness it brings to people."[72]

like to hire people from other industries and areas of expertise. For instance, when Geoffrey Ballard, founder of Ballard Power Systems, hired a chemist to develop a better battery, the chemist protested that he didn't know anything about batteries. Ballard replied: "That's fine. I don't want someone who knows batteries. They know what won't work."[70]

- *Independent imagination.* Creative people possess a cluster of personality traits and values that support an independent imagination: high openness to experience, moderately low need for affiliation, and strong values around self-direction and stimulation.[71] Openness to experience is a Big Five personality dimension representing the extent to which a person is imaginative, curious, sensitive, open-minded, and original (see Chapter 2). Creative people have a moderately low need for affiliation, so they are less embarrassed when making mistakes. Self-direction includes the values of creativity and independent thought; stimulation includes the values of excitement and challenge. Together, these values form openness to change—representing the motivation to pursue innovative ways (see Chapter 2).

ORGANIZATIONAL CONDITIONS SUPPORTING CREATIVITY

Intelligence, persistence, expertise, and independent imagination represent a person's creative potential, but the extent to which these characteristics produce more creative output depends on how well the work environment supports the creative process.[73] Several job and workplace characteristics have been identified in the literature, and different combinations of situations can equally support creativity; there isn't one best work environment.[74]

One of the most important conditions that supports creative practice is that the organization has a *learning orientation;* that is, leaders recognize that employees make reasonable mistakes as part of the creative process. "Creativity comes from failure," recently retired Samsung Electronics CEO Yun Jong-yong advised employees. "We should reform our corporate culture to forgive failure if workers did their best."[75] Motivation from the job itself is another important condition for creativity.[76] Employees tend to be more creative when they believe their work benefits the organization and/or larger society (i.e., task significance) and when they have the freedom to pursue novel ideas without bureaucratic delays (i.e., autonomy). Creativity is about changing things, and change is possible only when employees have the authority to experiment. More generally, jobs encourage creativity when they are challenging and aligned with the employee's competencies.

Along with supporting a learning orientation and intrinsically motivating jobs, companies foster creativity through open communication and sufficient resources. They also provide a comfortable degree of job security, which explains why creativity suffers during times of downsizing and corporate restructuring.[77] Some companies also support creativity by designing nontraditional workspaces, such as unique building designs or unconventional office areas.[78] Google is one example. The Internet innovator has funky offices in several countries that include hammocks, gondola- and hive-shaped privacy spaces, slides, and brightly painted walls.

To some degree, creativity also improves with support from leaders and coworkers. One study reported that effective product champions provide enthusiastic support for new ideas. Other studies suggest that coworker support can improve creativity in some situations, whereas competition among coworkers improves creativity in other situations.[79] Similarly, it

Nvidia's high-powered graphics cards and chipsets unleash the creative potential of its customers. But just as much creativity is needed to design these complex pieces of technology. NVidia cofounder and CEO Jen-Hsun Huang believes the Santa Clara, California, company supports this creative process through a learning orientation culture. "It's OK to try, and if it doesn't work, learn from it, adjust and keep failing forward," says Huang. "Mistakes and failures are kind of the negative space around success, right? And if we could take enough shots at it, we're going to figure out what success is going to look like."[80]

isn't clear how much pressure should be exerted on employees to produce creative ideas. Extreme time pressures are well-known creativity inhibitors, but lack of pressure doesn't seem to produce the highest creativity either.

ACTIVITIES THAT ENCOURAGE CREATIVITY

Hiring people with strong creative potential and providing a work environment that supports creativity are two cornerstones of a creative workplace. The third cornerstone consists of various activities that help employees think more creatively. One set of activities involves redefining the problem. Employees might be encouraged to revisit old projects that have been set aside. After a few months of neglect, these projects might be seen in new ways.[81] Another strategy involves asking people unfamiliar with the issue (preferably with different expertise) to explore the problem with you. You would state the objectives and give some facts and then let the other person ask questions to further understand the situation. By verbalizing the problem, listening to questions, and hearing what others think, you are more likely to form new perspectives on the issue.[82]

A second set of creativity activities, known as *associative play,* ranges from art classes to impromptu storytelling and acting. For example, British media giant OMD sends employees to two-day retreats in the countryside, where they play grapefruit croquet, chant like medieval monks, and pretend to be dog collars. "Being creative is a bit like an emotion; we need to be stimulated," explains Harriet Frost, one of OMD's specialists in

Creativity Is Important,
But Not So Valued[83]

32% of American employees say "not really" about whether management places a premium on people who are creative.

41% of U.S. federal government employees agree or strongly agree that creativity and innovation are rewarded in their workplace.

53% of Canadian federal government employees mostly or strongly agree that innovation is valued in their work unit.

60% of chief executive officers identify creativity as the most important leadership quality required over the next five years.

77% of American office workers believe business leaders need to take more risks to create innovation.

78% of American employees believe that creativity is very or extremely important for their job.

Sources: These statistics are from several recent surveys of 251,507 U.S. federal government employees; 169,600 Canadian federal government employees; 1,500 CEOs in several countries surveyed for IBM; 1,461 American employees; and a panel of 501 American office employees surveyed for Microsoft.

building creativity. "The same is true for our imagination and its ability to come up with new ideas. You can't just sit in a room and devise hundreds of ideas."[84] Another associative play activity, called *morphological analysis,* involves listing different dimensions of a system and the elements of each dimension and then looking at each combination. This encourages people to carefully examine combinations that initially seem nonsensical.

A third set of activities that promotes creative thinking falls under the category of *cross-pollination.*[85] Cross-pollination occurs when people from different areas of the organization exchange ideas or when new people are brought into an existing team. Mother, the London-based creative agency, has unusual policies and working conditions that apply this creative process. The company's 100 or so employees perform their daily work around one monster-size table—an 8-foot-wide, reinforced-concrete slab that extends 300 feet like a skateboard ramp around the entire floor. Every three weeks, employees are asked to relocate their laptop, portable telephone, and trolley to another area around the table. Why the musical-chairs exercise? "It encourages cross-pollination of ideas," explains Stef Calcraft, one of Mother's founding partners. "You have people working on the same problem from different perspectives. It makes problem-solving much more organic."[86]

Cross-pollination highlights the fact that creativity rarely occurs alone. Some creative people may be individualistic, but most creative ideas are generated through teams and informal social interaction. "This whole thing about the solitary tortured artist is nonsense I think," says John Collee, the screenwriter who penned such films as *Happy Feet* and *Master and Commander.* "All the great creative people I know have become great precisely because they know how to get along with people and swim around in the communal unconscious."[87] This notion of improving creativity through social interaction leads us to the final section of this chapter: employee involvement in decision making.

Employee Involvement in Decision Making

LO5

Nishith Desai Associates (NDA) isn't your typical law firm. About 60 percent of decisions at the 100-member Mumbai, India–based organization occur through consensus. Another 25 percent are reached through majority vote of the partners, and the remainder are determined by the executive committee or the CEO. The law firm also has representative committees. The compensation committee, for example, consists of staff voted into the position who have three or more years of professional experience. Overall, NDA strives to become a democratic organization by relying on various levels and forms of employee involvement in decision making.[88]

Employee involvement (also called *participative management*) refers to the degree to which employees influence how their work is organized and carried out.[89] Employee involvement has become a natural process in every organization, but the level of involvement varies with the situation. In some organizations, such as NDA, almost everyone has a high degree of involvement in some corporate-wide decisions during a given year, whereas other organizations might give employees only low levels of involvement. The main levels of involvement (from lowest to highest) include:[90]

- *Decide alone.* The decision maker relies on personal knowledge and insight to complete the entire decision process without conferring with anyone else.
- *Receive information from individuals.* The decision maker asks individuals for information. They do not make recommendations and might not even know what the problem is about.
- *Consult with individuals.* The decision maker describes the problem to selected individuals and seeks both their information and recommendations. The final decision is made by the decision maker, who may or may not take the advice of others into account.

Debating Point

SHOULD ORGANIZATIONS PRACTICE DEMOCRACY?

Most organizational experts recommend some degree of employee involvement, but a few go further by proposing that organizations should operate like democracies rather than hierarchical fiefdoms. Organizational democracy consists of the highest form of involvement, whereby employees have real institutionalized control—either directly or through representation—over organizational decisions. In addition, no one in a democratic enterprise holds higher authority except where such power is explicitly granted by the others (such as through employee election of the company's leaders). Democracy also gives all organizational members protection against arbitrary or unjust decisions (such as protection against being fired without cause).[91]

Some readers might think workplace democracy is an extreme way to run an organization, but advocates point out that it is the principle on which many societies have operated for centuries and most others aspire. Democratic governance has been established in several high-profile and successful companies, such as Semco SA and W.L. Gore & Associates, as well as many employee-owned firms and worker cooperatives. Legislation in several countries (particularly in continental Europe) requires companies to give employees control over some organizational decisions through work councils or board membership.[92]

Advocates point out that as a form of participation, workplace democracy can improve the quality of organizational decisions and employee commitment to those decisions. Indeed, democracy inherently advocates shared leadership (where everyone should be a leader in various ways), which is increasingly recommended for improved decision making and organizational effectiveness. Democratic enterprises might also be more flexible and innovative. Rather than obediently follow management's standard operating procedures, employees in democratic organizations have the opportunity—and likely the expectation—to adapt and experiment with new work practices as circumstances change. This form of organization also encourages more organizational learning.[93]

A final argument is that the democratic enterprise is ethically superior to the traditional hierarchical organization.[94] It respects individual rights and dignity, more fully satisfies the standards of ethical conduct, and is more likely than traditional management to adopt the multiple stakeholder approach expected by society. Indeed, some European governments have debated the notion that organizational democracy is a potentially effective way to minimize corporate wrongdoing because it actively monitors top decision makers and continually holds them accountable for their actions.

The democratic enterprise model has a number of vocal advocates, but few practitioners. There is somewhat more employee involvement today than a few decades ago, but still far from the democratic ideal. Most firms operate with the traditional model that management retains control and employees have few rights. There may be reasons for this intransigence. One argument against organizational democracy is that employees have a contractual rather than ownership relationship with the organization. Legally (and possibly morally), they have no right to assume citizenship rights or control over the business. A second consideration is that employees might emphasize their own interests to the detriment of other stakeholders. In contrast, traditional organizations give management an explicit obligation to serve multiple stakeholders to ensure the organization's survival and success.

Another concern is that workplace democracy might dilute accountability. Although moderate levels of employee involvement can improve decision-making quality and commitment, there is a real risk that no one will take responsibility for decisions when everyone has a say in them. In addition, democracy often results in slower decision making, which could lead to a lethargic corporate response to changes in the external environment. Finally, the democratic enterprise model presumes that employees want to control their organizations, but some research suggests that employees prefer a more moderate level of workplace involvement. For this reason (and the others noted above), employee-owned companies often maintain a more traditional hierarchical worker–management relationship.[95]

---

employee involvement
The degree to which employees influence how their work is organized and carried out.

- *Consult with the team.* The decision maker brings together a team of people (such as all staff in the department), who are told about the problem and provide their ideas and recommendations. The decision maker makes the final decision, which may or may not reflect the team's information.
- *Facilitate the team's decision.* The entire decision-making process is handed over to the team, where the original decision maker serves only as a facilitator to guide the team's decision process and keep everyone on track. The team identifies the problem, discovers alternative solutions, chooses the best alternative, and implements its choice.

connections 7.2

A Refinery Built on Involvement[96]

When the Great Financial Crisis hit the global economy, the Yabulu nickel and cobalt refinery in northern Queensland, Australia, faced almost certain closure. The refinery was losing more than $10 million per month, so its owner, BHP Billiton, quietly prepared to shut down operations while it skeptically searched for anybody to buy it. "We were all staring down the barrel of wholesale job losses, shutting the gate and closing the plant," recalls general manager Trefor Flood, shown here at the Yabulu refinery.

Mining and property magnate Clive Palmer took up the offer to buy Yabulu less than one month before the planned closure. Palmer likely took this calculated gamble believing that nickel prices would improve (they had fallen by 70 percent over the previous year). But Palmer also had faith in the capacity of Yabulu's workforce to improve the refinery's productivity enough to make it profitable.

"When we took over the plant we recognized that we didn't know how to run the plant as well as the workforce," Palmer explains. "Our strategy was to get the workforce onside and realize that we are all in this together. We let them go do what they thought was best."

When Palmer met with Yabulu's employees a few weeks later, he was symbolically wearing a Eureka Stockade cap. (The Eureka Stockade rebellion of 1854—in which miners opposed government taxation and corruption—is considered the birthplace of Australian democracy.) Along with encouraging employees to take ownership of the company's future, he immediately restructured their bonus plan from an annual payment based on intangible work processes to a quarterly payment based on measurable production and efficiency. Within the first month, and every month since, Yabulu's employees exceeded previous production

Yabulu nickel and cobalt refinery general manager Trefor Flood is all smiles because employee involvement boosted productivity and profitability. "We have given power to the people, and it is working."

records. In some months, employees produced 25 percent above previous records yet also produced higher-grade output.

Refinery manager Trefor Flood emphasizes that employee involvement is the main reason employees have smashed previous production records. "They haven't come about through millions of dollars of capital, they have come about through workers and maintenance crews coming forward with ideas," he says. "We are using the same equipment, same people, to make the same product. But we are making the big tonnes because we have handed control over to the veteran operators on the line. Under Clive Palmer, we have given power to the people, and it is working."

BENEFITS OF EMPLOYEE INVOLVEMENT

For the past half century, organizational behavior experts have advised that employee involvement potentially improves an organization's effectiveness.[97] Indeed, there are many examples of operations that have turned around when management gave employees more say in how to run the business. One of the most striking recent illustrations is the Yabulu nickel and cobalt refinery in northern Queensland, Australia, which is described in Connections 7.2.

How does employee involvement improve organizational effectiveness? One way is by improving the quality of organizational decisions. Employees are, in many respects, the sensors of the organization's environment, so they often recognize problems more quickly and define them more accurately. When the organization's activities misalign with customer expectations, for example, employees are usually the first to know. Employee involvement ensures that everyone in the organization is quickly alerted to such problems.[98] A second way is by potentially improving the number and quality of solutions generated. In a well-managed meeting, team members create synergy by pooling their knowledge to form new alternatives. In other words, several people working together can potentially generate better solutions than the same people working alone.

A third benefit of employee involvement is that, under specific conditions, it improves the evaluation of alternatives. Numerous studies on participative decision making, constructive conflict, and team dynamics have found that involvement brings out more diverse perspectives, tests ideas, and provides more valuable knowledge, all of which help the decision maker select the best alternative.[99] A mathematical theorem introduced in 1785 by the

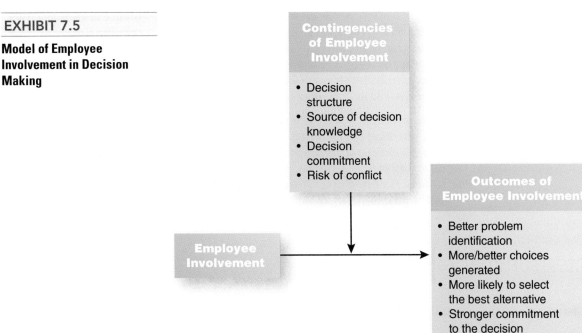

EXHIBIT 7.5

Model of Employee Involvement in Decision Making

Contingencies of Employee Involvement

- Decision structure
- Source of decision knowledge
- Decision commitment
- Risk of conflict

Employee Involvement

Outcomes of Employee Involvement

- Better problem identification
- More/better choices generated
- More likely to select the best alternative
- Stronger commitment to the decision

Marquis de Condorcet states that the alternative selected by the team's majority is more likely to be correct than is the alternative selected by any team member individually.[100]

Along with improving decision quality, employee involvement tends to strengthen employee commitment to the decision. Rather than viewing themselves as agents of someone else's decision, staff members who participate in a decision feel personally responsible for its success. Involvement also has positive effects on employee motivation, satisfaction, and turnover. It increases skill variety, feelings of autonomy, and task identity, all of which increase job enrichment and potentially employee motivation. Participation is also a critical practice in organizational change because employees are more motivated to implement the decision and less likely to resist changes resulting from the decision.[101]

CONTINGENCIES OF EMPLOYEE INVOLVEMENT

If employee involvement is so wonderful, why don't leaders leave all decisions to employees? The answer is that the optimal level of employee involvement depends on the situation. The employee involvement model shown in Exhibit 7.5 lists four contingencies: decision structure, source of decision knowledge, decision commitment, and risk of conflict in the decision process.[102]

- *Decision structure.* At the beginning of this chapter, we stated that some decisions are programmed, whereas others are nonprogrammed. Programmed decisions are less likely to need employee involvement because the solutions are already worked out from past incidents. In other words, the benefits of employee involvement increase with the novelty and complexity of the problem or opportunity.

- *Source of decision knowledge.* Subordinates should be involved in some level of decision making when the leader lacks sufficient knowledge and subordinates have additional information to improve decision quality. In many cases, employees are closer to customers and production activities, so they often know where the company can save money, improve product or service quality, and realize opportunities. This is particularly true for complex decisions where employees are more likely to possess relevant information.

- *Decision commitment.* Participation tends to improve employee commitment to the decision. If employees are unlikely to accept a decision made without their involvement, some level of participation is usually necessary.

- *Risk of conflict.* Two types of conflict undermine the benefits of employee involvement. First, if employee goals and norms conflict with the organization's goals, only a low level of employee involvement is advisable. Second, the degree of involvement depends on whether employees will agree with each other on the preferred solution. If conflict is likely to occur, high involvement (i.e., employees make the decision alone) would be difficult to achieve.

Employee involvement is an important component of the decision-making process. To make the best decisions, we need to involve people who have the most valuable information and who will increase commitment to implement the decision. Employee involvement is a formative stage of team dynamics, so it carries many of the benefits and challenges of working in teams. The next chapter provides a closer look at team dynamics, including processes for making decisions in teams.

[chapter summary]

LO1 Describe the rational choice paradigm.

Decision making is a conscious process of making choices among one or more alternatives with the intention of moving toward some desired state of affairs. The rational choice paradigm relies on subjective expected utility to identify the best choice. It also follows the logical process of identifying problems and opportunities, choosing the best decision style, discovering or developing alternative solutions, choosing the best solution, implementing the selected alternative, and evaluating decision outcomes.

LO2 Explain why people differ from the rational choice paradigm when identifying problems/opportunities, evaluating/choosing alternatives, and evaluating decision outcomes.

Stakeholder framing, perceptual defense, mental models, decisive leadership, and solution-oriented focus affect our ability to objectively identify problems and opportunities. We can minimize these challenges by being aware of the human limitations and discussing the situation with colleagues.

Evaluating and choosing alternatives is often challenging because organizational goals are ambiguous or in conflict, human information processing is incomplete and subjective, and people tend to satisfice rather than maximize. Decision makers also short-circuit the evaluation process when faced with an opportunity rather than a problem. People generally make better choices by systematically evaluating alternatives. Scenario planning can help make future decisions without the pressure and emotions that occur during real emergencies.

Confirmation bias and escalation of commitment make it difficult to accurately evaluate decision outcomes. Escalation is mainly caused by self-justification, the prospect theory effect, perceptual blinders, and closing costs. These problems are minimized by separating decision choosers from decision evaluators, establishing a preset level at which the decision is abandoned or reevaluated, relying on more systematic and clear feedback about the project's success, and involving several people in decision making.

LO3 Discuss the roles of emotions and intuition in decision making.

Emotions shape our preferences for alternatives and the process we follow to evaluate alternatives. We also listen in to our emotions for guidance when making decisions. This latter activity relates to intuition—the ability to know when a problem or opportunity exists and to select the best course of action without conscious reasoning. Intuition is both an emotional experience and a rapid nonconscious analytic process that involves both pattern matching and action scripts.

LO4 Describe employee characteristics, workplace conditions, and specific activities that support creativity.

Creativity is the development of original ideas that make a socially recognized contribution. The four creativity stages are preparation, incubation, illumination, and verification. Incubation assists divergent thinking, which involves reframing the problem in a unique way and generating different approaches to the issue.

Four of the main features of creative people are intelligence, persistence, expertise, and independent imagination. Creativity is also strengthened for everyone when the work environment supports a learning orientation, the job has high intrinsic motivation, the organization provides a reasonable level of job security, and project leaders provide appropriate goals, time pressure, and resources. Three types of activities that encourage creativity are redefining the problem, associative play, and cross-pollination.

LO5 Describe the benefits of employee involvement and identify four contingencies that affect the optimal level of employee involvement.

Employee involvement refers to the degree that employees influence how their work is organized and carried out. The level of participation may range from an employee providing specific information to management without knowing the problem or issue to complete involvement in all phases of the decision process. Employee involvement may lead to higher decision quality and commitment, but several contingencies need to be considered, including the decision structure, source of decision knowledge, decision commitment, and risk of conflict.

anchoring and adjustment heuristic, p. 200

availability heuristic, p. 200

bounded rationality, p. 199

creativity, p. 207

decision making, p. 194

divergent thinking, p. 208

employee involvement, p. 212

escalation of commitment, p. 206

implicit favorite, p. 200

intuition, p. 204

prospect theory effect, p. 206

rational choice paradigm, p. 194

representativeness heuristic, p. 200

satisficing, p. 201

scenario planning, p. 205

subjective expected utility, p. 194

(critical thinking questions)

1. A management consultant is hired by a manufacturing firm to determine the best site for its next production facility. The consultant has had several meetings with the company's senior executives regarding the factors to consider when making the recommendation. Discuss the decision-making problems that might prevent the consultant from choosing the best site location.

2. You have been asked to personally recommend a new travel agency to handle all airfare, accommodation, and related travel needs for your organization of 500 staff. One of your colleagues, who is responsible for the company's economic planning, suggests that the best travel agent could be selected mathematically by inputting the relevant factors for each agency and the weight (importance) of each factor. What decision-making approach is your colleague recommending? Is this recommendation a good idea in this situation? Why or why not?

3. Intuition is both an emotional experience and a nonconscious analytic process. One problem, however, is that not all emotions signaling that there is a problem or opportunity represent intuition. Explain how we would know if our "gut feelings" are intuition or not, and if not intuition, suggest what might be causing them.

4. A developer received financial backing for a new business financial center along a derelict section of the waterfront, a few miles from the current downtown area of a large European city. The idea was to build several high-rise structures, attract large tenants to those sites, and have the city extend transportation systems out to the new center. Over the next decade, the developer believed that others would build in the area, thereby attracting the regional or national offices of many financial institutions. Interest from potential tenants was much lower than

initially predicted, and the city did not build transportation systems as quickly as expected. Still, the builder proceeded with the original plans. Only after financial support was curtailed did the developer reconsider the project. Using your knowledge of escalation of commitment, discuss three possible reasons why the developer was motivated to continue with the project.

5. Ancient Book Company has a problem with new book projects. Even when others are aware that a book is far behind schedule and may engender little public interest, sponsoring editors are reluctant to terminate contracts with authors whom they have signed. The result is that editors invest more time with these projects than on more fruitful projects. As a form of escalation of commitment, describe two methods that Ancient Book Company can use to minimize this problem.

6. Think of a time when you experienced the creative process. Maybe you woke up with a brilliant (but usually sketchy and incomplete) idea, or you solved a baffling problem while doing something else. Describe this incident to your class and explain how the experience followed the creative process.

7. Two characteristics of creative people are that they have relevant experience and are persistent in their quest. Does this mean that people with the most experience and the highest need for achievement are the most creative? Explain your answer.

8. Employee involvement applies just as well to the classroom as to the office or factory floor. Explain how student involvement in classroom decisions typically made by the instructor alone might improve decision quality. What potential problems may occur in this process?

CASE STUDY 7.1 EMPLOYEE INVOLVEMENT CASES

Scenario 1: Social Media Decision for the State Government

As the director of disability services in a state government department, you have a high priority to recruit and retain young, well-educated, high-potential employees. During a recent recruiting drive at universities and polytechnics, some potential applicants candidly stated that the state government seems out of touch with the younger generation, particularly their use of technology. A few observed that the agency's web site doesn't provide much recruitment information, and they couldn't find the agency's Facebook or Twitter sites.

These comments led to you think about whether or to what degree you should encourage agency staff to have work-related Facebook sites, personal blogs, and Twitter sites. You personally know very little about these social media, although many of your direct reports (regional and functional managers) have varying degrees of knowledge about them. A few even have their own personal Facebook sites and one manager has her own blog on travel. Some direct reports are strongly opposed to social media in the workplace, whereas others are likely very supportive. However, you believe that all of their views are in the agency's best interests.

This social media decision would be within your mandate; the state government has no specific policy on this matter. However, some other government departments prohibit Facebook and texting activity during work and, due to concerns about breaches of confidentiality and employer reputation, do not allow employees to mention work-related matters in any social media.

Scenario 2: The Sugar Substitute Research Decision

You are the head of research and development (R&D) for a major beer company. While working on a new beer product, one of the scientists in your unit seems to have tentatively identified a new chemical compound that has few calories but tastes closer to sugar than current sugar substitutes. The company has no foreseeable need for this product, but it could be patented and licensed to manufacturers in the food industry.

The sugar-substitute discovery is in its preliminary stages and would require considerable time and resources before it would be commercially viable. This means that it would necessarily take some resources away from other projects in the lab. The sugar-substitute project is beyond your technical expertise, but some of the R&D lab researchers are familiar with that field of chemistry. As with most forms of research, it is difficult to determine the amount of research required to further identify and perfect the sugar substitute. You do not know how much demand is expected for this product. Your department has a decision process for funding projects that are behind schedule. However, there are no rules or precedents about funding projects that would be licensed but not used by the organization.

The company's R&D budget is limited, and other scientists in your work group have recently complained that they require more resources and financial support to get their projects completed. Some of these R&D projects hold promise for future beer sales. You believe that most researchers in the R&D unit are committed to ensuring that the company's interests are achieved.

Scenario 3: Coast Guard Cutter Decision Problem

You are the captain of a 200-foot Coast Guard cutter, with a crew of 16, including officers. Your mission is general at-sea search and rescue. At 2:00 a.m. this morning, while en route to your home port after a routine 28-day patrol, you received word from the nearest Coast Guard station that a small plane had crashed 60 miles offshore. You obtained all the available information concerning the location of the crash, informed your crew of the mission, and set a new course at maximum speed for the scene to commence a search for survivors and wreckage.

You have now been searching for 20 hours. Your search operation has been increasingly impaired by rough seas, and there is evidence of a severe storm building. The atmospherics associated with the deteriorating weather have made communications with the Coast Guard station impossible. A decision must be made shortly about whether to abandon the search and place your vessel on a course that would ride out the storm (thereby protecting the vessel and your crew, but relegating any possible survivors to almost certain death from exposure) or to continue a potentially futile search and the risks it would entail.

Before losing communications, you received an update weather advisory concerning the severity and duration of the storm. Although your crew members are extremely conscientious about their responsibility, you believe that they would be divided on the decision of leaving or staying.

Discussion Questions (for all three scenarios)

1. To what extent should your subordinates be involved in this decision? Select one of the following levels of involvement:

   - *Decide alone.* Use your personal knowledge and insight to complete the entire decision process without conferring with anyone else.

   - *Receive information from individuals.* Ask specific individuals for information. They do not make recommendations and might not even know what the problem is about.

   - *Consult with individuals.* Describe the problem to selected individuals and seek both their information and recommendations. The final decision is made by you, and you may or may not take the advice from these others into account.

   - *Consult with the team.* You bring together a team of people (all department staff or a representation of them if the department is large), who are told about the problem and provide their ideas and recommendations. You make the final decision, which may or may not reflect the team's information.

- *Facilitate the team's decision*. The entire decision-making process is handed over to a team or committee of subordinates. You serve only as a facilitator to guide the decision process and keep everyone on track. The team identifies the problem, discovers alternative solutions, chooses the best alternative, and implements their choice.

2. What factors led you to choose this level of employee involvement rather than the others?

3. What problems might occur if less or more involvement occurred in this case (where possible)?

Source: The Social Media Decision was written by Steven L. McShane and Sandra. L. Steen. The Sugar Substitute Research Decision: © 2002 Steven L. McShane. The Coast Guard Cutter case is adapted from V.H. Vroom and A.G. Jago, *The New Leadership: Managing Participation in Organizations* (Englewood Cliffs, NJ: Prentice Hall, 1988), © 1987 V.H. Vroom and A.G. Jago. Used with permission of the authors.

CASE STUDY 7.2 GOING FOR WOW AT NOTTINGHAM-SPIRK

You might say that creativity is a religious experience at Nottingham-Spirk Design Associates, Inc. A few years ago, the industrial-design company moved into an old church in Cleveland's university park area. Perched atop an escarpment on five acres of property, the 1920s octagon-shaped limestone building looks like a Roman temple. Inside, employees work in a large rotunda below a domed ceiling supported by 20 columns. Symbols of the original church remain, including a choir loft and soaring pipe organ. "You can't help but walk in here and say, 'I want to create something new,'" says John Nottingham, who cofounded Nottingham-Spirk with John Spirks three decades ago.

Along with an inspiring church building, Nottingham-Spirk supports creativity through its risk-tolerant learning orientation culture. "We stick our necks out," says Nottingham. "If we fail, we go down the wrong path, we dust ourselves off and go the other way. We understand that's innovation." The cofounders and their 70 employees also discover ideas by looking around store shelves. "We're trying to figure out what consumers will want two years down the road," explains Spirk. "We look and see what's not there," Nottingham adds. "We literally visualize an innovation sitting on the shelf next to the competition at a price point."

These activities produce sparks of insight, but they are only the starting point in the creative process. "Anyone can have a good idea," he says. "The difficult thing is to get it to market. You've got to make the idea work and prove its feasibility as a product." To transform ideas to profitable products, Nottingham-Spirk forms teams of up to 10 employees who hold two types of meetings. In the first meeting, called a *diverging session*, team members brainstorm ideas. "We start with a creative session, people from our team that can complement each other, and we come up with as many ideas as you can," says Nottingham. These ideas are documented as scribbles and sketches on slips of paper; up to 100 of them plaster the walls by the end of the session.

In the second round of meetings, called a *converging session*, each idea is systematically evaluated by the team. "I pass around notecards, each with a word or phrase on it that says, WHO CARES, NICE, or WOW," Nottingham explains. The person who introduced an idea can explain it further; then each person judges the idea by selecting one of the three cards. "If everyone holds up a WOW card, you know you've got something," says Nottingham. The WHO CARES ideas get tossed. Some of the NICE ideas are developed further by an idea champion. For example, the SwivelStraight one-minute Christmas tree stand received mainly NICE ratings when it was first proposed, but coworkers gave it WOW ratings after Nottingham-Spirk designer Craig Saunders refined it further. Almost 1 million SwivelStraight stands were sold in its first five years on the market.

Diverging and converging sessions are complemented by focus group meetings and client feedback to improve prototypes. Nottingham-Spirk's redesign of the round metal paint can, which has changed little over the past century, is a case in point. Employees knew from experience the frustration of working with traditional paint cans. "We couldn't think of another consumer product that you need a screwdriver to open and a hammer to close," says designer Craig Saunders. So Saunders and his coworkers created a paint can with a twist top and built-in no-drip pour spout. When shown an early prototype, potential users claimed the container wouldn't stack well in warehouses and stores, so the revised prototype was made wider and more stackable. Next, users were concerned that the plastic container would break if it was dropped. "So we took a bunch of them up on ladders and dropped them," says Nottingham. "They bounced." This feedback made the Twist and Pour paint can an instant success; Sherwin-Williams tripled sales of its Dutch Boy paint in the first six months.

Thanks to its creative work environment and innovation process, Nottingham-Spirk has registered close to 500 patents and helped clients achieve more than $30 billion in sales over the past three decades. Its most visible innovations include the Crest SpinBrush®, Invacare Corp. wheelchairs, Swiffer SweeperVac®, wide-oval shaped antiperspirant containers, MRI scanner designs, and the Twist and Pour paint can.[103]

Discussion Questions

1. What organizational conditions seem to support creative thinking at Nottingham-Spirk? Why do these conditions support creativity?

2. Explain how the converging–diverging sessions at Nottingham-Spirks aid employee and team creativity.

TEAM EXERCISE 7.3 WHERE IN THE WORLD ARE WE?

PURPOSE This exercise is designed to help you understand the potential advantages of involving others in decisions rather than making decisions alone.

MATERIALS You will require an unmarked copy of the map of the United States with grid marks (see Exhibit B). You may not look at any other maps or use any other materials. The instructor will provide a list of communities located somewhere on Exhibit B. The instructor will also provide copies of the answer sheet after you have individually and in teams estimated the locations of communities.

INSTRUCTIONS

Step 1: Write down in Exhibit A the list of communities identified by your instructor. Then, working alone, estimate the location in Exhibit B of these communities, all of which are in the United States. For example, mark a small "1" in Exhibit B on the spot where you believe the first community is located. Mark a small "2" where you think the second community is located, and so on. Please be sure to number each location clearly and with numbers small enough to fit within one grid space.

Step 2: The instructor will organize students into approximately equal sized teams (typically five or six people per team). Working with your team members, reach a consensus on the location of each community listed in Exhibit A. The instructor might provide teams with a separate copy of this map, or each member can identify the team's numbers using a different colored pen on their individual maps. The team's decision for each location should occur by consensus, not voting or averaging.

Step 3: The instructor will provide or display an answer sheet, showing the correct locations of the communities. Using this answer sheet, students will count the minimum number of grid squares between the location they individually marked and the true location of each community. Write the number of grid squares in the second column of Exhibit A; then add up the total. Next, count the minimum number of grid squares between the location the team marked and the true location of each community. Write the number of grid squares in the third column of Exhibit A; then add up the total.

Step 4: The instructor will ask for information about the totals, and the class will discuss the implications of these results for employee involvement and decision making.

EXHIBIT A List of Selected Communities in the United States

NUMBER	COMMUNITY	INDIVIDUAL DISTANCE IN GRID UNITS FROM THE TRUE LOCATION	TEAM DISTANCE IN GRID UNITS FROM THE TRUE LOCATION
1			
2			
3			
4			
5			
6			
7			
8			
		Total:	Total:

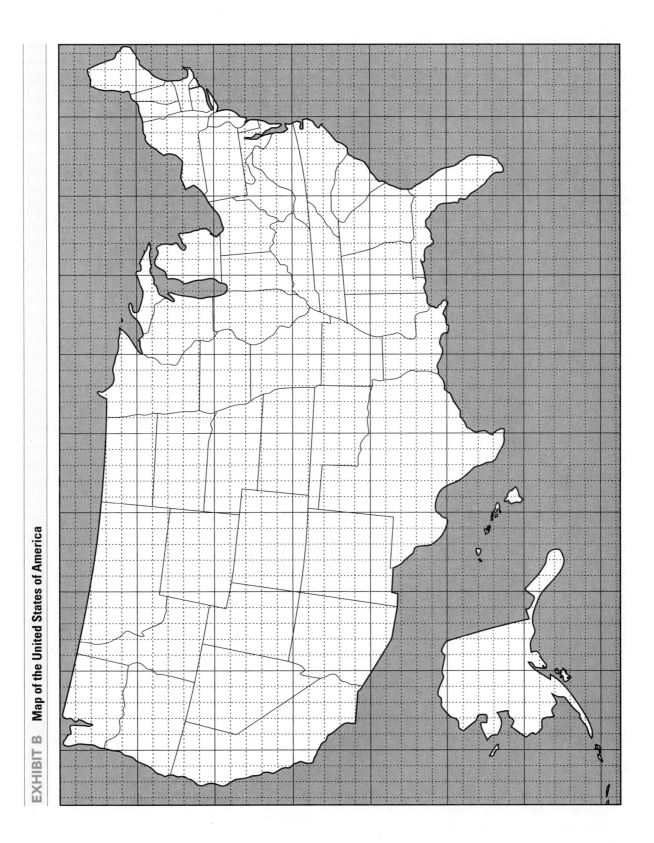

CLASS EXERCISE 7.4 THE HOPPING ORANGE

PURPOSE This exercise is designed to help you understand the dynamics of creativity and team problem solving.

INSTRUCTIONS You will be placed in teams of six students. One student serves as the official timer for the team and must have a stopwatch timer (such as on your watch or cell phone). The instructor will give each team an orange (or similar object) with a specific task involving the use of the orange. The objective is easy to understand and nonthreatening, and it will be described by the instructor at the beginning of the exercise. Each team will have a few opportunities to achieve the objective more efficiently. To maximize the effectiveness of this exercise, no other information is provided here.

CLASS EXERCISE 7.5 CREATIVITY BRAINBUSTERS

PURPOSE This exercise is designed to help you understand the dynamics of creativity and team problem solving.

INSTRUCTIONS (LARGE OR SMALL CLASS) The instructor will describe the problem, and you should figure out a solution working alone. When enough time has passed, the instructor may then ask specific students who believe they have the solution to describe (or show using overhead transparency) their answer. The instructor will review the solutions and discuss the implications of this exercise. In particular, be prepared to discuss what you needed to solve these puzzles and what may have prevented you from solving them more quickly

1. *Double-circle problem*. Draw two circles, one inside the other, with a single line and with neither circle touching the other (as shown below). In other words, you must draw both of these circles without lifting your pen (or other writing instrument).

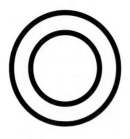

2. *Nine-dot problem*. Below are nine dots. Without lifting your pencil, draw no more than four straight lines that pass through all nine dots.

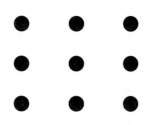

3. *Nine-dot problem revisited*. Referring to the nine-dot exhibit above, describe how, without lifting your pencil, you could pass a pencil line through all dots with three or fewer straight lines.

4. *Word search*. In the following line of letters, cross out five letters so that the remaining letters, without altering their sequence, spell a familiar English word.

   CFRIVEELATETITEVRSE

5. *Burning ropes*. You have two pieces of rope of unequal lengths and a box of matches. In spite of their different lengths, each piece of rope takes one hour to burn; however, parts of each rope burn at unequal speeds. For example, the first half of one piece might burn in 10 minutes. Use these materials to accurately determine when 45 minutes has elapsed.

SELF-ASSESSMENT 7.6 MEASURING YOUR CREATIVE PERSONALITY

PURPOSE This self-assessment is designed to help you measure the extent to which you have a creative personality.

INSTRUCTIONS Listed below is an adjective checklist with 30 words that may or may not describe you. Put a mark in the box beside each word that you think accurately describes you. Please do not mark the boxes for words that do not describe you. When finished, you can score the test using the scoring key in Appendix B at the end of the book. This exercise should be completed alone so that you can assess yourself without concerns of social comparison. Class discussion will focus on how this scale might be applied in organizations and on the limitations of measuring creativity in work settings.

ADJECTIVE CHECKLIST					
Affected	☐	Honest	☐	Reflective	☐
Capable	☐	Humorous	☐	Resourceful	☐
Cautious	☐	Individualistic	☐	Self-confident	☐
Clever	☐	Informal	☐	Sexy	☐
Commonplace	☐	Insightful	☐	Sincere	☐
Confident	☐	Intelligent	☐	Snobbish	☐
Conservative	☐	Inventive	☐	Submissive	☐
Conventional	☐	Mannerly	☐	Suspicious	☐
Dissatisfied	☐	Narrow interests	☐	Unconventional	☐
Egotistical	☐	Original	☐	Wide interests	☐

Source: Adapted from and based on information in H.G. Gough and A.B. Heilbrun Jr., *The Adjective Check List Manual* (Palo Alto, CA: Consulting Psychologists Press, 1965).

After reading this chapter go to www.mhhe.com/mcshane6e for more in-depth information and interactivities that correspond to the chapter.

Team Dynamics

learning objectives

After reading this chapter, you should be able to:

LO1 Discuss the benefits and limitations of teams, and explain why employees join informal groups.

LO2 Outline the team effectiveness model and discuss how task characteristics, team size, and team composition influence team effectiveness.

LO3 Discuss how the four team processes—team development,

norms, cohesion, and trust—influence team effectiveness.

LO4 Discuss the characteristics and factors required for the success of self-directed teams and virtual teams.

LO5 Identify four constraints on team decision making and discuss the advantages and disadvantages of four structures aimed at improving team decision making.

United Kingdom, is a model of efficiency, but you won't find many bosses around. The hypercompetitive facility's two production areas—one makes high-volume liquids (e.g., Woolite® detergent), the other is Europe's only aerosol products maker—operate through self-led teams. Teams are responsible for training, productivity improvement, and quality assurance. The plant employs 200 people and has only three production managers. Employees earn team-based bonuses based on product quality and how quickly they solve quality issues.

Self-directed teams are also the foundation of production at RB's health products manufacturing facility in Hull, UK. "The people on the lines decide how they are going to run over the next three to four weeks," says a team leader in the Hull plant, which makes Gaviscon® antacid tablets and other over-the-counter medicines. Another team leader proudly notes that his team has become "one of the most efficient in northern Europe" because "we were given the opportunity to take ownership of the line."

Reckitt Benckiser's team spirit extends throughout its marketing, research, and other functions, often through virtual teams. "For most projects I've participated in, the team members usually are sitting in different countries," explains Gaonan, who works in RB's information services (IS) group. "What do you think makes a global team?" Gaonan asks. "This essential element is trust. IS people sitting in one site trust that their team members sitting in another continent can fully understand and help resolve their problems."

RB's team-oriented culture is reinforced through socialization, rewards, and team-building events. For example, 65 employees from 34 countries recently teamed up in Brazil to renovate facilities for vulnerable preschool children and raise funds through a challenging hike. "Work was plentiful and we all worked brilliantly as a team—the RB way of course!" says Mmalorato Mabaso, an RB manager in South Africa who participated in the Brazil event. "The team came together with one goal in mind: To bring hope to children."[1]

From self-led production teams in the UK to volunteering and extreme hiking team-building activities in Brazil (as shown in this photo), household products manufacturer Reckitt Benckiser thrives on a team spirit.

Reckitt Benckiser's emphasis on teamwork is one reason it is a significant rival to Procter & Gamble and Unilever. But this UK-based global household and personal care products company isn't alone in leveraging the benefits of teams. More than half of the organizations polled in a recent survey use teams to a high or very high extent to conduct day-to-day business. Furthermore, 77 percent of those firms rely on teams for one-time projects and 67 percent rely on teams for ongoing projects. By comparison, a decade ago only 50 percent of executives said their work was done in teams. Two decades ago, only 20 percent of those executives said they worked in teams.[2]

Teamwork has also become more important in scientific research. A recent study of almost 20 million research publications reported that the percentage of journal articles written by teams rather than individuals has increased substantially over the past five decades. Team-based articles also had a much higher number of subsequent citations, suggesting that journal articles written by teams are superior to articles written by individuals.[3]

Why are teams becoming so important, and how can organizations strengthen their potential for organizational effectiveness? We find the answers to these and other questions in this chapter on team dynamics. This chapter begins by defining *teams* and examining the reasons organizations rely on teams and why people join informal groups in organizational settings. A large segment of this chapter examines a model of team effectiveness, which includes team and organizational environment, team design, and the team processes of development, norms, cohesion, and trust. We then turn our attention to two specific types of teams: self-directed teams and virtual teams. The final section of this chapter looks at the challenges and strategies for making better decisions in teams.

Teams and Informal Groups

Teams are groups of two or more people who interact and influence each other, are mutually accountable for achieving common goals associated with organizational objectives, and perceive themselves as a social entity within an organization.[4] This definition has a few important components worth repeating. First, all teams exist to fulfill some purpose, such as repairing electric power lines, assembling a product, designing a new social welfare program, or making an important decision. Second, team members are held together by their interdependence and need for collaboration to achieve common goals. All teams require some form of communication so that members can coordinate and share common objectives. Third, team members influence one another, although some members may be more influential than others regarding the team's goals and activities. Finally, a team exists when its members perceive themselves to be a team.

Exhibit 8.1 briefly describes various types of teams in organizations. Some teams are permanent, while others are temporary; some are responsible for making products or providing services, while others exist to make decisions or share knowledge. Each type of team has been created deliberately to serve an organizational purpose. Some teams, such as skunkworks teams, are not initially sanctioned by management, yet they are called "teams" because members work toward an organization objective.

INFORMAL GROUPS

For the most part, this chapter focuses on formal teams, but employees also belong to informal groups. All teams are groups, but many groups do not satisfy our definition of teams. Groups include people assembled together, whether or not they have any interdependence or organizationally focused objective. The friends you meet for lunch are an *informal group,* but they wouldn't be called a team because they have little or no interdependence (each person could just as easily eat lunch alone) and no organizationally mandated purpose. Instead, they exist primarily for the benefit of their members. Although the terms are used interchangeably, *teams* has largely replaced *groups* in the language of business when referring to employees who work together to complete organizational tasks.[5]

EXHIBIT 8.1   Types of Teams in Organizations

TEAM TYPE	DESCRIPTION
Departmental teams	Teams that consist of employees who have similar or complementary skills and are located in the same unit of a functional structure; usually minimal task interdependence because each person works with clients or employees in other departments.
Production/service/leadership teams	Typically multiskilled (employees have diverse competencies), team members collectively produce a common product/service or make ongoing decisions; production/service teams typically have an assembly-line type of interdependence, whereas leadership teams tend to have tight interactive (reciprocal) interdependence.
Self-directed teams	Similar to production/service teams except (1) they are organized around work processes that complete an entire piece of work requiring several interdependent tasks and (2) they have substantial autonomy over the execution of those tasks (i.e., they usually control inputs, flow, and outputs with little or no supervision).
Advisory teams	Teams that provide recommendations to decision makers; include committees, advisory councils, work councils, and review panels; may be temporary, but often permanent, some with frequent rotation of members.
Task force (project) teams	Usually multiskilled, temporary teams whose assignment is to solve a problem, realize an opportunity, or design a product or service.
Skunkworks	Multiskilled teams that are usually located away from the organization and are relatively free of its hierarchy; often initiated by an entrepreneurial team leader who borrows people and resources *(bootlegging)* to design a product or service.
Virtual teams	Teams whose members operate across space, time, and organizational boundaries and are linked through information technologies to achieve organizational tasks; may be a temporary task force or permanent service team.
Communities of practice	Teams (but often informal groups) bound together by shared expertise and passion for a particular activity or interest; main purpose is to share information; often rely on information technologies as the main source of interaction.

teams
Groups of two or more people who interact and influence each other, are mutually accountable for achieving common goals associated with organizational objectives, and perceive themselves as a social entity within an organization.

Why do informal groups exist? One reason is that human beings are social animals. Our drive to bond is hardwired through evolutionary development, creating a need to belong to informal groups.[6] This is evident by the fact that people invest considerable time and effort forming and maintaining social relationships without any special circumstances or ulterior motives. A second reason people join informal groups is provided by social identity theory, which states that individuals define themselves by their group affiliations (see Chapter 3). Thus, we join groups—particularly those that are viewed favorably by others and that have values similar to our own—because they shape and reinforce our self-concept.[7]

A third reason people are motivated to form informal groups is that such groups accomplish tasks that cannot be achieved by individuals working alone. For example, employees will sometimes congregate to oppose organizational changes because this collective effort has more power than individuals who try to oppose change alone. These informal groups, called coalitions, are discussed in Chapter 10. A fourth explanation for informal groups is that we are comforted by the mere presence of other people and are therefore motivated to be near them in stressful situations. When in danger, people congregate even though doing so serves no protective purpose. Similarly, employees tend to mingle more often after hearing rumors that the company might be acquired by a competitor. As Chapter 4 explained, this social support minimizes stress by providing emotional and/or informational support to buffer the stress experience.[8]

Informal Groups and Organizational Outcomes

Informal groups are not created to serve organizational objectives. Nevertheless, they have a profound influence on organizations and individual employees. Informal groups potentially minimize employee stress because, as mentioned above, group members provide emotional and informational social support. This stress-reducing capability of informal groups improves employee well-being, thereby improving organizational effectiveness. Informal groups are also the backbone of *social networks*, which are important sources of trust building, information sharing, power, influence, and employee well-being in the workplace.[9] Chapter 9 describes the growing significance of social networking sites similar to Facebook and LinkedIn to encourage the formation of informal groups and associated communication. Chapter 10 explains how social networks are a source of influence in organizational settings. Employees with strong informal networks tend to have more power and influence because they receive better information and preferential treatment from others and their talent is more visible to key decision makers.

Advantages and Disadvantages of Teams

Employees don't work alone very often at Menlo Innovations. The software development company in Ann Arbor, Michigan, organizes employees into pairs each week. Two employees share one computer while discussing ideas on the same part of a large project. Each Monday, the company's two dozen employees not only switch partners; they often switch to a different part of the project or to another project altogether. "Just the act of one person bringing the other up to speed, saying things out loud, brings out things people hadn't noticed before," explains Richard Sheridan, one of Menlo Innovations' four cofounders. "That makes them smarter."[10]

The musical chairs arrangement at Menlo Innovations indicates that teamwork is an important ingredient for the software company's business success. Why are teams so important? The answer to this question has a long history.[12] Early research on British coal mining in the 1940s, studies of the Japanese economic miracle of the 1970s, and a huge number of investigations since then, have revealed that *under the right conditions*, teams make better decisions,

Teams are the foundation on which Ergon Energy does business. The electricity distribution company for regional Queensland, Australia, organizes its employees around teams and rewards them for team safety and performance. Teamwork is also one of Ergon's six core values. "Teamwork is a way of life, and it's something you can feel from your first day on the job," says Ergon's careers website. "Our employees really value teamwork," says an Ergon Energy executive. "It is a real key to our success and there's a real family culture, a sort of feeling that everyone is your mate."[11]

develop better products and services, and create a more engaged workforce than do employees working alone.[13] Similarly, team members can quickly share information and coordinate tasks, whereas these processes are slower and prone to more errors in traditional departments led by supervisors. Teams typically provide superior customer service because they provide more breadth of knowledge and expertise to customers than individual "stars" can offer.

In many situations, people are potentially more motivated when working in teams than when working alone.[14] One reason for this motivation is that, as we mentioned a few paragraphs ago, employees have a drive to bond and are motivated to fulfill the goals of groups to which they belong. This motivation is particularly strong when the team is part of the employee's social identity.

Second, people are more motivated in teams because they are accountable to fellow team members, who monitor performance more closely than a traditional supervisor. This is particularly true where the team's performance depends on the worst performer, such as on an assembly line, where how fast the product is assembled depends on the speed of the slowest employee. Third, under some circumstances, performance improves when employees work near others because coworkers become benchmarks of comparison. Employees are also motivated to work harder because of apprehension that their performance will be compared to others' performance.

THE CHALLENGES OF TEAMS

In spite of their many benefits, teams are not always as effective as individuals working alone.[15] Teams are usually better suited to complex work, such as designing a building or auditing a company's financial records. Under these circumstances, one person rarely has all the necessary knowledge and skills. Instead, complex work is performed better by dividing its tasks into more specialized roles, with people in those specialized jobs coordinating with each other. In contrast, work is typically performed more effectively by individuals alone when they have all the necessary knowledge and skills and the work cannot be divided into specialized tasks or is not complex enough to benefit from specialization. Even where the work can and should be specialized, a team structure might not be necessary if the tasks performed by several people require minimal coordination.

The main problem with teams is that they have additional costs called **process losses** — resources (including time and energy) expended toward team development and maintenance rather than the task.[16] It is much more efficient for an individual to work out an issue alone than to resolve differences of opinion with other people. For a team to perform well, team members need to agree and have mutual understanding of their goals, the strategy for accomplishing those goals, their specific roles, and informal rules of conduct.[17] Team members need to divert time and energy away from performing the work so they can develop and maintain these team requirements. The process loss problem is particularly apparent when more people are added or replace others on the team. Team performance suffers when a team adds members, because those employees need to learn how the team operates and how to coordinate efficiently with other team members. Process losses also occur because the workload often needs to be redistributed.

The software industry even has a name for the problems of adding people to a team: **Brooks's law** (also called the "mythical man-month") says that adding more people to a late software project only makes it later! According to some sources, Apple, Inc. may have fallen into this trap in the recent development of its professional photography software program, called Aperture. When the project started to fall behind schedule, the manager in charge of the Aperture project increased the size of the team—some sources say it ballooned from 20 to almost 150 engineers and quality assurance staff within a few weeks. Unfortunately, adding so many people further bogged down the project. The result? When Aperture was finally released, it was nine months late and considered one of Apple's buggier software offerings.[18]

process losses
Resources (including time and energy) expended toward team development and maintenance rather than the task.

Brooks's law
The principle that adding more people to a late software project only makes it later. Also called the *mythical man-month.*

Social Loafing   Perhaps the best-known limitation of teams is the risk of productivity loss due to **social loafing.** Social loafing occurs when people exert less effort (and usually perform at a lower level) when working in teams than when working alone.[19] Social loafing tends to be more serious when the individual's performance is less likely to be noticed, such as when people work together in very large teams. The individual's output is also less noticeable where the team produces a single output (rather than each team member producing output), such as finding a single solution to a customer's problem. There is less social loafing when each team member's contribution is more noticeable; this can be achieved by reducing the size of the team, for example, or measuring each team member's performance. Strategic Investments & Holdings Inc., a buyout firm in Buffalo, New York, deliberately restricts the number of company directors for this reason. "When the group is smaller, there's nowhere to hide," explains Strategic Investments principal David Zebro. "You have to pull your weight."[20]

Social loafing also depends on the employee's motivation to perform the work. Social loafing is less prevalent when the task is interesting, because individuals are more motivated by the work itself to perform their duties. For example, one recent study revealed that student apathy explains some of the social loafing that occurs in college student teams. Social loafing is also less common when the team's objective is important, possibly because individuals experience more pressure from coworkers to perform well. Finally, social loafing occurs less frequently among members who value team membership and believe in working toward the team's objectives.[21]

In summary, teams can be very powerful forces for competitive advantage, or they can be much more trouble than they are worth, so much so that job performance and morale decline when employees are placed in teams. To understand when teams are better than individuals working alone, we need to more closely examine the conditions that make teams effective or ineffective. The next few sections of this chapter discuss the model of team effectiveness.

A Model of Team Effectiveness

LO2

Why are some teams effective while others fail? To answer this question, we first need to clarify the meaning of team effectiveness. A team is effective when it benefits the organization, its members, and its own survival.[22] First, teams exist to serve some organizational purpose, so effectiveness is partly measured by the achievement of those objectives. Second, a team's effectiveness relies on the satisfaction and well-being of its members. People join groups to fulfill their personal needs, so effectiveness is partly measured by this need fulfillment. Finally, team effectiveness includes the team's viability—its ability to survive. It must be able to maintain the commitment of its members, particularly during the turbulence of the team's development. Without this commitment, people leave and the team will fall apart. The team must also secure sufficient resources and find a benevolent environment in which to operate.

Researchers have developed several models over the years to identify the features or conditions that make some teams more effective than others.[23] Exhibit 8.2 integrates the main components of these team effectiveness models. We will closely examine each component over the next several pages. This model is best viewed as a template of several theories, because each component (team development, team cohesion, etc.) includes its own set of theories and models to explain how that component operates.

ORGANIZATIONAL AND TEAM ENVIRONMENT

The organizational and team environment represents all conditions beyond the team's boundaries that influence its effectiveness. Team members tend to work together more effectively when they are at least partly rewarded for team performance.[24] Another

social loafing
The problem that occurs when people exert less effort (and usually perform at a lower level) when working in teams than when working alone.

EXHIBIT 8.2   Team Effectiveness Model

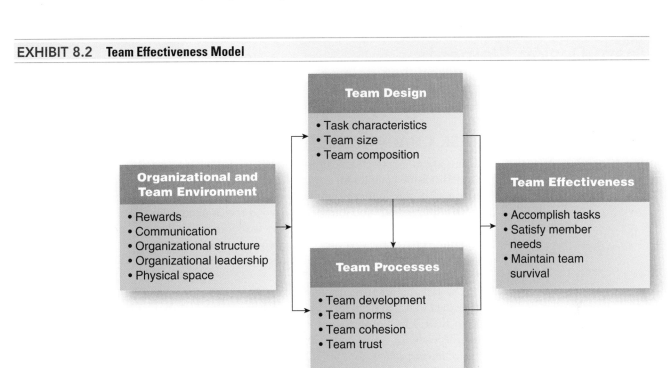

Team Design
- Task characteristics
- Team size
- Team composition

Organizational and Team Environment
- Rewards
- Communication
- Organizational structure
- Organizational leadership
- Physical space

Team Processes
- Team development
- Team norms
- Team cohesion
- Team trust

Team Effectiveness
- Accomplish tasks
- Satisfy member needs
- Maintain team survival

environmental factor is the organizational structure. Teams flourish when organized around work processes, because this structure increases interaction and interdependence among team members and reduces interaction with people outside the team. High-performance teams also depend on organizational leaders who provide support and strategic direction while team members focus on operational efficiency and flexibility.[25] The physical layout of the team's workspace can also make a difference. For example, Toyota Motor Company, PSA Peugeot Citroën, and other firms have an "obeya room" to bring together project members with diverse backgrounds to more quickly resolve problems.

PSA Peugeot Citroën, Europe's second largest automaker, has set up an "obeya room" (Japanese for "big room") to speed up team decision making. The walls are plastered with graphs and notes so team members can visualize key issues. The obeya room creates a unique team environment that encourages face-to-face interaction to quickly solve critical, focused decisions. At one session, for example, managers figured out how to significantly reduce accidents among temporary workers. "The themes for projects in progress are displayed on the walls, with red when something is wrong," explains PSA Peugeot Citroën chief executive Philippe Varin. "Everyone takes the same problem and tries to fix it."[26]

Team Design Elements

Along with setting up a team-friendly environment, leaders need to carefully design the team itself, including task characteristics, team size, team composition, and team roles.

TASK CHARACTERISTICS

Teams are more effective than individuals in specific types of tasks. They are better for work that is too complex for any individual to perform, such as launching the business in a new market, developing a computer operating system, or constructing a bridge. Complex work requires skills and knowledge beyond the competencies of one person. Teams are particularly well suited when the complex work can be divided into more specialized roles and the people in the specialized roles require frequent coordination. Some evidence also suggests that teams work best with well-structured tasks because it is easier to coordinate such work among several people.[27]

One task characteristic that is particularly important for teams is **task interdependence**—the extent to which team members must share materials, information, or expertise to perform their jobs.[28] Apart from complete independence, there are three levels of task interdependence, as illustrated in Exhibit 8.3. The lowest level of interdependence, called *pooled interdependence,* occurs when an employee or work unit shares a common resource, such as machinery, administrative support, or a budget, with other employees or work units. This would occur in a team setting where each member works alone but shares raw materials or machinery to perform her or his otherwise independent tasks. Interdependence is higher under *sequential interdependence,* in which the output of one person becomes the direct input for another person or unit. Sequential interdependence occurs where team members are organized in an assembly line.

Reciprocal interdependence, in which work output is exchanged back and forth among individuals, produces the highest degree of interdependence. People who design a new product or service would typically have reciprocal interdependence because their design decisions affect others involved in the design process. Any decision made by the design engineers would influence the work of the manufacturing engineer and purchasing specialist, and vice versa. Employees with reciprocal interdependence should be organized into teams to facilitate coordination in their interwoven relationship.

EXHIBIT 8.3

Levels of Task Interdependence

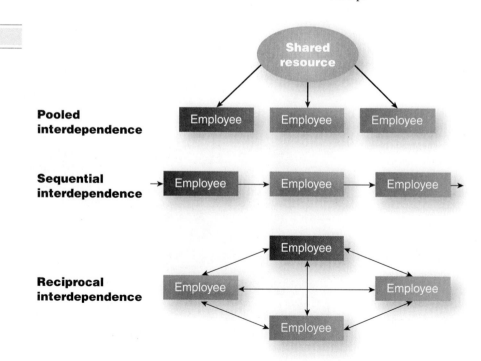

As a rule, the higher the level of task interdependence, the greater the need to organize people into teams rather than have them work alone. A team structure improves interpersonal communication and thus results in better coordination. High task interdependence also motivates most people to be part of the team. However, the rule that a team should be formed when employees have high interdependence applies when team members have the same task goals, such as serving the same clients or collectively assembling the same product. When team members have different goals (such as serving different clients) but must depend on other team members to achieve those unique goals, teamwork might create excessive conflict. Under these circumstances, the company should try to reduce the level of interdependence or rely on supervision as a buffer or mediator among employees.

TEAM SIZE

What is the ideal size for a team? Online retailer Amazon relies on the "two-pizza team" rule, namely, that a team should be small enough to be fed comfortably with two large pizzas. This works out to between five and seven employees. At the other extreme, a few experts suggest that tasks are becoming so complex that many teams need to have more than 100 members.[29] Unfortunately, the former piece of advice (two-pizza teams) is excessively simplistic, and the latter seems to have lost sight of the meaning and dynamics of real teams.

Generally, teams should be large enough to provide the necessary competencies and perspectives to perform the work, yet small enough to maintain the efficient coordination and meaningful involvement of each member.[30] "You need to have a balance between having enough people to do all the things that need to be done, while keeping the team small enough so that it is cohesive and can make decisions effectively and speedily," says Jim Hassell, a senior executive at NBN Co and previously with Sun and IBM.[31] Small teams (say, less than a dozen members) operate effectively because they have less process loss. Members of smaller teams also tend to feel more engaged because they get to know the other team members (which improves trust), have more influence on the group's norms and goals, and feel more responsible for the team's success and failure.

Should companies have 100-person teams if the task is highly complex? The answer is that a group this large probably isn't a team, even if management calls it one. A team exists when its members interact and influence one another, are mutually accountable for achieving common goals associated with organizational objectives, and perceive themselves as a social entity within an organization. It is very difficult for everyone in a 100-person work unit to influence one another and experience enough cohesion to perceive themselves as team members.

Executives at Whole Foods Market were aware that real teams are much smaller than 100 people when the food retailer opened its huge store in New York City's Columbus Circle. The store had 140 cashiers—far too many people for one cashier team—so Whole Foods Market divided the group into teams with a dozen employees each. All cashiers meet as one massive group every month to discuss production issues, but the smaller teams work effectively on a day-to-day basis.[32]

TEAM COMPOSITION

In most workplaces, employees must have more than technical skills; they must also be able and willing to work in a team environment. Team competencies are so important at Royal Dutch/Shell that the global energy giant hosts a special five-day "Gourami" exercise in Europe, North America, Asia, and the Middle East to observe how well university students (potential job applicants) work effectively under pressure in a team setting. "Dealing with the 'real-life' challenges of Gourami made us all aware of the value of other skills and aptitudes and the need to work as a team," says a mechanical engineering student who participated in one of these events.[33]

The most frequently mentioned characteristics or behaviors of effective team members are depicted in the "five C's" model illustrated in Exhibit 8.4: cooperating, coordinating, communicating, comforting, and conflict resolving. The first three competencies

task interdependence
The extent to which team members must share materials, information, or expertise in order to perform their jobs.

EXHIBIT 8.4

Five C's of Team Member Competency

Sources: Based on information in V. Rousseau, C. Aubé, and A. Savoie, "Teamwork Behaviors: A Review and an Integration of Frameworks," *Small Group Research* 37, no. 5 (2006), pp. 540–70; M.L. Loughry, M.W. Ohland, and D. D. Moore, "Development of a Theory-Based Assessment of Team Member Effectiveness," *Educational and Psychological Measurement* 67, no. 3 (2007), pp. 505–24.

are mainly (but not entirely) task-related, while the last two primarily assist team maintenance:[35]

- *Cooperating.* Effective team members are willing and able to work together rather than alone. This includes sharing resources and being sufficiently adaptive or flexible to accommodate the needs and preferences of other team members, such as rescheduling the use of machinery so that another team member with a tighter deadline can use it.

- *Coordinating.* Effective team members actively manage the team's work so that it is performed efficiently and harmoniously. For example, effective team members keep the team on track and help integrate the work performed by different members. This typically requires that effective team members know the work of other team members, not just their own.

- *Communicating.* Effective team members transmit information freely (rather than hoarding), efficiently (using the best channel and language), and respectfully (minimizing arousal of negative emotions). They also listen actively to coworkers.

- *Comforting.* Effective team members help coworkers maintain a positive and healthy psychological state. They show empathy, provide psychological comfort, and build coworker feelings of confidence and self-worth.

- *Conflict resolving.* Conflict is inevitable in social settings, so effective team members have the skills and motivation to resolve disagreements among team members. This requires the effective use of various conflict-handling styles as well as diagnostic skills to identify and resolve the structural sources of conflict.

Which employees tend to have these team competencies? The top of the list are those with high conscientiousness and extroversion personality traits, as well as with emotional

While many companies seek out star players with high IQs, recent studies suggest that they might get better performance out of employees who possess solid team competencies. One recent innovative study reported that the best predictors of a work unit's performance were the social sensitivity of its members (i.e., their emotional intelligence) and how equally they shared participation in the discussion (i.e., conversational turn-taking). General intelligence (IQ) did predict team effectiveness, but much less than the team competencies.[34]

intelligence. Furthermore, the old saying "One bad apple spoils the barrel" seems to apply to teams; one team member who lacks these teamwork competencies may undermine the dynamics of the entire team.[36]

Team Diversity   Another important dimension of team composition is diversity. Team diversity seems to have both positive and negative effects on team effectiveness.[37] Let's first look at the benefits of team diversity. Research suggests that, in specific situations, diverse teams are better than homogeneous teams at making decisions. One reason is that people from different backgrounds tend to see a problem or opportunity from different angles. Team members have different mental models, so they are more likely to identify viable solutions to difficult problems.

A second reason diverse teams tend to make better decisions is that they have a broader pool of technical competencies. For example, each team at Rackspace Hosting consists of more than a dozen people with diverse skills, such as account management, systems engineering, technical support, billing expertise, and data center support. The enterprise-level web infrastructure company requires these diverse technical competencies within each team to serve the needs of customers assigned to the team. A third reason favoring teams with diverse members is that they provide better representation of the team's constituents, such as other departments or clients from similarly diverse backgrounds. A team responsible for designing and launching a new service, for instance, should have representation from the organization's various specializations so that people in those work units will support the team's decisions.

Team diversity offers many advantages, but it also presents a number of opposing challenges.[38] Specifically, employees with diverse backgrounds take longer to become a high-performing team. This partly occurs because team members take longer to bond with people who are different from them, particularly when others hold different perspectives and values (i.e., deep-level diversity). Diverse teams are susceptible to "fault lines"—hypothetical dividing lines that may split a team into subgroups along gender, ethnic, professional, or other dimensions. These fault lines reduce team effectiveness by reducing the motivation to communicate and coordinate with teammates on the other side of the hypothetical divisions. In contrast, members of teams with minimal diversity experience higher satisfaction, less conflict, and better interpersonal relations. Consequently, homogeneous teams tend to be more effective for tasks requiring a high degree of cooperation and coordination, such as emergency response teams.

Team Processes

The third set of elements in the team effectiveness model, collectively known as *team processes*, includes team development, norms, cohesion, and trust. These elements represent characteristics of the team that continuously evolve.

TEAM DEVELOPMENT

Team members must resolve several issues and pass through several stages of development before emerging as an effective work unit. They need to get to know and trust each other, understand and agree on their respective roles, discover appropriate and inappropriate behaviors, and learn how to coordinate. The longer that team members work together, the better they develop common or complementary mental models, mutual

U.S. Air Force Security Forces Squadrons are deployed for special "outside-the-wire" operations, so their success depends on a high degree of team development. "I have 13 guys under me, and every single day I work with the same 13 guys," explains squad leader Staff Sergeant Eric Hammons. "They're going to know that when I go into a room I'm going to the right. And they know that since I'm going right they go left." These squadrons develop into high-performing teams through ongoing training in lifelike situations. This photo shows one of these "Ghostwalker" teams training in a simulated fire assignment.[39]

understanding, and effective performance routines to complete the work.

A popular model that captures many team development activities is shown in Exhibit 8.5.[40] The diagram shows teams moving systematically from one stage to the next, while the dashed lines illustrate that teams might fall back to an earlier stage of development as new members join or other conditions disrupt the team's maturity. *Forming,* the first stage of team development, is a period of testing and orientation in which members learn about one another and evaluate the benefits and costs of continued membership. People tend to be polite, will defer to authority, and try to find out what is expected of them and how they will fit into the team. The *storming* stage is marked by interpersonal conflict as members become more proactive and compete for various team roles. Members try to establish norms of appropriate behavior and performance standards.

During the *norming* stage, the team develops its first real sense of cohesion as roles are established and a consensus forms around group objectives and a common or complementary team-based mental model. By the *performing* stage, team members have learned to efficiently coordinate and resolve conflicts. In high-performance teams, members are highly cooperative, have a high level of trust in one another, are committed to group objectives, and identify with the team. Finally, the *adjourning* stage occurs when the team is about to disband. Team members shift their attention away from task orientation to a relationship focus.

The five-stage model is consistent with what students experience on team projects (as one study found), but it is far from a perfect representation of the team development process. For instance, it does not show that some teams remain in a particular stage longer than others. The five-stage model also masks two distinct processes during team development: developing team identity and developing team competence.[41]

- *Developing team identity.* This process involves the transition that individuals make from viewing the team as something "out there" to something that is part of themselves. In other words, team development occurs when employees shift their view of the team from "them" to "us." Developing team identity relates to becoming familiar with the team, making it part of their social identity, and shaping the team to better fit their prototype of an ideal team.

EXHIBIT 8.5   Stages of Team Development

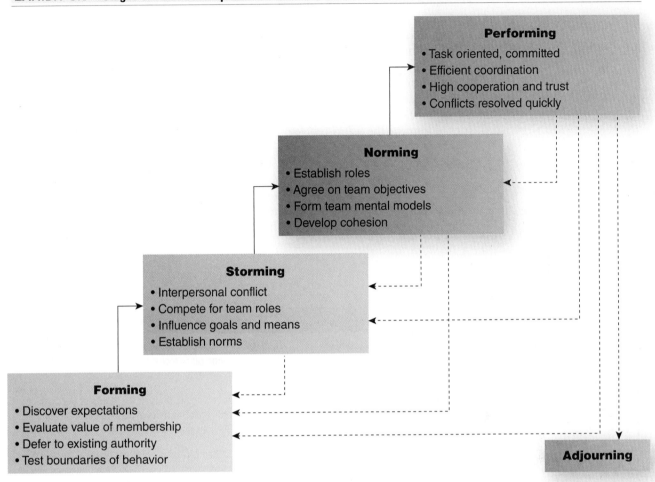

- *Developing team competence.* This process includes developing habitual routines with teammates and forming shared or complementary mental models.[42] Team mental models are visual or relational mental images that are shared by team members. For example, members of a newly formed team might have different views about customer service (quality of interaction, speed of service, technical expertise provided, etc.). As the team develops, these views converge into more of a shared mental model of customer service. One recent meta-analysis reported that teams are more effective when their members share common mental models of the work.[43]

Team Roles   An important part of the team development process is forming and reinforcing team roles. A **role** is a set of behaviors that people are expected to perform because they hold certain positions in a team and organization.[44] In a team setting, some roles help the team achieve its goals; other roles maintain relationships within the team. Some team roles are formally assigned to specific people. For example, team leaders are usually expected to initiate discussion, ensure that everyone has an opportunity to present his or her views, and help the team reach agreement on the issues discussed.

Team members are assigned specific roles within their formal job responsibilities. Yet team members also assume informal roles that suit their personality and values, as well as the wishes of other team members. These informal roles, which are negotiated throughout the team development process, range from supporting others to initiating new ideas. Informal team roles are shared, but many are eventually associated with one or two people on the team.[45]

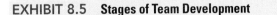

What team roles do you prefer?
Go to **www.mcgrawhillconnect.com** to assess the types of roles you like to be responsible for in teams.

role
A set of behaviors that people are expected to perform because of the positions they hold in a team and organization.

Accelerating Team Development Through Team Building   **Team building** consists of formal activities intended to improve the development and functioning of a work team.[46] To a large extent, team building attempts to speed up the team development process. This process may be applied to new teams, but it is more commonly introduced for existing teams that have regressed to earlier stages of team development due to membership turnover or loss of focus.

Some team-building interventions are task-focused. They clarify the team's performance goals, increase the team's motivation to accomplish these goals, and establish a mechanism for systematic feedback on the team's goal performance. A second type of team building tries to improve the team's problem-solving skills. A third category clarifies and reconstructs each member's perceptions of her or his role, as well as the role expectations that member has of other team members. Role definition team building also helps the team develop shared mental models—common internal representations of the external world, such as how to interact with clients, maintain machinery, and engage in meetings. Research studies indicate that team processes and performance depend on how well team members share common mental models about how they should work together.[47]

Popular Team-Building Activities[48]

TEAM-BUILDING ACTIVITY	DESCRIPTION	EXAMPLE
Team volunteering events	Teams of employees spend a day providing a public service to the community.	Timberland Co. employees work in teams to clean up the environment, plant trees, and work on community revitalization projects.
Team scavenger/treasure hunt competitions	Teams follow instructions to find clues or objects collected throughout the community.	With instructions and GPS devices, teams of Verizon Wireless employees track down 32 clues around Tampa within a three-hour time limit.
Team sports/exercise competitions	Wide variety of sports or health activities, ranging from volleyball tournaments across departments to teams competing globally in health activities.	More than 200 teams (7 employees per team) at Nestlé UK compete each year in the Global Corporate Challenge. Each team has the challenge of taking a virtual walk around the world in 125 days, which is about 10,000 steps per person.
Team cooking competitions	Employees work in teams to prepare a meal under the guidance of a master chef.	Employees at the Singapore operations of German engineering firm Siemens attend lessons at a bakery and then test their baking skills in teams.

A fourth—and likely the most common—type of team building is aimed at improving relations among team members. Its objective is to help team members learn more about one another, build trust, and develop ways to manage conflict within the team. Popular interventions such as wilderness team activities, paintball wars, and obstacle course challenges are typically offered to build trust. "If two colleagues hold the rope for you while you're climbing 10 meters up, that is truly team-building," suggests a partner in a German communications consulting firm who participated in that team-building event.[49]

Although team-building activities are popular, their success is less certain.[50] One problem is that team-building activities are used as general solutions to general team problems. A better approach is to begin with a sound diagnosis of the team's health and then select team-building interventions that address weaknesses.[51] Another problem is that team building is applied as a one-shot medical inoculation that every team should receive when it is formed. In truth, team building is an ongoing process, not a three-day jump start.[52] Finally, we must remember that team building occurs on the job, not just on an obstacle course or in a national park. Organizations should encourage team members to reflect on their work experiences and to experiment with just-in-time learning for team development.

TEAM NORMS

Norms are the informal rules and shared expectations that groups establish to regulate the behavior of their members. Norms apply only to behavior, not to private thoughts or feelings. Furthermore, norms exist only for behaviors that are important to the team.[53] Norms are enforced in various ways. Coworkers grimace if we are late for a meeting, or they make sarcastic comments if we don't have our part of the project completed on time. Norms are also directly reinforced through praise from high-status members, more access to valued resources, or other rewards available to the team. But team members often conform to prevailing norms without direct reinforcement or punishment because they identify with the group and want to align their behavior with the team's values. The more closely the person's social identity is connected to the group, the more the individual is motivated to avoid negative sanctions from that group.[54]

How Team Norms Develop

Norms develop when teams form because people need to anticipate or predict how others will act. Even subtle events during the team's formation, such as how team members initially greet each other and where they sit in the first few meetings, can initiate norms that are later difficult to change. Norms also form as team members discover behaviors that help them function more effectively (such as the need to respond quickly to e-mail). In particular, a critical event in the team's history can trigger formation of a norm or sharpen a previously vague one. A third influence on team norms is the experiences and values that members bring to the team. If members of a new team value work–life balance, norms are likely to develop that discourage long hours and work overload.[55]

Preventing and Changing Dysfunctional Team Norms

Team norms often become deeply anchored, so the best way to avoid norms that undermine organizational success or employee well-being is to establish desirable norms when the team is first formed. One way to do this is to clearly state desirable norms when the team is created. Another approach is to select people with appropriate values. If organizational leaders want their teams to have strong safety norms, they should hire people who already value safety and who clearly identify the importance of safety when the team is formed.

The suggestions so far refer to new teams, but how can organizational leaders maintain desirable norms in established teams? One solution comes from a recent study that showed leaders often have the capacity to alter existing norms.[56] By speaking up or actively coaching the team, they can often subdue dysfunctional norms while developing useful norms. A second suggestion is to introduce team-based rewards that counter dysfunction norms. However, studies report that employees might continue to adhere to a dysfunctional team norm (such as limiting output) even though this behavior reduces their paycheck. Finally, if dysfunctional norms are deeply ingrained and the previous solutions don't work, it may be necessary to disband the group and replace it with people with more favorable norms.

TEAM COHESION

Team cohesion refers to the degree of attraction people feel toward the team and their motivation to remain members. It is a characteristic of the team, including the extent to which its members are attracted to the team, are committed to the team's goals or tasks, and feel a collective sense of team pride.[57] Thus, team cohesion is an emotional experience, not just a calculation of whether to stay or leave the team. It exists when team members make the team part of their social identity. Team development tends to improve cohesion because members strengthen their identity to the team during the development process.

team building
A process that consists of formal activities intended to improve the development and functioning of a work team.

norms
The informal rules and shared expectations that groups establish to regulate the behavior of their members.

team cohesion
The degree of attraction people feel toward the team and their motivation to remain members.

Influences on Team Cohesion   Several factors influence team cohesion: member similarity, team size, member interaction, difficult entry, team success, and external competition or challenges. For the most part, these factors reflect the individual's social identity with the group and beliefs about how team membership will fulfill personal needs.

- *Member similarity.* Social scientists have long known that people are attracted to others who are similar to them.[58] This similarity-attraction effect occurs because we assume that people who look like us and have similar backgrounds are more trustworthy and are more likely to accept us. We also expect to have fewer negative experiences, such as conflicts and violations of our expectations and beliefs. Thus, teams have higher cohesion or become cohesive more quickly when members are similar. In contrast, it is more difficult and takes longer for teams with diverse members to become cohesive. This difficulty depends on the form of diversity, however. Teams consisting of people from different job groups seem to gel together just as well as teams of people from the same job.[59]

- *Team size.* Smaller teams tend to have more cohesion than larger teams because it is easier for a few people to agree on goals and coordinate work activities. However, small teams have less cohesion when they lack enough members to perform the required tasks.

- *Member interaction.* Teams tend to have more cohesion when team members interact fairly regularly. This occurs when team members perform highly interdependent tasks and work in the same physical area.

- *Somewhat difficult entry.* Teams tend to have more cohesion when entry to the team is restricted. Elite teams confer more prestige on their members, which increases the value of being a team member. At the same time, research suggests that severe initiations can weaken team cohesion because of the adverse effects of humiliation, even for those who successfully endure the initiation.[60]

- *Team success.* Cohesion is both emotional and instrumental, with the latter referring to the notion that people feel more cohesion to teams that fulfill their needs and goals. Consequently, cohesion increases with the team's level of success.[61] Furthermore, individuals are more likely to attach their social identity to successful teams than to those with a string of failures.[62]

Until recently, La-Z-Boy, Inc., production employees worked in functional groups. Upholsterers worked together in one area, and the frame makers worked in another area. Now, employees are organized into cross-functional teams. A La-Z-Boy chair team has three upholsterers, one frame maker, one person who does the stuffing, and one person who completes the assembly and packing. By working side-by-side to build an entire piece of furniture, these employees have more team cohesion as well as commitment to product quality. "The idea is to help make workers accountable, but also to give them a sense of ownership of what they do," says a La-Z-Boy production manager.[63]

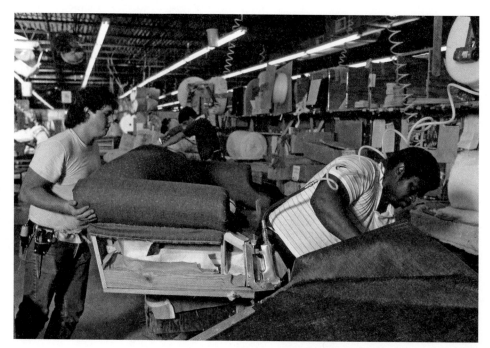

- *External competition and challenges.* Team cohesion tends to increase when members face external competition or a valued objective that is challenging. This might include a threat from an external competitor or friendly competition from other teams. Employees value their membership on the team because of its ability to overcome the threat or competition and as a form of social support. However, cohesion can dissipate when external threats are severe, because these threats are stressful and cause teams to make less effective decisions.[64]

Consequences of Team Cohesion   Every team must have some minimal level of cohesion to maintain its existence. People who belong to high-cohesion teams are motivated to maintain their membership and to help the team achieve its mutually agreed objectives. Compared with low-cohesion teams, high-cohesion team members spend more time together, share information more frequently, and are more satisfied with one another. They provide one another with better social support in stressful situations.[65] Members of high-cohesion teams are generally more sensitive to others' needs and develop better interpersonal relationships, thereby reducing dysfunctional conflict. When conflict does arise, members tend to resolve their differences swiftly and effectively. With better cooperation and more conformity to norms, high-cohesion teams usually perform better than low-cohesion teams.[66]

There are two important matters that need to be discussed regarding the cohesion–performance relationship, however. First, though we typically assume that increasing cohesion leads to higher team performance, we explained previously that team performance (success) is a predictor of cohesion. Indeed, one recent study estimated that team performance has a stronger effect on cohesion than vice versa. In other words, a team's performance will likely affect its cohesion, whereas a team's cohesion has less effect on its performance.[67]

Second, the weaker effect of cohesion on performance might be explained by another matter we need to address. As Exhibit 8.6 illustrates, team cohesion increases team performance only when the team's norms are compatible with organizational values and objectives. When team norms are counterproductive (such as when norms encourage absenteeism or discourage employees from working more productively), a cohesive team will typically perform worse than if the team has low cohesion. This effect occurs because cohesion motivates employees to perform at a level more consistent with team norms. When team norms undermine the organization's performance, high cohesion will motivate employees to reduce team performance.[68]

EXHIBIT 8.6

Effect of Team Cohesion on Task Performance

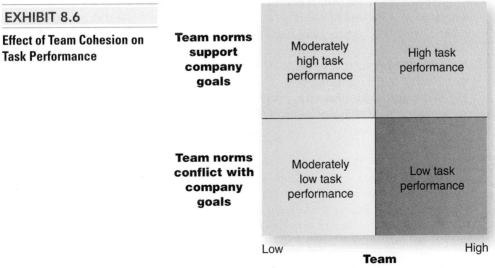

EXHIBIT 8.7

Three Foundations of Trust in Teams

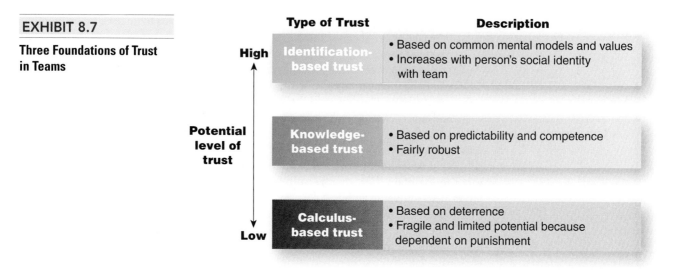

	Type of Trust	Description
High	Identification-based trust	• Based on common mental models and values • Increases with person's social identity with team
Potential level of trust	Knowledge-based trust	• Based on predictability and competence • Fairly robust
Low	Calculus-based trust	• Based on deterrence • Fragile and limited potential because dependent on punishment

TEAM TRUST

Any relationship—including the relationship among team members—depends on a certain degree of trust.[69] Trust refers to positive expectations one person has toward another person in situations involving risk (see Chapter 4).[70] A high level of trust occurs when others affect you in situations where you are at risk but you believe they will not harm you. Trust includes both your beliefs and conscious feelings about the relationship with other team members. In other words, a person both logically evaluates the situation as trustworthy and feels that it is trustworthy.[71] Trust is built on three foundations: calculus, knowledge, and identification (see Exhibit 8.7).

Calculus-based trust represents a logical calculation that other team members will act appropriately because they face sanctions if their actions violate reasonable expectations.[72] It offers the lowest potential trust and is easily broken by a violation of expectations. Generally, calculus-based trust alone cannot sustain a team's relationship, because it relies on deterrence. *Knowledge-based trust* is based on the predictability of another team member's behavior. Even if we don't agree with a particular team member's actions, his or her consistency generates some level of trust. Knowledge-based trust also relates to confidence in the other person's ability or competence, such as the confidence that exists when we trust a physician.[73] Knowledge-based trust offers a higher potential level of trust and is more stable because it develops over time.

Identification-based trust is based on mutual understanding and an emotional bond among team members. It occurs when team members think, feel, and act like one another. High-performance teams exhibit this level of trust because they share the same values and mental models. Identification-based trust is potentially the strongest and most robust of all three types of trust. The individual's self-concept is based partly on membership in the team, and he or she believes the members' values highly overlap, so any transgressions by other team members are quickly forgiven. People are more reluctant to acknowledge a violation of this high-level trust, because it strikes at the heart of their self-concept.

Dynamics of Team Trust

When joining a team, employees typically have a moderate or high level—not a low level—of trust in their new coworkers. The main explanation for the initially high trust (called *swift trust*) in organizational settings is that people usually believe fellow team members are reasonably competent (knowledge-based trust), and they tend to develop some degree of social identity with the team (identification-based trust). Even when working with strangers, most of us display some level of trust, if only because it supports our self-concept of being a good

self-directed teams (SDTs)
Cross-functional work groups that are organized around work processes, complete an entire piece of work requiring several interdependent tasks, and have substantial autonomy over the execution of those tasks.

person.[74] However, trust is fragile in new relationships, because it is based on assumptions rather than well-established experience. Consequently, studies report that trust tends to decrease rather than increase over time. This is unfortunate, because employees become less forgiving and less cooperative toward others as their level of trust decreases, and this undermines team and organizational effectiveness.[75]

The team effectiveness model is a useful template for understanding how teams work—and don't work—in organizations. With this knowledge in hand, let's briefly investigate two types of teams that have received considerable attention among OB experts and practitioners: self-directed teams and virtual teams.

Self-Directed Teams

LO4

The opening vignette to this chapter described two Reckitt Benckiser plants in the United Kingdom that operate with minimal management decision making or involvement in production line activities. These manufacturing facilities rely instead on self-directed teams. **Self-directed teams (SDTs)** are cross-functional groups organized around work processes, that complete an entire piece of work requiring several interdependent tasks, and that have substantial autonomy over the execution of those tasks.[76]

This definition captures two distinct features of SDTs. First, these teams complete an entire piece of work requiring several interdependent tasks. This type of work arrangement clusters the team members together while minimizing interdependence and interaction with employees outside the team. The result is a close-knit group of employees who depend on one another to accomplish their individual tasks. For example, Reckitt Benckiser employees responsible for manufacturing Lysol® disinfectant spray are responsible for that entire line of production—from receiving raw materials to packaging the product.

The second distinctive feature of SDTs is that they have substantial autonomy over the execution of their tasks. In particular, these teams plan, organize, and control work activities with little or no direct involvement of a higher-status supervisor. The teams at Reckitt Benckiser's plants, for instance, are considered self-directed because they have considerable autonomy and responsibility for decisions in their work area, including managing inventory, production efficiency, and related matters.

Whole Foods Market operates with self-directed teams. Each store has about 10 teams, such as the prepared foods team, the cashier/front-end team, and the seafood team. Teams are "self-directed" because team members make decisions about their work unit with minimal interference from management. "Each team is . . . responsible for managing its own business," explains Whole Foods Market cofounder John Mackey. "It gets a profit-and-loss statement; it's responsible for managing inventory, labor productivity, gross margins; and its members are responsible for many of the product placement decisions."[77]

Self-directed teams are found in several industries, ranging from petrochemical plants to aircraft parts manufacturing. Most of the top-rated manufacturing firms in North America apparently rely on SDTs.[78] Indeed, self-directed teams have become such a popular way to organize employees in manufacturing, services, and government work that many companies don't realize they have them. The popularity of SDTs is consistent with research indicating that they potentially increase both productivity and job satisfaction. For instance, one study found that car dealership service shops that organize employees into SDTs are significantly more profitable than shops where employees work without a team structure. Another study reported that both short- and long-term measures of customer satisfaction increased after street cleaners in a German city were organized into SDTs.[79]

SUCCESS FACTORS FOR SELF-DIRECTED TEAMS

The successful implementation of self-directed teams depends on several factors.[80] SDTs should be responsible for an entire work process, such as making an entire product or providing a service. This structure keeps each team sufficiently independent from other teams, yet it demands a relatively high degree of interdependence among employees within the team.[81] SDTs should also have sufficient autonomy to organize and coordinate their work. Autonomy allows them to respond more quickly and effectively to client and stakeholder demands. It also motivates team members through feelings of empowerment. Finally, SDTs are more successful when the work site and technology support coordination and communication among team members and increase job enrichment.[82] Too often, management calls a group of employees a "team," yet the work layout, assembly-line structure, and other technologies isolate the employees.

Virtual Teams

connect

To assist your learning and test your knowledge about virtual teams, go to **www.mcgrawhillconnect.com**, which has activities and test questions on this topic.

While many of its manufacturing plants are operated by self-directed teams, Reckitt Benckiser often relies on virtual teams in its marketing, information systems, and other office activities. **Virtual teams** are teams whose members operate across space, time, and organizational boundaries and are linked through information technologies to achieve organizational tasks.[83] Virtual teams differ from traditional teams in two ways: (1) They are not usually co-located (do not work in the same physical area), and (2) due to their lack of co-location, members of virtual teams depend primarily on information technologies rather than face-to-face interaction to communicate and coordinate their work effort.

Virtual teams have spread throughout most organizations, and this trend will continue. Two-thirds of human resource managers estimate that reliance on virtual teams will grow rapidly over the next few years.[84] In global companies such as IBM, almost everyone in knowledge work is part of a virtual team. One reason virtual teams have become so widespread is information technologies have made it easier than ever before to communicate and coordinate with people at a distance.[85] The shift from production-based to knowledge-based work is a second reason virtual teamwork is feasible. It isn't yet possible to make a physical product when team members are located apart, but most of us are now in jobs that mainly process knowledge.

Information technologies and knowledge-based work make virtual teams *possible*, but organizational learning and globalization are two reasons they are increasingly *necessary*. Virtual teams represent a natural part of the organizational learning process because they encourage employees to share and use knowledge where geography limits more direct forms of collaboration. Globalization makes virtual teams increasingly necessary because employees are spread around the planet rather than around one building or city. Thus, global businesses depend on virtual teamwork to leverage their human capital.

Debating Point

ARE VIRTUAL TEAMS MORE TROUBLE THAN THEY'RE WORTH?

Virtual teams were rare before the Internet was born. Two decades later, they are almost as commonplace as face-to-face teams. Virtual teams are increasingly possible because more of us are employed in knowledge work rather than physical production. Furthermore, information technologies make it easier to communicate instantaneously with coworkers around the globe. To some extent, virtual teams have even become "cool." It is almost a badge of honor to say that you are a member of a far-flung team of people from several continents.

But whether they are stylish or commonplace, virtual teams seem to be increasingly necessary for an organization's competitive advantage. This chapter points out that we need virtual teams to effectively engage in organizational learning. Knowledge has become the currency of organizational success, and globalization has ensured that such knowledge is scattered around the world. In short, organizations are at a disadvantage unless they use lots of virtual teams.

How could anyone claim that virtual teams aren't worth the effort, particularly when organizational learning is one of the four pillars of organizational effectiveness (see Chapter 1)? Well, actually, there are a few arguments against them. For the most part, critics don't deny the potential value of sharing knowledge through virtual teams. Rather, they have added up the negative features and concluded that they outweigh the benefits. In fact, when chief information officers were asked to identify the top challenges of globalization, 70 percent listed managing virtual teams as the top concern.[86]

One persistent problem with virtual teams is that they lack the richness of face-to-face communication. We'll provide more detail about this important matter in Chapter 9, but no information technology to date equals the volume and variety of information transmitted among people located in the same room. This is one reason Toyota, PSA Peugeot Citroën, and other companies arrange for teams to meet in the same physical space. They can exchange information in larger volumes, much faster, and more accurately compared with the clumsy methods currently available to virtual teams. Multiperson video chat is getting closer to face-to-face, but it requires considerable bandwidth and still falls short on communication richness.

Another problem with virtual teams is that people trust others more easily when they are nearby.[87] Various studies have reported that virtual team members either have lower trust compared with co-located team members, or their trust is much more fragile. In fact, experts offer one main recommendation to increase trust among virtual team members—have them spend time together as co-located teams. "When you're starting a company, everybody needs to be on the same page about what is important," warns Leonard Speiser, a serial Internet entrepreneur who has also worked at Yahoo and eBay. "You have to be able to get together and talk, get to know each other. It takes great effort to do that virtually."[88]

A third drawback with virtual teams is that the farther away people are located, the more they differ in experiences, beliefs, culture, and expectations. These differences can be advantageous for some decisions, of course, but they can also be a curse for team development and performance. "Everyone must have the same picture of what success looks like," advises Rick Maurer, a leadership consultant in Arlington, Virginia. "Without that laser-like focus, it is too easy for people in Bangalore to develop a different picture of success than the picture held by their colleagues in Brussels. Now multiply that by a couple more locations and you've got a mess."[89]

Here's one more reason why companies should think twice before relying on virtual teams: People seem to have less influence or control over distant than over co-located coworkers. A team member who stops by your cubicle to ask how your part of the report is coming along has much more effect than an impersonal—or even a flaming—e-mail from afar.

Perhaps that is why surveys reveal less satisfaction with virtual team members than co-located team members.[90] One study reported that distant colleagues received two to three times as many complaints as co-located colleagues about working half-heartedly (or not at all) on shared projects, falling behind on projects, not making deadlines, failing to warn about missing deadlines, making changes without warning, and providing misleading information. When asked how long it takes to resolve these problems, more than half of the respondents indicated a few days for co-located team members, whereas most estimated a few weeks or longer for distant team members.

virtual teams
Teams whose members operate across space, time, and organizational boundaries and are linked through information technologies to achieve organizational tasks.

SUCCESS FACTORS FOR VIRTUAL TEAMS

Virtual teams have all the challenges of traditional teams, along with the complications of distance and time. Fortunately, OB researchers have been keenly interested in virtual teams, and their studies are now yielding ways to improve virtual team effectiveness.[91] First, along with having the team competencies described previously in this chapter, members of successful virtual teams must have good communication technology skills, strong self-leadership skills to motivate and guide their behavior without peers or bosses nearby, and higher emotional intelligence so that they can decipher the feelings of other team members from e-mail and other limited communication media.

Second, virtual teams should have a toolkit of communication channels (e-mail, virtual whiteboards, video conferencing, etc.), as well as the freedom to choose the channels that work best for them. This may sound obvious, but unfortunately senior management tends to impose technology on virtual teams, often based on advice from external consultants, and expects team members to use the same communication technology throughout their work. In contrast, research suggests that specific communication channels gain and lose importance over time, depending on the task and level of trust.

Third, virtual teams need plenty of structure. In one recent review of effective virtual teams, many of the principles for successful virtual teams related mostly to creating these structures, such as clear operational objectives, documented work processes, and agreed upon roles and responsibilities.[92] The final recommendation is that virtual team members should meet face-to-face fairly early in the team development process. This idea may seem contradictory to the entire notion of virtual teams, but so far, no technology has replaced face-to-face interaction for high-level bonding and mutual understanding.[93]

Team Decision Making

Self-directed teams, virtual teams, and practically all other groups are expected to make decisions. Under certain conditions, teams are more effective than individuals at identifying problems, choosing alternatives, and evaluating their decisions. To leverage these benefits, however, we first need to understand the constraints on effective team decision making. Then, we look at specific team structures that try to overcome these constraints.

CONSTRAINTS ON TEAM DECISION MAKING

Anyone who has spent enough time in the workplace can recite several ways in which teams stumble in decision making. The four most common problems are time constraints, evaluation apprehension, pressure to conform, and some elements of groupthink.

Time Constraints   There's a saying that committees keep minutes and waste hours. This reflects the fact that teams take longer than individuals to make decisions.[94] Unlike individuals, teams require extra time to organize, coordinate, and maintain relationships. The larger the group, the more time is required to make a decision. Team members need time to learn about one another and build rapport. They need to manage an imperfect communication process so that there is sufficient understanding of one another's ideas. They also need to coordinate roles and rules of order within the decision process.

Another time-related constraint found in most team structures is that only one person can speak at a time.[95] This problem, known as **production blocking,** undermines idea generation in several ways. First, team members need to listen in on the conversation to find an opportune time to speak up, and this monitoring makes it difficult for them to concentrate on their own ideas. Second, ideas are fleeting, so the longer they wait to speak up, the more likely these flickering ideas will die out. Third, team members might remember their fleeting thoughts by concentrating on them, but this causes them to pay less attention to the conversation. By ignoring what others are saying, team members miss other potentially good ideas as well as the opportunity to convey their ideas to others in the group.

Evaluation Apprehension   Team members are often reluctant to mention ideas that seem silly because they believe (often correctly) that other team members are silently evaluating them.[96] This **evaluation apprehension** is based on the individual's desire to create a favorable self-presentation and need to protect self-esteem. It is most common when meetings are attended by people with different levels of status or expertise or when members formally evaluate others' performance throughout the year (as in 360-degree feedback). Creative ideas often sound bizarre or illogical when first presented, so evaluation apprehension tends to discourage employees from mentioning them in front of coworkers.

Pressure to Conform   Team cohesion leads employees to conform to the team's norms. This control keeps the group organized around common goals, but it may also cause team members to suppress their dissenting opinions, particularly when a strong team norm is related to the issue. When someone does state a point of view that violates the majority opinion, other members might punish the violator or try to persuade him or her that the opinion is incorrect. Conformity can also be subtle. To some extent, we depend on the opinions that others hold to validate our own views. If coworkers don't agree with us, we begin to question our own opinions even without overt peer pressure.

Groupthink   **Groupthink** refers to the tendency of highly cohesive groups to value consensus at the price of decision quality.[97] The concept includes the dysfunctional effects of conformity on team decision making, which we just described. It also includes the dysfunctional consequences of trying to maintain harmony within the team. This desire for harmony exists as a group norm and is most apparent when team members have a strong social identity with the group. Groupthink supposedly occurs most often when the team is isolated from outsiders, the team leader is opinionated (rather than impartial), the team is under stress due to an external threat, the team has experienced recent failures or other decision-making problems, and the team lacks clear guidance from corporate policies or procedures.

The term *groupthink* is now part of everyday language, but most experts have dismissed the concept. The main problem with the groupthink concept is that it consists of several elements that don't cluster together very well, and some of those elements actually improve rather than undermine decision making in some situations. Also, almost all support for the groupthink effect comes from case studies, most of which are flawed.[98]

Although the groupthink concept is on its last legs, there are specific elements that remain relevant as problems with team decision making. One of these elements, conformity, was identified earlier as a problem with team decision making. Overconfidence is another groupthink element that also deserves continued attention as a problem. Studies consistently report that highly confident teams have a false sense of invulnerability, which makes them less attentive in decision making than are moderately confident teams.[99] This overconfidence effect is related to problems with self-enhancement described in Chapter 3 and with the adverse effects of positive moods and emotions on the quality of decision making (see Chapter 7).

TEAM STRUCTURES TO IMPROVE DECISION MAKING

Team decision making is fraught with problems, but several solutions also emerge from these bad-news studies. Team members need to be confident in their decision making but not so confident that they collectively feel invulnerable. This calls for team norms that encourage critical thinking as well as team membership with sufficient diversity. Checks and balances need to be in place to prevent one or two people from dominating the discussion. The team should also be large enough to possess the collective knowledge to resolve the problem yet small enough that the team doesn't consume too much time or restrict individual input.

production blocking
A time constraint in team decision making due to the procedural requirement that only one person may speak at a time.

evaluation apprehension
A decision-making problem that occurs when individuals are reluctant to mention ideas that seem silly because they believe (often correctly) that other team members are silently evaluating them.

groupthink
The tendency of highly cohesive groups to value consensus at the price of decision quality.

Team structures also help minimize the problems described over the previous few pages. Four structures potentially improve team decision making in team settings: constructive conflict, brainstorming, electronic brainstorming, and nominal group technique.

Constructive Conflict   A popular way to improve team decision making at Corning Inc. is to assign promising ideas to two-person teams, who spend up to four months analyzing the feasibility of their assigned idea. The unique feature about this process at the ceramics and glass company is that the team is always composed of one person with marketing expertise and another person with technical expertise. This oil-and-water combination sometimes ruffles feathers, but it seems to generate better ideas and evaluations. "We find great constructive conflict this way," says Deborah Mills, who leads Corning's early-stage marketing team.[100]

Constructive conflict occurs when people focus on the issue and maintain respect for people having other points of view. This conflict is called "constructive" because it encourages people to present their divergent viewpoints so ideas and recommendations can be clarified, redesigned, and tested for logical soundness. This critical thinking and analysis helps participants reexamine their assumptions and logic. The main challenge with constructive conflict is that people get defensive when their ideas are questioned, even when those critiques are polite and logical. Consequently, constructive conflict often degenerates into defensive behavior and personal attacks. This tendency may explain why constructive conflict has not been consistently beneficial for team decision making across studies.[101] We explore this issue further in Chapter 11, along with specific strategies for minimizing the emotional effects of conflict while maintaining constructive debate.

Brainstorming   **Brainstorming** is a team event where participants try to think up as many ideas as possible. The process was introduced by advertising executive Alex Osborn in 1939 and has four simple rules to maximize the number and quality of ideas presented: (1) Speak freely—describe even the craziest ideas; (2) don't criticize others or their ideas; (3) provide as many ideas as possible—the quality of ideas increases with the quantity of ideas; and (4) build on the ideas that others have presented. These rules are supposed to encourage divergent thinking while minimizing evaluation apprehension and other team dynamics problems.[102]

Although brainstorming became immensely popular when first introduced, it lost credibility over the years—mostly for the wrong reasons. First, a business magazine article in the 1950s misrepresented and lampooned the process.[103] Second, numerous lab studies using college students concluded that brainstorming isn't very effective, mainly because production blocking and evaluation apprehension still interfere with team dynamics.[104]

These studies and the magazine article were unfortunate because subsequent work has found that brainstorming is potentially useful in real-world work settings.[105] Companies that use brainstorming emphasize that it takes considerable skill and experience to effectively lead brainstorming sessions, yet most lab studies have involved teams of college students who received minimal training and had no previous experience with these activities. Executives say that brainstorming requires a collaborative learning orientation culture where employees are not inhibited by evaluation apprehension, whereas the lab experiments involve students who often don't know one another and are sensitive about their image to others. Most studies also make the mistake of measuring brainstorming effectiveness by the number of ideas generated, whereas recent investigations indicate that brainstorming tends to generate more *creative* ideas (not necessarily a greater number of ideas).[106]

Lab studies also ignore other benefits of brainstorming reported by companies that claim they are effective. The positive focus of brainstorming (no criticizing) tends to increase team cohesion and participant commitment to the eventual decision. Brainstorming sessions also tend to spread enthusiasm—a condition that often generates creativity beyond these events. Overall, while brainstorming might not always be the best team structure, it seems more valuable than many lab studies have concluded.

Electronic Brainstorming   **Electronic brainstorming** is a variation of brainstorming that relies on networked computers to submit and share creative ideas. After receiving the question or issue, participants enter their ideas using special computer software. The ideas are distributed anonymously to other participants, who are encouraged to piggyback on those ideas. Team members eventually vote electronically on the ideas presented. Face-to-face discussion usually follows. Electronic brainstorming can be quite effective at generating creative ideas with

3M has a legendary reputation for creative thinking, but it has recently shifted some of its brainstorming activity to an online format called "Innovation Live." The intranet website's pilot project generated 736 ideas in two weeks from employees across 58 nations. 3M is now testing this online brainstorming process with marketing professionals in other companies. "Innovation is at the heart of 3M culture, and we are driven to search for new ideas," says Linda Siso, a 3M executive in South Africa. "We understand the power of a chain reaction—where one idea leads to numerous more."[108]

minimal production blocking, evaluation apprehension, or conformity problems.[107] Despite these numerous advantages, electronic brainstorming seems too structured and technology-bound for some executives. Some leaders may also feel threatened by the honesty of statements generated through this process and by their limited ability to control the discussion.

Nominal Group Technique   The **nominal group technique** is another variation of traditional brainstorming that tries to combine the benefits of team decision making without the problems mentioned earlier.[109] The method is called "nominal" because participants form a group in name only during two of its three stages. After the problem is described, team members silently and independently write down as many solutions as they can. In the second stage, participants describe their solutions to the other team members, usually in a round-robin format. As with brainstorming, there is no criticism or debate, though members are encouraged to ask for clarification of the ideas presented. In the third stage, participants silently and independently rank-order or vote on each proposed solution.

The nominal group technique has been applied in numerous laboratory and real-world settings, such as identifying ways to improve tourism in various countries.[110] For the most part, these studies endorse the use of this structured form of team decision making. It tends to generate a higher number of ideas and better-quality ideas than do traditional interacting and possibly brainstorming groups.[111] Due to its high degree of structure, the nominal group technique usually maintains a high task orientation and relatively low potential for conflict within the team. However, production blocking and evaluation apprehension still occur to some extent. At least one study also reports that participants require training to apply this structured approach to team decision making.[112]

---

constructive conflict
A type of conflict in which people focus their discussion on the issue while maintaining respect for people having other points of view.

brainstorming
A freewheeling, face-to-face meeting where team members aren't allowed to criticize but are encouraged to speak freely, generate as many ideas as possible, and build on the ideas of others.

electronic brainstorming
A form of brainstorming that relies on networked computers for submitting and sharing creative ideas.

nominal group technique
A variation of brainstorming consisting of three stages: Participants (1) silently and independently document their ideas, (2) collectively describe these ideas to the other team members without critique, and then (3) silently and independently evaluate the ideas presented.

LO1 Discuss the benefits and limitations of teams, and explain why employees join informal groups.

Teams are groups of two or more people who interact and influence each other, are mutually accountable for achieving common goals associated with organizational objectives, and perceive themselves as a social entity within an organization. All teams are groups, because they consist of people with a unifying relationship; not all groups are teams, because some groups do not exist to serve organizational objectives.

People join informal groups (and are motivated to be on formal teams) for four reasons: (1) They have an innate drive to bond, (2) group membership is an inherent ingredient in a person's self-concept, (3) some personal goals are accomplished better in groups, and (4) individuals are comforted in stressful situations by the mere presence of other people. Teams have become popular because they tend to make better decisions, support the knowledge management process, and provide superior customer service. People also tend to be more motivated working in teams. However, teams are not always as effective as individuals working alone. Process losses and social loafing are two particular concerns that drag down team performance.

LO2 Outline the team effectiveness model and discuss how task characteristics, team size, and team composition influence team effectiveness.

Team effectiveness includes the team's ability to achieve its objectives, fulfill the needs of its members, and maintain its survival. The model of team effectiveness considers the team and organizational environment, team design, and team processes. Three team design elements are task characteristics, team size, and team composition. Teams tend to be better suited for situations in which the work is complex and the tasks among employees have high interdependence. Teams should be large enough to perform the work yet small enough for efficient coordination and meaningful involvement. Effective teams are composed of people with the competencies and motivation to perform tasks in a team environment. Team member diversity has advantages and disadvantages for team performance.

LO3 Discuss how the four team processes—team development, norms, cohesion, and trust—influence team effectiveness.

Teams develop through the stages of forming, storming, norming, performing, and eventually adjourning. Within these stages are two distinct team development processes: developing team identity and developing team competence. Team development can be accelerated through team building—any formal activity intended to improve the development and functioning of a work team. Teams develop norms to regulate and guide member behavior. These norms may be influenced by initial experiences, critical events, and the values and experiences that team members bring to the group.

Team cohesion—the degree of attraction people feel toward the team and their motivation to remain members—increases with member similarity, smaller team size, higher degree of interaction, somewhat difficult entry, team success, and external challenges. Cohesion increases team performance when the team's norms are congruent with organizational goals. Trust refers to positive expectations one person has toward another person in situations involving risk. People trust others on the basis of three foundations: calculus, knowledge, and identification.

LO4 Discuss the characteristics and factors required for the success of self-directed teams and virtual teams.

Self-directed teams (SDTs) complete an entire piece of work requiring several interdependent tasks, and they have substantial autonomy over the execution of their tasks. Members of virtual teams operate across space, time, and organizational boundaries and are linked through information technologies to achieve organizational tasks. Virtual teams are more effective when the team members have certain competencies, the team has the freedom to choose the preferred communication channels, and the members meet face-to-face fairly early in the team development process.

LO5 Identify four constraints on team decision making and discuss the advantages and disadvantages of four structures aimed at improving team decision making.

Team decisions are impeded by time constraints, evaluation apprehension, conformity to peer pressure, and groupthink (specifically overconfidence). Four structures potentially improve decision making in team settings: constructive conflict, brainstorming, electronic brainstorming, and the nominal group technique.

{ key terms }

1. Informal groups exist in almost every form of social organization. What types of informal groups exist in your classroom? Why are students motivated to belong to these informal groups?

2. The late management guru Peter Drucker said: "The now-fashionable team in which everybody works with everybody on everything from the beginning rapidly is becoming a disappointment." Discuss three problems associated with teams.

3. You have been put in charge of a cross-functional task force that will develop enhanced Internet banking services for retail customers. The team includes representatives from marketing, information services, customer service, and accounting, all of whom will move to the same location at headquarters for three months. Describe the behaviors you might observe during each stage of the team's development.

4. You have just been transferred from the Kansas office to the Denver office of your company, a national sales organization of electrical products for developers and contractors. In Kansas, team members regularly called customers after a sale to ask whether the products arrived on time and whether they are satisfied. But when you moved to the Denver office, no one seemed to make these follow-up calls. A recently hired coworker explained that other coworkers discouraged her from making those calls. Later, another coworker suggested that your follow-up calls were making everyone else look lazy. Give three possible reasons why the norms in Denver might be different from those in the Kansas office, even though the customers, products, sales commissions, and other characteristics of the workplace are almost identical.

5. You have been assigned to a class project with five other students, none of whom you have met before, and some of whom come from different countries. To what extent would team cohesion improve your team's performance on this project? What actions would you recommend to build team cohesion among student team members in this situation?

6. Suppose that you were put in charge of a virtual team whose members are located in different cities around the world. What tactics could you use to build and maintain team trust and performance, as well as minimize the decline in trust and performance that often occurs in teams?

7. You are responsible for convening a major event in which senior officials from several state governments will try to come to an agreement on environmental issues. It is well known that some officials posture so that they appear superior, whereas others are highly motivated to solve the environmental problems that cross adjacent states. What team decision-making problems are likely to be apparent in this government forum, and what actions can you take to minimize these problems?

8. Sawgrass Widgets wants to use brainstorming with its employees and customers to identify new uses for its product. Advise Sawgrass's president about the potential benefits of brainstorming, as well as its potential limitations.

CASE STUDY 8.1 THE OUTSTANDING FACULTY AWARD

Adapted from a case by David J. Cherrington, Brigham Young University

I recently served on the Outstanding Faculty Award committee for the College of Business. This award is our college's highest honor for a faculty member, which is bestowed at a special reception ceremony. At the first meeting, our committee discussed the nomination process and decided to follow our traditional practice of inviting nominations from both the faculty and students. During the next month, we received six completed files with supporting documentation. Three of the nominations came from department chairs, two from faculty who recommended their colleagues, and one from a group of 16 graduate students.

At the second meeting, we agreed that we didn't know the six applicants well enough to make a decision that day, so we decided that we would read the applications on our own and rank them. There was no discussion about ranking criteria; I think I assumed that we shared a common definition of the word "outstanding."

During the third meeting, it quickly became apparent that each committee member had a different interpretation of what constitutes an "outstanding" faculty member. The discussion was polite, but we debated the extent to which this was an award for teaching, or research, or service to the college, or scholarly textbook writing, or consulting, or service to society, or some other factor. After three hours, we agreed on five criteria that we would apply to independently rate each candidate using a five-point scale.

When we reconvened the next day, our discussion was much more focused as we tried to achieve a consensus regarding how we judged each candidate on each criterion. After a lengthy discussion, we finally completed the task and averaged the ratings. The top three scores had an average rating (out of a maximum of 25) of 21, 19.5, and 18.75. I assumed the person with the highest total would receive the award. Instead, my colleagues began debating over the relevance of the five criteria that we had agreed on the previous day. Some committee members felt, in hindsight, that the criteria were incorrectly weighted or that other criteria should be considered. Although they did not actually say this, I sensed that at least two colleagues on the committee wanted the criteria or weights changed because their preferred candidate didn't get the highest score using the existing formula. When we changed the weights in various ways, a different candidate among the top three received the top score. The remaining three candidates received lower ratings every time. Dr. H always received the lowest score, usually around 12 on the 25-point range.

After almost two hours, the associate dean turned to one committee member and said, "Dolan, I sure would like to see Dr. H in your department receive this honor. He retires next year and this would be a great honor for him and no one has received this honor in your department recently."

Dolan agreed, "Yes, this is Dr. H's last year with us and it would be a great way for him to go out. I'm sure he would feel very honored by this award."

I sat there stunned at the suggestion while Dolan retold how Dr. H had been active in public service, his only real strength on our criteria. I was even more stunned when another committee member, who I think was keen to finish the meeting, said, "Well, I so move" and Dolan seconded it.

The associate dean, who was conducting the meeting, said, "Well, if the rest of you think this is a good idea, all in favor say aye." A few members said "Aye," and he quickly proceeded to explain what we needed to do to advertise the winner and arrange the ceremony without calling for nays.

During my conversations with other committee members over the next two weeks, I learned that everyone—including the two who said "Aye"—were as shocked as I was at our committee's decision. I thought we made a terrible decision, and I was embarrassed to be a member of the committee. A few weeks later, we were appropriately punished when Dr. H gave a 45-minute acceptance speech that started poorly and got worse.

Discussion Questions

1. What problems in team decision making likely caused the committee to select for the award the worst applicant on their list?

2. What would you recommend to future committees so they avoid the problems identified in this case?

3. Discuss what happened in this case using concepts and theories on individual decision making (Chapter 7).

CASE STUDY 8.2 PHILANTHROPIC TEAM BUILDING

The top dozen executives from Adolph Coors and Molson breweries wanted to accelerate their team development to kick off the postmerger integration of the two companies. But rather than the usual team building in the woods or a friendly game of golf, the Molson Coors leaders spent a full day helping build a house for Habitat for Humanity.

"We quickly got past the idea of a ropes course or golf outing," recalls Samuel D. Walker, Molson Coors' chief legal officer. "We really wanted something where we would give back to one of the communities where we do business." The volunteering experience exceeded everyone's expectations, says Walker. "We had to unload this truck full of cement roof tiles. We actually had to figure out how to have kind of a bucket line, handing these very heavy tiles from one person to the next. That's the ultimate team-building exercise."

Molson Coors and many other companies have discovered that volunteering is an effective way to build teams while giving back to the community. Devon County Council employees in southern England work after hours on various community projects, such as building a garden for a local children's center. Deputies at the sheriff's department in Chesapeake, Virginia, volunteer their time throughout the year to a program that develops leadership skills in young boys. Employees at the Belfast Telegraph participate in the Irish newspaper's Big Clean-Up campaign, which includes removing debris along beaches. "Our volunteering here today has not only given us the chance to link with some of the organizations our work supports, but also the time to engage in some valuable team building," says marketing manager Fidelma Glass.

ARAMARK, the world's largest food and professional services provider, launched its "Building Community" philanthropic and volunteer program a few years ago. For example, several hundred employees in Chicago have been working with the Jane Addams Hull House Association to educate families on how to live healthier lifestyles through better nutrition. "What started as a small volunteer event at a single Hull House location has turned into a great project that promotes team building among employees and showcases our company's commitment to the community and health and wellness," says Krista Wennerstrom, a food and nutrition services director at ARAMARK Healthcare.

Timberland Co. is a pioneer in donating employee time to community events. Since 1992, the New Hampshire–based footwear and apparel company has granted employees 40 hours of paid leave each year to work on community projects. Nearly half of Timberland's 5,000 employees around the world participate in more than 150 projects, many focusing on the environment and community revitalization. One popular event is Earth Day, when many Timberland employees participate in community projects and experience camaraderie with coworkers.

"It is a teambuilding event," says Lisa Rakaseder, a Timberland employee who participated in an Earth Day project at a YMCA camp, where she and coworkers built canoe racks and raked leaves. "It gets you to interact with other people at the company." Fabienne Verschoor, who organized the YMCA project, explains further: "You have senior staff, the loading dock crew, customer service, all working together. And you won't know the difference when you see a team working. They are all putting heart and soul into it."

John Pazzani, Timberland's vice president and corporate culture officer, has been involved in company volunteering events across a dozen states and 10 other countries over the years. These community service activities have included restoring buildings, improving trails, and cleaning up riverbanks. "People who care so much about their communities tend to care about their teammates and coworkers," says Pazzani. "If you work side by side with a coworker on a project cleaning up a riverbank, when you come back to work you can't help but be more collaborative."

Discussion Questions

1. What type of team building best describes these volunteering activities?

2. Explain how the corporate social responsibility element of volunteering contributes to team building.

3. Along with team building, in what other ways do these volunteering activities improve organizations?

Sources: M.C. White, "Doing Good on Company Time," *The New York Times*, May 8, 2007; A. Hall, "Timberland Shows Up," *Corporate Meetings & Incentives* 27 (July 2008), pp. 16–21; D. Moss, "The Value of Giving," *HRMagazine*, December 2009, p. 22; L. Stewart, "Beauty Spot Is Returned to Its Former Glory after Spruce-Up," *Belfast Telegraph* (Ireland), December 22, 2009, p. 12; "ARAMARK Employees Honored with Prestigious Jefferson Awards for Exceptional Public Service," *Obesity & Diabetes Week*, July 5, 2010, p. 5; "County Council Staff Transform Children's Centre Garden," Targeted News Service news release for Devon County Council (Exeter, England), August 24, 2010; V.L. Friedman, "Program Builds Leadership Skills," *Virginian-Pilot & The Ledger-Star*, May 22, 2011, p. 1.

TEAM EXERCISE 8.3 TEAM TOWER POWER

PURPOSE This exercise is designed to help you understand team roles, team development, and other issues in the development and maintenance of effective teams.

MATERIALS The instructor will provide enough Lego pieces or similar materials for each team to complete the assigned task. All teams should have identical (or very similar) amounts and types of pieces. The instructor will need a measuring tape and stopwatch. Students may use writing materials during the design stage (see step 2, below). The instructor will distribute a "Team Objectives Sheet" and "Tower Specifications Effectiveness Sheet" to all teams.

INSTRUCTIONS

1. The instructor will divide the class into teams. Depending on class size and space availability, teams may have between four and seven members, but all should be approximately equal size.

2. Each team has 20 minutes to design a tower that uses only the materials provided, is freestanding, and provides an optimal return on investment. Team members may wish to draw their tower on paper or a flipchart to facilitate the tower's design. Teams are free to practice building their tower during this stage. Preferably, each team will have a secluded space so that the design can be created privately. During this stage, each team will complete the Team Objectives Sheet distributed by the instructor. This sheet requires the Tower Specifications Effectiveness Sheet, also distributed by the instructor.

3. Each team will show the instructor that it has completed its Team Objectives Sheet. Then, with all teams in the same room, the instructor will announce the start of the construction phase. The time allowed for construction will be closely monitored, and the instructor will occasionally call out the time elapsed (particularly if there is no clock in the room).

4. Each team will advise the instructor as soon as it has completed its tower. The team will write down the time elapsed, as determined by the instructor. The team also may be asked to assist the instructor by counting the number of blocks used and measuring the height of the tower. This information gets added to the Team Objectives Sheet. Then the team calculates its profit.

5. After presenting the results, the class will discuss the team dynamics elements that contribute to team effectiveness. Team members will discuss their strategy, division of labor (team roles), expertise within the team, and other elements of team dynamics.

Source: Several published and online sources describe variations of this exercise, but there is no known origin to this activity.

TEAM EXERCISE 8.4 HUMAN CHECKERS

PURPOSE This exercise is designed to help you understand the importance and application of team dynamics and decision making.

MATERIALS None, but the instructor has more information about each team's task.

INSTRUCTIONS

1. Form teams of eight students. If possible, each team should have a private location, where team members can plan and practice the required task without being observed or heard by other teams.

2. All teams receive special instructions in class about their assigned task. All teams have the same task and the same amount of time to plan and practice the task. At the end of this planning and practice period, each team will be timed while completing the task in class. The team that completes the task in the least time wins.

3. No special materials are required or allowed (see rules below) for this exercise. Although the task is not described here, students should learn the following rules for planning and implementing the task:

   a. You cannot use any written form of communication or any props to assist in the planning or implementation of this task.

   b. You may speak to other students in your team at any time during the planning and implementation of this task.

   c. When performing the task, you can move only forward, not backward. (You are not allowed to turn around.)

   d. When performing the task, you can move forward to the next space, but only if it is vacant. In Exhibit 1, the individual (black dot) can move directly into an empty space (white dot).

   e. When performing the task, you can move forward two spaces if that space is vacant. In other words, you can move around a person who is one space in front of you to the next space if that space is vacant. (In Exhibit 2, two people occupy the black dots, and the white dot is an empty space. A person can move around the person in front to the empty space.)

Exhibit 1   **Exhibit 2**

4. When all teams have completed their task, the class will discuss the implications of this exercise for team dynamics and decision making.

Discussion Questions

1. Identify the team dynamics and decision-making concepts that the team applied to complete this task.

2. What personal theories of people and work teams were applied to complete this task?

3. What other organizational behavior issues occurred, and what actions were (or should have been) taken to solve them?

TEAM EXERCISE 8.5 MIST RIDGE

By Richard Field, University of Alberta, and Nicola Sutton

It is approximately 9:00 a.m. on August 23rd, and you and four friends are about to set off on an all day hike in the mountains of Southwestern Alberta, Canada. Having driven southwest from Calgary, Alberta, you have arrived at Kananaskis Provincial Park, located on the boundary between British Columbia and Alberta. Just off Highway 40, you turn into the Mist Creek day-use area and park the car. You can see a sign indicating the beginning of the Mist Ridge trail, which you have selected for your hike, but you know that from there on the trail proceeds along unmarked paths and logging roads. You can also see another sign that allows campfires only in designated rest areas.

Since it is mid-week, few others should be on the Mist Ridge trail. You and your friends are looking forward to an enjoyable day walking the long grass and rock ridge, as it is usually dry and sunny at this time of year, whereas a mere few kilometers (couple of miles) away, across the valley, Mist Mountain can be covered in rain clouds. Hiking from the parking lot to the ridge, along the whole top of the ridge to Rickert's Pass, and then returning at ground level alongside Mist Creek is a minimum eight-hour trip. In guidebooks it is classified as a long day hike, covering a total distance of 23 kilometers (14 miles), with a height gain of 808 meters (2,650 feet) and a maximum elevation of 2,515 meters (8,250 feet).

The weather at the moment is cool but not cold, and the sun is beaming down, beginning to heat the air. In general, the climate of Southwestern Alberta is cold continental, having long cold winters and cool summers, though summers do have brief hot spells. Annual precipitation peaks in the summer, and thunderstorms occur regularly. Hikers at this time of year must be prepared for rain or cold weather. Snow has been known to fall by the middle of August in this area, with accumulations on the ground of up to 20 centimeters (8 inches). Also, the weather can be somewhat changeable and unpredictable. What starts out as a warm sunny morning could easily change into a cold, snowy afternoon. Therefore, experienced hikers will make sure that they have adequate reserve clothing for the rain or snow that could develop. It is also known that temperatures are expected to be cooler at the top of the ridge, as temperatures decrease, in general, 2 degrees Celsius for every 300 meters (1,000 feet) of altitude.

There are a few dangers to watch out for during your hike. If you get soaked crossing a river, loss of body heat may result in hypothermia, even when temperatures are above freezing. Death from hypothermia is quite possible within a few hours of the first symptoms if proper care is not taken. On the other hand, the exertions of walking and climbing will probably cause you to sweat. Dehydration can increase your chance of sunstroke and hypothermia. In

Team Roles Preferences Scale   (*continued*)

CIRCLE THE NUMBER THAT BEST REFLECTS YOUR POSITION REGARDING EACH OF THESE STATEMENTS	DOES NOT DESCRIBE ME AT ALL	DOES NOT DESCRIBE ME VERY WELL	DESCRIBES ME SOMEWHAT	DESCRIBES ME WELL	DESCRIBES ME VERY WELL
10. Team members usually count on me to give everyone a chance to speak.	1	2	3	4	5
11. In most meetings, I am less likely than others to criticize the ideas of teammates.	1	2	3	4	5
12. I actively help teammates to resolve their differences in meetings.	1	2	3	4	5
13. I actively encourage quiet team members to describe their ideas about each issue.	1	2	3	4	5
14. People tend to rely on me to clarify the purpose of the meeting.	1	2	3	4	5
15. I like to be the person who takes notes or minutes of the meeting.	1	2	3	4	5

 After reading this chapter go to www.mhhe.com/mcshane6e for more in-depth information and interactivities that correspond to the chapter.

Communicating in Teams and Organizations

learning objectives

After reading this chapter, you should be able to:

LO1 Explain why communication is important in organizations, and discuss four influences on effective communication encoding and decoding.

LO2 Compare and contrast the advantages of and problems with electronic mail, other verbal communication media, and nonverbal communication.

LO3 Explain how social acceptance and media richness influence the preferred communication channel.

LO4 Discuss various barriers (noise) to effective communication, including cross-cultural and gender-based differences in communication.

LO5 Explain how to get messages across more effectively, and summarize the elements of active listening.

LO6 Summarize effective communication strategies in organizational hierarchies, and review the role and relevance of the organizational grapevine.

world's largest online retailers, Hsieh discovered that tweeting (transmitting 140-character maximum Twitter messages) is a powerful way to connect with his staff and the wider community. "What I found was that people really appreciated the openness and honesty [of tweets], and that led people to feel more of a personal connection with Zappos and me," Hsieh wrote in one of his weblogs.

Tweeting is so important at Zappos that new employees receive training on how to use the technology and are free to tweet to the public. One-third of Zappos's 1,500 employees have Twitter accounts to communicate with one another and with customers. Hsieh also encourages other forms of communication across the organization. He has a popular blog, and many employees share information through Facebook pages. "For us, Twitter, Facebook, YouTube, blogs, etc. are all ways we can connect with our customers and employees," Hsieh explains. "We're not looking at them as marketing channels, more as connection channels."

But if tweeting the top boss and reading his blogs seems too impersonal, Hsieh also has the ultimate open-door policy. His desk is located in an open office setting in an area where anyone can speak with him. "The best way to have an open-door policy is not to have a door in the first place," Hsieh explains. Hsieh's office space does have one distinguishing feature: Fake vines cascade from the ceiling and across partitions to create an area appropriately called "the jungle."

Hsieh is equally serious about encouraging face-to-face communication across the entire organization. When Zappos's head office moved to its current Las Vegas location, for example, Hsieh realized that the previous tenant installed several exits that allowed employees to enter and leave the building within their own area. This building design might get some people to the parking lot faster, but it also isolates them. Hsieh's solution was to lock most of the side exit doors so employees had to leave the building through the front-entrance reception area. "The reason for that is to create this kind of central hub that everyone has to pass through to help build community and culture," says Hsieh.[1]

Zappos CEO Tony Hsieh values open communication with staff, such as sending Twitter tweets, writing blogs, and having an office with no door.

Communication is the lifeblood of all organizations, so Zappos and other organizations are keeping pace by adopting social media and other emerging channels into their communication toolkit. Certainly, social media technologies such as Facebook, Twitter, and LinkedIn have transformed how we communicate in society, yet we may still be at the beginning of this revolution. Wire cablegrams and telephones introduced a century ago are giving way to e-mail, instant messaging, weblogs, and now social media sites. Each of these inventions creates fascinating changes in how people communicate with one another in the workplace, as well as new opportunities to improve organizational effectiveness and employee well-being.

Communication refers to the process by which information is transmitted and *understood* between two or more people. We emphasize the word "understood" because transmitting the sender's intended meaning is the essence of good communication. This chapter begins by discussing the importance of effective communication, outlining the communication process model, and discussing factors that improve communication coding and decoding. Next, we identify types of communication channels, including e-mail and social media sites, followed by factors to consider when choosing a communication medium. This chapter then identifies barriers to effective communication. The latter part of this chapter offers an overview of ways to communicate in organizational hierarchies and offers insight about the pervasive organizational grapevine.

The Importance of Communication

LO1

Effective communication is vital to all organizations, so much so that no company could exist without it. The reason? Recall from Chapter 1 that organizations are defined as groups of people who work interdependently toward some purpose. People work interdependently only when they can communicate. Although organizations rely on a variety of coordinating mechanisms (which we discuss in Chapter 13), frequent, timely, and accurate communication remains the primary means through which employees and work units effectively synchronize their work.[2] Chester Barnard, a telecommunications CEO and respected pioneer in organizational behavior theory, stated this point back in 1938: "An organization comes into being when there are persons able to communicate with each other."[3]

In addition to coordination, communication plays a central role in organizational learning. It is the means through which knowledge enters the organization and is distributed to employees.[4] A third function of communication is decision making. Imagine the challenge of

By making employee communication a priority, ESL Federal Credit Union has become one of the top medium-sized companies to work for in America. "We're always focused on employee communication," says Maureen Wolfe, vice president of people and organization development at the Rochester, NY–based financial institution. ESL relies on employee surveys, its intranet system, and plenty of face-to-face interaction between management and staff. "Employees feel they understand the expectations and have the tools they need to help in their day-to-day job while also keeping up on the latest business updates and fun activities going on as well."[5]

making a decision without any information about the decision context, the alternatives available, the likely outcomes of those options, or the extent to which the decision is achieving its objectives. All of these ingredients require communication from coworkers as well as from stakeholders in the external environment. For example, airline cockpit crews make much better decisions—and thereby cause far fewer accidents—when the captain encourages the crew to share information openly.[6]

A fourth function is to change behavior. When communicating to others, we are often trying to alter their beliefs and feelings and ultimately their behavior. This influence process might be passive, such as merely describing the situation more clearly and fully. Sometimes, the communication event is a deliberate attempt to change someone's thoughts and actions. We will discuss this function under the topic of persuasion later in this chapter.

Finally, communication supports employee well-being.[7] Informationally, communication conveys knowledge that helps employees better manage their work environment. For instance, research shows that new employees adjust much better to the organization when coworkers communicate subtle nuggets of wisdom, such as how to avoid office politics, complete work procedures correctly, find useful resources, handle difficult customers, and so on.[8] Emotionally, the communication experience itself is a soothing balm. Indeed, people are less susceptible to colds, cardiovascular disease, and other physical and mental illnesses when they have regular social interaction.[9] In essence, people have an inherent drive to bond, to validate their self-worth, and to maintain their social identity. Communication is the means through which these drives and needs are fulfilled.

A Model of Communication

To understand the key interpersonal features of effective communication, let's examine the model presented in Exhibit 9.1, which provides a useful "conduit" metaphor for thinking about the communication process.[10] According to this model, communication flows through channels between the sender and receiver. The sender forms a message and encodes it into words, gestures, voice intonations, and other symbols or signs. Next, the encoded message is transmitted to the intended receiver through one or more communication channels (media). The receiver senses the incoming message and decodes it into something meaningful. Ideally, the decoded meaning is what the sender had intended.

communication
The process by which information is transmitted and understood between two or more people.

EXHIBIT 9.1

The Communication Process Model

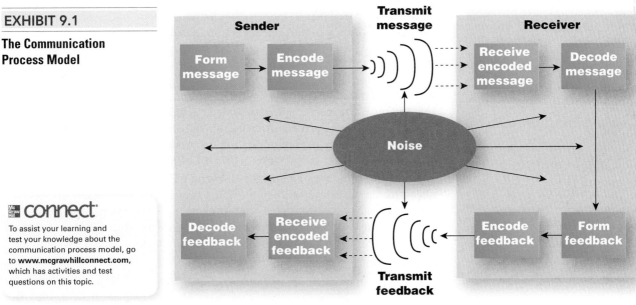

connect

To assist your learning and test your knowledge about the communication process model, go to **www.mcgrawhillconnect.com,** which has activities and test questions on this topic.

In most situations, the sender looks for evidence that the other person received and understood the transmitted message. This feedback may be a formal acknowledgment, such as "Yes, I know what you mean," or indirect evidence from the receiver's subsequent actions. Notice that feedback repeats the communication process. Intended feedback is encoded, transmitted, received, and decoded from the receiver to the sender of the original message. This model recognizes that communication is not a free-flowing conduit. Rather, the transmission of meaning from one person to another is hampered by *noise*—the psychological, social, and structural barriers that distort and obscure the sender's intended message. If any part of the communication process is distorted or broken, the sender and receiver will not have a common understanding of the message.

INFLUENCES ON EFFECTIVE ENCODING AND DECODING

The communication process model suggests that communication effectiveness depends on the ability of sender and receiver to efficiently and accurately encode and decode information. There are four main factors that influence the effectiveness of the encoding-decoding process.[11]

1. *Communication channel proficiency.* Communication effectiveness improves when the sender and receiver are both motivated and able to communicate through the communication channel. Some people are better and more motivated to communicate through face-to-face conversations. Others are awkward in conversations, yet are quite good at communicating via smartphone or text message technologies. Generally, the encoding–decoding process is more effective when both parties are skilled and enjoy using the selected communication channel.[12]

2. *Similar codebooks.* The sender and receiver rely on "codebooks," which are dictionaries of symbols, language, gestures, idioms, and other tools used to convey information. With similar codebooks, communication participants are able to encode and decode more accurately, because they both have the same or similar meaning. Communication efficiency also improves because there is less need for redundancy (such as saying the same thing in different ways) or confirmation feedback ("So, you are saying that . . . ?").

3. *Shared mental models of the communication context.* Mental models are internal representations of the external world that allow us to visualize elements of a setting and relationships among those elements (see Chapter 3). When sender and receiver have shared mental models, they have a common understanding of the environment relating to the information, so less communication is necessary to clarify meaning about that context. Notice that sharing the same codebook differs from sharing the same mental models of the topic context. Codebooks are symbols used to convey message content, whereas mental models are knowledge structures of the communication setting. For example, a Russian cosmonaut and American astronaut might have shared mental models about the design and technology onboard the international space station (communication context), yet they experience poor communication because of language differences (i.e., different codebooks).

4. *Experience encoding the message.* As people gain experience communicating the subject matter, they become more proficient at using the codebook of symbols to convey the message. For example, after speaking to several groups of employees about the company's new product development, you learn which words and phrases help to convey that particular message better to the audience. This is similar to the effect of job training or sports practice. The more experience and practice gained at communicating a subject, the more people learn how to effectively transmit that information to others.

Communication Channels

LO2

A critical part of the communication model is the channel or medium through which information is transmitted. There are two main types of channels: verbal and nonverbal. Verbal communication uses words and occurs through either spoken or written channels. Nonverbal communication is any part of communication that does not use words. Spoken and written communication are both verbal (i.e., they both use words), but they are quite different from each other and have different strengths and weaknesses in communication effectiveness, which we discuss later in this section. Also, written communication traditionally has been much slower than spoken communication at transmitting messages, though electronic mail, Twitter tweets, and other Internet-based communication channels have significantly improved written communication efficiency.

INTERNET-BASED COMMUNICATION

In the early 1960s, with funding from the U.S. Department of Defense, university researchers began discussing how to collaborate better by connecting their computers through a network. Their rough vision of connected computers became a reality in 1969 as the Advanced Research Projects Agency Network (ARPANET). ARPANET initially had only a dozen or so connections and was very slow and expensive by today's standards, but it marked the birth of the Internet. Two years later, a computer engineer developing ARPANET sent the first electronic mail (e-mail) message between different computers on a network. By 1973, most communication on ARPANET was through e-mail. ARPANET was mostly restricted to U.S. Defense Department–funded research centers, so in 1979, two graduate students at Duke University developed a public network system, called Usenet. Usenet allowed people to post information that could be retrieved by anyone else on the network, making it the first public computer-mediated social network.[13]

We have come a long way since the early days of ARPANET and Usenet. The medium of choice in most workplaces today is e-mail, because messages can be quickly written, edited, and transmitted. Information can be appended and conveyed to many people with a simple click of a mouse. E-mail is also asynchronous (messages are sent and received at different times), so there is no need to coordinate a communication session. With advances in computer search technology, e-mail software has also become an efficient filing cabinet.[14]

E-mail tends to be the preferred medium for sending well-defined information for decision making. It is also central for coordinating work, though text messaging and Twitter tweets might soon overtake e-mail for this objective. As e-mail has been introduced in the workplace over the past two decades, it has tended to increase the volume of communication and significantly alter the flow of that information within groups and throughout the organization.[15] Specifically, it has reduced some face-to-face and telephone communication but increased communication with people further up the hierarchy. Some social and organizational status differences still exist with e-mail,[16] but they are somewhat less apparent than in face-to-face communication. By hiding age, race, and other features, e-mail reduces stereotype biases. However, it also tends to increase reliance on stereotypes when we are already aware of the other person's personal characteristics.[17]

PROBLEMS WITH E-MAIL

In spite of the wonders of e-mail, anyone who has used this communication medium knows that it has its limitations. Here are the top four complaints:

Poor Medium for Communicating Emotions   People rely on facial expressions and other nonverbal cues to interpret the emotional meaning of words; e-mail lacks this parallel communication channel. People consistently and significantly underestimate the degree to which they understand the emotional tone of e-mail messages.[18] Senders try to clarify the emotional tone of their messages by using expressive language ("Wonderful to hear from you!"), highlighting phrases in boldface or quotation marks, and inserting graphic faces (called emoticons or "smileys") representing the desired emotion. Recent studies suggest that writers are getting better at using these emotion symbols. Still, they do not replace the full complexity of real facial expressions, voice intonation, and hand movements.[19]

Reduces Politeness and Respect   E-mail messages are often less diplomatic than written letters. The term "flaming" has entered our language to describe e-mail and other electronic messages that convey strong negative emotions to the receiver. People who receive e-mail are partly to blame, because they tend to infer a more negative or neutral interpretation of the e-mail than was intended by the sender.[20] Even so, e-mail flame wars occur mostly because senders are more likely to send disparaging messages by e-mail than by other communication channels. One reason for this tendency is that people can post e-mail messages before their emotions subside, whereas the sender of a traditional memo or letter would have time for sober second thoughts. A second reason is the low social presence (impersonal) of e-mail; people are more likely to write things that they would never say in face-to-face conversation. Fortunately, research has found that flaming decreases as teams move to later stages of development and when explicit norms and rules of communication are established.[21]

Poor Medium for Ambiguous, Complex, and Novel Situations   E-mail is usually fine for well-defined situations, such as giving basic instructions or presenting a meeting agenda, but it can be cumbersome in ambiguous, complex, and novel situations. As we will describe later in this section, these circumstances require communication channels that transmit a larger volume of information with more rapid feedback. In other words, when the issue gets messy, stop e-mailing and start talking, preferably face-to-face.

Contributes to Information Overload   E-mail contributes to information overload.[22] Approximately 20 trillion e-mails (excluding spam) are now transmitted annually around the world, up from just 1.1 trillion in 1998. The e-mail glut occurs because messages are created and copied to many people without much effort. The number of e-mail messages will probably decrease as people become more familiar with it; until then, e-mail volume continues to rise.

WORKPLACE COMMUNICATION THROUGH SOCIAL MEDIA

E-mail continues to dominate Internet-based communication in organizations, but a few corporate leaders believe that it undermines productivity and well-being rather than supporting these objectives. The opening vignette to this chapter described how Zappos employees already rely on Twitter, blogs, Facebook pages, and other social media to communicate. As Connections 9.1 describes, the Paris-based information technology consulting firm Atos Origin plans to replace e-mail altogether with social media and other communication technologies.

Social media include Internet-based tools (websites, applications, etc.) that allow users to generate and exchange information. This "user-generated content" is creative content (developed by the user), published on the Internet (perhaps with restricted access), and produced outside of professional routines and practices.[23] Social media take many forms—blogs, wikis, instant messages, Twitter tweets, personal presentation sites (e.g., Facebook), viewer feedback forums, and the like. Whereas previous Internet activity involved passively reading or watching content, these emerging activities are more interactive and dynamic.

One recent model suggests that social media serve several functions: presenting the individual's identity, enabling conversations, sharing information, sensing the presence of

connections 9.1

Good-Bye E-Mail, Hello Social Media!

Atos Origin is at war with e-mail. Executives at the Paris-based global information technology consulting firm believe the volume of e-mail transmitted around the company has created "information pollution" that stifles productivity and undermines employee well-being. "We are producing data on a massive scale that is fast polluting our working environments and also encroaching into our personal lives," says Atos Origin chief executive Thierry Breton. The company estimates that reading and writing e-mails consumes up to half of its managers' workweek. Furthermore, e-mail messages are irrelevant to about 70 percent of the people who receive them, according to a survey by Salesforce.com.

Other companies have fought e-mail overload by banning them for one day each week. Unfortunately, these "e-mail-free Fridays" often produce "e-mail-overload Mondays." Atos Origin's strategy is more radical: It plans to ban all e-mail among the company's 50,000 staff within the next couple of years. The company will encourage staff to share ideas, engage in communities, and have virtual team meetings through instant messaging, web conferences, and an enterprise-strength social media site.

"It is clearly going to be a big challenge for us because e-mail is everywhere," admits Atos Origin vice president for global innovation Marc-Henri Desportes. Desportes also notes

Paris-based information technology company Atos Origin plans to replace e-mail completely with other Internet-based communication tools within the next couple of years.

though that this transformation is less difficult for the company's Generation-Y employees. "These people do not use e-mail any more. They use social media tools."[24]

others in the virtual space, maintaining relationships, revealing reputation or status, and supporting communities (see Exhibit 9.2).[25] For instance, Facebook has a strong emphasis on maintaining relationships but relatively low emphasis on sharing information or forming communities (groups). Wikis, in contrast, focus on sharing information or forming communities but place much less emphasis on presenting the user's identity or reputation.

EXHIBIT 9.2   Functions of Communicating Through Social Media

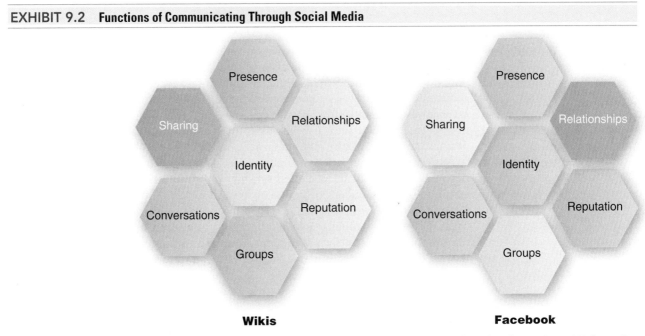

Wikis   Facebook

Source: Based on J.H. Kietzmann, K. Hermkens, I.P. McCarthy, and B.S. Silvestre, "Social Media? Get Serious! Understanding the Functional Building Blocks of Social Media," *Business Horizons* (in press).

CEMEX enables employees to communicate and collaborate more easily through its new technology-based platform, called Shift. "Shift combines some of the best elements from popular social networking platforms," says Sergio J. Escobedo Serna, vice president of innovation at the Monterrey, Mexico–based global building materials company. Along with traditional e-mail and scheduling, Shift incorporates wikis, blogs, web conferencing, and other team collaboration tools. "With Shift, we continue to empower our employees by promoting engagement and collaboration beyond traditional roles and titles, allowing the best ideas to resonate company-wide and effect real change," says CEMEX chairman and CEO Lorenzo H. Zambrano.[26]

A few studies conclude (with caution) that social media offer considerable versatility and potential in the workplace.[27] Even so, few companies have introduced these communication tools, mainly because they lack knowledge, staff/resources, and technical support to put them into practice.[28] However, a common tactic is simply to ban employee access to social media (usually after discovering excess employee activity on Facebook) without thinking through its potential. One exception is Serena Software, which has made Facebook its new corporate intranet. The Californian company introduced "Facebook Fridays," sessions in which it hires teenagers to teach older staff how to use Facebook. Most Serena employees now have Facebook pages, and the company's Facebook site links employees to confidential documents behind the company's firewall.[29]

NONVERBAL COMMUNICATION

Nonverbal communication includes facial gestures, voice intonation, physical distance, and even silence. This communication channel is necessary where noise or physical distance prevents effective verbal exchanges and the need for immediate feedback precludes written communication. But even in quiet, face-to-face meetings, most information is communicated nonverbally. Rather like a parallel conversation, nonverbal cues signal subtle information to both parties, such as reinforcing their interest in the verbal conversation or demonstrating their relative status in the relationship.[30]

Nonverbal communication differs from verbal (i.e., written and spoken) communication in a couple of ways. First, it is less rule-bound than verbal communication. We receive considerable formal training on how to understand spoken words, but very little on how to understand the nonverbal signals that accompany those words. Consequently, nonverbal cues are generally more ambiguous and susceptible to misinterpretation. At the same time, many facial expressions (such as smiling) are hardwired and universal, thereby providing the only reliable means of communicating across cultures.

The other difference between verbal and nonverbal communication is that the former is typically conscious, whereas most nonverbal communication is automatic and nonconscious. We normally plan the words we say or write, but we rarely plan every blink, smile, or other gesture during a conversation. Indeed, as we just mentioned, many of these facial expressions communicate the same meaning across cultures because they are hardwired, nonconscious responses to human emotions.[31] For example, pleasant emotions cause the brain center to widen the mouth, whereas negative emotions produce constricted facial expressions (squinting eyes, pursed lips, etc.).

Emotional Contagion   One of the most fascinating effects of emotions on nonverbal communication is the phenomenon called **emotional contagion,** which is the automatic process of "catching" or sharing another person's emotions by mimicking that person's facial expressions and other nonverbal behavior. Technically, human beings have brain receptors that cause them to mirror what they observe. In other words, to some degree our brain causes us to act as though we are the person we are watching.[32]

Consider what happens when you see a coworker accidentally bang his or her head against a filing cabinet. Chances are, you wince and put your hand on your own head as if you had hit the cabinet. Similarly, while listening to someone describe a positive event, you tend to smile and exhibit other emotional displays of happiness. While some of our nonverbal communication is planned, emotional contagion represents nonconscious behavior—we automatically mimic and synchronize our nonverbal behaviors with other people.[33]

Emotional contagion serves three purposes. First, mimicry provides continuous feedback, communicating that we understand and empathize with the sender. To consider the significance of this, imagine employees remaining expressionless after watching a coworker bang his or her head! The lack of parallel behavior conveys a lack of understanding or caring. Second, mimicking the nonverbal behaviors of other people seems to be a way of receiving emotional meaning from those people. If a coworker is angry with a client, your tendency to frown and show anger while listening helps you experience that emotion more fully. In other words, we receive meaning by expressing the sender's emotions, as well as by listening to the sender's words.

The third function of emotional contagion is to fulfill the drive to bond that was described in Chapter 5. Social solidarity is built on each member's awareness of a collective sentiment. Through nonverbal expressions of emotional contagion, people see others share the same emotions that they feel. This strengthens relations among team members as well as between leaders and followers by providing evidence of their similarity.[34]

Choosing the Best Communication Channel

LO3

Which communication channel is most appropriate in a particular situation? Two important sets of factors to consider are social acceptance and media richness.

SOCIAL ACCEPTANCE

Social acceptance refers to how well the communication medium is approved and supported by the organization, teams, and individuals.[35] One factor in social acceptance is organizational and team norms regarding the use of specific communication channels. Norms partly explain why face-to-face meetings are daily events among staff in some firms, whereas computer-based video conferencing (such as Skype) and Twitter tweets are the media of choice in other organizations. Communication channel norms also vary across cultures. One recent study reported that when communicating with people further up the hierarchy, Koreans are much less likely than Americans to use e-mail, because this medium is less respectful of the superior's status.[36]

A second social acceptance factor is individual preferences for specific communication channels.[37] You may have noticed that some coworkers ignore (or rarely check) voice mail, yet they quickly respond to text messages or Twitter tweets. These preferences are due to personality traits, as well as previous experience and reinforcement with particular channels.

A third social acceptance factor is the symbolic meaning of a channel. Some communication channels are viewed as impersonal, whereas others are more personal; some are considered professional, whereas others are casual; some are "cool," whereas

emotional contagion
The nonconscious process of "catching" or sharing another person's emotions by mimicking that person's facial expressions and other nonverbal behavior.

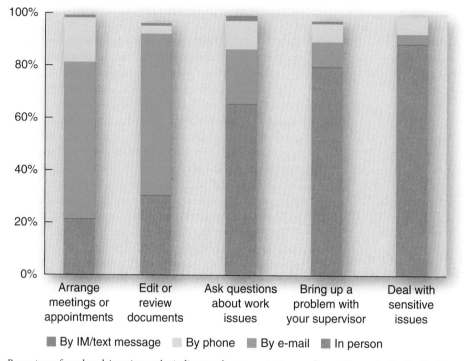

Some Things Are Better Communicated In Person[38]

Legend: ■ By IM/text message   ■ By phone   ■ By e-mail   ■ In person

Percentage of employed Americans who indicate each communication medium is the most effective for that workplace situation. N = 655. Sample includes only people who use e-mail at work. Numbers do not add up to 100 percent because some people did not give an answer.

others are old-fashioned. In one recent survey, 60 percent of employees said they used e-mail to arrange meetings, whereas less than 10 percent used this channel to communicate with their boss about problems.[39] The importance of a channel's symbolic meaning is perhaps most apparent in stories about managers who use e-mails or text messages to inform employees that they have been fired or laid off. These communication events make headlines because e-mail and text messages are considered inappropriate (too impersonal) for transmission of that particular information.[40]

MEDIA RICHNESS

Along with social acceptance, people need to determine the best level of **media richness** for their message. Media richness refers to the medium's data-carrying capacity—the volume and variety of information that can be transmitted during a specific time.[41] Exhibit 9.3 illustrates various communication channels arranged in a hierarchy of richness, with face-to-face interaction at the top and lean, data-only reports at the bottom. A communication channel has high richness when it is able to convey multiple cues (such as both verbal and nonverbal information), allows timely feedback from receiver to sender, allows the sender to customize the message to the receiver, and makes use of complex symbols (such as words and phrases with multiple meanings).

Face-to-face communication is at the top of media richness because it allows us to communicate both verbally and nonverbally at the same time, to receive feedback almost immediately from the receiver, to quickly adjust our message and style, and to use complex language such as metaphors and idioms (e.g., "spilling the beans").

According to media richness theory, rich media are better than lean media when the communication situation is nonroutine and ambiguous. In nonroutine situations (such as an unexpected and unusual emergency), the sender and receiver have little common experience, so they need to transmit a large volume of information with immediate feedback. Lean media work well in routine situations because the sender and receiver have common

EXHIBIT 9.3   **Media Richness Hierarchy**

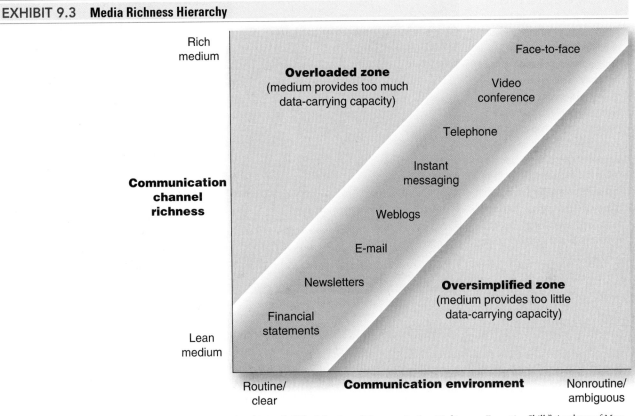

Source: Based on R. Lengel and R. Daft, "The Selection of Communication Media as an Executive Skill," *Academy of Management Executive* 2, no. 3 (August 1988), p. 226; R.L. Daft and R.H. Lengel, "Information Richness: A New Approach to Managerial Behavior and Organization Design," *Research in Organizational Behavior* 6 (1984), pp. 191–233.

expectations through shared mental models. Ambiguous situations also require rich media because the parties must share large amounts of information with immediate feedback to resolve multiple and conflicting interpretations of their observations and experiences.[42] Choosing the wrong medium reduces communication effectiveness. When the situation is routine or clear, using a rich medium—such as holding a special meeting—would seem like a waste of time. On the other hand, if a unique and ambiguous issue is handled through e-mail or another lean medium, then issues take longer to resolve, and misunderstandings are more likely to occur.

Exceptions to Media Richness Theory   Research generally supports the relevance of media richness for traditional channels (face-to-face, written memos, etc.). However, the model doesn't fit reality nearly as well when electronic communication channels are studied. Three factors seem to override or blur the medium's richness:

1. *Ability to multi-communicate.* It is usually difficult (as well as rude) to communicate face-to-face with someone while simultaneously transmitting messages to someone else using another medium. Most information technologies, on the other hand, require less social etiquette and attention, so employees can easily engage in two or more communication events at the same time. In other words, they can multi-communicate.[44] For example, people routinely scan web pages while carrying on telephone conversations. Some write text messages to a client while simultaneously listening to a discussion at a large meeting. People don't multitask as efficiently as they believe, but some are good enough that they likely exchange as much information through two or more lean media as through one high media richness channel.

2. *Communication proficiency.* Earlier in this chapter, we explained that communication effectiveness is partially determined by the sender's competency with the

media richness
A medium's data-carrying capacity, that is, the volume and variety of information that can be transmitted during a specific time.

Every day, employees at I Love Rewards Inc. meet face-to-face for 10 minutes to communicate priorities and share news. The Toronto-based incentive marketing company has these highly structured sessions because their high media richness provides a personal connection and highly interactive feedback on timely issues. The meeting includes "must-do" notices and "red flags" that staff need to be aware of. Employees also share a "Headline" summary of something important to them (e.g., a client meeting, last week's vacation).[43]

communication channel. People with higher proficiency can "push" more information through the channel, thereby increasing the channel's information flow. Experienced iPhone users, for instance, can whip through messages in a flash, whereas new users struggle to type notes and organize incoming messages. In contrast, there is less variation in the ability to communicate through casual conversation and other natural channels because most of us develop good levels of proficiency throughout life and possibly through hardwired evolutionary development.[45]

3. *Social presence effects.* Channels with high media richness tend to have more social presence; that is, the participants experience a stronger physical presence of each other.[46] However, high social presence also sensitizes both parties to their relative status and self-presentation, which can distort or divert attention away from the message.[47] Face-to-face communication has very high media richness, yet its high social presence can disrupt the efficient flow of information through that medium. During a personal meeting with the company's CEO, for example, you might concentrate more on how you come across than on what the CEO is saying to you. In other words, the benefits of channels with high media richness may be offset by their social presence distractions, whereas lean media have much less social presence to distract or distort the transmitted information.

COMMUNICATION CHANNELS AND PERSUASION

Media richness and social acceptance lay the foundation for understanding which communication channels are more effective for **persuasion,** that is, changing another person's beliefs and attitudes. Recent studies support the long-held view that spoken communication, particularly face-to-face interaction, is more persuasive than e-mails, websites, and other forms of written communication. There are three main reasons for this persuasive effect.[48] First, spoken communication is typically accompanied by nonverbal communication. People are often persuaded more when they receive both emotional and logical messages, and the combination of spoken with nonverbal communication provides this dual punch. A lengthy pause, raised voice tone, and animated hand gestures can amplify the emotional tone of the message, thereby signaling the vitality of the issue.

Second, spoken communication offers the sender high-quality, immediate feedback about whether the receiver understands and accepts the message (i.e., is being persuaded). This feedback allows the sender to adjust the content and emotional tone of the message more quickly than with written communication. Third, people are persuaded more under conditions of high social presence than low social presence. The sender can more easily monitor the receiver's listening in face-to-face conversations (high social presence), so listeners are more motivated to pay attention and consider the sender's ideas. When people receive persuasion attempts through a website, e-mail, or other source of written communication, they instead experience a higher degree of anonymity and psychological distance from the persuader. These conditions reduce the motivation to think about and accept the persuasive message.

Although spoken communication tends to be more persuasive, written communication can also persuade others to some extent. Written messages have the advantage of presenting more technical detail than can occur through conversation. This factual information is valuable when the issue is important to the receiver. Also, people experience a moderate degree of social presence in written communication when they are exchanging messages with close associates, so messages from friends and coworkers can be persuasive.

Communication Barriers (Noise)

LO4

In spite of the best intentions of sender and receiver to communicate, several barriers (called "noise" in Exhibit 9.1) inhibit the effective exchange of information. As George Bernard Shaw wrote, "The greatest problem with communication is the illusion that it has been accomplished." One barrier is the imperfect perceptual process of both sender and receiver. As receivers, we don't listen as well as senders assume, and our needs and expectations influence what signals get noticed and ignored. We aren't any better as senders, either. Some studies suggest that we have difficulty stepping out of our own perspectives and stepping into the perspectives of others, so we overestimate how well other people understand the message we are communicating.[49]

Language issues can be huge sources of communication noise because sender and receiver might not have the same codebook. They might not speak the same language, or they might have different meanings for particular words and phrases. The English language (among others) also has built-in ambiguities that cause misunderstandings. Consider the question, "Can you close the door?" You might assume the sender is asking whether shutting the door is permitted. However, the question might be asking whether you are physically able to shut the door or whether the door is designed such that it can be shut. In fact, this question might not be a question at all; the person could be politely *telling* you to shut the door.[50]

The ambiguity of language isn't always dysfunctional noise.[51] Corporate leaders are sometimes purposively obscure to reflect the ambiguity of the topic or to avoid using precise language that carries unwanted emotional responses. They might use metaphors to represent an abstract vision of the company's future or use obtuse phrases such as "rightsizing" and "restructuring" to obscure the underlying message that people would be fired or laid off. One study reported that people rely on more ambiguous language when communicating with people who have different values and beliefs. In these situations, ambiguity minimizes the risk of conflict.[52]

Jargon—specialized words and phrases for specific occupations or groups—is usually designed to improve communication efficiency. However, it is a source of communication noise when transmitted to people who do not possess the jargon codebook. Furthermore, people who use jargon excessively put themselves in an unflattering light. For example, former Chrysler CEO Robert Nardelli announced: "I'm blessed to have individuals with me who can take areas of responsibility and do vertical dives to really get the granularity and make sure that we're coupling horizontally across those functions so that we have a pure line of sight toward the customer." Business journalists weren't impressed, even if they did figure out what Nardelli meant.[53]

Another source of noise in the communication process is the tendency to filter messages. Filtering may involve deleting or delaying negative information or using less

persuasion
The use of facts, logical arguments, and emotional appeals to change another person's beliefs and attitudes, usually for the purpose of changing the person's behavior.

"That's my commendation for deciphering all the sales talk when we needed to upgrade the computer."

Credit: Copyright © Ted Goff.

harsh words so the message sounds more favorable.[54] Filtering is less likely to occur when corporate leaders create a "culture of candor." This culture develops when leaders themselves communicate truthfully, seek out diverse sources for information, and protect and reward those who speak openly and truthfully.[55]

INFORMATION OVERLOAD

Start with a daily avalanche of e-mail; then add in cell phone calls, text messages, pdf file downloads, web pages, hard copy documents, some Twitter tweets, blogs, wikis, and other sources of incoming information. Together, you have created a perfect recipe for **information overload**.[56] As Exhibit 9.4 illustrates, information overload occurs whenever the job's information load exceeds the individual's capacity to get through it. Employees have a certain *information processing capacity*—the amount of information that they are able to process in a fixed unit of time. At the same time, jobs have a varying *information load*—the amount of information to be processed per unit of time. Information overload creates noise in the communication system because information gets overlooked or misinterpreted when people can't process it fast enough. The result is poorer-quality decisions as well as higher stress.[57]

Information overload problems can be minimized by increasing our information processing capacity, reducing the job's information load, or a combination of both. Studies suggest that employees often increase their information processing capacity by temporarily reading faster, scanning through documents more efficiently, and removing distractions that slow information processing speed. Time management also increases information processing capacity. When information overload is temporary, information processing capacity can increase by working longer hours. Information load can be reduced by buffering, omitting, and summarizing. Buffering involves having incoming communication filtered,

EXHIBIT 9.4

Dynamics of Information Overload

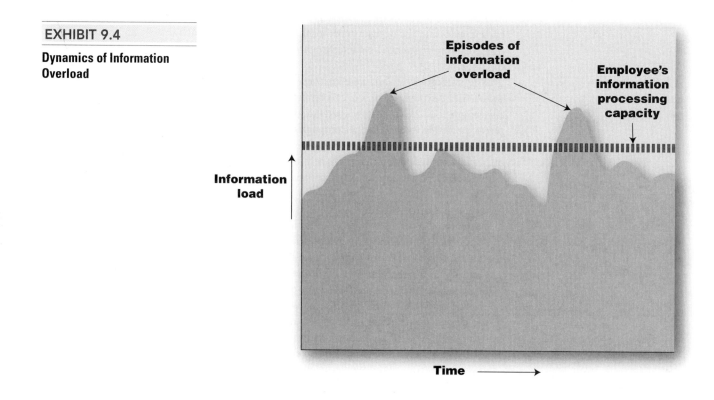

usually by an assistant. Omitting occurs when we decide to overlook messages, such as using software rules to redirect e-mails from distribution lists to folders that we never look at. An example of summarizing would be reading executive summaries rather than the full report.

Cross-Cultural and Gender Communication

Increasing globalization and cultural diversity have brought more cross-cultural communication issues.[58] Voice intonation is one form of cross-cultural communication barrier. How loudly, deeply, and quickly people speak varies across cultures, and these voice intonations send secondary messages that have different meaning in different cultures.

As mentioned earlier, language is an obvious cross-cultural communication challenge. Words are easily misunderstood in verbal communication, either because the receiver has a limited vocabulary or the sender's accent distorts the usual sound of some words. In one cross-cultural seminar, for example, participants at the German electronics company Siemens were reminded that a French coworker might call an event a "catastrophe" as a casual exaggeration, whereas someone in Germany usually interprets this word literally as an earth-shaking event. Similarly, KPMG staff from the United Kingdom sometimes referred to another person's suggestions as "interesting." They had to clarify to their German colleagues that "interesting" isn't always a compliment to the idea.[59]

Communication includes silence, but its use and meaning varies from one culture to another.[60] One study estimated that silence and pauses represented 30 percent of conversation time between Japanese doctors and patients, compared with only 8 percent of the time between U.S. doctors and patients. Why is there more silence in Japanese conversations? One reason is that interpersonal harmony and saving face are more important in Japanese culture, and silence is a way of disagreeing without upsetting that harmony or offending the other person.[61] In addition, silence symbolizes respect and indicates that the listener is thoughtfully contemplating what has just been said.[62] Empathy is very important in Japan, and this shared understanding is demonstrated without using words. In contrast, most people in the United States and many other cultures view silence as a *lack* of communication and often interpret long breaks as a sign of disagreement.

Conversational overlaps also send different messages in different cultures. Japanese people usually stop talking when they are interrupted, whereas talking over the other person's speech is more common in Brazil, France, and some other countries. The difference in communication behavior is, again, due to interpretations. Talking while someone is speaking to you is considered quite rude in Japan, whereas Brazilians and French are more likely to interpret it as the person's interest and involvement in the conversation.

NONVERBAL DIFFERENCES ACROSS CULTURES

Nonverbal communication represents another potential area for misunderstanding across cultures. Many nonconscious or involuntary nonverbal cues (such as smiling) have the same meaning around the world, but deliberate gestures often have different interpretations. For example, most of us shake our head from side to side to say "No," but a variation of head shaking means "I understand" to many people in India. Filipinos raise their eyebrows to give an affirmative answer, yet Arabs interpret this expression (along with clicking one's tongue) as a negative response. Most Americans are taught to maintain eye contact with the speaker to show interest and respect, whereas some North American native groups learn at an early age to show respect by looking down when an older or more senior person is talking to them.[63]

GENDER DIFFERENCES IN COMMUNICATION

Men and women have similar communication practices, but there are subtle distinctions that can occasionally lead to misunderstanding and conflict (see Exhibit 9.5).[64]

information overload
A condition in which the volume of information received exceeds the person's capacity to process it.

EXHIBIT 9.5   Gender Differences in Communication

WHEN MEN COMMUNICATE	WHEN WOMEN COMMUNICATE
• Report talk—giving advice, asserting power • Give advice directly • Dominate the conversation • Apologize less often • Tend to be less sensitive to nonverbal cues	• Rapport talk—relationship building • Give advice indirectly • Adopt a flexible conversation style • Apologize more often • Tend to be more sensitive to nonverbal cues

One distinction is that men are more likely than women to view conversations as negotiations of relative status and power. They assert their power by directly giving advice to others (e.g., "You should do the following") and using combative language. There is also evidence that men dominate the talk time in conversations with women, as well as interrupt more and adjust their speaking style less than do women.

Men engage in more "report talk," in which the primary function of the conversation is impersonal and efficient information exchange. Women also do report talk, particularly when conversing with men, but conversations among women have a higher incidence of relationship building through "rapport talk." Women make more use of indirect requests ("Do you think you should . . ."), apologize more often, and seek advice from others more quickly than do men. Finally, research fairly consistently indicates that women are more sensitive than men to nonverbal cues in face-to-face meetings.[65] Together, these conditions can create communication conflicts. Women who describe problems get frustrated that men offer advice rather than rapport, whereas men become frustrated because they can't understand why women don't appreciate their advice.

Gender differences are also emerging in the use of social media to communicate.[66] Specifically, women are more likely to visit social networking sites like Facebook and Twitter, spend more time online, and click on more web pages than their male counterparts. Women are also more active participants in photo sharing websites. Globally, women are outpacing men in signing up for Twitter accounts and are more active Twitter users. Their reasons for using this communication channel also differ. Women tend to use Twitter as a conversational rather than functional medium. Overall, women spend an average of 24.8 hours per month online, whereas men spend 22.9 hours per month online.

Improving Interpersonal Communication

LO5

Effective interpersonal communication depends on the sender's ability to get the message across and the receiver's performance as an active listener. In this section, we outline these two essential features of effective interpersonal communication.

GETTING YOUR MESSAGE ACROSS

This chapter began with the statement that effective communication occurs when the other person receives and understands the message. This is more difficult to accomplish than most people believe. To get your message across to the other person, you first need to empathize with the receiver, such as being sensitive to words that may be ambiguous or trigger the wrong emotional response. Second, be sure that you repeat the message, such as by rephrasing the key points a couple of times. Third, your message competes with other messages and noise, so find a time when the receiver is less likely to be distracted by these other matters. Finally, if you are communicating bad news or criticism, focus on the problem, not the person.

ACTIVE LISTENING

Almost 2,000 years ago, the Greek philosopher Epictetus wrote: "Nature gave us one tongue, but two ears, so we may listen twice as much as we speak."[67] This sage advice suggests that we need to recognize the value of active listening by actively sensing the sender's signals, evaluating them accurately, and responding appropriately. These three components of listening—sensing, evaluating, and responding—reflect the listener's side of the communication model described at the beginning of this chapter. Listeners receive the sender's signals, decode them as intended, and provide appropriate and timely feedback to the sender (see Exhibit 9.6). Active listeners constantly cycle through sensing, evaluating, and responding during the conversation and engage in various activities to improve these processes.[68]

Sensing   Sensing is the process of receiving signals from the sender and paying attention to them. Active listeners improve sensing in three ways. First, they postpone evaluation by not forming an opinion until the speaker has finished. Second, they avoid interrupting the speaker's conversation. Third, they remain motivated to listen to the speaker.

Evaluating   This component of listening includes understanding the message meaning, evaluating the message, and remembering the message. To improve their evaluation of the conversation, active listeners empathize with the speaker. They try to understand and be sensitive to the speaker's feelings, thoughts, and situation. Evaluation also improves listening by organizing the speaker's ideas during the communication episode.

EXHIBIT 9.6

Active Listening Process and Strategies

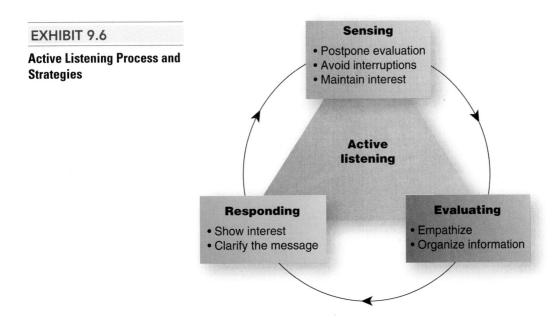

Responding   Responding, the third component of listening, is feedback to the sender, which motivates and directs the speaker's communication. Active listeners accomplish this by maintaining sufficient eye contact and sending back channel signals (e.g., "I see"), both of which show interest. They also respond by clarifying the message, such as by rephrasing the speaker's ideas at appropriate breaks ("So you're saying that . . . ?").

Improving Communication Throughout the Hierarchy

LO6

So far, we have focused on micro-level issues in the communication process, namely, the dynamics of sending and receiving information between two employees or the informal exchanges of information across several people. But in this era, when knowledge is a competitive advantage, corporate leaders also need to maintain an open flow of communication up, down, and across the organization. In this section, we discuss three communication strategies: workspace design, Internet-based communication, and direct communication with top management.

WORKSPACE DESIGN

Executives at the Brazilian branch of Diageo plc aren't cloistered into their own private offices. Instead, they sit together around a massive desk called the "Star Trek table" in an open plan workspace. The Sao Paulo executives of this global premium wine and spirits company also have an adjacent room that they share for private conversations. "They see it as a tremendous benefit," says John Pursell, Diageo's vice president of corporate real estate. "It encourages more dialogue and more feedback."[69]

Diageo and many other companies are improving communication by tearing down walls.[70] Diageo has created shared space for the executive team, whereas Zappos and some other firms have created an open office design for everybody. The location and design of hallways, offices, cubicles, and communal areas (cafeterias, elevators) all shape to whom we speak as well as the frequency of that communication. For instance, face-to-face communication increased when GlaxoSmithKline employees moved to its new open-office environment in Raleigh, North Carolina, whereas the volume of e-mail dropped significantly.

To improve information sharing and create a more sociable work environment, Intel is tearing down the cubicle walls at its microchip design center near Portland, Oregon. "We realized that we were inefficient and not as collaborative as we would have liked," acknowledges Neil Tunmore, Intel's director of corporate services. The refurbished building (shown here) includes more shared space where employees set up temporary work areas. There are also more meeting rooms where employees can collaborate in private.[71]

Although these open space arrangements increase the amount of face-to-face communication, they also potentially produce more noise, distractions, and loss of privacy.[72] For instance, one GlaxoSmithKline employee described the pharmaceutical company's recent transition to open offices as "a big adjustment. There were a lot of distractions, and it was hard to stay focused."[73] Employees at one eBay call center also experienced too much distraction, so they agreed to hush up when coworkers draped a colorful bandana on their desk lamps or around their heads.[74] Others claim that open offices have minimal noise problems because employees tend to speak more softly and white noise technology blocks out most voices. Still, the challenge is to increase social interaction without these stressors.

Another workspace strategy is to cloister employees into team spaces but also encourage sufficient interaction with people from other teams. Pixar Animation Studios constructed its campus in Emeryville, California, with these principles in mind. The building encourage communication among team members. At the same time, the campus encourages happenstance interactions with people on other teams. Pixar executives call this the "bathroom effect," because team members must leave their isolated team pods to fetch their mail, have lunch, or visit the restroom.[75]

INTERNET-BASED ORGANIZATIONAL COMMUNICATION

For decades, employees received official company news through hard copy newsletters and magazines. Some firms still use these communication devices, but most have supplemented or replaced them completely with web-based sources of information. The traditional company magazine is now typically published on web pages or distributed in PDF format. The advantage of these *e-zines* is that company news can be prepared and distributed quickly.

Employees are increasingly skeptical of information that has been screened and packaged by management, so a few companies such as IBM are encouraging employees to post their own news on internal blogs and wikis. Wikis are collaborative web spaces in which anyone in a group can write, edit, or remove material from the website. Wikipedia, the popular online encyclopedia, is a massive public example of a wiki. IBM's WikiCentral now hosts more than 20,000 wiki projects involving 100,000 employees. The accuracy of wikis depends on the quality of participants, but IBM experts say that errors are quickly identified by IBM's online community. Also, some wikis have failed to gain employee support, likely because wiki involvement takes time, and few companies reward or recognize those who provide this time for wiki development.[76]

DIRECT COMMUNICATION WITH TOP MANAGEMENT

"The best fertilizer in any field is that of the farmer's footsteps!" This old Chinese saying suggests that farmers have greater success when they spend more time in the fields directly observing the crop's development. Translated into an organizational context, it means that senior executives will understand their business better if they meet directly with employees and other stakeholders. Four decades ago, people at Hewlett-Packard coined a phrase for this communication strategy: **management by walking around (MBWA).** Brian Scudamore, founder and CEO of 1-800-Got-Junk?, takes this practice further. "I don't have my own office, and I very often move around to different departments for a day at a time," says Scudamore.[77]

Along with MBWA, executives communicate more directly with employees through town hall meetings. Some executives also conduct employee roundtable forums to hear opinions from a small representation of staff about various issues. At the departmental level, some companies (including I Love Rewards, described previously) hold daily or weekly "huddles"—brief, stand-up meetings in which staff and their manager discuss goals and hear good-news stories. These direct communication strategies potentially minimize filtering, because executives listen directly to employees. They also help

management by walking around (MBWA)
A communication practice in which executives get out of their offices and learn from others in the organization through face-to-face dialogue.

During the great financial crisis, employee satisfaction scores at the U.S. Department of Transportation were among the lowest in the federal government. U.S. Secretary of Transportation Ray LaHood is improving that situation through more open communication and other management practices. Morale is already improving. "This boost in employee satisfaction is no accident," says LaHood. "Since joining DOT, I initiated town hall meetings with employees around the country, and I have also held regular open-door office hours where employees are free to let me know what's on their minds." These photos show the Secretary of Transportation at one of those town hall meetings.[78]

executives acquire a deeper meaning and quicker understanding of internal organizational problems. A third benefit of direct communication is that employees might have more empathy for decisions made further up the corporate hierarchy.

Communicating Through the Grapevine

No matter how much organizational leaders try to get messages to employees quickly through e-zines, blogs, MBWA, Twitter tweets, and other means, employees still use the oldest communication channel: the corporate **grapevine.** The grapevine is an unstructured and informal network founded on social relationships rather than organizational charts or job descriptions. What do employees think about the grapevine? Surveys of employees in two firms—one in Florida, the other in California—found that almost all employees use the grapevine, but very few of them prefer this source of information. The California survey also reported that only one-third of employees believe grapevine information is credible. In other words, employees turn to the grapevine when they have few other options.[79]

GRAPEVINE CHARACTERISTICS

Research conducted several decades ago reported that the grapevine transmits information very rapidly in all directions throughout the organization. The typical pattern is a cluster chain, whereby a few people actively transmit rumors to many others. The grapevine works through informal social networks, so it is more active where employees have similar backgrounds and are able to communicate easily. Many rumors seem to have at least a kernel of truth, possibly because they are transmitted through media-rich communication channels (e.g., face to face) and employees are motivated to communicate effectively. Nevertheless, the grapevine distorts information by deleting fine details and exaggerating key points of the story.[80]

Some of these characteristics might still be true, but the grapevine almost certainly has changed as e-mail, social networking sites, and Twitter tweets have replaced the traditional water cooler as sources of gossip. For example, several Facebook sites are

Debating Point

SHOULD MANAGEMENT USE THE GRAPEVINE TO COMMUNICATE TO EMPLOYEES?

The grapevine has been the curse of management since modern-day organizations were invented. News flows with stealth-like efficiency below the surface, making it difficult to tell where information is traveling, what is being said to whom, or who is responsible for any misinformation. Although employees naturally flock to the grapevine for knowledge and social comfort in difficult times, its messages can be so distorted that they sometimes produce more stress than they alleviate. It is absurd to imagine management trying to systematically transmit important information—or any news whatsoever—through this uncontrollable, quirky communication channel.

But some communication experts are taking a second look at the grapevine, viewing it more as a resource than a nemesis. Their inspiration comes from marketing, where viral and word-of-mouth marketing have become hot topics.[81] Viral and word-of-mouth marketing occur when information seeded to a few people is transmitted to others based on patterns of friendship. In other words, information is passed along to others at the whim of those who first receive that information. Within organizations, this process is essentially the grapevine at work. Employees transmit information to other people within their sphere of everyday interaction.

The grapevine might seem to transmit information in strange and unreliable ways, but there are two contrary arguments. First, the grapevine channel is becoming more robust and reliable, thanks to social media and other emerging forms of electronic communication. These media have produced a stronger scaffolding than ever before, which potentially makes the grapevine more useful for transmitting information.

The second argument is that the grapevine tends to be more persuasive than traditional communication channels from management to employees. The grapevine is based on social networks, which we discuss in the next chapter. Social networks are an important source of organizational power because they are built on trust, and trust increases acceptance of information sent through those networks. Consequently, the grapevine tends to be far more persuasive than other communication channels.

The power of the grapevine as a communication tool was recently illustrated when Novo Nordisk tried to change the image of its regulatory affairs staff.[82] The European pharmaceutical company made limited progress after a year of using traditional communication channels. "We had posters, meetings, competitions, and everything else you would expect," recalls communication adviser Jakob Wolter. "By the end of it, we'd achieved something—a general awareness among our people—but very little else."

So, Novo Nordisk took another route. During the half-yearly gathering of all employees, nine regulatory staff were given wax-sealed confidential envelopes that assigned them to one of three "secret societies." Between conference sessions, these employees met with the managing director, who assigned their manifesto, including a mandate and budget. They were also told to keep their mission secret, saying to inquisitive coworkers, "I can't tell you."

"The rumor mill started right there that day," says Wolter. "People were already wondering what on earth was going on." The societies were allowed to recruit more employees, which they did in subsequent months. Many employees throughout Novo Nordisk became intrigued, spreading their opinions and news to others. Meanwhile, empowered to improve their image and work processes, members of the three secret societies introduced several initiatives that brought about improvements.

themed around specific companies, allowing employees and customers to vent their complaints about the organization. Along with altering the speed and network of corporate grapevines, the Internet has expanded these networks around the globe, not just around the next cubicle.

GRAPEVINE BENEFITS AND LIMITATIONS

grapevine
An unstructured and informal communication network founded on social relationships rather than organizational charts or job descriptions.

Should the grapevine be encouraged, tolerated, or quashed? The difficulty in answering this question is that the grapevine has both benefits and limitations.[83] One benefit, as was mentioned previously, is that employees rely on the grapevine when information is not available through formal channels. It is also the main conduit through which organizational stories and other symbols of the organization's culture are communicated. A third benefit of the grapevine is that this social interaction tends to relieve anxiety. This explains why rumor mills are most active during times of uncertainty.[84] Finally, the grapevine is associated with the drive to bond. Being a recipient of gossip is a sign of inclusion, according to evolutionary psychologists. Trying to quash the grapevine is, in some respects, an attempt to undermine the natural human drive for social interaction.[85]

While the grapevine offers these benefits, it is not a preferred communication medium. Grapevine information is sometimes so distorted that it escalates rather than reduces employee anxiety. Furthermore, employees develop more negative attitudes toward the organization when management is slower than the grapevine in communicating information. What should corporate leaders do with the grapevine? The best advice seems to be to listen to the grapevine as a signal of employee anxiety, then correct the cause of this anxiety. Some companies also listen to the grapevine and step in to correct blatant errors and fabrications. Most important, corporate leaders need to view the grapevine as a competitor and meet this challenge by directly informing employees of news before it spreads throughout the organizational grapevine.

[chapter summary]

LO1   Explain why communication is important in organizations, and discuss four influences on effective communication encoding and decoding.

Communication refers to the process by which information is transmitted and *understood* between two or more people. Communication supports work coordination, organizational learning, decision making, changing others' behavior, and employee well-being. The communication process involves forming, encoding, and transmitting the intended message to a receiver, who then decodes the message and provides feedback to the sender. Effective communication occurs when the sender's thoughts are transmitted to and understood by the intended receiver. Four ways to improve this process is for both sender and receiver to be proficient with the communication channel, have similar codebooks, have shared common mental models of the communication context, and for the sender to be experienced at sending that message.

LO2   Compare and contrast the advantages of and problems with electronic mail, other verbal communication media, and nonverbal communication.

The two main types of communication channels are verbal and nonverbal. Various forms of Internet-based communication are widely used in organizations, with e-mail as the most popular. Although an efficient and useful filing cabinet, e-mail is relatively poor at communicating emotions; it tends to reduce politeness and respect; it is an inefficient medium for communicating in ambiguous, complex, and novel situations; and it contributes to information overload. Facebook-like websites, wikis, virtual reality platforms, and other forms of social media are gaining popularity in the workplace. Social media include Internet-based tools (websites, applications, etc.) that allow users to generate and exchange information. They serve several functions, including presenting the individual's identity, enabling conversations, sharing information, sensing the presence of others in the virtual space, maintaining relationships, revealing reputation or status, and supporting communities. Nonverbal communication includes facial gestures, voice intonation, physical distance, and even silence. Unlike verbal communication, nonverbal communication is less rule bound and is mostly automatic and nonconscious. Some nonverbal communication is automatic, through a process called emotional contagion.

LO3   Explain how social acceptance and media richness influence the preferred communication channel.

The most appropriate communication medium partly depends on its social acceptance and media richness. Social acceptance refers to how well the communication medium is approved and supported by the organization, teams, and individuals. This contingency includes organization and team norms, individual preferences for specific communication channels, and the symbolic meaning of a channel. A communication medium should also be chosen for its data-carrying capacity (media richness). Nonroutine and ambiguous situations require rich media. However, technology-based lean media might be almost as effective as rich media for transferring information, particularly when users can multi-communicate and have high proficiency with that technology, and when the social distractions of high media richness channels reduce the efficient processing of information through those channels. These contingencies also should be considered when selecting the best channels for persuasion.

LO4   Discuss various barriers (noise) to effective communication, including cross-cultural and gender-based differences in communication.

Several barriers create noise in the communication process. People misinterpret messages because of misaligned codebooks due to different languages, jargon, and use of ambiguous phrases. Filtering messages and information overload are two other communication barriers. These problems are often amplified in cross-cultural settings in which these problems occur together with differences in the meaning of nonverbal cues, silence, and conversational overlaps. There are also some communication differences between men and women, such as the tendency for men to exert status and engage in report talk in conversations, whereas women use more rapport talk and are more sensitive than are men to nonverbal cues.

LO5 Explain how to get messages across more effectively, and summarize the elements of active listening.

To get a message across, the sender must learn to empathize with the receiver, repeat the message, choose an appropriate time for the conversation, and be descriptive rather than evaluative. Listening includes sensing, evaluating, and responding. Active listeners support these processes by postponing evaluation, avoiding interruptions, maintaining interest, empathizing, organizing information, showing interest, and clarifying the message.

LO6 Summarize effective communication strategies in organizational hierarchies, and review the role and relevance of the organizational grapevine.

Some companies try to encourage communication through workspace design, as well as through Internet-based communication channels. Some executives also meet directly with employees, such as through management by walking around (MBWA) and town hall meetings, to facilitate communication across the organization.

In any organization, employees rely on the grapevine, particularly during times of uncertainty. The grapevine is an unstructured and informal network founded on social relationships rather than organizational charts or job descriptions. Although early research identified several unique features of the grapevine, some of these features may be changing as the Internet plays an increasing role in grapevine communication.

[key terms]

communication, p. 260
emotional contagion, p. 267
grapevine, p. 278

information overload, p. 272
management by walking around (MBWA), p. 277

media richness, p. 268
persuasion, p. 270

[critical thinking questions]

1. You have been hired as a consultant to improve communication between the engineering and marketing staff in a large high-technology company. Use the communication model and the four ways to improve that process to devise strategies to improve communication effectiveness among employees between these two work units.

2. A company in a country that is just entering the information age intends to introduce e-mail for office staff at its three buildings located throughout the city. Describe two benefits and two potential problems that employees will likely experience with this medium.

3. Senior management at a consumer goods company wants you to investigate the feasibility of using a virtual reality platform (such as Second Life) for monthly online meetings involving its three dozen sales managers located in several cities and countries. Use the social acceptance and media richness factors described in this chapter to identify information you need to consider when conducting this evaluation.

4. Wikis are collaborative websites where anyone in the group can post, edit, or delete any information. Where might this communication technology be most useful in organizations?

5. Under what conditions, if any, do you think it is appropriate to use e-mail to notify an employee that he or she has been laid off or fired? Why is e-mail usually considered an inappropriate channel to convey this information?

6. Suppose that you are part of a virtual team and must persuade other team members on an important matter (such as switching suppliers or altering the project deadline). Assuming that you cannot visit these people in person, what can you do to maximize your persuasiveness?

7. Explain why men and women are sometimes frustrated with each other's communication behaviors.

8. In your opinion, has the introduction of e-mail and other information technologies increased or decreased the amount of information flowing through the corporate grapevine? Explain your answer.

CASE STUDY 9.1 COMMUNICATING ONE METLIFE

Suppose you had to get a message from your CEO to 70,000 employees in 64 countries. You could e-mail it. But what if you also had to make each recipient feel personally

addressed in a respectful way? You could do careful work with translators to get not just the overall message right but local nuances as well.

But what if you had to deliver the appropriately translated message; make each recipient feel understood and respected; welcome all of them as employees of a new, global company being created from their former employers; make it a two-way interaction; and deploy the whole enchilada by an immovable deadline?

Day One

That was the communications mountain Karen Horn faced when she and a team were charged with creating a campaign to integrate the 52,000 mainly U.S.-based employees of MetLife and the 18,000 worldwide employees of AIG-owned Alico, which MetLife announced its intention to acquire. It became known as the Day One campaign, a literal reference to the day the $16.2 billion deal was finalized.

"We wanted Alico employees, on day one, to feel welcome and to operate as part of MetLife," says Horn, the company's New York–based vice president, internal communications. "Likewise for MetLife legacy employees. We wanted them to understand that this made us a totally different company—a global company."

Horn partnered with event marketing agency TBA Global, and everyone's first instinct was to consider one worldwide event. But as tempting as it was to have 70,000 people sharing a moment, Horn and the team realized it would, in fact, send the wrong message. So rather than expecting all offices to tune in at an appointed time, MetLife and TBA Global reached out to contacts in the seven geographic regions and asked for advice on delivering the message of unity. "We said, 'Here's what we want people to think and feel. What would that take? A ballroom? Lunch around the office conference table?'" Horn explains. "The whole point was for everyone to feel, 'I'm a part of MetLife, and MetLife understands and cares about me.' It was important that we do things as it made sense in each location."

So instead of one event on November 1 (which had its own problems, since the day is a religious holiday in many countries), Horn worked to arrange 60-plus events held at times that best suited each office or region within a week or two after November 1.

Keeping It Simple

But what would they celebrate? Horn recalls meeting with Alico's regions and offering communications concepts: "What we came away thinking was, 'We knew they all would be different, but, wow, they're all really different.'"

The brand message, therefore, had to be "translatable, universal, and able to be internalized and embraced in any language," says Alison Jenks, vice president, marketing, at TBA Global. Creative, yes; complicated, no. "We realized it had to be as simple as possible," Horn says. "Everyone understands the concept of 'one.' We are one company. We are 'One MetLife.'"

The next challenge was how best to carry that message through at the local events. "Our solution was to make a

variety of materials and give them options," Horn says. Each of the 100 offices received a "digital toolkit" with elements (translated into 19 languages) that they could use in their own Day One events. Among the tools were logos, photos, brand identity guidelines, and videos.

One video, created by TBA Global from clips submitted by each region showing employees displaying a special One MetLife logo, was included for use as the opener for all of the Day One events worldwide. "From Uruguay to Athens to Tokyo, it was amazing to see what they did," Horn says.

TBA Global also produced a five-minute video called "Who is MetLife?" Leaders of every business area and region were included. "It's important that you hear 'your' person," Horn notes, "and for you to think, 'My leader is there. I'm a part of this.'"

The U.S. event was held with 600 legacy MetLife and former Alico employees gathering at the Sheraton New York. Many of the MetLife executives had just returned—in at least one case, coming directly from airport to stage—from attending Day One events in Japan, Chile, France, Dubai, and Mexico.

"Our goals were to create a welcoming environment that allowed attendees to mix and mingle, as well as feel recognized for their contributions to the acquisition and integration process," says Lori Allen, manager, global events, at MetLife in New York, who served as lead planner for the event. "We also wanted to showcase the fact that this was not the only event, merely the final event, in a weeklong series of international celebrations commemorating our new global presence."

As the meeting's technical director, Rich Young, meeting specialist, says, "Our goal was to 'wow' them with the graphics and videos that were being shown that night. We used a 60-by-20-foot screen that gave a lot of power to the room and enhanced the videos and images. It also was a dramatic backdrop for the presenters and for group photos during the evening."

Alico meeting professionals Trish Anderson and Darrell Drason were on hand as well. "The event was great exposure for them to MetLife associates, and they were familiar faces for the Alico attendees," Allen notes. "We've realigned our department as a result of our expanded international scope. Trish and Darrell now are senior planners in our Global Events Team."

Message Received

So did Horn successfully scale the mountain? In terms of engagement, yes: Every region participated in creating a video for the opening montage, and every employee was reached by a Day One event. In terms of retention, also yes: Two months post-acquisition, MetLife had met its goal of retaining 90 percent of target employees.

"Our regions exceeded our expectations because they added so much energy with their local interpretations of the event and its meaning," Horn says. "People were genuinely excited to see 'real people' in other locations saying with a big smile, 'One MetLife.' That made it all worth it."

Discussion Questions

1. Which communication channels were mainly used to communicate MetLife's message of "One MetLife"? Why were these channels used rather than others?

2. This organizational communication event occurred across many languages and cultures. What communication problems might potentially occur in this situation?

3. The process of acquiring another company is fraught with emotions, such as the loss of identity that Alico employees might feel. How would these emotions affect the communication activities used in MetLife's integration process?

Source: From A. Hall, "MetLife's Communication Challenge: Uniting Employees After An Acquisition," *Penton Insight*, Vol. 28, February 2011. Reprinted with permission of Penton Media, Inc.

CASE STUDY 9.2 COMMUNICATING WITH THE MILLENNIALS

The Millennials (including Generation Y) have arrived in the workplace, and they are bringing new ways to communicate. Surveys report that this generation lives by computer and cell phone communication. Three out of four Gen-Yers use instant messaging (including Twitter tweets); 15 percent of them are logged on to instant messaging 24/7! Most Gen-Yers either have a space on a social network site such as Facebook or frequent these sites where they have friends. These digital natives also get most of their news from the Internet rather than from television or newspapers.

"Employers are going to find this generation communicates differently. They IM [instant message], send text messages, and can't live without a cell phone," says Dave O'Brien, regional manager of Berbee, a company that helps businesses with their information technology needs. Frank Albi, president of Inacom, a technology and business consulting firm, agrees. "The way they [Millennials] exchange information is vastly different. It's all about IMs and text messages—nice and short."

Albi also notes that Millennials are much more active in multi-communicating. "You can be on the phone with someone and easily instant message someone who you see is online to answer a question or share an idea with," Albi says. However, managers also worry that too much of this multi-communication isn't work-related. "There's a fine line about what can be allowed at work and what can't," suggests Steve Hoeft, a recruiting manager at Time Warner Cable. "Instant messaging is very popular, but if it's affecting their work, that's when there's a problem."

Corporate leaders at BT, Britain's largest telecommunications company, are also aware that Millennials (and to some extent Gen-X employees) live in different communication channels from Baby Boomers. "Young people in BT communicate much more informally and in real-time," says Richard Dennison, BT's intranet and channel strategy manager. "They're not intimidated by hierarchy or status; to them BT is flat." Dennison adds that Generation-Y employees want bite-sized information, not long treatises.

Dennison also emphasizes that, more than previous generations, Millennials demand authentic communication, not marketing hype. "Corporate speak won't cut it anymore," Dennison warns. "First, people won't read it—if they ever did—and second, people won't believe it—if they ever did." Dennison also notices that if Gen-Yers receive corporate babble, they find ways to let the source know that it lacks authenticity. Remember, this is the generation that has always had a place to write comments after reading the original message.

From these observations, you might think that executive blogs are the answer to Gen-Y communication needs. Not so, argues Dennison. "Force all our senior managers to blog? My experience is that the more senior a manager is, the less likely they'll be able to blog successfully." He adds that executives have too little time to nurture a blog, and they tend to have communication experts who want to meddle (thereby undermining the blog's authenticity).

So how can the company's top dogs communicate effectively with Millennial employees? At BT, the chief executive has held 90-minute online web chats with BT staff every six weeks. This medium works well for young BT employees because the communication is in real time and authentic; the questions aren't screened and the CEO's answers aren't edited. "Thousands of people participate in these chats and it has helped to build up a significant amount of trust" in the CEO, says Dennison. These online web chats also work well with BT executives, because they represent a fixed chunk of time and provide direct contact with the concerns and issues facing employees throughout the hierarchy.

Discussion Questions

1. Take a poll of your class (at least, the Gen-X and Gen-Y members). At school or work, how many regularly (e.g., daily or every few days) send or receive information (not entertainment) using (a) e-mail, (b) instant messages or Twitter tweets, (c) cell phone text messages, (d) reading/writing blogs, (e) visiting/authoring social media sites (e.g., Facebook), (f) watching/creating online videos (e.g., YouTube)?

2. Even within this generation, there are different preferences for communication media. After conducting the poll, ask students who don't regularly use one or more of these methods why they don't like that particular communication medium. Ask those who very often use these sources to give their point of view.

3. Companies have been slow and reluctant to adopt social media channels, online videos, and similar forms of communication. If you were a senior manager, how would you introduce these communication technologies in the workplace to share information and knowledge more effectively?

Sources: MaryBeth Matzek, "R U on 2 Gen Y?" *Marketplace*, September 4, 2007, p. 10; Richard Dennison, "Encouraging BT's Authentic Voice of Leadership," *Strategic Communication Management* 12, no. 2 (2008), p. 12.

TEAM EXERCISE 9.3 ANALYZING BLOGS AND TWEETS

PURPOSE This exercise is designed to help you understand the dynamics of corporate blogs and microblogs as a way to communicate around organizations.

INSTRUCTIONS This exercise is usually conducted between classes as a team assignment (though it can also be conducted individually). The instructor will divide the class into teams, and each team will identify an executive who communicates using a corporate blog or microblog (e.g., Twitter) aimed at customers, employees, or the wider community.

Analyze content from the selected blog or microblog and answer the following questions in class (preferably with brief samples where applicable):

1. Who is the main intended audience of the selected blog or microblog?
2. What are the main topics in recent postings/tweets about this organization?
3. To what extent do you think this blog/microblog attracts the interest of its intended audience? Explain.

TEAM EXERCISE 9.4 ACTIVE LISTENING EXERCISE

Mary Gander, Winona State University

PURPOSE This exercise is designed to help you understand the dynamics of active listening in conversations and to develop active listening skills.

INSTRUCTIONS For each of the four vignettes presented here, either in teams or individually, compose three statements that demonstrate active listening. One statement will indicate that you show empathy for the situation; the second will ask for clarification and detail in a nonjudgmental way; and the third statement will provide nonevaluative feedback to the speaker. Here are some details about each of these three types of responses:

- *Showing empathy: Acknowledge feelings.* Sometimes it sounds like a speaker wants you to agree with him or her, but in reality the speaker mainly wants you to understand how he or she feels. "Acknowledging feelings" involves taking in the speaker's statements while looking at the "whole message," including body language, tone of voice, and level of arousal, and trying to determine what emotion the speaker is conveying. Then you let the speaker know that you realize what he or she is feeling by acknowledging it in a sentence.

- *Asking for clarification and detail while withholding judgment and opinions.* This step conveys that you are trying to understand and not just trying to push your opinions onto the speaker. To formulate a relevant question in asking for more clarification, you will have to listen carefully to what the speaker says. Frame your question as someone trying to understand in more detail; often asking for a specific example is useful. This also helps the speaker evaluate his or her own opinions and perspective.

- *Providing nonevaluative feedback: Feeding back the message you heard.* This will allow the speaker to determine if he or she has conveyed the message to you and will help prevent troublesome miscommunication.

It will also help the speaker become more aware of how he or she is coming across to another person (self-evaluation). Just think about what the speaker is conveying; paraphrase it in your own words, and say it back to the speaker (without judging the correctness or merit of what was said), asking him or her if that is what was meant.

After teams (or individual students) have prepared the three statements for each vignette, the instructor will ask you to present your statements and explain how these statements satisfy the active listening criteria.

VIGNETTE #1 A colleague stops by your desk and says, "I am tired of the lack of leadership around here. The boss is so wishy-washy; he can't get tough with some of the slackers around here. They just keep milking the company, living off the rest of us. Why doesn't management do something about these guys? And you are always so supportive of the boss; he's not as good as you make him out to be."

Develop three statements that respond to the speaker in this vignette by (a) showing empathy, (b) seeking clarification, and (c) providing nonevaluative feedback.

VIGNETTE #2 Your coworker stops by your cubicle; her voice and body language show stress, frustration, and even some fear. You know she has been working hard and has a strong need to get her work done on time and done well. You are trying to concentrate on some work and have had a number of interruptions already. She abruptly interrupts you and says, "This project is turning out to be a mess. Why can't the other three people on my team quit fighting with each other?"

Develop three statements that respond to the speaker in this vignette by (a) showing empathy, (b) seeking clarification, and (c) providing nonevaluative feedback.

VIGNETTE #3 One of your subordinates is working on an important project. He is an engineer who has good technical skills and knowledge and was selected for the project team for that reason. He stops by your office and appears to be quite agitated: His voice is loud and strained, and his face has a look of bewilderment. He says, "I'm supposed to be working with four other people from four other departments on this new project, but they never listen to my ideas and seem to hardly know I'm at the meeting!"

Develop three statements that respond to the speaker in this vignette by (a) showing empathy, (b) seeking clarification, and (c) providing nonevaluative feedback.

VIGNETTE #4 Your subordinate comes into your office in a state of agitation, asking if she can talk to you. She is polite and sits down. She seems calm and does not have an angry look on her face. However, she says, "It seems like you consistently make up lousy schedules; you are unfair and unrealistic in the kinds of assignments you give certain people, me included. Everyone else is so intimidated they don't complain, but I think you need to know that this isn't right and it's got to change."

Develop three statements that respond to the speaker in this vignette by (a) showing empathy, (b) seeking clarification, and (c) providing nonevaluative feedback.

TEAM EXERCISE 9.5 CROSS-CULTURAL COMMUNICATION GAME

PURPOSE This exercise is designed to develop and test your knowledge of cross-cultural differences in communication and etiquette.

MATERIALS The instructor will provide one set of question/answer cards to each pair of teams.

INSTRUCTIONS

Step 1: The class is divided into an even number of teams. Ideally, each team would have three students. (Two- or four-student teams are possible if matched with an equal-sized team.) Each team is then paired with another team and the paired teams (Team "A" and Team "B") are assigned a private space away from other matched teams.

Step 2: The instructor will hand each pair of teams a stack of cards with the multiple-choice questions face down. These cards have questions and answers about cross-cultural differences in communication and etiquette. No books or other aids are allowed.

Step 3: The exercise begins with a member of Team A picking up one card from the top of the pile and asking the question on that card to the members of Team B. The information given to Team B includes the question and all alternatives listed on the card. Team B has 30 seconds after the question and alternatives have been read to give an answer. Team B earns one point if the correct answer is given. If Team B's answer is incorrect, however, Team A earns that point. Correct answers to each question are indicated on the card and, of course, should not be revealed until the question is correctly answered or time is up. Whether or not Team B answers correctly, it picks up the next card on the pile and reads it to members of Team A. In other words, cards are read alternatively to each team. This procedure is repeated until all of the cards have been read or time has expired. The team receiving the most points wins.

Important note: The textbook provides very little information pertaining to the questions in this exercise. Rather, you must rely on past learning, logic, and luck to win.

© 2011, 2001 Steven L. McShane.

SELF-ASSESSMENT 9.6 ARE YOU AN ACTIVE LISTENER?

PURPOSE This self-assessment is designed to help you estimate your strengths and weaknesses on various dimensions of active listening.

INSTRUCTIONS Think back to face-to-face conversations you have had with a coworker or client in the office, hallway, factory floor, or other setting. Indicate the extent to which each item in the following table describes your behavior during those conversations. Answer each item as truthfully as possible so that you get an accurate estimate of where your active listening skills need improvement. Then use the scoring key in Appendix B to calculate your results for each scale. This exercise is completed alone so students assess themselves honestly without concerns of social comparison. However, class discussion will focus on the important elements of active listening.

Active Listening Skills Inventory

WHEN LISTENING TO OTHERS IN FACE-TO-FACE, TELEPHONE, OR SIMILAR CONVERSATIONS, HOW OFTEN DO YOU DO THE FOLLOWING?	NEVER OR RARELY	SELDOM	SOMETIMES	OFTEN	ALMOST ALWAYS
1. I keep an open mind when others describe their ideas.	☐	☐	☐	☐	☐
2. I organize the speaker's ideas while s/he is talking to me.	☐	☐	☐	☐	☐
3. I ask questions to show I understand and am focused on the speaker's message.	☐	☐	☐	☐	☐
4. I interrupt before the speaker sufficiently presents his/her views.	☐	☐	☐	☐	☐
5. While listening, I mentally sort out the speaker's ideas so s/he makes sense to me.	☐	☐	☐	☐	☐
6. I use gestures and words (nodding, agreeing) to show I am listening.	☐	☐	☐	☐	☐
7. I let my mind wander when listening to people.	☐	☐	☐	☐	☐
8. I try to visualize and feel the speaker's experience while s/he is describing those events.	☐	☐	☐	☐	☐
9. I summarize the speaker's ideas to confirm that I understand him/her correctly.	☐	☐	☐	☐	☐
10. I focus on what the speaker is saying to me even when it doesn't sound interesting.	☐	☐	☐	☐	☐
11. I see the topic from my perspective rather than from the speaker's perspective.	☐	☐	☐	☐	☐
12. I show interest while listening to others.	☐	☐	☐	☐	☐

 After reading this chapter go to www.mhhe.com/mcshane6e for more in-depth information and interactivities that correspond to the chapter.

Power and Influence in the Workplace

learning objectives

After reading this chapter, you should be able to:

LO1 Describe the dependence model of power as well as the five sources of power in organizations.

LO2 Discuss the four contingencies of power.

LO3 Explain how people and work units gain power through social networks.

LO4 Describe eight types of influence tactics, three consequences of influencing others, and three contingencies to consider when choosing an influence tactic.

LO5 Identify the organizational conditions and personal characteristics that support organizational politics, as well as ways to minimize organizational politics.

his executive decision process. "I do things based on intuition, so when I meet with my financial director I only need a one-page summary," says the managing director of services for Sodexo Motivation Solutions Ltd. in Surrey, England. Unfortunately, the financial director didn't initially figure out McMath's preferences. "She . . . was coming to the meetings with a file of 600 pages," McMath recalls. "I would then get frustrated because she gave me too much information, and she would get frustrated because she thought I didn't understand the importance of the data."

McMath's financial director eventually adjusted her behavior to fit her boss's preferences. This alignment not only reduced conflict and frustration; it helped the financial director manage her boss by creating a more favorable impression. Managing your boss is the process of improving the relationship with your manager for the benefit of both of you and the organization. It includes developing bases of power that enable you to influence the manager and thereby achieve organizational objectives. Most executives say it is a key factor in everyone's career success. "It is crucial to understand how to manage your manager," says Tracey Andrews, manager of learning and development at the British department store chain John Lewis. "Start by getting to know how your manager thinks and works and what his/her priorities are."

Along with aligning your behavior with the manager's preferred style, managing your boss involves becoming a valuable resource by making your manager's job easier. This begins by performing your own job well. "Managing your manager is all about going that extra step," advises Chris Barber, who leads a team of 12 people as director of a photography studio in Warwickshire, UK. "It doesn't mean manipulating people . . . it's about doing your job well and helping your manager to get the best results."

Managing your boss also requires some impression management. For example, you need to "be a 'problem solver' rather than a 'problem pyromaniac,'" says John Shetcliffe, managing director of John Shetcliffe Marketing in Hertfordshire, England. Problem pyromaniacs turn everything into problems for the boss to fix, whereas problem solvers offer the boss solutions when problems arise. Shetcliffe recommends a related impression management strategy for managing your boss: "Don't supply just bad news; announce good news too. Otherwise, little by little *you* become the bad news!"[1]

Most executives say that managing your boss is a key factor in everyone's career success.

Managing your boss may sound manipulative, but it is really a valuable process of gaining power for the benefit of the organization. All of us try to manage others—with varying levels of success. In the opening chapter to this book, we pointed out that people apply organizational behavior (OB) theories and practices to help them get things done in organizations. This includes improving relationships, developing power bases, and applying influence tactics that change the behavior of others. In fact, OB experts point out that power and influence are inherent in all organizations. They exist in every business and in every decision and action.

This chapter unfolds as follows: We first define power and present a basic model depicting the dynamics of power in organizational settings. The chapter then discusses the five bases of power, including the role of information in legitimate and expert power. Next, we look at the contingencies necessary to translate those sources into meaningful power. Our attention then turns to social networks and how they provide power to members through social capital. A later part of this chapter examines the various types of influence in organizational settings, as well as the contingencies of effective influence strategies. The final section of this chapter looks at situations in which influence becomes organizational politics, as well as ways to minimize dysfunctional politics.

The Meaning of Power

LO1

Power is the capacity of a person, team, or organization to influence others.[2] There are a few important features of this definition. First, power is not the act of changing someone's attitudes or behavior; it is only the *potential* to do so. People frequently have power they do not use; they might not even know they have power. Second, power is based on the target's *perception* that the power holder controls (i.e., possesses, has access to, or regulates) a valuable resource that can help him or her achieve goals.[3] People might generate power by convincing others that they control something of value, whether or not they actually control that resource. This perception is also formed from the power holder's behavior, such as those who are not swayed by authority or norms. For instance, one recent study found that people are perceived as more powerful just by their behavior—such as putting their feet on a table, taking coffee from someone else's container, and being less vigilant of bookkeeping rules.[4] Notice, too, that power is not a personal feeling of power. You might feel powerful or think you have power over others, but it is not power unless others believe you have that capacity.

Third, power involves the asymmetric (unequal) *dependence* of one party on another party.[5] This dependent relationship is illustrated in Exhibit 10.1. The line from Person B to the goal shows that he or she believes Person A controls a resource that can help or hinder Person B in achieving that goal. Person A, the power holder in this illustration, might have power over Person B by controlling a desired job assignment, useful information, rewards, or even the privilege of being associated with him or her! For example, if you believe a coworker has expertise (the resource) that would substantially help you write a better

EXHIBIT 10.1

Dependence in the Power Relationship

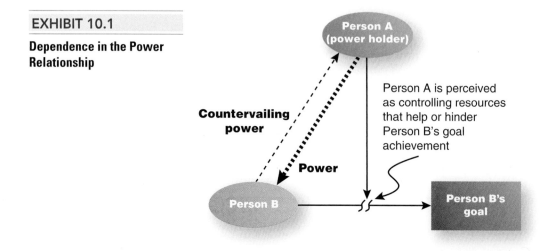

EXHIBIT 10.2

Sources and Contingencies of Power

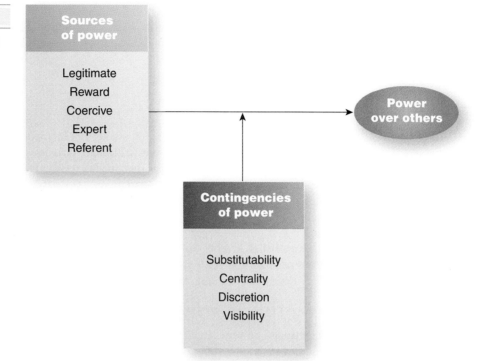

report (your goal), then that coworker has some power over you because you value that expertise to achieve your goal. Whatever the resource is, Person B is *dependent* on Person A (the power holder) to provide the resource so Person B can reach his or her goal.

Although dependence is a key element of power relationships, we use the phrase "asymmetric dependence" because the less powerful party still has some degree of power—called **countervailing power**—over the power holder. In Exhibit 10.1, Person A dominates the power relationship, but Person B has enough countervailing power to keep Person A in the exchange relationship and ensure that this person or department uses its dominant power judiciously. For example, though managers have power over subordinates in many ways (e.g., controlling job security, preferred work assignments), employees have countervailing power because they possess the skills and knowledge to keep production humming and customers happy, something that management can't accomplish alone.

Fourth, the power relationship depends on some minimum level of trust. Trust indicates a level of expectation that the more powerful party will deliver the resource. For example, you trust your employer to give you a paycheck at the end of each pay period. Even those in extremely dependent situations will usually walk away from the relationship if they lack a minimum level of trust in the more powerful party.

Let's look at this power dependence model in the context of managing your boss. You become a valuable resource to your manager by performing your job well, being solution-oriented, providing useful information, and adjusting your behavior to the manager's preferred work practices. Power exists only through your boss's awareness of your value, so managing your boss also involves some impression management. Furthermore, managing your boss builds countervailing power; only occasionally do employees have more power than their boss in the employment relationship. Finally, trust is an essential ingredient in managing your boss. Being reliable, productive, and showing empathy for the boss's needs are ways that managers increase their trust in subordinates.

The dependence model reveals only the core features of power dynamics between people and work units in organizations. We also need to learn about the specific sources of power and contingencies that allow that power to be effectively applied as influence. As Exhibit 10.2 illustrates, power is derived from five sources: legitimate, reward,

power
The capacity of a person, team, or organization to influence others.

countervailing power
The capacity of a person, team, or organization to keep a more powerful person or group in the exchange relationship.

coercive, expert, and referent. The model also identifies four contingencies of power: the employee's or department's substitutability, centrality, discretion, and visibility. Over the next few pages, we will discuss each of these sources and contingencies of power in the context of organizations.

Sources of Power in Organizations

A half-century ago, the social scientists John French and Bertrand Raven identified five sources of power in organizations. Although variations of this list have been proposed over the years, the original list has remained surprisingly intact.[6] Three sources of power—legitimate, reward, and coercive—originate mostly (but not completely) from the power holder's formal position or informal role. In other words, the person is granted these sources of power formally by the organization or informally by coworkers. Two other sources of power—expert and referent—originate mainly from the power holder's own characteristics; in other words, people carry these power bases around with them. However, even personal sources of power are not completely contained within the person, because they depend on how others perceive them.

LEGITIMATE POWER

Legitimate power is an agreement among organizational members that people in certain roles can request a set of behaviors from others. This perceived right or obligation originates from formal job descriptions, as well as informal rules of conduct. The most obvious example of legitimate power is a manager's right to tell employees what tasks to perform, whom to work with, what office resources they can use, and so forth. Employees follow the boss's requests because there is mutual agreement that employees will follow a range of directives from people in these positions of authority. Employees defer to this authority whether or not they will be rewarded or punished for complying with those requests.

Notice that legitimate power has restrictions; it only gives the power holder the right to ask for a *range* of behaviors from others. This range—known as the "zone of indifference"—is the set of behaviors that individuals are willing to engage in at the other person's request.[7] Although most employees accept the boss's right to deny them access to Facebook during company time, some might draw the line when the boss asks them to work several hours beyond the regular workday. There are also occasions in which employees actively oppose the boss's actions.

The size of the zone of indifference (and, consequently, the magnitude of legitimate power) increases with the level of trust in the power holder. Some values and personality traits also make people more obedient to authority. Those who value conformity and tradition and have high power distance (i.e., they accept an unequal distribution of power) tend to express higher deference to authority. The organization's culture represents another influence on the willingness of employees to follow orders. A 3M scientist might continue to work on a project after being told by superiors to stop working on it because the 3M culture supports an entrepreneurial spirit, which includes ignoring your boss's authority from time to time.[8]

Managers are not the only people with legitimate power in organizations. Employees also have legitimate power over their bosses and coworkers through legal and administrative rights, as well as informal norms.[9] For example, an organization might give employees the right to request information that is required for their job. Laws give employees the right to refuse work in unsafe conditions. More subtle forms of legitimate power also exist. Human beings have a **norm of reciprocity**—a feeling of obligation to help someone who has helped them.[10] If a coworker previously helped you handle a difficult client, that coworker has power because you feel an obligation to help the coworker on something of similar value in the future. The norm of reciprocity is a form of legitimate power because it is an informal rule of conduct that we are expected to follow.

Legitimate Power Through Information Control
A particularly potent form of legitimate power occurs where people have the right to control the information that others

A French television program recently revealed how far people are willing to follow orders. As a variation of the 1960s experiments conducted by Stanley Milgram, 80 contestants administered electric shocks whenever a volunteer (an actor who didn't receive the shocks at all) answered a question incorrectly. Shocks increased in 20-volt increments, from 20 volts for the first mistake through to 460 volts. Contestants often hesitated after hearing the volunteer screaming for them to stop, yet continued the shocks after the host reminded them of their duty. Only 16 of the 80 contestants refused to administer the strongest shocks.[11]

receive.[12] These information gatekeepers gain power in two ways. First, information is a resource, so those who need that information are dependent on the gatekeeper to provide that resource. For example, the maps department of a mining company has incredible power when other departments are dependent on the map department to deliver maps required for exploration projects.

Second, information gatekeepers gain power by selectively distributing information so those receiving the information perceive the situation differently.[13] Executives depend on middle managers and employees to provide an accurate picture of the company's operations. Yet, as we learned in the previous chapter on communication, information is often filtered as it flows up the hierarchy. Middle managers and employees filter information so it puts them in a more positive light and allows them to steers the executive team toward one decision rather than another. In other words, these information gatekeepers can potentially influence executive decisions by framing their reality through selective distribution of information.

REWARD POWER

Reward power is derived from the person's ability to control the allocation of rewards valued by others and to remove negative sanctions (i.e., negative reinforcement). Managers have formal authority that gives them power

legitimate power
An agreement among organizational members that people in certain roles can request certain behaviors of others.

norm of reciprocity
A felt obligation and social expectation of helping or otherwise giving something of value to someone who has already helped or given something of value to you.

over the distribution of organizational rewards such as pay, promotions, time off, vacation schedules, and work assignments. Employees also have reward power over their bosses through their feedback and ratings in 360-degree feedback systems. These ratings affect supervisors' promotions and other rewards, so supervisors tend to pay more attention to employee needs after a 360-degree feedback system is introduced.

COERCIVE POWER

Coercive power is the ability to apply punishment. For many of us, the first response to this definition is managers threatening employees with dismissal. Yet employees also have coercive power, such as being sarcastic toward coworkers or threatening to ostracize them if they fail to conform to team norms. Many firms rely on this coercive power to control coworker behavior in team settings. Nucor is one such example: "If you're not contributing with the team, they certainly will let you know about it," says an executive at the Charlotte, North Carolina, steelmaker. "The few poor players get weeded out by their peers." Similarly, when asked how AirAsia maintained attendance and productivity after the Malaysian discount airline removed time clocks, chief executive Tony Fernandes replied: "Simple. Peer pressure sees to that. The fellow employees, who are putting their shoulders to the wheel, will see to that."[14]

EXPERT POWER

For the most part, legitimate, reward, and coercive power originate from the position.[15] Expert power, on the other hand, originates mainly from within the power holder. It is an individual's or work unit's capacity to influence others by possessing knowledge or skills valued by others. One important form of expert power is the (perceived) ability to manage uncertainties in the business environment. Organizations are more effective when they operate in predictable environments, so they value people who can cope with turbulence in the consumer trends, societal changes, unstable supply lines, and so forth.

A groundbreaking study of breweries and container companies identified three types of expertise that cope with uncertainty. These coping strategies are arranged in a hierarchy of importance, with prevention being the most powerful:[16]

Colleen DeCourcy is a powerful force in the advertising industry because of her digital marketing expertise. She is "one of the most brilliant digital talents in the world," says David Jones, CEO of Havas Worldwide, which recently acquired a majority equity stake in DeCourcy's company, Socialistic. Creative agencies are struggling to adapt to the world of Twitter tweets and Facebook pages. "I think we have a long way to go before we're really using technology in marketing," she warns. DeCourcy has gained power by forecasting digital developments and helping creative agencies adapt to them.[17]

- *Prevention.* The most effective strategy is to prevent environmental changes from occurring. For example, financial experts acquire power by preventing the organization from experiencing a cash shortage or defaulting on loans.
- *Forecasting.* The next best strategy is to predict environmental changes or variations. In this respect, trendspotters and other marketing specialists gain power by predicting changes in consumer preferences.
- *Absorption.* People and work units also gain power by absorbing or neutralizing the impact of environmental shifts as they occur. An example is the ability of maintenance crews to come to the rescue when machines break down.

Many people respond to expertise just as they respond to authority: They mindlessly follow the guidance of these experts.[18] In one classic study, for example, a researcher posing as a hospital physician telephoned on-duty nurses to prescribe a specific dosage of medicine to a hospitalized patient. None of the nurses knew the person calling, and hospital policy forbade them from accepting treatment by telephone (i.e., they lacked legitimate power). Furthermore, the medication was unauthorized, and the prescription was twice the maximum daily dose. Yet, almost all 22 nurses who received the telephone call followed the "doctor's" orders until stopped by researchers.[19]

This doctor–nurse study is a few decades old, but the power of expertise remains just as strong today, sometimes with tragic consequences. The Canadian justice system recently discovered that one of its "star" expert witnesses, a forensic child pathology expert, had provided inaccurate cause of death evaluations in at least 20 cases, a dozen of which resulted in wrongful or highly questionable criminal convictions. The pathologist's reputation as a renowned authority was the main reason why his often weak evidence was accepted without question. "Experts in a courtroom—we give great deference to experts," admits a Canadian defense lawyer familiar with this situation.[20]

REFERENT POWER

People have **referent power** when others identify with them, like them, or otherwise respect them. As with expert power, referent power originates within the power holder. It is largely a function of the person's interpersonal skills and tends to develop slowly. Referent power is also associated with **charisma.** Experts have difficulty agreeing on the meaning of charisma, but it is most often described as a form of interpersonal attraction whereby followers ascribe almost magical powers to the charismatic individual.[21] Some writers describe charisma as a special "gift" or trait within the charismatic person, while others say it is mainly in the eyes of the beholder. However, all agree that charisma produces a high degree of trust, respect, and devotion toward the charismatic individual.

Contingencies of Power

LO2

Let's say that you have expert power because of your ability to forecast and possibly even prevent dramatic changes in the organization's environment. Does this expertise mean that you are influential? Not necessarily. As was illustrated in Exhibit 10.2, sources of power generate power only in certain conditions. Four important contingencies of power are substitutability, centrality, visibility, and discretion.[22]

SUBSTITUTABILITY

A key strategy for managing your boss is to become a valuable resource. As we mentioned in the opening story to this chapter, employees become valuable by performing their jobs well and by offering useful information and guidance that makes a manager's job easier (e.g., offering solutions, not just problems). But your power over your boss depends not only on providing something of value; it also depends on how many other people offer the same resource.

The key word here is **substitutability,** or the availability of alternatives. If you and no one else has expertise across the organization on an important issue, you would be more powerful than if several people in your company possessed this valued knowledge. Conversely, power decreases as the number of alternative sources of the critical resource increases. Substitutability refers not only to other sources that offer the resource but also to substitutions for the resource itself. For instance, labor unions are weakened when companies introduce technologies that replace the need for their union members. Technology is a substitute for employees and, consequently, reduces union power.

Nonsubstitutability is strengthened by controlling access to the resource. Professions and labor unions gain power by controlling knowledge, tasks, or labor to perform important activities. For instance,

connect

To assist your learning and test your knowledge about the contingencies of power, go to **www.mcgrawhillconnect.com,** which has activities and test questions on this topic.

referent power
The capacity to influence others on the basis of an identification with and respect for the power holder.

charisma
A personal characteristic or special "gift" that serves as a form of interpersonal attraction and referent power over others.

substitutability
A contingency of power pertaining to the availability of alternatives.

Developing your personal brand is one of the key drivers of career success. The first step is to identify your "DNA"—your distinct and notable attributes. This DNA is a talent or expertise that is both valuable *and* unique, which leverages the power of nonsubstitutability. "Be unique about something. Be a specialist in something. Be known for something. Drive something," advises Barry Salzberg, global chief executive of the accounting and consulting firm Deloitte Touche Tohmatsu. "That's very, very important for success in leadership because there are so many highly talented people. What's different about you—that's your personal brand."[23]

the medical profession is powerful because it controls who can perform specific medical procedures. Labor unions that dominate an industry effectively control access to labor needed to perform key jobs. Employees become nonsubstitutable when they possess knowledge (such as operating equipment or serving clients) that is not documented or readily available to others. Nonsubstitutability also occurs when people differentiate their resource from the alternatives. Some people claim that consultants use this tactic. They take skills and knowledge that many other consulting firms can provide and wrap them into a package (with the latest buzzwords, of course) so that it looks like a service that no one else can offer.

CENTRALITY

Centrality refers to the power holder's importance, based on the degree and nature of his or her interdependence with others.[24] Centrality increases with the number of people dependent on you, as well as with how quickly and severely they are affected by that dependence. Think about your own centrality for a moment: If you decided not to show up for work or school tomorrow, how many people would have difficulty performing their jobs because of your absence? How soon after they arrive at work would these coworkers notice that you are missing and have to adjust their tasks and work schedule as a result? If you have high centrality, most people in the organization would be adversely affected by your absence, and they would be affected quickly.

The extent to which centrality leverages power is apparent in well-timed labor union strikes, such as the New York City transit strike during the busy Christmas shopping season a few years ago. The illegal three-day work stoppage clogged roads and caused half the city workers to miss or arrive very late for work. "[The Metropolitan Transit Authority] told us we got no power, but we got power," said one striking transit worker. "We got the power to stop the city."[25]

VISIBILITY

Lucy Shadbolt and her team members work from home and other remote locations for most of the workweek. While the manager of British Gas New Energy enjoys this freedom, she also knows that working remotely can be a career liability due to the lack of visibility. "When I go into the office, where we hot-desk, I have to make an effort to position myself near my boss," says Shadbolt. "You need to consciously build relationships when you don't have those water-cooler moments naturally occurring."[26]

Shadbolt recognizes that power does not flow to unknown people in the organization. Instead, employees gain power when their talents remain in the forefront of the minds of their bosses, coworkers, and others. In other words, power increases with your visibility. One way to increase visibility is to take people-oriented jobs and work on projects that require frequent interaction with senior executives. "You can take visibility in steps," advises an executive at a pharmaceutical firm. "You can start by making yourself visible in

Debating Point
HOW MUCH POWER DO CEOS REALLY POSSESS?

Chief executive officers wield enormous power. They have legitimate power by virtue of their position at the top of the organizational hierarchy. They also have tremendous reward and coercive power because they direct budgets and other resources toward or away from various individuals and work units. Refusing to go along with the CEO's wishes can be an unfortunate career decision. Some CEOs also gain referent power because their lofty position creates an aura of reverence. Even in this era of egalitarianism, most employees further down the organization are in awe when visited by the top executive.

CEO power is equally apparent through various contingencies. Top executives are almost always visible; some amplify that visibility when they become synonymous with the company's brand.[27] CEOs also have high centrality. Few strategic decisions are put into motion unless the top dog is on board. CEOs are supposed to have replacements-in-waiting (to make them substitutable), yet more than a few don't take enough time to mentor an heir-apparent. Some CEOs create an image of being too unique to be replicated.

These points make it evident that CEOs have considerable power . . . except that many CEOs and a few experts don't agree.[28] New CEOs quickly discover that they no longer have expertise over a specific area of the company or subject matter. Instead, they oversee the entire organization and its vast external environment—a domain so broad that CEOs necessarily become jacks-of-all-trades and masters-of-none. Consequently, more than any other position, the CEO depends on the expertise of others to get things done. CEOs don't even have much knowledge about what goes on in the organization. Reliable sources of information become more guarded when communicating to the top dog; employees further down the hierarchy carefully filter information so the CEO hears more of the good and less of the bad news.

The main Achilles heel for CEO power is their discretion, which is much more restricted than most people realize. To begin with, CEOs are rarely at the top of the power pyramid. Instead, they report to the company board, which can reject their proposals and fire them for acting contrary to the board's wishes. The board's power over the CEO is particularly strong when the company has one or two dominant shareholders. But CEOs have been fired by the board even when the company's ownership is dispersed and the CEO is the company's founder! At one time, some CEOs had more power by serving as the board's chair and personally selecting board members. Today, corporate governance rules and laws have curtailed this practice, resulting in more power for the board and less power for the CEO.[29]

The CEO's discretion is also held in check by the power of various groups within the organization. One such group is the CEO's own executive team. These executives constantly monitor their boss, because their careers and reputation are affected by his or her actions, and some of them are eager to fill the top job themselves.[30] Similarly, the actions of hospital CEOs are restricted to some extent by the interests and preferences of physicians associated with the hospital.

One cross-cultural study found that the CEO's discretion is limited in countries where laws offer greater rights to many stakeholders (rather than just shareholders) and give employees more protection from dismissal and other company actions. The study also reported that the CEO's discretion is limited in cultures with high uncertainty avoidance, because these social values require executives to take measured rather than bold steps toward change.[31]

You might think that CEOs have one remaining form of discretion: They can still overrule their vice presidents. Technically they can, but one group of experts pointed out that doing so has nasty repercussions. It triggers resentment and sends morale into a tailspin. Worse, this action motivates direct reports to seek out the CEO's involvement much earlier, which overwhelms the CEO's schedule and leaves less time for other priorities. A related observation is that CEOs are the official voice of the organization, so they have much less discretion about what they can say in public or in private conversations.

Finally, though it seems safe to claim that CEOs have high centrality, a few executives see their situation differently. "I am the least important person in this building," claims Mike Brown, CEO of Provena United Samaritans Medical Center in Illinois. "This place would run without me for weeks, but the most important groups here are the people taking care of the patients."[32]

---

centrality
A contingency of power pertaining to the degree and nature of interdependence between the power holder and others.

a small group, such as a staff meeting. Then when you're comfortable with that, seek out larger arenas."[33]

Employees also gain visibility by being, quite literally, visible. Some people (such as Shadbolt) strategically locate themselves in more visible work areas, such as those closest to the boss or where other employees frequently pass by. People often use public symbols as subtle (and not-so-subtle) cues to make their power sources known to others. Many professionals display their educational diplomas and awards on office walls to remind visitors of their expertise. Medical professionals wear white coats with stethoscopes around their necks to symbolize their legitimate and expert power in hospital settings. Other people play the game of "face time"—spending more time at work and showing that they are working productively.

DISCRETION

The freedom to exercise judgment—to make decisions without referring to a specific rule or receiving permission from someone else—is another important contingency of power in organizations. Consider the plight of first-line supervisors. It may seem that they have legitimate, reward, and coercive power over employees, but this power is often curtailed by specific rules. The lack of discretion makes supervisors less powerful than their positions would indicate. "Middle managers are very much 'piggy-in-the-middle,'" complains a middle manager at Britain's National Health System. "They have little power, only what senior managers are allowed to give them."[34] More generally, research indicates that managerial discretion varies considerably across industries, and that managers with an internal locus of control are viewed as more powerful because they act as though they have considerable discretion in their job.[35]

The Power of Social Networks

LO3

"It's not what you know, but who you know that counts!" This often-heard statement reflects the idea that employees get ahead not just by developing their competencies, but by locating themselves within **social networks**—social structures of individuals or social units (e.g., departments, organizations) that are connected through one or more forms of interdependence.[36] Some networks are held together due to common interests, such as when employees who love fancy cars spend more time together. Other networks form around common status, expertise, kinship, or physical proximity. For instance, employees are more likely to form networks with coworkers located near them as well as with coworkers who are relatives or close neighbors.[37]

Social networks exist everywhere because people have a drive to bond. However, there are cultural differences in the norms of active network involvement. Several writers suggest that social networking is more of a central life activity in Asian cultures that emphasize *guanxi*, a Chinese term referring to an individual's network of social connections. Guanxi is an expressive activity because being part of a close-knit network of family and friends reinforces one's self-concept. Guanxi is also an instrumental activity because it is a strategy for receiving favors and opportunities from others. People across all cultures rely on social networks for both expressive and instrumental purposes, but these activities seem to be somewhat more explicit in Confucian cultures.[38]

Do you have a guanxi orientation? Go to **www.mcgrawhillconnect.com** to assess how well you nurture interpersonal connections.

SOCIAL CAPITAL AND SOURCES OF POWER

Social networks generate power through **social capital**—the goodwill and resulting resources shared among members in a social network.[39] Social networks produce trust, support, sympathy, forgiveness, and similar forms of goodwill among network members, and this goodwill motivates and enables network members to share resources with one another.[40]

Social networks offer a variety of resources, each of which potentially enhances the power of its members. Probably the best-known resource is information from other network members, which improves the individual's expert power.[41] The goodwill of social capital opens communication pipelines among those within the network. Network members receive valuable knowledge more easily and more quickly from fellow network members than do people outside that network.[42] With better information access and timeliness, members have more power because their expertise is a scarce resource; it is not widely available to people outside the network.

Increased visibility is a second contributor to a person's power through social networks. When asked to recommend someone for valued positions, other network members more readily think of you than people outside the network. Similarly, they are more likely to

connections 10.1

Powered by the Social Network

Engineering and environmental consulting firm MWH Global reorganized its information technology (IT) operations into a single global division and located its main service center in New Zealand. Ken Loughridge was transferred from England to manage the new service center, but he didn't know the key players in his New Zealand team. "By and large, the staff I'd adopted were strangers," he says.

Fortunately, Loughridge was able to consult a report displaying the informal social network of relationships among his staff. MWH Global had surveyed its IT employees a few months earlier about whom they communicated with most often for information. These data produced a web-like diagram of nodes (people) connected by a maze of lines (relationships). From this picture, Loughridge could identify the employees on whom others depend for information. "It's as if you took the top off an ant hill and could see where there's a hive of activity," he says of the map. "It really helped me understand who the players were."

Social network analysis has gained a following among some executives as they discover that visual displays of relationships and information flows can help them to tap into employees with expertise and influence. "You look at an org chart within a company and you see the distribution of power that should be," says Eran Barak, global head of marketing strategies at Thomson Reuters. "You look at the dynamics in the social networks [to] see the distribution of power that is. It reflects where information is flowing—who is really driving things."

Karl Arunski, director of Raytheon's engineering center in Colorado, can appreciate these words. The defense and technology company's organizational chart didn't show how mission management specialists influenced people across departmental boundaries. So Arunski asked two executives to identify the names of up to ten experts who didn't fit squarely in a particular department, and then he conducted social network analysis to see how these people collaborated with engineers throughout the organization.

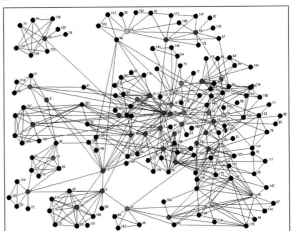

This is one of several social network analysis diagrams that helped Raytheon engineering director Karl Arunski determine who has the most social network power.

Credit: Courtesy of Karl J. Arunski, Raytheon.

The resulting maps (one of which is shown here) showed Arunski the influence and knowledge flow of various experts. It also highlighted problems: One cluster of employees is almost completely disconnected from the rest of the engineering group (top left of the diagram). The team's isolation was worrisome, because its members were experts in systems architecture, an important growth area for Raytheon. To increase the team's network power, Arunski encouraged the team leader to hold meetings where engineers could share information about systems architecture. The number of people attending eventually grew to 75 people and reduced the team's isolation from others. "Social network analysis helped Rocky Mountain Engineering understand how organizations develop architectures, and it enabled us to know how engineers become architects," says Arunski.[43]

---

mention your name when asked to identify people with expertise in your areas of knowledge. Referent power is a third source of power from networks. People tend to gain referent power because network members identify more with or at least have greater trust in network members. Referent power is also apparent by the fact that reciprocity increases among network members as they become more embedded in the network.[44]

A common misperception is that social networks are free spirits that cannot be orchestrated by corporate leaders. In reality, company structures and practices can shape these networks to some extent.[45] But even if organizational leaders don't try to manage social networks, they need to be aware of them. Indeed, people gain power in organizations by knowing what the social networks around them look like.[46] As Connections 10.1 describes, some leaders are discovering the hidden dynamics of these networks and tapping into their potential.

social networks
Social structures of individuals or social units that are connected to each other through one or more forms of interdependence.

social capital
The knowledge and other resources available to people or social units (teams, organizations) from a durable network that connects them to others.

GAINING POWER FROM SOCIAL NETWORKS

How do individuals (and teams and organizations) gain the most social capital from social networks? To answer this question, we need to consider the number, depth, variety, and centrality of connections that people have in their networks.

Strong Ties, Weak Ties, Many Ties

The volume of information, favors, and other social capital that people receive from networks usually increases with the number of people connected to them. Some people have an amazing capacity to maintain their connectivity with many people, and emerging communication technologies (Facebook, LinkedIn, etc.) have further amplified this capacity to maintain these numerous connections.[47] At the same time, the more people you know, the less time and energy you have to form "strong ties." Strong ties are close-knit relationships, which are evident from how often we interact with people, how much we share resources with them, and whether we have multiple- or single-purpose relationships with them (e.g., friend, coworker, and sports partner). The main advantages of having strong ties are that they offer resources more quickly and sometimes more plentifully than are available in weak ties (i.e., from acquaintances).

Some minimal connection strength is necessary to remain in any social network, but strong connections aren't necessarily the most valuable ties. Instead, having weak ties (i.e., being merely acquaintances) with people from diverse networks can be more valuable than having strong ties (i.e., close friendships) with people in similar networks.[48] Why is this so? Close ties—our close-knit circle of friends—tend to be similar to us, and similar people tend to have the same information and connections that we already have.[49] Weak ties, on the other hand, are acquaintances who are usually different from us and therefore offer resources we do not possess. Furthermore, by serving as a "bridge" across several unrelated networks, we receive unique resources from each network rather than more of the same resources.

The strength of weak ties is most apparent in job hunting and career development.[50] People with diverse networks tend to be more successful job seekers because they have a wider net to catch new job opportunities. In contrast, people who belong to similar overlapping networks tend to receive fewer leads, many of which they already knew about. Because careers require more movement across many organizations and industries, you need to establish connections with people across a diverse range of industries, professions, and other spheres of life.

Social Network Centrality

Earlier in this chapter, we explained that centrality is an important contingency of power. This contingency also applies to social networks.[51] The more centrally a person (or team or organization) is located in the network, the more social capital and therefore the more power he or she acquires. Centrality is your importance in the network. What conditions give you more centrality than others in social networks? One important factor is your "betweenness," which literally refers to how much you are located between others in the network. The more betweenness you have, the more you control the distribution of information and other resources to people on either side of you. In Exhibit 10.3, Person A has high betweenness centrality because he or she is a gatekeeper who controls the flow of information to and from many other people in the network. Person G has less betweenness, whereas Person F and several other network members in the diagram have no betweenness.

Another factor in centrality is the number or percentage of connections you have to others in the network (called "degree centrality"). Recall that the more people connected to you, the more resources (information, favors, etc.) will be available. The number of connections also increases centrality because you are more visible to other members of the network. Although being a member of a network gives you access to resources in that network, having a direct connection to people makes that resource sharing more fluid. Finally, centrality is a function of the "closeness" of the relationship. High closeness occurs when a member has shorter, more direct, and efficient paths or connections with others in the network. For example, Person A has fairly high closeness centrality because he or she has direct paths to most of the network, and many of these paths are short (implying efficient and high-quality communication links).

EXHIBIT 10.3

Centrality in Social Networks

Person A has high betweenness, closeness, and degree (number) centrality

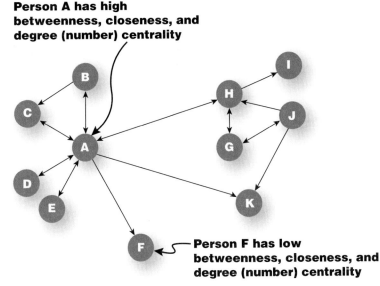

Person F has low betweenness, closeness, and degree (number) centrality

One last observation is that Exhibit 10.3 illustrates two clusters of people in the network. The gap between these two clusters is called a **structural hole**.[52] Notice that Person A provides the main bridge across this structural hole (connecting to H and K in the other cluster). This bridging role gives Person A additional power in the network. By bridging this gap, Person A becomes a broker—someone who connects two independent networks and controls information flow between them. Research shows that the more brokering relationships you have, the more likely you are to get early promotions and higher pay.

The Dark Side of Social Networks Social networks are natural elements of all organizations, yet they can create a formidable barrier to those who are not actively connected to it.[53] Women are often excluded from informal management networks because they do not participate in golf games and other male-dominated social events. Nina Smith, who leads Sage Software's Business Management Division, has had several conversations with female executives about these power dynamics. "I'm still trying to knock down the Boys Club and I still have women at Sage coming to me and saying, 'Nina, that's the boys' network and I can't get in.'"[54] Several years ago, executives at Deloitte Touche Tohmatsu discovered that inaccessibility to powerful social networks partly explained why many junior female employees left the accounting and consulting firm before reaching the partnership level. The global firm now relies on mentoring, formal women's network groups, and measurement of career progress to ensure that female staff members have the same career development opportunities as their male colleagues.[55]

Consequences of Power

structural hole
An area between two or more dense social network areas that lacks network ties.

How does power affect the power holder? The answer depends to some extent on the type of power.[56] When people feel empowered (high self-determination, meaning, competence, and impact), they believe they have power over themselves and freedom from being influenced by others. Empowerment tends to increase motivation, job satisfaction, organizational commitment, and job performance. However, this feeling of being in control and free from others' authority also increases automatic rather than mindful thinking. In particular, people who feel powerful usually are more likely to rely on stereotypes, have difficulty empathizing, and generally have less accurate perceptions compared to people with less power.[57]

The other type of power is one in which an individual has power over others, such as the legitimate, reward, and coercive power that managers have over employees in the workplace. This type of power is accompanied by a sense of duty or responsibility for the people over whom they have power. Consequently, people who have power over others tend to be more mindful of their actions and engage in less stereotyping.

Influencing Others

LO3

So far, this chapter has focused on the sources and contingencies of power, as well as power derived from social networks. But power is only the *capacity* to influence others. It represents the potential to change someone's attitudes and behavior. **Influence,** on the other hand, refers to any behavior that attempts to alter someone's attitudes or behavior.[58] Influence is power in motion. It applies one or more sources of power to get people to alter their beliefs, feelings, and activities. Consequently, our interest in the remainder of this chapter is on how people use power to influence others.

Influence tactics are woven throughout the social fabric of all organizations. This is because influence is an essential process through which people coordinate their effort and act in concert to achieve organizational objectives. Indeed, influence is central to the definition of leadership. Influence operates down, across, and up the corporate hierarchy. Executives ensure that subordinates complete required tasks. Employees influence coworkers to help them with their job assignments. And as the opening story to this chapter described, subordinates engage in upward influence tactics so bosses make decisions compatible with subordinates' needs and expectations.

TYPES OF INFLUENCE TACTICS

Organizational behavior researchers have devoted considerable attention to the various types of influence tactics found in organizational settings. They do not agree on a definitive list, but the most commonly discussed influence tactics are identified in Exhibit 10.4 and described over the next few pages.[59] The first five are known as "hard" influence tactics because they force behavior change through position power (legitimate, reward, and coercion).

connect

To assist your learning and test your knowledge about influence tactics, go to **www.mcgrawhillconnect.com**, which has activities and test questions on this topic.

EXHIBIT 10.4

Types of Influence Tactics in Organizations

INFLUENCE TACTIC	DESCRIPTION
Silent authority	Influencing behavior through legitimate power without explicitly referring to that power base.
Assertiveness	Actively applying legitimate and coercive power by applying pressure or threats.
Information control	Explicitly manipulating someone else's access to information for the purpose of changing his or her attitudes and/or behavior.
Coalition formation	Forming a group that attempts to influence others by pooling the resources and power of its members.
Upward appeal	Gaining support from one or more people with higher authority or expertise.
Persuasion	Using logical arguments, factual evidence, and emotional appeals to convince people of the value of a request.
Ingratiation/impression management	Attempting to increase liking by, or perceived similarity to, some targeted person.
Exchange	Promising benefits or resources in exchange for the target person's compliance.

The foreman at Otago Sheetmetal in New Zealand wasn't subtle about trying to improve staff performance. He often called the office administrator "useless" and, on one occasion, threatened to "plant her one." He also raised his voice and occasionally swore at other employees. One employee had his lawyer send a letter to Otago Sheetmetal urging the foreman to be less aggressive. These incidents are distressing, but not unique. One recent large survey reported that 24 percent of U.S. employees are yelled at by their boss in front of coworkers, 23 percent are belittled during meetings, and 38 percent are harshly criticized at work.[60]

The latter three—persuasion, ingratiation and impression management, and exchange—are called "soft" tactics because they rely more on personal sources of power (referent, expert) and appeal to the target person's attitudes and needs.

Silent Authority   The silent application of authority occurs when someone complies with a request because of the requester's legitimate power as well as the target person's role expectations.[61] This deference occurs when you comply with your boss's request to complete a particular task. If the task is within your job scope and your boss has the right to make this request, then this influence strategy operates without negotiation, threats, persuasion, or other tactics. Silent authority is the most common form of influence in high power distance cultures.[62]

Assertiveness   In contrast with silent authority, assertiveness might be called "vocal authority" because it involves actively applying legitimate and coercive power to influence others. Assertiveness includes persistently reminding the target of his or her obligations, frequently checking the target's work, confronting the target, and using threats of sanctions to force compliance. Assertiveness typically applies or threatens to apply punishment if the target does not comply. Explicit or implicit threats range from job loss to losing face by letting down the team. Extreme forms of assertiveness include blackmailing colleagues, such as by threatening to reveal the other person's previously unknown failures unless he or she complies with your request.

influence
Any behavior that attempts to alter someone's attitudes or behavior.

Information Control   Earlier in this chapter we explained that people with centrality in social networks have the power to control information. This power translates into influence when the power holder selectively distributes information, such that it reframes the situation and causes others to change their attitudes and/or behavior. Controlling information might include withholding information that is more

EXHIBIT 10.5

Elements of Persuasion

PERSUASION ELEMENT	CHARACTERISTICS OF EFFECTIVE PERSUASION
Persuader characteristics	• Expertise • Credibility • No apparent profit motive • Appears somewhat neutral (acknowledges benefits of the opposing view)
Message content	• Multiple viewpoints (not exclusively supporting the preferred option) • Limited to a few strong arguments (not many arguments) • Repeats arguments, but not excessively • Uses emotional appeals in combination with logical arguments • Offers specific solutions to overcome the stated problems • Inoculation effect—audience warned of counterarguments that the opposition will present
Communication medium	• Media-rich channels
Audience characteristics	• Lower self-esteem • Lower intelligence • Self-concept is not tied to the opposing view

critical or favorable or distributing information to some people but not to others. According to one major survey, almost half of employees believe coworkers keep others in the dark about work issues if it helps their own cause. Another study found that CEOs influence their board of directors by selectively feeding and withholding information.[63]

Coalition Formation   When people lack sufficient power alone to influence others in the organization, they might form a **coalition** of people who support the proposed change. A coalition is influential in three ways.[64] First, it pools the power and resources of many people, so the coalition potentially has more influence than any number of people operating alone. Second, the coalition's mere existence can be a source of power by symbolizing the legitimacy of the issue. In other words, a coalition creates a sense that the issue deserves attention because it has broad support. Third, coalitions tap into the power of the social identity process introduced in Chapter 3. A coalition is an informal group that advocates a new set of norms and behaviors. If the coalition has a broad-based membership (i.e., its members come from various parts of the organization), then other employees are more likely to identify with that group and, consequently, accept the ideas the coalition is proposing.

Upward Appeal   **Upward appeal** involves calling on higher authority or expertise, or symbolically relying on these sources, to support the influencer's position. It occurs when someone says, "The boss likely agrees with me on this matter; let's find out!" Upward appeal also occurs when relying on the authority of the firm's policies or values. By reminding others that your request is consistent with the organization's overarching goals, you are implying support from senior executives without formally involving them.

Persuasion   Persuasion is one of the most effective influence strategies for career success. The ability to present facts, logical arguments, and emotional appeals to change another person's attitudes and behavior is not just an acceptable way to influence others; in many societies, it is a noble art and a quality of effective leaders. The effectiveness of persuasion as an influence tactic

coalition
A group that attempts to influence people outside the group by pooling the resources and power of its members.

upward appeal
A type of influence in which someone with higher authority or expertise is called on in reality or symbolically to support the influencer's position.

depends on characteristics of the persuader, message content, communication medium, and the audience being persuaded (see Exhibit 10.5).[65] People are more persuasive when listeners believe they have expertise and credibility, such as when the persuader does not seem to profit from the persuasion attempt and states a few points against the position.

The message is more important than the messenger when the issue is important to the audience. Persuasive message content acknowledges several points of view so the audience does not feel cornered by the speaker. The message should also be limited to a few strong arguments, which are repeated a few times, but not too frequently. The message should use emotional appeals (such as graphically showing the unfortunate consequences of a bad decision), but only in combination with logical arguments and specific recommendations to overcome the threat. Finally, message content is more persuasive when the audience is warned about opposing arguments. This **inoculation effect** causes listeners to generate counterarguments to the anticipated persuasion attempts, which makes the opponent's subsequent persuasion attempts less effective.[66]

Two other considerations when persuading people are the medium of communication and characteristics of the audience. Generally, persuasion works best in face-to-face conversations and through other media-rich communication channels. The personal nature of face-to-face communication increases the persuader's credibility, and the richness of this channel provides faster feedback that the influence strategy is working. With respect to audience characteristics, it is more difficult to persuade people who have high self-esteem and intelligence, as well as a self-concept that is strongly tied to the opposing viewpoint.[67]

"Our task is to find out what management thinks we should be doing, and then to make management think we're doing it."

Credit: Copyright © Ted Goff.

Ingratiation and Impression Management Silent authority, assertiveness, information control, coalitions, and upward appeals are somewhat (or very!) forceful ways to influence other people. In contrast, a very "soft" influence tactic is **ingratiation**—any attempt to increase liking by, or perceived similarity to, some targeted person.[68] Ingratiation comes in several flavors. Employees might flatter their boss in front of others, demonstrate that they have similar attitudes as their boss (e.g., agreeing with the boss's proposal), and ask their boss for advice. Ingratiation is one of the more effective influence tactics for boosting a person's career success (i.e., performance appraisal feedback, salaries, and promotions).[69] However, people who engage in high levels of ingratiation are less (not more) influential and less likely to get promoted.[70] The explanation for the contrasting evidence is that those who engage in too much ingratiation are viewed as insincere and self-serving. The terms "apple polishing" and "brown-nosing" are applied to those who ingratiate to excess or in ways that suggest selfish motives for the ingratiation.

Ingratiation is part of a larger influence tactic known as impression management. **Impression management** is the practice of actively shaping our public images.[71] These public images might be crafted as important, vulnerable, threatening, or pleasant. For the most part, employees routinely engage in pleasant impression management behaviors to

inoculation effect
A persuasive communication strategy of warning listeners that others will try to influence them in the future and that they should be wary about the opponent's arguments.

ingratiation
Any attempt to increase liking by, or perceived similarity to, some targeted person.

impression management
The practice of actively shaping our public images.

satisfy the basic norms of social behavior, such as the way they dress and how they behave toward colleagues and customers.

Impression management is a common strategy for people trying to get ahead in the workplace. In fact, career professionals encourage people to develop a personal "brand" to demonstrate and symbolize a distinctive competitive advantage.[72] Furthermore, people who master the art of personal branding rely on impression management through distinctive personal characteristics such as black shirts, tinted hair, or unique signatures. "In today's economy, your personal brand is being judged every day," says Coca-Cola senior vice president Jerry Wilson. "Either position yourself, or others will position you."[73]

Unfortunately, a few individuals carry impression management beyond ethical boundaries by exaggerating their credentials and accomplishments. For instance, a Alcatel-Lucent executive lied about having a PhD from Stanford University and hid his criminal past involving forgery and embezzlement. Ironically, the executive was Alcatel's director of recruiting![74] One of the most elaborate misrepresentations occurred a few years ago when a Singaporean entrepreneur sent out news releases claiming to be a renowned artificial intelligence researcher, the author of several books, and the recipient of numerous awards from MIT and Stanford University (one of the awards was illustrated on his website). These falsehoods were so convincing that the entrepreneur almost received a real award, the "Internet Visionary of the Year" at the Internet World Asia Industry Awards.[75]

Exchange   Exchange activities involve the promise of benefits or resources in exchange for the target person's compliance with your request. Negotiation is an integral part of exchange influence activities. For instance, you might negotiate with your boss for a day off in return for working a less desirable shift at a future date. Exchange also includes applying the norm of reciprocity that we described previously, such as reminding the target person of past benefits or favors with the expectation that the target person will now make up for that debt. Earlier in this chapter we explained how people gain power through social networks. They also use norms of reciprocity to influence others in the network. Active networkers build up "exchange credits" by helping colleagues in the short term for reciprocal benefits in the long term.

CONSEQUENCES AND CONTINGENCIES OF INFLUENCE TACTICS

Faced with a variety of influence strategies, you are probably asking: Which ones are best? The best way to answer this question is to describe how people react when others try to influence them: resistance, compliance, or commitment.[76] *Resistance* occurs when people or work units oppose the behavior desired by the influencer by refusing, arguing, or delaying engagement in the behavior. *Compliance* occurs when people are motivated to implement the influencer's request at a minimal level of effort and for purely instrumental reasons. Without external sources to prompt the desired behavior, compliance would not occur. *Commitment* is the strongest outcome of influence, whereby people identify with the influencer's request and are highly motivated to implement it even when extrinsic sources of motivation are no longer present.

Generally, people react more favorably to "soft" tactics than to "hard" tactics (see Exhibit 10.6). Soft influence tactics rely on personal sources of power (expert and referent power), which tend to build commitment to the influencer's request. In contrast, hard tactics rely on position power (legitimate, reward, and coercion), so they tend to produce compliance or, worse, resistance. Hard tactics also tend to undermine trust, which can hurt future relationships.

Apart from the general preference for soft rather than hard tactics, the most appropriate influence strategy depends on a few contingencies. One obvious contingency is which sources of power are strongest. Those with expertise tend to have more influence using

**Consequences of Hard and
Soft Influence Tactics**

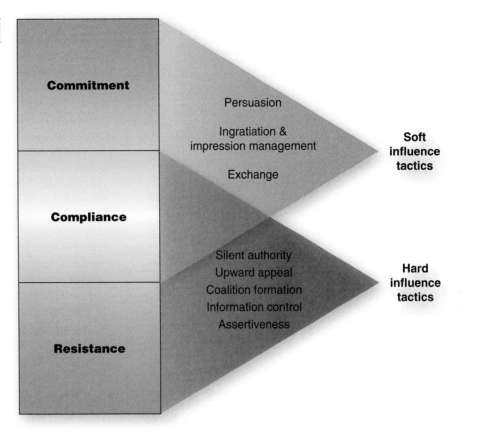

persuasion, whereas those with a strong legitimate power base are usually more successful applying silent authority.[77] A second contingency is whether the person being influenced is higher, lower, or at the same level in the organization. As an example, employees may face adverse career consequences by being too assertive with their boss. Meanwhile, supervisors who engage in ingratiation and impression management tend to lose the respect of their staff.

Finally, the most appropriate influence tactic depends on personal, organizational, and cultural values.[78] People with a strong power orientation might feel more comfortable using assertiveness, whereas those who value conformity might feel more comfortable with upward appeals. At an organizational level, firms with a competitive culture might foment more use of information control and coalition formation, whereas companies with a learning orientation would likely encourage more influence through persuasion. The preferred influence tactics also vary across societal cultures. Research indicates that ingratiation is much more common among managers in the United States than in Hong Kong, possibly because this tactic disrupts the more distant roles that managers and employees expect in high power distance cultures.

How politically charged is your school? Go to **www. mcgrawhillconnect.com** to assess the level of organizational politics, and to assist your learning about organizational politics and influence tactics.

Influence and Organizational Politics

LO4

You might have noticed that organizational politics has not been mentioned yet, even though some of the practices or examples described over the past few pages are usually considered political tactics. The phrase was carefully avoided because, for the most part, organizational politics is in the eye of the beholder. You might perceive a coworker's attempt to influence the boss as acceptable behavior for the good of the organization, whereas someone else might perceive the coworker's tactic as brazen organizational politics.

Office Politics
by the Numbers[79]

53%   of British managers polled feel that organizational politics is a major cause of stress at work (top-ranked cause of stress).

47%   of American employees polled say that office politics cuts into productive time (second highest cause, after fixing someone else's work).

36%   of Canadian employees polled recently say that office politics is one of the biggest roadblocks to productivity.

19%   of Canadian employees polled 10 years ago said that office politics is one of the biggest roadblocks to productivity.

29%   of American employees polled say a coworker has taken credit for one of their ideas.

58%   of Canadian employees polled say a coworker has taken credit for one of their ideas.

This perceptual issue explains why OB experts increasingly discuss influence tactics as behaviors and organizational politics as perceptions.[80] The influence tactics described earlier are perceived as **organizational politics** when they seem to be self-serving behaviors undertaken at the expense of others and possibly contrary to the interests of the entire organization. Of course, some tactics are so blatantly selfish and counterproductive that almost everyone correctly sees them as organizational politics. In other situations, however, a person's behavior might be viewed as political or in the organization's best interest, depending on your point of view.

Employees who experience organizational politics have lower job satisfaction, organizational commitment, organizational citizenship, and task performance, as well as higher levels of work-related stress and motivation to leave the organization.[81] And because political tactics serve individuals rather than organizations, they potentially divert resources away from the organization's effective functioning and potentially threaten its survival.

CONDITIONS SUPPORTING ORGANIZATIONAL POLITICS

Employees are more likely to engage in organizational politics (that is, use influence tactics for personal gain) in certain conditions.[83] One of those conditions is scarce resources. When budgets are slashed, people rely on political tactics to safeguard their resources and maintain the status quo. Office politics also flourish when resource allocation decisions are ambiguous, complex, or lack formal rules. This occurs because decision makers are given more discretion over resource allocation, so potential recipients of those resources use political tactics to influence the factors that should be considered in the decision. Organizational change encourages political behaviors for this reason. Change creates uncertainty

Over a two-year period, Philadelphia news co-anchor Alycia Lane was subject to malicious news stories from anonymous sources about her off-air behavior. Lane's co-anchor, Larry Mendte, showed concern when these stories emerged but, Lane claims, he recommended that she needed to move to another city. Soon after she lost her job (partly due to the rumors), Lane discovered why Mendte offered this advice: He was likely the person who fed private information about Lane to the media. The FBI discovered that Mendte used keystroke software to gain access to Lane's e-mail and that he looked at her e-mail at least 500 times. "[Alycia Lane's] star was climbing, while his was not climbing," claims Lane's attorney. "His conduct was designed to undermine her."[82]

and ambiguity as the company moves from an old set of rules and practices to a new set. During these times, employees apply political strategies to protect their valued resources, position, and self-concept.[84]

Personal Characteristics

Several personal characteristics affect an individual's motivation to engage in self-serving behavior.[85] This includes a strong need for personal as opposed to socialized power. Those with a need for personal power seek power for its own sake and try to acquire more power. Some individuals have strong **Machiavellian values.** Machiavellianism is named after Niccolò Machiavelli, the sixteenth-century Italian philosopher who wrote *The Prince*, a famous treatise about political behavior. People with high Machiavellian values are comfortable with getting more than they deserve, and they believe that deceit is a natural and acceptable way to achieve this goal. They seldom trust coworkers and tend to use cruder influence tactics, such as bypassing one's boss or being assertive, to get their own way.[86]

Minimizing Organizational Politics and Its Consequences

The conditions that fuel organizational politics also give us some clues about how to control dysfunctional political activities.[87] One strategy to keep organizational politics in check is to introduce clear rules and regulations that clarify the use of scarce resources. Organizational politics can become a problem during times of organizational change, so politics can be minimized through effective organizational change practices. Leaders also need to actively manage group norms to curtail self-serving influence activities. In particular, they can support organizational values that oppose political tactics, such as altruism and customer focus. One of the most important strategies is for leaders to become role models of organizational citizenship rather than symbols of successful organizational politicians.

Along with minimizing organizational politics, companies can limit the adverse effects of political perceptions by giving employees more control over their work and keeping them informed of organizational events. Research has found that employees who are kept informed of what is going on in the organization and who are involved in organizational decisions are less likely to experience organizational politics, which results in less stress, job dissatisfaction, and absenteeism.

organizational politics
Behaviors that others perceive as self-serving tactics at the expense of other people and possibly the organization.

Machiavellian values
The beliefs that deceit is a natural and acceptable way to influence others and that getting more than one deserves is acceptable.

[chapter summary]

LO1 Describe the dependence model of power as well as the five sources of power in organizations.

Power is the capacity to influence others. It exists when one party perceives that he or she is dependent on the other for something of value. However, the dependent person must also have countervailing power—some power over the dominant party—to maintain the relationship, and the parties must have some level of trust.

There are five power bases. Legitimate power is an agreement among organizational members that people in certain roles can request certain behaviors of others. This power has restrictions represented by the target person's zone of indifference. It also includes the norm of reciprocity (a feeling of obligation to help someone who has helped you). Reward power is derived from the ability to control the allocation of

rewards valued by others and to remove negative sanctions. Coercive power is the ability to apply punishment. Expert power is the capacity to influence others by possessing knowledge or skills that they value. An important form of expert power is the (perceived) ability to manage uncertainties in the business environment. People have referent power when others identify with them, like them, or otherwise respect them.

LO2 Discuss the four contingencies of power.

Four contingencies determine whether these power bases translate into real power. Individuals and work units are more powerful when they are nonsubstitutable; that is, there is a lack of alternatives. Employees, work units, and organizations reduce substitutability by controlling tasks, knowledge, and labor and by differentiating themselves from competitors. A second contingency is centrality. People have more power when they have high centrality; that is, the number of people affected is large and people are quickly affected by their actions. The third contingency, visibility, refers to the idea that power increases to the extent that a person's or work unit's competencies are known to others. Discretion, the fourth contingency of power, refers to the freedom to exercise judgment. Power increases when people have freedom to use their power.

LO3 Explain how people and work units gain power through social networks.

Social networks are social structures of individuals or social units (e.g., departments, organizations) that are connected to one another through one or more forms of interdependence. People receive power in social networks through social capital, which is the goodwill and resulting resources shared among members in a social network. Three main resources from social networks are information, visibility, and referent power.

Employees gain social capital through their relationship in the social network. Social capital tends to increase with the number of network ties. Strong ties (close-knit relationships) can also increase social capital because these connections offer more resources and offer them more quickly. However, having weak ties with people from diverse networks can be more valuable than having strong ties with people in similar networks. Weak ties provide more resources that we do not already possess. Another influence on social capital is the person's centrality in the network. Network centrality is determined in several ways, including the extent to which you are located between others in the network (betweenness), how many direct ties you have (degree), and the closeness of these ties. People also gain power by bridging structural holes—linking two or more clusters of people in a network.

LO4 Describe eight types of influence tactics, three consequences of influencing others, and three contingencies to consider when choosing an influence tactic.

Influence refers to any behavior that attempts to alter someone's attitudes or behavior. The most widely studied influence tactics are silent authority, assertiveness, information control, coalition formation, upward appeal, ingratiation and impression management, persuasion, and exchange. "Soft" influence tactics such as friendly persuasion and subtle ingratiation are more acceptable than "hard" tactics such as upward appeal and assertiveness. However, the most appropriate influence tactic also depends on the influencer's power base; whether the person being influenced is higher, lower, or at the same level in the organization; and personal, organizational, and cultural values regarding influence behavior.

LO5 Identify the organizational conditions and personal characteristics that support organizational politics, as well as ways to minimize organizational politics.

Organizational politics refers to influence tactics that others perceive to be self-serving behaviors at the expense of others and sometimes contrary to the interests of the organization. It is more common when ambiguous decisions allocate scarce resources and when the organization tolerates or rewards political behavior. Individuals with a high need for personal power and strong Machiavellian values have a higher propensity to use political tactics. Organizational politics can be minimized by providing clear rules for resource allocation, establishing a free flow of information, using education and involvement during organizational change, supporting team norms and a corporate culture that discourage dysfunctional politics, and having leaders who model organizational citizenship rather than political savvy.

[key terms]

centrality, p. 296
charisma, p. 295
coalition, p. 304
countervailing power, p. 291
impression management, p. 305
influence, p. 302
ingratiation, p. 305

inoculation effect, p. 305
legitimate power, p. 292
Machiavellian values, p. 309
norm of reciprocity, p. 292
organizational politics, p. 308
power, p. 290

referent power, p. 295
social capital, p. 298
social networks, p. 298
structural hole, p. 301
substitutability, p. 295
upward appeal, p. 304

[critical thinking questions]

1. What role does countervailing power play in the power relationship? Give an example of an encounter of your own with countervailing power at school or work.

2. Several years ago, the Major League Baseball players' association went on strike in September, just before the World Series started. The players' contract expired at the beginning of the season (May), but they held off the strike until September when they would lose only one-sixth of their salaries. In contrast, a September strike would hurt the owners financially because they earn a larger portion of their revenue during the playoffs. As one player explained: "If we strike next spring, there's nothing stopping [the club owners] from letting us go until next June or July because they don't have that much at stake." Use your knowledge of the sources and contingencies of power to explain why the baseball players' association had more power in negotiations by walking out in September rather than March.

3. You have just been hired as a toothpaste brand manager for a large consumer products company. Your job mainly involves encouraging the advertising and production groups to promote and manufacture your product more effectively. These departments aren't under your direct authority, though company procedures indicate that they must complete certain tasks requested by brand managers. Describe the sources of power you can use to ensure that the advertising and production departments will help you make and sell toothpaste more effectively.

4. How does social networking increase a person's power? What social networking strategies could you initiate now to enhance your future career success?

5. List the eight influence tactics described in this chapter in terms of how they are used by students to influence their university instructors. Which influence tactic is applied most often? Which is applied least often, in your opinion? To what extent is each influence tactic considered legitimate behavior or organizational politics?

6. How do cultural differences affect the following influence factors: (a) silent authority and (b) upward appeal?

7. A dozen or so years ago, the CEO of Apple Computer invited Steve Jobs (who was not associated with the company at the time) to serve as a special adviser and raise morale among Apple employees and customers. While doing this, Jobs spent more time advising the CEO on how to cut costs, redraw the organization chart, and hire new people. Before long, most of the top people at Apple were Jobs's colleagues, who began to systematically evaluate and weed out teams of Apple employees. While publicly supporting Apple's CEO, Jobs privately criticized him and, in a show of nonconfidence, sold 1.5 million shares of Apple stock he had received. This action caught the attention of Apple's board of directors, who soon after decided to replace the CEO with Steve Jobs. The CEO claimed Jobs was a conniving back-stabber who used political tactics to get his way. Others suggest that Apple would be out of business today if he hadn't taken over the company. In your opinion, were Steve Jobs's actions examples of organizational politics? Justify your answer.

8. This book frequently emphasizes that successful companies engage in organizational learning. How do political tactics interfere with organizational learning objectives?

CASE STUDY 10.1 RESONUS CORPORATION

By Steven L. McShane, based on an earlier case written by John A. Seeger

Frank Choy is normally a quiet person, but his patience has already been worn thin by interdepartmental battles. Choy joined Resonus Corporation, a hearing aid designer and manufacturer, eight months ago as director of engineering. Production of the latest product has been delayed by two months, and Choy's engineering services department (ESD)—which prepares final manufacturing specifications—is taking the heat as the main culprit for these delays. Similar delays have been occurring at Resonus for the past few years. The previous engineering director was fired after 18 months; the director before him quit after about the same amount of time.

Bill Hunt, CEO of Resonus for the past 15 years, responded to these problems by urging everyone to remain civil. "I'm sure we can resolve these differences if we just learn to get along better," he said whenever a dispute broke out. Hunt disliked firing anyone, but he felt the previous engineering director was too confrontational. "I spent too much time smoothing out arguments when he was here," Hunt thought to himself soon after Choy was hired. "Frank, on the other hand, seems to fit into our culture of collegiality."

Hunt was groomed by the company's founder and took great pride in preserving the organization's family spirit. He also discouraged bureaucracy, believing that Resonus operated best through informal relationships among its managers. Most Resonus executives were similarly informal, except Jacqui Blanc, the production director, who insisted on strict guidelines. Hunt tolerated Blanc's formal style because soon after joining Resonus five years ago, she

discovered and cleaned up fraudulent activity involving two production managers and a few suppliers.

The organizational chart shows that Frank Choy oversees two departments: ESD and research. In reality, "Doc" Kalandry, the research director, informally reports directly to the CEO (Hunt) and has never considered the director of engineering as his boss. Hunt actively supports this informal reporting relationship because of Doc's special status in the organization. "Doc Kalandry is a living genius," Hunt told Choy soon after he joined the firm. "With Doc at the helm of research, this company will continue to lead the field in innovation." Hunt's first job at Resonus was in the research group, and Choy suspected that Hunt still favored that group.

Everyone at Resonus seems to love Doc's successful products, his quirky style, and his over-the-top enthusiasm, but some of Choy's ESD staff are also privately concerned. Says one engineer: "Doc is like a happy puppy when he gets a new product idea. He delights in the discovery, but also won't let go of it. He also gets Hunt too enthusiastic. But Doc's too optimistic; we've had hundreds of production change orders already this year. If I were in Frank's shoes, I'd put my foot down on all this new development."

Soon after joining Resonus, Choy realized that ESD employees get most of the blame and little of the credit for their work. When production staff find a design fault, they directly contact the research design engineer who developed the technology, rather than the ESD group who prepare the specifications. Research engineers willingly work with production because they don't want to let go of their project. "The designers seem to feel they're losing something when one of us [ESD] tries to help," Choy explains.

Meanwhile, production supervisors regularly critique ESD staff, whereas they tend to accept explanations from the higher-status research department engineers. "Production routinely complains about every little specification error, many of which are due to design changes made by the research group," says one frustrated ESD technician. "Many of us have more than 15 years experience in this work. We shouldn't have to prove our ability all the time, but we spend as much time defending ourselves as we do getting the job done."

Choy's latest troubles occurred when Doc excitedly told Hunt, the CEO, about new nanoprocessor technology that he wanted to install in the forthcoming high-end hearing aid product. As with most of Doc's previous last-minute revisions, Hunt endorsed this change and asked Choy and Blanc (the production director) to show their commitment, even though production was scheduled to begin in less than three weeks. Choy wanted to protest, knowing that his department would have to tackle unexpected incompatibility design errors. Instead, he quietly agreed to Hunt's request to avoid acting like his predecessor and facing similar consequences (i.e., getting fired). Blanc curtly stated that her group was ready if Choy's ESD unit could get accurate production specifications ready on time and if the sales director would stop making wild delivery promises to customers.

When Doc's revised design specs arrived more than a week later, Choy's group discovered numerous incompatibilities that had to be corrected. Even though several ESD staff were assigned to 12-hour days on the revisions, the final production specifications weren't ready until a couple of days after the deadline. Production returned these specs two days later, noting a few elements that required revision because they were too costly or difficult to manufacture in their current form. By that time, the production director had to give priority to other jobs and move the new hearing aid product further down the queue. This meant that manufacturing of the new product was delayed by at least two months. The sales director was furious and implied that Frank Choy's incompetence was to blame for this catastrophe.

Discussion Questions

1. What sources and contingencies of power existed among the executives and departments at Resonus?

2. What influence tactics were evident in this case study? Would you define any of these influence activities as organizational politics? Why or why not?

3. Suppose you are a consultant invited to propose a solution to the problems facing this organization's product delays. What would you recommend, particularly regarding power dynamics among the executives and departments?

CASE STUDY 10.2 NAB'S ROGUE TRADER

For three long days, junior trader Dennis Gentilin received the cold shoulder from his boss, Luke Duffy. Duffy, who ran National Australia Bank's (NAB's) foreign currency options desk in Melbourne, had discovered that Gentilin complained to Duffy's boss, Gary Dillon, that Duffy was altering transaction records to "smooth" his group's profits. Smoothing (which includes carrying forward trading losses) was apparently common at one time, but traders had recently been warned to stop the practice.

On the fourth day, Duffy called Gentilin into a private meeting and, according to Gentilin, launched into a tirade: "I felt like . . . killing someone the other day," Duffy said pointedly to Gentilin. "If you want to stay in the team, I demand loyalty and don't want you going to Dillon about what's happening in the team."

Duffy was apparently accustomed to getting his way. Gentilin explained that Duffy, Dillon, and a few other senior traders were "untouchables" who were given free rein at NAB due to their expertise. "They just created this power base where they were laws unto themselves," claims Gentilin.

Anyone who interfered with Duffy's plans was apparently mocked into submission. For example, Duffy taunted a coworker in London who he thought was too skeptical and conservative. Duffy called him "the London stench boy" because he "was always making a stink about things

whether they were going on both good and bad, and you could smell the stink coming from London," Duffy admitted in court. Duffy's actions kept the London employee compliant with Duffy's activities.

Soon after his private meeting with Duffy, Gentilin was transferred to NAB's London office, still working in the foreign exchange group. Duffy's unit in Melbourne continued to fudge the numbers so upper management wouldn't notice any problems with the trading results. But when the group bet the wrong way against a rising Australian dollar, the cover-ups escalated, including the creation of fictitious trades to offset the losses. The idea was that they could recover the losses and receive their cherished bonuses by year end.

Fatefully, Gentilin got wind of the problems from London, so he asked Vanessa McCallum, a junior NAB trader in Melbourne, to have other people look into Duffy's transactions. McCallum later acknowledged that she was terrified about asking for the audit. "My greatest fear was, if nothing is wrong I'm going to have to leave the desk [move to a different division] because you had to be loyal to Luke [Duffy]," explained McCallum, who no longer works at the bank.

What senior NAB executives discovered shook the Australian bank to its core. Duffy and other senior traders had become a rogue team that amassed $350 million in losses in one year. They managed to keep everyone in line, resulting in countless transaction record irregularities and over 800 breaches of the bank's trading limits. Duffy and a few other traders were jailed for securities violations. Several executives, including both NAB's chief executive and chairman, lost their jobs due to these events.

Discussion Questions

1. What were the main sources of power that Luke Duffy used to keep everyone in line with his irregular business practices? Describe how he applied these power sources to influence subordinates and senior executives.

2. What contingencies strengthened Luke Duffy's power at NAB's foreign currency options desk?

3. What can companies do to minimize this sort of abuse of power and influence?

Sources: R. Gluyas, "Fear and Loathing in NAB's Forex Fiasco," *The Australian*, August 6, 2005, p. 35; E. Johnston, "'Anything Goes,' Ex-Trader Says," *Australian Financial Review*, August 2, 2005, p. 3; E. Johnston, "Expletives and Stench in Hothouse of NAB Dealers," *Australian Financial Review*, August 6, 2005, p. 3.

TEAM EXERCISE 10.3 IMPRESSION MANAGEMENT IN EMPLOYMENT INTERVIEWS

By Sandra Steen, University of Regina

PURPOSE This exercise is designed to help you examine impression management as it relates to employment interviews.

INSTRUCTIONS

Step 1: Form teams with four or five members.

   a) Identify specific principles or rules to help an interviewee guide the best response to each interviewer question.

   b) Provide specific statements the interviewee should say in the interview to represent that principle/rule in action.

For example:

> **Interview Question:** Why are you leaving your current job?
>
> **Principle/Rule:** Keep positive; don't criticize your current employer.
>
> **Possible Statement:** "I enjoyed working at XYZ, but I was looking for more personal growth and development, which your company has a great reputation for."

INTERVIEW QUESTIONS

- What interests you about this job?
- What are your greatest weaknesses?
- Describe a time when you had to deal with a professional disagreement or conflict with a coworker.
- Is there anything you would like to avoid in your next job?
- How many times do a clock's hands overlap in a day?

Step 2: The instructor will lead a class discussion about each of the interview questions.

1. What was your ideal answer?
2. What impression of your knowledge or skills were you attempting to create with your ideal answer?
3. What is an example of an unsuitable interview response?

Discussion Question

1. Why is it important that the personal brand you cultivate in an employment interview is an authentic representation of your knowledge and skills?

TEAM EXERCISE 10.4 DECIPHERING THE NETWORK

PURPOSE This exercise is designed to help you interpret social network maps, including their implications for organizational effectiveness.

MATERIALS The instructor will distribute several social network diagrams to each student.

INSTRUCTIONS (SMALLER CLASSES) The instructor will organize students into teams (typically four to seven people, depending on class size). Teams will examine each social network diagram to answer the following questions:

1. What aspects of this diagram suggest that the network is not operating as effectively as possible?

2. Which people in this network seem to be most powerful? Least powerful? What information or features of the diagram lead you to this conclusion?

3. If you were responsible for this group of people, how would you change this situation to improve their effectiveness?

After teams have diagnosed each social network map, the class will debrief by hearing each team's assessments and recommendations.

INSTRUCTIONS (LARGER CLASSES) This activity is also possible in large classes by projecting each social network diagram on a screen and giving students a minute or two to examine the diagram. The instructor can then ask specific questions to the class, such as pointing to a specific individual in the network and asking whether he or she has high or low power, what level of centrality is apparent, and whether the individual's connections are mainly strong or weak ties. The instructor might also ask which quadrant on the map indicates the most concern and then allow individual students to provide an explanation as to why.

SELF-ASSESSMENT 10.5 HOW DO YOU INFLUENCE COWORKERS AND OTHER PEERS?

PURPOSE This exercise is designed to help you understand different forms of influence when working with coworkers (i.e., people at the same organizational level), as well as estimate your preference for each influence tactic in this context.

INSTRUCTIONS Think about the occasions when a coworker disagreed with you, opposed your preference, or was reluctant to actively support your point of view about something at work. These conflicts might have been about company policy, assignment of job duties, distribution of resources, or any other matter. What did you do to try to get the coworker to support your preference?

The statements below describe ways that people try to influence coworkers. Thinking about your own behavior over the past six months, how often did you engage in each of these behaviors to influence coworkers (i.e., people at a similar level in the organization)?* Circle the most accurate number for each statement. When done, use the scoring key in Appendix B to calculate your results. This exercise is completed alone so students assess themselves honestly without concerns of social comparison. However, class discussion will focus on the types of influence in organizations and which influence tactics are most and least successful or popular when influencing coworkers.

*Note: If you have not been in the workforce recently, complete this instrument thinking about influencing another student instead of a coworker.

Coworker Influence Scale

OVER THE PAST SIX MONTHS, HOW OFTEN DID YOU USE THE FOLLOWING TACTICS TO INFLUENCE COWORKERS?	RARELY/ NEVER	SELDOM	SOMETIMES	OFTEN	ALMOST ALWAYS
1. Gave the coworker logical reasons why the matter should be decided in my favor.	1	2	3	4	5
2. Made my authority or expertise regarding the issue known without being obvious about it.	1	2	3	4	5
3. Tried to negotiate a solution, where I would offer something in return for the coworker's support.	1	2	3	4	5
4. Demanded that the matter should be resolved in my favor.	1	2	3	4	5
5. Avoided showing the coworker information that opposed my preference.	1	2	3	4	5
6. Enlisted the support of other employees so the coworker would see that I have the more popular preference.	1	2	3	4	5
7. Claimed or demonstrated that my preference has management support.	1	2	3	4	5
8. Said something positive about the coworker, hoping this would increase his/her support for my views.	1	2	3	4	5
9. Tried to convince the coworker using factual information and logic.	1	2	3	4	5

(*continued*)

Coworker Influence Scale (*continued*)

OVER THE PAST SIX MONTHS, HOW OFTEN DID YOU USE THE FOLLOWING TACTICS TO INFLUENCE COWORKERS?	RARELY/ NEVER	SELDOM	SOMETIMES	OFTEN	ALMOST ALWAYS
10. Subtly let the coworker know about my expertise on the matter.	1	2	3	4	5
11. Offered to support or assist the coworker on something if he/she would agree with me on this matter.	1	2	3	4	5
12. Showed impatience or frustration with the coworker's opposition to my preference.	1	2	3	4	5
13. Presented information in a way that looked better for my preference.	1	2	3	4	5
14. Claimed that other staff support my position on this matter.	1	2	3	4	5
15. Suggested or threatened to have the issue resolved by higher management.	1	2	3	4	5
16. Became friendlier toward the coworker, hoping this would create a more favorable opinion of my viewpoint.	1	2	3	4	5
17. Helped the coworker to see the benefits of my preference and/or the negative outcomes of other choices.	1	2	3	4	5
18. Quietly or indirectly showed the coworker my authority, expertise, or right to have this matter decided in my favor.	1	2	3	4	5
19. Mentioned that I had helped the coworker in the past, hoping that he/she would reciprocate by supporting me now.	1	2	3	4	5
20. Let the coworker know that I might be disagreeable or uncooperative in the future if he/she did not support me now.	1	2	3	4	5
21. Framed and selected information that mainly agreed with (rather than opposed) my preference.	1	2	3	4	5
22. Made sure that at least a few other people were on my side of this issue.	1	2	3	4	5
23. Pointed out that my view was consistent with the company's values or policies.	1	2	3	4	5
24. Showed more respect toward the coworker, hoping this would encourage him/her to support me.	1	2	3	4	5

© 2011 Steven L. McShane.

 After reading this chapter go to www.mhhe.com/mcshane6e for more in-depth information and interactivities that correspond to the chapter.

Conflict and Negotiation in the Workplace

learning objectives

After reading this chapter, you should be able to:

LO1 Define *conflict* and debate its positive and negative consequences in the workplace.

LO2 Distinguish constructive from relationship conflict and describe three strategies to minimize relationship conflict during constructive conflict episodes.

LO3 Diagram the conflict process model and describe six structural sources of conflict in organizations.

LO4 Outline the five conflict handling styles and discuss the circumstances in which each would be most appropriate.

LO5 Apply the six structural approaches to conflict management and describe the three types of third-party dispute resolution.

LO6 Describe the bargaining zone model and outline strategies that skilled negotiators use to claim value and create value in negotiations.

that the company's workforce would soon have equal portions of Baby Boomers, Generation-Xers, and Generation-Yers. As more Gen-Y employees joined the Montreal offices of the Paris-based beauty and personal care products firm, L'Oreal Canada executives discovered something else: Gen-Yers bring different beliefs, values, and behaviors to the workplace.

"This new generation is so candid about participating and a lot freer," says L'Oreal Canada Director of Learning and Development Marjolaine Rompré. "These people are very, very entrepreneurial so they want a workplace that's innovative, flexible and merit-driven. Individual development and early responsibility really resonate with them." From these observations, Rompré and other L'Oreal Canada executives also saw signs of intergenerational conflict brewing. "We realized we could be faced with an interesting problem. We called it Generation Shock."

Rather than have that generation shock turn into dysfunctional conflict, L'Oreal Canada introduced a half-day intergenerational seminar, called Valorizing Generational Differences, which aims to help employees across all generations share their perceptions, values, and expectations with each other. To date, 85 percent of L'Oreal Canada employees have participated in the voluntary, award-winning initiative.

As a major part of the session, employees sit together in their generational cohorts and are asked to answer questions; they then share their answers with the other cohorts. "Each group is interested and surprised to see what's important to the other group," says Rompré. For example, participants at several sessions learned that "security" meant different things to people across generations—a pension plan for Baby Boomers and a good résumé for Gen-Xers, whereas security has less significance for many Gen-Yers. These and other observations cleared up several misunderstandings. "The [Gen-]Ys told us they were so happy to learn why the baby boomers could be more conservative and why Gen X didn't want to share information with them," says Rompré.

Overall, Valorizing Generational Differences has been a huge success by improving mutual understanding and reducing dysfunctional conflict across the organization. It has also helped L'Oreal Canada to become one of the best places to work in Canada, as well as one of the country's best diversity employers.[1]

L'Oreal Canada executive Marjolaine Rompré (left in this photo, with CEO Javier San Juan and Garnier brand director Sheila Morin) introduced educational seminars to help employees across generations improve their mutual understanding and thereby minimize conflict.

L'Oreal Canada's awareness of intergenerational conflict, and its successful training program to manage that conflict, reflects ongoing issues about differences in the workplace. This chapter investigates these dynamics of conflict in organizational settings. It begins by defining conflict and discussing the age-old question: Is conflict good or bad? Next, we look at the conflict process and examine in detail the main factors that cause or amplify conflict. The five styles of handling conflict are then described, including gender and cross-cultural differences. Next, we look at structural approaches to conflict management, followed by the role of managers and others in third-party conflict resolution. The final section of this chapter reviews key issues in negotiating conflict resolution.

The Meaning and Consequences of Conflict

LO1, LO2

One of the facts of life is that organizations are continuously adapting to their external environment and introducing better ways to transform resources into outputs (see Chapter 1). There is no clear road map on how companies should change, and employees and other stakeholders rarely agree completely on the direction or form of these adjustments. Employees have divergent personal and work goals, which leads them to prefer different directions for the organization.

These differences in goals and viewpoints, along with a few other key factors described in this chapter, lead to conflict. **Conflict** is a process in which one party perceives that its interests are being opposed or negatively affected by another party.[2] It may occur when one party obstructs another's goals in some way, or just from one party's perception that the other party is going to do so. Conflict is ultimately based on perceptions; it exists whenever one party *believes* that another might obstruct its efforts, whether the other party actually intends to do so.

IS CONFLICT GOOD OR BAD?

One of the oldest debates in organizational behavior is whether conflict is good or bad—or, more recently, what forms of conflict are good or bad—for organizations.[3] The dominant view over most of this time has been that conflict is dysfunctional.[4] At the turn of the previous century, European administrative theorists Henri Fayol and Max Weber independently recommended organizational structures that depended on harmonious relations and systematically discouraged conflict. Elton Mayo, who founded Harvard University's human relations school and is considered one of the founders of organizational behavior, was convinced that employee–management conflict undermines organizational effectiveness. These and other critics warn that even moderately low levels of disagreement tatter the fabric of workplace relations and sap energy from productive activities. Disagreement with one's supervisor, for example, wastes productive time, violates the hierarchy of command, and questions the efficient assignment of authority (where managers make the decisions and employees followed them).

Although the "conflict-is-bad" perspective is now considered too simplistic, conflict can indeed have negative consequences in some circumstances (see Exhibit 11.1).[5] Conflict has

EXHIBIT 11.1

Consequences of Workplace Conflict

NEGATIVE CONSEQUENCES	POSITIVE CONSEQUENCES
Uses otherwise productive time	Better decision making
Less information sharing	• Tests logic of arguments
Higher stress, dissatisfaction, and turnover	• Questions assumptions
Increases organizational politics	More responsive to changing environment
Wastes resources	Stronger team cohesion (conflict between the team and outside opponents)
Weakens team cohesion (conflict among team members)	

been criticized for consuming otherwise productive time. For instance, almost one-third of the 5,000 employees recently surveyed across nine countries reported that they are frequently or always dealing with workplace conflict. More than half of the employees in Germany complained that conflict was consuming their workday.[6]

Conflict can undermine job performance in other ways.[7] It is often stressful, which consumes personal energy and distracts employees from their work. Conflict discourages people engaged in the dispute from sharing resources and coordinating with each other. It can reduce job satisfaction, resulting in higher turnover and lower customer service. Conflict fuels organizational politics, such as motivating employees to find ways to undermine the credibility of their opponents. Decision making suffers because people are less motivated to communicate valuable information. Ironically, with less communication, the feuding parties are more likely to escalate their disagreement, because each side relies increasingly on distorted perceptions and stereotypes of the other party. Finally, conflict among team members may undermine team cohesion.

Benefits of Conflict   In the 1920s, when most organizational scholars viewed conflict as inherently dysfunctional, educational philosopher and psychologist John Dewey praised its benefits: "Conflict is the gadfly of thought. It stirs us to observation and memory. It instigates to invention. It shocks us out of sheeplike passivity, and sets us at noting and contriving."[8] Three years later, political science and management theorist Mary Parker Follett similarly remarked that the "friction" of conflict should be put to use rather than treated as an unwanted consequence of differences.[9]

But it wasn't until the 1970s that conflict management experts began to embrace the "optimal conflict" perspective. According to this view, organizations are most effective when employees experience some level of conflict, but become less effective with high levels of conflict.[10] What are the benefits of conflict? As Dewey stated, conflict energizes people to debate issues and evaluate alternatives more thoroughly. The debate tests the logic of arguments and encourages participants to reexamine their basic assumptions about the problem and its possible solution. It prevents individuals and groups from making inferior decisions. As individuals and teams strive to reach agreement, they learn more about one another and come to understand the underlying issues that need to be addressed. This helps them develop more creative solutions that reflect the needs of multiple stakeholders. By generating active thinking, conflict also potentially improves creativity.[11]

A second potential benefit is that moderate levels of conflict prevent organizations from stagnating and becoming nonresponsive to their external environment. Through conflict, employees continuously question current practices and become more sensitive to dissatisfaction from stakeholders. In other words, conflict generates more vigilance.[12] Conflict offers a third positive consequence when team members have a dispute or competition with external sources. This form of conflict represents an external challenge that, as was noted in the team dynamics chapter (Chapter 8), potentially increases cohesion within the team. People are more motivated to work together when faced with an external threat, such as conflict with people outside the team.

THE EMERGING VIEW: CONSTRUCTIVE AND RELATIONSHIP CONFLICT

Although many writers still refer to the "optimal conflict" perspective, an emerging school of thought is that there are two types of conflict with opposing consequences: constructive conflict and relationship conflict.[13] Constructive conflict (also called *task-related conflict*) occurs when people focus their discussion around the issue while showing respect for people with other points of view. This conflict is called "constructive" because different positions are encouraged, so ideas and recommendations can be clarified, redesigned, and tested for logical soundness. By keeping the debate focused on the issue, participants calmly reexamine their assumptions and beliefs without having hostile emotions triggered by their drive to defend their self-concept. Research indicates that

conflict
A process in which one party perceives that his or her interests are being opposed or negatively affected by another party.

teams and organizations with very low levels of constructive conflict are less effective.[14] At the same time, there is likely an upper limit to the intensity of any disagreement, above which it would be difficult to remain constructive.

In contrast to constructive conflict, **relationship conflict** (also known as *socioemotional conflict*) focuses on the adversary rather than the issue as the source of conflict. The parties refer to "personality clashes" and other interpersonal incompatibilities rather than legitimate differences of opinion regarding tasks or decisions. They try to undermine the other person's argument by questioning his or her competency. Attacking a person's credibility or displaying an aggressive response toward him or her triggers defense mechanisms and a competitive orientation. Relationship conflict also reduces trust because the strong negative emotions that typically accompany this conflict undermine any identification with the other person, leaving the relationship held together mainly by calculus-based trust.[15] The conflict more easily escalates because the adversaries become less motivated to communicate and share information, making it more difficult for them to discover common ground and ultimately resolve the conflict. Instead, they rely more on distorted perceptions and stereotypes that, as we noted earlier, tend to further escalate the conflict.

Separating Constructive from Relationship Conflict

If there are two types of conflict, then the obvious advice is to encourage constructive conflict and minimize relationship conflict. This recommendation sounds good in theory, but separating these two types of conflict isn't easy. Research indicates that we experience some degree of relationship conflict whenever we are engaged in constructive debate.[16] No matter how diplomatically someone questions our ideas and actions, he or she potentially triggers our drive to defend our ideas, our sense of competence, and our public image. The stronger the level of debate and the more the issue is tied to our self-concept, the higher the chance that the constructive conflict will evolve into (or mix with) relationship conflict. As Connections 11.1 describes, Intel has benefited from its emphasis on constructive debate, but some employees also experience relationship conflict.

Fortunately, three strategies or conditions potentially minimize the level of relationship conflict during constructive conflict episodes.[17]

- *Emotional intelligence.* Relationship conflict is less likely to occur, or is less likely to escalate, when team members have high levels of emotional intelligence. Employees with higher emotional intelligence are better able to regulate their emotions during debate, which reduces the risk of escalating perceptions of interpersonal hostility. People with high emotional intelligence are also more likely to view a coworker's emotional reaction as valuable information about that person's needs and expectations, rather than as a personal attack.

- *Cohesive team.* Relationship conflict is suppressed when the conflict occurs within a highly cohesive team. The longer people work together, get to know each other, and develop mutual trust, the more latitude they give to each other to show emotions without being personally offended. Strong cohesion also allows each person to know about and anticipate the behaviors and emotions of his or her teammates. Another benefit is that cohesion produces a stronger social identity with the group, so team members are motivated to avoid escalating relationship conflict during otherwise emotionally turbulent discussions.

- *Supportive team norms.* Various team norms can hold relationship conflict at bay during constructive debate. When team norms encourage openness, for instance, team members learn to appreciate honest dialogue without personally reacting to any emotional display during the disagreements.[18] Other norms might discourage team members from displaying negative emotions toward coworkers. Team norms also encourage tactics that diffuse relationship conflict when it first appears. For instance, research has found that teams with low relationship conflict use humor to maintain positive group emotions, which offsets negative feelings team members might develop toward some coworkers during debate.

Constructive Confrontation Inside Intel

Until a few years ago, Intel engineers were obsessed with designing computer processors that were faster, smaller, and ultimately hotter and more power hungry. But key people at Intel's Israeli operations saw trouble brewing. Almost weekly, they would fly from Haifa to Intel's headquarters in California, "pestering" top executives with data and arguments that the company would soon hit the limits of chip speed. The Israeli crew also warned that Intel would lose out to competitors that could produce cooler and more efficient "mobility" chips for laptops and other mobility devices.

The conflict may have rankled some Intel bosses, but the Israeli staff convinced Intel to change direction. Their persistent arguing also demonstrated the value of "constructive confrontation"—the art of argument and respectful debate. "The goal of a leader should be to maximize resistance—in the sense of encouraging disagreement and dissent," says Dov Frohman, founder of Intel Israel.

Intel cofounder Andy Grove introduced and embedded constructive confrontation into the company's culture many years ago. "Constructive confrontation does not mean being loud, unpleasant or rude, and it is not designed to affix blame," warns Andy Grove. "The essence of it is to attack a problem by speaking up in a businesslike way." Grove points out that if you target the other person, then the benefits of constructive debate disintegrate.

Constructive confrontation is so important that new Intel employees are taught it through supervised debates and role plays. Still, this activity also has its challenges. One issue is that open disagreement is contrary to cultural norms in some parts of the world. "In the US, people who visit each other's homes regularly can get into a professional argument very easily at office. In India that's not so. One has to handle the situation differently here," explains Praveen Vishakantaiah, CEO of Intel India.

But even in the United States, some people claim that Intel's constructive confrontation has a heavy dose of relationship conflict. "I can tell you unequivocally that constructive

Constructive conflict is part of Intel's culture, but some people say the computer chipmaker's task-focused discussion descends into relationship conflict.

confrontation was a license for a**holes to be a**holes and express themselves," says former Intel employee Logan Shrine, who coauthored a book with Bob Coleman on Intel's changing culture. "Intel's culture is dysfunctional and anomalous to what's considered acceptable behavior in any other corporation."[19]

Conflict Process Model

Now that we have outlined the history and current knowledge about conflict and its outcomes, let's look at the model of the conflict process, shown in Exhibit 11.2.[20] This model begins with the sources of conflict, which we will describe in the next section. At some point, the sources of conflict lead one or both parties to perceive that conflict exists. They become aware that one party's statements and actions are incompatible with their own goals. These perceptions usually interact with emotions experienced about the conflict.[21] Conflict perceptions and emotions produce manifest conflict—the decisions and behaviors of one party toward the other. These *conflict episodes* may range from subtle nonverbal behaviors to warlike aggression. Particularly when people experience high levels of conflict-generated emotions, they have difficulty finding the words and expressions that communicate effectively without further irritating the relationship.[22] Conflict is also manifested by the style each side uses to resolve the

relationship conflict
A type of conflict in which people focus on characteristics of other individuals, rather than on the issues, as the source of conflict.

EXHIBIT 11.2   Model of the Conflict Process

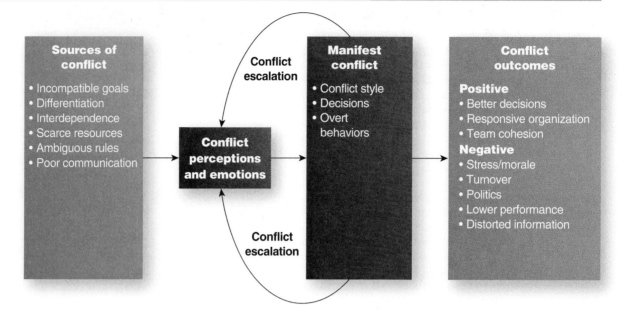

conflict. Some people tend to avoid the conflict, whereas others try to defeat those with opposing views.

Exhibit 11.2 shows arrows looping back from manifest conflict to conflict perceptions and emotions. These arrows illustrate that the conflict process is really a series of episodes that potentially cycle into conflict escalation.[23] It doesn't take much to start this conflict cycle—just an inappropriate comment, a misunderstanding, or action that lacks diplomacy. These behaviors cause the other party to perceive that conflict exists. Even if the first party did not intend to demonstrate conflict, the second party's response may create that perception.

Structural Sources of Conflict in Organizations

The conflict model starts with the sources of conflict, so we need to understand these sources to effectively diagnose conflict episodes and subsequently resolve the conflict or occasionally generate conflict where it is lacking. The six main conditions that cause conflict in organizational settings are incompatible goals, differentiation, interdependence, scarce resources, ambiguous rules, and communication problems.

INCOMPATIBLE GOALS

To assist your learning and test your knowledge about the structural sources of conflict, go to **www.mcgrawhillconnect.com,** which has activities and test questions on this topic.

Goal incompatibility occurs when the goals of one person or department seem to interfere with another person's or department's goals.[24] For example, the production department strives for cost efficiency by scheduling long production runs, whereas the sales team emphasizes customer service by delivering the client's product as quickly as possible. If the company runs out of a particular product, the production team would prefer to have clients wait until the next production run. This infuriates sales representatives who would rather change production quickly to satisfy consumer demand.

Goal incompatibility partly explains some of the "internecine warfare" reported at Microsoft in recent years. One former executive recounted how competition among Microsoft divisions effectively killed many great products because accepting another division's inventions was tantamount to giving it more budget. One example was ClearType, an innovative technology that makes screens more readable. Microsoft divisions gave questionable reasons why they wouldn't adopt the technology. The pocket devices group agreed to use ClearType, but only if the program and engineers were transferred to their division! A few years earlier, Microsoft's MSN group fought against the Microsoft Office Group over MSN's desire to connect their online calendar with the calendar in Office. The Office group balked because "then MSN could cannibalize Office," says an employee who left Microsoft. "Windows and Office would never let MSN have more budget or more control."[25]

DIFFERENTIATION

Another source of conflict is differentiation—differences among people and work units regarding their training, values, beliefs, and experiences. Differentiation can be distinguished from goal incompatibility; two people or departments may agree on a common goal (serving customers better) but have different beliefs about how to achieve that goal (e.g., standardize employee behavior versus give employees autonomy in customer interactions). Consider the opening story to this chapter. Intergenerational conflicts occur because younger and older employees have different needs, different expectations, and different workplace practices, which sometimes produce conflicting preferences and actions. Recent studies suggest that these intergenerational differences occur because people develop social identities around technological developments and other pivotal social events that are unique to their era.[26]

Differentiation also produces the classic tension between employees from two companies brought together through a merger. Even though everyone wants the company to succeed, they fight over the "right way" to do things because of their unique experiences in the separate companies. A mid-sized retail clothing chain experienced another variation of differentiation-based conflict when the founder and CEO hired several senior managers from large organizations to strengthen the experience levels of its senior management group. The newly hired managers soon clashed with long-time executives at the clothing chain. "We ended up with an old team and a new team and they weren't on the same wavelength," explains the company owner, who eventually fired most of the new managers.

INTERDEPENDENCE

Conflict tends to increase with the level of task interdependence. Task interdependence refers to the extent to which employees must share materials, information, or expertise to

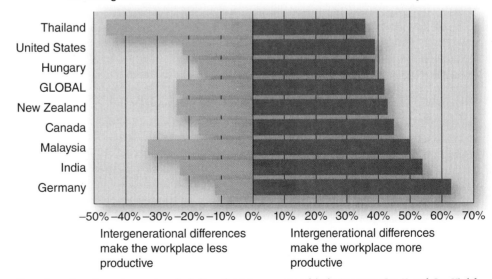

Do Intergenerational Differences Increase or Decrease Productivity?[27]

Intergenerational differences make the workplace less productive

Intergenerational differences make the workplace more productive

Percentage of employees by country who believe that intergenerational (Baby Boomers, Gen X, and Gen Y) differences have a positive or negative effect on workplace productivity. Percentages do not add up to 100 percent because some respondents reported that generational differences have no effect on productivity. Based on a survey of 100,000 employees in 33 countries.

Exxon Mobil's acquisition of natural gas producer XTO Energy immediately raised concerns about conflict. "It is very likely that there will be some culture clashes," advises Jacqueline Weaver, a university law professor who once worked at Exxon. Weaver and others point out that the two companies have diametrically opposing cultures. "Exxon is the proverbial mega-corporation. It's very slow moving and bureaucratic," explains energy analyst Pavel Molchanov, whereas XTO is an entrepreneurial company. "I think there are people who work at XTO who will think twice about working for Exxon."[28]

perform their jobs (see Chapter 8). This interdependence includes sharing common resources, exchanging work or clients back and forth, and receiving outcomes (such as rewards) that are partly determined by the performance of others.[29] Higher interdependence increases the risk of conflict because there is a greater chance that each side will disrupt or interfere with the other side's goals.[30]

Aside from complete independence, employees tend to have the lowest risk of conflict when working with others in a pooled interdependence relationship. Pooled interdependence occurs when individuals operate independently except for reliance on a common resource or authority. The potential for conflict is higher in sequential interdependence work relationships, such as an assembly line. The highest risk of conflict tends to occur in reciprocal interdependence situations. With reciprocal interdependence, employees have high mutual dependence on one another and consequently have a higher probability of interfering with one another's work and personal goals.

SCARCE RESOURCES

Resource scarcity generates conflict because each person or unit requiring the same resource necessarily undermines others who also need that resource to fulfill their goals. Most labor strikes, for instance, occur because there aren't enough financial and other resources for employees and company owners to each receive the outcomes they seek, such as higher pay (employees) and higher investment returns (shareholders). Budget deliberations within organizations also produce conflict because there aren't enough funds to satisfy the goals of each work unit. The more resources one group receives, the fewer resources other stakeholders will receive. Fortunately, these interests aren't perfectly opposing in complex negotiations, but limited resources are typically a major source of friction.

AMBIGUOUS RULES

Ambiguous rules—or the complete lack of rules—breed conflict. This occurs because uncertainty increases the risk that one party intends to interfere with the other party's goals. Ambiguity also encourages political tactics and, in some cases, employees enter a free-for-all battle to win decisions in their favor. This explains why conflict is more common during mergers and acquisitions. Employees from both companies have conflicting practices and values, and few rules have been developed to minimize the maneuvering for power and resources.[31] When clear rules exist, employees instead know what to expect and have agreed to abide by those rules.

COMMUNICATION PROBLEMS

Conflict often occurs due to the lack of opportunity, ability, or motivation to communicate effectively. Let's look at each of these causes. First, when two parties lack the opportunity to communicate, they tend to rely more on stereotypes to understand the other party in the conflict. Unfortunately, stereotypes are sufficiently subjective that emotions can negatively distort the meaning of an opponent's actions, thereby escalating perceptions of conflict. Second, some people lack the necessary skills to communicate in a diplomatic, nonconfrontational manner. When one party communicates its disagreement arrogantly, opponents are more likely to heighten their perception of the conflict. This may lead opponents to reciprocate with a similar response, which further escalates the conflict.[32]

A third problem is that relationship conflict is uncomfortable, so people are less motivated to communicate with others in a disagreement. Unfortunately, less communication can further escalate the conflict because each side has less accurate information about the other side's intentions. To fill in the missing pieces, they rely on distorted images and stereotypes of the other party. Perceptions are further distorted because people in conflict situations tend to engage in more differentiation with those who are different from them (see Chapter 3). This differentiation creates a more positive self-concept and a more negative image of the opponent. We begin to see competitors less favorably so that our self-concept remains positive during these uncertain times.[33]

Interpersonal Conflict Handling Styles

LO4

The six structural conditions described in the previous section lead to conflict perceptions and emotions, which in turn motivate people to take some sort of action to address the conflict. Along with her pioneering view that some conflict is beneficial, Mary Parker Follett suggested there are different conflict handling styles. Conflict management experts subsequently expanded and refined a taxonomy of conflict handling styles, with most of them adapting variations of the five-category model shown in Exhibit 11.3. This model recognizes

EXHIBIT 11.3

Interpersonal Conflict Handling Styles

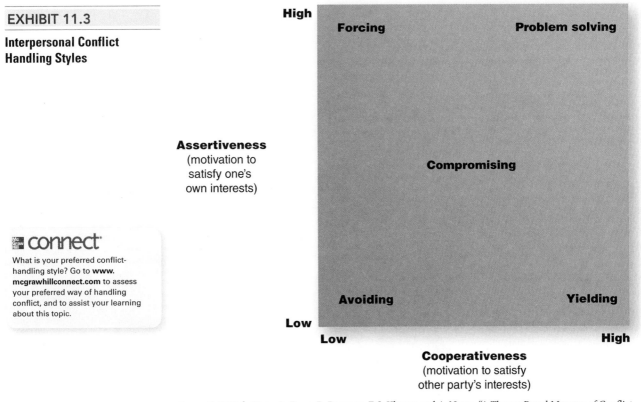

What is your preferred conflict-handling style? Go to **www.mcgrawhillconnect.com** to assess your preferred way of handling conflict, and to assist your learning about this topic.

Source: C.K.W. de Dreu, A. Evers, B. Beersma, E.S. Kluwer, and A. Nauta, "A Theory-Based Measure of Conflict Management Strategies in the Workplace," *Journal of Organizational Behavior* 22 (2001), pp. 645–68. For other variations of this model, see T.L. Ruble and K. Thomas, "Support for a Two-Dimensional Model of Conflict Behavior," *Organizational Behavior and Human Performance* 16 (1976), p. 145; R.R. Blake, H.A. Shepard, and J.S. Mouton. *Managing Intergroup Conflict in Industry* (Houston: Gulf Publishing, 1964); M.A. Rahim, "Toward a Theory of Managing Organizational Conflict," *International Journal of Conflict Management* 13, no. 3 (2002), pp. 206–35.

that how people approach a conflict situation depends on the relative importance they place on maximizing outcomes for themselves and maximizing outcomes for the other party.[34]

- *Problem solving.* Problem solving tries to find a solution that is beneficial for both parties. This is known as the **win–win orientation** because people using this style believe the resources at stake are expandable rather than fixed if the parties work together to find a creative solution. Information sharing is an important feature of this style, because both parties collaborate to identify common ground and potential solutions that satisfy everyone involved.

- *Forcing.* Forcing tries to win the conflict at the other's expense. People who use this style typically have a **win–lose orientation**—they believe the parties are drawing from a fixed pie, so the more one party receives, the less the other party will receive. Consequently, this style relies on some of the "hard" influence tactics described in Chapter 10, particularly assertiveness, to get one's own way.

- *Avoiding.* Avoiding tries to smooth over or avoid conflict situations altogether. It represents a low concern for both self and the other party; in other words, avoiders try to find ways to avoid thinking about the conflict.[35] Some employees rearrange their work area or tasks to minimize interaction with certain coworkers. According to one recent large survey across several countries, 67 percent of employees go out of their way to avoid seeing coworkers with whom they have a disagreement. A smaller number (14 percent) have missed a day of work to avoid workplace conflict.[36]

- *Yielding.* Yielding involves giving in completely to the other side's wishes, or at least cooperating with little or no attention to your own interests. This style involves making unilateral concessions and unconditional promises, as well as offering help with no expectation of reciprocal help.

- *Compromising.* Compromising involves looking for a position in which your losses are offset by equally valued gains. It involves matching the other party's concessions, making conditional promises or threats, and actively searching for a middle ground between the interests of the two parties.

CHOOSING THE BEST CONFLICT HANDLING STYLE

Chances are that you have a preferred conflict handling style. You might typically engage in avoiding or yielding because disagreement makes you feel uncomfortable and is contrary to

"We are really, really, really nice," emphasizes Xerox CEO Ursula Burns (left in this photo) about social relationships in the technology company. But she also believes this "terminal niceness" encourages too much of an avoidance conflict handling style. For example, Burns notes that employees don't raise objections in meetings even when employees present ideas that aren't workable. "When we're in the family, you don't have to be as nice as when you're outside of the family," says Burns. "I want us to stay civil and kind, but we have to be frank—and the reason we can be frank is because we are all in the same family."[37]

EXHIBIT 11.4   Conflict Handling Style Contingencies and Problems

CONFLICT HANDLING STYLE	PREFERRED STYLE WHEN . . .	PROBLEMS WITH THIS STYLE
Problem solving	• Interests are not perfectly opposing (i.e., not pure win–lose) • Parties have trust, openness, and time to share information • The issues are complex	• Sharing information that the other party might use to its advantage
Forcing	• You have a deep conviction about your position (e.g., believe the person's behavior is unethical) • Dispute requires a quick solution • The other party would take advantage of more cooperative strategies	• Highest risk of relationship conflict • May damage long-term relations, reducing future problem solving
Avoiding	• Conflict has become too emotionally charged • Cost of trying to resolve the conflict outweighs the benefits	• Doesn't usually resolve the conflict • May increase other party's frustration
Yielding	• Other party has substantially more power • Issue is much less important to you than to the other party • The value and logic of your position aren't as clear	• Increases other party's expectations in future conflict episodes
Compromising	• Parties have equal power • Time pressure to resolve the conflict • Parties lack trust/openness for problem solving	• Suboptimal solution when mutual gains are possible

your self-view as someone who likes to get along with everyone. Or perhaps you prefer the compromising and forcing strategies because they reflect your strong needs for achievement and to control your environment. People usually gravitate toward one or two conflict handling styles that match their personality, personal and cultural values, and past experience. However, the best style depends on the situation, so we need to understand and develop the capacity to use each style for the appropriate occasion.[38]

Exhibit 11.4 summarizes the main contingencies, as well as problems, with using each conflict handling style. Problem solving is widely recognized as the preferred conflict handling style, whenever possible. Why? This approach calls for dialogue and clever thinking, both of which help the parties discover a win-win solution. In addition, a problem solving style tends to improve long-term relationships, reduce stress, and minimize emotional defensiveness and other indications of relationship conflict.[39]

However, problem solving assumes there are opportunities for mutual gains, such as when the conflict is complex with multiple elements. If the conflict is simple and perfectly opposing (each party wants more of a single fixed pie), then this style will waste time and increase frustration. The problem solving approach also takes more time and requires a fairly high degree of trust, because there is a risk that the other party will take advantage of the information you have openly shared. As one study recently found, the problem solving style is more stressful when people experience strong feelings of conflict, likely because these negative emotions undermine trust in the other party.[40]

win–win orientation
The belief that conflicting parties will find a mutually beneficial solution to their disagreement.

win–lose orientation
The belief that conflicting parties are drawing from a fixed pie, so the more one party receives, the less the other party will receive.

The conflict avoidance style is often ineffective because it doesn't resolve the conflict and may increase the other party's frustration. However, avoiding may be the best strategy where conflict has become emotionally charged or where conflict resolution would cost more than its benefits.[41] The forcing style is usually inappropriate, because it commonly generates relationship conflict more quickly or intensely than other conflict handling styles. However, forcing may be necessary if you know you are correct (e.g., the other party's position is unethical or based on obviously flawed logic), the dispute requires a quick solution, or the other party would take advantage of a more cooperative conflict handling style.

The yielding style may be appropriate when the other party has substantially more power, the issue is not as important to you as to the other party, and you aren't confident that your position has superior logical or ethical justification. On the other hand, yielding behaviors may give the other side unrealistically high expectations, thereby motivating them to seek more from you in the future. In the long run, yielding may produce more conflict rather than resolve it. "Raised voices, red faces, and table thumping is a far less dysfunctional way of challenging each other than withdrawal, passivity and sullen acceptance," argues one conflict management consultant. "It doesn't mean that people agree with you: they just take their misgivings underground and spread them throughout the organization, which has a corrosive effect."[42]

The compromising style may be best when there is little hope for mutual gain through problem solving, both parties have equal power, and both are under time pressure to settle their differences. However, we rarely know whether the parties have perfectly opposing interests, yet the compromise approach assumes this win-lose orientation. Therefore, entering a conflict with the compromising style may cause the parties to overlook better solutions because they have not attempted to share enough information and creatively look for win-win alternatives.

CULTURAL AND GENDER DIFFERENCES IN CONFLICT HANDLING STYLES

Cultural differences are more than just a source of conflict. They also influence the preferred conflict handling style.[43] Some research suggests that people from collectivist cultures—where group goals are valued more than individual goals—are motivated to maintain harmonious relations and, consequently, are more likely than those from low collectivism cultures to manage disagreements through avoidance or problem solving. However, this view may be somewhat simplistic, because people in some collectivist cultures are also more likely to publicly shame those whose actions oppose their own.[44] Cultural values and norms influence the conflict handling style used most often in a society, but they also represent an important contingency when outsiders choose the preferred conflict handling approach. For example, people who frequently use the conflict avoidance style might have more problems in cultures where the forcing style is common.

According to some writers, men and women tend to rely on different conflict handling styles.[45] Compared with men, women often pay more attention to the relationship between the parties. Consequently, women tend to adopt a compromising or occasionally problem solving style in business settings and are more willing to compromise to protect the relationship. They also are slightly more likely to use the avoiding style. Men tend to be more competitive and take a short-term orientation to the relationship. In low collectivism cultures, men are more likely than women to use the forcing approach to conflict handling. We must be cautious about these observations however, because differences between men and women on preferred conflict handling styles are fairly small.

Structural Approaches to Conflict Management

LO5

Conflict handling styles describe how one party approaches the other party in a conflict situation. But conflict management also involves altering the underlying structural causes of potential conflict. The main structural approaches are emphasizing superordinate goals, reducing differentiation, improving communication and understanding, reducing task interdependence, increasing resources, and clarifying rules and procedures.

EMPHASIZING SUPERORDINATE GOALS

One of the oldest recommendations for resolving conflict is to refocus the parties' attention around superordinate goals and away from the conflicting subordinate goals.[46] **Superordinate goals** are goals that the conflicting employees or departments value and whose attainment requires the joint resources and effort of those parties.[47] These goals are called superordinate because they are higher-order aspirations, such as the organization's strategic objectives rather than objectives specific to the individual or work unit. Research indicates that the most effective executive teams frame their decisions as superordinate goals that rise above each executive's departmental or divisional goals. Similarly, one recent study reported that leaders reduce conflict through an inspirational vision that unifies employees and makes them less preoccupied with their subordinate goal differences.[48]

Suppose that marketing staff want a new product released quickly, whereas engineers want more time to test and add new features. Leaders can potentially reduce this interdepartmental conflict by reminding both groups of the company's mission to serve customers or by pointing out that competitors currently threaten the company's leadership in the industry. With increased commitment to corporate-wide goals (customer focus, competitiveness), engineering and marketing employees pay less attention to their competing departmental-level goals, which reduces their perceived conflict with coworkers. Superordinate goals also potentially reduce the problem of differentiation, because they establish feelings of a shared social identity (work for the same company).[49]

REDUCING DIFFERENTIATION

Another way to minimize dysfunctional conflict is to reduce the differences that generate conflict. As people develop common experiences and beliefs, they become more motivated to coordinate activities and resolve their disputes through constructive discussion.[50] SAP, the German enterprise software company, applied this approach when it recently acquired Business Objects, a French company with a strong American presence. Immediately after the merger, SAP began intermingling people from the two organizations. Several senior SAP executives transferred to Business Objects, and all of the acquired company's executives are on SAP's shared services team. "We also encourage cross-border, cross-functional teamwork on projects such as major product releases," says Business Objects CEO John Schwarz. "In this way team members come to depend on each other."[51] Essentially, SAP provided opportunities for managers and technical employees in the acquired firm to develop common experiences with their SAP counterparts by moving staff across the two companies or having them work together on joint projects.

IMPROVING COMMUNICATION AND MUTUAL UNDERSTANDING

A third way to resolve dysfunctional conflict is to give the conflicting parties more opportunities to communicate and understand each other. This recommendation applies two principles and practices introduced in Chapter 3: the Johari Window model and the contact hypothesis. Although both were previously described as ways to improve self-awareness, they are equally valuable to improve other-awareness. In the Johari Window process, you disclose more about yourself so others have a better understanding of the underlying causes of your behavior. The contact hypothesis is the proposition that we rely less on stereotypes to understand someone when we have more meaningful interaction with that person.[52] Through meaningful interaction, we develop a more person-specific and accurate understanding of others.

Exhibit 11.5 outlines the guidelines for resolving conflict through communication and mutual understanding. The parties need to remain open-minded and avoid defensive emotional responses throughout this process. The process begins when each party describes its perceptions of the situation to the other party. In the opening story to this chapter for example, L'Oreal Canada's intergenerational seminar asked each cohort to

---

connect

---

superordinate goals
Goals that the conflicting parties value and whose attainment requires the joint resources and effort of those parties.

EXHIBIT 11.5

Resolving Conflict through Dialogue[53]

1. Begin with an open, curious, and emotionally stable frame of mind.
2. Ask the other people in the conflict to describe their perspectives on the situation.
3. Listen actively to the stories told by the others, focusing on their perceptions, not on who is right or wrong.
4. Acknowledge and demonstrate that you understand the others' viewpoints as well as their feelings about the situation.
5. Present your perspective of the situation, describing it as your perception (not facts).
6. Refer to the others' viewpoints while you are describing your viewpoint.
7. Ask other people in the conflict for their ideas about how to overcome these differences.
8. Create solutions that incorporate ideas from everyone involved in the discussion.

describe its perspectives on key issues, such as security, performance, collaboration, and so forth. Throughout this process, each party actively listens to the other party's views and shows understanding of those views. Also, each side needs to present its views as perceptions, not as though its perspective is "the truth." As viewpoints become understood, the parties suggest ways to resolve their differences. The solutions need to incorporate various perspectives to ensure buy-in.

Although communication and mutual understanding can work well, there are two important warnings. First, these interventions should be applied only where differentiation is sufficiently low or *after* differentiation has been reduced. If perceived differentiation remains high, attempts to manage conflict through dialogue might escalate rather than reduce relationship conflict. The reason is that when forced to interact with people whom we believe are quite different and in conflict with us, we tend to select information that reinforces that view.[54] The second warning is that people in collectivist and high power distance cultures are less comfortable with the practice of resolving differences through direct and open communication.[55] As noted earlier, people in Confucian cultures prefer an avoidance conflict management style because it is the most consistent with harmony and face saving. Direct communication is a high-risk strategy because it easily threatens the need to save face and maintain harmony.

Mobiltel Bulgaria has one of the most engaged workforces in Bulgaria, partly because it minimizes dysfunctional conflict through initiatives that strengthen communication and mutual understanding. The Austrian-owned telecom introduced a "Don't be Apart, Be a Part!" program, which includes sessions in which employees share their ideas and concerns with CEO Andreas Maierhofer and other executives. The company also has "A Day With A Division Director" and "Visit A Colleague" initiatives, through which employees visit an executive or coworker in another department of their choice to better understand their workday and improve cooperation among the teams in the company.[56]

REDUCING INTERDEPENDENCE

Conflict occurs when people are dependent on one another, so another way to reduce dysfunctional conflict is to minimize the level of interdependence among the parties. Three ways to reduce interdependence among employees and work units are to create buffers, use integrators, and combine jobs.

- *Create buffers:* A buffer is any mechanism that loosens the coupling between two or more people or work units. This decoupling reduces the potential for conflict because the buffer reduces the effect of one party on the other. Building up inventories between people in an assembly line would be a buffer, for example, because each employee is less dependent in the short term on the previous person along that line.

- *Use integrators:* Integrators are employees who coordinate the activities of work units toward the completion of a common task. For example, an individual might be responsible for coordinating the efforts of the research, production, advertising, and marketing departments in launching a new product line. In some respects, integrators are human buffers; they reduce the frequency of direct interaction among work units that have diverse goals and perspectives. Integrators rarely have direct authority over the departments they integrate, so they must rely on referent power and persuasion to manage conflict and accomplish the work.

- *Combine jobs:* Combining jobs is both a form of job enrichment and a way to reduce task interdependence. Consider a toaster assembly system where one person inserts the heating element, another adds the sides, and so on. By combining these tasks so that each person assembles an entire toaster, the employees now have a pooled rather than sequential form of task interdependence, and the likelihood of dysfunctional conflict is reduced.

INCREASING RESOURCES

An obvious way to reduce conflict caused by resource scarcity is to increase the amount of resources available. Corporate decision makers might quickly dismiss this solution because of the costs involved. However, they need to carefully compare these costs with the costs of dysfunctional conflict arising out of resource scarcity.

CLARIFYING RULES AND PROCEDURES

Conflicts that arise from ambiguities can be minimized by establishing rules and procedures. If two departments are fighting over the use of a new laboratory, a schedule might be established that allocates the lab exclusively to each team at certain times of the day or week. Armstrong World Industries, Inc., applied the clarifying rules and procedures strategy when consultants and information systems employees clashed while working together on development of a client–server network. Information systems employees at the flooring and building materials company thought they should be in charge, whereas consultants believed they had the senior role. Also, the consultants wanted to work long hours and take Friday off to fly home, whereas Armstrong employees wanted to work regular hours. The company reduced these conflicts by having both parties agree on specific responsibilities and roles. The agreement also assigned two senior executives at the companies to establish rules if future disagreements arose.[57]

Third-Party Conflict Resolution

Most of this chapter has focused on people directly involved in a conflict, yet many disputes among employees and departments are resolved with the assistance of a manager. **Third-party conflict resolution** is any attempt by a relatively neutral person to help the parties resolve their differences. There are three main third-party dispute resolution activities: arbitration, inquisition, and mediation. These interventions can be classified by their level of control over the process and control over the decision (see Exhibit 11.6).[58]

- *Arbitration.* Arbitrators have high control over the final decision but low control over the process. Executives engage in this strategy by following previously agreed rules of due process, listening to arguments from the disputing employees, and making a binding decision. Arbitration is applied as the final stage of grievances by unionized employees in many countries, but it is also becoming more common in nonunion conflicts.

- *Inquisition.* Inquisitors control all discussion about the conflict. Like arbitrators, they have high decision control because they choose an action that will resolve the conflict. However, they also have high process control because they choose which information to examine and how to examine it, and they generally decide how the conflict resolution process will be handled.

third-party conflict resolution
Any attempt by a relatively neutral person to help conflicting parties resolve their differences.

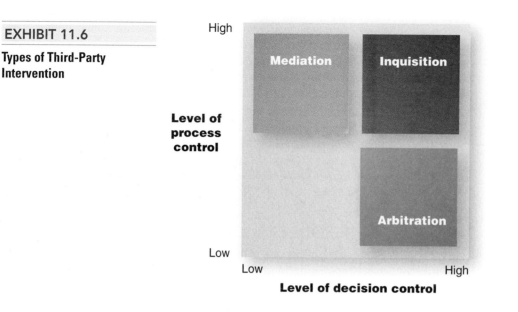

EXHIBIT 11.6

Types of Third-Party Intervention

High

Level of process control

Low

Mediation

Inquisition

Arbitration

Low   High

Level of decision control

- *Mediation.* Mediators have high control over the intervention process. In fact, their main purpose is to manage the process and context of interaction between the disputing parties. However, the parties make the final decision about how to resolve their differences. Thus, mediators have little or no control over the conflict resolution decision.

CHOOSING THE BEST THIRD-PARTY INTERVENTION STRATEGY

Team leaders, executives, and coworkers regularly intervene in workplace disputes. Sometimes they adopt a mediator role; other times they serve as arbitrators. Occasionally, they begin with one approach, then switch to another. However, research suggests that people in positions of authority (e.g., managers) usually adopt an inquisitional approach and dominate the intervention process, as well as make a binding decision.[60]

Managers tend to rely on the inquisition approach because it is consistent with the decision-oriented nature of managerial jobs, gives them control over the conflict process and outcome, and tends to resolve disputes efficiently. However, inquisition is usually the least effective third-party conflict resolution method in organizational settings.[61] One problem is that leaders who take an inquisitional role tend to collect limited information about the problem, so their imposed decision may produce an ineffective solution to the conflict. Another problem is that employees often view inquisitional procedures and outcomes as unfair because they have little control over this approach. In particular, the inquisitional approach potentially violates several practices required to support procedural justice (see Chapter 5).

Which third-party intervention is most appropriate in organizations? The answer partly depends on the situation, such as the type of dispute, the relationship between the manager and employees, and cultural values such as power distance.[62] But generally speaking, for everyday disagreements between two employees, the mediation approach is usually best because it gives employees more responsibility for resolving their own disputes. The third-party representative merely establishes an appropriate context for conflict resolution. Although not as efficient as other

The United States Postal Service has an innovative process to resolve workplace disputes through mediation. Called REDRESS® (Resolve Employment Disputes, Reach Equitable Solutions Swiftly), the program gives both parties more power and involvement in the process, with the aid of external professional mediators. The employee may bring a representative or engage in the process alone. The USPS employment mediation program is now the world's largest and has received favorable recognition from conflict resolution experts.[59]

strategies, mediation potentially offers the highest level of employee satisfaction with the conflict process and outcomes.[63] When employees cannot resolve their differences through mediation, arbitration seems to work best because the predetermined rules of evidence and other processes create a higher sense of procedural fairness.[64] Arbitration is also preferred where the organization's goals should take priority over individual goals.

Resolving Conflict through Negotiation

LO6

Think back through yesterday's events. Maybe you had to work out an agreement with other students about what tasks to complete for a team project. Chances are that you shared transportation with someone, so you had to agree on the timing of the ride. Then perhaps there was the question of who made dinner. Each of these daily events created potential conflict, and they were resolved through negotiation. **Negotiation** occurs whenever two or more conflicting parties attempt to resolve their divergent goals by redefining the terms of their interdependence. In other words, people negotiate when they think that discussion can produce a more satisfactory arrangement (at least for them) in their exchange of goods or services.

As you can see, negotiation is not an obscure practice reserved for labor and management bosses when hammering out a collective agreement. Everyone negotiates, every day. Most of the time, you don't even realize that you are in negotiations. Negotiation is particularly evident in the workplace because employees work interdependently with one another. They negotiate with their supervisors over next month's work assignments, with customers over the sale and delivery schedules of their product, and with coworkers over when to have lunch. And yes, they occasionally negotiate in labor disputes and collective agreements.

BARGAINING ZONE MODEL OF NEGOTIATIONS

One way to view the negotiation process is that each party moves along a continuum in opposite directions with an area of potential overlap called the *bargaining zone*.[65] Exhibit 11.7 displays one possible bargaining zone situation. This linear diagram illustrates a purely win–lose situation—one side's gain will be the other's loss. However, a different form of the bargaining zone model can also be applied to situations in which both sides potentially gain from the negotiations. As this model illustrates, the parties typically establish three main negotiating points. The *initial offer point* is the team's opening offer to the other party. This may be its best expectation or a pie-in-the-sky starting point. The *target point* is the team's realistic goal or expectation for a final agreement. The *resistance point* is the point beyond which the team will make no further concessions.

The parties begin negotiations by describing their initial offer point for each item on the agenda. In most cases, the participants know that this is only a starting point that will change as both sides offer concessions. In win–lose situations, neither the target nor the resistance point is revealed to the other party. However, people try to discover the other side's resistance point because this knowledge helps them determine how much they can gain without breaking off negotiations.

The bargaining zone model implies that the parties compete to reach their target point. Competition exists to varying degrees because constituents expect the negotiator to *claim value*, that is, to get the best possible outcomes for themselves. Yet the hallmark of successful negotiations is a combination of competition and cooperation. Negotiators need to cooperate to *create value*, that is, to discover ways to achieve mutually satisfactory outcomes for both parties.[68] Cooperation maintains a degree of trust necessary to share information. To some degree, it may also improve concessions so the negotiations are resolved more quickly and with greater mutual gains.

negotiation
The process whereby two or more conflicting parties attempt to resolve their divergent goals by redefining the terms of their interdependence.

EXHIBIT 11.7   Bargaining Zone Model of Negotiations

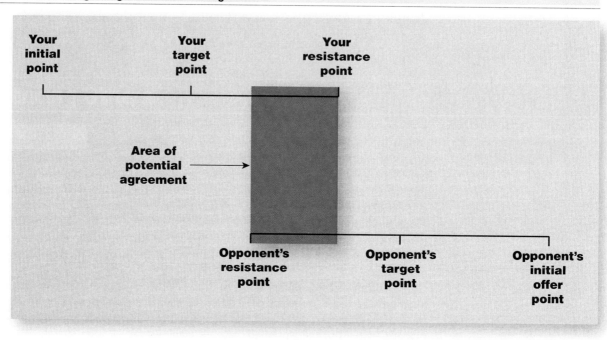

STRATEGIES FOR CLAIMING VALUE

Claiming value involves trying to obtain the best possible outcomes for yourself and your constituents. A purely competitive approach, in which you forcefully persuade the other party and assert your power (such as threatening to walk away from the negotiation), typically leads to failure because it generates negative emotions and undermines trust. Even so, some degree of value claiming is necessary to achieve a favorable outcome. Here are four skills to effectively claim value in negotiations.

Prepare and Set Goals   People negotiate more successfully when they carefully think through their three key positions in the bargaining zone model (initial, target, and resistance), consider alternative strategies to achieve those objectives, and test their underlying assumptions about the situation.[69] Equally important, they need to research what the other party wants from the negotiation. "You have to be prepared every which way about the people, the subject, and your fallback position," advises Paul Tellier, chairman of Global Container Terminals and the former president of CN Railway and Bombardier, Inc. "Before walking into the room for the actual negotiation, I ask my colleagues to throw some curve balls at me."[70]

Know Your BATNA   To determine whether the opponent's offers are favorable, negotiators need to understand what outcome they might achieve through some other means (such as negotiating with someone else). This comparison is called the **best alternative to a negotiated agreement (BATNA).** BATNA estimates your power in the negotiation, because it represents the estimated cost of walking away from the relationship. If others are willing to negotiate with you for the product or service you need, then you have a high BATNA and considerable power in the negotiation; it would not cost you much to walk away from the current negotiation. A common problem in negotiations, however, is that people tend to overestimate their BATNA; they wrongly believe there are plenty of other ways to achieve their objective rather than through this negotiation.

Manage Time

Negotiators make more concessions as the deadline gets closer.[71] This can be a liability if you are under time pressure, or it can be an advantage if the other party alone is under time pressure. Negotiators with more power in the relationship sometimes apply time pressure through an "exploding offer," whereby they give their opponent a very short time to accept their offer.[72] These time-limited offers are frequently found in consumer sales ("on sale today only!") and in some job offers. They produce time pressure, which can motivate the other party to accept the offer and forfeit the opportunity to explore their BATNA. Another time factor is that the more time someone has invested in the negotiation, the more committed he or she becomes to ensuring an agreement is reached. This commitment increases the tendency to make unwarranted concessions so that the negotiations do not fail.

Manage First Offers and Concessions

Negotiators who make the first offer have the advantage of creating a position around which subsequent negotiations are anchored. As we explained in Chapter 7, people tend to adjust their expectations around the initial point, so if your initial request is high, opponents might move more quickly toward their resistance point along the bargaining zone.[73] It may even cause opponents to lower their resistance point.

After the first offer, negotiators need to make concessions. Concessions serve at least three important purposes: (1) they enable the parties to move toward the area of potential agreement, (2) they symbolize each party's motivation to bargain in good faith, and (3) they tell the other party of the relative importance of the negotiating items.[74] However, concessions need to be clearly labeled as such and should be accompanied by an expectation that the other party will reciprocate. They should also be offered in installments because people experience more positive emotions from a few smaller concessions than from one large concession.[75] Generally, the best strategy is to be moderately tough and give just enough concessions to communicate sincerity and motivation to resolve the conflict.[76]

STRATEGIES FOR CREATING VALUE

Earlier in this section we pointed out that negotiations involve more than just claiming value; they also involve creating value—or trying to obtain the best possible outcomes for both parties. In other words, negotiators need to apply the problem solving approach to conflict handling. Information exchange is a critical feature of creating value, but it is also a potential pitfall. Information is power in negotiations, so information sharing gives the other party more power to leverage a better deal if the opportunity occurs.[77] Skilled negotiators address this dilemma by adopting a cautious problem solving style at the outset. They begin by sharing information slowly and determining whether the other side will reciprocate. In this way, they try to establish trust with the other party. Here are several ways that skilled negotiators reap the benefits of problem solving and value creation.

Gather Information

Information is the cornerstone of effective value creation.[78] Skilled negotiators heed the advice of management guru Stephen Covey: "Seek first to understand, then to be understood."[79] This means that we should present our case only after spending more time listening closely to the other party and asking for details. It is particularly important to look beyond the opponent's stated justifications to the unstated motivation for their claims. Probing questions (such as asking "why") and listening intently can reveal better solutions for both parties. Nonverbal communication can also convey important information about the other party's priorities. Negotiating in teams can aid the information gathering process, because some team members will hear information that others have ignored.

best alternative to a negotiated agreement (BATNA)
The best outcome you might achieve through some other course of action if you abandon the current negotiation.

Debating Point
IS CREATING VALUE REALLY SUCH A GOOD NEGOTIATION STRATEGY?

One of the bedrock principles of conflict management and negotiation is that the parties need to adopt a problem solving approach. In negotiation, this win–win perspective is called *creating value*—discovering ways to achieve mutually satisfactory outcomes for both parties. Creating value is important for several reasons. First, creating value produces more trust. Some experts suggest that trust is vital in negotiations because it enables each side to move forward with concessions and points of agreement.

Second, creating value involves sharing information, including a better understanding of each other's needs, so the parties can reach an optimal solution. This solution needs to figure out the relative value that each side assigns to aspects of the issues or items negotiated. By identifying which items are more important to one party than the other, the resources can be divided up in a way that gains the most value for both sides.

Experts agree with these and other benefits of creating value, but some also warn that this scholarly picture isn't always as rosy in real life. The most potent problem with creating value is that it requires the parties to share information. This sharing is fine if you know the other party will reveal any mutual gains discovered from the information sharing process, but this revelation doesn't always occur. Instead, Side B might discover something of value that could give it more of what it wants while making Side A think it has gained at great loss to Side B.

Consider the following true example:[66] Back in the days of the Model-T, the supplier of the car's door handles asked Ford for a 5 percent increase. Ford initially balked but then agreed to the higher price if the supplier would reconfigure the bolt holes in the lids of the wooden crates used to deliver the door handles. The supplier was both perplexed and delighted; it didn't cost anything to make the change, but what was the value to Ford? Back then, Model-T floorboards were made of wood, and Ford staff figured out how to modify the supplier's crate lids as floorboards.

In this incident, Ford might have told the curious supplier why it was willing to pay this higher price, but this doesn't always occur. Sometimes, one side falsely believes the other side is making a significant sacrifice when, in fact, that other side has received considerable gains.[67] If these gains had been revealed, the first party might have asked for even more!

Another concern is that it is sometimes difficult for each party to distinguish creating value from yielding—giving the other party what they want. In an attempt to show collaboration, you give one concession here, another there, and so forth. Eventually, your position lacks negotiation options because most of the concession space has been given away while the other party has given very little. Creating value is an inherent tension with gaining value because you must always keep your own interests equal to or greater than the interests of the other party.

Discover Priorities Through Offers and Concessions   Some types of offers and concessions are better than others at creating value. The key objective is to discover and signal which issues are more and less important to each side. Suppose another division is "seconding" (temporarily transferring) some of your best staff to their projects, whereas you need these people on site for other assignments and to coach junior staff. Through problem solving negotiation, you discover that the other division doesn't need those staff at their site; rather, the division head mainly needs some guarantee that these people will be available. The result is that your division keeps the staff (important to you), while the other division has some guarantee these people will be available at specific times for their projects (important to them).

One way to figure out the relative importance of the issues to each party is to make multi-issue offers rather than discussing one issue at a time.[80] You might offer a client a specific price, delivery date, and guarantee period, for example. The other party's counteroffer to multiple items signals which are more and which are less important to them. Your subsequent concessions similarly signal how important each issue is to your group.

Build the Relationship   Trust is critical for the problem solving style of conflict handling, as well as in the value creation objective of negotiations.[81] How do you build trust in negotiations? One approach is to discover common backgrounds and interests, such as places you have lived, favorite hobbies and sports teams, and so forth. If there are substantial differences between the parties (age, gender), consider having team members who more

He exuded calm to the chain bookstore buyer ...
but his tail betrayed him.

Credit: http://www.cartoonresource.com. Reprinted with permission of Cartoon Resource.

closely match the backgrounds of the other party. First impressions are also important. Recall from earlier chapters in this book that people attach emotions to incoming stimuli in a fraction of a second. Therefore, you need to be sensitive to your nonverbal cues, appearance, and initial statements.

Signaling that we are trustworthy also helps strengthen the relationship. We can do this by demonstrating that we are reliable and will keep our promises, as well as by identifying shared goals and values. Trustworthiness also increases by developing a shared understanding of the negotiation process, including its norms and expectations about speed and timing.[82] Finally, relationship building demands emotional intelligence.[83] This includes managing the emotions you display to the other party, particularly avoiding an image of superiority, aggressiveness, or insensitivity. Emotional intelligence also involves managing the other party's emotions. We can use well-placed flattery, humor, and other methods to keep everyone in a good mood and to break unnecessary tension.[84]

SITUATIONAL INFLUENCES ON NEGOTIATIONS

The effectiveness of negotiating depends to some extent on the environment in which the negotiations occur. Three key situational factors are location, physical setting, and audience.

Location   It is easier to negotiate on your own turf, because you are familiar with the negotiating environment and are able to maintain comfortable routines.[85] Also, there is no need to cope with travel-related stress or depend on others for resources during the negotiation. Of course, you can't walk out of negotiations as easily when on your own turf, but this is usually a minor issue. Considering these strategic benefits of home turf, many negotiators agree to neutral territory. Phone calls, videoconferences, and other forms of information technology potentially avoid territorial issues, but skilled negotiators usually prefer the media richness of face-to-face meetings. Frank Lowy, cofounder of the retail property giant Westfield Group, says that telephones are "too cold" for negotiating: "From a voice I don't get all the cues I need. I go by touch and feel and I need to see the other person."[86]

Physical Setting   The physical distance between the parties and formality of the setting can influence their orientation toward each other and the disputed issues. So can the seating arrangements. People who sit face-to-face are more likely to develop a win–lose orientation toward the conflict situation. In contrast, some negotiation groups deliberately intersperse participants around the table to convey a win–win orientation. Others arrange the seating so that both parties face a whiteboard, reflecting the notion that both parties face the same problem or issue.

Audience Characteristics   Most negotiators have audiences—anyone with a vested interest in the negotiation outcomes, such as executives, other team members, or the general public. Negotiators tend to act differently when their audience observes the negotiation or has detailed information about the process, compared with situations in which the audience sees only the end results.[87] When the audience has direct surveillance over the proceedings, negotiators tend to be more competitive, less willing to make concessions, and more likely to engage in assertive tactics against the other party. This "hard-line" behavior shows the audience that the negotiator is working for their interests. With their audience watching, negotiators also have more interest in saving face.

{ chapter summary }

LO1 Define *conflict* and debate its positive and negative consequences in the workplace.

Conflict is the process in which one party perceives that its interests are being opposed or negatively affected by another party. The earliest view of conflict was that it was dysfunctional for organizations. Even today, we recognize that conflict sometimes or to some degree consumes productive time, increases stress and job dissatisfaction, discourages coordination and resource sharing, undermines customer service, fuels organizational politics, and undermines team cohesion. But conflict can also be beneficial. It is known to motivate more active thinking about problems and possible solutions, encourage more active monitoring of the organization in its environment, and improve team cohesion (if the conflict source is external).

LO2 Distinguish constructive from relationship conflict and describe three strategies to minimize relationship conflict during constructive conflict episodes.

Constructive conflict occurs when people focus their discussion around the issue while showing respect for people with other points of view. Relationship conflict exists when people view each other, rather than the issue, as the source of conflict. It is apparent when people attack each other's credibility and display aggression toward the other party. It is difficult to separate constructive from relationship conflict. However, three strategies or conditions that minimize relationship conflict during constructive debate are (1) emotional intelligence of the participants, (2) team cohesion, and (3) supportive team norms.

LO3 Diagram the conflict process model and describe six structural sources of conflict in organizations.

The conflict process model begins with the six structural sources of conflict: incompatible goals, differentiation (different values and beliefs), interdependence, scarce resources, ambiguous rules, and communication problems. These sources lead one or more parties to perceive a conflict and to experience conflict emotions. This, in turn, produces manifest conflict, such as behaviors toward the other side. The conflict process often escalates through a series of episodes.

LO4 Outline the five conflict handling styles and discuss the circumstances in which each would be most appropriate.

There are five known conflict handling styles: problem solving, forcing, avoiding, yielding, and compromising. People who use problem solving have a win–win orientation. Other styles, particularly forcing, assume a win-lose orientation. In general, people gravitate toward one or two preferred conflict handling styles that match their personality, personal and cultural values, and past experience.

The best style depends on the situation. Problem solving is best when interests are not perfectly opposing, the parties trust each other, and the issues are complex. Forcing works best when you strongly believe in your position, the dispute requires quick action, and the other party would take advantage of a cooperative style. Avoiding is preferred when the conflict has become emotional or the cost of resolution is higher than its benefits. Yielding works well when the other party has substantially more power, the issue is less important to you, and you are not confident in the logical soundness of your position. Compromising is preferred when the parties have equal power, they are under time pressure, and they lack trust.

LO5 Apply the six structural approaches to conflict management and describe the three types of third-party dispute resolution.

Structural approaches to conflict management include emphasizing superordinate goals, reducing differentiation, improving communication and understanding, reducing interdependence, increasing resources, and clarifying rules and procedures.

Third-party conflict resolution is any attempt by a relatively neutral person to help the parties resolve their differences. The three main forms of third-party dispute resolution are mediation, arbitration, and inquisition. Managers tend to use an inquisition approach, though mediation and arbitration are more appropriate, depending on the situation.

LO6 Describe the bargaining zone model and outline strategies skilled negotiators use to claim value and create value in negotiations.

Negotiation occurs whenever two or more conflicting parties attempt to resolve their divergent goals by redefining the terms of their interdependence. The bargaining zone model identifies three strategic positions for each party (initial, target, resistance) and shows how each party moves along a continuum in opposite directions with an area of potential overlap. All negotiations consist of two divergent objectives: claiming value (getting the best personal outcome) and creating value (discover ways to achieve mutually satisfactory outcomes for both parties). Skilled negotiators claim more value by preparing and setting goals, knowing their alternatives to the negotiation (BATNA), managing time to their advantage, and managing first offers and concessions. Skilled negotiators create more value by gathering information, using offers and concessions to discover issue priorities, and building relationships with the other party. The situation is also an important consideration in negotiations, including location, physical setting, and audience characteristics.

{ key terms }

(critical thinking questions)

1. Distinguish constructive conflict from relationship conflict and explain how to apply the former with minimal levels of the latter.

2. The chief executive officer of Creative Toys, Inc., read about cooperation in Japanese companies and vowed to bring this same philosophy to the company. The goal is to avoid all conflict, so that employees would work cooperatively and be happier at Creative Toys. Discuss the merits and limitations of the CEO's policy.

3. Conflict among managers emerged soon after a French company acquired a Swedish firm. The Swedes perceived the French management as hierarchical and arrogant, whereas the French thought the Swedes were naive, cautious, and lacking an achievement orientation. Describe ways to reduce dysfunctional conflict in this situation.

4. This chapter describes three levels of interdependence that exist in interpersonal and intergroup relationships. Identify examples of these three levels in your work or school activities. How do these three levels affect potential conflict for you?

5. You are a special assistant to the commander-in-chief of a peacekeeping mission to a war-torn part of the world. The unit consists of a few thousand peacekeeping troops from the United States, France, India, and four other countries. The troops will work together for approximately one year. What strategies would you recommend to improve mutual understanding and minimize conflict among these troops?

6. The chief operating officer (COO) has noticed that production employees in the company's Mexican manufacturing operations are unhappy with some of the production engineering decisions made by engineers in the company's headquarters in Chicago. At the same time, the engineers complain that production employees aren't applying their engineering specifications correctly and don't understand why those specifications were put in place. The COO believes that the best way to resolve this conflict is to have a frank and open discussion between some of the engineers and employees representing the Mexican production crew. This open dialogue approach worked well recently among managers in the company's Chicago headquarters, so it should work equally well between the engineers and production staff. Based on your knowledge of communication and mutual understanding as a way to resolve conflict, discuss the COO's proposal.

7. Describe the inquisitional approach to resolve disputes between employees or work units. Discuss its appropriateness in organizational settings, including the suitability of its use with a multigenerational workforce.

8. Jane has just been appointed as purchasing manager of Tacoma Technologies, Inc. The previous purchasing manager, who recently retired, was known for his "winner-take-all" approach to suppliers. He continually fought for more discounts and was skeptical about any special deals that suppliers would propose. A few suppliers refused to do business with Tacoma Technologies, but senior management was confident that the former purchasing manager's approach minimized the company's costs. Jane wants to try a more collaborative approach to working with suppliers. Will her approach work? How should she adopt a more collaborative approach in future negotiations with suppliers?

9. You are a new program manager with responsibility for significant funding and external relations, and because of downsizing issues in your area, you have lost two valuable employees (actually 1.5, because the second is on half time now; she used to be your manager and was the one you trained under). You have been in the new job approximately two weeks; however, you have been in the unit for more than a year and have seen how systems are managed from your manager's perspective. You now have her job. Out of the blue, a senior person (not in your area) comes to you and says he is taking most of your space (when the company had to let the 1.5 people go). He doesn't ask your permission, nor does he seem the least bit concerned with what your response is. What do you do?

CASE STUDY 11.1 A MIR KISS?

By Steven L. McShane, University of Western Australia

A team of psychologists at Moscow's Institute for Biomedical Problems (IBMP) wanted to learn more about the dynamics of long-term isolation in space. This knowledge would be applied to the International Space Station, a joint project of several countries that would send people into space for more than six months. It would eventually include a trip to Mars, taking up to three years.

IBMP set up a replica in Moscow of the Mir space station. It then arranged for three international researchers from Japan, Canada, and Austria to spend 110 days isolated in a chamber the size of a train car. This chamber joined a smaller chamber, where four Russian cosmonauts had already completed half of their 240 days of isolation. This was the first time an international crew was involved in the studies. None of the participants spoke English as their first language, yet they communicated throughout their stay in English at varying levels of proficiency.

Judith Lapierre, a French-Canadian, was the only female in the experiment. Along with a PhD in public health and social medicine, Lapierre studied space sociology at the International Space University in France and conducted isolation research in the Antarctic. This was her fourth trip to Russia, where she had learned the language. The mission was supposed to have a second female participant from the Japanese space program, but she was not selected by IBMP.

The Japanese and Austrian participants viewed the participation of a woman as a favorable factor, says Lapierre. For example, to make the surroundings more comfortable, they rearranged the furniture, hung posters on the wall, and put a tablecloth on the kitchen table. "We adapted our environment, whereas the Russians just viewed it as something to be endured," she explains. "We decorated for Christmas, because I'm the kind of person who likes to host people."

New Year's Eve Turmoil

Ironically, it was at one of those social events, the New Year's Eve party, that events took a turn for the worse. After drinking vodka (allowed by the Russian space agency), two of the Russian cosmonauts got into a fistfight that left blood splattered on the chamber walls. At one point, a colleague hid the knives in the station's kitchen because of fears that the two Russians were about to stab each other. The two cosmonauts, who generally did not get along, had to be restrained by other men. Soon after that brawl, the Russian commander grabbed Lapierre, dragged her out of view of the television monitoring cameras, and kissed her aggressively—twice. Lapierre fought him off, but the message didn't register. He tried to kiss her again the next morning.

The next day, the international crew complained to IBMP about the behavior of the Russian cosmonauts. The Russian institute apparently took no action against any of the aggressors. Instead, the institute's psychologists replied that the incidents were part of the experiment. They wanted crew members to solve their personal problems with mature discussion, without asking for outside help. "You have to understand that Mir is an autonomous object, far away from anything," Vadim Gushin, the IBMP psychologist in charge of the project, explained after the experiment had ended in March: "If the crew can't solve problems among themselves, they can't work together."

Following IBMP's response, the international crew wrote a scathing letter to the Russian institute and the space agencies involved in the experiment. "We had never expected such events to take place in a highly controlled scientific experiment where individuals go through a multistep selection process," they wrote. "If we had known . . . we would not have joined it as subjects." The letter also complained about IBMP's response to their concerns.

Informed of the New Year's Eve incident, the Japanese space program convened an emergency meeting on January 2 to address the incidents. Soon after, the Japanese team member quit, apparently shocked by IBMP's inaction. He was replaced with a Russian researcher on the international team. Ten days after the fight—a little over a month after the international team began the mission—the doors between the Russian and international crew's chambers were barred at the request of the international research team. Lapierre later emphasized that this action was taken because of concerns about violence, not the incident involving her.

A Stolen Kiss or Sexual Harassment?

By the end of the experiment in March, news of the fistfight between the cosmonauts and the commander's attempts to kiss Lapierre had reached the public. Russian scientists attempted to play down the kissing incident by saying that it was one fleeting kiss, a clash of cultures, and a female participant who was too emotional.

"In the West, some kinds of kissing are regarded as sexual harassment. In our culture it's nothing," said Russian scientist Vadim Gushin in one interview. In another interview, he explained: "The problem of sexual harassment is given a lot of attention in North America but less in Europe. In Russia it is even less of an issue, not because we are more or less moral than the rest of the world; we just have different priorities."

Judith Lapierre says the kissing incident was tolerable compared with this reaction from the Russian scientists who conducted the experiment. "They don't get it at all," she complains. "They don't think anything is wrong. I'm more frustrated than ever. The worst thing is that they don't realize it was wrong."

Norbert Kraft, the Austrian scientist on the international team, also disagreed with the Russian interpretation of events. "They're trying to protect themselves," he says. "They're trying to put the fault on others. But this is not a cultural issue. If a woman doesn't want to be kissed, it is not acceptable."

Discussion Questions

1. Identify the different conflict episodes that exist in this case. Who was in conflict with whom?

2. What are the sources of conflict for these conflict incidents?

3. What conflict management style(s) did Lapierre, the international team, and Gushin use to resolve these conflicts? What style(s) would have worked best in these situations?

4. What conflict management interventions were applied here? Did they work? What alternative strategies would work best in this situation and in the future?

Source: The facts of this case were pieced together by Steven L. McShane from the following sources: G. Sinclair Jr., "If You Scream in Space, Does Anyone Hear?" *Winnipeg Free Press*, May 5, 2000, p. A4; S. Martin, "Reining in the Space Cowboys," *Globe & Mail*, April 19, 2000, p. R1; M. Gray, "A Space Dream Sours," *Maclean's*, April 17, 2000, p. 26; E. Niiler, "In Search of the Perfect Astronaut," *Boston Globe*, April 4, 2000, p. E4; J. Tracy, "110-Day Isolation Ends in Sullen . . . Isolation," *Moscow Times*, March 30, 2000, p. 1; M. Warren, "A Mir Kiss?" *Daily Telegraph (London)*, March 30, 2000, p. 22; G. York, "Canadian's Harassment Complaint Scorned," *Globe & Mail*, March 25, 2000, p. A2; S. Nolen, "Lust in Space," *Globe & Mail*, March 24, 2000, p. A3.

CASE STUDY 11.2 CAR WARS AT WOLFSBURG

By Steven L. McShane, University of Western Australia

Over the past 15 years, Volkswagen Group (VW) acquired several fiefdoms—Audi, Lamborghini, Bentley, Bugatti, Skoda, SEAT—that jealously guarded their brand and continuously rebelled against sharing knowledge. One member of VW's supervisory board (the German equivalent of a board of directors) commented that managing the company is "like trying to ride a chariot with four or five horses, each of which pulls in a different direction."

Then Porsche AG entered the fray. The luxury sports car company, which relies on VW for some of its production work, began acquiring stock in VW and eventually achieved a controlling interest. Porsche CEO Wendelin Wiedeking was aware of VW's internal rivalries. "If you mix the Porsche guys with the Audi guys and the VW guys you will have trouble," says Wiedeking. "Each is proud to belong to his own company."

Yet Wiedeking stirred up a different type of conflict as Porsche tightened its grip over VW's supervisory board. Through an unswerving drive for efficient production and astute marketing, Wiedeking and his executive team transformed Porsche into the world's most profitable and prestigious car company. Wiedeking wanted to apply those practices at VW by closing down inefficient operations and money-losing car lines.

"Wiedeking is a Porsche CEO from another corporate culture," says German auto analyst Christoph Stuermer. "He's out to maximize profits by cutting costs. And he snubbed everyone, telling off VW management, interfering with their way of doing business." Ferdinand Dudenhoeffer, director of Germany's Center of Automotive Research (CAR), agrees. "Porsche is very successful in being lean and profitable. It's not going to be harmonious."

Particularly offended by Wiedeking's plans was VW chairman Ferdinand Piëch, who had a different vision of Europe's largest automaker. Piëch, whose grandfather developed the VW Beetle, placed more emphasis on spectacular engineering than exceptional profits. For example, he supported the money-losing Bugatti brand, which VW acquired several years ago when Piëch was CEO. More recently, Piëch championed the Phaeton, VW's luxury car that broke new ground in innovation (it boasts 100 patents) but did not achieve commercial success.

Wiedeking, on the other hand, believed that VW could be more profitable if it stopped producing the Phaeton and Bugatti. "Piëch sees his vision endangered by Wiedeking," says Dudenhoeffer. "Wiedeking said that there are no holy cows at VW, no more Phaetons, no more Bugattis." These ideas made Piëch's blood boil. "Anyone who says that VW should pull the Phaeton doesn't understand the world," grumbled Piëch, explaining that luxury cars represent the only segment with double-digit growth.

There is an unusual twist in the conflict involving Piëch, Wiedeking, and Porsche. Piëch is a member of the Porsche family. He is a cousin of Porsche chairman Wolfgang Porsche and owns a 10 percent share of the Porsche company. Piëch began his career at Porsche and became its chief engineer before moving to Audi and later VW. Furthermore, in what many consider a blatant conflict of interest, Piëch supported Porsche's initial investment in VW. But when Piëch's and Wiedeking's plans ended up on a collision course, that initial friendly investment in the partnership turned into all-out corporate war. "There was always a cease-fire between Piëch and the Porsches, but now it's war," claims auto analyst Ferdinand Dudenhoeffer. "This is like *Dallas* and *Dynasty* in Wolfsburg [the city where VW has its headquarters]. No company in the world is so self-absorbed with its problems."

Postscript

Ironically, Porsche CEO Wendelin Wiedeking's plans backfired. Porsche had borrowed heavily to acquire its controlling interest in VW while maintaining its own business operations. Some estimate that Porsche had loans of more than US$14 billion. Furthermore, VW shares increased substantially during the takeover process, so Porsche owed massive taxes for the increased "paper profits" of the shares it owned. The timing couldn't have been worse. The great financial crisis hit the world, which cut Porsche sales and dried up funds, making it difficult for Porsche to pay interest on its loans and to renew loans that were coming due. In effect, it was on the brink of bankruptcy. In addition, a unique law allowed one German state (Lower Saxony), which had a 20 percent ownership in VW, to veto any important decisions in the company, including Porsche's control of VW.

Ultimately, Porsche agreed to give up its controlling interest in VW. Instead, it sold some of its business to VW and the Qatar government and, ultimately, agreed to be acquired by VW (rather than vice versa). Wiedeking lost his job as Porsche CEO, whereas Ferdinand Piëch (as chairman of VW's supervisory board) would effectively be head of both automakers. Complicated legal and financial matters have delayed the complete acquisition, but VW effectively manages Porsche today.

Discussion Questions

1. Identify and discuss the sources of conflict between Porsche and Volkswagen executives.

2. Describe the conflict handling styles used by Wendelin Wiedeking and Ferdinand Piëch. Were they appropriate in this situation?

Source: The facts of this case were pieced together by Steven L. McShane from the following sources: M. Landler, "Twist in the Intrigue at VW May Help Chief Keep His Job," *The New York Times*, April 21, 2006, p. 5; R. Hutton, "Porsche Ready to Swallow VW," *Autocar*, November 7, 2007; "German Carmaker Family Feud Plays Out in VW Boardroom,"

Deutsche Welle, September 18, 2008; D. Hawranek, "Clans, Executives Sharpen Knives Backstage at Porsche and VW," *Spiegel Online*, March 11, 2008; N.D. Schwartz, "Porsche Takes a Controlling Interest in VW," *The New York Times*, September 17, 2008; D. Hawranek, "German Carmaker Narrowly Averts Bankruptcy," *Spiegel Online*, May 25, 2009; C. Dougherty, "Porsche Chief Pays Full Price for His Overreach," *International Herald Tribune*, July 24, 2009, p. 1; D. Schäfer, "Porsche and VW Push on with Merger Plans," *Financial Times* (London), June 17, 2011.

CLASS EXERCISE 11.3 THE CONTINGENCIES OF CONFLICT HANDLING

Gerard A. Callanan and David F. Perri, West Chester University of Pennsylvania

PURPOSE This exercise is designed to help you understand the contingencies of applying conflict handling styles in organizational settings.

INSTRUCTIONS

Step 1: Read each of the five scenarios presented below and select the most appropriate response from among the five alternatives. Each scenario has a correct response for that situation.

Step 2 (Optional): The instructor may ask each student to complete the Conflict Handling Scale self-assessment in this chapter (Self-Assessment 11.5) or a similar instrument. This instrument will provide an estimate of your preferred conflict handling style.

Step 3: As a class, participants give their feedback on the responses to each of the scenarios, with the instructor guiding discussion on the contextual factors embodied in each scenario. For each scenario, the class should identify the response selected by the majority. In addition, you will discuss how you decided on the choices you made and the contextual factors you took into account in making your selections.

Step 4: Students will compare their responses to the five scenarios with the results from the conflict handling self-assessment. Discussion will focus on the extent to which each person's preferred conflict handling style influenced his or her alternatives in this activity, as well as the implications of this style preference for managing conflict in organizations.

SCENARIO #1

Setting

You are a manager of a division in the accounting department of a large eastern U.S. bank. Nine exempt-level analysts and six nonexempt clerical staff report to you. Recently, one of your analysts, Jane Wilson, has sought the bank's approval for tuition reimbursement for the cost of an evening MBA program specializing in organizational behavior. The bank normally encourages employees to seek advanced degrees on a part-time basis. Indeed, through your encouragement, nearly all of the members of your staff are pursuing additional schoolwork. You consult the bank's policy manual and discover that two approvals are necessary for reimbursement—yours and that of the manager of training and development, Kathy Gordon. Further, the manual states that approval for reimbursement will only be granted if the coursework is "reasonably job related." Based on your review of the matter, you decide to approve Jane's request for reimbursement. However, Kathy Gordon rejects it outright by claiming that coursework in organizational behavior is not related to an accounting analyst position. She states that the bank will only reimburse the analyst for a degree in either accounting or finance. In your opinion, however, the interpersonal skills and insights to be gained from a degree in organizational behavior are job related and can also benefit the employee in future assignments. The analyst job requires interaction with a variety of individuals at different levels in the organization, and it is important that interpersonal and communication skills be strong.

After further discussion it becomes clear that you and Kathy Gordon have opposite views on the matter. Since both of you are at the same organizational level and have equal status, it appears that you are at an impasse. Although the goal of reimbursement is important, you are faced with other pressing demands on your time. In addition, the conflict has diverted the attention of your work group away from its primary responsibilities. Because the school term is about to begin, it is essential that you and Kathy Gordon reach a timely agreement to enable Jane to pursue her coursework.

Action Alternatives for Scenario #1

Please indicate your first and second choices from among the following alternatives by writing the appropriate number in the space provided.

ACTION ALTERNATIVE	RANKING (1 AND 2)
1. You go along with Kathy Gordon's view and advise Jane Wilson to select either accounting or finance as a major for her MBA.	_____
2. You decide to withdraw from the situation completely and tell Jane to work it out with Kathy Gordon on her own.	_____
3. You decide to take the matter to those in higher management levels and argue forcefully for your point of view. You do everything in your power to ensure that a decision will be made in your favor.	_____
4. You decide to meet Kathy Gordon halfway to reach an agreement. You advise Jane to pursue her MBA in accounting or finance but also recommend she minor in organizational behavior by taking electives in that field.	_____
5. You decide to work more closely with Kathy Gordon by attempting to get a clear and flexible written policy that reflects both of your views. Of course, this will require a significant amount of your time.	_____

SCENARIO #2

Setting

You are the vice president of a relatively large division (80 employees) in a medium-sized consumer products company. Due to the recent turnover of minority staff, your division has fallen behind in meeting the company's goal for Equal Employment Opportunity (EEO) hiring. Because of a scarcity of qualified minority candidates, it appears that you may fall further behind in achieving stated EEO goals.

Although you are aware of the problem, you believe that the low level of minority hiring is due to increased attrition in minority staff, as well as the lack of viable replacement candidates. However, the EEO officer believes that your hiring criteria are too stringent, resulting in the rejection of minority candidates with the basic qualifications to do the job. You support the goals and principles of EEO; however, you are concerned that the hiring of less qualified candidates will weaken the performance of your division. The EEO officer believes that your failure to hire minority employees is damaging to the company in the short term, because corporate goals will not be met, and in the long term, because it will restrict the pool of minority candidates available for upward mobility. Both of you regard your concerns as important. Further, you recognize that both of you have the company's best interests in mind and that you have a mutual interest in resolving the conflict.

Action Alternatives for Scenario #2

Please indicate your first and second choices from among the following alternatives by writing the appropriate number in the space provided.

ACTION ALTERNATIVE	RANKING (1 & 2)
1. You conclude that the whole problem is too complex an issue for you to handle right now. You put it on the "back burner" and decide to reconsider the problem at a later date.	_____
2. You believe that your view outweighs the perspective of the EEO officer. You decide to argue your position more vigorously and hope that your stance will sway the EEO officer to agree with your view.	_____
3. You decide to accept the EEO officer's view. You agree to use less stringent selection criteria and thereby hire more minority employees.	_____
4. You give in to the EEO officer somewhat by agreeing to relax your standards a little bit. This would allow slightly more minority hiring (but not enough to satisfy the EEO goal) and could cause a small reduction in the overall performance of your division.	_____
5. You try to reach a consensus that addresses each of your concerns. You agree to work harder at hiring more minority applicants and request that the EEO officer agree to help find the most qualified minority candidates available.	_____

SCENARIO #3

Setting

You are the manager in charge of the financial reporting section of a large insurance company. It is the responsibility of your group to make periodic written and oral reports to senior management regarding the company's financial performance. The company's senior management has come to rely on your quick and accurate dissemination of financial data as a way to make vital decisions in a timely fashion. This has given you a relatively high degree of organizational influence. You rely on various operating departments to supply you with financial information according to a preestablished reporting schedule.

In two days, you must make your quarterly presentation to the company's Board of Directors. However, the Claims Department has failed to supply you with several key pieces of information that are critical to your presentation. You check the reporting schedule and realize that you should have had the information two days ago. When you call Bill Jones, the Claims Department manager, he informs you that he cannot possibly have the data to you within the next two days. He states that other pressing work has a higher priority. Although you explain the critical need for this data, he is unwilling to change his position. You believe that your presentation is vital to the company's welfare and explain this to Bill Jones. Although Bill has less status than you, he has been known to take advantage of individuals who are unwilling or unable to push their point of view. With your presentation less than two days away, it is critical that you receive information from the Claims Department within the next 24 hours.

Action Alternatives for Scenario #3

Please indicate your first and second choices from among the following alternatives by writing the appropriate number in the space provided.

ACTION ALTERNATIVE	RANKING (1 & 2)
1. Accept the explanation from Bill Jones and try to get by without the figures by using your best judgment as to what they would be.	_____
2. Tell Bill Jones that unless you have the data from his department on your desk by tomorrow morning, you will be forced to go over his head to compel him to give you the numbers.	_____
3. Meet Bill Jones halfway by agreeing to receive part of the needed figures and using your own judgment on the others.	_____
4. Try to get your presentation postponed until a later date, if possible.	_____
5. Forget about the short-term need for information and try to achieve a longer-term solution, such as adjusting the reporting schedule to better accommodate your mutual needs.	_____

SCENARIO #4

Setting

You are the production manager of a medium-sized building products company. You control a production line that runs on a three-shift basis. Recently, Ted Smith, the materials handling manager, requested that you accept a different packaging of the raw materials for the production process than has been customary. He states that new machinery he has installed makes it much easier to provide the material in 100-pound sacks instead of the 50-pound bags that you currently receive. Ted further explains that the provision of the material in the 50-pound bags would put an immense strain on his operation, and he therefore has a critical need for you to accept the change. You know that accepting materials in the new packaging will cause some minor disruption in your production process but should not cause long-term problems for any of the three shifts. However, you are a little annoyed by the proposed change because Ted did not consult with you before he installed the new equipment. In the past, you and he have been open in your communication. You do not think that this failure to consult you represents a change in your relationship.

Because you work closely with Ted, it is essential that you maintain the harmonious and stable working relationship that you have built over the past few years. In addition, you may need some help from him in the future, since you already know that your operation will have special material requirements in about two months. You also know that Ted has influence at higher levels of the organization.

Action Alternatives for Scenario #4

Please indicate your first and second choices from among the following alternatives by writing the appropriate number in the space provided.

ACTION ALTERNATIVE	RANKING (1 & 2)
1. Agree to accept the raw material in the different format.	_____
2. Refuse to accept the material in the new format because it would cause a disruption in your operation.	_____
3. Propose a solution where you accept material in the new format during the first shift but not during the second and third.	_____
4. Tell Ted Smith that you do not wish to deal with the issue at this time, but that you will consider his request and get back to him at a later date.	_____
5. You decide to tell Ted Smith of your concern regarding his failure to consult with you before installing new equipment. You inform him that you wish to find longer-term solutions to the conflict between you.	_____

SCENARIO #5

Setting

You are employed as supervisor of the compensation and benefits section in the human resources department of a medium-sized pharmaceutical company. Your staff of three clerks is responsible for maintaining contacts with the various benefits providers and answering related questions from the company's employees. Your section shares secretarial, word processing, and copier resources with the training and development section of the department. Recently, a disagreement has arisen between you and Beth Hanson, the training and development supervisor, over when the secretarial staff should take their lunch breaks. Beth would like the secretarial staff to take their lunch breaks an hour later to coincide with the time most of her people go to lunch. You know that the secretaries do not want to change their lunch times. Further, the current time is more convenient for your staff.

At this time, you are hard-pressed to deal with the situation. You have an important meeting with the provider of dental insurance in two days. It is critical that you are well prepared for this meeting, and these other tasks are a distraction.

Action Alternatives for Scenario #5

Please indicate your first and second choices from among the following alternatives by writing the appropriate number in the space provided.

ACTION ALTERNATIVE	RANKING (1 & 2)
1. Take some time over the next day and propose a solution whereby three days a week the secretaries take their lunch at the earlier time and two days at the later.	_____
2. Tell Beth Hanson you will deal with the matter in a few days, after you have addressed the more pressing issues.	_____
3. Let Beth Hanson have her way by agreeing to a later lunch hour for the secretarial staff.	_____
4. Flat out tell Beth Hanson that you will not agree to a change in the secretaries' lunch time.	_____
5. Devote more time to the issue. Attempt to achieve a broad-based consensus with Beth Hanson that meets her needs as well as yours and those of the secretaries.	_____

Source: G.A. Callanan and D.F. Perri, "Teaching Conflict Management Using a Scenario-Based Approach," *Journal of Education for Business* 81 (January/February 2006), pp. 131–39.

TEAM EXERCISE 11.4 UGLI ORANGE ROLE PLAY

PURPOSE This exercise is designed to help you understand the dynamics of interpersonal and intergroup conflict, as well as the effectiveness of negotiation strategies under specific conditions.

MATERIALS The instructor will distribute roles for Dr. Roland, Dr. Jones, and a few observers. Ideally, each negotiation should occur in a private area away from other negotiations.

INSTRUCTIONS
Step 1: The instructor will divide the class into an even number of teams of three people each, with one participant left over for each team formed (e.g., six observers if

there are six teams). Half of the teams will take the role of Dr. Roland, and the other half will be Dr. Jones. The instructor will distribute roles after these teams have been formed.

Step 2: Members within each team are given 10 minutes (or other time limit stated by the instructor) to learn their roles and decide negotiating strategy.

Step 3: After reading their roles and discussing strategy, each Dr. Jones team is matched with a Dr. Roland team to conduct negotiations. Observers will receive observation forms from the instructor, and two observers will be assigned to watch the paired teams during prenegotiations and subsequent negotiations.

Step 4: As soon as Roland and Jones reach agreement or at the end of the time allotted for the negotiation (whichever comes first), the Roland and Jones teams report to the instructor for further instruction.

Step 5: At the end of the exercise, the class will congregate to discuss the negotiations. Observers, negotiators, and instructors will then discuss their observations and experiences and the implications for conflict management and negotiation.

Source: This exercise was developed by Robert J. House, Wharton Business School, University of Pennsylvania. A variation of this incident involving sisters is also described in R. Fisher, W. Ury, and B. Patton, *Getting to Yes: Negotiating Agreement without Giving In,* 2nd ed. (New York: Harvard University, 1991).

SELF-ASSESSMENT 11.5 WHAT IS YOUR PREFERRED CONFLICT HANDLING STYLE?

PURPOSE This self-assessment is designed to help you to identify your preferred conflict management style.

INSTRUCTIONS Read each of the statements below and select the response that best indicates how often you handle conflict in the way described in that statement. Then use the scoring key in Appendix B to calculate your results for each conflict management style. This exercise is completed alone so you can assess yourself honestly without concerns of social comparison. However, class discussion will focus on the different conflict management styles and the situations in which each is most appropriate.

Conflict Handling Style Scale

OVER THE PAST SIX MONTHS, HOW OFTEN DID YOU DO THE FOLLOWING TO HANDLE CONFLICTS?	NEVER/ RARELY	SELDOM	SOMETIMES	OFTEN	ALMOST ALWAYS
1. I went along with the other party's wishes rather than my own.	☐	☐	☐	☐	☐
2. I compromised by accepting a middle ground solution.	☐	☐	☐	☐	☐
3. I tried to creatively find the best solution for everyone.	☐	☐	☐	☐	☐
4. I avoided differences of opinion as much as possible.	☐	☐	☐	☐	☐
5. I pushed my own ideas and preferences.	☐	☐	☐	☐	☐
6. I tried to make the dispute seem less important.	☐	☐	☐	☐	☐
7. I accommodated the other party's wishes.	☐	☐	☐	☐	☐
8. I did my best to get what I wanted.	☐	☐	☐	☐	☐
9. I tried to figure out how to satisfy both my interests and the other party's.	☐	☐	☐	☐	☐
10. I made sure that both sides gave in a little.	☐	☐	☐	☐	☐
11. I worked toward a 50–50 compromise.	☐	☐	☐	☐	☐
12. I fought for my own position.	☐	☐	☐	☐	☐
13. I searched for a solution that satisfied both parties.	☐	☐	☐	☐	☐
14. I delayed or avoided solving the disagreement.	☐	☐	☐	☐	☐

(continued)

Conflict Handling Style Scale   (*continued*)

OVER THE PAST SIX MONTHS, HOW OFTEN DID YOU DO THE FOLLOWING TO HANDLE CONFLICTS?	NEVER/ RARELY	SELDOM	SOMETIMES	OFTEN	ALMOST ALWAYS
15. I held my position.	☐	☐	☐	☐	☐
16. I let the other side have its way.	☐	☐	☐	☐	☐
17. I tried to settle the conflict with a half-way compromise.	☐	☐	☐	☐	☐
18. I tried to find a solution that benefited both sides.	☐	☐	☐	☐	☐
19. I avoided communicating with the people with whom I had the conflict.	☐	☐	☐	☐	☐
20. I gave the other party what it wanted.	☐	☐	☐	☐	☐

Sources: This scale was created by Steven L. McShane, based on information and instruments published in R.R. Blake, H.A. Shepard, and J.S. Mouton, *Managing Intergroup Conflict in Industry* (Houston, TX: Gulf Publishing, 1964); K.W. Thomas, "Conflict and Negotiation Processes in Organizations," in *Handbook of Industrial and Organizational Psychology*, 2nd ed., ed. M.D. Dunnette and L.M. Hough (Palo Alto, CA: Consulting Psychologists Press, 1992), pp. 651–718; C.K.W. de Dreu, A. Evers, B. Beersma, E.S. Kluwer, and A. Nauta, "A Theory-Based Measure of Conflict Management Strategies in the Workplace," *Journal of Organizational Behavior* 22 (2001), pp. 645–68; M.A. Rahim, *Managing Conflict in Organizations*, 4th ed. (New Brunswick, NJ: Transaction Publishers, 2011).

 After reading this chapter go to www.mhhe.com/mcshane6e for more in-depth information and interactivities that correspond to the chapter.

Leadership in Organizational Settings

learning objectives

After reading this chapter, you should be able to:

LO1 Define *leadership* and *shared leadership.*

LO2 Identify eight competencies associated with effective leaders, and describe authentic leadership.

LO3 Describe the key features of task-oriented, people-oriented, and servant leadership, and discuss their effects on followers.

LO4 Discuss the key elements of path-goal theory, Fiedler's contingency model, and leadership substitutes.

LO5 Describe the four elements of transformational leadership, and distinguish this theory from transactional and charismatic leadership.

LO6 Describe the implicit leadership perspective.

LO7 Discuss cultural and gender similarities and differences in leadership.

perfectionist. But was Steve Jobs, cofounder of Apple, Inc., and founder of Pixar Animation Studios, a great leader? Many of the world's top business publications think so. During his life, Jobs was awarded numerous honors, including CEO of the Year, CEO of the Decade, and even CEO of the Century.

Steve Jobs had an uncanny ability to form a strategic vision that boldly peeked around corners into an otherwise unknown future. This vision extended beyond customer expectations; he envisioned products and services that customers didn't even know they will wanted. When asked what consumer research Apple had done before launching the iPad, for example, Jobs candidly replied "None. It isn't the consumers' job to know what they want."

Jobs is famous for passionately communicating his vision in ways that inspired others. He created a "reality distortion field," in which people got caught in his visionary headlights. In this respect, Jobs is often cited as an example of charismatic leadership. Many people are understandably skeptical about cult-like leaders, but observers say Jobs's status is as much substance as style. "The cult of the chief executive exists, although whether or not it is overblown depends on the chief executive," explains one Wall Street analyst. "But in Steve Jobs' case, he really is a genius."

But while Jobs's talents as a visionary, charismatic leader are legendary, so were his apparent failings as a servant leader who nurtured individual potential. "The degree to which people in Silicon Valley are afraid of Jobs is unbelievable," says Stanford University professor Robert Sutton, who received many stories about Jobs while writing a recent book on corporate tyrants. "He made people feel terrible; he made people cry. But he was almost always right, and even when he was wrong, it was so creative it was still amazing." In the words of former Apple PR chief Laurence Clavere: "Working with Steve is incredibly challenging, incredibly interesting. It was also sometimes incredibly difficult."

Several CEOs of other major companies suggest that Steve Jobs's demanding high standards represented another of his strengths—not limitations—as a successful leader. "One remarkable thing about Steve is how he sets expectations on people," observed Disney CEO Bob Iger. "I worked for [the legendary ABC News chairman] Roone Arledge for 10 years. He demanded perfection, never accepted mediocrity. Steve is the same. I see that in the way he manages his people. He sets expectations for quality, challenging the status quo—and never accepts no for an answer."[1]

During his life, Steve Jobs was often described as a charismatic visionary as well as a demanding perfectionist. Was the Apple cofounder an effective leader?

A charismatic leader. A visionary leader. A demanding taskmaster (which might be good or bad leadership). People have described the leadership of Steve Jobs in many ways, and with considerably divergent attitudes toward that leadership. These diverse views illustrate that leadership is multidimensional; it exists in many ways and forms. Furthermore, people are not necessarily effective leaders from all of these perspectives. This chapter explores leadership from the five perspectives that are apparent in the huge volume of leadership literature: competency, behavioral, contingency, transformational, and implicit.[2] In the final section, we also consider cross-cultural and gender issues in organizational leadership. But first, we learn about the meaning of leadership and shared leadership.

What Is Leadership?

LO1

A few years ago, 54 leadership experts from 38 countries reached a consensus that **leadership** is about influencing, motivating, and enabling others to contribute toward the effectiveness and success of the organizations of which they are members.[3] This definition has two key components. First, leaders motivate others through persuasion and other influence tactics. They use their communication skills, rewards, and other resources to energize the collective to achieve challenging objectives. Second, leaders are enablers. They arrange the work environment—such as allocating resources and altering communication patterns—so employees can achieve organizational objectives more easily.

Leadership is one of the most researched and discussed topics in the field of organizational behavior. Google returns a whopping 724 million web pages that mention either "leader" or "leadership" (24 million of them have one of these words in the title). Google Scholar lists 173,000 journal articles and books that have one or both words in the title. Amazon, the online retailer, currently lists more than 55,000 printed leadership books. As Exhibit 12.1 illustrates, the number of leadership books and materials added to the U.S. Library of Congress catalog has grown exponentially over the past half-century. Why does the topic of leadership command so much attention? Possibly because leadership

EXHIBIT 12.1   Filling the U.S. Library of Congress with Leadership Books and Materials

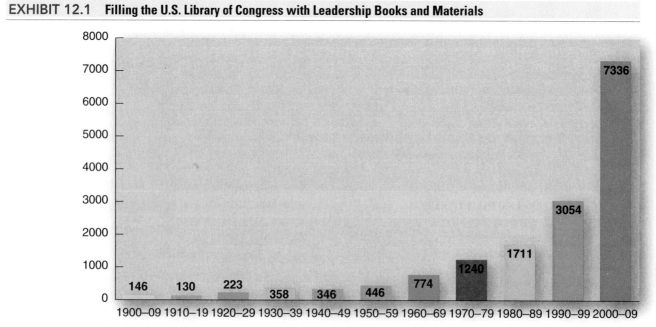

Number of books and other materials with "leader" or "leadership" in the title or citation cataloged by the U.S. Library of Congress and currently listed by decade that the item was published or produced. The U.S. Library of Congress is the world's largest library.

The Palo Verde Nuclear Generating Station is the largest nuclear power plant in the United States, producing enough electricity to serve 4 million people in California, Arizona, New Mexico, and Texas. Along with extensive technical and team-related training, Palo Verde Nuclear's 3,000 employees learn about the company's leadership model, which emphasizes safety, operational focus, long-term productivity, and cost-effectiveness. The overarching principle of that leadership model is: "Every employee is a leader, regardless of title or position." In other words, the company encourages shared leadership, whereby everyone is expected to serve as a leader to fulfill the company's key objectives.[4]

does make a difference to an organization's effectiveness. Furthermore, we are awed by individuals who influence and motivate others beyond expectations to build commitment to a better future.

SHARED LEADERSHIP

As part of its employee engagement initiative, Rolls-Royce Engine Services in Oakland, California, involved employees directly with clients, encouraged weekly huddles for information sharing, and accepted employee requests for less micromanagement. Employees at the aircraft engine repair facility not only experienced higher levels of engagement and empowerment; they also accepted more leadership responsibilities. "I saw people around me, all front-line employees, who were leaders," says a machine programmer at the Rolls-Royce Oakland plant. "They weren't actually leading the company, but they were people you would listen to and follow. We didn't have titles, but people had respect for what we did."[5]

Rolls-Royce Engine Services has moved toward greater **shared leadership,** in which employees throughout the organization informally assume leadership responsibilities in various ways and at various times.[6] Shared leadership is based on the idea that leadership is plural, not singular. It doesn't operate out of one formally assigned position, role, or individual. Instead, employees lead each other as the occasion arises. Shared leadership typically supplements formal leadership. However, W.L. Gore & Associates and Semco SA rely almost completely on shared leadership because there is no formal hierarchy or organizational chart.[7] In fact, when Gore employees are asked in annual surveys "Are you a leader?" more than 50 percent of them answer "Yes."

The late John Gardner, the former U.S. Secretary of Health, Education, and Welfare who introduced Medicare and public broadcasting, wrote more than two decades ago that the "vitality" of large organizations depends on shared leadership.[8] Employees across all levels of the organization need to seek out opportunities and solutions to problems rather than rely on formal leaders to serve these roles. Gardner observed, for example, that successful teams consist of individuals other than the formal leader

leadership
Influencing, motivating, and enabling others to contribute toward the effectiveness and success of the organizations of which they are members.

shared leadership
The view that leadership is broadly distributed, rather than assigned to one person, such that people within the team and organization lead each other.

who take responsibility for healing rifts when conflicts arise and for building confidence in others when events have turned for the worse. Various studies have also noted that employees who champion the introduction of new technologies and products are stepping unofficially into leadership positions.[9]

Shared leadership flourishes in organizations where the formal leaders are willing to delegate power and encourage employees to take initiative and risks without fear of failure (i.e., a learning orientation culture). Shared leadership also calls for a collaborative rather than internally competitive culture, because employees take on shared leadership roles when coworkers support them for their initiative. Furthermore, shared leadership lacks formal authority, so it operates best when employees learn to influence others through their enthusiasm, logical analysis, and involvement of coworkers in their idea or vision.

As we mentioned earlier, there is probably more writing on leadership than on any other topic in organizational behavior. Fortunately, most of this enormous volume of leadership literature can be distilled and organized into five perspectives: competency, behavioral, contingency, transformational, and implicit.[10] Although some of these perspectives are currently more popular than others, each helps us more fully understand the complex field of leadership.

connect

To assist your learning and test your knowledge about leadership perspectives, go to **www. mcgrawhillconnect.com**, which has activities and test questions about these different views of leadership.

Competency Perspective of Leadership

LO2

Since the beginning of recorded civilization, people have been interested in the personal characteristics that distinguish great leaders from the rest of us.[11] In the 6th century BCE, the Chinese philosopher Lao-tzu described effective leaders as selfless, honest, fair, and hardworking. The Greek philosopher Plato claimed that great leaders have wisdom and a superior capacity for logical thinking. For the past century, hundreds of leadership studies have tried to empirically identify the traits of effective leaders. However, a major review in the late 1940s concluded that no consistent list of traits could be distilled from this research. This conclusion was revised a decade later, suggesting that a few traits are associated with effective leaders.[12] These nonsignificant findings caused many scholars to give up their search for personal characteristics that distinguish effective leaders.

Over the past two decades, leadership experts have returned to the notion that effective leaders possess specific personal characteristics.[13] The earlier research was apparently plagued by methodological problems, lack of theoretical foundation, and inconsistent definitions of leadership. The emerging work has identified several leadership *competencies*, that is, skills, knowledge, aptitudes, and other personal characteristics that lead to superior performance (see Chapter 2). The main categories of leadership competencies are listed in Exhibit 12.2 and described below:[14]

connect

To assist your learning and test your knowledge about leadership competencies go to **www. mcgrawhillconnect.com**, which has activities and test questions about this topic.

- *Personality.* Most of the Big Five personality dimensions (see Chapter 2) are associated with effective leadership to some extent, but the strongest predictors are high levels of extroversion (outgoing, talkative, sociable, and assertive) and conscientiousness (careful, dependable, and self-disciplined). With high extroversion, effective leaders are comfortable having an influential role in social settings. With higher conscientiousness, effective leaders set higher goals for themselves (and others) are more motivated to pursue those goals, and have a sense of duty to others.

- *Self-concept.* Successful leaders have a complex, internally consistent, and clear self-concept of themselves as a leader (see Chapter 2). This "leader identity" also includes a positive self-evaluation, including high self-esteem, self-efficacy, and internal locus of control.[15] In short, effective leaders define themselves as leaders and are confident with this self-view.

- *Drive.* Related to their high conscientiousness and positive self-concept, successful leaders have a high need for achievement (see Chapter 5). This drive represents the inner motivation that leaders possess to pursue their goals and encourage others to

EXHIBIT 12.2 Competencies of Effective Leaders

LEADERSHIP COMPETENCY	DESCRIPTION
Personality	The leader's higher levels of extroversion (outgoing, talkative, sociable, and assertive) and conscientiousness (careful, dependable, and self-disciplined).
Self-concept	The leader's self-beliefs and positive self-evaluation about his or her own leadership skills and ability to achieve objectives.
Drive	The leader's inner motivation to pursue goals.
Integrity	The leader's truthfulness and tendency to translate words into deeds.
Leadership motivation	The leader's need for socialized power to accomplish team or organizational goals.
Knowledge of the business	The leader's tacit and explicit knowledge about the company's environment, enabling the leader to make more intuitive decisions.
Cognitive and practical intelligence	The leader's above-average cognitive ability to process information (cognitive intelligence) and ability to solve real-world problems by adapting to, shaping, or selecting appropriate environments (practical intelligence).
Emotional intelligence	The leader's ability to monitor his or her own and others' emotions, discriminate among them, and use the information to guide his or her thoughts and actions.

move forward with theirs. Drive inspires inquisitiveness, an action orientation, and boldness to take the organization or team into uncharted waters. This characteristic, among others, was quite apparent in Steve Jobs, whom we described at the beginning of this chapter.

- *Integrity.* Integrity involves truthfulness and consistency of words and actions, qualities that are related to honesty and ethical conduct. Leaders have a high moral capacity to judge dilemmas using sound values and to act accordingly. Notice that integrity is ultimately based on the leader's values, which provide an anchor for consistency. Several large-scale studies have reported that integrity and honesty are the most important characteristics of effective leaders.[16] Unfortunately, recent surveys report that employees don't trust their leaders and don't think they have integrity. For example, only 48 percent of employees in the United Kingdom/Ireland and 53 percent in North America trust senior management. Another survey reported that only 2 percent of Americans have a great deal of trust in the people who run big companies; 30 percent say they don't trust these leaders at all![17]

- *Leadership motivation.* Effective leaders are motivated to lead others. They have a strong need for *socialized power*, meaning that they want power as a means to accomplish organizational objectives and similar good deeds. This contrasts with a need for *personalized power*, which is the desire to have power for personal gain or for the thrill one might experience from wielding power over others (see Chapter 5).[18] Leadership motivation is also necessary because, even in collegial firms, leaders are in contests for positions further up the hierarchy. Effective leaders thrive rather than wither in the face of this competition.[19]

- *Knowledge of the business.* Effective leaders possess tacit and explicit knowledge of the business environment in which they operate. This competency partly explains why Steve Jobs excelled as CEO of Apple, Inc. Jobs was one of the pioneers of personal computing and has developed an uncanny ability to see the potential of this technology in emerging products such as the iPhone and iPad.

- *Cognitive and practical intelligence.* Leaders have above-average cognitive ability to process enormous amounts of information. Leaders aren't necessarily geniuses; rather, they have a superior ability to analyze many complex alternatives and opportunities.

EXHIBIT 12.3

Authentic Leadership

Know yourself

- Engage in self-reflection
- Receive feedback from trusted sources
- Understand your life story

Be yourself

- Develop your own style
- Apply your values
- Maintain a positive core self-evaluation

Furthermore, leaders have practical intelligence. Cognitive intelligence is assessed by performance on clearly defined problems with sufficient information and usually one best answer. In contrast, practical intelligence is assessed by performance in real-world settings, where problems are poorly defined, information is missing, and more than one solution may be plausible.[20]

- *Emotional intelligence.* Effective leaders have a high level of emotional intelligence.[21] They are able to perceive and express emotion, assimilate emotion in thought, understand and reason with emotion, and regulate emotion in themselves and others (see Chapter 4).

AUTHENTIC LEADERSHIP

What are the most important lessons about being a leader? For Nvidia CEO Jen-Hsun Huang, the answer is that successful leaders are authentic. "I appreciate people who are authentic," says Huang. "They are just who they are. They don't dress like a CEO because they think that's what CEOs dress like. They don't talk like CEOs because that's the way they think CEOs talk."[22]

Authentic leadership refers to how well leaders are aware of, feel comfortable with, and act consistently with their self-concept.[23] In other words, authenticity is knowing yourself and being yourself (Exhibit 12.3). Leaders learn more about their personality, values, thoughts, and habits by reflecting on various situations and personal experiences. They also improve this self-awareness by receiving feedback from trusted people inside and outside the organization. Both self-reflection and receptivity to feedback require high levels of emotional intelligence.

As people learn more about themselves, they gain a greater understanding of their inner purpose, which generates a long-term passion for achieving something worthwhile for the organization or society. Some leadership experts suggest that this inner purpose emerges from a life story, typically a critical event or experience earlier in life that provides guidance for their later career and energy.

Authentic leadership is more than self-awareness; it also involves behaving in ways that are consistent with that self-concept rather than pretending to be someone else. To be themselves, great leaders regulate their decisions

sure *we can*

TNT employs more than 150,000 people worldwide, yet the international express and mail delivery services company remains "humanized" through "honesty, authentic leadership, and truly connecting with staff." Herna Verhagen, global leader of human resources at the Netherlands-based firm, explains that authenticity is intrinsic in effective leaders. "You cannot make someone be authentic," suggests Verhagen. "What you can do as a company is emphasize that authentic leadership is key and explain what it entails." Furthermore, Verhagen believes that authentic leadership requires a "secure base," which includes taking pride in your company, team, boss, and yourself.[24]

Debating Point

SHOULD LEADERS *REALLY* BE AUTHENTIC ALL OF THE TIME?

According to popular business books and several scholarly articles, authentic leadership is one of the core attributes of effective leaders. Authentic leaders know themselves and act in accordance with that self-concept. They live their personal values and find a leadership style that best matches their personality. Furthermore, authentic leaders have a sense of purpose, often developed through a crisis or similar "crucible" event in their lives.

It makes sense that leaders should be authentic. After all, as singer Lisa Minnelli has often said: "I would rather be a first-rate version of myself than a second-rate version of anybody else."[25] In other words, leaders are better at acting out their natural beliefs and tendencies than by acting like someone else. Furthermore, authenticity results in consistency, which is a foundation of trust. So, by being authentic, leaders are more likely to be trusted by followers.[26]

But should leaders always be themselves and act consistently with their beliefs and personality? Not necessarily, according to a few experts. The concept of authentic leadership seems to be at odds with well-established research that people are evaluated as more effective leaders when they have a high rather than low self-monitoring personality.[27]

High "self-monitors" quickly understand their social environment and easily adapt their behavior to that environment. In other words, high self-monitors change their behavior to suit what others expect from them. In contrast, low self-monitors behave consistently with their personality and self-concept. They do not change their beliefs, style, or behaviors across social contexts. On the contrary, they feel much more content with high congruence between who they are and what they do, even when their natural style does not fit the situation.

Employees prefer an adaptive (i.e., high self-monitoring) leader because they have preconceived prototypes of how leaders should act.[28] (We discuss this theory—called implicit leadership—later in this chapter.) Authentic leaders are more likely to violate those prototypical expectations and, consequently, be viewed as less leader-like. The message from this is that leadership is a role requiring its incumbents to perform that role rather than to "act naturally" to some degree. Ironically, while applauding the virtues of authentic leadership, leadership guru Warren Bennis acknowledged that "leadership is a performance art." His point was that leaders are best when they act naturally in that role, but the reality of any performance is that people can never be fully themselves.[29]

Furthermore, while being yourself is authentic, it may convey the image of being inflexible and insensitive.[30] This problem was apparent to a management professor and consultant when recently working with a client. The executive's staff followed a work process that was comfortable to the executive but not many of her employees. When asked to consider adopting a process that was easier for her staff, the executive replied: "Look. This is just how I work." The executive was authentic, but the inflexibility undermined employee performance and morale.[31]

and behavior in several ways. First, they develop their own style and, where appropriate, place themselves into positions where that style is most effective. Although effective leaders adapt their behavior to the situation to some extent, they invariably understand and rely on decision methods and interpersonal styles that feel most comfortable to them.

Second, effective leaders continually think about and consistently apply their stable hierarchy of personal values to those decisions and behaviors. Leaders face many pressures and temptations, such as achieving short-term stock price targets at the cost of long-term profitability. Experts note that authentic leaders demonstrate self-discipline by remaining anchored to their values. Third, leaders maintain consistency around their self-concept by having a strong, positive core self-evaluation. They have high self-esteem and self-efficacy, as well as an internal locus of control (Chapter 2).

authentic leadership
The view that effective leaders need to be aware of, feel comfortable with, and act consistently with their values, personality, and self-concept.

COMPETENCY PERSPECTIVE LIMITATIONS AND PRACTICAL IMPLICATIONS

Although the competency perspective is gaining popularity (again), it has a few limitations.[32] First, it assumes that all effective leaders have the same personal characteristics that are equally important in all situations. This is probably a false assumption; leadership is far too complex to have a universal list of traits that apply to every condition. Some competencies might not be important all the time. Second, alternative combinations of competencies may be equally successful; two people with different sets of competencies might be equally good leaders. Third, the competency perspective views leadership as something within a person, yet experts emphasize that leadership is relational. People are effective leaders because of their favorable relationships with followers, so effective leaders cannot be identified without considering the quality of these relationships.[33]

Several leadership researchers have also warned that some personal characteristics might influence only our perception that someone is a leader, not whether the individual really makes a difference to the organization's success. People who exhibit self-confidence, extroversion, and other traits are called leaders because they fit our prototype of an effective leader. Or we might see a successful person, call that person a leader, and then attribute unobservable traits that we consider essential for great leaders. We will discuss this issue later in the implicit leadership perspective.

The competency perspective of leadership does not necessarily imply that leadership is a talent acquired at birth rather than developed throughout life. On the contrary, competencies indicate only leadership *potential*, not leadership performance. People with these characteristics become effective leaders only after they have developed and mastered the necessary leadership behaviors. People with somewhat lower leadership competencies may become very effective leaders because they have leveraged their potential more fully.

Behavioral Perspective of Leadership

LO3

In the 1940s and 1950s, leadership experts at several universities launched an intensive research investigation to answer the question, "What behaviors make leaders effective?" Questionnaires were administered to subordinates, asking them to rate their supervisors on a large number of behaviors. This study distilled two clusters of leadership behaviors from literally thousands of items (Exhibit 12.4).[34]

One cluster, called task-oriented leadership, includes behaviors that define and structure work roles. Task-oriented leaders assign employees to specific tasks, set goals and deadlines, clarify work duties and procedures, define work procedures, and plan work activities. The other cluster represents people-oriented behaviors. This cluster includes behaviors such as listening to employees for their opinions and ideas, creating a pleasant physical work environment, showing interest in staff, complimenting and recognizing employees for their effort, and showing consideration of employee needs.

CHOOSING TASK- VERSUS PEOPLE-ORIENTED LEADERSHIP

Should leaders be task-oriented or people-oriented? This is a difficult question to answer because each style has its advantages and disadvantages. Recent evidence suggests that both styles are positively associated with leader effectiveness, but in different ways.[35] Not surprisingly, increasing people-oriented leadership reduces employee absenteeism, grievances, turnover, and job dissatisfaction, whereas increasing task-oriented leadership results in higher job performance. Research suggests that university students value task-oriented

EXHIBIT 12.4

Task- and People-Oriented Leadership Styles

LEADERS ARE TASK-ORIENTED WHEN THEY . . .	LEADERS ARE PEOPLE-ORIENTED WHEN THEY . . .
• Assign work and clarify responsibilities.	• Show interest in others as people.
• Set goals and deadlines.	• Listen to employees.
• Evaluate and provide feedback on work quality.	• Make the workplace more pleasant.
• Establish well-defined best-work procedures.	• Compliment employees for their work.
• Plan future work activities.	• Are considerate of employee needs.

instructors because they want clear objectives and well-prepared lectures that abide by the unit's objectives.[36] Other research indicates that followers have fewer stress symptoms when leaders show empathy toward employees.[37]

One problem with the behavioral leadership perspective is that the two categories are broad generalizations that mask specific behaviors within each category. For instance, task-oriented leadership includes planning work activities, clarifying roles, and monitoring operations and performance. Each of these clusters of activities is fairly distinct and likely has different effects on employee well-being and performance. A second concern is that the behavioral approach assumes that high levels of both styles are best in all situations. In reality, the best leadership style depends on the situation.[38] On a positive note, the behavioral perspective lays the foundation for two of the main leadership styles—people-oriented and task-oriented—found in many contemporary leadership theories.

SERVANT LEADERSHIP

Servant leadership is an extension or variation of the people-oriented leadership style, because it defines leadership as serving others to encourage their need fulfillment and personal development and growth.[39] Servant leaders ask, "How can I help you?" rather than expect employees to serve them. People who epitomize servant leadership have been described as selfless, egalitarian, humble, nurturing, empathetic, and ethical coaches. The main objective of servant leadership is to help other stakeholders fulfill their needs and potential, particularly "to become healthier, wiser, freer, more autonomous, [and] more likely themselves to become servants."[40]

Servant leadership research suffers from ambiguous and conflicting definitions, but writers agree on a few features.[41] First, servant leaders have a natural desire or "calling" to serve others. This natural desire is a deep commitment to the growth of others for that purpose alone. It goes beyond the leader's role obligation to help others and is not merely an instrument to achieve company objectives. Second, servant leaders maintain a relationship with others that is humble, egalitarian, and accepting. Servant leaders do not view leadership as a position of power. Rather, they serve without drawing attention to themselves, without evoking superior status, and without being judgmental about others or defensive of criticisms received. Third, servant leaders anchor their decisions and actions in ethical principles and practices. They display sensitivity to and enactment of moral values and are not swayed by social pressures or expectations to deviate from those values. In this respect, servant leadership relies heavily on the idea of authentic leadership that we introduced a few pages ago.

Servant leadership was introduced four decades ago and has since gained a steady following, particularly among practitioners and religious leaders. Scholarly interest in this topic has bloomed within the past few years, but the concept still faces a number of conceptual hurdles. Although servant leadership writers generally agree on the three features we described above, many have included other characteristics that lack agreement and might confound the concept with its predictors and outcomes. Still, the notion of leader as servant has considerable currency and for many centuries has been embedded in the principles of most major religions.

LO4

Contingency Perspective of Leadership

servant leadership
The view that leaders serve followers, rather than vice versa; leaders help employees fulfill their needs and are coaches, stewards, and facilitators of employee development.

The contingency perspective of leadership is based on the idea that the most appropriate leadership style depends on the situation. Most (although not all) contingency leadership theories assume that effective leaders must be both insightful and flexible.[42] They must be able to adapt their behaviors and styles to the immediate situation. This isn't easy to do, however. Leaders typically have a preferred style. It takes considerable effort for leaders to choose and enact different styles to match the situation. As we noted earlier, leaders must have high emotional intelligence so that they can diagnose the circumstances and match their behaviors accordingly.

PATH-GOAL THEORY OF LEADERSHIP

Several contingency theories have been proposed over the years, but **path-goal leadership theory** has withstood scientific critique better than the others. Indeed, one recent study found that the path-goal theory explained more about effective leadership than did another popular perspective of leadership (transformational, which we describe later in this chapter).[43] Path-goal leadership theory has its roots in the expectancy theory of motivation (see Chapter 5), because leaders create paths (expectancies) to effective performance (goals) for their employees.[44] Path-goal theory states that effective leaders ensure that good performers receive more valued rewards than do poor performers. Effective leaders also provide the information, support, and other resources necessary to help employees complete their tasks.[45]

Path-Goal Leadership Styles   Exhibit 12.5 presents the path-goal theory of leadership. This model specifically highlights four leadership styles and several contingency factors leading to three indicators of leader effectiveness. The four leadership styles are:[46]

- *Directive.* This leadership style consists of clarifying behaviors that provide a psychological structure for subordinates. The leader clarifies performance goals, the means to reach those goals, and the standards against which performance will be judged. It also includes the judicious use of rewards and disciplinary actions. Directive leadership is the same as task-oriented leadership, described earlier, and echoes our discussion in Chapter 2 on the importance of clear role perceptions in employee performance.

- *Supportive.* In this style, the leader's behaviors provide psychological support for subordinates. The leader is friendly and approachable; makes the work more pleasant; treats employees with equal respect; and shows concern for the status, needs, and well-being of employees. Supportive leadership is the same as people-oriented leadership, described earlier, and reflects the benefits of social support to help employees cope with stressful situations.

- *Participative.* Participative leadership behaviors encourage and facilitate subordinate involvement in decisions beyond their normal work activities. The leader consults with employees, asks for their suggestions, and takes these ideas into serious consideration before making a decision. Participative leadership relates to involving employees in decisions (see Chapter 7).

- *Achievement-oriented.* This leadership style emphasizes behaviors that encourage employees to reach their peak performance. The leader sets challenging goals, expects employees to perform at their highest level, continuously seeks improvement in employee performance, and shows a high degree of confidence that employees will assume responsibility and accomplish challenging goals. Achievement-oriented leadership applies goal-setting theory as well as positive expectations in self-fulfilling prophecy.

EXHIBIT 12.5

Path-Goal Leadership Theory

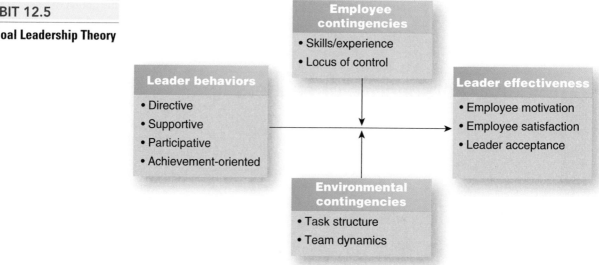

connections 12.1

Leading with a Steel Fist in a Velvet Glove

Leadership experts have long debated whether great leaders are people-oriented or task-oriented. Their conclusion? Great leaders apply one style or the other, depending on the situation. Even so, some of the world's most respected leaders have the uncanny ability to keep employees focused on the task while simultaneously being supportive. Anne Sweeney, co-chair of Disney Media Networks and president of Disney/ABC Television Group, is a case in point. News Corporation founder Rupert Murdoch once said that Sweeney has "a steel fist in a velvet glove."

Sweeney is renowned for her empathy and consideration. "She has been incredibly supportive through all the ups and downs of rebuilding a network schedule, which made it possible for us to achieve so much so fast," says one ABC executive. Albert Cheng echoes this view: "Anne makes it a point to engage with everyone," says the Disney Digital Media executive vice president. "She's very concerned about the people who work for her."

At the same time, Sweeney maintains a sharp focus on the future and ensures that her staff reach their potential. Rich Ross notes that Sweeney avoids micromanaging her staff but applies her analytic skill to challenge managers to think through their ideas. "[She] asks the tough questions. . . . It trains you to anticipate it," says the chairman of Walt Disney studios. Another ABC executive adds: "Anne draws upon her optimism and her grace in keeping her focus firmly on the future. None of us could wish for a better leader, through whatever may come our way."

Disney/ABC executive Anne Sweeney is renowned for applying both task- and people-oriented leadership styles to help her direct reports reach their potential.

Anne Sweeney's appropriate application of task- and people-oriented leadership has undoubtedly been a factor in the company's success. For example, the American television network ABC was floundering in fourth place and employee morale was low before Sweeney took the reins. Yet less than four years later, ABC was competing for the top spot with popular programs. Similar achievements occurred earlier when Sweeney was head of the Disney, Nickelodeon, and FX cable networks.[47]

The path-goal model contends that effective leaders are capable of selecting the most appropriate behavioral style (or styles) for each situation. Leaders might simultaneously use two or more styles. Disney/ABC executive Anne Sweeney applies this multi-style orientation, as Connections 12.1 describes.

Contingencies of Path-Goal Theory As a contingency theory, path-goal theory states that each of the four leadership styles will be effective in some situations but not in others. The path-goal leadership model specifies two sets of situational variables that moderate the relationship between a leader's style and effectiveness: (1) employee characteristics and (2) characteristics of the employee's work environment. Several contingencies have already been studied within the path-goal framework, and the model is open for more variables in the future.[48] However, only four contingencies are reviewed here.

- *Skill and experience.* A combination of directive and supportive leadership is best for employees who are (or perceive themselves to be) inexperienced and unskilled.[49] Directive leadership gives subordinates information about how to accomplish the task, whereas supportive leadership helps them cope with the uncertainties of unfamiliar work situations. Directive leadership is detrimental when employees are skilled and experienced, because it introduces too much supervisory control.

- *Locus of control.* People with an internal locus of control believe that they have control over their work environment (see Chapter 3). Consequently, these employees prefer participative and achievement-oriented leadership styles and may become

path-goal leadership theory
A contingency theory of leadership based on the expectancy theory of motivation that relates several leadership styles to specific employee and situational contingencies.

frustrated with a directive style. In contrast, people with an external locus of control believe that their performance is due more to luck and fate, so they tend to be more satisfied with directive and supportive leadership.

- *Task structure.* Leaders should adopt the directive style when the task is nonroutine, because this style minimizes role ambiguity that tends to occur in complex work situations (particularly for inexperienced employees).[50] The directive style is ineffective when employees have routine and simple tasks, because the manager's guidance serves no purpose and may be viewed as unnecessarily close control. Employees in highly routine and simple jobs may require supportive leadership to help them cope with the tedious nature of the work and lack of control over the pace of work. Participative leadership is preferred for employees performing nonroutine tasks, because the lack of rules and procedures gives them more discretion to achieve challenging goals. The participative style is ineffective for employees in routine tasks, because they lack discretion over their work.

- *Team dynamics.* Cohesive teams with performance-oriented norms act as a substitute for most leader interventions. High team cohesion substitutes for supportive leadership, whereas performance-oriented team norms substitute for directive and possibly achievement-oriented leadership. Thus, when team cohesion is low, leaders should use the supportive style. Leaders should apply a directive style to counteract team norms that oppose the team's formal objectives. For example, the team leader may need to use legitimate power if team members have developed a norm to "take it easy" rather than get a project completed on time.

Path-goal theory has received more research support than other contingency leadership models, but the evidence is far from complete. A few contingencies (e.g., task structure) have limited research support. Other contingencies and leadership styles in the path-goal leadership model haven't been investigated at all.[51] Another concern is that as path-goal theory expands, the model may become too complex for practical use. Few people would be able to remember all the contingencies and the appropriate leadership styles for those contingencies. In spite of these limitations, path-goal theory remains a relatively robust contingency leadership theory.

OTHER CONTINGENCY THEORIES

Many leadership theories have developed over the years, most of which are found in the contingency perspective of leadership. Some overlap with the path-goal model's leadership styles, but most use simpler and more abstract contingencies. We will briefly mention only two here because of their popularity and historical significance to the field.

Situational Leadership Theory   One of the most popular contingency theories among practitioners is the **situational leadership theory (SLT),** developed by Paul Hersey and Ken Blanchard.[52] The SLT suggests that effective leaders vary their style with the ability and motivation (or commitment) of followers. The earliest versions of the model compressed the employee's ability and motivation into a single situational condition called maturity or readiness. The most recent version uses four labels, such as "enthusiastic beginner" (low ability, high motivation) and "disillusioned learner" (moderate ability and low motivation).

The situational leadership model also identifies four leadership styles—telling, selling, participating, and delegating—that Hersey and Blanchard distinguish by the amount of directive and supportive behavior provided. For example, "telling" has high task behavior and low supportive behavior. The situational leadership model has four quadrants, with each quadrant showing the leadership style that is most appropriate under different circumstances.

In spite of its popularity, several studies and at least three reviews have concluded that the situational leadership model lacks empirical support.[53] Only one part of the model apparently works, namely, that leaders should use "telling" (i.e., directive style) when employees lack motivation and ability. This relationship is also documented in path-goal theory. The model's elegant simplicity is attractive and entertaining, but most parts don't represent reality very well.

Fiedler's Contingency Model

Fiedler's contingency model, developed by Fred Fiedler and his associates, is the earliest contingency theory of leadership.[54] According to this model, leader effectiveness depends on whether the person's natural leadership style is appropriately matched to the situation. The theory examines two leadership styles that essentially correspond to the previously described people-oriented and task-oriented styles. Unfortunately, Fiedler's model relies on a questionnaire that does not measure either leadership style very well.

Fiedler's model suggests that the best leadership style depends on the level of *situational control*, that is, the degree of power and influence the leader possesses in a particular situation. Situational control is affected by three factors in the following order of importance: leader–member relations, task structure, and position power.[55] *Leader–member relations* refer to how much employees trust and respect the leader and are willing to follow his or her guidance. *Task structure* refers to the clarity or ambiguity of operating procedures. *Position power* is the extent to which the leader possesses legitimate, reward, and coercive power over subordinates. These three contingencies form the eight possible combinations of *situation favorableness* from the leader's viewpoint. Good leader–member relations, high task structure, and strong position power create the most favorable situation for the leader, because he or she has the most power and influence under these conditions.

Fiedler has gained considerable respect for pioneering the first contingency theory of leadership, but his theory has fared less well. As mentioned, the leadership-style scale used by Fiedler has been widely criticized. There is no scientific justification for placing the three situational control factors in a hierarchy. Furthermore, the concept of leader–member relations is really an indicator of leader effectiveness (as in path-goal theory) rather than a situational factor. Finally, the theory considers only two leadership styles, whereas other models present a more complex and realistic array of behavior options. These concerns explain why the theory has limited empirical support.[56]

Changing the Situation to Match the Leader's Natural Style

Fiedler's contingency model may have become a historical footnote, but it does make an important and lasting contribution on one point. Fiedler argued that, contrary to most contingency theories, leaders can't change their style very easily to fit the situation. Instead, they tend to rely mainly on one style that is most consistent with their personality and values. Leaders with high agreeableness personality and benevolence values tend to prefer supportive leadership, for example, whereas leaders with high conscientiousness personality and achievement values feel more comfortable with the directive style of leadership.[57] A few scholars have recently proposed that leadership styles are "hardwired" more than most contingency leadership theories assume.[58] Leaders might be able to alter their style temporarily, but they tend to rely mainly on one style that is most consistent with their personality and values.

If leadership style is influenced by an individual's personality and values, organizations should engineer the situation to fit the leader's dominant style, rather than expect leaders to change their style with the situation. A directive leader might be assigned inexperienced newcomers who need direction rather than skilled employees who work less effectively under a directive style. Alternatively, companies might transfer supervisors to workplaces where their dominant style fits best. For instance, directive leaders might be parachuted into work teams

situational leadership theory
A commercially popular but poorly supported leadership model stating that effective leaders vary their style (telling, selling, participating, delegating) with the "readiness" of followers.

Fiedler's contingency model
Developed by Fred Fiedler, an early contingency leadership model that suggests that leader effectiveness depends on whether the person's natural leadership style is appropriately matched to the situation.

with counterproductive norms, whereas leaders who prefer a supportive style should be sent to departments in which employees face work pressures and other stressors.

LEADERSHIP SUBSTITUTES

So far, we have looked at theories that recommend using different leadership styles in various situations. But one theory, called **leadership substitutes,** identifies conditions that either limit the leader's ability to influence subordinates or make a particular leadership style unnecessary. Prior literature identifies several conditions that possibly substitute for task-oriented or people-oriented leadership. Task-oriented leadership might be less important when performance-based reward systems keep employees directed toward organizational goals. Similarly, increasing employee skill and experience might reduce the need for task-oriented leadership. This proposition is consistent with path-goal leadership theory, which states that directive leadership is unnecessary—and may be detrimental—when employees are skilled or experienced.[59]

Some research suggests that effective leaders help team members learn to lead themselves through leadership substitutes; in other words, coworkers substitute for leadership in high-involvement team structures.[60] Coworkers instruct new employees, thereby providing directive leadership. They also provide social support, which reduces stress among fellow employees. Teams with norms that support organizational goals may substitute for achievement-oriented leadership, because employees encourage (or pressure) coworkers to stretch their performance levels.[61] Self-leadership—the process of influencing oneself to establish the self-direction and self-motivation needed to perform a task (see Chapter 6)—might be a substitute for task-oriented and achievement-oriented leadership.[62]

The leadership substitutes model has intuitive appeal, but the evidence so far is mixed. Some studies show that a few substitutes do replace the need for task- or people-oriented leadership, but others do not. The difficulties of statistically testing for leadership substitutes may account for some problems, but a few writers contend that the limited support is evidence that leadership plays a critical role regardless of the situation.[63] At this point, we can conclude that leadership substitutes might reduce the need for leaders, but they do not completely replace leaders in these situations.

Transformational Perspective of Leadership

LO5

Transformational leadership is by far the most popular perspective of leadership today. Unlike the contingency and behavioral perspectives, which examine how leaders improve employee performance and well-being, the transformational leadership perspective views effective leaders as agents of change in the work unit or organization. They create, communicate, and model a shared vision for the team or organization, and they inspire followers to strive to achieve that vision.[64]

TRANSFORMATIONAL VERSUS TRANSACTIONAL LEADERSHIP

Leadership experts often contrast transformational leadership with **transactional leadership.**[65] Transactional leaders influence others mainly by using rewards and penalties, as well as by negotiating services from employees. James McGregor Burns, who coined the term four decades ago, describes transactional leadership with reference to political leaders who engage in vote buying or make transactional promises (e.g., "I'll have a new hospital built if you vote for me").[66] Managers in organizations are rarely elected, yet transactional leadership has become the focus of study in organizational behavior. The problem is compounded by a confusing and sometimes conflicting array of definitions and measures for transactional

connect

What are your transformational leadership tendencies? Go to **www.mcgrawhillconnect.com** to estimate your score on and assist your learning about transformational leadership.

leadership. For example, Burns acknowledges that transactional leaders can appeal to follower wants and convictions about morality and justice, which is similar to transformational leadership. [67]

What is your preferred managerial leadership style? Go to **www.mcgrawhillconnect.com** to assess your tendency to use one of three leadership styles.

For these reasons, we will avoid the "transactional leadership" concept. Instead, our main focus will be only on transformational leadership. Furthermore, we believe a more appropriate comparison to transformational leadership is **managerial leadership** or managing. Transformational leaders are change agents who energize and direct employees to a new vision and corresponding behaviors. Managerial leaders instead help employees become more proficient and satisfied in the current situation. [68] The contingency and behavioral leadership theories described earlier refer to managerial leadership, because they focus on leader behaviors that improve employee performance and well-being rather than on behaviors that move the organization and work unit to a new direction. As leadership expert Warren Bennis noted several years ago, "Managers are people who do things right, and leaders are people who do the right thing." [69]

Organizations require both managerial and transformational leadership. [70] Managing improves organizational efficiency, whereas transformational leadership steers companies onto a better course of action. Transformational leadership is particularly important in organizations that require significant alignment with the external environment. Unfortunately, too many leaders get trapped in the daily activities that represent managerial leadership. [71] They lose touch with the transformational aspect of effective leadership. Without transformational leaders, organizations stagnate and eventually become seriously misaligned with their environments.

TRANSFORMATIONAL VERSUS CHARISMATIC LEADERSHIP

Another topic that has generated some confusion and controversy is the distinction between transformational and charismatic leadership. Many researchers either use the words interchangeably, as if they have the same meaning, or view charismatic leadership as an essential ingredient of transformational leadership. Others take this notion further by suggesting that charismatic leadership is the highest degree of transformational leadership. [72]

However, the emerging view, which this book adopts, comes from a third group of experts who contend that charisma is distinct from transformational leadership. These scholars point out that charisma is a personal trait or relational quality that provides referent power over followers, whereas transformational leadership is a set of behaviors that engage followers toward a better future. [73] This view is most consistent with the original and ongoing scholarly definition of charisma as an inherent characteristic of one's character, not something that can be easily learned or mimicked. [74] Transformational leadership motivates followers through behaviors that persuade and earn trust, whereas charismatic leadership motivates followers directly through existing referent power. For instance, communicating an inspiration vision is a transformational leadership behavior that motivates followers to strive for that vision. This motivational effect exists separate from the leader's degree of charisma. If the leader is highly charismatic, however, his or her charisma will amplify follower motivation.

---

leadership substitutes
A theory identifying contingencies that either limit a leader's ability to influence subordinates or make a particular leadership style unnecessary.

transformational leadership
A leadership perspective that explains how leaders change teams or organizations by creating, communicating, and modeling a vision for the organization or work unit and inspiring employees to strive for that vision.

transactional leadership
The view that leaders influence employees mainly by using rewards and penalties, as well as through negotiation.

managerial leadership
A leadership perspective stating that effective leaders help employees improve their performance and well-being in the current situation.

Being charismatic is not inherently good or bad, but several writers have warned that it can have negative consequences in leadership.[75] One concern is that leaders who possess the gift of charisma may become intoxicated by this power, which leads to a greater focus on self-interest than on the common good. "Charisma becomes the undoing of leaders," warns Peter Drucker. "It makes them inflexible, convinced of their own infallibility, unable to change."[76] The late management guru witnessed the destructive effects of charismatic political leaders in Europe a century ago and foresaw that this personal or relational characteristic would create similar problems for organizations.

Another concern with charismatic leadership is that it tends to produce dependent followers. Transformational leadership has the opposite effect—it builds follower empowerment, which tends to reduce dependence on the leader. One study also found that charismatic leadership has a negative effect on follower self-efficacy, which would further increase dependence on the leader.

The main point here is that transformational leaders are not necessarily charismatic, and charismatic leaders are not necessarily transformational. Procter & Gamble CEO Alan G. Lafley is not known for being charismatic, but he has transformed the household goods company like no leader in recent memory. Similarly, IBM CEO Sam Palmisano has guided IBM's success without much inherent charisma. "I don't have much curb appeal," Palmisano admits. "I just try to lead them and get them to come together around a common point of view."[77] In other words, Palmisano and Lafley lead by applying transformational leadership behaviors.

ELEMENTS OF TRANSFORMATIONAL LEADERSHIP

There are several descriptions of transformational leadership, but most include the following four elements: Create a strategic vision, communicate the vision, model the vision, and build commitment toward the vision (see Exhibit 12.6).

Develop a Strategic Vision   A core element of transformational leadership is strategic vision—a realistic and attractive future that bonds employees together and focuses their energy toward a superordinate organizational goal.[78] Indeed, experts describe vision as the commodity or substance of transformational leadership. Strategic vision represents a "higher purpose" or superordinate goal that energizes and unifies employees and adds meaning to each person's self-concept.[79] It is typically described in a way that departs

EXHIBIT 12.6

Elements of Transformational Leadership

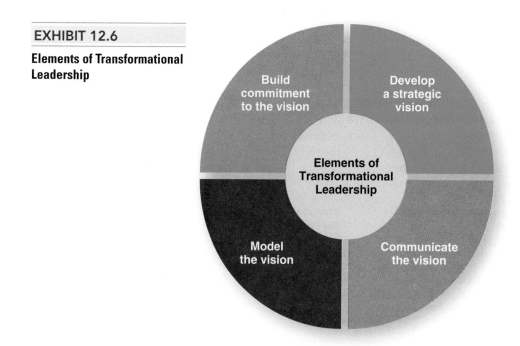

Edward Stack had plenty of doubters when he recommended rapid expansion of his father's two-store sporting goods business in upstate New York. His vision was to become the nation's leading retail sports store. "You'll have a lot of people who won't really share your vision and will tell you all of the reasons why it won't work," Stack advises. But he points out that a vision is critical to the company's success. "If you don't have a solid vision, you probably aren't going to be able to grow profitably." Today, Stack's company employs nearly 26,000 people in more than 500 Dick's Sporting Goods and Golf Galaxy stores through the United States.[81]

from the current situation and is both appealing and achievable. A strategic vision might originate with the leader, but it is just as likely to emerge from employees, clients, suppliers, or other stakeholders. When embraced by employees, a strategic vision plays an important role in organizational effectiveness.[80] It offers the same motivational benefits as goal setting (see Chapter 5), but it also serves as a source of a common bond that builds employee commitment to this collective purpose.

Communicate the Vision   If vision is the substance of transformational leadership, communicating that vision is the process. CEOs say that the most important leadership quality is being able to build and share their vision for the organization. "Part of a leader's role is to set the vision for the company and to communicate that vision to staff to get their buy-in," explains Dave Anderson, president of WorkSafeBC (the Workers' Compensation Board of British Columbia, Canada).[82]

Transformational leaders communicate meaning and elevate the importance of the visionary goal to employees. They frame messages around a grand purpose with emotional appeal that captivates employees and other corporate stakeholders. Framing generates positive emotions and motivation and establishes a common mental model so that the group or organization will act collectively toward the desirable goal.[83] Transformational leaders bring their visions to life through symbols, metaphors, stories, and other vehicles that transcend plain language. Metaphors borrow images of other experiences, thereby creating richer meaning of the vision that has not yet been experienced.

Model the Vision   Transformational leaders not only talk about a vision; they enact it. They "walk the talk" by stepping outside the executive suite and doing things that symbolize the vision.[84] "We hold our leaders to an even higher standard than our employees," says Nathan Bigler, human resource director at Eastern Idaho Regional Medical Center. "Leaders have to consistently walk the talk."[85]

Leaders walk the talk through significant events such as visiting customers, moving their offices closer to (or further from) employees, and holding ceremonies to destroy outdated policy manuals. However, they also alter mundane activities—meeting agendas, dress codes, executive schedules—so that the activities are more consistent with the vision and its underlying values. Modeling the vision is important because it legitimizes and demonstrates what the vision looks like in practice. Modeling is also important because it builds employee trust in the leader. The greater the consistency between the leader's words and actions, the more employees will believe in and be willing to follow the leader. In fact, one survey reported that leading by example is the most important characteristic of a leader.[86] "As an executive, you're always being watched by employees, and everything you say gets magnified—so you teach a lot by how you conduct yourself," advises Carl Bass, CEO of the California software company Autodesk.[87]

Build Commitment Toward the Vision   Transforming a vision into reality requires employee commitment, and transformational leaders build this commitment in several ways. Their words, symbols, and stories build a contagious enthusiasm that energizes people to adopt the vision as their own. Leaders demonstrate a "can-do" attitude by enacting their vision and staying on course. Their persistence and consistency reflect an image of honesty, trust, and integrity. Finally, leaders build commitment by involving employees in the process of shaping the organization's vision.

EVALUATING THE TRANSFORMATIONAL LEADERSHIP PERSPECTIVE

Transformational leaders do make a difference.[88] Subordinates are more satisfied and have higher affective organizational commitment under transformational leaders. They also perform their jobs better, engage in more organizational citizenship behaviors, and make better or more creative decisions. One study of bank branches reported that organizational commitment and financial performance seem to increase in branches whose manager had completed a transformational leadership training program.[89]

Transformational leadership is currently the most popular leadership perspective, but it faces a number of challenges. One problem is that some writers engage in circular logic.[90] They define and measure transformational leadership by how well the leader inspires and engages employees rather than by whether the leader engages in behaviors we call transformational (e.g., communicating a vision). This approach makes it impossible to evaluate transformational leadership, because by definition and measurement, all transformational leaders are effective!

Another concern is that transformational leadership is usually described as a universal rather than contingency-oriented model. Only very recently have writers begun to explore the idea that transformational leadership is more valuable in some situations than others.[91] For instance, transformational leadership is probably more appropriate when organizations need to adapt than when environmental conditions are stable. Preliminary evidence suggests that the transformational leadership perspective is relevant across cultures. However, there may be specific elements of transformational leadership, such as the way visions are formed and communicated, that are more appropriate in North America than other cultures.

Implicit Leadership Perspective

LO6

The competency, behavior, contingency, and transformational leadership perspectives make the basic assumption that leaders "make a difference." Certainly, there is evidence that senior executives influence organizational performance. However, leadership also involves followers' perceptions about the characteristics and influence of people they call leaders. This perceptual perspective of leadership, called **implicit leadership theory,** has two components: leader prototypes and the romance or attribution of leadership.[92]

PROTOTYPES OF EFFECTIVE LEADERS

One aspect of implicit leadership theory states that everyone has *leadership prototypes*—preconceived beliefs about the features and behaviors of effective leaders.[93] These prototypes, which develop through socialization within the family and society, shape the follower's expectations and acceptance of others as leaders, and this in turn affects their willingness to remain as a follower. For example, one study reported that inherited personality characteristics significantly influence the perception that someone is a leader in a leaderless situation.[94]

Leadership prototypes not only support a person's role as leader; they also form or influence our perception of the leader's effectiveness. In other words, people are more likely to believe a leader is effective when he or she looks like and acts consistently with their prototype of a leader.[95] This prototype comparison process occurs because people have an inherent need to quickly evaluate individuals as leaders, yet leadership effectiveness is often ambiguous and might not be apparent for a long time.

THE ROMANCE OF LEADERSHIP

Along with relying on implicit prototypes of effective leaders, followers tend to distort their perception of the influence that leaders have on the environment. This "romance of

As the CEO of a successful company (Semco SA) and the author of best-selling business books, Ricardo Semler is a giant among corporate leaders in South America. Yet he warns that "romance of leadership" problems can occur when employees are blinded by charismatic leadership. "People will naturally create and nurture a charismatic figure. The charismatic figure, on the other hand, feeds this," Semler explains. "The people at Semco don't look and act like me. They are not yes-men by any means. . . . [Yet] they credit me with successes that are not my own, and they don't debit me my mistakes."[96]

leadership" effect exists because in most cultures people want to believe that leaders make a difference. There are two basic reasons people inflate their perceptions of the leader's influence over the environment.[97]

First, leadership is a useful way for us to simplify life events. It is easier to explain organizational successes and failures in terms of the leader's ability than by analyzing a complex array of other forces. Second, there is a strong tendency in the United States and other Western cultures to believe that life events are generated more from people than from uncontrollable natural forces.[98] This illusion of control is satisfied by believing that events result from the rational actions of leaders. In other words, employees feel better believing that leaders make a difference, so they actively look for evidence that this is so.

One way that followers support their perceptions that leaders make a difference is through fundamental attribution error (see Chapter 3). Research has found that (at least in Western cultures) leaders are given credit or blame for the company's success or failure because employees do not readily see the external forces that also influence these events. Leaders reinforce this belief by taking credit for organizational successes.[99]

The implicit leadership perspective provides valuable advice to improve leadership acceptance. It highlights that leadership depends on the perception of followers as much as the actual behaviors and formal roles of people calling themselves leaders. Potential leaders must be sensitive to this fact, understand what followers expect, and act accordingly. Individuals who do not make an effort to fit leadership prototypes will have more difficulty bringing about necessary organizational change.

Cross-Cultural and Gender Issues in Leadership

Along with the five perspectives of leadership presented throughout this chapter, cultural values and practices affect what leaders do. Culture shapes the leader's values and norms, which influence his or her decisions and actions. Cultural values also shape the expectations that followers have of their leaders. An executive who acts inconsistently with cultural expectations is more likely to be perceived as an ineffective leader. Furthermore, leaders who deviate from those values may experience various forms of influence to get them to conform to the leadership norms and expectations of the society. In other words, implicit leadership theory, described in the previous section of this chapter, explains differences in leadership practices across cultures.

Over the past decade, 150 researchers from dozens of countries have worked together on Project GLOBE (Global Leadership and Organizational Behavior Effectiveness) to identify the effects of cultural values on leadership.[100] The project organized countries into 10 regional clusters, of which the United States, Canada, Great Britain, and similar countries are grouped into the "Anglo" cluster. The results of this massive investigation suggest that some features of leadership are universal and some differ across cultures. Specifically, the GLOBE project reports that "charismatic visionary" is

implicit leadership theory
A theory stating that people evaluate a leader's effectiveness in terms of how well that person fits preconceived beliefs about the features and behaviors of effective leaders (leadership prototypes) and that people tend to inflate the influence of leaders on organizational events.

Barloworld Logistics does business in 26 countries. Yet CEO Isaac Shongwe is keen to imprint Africa's unique ubuntu value throughout the company's far-flung operations. "My concern is how to create one company with one culture across all these borders," says the South African–born executive. "I am putting the concept of ubuntu at the heart of this and recognizing the humanity of us all, wherever we live, whether that's Germany or Dubai." Ubuntu is the notion of humanity and interdependence, that each of us is a person through others. Thus, ubuntu calls for leadership that emphasizes mutual respect, tolerance, and forgiveness.[101]

a universally recognized concept and that middle managers around the world believe it is characteristic of effective leaders. *Charismatic visionary* represents a cluster of concepts, including visionary, inspirational, performance orientation, integrity, and decisiveness.[102] In contrast, participative leadership is perceived as characteristic of effective leadership in low power distance cultures but less so in high power distance cultures. For instance, one study reported that Mexican employees expect managers to make decisions affecting their work. Mexico is a high power distance culture, so followers expect leaders to apply their authority rather than delegate their power most of the time.[103] In summary, there are similarities and differences in the concept and preferred practice of leadership across cultures.

GENDER AND LEADERSHIP

Studies in field settings have generally found that male and female leaders do not differ in their levels of task-oriented or people-oriented leadership. The main explanation is that real-world jobs require similar behavior from male and female job incumbents.[104] However, women adopt a participative leadership style more readily than their male counterparts. One possible reason is that, compared with boys, girls are often raised to be more egalitarian and less status-oriented, which is consistent with being participative. There is also some evidence that women have somewhat better interpersonal skills than men, and this translates into their relatively greater use of the participative leadership style. A third explanation is that subordinates, on the basis of their own gender stereotypes, expect female leaders to be more participative, so female leaders comply with follower expectations to some extent.

Surveys report that women are rated higher than men on the emerging leadership qualities of coaching, teamwork, and empowering employees.[105] Yet research also suggests that women are evaluated negatively when they try to apply the full range of leadership styles, particularly more directive and autocratic approaches. Thus, ironically, women may be well suited to contemporary leadership roles, yet they often continue to face limitations of leadership through the gender stereotypes and prototypes of leaders that are held by followers.[106] Overall, both male and female leaders must be sensitive to the fact that followers have expectations about how leaders should act, and negative evaluations may go to leaders who deviate from those expectations.

[chapter summary]

LO1 Define *leadership* and *shared leadership*.

Leadership is defined as the ability to influence, motivate, and enable others to contribute toward the effectiveness and success of the organizations of which they are members. Leaders use influence to motivate followers and arrange the work environment so that they do the job more effectively. Shared leadership views leadership as a role rather than a formal position, so employees throughout the organization act informally as leaders as the occasion arises. These situations include serving as champions for specific ideas or changes, as well as filling leadership roles as needed.

LO2 Identify eight competencies associated with effective leaders and describe authentic leadership.

The competency perspective tries to identify the characteristics of effective leaders. Recent writing suggests that leaders have specific personality characteristics, positive self-concept, drive, integrity, leadership motivation, knowledge of the business, cognitive and practical intelligence, and emotional intelligence. Authentic leadership refers to how well leaders are aware of, feel comfortable with, and act consistently with their self-concept. This concept consists mainly of two parts: self-awareness and engaging in behavior that is consistent with one's self-concept.

LO3 Describe the key features of task-oriented, people-oriented, and servant leadership, and discuss their effects on followers.

The behavioral perspective of leadership identifies two clusters of leader behavior, people-oriented and task-oriented. People-oriented behaviors include showing mutual trust and respect for subordinates, demonstrating a genuine concern for their needs, and having a desire to look out for their welfare. Task-oriented behaviors include assigning employees to specific tasks, clarifying their work duties and procedures, ensuring they follow company rules, and pushing them to reach their performance capacity.

Servant leadership defines leadership as serving others to help them achieve their need fulfillment and personal development and growth. Servant leaders have a natural desire or "calling" to serve others. They maintain a relationship with others that is humble, egalitarian, and accepting. Servant leaders also anchor their decisions and actions in ethical principles and practices.

LO4 Discuss the key elements of path-goal theory, Fiedler's contingency model, and leadership substitutes.

The contingency perspective of leadership takes the view that effective leaders diagnose the situation and adapt their style to fit that situation. The path-goal model is the prominent contingency theory that identifies four leadership styles—directive, supportive, participative, and achievement-oriented—and several contingencies relating to the characteristics of the employee and of the situation.

Two other contingency leadership theories include the situational leadership theory and Fiedler's contingency theory. Research support is quite weak for both theories. However, a lasting element of Fiedler's theory is the idea that leaders have natural styles and, consequently, companies need to change the leaders' environments to suit their style. Leadership substitutes theory identifies contingencies that either limit the leader's ability to influence subordinates or make a particular leadership style unnecessary.

LO5 Describe the four elements of transformational leadership, and distinguish this theory from transactional and charismatic leadership.

Transformational leaders create a strategic vision, communicate that vision through framing and use of metaphors, model the vision by walking the talk and acting consistently, and build commitment toward the vision. This contrasts with transactional leadership, which has ambiguous meaning but is usually viewed as an exchange relationship with followers. Transformational leadership is also distinguished from managerial leadership, which relates to the contingency theories of leadership. Some transformational leadership theories view charismatic leadership as an essential ingredient of transformational leadership. However, this view is inconsistent with the meaning of charisma and at odds with research on the dynamics and outcomes of charisma in leader–follower relationships.

LO6 Describe the implicit leadership perspective.

According to the implicit leadership perspective, people have leadership prototypes, which they use to evaluate the leader's effectiveness. Furthermore, people form a romance of leadership; they want to believe that leaders make a difference, so they engage in fundamental attribution error and other perceptual distortions to support this belief in the leader's impact.

LO7 Discuss cultural and gender similarities and differences in leadership.

Cultural values also influence the leader's personal values, which in turn influence his or her leadership practices. Women generally do not differ from men in the degree of people-oriented or task-oriented leadership. However, female leaders more often adopt a participative style. Research also suggests that people evaluate female leaders on the basis of gender stereotypes, which may result in higher or lower ratings.

{ key terms }

authentic leadership, p. 354
Fiedler's contingency model, p. 361
implicit leadership theory, p. 366
leadership, p. 350

leadership substitutes, p. 362
managerial leadership, p. 363
path-goal leadership theory, p. 358
servant leadership, p. 357

shared leadership, p. 351
situational leadership theory, p. 360
transactional leadership, p. 362
transformational leadership, p. 362

{ critical thinking questions }

1. Why is it important for top executives to value and support shared leadership?
2. Find two newspaper ads for management or executive positions. What leadership competencies are mentioned in these ads? If you were on the selection panel, what methods would you use to identify these competencies in job applicants?
3. Consider your favorite teacher. What people-oriented and task-oriented leadership behaviors did he or she use effectively? In general, do you think students prefer an instructor who is more people-oriented or task-oriented? Explain your preference.
4. Your employees are skilled and experienced customer service representatives who perform nonroutine tasks, such as

solving unique customer problems or meeting special needs with the company's equipment. Use path-goal theory to identify the most appropriate leadership style(s) you should use in this situation. Be sure to fully explain your answer, and discuss why other styles are inappropriate.

5. Transformational leadership is the most popular perspective of leadership. However, it is far from perfect. Discuss the limitations of transformational leadership.

6. This chapter distinguished charismatic leadership from transformational leadership. Yet charisma is identified by most employees and managers as a characteristic of effective leaders. Why is charisma commonly related to leadership? In your opinion, are the best leaders charismatic? Why or why not?

7. You hear two people debating the merits of women as leaders. One person claims that women make better leaders than do men because women are more sensitive to their employees' needs and involve them in organizational decisions. The other person counters that though these leadership styles may be increasingly important, most women have trouble gaining acceptance as leaders when they face tough situations in which a more autocratic style is required. Discuss the accuracy of the comments made in this discussion.

8. The theories discussed in this chapter seem to be more relevant for leaders in large companies or multinational firms. Please discuss how these theories relate to our political leadership. Do you think we need to have transformational leaders running our country, charismatic leaders, or transactional leaders? What would be the pros and cons associated with these different leadership styles?

CASE STUDY 12.1 PROFITEL INC.

By Steven L. McShane, University of Western Australia

As a formerly government-owned telephone monopoly, Profitel enjoyed many decades of minimal competition. Even today as a publicly traded enterprise, the company's almost exclusive control over telephone copper wiring across the country keeps its profit margins above 40 percent. Competitors in telephone and DSL broadband continue to rely on Profitel's wholesale business, which generates substantially more profit than similar wholesale services in many other countries. However, Profitel has stiff competition in the cellular (mobile) telephone business, and other emerging technologies (voice-over-Internet) threaten Profitel's dominance. Based on these threats, Profitel's board of directors decided to hire an outsider as the new chief executive.

Although several qualified candidates expressed an interest in Profitel's top job, the board selected Lars Peeters, who had been CEO for six years of a publicly traded European telephone company, followed by a brief stint as CEO of a cellular telephone company in the United States until it was acquired by a larger firm. Profitel's board couldn't believe its good fortune; Peeters brought extensive industry knowledge and global experience, a high-octane energy level, self-confidence, decisiveness, and a congenial yet strongly persuasive interpersonal style. He also had a unique "presence" that caused people to pay attention and respect his leadership. The board was also impressed with Peeters' strategy to bolster Profitel's profit margins. This included heavy investments in the latest wireless broadband technology (for both cellular telephone and computer Internet) before competitors could gain a foothold, cutting costs through layoffs and reduction of peripheral services, and putting pressure on government to deregulate its traditional and emerging businesses. When Peeters described his strategy to the board, one board member commented that this was the same strategy Peeters used in his previous

two CEO postings. Peeters dismissed the comment, saying that each situation is unique.

Peeters lived up to his reputation as a decisive executive. Almost immediately after taking the CEO job at Profitel, he hired two executives from the European company where he previously worked. Together over the next two years they cut the workforce by 5 percent and rolled out the new wireless broadband technology for cell phones and Internet. Costs increased somewhat due to the downsizing expenses and the wireless technology rollout. Profitel's wireless broadband subscriber list grew quickly because, in spite of its very high prices, the technology faced limited competition, and Profitel was pushing customers off the older technology to the new network. Profitel's customer satisfaction ratings fell, however. A national consumer research group reported that Profitel's broadband offered the country's worst value. Employee morale also declined due to layoffs and the company's public image problems. Some industry experts noted that Profitel selected its wireless technology without evaluating the alternative emerging wireless technology, which had been gaining ground in other countries. Peeters' aggressive campaign against government regulation also had unintended consequences. Rather than achieving less regulation, criticizing government and its telecommunications regulator made Profitel look even more arrogant in the eyes of both customers and government leaders.

Profitel's board was troubled by the company's lackluster share price, which had declined 20 percent since Peeters was hired. Some board members also worried that the company had bet on the wrong wireless technology and that subscription levels would stall far below the number necessary to achieve the profits stated in Peeters' strategic plan. This concern came closer to reality when a foreign-owned competitor won a $1 billion government contract to improve broadband services in regional areas of the country. Profitel's proposal for that regional broadband upgrade specified high prices and limited corporate investment, but Peeters was confident Profitel would be awarded the contract because of its market dominance and existing infrastructure with the new wireless network. When the government decided otherwise, Profitel's board fired Peeters, along with two executives he had hired from the European company where he previously worked. Now, the board had to figure out what went wrong and how to avoid this problem in the future.

Discussion Questions

1. Which perspective of leadership best explains the problems experienced in this case? Analyze the case using concepts discussed in that leadership perspective.

2. What can organizations do to minimize the leadership problems discussed above?

CASE STUDY 12.2 A WINDOW ON LIFE

By Steven L. McShane, University of Western Australia

For Gilbert LaCrosse, there is nothing quite as beautiful as a handcrafted wood-framed window. LaCrosse's passion for windows goes back to his youth in Eau Claire, Wisconsin, where he learned how to make residential windows from an elderly carpenter. He learned about the characteristics of good wood, the best tools to use, and how to choose the best glass from local suppliers. LaCrosse apprenticed with the carpenter in his small workshop and, when the carpenter retired, was given the opportunity to operate the business himself.

LaCrosse hired his own apprentice as he built up business in the local area. His small operation soon expanded as the quality of windows built by LaCrosse Industries, Inc., became better known. Within eight years, the company employed nearly 25 people, and the business had moved to larger facilities to accommodate the increased demand from Wisconsin. In these early years, LaCrosse spent most of his time in the production shop, teaching new apprentices the unique skills that he had mastered and applauding the journeymen for their accomplishments. He would constantly repeat the point that LaCrosse products had to be of the highest quality because they gave families a "window on life."

After 15 years, LaCrosse Industries employed over 200 people. A profit-sharing program was introduced to give employees a financial reward for their contribution to the organization's success. Due to the company's expansion, headquarters had to be moved to another area of the city, but the founder never lost touch with the workforce. Although new apprentices were now taught entirely by the master carpenters and other craftspeople, LaCrosse would still chat with plant and office employees several times each week.

When a second work shift was added, LaCrosse would show up during the evening break with coffee and boxes of donuts and discuss how the business was doing and how it became so successful through quality workmanship. Production employees enjoyed the times when he would gather them together to announce new contracts with developers from Chicago and New York. After each announcement, LaCrosse would thank everyone for making the business a success. They knew that LaCrosse quality had become a standard of excellence in window manufacturing across the Eastern part of the country.

It seemed that almost every time he visited, LaCrosse would repeat the now well-known phrase that LaCrosse products had to be of the highest quality because they provided a window on life to so many families. Employees never grew tired of hearing this from the company founder. However, it gained extra meaning when LaCrosse began posting photos of families looking through LaCrosse windows. At first, LaCrosse would personally visit developers and homeowners with a camera in hand. Later, as the "window on life" photos became known by developers and customers, people would send in photos of their own families looking through elegant front windows made by LaCrosse Industries. The company's marketing staff began using this idea, as well as LaCrosse's famous phrase, in their advertising. After one such marketing campaign, hundreds of photos were sent in by satisfied customers. Production and office employees took time after work to write personal letters of thanks to those who had submitted photos.

As the company reached the quarter-century mark, LaCrosse, now in his mid-fifties, realized that the organization's success and survival depended on expansion to other parts of the United States. After consulting with employees, LaCrosse made the difficult decision to sell a majority share to Build-All Products, Inc., a conglomerate with international marketing expertise in building products. As part of the agreement, Build-All brought in a vice president to oversee production operations while LaCrosse spent more time meeting with developers. LaCrosse would return to the plant and office at every opportunity, but often this would be only once a month.

Rather than visiting the production plant, Jan Vlodoski, the new production vice president, would rarely leave his office in the company's downtown headquarters. Instead, production orders were sent to supervisors by memorandum. Although product quality had been a priority throughout the company's history, less attention had been paid to inventory controls. Vlodoski introduced strict inventory guidelines and outlined procedures on using supplies for each shift. Goals were established for supervisors to meet specific inventory targets. Whereas employees previously could have tossed out several pieces of warped wood, they would now have to justify this action, usually in writing.

Vlodoski also announced new procedures for purchasing production supplies. LaCrosse Industries had highly trained purchasing staff who worked closely with senior craftspeople when selecting suppliers, but Vlodoski wanted to bring in Build-All's procedures. The new purchasing methods removed production leaders from the decision process and, in some cases, resulted in trade-offs that LaCrosse's employees would not have made earlier. A few employees quit during this time, saying that they did not feel comfortable about producing a window that would not stand the test of time. However, there were few jobs for carpenters at the time, so most staff members remained with the company.

After one year, inventory expenses decreased by approximately 10 percent, but the number of defective windows returned by developers and wholesalers had increased markedly. Plant employees knew that the number of defective windows would increase as they used somewhat lower-quality materials to reduce inventory costs. However, they heard almost no news about the seriousness of the problem until Vlodoski sent a memo to all production staff saying that quality must be maintained. During the latter part of the first year under Vlodoski, a few employees had the opportunity to personally ask LaCrosse about the changes and express their concerns. LaCrosse apologized, saying due to his travels to new regions, he had not heard about the problems, and that he would look into the matter.

Exactly 18 months after Build-All had become majority shareholder of LaCrosse Industries, LaCrosse called together five of the original staff in the plant. The company founder looked pale and shaken as he said that Build-All's actions were inconsistent with his vision of the company and, for the first time in his career, he did not know what to do. Build-All was not pleased with the arrangement either. Although LaCrosse windows still enjoyed a healthy market share and were competitive for the value, the company did not quite provide the minimum 18 percent return on equity that the conglomerate expected. LaCrosse asked his long-time companions for advice.

Discussion Questions

1. Identify the symptoms indicating that problems exist at LaCrosse Industries, Inc.

2. Use one or more leadership theories to analyze the underlying causes of the current problems at LaCrosse Industries. What other organizational behavior theories might also help explain some of the problems?

3. What should Gilbert LaCrosse do in this situation?

TEAM EXERCISE 12.3 LEADERSHIP DIAGNOSTIC ANALYSIS

PURPOSE To help students learn about the different path-goal leadership styles and when to apply each style.

INSTRUCTIONS

Step 1: Individually write down two incidents in which someone has been an effective manager or leader over you. The leader and situation might be from work, a sports team, a student work group, or any other setting where leadership might emerge. For example, you might describe how your supervisor in a summer job pushed you to reach higher performance goals than you would have done otherwise. Each incident should state the actual behaviors that the leader used, not just general statements (e.g., "My boss sat down with me and we agreed on specific targets and deadlines; then he said several times over the next few weeks that I was capable of reaching those goals.") Each incident requires only two or three sentences.

Step 2: After everyone has written their two incidents, the instructor will form small groups (typically of four or five students). Each team will answer the following questions for each incident presented in that team:

1. Which path-goal theory leadership style(s)—directive, supportive, participative, or achievement-oriented—did the leader apply in this incident?

2. Ask the person who wrote the incident about the conditions that made this leadership style (or these styles, if more than one was used) appropriate in this situation. The team should list these contingency factors clearly and, where possible, connect them to the contingencies described in path-goal theory. (Note: The team might identify path-goal leadership contingencies that are not described in the book. These, too, should be noted and discussed.)

Step 3: After the teams have diagnosed the incidents, each team will describe to the entire class the most interesting incidents, as well as its diagnosis of that incident. Other teams will critique the diagnosis. Any leadership contingencies not mentioned in the textbook should also be presented and discussed.

SELF-ASSESSMENT 12.4 DO LEADERS MAKE A DIFFERENCE?

PURPOSE This assessment is designed to help you assess your beliefs about the influence of leaders.

INSTRUCTIONS Read each of the statements below and circle the response that best indicates your personal belief about that statement. Then use the scoring key in Appendix B to calculate the results for each leadership dimension. After completing this assessment, be prepared to discuss in class the relevance and level of implicit leadership theory.

Romance of Leadership Scale

TO WHAT EXTENT DO YOU AGREE OR DISAGREE THAT ...	STRONGLY AGREE	AGREE	NEUTRAL	DISAGREE	STRONGLY DISAGREE
1. Even in an economic recession, a good leader can prevent a company from doing poorly.	☐	☐	☐	☐	☐
2. The quality of leadership is the single most important influence on how well the organization functions.	☐	☐	☐	☐	☐
3. The CEO and executive team have relatively little effect on the company's success or failure.	☐	☐	☐	☐	☐
4. Sooner or later, bad leadership at the top will result in declining organizational performance.	☐	☐	☐	☐	☐
5. The effect of a company's leaders on organizational performance is fairly weak.	☐	☐	☐	☐	☐
6. A company is only as good or as bad as its leaders.	☐	☐	☐	☐	☐
7. Even the best leaders can't help an organization very much when the economy is bad or competition is tough.	☐	☐	☐	☐	☐
8. It is impossible for an organization to do well when its leaders are average.	☐	☐	☐	☐	☐
9. Compared with the economy, competition, and other external forces, leaders have only a small influence on a firm's performance.	☐	☐	☐	☐	☐
10. The company's top executives have the power to make or break the organization.	☐	☐	☐	☐	☐

Source: Adapted and condensed by B. Schyns, J.R. Meindl, and M.A. Croon, "The Romance of Leadership Scale: Cross-Cultural Testing and Refinement," *Leadership,* Vol. 3, No. 1, (2007), pp. 29–46. Copyright © 2007. Reproduced with permission of Sage Publications.

 After reading this chapter go to www.mhhe.com/mcshane6e for more in-depth information and interactivities that correspond to the chapter.

Designing Organizational Structures

learning objectives

After reading this chapter, you should be able to:

LO1 Describe three types of coordination in organizational structures.

LO2 Discuss the role and effects of span of control, centralization, and formalization, and relate these elements to organic and mechanistic organizational structures.

LO3 Identify and evaluate six types of departmentalization.

LO4 Explain how the external environment, organizational size, technology, and strategy are relevant when designing an organizational structure.

a small business located in a tiny 450-foot store in Tulsa, Oklahoma. The couple were the only employees. "I would make cakes and Bobbie would come in and decorate them," Larry recalls. Sales were slow until they added cinnamon rolls and bought a doughnut shop around the corner one year later. The name changed to Merritt's Bakery. They hired a few employees to assist with sales as the business grew.

After a dozen years, Merritt's Bakery moved to a 6,000-foot location across the street. Business boomed as customers lined up down the sidewalk to buy its fresh-baked goods. "That looks like success to a lot of people, but that was failure," says Bobbie Merritt. The problem was that the couple couldn't produce their baked goods fast enough and didn't want to delegate production to employees. But after working too many 20-hour days, they recognized that they had to become managers rather than bakers. They devised a plan to grow the business and drew up an organizational structure that formalized roles and responsibilities.

When a second Merritt's Bakery store opened across town, each store was assigned a manager, a person in charge of baking production, another in charge of cake decorating and pastries, and someone responsible for sales. Larry worked on standardizing quality by training bakery staff at each store. "Because it is so difficult to find qualified bakers nowadays, I want to spend more time teaching and developing our products," he said at the time.

Christian Merritt, Larry and Bobbie's son, joined the business after several years in engineering and is now director of bakery operations. A third store was opened and bakery production was moved to a dedicated facility rather than at each store. Centralizing production helped the company improve quality and efficiency. Meanwhile, the stores have become restaurants with a menu that now includes hot breakfast and lunch meals.

Today, Merritt's Bakery employs more than 80 people and recently hired a marketing director. It has introduced more standardization, such as flowcharts that guide employees through most aspects of their job duties without the need for direct supervision. Training programs now develop employees for each specialized function in the store and bakery production.

"We're just now getting the pieces in place to start to treat Merritt's Bakery like a business, with a lot of parts that we manage from a distance," says Christian Merritt. "We're present but detached; we have our hands in a lot of things, but it's in managing stores instead of operating them."[1]

The organizational structure of Merritt's Bakery has evolved as the Tulsa, Oklahoma, company has grown over the years.

Merritt's Bakery has come a long way since its humble beginnings as a small cake shop in Tulsa, Oklahoma. Along the way, owners Larry and Bobbie Merritt discovered that successful business growth depends to some extent on creating an organizational structure that supports the business strategy and process. **Organizational structure** refers to the division of labor as well as the patterns of coordination, communication, workflow, and formal power that direct organizational activities. It formally dictates what activities receive the most attention, as well as financial, power, and information resources. For example, Merritt's Bakery grew into a functional structure and developed various coordinating mechanisms to ensure that everyone works in concert toward the organization's objectives.

Although the topic of organizational structure typically conjures up images of an organizational chart, this diagram is only part of the puzzle. Organizational structure includes these reporting relationships, but it also relates to job design, information flow, work standards and rules, team dynamics, and power relationships. As such, the organization's structure is an important instrument in an executive's toolkit for organizational change, because it establishes new communication patterns and aligns employee behavior with the corporate vision.[2]

For example, Merritt's Bakery reorganized reporting relationships and communication patterns when it moved bakery staff to a central production facility. With this organizational structure change, the company was able to specialize production jobs—for example, employees are now trained through different levels of decorating expertise. It was also able to increase efficiency through more standardized work and to improve supervisory control because bakery employees have common skill sets.

This chapter begins by introducing the two fundamental processes in organizational structure: division of labor and coordination. This is followed by a detailed investigation of the four main elements of organizational structure: span of control, centralization, formalization, and departmentalization. The latter part of this chapter examines the contingencies of organizational design, including external environment, organizational size, technology, and strategy.

Division of Labor and Coordination

LO1

All organizational structures include two fundamental requirements: the division of labor into distinct tasks and the coordination of that labor so that employees are able to accomplish common goals.[3] Organizations are groups of people who work interdependently toward some purpose. To efficiently accomplish their goals, these groups typically divide the work into manageable chunks, particularly when there are many different tasks to perform. They also introduce various coordinating mechanisms to ensure that everyone is working effectively toward the same objectives.

DIVISION OF LABOR

Division of labor refers to the subdivision of work into separate jobs assigned to different people. Subdivided work leads to job specialization, because each job now includes a narrow subset of the tasks necessary to complete the product or service. Merritt's Bakery organizes employees into a dozen or so specific jobs to effectively serve customers, bake cakes and pastries, and manage the restaurants. As companies get larger, horizontal division of labor is usually accompanied by a vertical division of labor: Some people are assigned the task of supervising employees, others are responsible for managing those supervisors, and so on.

Why do companies divide the work required to operate a bakery into several jobs? As we described earlier in this book, job specialization increases work efficiency.[4] Job incumbents can master their tasks quickly because work cycles are shorter. Less time is wasted changing from one task to another. Training costs are reduced because employees require fewer physical and mental skills to accomplish the assigned work. Finally, job

EXHIBIT 13.1   Coordinating Mechanisms in Organizations

FORM OF COORDINATION	DESCRIPTION	SUBTYPES/STRATEGIES
Informal communication	Sharing information on mutual tasks; forming common mental models to synchronize work activities	• Direct communication • Liaison roles • Integrator roles • Temporary teams
Formal hierarchy	Assigning legitimate power to individuals, who then use this power to direct work processes and allocate resources	• Direct supervision • Formal communication channels
Standardization	Creating routine patterns of behavior or output	• Standardized skills • Standardized processes • Standardized output

Sources: Based on information in J. Galbraith, *Designing Complex Organizations* (Reading, MA: Addison-Wesley, 1973), pp. 8–19; H. Mintzberg, *The Structuring of Organizations* (Englewood Cliffs, NJ: Prentice Hall, 1979), Ch. 1; D.A. Nadler and M.L. Tushman, *Competing by Design: The Power of Organizational Architecture* (New York: Oxford University Press, 1997), Ch. 6.

specialization makes it easier to match people with specific aptitudes or skills to the jobs for which they are best suited. Although one person working alone might be able to prepare, serve, and market food products at each Merritt's Bakery outlet, doing so would take much longer than having some people prepare the food, others serve it to customers, and still others take care of marketing, purchasing, accounting, and other functions. Some employees are talented at serving customers, whereas others are better at decorating wedding cakes.

COORDINATING WORK ACTIVITIES

When people divide work among themselves, they require coordinating mechanisms to ensure that everyone works in concert. Coordination is so closely connected to division of labor that the optimal level of specialization is limited by the feasibility of coordinating the work. In other words, an organization's ability to divide work among people depends on how well those people can coordinate with one another. Otherwise, individual effort is wasted due to misalignment, duplication, and mistiming of tasks. Coordination also tends to become more expensive and difficult as the division of labor increases. Therefore, companies specialize jobs only to the point where it is not too costly or challenging to coordinate the people in those jobs.[5]

Every organization—from the two-person corner convenience store to the largest corporate entity—uses one or more of the following coordinating mechanisms:[6] informal communication, formal hierarchy, and standardization (see Exhibit 13.1). These forms of coordination align the work of staff within the same department as well as across work units. These coordinating mechanisms are also critical when several organizations work together, such as in joint ventures and humanitarian aid programs.[7]

Coordination Through Informal Communication   All organizations rely on informal communication as a coordinating mechanism. This process includes sharing information on mutual tasks as well as forming common mental models so that employees synchronize work activities using the same mental road map.[8] Informal communication is vital in nonroutine and ambiguous situations because employees need to exchange a large volume of information through face-to-face communication and other media-rich channels.

Coordination through informal communication is easiest in small firms, though information technologies have further leveraged this coordinating mechanism in large

connect

To assist your learning and test your knowledge about coordinsting mechanisms, go to **www. mcgrawhillconnect.com,** which has activities and test questions on this and other organizational structure topics.

organizational structure
The division of labor as well as the patterns of coordination, communication, workflow, and formal power that direct organizational activities.

organizations.[9] Companies employing thousands of people also support informal communication by keeping each production site small. Magna International, the global auto parts manufacturer, keeps its plants to a maximum size of around 200 employees. Magna's leaders believe that employees have difficulty remembering one another's names in plants that are any larger, a situation that makes informal communication more difficult as a coordinating mechanism.[10]

Larger organizations also encourage coordination through informal communication by assigning *liaison roles* to employees, who are expected to communicate and share information with coworkers in other work units. Where coordination is required among several work units, companies create *integrator roles*. These people are responsible for coordinating a work process by encouraging employees in each work unit to share information and informally coordinate work activities. Integrators do not have authority over the people involved in that process, so they must rely on persuasion and commitment. Brand managers at Procter & Gamble have integrator roles because they coordinate work among marketing, production, and design groups.[11]

Another way that larger organizations encourage coordination through informal communication is by organizing employees from several departments into temporary teams. **Concurrent engineering** applies this coordinating strategy for the development of products or services. Concurrent engineering typically consists of a cross-functional project team of people from various functional departments, such as design engineering, manufacturing, marketing, and purchasing. By being assigned to a team, rather than working within their usual specialized departments, these employees have more authority and opportunity to coordinate using informal communication. When the design engineer begins to form the product specifications, representatives from manufacturing, engineering, marketing, purchasing, and other departments can offer feedback as well as begin their contribution to the process. By coordinating through information-rich informal communication, concurrent engineering teams tend to produce higher-quality products with dramatically less development time compared with situations in which employees work in their own departments and coordinate through other means.[12]

Coordination Through Formal Hierarchy   Informal communication is the most flexible form of coordination, but it can become chaotic as the number of employees increases. Consequently, as organizations grow, they rely increasingly on a second coordinating mechanism: formal hierarchy.[13] Hierarchy assigns legitimate power to individuals, who then use this power to direct work processes and allocate resources. In other words, work is coordinated through direct supervision—the chain of command. For instance, each Merritt's Bakery outlet has a manager and likely an assistant manager who is responsible for ensuring that employees perform their respective tasks as well as coordinate effectively with other staff on each work shift.

A century ago, management scholars applauded the formal hierarchy as the best coordinating mechanism for large organizations. They argued that organizations are most effective when managers exercise their authority and employees receive orders from only one supervisor. The chain of command—in which information flows across work units only through supervisors and managers—was viewed as the backbone of organizational strength.

Coordination Through
Micromanagement[14]

37%
of 524 American employees polled said they occasionally or frequently feel micromanaged by their boss.

25%
of 500 American employees said they work for a "micromanager."

17%
of 150 senior executives from the nation's 1,000 largest companies identified micromanaging as having the most negative impact on employee morale (third highest factor after lack of communication and recognition).

9%
of 11,045 American employees polled identified micromanagement as the most significant barrier to their productivity.

44%
of 434 human resource managers said younger employees complain that older managers micromanage them.

35%
of 434 human resource managers said older managers complain that younger employees lack respect for the organizational hierarchy.

Although still important, formal hierarchy is much less popular today. One concern is that it is not as agile for coordination in complex and novel situations. Communicating through the chain of command is rarely as fast or accurate as direct communication between employees. For instance, product development—typically a complex and novel activity—tends to occur more quickly and produce higher-quality results when people coordinate mainly through informal communication rather than formal hierarchy. Another concern with formal hierarchy is that managers are able to closely supervise only a limited number of employees. As the business grows, the number of supervisors and layers of management must increase, resulting in a costly bureaucracy. Finally, today's workforce demands more autonomy over work and more involvement in company decisions. Formal hierarchy coordination processes tend to conflict with employee autonomy and involvement.

Coordination Through Standardization   Standardization, the third means of coordination, involves creating routine patterns of behavior or output. This coordinating mechanism takes three distinct forms:

- *Standardized processes.* Quality and consistency of a product or service can often be improved by standardizing work activities through job descriptions and procedures.[15] Merritt's Bakery uses flowcharts that standardize work processes for many of its work activities. This coordinating mechanism is feasible when the work is routine (such as mass production) or simple (such as making cupcakes), but it is less effective in nonroutine and complex work such as product design.

- *Standardized outputs.* This form of standardization involves ensuring that individuals and work units have clearly defined goals and output measures (e.g., customer satisfaction, production efficiency). For instance, to coordinate the work of salespeople, companies assign sales targets rather than specific behaviors.

- *Standardized skills.* When work activities are too complex to standardize through processes or goals, companies often coordinate work effort by extensively training employees or hiring people who have learned precise role behaviors from educational programs. Merritt's Bakery relies on this coordinating mechanism to some extent. It trains production staff so cakes and pastries are produced to a high quality. It also trains store staff so customer interactions are consistent and professional. Training is particularly critical as a coordinating mechanism in hospital operating rooms. Surgeons, nurses, and other operating room professionals coordinate their work more through training than through goals or company rules.

Division of labor and coordination of work represent the two fundamental ingredients of all organizations. But how work is divided, which coordinating mechanisms are emphasized, who makes decisions, and other issues are related to the four elements of organizational structure.

Elements of Organizational Structure

Organizational structure has four elements that apply to every organization. This section introduces three of them: span of control, centralization, and formalization. The fourth element—departmentalization—is presented in the next section.

concurrent engineering
The organization of employees from several departments into a temporary team for the purpose of developing a product or service.

span of control
The number of people directly reporting to the next level in the hierarchy.

SPAN OF CONTROL

Span of control (also called *span of management*) refers to the number of people directly reporting to the next level in the hierarchy. A narrow span of control exists when very few people report directly to a manager, whereas a wide span exists when a manager has many direct reports.[16] A century ago, French engineer and management scholar Henri Fayol strongly recommended a relatively narrow span of control, typically no more than 20 employees per supervisor and 6 supervisors per manager. Fayol championed formal hierarchy as the primary coordinating mechanism, so he believed that supervisors should closely monitor and coach employees. His views were similar to those of Napoleon, who declared that 5 reporting officers is the maximum span of control for more senior leaders. These prescriptions were based on the belief that managers simply could not monitor and control any more subordinates closely enough.[17]

Today, we know better. The best-performing manufacturing plants currently have an average of 38 production employees per supervisor (see Exhibit 13.2).[18] What's the secret here? Did Fayol, Napoleon, and others miscalculate the optimal span of control? The answer is that those sympathetic to hierarchical control believed that employees should perform the physical tasks, whereas supervisors and other management personnel should make the decisions and monitor employees to make sure they performed their tasks. In contrast, the best-performing manufacturing operations today rely on self-directed teams, so direct supervision (formal hierarchy) is supplemented with other coordinating mechanisms. Self-directed teams coordinate mainly through informal communication and various forms of standardization (i.e., training and processes), so formal hierarchy plays more of a supporting role.

Many firms that employ doctors, lawyers, and other professionals also have a wider span of control because these staff members coordinate their work mainly through standardized skills. For example, more than two dozen people report directly to Cindy Zollinger, cofounder and president of the Boston-based litigation-consulting firm Cornerstone Research. Zollinger explains that this large number of direct reports is possible because she leads professional staff who don't require close supervision. "They largely run themselves," Zollinger explains. "I help them in dealing with obstacles they face, or in making the most of opportunities that they find."[19]

A second factor influencing the best span of control is whether employees perform routine tasks. A wider span of control is possible when employees perform routine jobs, because there is less frequent need for direction or advice from supervisors. A narrow span of control is necessary when employees perform novel or complex tasks, because these employees tend to require more supervisory decisions and coaching. This principle is

Which organizational structure do you prefer? Go to **www.mcgrawhillconnect.com** to estimate your preference for structures with a tall span of control, centralization, and formalization, as well as to assist your learning about these topics.

EXHIBIT 13.2

Recommended, Actual, and Enforced Spans of Control[20]

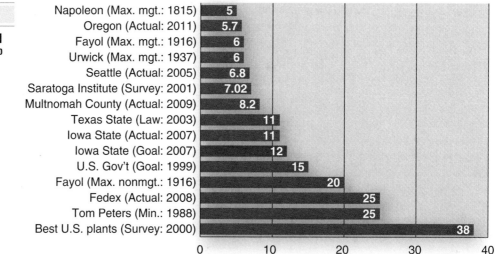

Figures represent the average number of direct reports per manager. "Max." figures represent the maximum spans of control recommended by Napoleon Bonaparte, Henri Fayol, and Lindall Urwick. "Min." figure represents the minimum span of control recommended by Tom Peters. "Goal" figures represent span of control targets that the U.S. government and the State of Iowa have tried to achieve. The State of Texas figure represents the span of control mandated by law. The Saratoga Institute figure is the average span of control among U.S. companies surveyed. The Best U.S. Plants figure is the average span of control in U.S. manufacturing facilities identified by *Industry Week* magazine as the most effective. "Actual" figures are spans of control in the city of Seattle, State of Oregon, Multnomah County (including Portland, Oregon), State of Iowa, and Fedex Corporation in the years indicated.

illustrated in a survey of property and casualty insurers. The average span of control in commercial policy processing departments is around 15 employees per supervisor, whereas the span of control is 6.1 in claims service and 5.5 in commercial underwriting. Staff members in the latter two departments perform more technical work, so they have more novel and complex tasks, which requires more supervisor involvement. Commercial policy processing is like production work. Tasks are routine and have few exceptions, so managers have less coordinating to do with each employee.[21]

A third influence on span of control is the degree of interdependence among employees within the department or team.[22] Generally, a narrow span of control is necessary when employees perform highly interdependent work with others. More supervision is required for highly interdependent jobs because employees tend to experience more conflict, which requires more of a manager's time to resolve. Also, employees are less clear on their personal work performance in highly interdependent tasks, so supervisors spend more time providing coaching and feedback.

Tall Versus Flat Structures   Span of control is interconnected with organizational size (number of employees) and the number of layers in the organizational hierarchy. Consider two companies with the same number of employees. If Company A has a wider span of control (more direct reports per manager) than Company B, then Company A necessarily has fewer layers of management (i.e., a flatter structure). The reason for this relationship is that a company with a wider span of control has more employees per supervisor, more supervisors for each middle manager, and so on. This larger number of direct reports, compared with a company with a narrower span of control, is possible only by removing layers of management.

The interconnection of span of control, organizational size (number of employees), and number of management layers has important implications for companies. As organizations employ more people, they must widen the span of control, build a taller hierarchy, or both. Most companies end up building taller structures, because they rely on direct supervision to some extent as a coordinating mechanism and there are limits to how many people each manager can coordinate.

Unfortunately, building a taller hierarchy (more layers of management) creates problems. One concern is that taller structures have higher overhead costs because they have more managers per employee. This means there are more people administering the company and fewer actually making the product or supplying the service. A second problem is that senior managers in tall structures tend to receive lower-quality and less timely information. People tend to filter, distort, and simplify information before it is passed to higher levels in the hierarchy, because they are motivated to frame the information in a positive light or to summarize it more efficiently. In contrast, information receives less manipulation in flat hierarchies and is often received much more quickly than in tall hierarchies. A third issue with tall hierarchies is that they tend to undermine employee empowerment and engagement. Hierarchies are power structures, so more levels of hierarchy tend to reduce the power distributed to people at the bottom of that hierarchy. Indeed, the size of the hierarchy itself tends to focus power around managers rather than employees.[23]

KenGen, Kenya's leading electricity generation company, had more than 15 layers of hierarchy a few years ago. Today, the company's 1,500 employees are organized in a hierarchy with only 6 layers: the chief executive, executive directors, senior managers, chief officers, frontline management, and nonmanagement staff. "This flatter structure has reduced bureaucracy and it has also improved teamwork," explains KenGen executive Simon Ngure.[24]

Debating Point
SHOULD ORGANIZATIONS CUT BACK MIDDLE MANAGEMENT?

Business leaders face the ongoing challenge of preventing their organization from ballooning into a fat bureaucracy with too many layers of middle managers. Indeed, it has become a mantra for incoming CEOs to state gallantly they will "delayer" or "flatten" the corporate hierarchy, usually as part of a larger mandate to "empower" the workforce.

As we describe in this chapter, there are several valid arguments for minimizing the corporate hierarchy, particularly by cutting back middle management. As companies employ more managers, they increase overhead costs and have a lower percentage of people actually generating revenue by making products or providing services. A taller hierarchy also undermines effective communication between frontline staff—who receive valuable knowledge about the external environment—and the top executive team. Middle managers have a tendency to distort, simplify, and filter information as it passes from them to higher authorities in the company. A third reason for cutting back middle management is that managers absorb organizational power. As companies add more layers, they remove more power that might have been assigned directly to frontline employees. In other words, tall hierarchies potentially undermine employee empowerment.

These concerns seem logical, but slashing the hierarchy can have several unexpected consequences that outweigh any benefits. In fact, a growing chorus of management experts warn about several negative long-term consequences of cutting out too much middle management.[25]

Critics of delayering point out that all companies need managers to translate corporate strategy into coherent daily operations.

"Middle managers are the link between your mission and execution," advises a senior hospital executive. "They turn our strategy into action and get everyone on the same page."[26] Furthermore, managers are needed to make quick decisions, coach employees, and help resolve conflicts. These valuable functions are underserved when the span of control becomes too wide.

Delayering increases the number of direct reports per manager and thus significantly increases management workload and corresponding levels of stress. Managers partly reduce the workload by learning to give subordinates more autonomy rather than micromanaging them. However, this role adjustment itself is stressful (same responsibility, less authority or control). Companies often increase the span of control beyond the point at which many managers are capable of coaching or leading their direct reports.

A third concern is that delayering results in fewer managerial jobs, so companies have less maneuverability to develop managerial skills. Promotions are also riskier because they involve a larger jump in responsibility in flatter, compared with taller, hierarchies. Furthermore, having fewer promotion opportunities means that managers experience more career plateauing, which reduces their motivation and loyalty. Chopping back managerial career structures also sends a signal that managers are no longer valued. "Delayering has had an adverse effect on morale, productivity and performance," argues a senior government executive. "Disenfranchising middle management creates negative perceptions and lower commitment to the organization with consequent reluctance to accept responsibility."[27]

These problems have prompted leaders to "delayer"—remove one or more levels in the organizational hierarchy.[28] For instance, Chrysler Corp. CEO Sergio Marchionne recently warned that the automaker needs to have a flatter corporate structure to improve innovation, responsiveness, and customer service. "We need to be able to respond quickly, whether it's to customer complaints or consumer needs. Any new idea condemned to struggle upward through multiple levels of rigidly hierarchical, risk averse management is an idea that won't see daylight until dusk—until it's too late." BASF's European Seal Sands plant came to the same conclusion several years ago; it was dramatically restructured around self-directed teams, cutting the hierarchy from seven to just two layers of management.[29]

CENTRALIZATION AND DECENTRALIZATION

For many years, Barrick Gold Corporation concentrated decision making at its global headquarters even though it was becoming the world's largest gold producer with far-flung operations around the world. "Barrick had always been run on this command-and-control model, a centrist approach that saw all the decision making made in Toronto," says Barrick's late CEO Greg Wilkins. "That worked while the company was small and operating only in North America. But all of a sudden we are in four continents and seven countries and it becomes pretty clear that you just can't do it any more." The solution that Wilkins and his

Samsonite, the Massachusetts-based luggage company, recently abandoned its centralized organizational structure by delegating more power to country managers. The reason? "We've learned that all of our customers are more different than similar," explains Samsonite chief financial officer Kyle Gendreau. Rather than follow global marketing and distribution practices dictated by head office, country managers are now "empowered" to apply practices that best serve their local markets. "Letting people be entrepreneurial on the ground drives growth," says Gendreau. "It's really paying off for us."[30]

senior leadership team implemented was a more decentralized structure in which Barrick's four regional business units are now responsible for their own operations and business growth. Headquarters provides the strategic guidance and oversight.[31]

This Barrick Gold story illustrates that a key decision in designing organizations is how much to centralize or decentralize decision-making power. **Centralization** means that formal decision-making authority is held by a small group of people, typically those at the top of the organizational hierarchy. Most organizations begin with centralized structures, as the founder makes most of the decisions and tries to direct the business toward his or her vision. As organizations grow, however, they diversify and their environments become more complex. Senior executives aren't able to process all the decisions that significantly influence the business. Consequently, larger organizations typically *decentralize*; that is, they disperse decision authority and power throughout the organization.

The optimal level of centralization or decentralization depends on several contingencies that we will examine later in this chapter. However, we also need to keep in mind that different degrees of decentralization can occur simultaneously in different parts of an organization. Nestlé, the Swiss-based food company, has decentralized marketing decisions to remain responsive to local markets, but it has centralized production, logistics, and supply chain management activities to improve cost efficiencies and avoid having too much complexity across the organization. "If you are too decentralized, you can become too complicated—you get too much complexity in your production system," explains a Nestlé executive.[32] On a much smaller scale, Merritt's Bakery in Tulsa, Oklahoma (see opening story), centralized bakery production yet has more decentralized restaurant operations.

Likewise, 7-Eleven relies on both centralization and decentralization in different parts of the organization. The convenience store chain leverages buying power and efficiencies by centralizing decisions about information technology and supplier purchasing. At the same time, it decentralizes local inventory decisions to store managers so that they can adapt quickly to changing circumstances at the local level. Along with receiving ongoing product training and guidance from regional consultants, store managers have the best information about their customers and can respond quickly to local market needs. "We could never predict a busload of football players on a Friday night, but the store manager can," explains a 7-Eleven executive.[33]

centralization
The degree to which formal decision authority is held by a small group of people, typically those at the top of the organizational hierarchy.

FORMALIZATION

Formalization is the degree to which organizations standardize behavior through rules, procedures, formal training, and related mechanisms.[34] In other words, companies become more formalized as they increasingly rely on various forms of standardization to coordinate work. The opening story to this chapter described how Christian Merritt has introduced some formalization through workflow charts that guide employees through the steps for various work activities. McDonald's Restaurants and most other efficient fast-food chains typically have a high degree of formalization because they rely on standardization of work processes as a coordinating mechanism. Employees have precisely defined roles, right down to how much mustard should be dispensed, how many pickles should be applied, and how long each hamburger should be cooked.

Older companies tend to become more formalized because work activities become routinized, making them easier to document into standardized practices. Larger companies also tend to have more formalization because direct supervision and informal communication among employees do not operate as easily when large numbers of people are involved. External influences, such as government safety legislation and strict accounting rules, also encourage formalization.

Formalization may increase efficiency and compliance, but it can also create problems.[35] Rules and procedures reduce organizational flexibility, so employees follow prescribed behaviors even when the situation clearly calls for a customized response. High levels of formalization tend to undermine organizational learning and creativity. Some work rules become so convoluted that organizational efficiency would decline if they were actually followed as prescribed. Formalization is also a source of job dissatisfaction and work stress. Finally, rules and procedures have been known to take on a life of their own in some organizations. They become the focus of attention, rather than the organization's ultimate objectives of producing a product or service and serving its dominant stakeholders.

MECHANISTIC VERSUS ORGANIC STRUCTURES

We discussed span of control, centralization, and formalization together because they cluster around two broader organizational forms: mechanistic and organic structures (see Exhibit 13.3).[36] A **mechanistic structure** is characterized by a narrow span of control and high degree of formalization and centralization. Mechanistic structures have many rules and procedures, limited decision making at lower levels, tall hierarchies of people in specialized roles, and vertical rather than horizontal communication flows. Tasks are rigidly defined and are altered only when sanctioned by higher authorities.

Companies with an **organic structure** have the opposite characteristics. They operate with a wide span of control, decentralized decision making, and little formalization. Tasks are fluid, adjusting to new situations and organizational needs. Connections 13.1 illustrates how TAXI, a top-ranked creative agency, relies on an organic structure to remain nimble.

As a general rule, mechanistic structures operate better in stable environments because they rely on efficiency and routine behaviors, whereas organic structures work better in rapidly

EXHIBIT 13.3

Contrasting Mechanistic and Organic Organizational Structures

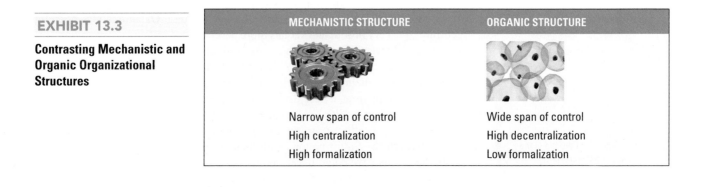

MECHANISTIC STRUCTURE	ORGANIC STRUCTURE
Narrow span of control	Wide span of control
High centralization	High decentralization
High formalization	Low formalization

connections 13.1

Growing an Organic TAXI

With more than 1,200 awards, including recent honors as Canada's creative agency of the decade, TAXI is a company like no other. The agency dreamed up the cute critters in Telus ads and the smiling man skipping to work in Pfizer's famous Viagra ad. Other creative agencies either burn out or become rigid hierarchies over time. TAXI, in contrast, has continued to amaze the world with its creative flair over the past two decades while it also expanded to 350 employees in several offices across Canada, the United States, and the Netherlands.

How has TAXI maintained this momentum? Leadership and talent are key factors, but perhaps equally important is the company's fanatical reliance on an organic organizational structure. This organic structure assigns each client or project to "a nimble, autonomous team that is both empowered and responsible for results," says TAXI's website. The company claims the TAXI name reflects this small-team mandate: "We believe a small team of experts should drive every piece of the business—as many as can fit into a cab."

TAXI's organic structure also accommodates growth. As the company expanded, it deliberately avoided creating work centers that had more than 150 staff members. "Ancient nomadic tribes observed that a population exceeding 150 people had a tendency to form factions, erode group harmony and render it dysfunctional," claims TAXI. Consequently, as the company has duplicated itself across several cities, each office has maintained an organic structure that actively collaborates with other offices. Even when the Toronto business outgrew its optimal size, TAXI opened a second location, called TAXI 2, within the same city.

TAXI's organic organizational structure contrasts with the rigid departmentalization found in many other creative agencies.

TAXI, Canada's agency of the decade, relies on an organic structure of small flexible teams, as well as limited-size work centers.

"[Other advertising firms] operated on a 19th-century model of many secular departments trying to integrate everything ad hoc. Most cultures were so layered that a great idea was easily crushed," explains TAXI cofounder Paul Lavoie (right in photo). "We needed a flexible infrastructure, able to move with the pace of change. TAXI started lean and nimble, and remains so today."[37]

changing (i.e., dynamic) environments because they are more flexible and responsive to changes. Organic structures are also more compatible with organizational learning, high-performance workplaces, and quality management, because they emphasize information sharing and an empowered workforce rather than hierarchy and status.[38] However, organic structures tend to be better than mechanistic structures in dynamic environments only when employees have developed well-established roles and expertise.[39] Without these conditions, employees are unable to coordinate effectively with one another, resulting in errors and gross inefficiencies.

Start-up companies often face this problem known as the *liability of newness*. Newness makes start-up firms more organic—they tend to have few rules and considerable delegation of authority. However, employees in new organizations often lack industry experience, and their teams have not developed sufficiently for peak performance. As a result, the organic structures of new companies cannot compensate for the poorer coordination and significantly lower efficiencies caused by the lack of structure from past experience and team mental models. Fortunately, companies can minimize the liability of newness by launching businesses with existing teams of people or with industry veterans guiding the novices.

formalization
The degree to which organizations standardize behavior through rules, procedures, formal training, and related mechanisms.

mechanistic structure
An organizational structure with a narrow span of control and a high degree of formalization and centralization.

organic structure
An organizational structure with a wide span of control, little formalization, and decentralized decision making.

Forms of Departmentalization

LO3

Span of control, centralization, and formalization are important elements of organizational structure, but most people think about organizational charts when the discussion of organizational structure arises. The organizational chart represents the fourth element in the structuring of organizations, called *departmentalization*. Departmentalization specifies how employees and their activities are grouped together. It is a fundamental strategy for coordinating organizational activities, because it influences organizational behavior in the following ways:[40]

- Departmentalization establishes the chain of command—the system of common supervision among positions and units within the organization. It frames the membership of formal work teams and typically determines which positions and units must share resources. Thus, departmentalization establishes interdependencies among employees and subunits.

- Departmentalization focuses people around common mental models or ways of thinking, such as serving clients, developing products, or supporting a particular skill set. This focus is typically anchored around the common budgets and measures of performance assigned to employees within each departmental unit.

- Departmentalization encourages specific people and work units to coordinate through informal communication. With common supervision and resources, members within each configuration typically work near one another, so they can use frequent and informal interaction to get the work done.

connect

To assist your learning and test your knowledge about the different forms of departmentalization, go to **www.mcgrawhillconnect.com,** which has activities and test questions on this topic.

There are almost as many organizational charts as there are businesses, but the six most common pure types of departmentalization are simple, functional, divisional, team-based, matrix, and network.

SIMPLE STRUCTURE

Most companies, including Merritt's Bakery, begin with a *simple structure*.[41] They employ only a few people and typically offer only one distinct product or service. There is minimal hierarchy—usually just employees reporting to the owners. Employees perform broadly defined roles because there are insufficient economies of scale to assign them to specialized jobs. The simple structure is highly flexible and minimizes the walls that form between employees in other structures. However, the simple structure usually depends on the owner's direct supervision to coordinate work activities, so it is very difficult to operate as the company grows and becomes more complex.

FUNCTIONAL STRUCTURE

Growing organizations usually introduce a functional structure at some level of the hierarchy or at some time in their history. A **functional structure** organizes employees around specific knowledge or other resources (see Exhibit 13.4). Employees with marketing expertise are grouped into a marketing unit, those with production skills are located in manufacturing, engineers are found in product development, and so on. Organizations with functional structures are typically centralized to coordinate their activities effectively.

functional structure
An organizational structure in which employees are organized around specific knowledge or other resources.

divisional structure
An organizational structure in which employees are organized around geographic areas, outputs (products or services), or clients.

Evaluating the Functional Structure   The functional structure creates specialized pools of talent that typically serve everyone in the organization. This provides more economies of scale than are possible if functional specialists are spread over different parts of the organization. It increases employee identity with the specialization or profession. Direct supervision is easier

EXHIBIT 13.4

A Functional Organizational Structure

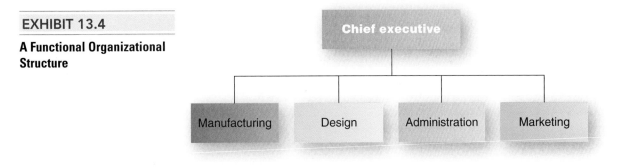

in functional structures because managers oversee people with common issues and expertise.[42]

The functional structure also has limitations.[43] Grouping employees around their skills tends to focus attention on those skills and related professional needs rather than on the company's product, service, or client needs. Unless people are transferred from one function to the next, they might not develop a broader understanding of the business. Compared with other structures, the functional structure usually produces higher dysfunctional conflict and poorer coordination in serving clients or developing products. These problems occur because employees need to work with coworkers in other departments to complete organizational tasks, yet they have different subgoals and mental models of ideal work. Together, these problems require substantial formal controls and coordination when people are organized around functions.

DIVISIONAL STRUCTURE

The **divisional structure** (sometimes called the *multidivisional* or *M-form* structure) groups employees around geographic areas, outputs (products or services), or clients. Exhibit 13.5 illustrates these three variations of divisional structure. The *geographic divisional structure* organizes employees around distinct regions of the country or world. Exhibit 13.5(*a*) illustrates a geographic divisional structure recently adopted by Barrick Gold Corporation, the world's largest gold-mining company. The *product/service divisional structure* organizes employees around distinct outputs. Exhibit 13.5(*b*) illustrates a simplified version of this type of structure at Philips. The Dutch electronics company divides its workforce mainly into three divisions: health care products, lighting products, and consumer products. (Philips also has a fourth organizational group consisting of the research and design functions.) The *client divisional structure* organizes employees around specific customer groups. Exhibit 13.5(*c*) illustrates a customer-focused divisional structure similar to one adopted by the U.S. Internal Revenue Service.[44]

Toyota Motor Company received scathing criticism for its ineffective handling of sticky gas pedals and other safety problems. A special panel of independent experts commissioned by Toyota concluded that the automaker's centralized functional organizational structure was partly to blame. Toyota was mainly organized around functional units (sales, engineering, manufacturing) that reported directly to headquarters in Japan. The panel concluded that this structure hindered information sharing, increased miscommunication, and "delayed response time to quality and safety issues." Toyota CEO Akio Toyoda agreed that this functional structure should be replaced with a geographic divisionalized structure. "Dealing with our overseas operations on a regional basis, rather than a functional basis, will enable us to conduct decision making on a more comprehensive basis," he asserted.[45]

EXHIBIT 13.5   Three Types of Divisional Structure

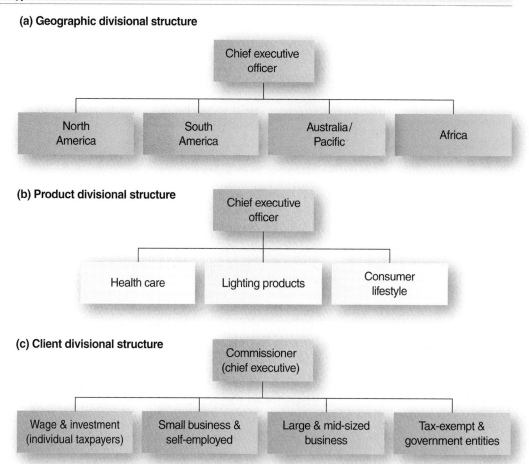

(a) Geographic divisional structure

Chief executive officer

North America | South America | Australia/Pacific | Africa

(b) Product divisional structure

Chief executive officer

Health care | Lighting products | Consumer lifestyle

(c) Client divisional structure

Commissioner (chief executive)

Wage & investment (individual taxpayers) | Small business & self-employed | Large & mid-sized business | Tax-exempt & government entities

Note: Diagram (a) shows a global geographic divisional structure similar to Barrick Gold Corp.; diagram (b) is similar to the product divisions at Philips; and diagram (c) is similar to the customer-focused structure at the U.S. Internal Revenue Service.

Which form of divisional structure should large organizations adopt? The answer depends mainly on the primary source of environmental diversity or uncertainty.[46] Suppose an organization has one type of product sold to people across the country. If customers have different needs across regions, or if state governments impose different regulations on the product, then a geographic structure would be best to be more vigilant of this diversity. On the other hand, if the company sells several types of products across the country and customer preferences and government regulations are similar everywhere, then a product structure would likely work best.

Coca-Cola, Nestlé, and many other food and beverage companies are organized mainly around geographic regions, because consumer tastes and preferred marketing strategies vary considerably around the world. Even though McDonald's makes the same Big Mac throughout the world, the company has more fish products in Hong Kong and more vegetarian products in India, in line with traditional diets in those countries. Philips, on the other hand, is organized around products because consumer preferences around the world are similar within each product group. Hospitals from Geneva, Switzerland, to Santiago, Chile, buy similar medical equipment from Philips, whereas the manufacturing and marketing of these products are quite different from those in Philips's consumer electronics business.

Many companies are moving away from structures that organize people around geographic clusters.[47] One reason is that clients can purchase products online and communicate with businesses almost anywhere in the world, so local representation is becoming less critical. Reduced geographic variation is another reason for the shift away from geographic structures; freer trade has reduced government intervention, and consumer preferences for many products and services are becoming more similar (converging) around the world. The third reason is that large companies increasingly have global business customers who demand one global point of purchase, not one in every country or region.

The Globally Integrated Enterprise   The shift away from geographic and toward product- or client-based divisional structures reflects the trend toward the **globally integrated enterprise.**[48] As the label implies, a globally integrated enterprise connects work processes around the world, rather than replicating them within each country or region. This type of organization typically organizes people around product or client divisions. Even functional units—production, marketing, design, human resources, and so on—serve the company worldwide rather than within specific geographic clusters. These functions are sensitive to cultural and market differences and have local representation to support that sensitivity, but local representatives are associates of a global function rather than a local subsidiary copied across several regions. Indeed, a globally integrated enterprise is marked by a dramatic increase in virtual teamwork, because employees are assigned global projects and ongoing responsibilities for work units that transcend geographic boundaries.

The globally integrated enterprise no longer orchestrates its business from a single headquarters in one "home" country. Instead, its divisional and functional operations are led from where the work is concentrated, and this concentration depends on economics (cost of labor, infrastructure, etc.), expertise, and openness (trade, capital flow, knowledge sharing, etc.). For example, IBM has moved toward the globally integrated enterprise structure by locating its global data centers in Colorado, website management in Ireland, back-office finance in Brazil, software in India, and procurement in China. IBM's vice president of worldwide engineering, responsible for procurement, moved from Armonk, New York, to China, where the procurement center is located. "These people are not leading teams focused on China or India or Brazil or Ireland—or Colorado or Vermont," says IBM CEO Sam Palmisano. "They are leading integrated global operations."[49]

Evaluating the Divisional Structure   The divisional organizational structure is a building block structure; it accommodates growth relatively easily and focuses employee attention on products or customers rather than tasks. Different products, services, or clients can be accommodated by sprouting new divisions. These advantages are offset by a number of limitations. First, the divisional structure tends to duplicate resources, such as production equipment and engineering or information technology expertise. Also, unless the division is quite large, resources are not used as efficiently as they are in functional structures where resources are pooled across the entire organization. The divisional structure also creates silos of knowledge. Expertise is spread across several autonomous business units, which reduces the ability and perhaps motivation of the people in one division to share their knowledge with counterparts in other divisions. In contrast, a functional structure groups experts together, thereby supporting knowledge sharing.

Finally, the preferred divisional structure depends on the company's primary source of environmental diversity or uncertainty. This principle seems to be applied easily enough at Coca-Cola, McDonald's, and Philips, but many global organizations experience diversity and uncertainty in terms of geography, product, *and* clients. Consequently, some organizations revise their structures back and forth or create complex structures that attempt to give all three dimensions equal status. This waffling and complexity generates further complications, because organizational structure decisions shift power and status among executives. If the company

globally integrated enterprise
An organizational structure in which work processes and executive functions are distributed around the world through global centers, rather than developed in a home country and replicated in satellite countries or regions.

switches from a geographic to product structure, people who lead the geographic fiefdoms suddenly get demoted under the product chiefs. In short, leaders of global organizations struggle to find the best divisional structure, often resulting in the departure of some executives and frustration among those who remain.

TEAM-BASED STRUCTURE

A **team-based organizational structure** is built around self-directed teams that complete an entire piece of work, such as manufacturing a product or developing an electronic game. This type of structure is usually organic. There is a wide span of control because teams operate with minimal supervision. In extreme situations, there is no formal leader, just someone selected by other team members to help coordinate the work and liaise with top management. Team structures are highly decentralized, because almost all day-to-day decisions are made by team members rather than someone further up the organizational hierarchy. Finally, many team-based structures have low formalization because teams are given relatively few rules about how to organize their work. Instead, executives assign quality and quantity output targets and often productivity improvement goals to each team. Teams are then encouraged to use available resources and their own initiative to achieve those objectives.

Team-based structures are usually found within the manufacturing or service operations of larger divisional structures. For example, several GE Aircraft Engines plants are organized as team-based structures, but these plants operate within GE's larger divisional structure. However, a small number of firms apply the team-based structure from top to bottom, including W. L. Gore & Associates and Semco SA, where almost all associates work in teams.

Evaluating the Team-Based Structure
The team-based structure has gained popularity because it tends to be flexible and responsive in turbulent environments.[50] It tends to reduce costs because teams have less reliance on a formal hierarchy (direct supervision). A cross-functional team structure improves communication and cooperation

W. L. Gore & Associates employs 7,000 people, but no managers. That's because the Newark, Delaware–based manufacturer of fabrics (Gore-Tex®), electronics, industrial, and medical products has adopted an organizational structure where most employees (called "associates") are organized around self-directed teams. Day-to-day decisions are decentralized to these teams, which are formed around idea champions and plenty of shared leadership. "Your team is your boss, because you don't want to let them down," says Diane Davidson, who works in Gore's fashion products group. "Everyone's your boss, and no one's your boss."[51]

across traditional boundaries. With greater autonomy, this structure also allows quicker and more informed decision making.[52] For this reason, some hospitals have shifted from functional departments to cross-functional teams. Teams composed of nurses, radiologists, anesthetists, a pharmacology representative, possibly social workers, a rehabilitation therapist, and other specialists communicate and coordinate more efficiently, thereby reducing delays and errors.[53]

Against these benefits, the team-based structure can be costly to maintain due to the need for ongoing interpersonal skill training. Teamwork potentially takes more time to coordinate than a formal hierarchy during the early stages of team development. Employees may experience more stress due to increased ambiguity in their roles. Team leaders also experience more stress due to increased conflict, loss of functional power, and unclear career progression ladders. In addition, team structures suffer from duplication of resources and potential competition (and lack of resource sharing) across teams.[54]

MATRIX STRUCTURE

When physicians Ray Muzyka and Greg Zeschuk and a third partner (who later returned to medical practice) founded BioWare ULC, they initially organized employees at the electronic games company into a simple structure in which everyone worked together on the first game, *Shattered Steel*. Soon after, Muzyka and Zeschuk decided to create a second game (*Baldur's Gate*), but they weren't sure what organizational structure would be best. Simply creating a second team might duplicate resources, undermine information sharing across teams, and weaken employee loyalty to the overall company. Alternatively, the game developer could adopt a functional structure by assigning employees to specialized departments such as art, programming, audio, quality assurance, and design. A functional structure would encourage employees within each specialization to share information, but it might undermine team dynamics on game projects and reduce employee commitment to the game they were developing.[55]

After carefully weighing the various organizational structure options, Muzyka and Zeschuk adopted a **matrix structure** to gain the benefits of both a functional structure and a project-based (team) structure. BioWare's matrix structure, which is similar to the diagram in Exhibit 13.6, is organized around both functions (art, audio, programming, etc.) and team-based game development projects. Employees are assigned to a cross-functional team responsible for a specific game project, yet they also belong to a permanent functional unit from which they are reassigned when their work is completed on a particular project.[56]

Muzyka and Zeschuk say the matrix structure focuses employees on the final product yet keeps them organized around their expertise to encourage knowledge sharing. "The matrix structure also supports our overall company culture where BioWare is the team, and everyone is always willing to help each other whether they are on the same project or not," they add. BioWare's matrix structure was a good choice, particularly as the company (which recently became an independent division of Electronic Arts) has grown to almost 800 employees working on numerous game projects at four centers around the United States and Canada.

BioWare's structure, in which project teams overlap with functional departments, is just one form of matrix structure. Another variation, found mainly in large global firms, has geographic divisions on one axis and products/services or client divisions on the other. Nestlé, Procter & Gamble, Shell, and many other global organizations have variations of a matrix structure that attempt to balance geography with products/services.

For instance, Nestlé Waters, a product division of Nestlé S.A., markets several brands of bottled water in more than three dozen countries. The brands vary from one country to the next; for example, Poland Springs is

team-based organizational structure
An organizational structure built around self-directed teams that complete an entire piece of work.

matrix structure
An organizational structure that overlays two structures (such as a geographic divisional and a functional structure) in order to leverage the benefits of both.

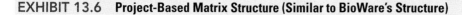

EXHIBIT 13.6   Project-Based Matrix Structure (Similar to BioWare's Structure)

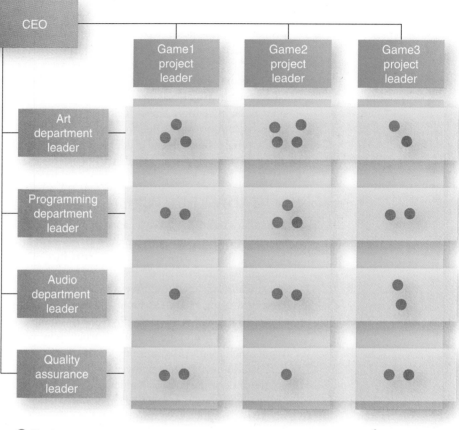

● Employee

unique to the United States (originating in Maine), and Santa Maria is unique to Mexico. The manager responsible for Nestlé's bottled water brands in Mexico, for instance, would report to both Nestlé's top country manager and the top Nestlé Waters executive at the company's headquarters in Switzerland. Similarly, the manager responsible for baby foods in Singapore would report to the country manager as well as to the headquarters executive responsible for that product group.[57]

A common error is the belief that everyone in a matrix organizational structure reports to two bosses. This two-boss situation exists for most employees in project-based matrix structures such as at BioWare, but not in global matrix structures such as at Nestlé. In multinational companies with matrix structures, only employees at one level in the organization (typically country-specific brand managers) report to two bosses. For example, the manager responsible for Nestlé's bottled water brands in Mexico would have two bosses: Nestlé's Mexican country manager and the world headquarters executive responsible for Nestlé Waters. In contrast, sales and marketing employees further down the hierarchy report only to a Mexican manager.

Evaluating the Matrix Structure   The matrix structure usually makes very good use of resources and expertise, making it ideal for project-based organizations with fluctuating workloads. When properly managed, it improves communication efficiency, project flexibility, and innovation, compared with purely functional or divisional designs. It focuses employees on serving clients or creating products yet keeps people organized around their specialization, so knowledge sharing improves and resources are used more efficiently. The

connections 13.2

Losing Data in the Matrix

Soon after Britain's Inland Revenue and Customs/Excise departments merged to become HM Revenue & Customs (HMRC), the combined department experienced a series of errors that violated individual privacy rights. The most serious of these incidents occurred when HMRC staff somehow lost two computer discs containing confidential details of 25 million child welfare claimants.

The UK government's investigation into the security lapse concluded that along with resulting from poor security procedures, the error was partly due to "muddled accountabilities" created by the matrix organizational structure under which the new department operated. The investigator's initial briefing stated that the matrix structure and numerous departments made it "difficult to relate roles and responsibilities amongst senior management to accountability." In fact, responsibility for data security was assigned to no less than five departments, each of which reported to different director generals.

The final report concluded that "[HMRC] is not suited to the so-called 'constructive friction' matrix type organization [that was] in place at the time of the data loss." HMRC has since changed to a more traditional, single-command organizational structure.[58]

Britain's Inland Revenue and Customs suffered from "muddled accountabilities" due to its matrix organizational structure.

---

matrix structure is also a logical choice when, as in the case of Nestlé, two different dimensions (regions and products) are equally important. Structures determine executive power and what is important; the matrix structure works when two different dimensions deserve equal attention.

In spite of these advantages, the matrix structure has several well-known problems.[59] One concern is that it increases conflict among managers who equally share power. Employees working at the matrix level have two bosses and, consequently, two sets of priorities that aren't always aligned. Project leaders might squabble with functional leaders regarding the assignment of specific employees to projects, as well as regarding the employee's technical competence. For example, Citigroup, Inc., recently adopted a geographic-product matrix structure and apparently is already experiencing dysfunctional conflict between the regional and product group executives.[60] Aware of these potential conflicts, BioWare holds several "synchronization meetings" each year involving all department directors (art, design, audio, etc.), producers (i.e., game project leaders), and the human resource manager. These meetings sort out differences and ensure that staff members are properly assigned to each game project.

Another challenge is that the existence of two bosses can dilute accountability. This problem, which is described in Connections 13.2, recently occurred at Britain's Inland Revenue and Customs/Excise department. In a functional or divisional structure, one manager is responsible for everything, even the most unexpected issues. But in a matrix structure, the unusual problems don't get resolved because neither manager takes ownership of them.[61]

Soon after Mark Hurd became CEO of Hewlett-Packard, he replaced the technology company's matrix structure because of concerns about accountability. "The more accountable I can make you, the easier it is for you to show you're a great performer," declared Hurd, who is now with Oracle, Inc. "The more I use a matrix, the easier I make it to blame someone else."[62] The combination of dysfunctional conflict and ambiguous accountability in matrix structures also explains why some employees experience more stress and some managers are less satisfied with their work arrangements.

NETWORK STRUCTURE

BMW AG and Daimler AG aren't eager to let you know this, but some of their vehicles designed and constructed with Germanic precision are neither designed nor constructed by them or in Germany. Much of BMW's X3, for example, was designed by Magna Steyr in Austria. Magna also manufactured the vehicle in Austria, until BMW transferred this work to its manufacturing plant in the United States. The contract manufacturer also builds Daimler's off-road G-class Mercedes. Both BMW and Daimler Benz are hub organizations that own and market their respective brands, whereas Magna and other suppliers are spokes around the hub that provide production, engineering, and other services that get the auto firms' luxury products to customers.[63]

BMW, Daimler, and many other organizations are moving toward a **network structure** as they design and build a product or serve a client through an alliance of several organizations.[64] As Exhibit 13.7 illustrates, this collaborative structure typically consists of several satellite organizations bee-hived around a hub or core firm. The core firm orchestrates the network process and provides one or two other core competencies, such as marketing or product development. In our example, BMW or Mercedes is the hub that provides marketing and management, whereas other firms perform many other functions. The core firm might be the main contact with customers, but most of the product or service delivery and support activities are farmed out to satellite organizations located anywhere in the world. Extranets (web-based networks with partners) and other technologies ensure that information flows easily and openly between the core firm and its array of satellites.[65]

One of the main forces pushing toward a network structure is the recognition that an organization has only a few *core competencies*. A core competency is a knowledge base that resides throughout the organization and provides a strategic advantage. As companies

EXHIBIT 13.7

A Network Organizational Structure

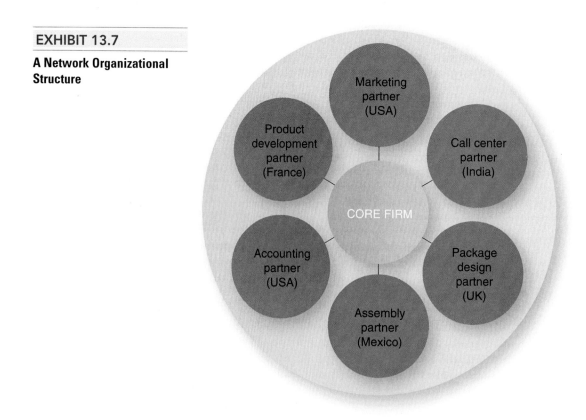

discover their core competency, they "unbundle" noncritical tasks to other organizations that have a core competency at performing those tasks. For instance, BMW decided long ago that facilities management is not one of its core competencies, so it outsourced this function from its British engine plant to Dalkia, which specializes in facility maintenance and energy management.[66]

Companies are also more likely to form network structures when technology is changing quickly and production processes are complex or varied.[67] Many firms cannot keep up with the hyperfast changes in information technology, so they have outsourced their entire information system departments to IBM, HP Enterprise Business, and other firms that specialize in information system services. Similarly, many high-technology firms form networks with Flextronics, Celestica, and other electronic equipment manufacturers that have expertise in diverse production processes.

Evaluating the Network Structure   For several years, organizational behavior theorists have argued that organizational leaders must develop a metaphor of organizations as plasma-like organisms rather than rigid machines.[68] Network structures come close to the organism metaphor because they offer the flexibility to realign their structure with changing environmental requirements. If customers demand a new product or service, the core firm forms new alliances with other firms offering the appropriate resources. For example, by working with Magna International, BMW was probably able to develop and launch the X3 vehicle much sooner than would have been the case if it had performed these tasks on its own. When BMW needs a different type of manufacturing, it isn't saddled with nonessential facilities and resources. Network structures also offer efficiencies because the core firm becomes globally competitive as it shops worldwide for subcontractors with the best people and the best technology at the best price. Indeed, the pressures of global competition have made network structures more vital, and computer-based information technology has made them possible.[69]

A potential disadvantage of network structures is that they expose the core firm to market forces. Other companies may bid up the price for subcontractors, whereas the short-term cost would be lower if the company hired its own employees to perform the same function. Another problem is that though information technology makes worldwide communication much easier, it will never replace the degree of control organizations have when manufacturing, marketing, and other functions are in-house. The core firm can use arm's-length incentives and contract provisions to maintain the subcontractor's quality, but these actions are relatively crude compared with maintaining the quality of work performed by in-house employees.

Contingencies of Organizational Design

LO4

Most organizational behavior theories and concepts have contingencies: Ideas that work well in one situation might not work as well in another situation. This contingency approach is certainly relevant when choosing the most appropriate organizational structure.[70] In this section, we introduce four contingencies of organizational design: external environment, size, technology, and strategy.

EXTERNAL ENVIRONMENT

network structure
An alliance of several organizations for the purpose of creating a product or serving a client.

The best structure for an organization depends on its external environment. The external environment includes anything outside the organization, including most stakeholders (e.g., clients, suppliers, government), resources (e.g., raw materials, human resources, information, finances), and competitors. Four characteristics of external environments influence the type of organizational structure best suited to a particular situation: dynamism, complexity, diversity, and hostility.[71]

Dynamic Versus Stable Environments

Dynamic environments have a high rate of change, leading to novel situations and a lack of identifiable patterns. Organic structures are better suited to this type of environment so that the organization can adapt more quickly to changes, but only if employees are experienced and coordinate well in teamwork.[72] In contrast, stable environments are characterized by regular cycles of activity and steady changes in supply and demand for inputs and outputs. Events are more predictable, enabling the firm to apply rules and procedures. Mechanistic structures are more efficient when the environment is predictable, so they tend to work better than organic structures.

Complex Versus Simple Environments

Complex environments have many elements, whereas simple environments have few things to monitor. As an example, a major university library operates in a more complex environment than a small-town public library. The university library's clients require several types of services—book borrowing, online full-text databases, research centers, course reserve collections, and so on. A small-town public library has fewer of these demands placed on it. The more complex the environment, the more decentralized the organization should become. Decentralization is a logical choice in complex environments because decisions are pushed down to people and subunits with the necessary information to make informed choices.

Diverse Versus Integrated Environments

Organizations located in diverse environments have a greater variety of products or services, clients, and regions. In contrast, an integrated environment has only one client, product, and geographic area. The more diversified the environment, the more the firm needs to use a divisional structure aligned with that diversity. If it sells a single product around the world, a geographic divisional structure would align best with the firm's geographic diversity, for example.

Hostile Versus Munificent Environments

Firms located in a hostile environment face resource scarcity and more competition in the marketplace. Hostile environments are typically dynamic ones because they reduce the predictability of access to resources and demand for outputs. Organic structures tend to be best in hostile environments. However, when the environment is extremely hostile—such as one that involves a severe shortage of supplies or lower market share—organizations tend to temporarily centralize so that decisions can be made more quickly and executives feel more comfortable being in control.[73] Ironically, centralization may result in lower-quality decisions during organizational crises, because top management has less information, particularly when the environment is complex.

connect

To assist your learning and test your knowledge about the contingencies of organizational structure, go to **www.mcgrawhillconnect.com,** which has activities and test questions on this topic.

For more than four decades, Nucor Corporation proudly maintained a lean, flat organizational structure with only four management layers: supervisors, functional managers, plant managers, and CEO. The CEO could directly manage more than two dozen plant managers because they operated as independent businesses. Today, Nucor is America's largest steelmaker, employing 20,000 people at more than four dozen facilities worldwide. Managing so many direct reports would overwhelm most executives, so Nucor CEO Dan DiMicco reluctantly added five executive vice presidents, creating another layer of management. "I needed to be free to make decisions on trade battles," says DiMicco apologetically.[74]

ORGANIZATIONAL SIZE

Larger organizations should have different structures from smaller organizations.[75] As the number of employees increases, job specialization increases due to a greater division of labor. The greater division of labor requires more elaborate coordinating mechanisms. Thus, larger firms make greater use of standardization (particularly work processes and outcomes) to coordinate work activities. These coordinating mechanisms create an administrative hierarchy and greater formalization. Historically, larger organizations make less use of informal communication as a coordinating mechanism. However, emerging information technologies and increased emphasis on empowerment have caused informal communication to regain its importance in large firms.[76]

Larger organizations also tend to be more decentralized. Executives have neither sufficient time nor expertise to process all the decisions that significantly influence the business as it grows. Therefore, decision-making authority is pushed down to lower levels, where incumbents are able to cope with the narrower range of issues under their control.

TECHNOLOGY

Technology is another factor to consider when designing the best organizational structure for the situation.[77] *Technology* refers to the mechanisms or processes by which an organization turns out its product or service. One technological contingency is *variability*—the number of exceptions to standard procedure that tend to occur. In work processes with low variability, jobs are routine and follow standard operating procedures. Another contingency is *analyzability*—the predictability or difficulty of the required work. The less analyzable the work, the more it requires experts with sufficient discretion to address the work challenges. An organic, rather than a mechanistic, structure should be introduced where employees perform tasks with high variability and low analyzability, such as in a research setting. The reason is that employees face unique situations with little opportunity for repetition. In contrast, a mechanistic structure is preferred where the technology has low variability and high analyzability, such as an assembly line. The work is routine and highly predictable, an ideal situation for a mechanistic structure to operate efficiently.

ORGANIZATIONAL STRATEGY

Organizational strategy refers to the way the organization positions itself in its setting in relation to its stakeholders, given the organization's resources, capabilities, and mission.[78] In other words, strategy represents the decisions and actions applied to achieve the organization's goals. Although size, technology, and environment influence the optimal organizational structure, these contingencies do not necessarily determine structure. Instead, corporate leaders formulate and implement strategies that shape the characteristics of these contingencies, as well as the organization's resulting structure.

This concept is summed up with the simple phrase, "Structure follows strategy."[79] Organizational leaders decide how large to grow and which technologies to use. They take steps to define and manipulate their environments, rather than let the organization's fate be entirely determined by external influences. Furthermore, organizational structures don't evolve as a natural response to environmental conditions; they result from conscious human decisions. Thus, organizational strategy influences both the contingencies of structure and the structure itself.

If a company's strategy is to compete through innovation, a more organic structure would be preferred because it is easier for employees to share knowledge and be creative. If a company chooses a low-cost strategy, a mechanistic structure is preferred because it maximizes production and service efficiency.[80] Overall, it is now apparent that organizational structure is influenced by size, technology, and environment, but the organization's strategy may reshape these elements and loosen their connection to organizational structure.

organizational strategy
The way the organization positions itself in its setting in relation to its stakeholders, given the organization's resources, capabilities, and mission.

LO1 Describe three types of coordination in organizational structures.

Organizational structure is the division of labor, as well as the patterns of coordination, communication, workflow, and formal power that direct organizational activities. All organizational structures divide labor into distinct tasks and coordinate that labor to accomplish common goals. The primary means of coordination are informal communication, formal hierarchy, and standardization.

LO2 Discuss the role and effects of span of control, centralization, and formalization, and relate these elements to organic and mechanistic organizational structures.

The four basic elements of organizational structure are span of control, centralization, formalization, and departmentalization. The optimal span of control—the number of people directly reporting to the next level in the hierarchy—depends on what coordinating mechanisms are present other than formal hierarchy, whether employees perform routine tasks, and how much interdependence there is among employees within the department.

Centralization occurs when formal decision authority is held by a small group of people, typically senior executives. Many companies decentralize as they become larger and more complex, but some sections of the company may remain centralized while other sections decentralize. Formalization is the degree to which organizations standardize behavior through rules, procedures, formal training, and related mechanisms. Companies become more formalized as they get older and larger. Formalization tends to reduce organizational flexibility, organizational learning, creativity, and job satisfaction.

Span of control, centralization, and formalization cluster into mechanistic and organic structures. Mechanistic structures are characterized by a narrow span of control and a high degree of formalization and centralization. Companies with an organic structure have the opposite characteristics.

LO3 Identify and evaluate six types of departmentalization.

Departmentalization specifies how employees and their activities are grouped together. It establishes the chain of command,

focuses people around common mental models, and encourages coordination through informal communication among people and subunits. A simple structure employs few people, has minimal hierarchy, and typically offers one distinct product or service. A functional structure organizes employees around specific knowledge or other resources. This structure fosters greater specialization and improves direct supervision, but it weakens the focus on serving clients or developing products.

A divisional structure groups employees around geographic areas, clients, or outputs. This structure accommodates growth and focuses employee attention on products or customers rather than tasks. However, this structure also duplicates resources and creates silos of knowledge. Team-based structures are very flat, with low formalization, and organize self-directed teams around work processes rather than functional specialties. The matrix structure combines two structures to leverage the benefits of both types. However, this approach requires more coordination than functional or pure divisional structures, may dilute accountability, and increases conflict. A network structure is an alliance of several organizations for the purpose of creating a product or serving a client.

LO4 Explain how the external environment, organizational size, technology, and strategy are relevant when designing an organizational structure.

The best organizational structure depends on the firm's external environment, size, technology, and strategy. The optimal structure depends on whether the environment is dynamic or stable, complex or simple, diverse or integrated, and hostile or munificent. As organizations increase in size, they become more decentralized and more formalized. The work unit's technology—including variability of work and analyzability of problems—influences whether it should adopt an organic or mechanistic structure. These contingencies influence but do not necessarily determine structure. Instead, corporate leaders formulate and implement strategies that shape both the characteristics of these contingencies and the organization's resulting structure.

{ key terms }

centralization, p. 383

concurrent engineering, p. 378

divisional structure, p. 387

formalization, p. 384

functional structure, p. 386

globally integrated enterprise, p. 389

matrix structure, p. 391

mechanistic structure, p. 384

network structure, p. 394

organic structure, p. 385

organizational strategy, p. 397

organizational structure, p. 376

span of control, p. 379

team-based organizational structure, p. 390

{ critical thinking questions }

1. Merritt's Bakery's organizational structure was described at the beginning of this chapter. What coordinating mechanism is likely most common in this organization? Describe the extent and form in which the other two types of coordination might be apparent in this company.

2. Think about the business school or other organizational unit whose classes you are currently attending. What is the dominant coordinating mechanism used to guide or control the instructor? Why is this coordinating mechanism used the most here?

3. Administrative theorists concluded many decades ago that the most effective organizations have a narrow span of control. Yet today's top-performing manufacturing firms have a wide span of control. Why is this possible? Under what circumstances, if any, should manufacturing firms have a narrow span of control?

4. Leaders of large organizations struggle to identify the best level and types of centralization and decentralization. What should companies consider when determining the degree of decentralization?

5. Diversified Technologies, Inc. (DTI), makes four types of products, each type to be sold to different types of clients. For example, one product is sold exclusively to automobile repair shops, whereas another is used mainly in hospitals. Expectations within each client group are surprisingly similar throughout the world. The company has separate marketing, product design, and manufacturing facilities in Asia, North America, Europe, and South America because, until recently, each jurisdiction had unique regulations governing the production and sales of these products. However, several governments have begun the process of deregulating the products that DTI designs and manufactures, and trade agreements have opened several markets to foreign-made products. Which form of departmentalization might be best for DTI if deregulation and trade agreements occur?

6. IBM is becoming a globally integrated enterprise. What does this organization look like in terms of its departmentalization? What challenges might face companies that try to adopt the globally integrated enterprise model?

7. From an employee perspective, what are the advantages and disadvantages of working in a matrix structure?

8. Suppose you have been hired as a consultant to diagnose the environmental characteristics of your college or university. How would you describe the school's external environment? Is the school's existing structure appropriate for this environment?

9. Suppose you live in a very densely populated city, like Hong Kong or Beijing or even New York City. Your business is doing extremely well and you need to hire people, but you have nowhere to put them. What do you do? Would you consider outsourcing them? Building existing layers on an already tall high-rise building? Letting them work at home or at some other off-site facility? What do you know about these various structural solutions to solving the need to add more people? Conversely, if you had to downsize, what could be done with the structural space?

CASE STUDY 13.1 NOKIA'S EVOLVING ORGANIZATIONAL STRUCTURE

Nokia Corporation has experienced considerable change over the past three decades, and its organizational structure has changed just as dramatically. In the early 1990s, the Finnish company had a product-based organizational structure designed around its diversified businesses: consumer electronics (televisions, audio equipment), cable for construction and power transmission, industrial rubber (tires, footwear), and a recently acquired telecommunications business that would soon evolve into cell phones.

Nokia became the market leader in cell phones by 1998 (overtaking Motorola), so it sold most other divisions and designed a new organizational structure that highlighted its cell phone and consumer electronics businesses, as well as several function groups (finance, human resources, etc.). The consumer electronics business was not sufficiently profitable, so it was sold, and Nokia drew a new organizational chart in 1999 centered on cell phones, the emerging business of mobile networks, ventures (emerging Internet mobile technology), and communication products (digital terminals).

By 2003, the cell phone market was converging with photography, games, music, and other multimedia content, so Nokia added a new "multimedia" division to keep the company at the forefront. In 2006, the company's burgeoning network division was spun off as a joint venture with a similar product group at Siemens.

Nokia's earlier organizational structures gave some priority to Internet and multimedia technologies, enough to keep the company on pace with the quickly emerging smartphone market. But Nokia was caught off guard by the rapid development of smartphones, initially by Research in Motion (which makes the BlackBerry) and more recently by Apple (iPhone) and Google (Android operating system). Faced with declining sales, Nokia recently announced a new organizational structure that would focus on smartphones and traditional cell phones.

"Nokia is at a critical juncture, where significant change is necessary and inevitable in our journey forward," said Nokia president and CEO Stephen Elop when the new structure was announced. "Today, we are accelerating that change through a new path, aimed at regaining our smartphone leadership, reinforcing our mobile device platform, and realizing our investments in the future."

The new chart (shown at the end of this case) emphasizes two central product divisions: Smart Devices and Mobile Phones. The smartphones division competes against Apple's iPhone and similar products. The mobile phone division covers traditional cell phone products with a particular emphasis on growing business in emerging markets. The chart also features a "Markets" division, which is a functional group responsible for global sales and supply chain operations. There are several other functional groups in the chart too. NAVTEC and Nokia Siemens Networks are separate organizations, of which Nokia is a joint partner.

Nokia's new structure also imposes three other units—services and developer experience, design, and chief technology officer (CTO) office—across the two product divisions and "Markets" group. These functions represent a type of matrix structure to ensure that the company offers consistent user experiences and shares design and research resources across products.

Nokia's Organizational Structure

NAVTEQ	CEO		Nokia Siemens Networks
Corporate development	Mobile phones	Smart devices	Markets
CFO office			
Human resources			
Legal & intellectual property			
Corporate relations and responsibility	Services & developer experience		
Quality & capability development	Design		
Workplace resources	CTO office		

Discussion Questions

1. What form of departmentalization has Nokia relied on throughout most of the past three decades? Why have these forms of departmentalization been adopted?

2. Evaluate Nokia's changing organizational structure against the changing characteristics of the external environment over this time. Has the structure mostly contributed to Nokia's success or been a hindrance to it?

3. Although not explicitly described in this case, in your opinion, in what parts of Nokia would you expect to find the most organic organizational structure, particularly low formalization and high decentralization? What parts of Nokia would be most mechanistic?

Sources: "Nokia in Major Reorganization Plan," *Warren's Consumer Electronics Daily,* September 29, 2003; K.J. O'Brien, "Head of Nokia's Mobile Phone Unit Is Leaving," *The New York Times,* May 12, 2010, p. 5; "Nokia Outlines New Strategy, Introduces New Leadership, Operational Structure," news release, February 11, 2011.

CASE STUDY 13.2 FINDING A HOME FOR DIGITAL IN THE CREATIVE ENTERPRISE

A few years ago, TBWA Worldwide hired Colleen DeCourcy to fill its newly created chief digital officer position. Soon thereafter, she unveiled a new organizational unit, TBWA\ Digital Arts. DeCourcy's announcement came in a decidedly new-school way: She tweeted it. With this unit, TBWA would use its roving band of digital geniuses as a center of excellence and thereby catapult the organization's traditional creative talent into the digital age. In DeCourcy's words, it was to be "advertising at the speed of culture."

What DeCourcy and chief digital officers at other mega-agencies failed to anticipate were the number of barriers. DeCourcy's Digital Arts group never integrated well with TBWA, beset as it was by the typical agency bureaucratic infighting, turf wars, and the realization that injecting digital into hulking organizations like TBWA would need more than just hiring a crew of hotshots. According to one source, "I don't think everyone in the company had clarity about how it was to work."

Even the CEO of TBWA Worldwide, Tom Carroll, acknowledged that Digital Arts hit some bumps in the road: "We played with certain things, we experimented with certain things, and some of it has worked and some of it hasn't," he noted. "We get better every day. We learn more every day."

But perhaps the most important thing that Carroll and other corporate heads learned was that chief digital officers do not fit easily into traditional creative giants. DeCourcy recently left TBWA, as did her counterparts at the creative agencies Ogilvy & Mather and Young & Rubicam. None of the companies has since filled these positions with new staff. The remaining digital geniuses have been folded into existing media departments. In effect, the experiment of creating an organizational structure with an elite digital SWAT team has come to an end.

Perhaps the main problem with a chief digital officer and a team of digital geniuses is that the unit will never match a sprawling organizational structure. DeCourcy's Digital Arts group operated at the worldwide level, as part of the Media Arts unit. Thus, financial questions arose when it plugged in to local agencies, such as whether billing for the well-compensated digital artists would come out of a local office's budget. The New York–based digital units also faced resistance from local offices that were wary of losing client revenue to headquarters. They appeared to "parachute in" on projects and take too much credit.

Another problem was that the digital leaders found themselves pulled in different ways. It was unrealistic to expect a single digital leader to take responsibility for the entire agency's digital success or failure. "It's just one person," said Ogilvy North America CEO John Seifert. "What I think the flaw has been is that too much has been assumed or made of a single person in that role," which meant that the digital chiefs were "just stretched in a million directions."

Finally, digital was never a centerpiece in the competitive strategy of traditional agencies. Although they wanted greater digital know-how, such all-purpose shops mainly tout their breadth of services, not their digital prowess. "The reality is there is a degree to which these agencies feel the need to get digital," said one source. "And if we remember at their heart that they're advertising agencies, then there's probably only a certain degree [of digital expertise] that they need to have as creative services companies."

This reality seemingly has sunk in. Chief executives claim their agencies no longer need chief digital officers, and they assert that digital is "not all or nothing," in TBWA's Tom Carroll's words. "Our guys get closer and closer to doing what [digital agencies do]. We get closer every day—and that's enough."

In response, Ogilvy's John Seifert argues for closer digital integration rather than a distinct corporate structure for digital experts, because the rank and file "have to be part of this digital revolution." The chief digital officers who have departed generally agree, noting "Digital needs to be so integral to the organization that it's not distinguished by a group or individual leaders." In effect, traditional creative agencies are taking a bottom-up rather than top-down approach to their digital transformation.

Discussion Questions

1. List the main reasons organizational structures with chief digital officers did not work well at TBWA and other major creative agencies.

2. What form of departmentalization best represents the Digital Arts group at TBWA and similar digital genius SWAT teams?

3. Suppose you were head of a very large, traditional advertising agency. Having read this case study, what organizational structure would you use to encourage more emphasis on digital media across the organization?

Sources: B. Morrissey and A. McMains, "The Twisting Path to New Agency Models," *AdWeek*, May 10, 2010; A. McMains, "New Strategies Replace Solo Acts," *AdWeek*, June 28, 2010.

TEAM EXERCISE 13.3 THE CLUB ED EXERCISE

Cheryl Harvey and Kim Morouney, Wilfred Laurier University

PURPOSE This exercise is designed to help you understand the issues to consider when designing organizations at various stages of growth.

MATERIALS Each student team should have enough overhead transparencies or flip chart sheets to display several organizational charts.

INSTRUCTIONS Each team discusses the scenario presented. The instructor will facilitate discussion and notify teams when to begin the next step. The exercise and debriefing require approximately 90 minutes, though fewer scenarios can reduce the time somewhat.

Step 1: Students are placed in teams (typically four or five people).

Step 2: After reading Scenario #1, each team will design an organizational chart (departmentalization) that is most appropriate for this situation. Students should be able to describe the type of structure drawn and explain why it is appropriate. The structure should be drawn on an overhead transparency or flip chart for others to see during subsequent class discussion. The instructor will set a fixed time (e.g., 15 minutes) to complete this task.

Scenario #1. Determined never to shovel snow again, you are establishing a new resort business on a small Caribbean island. The resort is under construction and is scheduled to open one year from now. You decide it is time to draw up an organizational chart for this new venture, called Club Ed.

Step 3: At the end of the time allowed, the instructor will present Scenario #2, and each team will be asked to draw another organizational chart to suit that situation. Again, students should be able to describe the type of structure drawn and explain why it is appropriate.

Step 4: At the end of the time allowed, the instructor will present Scenario #3, and each team will be asked to draw another organizational chart to suit that situation.

Step 5: Depending on the time available, the instructor might present a fourth scenario. The class will gather to present their designs for each scenario. During each presentation, teams should describe the type of structure drawn and explain why it is appropriate.

Source: Adapted from C. Harvey and K. Morouney, *Journal of Management Education* 22 (June 1998), pp. 425–29. Used with permission of the authors.

SELF-ASSESSMENT 13.4 WHAT ORGANIZATIONAL STRUCTURE DO YOU PREFER?

PURPOSE This exercise is designed to help you understand how an organization's structure influences the personal needs and values of people working in that structure.

INSTRUCTIONS Personal values influence how comfortable you are working in different organizational structures. You might prefer an organization with clearly defined rules or no rules at all. You might prefer a firm where almost any employee can make important decisions or one where important decisions are screened by senior executives. Read each statement below and indicate the extent to which you would like to work in an organization with that characteristic. When finished, use the scoring key in Appendix B at the end of the book to calculate your results. This self-assessment should be completed alone so that you can assess yourself honestly without concerns of social comparison. Class discussion will focus on the elements of organizational design and their relationship to personal needs and values.

Organizational Structure Preference Scale

I WOULD LIKE TO WORK IN AN ORGANIZATION WHERE . . .	NOT AT ALL	A LITTLE	SOMEWHAT	VERY MUCH	SCORE
1. A person's career ladder has several steps toward higher status and responsibility.	☐	☐	☐	☐	_____
2. Employees perform their work with few rules to limit their discretion.	☐	☐	☐	☐	_____
3. Responsibility is pushed down to employees who perform the work.	☐	☐	☐	☐	_____
4. Supervisors have few employees, so they work closely with each person.	☐	☐	☐	☐	_____
5. Senior executives make most decisions to ensure that the company is consistent in its actions.	☐	☐	☐	☐	_____
6. Jobs are clearly defined so that there is no confusion over who is responsible for various tasks.	☐	☐	☐	☐	_____
7. Employees have their say on issues, but senior executives make most of the decisions.	☐	☐	☐	☐	_____
8. Job descriptions are broadly stated or nonexistent.	☐	☐	☐	☐	_____
9. Everyone's work is tightly synchronized around top-management operating plans.	☐	☐	☐	☐	_____

(continued)

Organizational Structure Preference Scale (*continued*)

I WOULD LIKE TO WORK IN AN ORGANIZATION WHERE . . .	NOT AT ALL	A LITTLE	SOMEWHAT	VERY MUCH	SCORE
10. Most work is performed in teams without close supervision.	☐	☐	☐	☐	_____
11. Work gets done through informal discussion with coworkers rather than through formal rules.	☐	☐	☐	☐	_____
12. Supervisors have so many employees that they can't watch anyone very closely.	☐	☐	☐	☐	_____
13. Everyone has clearly understood goals, expectations, and job duties.	☐	☐	☐	☐	_____
14. Senior executives assign overall goals, but leave daily decisions to frontline teams.	☐	☐	☐	☐	_____
15. Even in a large company, the CEO is only three or four levels above the lowest position.	☐	☐	☐	☐	_____

After reading this chapter go to www.mhhe.com/mcshane6e for more in-depth information and interactivities that correspond to the chapter.

Organizational Culture

learning objectives

After reading this chapter, you should be able to:

LO1 Describe the elements of organizational culture and discuss the importance of organizational subcultures.

LO2 List four categories of artifacts through which corporate culture is deciphered.

LO3 Discuss the importance of organizational culture and the conditions in which organizational culture strength improves organizational performance.

LO4 Compare and contrast four strategies for merging organizational cultures.

LO5 Identify four strategies for changing or strengthening an organization's culture, including the application of attraction–selection–attrition theory.

LO6 Describe the organizational socialization process and identify strategies to improve that process.

125 staff work there, making Austin the company's second largest U.S. office outside its headquarters in Palo Alto, California. The booming social network company has also opened operations in Dublin, Ireland, and Hyderabad, India.

In each country, Facebook has been able to instill its unique corporate culture: focus on impact, be bold, and move fast (and break things). "There is a really great culture of empowerment here," says Charlton Gholson, a Facebook employee in Austin. "We want people to take risks and be bold and really strive to make a huge impact, because that is what the company is trying to do."

Keeping its culture intact during rapid expansion has been one of Facebook's key concerns. "Maintaining culture is one of the top priorities we have as a company," says Sarah Smith, head of online operations in Austin. "So we're focused on building a few offices, but making sure they are really tied into the culture."

Facebook carefully selects a handful of current employees—called the Landing Team—to open each site and serve as the company's culture carriers. The objective of the landing team is "a transfer of knowledge and of culture to make sure we're spreading our own unique Facebook culture in different offices around the world," says Joanna Lee, a Landing Team member who opened the office in Hyderabad. "So the India landing team had seven members across three different teams in operations—advertisers, developers, and testers."

The Landing Team embeds Facebook's culture at each site by carefully selecting applicants for their compatibility with that culture and coaching newcomers on the Facebook way of life. The team also introduces one of Facebook's most notable cultural symbols: Hackathons. These special one-day events allow employees to work on interesting projects of their choosing that they would not normally do in their daily jobs.

Facebook's culture is further reinforced through its office layout: open-space work areas with wooden tables and no partitions, plenty of recreational activities, free food, and conference rooms named after cultural icons. Facebook's offices also have an unfinished look, which Sarah Smith says is consistent with its fast-moving culture. "We talk about this idea that we are 1 percent done with this journey as a company," says Smith. "We are just at the beginning of building this office."[1]

"Maintaining culture is one of the top priorities we have as a company," says Sarah Smith (shown in this photo), head of Facebook's operations in Austin, Texas.

Facebook has a distinctive organizational culture and, in spite of its exponential growth, has discovered ways to maintain and perhaps even strengthen that culture throughout its global offices. **Organizational culture** consists of the values and assumptions shared within an organization.[2] It defines what is important and unimportant in the company and consequently directs everyone in the organization toward the "right way" of doing things. You might think of organizational culture as the company's DNA; it's invisible to the naked eye, yet provides a powerful template that shapes what happens in the workplace.

This chapter begins by identifying the elements of organizational culture and then describing how culture is deciphered through artifacts. This is followed by a discussion of the relationship between organizational culture and performance, including the effects of cultural strength, fit, and adaptability. We then turn our attention to the challenges of and solutions to merging organizational cultures. The latter part of this chapter examines ways to change and strengthen organizational culture, including a closer look at the related topic of organizational socialization.

Elements of Organizational Culture

LO1

As its definition states, organizational culture consists of shared values and assumptions. Exhibit 14.1 illustrates how these shared values and assumptions relate to one another and are associated with artifacts, discussed later in this chapter. *Values* are stable, evaluative beliefs that guide our preferences for outcomes or courses of action in a variety of situations (see Chapters 1 and 2).[3] They are conscious perceptions about what is good or bad, right or wrong. In the context of organizational culture, values are discussed as *shared values,* which are values that people within the organization or work unit have in common and place near the top of their hierarchy of values.[4] At Facebook, most employees embrace the shared values of making a difference (focus on impact), taking risks (be bold), and being entrepreneurial (moving fast).

Organizational culture also consists of *shared assumptions*—a deeper element that some experts believe is the essence of corporate culture. Shared assumptions are nonconscious, taken-for-granted perceptions or ideal prototypes of behavior that are considered the correct way to think and act toward problems and opportunities. Shared assumptions are so deeply ingrained that you probably wouldn't discover them by surveying employees. Only by observing employees, analyzing their decisions, and debriefing them on their actions would these assumptions rise to the surface.

It has become a popular practice for leaders to identify and publicly state their organization's shared values. Online retailer Zappos lists 10 core values, such as "Deliver WOW through Service," "Embrace and Drive Change," and "Create Fun and A Little Weirdness." Gap Adventures, the Toronto-based outdoor adventure company, describes its five values: We love changing people's lives, embrace the bizarre, lead with service, do the right thing, and create happiness and community.[5]

Do these values really represent the cultural content of Zappos and Gap Adventures? Very probably in the case of these two organizations, because their cultures are well known and deeply entrenched. However, the values statements of many organizations do not necessarily reflect the values that are widely shared and practiced in the organization. This distinction occurs because corporate leaders typically describe *espoused values*—the values that they want others to believe guide the organization's decisions and actions.[6] Espoused values are usually socially desirable, so they present a positive public image. Even if top management acts consistently with the espoused values, lower-level employees might not do so. Employees bring diverse personal values to the organization, some of which might conflict with the organization's espoused values.

Organizational culture is not represented by espoused values. Instead, it consists of shared *enacted values*—the values that most leaders and employees truly rely on to guide their decisions and behavior. These "values-in-use" are apparent by watching executives

EXHIBIT 14.1   Organizational Culture Assumptions, Values, and Artifacts

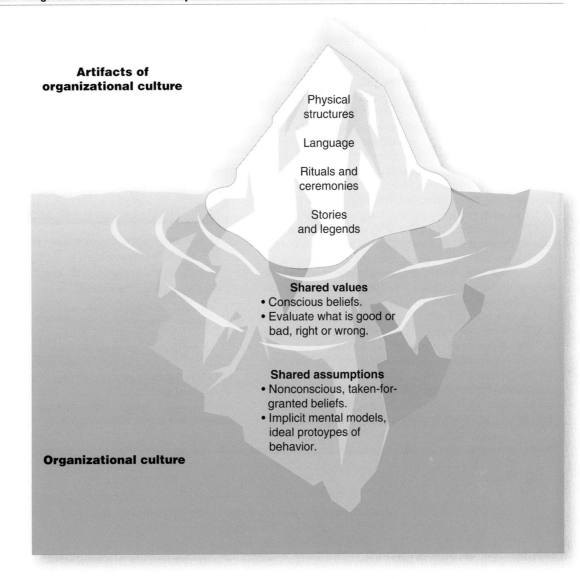

Artifacts of organizational culture

Physical structures

Language

Rituals and ceremonies

Stories and legends

Shared values
- Conscious beliefs.
- Evaluate what is good or bad, right or wrong.

Shared assumptions
- Nonconscious, taken-for-granted beliefs.
- Implicit mental models, ideal protoypes of behavior.

Organizational culture

and other employees in action, including their decisions, where they focus their attention and resources, and how they behave toward stakeholders. For example, Connections 14.1 describes how BP's stated (espoused) value of responsibility seems to be wildly at odds with the decisions, priorities, and behavior of its leaders and many employees.

CONTENT OF ORGANIZATIONAL CULTURE

Organizations differ in their cultural content, that is, the relative ordering of shared values. Facebook has an entrepreneurial culture where employees are encouraged to take risks to make a difference to the company and society. The company also recognizes that employees make mistakes (break things) along that innovation journey. The culture at Netflix is considerably different.[7] Executives at the on-demand and mail-order movie rental company view themselves as a sports team. "Netflix leaders hire, develop, and cut smartly, so we have stars in every position," a Netflix slideshow candidly states. The company even asks managers to regularly apply the "keeper test": Determine which employees they would fight hard to prevent from leaving. And the others? "[They] should get a generous severance package now, so we can open a slot to try to find a star for that

organizational culture
The values and assumptions shared within an organization.

connections 14.1

BP's Espoused vs. Enacted Values

BP, the British energy giant, lists four core values: progressive, responsible, innovative, and performance-driven. The company says that these values "guide us in the conduct of our business." In other words, BP claims these four core values are enacted; they are evident in the company's decisions and allocation of resources, as well as in the daily behavior of its employees.

Most people around the Gulf of Mexico and in Alaska would quickly dismiss those claims. In particular, BP describes its "responsibility" value as being "committed to the safety and development of our people and the communities and societies in which we operate. We aim for no accidents, no harm to people and no damage to the environment." Yet, the energy company's track record on safety and environmentalism suggests otherwise.

BP is at the center of the Gulf of Mexico oil spill, now considered the worst environmental disaster in recent history. A few months before the spill occurred, the U.S. government's Occupational Safety and Health Administration (OSHA) penalized BP with the largest fine in OSHA's history for failing to sufficiently improve safety at its Texas City refinery. Four years earlier, 15 employees died in an explosion at that refinery. A U.S. government report on that explosion concluded that BP "did not provide effective safety culture leadership."

BP's "responsibility" value has been around for a few years, yet the company's environmental and safety problems were well known long before the Gulf and Texas disasters. In 2003, the Norwegian government concluded that "a poor HES (Health, Environment, and Safety) culture" contributed to a fatality on a

BP describes one of its four core values as aiming "for no accidents, no harm to people and no damage to the environment," yet the British energy company's track record indicates that this value is espoused, not enacted.

BP oil platform. A few years earlier, a prominent newspaper concluded that a series of spills, accidents, and alleged hushups at the Alaskan operations managed by BP "raises serious questions about BP's safety culture." In short, being safety and environmentally "responsible" is an espoused value at BP but not likely part of the company's current or recent culture.[8]

---

role." So, while Netflix has a winner-take-all performance culture, Facebook's culture is more entrepreneurial: empowering employees to have an impact, taking risks, and receiving support for reasonable mistakes along the way.

How many corporate cultures are there? Several models and measures classify organizational culture into a handful of easy-to-remember categories. One of these, shown in Exhibit 14.2, identifies seven corporate cultures. Another popular model identifies four organizational cultures organized in a two-by-two table representing internal versus external focus and flexibility versus control. Other models organize cultures around a circle with 8 or 12 categories. These circumplex models suggest that some cultures are opposite to others, such as an avoidance culture versus a self-actualization culture, or a power culture versus a collegial culture.[9]

These organizational culture models and surveys are popular with corporate leaders faced with the messy business of diagnosing their company's culture and identifying what kind of culture they want to develop. Unfortunately, they oversimplify the diversity of cultural values in organizations. There are dozens of individual values, and many more combinations of values, so the number of organizational cultures that these models describe likely falls considerably short of the full set. A second concern is that organizational culture includes shared assumptions, not just shared values. Most organizational culture measures ignore assumptions because they represent a more subterranean aspect of culture.

A third concern is that many organizational culture models and measures incorrectly assume that organizations have a fairly clear, unified culture that is easily decipherable.[10] This "integration" perspective, as it is called, further assumes that when an organization's culture changes, it shifts from one unified condition to a new unified condition with only

connect

Which corporate culture do you prefer? Go to **www. mcgrawhillconnect.com** to estimate your preference among a small set of common cultures, as well as to assist your learning about organizational culture and effectiveness.

EXHIBIT 14.2

Organizational Culture Profile Dimensions and Characteristics

ORGANIZATIONAL CULTURE DIMENSION	CHARACTERISTICS OF THE DIMENSION
Innovation	Experimenting, opportunity seeking, risk taking, few rules, low cautiousness
Stability	Predictability, security, rule oriented
Respect for people	Fairness, tolerance
Outcome orientation	Action oriented, high expectations, results oriented
Attention to detail	Precise, analytic
Team orientation	Collaboration, people oriented
Aggressiveness	Competitive, low emphasis on social responsibility

Source: Based on information in C.A. O'Reilly III, J. Chatman, and D.F. Caldwell, "People and Organizational Culture: A Profile Comparison Approach to Assessing Person-Organization Fit," *Academy of Management Journal* 34, no. 3 (1991), pp. 487–518.

temporary ambiguity or weakness during the transition. These assumptions are probably incorrect or, at best, oversimplified. An organization's culture is usually quite blurry, so much so that it cannot be estimated through employee surveys alone. As we discuss next, organizations consist of diverse subcultures, because employees across the organization have different clusters of experiences and backgrounds that have shaped their values and priorities. For example, after BP's Texas refinery explosion a few years ago, an independent panel investigated the energy company's safety culture across the United States. The panel concluded that a few of BP's sites embraced the importance of safety, but most required a much stronger safety culture.[11]

Even these subcultural clusters can be ill-defined because values and assumptions ultimately vary from one employee to the next. As long as employees differ, an organization's culture will have noticeable variability. Thus, many of the popular organizational culture models and measures oversimplify the variety of organizational cultures and falsely presume that it is relatively easy to fit organizations into these categories.

ORGANIZATIONAL SUBCULTURES

When discussing organizational culture, we are really referring to the *dominant culture*, that is, the values and assumptions shared most consistently and widely by the organization's members. The dominant culture is usually supported by senior management, but cultures can also persist in spite of senior management's desire for another culture. Furthermore, organizations are composed of *subcultures* located throughout their various divisions, geographic regions, and occupational groups.[12] Some subcultures enhance the dominant culture by espousing parallel assumptions and values. Others differ from but do not conflict with the dominant culture. Still others are called *countercultures* because they embrace values or assumptions that directly oppose the organization's dominant culture. It is also possible that some organizations (including some universities, according to one study) consist of subcultures with no decipherable dominant culture at all.[13]

Subcultures, particularly countercultures, potentially create conflict and dissension among employees, but they also serve two important functions.[14] First, they maintain the organization's standards of performance and ethical behavior. Employees who hold countercultural values are an important source of surveillance and critical review of the dominant order. They encourage constructive conflict and more creative thinking about how the organization should interact with its environment. Subcultures potentially support ethical conduct by preventing employees from blindly following one set of values. Subculture members continually question the "obvious" decisions and actions of the majority, thereby making everyone more mindful of the consequences of their actions.

The second function of subcultures is that they are the spawning grounds for emerging values that keep the firm aligned with the evolving needs and expectations of customers, suppliers, communities, and other stakeholders. Companies eventually need to replace their dominant values with ones that are more appropriate for the changing environment. If subcultures are suppressed, the organization may take longer to discover and adopt values aligned with the emerging environment.

Deciphering Organizational Culture Through Artifacts

LO2

Shared values and assumptions are not easily measured through surveys and might not be accurately reflected in the organization's values statements. Instead, as Exhibit 14.1 illustrated previously, an organization's culture must be deciphered through a detailed investigation of artifacts. **Artifacts** are the observable symbols and signs of an organization's culture, such as the way visitors are greeted, the organization's physical layout, and how employees are rewarded.[15] A few experts suggest that artifacts are the essence of organizational culture, whereas most others (including the authors of this book) view artifacts as symbols or indicators of culture. In other words, culture is cognitive (values and assumptions inside people's heads), whereas artifacts are observable manifestations of that culture. Either way, artifacts are important because they represent and reinforce an organization's culture.

Artifacts provide valuable evidence about a company's culture.[16] An organization's ambiguous (fragmented) culture is best understood by observing workplace behavior, listening to everyday conversations among staff and with customers, studying written documents and e-mails, viewing physical structures and settings, and interviewing staff about corporate stories. In other words, to truly understand an organization's culture, we need to sample information from a variety of organizational artifacts.

The Mayo Clinic conducted such an assessment a few years ago. An anthropologist was hired to decipher the medical organization's culture at its headquarters in Minnesota and to identify ways to transfer that culture to its two newer sites in Florida and Arizona. For six weeks, the anthropologist shadowed employees, posed as a patient in waiting rooms, did countless interviews, and accompanied physicians on patient visits. The final report outlined Mayo's dominant culture and how its satellite operations varied from that culture.[17]

In this section, we review the four broad categories of artifacts: organizational stories and legends, rituals and ceremonies, language, and physical structures and symbols.

ORGANIZATIONAL STORIES AND LEGENDS

David Ogilvy is a legend in the advertising industry, but equally significant are the stories about him that have continued to reinforce the values that he instilled. One story recounts how Ogilvy's board of directors arrived at a meeting to discover a Russian matryoshka doll at each of their seats. The directors opened each doll, one nested inside the other, until they discovered this message inside the tiniest doll: "If you hire people who are smaller than you are, we shall become a company of dwarfs. If you hire people who are bigger than you are, we shall become a company of giants." The Russian dolls became part of Ogilvy's culture, which demands hiring talent, not subservience.[18]

Stories such as Ogilvy's Russian dolls permeate strong organizational cultures. Some tales recount heroic deeds, whereas others ridicule past events that deviate from the firm's core values. Organizational stories and legends serve as powerful social prescriptions of the way things should (or should not) be done. They add human realism to corporate expectations, individual performance standards, and the criteria for getting fired. Stories also produce emotions in listeners, and these emotions tend to improve listeners' memory of the lesson within the story.[19] Stories have the greatest effect on communicating corporate culture when they describe real people, are assumed to be true, and are known by employees throughout the organization. Stories are also prescriptive—they advise people what to do or not to do.[20]

Zappos is renowned for its "Wow" service. The online shoe and apparel company's customer-focused culture is equally apparent (as is a bit of weirdness) in the artifacts at its headquarters in Nevada. Visitors are cheered by staff as they walk by. Employees seem perpetually upbeat. Probably the most unusual artifact at Zappos is a ceremony in which guests have their picture taken while seated on a royal throne wearing a regal crown.[23]

RITUALS AND CEREMONIES

Rituals are the programmed routines of daily organizational life that dramatize an organization's culture.[21] They include how visitors are greeted, how often senior executives visit frontline staff, how people communicate with one another, how much time employees take for lunch, and so on. These rituals are repetitive, predictable events that have symbolic meanings reflecting underlying cultural values and assumptions. For instance, BMW's fast-paced culture is quite literally apparent in the way employees walk around the German automaker's offices. "When you move through the corridors and hallways of other companies' buildings, people kind of crawl, they walk slowly," observes a BMW executive. "But BMW people tend to move faster."[22] **Ceremonies** are more formal artifacts than rituals. Ceremonies are planned activities conducted specifically for the benefit of an audience. This would include publicly rewarding (or punishing) employees or celebrating the launch of a new product or newly won contract.

ORGANIZATIONAL LANGUAGE

The language of the workplace speaks volumes about the company's culture. How employees talk to one another, describe customers, express anger, and greet stakeholders are all verbal symbols of cultural values. The language of culture is apparent at The Container Store, where employees compliment each other for "being Gumby," meaning that they are as flexible as the once-popular green toy when helping a customer or another employee.[24] Language also highlights values held by organizational subcultures. Consultants working at Whirlpool kept hearing employees talk about the appliance company's "PowerPoint culture." This phrase, which refers to Microsoft's presentation software, implied that Whirlpool had a hierarchical culture in which communication was one-way (from executives to employees).[25]

PHYSICAL STRUCTURES AND SYMBOLS

Winston Churchill once said: "We shape our buildings; thereafter, they shape us."[26] The former British prime minister was reminding us that buildings both reflect and influence an organization's culture. The size, shape, location, and age of buildings might suggest a company's emphasis on teamwork, environmental friendliness, hierarchy, or any other set of values.[27] An extreme example is the "interplanetary headquarters" of Oakley, Inc. The ultra hip eyewear and clothing company built a vault-like structure in Foothills Ranch, California, complete with towering metallic walls studded with oversize bolts, to represent its secretive and protective culture. "We've always had a fortress mentality," says an Oakley executive. "What we make is gold, and people will do anything to get it, so we protect it."[28]

Even if the building doesn't make much of a statement, there is a treasure trove of physical artifacts inside. Desks, chairs, office space, and wall hangings (or lack of them) are just a few of the items that might convey cultural meaning.[29] Consider the physical artifacts that you might notice when visiting Facebook's offices. As described in the opening story to this

artifacts
The observable symbols and signs of an organization's culture.

rituals
The programmed routines of daily organizational life that dramatize the organization's culture.

ceremonies
Planned displays of organizational culture, conducted specifically for the benefit of an audience.

chapter, all of Facebook's offices have a similar open-space layout where employees work at wooden desks without any partitions. Many of these workspaces have an unfinished look. Each of these physical artifacts alone might not say much, but put enough of them together, and you can see how they symbolize Facebook's early-stage, fast-paced, creative culture with a strong collegial orientation.[30]

Is Organizational Culture Important?

LO3

Does organizational culture improve organizational effectiveness? Leaders at Facebook, Zappos, Mayo Clinic, and other companies think so. "Culture is one of the most precious things a company has, so you must work harder on it than anything else," says Herb Kelleher, founder of Southwest Airlines. Gap Adventures founder Bruce Poon Tip agrees: "If you want to maintain the brightest and the best, then corporate culture is everything."[31] Many writers of popular press management books also assert that the most successful companies have strong cultures. In fact, one popular management book, *Built to Last*, suggests that successful companies are "cult like" (though not actually cults, the authors are careful to point out).[32]

So, are companies more effective when they have a strong culture? Possibly, but research evidence indicates that the answer depends on a few conditions.[33] Before discussing these contingencies, let's examine the meaning of a "strong" organizational culture and its potential benefits. The strength of an organization's culture refers to how widely and deeply employees hold the company's dominant values and assumptions. In a strong organizational culture, most employees across all subunits understand and embrace the dominant values. These values and assumptions are also institutionalized through well-established artifacts, which further entrench the culture. In addition, strong cultures tend to be long-lasting; some can be traced back to the values and assumptions established by the company's founder. In contrast, companies have weak cultures when the dominant values are held mainly by a few people at the top of the organization, are barely discernible from artifacts, and are in flux.

As mentioned, companies with stronger cultures are potentially more effective, and this occurs through the three important functions listed in Exhibit 14.3 and described below:

1. *Control system.* Organizational culture is a deeply embedded form of social control that influences employee decisions and behavior.[34] Culture is pervasive and operates nonconsciously. You might think of it as an automatic pilot, directing employees in ways that are consistent with organizational expectations.

2. *Social glue.* Organizational culture is the "social glue" that bonds people together and makes them feel like part of the organizational experience.[35] Employees are motivated to internalize the organization's dominant culture because it fulfills their need

Lee Kum Kee Health Products Co., Ltd., a subsidiary of the Hong Kong–based food products company Lee Kum Kee (LKK), has a secret sauce that makes it one of the best places to work in Asia. "Two words explain why we are a Best Employer: corporate culture," says Raymond Lo, human resource vice president of the LKK health products group. "Our unique culture is our competitive edge. It plays a major role in the success of our organization." Lo explains that a strong culture begins with buy-in from the executive team. "Unless the chief executive and management truly believe in the culture, it won't work."[36]

for social identity. This social glue is increasingly important as a way to attract new staff and retain top performers. It also becomes the common thread that holds together employees in global organizations. "The values of the company are really the bedrock—the glue which holds the firm together," says Nandan Nilekani, the head of the government of India's technology committee and former CEO of Infosys.[37]

3. *Sense making.* Organizational culture helps employees make sense of what goes on and why things happen in the company.[38] Corporate culture also makes it easier for employees to understand what is expected of them. For instance, research has found that sales staff in companies with stronger organizational cultures have clearer role perceptions and less role-related stress.[39]

CONTINGENCIES OF ORGANIZATIONAL CULTURE AND EFFECTIVENESS

Studies have found only a modestly positive relationship between culture strength and organizational effectiveness. Why is there such a weak link? The answer is that strong cultures improve organizational effectiveness only under specific conditions (see Exhibit 14.3). Three important contingencies are whether (1) the culture content is aligned with the environment; (2) the culture is moderately strong, not cult-like; and (3) the culture incorporates an adaptive culture.

Culture Content Alignment with Environment   One contingency between cultural strength and organizational effectiveness is whether the organization's culture content—its dominant values and assumptions—is aligned with the external environment. Consider the challenges that Dell, Inc., faced a few years ago. The computer manufacturer's culture gave the highest priority to cost efficiency and competitiveness, yet these values and assumptions were no longer sufficient for the marketplace. Low-cost computers are still popular, but consumers increasingly demand computers that are innovative with elegant styling. Dell had a strong culture, but it was no longer the best culture for the external environment. "Dell's culture is not inspirational or aspirational," suggests one industry expert. "[Its] culture only wants to talk about execution."[40]

Avoiding a Corporate Cult   A second contingency is the degree of cultural strength. Various experts suggest that companies with very strong cultures (i.e., corporate "cults") may be less effective than companies with moderately strong cultures.[41] One reason corporate cults may undermine organizational effectiveness is that they lock people into mental models, which can blind them to new opportunities and unique problems. The

---

EXHIBIT 14.3   Potential Benefits and Contingencies of Culture Strength

Benefits of culture strength depend upon . . .
- Whether culture content fits the environment
- Moderate, not cult-like, strength
- An adaptive culture

Functions of strong cultures
- Control system
- Social glue
- Sense making

Organizational outcomes
- Organizational performance
- Employee well-being

Debating Point

IS CORPORATE CULTURE AN OVERUSED PHRASE?

Corporate culture is likely one of the most commonly uttered phrases in organizations these days. That's quite an accomplishment for two words that were rarely paired together prior to 1982.[42] Executives say they have crafted the company's culture to attract top talent and better serve clients. Job applicants have made organizational culture one of the top factors in their decision whether to join the company. Journalists routinely blame corporate culture for business failures, deviant activities, and quirky employee conduct.

This chapter offers plenty of ammunition to defend the argument that organizational culture explains employee decisions and behavior. A strong culture is a control system that directs employee decisions and behavior. It is, after all, the "way we do things around here." The underlying assumptions of a company's culture also guide employee behavior without conscious awareness. Furthermore, a strong culture is "social glue" that strengthens cohesion among employees. In other words, employees in strong cultures have similar beliefs and values, which in turn increase their motivation to follow the corporate herd.

Organizational culture can be a useful concept to explain workplace activities, but there are also grounds to argue that the phrase is overused. To begin with, corporate culture is usually presented as a singular thing within the company. This presumption of a homogeneous culture—in which every employee understands and embraces the same few dominant values—just doesn't exist. Every organization's culture is fragmented to some degree. Furthermore, many employees engage in façades of conformity. They pretend to live the company's values but don't actually do so because they don't believe in them.[43] Fragmentation and façades suggest that culture is not a singular force field that manipulates people like mindless robots. Instead, employees ultimately make decisions based on a variety of influences, only one of which is the organization's shared (or espoused) values and assumptions.

Another argument that the phrase "corporate culture" is overused is that values don't drive behavior as often as many people believe. Instead, employees pay attention to their values only when they are reminded of them or when the situation produces fairly obvious conflicts.[44] Most of the time, frontline staff perform their jobs without much thought to their values. Their decisions are usually technical rather than values-based matters. As such, corporate culture has a fairly peripheral role in the workplace.

A third problem is that organizational culture is a blunt instrument for explaining workplace behavior and for recommending how to change those behaviors. "Fix the culture" is almost meaningless because the problems prompting this advice could be due to any number of artifacts. Furthermore, some problems attributed to a poor corporate culture may be due to more mundane and precise dysfunctions—unintended consequences of poorly designed rewards, ineffective leadership, misaligned corporate strategy, biased information systems, and a host of other conditions. Rather than blame the company's culture, we should pay more attention to specific systems, structures, behaviors, and attitudes that explain what went wrong.

effect of these very strong cultures is that people overlook or incorrectly dismiss subtle misalignments between the organization's activities and the changing environment.

The other reason very strong cultures may be dysfunctional is that they suppress dissenting subcultural values. The challenge for organizational leaders is to maintain not only a strong culture but one that allows subcultural diversity. Subcultures encourage constructive conflict, which improves creative thinking and offers some level of ethical vigilance over the dominant culture. In the long run, a subculture's nascent values could become important dominant values as the environment changes. Corporate cults suppress subcultures, thereby undermining these benefits.

Culture Is an Adaptive Culture   A third contingency determining the influence of cultural strength on organizational effectiveness is whether the culture content includes an **adaptive culture.**[45] Facebook, described at the beginning of this chapter, has an adaptive culture because it encourages employees to be innovative and receptive to change. Employees who embrace an adaptive culture see things from an open-systems perspective. They view the organization's survival and success in terms of ongoing adaptation to the external environment, which itself is continuously changing. They assume that their future depends on monitoring the external environment and serving stakeholders with the resources available. Thus, employees in adaptive cultures have a strong sense of ownership. They take responsibility for the organization's performance and alignment with the external environment.

In an adaptive culture, receptivity to change extends to internal processes and roles. Employees recognize that satisfying stakeholder needs calls for continuous improvement of internal work processes, as well as flexibility in their own work roles. The phrase, "That's not my job," is found in nonadaptive cultures. Finally, an adaptive culture has a strong *learning orientation* because being receptive to change necessarily means that the company also supports action-oriented discovery. With a learning orientation, employees welcome new learning opportunities, actively experiment with new ideas and practices, view reasonable mistakes as a natural part of the learning process, and continuously question past practices.[46]

ORGANIZATIONAL CULTURE AND BUSINESS ETHICS

An organization's culture influences the ethical conduct of its employees. This makes sense because good behavior is driven by ethical values, and ethical values become embedded in an organization's dominant culture. Consider the recent unraveling of News Corp., the media giant that owns the *New York Post*, *The Wall Street Journal*, Fox Broadcasting, 20th Century Fox, and numerous other media around the world. Critics claim that for many years, News Corp.'s news tabloids have had a culture that rewards aggressive, partisan, and sensationalistic tactics. This culture may have uncovered news, but it allegedly also pushed some segments of the company over the ethical line.[47]

In particular, one of News Corp.'s British tabloids, *News of the World*, was caught illegally hacking into the phones of celebrities, victims, and politicians. When the first incident was discovered, the corporate chiefs swore that a rogue reporter alone was responsible. Yet over the next five years, News Corp. paid out more than (USD) $3.3 million to victims of other phone hacking incidents. Similar payouts occurred at one or more of News Corp.'s New York newspapers. News Corp. shut down *News of the World* when the extent of journalistic wrongdoing recently became public, but critics say that this dysfunctional culture still exists in other parts of the company. "Phone hacking is done by employees within the corporate culture of 'whatever it takes,'" concluded one journalist.

Merging Organizational Cultures

LO4

connect

To assist your learning and test your knowledge about merging organizational cultures, go to **www.mcgrawhillconnect.com**, which has activities and test questions on this topic.

adaptive culture
An organizational culture in which employees are receptive to change, including the ongoing alignment of the organization to its environment and continuous improvement of internal processes.

4C Corporate Culture Clash and Chemistry is a company with an unusual name and mandate. The Dutch consulting firm helps clients determine whether their culture is aligned ("chemistry") or incompatible ("clash") with a potential acquisition or merger partner. The firm also compares the company's culture with its strategy. There should be plenty of demand for 4C's expertise. One study estimated that only half of all corporate acquisitions add value, whereas two other studies report that only 30 percent of these acquisitions produce financial gains.[48] Meanwhile, mergers have a substantial disruptive effect on the organizations involved, often leading to neglected strategy, employee stress, and customer problems.

Mergers and acquisitions fail partly because corporate leaders are so focused on the financial or marketing logistics of the merging organizations that they do not conduct due diligence audits on their respective corporate cultures.[49] Some forms of integration may allow successful mergers between companies with different cultures. However, research concludes that mergers typically suffer when organizations with significantly divergent corporate cultures merge into a single entity with a high degree of integration.[50]

One recent corporate culture clash occurred when Bank of America (BofA) hastily acquired Merrill Lynch during the great financial crisis. BofA's "Main Street" culture is about serving middle America with broad-based, accessible services, whereas Merrill Lynch had a much more exclusive culture catering to wealthy clients. Consistent with these divergent client orientations, BofA's culture embraces cost efficiencies and penny pinching, whereas Merrill Lynch had more of an "entitlement" culture that encouraged big spending and bigger bonuses. To illustrate, in spite of the company's staggering losses during the previous year, Merrill Lynch's CEO spent more than $1 million renovating his office, hired an executive with a $25 million signing bonus, and handed out billions in bonuses. BofA's culture is also more cautious and bureaucratic, requiring more signatures and higher-level authority, whereas Merrill Lynch's "thundering herd" culture was more aggressive, entrepreneurial, and, some say, more likely to venture into ethically questionable territory.[51]

BICULTURAL AUDIT

Organizational leaders can minimize these cultural collisions and fulfill their duty of due diligence by conducting a bicultural audit.[52] A **bicultural audit** diagnoses cultural relations between the companies and determines the extent to which cultural clashes will likely occur. The bicultural audit process begins by identifying cultural differences between the merging companies. Next, the bicultural audit data are analyzed to determine which differences between the two firms will result in conflict and which cultural values provide common ground on which to build a cultural foundation in the merged organization. The final stage involves identifying strategies and preparing action plans to bridge the two organizations' cultures.

SABMiller plc and Molson Coors Brewing Company relied on a bicultural audit prior to forming their joint venture, MillerCoors. The due diligence analysis revealed that the two companies had different working styles but similar employee goals. The bicultural audit also helped SABMiller and Molson Coors executives discover cultural differences and thereby anticipate potential culture clashes in the joint venture.[53]

STRATEGIES FOR MERGING DIFFERENT ORGANIZATIONAL CULTURES

In some cases, the bicultural audit results in a decision to end merger talks because the two cultures are too different to merge effectively. However, even with substantially different cultures, two companies may form a workable union if they apply the appropriate merger strategy. The four main strategies for merging different corporate cultures are assimilation, deculturation, integration, and separation (see Exhibit 14.4).[54]

Assimilation   Assimilation occurs when employees at the acquired company willingly embrace the cultural values of the acquiring organization. Typically, this strategy works best when the acquired company has a weak, dysfunctional culture and the acquiring company's culture is strong and aligned with the external environment. Culture clash is rare with assimilation, because the acquired firm's culture is weak and employees are looking for better cultural alternatives. Research in Motion (RIM), the company that produces BlackBerry wireless devices, applies the assimilation strategy by deliberately acquiring only small start-up

EXHIBIT 14.4   Strategies for Merging Different Organizational Cultures

MERGER STRATEGY	DESCRIPTION	WORKS BEST WHEN:
Assimilation	Acquired company embraces acquiring firm's culture.	Acquired firm has a weak culture.
Deculturation	Acquiring firm imposes its culture on unwilling acquired firm.	Rarely works—may be necessary only when acquired firm's culture doesn't work but employees don't realize it.
Integration	Merging companies combine the two or more cultures into a new composite culture.	Existing cultures can be improved.
Separation	Merging companies remain distinct entities with minimal exchange of culture or organizational practices.	Firms operate successfully in different businesses requiring different cultures.

Sources: Based on ideas in A.R. Malekzedeh and A. Nahavandi, "Making Mergers Work by Managing Cultures," *Journal of Business Strategy* 11 (May–June 1990), pp. 55–57; K.W. Smith, "A Brand-New Culture for the Merged Firm," *Mergers and Acquisitions* 35 (June 2000), pp. 45–50.

Southwest Airlines has maintained a strong, distinctive culture throughout its dramatic growth to become America's largest airline for domestic travel. But most of that growth occurred organically, whereas cultural assimilation practices were needed to help AirTran Airways employees, which Southwest recently acquired, to understand the "Southwest Way." Southwest executive Bob Jordan also believes the success and popularity of Southwest's culture will assist this assimilation process. "It's helpful that Southwest has a great cultural reputation," says Jordan.[55]

firms. "Small companies . . . don't have cultural issues," says RIM co-CEO Jim Balsillie, adding that they are typically absorbed into RIM's culture with little fuss or attention.[56]

Deculturation   Assimilation is rare. Employees usually resist organizational change, particularly when they are asked to throw away personal and cultural values. In these conditions, some acquiring companies apply a *deculturation* strategy by imposing their culture and business practices on the acquired organization. The acquiring firm strips away artifacts and reward systems that support the old culture. People who cannot adopt the acquiring company's culture often lose their jobs. Deculturation may be necessary when the acquired firm's culture doesn't work, even when employees in the acquired company aren't convinced of it. However, this strategy is difficult to apply effectively because the acquired firm's employees resist the cultural intrusions from the buying firm, thereby delaying or undermining the merger process.

Integration   A third strategy is to combine the two or more cultures into a new composite culture that preserves the best features of the previous cultures. Integration is slow and potentially risky because there are many forces preserving the existing cultures. Still, this strategy should be considered when the companies have relatively weak cultures or when their cultures include several overlapping values. Integration also works best when people realize that their existing cultures are not good enough, which motivates them to adopt a new set of dominant values.

Separation   A separation strategy occurs when the merging companies agree to remain distinct entities with minimal exchange of culture or organizational practices. This strategy is most appropriate when the two merging companies are in unrelated industries or operate in different countries, because the most appropriate cultural values tend to differ by industry and national culture. This strategy is also relevant advice for the corporate cultures of diversified conglomerates.

bicultural audit
A process of diagnosing cultural relations between companies and determining the extent to which cultural clashes will likely occur.

For example, Amazon has applied a separation strategy in its acquisition of Zappos. "The Amazon deal got us the best of all worlds," explains Zappos CEO Tony Hsieh. "We can continue to run independently and grow the Zappos brand and culture."[57] Amazon's cultural separation approach is rare, however. Executives in acquiring firms usually have difficulty keeping their hands off the acquired firm. According to one estimate, only 15 percent of mergers leave the acquired company as a stand-alone unit.[58]

Changing and Strengthening Organizational Culture

LO5

Is it possible to change an organization's culture? Yes, but doing so isn't easy, the change rarely occurs quickly, and often the culture ends up changing (or replacing) corporate leaders. A few experts argue that an organization's culture "cannot be managed," so attempting to change the company's values and assumptions is a waste of time.[59] This may be an extreme view, but organizational culture experts generally agree that changing an organization's culture is a monumental challenge. At the same time, it is sometimes necessary to change one or more shared values and assumptions because the alignment of that culture with the external environment can influence the organization's survival and success. Over the next few pages, we will highlight four strategies that have had some success at altering corporate cultures. These strategies, illustrated in Exhibit 14.5, are not exhaustive, but each seems to work well in the right circumstances.

ACTIONS OF FOUNDERS AND LEADERS

In the early 1970s, the Four Seasons Hotels & Resorts was a small enterprise with just four properties in Canada and one in London, England. Even so, founder Isadore Sharp believed the Toronto-based company could become "the world's best hotel company." But achieving this lofty vision required mechanisms to build and maintain a strong focus on service, so Sharp searched for these methods in other companies with excellent service. One day, while attending an orientation program for new recruits at McDonald's Restaurants, Sharp realized that the fast-food chain's ability to maintain quality and service was based on well-entrenched and unwavering values. This was particularly apparent by the fact that the film McDonald's showed to new hires was at least 15 years old. "It struck me then that when you have something people can identify with, you don't have to keep reinventing it," Sharp recalls. "Once it's rooted, it sticks."[60]

Isadore Sharp and other great leaders form their organizations' culture during their early stages and introduce ways to make that culture "stick."[61] Founders are often visionaries who provide a powerful role model for others to follow. The company's culture sometimes reflects the founder's personality, and this cultural imprint can remain with the organization for decades. The founder's activities are later retold as organizational stories to further

EXHIBIT 14.5

Strategies for Changing and Strengthening Organizational Culture

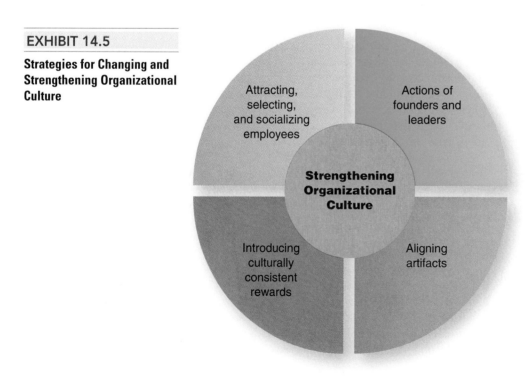

Organizational culture is so important at Rising Medical Solutions Inc. that the annual performance review is based partly on how well employees live the company values. "If the employee is observed helping coworkers on a specific project, this can be used to support that value," explains an executive at the Chicago-based company. Employees also receive guidance during daily morning huddles on how to enact the company's values. This photo shows Rising's Talent Management & Corporate Administration team's daily huddle with (from left) Kristyn Mullikin, Rick Thompson, Kathleen Dumlao, and Sarah Hulse.[66]

reinforce the culture. In spite of the founder's cultural imprint, subsequent leaders are sometimes able to reshape that culture by applying transformational leadership and organizational change practices.[62]

ALIGNING ARTIFACTS

Artifacts represent more than just the visible indicators of a company's culture. They are also mechanisms that keep the culture in place. By altering artifacts—or creating new ones—leaders can potentially adjust shared values and assumptions. Corporate cultures are also altered and strengthened through the artifacts of stories and behaviors. According to Max De Pree, former CEO of furniture manufacturer Herman Miller Inc., every organization needs "tribal storytellers" to keep the organization's history and culture alive.[63] Leaders play a role by creating memorable events that symbolize the cultural values they want to develop or maintain. Companies also strengthen culture in new operations by transferring current employees who abide by the culture.

INTRODUCING CULTURALLY CONSISTENT REWARDS

Reward systems are artifacts that often have a powerful effect on strengthening or reshaping an organization's culture.[64] Robert Nardelli used rewards to change Home Depot's freewheeling culture. Nardelli introduced precise measures of corporate performance and drilled managers with weekly performance objectives related to those metrics. A two-hour weekly conference call became a ritual in which Home Depot's top executives were held accountable for the previous week's goals. These actions reinforced a more disciplined (and centralized) performance-oriented culture.[65]

ATTRACTING, SELECTING, AND SOCIALIZING EMPLOYEES

The opening story to this chapter described how Facebook transfers and embeds its unique culture at new locations through a Landing Team that consists of current employees. One of the first strategies—and arguably the most important strategy—for embedding Facebook's culture in a new location is to attract and hire people whose values are consistent with that culture. This process, along with weeding out people who don't fit the culture, is explained by **attraction–selection–attrition (ASA) theory.**[67] ASA theory states that

attraction–selection–attrition (ASA) theory
A theory which states that organizations have a natural tendency to attract, select, and retain people with values and personality characteristics that are consistent with the organization's character, resulting in a more homogeneous organization and a stronger culture.

"You seem intelligent, capable, level-headed and mature. That's a shame because I was really hoping you'd fit in here."

Credit: Copyright © Randy Glasbergen, www.glasbergen.com. Reprinted with permission.

organizations have a natural tendency to attract, select, and retain people with values and personality characteristics that are consistent with the organization's character, resulting in a more homogeneous organization and a stronger culture.

- *Attraction.* Job applicants engage in self-selection by avoiding employment in companies whose values seem incompatible with their own values.[68] They look for subtle artifacts during interviews and through public information that communicate the company's culture. Some organizations often encourage this self-selection by actively describing their cultures. At Reckitt Benckiser, for instance, applicants can complete an online simulation that estimates their fit with the British household products company's hard-driving culture. Participants indicate how they would respond to a series of business scenarios. The exercise then calculates their cultural fit score and asks them to decide whether to continue pursuing employment with the company.[69]

- *Selection.* How well the person "fits" in with the company's culture is often a factor in deciding which job applicants to hire. Companies with strong cultures often put applicants through several interviews and other selection tests, in part to better gauge the applicant's values and their congruence with the company's values.[70] Consider Park Place Dealerships. As one of the top-rated luxury car dealerships in the United States, the Dallas–Fort Worth company relies on interviews and selection tests to carefully screen applicants for their culture fit. "Testing is one piece of our hiring process that enables us to find people who will not only be successful in our culture, but thrive and enjoy our culture," says Park Place chairman Ken Schnitzer. "It's not easy to get hired by Park Place."[71]

- *Attrition.* People are motivated to seek environments that are sufficiently congruent with their personal values and to leave environments that are a poor fit. This occurs because person–organization values congruence supports their social identity and minimizes internal role conflict. Even if employees aren't forced out, many quit when the values incongruence is sufficiently high.[72]

Organizational Culture
During the Hiring Process[73]

58%
of 1,500 American job seekers polled wanted to know, during the hiring process, about the **company's culture.**

68%
of Fortune 500 high-tech companies take steps to describe their corporate culture to job seekers.

75%
of 500 Canadian executives polled say **cultural fit** is more important than skills for selecting external candidates.

44%
of Fortune 500 companies take steps to describe their **corporate culture** to job seekers.

Organizational Socialization

Along with their use of attraction, selection, and attrition, organizations rely on organizational socialization to maintain a strong corporate culture. **Organizational socialization** is the process by which individuals learn the values, expected behaviors, and social knowledge necessary to assume their roles in the organization.[74] This process can potentially change employee values to be more aligned with the company's culture, though this is much more difficult than is often assumed. An individual's values do not change much past young adulthood. More likely, effective socialization gives newcomers clearer understanding about the company's values and how they translate into specific on-the-job behaviors.[75]

Along with supporting the organization's culture, socialization helps newcomers adjust to coworkers, work procedures, and other corporate realities. Research indicates that when employees are effectively socialized into the organization, they tend to perform better, have higher job satisfaction, and remain longer with the organization.[76]

ORGANIZATIONAL SOCIALIZATION AS A LEARNING AND ADJUSTMENT PROCESS

Organizational socialization is a process of both learning and adjustment. It is a learning process because newcomers try to make sense of the company's physical workplace, social dynamics, and strategic and cultural environment. They learn about the organization's performance expectations, power dynamics, corporate culture, company history, and jargon. They also need to form successful and satisfying relationships with other people from whom they can learn the ropes.[77] Thus, effective socialization enables new employees to form a cognitive map of the physical, social, and strategic and cultural dynamics of the organization without information overload.

Organizational socialization is also a process of adjustment, because individuals need to adapt to their new work environment. They develop new work roles that reconfigure their social identity, adopt new team norms, and practice new behaviors.[78] Research reports that the adjustment process is fairly rapid for many people, usually occurring within a few months. However, newcomers with diverse work experience seem to adjust better than those with limited previous experience, possibly because they have a larger toolkit of knowledge and skills to make the adjustment possible.[79]

ORGANIZATIONAL SOCIALIZATION AND PSYCHOLOGICAL CONTRACTS

For 14 years, John Kolliopoulos was a loyal employee at a major department store chain. The information technology (IT) expert was proud to be employed there, and he worked hard to perform his job. Then one day, he and other IT department employees learned that management had outsourced the entire IT department. "All those feelings of loyalty went away when we were shown the door," recalls Kolliopoulos, who now works for an IT company. "Now I no longer have any sense of faith or trust in any employer."[80]

Kolliopoulos and his coworkers experienced the shock of having their psychological contract violated. The **psychological contract** refers to the individual's beliefs about the terms and conditions of a reciprocal exchange agreement between that person and another party (the employer in most work situations). The psychological contract is a perception formed during recruitment and throughout the organizational socialization process about what the employee is entitled to receive and is obliged to offer the employer in return.[81]

Job applicants form perceptions of what the company will offer them by way of career and learning opportunities,

organizational socialization
The process by which individuals learn the values, expected behaviors, and social knowledge necessary to assume their roles in the organization.

psychological contract
The individual's beliefs about the terms and conditions of a reciprocal exchange agreement between that person and another party (typically an employer).

job resources, pay and benefits, quality of management, job security, and so forth. They also form perceptions about what the company expects from them, such as hours of work, continuous skill development, and demonstrated loyalty. For example, John Kolliopoulos believed that his psychological contract included long-term employment in return for hard work and loyalty to his employer. The psychological contract continues to develop and evolve after job applicants become employees, but they are also continuously testing the employer's fulfillment of that exchange relationship.

Types of Psychological Contracts

Some psychological contracts are more transactional, whereas others are more relational.[82] Transactional contracts are primarily short-term economic exchanges. Responsibilities are well defined around a fairly narrow set of obligations that do not change over the life of the contract. People hired in temporary positions and as consultants tend to have transactional contracts. To some extent, new employees also form transactional contracts until they develop a sense of continuity with the organization.

In contrast, relational contracts are rather like marriages; they are long-term attachments that encompass a broad array of subjective mutual obligations. Employees with a relational psychological contract are more willing to contribute their time and effort without expecting the organization to pay back this debt in the short term. Relational contracts are also dynamic, meaning that the parties tolerate and expect that mutual obligations are not necessarily balanced in the short run. Not surprisingly, organizational citizenship behaviors are more likely to prevail under relational than transactional contracts. Permanent employees are more likely to believe they have a relational contract.

STAGES OF ORGANIZATIONAL SOCIALIZATION

Organizational socialization is a continuous process, beginning long before the first day of employment and continuing throughout one's career within the company. However, it is most intense when people move across organizational boundaries, such as when they first join a company or get transferred to an international assignment. Each of these transitions is a process that can be divided into three stages. Our focus here is on the socialization of new employees, so the three stages are called preemployment socialization, encounter, and role management (see Exhibit 14.6). These stages parallel the individual's transitions from outsider to newcomer and then to insider.[83]

Stage 1: Preemployment Socialization

Think back to the months and weeks before you began working in a new job (or attending a new school). You actively searched for information about the company, formed expectations about working there, and felt some anticipation about fitting into that environment. The preemployment socialization

---

EXHIBIT 14.6   Stages of Organizational Socialization

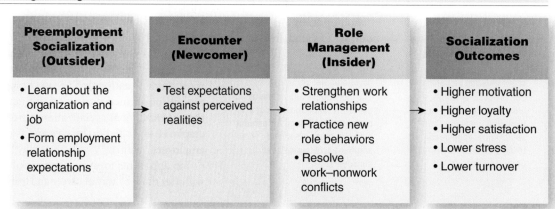

stage encompasses all the learning and adjustment that occurs before the first day of work. In fact, a large part of the socialization adjustment process occurs during this stage.[84]

The main problem with preemployment socialization is that outsiders rely on indirect information about what it is like to work in the organization. This information is often distorted by inherent conflicts during the mating dance between employer and applicant.[85] One conflict occurs between the employer's need to attract qualified applicants and the applicant's need for complete information to make accurate employment decisions. Many firms use a "flypaper" approach by describing only positive aspects of the job and company, causing applicants to accept job offers based on incomplete or false expectations. Another conflict that prevents the accurate exchange of information occurs when applicants avoid asking important questions about the company because they want to convey a favorable image to their prospective employer. For instance, applicants usually don't like to ask about starting salaries and promotion opportunities because it makes them seem greedy or aggressive. Yet unless the employer provides this information, applicants might fill in the missing information with false assumptions that produce an inaccurate psychological contract.

Two other types of conflict tend to distort preemployment information for employers. Applicants engage in impression management when seeking employment, and this tends to motivate them to hide negative information, act out of character, and occasionally embellish information about their past accomplishments. At the same time, employers are sometimes reluctant to ask certain questions or use potentially valuable selection devices because they might scare off applicants. Unfortunately, exaggerated résumés from applicants and reluctance to ask for some information cause employers to form a less accurate opinion of the job candidate's potential as an employee.

Stage 2: Encounter   The first day on the job typically marks the beginning of the encounter stage of organizational socialization. This is the stage in which newcomers test how well their preemployment expectations fit reality. Many companies fail the test, resulting in **reality shock**—the stress that results when employees perceive discrepancies between their preemployment expectations and the on-the-job reality.[86] Reality shock doesn't necessarily occur on the first day; it might develop over several weeks or even months as newcomers form a better understanding of their new work environment.

Reality shock is common in many organizations.[87] Unmet expectations sometimes occur because the employer is unable to live up to its promises, such as failing to provide challenging projects or the resources to get the work done. Reality shock also occurs because new hires develop distorted work expectations through the information exchange conflicts described previously. Whatever the cause, reality shock impedes the socialization process because the newcomer's energy is directed toward managing the stress rather than learning and accepting organizational knowledge and roles.[88]

Stage 3: Role Management   Role management, the third stage of organizational socialization, really begins during preemployment socialization, but it is most active as employees make the transition from newcomers to insiders. They strengthen relationships with coworkers and supervisors, practice new role behaviors, and adopt attitudes and values consistent with their new positions and the organization. Role management also involves resolving the conflicts between work and nonwork activities, including resolving discrepancies between their existing values and those emphasized by the organizational culture.

reality shock
The stress that results when employees perceive discrepancies between their preemployment expectations and on-the-job reality.

realistic job preview (RJP)
A method of improving organizational socialization in which job applicants are given a balance of positive and negative information about the job and work context.

IMPROVING THE SOCIALIZATION PROCESS

One potentially effective way to improve the socialization process is through a **realistic job preview (RJP),** which provides applicants with a balance of positive and negative information about the job and work context.[89] Unfortunately, as mentioned previously, many companies

Lindblad Expeditions can't afford to have crew members jump ship soon after starting the job. To minimize their reality shock, the adventure cruise company gives applicants a realistic picture of what it's like to work on board. Applicants watch a video program that shows exciting aspects of the work, as well as the challenges (such as cleaning toilets and sleeping in small quarters). The video is meant to scare off some applicants, but Lindblad human resource manager Kris Thompson points out that this attrition is well worth it if it reduces turnover soon after staff are hired. "If [new recruits] get on board and say, 'This is not what I expected,' then shame on us," says Thompson.[90]

overpromise. They often exaggerate positive features of the job and neglect to mention the undesirable elements in the hope that the best applicants will be attracted to the organization.

In contrast, an RJP helps job applicants to decide for themselves whether their skills, needs, and values are compatible with the job and organization. RJPs scare away some applicants, but they also tend to reduce turnover and increase job performance.[91] This occurs because RJPs help applicants develop more accurate preemployment expectations, which minimize reality shock. RJPs represent a type of vaccination by preparing employees for the more challenging and troublesome aspects of work life. There is also some evidence that RJPs increase organizational loyalty. A possible explanation is that companies providing candid information are easier to trust. They also show respect for the psychological contract and concern for employee welfare.[92]

Socialization Agents   Ask new employees what most helped them adjust to their jobs, and chances are they will mention helpful coworkers, bosses, or friends who work elsewhere in the organization. The fact is that socialization occurs mainly through these socialization agents.[93] Supervisors tend to provide technical information, performance feedback, and information about job duties. They also improve the socialization process by giving newcomers reasonably challenging first assignments, buffering them from excessive demands, and helping them form social ties with coworkers.

Coworkers are important socialization agents because they are easily accessible, can answer questions when problems arise, and serve as role models for appropriate behavior. New employees tend to receive this information and support when coworkers integrate them into the work team. Coworkers also aid the socialization process by being flexible and tolerant in their interactions with new hires.

The challenge for some companies is the socialization of newcomers when opening new offices or stores or after acquiring another company. Facebook addresses this issue through its Landing Teams. As we described at the beginning of this chapter, these specially selected teams of current employees are parachuted into the new site to hire and train local staff. The Landing Team members are also socialization agents because they actively coach newcomers about the values and corresponding desired behaviors that represent the organization's culture.

Several organizations rely on a "buddy system," whereby newcomers are assigned to coworkers for sources of information and social support. Meridian Technology Center in Stillwater, Oklahoma, relies on a buddy system. Buddies introduce new hires to other employees, give them campus tours, and generally familiarize them with the physical layout of the workplace. They have lunch with employees on their first day and meet weekly with them for their first two months. CXtec, a networking and voice technology company in Syracuse, New York, helps new staff meet other employees through food. On the first Friday of each month, new staff members take charge of the doughnut cart, introducing themselves as they distribute the morning snack to the company's 350 employees.[94] Collectively, these practices help newcomers form social networks, which are powerful means of gaining information and influence in the organization.

[chapter summary]

LO1 Describe the elements of organizational culture and discuss the importance of organizational subcultures.

Organizational culture consists of the values and assumptions shared within an organization. Shared assumptions are nonconscious, taken-for-granted perceptions or beliefs that have worked so well in the past that they are considered the correct way to think and act toward problems and opportunities. Values are stable, evaluative beliefs that guide our preferences for outcomes or courses of action in a variety of situations.

Organizations differ in their cultural content, that is, the relative ordering of values. There are several classifications of organizational culture, but they tend to oversimplify the wide variety of cultures and completely ignore the underlying assumptions of culture. Organizations have subcultures as well as a dominant culture. Subcultures maintain the organization's standards of performance and ethical behavior. They are also the source of emerging values that replace aging core values.

LO2 List four categories of artifacts through which corporate culture is deciphered.

Artifacts are the observable symbols and signs of an organization's culture. Four broad categories of artifacts are organizational stories and legends, rituals and ceremonies, language, and physical structures and symbols. Understanding an organization's culture requires assessment of many artifacts because they are subtle and often ambiguous.

LO3 Discuss the importance of organizational culture and the conditions in which organizational culture strength improves organizational performance.

Organizational culture has three main functions: a form of social control, the "social glue" that bonds people together, and a way to help employees make sense of the workplace. Companies with strong cultures generally perform better than those with weak cultures, but only when the cultural content is appropriate for the organization's environment. Also, the culture should not be so strong that it drives out dissenting values, which may form emerging values for the future. Organizations should have adaptive cultures so that employees support ongoing change in the organization and their own roles.

LO4 Compare and contrast four strategies for merging organizational cultures.

Organizational culture clashes are common in mergers and acquisitions. This problem can be minimized by performing a bicultural audit to diagnose the compatibility of the organizational cultures. The four main strategies for merging different corporate cultures are integration, deculturation, assimilation, and separation.

LO5 Identify four strategies for changing or strengthening an organization's culture, including the application of attraction–selection–attrition theory.

Organizational culture is very difficult to change, but cultural change is possible and sometimes necessary for a company's continued survival. Four strategies for changing and strengthening an organization's culture are the actions of founders and leaders; aligning artifacts with the desired culture; introducing culturally consistent rewards; and attracting, selecting, and socializing employees.

Attraction–selection–attrition (ASA) theory states that organizations have a natural tendency to attract, select, and retain people with values and personality characteristics that are consistent with the organization's character, resulting in a more homogeneous organization and a stronger culture. Organizational socialization is the process by which individuals learn the values, expected behaviors, and social knowledge necessary to assume their roles in the organization. It is a process of both learning about the work context and adjusting to new work roles, team norms, and behaviors.

LO6 Describe the organizational socialization process and identify strategies to improve that process.

Organizational socialization is the process by which individuals learn the values, expected behaviors, and social knowledge necessary to assume their roles in the organization. It is a process of both learning and adjustment. During this process, job applicants and newcomers develop and test their psychological contract—personal beliefs about the terms and conditions of a reciprocal exchange agreement between that person and another party (the employer).

Employees typically pass through three socialization stages: preemployment, encounter, and role management. To manage the socialization process, organizations should introduce realistic job previews (RJPs) and recognize the value of socialization agents in the process. RJPs give job applicants a realistic balance of positive and negative information about the job and work context. Socialization agents provide information and social support during the socialization process.

adaptive culture, p. 414

artifacts, p. 410

attraction–selection–attrition (ASA) theory, p. 419

bicultural audit, p. 416

ceremonies, p. 411

organizational culture, p. 406

organizational socialization, p. 421

psychological contract, p. 421

realistic job preview (RJP), p. 423

reality shock, p. 423

rituals, p. 411

critical thinking questions

1. Superb Consultants has submitted a proposal to analyze your organization's culture. The proposal states that Superb has developed a revolutionary new survey to tap the company's true culture. The survey takes just 10 minutes to complete, and the consultants say the results can be based on a small sample of employees. Discuss the merits and limitations of this proposal.

2. Some people suggest that the most effective organizations have the strongest cultures. What do we mean by the "strength" of organizational culture, and what possible problems are there with a strong organizational culture?

3. The CEO of a manufacturing firm wants everyone to support the organization's dominant culture of lean efficiency and hard work. The CEO has introduced a new reward system to reinforce this culture and personally interviews all professional and managerial applicants to ensure that they bring similar values to the organization. Some employees who criticized these values had their careers sidelined until they left. Two midlevel managers were fired for supporting contrary values, such as work–life balance. Based on your knowledge of organizational subcultures, what potential problems is the CEO creating?

4. Identify at least two artifacts from each of the four broad categories that you have observed in your department or school: (a) organizational stories and legends, (b) rituals and ceremonies, (c) language, and (d) physical structures and symbols.

5. "Organizations are more likely to succeed when they have an adaptive culture." What can an organization do to foster an adaptive culture?

6. Suppose you are asked by senior officers of a city government to identify ways to reinforce a new culture of teamwork and collaboration. The senior executive group clearly supports these values, but it wants everyone in the organization to embrace them. Identify four types of activities that would strengthen these cultural values.

7. Socialization is most intense when people pass through organizational boundaries. One example is your entry into the college or university that you are now attending. What learning and adjustment occurred as you moved from outsider to newcomer to insider as a student here?

8. Acme Corp. is planning to acquire Beta Corp., which operates in a different industry. Acme's culture is entrepreneurial and fast-paced, whereas Beta employees value slow, deliberate decision making by consensus. Which merger strategy would you recommend to minimize culture shock when Acme acquires Beta? Explain your answer.

9. How do you think organizational culture differs from and is similar to that of country culture? In Chapter 2 we discussed "values across cultures" when we discussed individualism versus collectivism, power distance, uncertainty avoidance, and several other dimensions. Please discuss these issues relative to organizational culture.

CASE STUDY 14.1 HILLTON'S TRANSFORMATION

Twenty years ago, Hillton was a small city (about 70,000 residents) that served as an outer suburb to a large metropolitan city. Hillton treated city employees like family and gave them a great deal of autonomy in their work. Everyone in the organization (including the two labor unions representing employees) implicitly agreed that the leaders and supervisors of the organization should rise through the ranks based on their experience. Few people were ever hired from the outside into middle or senior positions. The rule of employment at Hillton was to learn the job skills, maintain a reasonably good work record, and wait your turn for promotion.

Hillton has grown rapidly since the mid-1960s. As the population grew, so did the municipality's workforce, to keep pace with the increasing demand for municipal services.

This meant that employees were promoted fairly quickly and were almost assured lifetime employment. Until recently, Hillton had never laid off any employee. The organization's culture could be described as one of entitlement and comfort. Neither the elected city councilors nor the city manager bothered departmental managers about their work. There were few cost controls, because the rapid growth placed more emphasis on keeping up with the population expansion. The public became somewhat more critical of the city's poor service, including road construction at inconvenient times and the apparent lack of respect some employees showed toward taxpayers.

During these expansion years, Hillton put most of its money into "outside" (also called "hard") municipal services. These included road building, utility construction and maintenance, fire and police protection, recreational facilities, and land use control. This emphasis occurred because an expanding population demanded more of these services, and most of Hillton's senior people came from the outside services group. For example, Hillton's city manager for many years was a road development engineer. The "inside" workers (taxation, community services, etc.) tended to have less seniority, and their departments were given less priority.

As commuter and road systems developed, Hillton attracted more upwardly mobile professionals into the community. Some infrastructure demands continued, but now these suburban dwellers wanted more of the "soft" services, such as libraries, social activities, and community services. They also began complaining about the way the municipality was being run. The population had more than tripled between the 1960s and 1990s, and it was increasingly apparent that the organization needed more corporate planning, information systems, organization development, and cost control systems. In various ways, residents voiced their concerns that the municipality was not providing the quality of management that they would expect from a city of its size.

In 1996, a new mayor and council replaced most of the previous incumbents, mainly on the platform of improving the municipality's management structure. The new council gave the city manager, along with two other senior managers, an early retirement buyout package. Rather than promoting from the lower ranks, council decided to fill all three positions with qualified candidates from large municipal corporations in the region. The following year, several long-term managers left Hillton, and at least half of those positions were filled by people from outside the organization.

In less than two years, Hillton had eight senior or departmental managers hired from other municipalities who played a key role in changing the organization's value system. These eight managers became known (often with negative connotations) as the "professionals." They worked closely with one another to change the way middle- and lower-level managers had operated for many years. They brought in a new computer system and emphasized cost controls where managers previously had complete autonomy. Promotions were increasingly based more on merit than seniority.

The "professionals" frequently announced in meetings and newsletters that municipal employees must provide superlative customer service and that Hillton would become one of the most customer-friendly places for citizens and those who do business with the municipality. To this end, these managers were quick to support the public's increasing demand for more "soft" services, including expanded library services and recreational activities. And when population growth recently flattened out for a few years, the city manager and other professionals gained council support to lay off a few of the outside workers due to lack of demand for hard services.

One of the most significant changes was that the "outside" departments no longer held dominant positions in city management. Most of the "professional" managers had worked exclusively in administrative and related inside jobs. Two had Master's of Business Administration degrees. This led to some tension between the professional managers and the older outside managers.

Even before the layoffs, managers of outside departments resisted the changes more than others. These managers complained that their employees with the highest seniority were turned down for promotions. They argued for more budget and warned that infrastructure problems would cause liability problems. Informally, these outside managers were supported by the labor union representing outside workers. The union leaders tried to bargain for more job guarantees, whereas the union representing inside workers focused more on improving wages and benefits. Leaders of the outside union made several statements in the local media that the city had "lost its heart" and that the public would suffer from the actions of the new professionals.

Discussion Questions

1. Contrast Hillton's earlier corporate culture with the emerging set of cultural values.

2. Considering the difficulty in changing organizational culture, why does Hillton's management seem to have been successful in this transformation?

3. Identify two other strategies that the city might consider to reinforce the new set of corporate values.

CASE STUDY 14.2 SEPARATING THE STEAM FROM THE HAZE

"We need more steam mix for our hamburger buns," a veteran employee calls out to the new hire at a McDonald's Restaurant. "Get another package of mix, please."

For the newly hired McDonald's employee, this is just another task to learn in the confusing world of fast-food restaurants. For seasoned employees, it is a ritual for newcomers that usually brings hilarity to the otherwise serious work-oriented setting.

Some new employees get the joke immediately, but most scurry to the food storage area in search of the elusive package of steam mix. They check among the stacks of hamburger buns and in the freezer around the boxes of french fries for any package that says "steam mix" on it. After five or ten minutes, the discouraged recruits return empty-handed and ask for further directions.

Sometimes, if it isn't too busy, coworkers might say: "It's the big bag clearly marked 'Steam Mix'! The one with the picture of a kettle on it." Occasionally, the hazing might go one step further. With a straight face, an employee might reply, "Oh, that's right. We're out of steam mix. Here, take this bucket and go next door to Burger King. We often borrow some of their mix."

Eager to please their fellow employees, newcomers scurry across the parking lot with a McDonald's bucket in hand and politely ask a Burger King employee for some of their steam mix. A few Burger King staff members have learned to play along with the game by telling the visitor that their steam mix is different than what McDonald's uses. More often, the new McDonald's worker is politely reminded that steam comes from boiled water and doesn't require any other ingredients.

Across the parking lot, coworkers watch the embarrassed (and occasionally angry) newcomer return with the empty McDonald's bucket. Somehow, the hazing ritual never loses its appeal, maybe because it provides a welcome break from the work. No one has quit over the experience, though most newcomers are subsequently cautious whenever coworkers ask them to retrieve anything from the storage area.

Discussion Questions

1. What negative effects, if any, does this hazing activity have on the socialization of new employees? Why? Would this type of hazing have a positive effect on socialization in any way?

2. What hazing rituals are you aware of in organizational settings? Why do they occur? Should they be discouraged, or are they of some value?

3. Identify any organizational behavior topics that would explain why this hazing activity occurs and what consequences it has for the employee, coworkers, and restaurant.

Source: Based on information provided to Steven L. McShane by a student in Vancouver, Canada who survived this hazing ritual and watched many others experience it.

TEAM EXERCISE 14.3 ORGANIZATIONAL CULTURE METAPHORS

By David L. Luechauer, Butler University, and Gary M. Shulman, Miami University

PURPOSE Both parts of this exercise are designed to help you understand, assess, and interpret organizational culture using metaphors.

PART A: ASSESSING YOUR SCHOOL'S CULTURE

Instructions A metaphor is a figure of speech that contains an implied comparison between a word or phrase that is ordinarily used for one thing but can be applied to another. Metaphors also carry a great deal of hidden meaning—they say a lot about what we think and feel about that object. Therefore, this activity asks you to use several metaphors to define the organizational culture of your university, college, or institute. (Alternatively, the instructor might ask students to assess another organization that most students know about.)

Step 1: The class will be divided into teams of four to six members.

Step 2: Each team will reach consensus on which words or phrases should be inserted in the blanks of the statements presented below. This information should be recorded on a flip chart or overhead for class presentation. The instructor will provide 15 to 20 minutes for teams to determine which words best describe the college's culture.

If our school was an animal, it would be a _____ because _____.

If our school was a food, it would be _____ because _____.

If our school was a place, it would be _____ because _____.

If our school was a season, it would be _____ because _____.

If our school was a TV show or movie, it would be _____ because _____.

Step 3: The class will listen to each team present the metaphors that it believes symbolize the school's culture. For example, a team that picks winter for a season might explain they are feeling cold or distant about the school and its people.

Step 4: The class will discuss the following discussion questions.

Discussion Questions for Part A

1. How easy was it for your group to reach consensus regarding these metaphors? What does that imply about the culture of your school?

2. How do you see these metaphors in action? In other words, what are some critical school behaviors or other artifacts that reveal the presence of your culture?

3. Think of another organization to which you belong (e.g., work, religious congregation). What are its dominant cultural values, how do you see them in action, and how do they affect the effectiveness of that organization?

PART B: ANALYZING AND INTERPRETING CULTURAL METAPHORS

Instructions Previously, you completed a metaphor exercise to describe the corporate culture of your school. That exercise gave you a taste of how to administer such a diagnostic tool and draw inferences from the results generated. This activity builds on that experience and is designed to help refine your ability to analyze such data and make suggestions for improvement. Five work teams (four to seven members, mixed gender in all groups) of an organization located in Cincinnati completed the metaphor exercise similar to the exercise in which you participated in class (see Part A). Their responses are shown in the table below. Working in teams, analyze the information in this table and answer these questions:

Discussion Questions for Part B

1. In your opinion, what are the dominant cultural values in this organization? Explain your answer.

2. What are the positive aspects of this type of culture?
3. What are the negative aspects of this type of culture?
4. What is this organization's main business, in your opinion? Explain your answer.
5. These groups all reported to one manager. What advice would you give to the manager about this unit?

Metaphor Results of Five Teams in a Cincinnati Organization

TEAM	ANIMAL	FOOD	PLACE	TV SHOW	SEASON
1	Rabbit	Big Mac	Casino	*48 Hrs.* (movie)	Spring
2	Horse	Taco	Racetrack	*Miami Vice*	Spring
3	Elephant	Ribs	Circus	*Roseanne*	Summer
4	Eagle	Big Mac	Las Vegas	CNN	Spring
5	Panther	Chinese	New York	*LA Law*	Racing

Source: Adapted from D.L. Luechauer and G.M. Shulman, "Using a Metaphor Exercise to Explore the Principles of Organizational Culture," *Journal of Management Education* 22 (December 1998), pp. 736–44. Used with permission of the authors.

CLASS EXERCISE 14.4 DIAGNOSING CORPORATE CULTURE PROCLAMATIONS

PURPOSE This exercise is designed to help you understand the importance and context in which corporate culture is identified and discussed in organizations.

INSTRUCTIONS This exercise is a take-home activity, though it can be completed in classes where computers and Internet connections are available. The instructor will divide the class into small teams (typically four or five people per team). Each team is assigned a specific industry—such as energy, biotechnology, or computer hardware.

The team's task is to search the websites of several companies in the selected industry for company statements about their corporate cultures. Use company website search engines (if they exist) to find documents with key phrases such as "corporate culture" or "company values."

In the next class, or at the end of the time allotted in the current class, report on your observations by answering the following three discussion questions.

Discussion Questions

1. What values seem to dominate the corporate cultures of the companies you searched? Are these values similar or diverse across companies in the industry?

2. What was the broader content of the web pages on which these companies described or mentioned their corporate cultures?

3. Do companies in this industry refer to their corporate cultures on their websites more or less than companies in other industries searched by teams in this class?

SELF-ASSESSMENT 14.5 WHICH CORPORATE CULTURE DO YOU PREFER?

PURPOSE This self-assessment is designed to help you identify the corporate culture that fits most closely with your personal values and assumptions.

INSTRUCTIONS Read each pair of statements in the Corporate Culture Preference Scale and circle the statement that describes the organization you would prefer to work for. Then use the scoring key in Appendix B at the end of the book to calculate your results for each subscale.

The scale does not attempt to measure your preference for every corporate culture—just a few of the more common varieties. Also, keep in mind that none of these corporate cultures is inherently good or bad. The focus here is on how well you fit within each of them. This exercise should be completed alone so that you can assess yourself honestly without concerns of social comparison. Class discussion will focus on the importance of matching job applicants to the organization's dominant values.

Corporate Culture Preference Scale

I WOULD PREFER TO WORK IN AN ORGANIZATION:		
1a. Where employees work well together in teams.	*or*	1b. That produces highly respected products or services.
2a. Where top management maintains a sense of order in the workplace.	*or*	2b. Where the organization listens to customers and responds quickly to their needs.
3a. Where employees are treated fairly.	*or*	3b. Where employees continuously search for ways to work more efficiently.
4a. Where employees adapt quickly to new work requirements.	*or*	4b. Where corporate leaders work hard to keep employees happy.
5a. Where senior executives receive special benefits not available to other employees.	*or*	5b. Where employees are proud when the organization achieves its performance goals.
6a. Where employees who perform the best get paid the most.	*or*	6b. Where senior executives are respected.
7a. Where everyone gets her or his job done like clockwork.	*or*	7b. That is on top of innovations in the industry.
8a. Where employees receive assistance to overcome any personal problems.	*or*	8b. Where employees abide by company rules.
9a. That is always experimenting with new ideas in the marketplace.	*or*	9b. That expects everyone to put in 110 percent for peak performance.
10a. That quickly benefits from market opportunities.	*or*	10b. Where employees are always kept informed about what's happening in the organization.
11a. That can quickly respond to competitive threats.	*or*	11b. Where most decisions are made by the top executives.
12a. Where management keeps everything under control.	*or*	12b. Where employees care for each other.

 After reading this chapter go to www.mhhe.com/mcshane6e for more in-depth information and interactivities that correspond to the chapter.

Organizational Change

learning objectives

After reading this chapter, you should be able to:

LO1 Describe the elements of Lewin's force field analysis model.

LO2 Discuss the reasons people resist organizational change and how change agents should view this resistance.

LO3 Outline six strategies for minimizing resistance to change, and debate ways to effectively create an urgency for change.

LO4 Discuss how leadership, coalitions, social networks, and pilot projects influence organizational change.

LO5 Describe and compare action research, appreciative inquiry, large group interventions, and parallel learning structures as formal approaches to organizational change.

LO6 Discuss two cross-cultural and three ethical issues in organizational change.

CEO a few years ago. The company recorded massive losses as its sales and reputation plummeted. Today, despite the worst economic downturn in 50 years, Ford's production efficiency, customer satisfaction ratings, and market share are soaring. Five out of six Ford employees say their company is heading in the right direction. Mulally has been hailed as a turnaround champion by transforming Ford into the most successful and competitive automaker in America.

How did this remarkable corporate transformation occur? Most observers point to Mulally's vision for change ("One Ford—One Team, One Plan, One Goal"), which focused everyone on one brand (Ford) with a few models that have global platforms. This change was difficult because executives jealously guarded their vehicle badges and built their products mainly for the North American market. Ford's transformation was also painful. It shuttered 16 manufacturing facilities, laid off many staff, sold off peripheral brands (e.g., Land Rover, Jaguar), and negotiated lower labor costs.

Mulally, previously a senior executive at Boeing, took a hands-on role to change Ford's defensive and territorial culture. He joined staff in visiting customers and industry groups. He held numerous town hall meetings, repeating the same message: Everyone needs to cooperate more across divisions and focus more on customers than on careers. He also emphasized the urgency for change: "We have been going out of business for 40 years," Mulally quipped at several sessions.

Mulally shook up Ford's bureaucratic defensiveness by persistently challenging Ford engineers and executives to answer tough questions about quality and profitability. "Why haven't you figured out a way to make a profit?" he asked one group about losses of the Ford Focus. When a few offered lame answers about costs and sales quotas, Mulally shot back: "That's not what I asked! I want to know why no one figured a way to build this car at a profit." To reinforce this change, Mulally created a pilot project—a special global task force that designed and engineered a new Focus with the same chassis, features, and name around the world. Today, the Ford Focus is Mulally's "proof point"—a beacon of his "One Ford" vision.

Mulally's toughest challenge was to nurture an executive team that focused on "One Ford" rather than departmental fiefdoms. He partially accomplished this goal through weekly business planning review meetings, where his 16 direct reports are required to pay close attention to each other's presentation slides. Private chats and other distractions are prohibited. "If you aren't comfortable with that, you might be more comfortable leaving the company," said Mulally with a friendly, yet meaningful, tone.[1]

Alan Mulally applied several key change management practices to turn around an ailing Ford Motor Company.

The transformation of Ford Motor Company illustrates many of the strategies and practices necessary to change organizations. It reveals how CEO Alan Mulally created an urgency for change, revised systems and structures to support the change, introduced a pilot project (the Ford Focus development team) to spearhead the company's new global approach, and continuously communicated the change process. Although Ford's turnaround sounds like an smooth-running process, most organizational change is messy, requiring considerable leadership effort and vigilance. As we will describe throughout this chapter, the challenge of change is not just in deciding which way to go; the challenge is in the execution of this strategy. When leaders discover the need for change and identify preferred paths that will take the company to a better future, the change process involves navigating around the numerous obstacles and gaining organization-wide support for that change.

This chapter unfolds as follows. We begin by introducing Lewin's model of change and its component parts. Our discussion includes sources of resistance to change, ways to minimize this resistance, and ways to stabilize desired behaviors. Next, the chapter examines four approaches to organizational change—action research, appreciative inquiry, large group interventions, and parallel learning structures. The last section of this chapter considers both cross-cultural and ethical issues in organizational change.

Lewin's Force Field Analysis Model

LO1

"The velocity of change is so rapid, so quick, that if you don't accept the change and move with the change, you're going to be left behind."[2] This statement by BHP Billiton Chairman (and former Ford CEO) Jacques Nasser reflects the notion that organizations need to keep pace with ongoing changes in their external environment. Organizations are, after all, open systems that need to remain compatible with their external environments (see Chapter 1), such as consumer needs, global competition, technology, community expectations, government (de)regulation, and environmental standards. Successful organizations monitor their environments and take appropriate steps to maintain a compatible fit with new external conditions. Rather than resisting change, employees in successful companies embrace change as an integral part of organizational life. "I've always believed that when the rate of change inside an institution becomes slower than the rate of change outside, the end is in sight," says former General Electric CEO Jack Welch. "The only question is when."[3]

It is easy to see that environmental forces push companies to change the way they operate. What is more difficult to see is the complex interplay of these forces with the internal dynamics of organizations. Social psychologist Kurt Lewin developed the force field analysis model to describe this process using the metaphor of a force field (see Exhibit 15.1).[4] Although it was developed more than 50 years ago, recent reviews affirm that Lewin's **force field analysis** model remains one of the most widely respected ways of viewing the change process.[5]

One side of the force field model represents the *driving forces* that push organizations toward a new state of affairs. These might include new competitors or technologies, evolving workforce expectations, or a host of other environmental changes. Corporate leaders also produce driving forces even when external forces for change aren't apparent. For instance, some experts call for "divine discontent" as a key feature of successful organizations, meaning that leaders continually urge employees to strive for higher standards or better practices even when the company outshines the competition. "We have a habit of divine discontent with our performance," says creative agency Ogilvy & Mather about its corporate culture. "It is an antidote to smugness."[6]

The other side of Lewin's model represents the *restraining forces* that maintain the status quo. These restraining forces are commonly called "resistance to change" because they

connect®

To assist your learning and test your knowledge about Lewin's force field model of change, go to **www.mcgrawhillconnect.com**, which has activities and test questions on this topic.

EXHIBIT 15.1

Lewin's Force Field Analysis Model

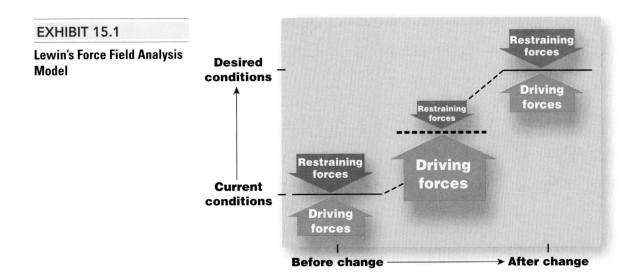

appear to block the change process. Stability occurs when the driving and restraining forces are roughly in equilibrium—that is, they are of approximately equal strength in opposite directions.

Lewin's force field model emphasizes that effective change occurs by **unfreezing** the current situation, moving to a desired condition, and then **refreezing** the system so it remains in the desired state. Unfreezing involves producing disequilibrium between the driving and restraining forces. As we will describe later, this process may occur by increasing the driving forces, reducing the restraining forces, or using a combination of both. Refreezing occurs when the organization's systems and structures are aligned with the desired behaviors. They must support and reinforce the new role patterns and prevent the organization from slipping back into the old way of doing things. Over the next few pages, we use Lewin's model to understand why change is blocked and how the process can evolve more smoothly.

Understanding Resistance to Change

LO2

Robert Nardelli pushed hard to transform Home Depot from a loose configuration of fiefdoms to a more performance-oriented operation that delivered a consistent customer experience. Change did occur at the world's largest home improvement retailer, but at a price. A large number of talented managers and employees left the company, and some of those remaining continued to resent Nardelli's transformation. Disenchanted staff referred to the company as "Home Despot" because the changes took away their autonomy. Others named it "Home GEpot," a disparaging reference to the many former GE executives that Nardelli hired into top positions. After five years, the Home Depot board decided to replace Nardelli, partly because he made some unsuccessful strategic decisions and partly because of the aftereffects of Nardelli's changes.[7]

Robert Nardelli experienced considerable *resistance to change* at Home Depot. He has plenty of company. One survey reported that 43 percent of U.S. managers identified resistance to change as a primary barrier to workplace

force field analysis
Kurt Lewin's model of systemwide change that helps change agents diagnose the forces that drive and restrain proposed organizational change.

unfreezing
The first part of the change process, in which the change agent produces disequilibrium between the driving and restraining forces.

refreezing
The latter part of the change process, in which systems and structures are introduced that reinforce and maintain the desired behaviors.

How Effectively Do Organizations around the World Handle Change?[8]

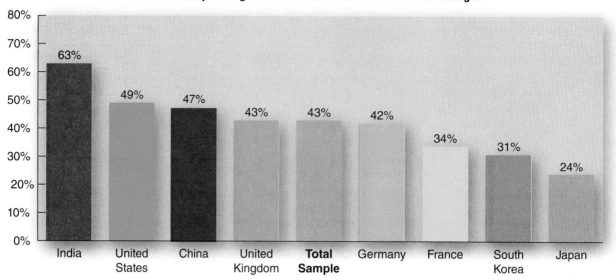

Percentage of employees, by selected countries, who agree or strongly agree that "change is handled effectively in my organization." Not all 28,810 employees across the 15 countries surveyed are shown here, but all are included in the "total sample" figure.

productivity. This resistance is not short-lived. Twenty-one percent of 1,700 change agents surveyed across more than 40 countries acknowledged that employees still resisted a specific major change one or two years after it was implemented.[9]

Resistance to change takes many forms, ranging from overt work stoppages to subtle attempts to continue the old ways.[10] A study of bank employees reported that subtle resistance is much more common than overt resistance. Some employees in that study avoided the desired changes by moving into different jobs. Others continued to perform tasks the old way as long as management didn't notice. Even when employees complied with the planned changes, they engaged in resistance by performing their work without corresponding cognitive or emotional support for the change.[11] In other words, they resisted by letting customers know that they disapproved of the changes forced on them.

Subtle forms of resistance potentially create the greatest obstacles to change because they are not as visible. In the words of one manager, "[Change efforts] never die because of direct confrontation. Direct confrontation you can work with because it is known. Rather, they die a death of a thousand cuts. People and issues you never confront drain the life out of important [initiatives] and result in solutions that simply do not have the performance impact that they should have."[12] This resistance is not unique to North America. As Connections 15.1 describes, Mina Ishiwatari experienced various forms of resistance to her innovative marketing ideas at Hoppy, the Japanese beverage company.

EMPLOYEE RESISTANCE AS A RESOURCE FOR CHANGE

Although change agents are understandably frustrated by passive or active resistance to change, they need to realize that resistance is a common and natural human response. As economist John Kenneth Galbraith once quipped: "Faced with the choice between changing one's mind and proving that there is no need to do so, almost everyone gets busy on the proof."[13] Even when people support change, they typically assume that it is others—not themselves—who need to change. The problem, however, isn't so much that resistance to change exists. The main problem is that change agents typically view resistance as an unreasonable, dysfunctional, and irrational response to a desirable initiative. They often form an "us versus them" perspective without considering that the causes of resistance may, in fact, be traced back to their own actions or inaction.[14]

The emerging view among change management experts is that resistance to change is a useful indicator rather than an impediment to change. Resistance aids change agents in

connections 15.1

Not Hoppy About Change

Hoppy, a carbonated, low-alcohol, malt-and-hops beverage, was popular around Tokyo after World War II as a cheap alternative to expensive beer, but it fell out of favor as beer became affordable. Mina Ishiwatari, granddaughter of Hoppy Beverage Co.'s founder, was determined to improve Hoppy's image when she joined the company a decade ago. Unfortunately, the company's 30 employees—mostly men in their fifties who were family relatives—didn't want to disturb their cozy jobs.

"It was a turbulent decade of eliminating evils from the company and rebuilding a new organization from scratch," recalls Ishiwatari, who began as a rank-and-file employee and is now the company's executive vice president. "I tried to take a new marketing approach to change the image of Hoppy ... but no one would listen to me."

With limited support and budget, Ishiwatari developed a website that informed the public about the product, sold it online, and documented Ishiwatari's views in an early weblog. As the contemporary marketing caught the attention of health-conscious young people, Ishiwatari pushed for further changes. Most managers who opposed Ishiwatari's radical ideas eventually left the company.

But Ishiwatari experienced resistance even among those who remained. One day, the factory manager presented her with resignations from all of the factory workers. Ishiwatari resolved the dispute, acknowledging that she was pushing

Mina Ishiwatari (center) faced, and overcame, resistance to change in the company that her grandfather founded.

change through too quickly and without enough consideration for employee feelings.

In the seven years since Ishiwatari began introducing these changes, Hoppy's annual sales have increased fourfold to about US$42 million, even though it is sold mainly around Tokyo. The company's workforce has expanded to more than 50 people.[15]

three ways. First, it is a signal—a warning system—that the change agent has not sufficiently addressed the underlying conditions that support effective organizational change.[16] In some situations, employees may be worried about the *consequences* of change, such as how the new conditions will take away their power and status. In other situations, employees show resistance because of concerns about the *process* of change itself, such as the effort required to break old habits and learn new skills.

Second, resistance is a form of constructive conflict that can potentially improve decision making, including identifying better ways to improve the organization's success. However, constructive conflict is typically accompanied by dysfunctional relationship conflict. This appears to be the case when change agents see resistance to change as an impediment rather than a resource. They describe the people who oppose them as the problem, whereas their focus should be on understanding the reasons why these people resist. Thus, by viewing resistance as a form of constructive conflict, change agents may be able to improve the change strategy or change process.

Third, resistance should be viewed in the context of justice and motivation. Resistance is a form of voice, so it potentially improves procedural justice (see Chapter 5). By redirecting initial forms of resistance into constructive conversations, change agents can increase employee perceptions and feelings of fairness. Furthermore, resistance is motivational; it potentially engages people to think about the change strategy and process. Change agents can harness that motivational force to ultimately strengthen commitment to the change initiative.

WHY EMPLOYEES RESIST CHANGE

Change management experts have developed a long list of reasons people do not embrace change. Some people resist change because of their personality and values.[17] Aside from these dispositional factors, however, employees often lack the motivation or commitment

connect

Are you tolerant of change? Go to **www.mcgrawhillconnect.com** or the end of this chapter to assess your natural tendency to tolerate change, as well as to assist your learning about the sources of resistance to change.

to change when they believe the change will fail, is the wrong action for the situation, or will be costly to them personally.[18] This cost might be in the form of lost rewards and status, or it might represent negative consequences if they attempt to support the change. Another reason for resistance is the person's inability (or perceived inability) to change due to inadequate skills and knowledge. A third reason is that employees lack role clarity about the change. This lack of role clarity occurs when people misunderstand or magnify what is expected of them in the future. These three factors—motivation, ability, and role (mis) perceptions—are the foundations of the six most commonly cited reasons people resist change, which are summarized here.[19]

Direct Costs   Employees lack commitment to (or even compliance with) a change initiative when their personal cost–benefit analysis calculation is negative rather than positive. They might believe the benefits for them (and possibly for the organization) are trivial (i.e., some pain for little gain). They might anticipate benefits from the change but also believe that they will be worse off overall. For example, the Malaysian government has introduced sweeping changes in which managers are expected to delegate more power and responsibility to staff. However, many government managers believe these reforms will give them less power and prestige, so they have hindered the change by delegating responsibility slowly.

Saving Face   Several years ago, Rob McEwan, CEO of Goldcorp and USGold, decided to post the mining company's confidential geological data online and offer a handsome reward to anyone who could help find more gold on the property. The Goldcorp Challenge was a huge success, but the firm's geological staff complained just before the event was launched. "We have real concerns," they told McEwen. "You're going to ask the rest of the world to tell you where we're going to find gold in our mine, and we think they're going to think we're really dumb and that you don't have any confidence in us."[20]

Goldcorp's geological staff resisted the global challenge because it threatened their self-esteem. Although McEwan eased those concerns, employees often continue to quietly attack changes that did not originate from them. Due to this "not-invented-here" syndrome, staff sometimes deliberately inflate problems with changes that they did not initiate, just to "prove" that those ideas were not superior to their own. This form of resistance is widespread, according to change experts. Says one consultant, "Unless they're scared enough to listen, they'll never forgive you for being right and for knowing something they don't."[21]

Fear of the Unknown   All change includes some degree of uncertainty. This uncertainty puts employees at risk. Their knowledge and skills might become obsolete; their

Ray Davis, CEO of Umpqua Bank, warns that employees tend to fall back into their old ways unless the change is reinforced through systems and structures. "When you are leading for growth, you know you are going to disrupt comfortable routines and ask for new behavior, new priorities, new skills," says Davis, whose Oregon-based bank is regarded as one of America's most innovative financial institutions. "Even when we want to change, and do change, we tend to relax and the rubber band snaps us back into our comfort zones."[23]

valued work space, perquisites, or even social relationships might be disrupted and re-moved. Thus, people resist change out of worry that they cannot adjust to the new work requirements or that they will produce unknown costs. Overall, this uncertainty is usually considered less desirable than the relative certainty of the status quo.

Breaking Routines People typically resist initiatives that force them out of their comfort zones and require them to invest time and energy in learning new role patterns. Indeed, most employees in one Australian survey admitted they don't follow through with organizational changes because they "like to keep things the way they are" or the changes seem to be too complicated or time wasting.[22]

Incongruent Team Dynamics Teams develop and enforce conformity to a set of norms that guide behavior. However, conformity to existing team norms may discourage employees from accepting organizational change. This form of resistance occurred at electronics retailer Best Buy when it introduced the results-only work environment (ROWE). ROWE evaluates employees by their results, not their face time, so employees can come to work and leave when they want. Yet coworkers often responded to deviations from the standard work schedule with half-humorous barbs such as "Forgot to set your alarm clock again?" These jibes supported the old employment model but undermined the ROWE program. Best Buy's consultants eventually set up sessions that warned employees about these taunts, which they called "sludge."[24]

Incongruent Organizational Systems Rewards, information systems, patterns of authority, career paths, selection criteria, and other systems and structures are both friends and foes of organizational change. When properly aligned, they reinforce desired behaviors. When misaligned, they pull people back into their old attitudes and behavior. Even enthusiastic employees lose momentum after failing to overcome the structural confines of the past.

Unfreezing, Changing, and Refreezing

LO3

According to Lewin's force field analysis model, effective change occurs by unfreezing the current situation, moving to a desired condition, and then refreezing the system so it remains in this desired state. Unfreezing occurs when the driving forces are stronger than the restraining forces. This happens by making the driving forces stronger, weakening or removing the restraining forces, or both.

The first option is to increase the driving forces, motivating employees to change through fear or threats (real or contrived). This strategy rarely works, however, because the action of increasing the driving forces alone is usually met with an equal and opposing increase in the restraining forces. A useful metaphor is pushing against the coils of a mattress. The harder corporate leaders push for change, the stronger the restraining forces push back. This antagonism threatens the change effort by producing tension and conflict within the organization.

The second option is to weaken or remove the restraining forces. The problem with this change strategy is that it provides no motivation for change. To some extent, weakening the restraining forces is like clearing a pathway for change. An unobstructed road makes it easier to travel to the destination but does not motivate anyone to go there. The preferred option, therefore, is to both increase the driving forces and reduce or remove the restraining forces. Increasing the driving forces creates an urgency for change, while reducing the restraining forces lessens motivation to oppose the change and removes obstacles such as lack of ability or situational constraints.

CREATING AN URGENCY FOR CHANGE

The opening story to this chapter described how Alan Mulally began the change process at Ford Motor Company by warning staff that the company would die if it didn't change quickly. The fact is, organizational change requires employees to have an urgency for change.[25] "I think there are two attributes for every successful company," says Warren Erhart, CEO of White

A few months after he became CEO of Nokia Corp, Stephen Elop sent employees a scorching e-mail, warning them about the urgency for change. "I have learned that we are standing on a burning platform," wrote Elop. "And, we have more than one explosion—we have multiple points of scorching heat that are fueling a blazing fire around us." Elop described strong competition from Apple and Google, Nokia's falling brand preference, and its declining credit rating. "We poured gasoline on our own burning platform," he suggested, pointing to the company's poor accountability and leadership.[27]

Spot, western Canada's oldest (since 1928) and most successful restaurant chain. "One is a sense of urgency, the other is a dedication to continuous improvement." Erhart explains the importance of these two attributes: "We know that success is fleeting. We have to keep working at it and keep focused all the time."[26]

Creating an urgency to change typically occurs by informing employees about competitors, changing consumer trends, impending government regulations, and other forms of turbulence in the external environment. These are the main driving forces in Lewin's model. They push people out of their comfort zones, energizing them to face the risks that change creates. In many organizations, however, leaders buffer employees from the external environment to such an extent that these driving forces are hardly felt by anyone below the top executive level. The result is that employees don't understand why they need to change and leaders are surprised when their change initiatives do not have much effect.

Customer-Driven Change   Some companies fuel the urgency to change by putting employees in direct contact with customers. Dissatisfied customers represent a compelling driving force for change because the organization's survival typically depends on having customers who are satisfied with the product or service. Customers also provide a human element that further energizes employees to change current behavior patterns.[28]

Executives at Shell Europe applied customer-driven change a few years ago. Many middle managers at the energy company seemed blissfully unaware that Shell wasn't achieving either its financial goals or its customer needs; so to create an urgency for change, the European managers were loaded onto buses and taken out to talk with customers and employees who work with customers every day. "We called these 'bus rides.' The idea was to encourage people to think back from the customer's perspective rather than from the head office," explains Shell Europe's vice president of retailing. "The bus rides were difficult for a lot of people who, in their work history, had hardly ever had to talk to a customer and find out what was good and not so good about Shell from the customer's standpoint."[29]

Creating an Urgency for Change Without External Forces   Exposing employees to external forces can strengthen the urgency for change, but leaders often need to begin the change process before problems come knocking at the company's door. "You want to create a burning platform for change even when there isn't a need for one," says Steve Bennett, former CEO of financial software company Intuit.[30] Creating an urgency for change when the organization is riding high requires rare persuasive capability that helps employees visualize future competitive threats and environmental shifts.

For instance, Apple Computer's iPod dominates the digital music market, but the late Steve Jobs wanted the company to be its own toughest competitor. Just when sales of the iPod Mini were soaring, Jobs challenged a gathering of 100 top executives and engineers to develop a better product to replace it. "Playing it safe is the most dangerous thing we can do," Jobs warned. Nine months later the company launched the iPod Nano, which replaced the still-popular iPod Mini before competitors could offer a better alternative.[31]

Experts warn, however, that employees may see the burning-platform strategy as manipulative—a view that produces cynicism about change and undermines trust in the change agent.[32] Also, the urgency for change doesn't need to originate from problems or threats to the company; this motivation can also develop through a change champion's vision of a more appealing future. By creating a future vision of a better organization, leaders effectively make the current situation less appealing. When the vision connects to employee values and needs, it can be a motivating force for change even when external problems are not strong.

EXHIBIT 15.2 **Strategies for Minimizing Resistance to Change**

STRATEGY	EXAMPLE	WHEN APPLIED	PROBLEMS
Communication	Customer complaint letters are shown to employees.	When employees don't feel an urgency for change, don't know how the change will affect them, or resist change due to a fear of the unknown.	Time-consuming and potentially costly.
Learning	Employees learn how to work in teams as company adopts a team-based structure.	When employees need to break old routines and adopt new role patterns.	Time consuming, potentially costly, and some employees might be unable to learn the new skills.
Employee involvement	Company forms a task force to recommend new customer service practices.	When the change effort needs more employee commitment, some employees need to save face, and/or employee ideas would improve decisions about the change strategy.	Very time-consuming. Might lead to conflict and poor decisions if employees' interests are incompatible with organizational needs.
Stress management	Employees attend sessions to discuss their worries about the change.	When communication, training, and involvement do not sufficiently ease employee worries.	Time-consuming and potentially expensive. Some methods may not reduce stress for all employees.
Negotiation	Employees agree to replace strict job categories with multiskilling in return for increased job security.	When employees will clearly lose something of value from the change and would not otherwise support the new conditions. Also necessary when the company must change quickly.	May be expensive, particularly if other employees want to negotiate their support. Also tends to produce compliance but not commitment to the change.
Coercion	Company president tells managers to "get on board" the change or leave.	When other strategies are ineffective and the company needs to change quickly.	Can lead to more subtle forms of resistance, as well as long-term antagonism with the change agent.

Sources: Adapted from J.P. Kotter and L.A. Schlesinger, "Choosing Strategies for Change," *Harvard Business Review* 57 (1979), pp. 106–14; P.R. Lawrence, "How to Deal with Resistance to Change," *Harvard Business Review*, May–June 1954, pp. 49–57.

REDUCING THE RESTRAINING FORCES

Employee resistance should be viewed as a resource, but its underlying causes—the restraining forces—still need to be addressed. As we explained earlier using the mattress coil metaphor, increasing the driving forces alone will not bring about change, because employees often push back harder to offset the opposing forces. Instead, change agents need to address each of the sources of resistance. Six of the main strategies are outlined in Exhibit 15.2. If feasible, communication, learning, employee involvement, and stress management should be attempted first.[33] However, negotiation and coercion are necessary for people who will clearly lose something from the change and in cases where the speed of change is critical.

Communication   Communication is the highest priority and first strategy required for any organizational change. According to one recent survey, communication (together with involvement) is considered the top strategy for engaging employees in the change process.[34] Communication improves the change process in at least two ways.[35] One way, which we described earlier, is by generating an urgency to change. Leaders motivate employees to support the change by candidly telling them about the external threats and opportunities that make change so important. Whether through town hall meetings with senior management or by directly meeting with disgruntled customers, employees become energized to change when they understand and visualize those external forces.

The second way that communication minimizes resistance to change is by illuminating the future and thereby reducing fear of the unknown. The more corporate leaders communicate their vision, particularly details about that future and milestones already achieved toward that future, the more easily employees can understand their own roles in that future. Similarly, as the leader communicates the future state more clearly, employees form a clearer picture about how the change relates to their jobs and responsibilities. "No. 1 is to always communicate, communicate, communicate," advises Randall Dearth, CEO of chemical manufacturer Lanxess Corp. "If you're bringing in change, you need to be able to make a very compelling case of what change looks like and why change is necessary."[36]

Learning　　Learning is an important process in most change initiatives because employees require new knowledge and skills to fit the organization's evolving requirements. For example, learning was an important strategy for change at CSC. The U.S. business and technology consulting and services firm's executive team recognized that the company's culture required better alignment with its growth strategy. To achieve this, CSC launched a leadership development program, which would minimize resistance to the change by equipping managers with the skills to coach employees toward emerging attitudes and values.[37]

Employee Involvement　　Unless the change must occur quickly or employee interests are highly incompatible with the organization's needs, employee involvement is almost an essential part of the change process. In the chapter on decision making (Chapter 7), we described several potential benefits of employee involvement, all of which are relevant to organizational change. Employees who participate in decisions about a change tend to feel more personal responsibility for its successful implementation, rather than being disinterested agents of someone else's decisions.[38] This sense of ownership also minimizes the problems of saving face and fear of the unknown. Furthermore, the complexity of today's work environment demands that more people provide ideas regarding the best direction of the change effort. Employee involvement is such an important component of organizational change that special initiatives have been developed to allow participation in large groups. These change interventions are described later in the chapter.

Stress Management　　Organizational change is a stressful experience for many people because it threatens self-esteem and creates uncertainty about the future.[39] Communication, learning, and employee involvement can reduce some of the stressors. However, research indicates that companies also need to introduce stress management practices to help employees cope with changes.[40] In particular, stress management minimizes resistance by removing some of the direct costs and fear of the unknown about the change process. Stress also saps energy, so minimizing stress potentially increases employee motivation to support the change process.

With brand-name clients and more than $500 million in sales, Lopez Foods Inc. has become the 10th largest Hispanic-owned company in America. To further improve its quality and efficiency, the Oklahoma City–based beef patty and sausage manufacturer recently involved employees in the change process. The current production process was mapped out on a large wall of brown paper, and employees were asked for ways to make it better. To management's surprise, employees were enthusiastic about suggesting productivity improvements. "Things we thought would be a hard sell on the employees, they themselves have come up to us and said, 'We can do this better,' or 'We don't need five people here, we only need three,'" says CEO Eduardo Sanchez.[41]

Negotiation   As long as people resist change, organizational change strategies will require a variety of influence tactics. Negotiation is a form of influence that involves the promise of benefits or resources in exchange for the target person's compliance with the influencer's request. This strategy potentially gains support from those who would otherwise lose out from the change. However, this support is mostly compliance with, rather than commitment to, the change effort, so it might not be effective in the long term.

Coercion   If all else fails, leaders rely on coercion to change organizations. Coercion can include persistently reminding people of their obligations, frequently monitoring behavior to ensure compliance, confronting people who do not change, and using threats of sanctions to force compliance. Replacing people who will not support the change is an extreme step, but it is fairly common. For instance, one year after Robert Nardelli was hired as CEO of Home Depot, most of the retailer's top management team had voluntarily or involuntarily left the company. Several years earlier, StandardAero CEO Bob Hamaberg threatened to fire senior managers who opposed his initiative to introduce lean management. "You must have senior management commitment," Hamaberg said bluntly at the time. "I had some obstacles. I removed the obstacles." Today, StandardAero is a world leader in the aircraft engine repair and overhaul business.[42]

Firing people is the least desirable way to change organizations. However, dismissals and other forms of coercion are sometimes necessary when speed is essential and other tactics are ineffective. For example, it may be necessary to remove several members of an executive team who are unwilling or unable to change their existing mental models of the ideal organization. This is also a radical form of organizational "unlearning" (see Chapter 1) because when executives leave, they remove knowledge of the organization's past routines that have become dysfunctional.[43] Even so, coercion is a risky strategy because survivors (employees who do not leave) may have less trust in corporate leaders and engage in more political tactics to protect their own job security.

REFREEZING THE DESIRED CONDITIONS

Unfreezing and changing behavior won't produce lasting change. People are creatures of habit, so they easily slip back into past patterns. Therefore, leaders need to refreeze the new behaviors by realigning organizational systems and team dynamics with the desired changes.[44] The desired patterns of behavior can be "nailed down" by changing the physical structure and situational conditions. Organizational rewards are also powerful systems that refreeze behaviors.[45] If the change process is supposed to encourage efficiency, then rewards should be realigned to motivate and reinforce efficient behavior. Information systems play a complementary role in the change process, particularly as conduits for feedback.[46] Feedback mechanisms help employees learn how well they are moving toward the desired objectives, and they provide a permanent architecture to support the new behavior patterns in the long term. The adage, "What gets measured, gets done," applies here. Employees concentrate on the new priorities when they receive a continuous flow of feedback about how well they are achieving those goals.

Bank of New Zealand BNZ applied this refreezing strategy by changing the feedback and reward system at its call centers. Previously, call center employees received feedback and were rewarded for answering and completing calls quickly. However, management concluded that customers wanted efficient calls, not fast talkers. "What do fast calls have to do with great conversations?" asks Susan Basile, BNZ's managing director of direct sales and service. "Sure, we don't want to waste the customer's time. But if we were to ask them what they most wanted from our call center, they might well say they want fast answers, but we'd be wrong to conclude they want fast talkers or hurried conversations." Now, BNZ provides employee feedback and rewards around "great conversations," not how quickly the call is completed. Employees are recognized for addressing customer needs rather than for how long it takes them to complete the call.[47]

Leadership, Coalitions, and Pilot Projects

Kurt Lewin's force field analysis model is a useful template to explain the dynamics of organizational change. But it overlooks three ingredients in effective change processes: leadership, coalitions, and pilot projects.

TRANSFORMATIONAL LEADERSHIP AND CHANGE

The opening vignette to this chapter described how Ford Motor Company came back from the brink through a tremendous change initiative. Perhaps the most important aspect of Ford's turnaround has been the transformational leadership of chief executive Alan Mulally. As we learned in the chapter about leadership (Chapter 12), transformational leaders are agents of change.[48] At Ford, Mulally developed and championed a vision of a better future for the troubled automaker, communicated that vision in ways that were meaningful to others, made decisions and acted in ways that were consistent with that vision, and built commitment to that vision.

A key element of leading change is a strategic vision.[49] A leader's vision provides a sense of direction and establishes the critical success factors against which the real changes are evaluated. Furthermore, a vision provides an emotional foundation to the change because it links the individual's values and self-concept to the desired change.[50] A strategic vision also minimizes employee fear of the unknown and provides a better understanding of what behaviors employees must learn for the desired future.

COALITIONS, SOCIAL NETWORKS, AND CHANGE

One of the great truths of organizational change is that change agents cannot lead the initiative alone. They need the assistance of several people with a similar degree of commitment to the change.[51] Indeed, one recent study concluded that this group—often called a *guiding coalition*—is the most important factor in the success of public sector organizational change programs.[52]

Membership in the guiding coalition extends beyond the executive team. Ideally, it includes a diagonal swath of employees representing different functions and most levels in the organization. In some cases, the guiding coalition is formed from a special task force that initially investigated the opportunities for change. Members of the guiding coalition should also be influence leaders; that is, they should be highly respected by peers in their area of the organization. At the same time, one recent report on organizational change warned that it takes more than a few dedicated disciples to generate widespread change.[53] Guiding coalitions may be very important, but they alone do not generate commitment to change in the rest of the workforce.

Social Networks and Viral Change   A guiding coalition is a formally structured group, but change also occurs more informally through social networks. To some extent, coalition members support the change process by feeding in to these networks. But social networks play a role in organizational change, whether or not the change process includes a formal coalition. Social networks are social structures of individuals or social units (e.g., departments, organizations) that are connected to each other through one or more forms of interdependence (see Chapter 10). They have an important role in communication and influence, both of which are key ingredients for organizational change.

The problem is that social networks are not easily controlled. Even so, some change agents have tapped into social networks to build a groundswell of support for a change initiative. This *viral change* process adopts principles found in word-of-mouth and viral marketing.[54] Viral and word-of-mouth marketing occur when information seeded to a few people is transmitted to others based on patterns of friendship. Within organizations, social networks represent the channels through which news and opinion about change initiatives are transmitted. Participants in that network have relatively high trust, so their information and views are more persuasive than many traditional ways that change is communicated. Social networks also provide opportunities for behavioral observation: Employees observe one another's

One of the more novel strategies to transformation work units and organizations is through viral change. Based on the power and influence of social networks, viral change begins by gaining support from key influencers. As these people change their behavior, others in the network eventually change their behavior. This occurs partly because of the influencer's referent power and partly because social networks make it easier for coworkers to observe and mimic the influencer's changed behavior. Although the viral change process is difficult to manage, Pfizer, Novo Nordisk, and a few other firms have been reasonably successful at using social networks to change employee attitudes and behavior.[56]

behavior and often adopt that behavior themselves. So when a change initiative causes change in the behavior of some employees, the social network potentially spreads this behavior change to others in that network.[55]

PILOT PROJECTS AND DIFFUSION OF CHANGE

Earlier in this chapter we mentioned that the U.S. retailer Best Buy introduced a results-only work environment (ROWE) initiative to support work–life balance and employment expectations of a younger workforce. ROWE evaluates employees by their results, not their face time. This new arrangement gives employees at the electronics retailer the freedom to come to work when it suits them. ROWE is a significant departure from the traditional employment relationship, so Best Buy wisely introduced an early version of this initiative as a pilot project. Specifically, the program was first tested with a retail division of 320 employees that suffered from low morale and high turnover. The ROWE program expanded to other parts of the organization only after employee engagement scores increased and turnover fell over several months.[57]

Best Buy and many other companies often introduce change through a pilot project. This cautious approach tests the effectiveness of the change as well as the strategies to gain employee support for the change without the enormous costs and risk of company-wide initiatives. Unlike centralized, systemwide changes, pilot projects are more flexible and less risky.[58] They also make it easier to select organizational groups that are most ready for change, thus increasing the chances of the pilot project's success.

But how do we diffuse the pilot project's change to other parts of the organization? Using the MARS model as a template (see Chapter 2), Exhibit 15.3 outlines several strategies to diffuse pilot projects. First, employees are more likely to adopt the practices of a pilot project when they are motivated to do so.[59] This occurs when they see that the pilot project is successful and people in the pilot project receive recognition and rewards for changing their previous work practices. Diffusion also occurs more successfully when managers support and reinforce the desired behaviors. More generally, change agents need to minimize the sources of resistance to change that we discussed earlier in this chapter.

Second, employees must have the ability—the required skills and knowledge—to adopt the practices introduced in the pilot project. According to innovation diffusion studies, people adopt ideas more readily when they have an opportunity to interact with and learn from others who have already applied the new practices.[60] Thus pilot projects get diffused when employees in the original pilot are dispersed to other work units as role models and knowledge sources.

Third, pilot projects get diffused when employees have clear role perceptions—that is, when they understand how the practices in a pilot project apply to them even though they are in a completely different functional area. For instance, accounting department employees won't easily recognize how they can adopt quality improvement practices developed by employees in the production department. The challenge here is for change agents to provide guidance that is not too specific (not too narrowly defined around the pilot project environment), because it might not seem relevant to other areas of the organization. At the same time, the pilot project intervention should not be described too broadly or abstractly to other employees because this makes the information and role model too vague. Fourth, employees require supportive situational factors, including the resources and time necessary to adopt the practices demonstrated in the pilot project.

EXHIBIT 15.3

Strategies for Diffusing Change from a Pilot Project

MOTIVATION

- Widely communicate and celebrate the pilot project's success.
- Reward and recognize pilot project employees, as well as those who work at transferring that change to other parts of the organization.
- Ensure that managers support and reinforce the desired behaviors related to the pilot project's success.
- Identify and address potential sources of resistance to change.

ABILITY

- Give employees the opportunity to interact with and learn from those in the pilot project.
- Reassign or temporarily transfer some pilot project employees to other work units, where they can coach and serve as role models.
- Give employees technical training to implement practices identified in the pilot project.

ROLE PERCEPTIONS

- Communicate and teach employees to discover how the pilot project practices are relevant for their own functional areas.
- Ensure that the pilot project is described in a way that is neither too specific nor too general.

SITUATIONAL FACTORS

- Give staff sufficient time and resources to learn and implement the pilot project practices in their work units.

Four Approaches to Organizational Change

LO5

So far, this chapter has examined the dynamics of change that occur every day in organizations. However, organizational change agents and consultants also apply various structured approaches to organizational change. This section introduces four of the leading approaches: action research, appreciative inquiry, large group interventions, and parallel learning structures.

ACTION RESEARCH APPROACH

connect

To assist your learning and test your knowledge about the four main approaches to organizational change, go to **www.mcgrawhillconnect.com,** which has activities and test questions on these topics.

Along with introducing the force field model, Kurt Lewin recommended an **action research** approach to the change process. The philosophy of action research is that meaningful change is a combination of action orientation (changing attitudes and behavior) and research orientation (testing theory).[61] On the one hand, the change process needs to be action-oriented because the ultimate goal is to change the workplace. An action orientation involves diagnosing current problems and applying interventions that resolve those problems. On the other hand, the change process is a research study because change agents apply a conceptual framework (such as team dynamics or organizational culture) to a real situation. As with any good research, the change process involves collecting data to diagnose problems more effectively and systematically evaluating how well the theory works in practice.[62]

Within this dual framework of action and research, the action research approach adopts an open-systems view. It recognizes that organizations have many interdependent parts, so change agents need to anticipate both the intended and the unintended consequences of their interventions. Action research is also a highly participative process because open-systems change requires both the knowledge and the commitment of members within that system. Indeed, employees are essentially co-researchers as well as participants in the intervention. Overall, action research is a data-based, problem-oriented process that

EXHIBIT 15.4   The Action Research Process

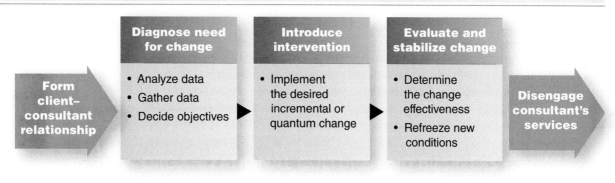

diagnoses the need for change, introduces the intervention, and then evaluates and stabilizes the desired changes. The main phases of action research are illustrated in Exhibit 15.4 and described here.[63]

1. *Form client–consultant relationship.* Action research usually assumes that the change agent originates outside the system (such as a consultant), so the process begins by forming the client–consultant relationship. Consultants need to determine the client's readiness for change, including whether people are motivated to participate in the process, are open to meaningful change, and possess the abilities to complete the process.

2. *Diagnose the need for change.* Action research is a problem-oriented activity that carefully diagnoses the problem through systematic analysis of the situation. Organizational diagnosis identifies the appropriate direction for the change effort by gathering and analyzing data about an ongoing system, such as through interviews and surveys of employees and other stakeholders. Organizational diagnosis also includes employee involvement in agreeing on the appropriate change method, the schedule for the actions involved, and the expected standards of successful change.

3. *Introduce intervention.* This stage in the action research model applies one or more actions to correct the problem. It may include any of the prescriptions mentioned in this book, such as building more effective teams, managing conflict, building a better organizational structure, or changing the corporate culture. An important issue is how quickly the changes should occur.[64] Some experts recommend *incremental change*, in which the organization fine-tunes the system and takes small steps toward a desired state. Others claim that *quantum change* is often required, in which the system is overhauled decisively and quickly.

4. *Evaluate and stabilize change.* Action research recommends evaluating the effectiveness of the intervention against the standards established in the diagnostic stage. Unfortunately, even when these standards are clearly stated, the effectiveness of an intervention might not be apparent for several years or might be difficult to separate from other factors. If the activity has the desired effect, the change agent and participants need to stabilize the new conditions. This refers to the refreezing process described earlier. Rewards, information systems, team norms, and other conditions are redesigned so they support the new values and behaviors.

action research
A problem-focused change process that combines action orientation (changing attitudes and behavior) and research orientation (testing theory through data collection and analysis).

The action research approach has dominated organizational change thinking since it was introduced in the 1940s. However, some experts are concerned that the problem-oriented nature of action research—in which something is wrong that must be fixed—focuses on the negative dynamics of the group or system rather than its positive opportunities and potential. This concern with action research has led to the development of a more positive approach to organizational change, called *appreciative inquiry.*[65]

Debating Point
WHAT'S THE BEST SPEED FOR ORGANIZATIONAL CHANGE?

One of the great debates among organizational change experts is how quickly the change should occur. One view is that slow, incremental change is better because it gives employees more time to adjust to the new realities, to keep up with what needs to be learned, and to manage their stress in this process. Incremental change is also preferred because it gives change champions more time to change course if the current direction isn't working as hoped.

The value of incremental change was recently illustrated at Ergon Energy. Government legislation required companies to upgrade their record-keeping system, but the Australian energy provider decided to make the changes incrementally because employees had already experienced constant change over the previous couple of years. "Even resilient staff such as those employed at Ergon Energy have a change tolerance level," explains Petá Sweeney, a consultant who worked with Ergon staff during this transition. "Consequently this led deliberately to discounting a revolutionary 'big bang' approach to record-keeping improvements." Sweeney reports that incremental change significantly improved employee engagement in the process. "Staff are more willing to participate in the change journey as well as offering suggestions for improvements. They do so knowing that changes will take place gradually and allow for time to fully bed down new practices and that effective enterprise-wide changes require their help."[66]

In spite of these apparent virtues of incremental change, some experts claim that rapid ("quantum") change is usually much better. They do not say that change needs to be radical or evenly rapid all of the time. Rather, they suggest that most change initiatives need to be, on average, much quicker than incremental. One argument is that companies operate in such a fast-paced environment that any speed less than "rapid" is risky; an incremental change initiative will put them further behind, to the point that any change seems futile.

A second argument is that quantum change creates a collective sense of momentum, whereas inertia eventually catches up with incremental change.[67] In other words, employees feel the sense of progress when change occurs quickly. This forward movement generates its own energy that helps motivate employees toward the vision. Incremental change, by comparison, is sluggish and lethargic. A related argument is that any organizational change requires plenty of energy, particularly from the leaders who must continually communicate, role model, coach, and otherwise support and influence employees toward the new state of affairs.[68] This energy is finite, and it is more likely to run out when the change is spread over a long rather than a short period of time.

Third, incremental change doesn't necessarily give employees more time to adjust; instead, it typically gives them more time to dig in their heels! Quantum change instead happens at such speed that employees don't have the opportunity to find ways to hold back, retrench, or even think about strategies to oppose the change effort. Finally, proponents of incremental change point to its benefits for minimizing stress, yet there is reason to believe that it often has the opposite effect. Changing slowly can feel like a slow train wreck: The more you see it coming, the more painful it feels. Quicker change, particularly when there are support systems to help employees through the process, may be less painful than changing incrementally.

APPRECIATIVE INQUIRY APPROACH

Appreciative inquiry tries to break out of the problem-solving mentality of traditional change management practices by reframing relationships around the positive and the possible. It searches for organizational (or team) strengths and capabilities and then applies or adapts that knowledge for further success and well-being. Appreciative inquiry is therefore deeply grounded in the emerging philosophy of *positive organizational behavior*, which suggests that focusing on the positive rather than the negative aspects of life will improve organizational success and individual well-being. In other words, this approach emphasizes building on strengths rather than trying to directly correct problems.[69]

Appreciative inquiry typically examines successful events, organizations, and work units. This focus becomes a form of behavioral modeling, but it also increases open dialogue by redirecting the group's attention away from its own problems. Appreciative inquiry is especially useful when participants are aware of their problems or already suffer from negativity in their relationships. The positive orientation of appreciative inquiry enables groups to overcome these negative tensions and build a more hopeful perspective of their future by focusing on what is possible.[70]

appreciative inquiry
An organizational change strategy that directs the group's attention away from its own problems and focuses participants on the group's potential and positive elements.

I Spy Marketing wanted to move to the next level of success. To accomplish this, the London-based digital marketing agency held workshops where staff identified and reflected on the features of several famous teams—Apple's Macintosh team, an F1 race car team, a famous West Indies cricket team, and television's A-Team. This discussion created positive energy in the participants and subsequently guided them to award-winning accomplishments in a difficult economic climate. "Fueled by these pictures of success, happy in clearly defined roles, consciously thinking about choices and consequences and ensuring clear contracting on a daily basis, we became the A Team," says I Spy managing director Nick Jones.[71]

Appreciative inquiry's positive focus is illustrated by the intervention conducted a few years ago by the British Broadcasting Corporation.[72] Almost 40 percent of BBC's workforce attended one of 200 appreciative inquiry meetings held over six months. Participants at each session were organized into pairs, where they asked each other three questions: (1) What has been the most creative/valued experience in your time at the BBC? (2) What were the conditions that made that experience possible? (3) If those experiences were to become the norm, how would the BBC have to change? These questions focused participants on the positive and the possible rather than on problems. They also produced 98,000 ideas, which were distilled into 15,000 unique suggestions and ultimately 35 concrete initiatives.

Appreciative Inquiry Principles   Appreciative inquiry embraces five key principles (see Exhibit 15.5).[73] One of these is the positive principle, which we described above. A second principle, called the *constructionist principle*, takes the position that conversations don't describe reality; they shape that reality. In other words, how we come to understand something depends on the questions we ask and the language we use. Thus appreciative inquiry requires sensitivity to and proactive management of the words and language used, as well as the thoughts and feelings behind that communication. This relates to a third principle, called the *simultaneity principle*, which states that inquiry and change are simultaneous, not sequential. The moment we ask questions of others, we are changing those people.

EXHIBIT 15.5   Five Principles of Appreciative Inquiry

APPRECIATIVE INQUIRY PRINCIPLE	DESCRIPTION
Positive principle	Focusing on positive events and potential produces more positive, effective, and enduring change.
Constructionist principle	How we perceive and understand the change process depends on the questions we ask and language we use throughout that process.
Simultaneity principle	Inquiry and change are simultaneous, not sequential.
Poetic principle	Organizations are open books, so we have choices in how they may be perceived, framed, and described.
Anticipatory principle	People are motivated and guided by the vision they see and believe in for the future.

Source: Based on D.L. Cooperrider and D.K. Whitney, *Appreciative Inquiry: A Positive Revolution in Change* (San Francisco, CA: Berrett-Koehler, 2005), Ch. 7; D.K. Whitney and A. Trosten-Bloom, *The Power of Appreciative Inquiry: A Practical Guide to Positive Change*, 2nd ed. (San Francisco, CA: Berrett-Koehler Publishers, 2010), Ch. 3.

Furthermore, the questions we ask determine the information we receive, which in turn affects which change intervention we choose. The key learning point from this principle is to be mindful of effects that the inquiry has on the direction of the change process.

A fourth principle, called the *poetic principle*, states that organizations are open books, so we have choices in how they may be perceived, framed, and described. The poetic principle is reflected in the notion that a glass of water can be viewed as half full or half empty. Thus appreciative inquiry actively frames reality in a way that provides constructive value for future development. *The anticipatory principle,* the fifth principle of appreciative inquiry, emphasizes the importance of a positive collective vision of the future state. People are motivated and guided by the vision they see and believe in for the future. Images that are mundane or disempowering will affect current effort and behavior differently than will images that are inspiring and engaging. We noted the importance of visions earlier in this chapter (change agents) and in our discussion of transformational leadership (Chapter 12).

The Four-D Model of Appreciative Inquiry   Built on these five principles, appreciative inquiry generally follows the "Four-D" process (named after its four stages) shown in Exhibit 15.6. Appreciative inquiry begins with *discovery*—identifying the positive elements of the observed events or organization.[74] This might involve documenting positive customer experiences elsewhere in the organization. Or it might include interviewing members of another organization to discover its fundamental strengths. As participants discuss their findings, they shift into the *dreaming* stage by envisioning what might be possible in an ideal organization. By pointing out a hypothetical ideal organization or situation, participants feel safer revealing their hopes and aspirations than they would if they were discussing their own organization or predicament.

As participants make their private thoughts public to the group, the process shifts into the third stage, called *designing*. Designing involves dialogue in which participants listen with selfless receptivity to one another's models and assumptions and eventually form a collective model for thinking within the team. In effect, they create a common image of what should be. As this model takes shape, group members shift the focus back to their own situation. In the final stage of appreciative inquiry, called *delivering* (also known as *destiny*), participants establish specific objectives and direction for their own organization on the basis of their model of what will be.

Appreciative inquiry was introduced more than two decades ago, but it really gained popularity only within the past few years. Several success stories of organizational change from appreciative inquiry have emerged in a variety of organizational settings, including the BBC, Castrol Marine, Canadian Tire, AVON Mexico, American Express, Green Mountain Coffee Roasters, and Hunter Douglas.[75]

EXHIBIT 15.6   The Four-D Model of Appreciative Inquiry

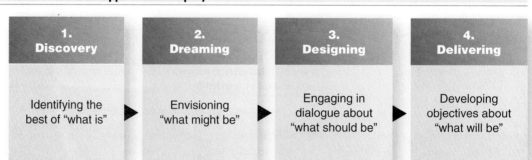

1. Discovery		2. Dreaming		3. Designing		4. Delivering
Identifying the best of "what is"	▶	Envisioning "what might be"	▶	Engaging in dialogue about "what should be"	▶	Developing objectives about "what will be"

Sources: Based on F.J. Barrett and D.L. Cooperrider, "Generative Metaphor Intervention: A New Approach for Working with Systems Divided by Conflict and Caught in Defensive Perception," *Journal of Applied Behavioral Science* 26 (1990), p. 229; D. Whitney and C. Schau, "Appreciative Inquiry: An Innovative Process for Organization Change," *Employment Relations Today* 25 (Spring 1998), pp. 11–21; D.L. Cooperrider and D.K. Whitney, *Appreciative Inquiry: A Positive Revolution in Change* (San Francisco, CA: Berrett-Koehler, 2005), Ch. 3.

Although appreciative inquiry has much to offer, it is not always the best approach to changing teams or organizations, and, indeed, it has not always been successful. This approach depends on participants' ability to let go of the problem-oriented approach, including the "blame game" of determining who may have been responsible for past failures. It also requires leaders who are willing to accept appreciative inquiry's less structured process.[76] Another concern is that research has not yet examined the contingencies of this approach.[77] In other words, we don't yet know under what conditions appreciative inquiry is a useful approach to organizational change and under what conditions it is less effective. Overall, appreciative inquiry can be an effective approach to organizational change, but we are just beginning to understand its potential and limitations.

LARGE GROUP INTERVENTION APPROACH

Appreciative inquiry can occur in small teams, but it is often designed to involve a large number of people, such as the 10,000 employees who participated in the process at the BBC. As such, appreciative inquiry is often identified as one of several large group organizational change interventions. Another large group intervention, known as **future search** (and its variations—*search conferences* and *open-space technology*), "puts the entire system in the room," meaning that the process tries to involve as many employees and other stakeholders as possible who are associated with the organizational system.[78] Future search conferences are typically held over a few days and involve participants in the search for trends or issues that are emerging. These events also ask participants to develop strategic solutions for those future conditions.

For example, Emerson & Cuming's chemical manufacturing facility in Canton, Massachusetts, relied on a future search conference in which managers, supervisors, and production employees were organized into five stakeholder teams to identify initiatives that would improve the plant's safety, efficiency, and cooperation. Lawrence Public Schools in Kansas conducted a future search conference involving parents, teachers, students, community partners, and other stakeholders to help the board allocate resources more effectively. "The goals that were developed at the future search conference reflect what the community envisioned for its school district," says superintendent Randy Weseman. Those goals have since become the foundation of the board's strategic decision making.[79]

Future search meetings and similar large group change events potentially minimize resistance to change and assist the quality of the change process, but they also have limitations.[80] One problem is that involving so many people invariably limits the opportunity to contribute and increases the risk that a few people will dominate the process. Another concern is that these events focus on finding common ground, which may prevent the participants from discovering substantive differences that interfere with future progress. A third issue is that these events generate high expectations about an ideal future state that are difficult to satisfy in practice. Employees become even more cynical and resistant to change if they do not see meaningful decisions and actions resulting from these meetings.

PARALLEL LEARNING STRUCTURE APPROACH

Parallel learning structures are highly participative arrangements composed of people from most levels of the organization who follow the action research model to produce meaningful organizational change. They are social structures developed alongside the formal hierarchy with the purpose of increasing the organization's learning.[81] Ideally, participants in parallel learning structures are sufficiently free from the constraints of the larger organization that they can effectively solve organizational issues.

Royal Dutch/Shell relied on a parallel learning structure to introduce a more customer-focused organization.[82]

future search
An organizational change strategy that consists of systemwide group sessions, usually lasting a few days, in which participants identify trends and establish ways to adapt to those changes.

parallel learning structure
A highly participative arrangement composed of people from most levels of the organization who follow the action research model to produce meaningful organizational change.

Rather than try to change the entire organization at once, executives held weeklong "retail boot camps" with six country teams of frontline people (such as gas station managers, truck drivers, and marketing professionals). Participants learned about competitive trends in their regions and were taught powerful marketing tools to identify new opportunities. The teams then returned home to study their markets and develop proposals for improvement. Four months later, boot camp teams returned for a second workshop, where each proposal was critiqued by Royal/Dutch Shell executives. Each team had 60 days to put its ideas into action; then the teams returned for a third workshop to analyze what worked and what didn't. This parallel learning process did much more than introduce new marketing ideas. It created enthusiasm in participants that spread contagiously to their coworkers, including managers above them, when they returned to their home countries.

Cross-Cultural and Ethical Issues in Organizational Change

LO6

Throughout this chapter, we have emphasized that change is an inevitable and often continuous phenomenon because organizations need to remain aligned with the dynamic external environment. Yet we also need to be aware of cross-cultural and ethical issues with any change process. Many organizational change practices are built around Western cultural assumptions and values, which may differ from and sometimes conflict with assumptions and values in other cultures.[83] One possible cross-cultural limitation is that Western organizational change models, such as Lewin's force field analysis, often assume that change has a beginning and an ending in a logical linear sequence (that is, a straight line from point A to point B). Yet change is viewed more as a cyclical phenomenon in some cultures, such as the earth's revolution around the sun or a pendulum swinging back and forth. Other cultures have more of an interconnected view of change, whereby one change leads to another (often unplanned) change, which leads to another change, and so on, until the change objective is ultimately achieved in a more circuitous way.

Another cross-cultural issue with some organizational change interventions is their assumption that effective organizational change is necessarily punctuated by tension and overt conflict. Indeed, some change interventions encourage such conflict. But this direct confrontation view is incompatible with cultures that emphasize harmony and equilibrium. These cross-cultural differences suggest that a more contingency-oriented perspective is required for organizational change to work effectively in this era of globalization.

Some organizational change practices also face ethical issues.[84] One ethical concern is the risk of violating individual privacy rights. The action research model is built on the idea of collecting information from organizational members, yet this requires that employees provide personal information and reveal emotions that they may not want to divulge.[85] A second ethical concern is that some change activities potentially increase management's power by inducing compliance and conformity in organizational members. For instance, action research is a systemwide activity that requires employee participation rather than allowing individuals to get involved voluntarily. A third concern is that some organizational change interventions undermine the individual's self-esteem. The unfreezing process requires that participants disconfirm their existing beliefs, sometimes including their own competence at certain tasks or interpersonal relations.

Organizational change is usually more difficult than it initially seems. Yet the dilemma is that most organizations operate in hyperfast environments that demand continuous and rapid adaptation. Organizations survive and gain competitive advantage by mastering the complex dynamics of moving people through the continuous process of change as quickly as the external environment is changing.

Organizational Behavior: The Journey Continues

Nearly 100 years ago, U.S. industrialist Andrew Carnegie said, "Take away my people, but leave my factories, and soon grass will grow on the factory floors. Take away my factories, but leave my people, and soon we will have a new and better factory."[86] Carnegie's statement reflects the message woven throughout this textbook: Organizations are not buildings or machinery or financial assets; rather, they are the people in them. Organizations are human entities—full of life, sometimes fragile, and always exciting.

> "Take away my people, but leave my factories, and soon grass will grow on the factory floors. Take away my factories, but leave my people, and soon we will have a new and better factory."
>
> —Attributed to Andrew Carnegie

(chapter summary)

LO1 Describe the elements of Lewin's force field analysis model.

Lewin's force field analysis model states that all systems have driving and restraining forces. Change occurs through the process of unfreezing, changing, and refreezing. Unfreezing produces disequilibrium between the driving and restraining forces. Refreezing realigns the organization's systems and structures with the desired behaviors.

LO2 Discuss the reasons people resist organizational change and how change agents should view this resistance.

Restraining forces are manifested as employee resistance to change. The main reasons people resist change are direct costs, saving face, fear of the unknown, breaking routines, incongruent team dynamics, and incongruent organizational systems. Resistance to change should be viewed as a resource, not an inherent obstacle to change. Employee resistance is a resource in three ways: (1) it is a signal that the conditions for effective change are not yet in place; (2) it is a form of constructive conflict; and (3) it is a form of voice, so it may improve procedural justice.

LO3 Outline six strategies for minimizing resistance to change, and debate ways to effectively create an urgency for change.

Organizational change requires employees to have an urgency for change. This typically occurs by informing them about driving forces in the external environment. Urgency to change also develops by putting employees in direct contact with customers. Leaders often need to create an urgency to change before the external pressures are felt, and this can occur through a vision of a more appealing future.

Resistance to change may be minimized by keeping employees informed about what to expect from the change effort (communicating); teaching employees valuable skills for the desired future (learning); involving them in the change process; helping employees cope with the stress of change; negotiating trade-offs with those who will clearly lose from the change effort; and using coercion (sparingly and as a last resort).

LO4 Discuss how leadership, coalitions, social networks, and pilot projects influence organizational change.

Every successful change also requires transformational leaders with a clear, well-articulated vision of the desired future state. They also need the assistance of several people (a guiding coalition) who are located throughout the organization. Change also occurs more informally through social networks. Viral change operates through social networks using influencers.

Many organizational change initiatives begin with a pilot project. The success of the pilot project is then diffused to other parts of the organization. This occurs by applying the MARS model, including motivating employees to adopt the pilot project's methods, training people to know how to adopt these practices, helping clarify how the pilot can be applied to different areas, and providing time and resources to support this diffusion.

LO5 Describe and compare action research, appreciative inquiry, large group interventions, and parallel learning structures as formal approaches to organizational change.

Action research is a highly participative, open-systems approach to change management that combines an action orientation (changing attitudes and behavior) with a research orientation (testing theory). It is a data-based, problem-oriented process that diagnoses the need for change, introduces the intervention, and then evaluates and stabilizes the desired changes.

Appreciative inquiry embraces the positive organizational behavior philosophy by focusing participants on the positive and possible. Along with this positive principle, this approach to change applies the constructionist, simultaneity, poetic, and anticipatory principles. The four stages of appreciative inquiry include discovery, dreaming, designing, and delivering.

Large-group interventions, such as future search conferences, are highly participative events that typically try to get the entire system into the room. Parallel learning structures rely on social structures developed alongside the formal hierarchy with the purpose of increasing the organization's learning. They are highly participative arrangements, composed of people from most levels of the organization who follow the action research model to produce meaningful organizational change.

LO6 Discuss two cross-cultural and three ethical issues in organizational change.

One significant concern is that organizational change theories developed with a Western cultural orientation potentially conflict with cultural values in some other countries. Also, organizational change practices can raise one or more ethical concerns, including increasing management's power over employees, threatening individual privacy rights, and undermining individual self-esteem.

{ key terms }

{ critical thinking questions }

1. Chances are that the school you are attending is currently undergoing some sort of change to adapt more closely with its environment. Discuss the external forces that are driving the change. What internal drivers for change also exist?

2. Use Lewin's force field analysis to describe the dynamics of organizational change at Ford Motor Company. The chapter's opening story about Ford's transformation provides some information, but think about other forces for and against change beyond the information provided in this vignette.

3. Employee resistance is a symptom, not a problem, in the change process. What are some of the real problems that may underlie employee resistance?

4. Senior management of a large multinational corporation is planning to restructure the organization. Currently, the organization is decentralized around geographic areas so that the executive responsible for each area has considerable autonomy over manufacturing and sales. The new structure will transfer power to the executives responsible for different product groups; the executives responsible for each geographic area will no longer be responsible for manufacturing in their area but will retain control over sales activities. Describe two types of resistance senior management might encounter from this organizational change.

5. Discuss the role of reward systems in organizational change. Specifically, identify where reward systems relate to Lewin's force field model and where they undermine the organizational change process.

6. Web Circuits is a Malaysian-based custom manufacturer for high-technology companies. Senior management wants to introduce lean management practices to reduce production costs and remain competitive. A consultant has recommended that the company start with a pilot project in one department and, when successful, diffuse these practices to other areas of the organization. Discuss the advantages of this recommendation, and identify three ways (other than the pilot project's success) to make diffusion of the change effort more successful.

7. Suppose that you are vice president of branch services at the Bank of East Lansing. You notice that several branches have consistently low customer service ratings even though there are no apparent differences in resources or staff characteristics. Describe an appreciative inquiry process in one of these branches that might help overcome this problem.

8. This chapter suggests that some organizational change activities face ethical concerns. Yet several consultants actively use these processes because they believe they benefit the organization and do less damage to employees than it seems on the surface. For example, some activities try to open up the employee's hidden area (review the Johari Window discussion in Chapter 3) so that there is better mutual understanding with coworkers. Discuss this argument, and identify where you think organizational change interventions should limit this process.

9. Change is often unwelcome, and we used to say that individuals, like organizations, do not like to change. For example, who wants to change from a comfortable to an uncomfortable pair of shoes? However, we have seen recently that individuals (perhaps like organizations) are embracing change. Please give several concrete examples of this phenomenon, and suggest reasons as to why this might be the case.

CASE STUDY 15.1 TRANSACT INSURANCE CORPORATION

TransAct Insurance Corporation (TIC) provides automobile insurance throughout the southeastern United States. Last year, a new president was hired by TIC's Board of Directors to improve the company's competitiveness and customer service. After spending several months assessing the situation, the new president introduced a strategic plan to strengthen TIC's competitive position. He also replaced three vice presidents. Jim Leon was hired as vice president of claims, TIC's largest division, with 1,500 employees, 50 claims center managers, and 5 regional directors.

Jim immediately met with all claims managers and directors and visited employees at TIC's 50 claims centers. As an outsider, this was a formidable task, but his strong interpersonal skills and uncanny ability to remember names and ideas helped him through the process. Through these visits and discussions, Jim discovered that the claims division had been managed in a relatively authoritarian, top-down manner. He could also see that morale was very low and employee–management relations were guarded. High workloads and isolation (adjusters work in tiny cubicles) were two other common complaints. Several managers acknowledged that the high turnover among claims adjusters was partly due to these conditions.

Following discussions with TIC's president, Jim decided to make morale and supervisory leadership his top priority. He initiated a divisional newsletter with a tear-off feedback form for employees to register their comments. He announced an open-door policy in which any claims division employee could speak to him directly and confidentially without going first to the immediate supervisor. Jim also fought organizational barriers to initiate a flex-time program so that employees could design work schedules around their needs. This program later became a model for other areas of TIC.

One of Jim's most pronounced symbols of change was the "Claims Management Credo," outlining the philosophy that every claims manager would follow. At his first meeting with the complete claims management team, Jim presented a list of what he thought were important philosophies and actions of effective managers. The management group was asked to select and prioritize items from this list. They were told that the resulting list would be the division's management philosophy and all managers would be held accountable for abiding by its principles. Most claims managers were uneasy about this process, but they also understood that the organization was under competitive pressure and that Jim was using this exercise to demonstrate his leadership.

The claims managers developed a list of 10 items, such as encouraging teamwork, fostering a trusting work environment, setting clear and reasonable goals, and so on. The list was circulated to senior management in the organization for their comment and approval and sent back to all claims managers for their endorsement. Once this was done, a copy of the final document was sent to every claims division employee. Jim also announced plans to follow up with an annual survey to evaluate each claims manager's performance. This announcement concerned the managers, but most of them believed the credo exercise was a result of Jim's initial enthusiasm and that he would be too busy to introduce a survey after settling into the job.

One year after the credo had been distributed, Jim announced that the first annual survey would be conducted. All claims employees would complete the survey and return it confidentially to the human resources department, where the survey results would be compiled for each claims center manager. The survey asked the extent to which the manager had lived up to each of the 10 items in the credo. Each form also provided space for comments.

Claims center managers were surprised that a survey would be conducted, but they were even more worried about Jim's statement that the results would be shared with employees. What "results" would employees see? Who would distribute these results? What happens if a manager gets poor ratings from his or her subordinates? "We'll work out the details later," said Jim in response to these questions. "Even if the survey results aren't great, the information will give us a good baseline for next year's survey."

The claims division survey had a high response rate. In some centers, every employee completed and returned a form. Each report showed the claim center manager's average score for each of the 10 items, as well as how many employees rated the manager at each level of the five-point scale. The reports also included every comment made by employees at that center.

No one was prepared for the results of the first survey. Most managers received moderate or poor ratings on the 10 items. Very few managers averaged above 3.0 (out of a five-point scale) on more than a couple of items. This suggested that, at best, employees were ambivalent about whether their claims center manager had abided by the 10 management philosophy items. The comments were even more devastating than the ratings. Comments ranged from mildly disappointed to extremely critical of their claims manager. Employees also described their long-standing frustration with TIC, high workloads, and isolated working conditions. Several people bluntly stated that they were skeptical about the changes that Jim had promised. "We've heard the promises before, but now we've lost faith," wrote one claims adjuster.

The survey results were sent to each claims manager, the regional director, and employees at the claims center. Jim instructed managers to discuss the survey data and comments with their regional manager and directly with employees. The claims center managers, who thought employees only received average scores, went into shock when they realized that the reports included individual comments. Some managers went to their regional director, complaining that revealing the personal comments would ruin their careers. Many directors sympathized, but the results were already available to employees.

When Jim heard about these concerns, he agreed that the results were lower than expected and that the comments should not have been shown to employees. After discussing the situation with his directors, he decided that the discussion meetings between claims managers and their employees should proceed as planned. To delay or withdraw the reports would undermine the credibility and trust that Jim was trying to develop with employees. However, the regional director attended the meeting in each claims center to minimize direct conflict between the claims center manager and employees.

Although many of these meetings went smoothly, a few created harsh feelings between managers and their employees. The sources of some comments were easily identified by their content, and this created a few delicate moments in several sessions. A few months after these meetings, two claims center managers quit and three others asked for transfers back to nonmanagement positions in TIC. Meanwhile, Jim wondered how to manage this process more effectively, particularly since employees expected another survey the following year.

Discussion Questions

1. What symptom(s) exist in this case to suggest that something has gone wrong?

2. What are the main causes of these symptoms?

3. What actions should the company take to correct these problems?

TEAM EXERCISE 15.2 STRATEGIC CHANGE INCIDENTS

PURPOSE This exercise is designed to help you identify strategies for facilitating organizational change in various situations.

INSTRUCTIONS

1. The instructor will place students into teams, and each team will be assigned one of the scenarios presented below.

2. Each team will diagnose its assigned scenario to determine the most appropriate set of change management practices. Where appropriate, these practices should (a) create an urgency for change, (b) minimize resistance to change, and (c) refreeze the situation to support the change initiative. Each of these scenarios is based on real events.

3. Each team will present and defend its change management strategy. Class discussion regarding the appropriateness and feasibility of each strategy will occur after all teams assigned the same scenario have presented. The instructor will then describe what the organizations actually did in these situations.

SCENARIO 1: LATTÉ TROUBLES Stock prices have just tumbled to a new 52-week low, and the market outlook for Starbucks is weak as consumers look to stretch their paychecks by passing on $4 lattés. Competitors are rapidly gaining market share in this high-margin industry. Input costs for coffee and dairy products have risen sharply, and widespread price increases have been passed on to customers. The performance of the most recently opened stores is much lower than of established stores. Executives have been reshuffled, and promises have been made to introduce new beverages to the menu. To cut costs, Starbucks stores are being closed and employees are being laid off. In their wake, loyal customers are complaining about their in-store experiences, citing long lines, lengthy waits, inexperienced baristas, and a loss of the coffeehouse ambience the retail chain previously was known for. The company founder has just returned as CEO to initiate a turnaround for his troubled organization. What should he do?

SCENARIO 2: GREENER TELCO The board of directors at a large telephone company wants its executives to make the organization more environmentally friendly by encouraging employees to reduce waste in the workplace. Government and other stakeholders expect the company to take this action and be publicly successful. Consequently, the chief executive officer wants to significantly reduce paper usage, trash, and other waste throughout the company's many widespread offices. Unfortunately, a survey indicates that employees do not value environmental objectives and do not know how to "reduce, reuse, recycle." As the executive responsible for this change, you have been asked to develop a strategy that might bring about meaningful behavioral change toward this environmental goal. What would you do?

SCENARIO 3: GO FORWARD AIRLINE A major airline had experienced a decade of rough turbulence, including two bouts of bankruptcy protection, 10 managing directors, and morale so low that employees had ripped off company logos from their uniforms out of embarrassment. Service was terrible, and the airplanes rarely arrived or left the terminal on time. This was costing the airline significant amounts of money in passenger layovers. Managers were paralyzed by anxiety, and many had been with the firm so long that they didn't know how to set strategic goals that worked. One-fifth of all flights were losing money, and the company overall was near financial collapse (just three months from defaulting on payroll obligations). You and the chief executive officer must get employees to improve operational efficiency and customer service quickly. What actions would you take to bring about these changes in time?

SELF-ASSESSMENT 15.3 ARE YOU TOLERANT OF CHANGE?

PURPOSE This exercise is designed to help you understand how people differ in their tolerance of change.

INSTRUCTIONS Read each of the statements below and circle the response that best fits your personal belief. Then use the scoring key in Appendix B at the end of this book to calculate your results. This self-assessment should be completed alone so that you can rate yourself honestly without concerns of social comparison. Class discussion will focus on the meaning of the concept measured by this scale and its implications for managing change in organizational settings.

Tolerance of Change Scale

TO WHAT EXTENT DOES EACH STATEMENT DESCRIBE YOU? INDICATE YOUR LEVEL OF AGREEMENT BY MARKING THE APPROPRIATE RESPONSE ON THE RIGHT	STRONGLY AGREE	MODERATELY AGREE	SLIGHTLY AGREE	NEUTRAL	SLIGHTLY DISAGREE	MODERATELY DISAGREE	STRONGLY DISAGREE
1. I generally prefer the unexpected to the predictable.	☐	☐	☐	☐	☐	☐	☐
2. I am much more comfortable at events where I know most of the people there.	☐	☐	☐	☐	☐	☐	☐
3. I don't consider new situations any more threatening than familiar situations.	☐	☐	☐	☐	☐	☐	☐
4. I prefer solving problems that have only one "best" solution rather than many solutions.	☐	☐	☐	☐	☐	☐	☐
5. I dislike ambiguous situations.	☐	☐	☐	☐	☐	☐	☐
6. I avoid situations that are too complicated for me to easily understand.	☐	☐	☐	☐	☐	☐	☐
7. I like situations that can be interpreted in more than one way.	☐	☐	☐	☐	☐	☐	☐
8. I cope well with unexpected events.	☐	☐	☐	☐	☐	☐	☐
9. Familiar situations are always preferable to me than unfamiliar situations.	☐	☐	☐	☐	☐	☐	☐
10. I enjoy working in ambiguous situations.	☐	☐	☐	☐	☐	☐	☐

Source: Adapted from D.L. Mclain, "The Mstat-I: A New Measure of an Individual's Tolerance for Ambiguity," *Educational and Psychological Measurement* 53, no. 1 (1993), pp. 183–89; S. Budner, "Intolerance of Ambiguity as a Personality Variable," *Journal of Personality* 30 (1962), pp. 29–50.

 After reading this chapter go to www.mhhe.com/mcshane6e for more in-depth information and interactivities that correspond to the chapter.

additional cases

CASE 1: ARCTIC MINING CONSULTANTS

By Steven L. McShane, University of Western Australia, and Tim Neale

Tom Parker enjoyed working outdoors. At various times in the past, he worked as a ranch hand, high steel rigger, headstone installer, prospector, and geological field technician. Now 43, Parker is a geological field technician and field coordinator with Arctic Mining Consultants. He has specialized knowledge and experience in all nontechnical aspects of mineral exploration, including claim staking, line cutting and grid installation, soil sampling, prospecting, and trenching. He is responsible for hiring, training, and supervising field assistants for all of Arctic Mining Consultants' programs. Field assistants are paid a fairly low daily wage (no matter how long they work, which may be up to 12 hours or more) and are provided meals and accommodation. Many of the programs are operated by a project manager who reports to Parker.

Parker sometimes acts as a project manager, as he did on a job that involved staking 15 claims near Eagle Lake, Alaska. He selected John Talbot, Greg Boyce, and Brian Millar, all of whom had previously worked with Parker, as the field assistants. To stake a claim, the project team marks a line with flagging tape and blazes along the perimeter of the claim, cutting a claim post every 500 yards (called a "length"). The 15 claims would require almost

60 miles of line in total. Parker had budgeted seven days (plus mobilization and demobilization) to complete the job. This meant that each of the four stakers (Parker, Talbot, Boyce, and Millar) would have to complete a little over seven "lengths" each day. The following is a chronology of the project.

DAY 1

The Arctic Mining Consultants crew assembled in the morning and drove to Eagle Lake, from where they were flown by helicopter to the claim site. On arrival, they set up tents at the edge of the area to be staked and agreed on a schedule for cooking duties. After supper, they pulled out the maps and discussed the job—how long it would take, the order in which the areas were to be staked, possible helicopter landing spots, and areas that might be more difficult to stake.

Parker pointed out that with only a week to complete the job, everyone would have to average seven and a half lengths per day. "I know that is a lot," he said, "but you've all staked claims before and I'm confident that each of you is capable of it. And it's only for a week. If we get the job done in time, there's a $300 bonus for each man." Two hours later, Parker and his crew members had developed what seemed to be a workable plan.

DAY 2

Millar completed six lengths, Boyce six lengths, Talbot eight, and Parker eight. Parker was not pleased with Millar's or Boyce's production. However, he didn't make an issue of it, thinking that they would develop their "rhythm" quickly.

DAY 3

Millar completed five and a half lengths, Boyce four, and Talbot seven. Parker, who was nearly twice as old as the other three, completed eight lengths. He also had enough time remaining to walk over and check the quality of stakes that Millar and Boyce had completed and then walk back to his own area for the helicopter pickup back to the tent site.

That night Parker exploded with anger. "I thought I told you that I wanted seven and a half lengths a day!" he shouted at Boyce and Millar. Boyce said that he was slowed down by unusually thick underbrush in his assigned area. Millar said that he had done his best and would try to pick up the pace. Parker did not mention that he had inspected their work. He explained that as far as he was concerned, the field assistants were supposed to finish their assigned area for the day, no matter what.

Talbot, who was sharing a tent with Parker, talked to him later. "I think that you're being a bit hard on them, you know. I know that it has been more by luck than anything else that I've been able to do my quota. Yesterday I only had five lengths done after the first seven hours and there was only an hour before I was supposed to be picked up. Then I hit a patch of really open bush, and was able to do three lengths in 70 minutes. Why don't I take Millar's area tomorrow and he can have mine? Maybe that will help."

"Conditions are the same in all of the areas," replied Parker, rejecting Talbot's suggestion. "Millar just has to try harder."

DAY 4

Millar did seven lengths and Boyce completed six and a half. When they reported their production that evening, Parker grunted uncommunicatively. Parker and Talbot did eight lengths each.

DAY 5

Millar completed six lengths, Boyce six, Talbot seven and a half, and Parker eight. Once again Parker blew up, but he concentrated his diatribe on Millar. "Why don't you do what you say you are going to do? You know that you have to do seven and a half lengths a day. We went over that when we first got here, so why don't you do it? If you aren't willing to do the job then you never should have taken it in the first place!"

Millar replied by saying that he was doing his best, that he hadn't even stopped for lunch, and that he didn't know how he could possibly do any better. Parker launched into him again: "You have got to work harder! If you put enough effort into it, you will get the area done!"

Later Millar commented to Boyce, "I hate getting dumped on all the time! I'd quit if it didn't mean that I'd have to walk 50 miles to the highway. And besides, I need the bonus money. Why doesn't he pick on you? You don't get any more done than me; in fact, you usually get less. Maybe if you did a bit more he wouldn't be so bothered about me."

"I only work as hard as I have to," Boyce replied.

DAY 6

Millar raced through breakfast, was the first one to be dropped off by the helicopter, and arranged to be the last one picked up. That evening the production figures were Millar eight and a quarter lengths, Boyce seven, and Talbot and Parker eight each. Parker remained silent when the field assistants reported their performance for the day.

DAY 7

Millar was again the first out and last in. That night, he collapsed in an exhausted heap at the table, too tired to eat. After a few moments, he announced in an abject tone, "Six lengths. I worked like a dog all day and I only got a lousy six lengths!" Boyce completed five lengths, Talbot seven, and Parker seven and a quarter.

Parker was furious. "That means we have to do a total of 34 lengths tomorrow if we are to finish this job on time!" With his eyes directed at Millar, he added: "Why is it that you never finish the job? Don't you realize that you are part of a team, and that you are letting the rest of the team down? I've been checking your lines and you're doing too much blazing and wasting too much time making picture-perfect claim posts! If you worked smarter, you'd get a lot more done!"

DAY 8

Parker cooked breakfast in the dark. The helicopter dropoffs began as soon as morning light appeared on the horizon. Parker instructed each assistant to complete eight lengths and, if they finished early, to help the others. Parker said that he would finish the other 10 lengths. Helicopter pickups were arranged for one hour before dark.

By noon, after working as hard as he could, Millar had only completed three lengths. "Why bother," he thought to himself, "I'll never be able to do another five lengths before the helicopter comes, and I'll catch the same amount of abuse from Parker for doing six lengths as for seven and a half." So he sat down and had lunch and a rest. "Boyce won't finish his eight lengths either, so even if I did finish mine, I still wouldn't get the bonus. At least I'll get one more day's pay this way."

That night, Parker was livid when Millar reported that he had completed five and a half lengths. Parker had done ten and a quarter lengths, and Talbot had completed eight. Boyce proudly announced that he finished seven and a half lengths, but sheepishly added that Talbot had helped him with some of it. All that remained were the two and a half lengths that Millar had not completed.

The job was finished the next morning and the crew demobilized. Millar has never worked for Arctic Mining Consultants again, despite being offered work several times by Parker. Boyce sometimes does staking for Arctic, and Talbot works full time with the company.

CASE 2: BRIDGING THE TWO WORLDS—THE ORGANIZATIONAL DILEMMA

By William Todorovic, Indiana-Purdue University, Fort Wayne

I had been hired by Aluminum Elements Corp. (AEC), and it was my first day of work. I was 26 years old, and I was now the manager of AEC's customer service group, which looked after customers, logistics, and some of the raw material purchasing. My superior, George, was the vice president of the company. AEC manufactured most of its products from aluminum, a majority of which were destined for the construction industry.

As I walked around the shop floor, the employees appeared to be concentrating on their jobs, barely noticing me. Management held daily meetings, in which various production issues were discussed. No one from the shop floor was invited to the meetings, unless there was a specific problem. Later I also learned that management had separate washrooms, separate lunchrooms, as well as other perks that floor employees did not have. Most of the floor employees felt that management, though polite on the surface, did not really feel they had anything to learn from the floor employees.

John, who worked on the aluminum slitter—a crucial operation required before any other operations could commence—had a number of unpleasant encounters with George. As a result, George usually sent written memos to the floor to avoid a direct confrontation with John. Because the directions in the memos were complex, these memos were often more than two pages in length.

One morning, as I was walking around, I noticed that John was very upset. Feeling that perhaps there was something I could do, I approached John and asked him if I could help. He indicated that everything was just fine. From the looks of the situation, and John's body language, I felt that he was willing to talk, but John knew that this was not the way things were done at AEC. Tony, who worked at the machine next to John's, then cursed and said that the office guys only cared about schedules, not about the people down on the floor. I just looked at him, and then said that I only began working here last week, but I thought that I could address some of their issues. Tony gave me a strange look, shook his head, and went back to his machine. I could

hear him still swearing as I left. Later I realized that most of the office staff were also offended by Tony's language.

On the way back to my office, Lesley, a recently hired engineer from Russia, approached me and pointed out that the employees were not accustomed to management talking to them. Management only issued orders and made demands. As we discussed the different perceptions between office and floor staff, we were interrupted by a very loud lunch bell, which startled me. I was happy to join Lesley for lunch, but she asked me why I was not eating in the office lunchroom. I replied that if I was going to understand how AEC worked, I had to get to know all the people better. In addition, I realized that this was not how things were done and wondered about the nature of this apparent division between the management and the floor. In the lunchroom, the other workers were amazed to see me there, commenting that I was just new and had not learned the ropes yet.

After lunch, when I asked George, my supervisor, about his recent confrontation with John, George was surprised that John got upset, and exclaimed, "I just wanted John to know that he did a great job, and as a result, we will be able to ship on time one large order to the West Coast. In fact, I thought I was complimenting him."

Earlier, Lesley had indicated that certain behavior was expected from management, and therefore from me. I reasoned that I did not think that this behavior works, and besides that, it was not what I believed or how I cared to behave. For the next couple of months, I simply walked around the floor and took every opportunity to talk to the shop floor employees. Often, when the employees related specific information about their workplaces, I felt that it went over my head. Frequently, I had to write down the information and revisit it later. I made a point of listening to them, identifying where they were coming from, and trying to understand them. I needed to keep my mind open to new ideas. Because the shop employees expected me to make requests and demands, I made a point of not doing any of that. Soon enough, the employees became friendly, and started to accept me as one of their own, or at least as a different type of a management person.

During my third month of work, the employees showed me how to improve the scheduling of jobs, especially those on the aluminum slitter. In fact, the greatest contribution was made by John, who demonstrated better ways to combine the most common slitting sizes and reduce waste by retaining some of the "common-sized" material for new orders. Seeing the opportunity, I programmed a spreadsheet to calculate and track inventory. This, in addition to better planning and forecasting, allowed us to reduce our new order turnarounds from four to five weeks to in by 10:00 a.m. and out by 5:00 p.m. on the same day.

By the time I was employed for four months, I realized that members from other departments came to me and asked me to relay messages to the shop employees. When I asked why they were delegating this task to me, they stated that I spoke the same language as the shop employees. Increasingly, I became the messenger for the office-to-shop floor communication.

One morning, George called me into his office and complimented me on the levels of customer service and the improvements that had been achieved. As we talked, I mentioned that we could not have done it without John's help. "He really knows his stuff, and he is good," I said. I suggested that we consider him for some type of promotion. Also, I hoped that this would be a positive gesture that would improve the communication between the office and shop floor.

George turned and pulled a flyer out of his desk. "Here is a management skills seminar. Do you think we should send John to it?"

"That is a great idea," I exclaimed, "Perhaps it would be good if he were to receive the news from you directly, George." George agreed, and after discussing some other issues, we parted company.

That afternoon, John came into my office, upset and ready to quit. "After all my effort and work, you guys are sending me for training seminars. So, am I not good enough for you?"

CASE 3: CHENGDU BUS GROUP

By Runtian Jing, University of Electronic Science and Technology of China

The Chengdu Bus Group (CBG) is a Chinese, state-owned enterprise with more than 4,000 buses and 14,000 employees. A few years ago, CBG encountered serious problems. The primary issue was the company's management systems, but it also faced a considerable financial crisis. Complaints against CBG from its many customers were becoming increasingly common, and the operations of the company were in disarray.

At the end of a troubled year, Dr. She Chen was appointed the director (CEO) of CBG. Dr. Chen had proven himself in previous positions as a thoughtful and insightful manager. He had accumulated a wealth of experience in not only effective leadership in Chinese society but also the field of management theory. In addition, he had earned a PhD—a very rare achievement in the Chinese business community.

Due to the seriousness of CBG's problems, the mayor of Chengdu gave Dr. Chen just three years to reform CBG—too short a time to gradually transform the organization, including the critically flawed management system and financial situation. Therefore, Dr. Chen had to implement rapid change and take risks to carry out a successful reform in the required time frame, even though he knew it would be met with great resistance from CBG's employees and many stakeholders.

After taking up his new position, Dr. Chen conducted a careful investigation into the functioning of CBG, after which he formulated a series of reform measures. He then discussed his ideas and proposed changes with the mayor and leaders of Chengdu city, obtaining full support in both authorization and funding, before implementing the organizational changes in the company.

FAST-PACED MANAGERIAL REFORM

Because CBG is an old, state-owned enterprise, very complicated working relationships and politics existed among the 14,000 employees. Dr. Chen knew that this situation would make it very difficult to carry out large-scale organizational reforms within the company. However, after two months of examination, Dr. Chen felt he had accurately grasped the important characteristics of the 533 managers in the company. He then carefully designed a reform plan and schedule for the managers and their positions. To avoid the influence of complicated *guanxi* (special relationships) among the managers, and to avoid the managers forming solid opposition to his changes, Dr. Chen implemented the reforms with a fast, accurate, and ambitious strategy. The changes were made quickly, precisely, and without compromise.

This strategy meant that adjustments to the managerial positions were completed before the managers could effectively react to what was happening and potentially disrupt the process. Nonetheless, when they realized what had happened, they began to protest. Dr. Chen was very calm and simply said to them: "After all these events have passed by, you will have many different impressions about me and my reforms. Although such an adjustment may bring some loss to you, in the future the commendation from others will be greater than the condemnation. All change must face resistance, complaint, and even rejection. What I have done is not for myself, but for the company."

SIMPLIFYING THE BRANCH COMPANY STRUCTURE

Another notable reform that Dr. Chen implemented involved the branch companies of CBG. The organization had four branch companies; two were wholly state-owned, whereas the other two were joint ventures with external investors. In addition to operating bus routes, each company owned buses, bus stations, repair workshops, and other facilities and equipment required to run their bus services. However, this organization created significant problems and inefficiencies as each company ran its operations independently of the other companies and did not share stations or repair workshops—essentially, the four companies were in direct competition.

Furthermore, different routes throughout the city had quite different profit rates. Without any formal authority coordinating the companies or implementing policies and rules, there was overcompetition for the desirable high-profit routes, resulting in inefficiencies and losses for all of the companies. To rectify this situation, Dr. Chen arranged for CBG to buy back the external equity of the joint ventures and changed the branch operations to purely state-owned subsidiaries. He then removed overservicing on the high-profit routes and redeployed the surplus buses and employees from these routes to develop the potential profitability of other routes, under the principle of optimization.

All the routes were rezoned to fall under the operations of four specific areas of the city, forming the eastern, western, southern, and northern bus companies. All bus stations were amalgamated into a single station company, and all the repair workshops amalgamated into a single repair company. These reforms made it possible for each of the four bus companies to obtain services from the station company or repair company anywhere in the city, which greatly reduced resource waste, overcompetition, and operating costs.

SALARIES AND REWARDS

Dr. Chen found that the salary system of CBG was questionable in both fairness and efficiency. For example, the frontline staff generally worked very hard, but their salaries were lower than the backup staff who did not work as hard, resulting in low job satisfaction and high turnover rates among the frontline staff. After careful evaluation of the different jobs' tasks and demands, Dr. Chen distinguished the tasks and demands of the frontline and backup staff. Despite criticism from backup staff and some managers, he insisted on increasing the wages and bonuses of the frontline staff.

To reduce frequent accidents by bus drivers, Dr. Chen linked the wage system to each driver's "safe mileage accumulation program." After an accident, the driver's safe mileage accumulation decreased, which affected the driver's wages. Conversely, if a driver had few accidents, or none at all, his or her wages would increase. A driver who had not been involved in any accidents could earn an even higher wage than the average middle manager! Such a policy quickly improved the safety awareness and practices of the drivers. Furthermore, Dr. Chen encouraged managers to use rewards instead of punishments to motivate their employees and abolished more than 50 penalty provisions.

THE RESULTS OF REFORM

After just two years of Dr. Chen's reforms, the Chengdu Bus Group achieved remarkable results. The management was greatly improved, the efficiency and profitability of CBG were enhanced, and the employees were performing better and were significantly happier. Through the safe mileage accumulation system, drivers' safety awareness and quality of service substantially improved, and the rate of accidents decreased greatly. The public attitude toward the company and its social evaluation also improved significantly. CBG received an award for its successful reform from the state-owned Assets Supervision and Administration Commission (SASAC) of Chengdu city in 2008.

CASE 4: FRAN HAYDEN JOINS DAIRY ENGINEERING

By Glyn Jones, University of Waikato, New Zealand

BACKGROUND

Dairy Engineering (NZ) Ltd. has its headquarters in Hamilton, New Zealand, with manufacturing plants in South Auckland and Christchurch. The company manufactures equipment for the dairy industry. In its early years it focused on the domestic market, but in the past five years it has expanded into exports. The company employs 450 people, which makes it a large company by New Zealand standards.

This case focuses on events in the Accounting Department at the head office, which consists of two sections, Cost Accounting and Management Information Services (MIS).

FRAN, THE NEW GRADUATE

Fran Hayden is in the final year of her Bachelor of Management Studies (BMS) degree at the University of Waikato, where she has proved to be a high achiever.

Fran was interested in a position with Dairy Engineering because of the opportunity to gain practical experience, the high starting salary offered in industry, and the proximity to her boyfriend.

Fran sent her curriculum vitae to the company and two weeks later was invited to an interview with the chief accountant. She was surprised at the end of the interview to be offered the position of assistant cost accountant. Fran said she would like to think it over. Two weeks later, when she had still not replied, she received a telephone call from Rob asking if she was going to take the position. Still not totally convinced, Fran decided to accept the offer.

THE FIRST DAY AT WORK

Like many of her peers, Fran was glad to be leaving university after four years of study. She was looking forward to having money to spend, as well as reducing her student debt. To "look the part," she had gone further into debt to buy some new "corporate clothing." On reporting to the Accounting Department, she got her first real-world shock: No one was expecting her! Even worse, she found that there was no vacancy for her in Cost Accounting; instead, she had been assigned to management information systems (MIS).

Fran was taken to MIS by one of her new colleagues, Mike, who introduced her to other colleagues, including Tom and Adrian. They seemed to be a friendly bunch, as apparently was her boss, Peter Bruton, who explained that her main duties were to assist with compiling information for the monthly management report, known as "Big Brother."

After two weeks later, the time arrived to compile Big Brother. Fran found that her part was almost entirely clerical and consisted of photocopying, collating, binding, punching, and stamping the pages of the report. She then had to hand-deliver copies of the report to the senior manager at headquarters. After Big Brother was completed, Fran found she had little to do. She began to wonder why MIS needed four people.

THE BIG OPPORTUNITY

One afternoon, out of the blue, the chief accountant called Fran to his office to tell her about an upcoming management workshop to be held in Auckland on performance measurement. Rob talked about the importance of staff development and indicated that he would like to see one of his younger staff attending the workshop. He then asked Fran if she would be interested. She jumped at the opportunity. Unfortunately her boss was away on two weeks' leave at the time, but Rob said he would talk with Peter.

Fran enjoyed the workshop, particularly rubbing shoulders with experienced managers, living in an Auckland hotel, and generally acting the management part. Even before returning to Hamilton, she wrote a detailed report on the workshop for the chief accountant. But on her return to Hamilton, she found that all was far from well.

On Sunday evening, Fran received a telephone call from her colleague Mike with some disturbing news. When Peter returned to work to find that Fran was in Auckland, he was furious, complaining that he had not been consulted and that his authority was being undermined.

Peter: Fran is no longer employed in his section.

Fran returned to work full of trepidation, only to find that the expected encounter with her boss did not take place because he was in Christchurch. She handed two copies of her report on the workshop to the chief accountant's secretary before taking the opportunity of her boss's absence to seek the advice of her colleagues:

Fran: I am really worried. What do you think I should do?

Adrian: Stop worrying about it. He's just letting off steam. I have seen this all before. He'll get over it.

Fran: Come on; get serious. He is my boss! He can make things very difficult for me.

Mike: I think you should talk with Rob. After all, he's the one who suggested you go. It's not like it was your idea. He has to stick up for you.

The next day, Fran managed to get an appointment with the chief accountant. She started by saying that she found the workshop very useful. She then brought up her fears about Peter's displeasure with her attendance at the workshop, to which Rob responded:

Rob: Well yes, he was a bit upset but don't worry, I will sort it out. The report was really good. By the way, I think you should treat it as confidential. Don't show it to anyone or discuss it with anyone. Is that ok? Don't worry about this. I assure you that I will sort it out.

Fran left the meeting feeling reassured but also a bit puzzled, wondering how Rob could have read her report in such a short time.

On Thursday Peter returned to work and just before lunch called Fran into his office, where he proceeded to attack her verbally, saying that she had "connived" behind his back to attend the workshop and that she had never asked for his permission. He said that he realized she was an intelligent "girl" but that she was "sneaky." He went on:

Peter: You had better know which side your bread is buttered on—that for better or worse, you are in my section. No other section would want you.

He then called Mike in and told him:

Peter: I don't want Fran wasting any more time—she is not to make any private calls from work.

Later in "confidence," he also told Janet, one of the administration clerks:

> **Peter:** Don't go talking with Fran—she has far too much work to catch up on.

Naturally, Janet did tell Fran.

The following week, Vernon happened to pass Fran in the corridor and stopped to talk with her. Fran had met Vernon only briefly during her first week in the company and was surprised when he asked her why she looked so miserable. After she explained, he suggested a talk with the chief accountant. Taking Fran with him, he went straight to Rob's office. Vernon said that they needed a word, and Fran listened as Vernon outlined the situation to Rob. Fran made it clear that if Peter continued to treat her this way, she would have to ask for a transfer. She also mentioned that there was not enough work in MIS to keep her occupied for more than a day or so each week.

The chief accountant listened and then asked her to give him a written report of what had happened since she had joined the company, including the latest incident with her boss. This account, he said, would be brought up at the next senior management meeting. Over the weekend, Fran wrote the report, which included a request for a transfer out of MIS on the basis of the lack of work and her boss's attitude toward her. On Monday morning, she handed her report to the chief accountant's secretary.

Fran expected a reply but by early afternoon still had heard nothing. At the end of the day, Peter called all his staff into his office. He was obviously in a good mood and told them that he had put his plan for revising Big Brother to the management meeting and had received an enthusiastic response. As he spoke, Fran noticed the color draining out of Mike's face. On the way out, Mike explained that what Peter was describing were his revision plans, not his own. Mike resolved never to give his boss another of his ideas, telling Fran:

> **Mike:** He just uses other people's brains—but that's the last time he uses mine.

Fran drove home from work feeling despondent. She wished she had never joined the company. Her job was boring, almost entirely clerical, and certainly not demanding enough to require her degree. She was also taking the stresses home, resulting in quarrels with her boyfriend and flat mates.

Fran concluded that she had two alternatives: transfer or resign. But to leave her job after less than five months would hardly impress any future employer. In desperation, she went to talk with Vernon, who she thought would be sympathetic, only to receive more unwelcome news about the outcome of the senior management meeting. Contrary to Fran's expectation, the chief accountant had not confronted Peter. In fact, it appeared he had been eclipsed by Peter's presentation for the revision of Big Brother and never attempted to raise the issue.

Vernon was frank: He agreed that she must either transfer or resign. Then, to Fran's surprise, he suggested she apply for a position in his section that would become vacant in three weeks' time. One of his assistant accountants was leaving to go overseas at short notice, and he did not have a replacement. Vernon cautioned however that Fran's only chance was to apply directly to the chief accountant, which would force the issue. With a formal, written application before him, the chief accountant would have to make a decision. Peter would resist the request. Later Fran drafted a letter to Rob, requesting that she be transferred from MIS to the upcoming position in Cost Accounting.

THE CONFRONTATION

The next morning, Fran took her request to the chief accountant, but after reading it, he said:

> **Rob:** You really needn't have done this, you know—I intended dealing with the situation.

Fran left Rob's office wondering what to believe. From her desk, she watched as Peter made his way across to the chief accountant's office. The meeting was brief. Five minutes later, he left Rob's office and, as he passed by, said in a loud voice:

> **Peter:** Fran, you are finished in this company.

Fran saw her colleagues duck their heads down and pretend to be working. No one envied her position. She wondered how, in such a short time, she had ended up in such a situation.

CASE 5: GOING TO THE X-STREAM

By Roy Smollan, Auckland University of Technology, New Zealand

Gil Reihana was the chief executive officer of X-Stream, a company he launched in Auckland, New Zealand, six years ago at the age of 25, after graduating with a bachelor's degree in information technology and management. He had inherited $300,000 and persuaded various family members to invest additional money. X-Stream assembled personal computers for the New Zealand and Australian markets and sold them through a number of chain stores and independent retailers. The company had soon established a reputation for quality hardware, customized products, excellent delivery times, and after-sales service. Six months ago, it had started a software division, specializing in web-page design and consulting on various applications for the development of electronic business.

Gil was driven by a desire to succeed. He had started working part-time at an electronics retailer at age 16 and in his spare time took apart old computers in his garage to see how they were made. He was extroverted, energetic, and enthusiastic, often arriving at work before 5:00 a.m. and seldom leaving before 7:00 p.m. He felt that work should be challenging but fun too. He had initially picked a young senior management team that he thought shared his outlook. A casual, almost irreverent atmosphere developed. However, a poorly organized accounting department led to the replacement of the first accountant after two years. Gil believed that major decisions should be made by consensus and that individuals should then be empowered to implement these decisions in their own way. In the beginning he had met with each staff member in January to discuss with them how happy they were in their jobs, what their ambitions were, and what plans they would like to make for the coming year in terms of their own professional development. These one-on-one meetings became more difficult as the company grew, so senior management team members were eventually delegated the task of conducting reviews with their own staff. However, Gil was unsure whether every manager was actually performing the reviews or how well they were working. Now he tried to keep in touch with staff by having lunch with them in the cafeteria occasionally.

Denise Commins (affectionately known to all staff as Dot Com) was the chief financial officer. She and Gil could not be more different. Denise was quiet, methodical, and very patient. Her superb interpersonal skills complemented a highly analytical mind. At 55 years old, she was considerably older than most of the employees and often showed a strong maternal side. Many of her team (and several from other departments as well) frequently consulted her on work issues and personal problems too. She enjoyed the informal relationships she had built up but found that the technical aspects of her role were becoming less rewarding.

Don Head, the marketing manager, was considered a rather ruthless operator, often undercutting the competition in terms of price and, on more than one occasion, by circulating false rumors of defects in their products. He deemed himself "a ladies' man" and was known to flirt with a number of the staff. A case of sexual harassment had been dropped after a 22-year-old secretary had been paid a sizeable sum of money. Gil and the members of the senior management team had been furious, but Don had denied any wrongdoing, claiming that she had "led him on." Don had been at university with Gil, and they spent many hours after work at a pub around the corner from the factory. With sales rising year after year, his marketing expertise and cunning were regarded as essential to the company's continuing growth. He had a department of eight whom he had carefully screened to be ambitious self-starters. They were required to set and achieve their own targets, as long as they were "big hairy ambitious goals," a phrase he had heard at a seminar.

Jason Palu, the production manager, was a soft-spoken man who had started as a supervisor and quickly worked his way up to a top position. He set extremely high standards for the production staff and was considered a perfectionist. He was highly regarded by his colleagues for his efficiency and reliability. There were very few occasions when an order could not be fulfilled on time, and his goal was zero defects. He tended to be autocratic; some people complained that he never listened to them and allocated work hours that did not suit people, often insisting on (paid) overtime at very short notice. When one production worker complained, Jason tersely responded, "We have a job to do and we just have to get on with it. The company depends on us."

Heather Berkowitz was the chief webpage designer. She had blue hair, a ring through her nose, and a variety of exotic clothes that had been sourced from various second-hand stores. She seldom arrived at work much before 11:00 a.m. and often left before 4:00 p.m. She said she did her best work at home, often at night, so why should she "punch the clock like the drones on the assembly line"? Gil and others had often received e-mails from her, sent at all hours of the night. She had established a reputation as a top webpage designer, and though her physical appearance did not go down too well with some of the company's clients (or staff), the quality and quantity of her work was extremely high.

On Tuesdays at 9:00 a.m., the senior staff met to discuss weekly plans and any significant issues that had arisen. All employees were invited to the meeting, and some accepted this opportunity to attend. Gil trusted all staff to keep confidential matters within the company. He believed that if the organization shared information with employees, they would be more likely to support management decisions. The meetings lacked formality and usually started with some jokes, usually at the expense of some members of staff. By and large the jokes were meant to be inoffensive but were not always taken that way. Nicknames were often assigned to staff, mostly by Don Head, some quite derogatory. You were thought to be a "wet blanket" if you objected. Don seemed oblivious to the unflattering nickname he had been given, preferring to call himself Braveheart, sometimes even signing memos in this fashion.

Although employment agreements referred to a 40-hour workweek, there was an expectation that staff would put in substantially more than that. Only the assembly line workers had to clock in and out, due, Jason explained, to the overtime that assembly staff were required to work to meet deadlines. The overtime pay was welcomed by some production staff and resented by some employees in other departments who believed they should be entitled to the same benefits.

Recently a conflict had arisen between Jason and Don. The company had been developing a top-of-the-range laptop, scheduled to launch in two weeks' time. Jason had been urging senior management to delay the introduction of the new X-MH until some glitches had been resolved. A batch of chips acquired from abroad had contained some defective features. Jason wanted to postpone the new model until these problems had been completely sorted out, a process that he believed would take another month. Don found the delay unacceptable. A former All Blacks (New Zealand rugby) captain had been contracted to attend the launch and market the new model on a roadshow that would travel throughout New Zealand's and Australia's main cities. He would not be available at the time Jason was prepared to release the X-MH. At a heated staff meeting, some of the senior staff backed Don, and some agreed with Jason. Don had urged all of his department to attend the meeting, to present a united front and convey an image of power.

Heather Berkowitz had arrived halfway through the meeting and, with a mouthful of muffin, proclaimed that there was no rush to get out the "new toy." The company had plenty of other issues to which it could devote its energy. She said she had met the head of information technology of a chain of fast-food restaurants that wanted to revitalize its website. She maintained she needed three extra staff to get this up and running. She left the meeting five minutes later. Don was fuming at the interruption and demanded that Gil should stick to the original launch date of the X-MH. Gil calmly replied that he understood Don's frustration but that more consultation was necessary. He said that it would be discussed by the parties concerned during the week and a final decision would be made at the following Tuesday's staff meeting.

Don spent the rest of the day lobbying other members of the senior staff. He offered Dorothy the use of his beach cottage if she backed him and promised to support her on the acquisition of expensive new accounting software. She just laughed and said that she was convinced the senior management team would approve the new software. She also informed Don that a member of her staff had seen one of his sales representatives entering a strip joint the previous week at a time when the sales force had been engaged in a staff meeting.

Other problems had arisen in recent months. Ramesh Patel, the newly recruited head of e-business applications had, with help from a personal contact, developed a software program that would help hotels and restaurants source products and services over the Internet. It was beginning to generate useful revenue. His contact had now billed X-Stream for $25,000 in consultancy fees and

development costs. Ramesh claimed that his contact had owed him a favor and that no mention of money had ever been made. X-Stream had referred the matter to its legal counsel.

Les Kong, the research and development manager (hardware), had complained to Gil that he could no longer work under Jason Palu. While he considered him a very pleasant man, and a very capable production manager, he could no longer tolerate his strict control style. "You can't do creative work on command!" was his lament. He loved his job and had spent hours over several weekends developing and refining a new product.

There was considerable resentment from Jason and Don about the resources that had been invested in the software division, partly because they did not see the need for the company to diversify, and partly because they claimed that money was being diverted from their departments to fund the new ventures. Ramesh claimed that "a good e-business starts at home—we should open up all our procurement via the Internet." His suggestion did not go down well with Jason and Don.

Gil had been pondering the structure of X-Stream for some time. The old functional structure no longer seemed appropriate. "Silo" mentality and departmental interests seemed to predominate, and turf wars were raging. The company had grown to 64 staff in New Zealand and 8 in Australia. The ongoing development of new hardware and the introduction of the software side of the business had made management somewhat complicated. He missed the old days when he knew every member of staff. The informal decision making that was characteristic of the business might have to give way to more formal processes. Yet he did not want to lose the creativity that underpinned its success. Despite the open invitation to attend the management meetings, many staff complained that they never knew what was going on. He expected all senior managers to keep their departmental staff informed of developments. Some had done this admirably, while others had virtually ignored his wishes.

A human resources manager, Alkina Bennelong, had been appointed a month previously and reported to Denise Commins. She had been reviewing the company's loosely worded job descriptions, personnel specifications, and recruitment and selection systems and had suggested more professional and elaborate approaches. She had also suggested the introduction of a performance management system, including feedback from peers, direct reports, and outsiders, such as suppliers and customers. "Over my dead body!" was the retort of Don Head. "How can you allow subordinates to tell you how to do your job?" queried Jason Palu. "Can't see what the fuss is all about," said Heather Berkowitz. "Everybody keeps telling me what to do anyway, even though they don't understand the first thing about my job! But it doesn't worry me."

CASE 6: KEEPING SUZANNE CHALMERS

By Steven L. McShane, University of Western Australia

Thomas Chan hung up the telephone and sighed. The vice president of software engineering at Advanced Photonics Inc. (API) had just spoken to Suzanne Chalmers, who called to arrange a meeting with him later that day. She didn't say what the meeting was about, but Chan almost instinctively knew that Chalmers was going to quit after working at API for the past four years. Chalmers is a software engineer in Internet Protocol (IP), the software that directs fiber-optic light through API's routers. It is very specialized work, and Chalmers is one of API's top talents in that area.

Thomas Chan had been through this before. A valued employee would arrange a private meeting. The meeting would begin with a few pleasantries; then the employee would announce that he or she wants to quit. Some employees say they are leaving because of the long hours and stressful deadlines. They say they need to decompress, get to know the kids again, or whatever. But that's not usually the real reason. Almost every organization in this industry is scrambling to keep up with technological advances and the competition. Employees would just leave one stressful job for another one.

Also, many of the people who leave API join a start-up company a few months later. These start-up firms can be pressure cookers where everyone works 16 hours each day and has to perform a variety of tasks. For example, engineers in these small firms might have to meet customers or work on venture capital proposals rather than focus on specialized tasks related to their knowledge. API now has over 6,000 employees, so it is easier to assign people to work that matches their technical competencies.

No, the problem isn't the stress or long hours, Chan thought. The problem is money—too much money. Most of the people who leave are millionaires. Suzanne Chalmers is one of them. Thanks to generous stock options that have skyrocketed on the stock markets, many employees at API have more money than they can use. Most are under 40 years old, so it's too early for them to retire. But their financial independence gives them less reason to remain with API.

THE MEETING

The meeting with Suzanne Chalmers took place a few hours after the telephone call. It began like the others, with the initial pleasantries and brief discussion about progress on the latest fiber-optic router project. Then Chalmers made her well-rehearsed statement: "Thomas, I've really enjoyed working here, but I'm going to leave Advanced Photonics." Chalmers took a breath and then looked at Chan. When he didn't reply after a few seconds, she continued: "I need to take time off. You know, get away to recharge my batteries. The project's nearly done and the team can complete it without me. Well, anyway, I'm thinking of leaving."

Chan spoke in a calm voice. He suggested that Chalmers should take an unpaid leave for two or maybe three months, complete with paid benefits, and then return refreshed. Chalmers politely rejected that offer, saying that she needed to get away from work for a while. Chan then asked Chalmers whether she was unhappy with her work environment—whether she was getting the latest computer technology to do her work and whether there were problems with co-workers. The workplace was fine, Chalmers replied. The job was getting a bit routine, but she had a comfortable workplace with excellent coworkers.

Chan then apologized for the cramped workspace, due mainly to the rapid increase in the number of people hired over the past year. He suggested that if Chalmers took a couple of months off, API would give her special treatment with a larger work space and a better view of the park behind the campus-like building when she returned. She politely thanked Chan for that offer, but it wasn't what she needed. Besides, it wouldn't be fair to have a large work space when other team members work in smaller quarters.

Chan was running out of tactics, so he tried his last hope: money. He asked whether Chalmers had higher offers. She replied that she regularly received calls from other companies, and some of them offered more money. Most were start-up firms that offered a lower salary but higher potential gains in stock options. Chan knew from market surveys that Chalmers was already paid well in the industry. He also knew that API couldn't compete on stock option potential. Employees working in start-up firms sometimes saw their stocks increase by five or ten times their initial value, whereas stocks at API and other large firms increased more slowly. However, Chan promised Chalmers that he would recommend that she receive a significant raise—maybe 25 percent more—and more stock options. Chan added that Chalmers was one of API's most valuable employees and that the company would suffer if she left the firm.

The meeting ended with Chalmers promising to consider Chan's offer of higher pay and stock options. Two days later, Chan received her resignation in writing. Five months later, Chan learned that after a few months traveling with her husband, Chalmers joined a start-up software firm in the area.

CASE 7: THE REGENCY GRAND HOTEL

By Elizabeth Ho, Gucci Group, under the supervision of Steven L. McShane, University of Western Australia

The Regency Grand Hotel is a five-star hotel in Bangkok, Thailand. The hotel was established 15 years ago by a local consortium of investors and has been operated by a Thai general manager throughout this time. The hotel is one of Bangkok's most prestigious hotels, and its 700 employees enjoy the prestige being associated with it. The hotel provides good welfare benefits, above-market-rate salaries, and job security. In addition, employees received a year-end bonus amounting to four months' salary, regardless of the hotel's overall performance during the year.

Recently, the Regency was sold to a large U.S. hotel chain that was very keen to expand its operations into Thailand. When the acquisition was announced, the general manager decided to take early retirement when the hotel changed ownership. The U.S. hotel chain kept all the Regency employees, though a few were transferred to other positions. John Becker, an American with 10 years of management experience with the hotel chain, was appointed as the new general manager of Regency Palace Hotel, due to his previous successes integrating newly acquired hotels in the United States. In most of the previous acquisitions, Becker took over operations with poor profitability and low morale.

Becker is a strong believer in empowerment. He expects employees to go beyond the guidelines and standards to consider guest needs on a case-to-case basis. He believes employees must be guest-oriented at all times to provide excellent customer service. From his U.S. experience, Becker has found that empowerment increases employee motivation, performance, and job satisfaction, all of which contribute to the hotel's profitability and customer service ratings. Soon after becoming general manager in Regency Palace, Becker introduced the practice of empowerment to replicate the successes that he had achieved back home.

The Regency Grand Hotel has been very profitable throughout its 15-year history. Employees have always worked according to management's instructions. Their responsibility was to ensure that the instructions from their managers were carried out diligently and conscientiously. Innovation and creativity were discouraged under the previous management. Indeed, employees were punished for their mistakes and discouraged from trying out ideas that had not been approved by management. As a result, employees were afraid to be innovative or take risks.

Becker met with the Regent's managers and department heads to explain that empowerment would be introduced in the hotel. He told them that employees must be empowered with decision-making authority so that they could use their initiative, creativity, and judgment to satisfy guest needs or handle problems effectively and efficiently. However, he stressed that the more complex issues and decisions were to be referred to superiors, who were to coach and assist rather than provide direct orders. Furthermore, Becker stressed that mistakes were allowed but he could not tolerate that the same mistakes be made more than twice. He advised managers and department heads not to discuss minor issues, problems, or decisions with him; however, they were to bring important and major issues and decisions to him. He concluded the meeting by asking for feedback. Several managers and department heads told him that they liked the idea and would support it, while others simply nodded their heads. Becker was pleased with the response and eager to have his plan implemented.

In the past, the Regency had emphasized administrative control, resulting in many bureaucratic procedures throughout the organization. For example, the front counter employees needed to seek approval from their manager before they could upgrade guests to another category of room. The front counter manager would then write and submit a report to the general manager justifying the upgrade. Soon after his meeting with managers, Becker reduced the number of bureaucratic rules at the Regency and allocated more decision-making authority to frontline employees. This action upset those who previously had decision-making power over these issues. As a result, several of these managers left the hotel.

Becker also began spending most of his time observing and interacting with the employees at the front desk, lobby, restaurants, and various departments. This direct interaction with Becker helped many employees understand what he wanted and expected of them. However, the employees had difficulty trying to distinguish between a major and minor issue or decision. More often than not, supervisors would reverse employee decisions by stating that they were major issues requiring management approval. Employees who displayed initiative and made good decisions in satisfying the needs of the guests rarely received any positive feedback from their supervisors. Eventually, most of these employees lost confidence in making decisions and reverted back to relying on their superiors for decision making.

Not long after the implementation of the practice of empowerment, Becker realized that his subordinates were consulting him more frequently than before. Most of them came to him with minor issues and consulted with him on about minor decisions. He had to spend most of his time attending to his subordinates. Soon he began to feel highly frustrated and exhausted, and often he would tell his secretary that "unless the hotel is on fire, don't let anyone disturb me."

Becker thought that the practice of empowerment would benefit the overall performance of the hotel. However, contrary to his expectation, the business and overall performance of the hotel began to deteriorate. There had been an increasing number of guest complaints. In the past, the hotel had minimal guest complaints. Now there were a significant number of formal written complaints every month. Many other guests voiced their dissatisfaction verbally to hotel employees. The number of mistakes made by employees had been on an increase. Becker was very upset when he realized that two local newspapers and an overseas newspaper had published negative feedback about the hotel in terms of service standards. He was most distressed when an international travel magazine had voted it "one of Asia's nightmare hotels."

The stress levels of the employees were continuously mounting since the introduction of empowerment. Absenteeism due to illness was increasing at an alarming rate. In addition, employee turnover rates had reached an all-time high. The good working relationships that were established under the old management had been severely strained. The employees were no longer united and supportive of one another; instead, they were quick to point fingers and backstab when mistakes were made or problems arose.

Note: This case is based on true events, but the industry and names have been changed.

CASE 8: THE SHIPPING INDUSTRY ACCOUNTING TEAM

By Steven L. McShane, University of Western Australia

For the past five years, I have been working at McKay, Sanderson, and Smith Associates, a mid-sized accounting firm in Boston that specializes in commercial accounting and audits. My particular specialty is accounting practices for shipping companies, ranging from small fishing fleets to a couple of the big firms with ships along the east coast.

About 18 months ago, McKay, Sanderson, and Smith Associates became part of a large merger involving two other accounting firms. These firms have offices in Miami, Seattle, Baton Rouge, and Los Angeles. Although the other two accounting firms were much larger than McKay, all three firms agreed to avoid centralizing the business around one office in Los Angeles. Instead, the new firm—called Goldberg, Choo, and McKay Associates—would rely on teams across the country to "leverage the synergies of our collective knowledge" (an often-cited statement from the managing partner soon after the merger).

The merger had its greatest effect on me a year ago when my boss (a senior partner and vice-president of the merger firm) announced that I would be working more closely with three people from the other two firms to become the firm's new shipping industry accounting team. The other "team members" were Elias in Miami, Susan in Seattle, and Brad in Los Angeles. I had met Elias briefly at a meeting in New York City during the merger but have never met Susan or Brad, though I knew they were shipping accounting professionals at the other firms.

Initially, the shipping "team" activities involved e-mailing each other about new contracts and prospective clients. Later, we were asked to submit joint monthly reports on accounting statements and issues. Normally, I submitted my own monthly reports to summarize activities involving my own clients. Coordinating the monthly report with three other people took much more time, particularly because the different accounting documentation procedures across the three firms were still being resolved. It took numerous e-mails and a few telephone calls to work out a reasonable monthly report style.

During this aggravating process, it became apparent—to me at least—that this "team" business was costing me more time than it was worth. Moreover, Brad in Los Angeles didn't have a clue as to how to communicate with the rest of us. He rarely replied to e-mails. Instead, he often used the telephone voice mail system, which resulted in lots of telephone tag. Brad arrives at work at 9:30 a.m. in Los Angeles (and is often late!), which is early afternoon in Boston. I typically have a flexible work schedule from 7:30 a.m. to 3:30 p.m. so I can chauffeur my kids after school to sports and music lessons. So Brad and I have a window of less than three hours to share information.

The biggest nuisance with the shipping specialist accounting team started two weeks ago when the firm asked the four of us to develop a new strategy for attracting more shipping firm business. This new strategic plan is a messy business. Somehow, we have to share our thoughts on various approaches, agree on a new plan, and write a unified submission to the managing partner. Already, the project is taking most of my time just writing and responding to e-mails and talking in conference calls (which none of us did much before the team formed).

Susan and Brad have already had two or three "misunderstandings" via e-mail about their different perspectives on delicate matters in the strategic plan. The worst of these disagreements required a conference call with all of us to resolve. Except for the most basic matters, it seems that we can't understand each other, let alone agree on key issues. I have come to the conclusion that I would never want Brad to work in my Boston office (thank goodness, he's on the other side of the country). While Elias and I seem to agree on most points, the overall team can't form a common vision or strategy. I don't know how Elias, Susan, or Brad feels, but I would be quite happy to work somewhere that did not require any of these long-distance team headaches.

© 2004 Steven L. McShane.

CASE 9: SIMMONS LABORATORIES

Adapted by William Starbuck from a case written by Alex Bavelas

Brandon Newbridge was sitting alone in the conference room of the laboratory. The rest of the group had gone. One of the secretaries had stopped and talked for a while about her husband's coming enrollment in graduate school and had finally left. Brandon, alone in the laboratory, slid a little farther down in his chair, looking with satisfaction at the results of the first test run of the new photon unit.

He liked to stay after the others had gone. His appointment as project head was still new enough to give him a deep sense of pleasure. His eyes were on the graphs before him, but in his mind, he could hear Dr. William Goh, the project head, saying again, "There's one thing about this place you can bank on. The sky is the limit for anyone who can produce!" Newbridge felt again the tingle of happiness and embarrassment. Well, dammit, he said to himself, he had produced. He wasn't kidding anybody. He had come to the Simmons Laboratories two years ago. During a routine test of some rejected Clanson components, he had stumbled on the idea of the photon correlator, and the rest just happened. Goh had been enthusiastic: A separate project had been set up for further research and development of the device, and he had gotten the job of running it. The whole sequence of events still seemed a little miraculous to Newbridge.

He shrugged out of the reverie and bent determinedly over the sheets when he heard someone come into the room behind him. He looked up expectantly; Goh often stayed late himself and now and then dropped in for a chat. This always made the day's end especially pleasant for Newbridge. The man who had entered wasn't Goh. He was a tall, thin stranger who wore steel-rimmed glasses and had a very wide leather belt with a large brass buckle.

The stranger smiled and introduced himself. "I'm Lester Zapf. Are you Brandon Newbridge?" They shook hands. "Dr. Goh said I might find you in. We were talking about your work, and I'm very much interested in what you are doing." Newbridge waved to a chair.

Zapf didn't seem to belong in any of the standard categories of visitors: customer, visiting fireman, stockholder. Newbridge pointed to the sheets on the table. "There are the preliminary results of a test we're running. We have a new gadget by the tail and we're trying to understand it. It's not finished, but I can show you the section we're testing."

He stood up, but Zapf was deep in the graphs. After a moment, he looked up with an odd grin. "These look like plots of a Jennings surface. I've been playing around with some autocorrelation functions of surfaces—you know that stuff." Newbridge, who had no idea what he was referring to, grinned back and nodded, and immediately felt uncomfortable. "Let me show you the monster," he said, and led the way to the workroom.

After Zapf left, Newbridge slowly put the graphs away, feeling vaguely annoyed. Then, as if he had made a decision, he quickly locked up and took the long way out so that he would pass Goh's office. But the office was locked. Newbridge wondered whether Goh and Zapf had left together.

The next morning, Newbridge dropped into Goh's office, mentioned that he had talked with Zapf, and asked who he was.

"Sit down for a minute," Goh said. "I want to talk to you about him. What do you think of him?" Newbridge replied truthfully that he thought Zapf was very bright and probably very competent. Goh looked pleased.

"We're taking him on," he said. "He's had a very good background in a number of laboratories, and he seems to have ideas about the problems we're tackling here." Newbridge nodded in agreement, instantly wishing that Zapf would not be placed with him.

"I don't know yet where he will finally land," Goh continued, "but he seems interested in what you are doing. I thought he might spend a little time with you by way of getting started." Newbridge nodded thoughtfully. "If his interest in your work continues, you can add him to your group."

"Well, he seemed to have some good ideas even without knowing exactly what we are doing," Newbridge answered. "I hope he stays; we'd be glad to have him."

Newbridge walked back to the lab with mixed feelings. He told himself that Zapf would be good for the group. He was no dunce; he'd produce. Newbridge thought again of

Goh's promise when he had promoted him—"The person who produces gets ahead in this outfit." The words seemed to carry the overtones of a threat now.

That day Zapf didn't appear until midafternoon. He explained that he had had a long lunch with Goh, discussing his place in the lab. "Yes," said Newbridge, "I talked with Jerry this morning about it, and we both thought you might work with us for a while."

Zapf smiled in the same knowing way that he had smiled when he mentioned the Jennings surfaces. "I'd like to," he said.

Newbridge introduced Zapf to the other members of the lab. Zapf and Link, the group's mathematician, hit it off well and spent the rest of the afternoon discussing a method for analyzing patterns that Link had been worrying over the last month.

It was 6:30 p.m. when Newbridge finally left the lab that night. He had waited almost eagerly for the end of the day to come—when they would all be gone and he could sit in the quiet rooms, relax, and think it over. "Think what over?" he asked himself. He didn't know. Shortly after 5:00 p.m., they had almost all gone except Zapf, and what followed was almost a duel. Newbridge was annoyed that he was being cheated out of his quiet period and finally resentfully determined that Zapf should leave first.

Zapf was sitting at the conference table reading, and Newbridge was sitting at his desk in the little glass-enclosed cubby he used during the day when he needed to be undisturbed. Zapf had gotten the last year's progress reports out and was studying them carefully. The time dragged. Newbridge doodled on a pad, the tension growing inside him. What the hell did Zapf think he was going to find in the reports?

Newbridge finally gave up, and they left the lab together. Zapf took several of the reports with him to study in the evening. Newbridge asked him if he thought the reports gave a clear picture of the lab's activities.

"They're excellent," Zapf answered with obvious sincerity. "They're not only good reports; what they report is damn good, too!" Newbridge was surprised at the relief he felt and grew almost jovial as he said good-night.

Driving home, Newbridge felt more optimistic about Zapf's presence in the lab. He had never fully understood the analysis that Link was attempting. If there was anything wrong with Link's approach, Zapf would probably spot it. "And if I'm any judge," he murmured, "he won't be especially diplomatic about it."

He described Zapf to his wife, who was amused by the broad leather belt and brass buckle. "It's the kind of belt that Pilgrims must have worn," she laughed.

"I'm not worried about how he holds his pants up," he laughed with her. "I'm afraid that he's the kind that just has to make like a genius twice each day. And that can be pretty rough on the group."

Newbridge had been asleep for several hours when he was jerked awake by the telephone. He realized it had rung several times. He swung off the bed muttering about damn fools and telephones. It was Zapf. Without any excuses, apparently oblivious of the time, he plunged into an excited recital of how Link's patterning problem could be solved.

Newbridge covered the mouthpiece to answer his wife's stage-whispered "Who is it?" "It's the genius," replied Newbridge.

Zapf, completely ignoring the fact that it was 2:00 in the morning, went on in a very excited way, starting in the middle of an explanation of a completely new approach to certain photon lab problems that he had stumbled on while analyzing past experiments. Newbridge managed to put some enthusiasm in his own voice and stood there, half-dazed and very uncomfortable, listening to Zapf talk endlessly about what he had discovered. It was probably not only a new approach but also an analysis that showed the inherent weakness of the previous experiment and how experimentation along that line would certainly have been inconclusive. The following day Newbridge spent the entire morning with Zapf and Link, the mathematician, the customary group morning meeting having been called off so that Zapf's work of the previous night could be gone over intensively. Zapf was very anxious that this be done, and Newbridge was not too unhappy to call the meeting off for reasons of his own.

For the next several days Zapf sat in the back office that had been turned over to him and did nothing but read the progress reports of the work that had been done in the last six months. Newbridge caught himself feeling apprehensive about the reaction that Zapf might have to some of his work. He was a little surprised at his own feelings. He had always been proud—though he had put on a convincingly modest face—of the way in which new ground in the study of photon measuring devices had been broken in his group. Now he wasn't sure, and it seemed to him that Zapf might easily show that the line of research they had been following was unsound or even unimaginative.

The next morning (as was the custom) the members of the lab, including the secretaries, sat around a conference table. Newbridge always prided himself on the fact that the work of the lab was guided and evaluated by the group as a whole, and he was fond of repeating that it was not a waste of time to include secretaries in such meetings. Often, what started out as a boring recital of fundamental assumptions to a naive listener uncovered new ways of regarding these assumptions that would not have occurred to the researcher who had long ago accepted them as a necessary basis for his work.

These group meetings also served Newbridge in another sense. He admitted to himself that he would have felt far less secure if he had had to direct the work out of his own mind, so to speak. With the group meeting as the principle of leadership, it was always possible to justify the exploration of blind alleys because of the general educative effect on the team. Zapf was there; Link was sitting next to Zapf, their conversation about Link's mathematical study apparently continuing from yesterday. The other members, Bob Davenport, Georgia Thurlow, and Arthur Oliver, were waiting quietly.

Newbridge, for reasons that he didn't quite understand, proposed for discussion this morning a problem that all of them had spent a great deal of time on previously, before coming to the conclusion that a solution was impossible, that there was no feasible way of treating it in an experimental fashion. When Newbridge proposed the problem, Davenport remarked that there was hardly any use going over it again; he was satisfied that there was no way of approaching the problem with the equipment and the physical capacities of the lab.

This statement had the effect of a shot of adrenaline on Zapf. He said he would like to know what the problem was in detail and, walking to the blackboard, began setting down the "factors" as various members of the group noted the problem and simultaneously listed the reasons it had been abandoned.

Very early in the description of the problem, it was evident that Zapf was going to disagree about the impossibility of attacking it. The group realized this, and their descriptions and recounting of the reasoning that had led to its abandonment dwindled away. Zapf began his statement, which seemingly had to have been prepared in advance, though Newbridge knew this was impossible. He couldn't help being impressed with the organized and logical way that Zapf was presenting ideas that must have occurred to him only a few minutes before.

What Zapf had to say, however, left Newbridge feeling a mixture of annoyance, irritation, and smug superiority over Zapf, in at least one area. Zapf held the opinion that the way that the problem had been analyzed was very typical of group thinking. With an air of sophistication that made it difficult for a listener to dissent, he proceeded to comment on the American emphasis on team ideas, satirically describing the ways in which they led to a "high level of mediocrity."

During this time, Newbridge observed that Link stared studiously at the floor, and he was very conscious of Georgia Thurlow's and Bob Davenport's glances toward him at several points of Zapf's little speech. Inwardly, Newbridge couldn't help feeling that this was one point at least in which Zapf was off on the wrong foot. The whole lab, following Goh's lead, talked and practiced the theory of small research teams as the basic organization for effective research. Zapf insisted that the problem could be approached and that he would like to study it for a while himself.

Newbridge ended the morning session by remarking that the meetings would continue and that the very fact that a supposedly insoluble experimental problem was now going to get another chance was another indication of the value of such meetings. Zapf immediately remarked that he was not at all averse to meetings to inform the group about the progress of its members. The point he wanted to make was that creative advances were seldom accomplished in such meetings, that they were made by an individual "living with" a problem closely and continuously, in a rather personal relationship to it.

Newbridge went on to say to Zapf that he was very glad that Zapf had raised these points and that he was sure the group would profit by reexamining the basis on which they had been operating. Newbridge agreed that individual effort was probably the basis for making major advances. He considered the group meetings useful primarily because they kept the group together and they helped the weaker members of the group keep up with the ones who were able to advance more easily and quickly in the analysis of problems.

It was clear as days went by and meetings continued that Zapf came to enjoy them because of the pattern that the meetings assumed. It became typical for Zapf to hold forth, and it was unquestionably clear that he was more brilliant, better prepared on the various subjects that were germane to the problem being studied, and more capable of going ahead than anyone there. Newbridge grew increasingly disturbed as he realized that his leadership of the group had been, in fact, taken over.

Whenever the subject of Zapf was mentioned in occasional meetings with Dr. Goh, Newbridge would comment only on the ability and obvious capacity for work that Zapf had. Somehow he never felt that he could mention his own discomforts, not only because they revealed a weakness on his part, but also because it was quite clear that Goh himself was considerably impressed with Zapf's work and with the contacts he had outside the photon laboratory.

Newbridge now began to feel that perhaps the intellectual advantages that Zapf had brought to the group did not quite compensate for what he felt was evidence of a breakdown in the cooperative spirit they had enjoyed before Zapf's arrival. More and more of the morning meetings were skipped. Zapf's opinion concerning the abilities of others of the group, except for Link, was obviously low. At times during morning meetings or in smaller discussions, he had been come close to the point of rudeness, refusing to pursue an argument when he claimed it was based on another person's ignorance of the facts involved. His impatience of others led him to also make similar remarks to Dr. Goh. Newbridge inferred this from a conversation with Goh in which Goh asked whether Davenport and Oliver were going to be kept on;

his failure to mention Link led Newbridge to feel that his comments were the result of private conversations between Zapf and Goh.

It was not difficult for Newbridge to make a quite convincing case about whether the brilliance of Zapf was sufficient recompense for the breakup of the group. He spoke privately with Davenport and Oliver, and it was quite clear that both were uncomfortable because of Zapf. Newbridge didn't press the discussion beyond the point of hearing them say that they did feel awkward and that it was sometimes difficult to understand the arguments Zapf advanced, but often embarrassing to ask him to fill in the basis for his arguments. Newbridge did not interview Link in this manner.

About six months after Zapf's arrival at the photon lab, a meeting was scheduled to give the sponsors of the research some idea of the work and its progress. It was customary at these meetings for project heads to present the research being conducted in their groups. The members of each group were invited to other meetings, held later in the day and open to all, but the special meetings were usually attended only by project heads, the head of the laboratory, and the sponsors.

As the time for the special meeting approached, it seemed to Newbridge that he must avoid the presentation at all cost. He felt that he could not trust himself to present the ideas and work that Zapf had advanced, because of his apprehension about whether he could present them in sufficient detail and answer questions about them. However, he also did not feel he could ignore these newer lines of work and present only the material that he had done or that had been started before Zapf's arrival. He believed also that it would not be beyond Zapf at all, in his blunt and undiplomatic way—if he were at the meeting, that is—to comment on Newbridge's presentation and reveal his inadequacy. It also seemed quite clear that it would not be easy to keep Zapf from attending the meeting, even though he was not on the administrative level of those invited.

Newbridge found an opportunity to speak to Goh and raised the question. He told Goh that, with the meetings coming up and with the interest in the work and with Zapf's contributions to the work, Zapf would probably like to come to the meetings, but there was a question of how the others in the group would feel if only Zapf were invited. Goh passed this over very lightly by saying that he didn't think the group would fail to understand Zapf's rather different position and that Zapf certainly should be invited. Newbridge immediately said he agreed: Zapf should present the work because much of it was work he had done, and this would be a nice way to recognize Zapf's contributions and to reward him, because he was eager to be recognized as a productive member of the lab. Goh agreed, and so the matter was decided.

Zapf's presentation was very successful and in some ways dominated the meeting. He attracted the interest and attention of many of those who had come, and a long discussion followed his presentation. Later in the evening, during the cocktail period before dinner, with the entire laboratory staff present, a little circle of people formed about Zapf. One of them was Goh himself, and a lively discussion took place regarding the application of Zapf's theory. All of this disturbed Newbridge, but his reaction and behavior were characteristic. He joined the circle, praised Zapf to Goh and to others, and remarked on the brilliance of the work.

Newbridge, without consulting anyone, began at this time to take some interest in the possibility of a job elsewhere. After a few weeks, he found that a new laboratory of considerable size was being organized in a nearby city and that the kind of training he had would enable him to get a project-head job, equivalent to the one he had at the lab with slightly more money.

He immediately accepted it and notified Goh by letter, which he mailed on a Friday night to Goh's home. The letter was quite brief, and Goh was stunned. The letter merely said that he had found a better position, that he didn't want to appear at the lab anymore for personal reasons, that he would be glad to come back at a later time to assist if there was any mix-up in the past work, that he felt sure Zapf could supply any leadership that the group required, and that his decision to leave so suddenly was based on personal problems—he hinted at problems of health in his family, his mother and father. All of this was fictitious, of course. Goh took it at face value but still felt that this was very strange behavior and quite unaccountable, for he had always felt his relationship with Newbridge had been warm and that Newbridge was satisfied and, in fact, quite happy and productive.

Goh was considerably disturbed, because he had already decided to place Zapf in charge of another project that was going to be set up very soon. He had been wondering how to explain this to Newbridge, in view of the obvious help Newbridge was getting from Zapf and the high regard in which Newbridge held him. Goh had even considered the possibility that Newbridge would want to add another person to his staff with the same kind of background and training that Zapf had, which had proved so valuable.

Goh did not make any attempt to meet Newbridge. In a way, he felt aggrieved about the whole thing. Zapf, too, was surprised at the suddenness of Newbridge's departure. When Goh asked Zapf whether he preferred to stay with the photon group instead of the new project for the Air Force, he chose the Air Force project and went on to that job the following week. The photon lab was hard hit. The leadership of the lab was given to Link, with the understanding that it would be temporary until someone could come in to take over.

CASE 10: TAMARACK INDUSTRIES

By David J. Cherrington, Brigham Young University

Tamarack Industries manufactures motorboats primarily used for water skiing. Students are hired during summer months to fill in for permanent employees on vacation. In past years, students worked alongside permanent employees, but a few staff complained that the students were inexperienced, slow, and arrogant. In general, permanent staff disliked the students' behavior, such as listening to music with earphones while working. This summer, the company reorganized all permanent employees into three production teams (they usually have four teams, but 25 percent are on holiday at any given time) and assigned the 16 summer students to their own team on the fourth production line.

The supervisor, Dan Jensen, decided to try a different strategy this summer and have all the college students work on the new line. He asked Mark Allen to supervise the new crew because Mark claimed that he knew everything about boats and could perform every job "with my eyes closed." Mark was happy to accept the new job and participated in selecting the student hires. Mark's crew was called "the Geek Team," because all the college students were savvy with computers, unlike most of the permanent employees.

Mark spent many hours training his student team to get the line running at full production. The college students learned quickly, and by the end of June their production rate was up to standard, with an error rate that was only slightly above normal. To simplify the learning process, Dan Jensen assigned the Geek Team long production runs that generally consisted of 30 to 40 identical units. Thus the training period was shortened and errors were reduced. Shorter production runs were assigned to the experienced teams.

By the middle of July, a substantial rivalry had been created between the Geek Team and the older workers. At first, the rivalry was good-natured. But after a few weeks, the older workers became resentful of the remarks made by the college students. The Geek Team often met its production schedules with time to spare at the end of the day for goofing around. It wasn't uncommon for someone from the Geek Team to go to another line pretending to look for materials, just to make demeaning comments. The experienced workers resented having to perform all the shorter production runs and began to retaliate with sabotage. They would sneak over during breaks and hide tools, dent materials, install something crooked, and in other small ways do something that would slow production for the Geek Team.

Dan felt good about his decision to form a separate crew of college students, but when he heard reports of sabotage and rivalry, he became very concerned. Because of complaints from the experienced workers, Dan equalized the production so that all of the crews had similar production runs. The rivalry, however, did not stop. The Geek Team continued to finish early and flaunt their performance in front of the other crews.

One day the Geek Team suspected that one of their assemblies was going to be sabotaged during the lunch break by one of the experienced crews. By skillful deception, they were able to substitute an assembly from the other experienced line for theirs. By the end of the lunch period, the Geek Team was laughing wildly because of their deception, while one experienced crew was very angry with the other one.

Dan Jensen decided that the situation had to be changed and announced that the job assignments between the different crews would be shuffled. The employees were told that when they appeared for work the next morning, the names of the workers assigned to each crew would be posted on the bulletin board. The announcement was not greeted with much enthusiasm, and Mark Allen decided to talk Dan out of his idea. Mark suspected that many of the college students would quit if their team was broken up.

CASE 11: TREETOP FOREST PRODUCTS

By Steven L. McShane, University of Western Australia, and David Lebeter

Treetop Forest Products Ltd. is a sawmill operation in Oregon, owned by a major forest products company, though it operates independently of headquarters. It was built 30 years ago and completely updated with new machinery 5 years ago. Treetop receives raw logs from the area for cutting and planing into building-grade lumber, mostly 2-by-4 and 2-by-6 pieces of standard lengths. Higher-grade logs leave Treetop's sawmill department in finished form and are sent directly to the packaging department. The remaining 40 percent of sawmill output is cuts from lower-grade logs, requiring further work by the planing department.

Treetop has 1 general manager, 16 supervisors and support staff, and 180 unionized employees. The unionized employees are paid an hourly rate specified in the collective agreement, whereas management and support staff are paid a monthly salary. The mill is divided into six operating departments: boom, sawmill, planer, packaging, shipping, and maintenance. The sawmill, boom, and packaging departments operate a morning shift starting at 6:00 a.m. and an afternoon shift starting at 2:00 p.m. Employees in these departments rotate shifts every two weeks. The planer and shipping departments operate only morning shifts. Maintenance employees work the night shift (starting at 10:00 p.m.).

Each department, except for packaging, has a supervisor on every work shift. The planer supervisor is responsible for the packaging department on the morning shift, and the sawmill supervisor is responsible for the packaging department on the afternoon shift. However, the packaging operation is housed in a separate building from the other departments, so supervisors seldom visit the packaging department—particularly in the afternoon shift, because the sawmill supervisor is the farthest distance from the packaging building.

PACKAGING QUALITY

Ninety percent of Treetop's product is sold on the international market through Westboard Co., a large marketing agency. Westboard represents all forest products mills owned by Treetop's parent company, as well as several other clients in the region. The market for building-grade lumber is very price competitive, because there are numerous mills selling a relatively undifferentiated product. However, some differentiation does occur in product packaging and presentation. Buyers will look closely at the packaging when deciding whether to buy from Treetop or another mill.

To encourage its clients to package their products better, Westboard sponsors a monthly package quality award. The marketing agency samples and rates its clients' packages daily, and the sawmill with the highest score at the end of the month is awarded a plaque. Package quality is a combination of how the lumber is piled (e.g., defects turned in), where the bands and dunnage are placed, how neatly the stencil and seal are applied, the stencil's accuracy, and how neatly and tightly the plastic wrap is attached.

Treetop Forest Products won Westboard's packaging quality award several times over the past five years and received high ratings even in the months that it didn't win. However, the mill's ratings have started to decline over the past year or two, and several clients have complained about the appearance of the finished product. A few large customers switched to competitors' lumber, saying that the decision was based on the substandard appearance of Treetop's packaging when it arrived in their lumber yard.

BOTTLENECK IN PACKAGING

The planing and sawmilling departments have significantly increased productivity over the past couple of years. The sawmill operation recently set a new productivity record on a single day. The planer operation has increased productivity to the point where last year it reduced operations to just one (rather than two) shifts per day. These productivity improvements are due to better operator training, fewer machine breakdowns, and better selection of raw logs. (Sawmill cuts from high-quality logs usually do not require planing work.)

Productivity levels in the boom, shipping, and maintenance departments have remained constant. However, the packaging department has recorded decreasing productivity over the past couple of years, with the result that a large backlog of finished product is typically stockpiled outside the packaging building. The morning shift of the packaging department is unable to keep up with the combined production of the sawmill and planer departments, so the unpackaged output is left for the afternoon shift. Unfortunately, the afternoon shift packages even less product than the morning shift, so the backlog continues to build. The backlog adds to Treetop's inventory costs and increases the risk of damaged stock.

Treetop has added Saturday overtime shifts as well as extra hours before and after the regular shifts for the packaging department employees to process this backlog. Last month, the packaging department employed 10 percent of the work force but accounted for 85 percent of the overtime. This is frustrating to Treetop's management, because time and motion studies recently confirmed that the packaging department is capable of processing all of the daily sawmill and planer production without overtime. Moreover, with employees earning one and a half or two times their regular pay on overtime, Treetop's cost competitiveness suffers.

Employees and supervisors at Treetop are aware that people in the packaging department tend to extend lunch by 10 minutes and coffee breaks by 5 minutes. They also typically leave work a few minutes before the end of the shift. This abuse has worsened recently, particularly on the afternoon shift. Employees who are temporarily assigned to the packaging department also seem to participate in this time loss pattern after a few days. Although they are punctual and productive in other departments, these temporary employees soon adopt the packaging crew's informal schedule when assigned to that department.

CASE 12: VÊTEMENTS LTÉE

By Steven L. McShane, University of Western Australia

Vêtements Ltée is a chain of men's retail clothing stores located throughout the province of Quebec, Canada. Two years ago, the company introduced new incentive systems for both store managers and sales employees. Each store managers receives a salary with annual merit increases based on sales above targeted goals, store appearance, store inventory management, customer complaints, and several other performance measures. Some of this information (e.g., store appearance) is gathered during visits by senior management, while other information is based on company records (e.g., sales volume).

Sales employees are paid a fixed salary plus a commission based on the percentage of sales credited to that employee over the pay period. The commission represents about 30 percent of a typical paycheck and is intended to encourage employees to actively serve customers and increase sales volume. Because returned merchandise is discounted from commissions, sales employees are discouraged from selling products that customers do not really want.

Soon after the new incentive systems were introduced, senior management began to receive complaints from store managers regarding the performance of their sales staff. They observed that sales employees tended to stand near the store entrance waiting to "tag" customers as their own. Occasionally, sales staff would argue over "ownership" of the customer. Managers were concerned that this aggressive behavior intimidated some customers. It also tended to leave some parts of the store unattended by staff.

Many managers were also concerned about inventory duties. Previously, sales staff would share responsibility for restocking inventory and completing inventory reorder forms. Under the new compensation system, however, few employees were willing to do these essential tasks. On several occasions, stores have faced stock shortages because merchandise was not stocked or reorder forms were not completed in a timely manner. Potential sales have suffered from empty shelves when plenty of merchandise was available in the back storeroom or at the warehouse. The company's new automatic inventory system could reduce some of these problems, but employees must still stock shelves and assist in other aspects of inventory management.

Store managers have tried to correct the inventory problem by assigning employees to inventory duty, but this has created resentment among the employees selected. Other managers have threatened sales staff with dismissals if they do not do their share of inventory management. This strategy has been somewhat effective when the manager is in the store, but staff members sneak back onto the floor when the manager is away. It also has hurt staff morale, particularly relations with the store manager.

To reduce the tendency of sales staff to hoard customers at the store entrance, some managers have assigned employees to specific areas of the store, creating resentment among employees stationed in areas with less traffic or lower-priced merchandise. Some staff have openly complained of lower paychecks because they have been placed in a slow area of the store or have been given more than their share of inventory duties.

Theory Building and Systematic Research Methods

THEORY BUILDING

People need to make sense of their world, so they form theories about the way the world operates. A **theory** is a general set of propositions that describes interrelationships among several concepts. We form theories for the purpose of predicting and explaining the world around us.[1] What does a good theory look like? First, it should be stated as clearly and simply as possible so that the concepts can be measured and there is no ambiguity regarding the theory's propositions. Second, the elements of the theory must be logically consistent with each other, because we cannot test anything that doesn't make sense. Third, a good theory provides value to society; it helps people understand their world better than they would without the theory.[2]

Theory building is a continuous process that typically includes the inductive and deductive stages shown in Exhibit A.1.[3] The inductive stage draws on personal experience to form a preliminary theory, whereas the deductive stage uses the scientific method to test the theory.

The inductive stage of theory building involves observing the world around us, identifying a pattern of relationships, and then forming a theory from these personal observations. For example, you might casually notice that new employees want their supervisor to give direction, whereas this leadership style irritates long-service employees. From these observations, you form a theory about the

effectiveness of directive leadership. (See Chapter 12 for a discussion of this leadership style.)

POSITIVISM VERSUS INTERPRETIVISM

Research requires an interpretation of reality, and researchers tend to perceive reality in one of two ways. A common view, called **positivism,** is that reality exists independent of people. It is "out there" to be discovered and tested. Positivism is the foundation for most quantitative research (statistical analysis). It assumes that we can measure variables and those variables have fixed relationships with other variables. For example, the positivist perspective says that we could study whether a supportive style of leadership reduces stress. If we find evidence that it does, then someone else studying leadership and stress would "discover" the same relationship.

Interpretivism takes a different view of reality. It suggests that reality comes from shared meaning among people in a particular environment. For example, supportive leadership is a personal interpretation of reality, not something that can be measured across time and people. Interpretivists rely mainly on qualitative data, such as observation and nondirective interviews. They particularly listen to the language people use to understand the common meaning that people assign to various events or phenomena. For example, they might argue that you need to experience and

---

EXHIBIT A.1   Theory Building and Theory Testing

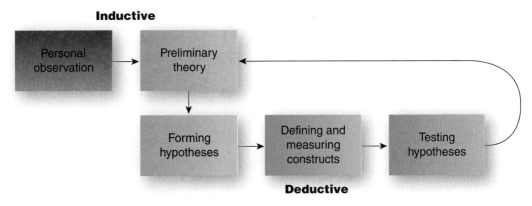

477

observe supportive leadership to effectively study it. Moreover, you can't really predict relationships because the specific situation shapes reality.[4]

Most OB scholars identify themselves somewhere between the extreme views of positivism and interpretivism. Many believe that inductive research should begin with an interpretivist angle. We should consider a new topic with an open mind and search for shared meaning among people in the situation being studied. In other words, researchers should let the participants define reality rather than let the researcher's preconceived notions shape that reality. This process involves gathering qualitative information and letting this information shape their theory.[5] After the theory emerges, researchers shift to the positivist perspective by quantitatively testing relationships in that theory.

THEORY TESTING: THE DEDUCTIVE PROCESS

Once a theory has been formed, we shift into the deductive stage of theory building. This process includes forming hypotheses, defining and measuring constructs, and testing hypotheses (see Exhibit A.1). **Hypotheses** make empirically testable declarations that certain variables and their corresponding measures are related in a specific way proposed by the theory. For instance, to find support for directive leadership theory, we need to form and then test a specific hypothesis from that theory. One such hypothesis might be: "New employees are more satisfied with supervisors who exhibit a directive rather than nondirective leadership style." Hypotheses are indispensable tools of scientific research, because they provide the vital link between the theory and empirical verification.

Defining and Measuring Constructs   Hypotheses are testable only if we can define and then form measurable indicators of the concepts stated in those hypotheses. Consider the hypothesis in the previous paragraph about new employees and directive leadership. To test this hypothesis, we first need to define the concepts, such as "new employees," "directive leadership," and "supervisor." These are known as **constructs,** because they are abstract ideas constructed by the researcher that can be linked to observable information. Organizational behavior researchers developed the construct called *directive leadership* to help them understand the different effects that leaders have on followers. We can't directly see, taste, or smell directive leadership; instead, we rely on indirect indicators of its existence, such as observing someone giving directions, maintaining clear performance standards, and ensuring that procedures and practices are followed.

As you can see, defining constructs well is very important, because these definitions become the foundation for finding or developing acceptable measures of those constructs. We can't measure directive leadership if we have only a vague idea about what this concept means. The better the construct is defined, the better our chances of finding or developing a good measure of that construct. However, even with a good definition, constructs can be difficult to measure, because the empirical representation must capture several elements in the definition. A measure of directive leadership must be able to identify not only people who give directions but also those who maintain performance standards and ensure that procedures are followed.

Testing Hypotheses   The third step in the deductive process is to collect data for the empirical measures of the variables. Following our directive leadership example, we might conduct a formal survey in which new employees indicate the behavior of their supervisors and their attitudes toward their supervisors. Alternatively, we might design an experiment in which people work with someone who applies either a directive or a nondirective leadership style. When the data have been collected, we can use various procedures to statistically test our hypotheses.

A major concern in theory building is that some researchers might inadvertently find support for their theory simply because they use the same information used to form the theory during the inductive stage. Consequently, the deductive stage must collect new data that are completely independent of the data used during the inductive stage. For instance, you might decide to test your theory of directive leadership by studying employees in another organization. Moreover, the inductive process may have relied mainly on personal observation, whereas the deductive process might use survey questionnaires. By studying different samples and using different measurement tools, we minimize the risk of conducting circular research.

USING THE SCIENTIFIC METHOD

Earlier, we said that the deductive stage of theory building follows the scientific method. The **scientific method** is a systematic, controlled, empirical, and critical investigation of hypothetical propositions about the presumed relationships among natural phenomena.[6] There are several elements to this definition, so let's look at each one. First, scientific research is *systematic and controlled*, because researchers want to rule out all but one explanation for a set of interrelated events. To rule out alternative explanations, we need to control them in some way, such as by keeping them constant or removing them entirely from the environment.

Second, we say that scientific research is *empirical* because researchers need to use objective reality—or as close as we can get to it—to test a theory. They measure observable elements of the environment, such as what a person says or does, rather than relying on their own subjective opinion to draw conclusions. Moreover, scientific research analyzes these data using acceptable principles of mathematics and logic.

Third, scientific research involves *critical investigation*. This means that the study's hypotheses, data, methods, and results are openly described so that other experts in the field can properly evaluate the research. It also means that scholars are encouraged to critique and build on previous research. The scientific method encourages the refinement and eventually the replacement of a particular theory with one that better suits our understanding of the world.

GROUNDED THEORY: AN ALTERNATIVE APPROACH

The scientific method dominates the quantitative approach to systematic research, but another approach, called **grounded theory,** dominates research using qualitative methods.[7] Grounded theory is a process of developing knowledge through the constant interplay of data collection, analysis, and theory development. It relies mainly on qualitative methods to form categories and variables, analyze relationships among these concepts, and form a model based on the observations and analysis. Grounded theory combines the inductive stages of theory development by cycling back and forth between data collection and analysis to converge on a robust explanatory model. This ongoing reciprocal process results in theory that is grounded in the data (hence the name grounded theory).

Like the scientific method, grounded theory is a systematic and rigorous process of data collection and analysis. It requires specific steps and documentation and adopts a positivist view by assuming that the results are generalizable to other settings. However, grounded theory also takes an interpretivist view by building categories and variables from the perceived realities of the subjects rather than from an assumed universal truth.[8] It also recognizes that personal biases are not easily removed from the research process.

SELECTED ISSUES IN ORGANIZATIONAL BEHAVIOR RESEARCH

There are many issues to consider in theory building, particularly when we use the deductive process to test hypotheses. Some of the more important issues are sampling, causation, and ethical practices in organizational research.

SAMPLING IN ORGANIZATIONAL RESEARCH

To find out why things happen in organizations, we typically gather information from a few sources and then draw conclusions about the larger population. If we survey several employees and determine that older employees are more loyal to their company, then we would like to generalize this statement to all older employees in our population, not just those whom we surveyed. Scientific inquiry generally requires that researchers engage in **representative**

sampling—that is, sampling a population in such a way that we can extrapolate the results of the sample to the larger population.

One factor that influences representativeness is whether the sample is selected in an unbiased way from the larger population. Let's suppose that you want to study organizational commitment among employees in your organization. A casual procedure might result in sampling too few employees from the head office and too many located elsewhere in the country. If head office employees actually have higher loyalty than employees located elsewhere, the biased sampling would cause the results to underestimate the true level of loyalty among employees in the company. If you repeat the process again next year but somehow overweight employees from the head office, the results might wrongly suggest that employees have increased their organizational commitment over the past year. In reality, the only change may be the direction of sampling bias.

How do we minimize sampling bias? The answer is to randomly select the sample. A randomly drawn sample gives each member of the population an equal probability of being chosen, so there is less likelihood that a subgroup within that population will dominate the study's results.

The same principle applies to the random assignment of participants to groups in experimental designs. If we want to test the effects of a team development training program, we need to randomly place some employees in the training group and randomly place others in a group that does not receive training. Without this random selection, each group might have different types of employees, so we wouldn't know whether the training explains the differences between the two groups. Moreover, if employees respond differently to the training program, we couldn't be sure that the training program results are representative of the larger population. Of course, random sampling does not necessarily produce a perfectly representative sample, but we do know that it is the best approach to ensure unbiased selection.

The other factor that influences representativeness is sample size. Whenever we select a portion of the population, there will be some error in our estimate of the population values. The larger the sample, the less error will occur in our estimate. Let's suppose that you want to find out how employees in a 500-person firm feel about smoking in the workplace. If you asked 400 of those employees, the information would provide a very good estimate of how the entire workforce in that organization feels. If you survey only 100 employees, the estimate might deviate more from the true population. If you ask only 10 people, the estimate could be quite different from what all 500 employees feel.

Notice that sample size goes hand in hand with random selection. You must have a sufficiently large sample size for the principle of randomization to work effectively. In our example of attitudes toward smoking, we would do a poor job of random selection if our sample consisted of only 10 employees from the 500-person organization. The reason is that these 10 people probably wouldn't capture the diversity of employees throughout the organization. In fact, the more diverse the population, the larger the sample size should be, to provide adequate representation through random selection.

CAUSATION IN ORGANIZATIONAL RESEARCH

Theories present notions about relationships among constructs. Often, these propositions suggest a causal relationship, namely, that one variable has an effect on another variable. When discussing causation, we refer to variables as being independent or dependent. *Independent variables* are the presumed causes of *dependent variables*, which are the presumed effects. In our earlier example of directive leadership, the main independent variable (there might be others) would be the supervisor's directive or nondirective leadership style, because we presume that it causes the dependent variable (satisfaction with supervision).

In laboratory experiments (described later), the independent variable is always manipulated by the experimenter. In our research on directive leadership, we might have subjects (new employees) work with supervisors who exhibit directive or nondirective leadership behaviors. If subjects are more satisfied under the directive leaders, we would be able to infer an association between the independent and dependent variables.

Researchers must satisfy three conditions to provide sufficient evidence of causality between two variables.[9] The first condition of causality is that the variables are empirically associated with each other. An association exists whenever one measure of a variable changes systematically with a measure of another variable. This condition of causality is the easiest to satisfy, because there are several well-known statistical measures of association. A research study might find, for instance, that heterogeneous groups (in which members come from diverse backgrounds) produce more creative solutions to problems. This might be apparent because the measure of creativity (such as number of creative solutions produced within a fixed time) is higher for teams that have a high score on the measure of group heterogeneity. They are statistically associated or correlated.

The second condition of causality is that the independent variable precedes the dependent variable in time. Sometimes, this condition is satisfied through simple logic. In our group heterogeneity example, it doesn't make sense to say that the number of creative solutions caused the group's heterogeneity, because the group's heterogeneity existed before the group produced the creative solutions. In other situations, however, the temporal relationship among variables is less clear. One example is the ongoing debate about job satisfaction and organizational commitment. Do companies develop more loyal employees by increasing their job satisfaction, or do changes in organizational loyalty cause changes in job satisfaction? Simple logic does not answer these questions; instead, researchers must use sophisticated longitudinal studies to build up evidence of a temporal relationship between the two variables.

The third requirement for evidence of a causal relationship is that the statistical association between two variables cannot be explained by a third variable. There are many associations that we quickly dismiss as causally related. For example, there is a statistical association between the number of storks in an area and the birth rate in that area. We know that storks don't bring babies, so something else must cause the association between these two variables. The real explanation is that both storks and birth rates have a higher incidence in rural areas.

In other studies, the third variable effect is less apparent. Many years ago, before polio vaccines were available, a study in the United States reported a surprisingly strong association between consumption of a certain soft drink and the incidence of polio. Was polio caused by drinking this pop, or did people with polio have a unusual craving for this beverage? Neither. Both polio and consumption of the pop drink were caused by a third variable: climate. There was a higher incidence of polio in the summer months and in warmer climates, and people drink more liquids in these climates.[10] As you can see from this example, researchers have a difficult time supporting causal inferences, because third-variable effects are sometimes difficult to detect.

ETHICS IN ORGANIZATIONAL RESEARCH

Organizational behavior researchers need to abide by the ethical standards of the society in which the research is conducted. One of the most important ethical considerations is the individual respondent's freedom to participate in the study. For example, it is inappropriate to force employees to fill out a questionnaire or attend an experimental intervention for research purposes only. Moreover, researchers have an obligation to tell potential subjects about any possible risks inherent in the study so that participants can make an informed choice about whether to be involved.

Finally, researchers must be careful to protect the privacy of those who participate in the study. This usually includes letting people know when they are being studied as well as guaranteeing that their individual information will remain confidential (unless publication of identities is otherwise granted). Researchers maintain anonymity through careful security of data. The research results usually aggregate data in numbers large enough that they do not reveal the opinions or characteristics of any specific individual. For example, we would report the average absenteeism of employees in a department rather than state the absence rates of each person. When researchers are sharing data with other researchers, it is usually necessary to code each case so that individual identities are not known.

RESEARCH DESIGN STRATEGIES

So far, we have described how to build a theory, including the specific elements of empirically testing the theory within the standards of scientific inquiry. But what are the different ways to design a research study so that we get the data necessary to achieve our research objectives? There are many strategies, but they mainly fall under three headings: laboratory experiments, field surveys, and observational research.

LABORATORY EXPERIMENTS

A **laboratory experiment** is any research study in which independent variables and variables outside the researcher's main focus of inquiry can be controlled to some extent. Laboratory experiments are usually located outside the everyday work environment, such as in a classroom, simulation lab, or any other artificial setting in which the researcher can manipulate the environment. Organizational behavior researchers sometimes conduct experiments in the workplace (called *field experiments*) in which the independent variable is manipulated. However, researchers have less control over the effects of extraneous factors in field experiments than they have in laboratory situations.

Advantages of Laboratory Experiments   There are many advantages of laboratory experiments. By definition, this research method offers a high degree of control over extraneous variables that would otherwise confound the relationships being studied. Suppose we wanted to test the effects of directive leadership on the satisfaction of new employees. One concern might be that employees are influenced by how much leadership is provided, not just the type of leadership style. An experimental design would allow us to control how often the supervisor exhibited this style so that this extraneous variable does not confound the results.

A second advantage of lab studies is that the independent and dependent variables can be developed more precisely than is possible in a field setting. For example, the researcher can ensure that supervisors in a lab study apply specific directive or nondirective behaviors, whereas real-life supervisors would use a more complex mixture of leadership behaviors. By using more precise measures, we are more certain that we are measuring the intended construct. Thus, if new employees are more satisfied with supervisors in the directive leadership condition, we are more confident that the independent variable was directive leadership rather than some other leadership style.

A third benefit of laboratory experiments is that the independent variable can be distributed more evenly among participants. In our directive leadership study, we can en-

sure that approximately half of the subjects have a directive supervisor, whereas the other half have a nondirective supervisor. In natural settings, we might have trouble finding people who have worked with a nondirective leader and, consequently, we couldn't determine the effects of this condition.

Disadvantages of Laboratory Experiments   With these powerful advantages, you might wonder why laboratory experiments are the least appreciated form of organizational behavior research.[11] One obvious limitation of this research method is that it lacks realism, and thus the results might be different in the real world. One argument is that laboratory experiment subjects are less involved than their counterparts in an actual work situation. This is sometimes true, though many lab studies have highly motivated participants. Another criticism is that the extraneous variables controlled in the lab setting might produce a different effect of the independent variable on the dependent variables. This might also be true, but remember that the experimental design controls variables in accordance with the theory and its hypotheses. Consequently, this concern is really a critique of the theory, not the lab study.

Finally, there is the well-known problem that participants are aware they are being studied, which causes them to act differently than they normally would. Some participants try to figure out how the researcher wants them to behave and then deliberately try to act that way. Other participants try to upset the experiment by doing just the opposite of what they believe the researcher expects. Still others might act unnaturally simply because they know they are being observed. Fortunately, experimenters are well aware of these potential problems and are usually (though not always) successful at disguising the study's true intent.

FIELD SURVEYS

Field surveys collect and analyze information in a natural environment—an office, a factory, or some other existing location. The researcher takes a snapshot of reality and tries to determine whether elements of that situation (including the attitudes and behaviors of people in that situation) are associated as hypothesized. Everyone does some sort of field research. You might think that people from some states are better drivers than others, so you "test" your theory by looking at the way people with out-of-state license plates drive. Although your methods of data collection might not satisfy scientific standards, this is a form of field research because it takes information from a naturally occurring situation.

One advantage of field surveys is that the variables often have a more powerful effect than they would in a laboratory experiment. Consider the effect of peer pressure on the behavior of members within the team. In a natural environment, team members would form very strong cohesive bonds over time, whereas a researcher would have difficulty replicating this level of cohesiveness and corresponding peer pressure in a lab setting.

Another advantage of field surveys is that the researcher can study many variables simultaneously, thereby permitting a fuller test of more complex theories. Ironically, this is also a disadvantage of field surveys, because it is difficult for the researcher to contain his or her scientific inquiry. There is a tendency to shift from deductive hypothesis testing to more inductive exploratory browsing through the data. If these two activities become mixed together, the researcher can lose sight of the strict covenants of scientific inquiry.

The main weakness with field surveys is that it is very difficult to satisfy the conditions for causal conclusions. One reason is that the data are usually collected at one point in time, so the researcher must rely on logic to decide whether the independent variable really preceded the dependent variable. Contrast this with the lab study in which the researcher can usually be confident that the independent variable was applied before the dependent variable occurred. Increasingly, organizational behavior studies use longitudinal research to provide a better indicator of temporal relations among variables, but it is still not as precise as the lab setting. Another reason causal analysis is difficult in field surveys is that extraneous variables are not controlled as they are in lab studies. Without this control, there is a higher chance that a third variable might explain the relationship between the hypothesized independent and dependent variables.

OBSERVATIONAL RESEARCH

In their study of brainstorming and creativity, Robert Sutton and Andrew Hargadon observed 24 brainstorming sessions at IDEO, a product design firm in Palo Alto, California. They also attended a dozen "Monday morning meetings," conducted 60 semi-structured interviews with IDEO executives and designers, held hundreds of informal discussions with these people, and read through several dozen magazine articles about the company.[12]

Sutton and Hargadon's use of observational research and other qualitative methods was quite appropriate for their research objective, which was to reexamine the effectiveness of brainstorming beyond the number of ideas generated. Observational research generates a wealth of descriptive accounts about the drama of human existence in organizations. It is a useful vehicle for learning about the complex dynamics of people and their activities, such as brainstorming. (Sutton and Hargadon's study is cited in the chapter on team decision making.)

Participant observation takes the observation method one step further by having the observer take part in the organization's activities. This experience gives the researcher a fuller understanding of the activities compared with just watching others participate in those activities.

Despite its intuitive appeal, observational research has a number of weaknesses. The main problem is that the observer is subject to the perceptual screening and organizing biases that we discuss in Chapter 3 of this textbook. There is a tendency to overlook the routine aspects of organizational life, even though they may prove to be the most important data for research purposes. Instead, observers tend to focus on unusual information, such as activities that deviate from what the observer expects. Because observational research usually records only what the observer notices, valuable information is often lost.

Another concern with the observation method is that the researcher's presence and involvement may influence the people whom he or she is studying. This can be a problem in short-term observations, but in the long term people tend to return to their usual behavior patterns. With ongoing observations, such as Sutton and Hargadon's study of brainstorming sessions at IDEO, employees eventually forget that they are being studied.

Finally, observation is usually a qualitative process, so it is more difficult to empirically test hypotheses with the data. Instead, observational research provides rich information for the inductive stages of theory building. It helps us form ideas about the way things work in organizations. We begin to see relationships that lay the foundation for new perspectives and theory. We must not confuse this inductive process of theory building with the deductive process of theory testing.

{ key terms }

constructs, p. 478	interpretivism, p. 477	representative sampling, p. 479
field surveys, p. 481	laboratory experiment, p. 481	scientific method, p. 478
grounded theory, p. 479	positivism, p. 477	theory, p. 477
hypotheses, p. 478		

(endnotes)

1. F.N. Kerlinger, *Foundations of Behavioral Research* (New York: Holt, Rinehart, & Winston, 1964), p. 11.

2. J.B. Miner, *Theories of Organizational Behavior* (Hinsdale, IL: Dryden, 1980), pp. 7–9.

3. Ibid., pp. 6–7.

4. J. Mason, *Qualitative Researching* (London: Sage, 1996).

5. A. Strauss and J. Corbin (eds.), *Grounded Theory in Practice* (London: Sage Publications, 1997); B.G. Glaser and A. Strauss, *The Discovery of Grounded Theory: Strategies for Qualitative Research* (Chicago, IL: Aldine Publishing Co, 1967).

6. Kerlinger, *Foundations of Behavioral Research*, p. 13.

7. Strauss and Corbin, *Grounded Theory in Practice*; Glaser and Strauss, *The Discovery of Grounded Theory*.

8. W.A. Hall and P. Callery, "Enhancing the Rigor of Grounded Theory: Incorporating Reflexivity and Relationality," *Qualitative Health Research*, 11 (March 2001), pp. 257–72.

9. P. Lazarsfeld, *Survey Design and Analysis* (New York: The Free Press, 1955).

10. This example is cited by D.W. Organ and T.S. Bateman, *Organizational Behavior*, 4th ed. (Homewood, IL: Irwin, 1991), p. 42.

11. Ibid., p. 45.

12. R.I. Sutton and A. Hargadon, "Brainstorming Groups in Context: Effectiveness in a Product Design Firm," *Administrative Science Quarterly*, 41 (1996), pp. 685–718.

appendix B

Scoring Keys for Self-Assessment Activities

The following pages provide the scoring keys for the self-assessments that are presented in each chapter of this textbook. These self-assessments, as well as the self-assessments summarized in this book, can be scored automatically in the Connect Library.

CHAPTER 2: SCORING KEY FOR THE EXTRAVERSION–INTROVERSION SCALE

Scoring Instructions: Use the table below to assign numbers to each box you checked. For example, if you checked "Moderately Inaccurate" for statement #1 ("I feel comfortable around people"), you would assign a "1" to that statement. After assigning numbers for all 10 statements, add up the numbers to estimate your extraversion–introversion personality.

FOR STATEMENT ITEMS 1, 2, 6, 8, 9:	FOR STATEMENT ITEMS 3, 4, 5, 7, 10:
Very accurate description of me = 4	Very accurate description of me = 0
Moderately accurate = 3	Moderately accurate = 1
Neither accurate nor inaccurate = 2	Neither accurate nor inaccurate = 2
Moderately inaccurate = 1	Moderately inaccurate = 3
Very inaccurate description of me = 0	Very inaccurate description of me = 4

Interpreting Your Score: Extraversion characterizes people who are outgoing, talkative, sociable, and assertive. It includes several facets, such as friendliness, gregariousness, assertiveness, activity level, excitement-seeking, and cheerfulness. The opposite of extraversion is introversion, which refers to the personality characteristics of being quiet, shy, and cautious. Extraverts get their energy from the outer world (people and things around them), whereas introverts get their energy from the internal world, such as personal reflection on concepts and ideas. Introverts are more inclined to direct their interests to ideas rather than to social events.

This is the short version of the IPIP Introversion-Extraversion Scale, so it estimates overall introversion-extraversion but not specific facets within the personality dimension. Scores range from 0 to 40. Low scores indicate

introversion; high scores indicate extraversion. The norms in the following table are estimated from results of early adults (under 30 years old) in Scotland and undergraduate psychology students in the United States. However, introversion–extraversion norms vary from one group to the next; the best norms are likely based on the entire class you are attending or on past students in this course.

IPIP Extraversion–Introversion Norms

IPIP EXTRAVERSION–INTROVERSION	INTERPRETATION
35–40	High extraversion
28–34	Moderate extraversion
21–27	In-between extraversion and introversion
7–20	Moderate introversion
0–6	High introversion

CHAPTER 3: SCORING KEY FOR THE WORK CENTRALITY SCALE

Scoring Instructions: Use the table below to assign numbers to each box you checked. For example, if you checked "Moderately Disagree" for statement #3 ("Work should be only a small part of one's life"), you would assign a "5" to that statement. After assigning numbers for all 6 statements, add up your scores to estimate your level of work centrality.

FOR STATEMENT ITEMS 1, 2, 4, 5, 6:	FOR STATEMENT ITEM 3:
Strongly Agree = 6	Strongly Agree = 1
Moderately Agree = 5	Moderately Agree = 2
Slightly Agree = 4	Slightly Agree = 3
Slightly Disagree = 3	Slightly Disagree = 4
Moderately Disagree = 2	Moderately Disagree = 5
Strongly Disagree = 1	Strongly Disagree = 6

Interpreting Your Score: The work centrality scale measures the extent that work is an important part of the individual's self-concept. People with high work centrality define themselves mainly by their work roles and view nonwork roles as much less significant. Consequently, people with a high work centrality score likely have lower complexity in their self-concept. This can be a concern because if something goes wrong with their work role, their nonwork roles are not of sufficient value to maintain a positive self-evaluation. At the same time, work dominates our work lives, so those with very low scores would be more of the exception than the rule in most societies.

Scores range from 6 to 36 with higher scores indicating higher work centrality. The norms in the following table are based on a large sample of Canadian employees (average score was 20.7). However, work centrality norms vary from one group to the next. For example, the average score in a sample of nurses was around 17 (translated to the scale range used here).

Work Centrality Norms

WORK CENTRALITY SCORE	INTERPRETATION
29–36	High work centrality
24–28	Above average work centrality
18–23	Average work centrality
13–17	Below average work centrality
6–12	Low work centrality

CHAPTER 4: SCORING KEY FOR THE EMOTIONAL INTELLIGENCE SELF-ASSESSMENT

Scoring Instructions: Use the table below to assign numbers to each box you checked. Insert the number for each statement on the appropriate line in the scoring key below the table. For example, if you checked "Moderately disagree" for statement #1 ("I tend to describe my emotions accurately"), you would write a "2" on the line with "(1)" underneath it. After assigning numbers for all 16 statements, add up your scores to estimate your self-assessed emotional intelligence on the four dimensions and overall score.

FOR STATEMENT ITEMS 1, 2, 3, 4, 6, 7, 9, 10, 11, 13, 14, 16:	FOR STATEMENT ITEMS 5, 8, 12, 15:
Strongly Agree = 6	Strongly Agree = 1
Moderately Agree = 5	Moderately Agree = 2
Slightly Agree = 4	Slightly Agree = 3
Slightly Disagree = 3	Slightly Disagree = 4
Moderately Disagree = 2	Moderately Disagree = 5
Strongly Disagree = 1	Strongly Disagree = 6

EMOTIONAL INTELLIGENCE DIMENSION	CALCULATION	YOUR SCORE
Self-awareness of emotions	____ + ____ + ____ + ____ = (1) (7) (9) (12)	_____
Self-management of emotions	____ + ____ + ____ + ____ = (2) (5) (10) (14)	_____
Awareness of others' emotions	____ + ____ + ____ + ____ = (3) (6) (13) (15)	_____
Management of others' emotions	____ + ____ + ____ + ____ = (4) (8) (11) (16)	_____
Emotional Intelligence Total	Add up all dimension scores =	_____

Interpreting Your Scores: This scale measures the four dimensions of emotional intelligence described in this book. The four dimensions are defined as follows:

- **Self-awareness of emotions.** The ability to perceive and understand the meaning of your own emotions.
- **Self-management of emotions.** The ability to manage your own emotions. It includes generating or suppressing emotions and displaying behaviors that represent desired emotions in a particular situation.
- **Awareness of others' emotions.** The ability to perceive and understand the emotions of other people, including the practices of empathy and awareness of social phenomena such as organizational politics.
- **Management of others' emotions.** The ability to manage other people's emotions. It includes generating or

suppressing emotions in other people, such as reducing their sadness and increasing their motivation.

Scores on the four emotional intelligence self-assessment dimensions range from 4 to 20. The overall score ranges from 16 to 80. Norms vary from one group to the next. The following table shows norms from a sample of 100 MBA students in two countries (Australia and Singapore). For example, the top 10th percentile for self-awareness is 19, indicating that 10 percent of people score 19 or 20, and 90 percent score below 19 on this dimension. Keep in mind that these scores represent self-perceptions. Evaluations from others (such as through 360-degree feedback) may provide a more accurate estimate of your emotional intelligence on some (not necessarily all) dimensions.

Emotional Intelligence Self-Assessment Norms

PERCENTILE	SELF-AWARENESS OF EMOTIONS	MANAGEMENT OF OWN EMOTIONS	AWARENESS OF OTHERS' EMOTIONS	MANAGEMENT OF OTHERS' EMOTIONS	TOTAL
Average Score	16.3	14.8	14.5	14.7	60.3
Top 10th percentile	19	18	17	18	70
Top 25th percentile	18	17	16	16	66
Median (50th percentile)	16	15	15	15	60
Bottom 25th percentile	15	13	13	13	56
Bottom 10th percentile	14	11	11	10	51

CHAPTER 5: SCORING KEY FOR THE PERSONAL NEEDS QUESTIONNAIRE

Scoring Instructions: Use the table at the right to assign numbers to each box you checked. Insert the number for each statement on the appropriate line in the scoring key below. For example, if you checked "Moderately inaccurate" for statement #1 ("I would rather be myself than be well thought of"), you would write a "3" on the line with "(1)" underneath it. After assigning numbers for all 15 statements, add up your scores to estimate your results for the two learned needs measured by this scale.

FOR STATEMENT ITEMS 2, 3, 4, 5, 6, 8, 9, 12, 14, 15:	FOR STATEMENT ITEMS 1, 7, 10, 11, 13:
Very accurate description of me = 4	Very accurate description of me = 0
Moderately accurate = 3	Moderately accurate = 1
Neither accurate nor inaccurate = 2	Neither accurate nor inaccurate = 2
Moderately inaccurate = 1	Moderately inaccurate = 3
Very inaccurate description of me = 0	Very inaccurate description of me = 4

PERSONAL NEEDS DIMENSION	CALCULATION	YOUR SCORE
Need for achievement:	___ + ___ + ___ + ___ + ___ + ___ + ___ = ___ (2) (3) (6) (7) (9) (12) (14)	___
Need for social approval:	___ + ___ + ___ + ___ + ___ + ___ + ___ + ___ = ___ (1) (4) (5) (8) (10) (11) (13) (15)	___

Although everyone has the same innate drives, our secondary or learned needs vary based on our personality, values, and self-concept. This self-assessment provides an estimate of your need strength on two learned needs: need for achievement and need for social approval.

Interpreting Your Need for Achievement Score: This scale, formally called "achievement striving," estimates the extent to which you are motivated to take on and achieve challenging personal goals. This includes a desire to perform better than others and to reach one's potential. The scale ranges from 0 to 28. How high or low is your need for achievement? The ideal would be to compare your score with the collective results of other students in your class. Otherwise, the table at the right offers a rough set of norms with which you can compare your score on this scale.

Need for Achievement Norms

NEED FOR ACHIEVEMENT SCORE	INTERPRETATION
24–28	High need for achievement
18–23	Above average need for achievement
12–17	Average need for achievement
6–11	Below average need for achievement
0–5	Low need for achievement

Interpreting Your Need for Social Approval Score: The need for social approval scale estimates the extent to which you are motivated to seek favorable evaluation from others. Founded on the drive to bond, the need for social approval is a secondary need, because people vary in this need based on their self-concept, values, personality, and possibly social norms. This scale ranges from 0 to 32. How high or low is your need for social approval? The ideal would be to compare your score with the collective results of other students in your class. Otherwise, the following table offers a rough set of norms on which you can compare your score on this scale.

Need for Social Approval Norms

NEED FOR SOCIAL APPROVAL SCORE	INTERPRETATION
28–32	High need for social approval
20–27	Above average need for social approval
12–19	Average need for social approval
6–11	Below average need for social approval
0–5	Low need for social approval

CHAPTER 6: SCORING KEY FOR THE MONEY ATTITUDE SCALE

Scoring Instructions: This instrument presents three dimensions with a smaller number of items from the original Money Attitude Scale. To calculate your score on each dimension, write the number that you circled in the scale over the corresponding item number in the scoring key at the top of the right column. For example, write the number you circled for the scale's first statement ("I sometimes purchase things . . .") on the line above "Item 1." Then add up the numbers for that dimension. The money attitude total score is calculated by adding up all scores on all dimensions.

MONEY ATTITUDE DIMENSION	CALCULATION				YOUR SCORE
Money as Power/ Prestige	—— + (1)	—— + (4)	—— + (7)	—— = (10)	——
Retention Time	—— + (2)	—— + (5)	—— + (8)	—— = (11)	——
Money Anxiety	—— + (3)	—— + (6)	—— + (9)	—— = (12)	——
Total score	Add up all dimension scores =				——

Interpreting Your Score: The three Money Attitude Scale dimensions measured here, as well as the total score, are defined as follows:

- **Money as Power/Prestige:** People with higher scores on this dimension tend to use money to influence and impress others.
- **Retention Time:** People with higher scores on this dimension tend to be careful financial planners.
- **Money Anxiety:** People with higher scores on this dimension tend to view money as a source of anxiety.
- **Money Attitude Total:** This is a general estimate of how much respect and attention you give to money.

Scores on the three Money Attitude Scale dimensions range from 4 to 20. The overall score ranges from 12 to 60. Norms vary from one group to the next. The following table shows how a sample of MBA students scored on the Money Attitude Scale. The table shows percentiles, that is, the percentage of people with the same or lower score. For example, the table indicates that a score of "13" on the retention scale is quite low because only 25 percent of students would have scored at this level or lower (75 percent scored higher). However, a score of "12" on the prestige scale is quite high because 75 percent of students score at or below this number (only 25 percent scored higher).

PERCENTILE	PRESTIGE SCORE	RETENTION SCORE	ANXIETY SCORE	TOTAL SCORE
Average Score	9.89	14.98	12.78	37.64
Top 10th percentile	13	18	16	44
Top 25th percentile	12	17	15	41
Median (50th percentile)	10	15	13	38
Bottom 25th percentile	8	13	11	33
Bottom 10th percentile	7	11	8	29

CHAPTER 7: SCORING KEY FOR THE CREATIVE PERSONALITY SCALE

Scoring Instructions: Assign a positive point (+1) after each of the following words that you checked off in the self-assessment:

_____ Capable	_____ Inventive
_____ Clever	_____ Original
_____ Confident	_____ Reflective
_____ Egotistical	_____ Resourceful
_____ Humorous	_____ Self-confident
_____ Individualistic	_____ Sexy
_____ Informal	_____ Snobbish
_____ Insightful	_____ Unconventional
_____ Intelligent	_____ Wide interests

Assign a negative point (–1) after each of the following words that you checked off in the self-assessment:

_____ Affected	_____ Honest
_____ Cautious	_____ Mannerly
_____ Commonplace	_____ Narrow interests
_____ Conservative	_____ Sincere
_____ Conventional	_____ Submissive
_____ Dissatisfied	_____ Suspicious

Next, sum the positive and negative points.

Interpreting Your Score: This instrument estimates your creative potential as a personal characteristic. The scale recognizes that creative people are intelligent and persistent and possess an inventive thinking style. Creative personality varies somewhat from one occupational group to the next. The table below provides norms based on undergraduate and graduate university/college students.

CREATIVE PERSONALITY SCORE	INTERPRETATION
Above +9	You have a high creative personality
+1 to +9	You have an average creative personality
Below +1	You have a low creative personality

CHAPTER 8: SCORING KEY FOR THE TEAM ROLES PREFERENCE SCALE

Scoring Instructions: Write the scores circled for each item on the appropriate line in the scoring key at the top of the right column (statement numbers are in parentheses), and add up each scale.

TEAM ROLES DIMENSION	CALCULATION	YOUR SCORE
Encourager	—— + —— + —— = (6) (9) (11)	——
Gatekeeper	—— + —— + —— = (4) (10) (13)	——
Harmonizer	—— + —— + —— = (3) (8) (12)	——
Initiator	—— + —— + —— = (1) (5) (14)	——
Summarizer	—— + —— + —— = (2) (7) (15)	——

Interpreting Your Score: The five team roles measured here are based on scholarship over the years. The following table defines these five roles and presents the range of scores for high, medium, and low levels of each role. These norms are based on results from a sample of MBA students.

Team Role Preference Definitions and Norms

TEAM ROLE AND DEFINITION	INTERPRETATION
Encourager: People who score high on this dimension have a strong tendency to praise and support the ideas of other team members, thereby showing warmth and solidarity with the group.	High: 12 and above Medium: 9 to 11 Low: 8 and below
Gatekeeper: People who score high on this dimension have a strong tendency to encourage all team members to participate in the discussion.	High: 12 and above Medium: 9 to 11 Low: 8 and below
Harmonizer: People who score high on this dimension have a strong tendency to mediate intragroup conflicts and reduce tension.	High: 11 and above Medium: 9 to 10 Low: 8 and below
Initiator: People who score high on this dimension have a strong tendency to identify goals for the meeting, including ways to work on those goals.	High: 12 and above Medium: 9 to 11 Low: 8 and below
Summarizer: People who score high on this dimension have a strong tendency to keep track of what was said in the meeting (i.e., act as the team's memory).	High: 10 and above Medium: 8 to 9 Low: 7 and below

CHAPTER 9: SCORING KEY FOR THE ACTIVE LISTENING SKILLS INVENTORY

Scoring Instructions: Use the first table below to score the response you marked for each statement. Then, in the scoring key, write that score on the line corresponding to the statement number (statement numbers are in parentheses) and add up each subscale. For example, if you checked "Seldom" for statement #1 ("I keep an open mind . . ."), you would write a "2" on the line with "(1)" underneath it. Calculate the overall Active Listening Inventory score by summing all subscales.

FOR STATEMENT ITEMS 4, 7, 11:	FOR STATEMENT ITEMS 1, 2, 3, 5, 6, 8, 9, 10, 12:
Rarely/never = 5	Rarely/never = 1
Seldom = 4	Seldom = 2
Sometimes = 3	Sometimes = 3
Often = 2	Often = 4
Almost always = 1	Almost always = 5

ACTIVE LISTENING DIMENSION	CALCULATION	YOUR SCORE
Sensing	—— + —— + —— + —— = (1) (4) (7) (10)	——
Evaluating	—— + —— + —— + —— = (2) (5) (8) (11)	——
Responding	—— + —— + —— + —— = (3) (6) (9) (12)	——
Active listening total	Add up all dimension scores =	——

Interpreting Your Score: The three active listening dimensions are defined as follows:

- **Sensing:** Sensing is the process of receiving signals from the sender and paying attention to them. Active listeners improve sensing in three ways. They postpone evaluation by not forming an opinion until the speaker has finished, avoid interrupting the speaker's conversation, and remain motivated to listen to the speaker.

- **Evaluating:** This dimension of active listening includes understanding the message meaning, evaluating the message, and remembering the message. To improve their evaluation of the conversation, active listeners empathize with the speaker—they try to understand and be sensitive to the speaker's feelings, thoughts, and situation. Evaluation also improves by organizing the speaker's ideas during the communication episode.

- **Responding:** Responding, the third dimension of active listening, is feedback to the sender, which motivates and directs the speaker's communication. Active listeners show interest through nonverbal cues (eye contact, nodding, symbiotic facial expression) and by sending back channel signals (e.g., "I see"). They also clarify the message, such as by summarizing or rephrasing the speaker's ideas at appropriate breaks ("So you're saying that . . . ?").

Scores on the three Active Listening dimensions range from 4 to 20. The overall score ranges from 12 to 60. Norms vary from one group to the next. The following table shows norms from a sample of 80 MBA students in two countries (Australia and Singapore). For example, the top 10th percentile for sensing is 17, indicating that 10 percent of people score 17 or above and 90 percent score below 17 on this dimension. Keep in mind that these scores represent self-perceptions. Evaluations from others (such as through 360-degree feedback) may provide a more accurate estimate of your active listening on one or more dimensions, particularly the responding dimension, which is visible to others.

Active Listening Norms

PERCENTILE	SENSING SCORE	EVALUATING SCORE	RESPONDING SCORE	TOTAL SCORE
Average Score	14.6	14.4	16.6	45.6
Top 10th percentile	17	17	19	52
Top 25th percentile	16	16	18	48
Median (50th percentile)	14	14	16	45
Bottom 25th percentile	13	13	15	42
Bottom 10th percentile	11	12	14	39

CHAPTER 10: SCORING KEY FOR THE COWORKER INFLUENCE SCALE

Scoring Instructions: To calculate your scores on the Coworker Influence Scale, write the number circled for each statement on the appropriate line in the scoring key below (statement numbers are in parentheses), and add up each scale.

Interpreting Your Score: Influence refers to any behavior that attempts to alter someone's attitudes or behavior. There are several types of influence, including the eight measured by this instrument. This instrument assesses your preference for using each type of influence on coworkers and other people at a similar level as your position in the organization.

- **Persuasion:** Persuasion refers to using logical and emotional appeals to change others' attitudes. This is one of

TEAM ROLES DIMENSION	CALCULATION	YOUR SCORE
Persuasion	—— + —— + —— = (1) (9) (17)	——
Silent Authority	—— + —— + —— = (2) (10) (18)	——
Exchange	—— + —— + —— = (3) (11) (19)	——
Assertiveness	—— + —— + —— = (4) (12) (20)	——
Information Control	—— + —— + —— = (5) (13) (21)	——
Coalition Formation	—— + —— + —— = (6) (14) (22)	——
Upward Appeal	—— + —— + —— = (7) (15) (23)	——
Ingratiation	—— + —— + —— = (8) (16) (24)	——

the most widely used influence strategies toward others in any position (e.g., coworkers, bosses, subordinates).

- **Silent Authority:** The silent application of authority occurs when someone complies with a request because her or she is aware of the requester's legitimate or expert power. This influence tactic is very subtle, such as making the target person aware of the status or expertise of the person making the request.
- **Exchange:** Exchange involves the promise of benefits or resources in exchange for the target person's compliance with your request. This tactic also includes reminding the target of past benefits or favors, with the expectation that the target will now make up for that debt. Negotiation is also part of the exchange strategy.
- **Assertiveness:** Assertiveness involves actively applying legitimate and coercive power to influence others. This tactic includes demanding that the other person comply with your wishes, showing frustration or impatience with the other person, and using threats of sanctions to force compliance.

- **Information Control:** Information control involves explicitly manipulating others' access to information for the purpose of changing their attitudes and/or behavior. It includes screening out information that might oppose your preference and embellishing or highlighting information that supports your position. According to one survey, more than half of employees believe their coworkers engage in this tactic.
- **Coalition Formation:** Coalition formation occurs when a group of people with common interests band together to influence others. It also exists as a perception, such as when you convince someone else that several people are on your side and support your position.
- **Upward Appeal:** Upward appeal occurs when you rely on support from people higher up the organizational hierarchy. This support may be real (senior management shows support) or logically argued (you explain how your position is consistent with company policy).
- **Ingratiation:** Ingratiation is a special case of impression management in which you attempt to increase the perception of liking or similarity to another person in the hope that he or she will become more supportive of your ideas. Flattering the coworker, becoming friendlier with the coworker, helping the coworker (with expectation of reciprocity), showing support for the coworker's ideas, and asking for the coworker's advice are all examples of ingratiation.

Scores on the eight Coworker Influence Scale dimensions range from 3 to 15. Higher scores indicate that the person has a higher preference for and use of that particular tactic. Norms vary from one group to the next. The following table shows norms from a sample of 70 MBA students in two countries (Australia and Singapore). For example, the top 10th percentile for assertiveness is 9, indicating that 10 percent of people score 9 or above and 90 percent score below 9 on this dimension. Keep in mind that these scores represent self-perceptions. Evaluations from others (such as through 360-degree feedback) may provide a more accurate estimate of your preferred influence tactics.

Coworker Influence Scale Norms

PERCENTILE	PERSUASION	SILENT AUTHORITY	EXCHANGE	ASSERTIVENESS
Average Score	12.6	10.0	7.3	5.4
Top 10th percentile	15	13	10	9
Top 25th percentile	14	12	9	6
Median (50th percentile)	13	10	8	5
Bottom 25th percentile	12	9	6	4
Bottom 10th percentile	10	7	4	3

(continued)

PERCENTILE	INFORMATION CONTROL	COALITION FORMATION	UPWARD APPEAL	INGRATIATION
Average Score	6.8	7.4	8.1	8.9
Top 10th percentile	10	10	11	13
Top 25th percentile	9	9	10	12
Median (50th percentile)	7	8	8	10
Bottom 25th percentile	5	6	6	7
Bottom 10th percentile	4	4	5	4

CHAPTER 11: SCORING KEY FOR THE CONFLICT HANDLING SCALE

Scoring Instructions: To estimate your preferred conflict handling styles, use the first table below to score the response you marked for each statement. Then, in the scoring key below, write that score on the line corresponding to the statement number (statement numbers are in parentheses) and add up each subscale. For example, if you checked "Seldom" for statement #1 ("I went along with the others . . ."), you would write a "2" on the line with "(1)" underneath it.

FOR ALL STATEMENT ITEMS
Rarely/never = 1
Seldom = 2
Sometimes = 3
Often = 4
Almost always = 5

CONFLICT HANDLING DIMENSION	CALCULATION	YOUR SCORE
Yielding	___ + ___ + ___ + ___ = (1) (7) (16) (20)	___
Compromising	___ + ___ + ___ + ___ = (2) (10) (11) (17)	___
Forcing	___ + ___ + ___ + ___ = (5) (8) (12) (15)	___
Problem solving	___ + ___ + ___ + ___ = (3) (9) (13) (18)	___
Avoiding	___ + ___ + ___ + ___ = (4) (6) (14) (19)	___

Interpreting Your Score: This instrument measures your preference for and use of the five conflict handling dimensions:

- **Yielding:** Yielding involves giving in completely to the other side's wishes, or at least cooperating with little or no attention to your own interests. This style involves making unilateral concessions, unconditional promises, and offering help with no expectation of reciprocal help.
- **Compromising:** Compromising involves looking for a position in which your losses are offset by equally valued gains. It involves matching the other party's concessions, making conditional promises or threats, and actively searching for a middle ground between the interests of the two parties.
- **Avoiding:** Avoiding tries to smooth over or avoid conflict situations altogether. It represents a low concern for both self and the other party. In other words, avoiders try to suppress thinking about the conflict.
- **Forcing:** Forcing tries to win the conflict at the other's expense. It includes "hard" influence tactics, particularly assertiveness, to get one's own way.
- **Problem Solving:** Problem solving tries to find a mutually beneficial solution for both parties. Information sharing is an important feature of this style, because both parties need to identify common ground and potential solutions that satisfy both (or all) of them.

Scores on the five Conflict Handling Scale dimensions range from 4 to 20. Higher scores indicate that the person has a higher preference for and use of that particular conflict handling style. Norms vary from one group to the next. The following table shows norms from a sample of 70 MBA students in two countries (Australia and Singapore). For example, the top 10th percentile for yielding is 14, indicating that 10 percent of people score 14 or above and 90 percent score below 14 on this dimension. Keep in mind that these scores represent self-perceptions. Evaluations from others (such as through 360-degree feedback) may provide a more accurate estimate of your preferred conflict handling style.

Conflict Handling Scale Norms

PERCENTILE	YIELDING	COMPROMISING	AVOIDING	FORCING	PROBLEM SOLVING
Average Score	11.0	13.8	10.2	13.5	15.9
Top 10th percentile	14	17	14	17	19
Top 25th percentile	12	16	12	15	17
Median (50th percentile)	11	14	10	13	16
Bottom 25th percentile	10	12	8	12	15
Bottom 10th percentile	8	10	6	10	13

CHAPTER 12: SCORING KEY FOR THE ROMANCE OF LEADERSHIP SCALE

Scoring Instructions: Use the table below to score the response you marked for each statement. Then, add up the scores to calculate your Romance of Leadership score. For example, if you marked "Disagree" for statement #1 ("Even in an economic . . ."), you would write a "2" on the line with "(1)" underneath it.

FOR STATEMENT ITEMS 3, 5, 7, 9:	FOR STATEMENT ITEMS 1, 2, 4, 6, 8, 10:
Strongly disagree = 5	Strongly disagree = 1
Disagree = 4	Disagree = 2
Neutral = 3	Neutral = 3
Agree = 2	Agree = 4
Strongly agree = 1	Strongly agree = 5

Total score:

$$\underline{\hspace{1cm}} + \underline{\hspace{1cm}} + \underline{\hspace{1cm}} + \underline{\hspace{1cm}} + \underline{\hspace{1cm}}$$
(1)   (2)   (3)   (4)   (5)

$$+ \underline{\hspace{1cm}} + \underline{\hspace{1cm}} + \underline{\hspace{1cm}} + \underline{\hspace{1cm}} + \underline{\hspace{1cm}}$$
(6)   (7)   (8)   (9)   (10)

$$= \underline{\hspace{1cm}}$$

Interpreting Your Score: Romance of leadership is a phenomenon in which followers (and possibly other stakeholders) want to believe that leaders make a difference in the organization's success. People with a high romance of leadership score attribute the causes of organizational events much more to its leaders and much less to the economy, competition, and other factors beyond the leader's short-term control. This scale ranges from 10 to 50, with higher scores indicating that the person has a higher romance of leadership. The following norms are derived from a large sample of European employees with an average age in their mid-30s and work experience averaging about 15 years. However, these norms should be viewed with caution, because the romance of leadership scale is a recent development and norms for any instrument can vary from one group to the next.

Romance of Leadership Norms

ROMANCE OF LEADERSHIP SCORE	INTERPRETATION
38–50	Above average romance of leadership
27–37	Average romance of leadership
10–26	Below average romance of leadership

CHAPTER 13: SCORING KEY FOR ORGANIZATIONAL STRUCTURE PREFERENCE SCALE

Scoring Instructions: Use the table below to assign numbers to each response you marked. Insert the number for each statement on the appropriate line in the scoring key. For example, if you checked "Not at all" for item #1 ("A person's career ladder . . ."), you would write a "0" on the line with "(1)" underneath it. After assigning numbers for all 15 statements, add up the scores to estimate your degree of preference for a tall hierarchy, formalization, and centralization. Then calculate the overall score by summing all scales.

FOR STATEMENT ITEMS 2, 3, 8, 10, 11, 12, 14, 15	FOR STATEMENT ITEMS 1, 4, 5, 6, 7, 9, 13
Not at all = 3	Not at all = 0
A little = 2	A little = 1
Somewhat = 1	Somewhat = 2
Very much = 0	Very much = 3

CONFLICT HANDLING DIMENSION	CALCULATION	YOUR SCORE
Tall Hierarchy (H)	$\underline{\hspace{0.5cm}} + \underline{\hspace{0.5cm}} + \underline{\hspace{0.5cm}} + \underline{\hspace{0.5cm}} + \underline{\hspace{0.5cm}} =$ (1) (4) (10) (12) (15)	$\underline{\hspace{0.5cm}}$ (H)
Formalization (F)	$\underline{\hspace{0.5cm}} + \underline{\hspace{0.5cm}} + \underline{\hspace{0.5cm}} + \underline{\hspace{0.5cm}} + \underline{\hspace{0.5cm}} =$ (2) (6) (8) (11) (13)	$\underline{\hspace{0.5cm}}$ (F)
Centralization (C)	$\underline{\hspace{0.5cm}} + \underline{\hspace{0.5cm}} + \underline{\hspace{0.5cm}} + \underline{\hspace{0.5cm}} + \underline{\hspace{0.5cm}} =$ (3) (5) (7) (9) (14)	$\underline{\hspace{0.5cm}}$ (C)
Total score (Mechanistic)	Add up all dimension scores (H + F + C) =	$\underline{\hspace{0.5cm}}$ Total

Interpreting Your Score: The three organizational structure dimensions and the overall score are defined below, along with the range of scores for high, medium, and low levels of each dimension based on a sample of MBA students.

Organizational Structure Preference Subscale Definitions and Norms

ORGANIZATIONAL STRUCTURE PREFERENCE SUBSCALE DEFINITION	INTERPRETATION
Tall hierarchy: People with high scores on this dimension prefer to work in organizations with several levels of hierarchy and a narrow span of control (few employees per supervisor).	High: 11 to 15 Medium: 6 to 10 Low: Below 6

(continued)

ORGANIZATIONAL STRUCTURE PREFERENCE SUBSCALE DEFINITION	INTERPRETATION
Formalization: People with high scores on this dimension prefer to work in organizations where jobs are clearly defined with limited discretion.	High: 12 to 15 Medium: 9 to 11 Low: Below 9
Centralization: People with high scores on this dimension prefer to work in organizations where decision making occurs mainly among top management rather than spread out to lower-level staff.	High: 10 to 15 Medium: 7 to 9 Low: Below 7
Total Score (Mechanistic): People with high scores on this dimension prefer to work in mechanistic organizations, whereas those with low scores prefer to work in organic organizational structures. Mechanistic structures are characterized by a narrow span of control and high degree of formalization and centralization. Organic structures have a wide span of control, little formalization, and decentralized decision making.	High: 30 to 45 Medium: 22 to 29 Low: Below 22

Corporate Culture Preference Subscale Definitions and Norms

CORPORATE CULTURE DIMENSION AND DEFINITION	SCORE INTERPRETATION
Control Culture: This culture values the role of senior executives to lead the organization. Its goal is to keep everyone aligned and under control.	High: 3 to 6 Medium: 1 to 2 Low: 0
Performance Culture: This culture values individual and organizational performance and strives for effectiveness and efficiency.	High: 5 to 6 Medium: 3 to 4 Low: 0 to 2
Relationship Culture: This culture values nurturing and well-being. It considers open communication, fairness, teamwork, and sharing a vital part of organizational life.	High: 6 Medium: 4 to 5 Low: 0 to 3
Responsive Culture: This culture values its ability to keep in tune with the external environment, including being competitive and realizing new opportunities.	High: 6 Medium: 4 to 5 Low: 0 to 3

CHAPTER 14: SCORING KEY FOR THE CORPORATE CULTURE PREFERENCE SCALE

Scoring Instructions: On each line below, write in a "1" if you circled the statement and a "0" if you did not. Then add up the scores for each subscale.

Control Culture   —— + —— + —— + —— + —— + —— = ——
                   (2a)   (5a)   (6b)   (8b)   (11b) (12a)

Performance Culture —— + —— + —— + —— + —— + —— = ——
                   (1b)   (3b)   (5b)   (6a)   (7a)   (9b)

Relationship Culture —— + —— + —— + —— + —— + —— = ——
                   (1a)   (3a)   (4b)   (8a)   (10b) (12b)

Responsive Culture   —— + —— + —— + —— + —— + —— = ——
                   (2b)   (4a)   (7b)   (9a)   (10a) (11a)

CHAPTER 15: SCORING KEY FOR THE TOLERANCE OF CHANGE SCALE

Scoring Instructions: Use the table below to assign numbers to each box you checked. For example, if you checked "Moderately disagree" for statement #1 ("I generally prefer the unexpected . . ."), you would write a "2" beside that statement. After assigning numbers for all 10 statements, add up your scores to estimate your tolerance for change.

Interpreting Your Score: These corporate cultures may be found in many organizations, but they represent only four of many possible organizational cultures. Also, keep in mind that none of these cultures is inherently good or bad. Each is effective in different situations. The four corporate cultures are defined in the table at the top of the right column, along with the range of scores for high, medium, and low levels of each dimension based on a sample of MBA students.

FOR STATEMENT ITEMS 1, 3, 7, 8, 10:	FOR STATEMENT ITEMS 2, 4, 5, 6, 9:
Strongly Agree = 7	Strongly Agree = 1
Moderately Agree = 6	Moderately Agree = 2
Slightly Agree = 5	Slightly Agree = 3
Neutral = 4	Neutral = 4
Slightly Disagree = 3	Slightly Disagree = 5
Moderately Disagree = 2	Moderately Disagree = 6
Strongly Disagree = 1	Strongly Disagree = 7

Interpreting Your Score: This instrument is formally known as the "tolerance of ambiguity" scale. The original scale, developed 50 years ago, has since been revised and adapted. The instrument presented here is an adaptation of these revised instruments. People with a high tolerance for ambiguity are comfortable with uncertainty and new situations. These are characteristics of the hyperfast changes occurring in many organizations today. This instrument ranges from 10 to 70, with higher scores indicating a higher tolerance for change (i.e., higher tolerance for ambiguity). The table at the right indicates the range of scores for high, medium, and low tolerance for change. These norms are estimates from recent studies using some or all of these items.

TOLERANCE FOR CHANGE SCORE	INTERPRETATION
50–70	You seem to have a high tolerance for change.
30–49	You seem to have a moderate level of tolerance for change.
10–29	You seem to have a low degree of tolerance for change. Instead, you prefer stable work environments.

(endnotes)

CHAPTER 1

1. J.C. Barbieri and A.C.T. Álvares, "Innovation in Mature Industries: The Case of Brasilata S.A. Metallic Packaging," paper presented at International Conference on Technology Policy and Innovation, Curitiba, Brazil, August 31, 2000; "Participaçoaõ É Desafio Nas Empresas [Participation Is a Challenge in Business]," *Gazeta do Povo*, November 16, 2008; "Brasilata Internal Suggestion System Is a Benchmark in Innovation in the Brazilian Market," (São Paulo, Brazil: Brazilata, 2010), http://brasilata.jp/en/noticias_detalhada.php?cd_noticia=219; C. Heath and D. Heath, *Switch: How to Change Things When Change Is Hard* (New York: Broadway Books, 2010); "Brasilata Inventors Turned in 205,536 Innovative Suggestions in 2010," (São Paulo, Brazil: Brasilata, 2011), http://brasilata.jp/en/noticias_detalhada.php?cd_noticia=264; "Simplification Project," (São Paulo, Brazil: Brasilata, 2011), http://brasilata.jp/en/projeto_cronologia.php; "Business Management," (São Paulo, Brazil: Brasilata, 2011), http://brasilata.jp/en/pessoal_negocios.php.

2. M. Warner, "Organizational Behavior Revisited," *Human Relations* 47 (October 1994), pp. 1151–66; R. Westwood and S. Clegg, "The Discourse of Organization Studies: Dissensus, Politics, and Peradigms," in *Debating Organization: Point-Counterpoint in Organization Studies*, ed. R. Westwood and S. Clegg (Malden, MA: Blackwood, 2003), pp. 1–42.

3. D. Katz and R.L. Kahn, *The Social Psychology of Organizations* (New York: Wiley, 1966), Ch. 2; R.N. Stern and S.R. Barley, "Organizations as Social Systems: Organization Theory's Neglected Mandate," *Administrative Science Quarterly* 41 (1996), pp. 146–62.

4. L.E. Greiner, "A Recent History of Organizational Behavior," in *Organizational Behaviour*, ed. S. Kerr (Columbus, Ohio: Grid, 1979), pp. 3–14; J. Micklethwait and A. Wooldridge, *The Company: A Short History of a Revolutionary Idea* (New York: Random House, 2003).

5. B. Schlender, "The Three Faces of Steve," *Fortune*, November 9, 1998, pp. 96–101.

6. J.A. Conger, "Max Weber's Conceptualization of Charismatic Authority: Its Influence on Organizational Research," *The Leadership Quarterly* 4, no. 3–4 (1993), pp. 277–88; R. Kanigel, *The One Best Way: Frederick Winslow Taylor and the Enigma of Efficiency* (New York: Viking, 1997); T. Takala, "Plato on Leadership," *Journal of Business Ethics* 17 (May 1998), pp. 785–98; J.A. Fernandez, "The Gentleman's Code of Confucius: Leadership by Values," *Organizational Dynamics* 33, no. 1 (February 2004), pp. 21–31.

7. C.D. Wrege, "Solving Mayo's Mystery: The First Complete Account of the Origin of the Hawthorne Studies—The Forgotten Contributions of C.E. Snow and H. Hibarger," in *Academy of Management Proceedings*, August 1976, pp. 12–16; J.A. Sonnenfeld, "Shedding Light on the Hawthorne Studies," *Journal of Occupational Behaviour* 6, no. 2 (1985), pp. 111–30; O'Connor, "Minding the Workers"; "A Field Is Born," *Harvard Business Review* 86, no. 7/8 (2008), pp. 164–164.

8. W.L.M. King, *Industry and Humanity: A Study in the Principles Underlying Industrial Reconstruction* (Toronto: Thomas Allen, 1918); H.C. Metcalf and L. Urwick, *Dynamic Administration: The Collected Papers of Mary Parker Follett* (New York: Harper & Brothers, 1940); J. Smith, "The Enduring Legacy of Elton Mayo," *Human Relations* 51, no. 3 (1998), pp. 221–49; E. O'Connor, "Minding the Workers: The Meaning of 'Human' and 'Human Relations' in Elton Mayo," *Organization* 6, no. 2 (May 1999), pp. 223–46; K. Hallahan, "W.L. Mackenzie King: Rockefeller's 'Other' Public Relations Counselor in Colorado," *Public Relations Review* 29, no. 4 (2003), pp. 401–14.

9. S.L. Rynes et al., "Behavioral Coursework in Business Education: Growing Evidence of a Legitimacy Crisis," *Academy of Management*

Learning & Education 2, no. 3 (2003), pp. 269–83; R.P. Singh and A.G. Schick, "Organizational Behavior: Where Does It Fit in Today's Management Curriculum?" *Journal of Education for Business* 82, no. 6 (July 2007), p. 349.

10. P.R. Lawrence and N. Nohria, *Driven: How Human Nature Shapes Our Choices* (San Francisco: Jossey-Bass, 2002), Ch. 6.

11. J.A.C. Baum, "Companion to Organizations: An Introduction," in *The Blackwell Companion to Organizations*, ed. J.A.C. Baum (Oxford, UK: Blackwell, 2002), pp. 1–34.

12. Organizational behavior scholars are currently in a heated debate regarding the field's relevance to practitioners. See, for example, P.R. Lawrence, "Historical Development of Organizational Behavior," in *Handbook of Organizational Behavior*, ed. L.W. Lorsch (Englewood Cliffs, NJ: Prentice Hall, 1987), pp. 1–9; R. Gulati, "Tent Poles, Tribalism, and Boundary Spanning: The Rigor-Relevance Debate in Management Research," *Academy of Management Journal* 50, no. 4 (August 2007), pp. 775–82; J.P. Walsh et al., "On the Relationship between Research and Practice: Debate and Reflections," *Journal of Management Inquiry* 16, no. 2 (June 2007), pp. 128–54; D. Palmer, B. Dick, and N. Freiburger, "Rigor and Relevance in Organization Studies," *Journal of Management Inquiry* 18, no. 4 (December 2009), pp. 265–72; A. Nicolai and D. Seidl, "That's Relevant! Different Forms of Practical Relevance in Management Science," *Organization Studies* 31, no. 9–10 (September 2010), pp. 1257–85; S.A. Mohrman and E.E. Lawler III, eds., *Useful Research: Advancing Theory and Practice* (San Francisco: Berrett-Koehler, 2011). At least one source argues that organizational scholarship does not need to be relevant to practitioners: M.W. Peng and G.G. Dess, "In the Spirit of Scholarship," *Academy of Management Learning & Education* 9, no. 2 (June 2010), pp. 282–98.

13. M.S. Myers, *Every Employee a Manager* (New York: McGraw Hill, 1970).

14. B.N. Pfau and I.T. Kay, *The Human Capital Edge* (New York: McGraw-Hill, 2002); I.S. Fulmer, B. Gerhart, and K.S. Scott, "Are the 100 Best Better? An Empirical Investigation of the Relationship between Being a 'Great Place to Work' and Firm Performance," *Personnel Psychology* 56, no. 4 (Winter 2003), pp. 965–93; Y.-H. Ling and B.-S. Jaw, "The Influence of International Human Capital on Global Initiatives and Financial Performance," *International Journal of Human Resource Management* 17, no. 3 (2006), pp. 379–98; M.A. West et al., "Reducing Patient Mortality in Hospitals: The Role of Human Resource Management," *Journal of Organizational Behavior* 27, no. 7 (2006), pp. 983–1002. However, one study warns that firm performance seems to predict the presence of OB practices as much as vice versa. See P.M. Wright et al., "The Relationship between HR Practices and Firm Performance: Examining Causal Order," *Personnel Psychology* 58, no. 2 (2005), pp. 409–46.

15. Deloitte & Touche, *Human Capital ROI Study: Creating Shareholder Value through People* (Toronto: Deloitte & Touche, 2002); D. Wheeler and J. Thomson, *Human Capital Based Investment Criteria for Total Shareholder Returns: A Canadian and International Perspective* (Toronto: Schulich School of Business, York University, June 2004); P. Shokeen, T.M. Woodward, and D. Wheeler, "Refining the York Index Investment Criteria," *SSRN eLibrary* (December 13, 2006); L. Bassi and D. McMurrer, "Maximizing Your Return on People," *Harvard Business Review* 85, no. 3 (March 2007), pp. 115–23, 144.

16. E.A. Robinson, "America's Most Admired Companies," *Fortune*, March 3, 1997, pp. 68–76; J. Kahn, "The World's Most Admired Companies," *Fortune*, October 26, 1998, pp. 206–16; A. Bernasek,

"The World's Most Admired Companies," *Fortune*, March 22, 2010, pp. 121–26.

17. Mohrman and Lawler III, eds., *Useful Research*. Similarly, in 1961, Harvard business professor Fritz Roethlisberger proposed that the field of OB is concerned with human behavior "from the points of view of both (a) its determination . . . and (b) its improvement." See P.B. Vaill, "F.J. Roethlisberger and the Elusive Phenomena of Organizational Behavior," *Journal of Management Education* 31, no. 3 (June 2007), pp. 321–38.

18. R.H. Hall, "Effectiveness Theory and Organizational Effectiveness," *Journal of Applied Behavioral Science* 16, no. 4 (October 1980), pp. 536–45; K. Cameron, "Organizational Effectiveness: Its Demise and Re-Emergence through Positive Organizational Scholarship," in *Great Minds in Management*, ed. K.G. Smith and M.A. Hitt (New York: Oxford University Press, 2005), pp. 304–30.

19. Bernasek, "The World's Most Admired Companies"; L. Daniel, "Apple's Shuffle," *Newsweek* 156, no. 11 (September 13, 2010); F. Manjoo and J. Caplan, "Apple Nation," *Fast Company*, no. 147 (July-August 2010), pp. 69–76; "The World's 50 Most Innovative Companies," *Fast Company*, no. 153 (2011), p. 67.

20. J.L. Price, "The Study of Organizational Effectiveness," *Sociological Quarterly* 13 (1972), pp. 3–15.

21. S.C. Selden and J.E. Sowa, "Testing a Multi-Dimensional Model of Organizational Performance: Prospects and Problems," *Journal of Public Administration Research and Theory* 14, no. 3 (July 2004), pp. 395–416.

22. Chester Barnard gives one of the earliest descriptions of organizations as systems interacting with external environments that are composed of subsystems. See C. Barnard, *The Functions of the Executive* (Cambridge, MA: Harvard University Press, 1938), especially Ch. 6. Also see F.E. Kast and J.E. Rosenzweig, "General Systems Theory: Applications for Organization and Management," *Academy of Management Journal* 15, no. 4 (1972), pp. 447–65; P.M. Senge, *The Fifth Discipline: The Art and Practice of the Learning Organization* (New York: Doubleday Currency, 1990); G. Morgan, *Images of Organization*, 2d ed. (Newbury Park: Sage, 1996); A. De Geus, *The Living Company* (Boston: Harvard Business School Press, 1997).

23. D.P. Ashmos and G.P. Huber, "The Systems Paradigm in Organization Theory: Correcting the Record and Suggesting the Future," *Academy of Management Review* 12, no. 4 (1987), pp. 607–21.

24. Katz and Kahn, *The Social Psychology of Organizations*; V.P. Rindova and S. Kotha, "Continuous 'Morphing': Competing through Dynamic Capabilities, Form, and Function," *Academy of Management Journal* 44 (2001), pp. 1263–80; J. McCann, "Organizational Effectiveness: Changing Concepts for Changing Environments," *Human Resource Planning* 27, no. 1 (2004), pp. 42–50.

25. D. Steinbok, *The Nokia Revolution: The Story of an Extraordinary Company That Transformed an Industry* (New York: AMACOM, 2001).

26. C. Ostroff and N. Schmitt, "Configurations of Organizational Effectiveness and Efficiency," *Academy of Management Journal* 36, no. 6 (1993), p. 1345.

27. P.S. Adler et al., "Performance Improvement Capability: Keys to Accelerating Performance Improvement in Hospitals," *California Management Review* 45, no. 2 (2003), pp. 12–33; J. Jamrog, M. Vickers, and D. Bear, "Building and Sustaining a Culture That Supports Innovation," *Human Resource Planning* 29, no. 3 (2006), pp. 9–19.

28. K.E. Weick, *The Social Psychology of Organizing* (Reading, MA: Addison-Wesley, 1979); S. Brusoni and A. Prencipe, "Managing Knowledge in Loosely Coupled Networks: Exploring the Links between Product and Knowledge Dynamics," *Journal of Management Studies* 38, no. 7 (November 2001), pp. 1019–35.

29. T.A. Stewart, *Intellectual Capital: The New Wealth of Organizations* (New York: Currency/Doubleday, 1997); H. Saint-Onge and D. Wallace, *Leveraging Communities of Practice for Strategic Advantage* (Boston: Butterworth-Heinemann, 2003), pp. 9–10; J.-A. Johannessen, B. Olsen, and J. Olaisen, "Intellectual Capital as a Holistic Management Philosophy: A Theoretical Perspective," *International Journal of Information Management* 25, no. 2 (2005), pp. 151–71; L. Striukova, J. Unerman, and J. Guthrie, "Corporate Reporting of Intellectual Capital: Evidence from UK Companies," *British Accounting Review* 40, no. 4 (2008), pp. 297–313.

30. J. Barney, "Firm Resources and Sustained Competitive Advantage," *Journal of Management* 17, no. 1 (1991), pp. 99–120.

31. "Jim Goodnight, Chief Executive Officer, SAS," (Cary, NC, 2011), http://www.sas.com/company/about/bios/jgoodnight.html.

32. S.-C. Kang and S.A. Snell, "Intellectual Capital Architectures and Ambidextrous Learning: A Framework for Human Resource Management," *Journal of Management Studies* 46, no. 1 (2009), pp. 65–92; L.-C. Hsu and C.-H. Wang, "Clarifying the Effect of Intellectual Capital on Performance: The Mediating Role of Dynamic Capability," *British Journal of Management* (2011), in press.

33. Some organizational learning researchers use the label "social capital" instead of relationship capital. Social capital is discussed later in this book as the goodwill and resulting resources shared among members in a social network. The two concepts may be identical (as those writers suggest). However, we continue to use "relationship capital" for intellectual capital because social capital typically refers to individual relationships, whereas relationship capital also includes value not explicit in social capital, such as the organization's goodwill and brand value.

34. G. Huber, "Organizational Learning: The Contributing Processes and Literature," *Organizational Science* 2 (1991), pp. 88–115; D.A. Garvin, *Learning in Action: A Guide to Putting the Learning Organization to Work* (Boston: Harvard Business School Press, 2000); H. Shipton, "Cohesion or Confusion? Towards a Typology for Organizational Learning Research," *International Journal of Management Reviews* 8, no. 4 (2006), pp. 233–52; W.C. Bogner and P. Bansal, "Knowledge Management as the Basis of Sustained High Performance," *Journal of Management Studies* 44, no. 1 (2007), pp. 165–88; D. Jiménez-Jiménez and J.G. Cegarra-Navarro, "The Performance Effect of Organizational Learning and Market Orientation," *Industrial Marketing Management* 36, no. 6 (2007), pp. 694–708.

35. R. Garud and A. Kumaraswamy, "Vicious and Virtuous Circles in the Management of Knowledge: The Case of Infosys Technologies," *MIS Quarterly* 29, no. 1 (March 2005), pp. 9–33; S.L. Hoe and S.L. McShane, "Structural and Informal Knowledge Acquisition and Dissemination in Organizational Learning: An Exploratory Analysis," *The Learning Organization* 17, no. 4 (2010), pp. 364–86.

36. Centre for Education and Work, *The Learning Organization Video*, (Winnipeg: Centre for Education and Work, 2009); C. Hawkins, *Duha Color Group*, Weslat Case Studies (Winnipeg: Centre for Education and Work, 2009).

37. W. Cohen and D. Levinthal, "Absorptive Capacity: A New Perspective on Learning and Innovation," *Administrative Science Quarterly* 35 (1990), pp. 128–52; G. Todorova and B. Durisin, "Absorptive Capacity: Valuing a Reconceptualization," *Academy of Management Review* 32, no. 3 (2007), pp. 774–86.

38. M.N. Wexler, "Organizational Memory and Intellectual Capital," *Journal of Intellectual Capital* 3, no. 4 (2002), pp. 393–414.

39. "A Cornerstone for Learning," *T&D*, October 2008, pp. 66–89.

40. M.E. McGill and J.W. Slocum Jr., "Unlearn the Organization," *Organizational Dynamics* 22, no. 2 (1993), pp. 67–79; A.E. Akgün, G.S. Lynn, and J.C. Byrne, "Antecedents and Consequences of Unlearning in New Product Development Teams," *Journal of Product Innovation Management* 23 (2006), pp. 73–88.

41. E. Appelbaum et al., *Manufacturing Advantage: Why High-Performance Work Systems Pay Off* (Ithaca, NY: Cornell University Press, 2000); A. Zacharatos, J. Barling, and R.D. Iverson, "High-Performance Work Systems and Occupational Safety," *Journal of Applied Psychology* 90, no. 1 (2005), pp. 77–93; G.S. Benson, S.M. Young, and E.E. Lawler III, "High-Involvement Work Practices and Analysts' Forecasts of Corporate Earnings," *Human Resource Management* 45, no. 4 (2006), pp. 519–37; L. Sels et al., "Unravelling the HRM–Performance Link: Value-Creating and Cost-Increasing Effects of Small Business HRM," *Journal of Management Studies* 43, no. 2 (2006), pp. 319–42.

42. M.A. Huselid, "The Impact of Human Resource Management Practices on Turnover, Productivity, and Corporate," *Academy of Management Journal* 38, no. 3 (1995), p. 635; B.E. Becker and M.A. Huselid, "Strategic Human Resources Management: Where Do We Go from Here?" *Journal of Management* 32, no. 6 (December 2006), pp. 898–925; J. Combs et al., "How Much Do High-Performance Work Practices Matter? A Meta-Analysis of Their Effects on Organizational Performance," *Personnel Psychology* 59, no. 3 (2006), pp. 501–28.

43. E.E. Lawler III, S.A. Mohrman, and G.E. Ledford Jr., *Strategies for High Performance Organizations* (San Francisco: Jossey-Bass, 1998); S.H. Wagner, C.P. Parker, and D. Neil, "Employees That Think and Act Like Owners: Effects of Ownership Beliefs and Behaviors on Organizational Effectiveness," *Personnel Psychology* 56, no. 4 (Winter 2003), pp. 847–71; P.J. Gollan, "High Involvement Management and Human Resource Sustainability: The Challenges and Opportunities," *Asia Pacific Journal of Human Resources* 43, no. 1 (April 2005), pp. 18–33; Y. Liu et al., "The Value of Human Resource Management for Organizational Performance," *Business Horizons* 50 (2007), pp. 503–11; P. Tharenou, A.M. Saks, and C. Moore, "A Review and Critique of Research on Training and Organizational-Level Outcomes," *Human Resource Management Review* 17, no. 3 (2007), pp. 251–73.

44. M. Subramony, "A Meta-Analytic Investigation of the Relationship between HRM Bundles and Firm Performance," *Human Resource Management* 48, no. 5 (2009), pp. 745–68.

45. R. Bostelaar, "Call Centres, Unscripted," *Ottawa Citizen*, August 28, 2010; E. Frauenheim, "Making the Call for Themselves," *Workforce Management*, August 2010, p. 16.

46. S. Fleetwood and A. Hesketh, "HRM–Performance Research: Under-Theorized and Lacking Explanatory Power," *International Journal of Human Resource Management* 17, no. 12 (December 2006), pp. 1977–93.

47. R. Takeuchi et al., "An Empirical Examination of the Mechanisms Mediating between High-Performance Work Systems and the Performance of Japanese Organizations," *Journal of Applied Psychology* 92, no. 4 (2007), pp. 1069–83; L.-Q. Wei and C.-M. Lau, "High Performance Work Systems and Performance: The Role of Adaptive Capability," *Human Relations* 63, no. 10 (2010), pp. 1487–1511; J. Camps and R. Luna-Arocas, "A Matter of Learning: How Human Resources Affect Organizational Performance," *British Journal of Management* (in press).

48. J. Godard, "High Performance and the Transformation of Work? The Implications of Alternative Work Practices for the Experience and Outcomes of Work," *Industrial and Labor Relations Review* 54, no. 4 (July 2001), pp. 776–805; G. Murray et al., eds., *Work and Employment Relations in the High-Performance Workplace* (London: Continuum, 2002); B. Harley, "Hope or Hype? High Performance Work Systems," in *Participation and Democracy at Work: Essays in Honour of Harvie Ramsay*, ed. B. Harley, J. Hyman, and P. Thompson (Houndsmills, UK: Palgrave Macmillan, 2005), pp. 38–54.

49. A.L. Friedman and S. Miles, *Stakeholders: Theory and Practice* (New York: Oxford University Press, 2006); M.L. Barnett, "Stakeholder Influence Capacity and the Variability of Financial Returns to Corporate Social Responsibility," *Academy of Management Review* 32, no. 3 (2007), pp. 794–816; R.E. Freeman, J.S. Harrison, and A.C.

Wicks, *Managing for Stakeholders: Survival, Reputation, and Success* (New Haven, CT: Yale University Press, 2007).

50. C. Eden and F. Ackerman, *Making Strategy: The Journey of Strategic Management* (London: Sage, 1998).

51. T.A. Hemphill, "Rejuvenating Wal-Mart's Reputation," *Business Horizons* 48, no. 1 (2005), pp. 11–21; A. Bianco, *The Bully of Bentonville: How the High Cost of Wal-Mart's Everyday Low Prices Is Hurting America* (New York: Random House, 2006); C. Fishman, *The Wal-Mart Effect* (New York: Penguin, 2006). For a description of Walmart's recent corrective actions on environmentalism, see E.L. Plambeck and L. Denend, "Wal * Mart," *Stanford Social Innovation Review* 6, no. 2 (Spring 2008), pp. 53–59.

52. G.R. Salancik and J. Pfeffer, *The External Control of Organizations: A Resource Dependence Perspective* (New York: Harper & Row, 1978); T. Casciaro and M.J. Piskorski, "Power Imbalance, Mutual Dependence, and Constraint Absorption: A Closer Look at Dependence Theory," *Administrative Science Quarterly* 50 (2005), pp. 167–99; N. Roome and F. Wijen, "Stakeholder Power and Organizational Learning in Corporate Environmental Management," *Organization Studies* 27, no. 2 (2005), pp. 235–63.

53. R.E. Freeman, A.C. Wicks, and B. Parmar, "Stakeholder Theory and 'The Corporate Objective Revisited,'" *Organization Science* 15, no. 3 (May-June 2004), pp. 364–69; Friedman and Miles, *Stakeholders*, Ch. 3; B.L. Parmar et al., "Stakeholder Theory: The State of the Art," *Academy of Management Annals* 4, no. 1 (2010), pp. 403–45.

54. B.M. Meglino and E.C. Ravlin, "Individual Values in Organizations: Concepts, Controversies, and Research," *Journal of Management* 24, no. 3 (1998), pp. 351–89; B.R. Agle and C.B. Caldwell, "Understanding Research on Values in Business," *Business and Society* 38, no. 3 (September 1999), pp. 326–87; A. Bardi and S.H. Schwartz, "Values and Behavior: Strength and Structure of Relations," *Personality and Social Psychology Bulletin* 29, no. 10 (October 2003), pp. 1207–20; S. Hitlin and J.A. Pilavin, "Values: Reviving a Dormant Concept," *Annual Review of Sociology* 30 (2004), pp. 359–93.

55. Some popular books that emphasize the importance of values include the following: J.C. Collins and J.I. Porras, *Built to Last: Successful Habits of Visionary Companies* (London: Century, 1995); C.A. O'Reilly III and J. Pfeffer, *Hidden Value* (Cambridge, MA: Harvard Business School Press, 2000); R. Barrett, *Building a Values-Driven Organization: A Whole System Approach to Cultural Transformation* (Burlington, MA: Butterworth-Heinemann, 2006); J.M. Kouzes and B.Z. Posner, *The Leadership Challenge*, 4th ed. (San Francisco: Jossey-Bass, 2007).

56. T. Hsieh, *Delivering Happiness: A Path to Profits, Passion, and Purpose* (New York: Hachette Book Group, 2010), pp. 155–59.

57. Aspen Institute, *Where Will They Lead? MBA Student Attitudes about Business & Society* (Washington, DC: Aspen Institute, April 2008).

58. M. van Marrewijk, "Concepts and Definitions of CSR and Corporate Sustainability: Between Agency and Communion," *Journal of Business Ethics* 44 (May 2003), pp. 95–105; Barnett, "Stakeholder Influence Capacity."

59. L.S. Paine, *Value Shift* (New York: McGraw-Hill, 2003); A. Mackey, T.B. Mackey, and J.B. Barney, "Corporate Social Responsibility and Firm Performance: Investor Preferences and Corporate Strategies," *Academy of Management Review* 32, no. 3 (2007), pp. 817–35.

60. S. Zadek, *The Civil Corporation: The New Economy of Corporate Citizenship* (London: Earthscan, 2001); S. Hart and M. Milstein, "Creating Sustainable Value," *Academy of Management Executive* 17, no. 2 (2003), pp. 56–69.

61. M. Friedman, *Capitalism and Freedom*, 40th anniversary ed. (Chicago: University of Chicago Press, 2002), Ch. 8; N. Vorster, "An Ethical Critique of Milton Friedman's Doctrine on Economics and Freedom," *Journal for the Study of Religions and Ideologies* 9, no. 26 (Summer 2010), pp. 163–88.

62. M. Johne, "Show Us the Green, Workers Say," *Globe & Mail*, October 10, 2007, p. C1.

63. MTN Group Limited, *2009 Sustainability Report* (Fairlands, South Africa: MTN Group, June 26, 2010); "21daysuganada," June 2, 2011, http://21daysuganda.wordpress.com/; "MTN Plants 5,800 Trees in 21 Days of Y'ello Care," *Spy Ghana*, June 10, 2011.

64. A. Fox, "Corporate Social Responsibility Pays Off," *HRMagazine* 52, no. 8 (August 2007), pp. 42–47.

65. Aspen Institute, *Where Will They Lead?*; A.E. Herman, *Corporate Social Responsibility to Employees and Creating Sustainable Business* (Wayne, PA: Kenexa Research Institute, October 2008); F. Smith, "Staff Care about the Company They Keep," *CIO New Zealand*, July 30, 2008; Kelly Services, *Generational Crossovers in the Workforce—Opinions Revealed* (Troy, MI: Kelly Services, 2010).

66. W. Immen, "On the Move for Work," *Globe & Mail*, May 15, 2010, p. B16.

67. S. Fischer, "Globalization and Its Challenges," *American Economic Review* (May 2003), pp. 1–29. For discussion of the diverse meanings of globalization, see M.F. Guillén, "Is Globalization Civilizing, Destructive or Feeble? A Critique of Five Key Debates in the Social Science Literature," *Annual Review of Sociology* 27 (2001), pp. 235–60.

68. The ongoing debate regarding the advantages and disadvantages of globalization is discussed by Guillén, "Is Globalization Civilizing, Destructive or Feeble?"; D. Doane, "Can Globalization Be Fixed?" *Business Strategy Review* 13, no. 2 (2002), pp. 51–58; J. Bhagwati, *In Defense of Globalization* (New York: Oxford University Press, 2004); M. Wolf, *Why Globalization Works* (New Haven, CT: Yale University Press, 2004).

69. K. Ohmae, *The Next Global Stage* (Philadelphia, PA: Wharton School Publishing, 2005).

70. "No. 3: Millennium: The Takeda Oncology Co.," Boston.com, 2010, http://www.boston.com/bostonworks/topplaces/2010/topplaces2010?pg=4.

71. "Verizon Again Named to Black Enterprise Magazine's List of 40 Best Companies for Diversity," M2 Presswire news release, June 29, 2010; "Working Mother Magazine Ranks Verizon among the Best Companies for Multicultural Women," PR Newswire news release, May 26, 2011; "No. 22: Verizon Communications," DiversityInc, 2011, http://diversityinc.com/article/8294/No-22-Verizon-Communications/.

72. M.F. Riche, "America's Diversity and Growth: Signposts for the 21st Century," *Population Bulletin* (June 2000), pp. 3–43; U.S. Census Bureau, *Statistical Abstract of the United States: 2004–2005*, (Washington, DC: U.S. Census Bureau, May 2005).

73. D.A. Harrison et al., "Time, Teams, and Task Performance: Changing Effects of Surface- and Deep-Level Diversity on Group Functioning," *Academy of Management Journal* 45, no. 5 (2002), pp. 1029–46.

74. R. Zemke, C. Raines, and B. Filipczak, *Generations at Work: Managing the Clash of Veterans, Boomers, Xers, and Nexters in Your Workplace* (New York: Amacom, 2000); S.H. Applebaum, M. Serena, and B.T. Shapiro, "Generation X and the Boomers: Organizational Myths and Literary Realities," *Management Research News* 27, no. 11/12 (2004), pp. 1–28; N. Howe and W. Strauss, "The Next 20 Years: How Customer and Workforce Attitudes Will Evolve," *Harvard Business Review* (July-August 2007), pp. 41–52.

75. U.S. Bureau of Labor Statistics, *Household Data, Annual Averages: Employment Status of the Civilian Noninstitutional Population by Age, Sex, and Race* (Washington, DC: U.S. Bureau of Labor Statistics, 2010).

76. E. Parry and P. Urwin, "Generational Differences in Work Values: A Review of Theory and Evidence," *International Journal of Management Reviews* 13 (2011), pp. 79–96.

77. E. Ng, L. Schweitzer, and S. Lyons, "New Generation, Great Expectations: A Field Study of the Millennial Generation," *Journal of Business and Psychology* 25, no. 2 (2010), pp. 281–92.

78. J.M. Twenge and S.M. Campbell, "Generational Differences in Psychological Traits and Their Impact on the Workplace," *Journal of Managerial Psychology* 23, no. 8 (2008), pp. 862–77; M. Wong et al., "Generational Differences in Personality and Motivation," *Journal of Managerial Psychology* 23, no. 8 (2008), pp. 878–90; J. Deal, D. Altman, and S. Rogelberg, "Millennials at Work: What We Know and What We Need to Do (If Anything)," *Journal of Business and Psychology* 25, no. 2 (2010), pp. 191–99; B. Kowske, R. Rasch, and J. Wiley, "Millennials' (Lack of) Attitude Problem: An Empirical Examination of Generational Effects on Work Attitudes," *Journal of Business and Psychology* 25, no. 2 (2010), pp. 265–79; J. Twenge, "A Review of the Empirical Evidence on Generational Differences in Work Attitudes," *Journal of Business and Psychology* 25, no. 2 (2010), pp. 201–10.

79. J.M. Twenge et al., "Generational Differences in Work Values: Leisure and Extrinsic Values Increasing, Social and Intrinsic Values Decreasing," *Journal of Management* 36, no. 5 (September 2010), pp. 1117–42. Another temporal cohort study also reports an increasing preference for leisure, though these differences were not significant. See J. Meriac, D. Woehr, and C. Banister, "Generational Differences in Work Ethic: An Examination of Measurement Equivalence across Three Cohorts," *Journal of Business and Psychology* 25, no. 2 (2010), pp. 315–24.

80. O.C. Richard, "Racial Diversity, Business Strategy, and Firm Performance: A Resource-Based View," *Academy of Management Journal* 43 (2000), pp. 164–77; T. Kochan et al., "The Effects of Diversity on Business Performance: Report of the Diversity Research Network," *Human Resource Management* 42 (2003), pp. 3–21; R.J. Burke and E. Ng, "The Changing Nature of Work and Organizations: Implications for Human Resource Management," *Human Resource Management Review* 16 (2006), pp. 86–94; M.-E. Roberge and R. van Dick, "Recognizing the Benefits of Diversity: When and How Does Diversity Increase Group Performance?" *Human Resource Management Review* 20, no. 4 (2010), pp. 295–308.

81. D. Porras, D. Psihountas, and M. Griswold, "The Long-Term Performance of Diverse Firms," *International Journal of of Diversity* 6, no. 1 (2006), pp. 25–34; R.A. Weigand, "Organizational Diversity, Profits and Returns in U.S. Firms," *Problems & Perspectives in Management* 3 (2007), pp. 69–83.

82. "Working Mother Magazine Ranks Verizon," news release.

83. R.J. Ely and D.A. Thomas, "Cultural Diversity at Work: The Effects of Diversity Perspectives on Work Group Processes and Outcomes," *Administrative Science Quarterly* 46 (June 2001), pp. 229–73; Kochan et al., "The Effects of Diversity on Business Performance: Report of the Diversity Research Network"; D. van Knippenberg and S.A. Haslam, "Realizing the Diversity Dividend: Exploring the Subtle Interplay between Identity, Ideology and Reality," in *Social Identity at Work: Developing Theory for Organizational Practice*, ed. S.A. Haslam et al. (New York: Taylor and Francis, 2003), pp. 61–80; D. van Knippenberg, C.K.W. De Dreu, and A.C. Homan, "Work Group Diversity and Group Performance: An Integrative Model and Research Agenda," *Journal of Applied Psychology* 89, no. 6 (2004), pp. 1008–22; E. Molleman, "Diversity in Demographic Characteristics, Abilities and Personality Traits: Do Faultlines Affect Team Functioning?" *Group Decision and Negotiation* 14, no. 3 (2005), pp. 173–93.

84. A. Birritteri, "Workplace Diversity: Realizing the Benefits of an All-Inclusive Employee Base," *New Jersey Business*, November 2005, p. 36.

85. W.G. Bennis and R.J. Thomas, *Geeks and Geezers* (Boston: Harvard Business School Press, 2002), pp. 74–79; E.D.Y. Greenblatt, "Work/Life Balance: Wisdom or Whining," *Organizational Dynamics* 31, no. 2 (2002), pp. 177–93.

86. WorldatWork, *Telework Trendlines 2009* (Scottsdale, AZ: Worldat-Work, February 2009).

87. D. Meinert, "Make Telecommuting Pay Off," *HRMagazine*, June 2011, p. 33. Deloitte's telework program, part of its mass career customization initiative, is described in C. Benko and M. Anderson, *The Corporate Lattice: Achieving High Performance in the Changing World of Work* (Boston: Harvard Business School Press, 2010).

88. M. Conlin, "The Easiest Commute of All," *BusinessWeek*, December 12, 2005, p. 78; "Increased Productivity Due to Telecommuting Generates an Estimated $277 Million in Annual Savings for Company," news release, Cisco Systems, June 25, 2009; Meinert, "Make Telecommuting Pay Off."

89. A. Bourhis and R. Mekkaoui, "Beyond Work–Family Balance: Are Family-Friendly Organizations More Attractive?" *Industrial Relations* 65, no. 1 (Winter 2010), pp. 98–117; E.J. Hill et al., "Workplace Flexibility, Work Hours, and Work-Life Conflict: Finding an Extra Day or Two," *Journal of Family Psychology* 24, no. 3 (June 2010), pp. 349–58.

90. "Increased Productivity Due to Telecommuting," news release; "Rep. Sarbane's Telework Improvements Act Passes House," news release, U.S. Federal News Service, July 15, 2010); Meinert, "Make Telecommuting Pay Off."

91. J. Bednar, "Beyond the 9-to-5," *BusinessWest*, February 15, 2010, p. 18.

92. D.E. Bailey and N.B. Kurland, "A Review of Telework Research: Findings, New Directions, and Lessons for the Study of Modern Work," *Journal of Organizational Behavior* 23 (2002), pp. 383–400; D.W. McCloskey and M. Igbaria, "Does 'Out of Sight' Mean 'Out of Mind'? An Empirical Investigation of the Career Advancement Prospects of Telecommuters," *Information Resources Management Journal* 16 (April-June 2003), pp. 19–34.

93. Most of these anchors are mentioned by J.D. Thompson, "On Building an Administrative Science," *Administrative Science Quarterly* 1, no. 1 (1956), pp. 102–11.

94. This anchor has a colorful history dating back to critiques of business schools in the 1950s. Soon after, systematic research became a mantra by many respected scholars. See ibid.

95. J. Pfeffer and R.I. Sutton, *Hard Facts, Dangerous Half-Truths, and Total Nonsense* (Boston: Harvard Business School Press, 2006); D.M. Rousseau and S. McCarthy, "Educating Managers from an Evidence-Based Perspective," *Academy of Management Learning & Education* 6, no. 1 (2007), pp. 84–101; R.B. Briner and D.M. Rousseau, "Evidence-Based I-O Psychology: Not There Yet," *Industrial and Organizational Psychology* 4, no. 1 (2011), pp. 3–22.

96. J.M. Bartunek, "Evidence-Based Approaches in I-O Psychology Should Address Worse Grumbles," *Industrial and Organizational Psychology* 4, no. 1 (2011), pp. 72–75; M.J. Burke, "Is There a Fly in the 'Systematic Review' Ointment?" *Industrial and Organizational Psychology* 4, no. 1 (2011), pp. 36–39; M.A. Cronin and R. Klimoski, "Broadening the View of What Constitutes 'Evidence,'" *Industrial and Organizational Psychology* 4, no. 1 (2011), pp. 57–61.

97. D.J. Cohen, "The Very Separate Worlds of Academic and Practitioner Publications in Human Resource Management: Reasons for the Divide and Concrete Solutions for Bridging the Gap," *Academy of Management Journal* 50, no. 5 (October 2007), pp. 1013–19; E.E. Lawler, "Why HR Practices Are Not Evidence-Based," *Academy of Management Journal* 50, no. 5 (October 2007), pp. 1033–36; S.L. Rynes, T.L. Giluk, and K.G. Brown, "The Very Separate Worlds of Academic and Practitioner Periodicals in Human Resource Management: Implications for Evidence-Based Management," *Academy of Management Journal* 50, no. 5 (October 2007), pp. 987–1008.

98. J. Greenberg and E.C. Tomlinson, "Situated Experiments in Organizations: Transplanting the Lab to the Field," *Journal of Management* 30, no. 5 (2004), pp. 703–24.

99. M.N. Zald, "More Fragmentation? Unfinished Business in Linking the Social Sciences and the Humanities," *Administrative Science Quarterly* 41 (1996), pp. 251–61; C. Heath and S.B. Sitkin, "Big-B versus Big-O: What Is Organizational about Organizational Behavior?" *Journal of Organizational Behavior* 22 (2001), pp. 43–58; C. Oswick, P. Fleming, and G. Hanlon, "From Borrowing to Blending: Rethinking the Processes of Organizational Theory Building," *Academy of Management Review* 36, no. 2 (April 2011), pp. 318–37.

100. D.M. Rousseau and Y. Fried, "Location, Location, Location: Contextualizing Organizational Research," *Journal of Organizational Behavior* 22, no. 1 (2001), pp. 1–13; C.M. Christensen and M.E. Raynor, "Why Hard-Nosed Executives Should Care about Management Theory," *Harvard Business Review*, September 2003, pp. 66–74. For an excellent critique of the "one best way" approach in early management scholarship, see P.F. Drucker, "Management's New Paradigms," *Forbes*, October 5, 1998, pp. 152–77.

101. H.L. Tosi and J.W. Slocum Jr., "Contingency Theory: Some Suggested Directions," *Journal of Management* 10 (1984), pp. 9–26.

102. D.M. Rousseau, "Meso Organizational Behavior: Avoiding Three Fundamental Biases," in *Trends in Organizational Behavior*, ed. C.L. Cooper and D.M. Rousseau (Chichester, UK: John Wiley & Sons, 1994), pp. 13–30.

103. "NHS Chief Vows to Cut Waste and Look to Toyota in Efficiency Drive," NHS Federation news release, June 14, 2006; D. Jones and A. Mitchell, *Lean Thinking for the NHS* (London: NHS Confederation, 2006); M. McCarthy, "Can Car Manufacturing Techniques Reform Health Care?" *Lancet* 367, no. 9507 (January 28, 2006), pp. 290–91; "Nissan 'Shot in the Arm' for Healthcare Sector," *Newcarinfo.co.uk*, February 13, 2007; I. Green, "Drive for Success," *Nursing Standard* 21, no. 38 (May 30, 2007), pp. 62–63; A.-M. Kelly et al., "Improving Emergency Department Efficiency by Patient Streaming to Outcomes-Based Teams," *Australian Health Review* 31, no. 1 (2007), pp. 16–21.

104. "The Pixar Principle," *The Age (Melbourne, AU)*, May 28, 2006; C. Eller, "Ed Catmull: Pixar's Superhero Shakes Up Disney," *Los Angeles Times*, June 12, 2006; W.C. Taylor and P. LaBarre, "How Pixar Adds a New School of Thought to Disney," *The New York Times*, January 29, 2006; B. Barnes, "Disney and Pixar: The Power of the Prenup," *The New York Times*, June 1, 2008; S. Leith, "How Pixar Found Its Shiny Metal Soul," *Sunday Telegraph (London)*, June 22, 2008; H. Rao and R.I. Sutton, "Innovation Lessons from Pixar: An Interview with Oscar-Winning Director Brad Bird," *McKinsey Quarterly*, April 2008, pp. 1–9.

CHAPTER 2

1. L. Beattie, "Top Hospitals Recognized as 'Best Places to Work' in the U.S.," (San Diego: AMN Healthcare, 2009), http://www.nursingjobs.com/healthcareleaders.asp?id=10826; "Developing a Culture of Revenue Cycle Excellence," *Healthcare Financial Management* 2010, pp. C5–C9; H. Poturalski, "Shopping Salute," *Columbus Dispatch (Ohio)*, June 23, 2010; J. Waddell, "Streamline Your Front-End Processes," *Health Management Technology*, April 2011, p. 24.

2. L.L. Thurstone, "Ability, Motivation, and Speed," *Psychometrika* 2, no. 4 (1937), pp. 249–54; N.R.F. Maier, *Psychology in Industry*, 2d ed. (Boston: Houghton Mifflin Company, 1955); V.H. Vroom, *Work and Motivation* (New York: John Wiley & Sons, 1964); J.P. Campbell et al., *Managerial Behavior, Performance, and Effectiveness* (New York: McGraw-Hill, 1970).

3. U.-C. Klehe and N. Anderson, "Working Hard and Working Smart: Motivation and Ability during Typical and Maximum Performance," *Journal of Applied Psychology* 92, no. 4 (2007), pp. 978–92; J.S. Gould-Williams and M. Gatenby, "The Effects of Organizational Context and Teamworking Activities on Performance Outcomes—A Study Conducted in England Local Government," *Public Management Review* 12, no. 6 (2010), pp. 759–87.

4. E.E.I. Lawler and L.W. Porter, "Antecedent Attitudes of Effective Managerial Performance," *Organizational Behavior and Human Performance* 2 (1967), pp. 122–42; M.A. Griffin, A. Neal, and S.K. Parker, "A New Model of Work Role Performance: Positive Behavior in Uncertain and Interdependent Contexts," *Academy of Management Journal* 50, no. 2 (April 2007), pp. 327–47.

5. Only a few literature reviews have included all four factors. These include J.P. Campbell and R.D. Pritchard, "Motivation Theory in Industrial and Organizational Psychology," in *Handbook of Industrial and Organizational Psychology,* ed. M. D. Dunnette (Chicago: Rand McNally, 1976), pp. 62–130; T.R. Mitchell, "Motivation: New Directions for Theory, Research, and Practice," *Academy of Management Review* 7, no. 1 (January 1982), pp. 80–88; G.A.J. Churchill et al., "The Determinants of Salesperson Performance: A Meta-Analysis," *Journal of Marketing Research* 22, no. 2 (1985), pp. 103–18; R.E. Plank and D.A. Reid, "The Mediating Role of Sales Behaviors: An Alternative Perspective of Sales Performance and Effectiveness," *Journal of Personal Selling & Sales Management* 14, no. 3 (Summer 1994), pp. 43–56. The *MARS* acronym was coined by senior officers in the Singapore armed forces. Chris Perryer at University of Western Australia suggests the full model should be called the "MARS BAR," because the outcomes might be labeled "behavior and results"!

6. Technically, the model proposes that situational factors moderate the effects of the three within-person factors. For instance, the effect of employee motivation on behavior and performance depends on (is moderated by) the situation.

7. C.C. Pinder, *Work Motivation in Organizational Behavior* (Upper Saddle River, NJ: Prentice-Hall, 1998); G.P. Latham and C.C. Pinder, "Work Motivation Theory and Research at the Dawn of the Twenty-First Century," *Annual Review of Psychology* 56 (2005), pp. 485–516.

8. L.M. Spencer and S.M. Spencer, *Competence at Work: Models for Superior Performance* (New York: Wiley, 1993); R. Kurz and D. Bartram, "Competency and Individual Performance: Modelling the World of Work," in *Organizational Effectiveness: The Role of Psychology,* ed. I. T. Robertson, M. Callinan, and D. Bartram (Chichester, UK: John Wiley & Sons, 2002), pp. 227–58; H. Heinsman et al., "Competencies through the Eyes of Psychologists: A Closer Look at Assessing Competencies," *International Journal of Selection and Assessment* 15, no. 4 (December 2007), pp. 412–27.

9. D. Bartram, "The Great Eight Competencies: A Criterion-Centric Approach to Validation," *Journal of Applied Psychology* 90, no. 6 (2005), pp. 1185–1203.

10. P. Tharenou, A.M. Saks, and C. Moore, "A Review and Critique of Research on Training and Organizational-Level Outcomes," *Human Resource Management Review* 17, no. 3 (2007), pp. 251–73; T.W.H. Ng and D.C. Feldman, "How Broadly Does Education Contribute to Job Performance?" *Personnel Psychology* 62, no. 1 (Spring 2009), pp. 89–134.

11. H. Cho, "Super Bowl of Retail Days," *Baltimore Sun,* November 23, 2006; A. Cheng, "Black Friday Kicks Off Retailers' Biggest Selling Season," *Dow Jones Business News,* November 24, 2007; J. Davis, "Training Helps Sales Staff Cope with Black Friday," *Rocky Mountain News (Denver),* November 20, 2007, p. B3; A.K. Walker, "Stores Looking Hard at Crowd Control for Post-Thanksgiving Rush," *Baltimore Sun,* November 26, 2009. This day is called Black Friday because in theory the typical retailer starts to make a profit (go in the black) around this time of year.

12. "Canadian Organizations Must Work Harder to Productively Engage Employees," news release, Watson Wyatt Canada (Toronto: January 25, 2005); BlessingWhite, *Employee Engagement Report 2011* (Princeton, NJ: BlessingWhite, January 2011).

13. J. Becker and L. Layton, "Safety Warnings Often Ignored at Metro," *Washington Post,* June 6, 2005, p. A01.

14. W.H. Cooper and M.J. Withey, "The Strong Situation Hypothesis," *Personality and Social Psychology Review* 13, no. 1 (February 2009), pp. 62–72; D.C. Funder, "Persons, Behaviors and Situations: An Agenda for Personality Psychology in the Postwar Era," *Journal of Research in Personality* 43, no. 2 (2009), pp. 120–26; R.D. Meyer, R.S. Dalal, and R. Hermida, "A Review and Synthesis of Situational Strength in the Organizational Sciences," *Journal of Management* 36, no. 1 (January 2010), pp. 121–40; R.A. Sherman, C.S. Nave, and D.C. Funder, "Situational Similarity and Personality Predict Behavioral Consistency," *Journal of Personality and Social Psychology* 99, no. 2 (2010), pp. 330–43.

15. K.F. Kane, "Special Issue: Situational Constraints and Work Performance," *Human Resource Management Review* 3 (Summer 1993), pp. 83–175; S.B. Bacharach and P. Bamberger, "Beyond Situational Constraints: Job Resources Inadequacy and Individual Performance at Work," *Human Resource Management Review* 5, no. 2 (1995), pp. 79–102; G. Johns, "Commentary: In Praise of Context," *Journal of Organizational Behavior* 22 (2001), pp. 31–42.

16. Meyer, Dalal, and Hermida, "A Review and Synthesis."

17. J.P. Campbell, "The Definition and Measurement of Performance in the New Age," in *The Changing Nature of Performance: Implications for Staffing, Motivation, and Development,* ed. D.R. Ilgen and E.D. Pulakos (San Francisco: Jossey-Bass, 1999), pp. 399–429; R.D. Hackett, "Understanding and Predicting Work Performance in the Canadian Military," *Canadian Journal of Behavioural Science* 34, no. 2 (2002), pp. 131–40.

18. O. Varela and R. Landis, "A General Structure of Job Performance: Evidence from Two Studies," *Journal of Business and Psychology* 25, no. 4 (2010), pp. 625–38.

19. D.W. Organ, "Organizational Citizenship Behavior: It's Construct Clean-Up Time," *Human Performance* 10 (1997), pp. 85–97; J.A. LePine, A. Erez, and D.E. Johnson, "The Nature and Dimensionality of Organizational Citizenship Behavior: A Critical Review and Meta-Analysis," *Journal of Applied Psychology* 87 (February 2002), pp. 52–65; R.S. Dalal, "A Meta-Analysis of the Relationship between Organizational Citizenship Behavior and Counterproductive Work Behavior," *Journal of Applied Psychology* 90, no. 6 (2005), pp. 1241–55.

20. K. Lee and N.J. Allen, "Organizational Citizenship Behavior and Workplace Deviance: The Role of Affect and Cognitions," *Journal of Applied Psychology* 87, no. 1 (2002), pp. 131–42.

21. S. Majumdar, "Meaningful Engagement," *Business Standard (India),* March 5, 2009, p. 8.

22. M. Rotundo and P. Sackett, "The Relative Importance of Task, Citizenship, and Counterproductive Performance to Global Ratings of Job Performance: A Policy-Capturing Approach," *Journal of Applied Psychology* 87 (February 2002), pp. 66–80; P.D. Dunlop and K. Lee, "Workplace Deviance, Organizational Citizenship Behaviour, and Business Unit Performance: The Bad Apples Do Spoil the Whole Barrel," *Journal of Organizational Behavior* 25 (2004), pp. 67–80; Dalal, "A Meta-Analysis"; N.A. Bowling and M.L. Gruys, "Overlooked Issues in the Conceptualization and Measurement of Counterproductive Work Behavior," *Human Resource Management Review* 20, no. 1 (2010), pp. 54–61.

23. P.I. Buerhaus, D.I. Auerbach, and D.O. Staiger, "The Recent Surge in Nurse Employment: Causes and Implications," *Health Affairs* 28, no. 4 (July 1, 2009), pp. w657–68; W. Dunham, "U.S. Healthcare System Pinched by Nursing Shortage," *Reuters (Washington, DC),* March 8, 2009; J. Skerritt, "Nursing Shortages Plague Reserves," *Winnipeg Free Press,* November 13, 2009, p. A4; S. Goodchild, "Babies Turned Away in Hospital Bed Crisis," *Evening Standard (London),* November 2, 2010.

24. N. Chaudhury et al., "Missing in Action: Teacher and Health Worker Absence in Developing Countries," *Journal of Economic Perspectives* 20, no. 1 (2006), pp. 91–116.

25. A. Furnham and M. Bramwell, "Personality Factors Predict Absenteeism in the Workplace," *Individual Differences Research* 4, no. 2 (2006), pp. 68–77.

26. D.A. Harrison and J.J. Martocchio, "Time for Absenteeism: A 20-Year Review of Origins, Offshoots, and Outcomes," *Journal of Management* 24 (Spring 1998), pp. 305–50; C.M. Mason and M.A. Griffin, "Group Absenteeism and Positive Affective Tone: A Longitudinal Study," *Journal of Organizational Behavior* 24 (2003), pp. 667–87; A. Vaananen et al., "Job Characteristics, Physical and Psychological Symptoms, and Social Support as Antecedents of Sickness Absence among Men and Women in the Private Industrial Sector," *Social Science & Medicine* 57, no. 5 (2003), pp. 807–24.

27. R. Lombardi, "Walking Wounded," *Canadian Occupational Safety,* November/December 2009, pp. 14–15; G. Johns, "Presenteeism in the Workplace: A Review and Research Agenda," *Journal of Organizational Behavior* 31, no. 4 (2010), pp. 519–42.

28. C. Crawshaw, "Personality Testing Can Be a Sticky Subject," *Edmonton Journal,* March 29, 2008, p. D14.

29. Personality researchers agree on one point about the definition of personality: It is difficult to pin down. A definition necessarily captures one perspective of the topic more than others, and the concept of personality is itself very broad. The definition presented here is based on C.S. Carver and M.F. Scheier, *Perspectives on Personality,* 6th ed. (Boston: Allyn & Bacon, 2007); D.C. Funder, *The Personality Puzzle,* 4th ed. (New York: W. W. Norton & Company, 2007).

30. D.P. McAdams and J.L. Pals, "A New Big Five: Fundamental Principles for an Integrative Science of Personality," *American Psychologist* 61, no. 3 (2006), pp. 204–17.

31. B. Reynolds and K. Karraker, "A Big Five Model of Disposition and Situation Interaction: Why a 'Helpful' Person May Not Always Behave Helpfully," *New Ideas in Psychology* 21 (April 2003), pp. 1–13; W. Mischel, "Toward an Integrative Science of the Person," *Annual Review of Psychology* 55 (2004), pp. 1–22.

32. B.W. Roberts and A. Caspi, "Personality Development and the Person-Situation Debate: It's Déjà Vu All Over Again," *Psychological Inquiry* 12, no. 2 (2001), pp. 104–109.

33. K.L. Jang, W.J. Livesley, and P.A. Vernon, "Heritability of the Big Five Personality Dimensions and Their Facets: A Twin Study," *Journal of Personality* 64, no. 3 (1996), pp. 577–91; N.L. Segal, *Entwined Lives: Twins and What They Tell Us about Human Behavior* (New York: Plume, 2000); T. Bouchard and J. Loehlin, "Genes, Evolution, and Personality," *Behavior Genetics* 31, no. 3 (May 2001), pp. 243–73; G. Lensvelt-Mulders and J. Hettema, "Analysis of Genetic Influences on the Consistency and Variability of the Big Five across Different Stressful Situations," *European Journal of Personality* 15, no. 5 (2001), pp. 355–71; P. Borkenau et al., "Genetic and Environmental Influences on Person X Situation Profiles," *Journal of Personality* 74, no. 5 (2006), pp. 1451–80.

34. Segal, *Entwined Lives,* pp. 116–18. For critiques of the genetics perspective of personality, see J. Joseph, "Separated Twins and the Genetics of Personality Differences: A Critique," *American Journal of Psychology* 114, no. 1 (Spring 2001), pp. 1–30; P. Ehrlich and M. W. Feldman, "Genes, Environments & Behaviors," *Daedalus* 136, no. 2 (Spring 2007), pp. 5–12.

35. B.W. Roberts and W.F. DelVecchio, "The Rank-Order Consistency of Personality Traits from Childhood to Old Age: A Quantitative Review of Longitudinal Studies," *Psychological Bulletin* 126, no. 1 (2000), pp. 3–25; A. Terracciano, P.T. Costa, and R.R. McCrae, "Personality Plasticity after Age 30," *Personality and Social Psychology Bulletin* 32, no. 8 (August 2006), pp. 999–1009.

36. M. Jurado and M. Rosselli, "The Elusive Nature of Executive Functions: A Review of Our Current Understanding," *Neuropsychology Review* 17, no. 3 (2007), pp. 213–33.

37. B.W. Roberts and E.M. Pomerantz, "On Traits, Situations, and Their Integration: A Developmental Perspective," *Personality & Social Psychology Review* 8, no. 4 (2004), pp. 402–16; W. Fleeson, "Situation-Based Contingencies Underlying Trait-Content Manifestation in Behavior," *Journal of Personality* 75, no. 4 (2007), pp. 825–62.

38. J.M. Digman, "Personality Structure: Emergence of the Five-Factor Model," *Annual Review of Psychology* 41 (1990), pp. 417–40; O.P. John and S. Srivastava, "The Big Five Trait Taxonomy: History, Measurement, and Theoretical Perspectives," in *Handbook of Personality: Theory and Research,* ed. L.A. Pervin and O.P. John (New York: Guildford Press, 1999), pp. 102–38; A. Caspi, B.W. Roberts, and R.L. Shiner, "Personality Development: Stability and Change," *Annual Review of Psychology* 56, no. 1 (2005), pp. 453–84; McAdams and Pals, "A New Big Five."

39. J. Hogan and B. Holland, "Using Theory to Evaluate Personality and Job-Performance Relations: A Socioanalytic Perspective," *Journal of Applied Psychology* 88, no. 1 (2003), pp. 100–12; D.S. Ones, C. Viswesvaran, and S. Dilchert, "Personality at Work: Raising Awareness and Correcting Misconceptions," *Human Performance* 18, no. 4 (2005), pp. 389–404; I.-S. Oh and C.M. Berry, "The Five-Factor Model of Personality and Managerial Performance: Validity Gains through the Use of 360 Degree Performance Ratings," *Journal of Applied Psychology* 94, no. 6 (2009), pp. 1498–513.

40. M.R. Barrick and M.K. Mount, "Yes, Personality Matters: Moving On to More Important Matters," *Human Performance* 18, no. 4 (2005), pp. 359–72; D. S. Ones et al., "In Support of Personality Assessment in Organizational Settings," *Personnel Psychology* 60, no. 4 (2007), pp. 995–1027; S.J. Perry et al., "$P = F$ (Conscientiousness $\times$ Ability): Examining the Facets of Conscientiousness," *Human Performance* 23, no. 4 (2010), pp. 343–60.

41. M.R. Barrick, M.K. Mount, and T.A. Judge, "Personality and Performance at the Beginning of the New Millennium: What Do We Know and Where Do We Go Next?" *International Journal of Selection and Assessment* 9, nos. 1 & 2 (2001), pp. 9–30; T. A. Judge and R. Ilies, "Relationship of Personality to Performance Motivation: A Meta-Analytic Review," *Journal of Applied Psychology* 87, no. 4 (2002), pp. 797–807; A. Witt, L.A. Burke, and M.R. Barrick, "The Interactive Effects of Conscientiousness and Agreeableness on Job Performance," *Journal of Applied Psychology* 87 (February 2002), pp. 164–69; J. Moutafi, A. Furnham, and J. Crump, "Is Managerial Level Related to Personality?" *British Journal of Management* 18, no. 3 (2007), pp. 272–80.

42. S. Vazire and S.D. Gosling, "E-Perceptions: Personality Impressions Based on Personal Websites," *Journal of Personality and Social Psychology* 87, no. 1 (2004), pp. 123–32; A.J. Gill, J. Oberlander, and E. Austin, "Rating E-Mail Personality at Zero Acquaintance," *Personality and Individual Differences* 40, no. 3 (2006), pp. 497–507; R.E. Guadagno, B.M. Okdie, and C.A. Eno, "Who Blogs? Personality Predictors of Blogging," *Computers in Human Behavior* 24, no. 5 (2008), pp. 1993–2004; D.H. Kluemper and P.A. Rosen, "Future Employment Selection Methods: Evaluating Social Networking Web Sites," *Journal of Managerial Psychology* 24, no. 6 (2009), pp. 567–80; C. Ross et al., "Personality and Motivations Associated with Facebook Use," *Computers in Human Behavior* 25, no. 2 (2009), pp. 578–86; M.D. Back et al., "Facebook Profiles Reflect Actual Personality, Not Self-Idealization," *Psychological Science,* January 2010; T. Yarkoni, "Personality in 100,000 Words: A Large-Scale Analysis of Personality and Word Use among Bloggers," *Journal of Research in Personality* 44, no. 3 (2010), pp. 363–73.

43. R. Ilies, M.W. Gerhardt, and H. Le, "Individual Differences in Leadership Emergence: Integrating Meta-Analytic Findings and Behavioral Genetics Estimates," *International Journal of Selection and Assessment* 12, no. 3 (September 2004), pp. 207–19; Oh and Berry, "The Five-Factor Model."

44. K.M. DeNeve and H. Cooper, "The Happy Personality: A Meta-Analysis of 137 Personality Traits and Subjective Well-Being," *Psychological Bulletin* 124 (September 1998), pp. 197–229; M.L. Kern and H.S. Friedman, "Do Conscientious Individuals Live Longer? A Quantitative Review," *Health Psychology* 27, no. 5 (2008), pp. 505–512; P.S. Fry and D.L. Debats, "Perfectionism and the Five-Factor Personality Traits as Predictors of Mortality in Older Adults," *Journal of Health Psychology* 14, no. 4 (May 1, 2009), pp. 513–24; F.C.M. Geisler, M. Wiedig-Allison, and H. Weber, "What Coping Tells about Personality," *European Journal of Personality* 23, no. 4 (2009), pp. 289–306; H.S. Friedman, M.L. Kern, and C.A. Reynolds, "Personality and Health, Subjective Well-Being, and Longevity," *Journal of Personality* 78, no. 1 (2010), pp. 179–216.

45. C.G. Jung, *Psychological Types,* trans. H.G. Baynes (Princeton, NJ: Princeton University Press, 1971); I.B. Myers, *The Myers-Briggs Type Indicator* (Palo Alto, CA: Consulting Psychologists Press, 1987).

46. Adapted from an exhibit found at http://www.16-personality-types.com.

47. M. Gladwell, "Personality Plus," *The New Yorker,* September 20, 2004, pp. 42–48; R.B. Kennedy and D.A. Kennedy, "Using the Myers-Briggs Type Indicator in Career Counseling," *Journal of Employment Counseling* 41, no. 1 (March 2004), pp. 38–44.

48. R.M. Capraro and M.M. Capraro, "Myers-Briggs Type Indicator Score Reliability across Studies: A Meta-Analytic Reliability Generalization Study," *Educational and Psychological Measurement* 62 (August 2002), pp. 590–602; J. Michael, "Using the Myers-Briggs Type Indicator as a Tool for Leadership Development? Apply with Caution," *Journal of Leadership & Organizational Studies* 10 (Summer 2003), pp. 68–81; Moutafi, Furnham, and Crump, "Is Managerial Level Related to Personality?"; F.W. Brown and M.D. Reilly, "The Myers-Briggs Type Indicator and Transformational Leadership," *Journal of Management Development* 28, no. 10 (2009), pp. 916–32; B.S. Kuipers et al., "The Influence of Myers-Briggs Type Indicator Profiles on Team Development Processes," *Small Group Research* 40, no. 4 (August 2009), pp. 436–64.

49. R.R. McCrae and P.T. Costa, "Reinterpreting the Myers-Briggs Type Indicator from the Perspective of the Five-Factor Model of Personality," *Journal of Personality* 57 (1989), pp. 17–40; A. Furnham, "The Big Five versus the Big Four: The Relationship between the Myers-Briggs Type Indicator (MBTI) and NEO-PI Five Factor Model of Personality," *Personality and Individual Differences* 21, no. 2 (1996), pp. 303–07.

50. K.M. Butler, "Using Positive Four-Letter Words," *Employee Benefit News,* April 2007; M. Weinstein, "Personality Assessment Soars at Southwest," *Training,* January 3, 2008.

51. "Metrolink Train Crews in Southern California Threaten Boycott over New Personality Tests," *Associated Press,* April 1, 2010; R.J. Lopez, D. Weikel, and R. Connell, "NTSB Blames Engineer for 2008 Metrolink Crash," *Los Angeles Times,* January 22, 2010.

52. R. Hogan, "In Defense of Personality Measurement: New Wine for Old Whiners," *Human Performance* 18, no. 4 (2005), pp. 331–41; K. Murphy and J.L. Dziewczynski, "Why Don't Measures of Broad Dimensions of Personality Perform Better as Predictors of Job Performance?" *Human Performance* 18, no. 4 (2005), pp. 343–57; F.P. Morgeson et al., "Reconsidering the Use of Personality Tests in Personnel Selection Contexts," *Personnel Psychology* 60, no. 3 (2007), pp. 683–729; R.P. Tett and C.N.D., "Personality Tests at the Crossroads: A Response to Morgeson, Campion, Dipboye, Hollenbeck, Murphy, and Schmitt (2007)," *Personnel Psychology* 60, no. 4 (2007), pp. 967–93.

53. D.L. Whetzel et al., "Linearity of Personality–Performance Relationships: A Large-Scale Examination," *International Journal of Selection and Assessment* 18, no. 3 (2010), pp. 310–20; H. Le et al., "Too Much of a Good Thing: Curvilinear Relationships between Personality Traits and Job Performance," *Journal of Applied Psychology* 96, no. 1 (2011), pp. 113–33.

54. L.A. Witt, M.C. Andrews, and D.S. Carlson, "When Conscientiousness Isn't Enough: Emotional Exhaustion and Performance among Call Center Customer Service Representatives," *Journal of Management* 30, no. 1 (2004), pp. 149–60; J. Stoeber, K. Otto, and C. Dalbert, "Perfectionism and the Big Five: Conscientiousness Predicts Longitudinal Increases in Self-Oriented Perfectionism," *Personality and Individual Differences* 47, no. 4 (2009), pp. 363–68; C.J. Boyce, A.M. Wood, and G.D.A. Brown, "The Dark Side of Conscientiousness: Conscientious People Experience Greater Drops in Life Satisfaction Following Unemployment," *Journal of Research in Personality* 44, no. 4 (2010), pp. 535–39.

55. S.D. Risavy and P.A. Hausdorf, "Personality Testing in Personnel Selection: Adverse Impact and Differential Hiring Rates," *International Journal of Selection and Assessment* 19, no. 1 (2011), pp. 18–30.

56. N.S. Hartman and W.L. Grubb, "Deliberate Faking on Personality and Emotional Intelligence Measures," *Psychological Reports* 108, no. 1 (2011), pp. 120–38.

57. B.S. Connelly and D.S. Ones, "An Other Perspective on Personality: Meta-Analytic Integration of Observers' Accuracy and Predictive Validity," *Psychological Bulletin* 136, no. 6 (2010), pp. 1092–122.

58. V. Baker, "Why Men Can't Manage Women," *The Guardian,* April 14, 2007, p. 1.

59. K.C. Neel, "Abdoulah Sets Wow Apart," *Multichannel News,* January 29, 2007, p. 2; D. Graham, "She Walks the Talk," *Denver Woman,* April 2009; "Wow! Management Team," (2010), http://www.wowway.com/internet-cable-phone-company/wow-management-executive-bios/.

60. B.M. Meglino and E.C. Ravlin, "Individual Values in Organizations: Concepts, Controversies, and Research," *Journal of Management* 24, no. 3 (1998), pp. 351–89; B.R. Agle and C.B. Caldwell, "Understanding Research on Values in Business," *Business and Society* 38, no. 3 (September 1999), pp. 326–87; S. Hitlin and J.A. Pilavin, "Values: Reviving a Dormant Concept," *Annual Review of Sociology* 30 (2004), pp. 359–93.

61. D. Lubinski, D.B. Schmidt, and C.P. Benbow, "A 20-Year Stability Analysis of the Study of Values for Intellectually Gifted Individuals from Adolescence to Adulthood," *Journal of Applied Psychology* 81 (1996), pp. 443–51.

62. L. Parks and R.P. Guay, "Personality, Values, and Motivation," *Personality and Individual Differences* 47, no. 7 (2009), pp. 675–84.

63. Hitlin and Pilavin, "Values: Reviving a Dormant Concept"; A. Pakizeh, J.E. Gebauer, and G.R. Maio, "Basic Human Values: Inter-Value Structure in Memory," *Journal of Experimental Social Psychology* 43, no. 3 (2007), pp. 458–65.

64. S.H. Schwartz, "Universals in the Content and Structure of Values: Theoretical Advances and Empirical Tests in 20 Countries," *Advances in Experimental Social Psychology* 25 (1992), pp. 1–65; S.H. Schwartz, "Are There Universal Aspects in the Structure and Contents of Human Values?" *Journal of Social Issues* 50 (1994), pp. 19–45; D. Spini, "Measurement Equivalence of 10 Value Types from the Schwartz Value Survey across 21 Countries," *Journal of Cross-Cultural Psychology* 34, no. 1 (January 2003), pp. 3–23; S.H. Schwartz and K. Boehnke, "Evaluating the Structure of Human Values with Confirmatory Factor Analysis," *Journal of Research in Personality* 38, no. 3 (2004), pp. 230–55.

65. G.R. Maio and J.M. Olson, "Values as Truisms: Evidence and Implications," *Journal of Personality and Social Psychology* 74, no. 2 (1998), pp. 294–311; G.R. Maio et al., "Addressing Discrepancies between Values and Behavior: The Motivating Effect of Reasons," *Journal of Experimental Social Psychology* 37, no. 2 (2001), pp. 104–17; B. Verplanken and R.W. Holland, "Motivated Decision Making: Effects of Activation and Self-Centrality of Values on Choices and

Behavior," *Journal of Personality and Social Psychology* 82, no. 3 (2002), pp. 434–47; A. Bardi and S.H. Schwartz, "Values and Behavior: Strength and Structure of Relations," *Personality and Social Psychology Bulletin* 29, no. 10 (October 2003), pp. 1207–20; M.M. Bernard and G.R. Maio, "Effects of Introspection about Reasons for Values: Extending Research on Values-as-Truisms," *Social Cognition* 21, no. 1 (2003), pp. 1–25.

66. N. Mazar, O. Amir, and D. Ariely, "The Dishonesty of Honest People: A Theory of Self-Concept Maintenance," *Journal of Marketing Research* 45 (December 2008), pp. 633–44.

67. A.L. Kristof, "Person-Organization Fit: An Integrative Review of Its Conceptualizations, Measurement, and Implications," *Personnel Psychology* 49, no. 1 (Spring 1996), pp. 1–49; M.L. Verquer, T.A. Beehr, and S.H. Wagner, "A Meta-Analysis of Relations between Person-Organization Fit and Work Attitudes," *Journal of Vocational Behavior* 63 (2003), pp. 473–89; J.W. Westerman and L.A. Cyr, "An Integrative Analysis of Person-Organization Fit Theories," *International Journal of Selection and Assessment* 12, no. 3 (September 2004), pp. 252–61; D. Bouckenooghe et al., "The Prediction of Stress by Values and Value Conflict," *Journal of Psychology* 139, no. 4 (2005), pp. 369–82.

68. K. Hornyak, "Upward Move: Cynthia Schwalm," *Medical Marketing & Media*, June 2008, p. 69. For research on the consequences on values congruence, see Kristof, "Person-Organization Fit"; Verquer, Beehr, and Wagner, "A Meta-Analysis of Relations"; Westerman and Cyr, "An Integrative Analysis of Person-Organization Fit Theories"; Bouckenooghe et al., "The Prediction of Stress by Values and Value Conflict."

69. H. Oliviero, "Chicken Chain Attracts Relatives," *Atlanta Journal-Constitution*, May 15, 2011, p. D1.

70. T. Simons, "Behavioral Integrity: The Perceived Alignment between Managers' Words and Deeds as a Research Focus," *Organization Science* 13, no. 1 (January-February 2002), pp. 18–35; Watson Wyatt, "Employee Ratings of Senior Management Dip, Watson Wyatt Survey Finds," news release, January 4, 2007.

71. Z. Aycan, R.N. Kanungo, and J.B.P. Sinha, "Organizational Culture and Human Resource Management Practices: The Model of Culture Fit," *Journal of Cross-Cultural Psychology* 30 (July 1999), pp. 501–26; M. Naor, K. Linderman, and R. Schroeder, "The Globalization of Operations in Eastern and Western Countries: Unpacking the Relationship between National and Organizational Culture and Its Impact on Manufacturing Performance," *Journal of Operations Management* 28, no. 3 (2010), pp. 194–205. This type of values incongruence can occur even when the company is founded in that country, that is, when a local company tries to introduce a culture incompatible with the national culture. See for example A. Danisman, "Good Intentions and Failed Implementations: Understanding Culture-Based Resistance to Organizational Change," *European Journal of Work and Organizational Psychology* 19, no. 2 (2010), pp. 200–220.

72. C. Savoye, "Workers Say Honesty Is Best Company Policy," *Christian Science Monitor*, June 15, 2000; J.M. Kouzes and B.Z. Posner, *The Leadership Challenge*, 3d ed. (San Francisco: Jossey-Bass, 2002); J. Schettler, "Leadership in Corporate America," *Training & Development*, September 2002, pp. 66–73; Ekos Politics, *Women See It Differently* (Ottawa: Ekos Politics, 2010).

73. Ethics Resource Center, *The 2009 National Business Ethics Survey: Ethics in the Recession* (Arlington, VA: Ethics Resource Center, 2009).

74. Transparency International, *Transparency International Corruption Perceptions Index 2010* (Berlin, Germany: Transparency International, 2010).

75. P.L. Schumann, "A Moral Principles Framework for Human Resource Management Ethics," *Human Resource Management Review* 11 (Spring-Summer 2001), pp. 93–111; J. Boss, *Analyzing Moral Issues,* 3d ed. (New York: McGraw-Hill, 2005), Ch. 1; M.G. Velasquez, *Business Ethics: Concepts and Cases,* 6th ed. (Upper Saddle River, NJ: Prentice-Hall, 2006), Ch. 2.

76. For a recent analysis of these predictors of ethical conduct, see J.J. Kish-Gephart, D.A. Harrison, and L.K. Treviño, "Bad Apples, Bad Cases, and Bad Barrels: Meta-Analytic Evidence about Sources of Unethical Decisions at Work," *Journal of Applied Psychology* 95, no. 1 (2010), pp. 1–31.

77. T.J. Jones, "Ethical Decision Making by Individuals in Organizations: An Issue Contingent Model," *Academy of Management Review* 16 (1991), pp. 366–95; B.H. Frey, "The Impact of Moral Intensity on Decision Making in a Business Context," *Journal of Business Ethics* 26 (August 2000), pp. 181–95; D.R. May and K.P. Pauli, "The Role of Moral Intensity in Ethical Decision Making," *Business and Society* 41 (March 2002), pp. 84–117.

78. J.R. Sparks and S.D. Hunt, "Marketing Researcher Ethical Sensitivity: Conceptualization, Measurement, and Exploratory Investigation," *Journal of Marketing* 62 (April 1998), pp. 92–109.

79. K.F. Alam, "Business Ethics in New Zealand Organizations: Views from the Middle and Lower Level Managers," *Journal of Business Ethics* 22 (November 1999), pp. 145–53; Human Resource Institute, *The Ethical Enterprise: State-of-the-Art* (St. Petersburg, FL: Human Resource Institute, 2006).

80. S.J. Reynolds, K. Leavitt, and K.A. DeCelles, "Automatic Ethics: The Effects of Implicit Assumptions and Contextual Cues on Moral Behavior," *Journal of Applied Psychology* 95, no. 4 (2010), pp. 752–60.

81. D.R. Beresford, N.D. Katzenbach, and C.B. Rogers Jr., *Report of Investigation by the Special Investigative Committee of the Board of Directors of Worldcom, Inc.,* March 31, 2003.

82. H. Donker, D. Poff, and S. Zahir, "Corporate Values, Codes of Ethics, and Firm Performance: A Look at the Canadian Context," *Journal of Business Ethics* 82, no. 3 (2008), pp. 527–37; L. Preuss, "Codes of Conduct in Organisational Context: From Cascade to Lattice-Work of Codes," *Journal of Business Ethics* 94, no. 4 (2010), pp. 471–87.

83. B. Farrell, D.M. Cobbin, and H.M. Farrell, "Codes of Ethics: Their Evolution, Development and Other Controversies," *Journal of Management Development* 21, no. 2 (2002), pp. 152–63; G. Wood and M. Rimmer, "Codes of Ethics: What Are They Really and What Should They Be?" *International Journal of Value-Based Management* 16, no. 2 (2003), p. 181.

84. S. Greengard, "Golden Values," *Workforce Management,* March 2005, pp. 52–53; K. Tyler, "Do the Right Thing," *HRMagazine,* February 2005, pp. 99–102.

85. Texas Instruments, *2009 Corporate Citizenship Report,* 2009, 2010; "Texas Instruments among 2011 'World's Most Ethical Companies,'" *Politics & Government Week,* March 31, 2011, p. 66; Texas Instruments, *The Values and Ethics of TI,* February 18, 2011.

86. G. Svensson et al., "Ethical Structures and Processes of Corporations Operating in Australia, Canada, and Sweden: A Longitudinal and Cross-Cultural Study," *Journal of Business Ethics* 86, no. 4 (2009), pp. 485–506.

87. E. Aronson, "Integrating Leadership Styles and Ethical Perspectives," *Canadian Journal of Administrative Sciences* 18 (December 2001), pp. 266–76; D.R. May et al., "Developing the Moral Component of Authentic Leadership," *Organizational Dynamics* 32 (2003), pp. 247–60. The Vodafone director quotation is from R. Van Lee, L. Fabish, and N. McGaw, "The Value of Corporate Values," *strategy+business*, no. 39 (Summer 2005), pp. 1–13.

88. V. Galt, "A World of Opportunity for Those in Mid-Career," *Globe & Mail,* June 7, 2006, p. C1.

89. L. Gettler, "The New Global Manager Needs to Understand Different Work Cultures," *The Age,* February 6, 2008.

90. Individualism and collectivism information are from the meta-analysis by D. Oyserman, H.M. Coon, and M. Kemmelmeier, "Rethinking Individualism and Collectivism: Evaluation of Theoretical Assumptions and Meta-Analyses," *Psychological Bulletin* 128 (2002), pp. 3–72, not earlier findings by Hofstede. Consistent with Oyserman et al., a recent study found high rather than low individualism among Chileans. See A. Kolstad and S. Horpestad, "Self-Construal in Chile and Norway," *Journal of Cross-Cultural Psychology* 40, no. 2 (March 2009), pp. 275–81.

91. C.P. Earley and C.B. Gibson, "Taking Stock in Our Progress on Individualism-Collectivism: 100 Years of Solidarity and Community," *Journal of Management* 24 (May 1998), pp. 265–304; F.S. Niles, "Individualism-Collectivism Revisited," *Cross-Cultural Research* 32 (November 1998), pp. 315–41; C.L. Jackson et al., "Psychological Collectivism: A Measurement Validation and Linkage to Group Member Performance," *Journal of Applied Psychology* 91, no. 4 (2006), pp. 884–99.

92. Oyserman, Coon, and Kemmelmeier, "Rethinking Individualism and Collectivism"; also see F. Li and L. Aksoy, "Dimensionality of Individualism–Collectivism and Measurement Equivalence of Triandis and Gelfand's Scale," *Journal of Business and Psychology* 21, no. 3 (2007), pp. 313–29. The relationship between individualism and collectivism is still being debated, but most experts now agree that individualism and collectivism have serious problems in their conceptualization and measurement.

93. M. Voronov and J.A. Singer, "The Myth of Individualism–Collectivism: A Critical Review," *Journal of Social Psychology* 142 (August 2002), pp. 461–80; Y. Takano and S. Sogon, "Are Japanese More Collectivistic than Americans?" *Journal of Cross-Cultural Psychology* 39, no. 3 (May 1, 2008), pp. 237–50; D. Dalsky, "Individuality in Japan and the United States: A Cross-Cultural Priming Experiment," *International Journal of Intercultural Relations* 34, no. 5 (2010), pp. 429–35.

94. G. Hofstede, *Culture's Consequences: Comparing Values, Behaviors, Institutions, and Organizations across Nations,* 2d ed. (Thousand Oaks, CA: Sage, 2001).

95. S. Klie, "Program Breaks Cultural Barriers," *Canadian HR Reporter,* September 10, 2007.

96. Hofstede, *Culture's Consequences*. Hofstede used the terms *masculinity* and *femininity* to refer to *achievement* and *nurturing orientation,* respectively. We (along with other writers) have adopted the latter two terms to minimize the sexist perspective of these concepts. Also, readers need to be aware that achievement orientation is assumed to be the opposite of nurturing orientation, though this opposing relationship might be questioned.

97. V. Taras, J. Rowney, and P. Steel, "Half a Century of Measuring Culture: Review of Approaches, Challenges, and Limitations Based on the Analysis of 121 Instruments for Quantifying Culture," *Journal of International Management* 15, no. 4 (2009), pp. 357–73.

98. R.L. Tung and A. Verbeke, "Beyond Hofstede and GLOBE: Improving the Quality of Cross-Cultural Research," *Journal of International Business Studies* 41, no. 8 (2010), pp. 1259–74.

99. W.K.W. Choy, A.B.E. Lee, and P. Ramburuth, "Multinationalism in the Workplace: A Myriad of Values in a Singaporean Firm," *Singapore Management Review* 31, no. 1 (January 2009).

100. N. Jacob, "Cross-Cultural Investigations: Emerging Concepts," *Journal of Organizational Change Management* 18, no. 5 (2005), pp. 514–28; V. Taras, B.L. Kirkman, and P. Steel, "Examining the Impact of Culture's Consequences: A Three-Decade, Multilevel, Meta-Analytic Review of Hofstede's Cultural Value Dimensions," *Journal of Applied Psychology* 95, no. 3 (2010), pp. 405–39.

101. M. Adams, "New Canadians, Old Values?" *Globe & Mail,* March 2, 2005, p. A17.

102. Oyserman, Coon, and Kemmelmeier, "Rethinking Individualism and Collectivism."

103. V.C. Plaut, H. Rose Markus, and M.E. Lachman, "Place Matters: Consensual Features and Regional Variation in American Well-Being and Self," *Journal of Personality and Social Psychology* 83, no. 1 (2002), pp. 160–84; S. Kitayama et al., "Ethos of Independence across Regions in the United States: The Production-Adoption Model of Cultural Change," *American Psychologist* 65, no. 6 (2010), pp. 559–74; J. Lieske, "The Changing Regional Subcultures of the American States and the Utility of a New Cultural Measure," *Political Research Quarterly* 63, no. 3 (September 2010), pp. 538–52; P.J. Rentfrow, "Statewide Differences in Personality: Toward a Psychological Geography of the United States," *American Psychologist* 65, no. 6 (2010), pp. 548–58.

104. D.S. Berry, G.M. Jones, and S.A. Kuczaj, "Differing States of Mind: Regional Affiliation, Personality Judgment, and Self-View," *Basic and Applied Social Psychology* 22, no. 1 (2000), pp. 43–56; K.H. Rogers and D. Wood, "Accuracy of United States Regional Personality Stereotypes," *Journal of Research in Personality* 44, no. 6 (2010), pp. 704–13.

105. J.A. Vandello and D. Cohen, "Patterns of Individualism and Collectivism across the United States," *Journal of Personality and Social Psychology* 77, no. 2 (1999), pp. 279–92.

106. Lieske, "The Changing Regional Subcultures of the American States and the Utility of a New Cultural Measure"; Rentfrow, "Statewide Differences in Personality."

CHAPTER 3

1. E. Barajas, "New Discrimination Claims from Firefighters," *KTRK-TV (Texas)*, July 29, 2009; C. Kittle, "Camp Teaches Girls Firefighting," *The Telegraph (Nashua, New Hampshire)*, August 15, 2010; K. Morgan, "Camp Houston Fire," *Houston Chronicle*, March 7, 2010, p. 1; T. Langford, "EEOC: Draycott Subjected to 'Hostile Work Environment,'" *Houston Chronicle*, January 17, 2011. Firefighter statistics are reported by the U.S. Census Bureau, *Table 615. Employed Civilians by Occupation, Sex, Race, and Hispanic Origin: 2009*, Statistical Abstract of the United States (Washington, DC: U.S. Census Bureau, 2011).

2. "Kate's Just One of a Growing Number of Female Firefighters," *Express & Echo (Exeter, UK)*, April 28, 2008, p. 24; C. Foran, "It's Not Just a Man's Job," *Odessa American (Texas)*, March 13, 2008.

3. J.D. Campbell, S. Assanand, and A. Di Paula, "The Structure of the Self-Concept and Its Relation to Psychological Adjustment," *Journal of Personality* 71, no. 1 (2003), pp. 115–40; M.J. Constantino et al., "The Direct and Stress-Buffering Effects of Self-Organization on Psychological Adjustment," *Journal of Social & Clinical Psychology* 25, no. 3 (2006), pp. 333–60.

4. E.J. Koch and J.A. Shepperd, "Is Self-Complexity Linked to Better Coping? A Review of the Literature," *Journal of Personality* 72, no. 4 (2004), pp. 727–60; A.R. McConnell, R.J. Rydell, and C.M. Brown, "On the Experience of Self-Relevant Feedback: How Self-Concept Organization Influences Affective Responses and Self-Evaluations," *Journal of Experimental Social Psychology* 45, no. 4 (2009), pp. 695–707.

5. J. Lodi-Smith and B.W. Roberts, "Getting to Know Me: Social Role Experiences and Age Differences in Self-Concept Clarity during Adulthood," *Journal of Personality* 78, no. 5 (2010), pp. 1383–410.

6. Koch and Shepperd, "Is Self-Complexity Linked to Better Coping?"; A.R. McConnell et al., "The Simple Life: On the Benefits of Low Self-Complexity," *Personality and Social Psychology Bulletin* 35, no. 7 (July 2009), pp. 823–35. On the process of self-concept repair, see S. Chen and H.C. Boucher, "Relational Selves as Self-Affirmational Resources," *Journal of Research in Personality* 42, no. 3 (2008), pp. 716–33.

7. A.T. Brook, J. Garcia, and M.A. Fleming, "The Effects of Multiple Identities on Psychological Well-Being," *Personality and Social Psychology Bulletin* 34, no. 12 (December 2008), pp. 1588–600.

8. J.D. Campbell, "Self-Esteem and Clarity of the Self-Concept," *Journal of Personality and Social Psychology* 59, no. 3 (1990).

9. T.W.H. Ng, K.L. Sorensen, and D.C. Feldman, "Dimensions, Ante-cedents, and Consequences of Workaholism: A Conceptual Integra-tion and Extension," *Journal of Organizational Behavior* 28 (2007), pp. 111–36; S. Pachulicz, N. Schmitt, and G. Kuljanin, "A Model of Career Success: A Longitudinal Study of Emergency Physicians," *Journal of Vocational Behavior* 73, no. 2 (2008), pp. 242–53.

10. B. George, *Authentic Leadership* (San Francisco: Jossey-Bass, 2004); S.T. Hannah and B.J. Avolio, "Ready or Not: How Do We Accelerate the Developmental Readiness of Leaders?" *Journal of Organizational Behavior* 31, no. 8 (2010), pp. 1181–87.

11. C. Sedikides and A.P. Gregg, "Portraits of the Self," in *The Sage Handbook of Social Psychology*, ed. M.A. Hogg and J. Cooper (London: Sage Publications, 2003), pp. 110–38; M.D. Alicke and C. Sedikides, "Self-Enhancement and Self-Protection: What They Are and What They Do," *European Review of Social Psychology* 20 (2009), pp. 1–48; C.L. Guenther and M.D. Alicke, "Deconstructing the Better-Than-Average Effect," *Journal of Personality and Social Psychology* 99, no. 5 (2010), pp. 755–70; S. Loughnan et al., "Univer-sal Biases in Self-Perception: Better and More Human Than Average," *British Journal of Social Psychology* 49 (2010), pp. 627–36.

12. K.P. Cross, "Not Can, but *Will* College Teaching Be Improved?" *New Directions for Higher Education* 17 (Spring 1977), pp. 1–15; U.S. Merit Systems Protection Board, *Accomplishing Our Mission: Results of the 2005 Merit Principles Survey* (Washington, DC: U.S. Merit Systems Protection Board, December 6, 2007).

13. D.A. Moore, "Not So Above Average after All: When People Believe They Are Worse Than Average and Its Implications for Theories of Bias in Social Comparison," *Organizational Behavior and Human Decision Processes* 102, no. 1 (2007), pp. 42–58.

14. M.S. Horswill, A.E. Waylen, and M.I. Tofield, "Drivers' Ratings of Different Components of Their Own Driving Skill: A Greater Illu-sion of Superiority for Skills That Relate to Accident Involvement," *Journal of Applied Social Psychology* 34, no. 1 (2004), pp. 177–95; N.J. Hiller and D.C. Hambrick, "Conceptualizing Executive Hubris: The Role of (Hyper-)Core Self-Evaluations in Strategic Decision-Making," *Strategic Management Journal* 26, no. 4 (2005), pp. 297–319; U. Malmendier and G. Tate, "CEO Overconfidence and Corporate Investment," *Journal of Finance* 60, no. 6 (2005), pp. 2661–700; J.A. Doukas and D. Petmezas, "Acquisitions, Overconfident Managers and Self-Attribution Bias," *European Financial Management* 13, no. 3 (2007), pp. 531–77; N. Harrè and C.G. Sibley, "Explicit and Implicit Self-Enhancement Biases in Drivers and Their Relationship to Driv-ing Violations and Crash-Risk Optimism," *Accident Analysis & Pre-vention* 39, no. 6 (2007), pp. 1155–61; D.A. Moore and P.J. Healy, "The Trouble with Overconfidence," *Psychological Review* 115, no. 2 (2008), pp. 502–17.

15. A. Finch, "High Climber," *Indianapolis Business Journal* 2011, p. A3.

16. W.B. Swann Jr., "To Be Adored or to Be Known? The Interplay of Self-Enhancement and Self-Verification," in *Foundations of Social Behavior*, ed. R.M. Sorrentino and E.T. Higgins (New York: Guildford, 1990), pp. 408–48; W.B. Swann Jr., P.J. Rentfrow, and J.S. Guinn, "Self-Verification: The Search for Coherence," in *Handbook of Self and Identity*, ed. M.R. Leary and J. Tagney (New York: Guildford, 2002), pp. 367–83.

17. F. Anseel and F. Lievens, "Certainty as a Moderator of Feedback Reactions? A Test of the Strength of the Self-Verification Motive," *Journal of Occupational & Organizational Psychology* 79, no. 4 (2006), pp. 533–51; T. Kwang and W.B. Swann, "Do People Embrace Praise Even When They Feel Unworthy? A Review of Critical Tests of Self-Enhancement versus Self-Verification," *Personality and Social Psychology Review* 14, no. 3 (August 2010), pp. 263–80.

18. M.R. Leary, "Motivational and Emotional Aspects of the Self," *Annual Review of Psychology* 58, no. 1 (2007), pp. 317–44.

19. T.A. Judge and J.E. Bono, "Relationship of Core Self-Evaluations Traits—Self-Esteem, Generalized Self-Efficacy, Locus of Control, and Emotional Stability—with Job Satisfaction and Job Performance: A Meta-Analysis," *Journal of Applied Psychology* 86, no. 1 (2001), pp. 80–92; T.A. Judge and C. Hurst, "Capitalizing on One's Advan-tages: Role of Core Self-Evaluations," *Journal of Applied Psychology* 92, no. 5 (2007), pp. 1212–27. We have described the three most commonly noted components of self-evaluation. The full model also includes emotional stability (low neuroticism). However, the core self-evaluation model has received limited research, and its dimensions are being debated. For example, see T.W. Self, "Evaluat-ing Core Self-Evaluations: Application of a Multidimensional, Latent-Construct, Evaluative Framework to Core Self-Evaluations Research," doctoral dissertation, University of Houston, 2007; R.E. Johnson, C.C. Rosen, and P.E. Levy, "Getting to the Core of Core Self-Evaluation: A Review and Recommendations," *Journal of Organizational Behavior* 29 (2008), pp. 391–413.

20. R.F. Baumeister and J.M. Twenge, The Social Self, *Handbook of Psychology* (New York: John Wiley & Sons, 2003); W.B. Swann Jr., C. Chang-Schneider, and K.L. McClarty, "Do People's Self-Views Matter? Self-Concept and Self-Esteem in Everyday Life," *American Psychologist* 62, no. 2 (2007), pp. 84–94.

21. A. Bandura, *Self-Efficacy: The Exercise of Control* (New York: W.H. Freeman, 1997). However, one recent review found that self-efficacy's effect on task and job performance is much lower in the presence of the effects of personality traits on performance. See T.A. Judge et al., "Self-Efficacy and Work-Related Performance: The Integral Role of Individual Differences," *Journal of Applied Psychol-ogy* 92, no. 1 (2007), pp. 107–27.

22. G. Chen, S.M. Gully, and D. Eden, "Validation of a New General Self-Efficacy Scale," *Organizational Research Methods* 4, no. 1 (January 2001), pp. 62–83.

23. J.B. Rotter, "Generalized Expectancies for Internal versus External Control of Reinforcement," *Psychological Monographs* 80, no. 1 (1966), pp. 1–7.

24. P.E. Spector, "Behavior in Organizations as a Function of Employee's Locus of Control," *Psychological Bulletin* 91 (1982), pp. 482–97; K. Hattrup, M.S. O'Connell, and J.R. Labrador, "Incremental Validity of Locus of Control after Controlling for Cognitive Ability and Con-scientiousness," *Journal of Business and Psychology* 19, no. 4 (2005), pp. 461–81; T.W.H. Ng, K.L. Sorensen, and L.T. Eby, "Locus of Con-trol at Work: A Meta-Analysis," *Journal of Organizational Behavior* 27 (2006), pp. 1057–87; Kwang and Swann, "Do People Embrace Praise Even When They Feel Unworthy?"

25. J.M. Twenge, L. Zhang, and C. Im, "It's Beyond My Control: A Cross-Temporal Meta-Analysis of Increasing Externality in Locus of Con-trol, 1960–2002," *Personality and Social Psychology Review* 8, no. 3 (August 2004), pp. 308–19.

26. H. Tajfel, *Social Identity and Intergroup Relations* (Cambridge: Cambridge University Press, 1982); B.E. Ashforth and F. Mael, "Social Identity Theory and the Organization," *Academy of Management Re-view* 14 (1989), pp. 20–39; M.A. Hogg and D.J. Terry, "Social Identity and Self-Categorization Processes in Organizational Contexts," *Academy of Management Review* 25 (January 2000), pp. 121–40; L.L. Gaertner et al., "The 'I,' the 'We,' and the 'When': A Meta-Analysis of Motivational Primacy in Self-Definition," *Journal of Personality and Social Psychology* 83, no. 3 (2002), p. 574; S.A. Haslam, R.A. Eggins, and K.J. Reynolds, "The Aspire Model: Actualizing Social and Per-sonal Identity Resources to Enhance Organizational Outcomes," *Journal of Occupational and Organizational Psychology* 76 (2003), pp. 83–113.

27. Sedikides and Gregg, "Portraits of the Self." The history of the social self in human beings is described in M.R. Leary and N.R. Butter-more, "The Evolution of the Human Self: Tracing the Natural His-tory of Self-Awareness," *Journal for the Theory of Social Behaviour* 33, no. 4 (2003), pp. 365–404.

28. M.R. Edwards, "Organizational Identification: A Conceptual and Operational Review," *International Journal of Management Reviews* 7, no. 4 (2005), pp. 207–30; D.A. Whetten, "Albert and Whetten Revisited: Strengthening the Concept of Organizational Identity," *Journal of Management Inquiry* 15, no. 3 (September 2006), pp. 219–34.

29. M.B. Brewer, "The Social Self: On Being the Same and Different at the Same Time," *Personality and Social Psychology Bulletin* 17, no. 5 (October 1991), pp. 475–82; R. Imhoff and H.-P. Erb, "What Motivates Nonconformity? Uniqueness Seeking Blocks Majority Influence," *Personality and Social Psychology Bulletin* 35, no. 3 (March 1, 2009), pp. 309–20; M.G. Mayhew, J. Gardner, and N.M. Ashkanasy, "Measuring Individuals' Need for Identification: Scale Development and Validation," *Personality and Individual Differences* 49, no. 5 (2010), pp. 356–61; K.R. Morrison and S.C. Wheeler, "Nonconformity Defines the Self: The Role of Minority Opinion Status in Self-Concept Clarity," *Personality and Social Psychology Bulletin* 36, no. 3 (March 2010), pp. 297–308.

30. See, for example, W.B. Swann Jr., R.E. Johnson, and J.K. Bosson, "Identity Negotiation at Work," *Research in Organizational Behavior* 29 (2009), pp. 81–109; M.N. Bechtoldt et al., "Self-Concept Clarity and the Management of Social Conflict," *Journal of Personality* 78, no. 2 (2010), pp. 539–74; Hannah and Avolio, "Ready or Not"; H.-L. Yang and C.-Y. Lai, "Motivations of Wikipedia Content Contributors," *Computers in Human Behavior* 26, no. 6 (2010), pp. 1377–83.

31. G. Joseph, "Man of the People," *Business Times Singapore*, November 13, 2010.

32. The effect of the target in selective attention is known as "bottom-up selection"; the effect of the perceiver's psychodynamics on this process is known as "top-down selection." See C.E. Connor, H.E. Egeth, and S. Yantis, "Visual Attention: Bottom-up versus Top-Down," *Current Biology* 14, no. 19 (2004), pp. R850–52; E.I. Knudsen, "Fundamental Components of Attention," *Annual Review of Neuroscience* 30 (2007), pp. 57–78.

33. A. Mack et al., "Perceptual Organization and Attention," *Cognitive Psychology* 24, no. 4 (1992), pp. 475–501; A.R. Damasio, *Descartes' Error: Emotion, Reason, and the Human Brain* (New York: Putnam Sons, 1994); C. Frith, "A Framework for Studying the Neural Basis of Attention," *Neuropsychologia* 39, no. 12 (2001), pp. 1367–71; N. Lavie, "Distracted and Confused? Selective Attention under Load," *Trends in Cognitive Sciences* 9, no. 2 (2005), pp. 75–82; M. Shermer, "The Political Brain," *Scientific American* 295, no. 1 (July 2006), p. 36; D. Westen, *The Political Brain: The Role of Emotion in Deciding the Fate of the Nation* (Cambridge, MA: PublicAffairs, 2007).

34. Plato, *The Republic*, trans. D. Lee (Harmondsworth, England: Penguin, 1955).

35. D.J. Simons and C.F. Chabris, "Gorillas in Our Midst : Sustained Inattentional Blindness for Dynamic Events," *Perception* 28 (1999), pp. 1059–74.

36. Confirmation bias is defined as "unwitting selectivity in the acquisition and use of evidence" by R.S. Nickerson, "Confirmation Bias: A Ubiquitous Phenomenon in Many Guises," *Review of General Psychology* 2, no. 2 (1998), pp. 175–220. It occurs in a variety of ways, including overweighting positive information, perceiving only positive information, or restricting cognitive attention to a favored hypothesis. Research has found that confirmation bias is typically nonconscious and driven by emotions.

37. K.A. Lane, J. Kang, and M.R. Banaji, "Implicit Social Cognition and Law," *Annual Review of Law and Social Science* 3 (2007).

38. The Sherlock Holmes quotation is from Sir A. Conan Doyle, "A Study in Scarlet," in *The Complete Sherlock Holmes* (New York: Fine Creative Media, 2003), pp. 3–96. Sherlock Holmes offers similar advice in "A Scandal in Bohemia," p. 189. The West Virginia case is reported in K. Gregory, "Unsolved Case: Police Still Looking for Kathy Goble, Missing since 2010," *Charleston Gazette*, April 24, 2011, p. 1A.

39. A. Cromer, "Pathological Science: An Update," *The Skeptical Inquirer* 17, no. 4 (Summer 1993), pp. 400–07.

40. C.N. Macrae and G.V. Bodenhausen, "Social Cognition: Thinking Categorically about Others," *Annual Review of Psychology* 51 (2000), pp. 93–120. For literature on the automaticity of the perceptual organization and interpretation process, see J.A. Bargh, "The Cognitive Monster: The Case against the Controllability of Automatic Stereotype Effects," in *Dual Process Theories in Social Psychology*, ed. S. Chaiken and Y. Trope (New York: Guilford, 1999), pp. 361–82; J.A. Bargh and M.J. Ferguson, "Beyond Behaviorism: On the Automaticity of Higher Mental Processes," *Psychological Bulletin* 126, no. 6 (2000), pp. 925–45; M. Gladwell, *Blink: The Power of Thinking without Thinking* (New York: Little, Brown, 2005).

41. E.M. Altmann and B.D. Burns, "Streak Biases in Decision Making: Data and a Memory Model," *Cognitive Systems Research* 6, no. 1 (2005), pp. 5–16. For a discussion of cognitive closure and perception, see A.W. Kruglanski, *The Psychology of Closed Mindedness* (New York: Psychology Press, 2004).

42. J. Willis and A. Todorov, "First Impressions: Making Up Your Mind after a 100-Ms Exposure to a Face," *Psychological Science* 17, no. 7 (July 2006), pp. 592–98; A. Todorov, M. Pakrashi, and N.N. Oosterhof, "Evaluating Faces on Trustworthiness after Minimal Time Exposure," *Social Cognition* 27, no. 6 (December 2009), pp. 813–33; C. Olivola and A. Todorov, "Elected in 100 Milliseconds: Appearance-Based Trait Inferences and Voting," *Journal of Nonverbal Behavior* 34, no. 2 (2010), pp. 83–110. For related research on thin slices, see N. Ambady et al., "Surgeons' Tone of Voice: A Clue to Malpractice History," *Surgery* 132, no. 1 (July 2002), pp. 5–9; D. J. Benjamin and J. M. Shapiro, "Thin-Slice Forecasts of Gubernatorial Elections," *Review of Economics and Statistics* 91, no. 3 (2009), pp. 523–36.

43. P.M. Senge, *The Fifth Discipline: The Art and Practice of the Learning Organization* (New York: Doubleday Currency, 1990), Ch. 10; P.N. Johnson-Laird, "Mental Models and Deduction," *Trends in Cognitive Sciences* 5, no. 10 (2001), pp. 434–42; A.B. Markman and D. Gentner, "Thinking," *Annual Review of Psychology* 52 (2001), pp. 223–47; T.J. Chermack, "Mental Models in Decision Making and Implications for Human Resource Development," *Advances in Developing Human Resources* 5, no. 4 (2003), pp. 408–22.

44. G.W. Allport, *The Nature of Prejudice* (Reading, MA: Addison-Wesley, 1954); J.C. Brigham, "Ethnic Stereotypes," *Psychological Bulletin* 76, no. 1 (1971), pp. 15–38; D.J. Schneider, *The Psychology of Stereotyping* (New York: Guilford, 2004); S. Kanahara, "A Review of the Definitions of Stereotype and a Proposal for a Progressional Model," *Individual Differences Research* 4, no. 5 (2006), pp. 306–21.

45. C.N. Macrae, A.B. Milne, and G.V. Bodenhausen, "Stereotypes as Energy-Saving Devices: A Peek inside the Cognitive Toolbox," *Journal of Personality and Social Psychology* 66 (1994), pp. 37–47; J.W. Sherman et al., "Stereotype Efficiency Reconsidered: Encoding Flexibility under Cognitive Load," *Journal of Personality and Social Psychology* 75 (1998), pp. 589–606; Macrae and Bodenhausen, "Social Cognition."

46. J.C. Turner and S.A. Haslam, "Social Identity, Organizations, and Leadership," in *Groups at Work: Theory and Research*, ed. M.E. Turner (Mahwah, NJ: Lawrence Erlbaum Associates, 2001), pp. 25–65; M.A. Hogg et al., "The Social Identity Perspective: Intergroup Relations, Self-Conception, and Small Groups," *Small Group Research* 35, no. 3 (June 2004), pp. 246–76; J. Jetten, R. Spears, and T. Postmes, "Intergroup Distinctiveness and Differentiation: A Meta-Analytic Integration," *Journal of Personality and Social Psychology* 86, no. 6 (2004), pp. 862–79; K. Hugenberg and D.F. Sacco, "Social Categorization and Stereotyping: How Social Categorization Biases Person Perception and Face Memory," *Social and Personality Psychology Compass* 2, no. 2 (2008), pp. 1052–72.

47. J.W. Jackson and E.R. Smith, "Conceptualizing Social Identity: A New Framework and Evidence for the Impact of Different

Dimensions," *Personality & Social Psychology Bulletin* 25 (January 1999), pp. 120–35.

48. S.N. Cory, "Quality and Quantity of Accounting Students and the Stereotypical Accountant: Is There a Relationship?" *Journal of Accounting Education* 10, no. 1 (1992), pp. 1–24; P.D. Bougen, "Joking Apart: The Serious Side to the Accountant Stereotype," *Accounting, Organizations and Society* 19, no. 3 (1994), pp. 319–35; A.L. Friedman and S.R. Lyne, "The Beancounter Stereotype: Towards a General Model of Stereotype Generation," *Critical Perspectives on Accounting* 12, no. 4 (2001), pp. 423–51; A. Hoffjan, "The Image of the Accountant in a German Context," *Accounting and the Public Interest* 4 (2004), pp. 62–89; T. Dimnik and S. Felton, "Accountant Stereotypes in Movies Distributed in North America in the Twentieth Century," *Accounting, Organizations and Society* 31, no. 2 (2006), pp. 129–55.

49. I.M. O'Bannon, "The 'Certifiable' Public Accountant," *CPA Technology Advisor* 20, no. 7 (November 2010), pp. 28–29. Blumer's comment can be found in a response to Joey Brannon's blog. See J. Brannon, "10 Ways You Know You Were Born to Be an Accountant (or Not)," (Bradenton, FL: Axiom CPA, 2010).

50. "Employers Face New Danger: Accidental Age Bias," *Omaha World-Herald*, October 10, 2005, p. D1; "Tiptoeing through the Employment Minefield of Race, Sex, and Religion? Here's Another One," *North West Business Insider (Manchester, UK)*, February 2006.

51. S.O. Gaines and E.S. Reed, "Prejudice: From Allport to Dubois," *American Psychologist* 50 (February 1995), pp. 96–103; S.T. Fiske, "Stereotyping, Prejudice, and Discrimination," in *Handbook of Social Psychology*, 4th ed., ed. D.T. Gilbert, S.T. Fiske, and G. Lindzey (New York: McGraw-Hill, 1998), pp. 357–411; M. Hewstone, M. Rubin, and H. Willis, "Intergroup Bias," *Annual Review of Psychology* 53 (2002), pp. 575–604.

52. E. Rosell, K. Miller, and K. Barber, "Firefighting Women and Sexual Harassment," *Public Personnel Management* 24, no. 3 (Fall 1995), pp. 339–50.

53. P. Gumbel, "The French Exodus," *Time International*, April 16, 2007, p. 18; E. Cediey and F. Foroni, *Discrimination in Access to Employment on Grounds of Foreign Origin in France* (Geneva: International Labour Organization, 2008); "Study Finds Major Discrimination against Turkish Job Applicants," *The Local (Germany) (Berlin)*, February 9, 2010.

54. J.A. Bargh and T.L. Chartrand, "The Unbearable Automaticity of Being," *American Psychologist* 54, no. 7 (July 1999), pp. 462–79; S.T. Fiske, "What We Know Now about Bias and Intergroup Conflict, the Problem of the Century," *Current Directions in Psychological Science* 11, no. 4 (August 2002), pp. 123–28. For recent evidence that shows that intensive training can minimize stereotype activation, see K. Kawakami et al., "Just Say No (to Stereotyping): Effects of Training in the Negation of Stereotypic Associations on Stereotype Activation," *Journal of Personality and Social Psychology* 78, no. 5 (2000), pp. 871–88; E.A. Plant, B.M. Peruche, and D.A. Butz, "Eliminating Automatic Racial Bias: Making Race Non-Diagnostic for Responses to Criminal Suspects," *Journal of Experimental Social Psychology* 41, no. 2 (2005), p. 141. On the limitations of some stereotype training, see B. Gawronski et al., "When 'Just Say No' Is Not Enough: Ayrmation versus Negation Training and the Reduction of Automatic Stereotype Activation," *Journal of Experimental Social Psychology* 44 (2008), pp. 370–77.

55. H.H. Kelley, *Attribution in Social Interaction* (Morristown, NJ: General Learning Press, 1971).

56. J.M. Feldman, "Beyond Attribution Theory: Cognitive Processes in Performance Appraisal," *Journal of Applied Psychology* 66 (1981), pp. 127–48.

57. J.M. Crant and T.S. Bateman, "Assignment of Credit and Blame for Performance Outcomes," *Academy of Management Journal* 36 (1993), pp. 7–27; B. Weiner, "Intrapersonal and Interpersonal Theories of Motivation from an Attributional Perspective," *Educational Psychology Review* 12 (2000), pp. 1–14; N. Bacon and P. Blyton, "Worker Responses to Teamworking: Exploring Employee Attributions of Managerial Motives," *International Journal of Human Resource Management* 16, no. 2 (February 2005), pp. 238–55.

58. Fundamental attribution error is part of a larger phenomenon known as correspondence bias. See D.T. Gilbert and P.S. Malone, "The Correspondence Bias," *Psychological Bulletin* 117, no. 1 (1995), pp. 21–38.

59. I. Choi, R.E. Nisbett, and A. Norenzayan, "Causal Attribution across Cultures: Variation and Universality," *Psychological Bulletin* 125, no. 1 (1999), pp. 47–63; D.S. Krull et al., "The Fundamental Fundamental Attribution Error: Correspondence Bias in Individualist and Collectivist Cultures," *Personality and Social Psychology Bulletin* 25, no. 10 (October 1999), pp. 1208–19; R.E. Nisbett, *The Geography of Thought: How Asians and Westerners Think Differently—and Why* (New York: The Free Press, 2003), Ch. 5.

60. D.T. Miller and M. Ross, "Self-Serving Biases in the Attribution of Causality: Fact or Fiction?" *Psychological Bulletin* 82, no. 2 (1975), pp. 213–25; J. Shepperd, W. Malone, and K. Sweeny, "Exploring Causes of the Self-Serving Bias," *Social and Personality Psychology Compass* 2, no. 2 (2008), pp. 895–908. The Philo Vance quotation is from S.S. Van Dine (Willard Huntington Wright), *The Benson Murder Mystery* (New York: Charles Scribner's Sons, 1926), Ch. 6.

61. E.W.K. Tsang, "Self-Serving Attributions in Corporate Annual Reports: A Replicated Study," *Journal of Management Studies* 39, no. 1 (January 2002), pp. 51–65; N.J. Roese and J.M. Olson, "Better, Stronger, Faster: Self-Serving Judgment, Affect Regulation, and the Optimal Vigilance Hypothesis," *Perspectives on Psychological Science* 2, no. 2 (2007), pp. 124–41; R. Hooghiemstra, "East–West Differences in Attributions for Company Performance: A Content Analysis of Japanese and U.S. Corporate Annual Reports," *Journal of Cross-Cultural Psychology* 39, no. 5 (September 1, 2008), pp. 618–29; M. Franco and H. Haase, "Failure Factors in Small and Medium-Sized Enterprises: Qualitative Study from an Attributional Perspective," *International Entrepreneurship and Management Journal* 6, no. 4 (2010), pp. 503–21.

62. A. Davis, "Moving to Greener Pastures," *Employee Benefit News*, December 2010, p. 18.

63. Similar models are presented in D. Eden, "Self-Fulfilling Prophecy as a Management Tool: Harnessing Pygmalion," *Academy of Management Review* 9 (1984), pp. 64–73; R.H.G. Field and D.A. Van Seters, "Management by Expectations (MBE): The Power of Positive Prophecy," *Journal of General Management* 14 (Winter 1988), pp. 19–33; D.O. Trouilloud et al., "The Influence of Teacher Expectations on Student Achievement in Physical Education Classes: Pygmalion Revisited," *European Journal of Social Psychology* 32 (2002), pp. 591–607.

64. D. Eden, "Interpersonal Expectations in Organizations," in *Interpersonal Expectations: Theory, Research, and Applications* (Cambridge, UK: Cambridge University Press, 1993), pp. 154–78.

65. D. Eden, "Pygmalion Goes to Boot Camp: Expectancy, Leadership, and Trainee Performance," *Journal of Applied Psychology* 67 (1982), pp. 194–99; R.P. Brown and E.C. Pinel, "Stigma on My Mind: Individual Differences in the Experience of Stereotype Threat," *Journal of Experimental Social Psychology* 39, no. 6 (2003), pp. 626–33.

66. S. Madon, L. Jussim, and J. Eccles, "In Search of the Powerful Self-Fulfilling Prophecy," *Journal of Personality and Social Psychology* 72, no. 4 (April 1997), pp. 791–809; A.E. Smith, L. Jussim, and J. Eccles, "Do Self-Fulfilling Prophecies Accumulate, Dissipate, or Remain Stable over Time?" *Journal of Personality and Social Psychology* 77, no. 3 (1999), pp. 548–65; S. Madon et al., "Self-Fulfilling Prophecies: The Synergistic Accumulative Effect of Parents' Beliefs on Children's Drinking Behavior," *Psychological Science* 15, no. 12 (2005), pp. 837–45.

67. W.H. Cooper, "Ubiquitous Halo," *Psychological Bulletin* 90 (1981), pp. 218–44; K.R. Murphy, R.A. Jako, and R.L. Anhalt, "Nature and Consequences of Halo Error: A Critical Analysis," *Journal of Applied Psychology* 78 (1993), pp. 218–25; T.H. Feeley, "Comment on Halo Effects in Rating and Evaluation Research," *Human Communication Research* 28, no. 4 (October 2002), pp. 578–86. For a variation of the classic halo effect in business settings, see P. Rosenzweig, *The Halo Effect . . . And the Eight Other Business Delusions That Deceive Managers* (New York: The Free Press, 2007).

68. B. Mullen et al., "The False Consensus Effect: A Meta-Analysis of 115 Hypothesis Tests," *Journal of Experimental Social Psychology* 21, no. 3 (1985), pp. 262–83; G. Marks and N. Miller, "Ten Years of Research on the False-Consensus Effect: An Empirical and Theoretical Review," *Psychological Bulletin* 102, no. 1 (1987), pp. 72–90; R.L. Cross and S.E. Brodt, "How Assumptions of Consensus Undermine Decision Making," *MIT Sloan Management Review* 42, no. 2 (Winter 2001), pp. 86–94; F.J. Flynn and S.S. Wiltermuth, "Who's with Me? False Consensus, Brokerage, and Ethical Decision Making in Organizations," *Academy of Management Journal* 53, no. 5 (October 2010), pp. 1074–89; S. Goel, W. Mason, and D.J. Watts, "Real and Perceived Attitude Agreement in Social Networks," *Journal of Personality and Social Psychology* 99, no. 4 (2010), pp. 611–21.

69. C.L. Kleinke, *First Impressions: The Psychology of Encountering Others* (Englewood Cliffs, NJ: Prentice Hall, 1975); E.A. Lind, L. Kray, and L. Thompson, "Primacy Effects in Justice Judgments: Testing Predictions from Fairness Heuristic Theory," *Organizational Behavior and Human Decision Processes* 85 (July 2001), pp. 189–210; O. Ybarra, "When First Impressions Don't Last: The Role of Isolation and Adaptation Processes in the Revision of Evaluative Impressions," *Social Cognition* 19 (October 2001), pp. 491–520; S.D. Bond et al., "Information Distortion in the Evaluation of a Single Option," *Organizational Behavior and Human Decision Processes* 102, no. 2 (2007), pp. 240–54.

70. D.D. Steiner and J.S. Rain, "Immediate and Delayed Primacy and Recency Effects in Performance Evaluation," *Journal of Applied Psychology* 74 (1989), pp. 136–42; K.T. Trotman, "Order Effects and Recency: Where Do We Go from Here?" *Accounting & Finance* 40 (2000), pp. 169–82; W. Green, "Impact of the Timing of an Inherited Explanation on Auditors' Analytical Procedures Judgements," *Accounting and Finance* 44 (2004), pp. 369–92.

71. L. Roberson, C.T. Kulik, and M.B. Pepper, "Using Needs Assessment to Resolve Controversies in Diversity Training Design," *Group & Organization Management* 28, no. 1 (March 2003), pp. 148–74; D.E. Hogan and M. Mallott, "Changing Racial Prejudice through Diversity Education," *Journal of College Student Development* 46, no. 2 (March/April 2005), pp. 115–25; Gawronski et al., "When 'Just Say No' Is Not Enough."

72. A. Kalev, F. Dobbin, and E. Kelly, "Best Practices or Best Guesses? Assessing the Efficacy of Corporate Affirmative Action and Diversity Policies," *American Sociological Review* 71 (August 2006), pp. 589–617; A. Nancherla, "Why Diversity Training Doesn't Work . . . Right Now," *T&D*, November 2008, pp. 52–61; J. Watson, "When Diversity Training Goes Awry," *Black Issues in Higher Education*, January 24, 2008, p. 11; E.L. Paluck and D.P. Green, "Prejudice Reduction: What Works? A Review and Assessment of Research and Practice," *Annual Review of Psychology* 60 (2009), pp. 339–67; A. Carrns, "Training in Trouble," *Boston Globe*, December 5, 2010, p. 8.

73. Eden, "Self-Fulfilling Prophecy as a Management Tool"; S.S. White and E.A. Locke, "Problems with the Pygmalion Effect and Some Proposed Solutions," *Leadership Quarterly* 11 (Autumn 2000), pp. 389–415.

74. T.W. Costello and S.S. Zalkind, *Psychology in Administration: A Research Orientation* (Englewood Cliffs, NJ: Prentice Hall, 1963), pp. 45–46; J.M. Kouzes and B.Z. Posner, *The Leadership Challenge*, 4th ed. (San Francisco: Jossey-Bass, 2007), Ch. 3.

75. George, *Authentic Leadership*; W.L. Gardner et al., "'Can You See the Real Me?' A Self-Based Model of Authentic Leader and Follower Development," *Leadership Quarterly* 16 (2005), pp. 343–72; B. George, *True North* (San Francisco: Jossey-Bass, 2007).

76. For a discussion of the implicit association test, including some critiques, see H. Blanton et al., "Decoding the Implicit Association Test: Implications for Criterion Prediction," *Journal of Experimental Social Psychology* 42, no. 2 (2006), pp. 192–212; A.G. Greenwald, B.A. Nosek, and N. Sriram, "Consequential Validity of the Implicit Association Test: Comment on Blanton and Jaccard (2006)," *American Psychologist* 61, no. 1 (2006), pp. 56–61; W. Hofmann et al., "Implicit and Explicit Attitudes and Interracial Interaction: The Moderating Role of Situationally Available Control Resources," *Group Processes Intergroup Relations* 11, no. 1 (January 2008), pp. 69–87.

77. Hofmann et al., "Implicit and Explicit Attitudes and Interracial Interaction"; J.T. Jost et al., "The Existence of Implicit Bias Is Beyond Reasonable Doubt: A Refutation of Ideological and Methodological Objections and Executive Summary of Ten Studies That No Manager Should Ignore," *Research in Organizational Behavior* 29 (2009), pp. 39–69.

78. J. Luft, *Of Human Interaction* (Palo Alto, CA: National Press, 1969). For a variation of this model, see J. Hall, "Communication Revisited," *California Management Review* 15 (Spring 1973), pp. 56–67.

79. S. Vazire and M.R. Mehl, "Knowing Me, Knowing You: The Accuracy and Unique Predictive Validity of Self-Ratings and Other-Ratings of Daily Behavior," *Journal of Personality and Social Psychology* 95, no. 5 (2008), pp. 1202–16; S. Vazire, "Who Knows What about a Person? The Self-Other Knowledge Asymmetry (SOKA) Model," *Journal of Personality and Social Psychology* 98, no. 2 (2010), pp. 281–300.

80. J. Dixon and K. Durrheim, "Contact and the Ecology of Racial Division: Some Varieties of Informal Segregation," *British Journal of Social Psychology* 42 (March 2003), pp. 1–23; P.J. Henry and C.D. Hardin, "The Contact Hypothesis Revisited: Status Bias in the Reduction of Implicit Prejudice in the United States and Lebanon," *Psychological Science* 17, no. 10 (2006), pp. 862–68; T.F. Pettigrew and L.R. Tropp, "A Meta-Analytic Test of Intergroup Contact Theory," *Journal of Personality and Social Psychology* 90, no. 5 (2006), pp. 751–83; C. Tredoux and G. Finchilescu, "The Contact Hypothesis and Intergroup Relations 50 Years On: Introduction to the Special Issue," *South African Journal of Psychology* 37, no. 4 (2007), pp. 667–78; T.F. Pettigrew, "Future Directions for Intergroup Contact Theory and Research," *International Journal of Intercultural Relations* 32, no. 3 (2008), pp. 187–99.

81. The contact hypothesis was first introduced by Allport, *The Nature of Prejudice*, Ch. 16.

82. C. Duan and C.E. Hill, "The Current State of Empathy Research," *Journal of Counseling Psychology* 43 (1996), pp. 261–74; W.G. Stephen and K.A. Finlay, "The Role of Empathy in Improving Intergroup Relations," *Journal of Social Issues* 55 (Winter 1999), pp. 729–43; S.K. Parker and C.M. Axtell, "Seeing Another Viewpoint: Antecedents and Outcomes of Employee Perspective Taking," *Academy of Management Journal* 44 (December 2001), pp. 1085–1100; G.J. Vreeke and I.L. van der Mark, "Empathy, an Integrative Model," *New Ideas in Psychology* 21, no. 3 (2003), pp. 177–207.

83. "Domino's Pizza Named One of Michigan's 'Cool Places to Work,'" PR Newswire news release, September 10, 2007; K.C. Neel, "Abdoulah Sets Wow Apart," *Multichannel News*, January 29, 2007, p. 2; G. Thomas, "Fye Rewrites the Tune at ANZ," *Air Transport World*, September 2007, p. 61; "Too Many Signatures," *McKinsey Quarterly*, no. 4 (2009); L. Buchanan, "The Un-Factory," *Inc.* 32, no. 5 (June 2010), pp. 62–67; J. Manby, "A CEO Goes Undercover," *HBS Alumni Bulletin*, September 2010.

84. D. Calderwood-Smith, "Degroote Grad Uses MBA Training to Aid a Developing Economy," *McMaster Daily News (Hamilton, Ont.)*, June 15, 2010.

85. S.J. Black, W.H. Mobley, and E. Weldon, "The Mindset of Global Leaders: Inquisitiveness and Duality," in *Advances in Global Leadership* (Stamford, CT: JAI Press, 2006), pp. 181–200; O. Levy et al., "What We Talk about When We Talk about 'Global Mindset': Managerial Cognition in Multinational Corporations," *Journal of International Business Studies* 38, no. 2 (2007), pp. 231–58; S. Beechler and D. Baltzley, "Creating a Global Mindset," *Chief Learning Officer* 7, no. 6 (2008), pp. 40–45.

86. A.K. Gupta and V. Govindarajan, "Cultivating a Global Mindset," *Academy of Management Executive* 16, no. 1 (2002), pp. 116–26.

87. M. Jackson, "Corporate Volunteers Reaching Worldwide," *Boston Globe*, May 4, 2008, p. 3.

88. "Sam Palmisano Discusses IBM's New Corporate Service Corps," news release, July, 25, 2007; "IBM's Corporate Service Corps Heading to Six Emerging Countries to Spark Socio-Economic Growth While Developing Global Leaders," news release, March 26, 2008; C. Hymowitz, "IBM Combines Volunteer Service, Teamwork to Cultivate Emerging Markets," *The Wall Street Journal*, August 4, 2008, p. B6.

89. U. Hedquist, "Kiwi Volunteer in Tanzania Project Receives Lessons in Life," *Computerworld (NZ)*, January 22, 2009.

CHAPTER 4

1. S. Edge, "I'm the World Famous Jet Rebel," *Daily Express (U.K.)*, August 13, 2010, pp. 32–33; C. Jones and M.T. Moore, "Jetblue Flight Attendant Strikes a Nerve with Stressed Workers," *USA Today*, August 11, 2010; A. Newman and R. Rivera, "Fed-Up Flight Attendant Lets Curses Fly, Then Makes Sliding Exit," *The New York Times*, August 10, 2010; T. Rochester, "T.O. Mother of Jetblue Flight Attendant Understands Meltdown," *Ventura County Star (CA)*, August 11, 2010; E. Vargas, "Did Flight Attendant Start Fight?" *Good Morning America*, August 13, 2010.

2. Emotions are also cognitive processes. However, we use the narrower definition of cognition that refers only to reasoning processes. Also, this and other chapters emphasize that emotional and cognitive processes are intertwined.

3. For a discussion of emotions in marketing, economics, sociology, and political science, see G. Loewenstein, "Emotions in Economic Theory and Economic Behavior," *American Economic Review* 90, no. 2 (May 2000), pp. 426–32; D.S. Massey, "A Brief History of Human Society: The Origin and Role of Emotion in Social Life," *American Sociological Review* 67 (February 2002), pp. 1–29; J. O'Shaughnessy and N.J. O'Shaughnessy, *The Marketing Power of Emotion* (New York: Oxford University Press, 2003); J. Druckman and R. McDermott, "Emotion and the Framing of Risky Choice," *Political Behavior* 30, no. 3 (2008), pp. 297–321; E. Petit, "The Role of Affects in Economics," *Revue d'Economie Politique* 119, no. 6 (2009), pp. 859–97; M. Hubert, "Does Neuroeconomics Give New Impetus to Economic and Consumer Research?" *Journal of Economic Psychology* 31, no. 5 (2010), pp. 812–17.

4. The definition presented here is constructed from the following sources: N.M. Ashkanasy, W.J. Zerbe, and C.E.J. Hartel, "Introduction: Managing Emotions in a Changing Workplace," in *Managing Emotions in the Workplace*, ed. N.M. Ashkanasy, W.J. Zerbe, and C.E.J. Hartel (Armonk, NY: M.E. Sharpe, 2002), pp. 3–18; H.M. Weiss, "Conceptual and Empirical Foundations for the Study of Affect at Work," in *Emotions in the Workplace*, ed. R.G. Lord, R.J. Klimoski, and R. Kanfer (San Francisco: Jossey-Bass, 2002), pp. 20–63. However, the meaning of emotions is still being debated. See, for example, M. Cabanac, "What Is Emotion?" *Behavioral Processes* 60 (2002), pp. 69–83; J. Gooty, M. Gavin, and N.M. Ashkanasy, "Emotions Research in OB: The Challenges That Lie Ahead," *Journal of Organizational Behavior* 30, no. 6 (2009), pp. 833–38.

5. R. Kanfer and R.J. Klimoski, "Affect and Work: Looking Back to the Future," in *Emotions in the Workplace*, ed. R.G. Lord, R.J. Klimoski, and R. Kanfer (San Francisco: Jossey-Bass, 2002), pp. 473–90; J.A. Russell, "Core Affect and the Psychological Construction of Emotion," *Psychological Review* 110, no. 1 (2003), pp. 145–72.

6. R.B. Zajonc, "Emotions," in *Handbook of Social Psychology*, ed. D.T. Gilbert, S.T. Fiske, and L. Gardner (New York: Oxford University Press, 1998), pp. 591–634.

7. N.A. Remington, L.R. Fabrigar, and P.S. Visser, "Reexamining the Circumplex Model of Affect," *Journal of Personality and Social Psychology* 79, no. 2 (2000), pp. 286–300; R.J. Larson, E. Diener, and R.E. Lucas, "Emotion: Models, Measures, and Differences," in *Emotions in the Workplace*, ed. R. G. Lord, R.J. Klimoski, and R. Kanfer (San Francisco: Jossey- Bass, 2002), pp. 64–113; L.F. Barrett et al., "The Experience of Emotion," *Annual Review of Psychology* 58 (2007), pp. 373–403.

8. A.H. Eagly and S. Chaiken, *The Psychology of Attitudes* (Orlando, FL: Harcourt Brace Jovanovich, 1993); A.P. Brief, *Attitudes in and around Organizations* (Thousand Oaks, CA: Sage, 1998). There is an amazing lack of consensus on the definition of attitudes. This book adopts the three-component model, whereas some experts define attitude as only the "feelings" component, with "beliefs" as a predictor and "intentions" as an outcome. Some writers specifically define attitudes as an "evaluation" of an attitude object, whereas others distinguish attitudes from evaluations of an attitude object. Some even define specific attitudes as "affects" (emotions), though there is also confusion about whether affect is emotional as well as cognitive feelings. For some of these variations, see I. Ajzen, "Nature and Operation of Attitudes," *Annual Review of Psychology* 52 (2001), pp. 27–58; D. Albarracín et al., "Attitudes: Introduction and Scope," in *The Handbook of Attitudes*, ed. D. Albarracín, B.T. Johnson, and M.P. Zanna (Mahwah, NJ: Lawrence Erlbaum Associates, 2005), pp. 3–20; W.A. Cunningham and P.D. Zelazo, "Attitudes and Evaluations: A Social Cognitive Neuroscience Perspective," *TRENDS in Cognitive Sciences* 11, no. 3 (2007), pp. 97–104.

9. Neuroscience has a slightly more complicated distinction, in that conscious awareness is "feeling a feeling" whereas "feeling" is a nonconscious sensing of the body state created by emotion, which itself is a nonconscious neural reaction to a stimulus. However, this distinction is not significant for scholars focused more on human behavior than on brain activity, and the labels collide with popular understanding of "feeling." See A.R. Damasio, *The Feeling of What Happens: Body and Emotion in the Making of Consciousness* (New York: Harcourt Brace and Company, 1999); T. Bosse, C.M. Jonker, and J. Treur, "Formalisation of Damasio's Theory of Emotion, Feeling and Core Consciousness," *Consciousness and Cognition* 17, no. 1 (2008), pp. 94–113.

10. C.D. Fisher, "Mood and Emotions While Working: Missing Pieces of Job Satisfaction?" *Journal of Organizational Behavior* 21 (2000), pp. 185–202; Cunningham and Zelazo, "Attitudes and Evaluations"; M.D. Lieberman, "Social Cognitive Neuroscience: A Review of Core Processes," *Annual Review of Psychology* 58 (2007), pp. 259–89; M. Fenton-O'Creevy et al., "Thinking, Feeling and Deciding: The Influence of Emotions on the Decision Making and Performance of Traders," *Journal of Organizational Behavior* (2010). The dual emotion-cognition processes are likely the same as the implicit-explicit attitude processes reported by a few scholars. See W.J. Becker and R. Cropanzano, "Organizational Neuroscience: The Promise and Prospects of an Emerging Discipline," *Journal of Organizational Behavior* 31, no. 7 (2010), pp. 1055–59.

11. S. Orbell, "Intention-Behavior Relations: A Self-Regulation Perspective," in *Contemporary Perspectives on the Psychology of Attitudes*, ed. G. Haddock and G. R. Maio (East Sussex, UK: Psychology Press, 2004), pp. 145–68.

12. H.M. Weiss and R. Cropanzano, "Affective Events Theory: A Theoretical Discussion of the Structure, Causes and Consequences of Affective Experiences at Work," *Research in Organizational Behavior*

18 (1996), pp. 1–74; H.A. Elfenbein, "Chapter 7: Emotion in Organizations," *Academy of Management Annals* 1 (2007), pp. 315–86.

13. J.A. Bargh and M.J. Ferguson, "Beyond Behaviorism: On the Automaticity of Higher Mental Processes," *Psychological Bulletin* 126, no. 6 (2000), pp. 925–45; P. Winkielman and K.C. Berridge, "Unconscious Emotion," *Current Directions in Psychological Science* 13, no. 3 (2004), pp. 120–23; J.M. George, "The Illusion of Will in Organizational Behavior Research: Nonconscious Processes and Job Design," *Journal of Management* 35, no. 6 (December 1, 2009), pp. 1318–39; K.I. Ruys and D.A. Stapel, "The Unconscious Unfolding of Emotions," *European Review of Social Psychology* 20 (2009), pp. 232–71.

14. A.R. Damasio, *Descartes' Error: Emotion, Reason, and the Human Brain* (New York: Putnam Sons, 1994); Damasio, *The Feeling of What Happens*; P. Ekman, "Basic Emotions," in *Handbook of Cognition and Emotion*, ed. T. Dalgleish and M. Power (San Francisco: Jossey-Bass, 1999), pp. 45–60; J.E. LeDoux, "Emotion Circuits in the Brain," *Annual Review of Neuroscience* 23 (2000), pp. 155–84; R.J. Dolan, "Emotion, Cognition, and Behavior," *Science* 298, no. 5596 (November 8, 2002), pp. 1191–94.

15. N. Schwarz, "Emotion, Cognition, and Decision Making," *Cognition and Emotion* 14, no. 4 (2000), pp. 433–40; M.T. Pham, "The Logic of Feeling," *Journal of Consumer Psychology* 14, no. 4 (2004), pp. 360–69. One recent proposition is that a person's confidence in his or her beliefs is also influenced by his or her emotional experiences with those beliefs. See Z. Memon and J. Treur, "On the Reciprocal Interaction between Believing and Feeling: An Adaptive Agent Modelling Perspective," *Cognitive Neurodynamics* 4, no. 4 (2010), pp. 377–94.

16. G.R. Maio, V.M. Esses, and D.W. Bell, "Examining Conflict between Components of Attitudes: Ambivalence and Inconsistency Are Distinct Constructs," *Canadian Journal of Behavioural Science* 32, no. 2 (2000), pp. 71–83.

17. P.C. Nutt, *Why Decisions Fail* (San Francisco, CA: Berrett-Koehler, 2002); S. Finkelstein, *Why Smart Executives Fail* (New York: Viking, 2003); P.C. Nutt, "Search during Decision Making," *European Journal of Operational Research* 160 (2005), pp. 851–76.

18. M. Tierney, "They're All in It Together," *Atlanta Journal-Constitution,* April 16, 2011, p. G7.

19. S. Bolton and M. Houlihan, "Are We Having Fun Yet? A Consideration of Workplace Fun and Engagement," *Employee Relations* 31, no. 6 (2009), pp. 556–68.

20. D.L. Collinson, "Managing Humour," *Journal of Management Studies* 39, no. 3 (2002), pp. 269–88; K. Owler, R. Morrison, and B. Plester, "Does Fun Work? The Complexity of Promoting Fun at Work," *Journal of Management and Organization* 16, no. 3 (2010), pp. 338–52.

21. E. Lamm and M.D. Meeks, "Workplace Fun: The Moderating Effects of Generational Differences," *Employee Relations* 31, no. 6 (2009), pp. 613–31; "Schumpeter: Down with Fun," *Economist Intelligence Unit–Executive Briefing (London),* September 22, 2010; M. McLaughlin, "Bosses Blind to Horrors of 'Fun Days,'" *Scotland on Sunday,* January 3, 2010, p. 10; E. Parry and P. Urwin, "Generational Differences in Work Values: A Review of Theory and Evidence," *International Journal of Management Reviews* 13, no. 1 (2011), pp. 79–96.

22. E. Maltby, "Boring Meetings? Get Out the Water Guns," *The Wall Street Journal,* January 7, 2010; E. Shearing, "Dixon Schwabl Focuses on Having Fun at Its Office Playground," *Democrat & Chronicle (Rochester, NY),* September 5, 2010.

23. C. Foster, "Turning Ha-Ha into A-Ha!" *Employee Benefit News Canada,* December 2007; S. Davies, "Razer Employees Wear Shorts, T-Shirts and Flip-Flops to Work," *Straits Times (Singapore),* May 10, 2008.

24. C. Cooper, "Elucidating the Bonds of Workplace Humor: A Relational Process Model," *Human Relations* 61, no. 8 (August 1, 2008), pp. 1087–1115; B. Plester and M. Orams, "Send in the Clowns: The Role of the Joker in Three New Zealand IT Companies," *Humor: International Journal of Humor Research* 21, no. 3 (2008), pp. 253–81.

25. Weiss and Cropanzano, "Affective Events Theory."

26. L. Festinger, *A Theory of Cognitive Dissonance* (Evanston, IL: Row, Peterson, 1957); G.R. Salancik, "Commitment and the Control of Organizational Behavior and Belief," in *New Directions in Organizational Behavior,* ed. B.M. Staw and G.R. Salancik (Chicago: St. Clair, 1977), pp. 1–54; A.D. Galinsky, J. Stone, and J. Cooper, "The Reinstatement of Dissonance and Psychological Discomfort Following Failed Affirmation," *European Journal of Social Psychology* 30, no. 1 (2000), pp. 123–47.

27. J. Cooper, *Cognitive Dissonance: Fifty Years of a Classic Theory* (London: Sage, 2007); A.R. McConnell and C.M. Brown, "Dissonance Averted: Self-Concept Organization Moderates the Effect of Hypocrisy on Attitude Change," *Journal of Experimental Social Psychology* 46, no. 2 (2010), pp. 361–66; J.M. Jarcho, E.T. Berkman, and M.D. Lieberman, "The Neural Basis of Rationalization: Cognitive Dissonance Reduction during Decision-Making," *Social Cognitive and Affective Neuroscience* (2011), in press.

28. T.A. Judge, E.A. Locke, and C.C. Durham, "The Dispositional Causes of Job Satisfaction: A Core Evaluations Approach," *Research in Organizational Behavior* 19 (1997), pp. 151–88; T.W.H. Ng and K.L. Sorensen, "Dispositional Affectivity and Work-Related Outcomes: A Meta-Analysis," *Journal of Applied Social Psychology* 39, no. 6 (2009), pp. 1255–87.

29. C.M. Brotheridge and A.A. Grandey, "Emotional Labor and Burnout: Comparing Two Perspectives of 'People Work,'" *Journal of Vocational Behavior* 60 (2002), pp. 17–39; P.G. Irving, D.F. Coleman, and D.R. Bobocel, "The Moderating Effect of Negative Affectivity in the Procedural Justice–Job Satisfaction Relation," *Canadian Journal of Behavioural Science* 37, no. 1 (January 2005), pp. 20–32.

30. J. Schaubroeck, D.C. Ganster, and B. Kemmerer, "Does Trait Affect Promote Job Attitude Stability?" *Journal of Organizational Behavior* 17 (1996), pp. 191–96; C. Dormann and D. Zapf, "Job Satisfaction: A Meta-Analysis of Stabilities," *Journal of Organizational Behavior* 22 (2001), pp. 483–504.

31. R. Corelli, "Dishing Out Rudeness," *Maclean's,* January 11, 1999, pp. 44–47; D. Matheson, "A Vancouver Cafe Where Rudeness Is Welcomed," *Canada AM, CTV Television* (January 11, 2000); A. Crossan, "Get Abused in the Elbow Room Café," *PRI's The World (Boston),* February 23, 2010.

32. B.E. Ashforth and R.H. Humphrey, "Emotional Labor in Service Roles: The Influence of Identity," *Academy of Management Review* 18 (1993), pp. 88–115. For a recent review of the emotional labor concept, see T.M. Glomb and M.J. Tews, "Emotional Labor: A Conceptualization and Scale Development," *Journal of Vocational Behavior* 64, no. 1 (2004), pp. 1–23.

33. J.A. Morris and D.C. Feldman, "The Dimensions, Antecedents, and Consequences of Emotional Labor," *Academy of Management Review* 21 (1996), pp. 986–1010; D. Zapf, "Emotion Work and Psychological Well-Being: A Review of the Literature and Some Conceptual Considerations," *Human Resource Management Review* 12 (2002), pp. 237–68.

34. "Reach for the Sky," *New Sunday Times (Kuala Lumpur),* November 16, 2008, p. 4; C. Platt, "Inside Flight Attendant School," *WA Today (Perth),* February 24, 2009.

35. L. Pivot, "Objectif Canada: A Vos Marques, Prêts . . . Partez!" *L'Express,* June 4, 2008; P. O'Neil, "Canada a Top Draw for French Seeking Jobs," *Montreal Gazette,* November 18, 2010, p. B2.

36. A.E. Raz and A. Rafaeli, "Emotion Management in Cross-Cultural Perspective: 'Smile Training' in Japanese and North American

Service Organizations," *Research on Emotion in Organizations* 3 (2007), pp. 199–220; D. Matsumoto, Seung Hee Yoo, and J. Fontaine, "Mapping Expressive Differences around the World," *Journal of Cross-Cultural Psychology* 39, no. 1 (January 1, 2008), pp. 55–74; S. Ravid, A. Rafaeli, and A. Grandey, "Expressions of Anger in Israeli Workplaces: The Special Place of Customer Interactions," *Human Resource Management Review* 20, no. 3 (2010), pp. 224–34. Emotional display norms might also explain differences in aggression across cultures. See N. Bergeron and B.H. Schneider, "Explaining Cross-National Differences in Peer-Directed Aggression: A Quantitative Synthesis," *Aggressive Behavior* 31, no. 2 (2005), pp. 116–37.

37. F. Trompenaars and C. Hampden-Turner, *Riding the Waves of Culture,* 2nd ed. (New York: McGraw-Hill, 1998), Ch. 6. One recent study reveals cultural differences in emotional display norms among American, Canadian, and Japanese students. See S. Safdar et al., "Variations of Emotional Display Rules within and across Cultures: A Comparison between Canada, USA, and Japan," *Canadian Journal of Behavioural Science* 41, no. 1 (2009), pp. 1–10.

38. This relates to the automaticity of emotion, which is summarized in Winkielman and Berridge, "Unconscious Emotion"; K.N. Ochsner and J.J. Gross, "The Cognitive Control of Emotions," *TRENDS in Cognitive Sciences* 9, no. 5 (May 2005), pp. 242–49.

39. W.J. Zerbe, "Emotional Dissonance and Employee Well-Being," in *Managing Emotions in the Workplace,* ed. N.M. Ashkanasy, W.J. Zerbe, and C.E.J. Hartel (Armonk, NY: M. E. Sharpe, 2002), pp. 189–214; R. Cropanzano, H.M. Weiss, and S.M. Elias, "The Impact of Display Rules and Emotional Labor on Psychological Well-Being at Work," *Research in Occupational Stress and Well Being* 3 (2003), pp. 45–89.

40. Brotheridge and Grandey, "Emotional Labor and Burnout"; Zapf, "Emotion Work and Psychological Well-Being"; J.M. Diefendorff, M.H. Croyle, and R.H. Gosserand, "The Dimensionality and Antecedents of Emotional Labor Strategies," *Journal of Vocational Behavior* 66, no. 2 (2005), pp. 339–57.

41. M. Weinstein, "Emotional Evaluation," *Training,* July 29, 2009.

42. J.D. Mayer, P. Salovey, and D.R. Caruso, "Models of Emotional Intelligence," in *Handbook of Human Intelligence,* ed. R.J. Sternberg, 2nd ed. (New York: Cambridge University Press, 2000), pp. 396–420. This definition is also recognized by C. Cherniss, "Emotional Intelligence and Organizational Effectiveness," in *The Emotionally Intelligent Workplace,* ed. C. Cherniss and D. Goleman (San Francisco: Jossey-Bass, 2001), pp. 3–12; M. Zeidner, G. Matthews, and R.D. Roberts, "Emotional Intelligence in the Workplace: A Critical Review," *Applied Psychology: An International Review* 53, no. 3 (2004), pp. 371–99.

43. This model is very similar to Goleman's revised emotional intelligence model. See R. Boyatzis, D. Goleman, and K.S. Rhee, "Clustering Competence in Emotional Intelligence," in *The Handbook of Emotional Intelligence,* ed. R. Bar-On and J.D.A. Parker (San Francisco: Jossey-Bass, 2000), pp. 343–62; D. Goleman, "An EI-Based Theory of Performance," in *The Emotionally Intelligent Workplace,* ed. C. Cherniss and D. Goleman (San Francisco: Jossey-Bass, 2001), pp. 27–44; D. Goleman, R. Boyatzis, and A. McKee, *Primal Leadership* (Boston: Harvard Business School Press, 2002), Ch. 3. Goleman's revised model received a cool reception by most scholars. Yet recent studies indicate that variations of this model (when properly framed as a set of abilities) provide a better fit than other models. See, in particular, C.-S. Wong and K.S. Law, "The Effects of Leader and Follower Emotional Intelligence on Performance and Attitude: An Exploratory Study," *Leadership Quarterly* 13 (2002), pp. 243–74; R.P. Tett and K.E. Fox, "Confirmatory Factor Structure of Trait Emotional Intelligence in Student and Worker Samples," *Personality and Individual Differences* 41 (2006), pp. 1155–68; P.J. Jordan and S.A. Lawrence, "Emotional Intelligence in Teams: Development and Initial Validation of the Short Version of the Workgroup Emotional

Intelligence Profile (WEIP-S)," *Journal of Management & Organization* 15 (2009), pp. 452–69; D.L. Joseph and D.A. Newman, "Emotional Intelligence: An Integrative Meta-Analysis and Cascading Model," *Journal of Applied Psychology* 95, no. 1 (2010), pp. 54–78.

44. H.A. Elfenbein and N. Ambady, "Predicting Workplace Outcomes from the Ability to Eavesdrop on Feelings," *Journal of Applied Psychology* 87, no. 5 (2002), pp. 963–71.

45. The hierarchical nature of the four EI dimensions is discussed by Goleman, but it is more explicit in the Salovey and Mayer model. See D.R. Caruso and P. Salovey, *The Emotionally Intelligent Manager* (San Francisco: Jossey-Bass, 2004). This hierarchy is also identified (without the self–other distinction) as a sequence in Joseph and Newman, "Emotional Intelligence."

46. P.N. Lopes et al., "Emotional Intelligence and Social Interaction," *Personality and Social Psychology Bulletin* 30, no. 8 (August 2004), pp. 1018–34; C.S. Daus and N.M. Ashkanasy, "The Case for the Ability-Based Model of Emotional Intelligence in Organizational Behavior," *Journal of Organizational Behavior* 26 (2005), pp. 453–66; J.E. Barbuto Jr. and M.E. Burbach, "The Emotional Intelligence of Transformational Leaders: A Field Study of Elected Officials," *Journal of Social Psychology* 146, no. 1 (2006), pp. 51–64; M.A. Brackett et al., "Relating Emotional Abilities to Social Functioning: A Comparison of Self-Report and Performance Measures of Emotional Intelligence," *Journal of Personality and Social Psychology* 91, no. 4 (2006), pp. 780–95; D.L. Reis et al., "Emotional Intelligence Predicts Individual Differences in Social Exchange Reasoning," *NeuroImage* 35, no. 3 (2007), pp. 1385–91; S.K. Singh, "Role of Emotional Intelligence in Organisational Learning: An Empirical Study," *Singapore Management Review* 29, no. 2 (2007), pp. 55–74.

47. Some studies have reported situations in which EI has a limited effect on individual performance. For example, see A.L. Day and S.A. Carroll, "Using an Ability-Based Measure of Emotional Intelligence to Predict Individual Performance, Group Performance, and Group Citizenship Behaviors," *Personality and Individual Differences* 36 (2004), pp. 1443–58; Z. Ivcevic, M.A. Brackett, and J.D. Mayer, "Emotional Intelligence and Emotional Creativity," *Journal of Personality* 75, no. 2 (2007), pp. 199–236; J.C. Rode et al., "Emotional Intelligence and Individual Performance: Evidence of Direct and Moderated Effects," *Journal of Organizational Behavior* 28, no. 4 (2007), pp. 399–421.

48. R. Bar-On, R. Handley, and S. Fund, "The Impact of Emotional Intelligence on Performance," in *Linking Emotional Intelligence and Performance at Work,* ed. V.U. Druskat, F. Sala, and G. Mount (Mahwah, NJ: Lawrence Erlbaum, 2006), pp. 3–19. However, the most important predictor of recruiter success was "assertiveness," which is a motivational disposition, so it probably would not be considered emotional intelligence ability.

49. "Occupational Analysts Influence Air Force Decision Makers," *US Fed News,* 3 November 2010; R. Bar-On, *Preliminary Report: A New Us Air Force Study Explores the Cost-Effectiveness of Applying the Bar-on EQ-I* (eiconsortium, August 2010); W. Gordon, "Climbing High for EI," *T + D* 64, no. 8 (August 2010), pp. 72–73.

50. L.J.M. Zijlmans et al., "Training Emotional Intelligence Related to Treatment Skills of Staff Working with Clients with Intellectual Disabilities and Challenging Behaviour," *Journal of Intellectual Disability Research* 55, no. 2 (February 2011), pp. 219–30.

51. R. Johnson, "Can You Feel It?" *People Management,* August 23, 2007, pp. 34–37; K.K. Spors, "Top Small Workplaces 2007," *The Wall Street Journal,* October 1, 2007, p. R1. Also see S.C. Clark, R. Callister, and R. Wallace, "Undergraduate Management Skills Courses and Students' Emotional Intelligence," *Journal of Management Education* 27, no. 1 (February 2003), pp. 3–23; D. Nelis et al., "Increasing Emotional Intelligence: (How) Is It Possible?" *Personality and Individual Differences* 47, no. 1 (2009), pp. 36–41.

52. Goleman, Boyatzis, and McKee, *Primal Leadership*; Lopes et al., "Emotional Intelligence and Social Interaction"; H.A. Elfenbein, "Learning in Emotion Judgments: Training and the Cross-Cultural Understanding of Facial Expressions," *Journal of Nonverbal Behavior* 30, no. 1 (2006), pp. 21–36; C.-S. Wong et al., "The Feasibility of Training and Development of EI: An Exploratory Study in Singapore, Hong Kong and Taiwan," *Intelligence* 35, no. 2 (2007), pp. 141–50.

53. E.A. Locke, "Why Emotional Intelligence Is an Invalid Concept," *Journal of Organizational Behavior* 26 (2005), pp. 425–31; J. Antonakis, "'Emotional Intelligence': What Does It Measure and Does It Matter for Leadership?" in *LMX Leadership–Game-Changing Designs: Research-Based Tools*, ed. G.B. Graen (Greenwich, CT: Information Age Publishing, 2009), pp. 163–92; J. Antonakis, N.M. Ashkanasy, and M.T. Dasborough, "Does Leadership Need Emotional Intelligence?" *Leadership Quarterly* 20 (2009), pp. 247–61; M. Fiori and J. Antonakis, "The Ability Model of Emotional Intelligence: Searching for Valid Measures," *Personality and Individual Differences* 50, no. 3 (2011), pp. 329–34.

54. D.A. Harrison, D.A. Newman, and P.L. Roth, "How Important Are Job Attitudes? Meta-Analytic Comparisons of Integrative Behavioral Outcomes and Time Sequences," *Academy of Management Journal* 49, no. 2 (2006), pp. 305–25. Another recent study concluded that job satisfaction and organizational commitment are so highly correlated that they represent the same construct. See H. Le et al., "The Problem of Empirical Redundancy of Constructs in Organizational Research: An Empirical Investigation," *Organizational Behavior and Human Decision Processes* 112, no. 2 (2010), pp. 112–25. They are also considered the two central work-related variables in the broader concept of happiness at work. See C.D. Fisher, "Happiness at Work," *International Journal of Management Reviews* 12, no. 4 (2010), pp. 384–412.

55. E.A. Locke, "The Nature and Causes of Job Satisfaction," in *Handbook of Industrial and Organizational Psychology*, ed. M. Dunnette (Chicago: Rand McNally, 1976), pp. 1297–1350; H.M. Weiss, "Deconstructing Job Satisfaction: Separating Evaluations, Beliefs and Affective Experiences," *Human Resource Management Review*, no. 12 (2002), pp. 173–94. Some definitions still include emotion as an element of job satisfaction, whereas the definition presented in this book views emotion as a cause of job satisfaction. Also, this definition views job satisfaction as a collection of attitudes, not several facets of job satisfaction.

56. Ipsos-Reid, "Ipsos-Reid Global Poll Finds Major Differences in Employee Satisfaction around the World," news release, January 8, 2001; International Survey Research, *Employee Satisfaction in the World's 10 Largest Economies: Globalization or Diversity?* (Chicago: International Survey Research, 2002); Watson Wyatt Worldwide, "Malaysian Workers More Satisfied with Their Jobs than Their Companies' Leadership and Supervision Practices," news release, November 30, 2004; Kelly Global Workforce Index, *American Workers Are Happy with Their Jobs and Their Bosses* (Troy, MI: Kelly Services, November 2006).

57. T.W. Smith, *Job Satisfaction in America: Trends and Socio-Demographic Correlates* (Chicago: National Opinion Research Center at the University of Chicago, August 2007); T.W. Smith, *Trends in Well-Being, 1972–2010*, General Social Survey (Chicago: National Opinion Research Center at the University of Chicago, March 2011). Similar and consistently high levels of job satisfaction are reported by other major surveys. For a review, see K. Bowman and A. Rugg, *The State of the American Workers 2010: Attitudes about Work in America* (Washington, DC: American Enterprise Institute for Public Policy Research, August 2010).

58. L. Saad, *Job Security Slips in U.S. Worker Satisfaction Rankings* (Princeton, NJ: Gallup, Inc., August 27, 2009); *Employee Engagement Report 2011* (Princeton, NJ: BlessingWhite, 2011).

59. The problems with measuring attitudes and values across cultures are discussed by G. Law, "If You're Happy & You Know It, Tick the Box," *Management-Auckland* 45 (March 1998), pp. 34–37; P.E. Spector et al., "Do National Levels of Individualism and Internal Locus of Control Relate to Well-Being? An Ecological Level International Study," *Journal of Organizational Behavior*, no. 22 (2001), pp. 815–32; L. Saari and T.A. Judge, "Employee Attitudes and Job Satisfaction," *Human Resource Management* 43, no. 4 (Winter 2004), pp. 395–407.

60. H. Rao and R.I. Sutton, "Innovation Lessons from Pixar: An Interview with Oscar-Winning Director Brad Bird," *McKinsey Quarterly* (April 2008), pp. 1–9.

61. M.J. Withey and W.H. Cooper, "Predicting Exit, Voice, Loyalty, and Neglect," *Administrative Science Quarterly*, no. 34 (1989), pp. 521–39; W.H. Turnley and D.C. Feldman, "The Impact of Psychological Contract Violations on Exit, Voice, Loyalty, and Neglect," *Human Relations*, no. 52 (July 1999), pp. 895–922. Subdimensions of silence and voice also exist. See L. van Dyne, S. Ang, and I.C. Botero, "Conceptualizing Employee Silence and Employee Voice as Multidimensional Constructs," *Journal of Management Studies* 40, no. 6 (September 2003), pp. 1359–92.

62. T.R. Mitchell, B.C. Holtom, and T.W. Lee, "How to Keep Your Best Employees: Developing an Effective Retention Policy," *Academy of Management Executive* 15 (November 2001), pp. 96–108; C.P. Maertz and M.A. Campion, "Profiles of Quitting: Integrating Process and Content Turnover Theory," *Academy of Management Journal* 47, no. 4 (2004), pp. 566–82; K. Morrell, J. Loan-Clarke, and A. Wilkinson, "The Role of Shocks in Employee Turnover," *British Journal of Management* 15 (2004), pp. 335–49; B.C. Holtom, T.R. Mitchell, and T.W. Lee, "Increasing Human and Social Capital by Applying Job Embeddedness Theory," *Organizational Dynamics* 35, no. 4 (2006), pp. 316–31.

63. A.A. Luchak, "What Kind of Voice Do Loyal Employees Use?" *British Journal of Industrial Relations* 41 (March 2003), pp. 115–34. For a critique and explanation for historical errors in the EVLN model's development, see S.L. McShane, "Reconstructing the Meaning and Dimensionality of Voice in the Exit-Voice-Loyalty-Neglect Model," Voice and Loyalty Symposium, Annual Conference of the Administrative Sciences Association of Canada, Organizational Behaviour Division, Halifax, May 21, 2008.

64. A.O. Hirschman, *Exit, Voice, and Loyalty: Responses to Decline in Firms, Organizations, and States* (Cambridge, MA: Harvard University Press, 1970); E.A. Hoffmann, "Exit and Voice: Organizational Loyalty and Dispute Resolution Strategies," *Social Forces* 84, no. 4 (June 2006), pp. 2313–30.

65. J.D. Hibbard, N. Kumar, and L.W. Stern, "Examining the Impact of Destructive Acts in Marketing Channel Relationships," *Journal of Marketing Research* 38 (February 2001), pp. 45–61; J. Zhou and J.M. George, "When Job Dissatisfaction Leads to Creativity: Encouraging the Expression of Voice," *Academy of Management Journal* 44 (August 2001), pp. 682–96.

66. M.J. Withey and I.R. Gellatly, "Situational and Dispositional Determinants of Exit, Voice, Loyalty and Neglect," *Proceedings of the Administrative Sciences Association of Canada, Organizational Behaviour Division*, June 1998; D.C. Thomas and K. Au, "The Effect of Cultural Differences on Behavioral Responses to Low Job Satisfaction," *Journal of International Business Studies* 33, no. 2 (2002), pp. 309–26; S.F. Premeaux and A.G. Bedeian, "Breaking the Silence: The Moderating Effects of Self-Monitoring in Predicting Speaking up in the Workplace," *Journal of Management Studies* 40, no. 6 (2003), pp. 1537–62.

67. V. Venkataramani and S. Tangirala, "When and Why Do Central Employees Speak Up? An Examination of Mediating and Moderating Variables," *Journal of Applied Psychology* 95, no. 3 (2010), pp. 582–91.

68. T.A. Judge et al., "The Job Satisfaction–Job Performance Relationship: A Qualitative and Quantitative Review," *Psychological Bulletin* 127, no. 3 (2001), pp. 376–407; C.-D. Fisher, "Why Do Lay People Believe That Satisfaction and Performance Are Correlated? Possible Sources of a Commonsense Theory," *Journal of Organizational Behavior* 24, no. 6 (2003), pp. 753–77; Saari and Judge, "Employee Attitudes and Job Satisfaction." Other studies report stronger correlations with job performance when both the belief and feeling components of job satisfaction are consistent with each other and when overall job attitude (satisfaction and commitment combined) is being measured. See D.J. Schleicher, J.D. Watt, and G.J. Greguras, "Reexamining the Job Satisfaction–Performance Relationship: The Complexity of Attitudes," *Journal of Applied Psychology* 89, no. 1 (2004), pp. 165–77; Harrison, Newman, and Roth, "How Important Are Job Attitudes?" The positive relationship between job satisfaction and employee performance is also consistent with emerging research on the outcomes of positive organizational behavior. For example, see J.R. Sunil, "Enhancing Employee Performance through Positive Organizational Behavior," *Journal of Applied Social Psychology* 38, no. 6 (2008), pp. 1580–1600.

69. However, panel studies suggest that satisfaction has a stronger effect on performance than the other way around. For a summary, see Fisher, "Happiness at Work."

70. "The Greatest Briton in Management and Leadership," *Personnel Today,* February 18, 2003, p. 20; J. Bonasia, "When Employees Occupy the Top Spot at Work," *Investor's Business Daily,* November 5, 2007; S.R. Ezzedeen, C.M. Hyde, and K.R. Laurin, "Is Strategic Human Resource Management Socially Responsible? The Case of Wegman's Food Markets, Inc.," *Employee Rights and Responsibilities Journal* 18 (2007), pp. 295–307.

71. J.I. Heskett, W.E. Sasser, and L.A. Schlesinger, *The Service Profit Chain* (New York: The Free Press, 1997); R.W.Y. Yee et al., "The Service-Profit Chain: A Review and Extension," *Total Quality Management & Business Excellence* 20, no. 6 (2009), pp. 617–32. Several studies and meta-analyses have found substantial support for most parts of this model. See G.A. Gelade and S. Young, "Test of a Service Profit Chain Model in the Retail Banking Sector," *Journal of Occupational & Organizational Psychology* 78 (2005), pp. 1–22; S.P. Brown and S.K. Lam, "A Meta-Analysis of Relationships Linking Employee Satisfaction to Customer Responses," *Journal of Retailing* 84, no. 3 (2008), pp. 243–55; C.G. Chi and D. Gursoy, "Employee Satisfaction, Customer Satisfaction, and Financial Performance: An Empirical Examination," *International Journal of Hospitality Management* 28, no. 2 (2009), pp. 245–53; R.G. Netemeyer, J.G. Maxham III, and D.R. Lichtenstein, "Store Manager Performance and Satisfaction: Effects on Store Employee Performance and Satisfaction, Store Customer Satisfaction, and Store Customer Spending Growth," *Journal of Applied Psychology* 95, no. 3 (2010), pp. 530–45; T.J. Gerpott and M. Paukert, "The Relationship between Employee Satisfaction and Customer Satisfaction: A Meta-Analysis [Der Zusammenhang Zwischen Mitarbeiter-Und Kundenzufriedenheit: Eine Metaanalyse]," *Zeitschrift für Personalforschung* 25, no. 1 (2011), pp. 28–54.

72. W.-C. Tsai and Y.-M. Huang, "Mechanisms Linking Employee Affective Delivery and Customer Behavioral Intentions," *Journal of Applied Psychology* 87, no. 5 (2002), pp. 1001–08; P. Guenzi and O. Pelloni, "The Impact of Interpersonal Relationships on Customer Satisfaction and Loyalty to the Service Provider," *International Journal of Service Industry Management* 15, no. 3–4 (2004), pp. 365–84; S.J. Bell, S. Auh, and K. Smalley, "Customer Relationship Dynamics: Service Quality and Customer Loyalty in the Context of Varying Levels of Customer Expertise and Switching Costs," *Journal of the Academy of Marketing Science* 33, no. 2 (Spring 2005), pp. 169–83; P.B. Barger and A.A. Grandey, "Service with a Smile and Encounter Satisfaction: Emotional Contagion and Appraisal

Mechanisms," *Academy of Management Journal* 49, no. 6 (2006), pp. 1229–38.

73. "CCW-Update," Customer Contact Management Association news release, December 7, 2007; E.G. Brown and J. Lubahn, "We Need 'to Talk,'" *Bank Marketing* 39, no. 7 (2007), pp. 32–36; J. Penman, "Clydesdale Rings the Changes," *Sunday Times (London),* February 4, 2007, p. 13; T. Russell, "Centres of Excellence," *Personnel Today,* January 23, 2007, pp. 24–25.

74. R.T. Mowday, L.W. Porter, and R.M. Steers, *Employee Organization Linkages: The Psychology of Commitment, Absenteeism, and Turnover* (New York: Academic Press, 1982); J.P. Meyer, "Organizational Commitment," *International Review of Industrial and Organizational Psychology* 12 (1997), pp. 175–228. Along with affective and continuance commitment, Meyer identifies "normative commitment," which refers to employee feelings of obligation to remain with the organization. This commitment has been excluded so that students focus on the two most common perspectives of commitment. Also, there is some question whether continuance and normative commitment are comparable to affective commitment; they are attitudes toward quitting and repaying a debt, respectively, rather than toward the organization. See O.N. Solinger, W. van Olffen, and R.A. Roe, "Beyond the Three-Component Model of Organizational Commitment," *Journal of Applied Psychology* 93, no. 1 (2008), pp. 70–83.

75. R.D. Hackett, P. Bycio, and P.A. Hausdorf, "Further Assessments of Meyer and Allen's (1991) Three-Component Model of Organizational Commitment," *Journal of Applied Psychology* 79 (1994), pp. 15–23.

76. J.P. Meyer et al., "Affective, Continuance, and Normative Commitment to the Organization: A Meta-Analysis of Antecedents, Correlates, and Consequences," *Journal of Vocational Behavior* 61 (2002), pp. 20–52; M. Riketta, "Attitudinal Organizational Commitment and Job Performance: A Meta-Analysis," *Journal of Organizational Behavior* 23 (2002), pp. 257–66; J.P. Meyer, T.E. Becker, and C. Vandenberghe, "Employee Commitment and Motivation: A Conceptual Analysis and Integrative Model," *Journal of Applied Psychology* 89, no. 6 (2004), pp. 991–1007; J.P. Meyer and E.R. Maltin, "Employee Commitment and Well-Being: A Critical Review, Theoretical Framework and Research Agenda," *Journal of Vocational Behavior* 77, no. 2 (2010), pp. 323–37.

77. J.P. Meyer et al., "Organizational Commitment and Job Performance: It's the Nature of the Commitment That Counts," *Journal of Applied Psychology* 74 (1989), pp. 152–56; A.A. Luchak and I.R. Gellatly, "What Kind of Commitment Does a Final-Earnings Pension Plan Elicit?" *Relations Industrielles* 56 (Spring 2001), pp. 394–417; Z.X. Chen and A.M. Francesco, "The Relationship between the Three Components of Commitment and Employee Performance in China," *Journal of Vocational Behavior* 62, no. 3 (2003), pp. 490–510; D.M. Powell and J.P. Meyer, "Side-Bet Theory and the Three-Component Model of Organizational Commitment," *Journal of Vocational Behavior* 65, no. 1 (2004), pp. 157–77.

78. J.E. Finegan, "The Impact of Person and Organizational Values on Organizational Commitment," *Journal of Occupational and Organizational Psychology* 73 (June 2000), pp. 149–69; A. Panaccio and C. Vandenberghe, "Perceived Organizational Support, Organizational Commitment and Psychological Well-Being: A Longitudinal Study," *Journal of Vocational Behavior* 75, no. 2 (2009), pp. 224–36.

79. J.W. Westerman and L.A. Cyr, "An Integrative Analysis of Person-Organization Fit Theories," *International Journal of Selection and Assessment* 12, no. 3 (September 2004), pp. 252–61; A.L. Kristof-Brown, R.D. Zimmerman, and E.C. Johnson, "Consequences of Individuals' Fit at Work: A Meta-Analysis of Person–Job, Person–Organization, Person–Group, and Person–Supervisor Fit," *Personnel Psychology* 58, no. 2 (2005), pp. 281–342; J.R. Edwards, "Chapter 4: Person–Environment Fit in Organizations: An Assessment of

Theoretical Progress," *Academy of Management Annals* 2 (2008), pp. 167–230.

80. D.M. Rousseau et al., "Not So Different after All: A Cross-Discipline View of Trust," *Academy of Management Review* 23 (1998), pp. 393–404.

81. A. Travaglione and B. Cross, "Diminishing the Social Network in Organizations: Does There Need to Be Such a Phenomenon as 'Survivor Syndrome' after Downsizing?" *Strategic Change* 15 (January-February 2006), pp. 1–13; D.K. Datta et al., "Causes and Effects of Employee Downsizing: A Review and Synthesis," *Journal of Management* 36, no. 1 (January 2010), pp. 281–348.

82. Similar concepts on information acquisition are found in socialization and organizational change research. See for example P. Bordia et al., "Uncertainty during Organizational Change: Types, Consequences, and Management Strategies," *Journal of Business and Psychology* 18, no. 4 (2004), pp. 507–32; H.D. Cooper-Thomas and N. Anderson, "Organizational Socialization: A Field Study into Socialization Success and Rate," *International Journal of Selection and Assessment* 13, no. 2 (2005), pp. 116–28; T.N. Bauer, "Newcomer Adjustment during Organizational Socialization: A Meta-Analytic Review of Antecedents, Outcomes, and Methods," *Journal of Applied Psychology* 92, no. 3 (2007), pp. 707–21.

83. T.S. Heffner and J.R. Rentsch, "Organizational Commitment and Social Interaction: A Multiple Constituencies Approach," *Journal of Vocational Behavior* 59 (2001), pp. 471–90.

84. J. Pierce, L.T. Kostova, and K.T. Dirks, "Toward a Theory of Psychological Ownership in Organizations," *Academy of Management Review* 26, no. 2 (2001), pp. 298–310; M. Mayhew et al., "A Study of the Antecedents and Consequences of Psychological Ownership in Organizational Settings," *Journal of Social Psychology* 147, no. 5 (2007), pp. 477–500; T.-S. Han, H.-H. Chiang, and A. Chang, "Employee Participation in Decision Making, Psychological Ownership and Knowledge Sharing: Mediating Role of Organizational Commitment in Taiwanese High-Tech Organizations," *International Journal of Human Resource Management* 21, no. 12 (2010), pp. 2218–33.

85. H. Samuel, "Why Have 24 France Telecom Workers Killed Themselves in the Past 19 Months?" *The Telegraph (London),* October 4, 2009; "Doctor or Decorator?" *The Economist,* April 8, 2010; F. Aizicovici, "France Telé Com: La Lutte Contre le Stress au Travail se Met en Place Lentement," *Le Monde (Paris),* January 26, 2010; R. Tomlinson and G. Viscusi, "Suicides inside France Telecom Prompting Sarkozy Stress Testing," *BusinessWeek,* January 25, 2010; A. Chrisafis, "France Telecom Worker Sets Himself Alight," *Guardian (London),* April 27, 2011, p. 22.

86. J.C. Quick et al., *Preventive Stress Management in Organizations* (Washington, DC: American Psychological Association, 1997), pp. 3–4; R.S. DeFrank and J.M. Ivancevich, "Stress on the Job: An Executive Update," *Academy of Management Executive* 12 (August 1998), pp. 55–66; A. L. Dougall and A. Baum, "Stress, Coping, and Immune Function," in *Handbook of Psychology,* ed. M. Gallagher and R.J. Nelson (Hoboken, NJ: John Wiley & Sons, 2003), pp. 441–55. There are at least three schools of thought regarding the meaning of stress, and some reviews of stress literature describe these schools without pointing to any one as the preferred definition. One reviewer concluded that the stress concept is so broad that it should be considered an umbrella concept, capturing a broad array of phenomena and providing a simple term for the public to use. See T.A. Day, "Defining Stress as a Prelude to Mapping Its Neurocircuitry: No Help from Allostasis," *Progress in Neuro-Psychopharmacology and Biological Psychiatry* 29, no. 8 (2005), pp. 1195–1200; R. Cropanzano and A. Li, "Organizational Politics and Workplace Stress," in *Handbook of Organizational Politics,* ed. E. Vigoda-Gadot and A. Drory (Cheltenham, UK: Edward Elgar, 2006), pp. 139–60; R.L. Woolfolk, P.M. Lehrer, and L.A. Allen, "Conceptual Issues Underlying Stress Management," in *Principles and Practice of Stress Management,* ed. P.M. Lehrer, R.L. Woolfolk, and W.E. Sime (New York: Guilford Press, 2007), pp. 3–15.

87. Finegan, "The Impact of Person and Organizational Values on Organizational Commitment"; Dougall and Baum, "Stress, Coping, and Immune Function"; R.S. Lazarus, *Stress and Emotion: A New Synthesis* (New York: Springer Publishing, 2006); L.W. Hunter and S.M.B. Thatcher, "Feeling the Heat: Effects of Stress, Commitment, and Job Experience on Job Performance," *Academy of Management Journal* 50, no. 4 (2007), pp. 953–68.

88. W. Lester, "Poll: Stress Knows Few Boundaries for People in Industrial Democracies," *USA Today,* December 20, 2006; "Hungarians Say Work Conditions Contribute to Poor Health," news release, Kelly Services, 2008; "Survey Reveals 77% of Americans Stressed about Something at Work," PR Newswire news release, March 30, 2011.

89. Quick et al., *Preventive Stress Management in Organizations,* pp. 5–6; B.L. Simmons and D.L. Nelson, "Eustress at Work: The Relationship between Hope and Health in Hospital Nurses," *Health Care Management Review* 26, no. 4 (October 2001), pp. 7ff. The eustress survey is reported in Towers Watson, "Debunking Workforce Myths," news release, March 2008.

90. H. Selye, "A Syndrome Produced by Diverse Nocuous Agents," *Nature* 138, no. 1 (July 4, 1936), p. 32; H. Selye, *Stress without Distress* (Philadelphia, PA: J.B. Lippincott, 1974). The earliest use of the word *stress* is described in R.M.K. Keil, "Coping and Stress: A Conceptual Analysis," *Journal of Advanced Nursing* 45, no. 6 (2004), pp. 659–65.

91. S.E. Taylor, R.L. Repetti, and T. Seeman, "Health Psychology: What Is an Unhealthy Environment and How Does It Get under the Skin?" *Annual Review of Psychology* 48 (1997), pp. 411–47.

92. D. Ganster, M. Fox, and D. Dwyer, "Explaining Employees' Health Care Costs: A Prospective Examination of Stressful Job Demands, Personal Control, and Physiological Reactivity," *Journal of Applied Psychology* 86 (May 2001), pp. 954–64; M. Kivimaki et al., "Work Stress and Risk of Cardiovascular Mortality: Prospective Cohort Study of Industrial Employees," *British Medical Journal* 325 (October 19, 2002), pp. 857–60; S. Andrew and S. Ayers, "Stress, Health, and Illness," in *The Sage Handbook of Health Psychology,* ed. S. Sutton, A. Baum, and M. Johnston (London: Sage, 2004), pp. 169–96; A. Rosengren et al., "Association of Psychosocial Risk Factors with Risk of Acute Myocardial Infarction in 11,119 Cases and 13,648 Controls from 52 Countries (the Interheart Study): Case-Control Study," *The Lancet* 364, no. 9438 (September 11, 2004), pp. 953–62.

93. R.C. Kessler, "The Effects of Stressful Life Events on Depression," *Annual Review of Psychology* 48 (1997), pp. 191–214; L. Greenburg and J. Barling, "Predicting Employee Aggression against Coworkers, Subordinates and Supervisors: The Roles of Person Behaviors and Perceived Workplace Factors," *Journal of Organizational Behavior* 20 (1999), pp. 897–913; M. Jamal and V.V. Baba, "Job Stress and Burnout among Canadian Managers and Nurses: An Empirical Examination," *Canadian Journal of Public Health* 91, no. 6 (November-December 2000), pp. 454–58; L. Tourigny, V.V. Baba, and T.R. Lituchy, "Job Burnout among Airline Employees in Japan: A Study of the Buffering Effects of Absence and Supervisory Support," *International Journal of Cross Cultural Management* 5, no. 1 (April 2005), pp. 67–85; M.S. Hershcovis et al., "Predicting Workplace Aggression: A Meta-Analysis," *Journal of Applied Psychology* 92, no. 1 (2007), pp. 228–38.

94. C. Maslach, W.B. Schaufeli, and M.P. Leiter, "Job Burnout," *Annual Review of Psychology* 52 (2001), pp. 397–422; J.R.B. Halbesleben and M.R. Buckley, "Burnout in Organizational Life," *Journal of Management* 30, no. 6 (2004), pp. 859–79.

95. K. Danna and R.W. Griffin, "Health and Well-Being in the Work-place: A Review and Synthesis of the Literature," *Journal of Management* (Spring 1999), pp. 357–84.

96. This is a slight variation of the definition in the Quebec antiharass-ment legislation. See http://www.cnt.gouv.qc.ca/en/in-case-of/psychological-harassment-at-work/index.html. For related defini-tions and discussion of workplace incivility, see H. Cowiea et al., "Measuring Workplace Bullying," *Aggression and Violent Behavior* 7 (2002), pp. 33–51; C.M. Pearson and C.L. Porath, "On the Nature, Consequences and Remedies of Workplace Incivility: No Time for 'Nice'? Think Again," *Academy of Management Executive* 19, no. 1 (February 2005), pp. 7–18. For recent discussion of workplace harassment legislation in the United States, see D.C. Yamada, "Workplace Bully and American Employment Law: A Ten-Year Progress Report and Assessment," *Comparative Labor Law and Policy Journal* 32, no. 1 (2010), pp. 251–84.

97. Pearson and Porath, "On the Nature, Consequences and Remedies of Workplace Incivility"; J. Przybys, "How Rude!" *Las Vegas Review-Journal,* April 25, 2006, p. 1E; J. Scott, C. Blanshard, and S. Child, "Workplace Bullying of Junior Doctors: A Cross-Sectional Ques-tionnaire Survey," *New Zealand Medical Journal* 121, no. 1282 (September 19, 2008), pp. 10–14; A. Yeung and B. Griffin, "Work-place Incivilty: Does It Matter in Asia?" *People & Strategy* 31, no. 1 (December 2008), pp. 14–19; "Power Harassment Cases Rising," *Daily Yomiuri (Tokyo),* June 10, 2009, p. 2.

98. For a legal discussion of types of sexual harassment, see B. Lindemann and D. D. Kadue, *Sexual Harassment in Employment Law* (Washington: BNA Books, 1999), pp. 7–9.

99. D. Ulrich and W. Ulrich, *The Why of Work: How Great Leaders Build Abundant Organizations That Win* (New York: McGraw-Hill, 2010), p. v.

100. "Worker at Centre of Abuse Storm Paid More than Mayor," *CBC News (Toronto),* June 3, 2010; "Mississauga Hazing Probe Ends with Suspensions," *CBC News (Toronto),* June 9, 2010.

101. E. Galinsky et al., *Overwork in America: When the Way We Work Becomes Too Much* (New York: Families and Work Institute, March 2005); J. MacBride-King, *Wrestling with Workload: Organizational Strategies for Success* (Ottawa: Conference Board of Canada, 2005); "Canadian Workers Feel More Stressed and Less Appreciated, Desjardins Financial Security National Survey on Canadian Health Finds," Canada NewsWire news release, September 8, 2010; A. Fung, "Poll: 40% Haven't Vacationed in 2 Years," *Richmond Times-Dispatch,* July 1, 2010, p. B3.

102. R. Drago, D. Black, and M. Wooden, *The Persistence of Long Work Hours* (Melbourne: Melbourne Institute of Applied Economic and Social Research, University of Melbourne, August 2005); L. Golden, "A Brief History of Long Work Time and the Contemporary Sources of Overwork," *Journal of Business Ethics* 84 (2009), pp. 217–27.

103. C.B. Meek, "The Dark Side of Japanese Management in the 1990s: Karoshi and Ijime in the Japanese Workplace," *Journal of Managerial Psychology* 19, no. 3 (2004), pp. 312–31; "Nagoya Court Rules Toyota Employee Died from Overwork," *Japan Times,* December 1, 2007; Y. Kageyama, "Questions Rise about Temps, Overwork at Toyota," *Associated Press Newswires,* September 10, 2008; Y. Kawanishi, "On Karo-Jisatsu (Suicide by Overwork)," *International Journal of Men-tal Health* 37, no. 1 (Spring 2008), pp. 61–74; P. Novotny, "Overwork a Silent Killer in Japan," *Agence France Presse,* January 11, 2009.

104. R. Karasek and T. Theorell, *Healthy Work: Stress, Productivity, and the Reconstruction of Working Life* (New York: Basic Books, 1990); N. Turner, N. Chmiel, and M. Walls, "Railing for Safety: Job Demands, Job Control, and Safety Citizenship Role Defini-tion," *Journal of Occupational Health Psychology* 10, no. 4 (2005), pp. 504–12.

105. Lazarus, *Stress and Emotion,* Ch. 5.

106. M. Zuckerman and M. Gagne, "The Cope Revised: Proposing a 5-Factor Model of Coping Strategies," *Journal of Research in Person-ality* 37 (2003), pp. 169–204; S. Folkman and J.T. Moskowitz, "Cop-ing: Pitfalls and Promise," *Annual Review of Psychology* 55 (2004), pp. 745–74; C.A. Thompson et al., "On the Importance of Coping: A Model and New Directions for Research on Work and Family," *Research in Occupational Stress and Well-Being* 6 (2007), pp. 73–113.

107. S.E. Taylor et al., "Psychological Resources, Positive Illusions, and Health," *American Psychologist* 55, no. 1 (January 2000), pp. 99–109; F. Luthans and C.M. Youssef, "Emerging Positive Organizational Behavior," *Journal of Management* 33, no. 3 (June 1, 2007), pp. 321–49; P. Steel, J. Schmidt, and J. Shultz, "Refining the Relationship be-tween Personality and Subjective Well-Being," *Psychological Bulletin* 134, no. 1 (2008), pp. 138–61; G. Alarcon, K.J. Eschleman, and N.A. Bowling, "Relationships between Personality Variables and Burnout: A Meta-Analysis," *Work & Stress* 23, no. 3 (2009), pp. 244–63; R. Kotov et al., "Linking 'Big' Personality Traits to Anxiety, Depressive, and Substance Use Disorders: A Meta-Analysis," *Psychological Bulletin* 136, no. 5 (2010), pp. 768–821.

108. G.A. Bonanno, "Loss, Trauma, and Human Resilience: Have We Underestimated the Human Capacity to Thrive after Extremely Aversive Events?" *American Psychologist* 59, no. 1 (2004), pp. 20–28; F. Luthans, C.M. Youssef, and B.J. Avolio, *Psychological Capital: Developing the Human Competitive Edge* (New York: Oxford University Press, 2007).

109. J.T. Spence and A.S. Robbins, "Workaholism: Definition, Measure-ment and Preliminary Results," *Journal of Personality Assessment* 58 (1992), pp. 160–178; R.J. Burke, "Workaholism in Organizations: Psychological and Physical Well-Being Consequences," *Stress Medi-cine* 16, no. 1 (2000), pp. 11–16; I. Harpaz and R. Snir, "Workaholism: Its Definition and Nature," *Human Relations* 56 (2003), pp. 291–319; R.J. Burke, A.M. Richardson, and M. Martinussen, "Workaholism among Norwegian Senior Managers: New Research Directions," *International Journal of Management* 21, no. 4 (December 2004), pp. 415–26; T.W.H. Ng, K.L. Sorensen, and D.C. Feldman, "Dimen-sions, Antecedents, and Consequences of Workaholism: A Concep-tual Integration and Extension," *Journal of Organizational Behavior* 28 (2007), pp. 111–36.

110. M. Siegall and L.L. Cummings, "Stress and Organizational Role Conflict," *Genetic, Social, and General Psychology Monographs* 12 (1995), pp. 65–95.

111. L.T. Eby et al., "Work and Family Research in IO/OB: Content Analysis and Review of the Literature (1980–2002)," *Journal of Vocational Behavior* 66, no. 1 (2005), pp. 124–97.

112. N. Davidson, "Vancouver Developer Looks to Make Video Games without Burning Out Staff," *Canadian Press,* February 21, 2006; F. Jossi, "Clocking Out," *HRMagazine,* June 2007, pp. 46–50; American Psychological Association, "San Jorge Children's Hospital: A Culture of Collaboration and Care," news release, 2011.

113. S.R. Madsen, "The Effects of Home-Based Teleworking on Work-Family Conflict," *Human Resource Development Quarterly* 14, no. 1 (2003), pp. 35–58; S. Raghuram and B. Wiesenfeld, "Work-Nonwork Conflict and Job Stress among Virtual Workers," *Human Resource Management* 43, no. 2/3 (Summer/Fall 2004), pp. 259–77.

114. Organization for Economic Co-operation and Development, *Babies and Bosses: Reconciling Work and Family Life,* Vol. 4 (Canada, Finland, Sweden and the United Kingdom) (Paris: OECD Publishing, 2005); J. Heymann et al., *The Work, Family, and Equity Index: How Does the United States Measure Up?* (Montreal: Institute for Health and Social Policy, June 2007).

115. M. Secret, "Parenting in the Workplace: Child Care Options for Consideration," *Journal of Applied Behavioral Science* 41, no. 3 (September 2005), pp. 326–47.

116. V. Bland, "Sabbaticals Ideal Refresher," *New Zealand Herald,* August 31, 2005; A.E. Carr and T.L.-P. Tang, "Sabbaticals and Employee

Motivation: Benefits, Concerns, and Implications," *Journal of Education for Business* 80, no. 3 (January/February 2005), pp. 160–64; S. Overman, "Sabbaticals Benefit Companies as Well as Employees," *Employee Benefit News,* April 15, 2006; O.B. Davidson et al., "Sabbatical Leave: Who Gains and How Much?" *Journal of Applied Psychology* 95, no. 5 (2010), pp. 953–64. For discussion of psychological detachment and stress management, see C. Fritz et al., "Happy, Healthy, and Productive: The Role of Detachment from Work during Nonwork Time," *Journal of Applied Psychology* 95, no. 5 (2010), pp. 977–83.

117. M. Conlin, "Smashing the Clock," *BusinessWeek,* December 11, 2006, pp. 60–68; L. Gresham, "A New Dawn," *Employee Benefits News,* March 2007; B. Ward, "Power to the People," *Star-Tribune (Minneapolis-St. Paul),* June 1, 2008, p. 1E.

118. M.H. Abel, "Humor, Stress, and Coping Strategies," *Humor: International Journal of Humor Research* 15, no. 4 (2002), pp. 365–81; N.A. Kuiper et al., "Humor Is Not Always the Best Medicine: Specific Components of Sense of Humor and Psychological Well-Being," *Humor: International Journal of Humor Research* 17, no. 1/2 (2004), pp. 135–68; E.J. Romero and K.W. Cruthirds, "The Use of Humor in the Workplace," *Academy of Management Perspectives* 20, no. 2 (2006), pp. 58–69; M. McCreaddie and S. Wiggins, "The Purpose and Function of Humor in Health, Health Care and Nursing: A Narrative Review," *Journal of Advanced Nursing* 61, no. 6 (2008), pp. 584–95.

119. W.M. Ensel and N. Lin, "Physical Fitness and the Stress Process," *Journal of Community Psychology* 32, no. 1 (January 2004), pp. 81–101.

120. S. Armour, "Rising Job Stress Could Affect Bottom Line," *USA Today,* July 29, 2003; V.A. Barnes, F.A. Treiber, and M.H. Johnson, "Impact of Transcendental Meditation on Ambulatory Blood Pressure in African-American Adolescents," *American Journal of Hypertension* 17, no. 4 (2004), pp. 366–69; P. Manikonda et al., "Influence of Non-Pharmacological Treatment (Contemplative Meditation and Breathing Technique) on Stress Induced Hypertension—A Randomized Controlled Study," *American Journal of Hypertension* 18, no. 5, Supplement 1 (2005), pp. A89–90.

121. C. Viswesvaran, J.I. Sanchez, and J. Fisher, "The Role of Social Support in the Process of Work Stress: A Meta-Analysis," *Journal of Vocational Behavior* 54, no. 2 (1999), pp. 314–34; S.E. Taylor et al., "Biobehavioral Responses to Stress in Females: Tend-and-Befriend, Not Fight-or-Flight," *Psychological Review* 107, no. 3 (July 2000), pp. 411–29; R. Eisler and D.S. Levine, "Nurture, Nature, and Caring: We Are Not Prisoners of Our Genes," *Brain and Mind* 3 (2002), pp. 9–52; T.A. Beehr, N.A. Bowling, and M.M. Bennett, "Occupational Stress and Failures of Social Support: When Helping Hurts," *Journal of Occupational Health Psychology* 15, no. 1 (January 2010), pp. 45–59; B.A. Scott et al., "A Daily Investigation of the Role of Manager Empathy on Employee Well-Being," *Organizational Behavior and Human Decision Processes* 113, no. 2 (2010), pp. 127–40.

CHAPTER 5

1. Corporate Research Forum, *Workshop Review: Using Strengths-Based Approaches to Improve Individual and Organisational Performance* (London: Corporate Research Forum, July 10, 2007); P. Flade, "Employee Engagement Drives Shareholder Value," *Director of Finance Online,* February 13, 2008; Standard Chartered, *Sustainability Review 2007: Leading the Way in Asia, Africa, and the Middle East,* (London: Standard Chartered Bank, March 17, 2008); M. Berry, "Tim Miller Is That Rare Beast—An HR Director at a Successful Bank," *Personnel Today,* January 26, 2010, pp. 10–11; Standard Chartered Bank, *2010 Annual Report* (London: Standard Chartered Bank, 2010).

2. C.C. Pinder, *Work Motivation in Organizational Behavior* (Upper Saddle River, NJ: Prentice-Hall, 1998); R.M. Steers, R.T. Mowday,

and D.L. Shapiro, "The Future of Work Motivation Theory," *Academy of Management Review* 29 (2004), pp. 379–87.

3. A.B. Bakker and W.B. Schaufeli, "Positive Organizational Behavior: Engaged Employees in Flourishing Organizations," *Journal of Organizational Behavior* 29, no. 2 (2008), pp. 147–54; W.H. Macey and B. Schneider, "The Meaning of Employee Engagement," *Industrial and Organizational Psychology* 1 (2008), pp. 3–30.

4. J. Engen, "Are Your Employees Truly Engaged?" *Chief Executive,* March 2008, p. 42; S. Flander, "Terms of Engagement," *Human Resource Executive Online,* January 2008; D. Macleod and N. Clarke, *Engaging for Success: Enhancing Performance through Employee Engagement* (London: July 2009).

5. Gallup Consulting, *The Gallup Q12-Employee Engagement-Poll 2008 Results* (Gallup Consulting, February 2009); A. Fox, "Raising Engagement," *HRMagazine,* May 2010, p. 34; BlessingWhite, *Employee Engagement Report 2011* (Princeton, NJ: BlessingWhite, January 2011).

6. Several sources have attempted to identify and organize the drivers of employee engagement. See, for example, D. Robinson, S. Perryman, and S. Hayday, *The Drivers of Employee Engagement* (Brighton, UK: Institute for Employment Studies, 2004); W.H. Macey et al., *Employee Engagement: Tools for Analysis, Practice, and Competitive Advantage* (Malden, MA: Wiley-Blackwell, 2009); Macleod and Clarke, *Engaging for Success*; M. Stairs and M. Galpin, "Positive Engagement: From Employee Engagement to Workplace Happiness," in *Oxford Handbook of Positive Psychology of Work,* ed. P.A. Linley, S. Harrington, and N. Garcea (New York: Oxford University Press, 2010), pp. 155–72.

7. The confusing array of definitions of drives and needs has been a subject of criticism for a half century. See, for example, R.S. Peters, "Motives and Motivation," *Philosophy* 31 (1956), pp. 117–30; H. Cantril, "Sentio, Ergo Sum: 'Motivation' Reconsidered," *Journal of Psychology* 65, no. 1 (January 1967), pp. 91–107; G.R. Salancik and J. Pfeffer, "An Examination of Need-Satisfaction Models of Job Attitudes," *Administrative Science Quarterly* 22, no. 3 (September 1977), pp. 427–56.

8. A. Blasi, "Emotions and Moral Motivation," *Journal for the Theory of Social Behaviour* 29, no. 1 (1999), pp. 1–19; D.W. Pfaff, *Drive: Neurobiological and Molecular Mechanisms of Sexual Motivation* (Cambridge, MA: MIT Press, 1999); T.V. Sewards and M.A. Sewards, "Fear and Power-Dominance Drive Motivation: Neural Representations and Pathways Mediating Sensory and Mnemonic Inputs, and Outputs to Premotor Structures," *Neuroscience and Biobehavioral Reviews* 26 (2002), pp. 553–79; K.C. Berridge, "Motivation Concepts in Behavioral Neuroscience," *Physiology & Behavior* 81, no. 2 (2004), pp. 179–209. We distinguish drives from emotions, but future research may find that the two concepts are not so different as is stated here. Woodworth is credited with either coining or popularizing the term "drives" in the context of human motivation. His classic book is certainly the first source to discuss the concept in detail. See R.S. Woodworth, *Dynamic Psychology* (New York: Columbia University Press, 1918).

9. "Come and Join Our Mob!" *St. Helens Reporter (UK),* March 2, 2011; B. Gibson, "Huddersfield B&Q Customers Surprised by Staff Flash Mob," *Huddersfield Daily Examiner (UK),* March 7, 2011.

10. G. Loewenstein, "The Psychology of Curiosity: A Review and Reinterpretation," *Psychological Bulletin* 116, no. 1 (1994), pp. 75–98; R.E. Baumeister and M.R. Leary, "The Need to Belong: Desire for Interpersonal Attachments as a Fundamental Human Motivation," *Psychological Bulletin* 117 (1995), pp. 497–529; A.E. Kelley, "Neurochemical Networks Encoding Emotion and Motivation: An Evolutionary Perspective," in *Who Needs Emotions? The Brain Meets the Robot,* ed. J.-M. Fellous and M.A. Arbib (New York: Oxford University Press, 2005), pp. 29–78; L.A. Leotti, S.S. Iyengar, and K.N. Ochsner, "Born to Choose: The Origins and Value of the Need for Control," *Trends in Cognitive Sciences* 14, no. 10 (2010), pp. 457–63.

11. K. Passyn and M. Sujan, "Self-Accountability Emotions and Fear Appeals: Motivating Behavior," *Journal of Consumer Research* 32, no. 4 (2006), pp. 583–89; S.G. Barsade and D.E. Gibson, "Why Does

Affect Matter in Organizations?" *Academy of Management Perspectives* 21, no. 2 (February 2007), pp. 36–59.

12. A.R. Damasio, *The Feeling of What Happens: Body and Emotion in the Making of Consciousness* (New York: Harcourt Brace & Company, 1999), p. 286.

13. S. Hitlin, "Values as the Core of Personal Identity: Drawing Links between Two Theories of Self," *Social Psychology Quarterly* 66, no. 2 (2003): 118–37; D. D. Knoch and E. E. Fehr, "Resisting the Power of Temptations. The Right Prefrontal Cortex and Self-Control," *Annals of the New York Academy of Sciences* 1104, no. 1 (2007), p. 123; B. Monin, D. A. Pizarro, and J. S. Beer, "Deciding versus Reacting: Conceptions of Moral Judgment and the Reason-Affect Debate," *Review of General Psychology* 11, no. 2 (2007), pp. 99–111.

14. A. H. Maslow, "A Theory of Human Motivation," *Psychological Review* 50 (1943), pp. 370–96; A. H. Maslow, *Motivation and Personality* (New York: Harper & Row, 1954).

15. D.T. Hall and K.E. Nougaim, "An Examination of Maslow's Need Hierarchy in an Organizational Setting," *Organizational Behavior and Human Performance* 3, no. 1 (1968), p. 12; M.A. Wahba and L.G. Bridwell, "Maslow Reconsidered: A Review of Research on the Need Hierarchy Theory," *Organizational Behavior and Human Performance* 15 (1976), pp. 212–40; E.L. Betz, "Two Tests of Maslow's Theory of Need Fulfillment," *Journal of Vocational Behavior* 24, no. 2 (1984), pp. 204–20; P.A. Corning, "Biological Adaptation in Human Societies: A 'Basic Needs' Approach," *Journal of Bioeconomics* 2, no. 1 (2000), pp. 41–86. For a recent proposed revision of the model, see D.T. Kenrick et al., "Renovating the Pyramid of Needs: Contemporary Extensions Built upon Ancient Foundations," *Perspectives on Psychological Science* 5, no. 3 (May 2010), pp. 292–314.

16. K. Dye, A.J. Mills, and T.G. Weatherbee, "Maslow: Man Interrupted–Reading Management Theory in Context," *Management Decision* 43, no. 10 (2005), pp. 1375–95.

17. A.H. Maslow, "A Preface to Motivation Theory," *Psychsomatic Medicine* 5 (1943), pp. 85–92.

18. S. Kesebir, J. Graham, and S. Oishi, "A Theory of Human Needs Should Be Human-Centered, Not Animal-Centered," *Perspectives on Psychological Science* 5, no. 3 (May 2010), pp. 315–19.

19. A.H. Maslow, *Maslow on Management* (New York: John Wiley & Sons, 1998).

20. F.F. Luthans, "Positive Organizational Behavior: Developing and Managing Psychological Strengths," *Academy of Management Executive* 16, no. 1 (2002), pp. 57–72; S.L. Gable and J. Haidt, "What (and Why) Is Positive Psychology?" *Review of General Psychology* 9, no. 2 (2005), pp. 103–10; M.E.P. Seligman et al., "Positive Psychology Progress: Empirical Validation of Interventions," *American Psychologist* 60, no. 5 (2005), pp. 410–21.

21. L. Parks and R.P. Guay, "Personality, Values, and Motivation," *Personality and Individual Differences* 47, no. 7 (2009), pp. 675–84.

22. B.A. Agle and C.B. Caldwell, "Understanding Research on Values in Business," *Business and Society* 38 (September 1999), pp. 326–87; B. Verplanken and R.W. Holland, "Motivated Decision Making: Effects of Activation and Self-Centrality of Values on Choices and Behavior," *Journal of Personality and Social Psychology* 82, no. 3 (2002), pp. 434–47; S. Hitlin and J.A. Pilavin, "Values: Reviving a Dormant Concept," *Annual Review of Sociology* 30 (2004), pp. 359–93.

23. D.C. McClelland, *The Achieving Society* (New York: Van Nostrand Reinhold, 1961); D.C. McClelland and D.H. Burnham, "Power Is the Great Motivator," *Harvard Business Review* 73 (January–February 1995), pp. 126–39; D. Vredenburgh and Y. Brender, "The Hierarchical Abuse of Power in Work Organizations," *Journal of Business Ethics* 17 (September 1998), pp. 1337–47; S. Shane, E.A. Locke, and C.J. Collins, "Entrepreneurial Motivation," *Human Resource Management Review* 13, no. 2 (2003), pp. 257–79.

24. McClelland, *The Achieving Society.*

25. Shane, Locke, and Collins, "Entrepreneurial Motivation."

26. S. Adams, "Entrepreneurs: The 'Business' Gene," *Forbes,* May 23, 2011, p. 74.

27. McClelland and Burnham, "Power Is the Great Motivator"; J.L. Thomas, M.W. Dickson, and P.D. Bliese, "Values Predicting Leader Performance in the U.S. Army Reserve Officer Training Corps Assessment Center: Evidence for a Personality-Mediated Model," *The Leadership Quarterly* 12, no. 2 (2001), pp. 181–96.

28. Vredenburgh and Brender, "The Hierarchical Abuse of Power in Work Organizations."

29. D. Miron and D.C. McClelland, "The Impact of Achievement Motivation Training on Small Business," *California Management Review* 21 (1979), pp. 13–28.

30. P. R. Lawrence and N. Nohria, *Driven: How Human Nature Shapes Our Choices* (San Francisco, CA: Jossey-Bass, 2002). On the application of four-drive theory to leadership, see P.R. Lawrence, *Driven to Lead* (San Francisco, CA: Jossey-Bass, 2010).

31. The drive to acquire is likely associated with research on getting ahead, desire for competence, the selfish gene, and desire for social distinction. See R.H. Frank, *Choosing the Right Pond: Human Behavior and the Quest for Status* (New York: Oxford University Press, 1985); L. Gaertner et al., "The 'I,' the 'We,' and the 'When': A Meta-Analysis of Motivational Primacy in Self-Definition," *Journal of Personality and Social Psychology* 83, no. 3 (2002), pp. 574–91; J. Hogan and B. Holland, "Using Theory to Evaluate Personality and Job-Performance Relations: A Socioanalytic Perspective," *Journal of Applied Psychology* 88, no. 1 (2003), pp. 100–12; R. Dawkins, *The Selfish Gene,* 30th anniversary ed. (Oxford, UK: Oxford University Press, 2006); B.S. Frey, "Awards as Compensation," *European Management Journal* 4 (2007), pp. 6–14; M.R. Leary, "Motivational and Emotional Aspects of the Self," *Annual Review of Psychology* 58, no. 1 (2007), pp. 317–44.

32. Baumeister and Leary, "The Need to Belong."

33. J. Litman, "Curiosity and the Pleasures of Learning: Wanting and Liking New Information," *Cognition and Emotion* 19, no. 6 (2005), pp. 793–814; T.G. Reio Jr. et al., "The Measurement and Conceptualization of Curiosity," *Journal of Genetic Psychology* 167, no. 2 (2006), pp. 117–35.

34. W.H. Bexton, W. Heron, and T.H. Scott, "Effects of Decreased Variation in the Sensory Environment," *Canadian Journal of Psychology* 8 (1954), pp. 70–76; Loewenstein, "The Psychology of Curiosity."

35. A.R. Damasio, *Descartes' Error: Emotion, Reason, and the Human Brain* (New York: Putnam, 1994); J.E. LeDoux, "Emotion Circuits in the Brain," *Annual Review of Neuroscience* 23 (2000), pp. 155–84; P. Winkielman and K.C. Berridge, "Unconscious Emotion," *Current Directions in Psychological Science* 13, no. 3 (2004), pp. 120–23.

36. Lawrence and Nohria, *Driven,* pp. 145–47.

37. S.H. Schwartz, B.A. Hammer, and M. Wach, "Les Valeurs de Base de la Personne: Théorie, Mesures et Applications," *Revue Française de Sociologie* 47, no. 4 (October–December 2006), pp. 929–68.

38. Lawrence and Nohria, *Driven,* Ch. 11.

39. D. Nebenzahl, "At Radialpoint, Innovation Is Key," *Montreal Gazette,* October 20, 2009, p. F16; "Polish Those Résumés: Here Are the Top 50," *Globe & Mail (Toronto),* June 2, 2010, p. B6.

40. The expectancy theory of motivation in work settings originated in V.H. Vroom, *Work and Motivation* (New York: Wiley, 1964). The version of expectancy theory presented here was developed by Edward Lawler. Lawler's model provides a clearer presentation of the model's three components. P-to-O expectancy is similar to "instrumentality" in Vroom's original expectancy theory model. The difference is that instrumentality is a correlation, whereas P-to-O expectancy is a probability. See J.P. Campbell et al., *Managerial Behavior, Performance, and Effectiveness* (New York: McGraw-Hill, 1970); E.E. Lawler III, *Motivation in Work Organizations* (Monterey,

CA: Brooks-Cole, 1973); D.A. Nadler and E.E. Lawler, "Motivation: A Diagnostic Approach," in *Perspectives on Behavior in Organizations*, ed. J.R. Hackman, E.E. Lawler III, and L.W. Porter, 2nd ed. (New York: McGraw-Hill, 1983), pp. 67–78.

41. M. Zeelenberg et al., "Emotional Reactions to the Outcomes of Decisions: The Role of Counterfactual Thought in the Experience of Regret and Disappointment," *Organizational Behavior and Human Decision Processes* 75, no. 2 (1998), pp. 117–41; B.A. Mellers, "Choice and the Relative Pleasure of Consequences," *Psychological Bulletin* 126, no. 6 (November 2000), pp. 910–24; R.P. Bagozzi, U.M. Dholakia, and S. Basuroy, "How Effortful Decisions Get Enacted: The Motivating Role of Decision Processes, Desires, and Anticipated Emotions," *Journal of Behavioral Decision Making* 16, no. 4 (October 2003), pp. 273–95.

42. Nadler and Lawler, "Motivation: A Diagnostic Approach."

43. B. Moses, "Time to Get Serious about Rewarding Employees," *Globe & Mail*, April 28, 2010, p. B16.

44. T. Matsui and T. Terai, "A Cross-Cultural Study of the Validity of the Expectancy Theory of Motivation," *Journal of Applied Psychology* 60 (1975), pp. 263–65; D.H.B. Welsh, F. Luthans, and S.M. Sommer, "Managing Russian Factory Workers: The Impact of U.S.-Based Behavioral and Participative Techniques," *Academy of Management Journal* 36 (1993), pp. 58–79.

45. This limitation was recently acknowledged by Victor Vroom, who introduced expectancy theory in his 1964 book. See G.P. Latham, *Work Motivation: History, Theory, Research, and Practice* (Thousand Oaks, CA: Sage, 2007), pp. 47-48.

46. J.B. Watson, *Behavior: An Introduction to Comparative Psychology* (New York: Henry Holt & Co., 1914).

47. B.F. Skinner, *About Behaviorism* (New York: Alfred A. Knopf, 1974); J. Komaki, T. Coombs, and S. Schepman, "Motivational Implications of Reinforcement Theory," in *Motivation and Leadership at Work*, ed. R. M. Steers, L. W. Porter, and G. A. Bigley (New York: McGraw-Hill, 1996), pp. 34–52; R.G. Miltenberger, *Behavior Modification: Principles and Procedures* (Pacific Grove, CA: Brooks/Cole, 1997).

48. T.K. Connellan, *How to Improve Human Performance* (New York: Harper & Row, 1978), pp. 48–57; F. Luthans and R. Kreitner, *Organizational Behavior Modification and Beyond* (Glenview, IL: Scott, Foresman, 1985), pp. 85–88.

49. B.F. Skinner, *Science and Human Behavior* (New York: The Free Press, 1965); Miltenberger, *Behavior Modification: Principles and Procedures*, Ch. 4–6.

50. T.R. Hinkin and C.A. Schriesheim, "If You Don't Hear from Me You Know You Are Doing Fine," *Cornell Hotel & Restaurant Administration Quarterly* 45, no. 4 (November 2004), pp. 362–72.

51. "10,000 Steps in the Right Direction," *Our City (Stoke-on-Kent)*, January 2009, p. 11; D. Blackhurst, "£1m Bill to Get Council and NHS Staff Walking," *The Sentinel (Staffordshire)*, February 2, 2009, p. 13.

52. L.K. Trevino, "The Social Effects of Punishment in Organizations: A Justice Perspective," *Academy of Management Review* 17 (1992), pp. 647–76; L.E. Atwater et al., "Recipient and Observer Reactions to Discipline: Are Managers Experiencing Wishful Thinking?" *Journal of Organizational Behavior* 22, no. 3 (May 2001), pp. 249–70.

53. G.P. Latham and V.L. Huber, "Schedules of Reinforcement: Lessons from the Past and Issues for the Future," *Journal of Organizational Behavior Management* 13 (1992), pp. 125–49; B.A. Williams, "Challenges to Timing-Based Theories of Operant Behavior," *Behavioural Processes* 62 (April 2003), pp. 115–23.

54. A.C. Giusti, "Employers in Louisiana Work Exercise into Daily Schedule to Save on Health Care," *New Orleans CityBusiness*, September 28, 2010; J.K. Mollohan, "Clear Incentives, Communication Help Louisiana Health System Find Wellness Success," *Employee Benefit News*, June 15, 2010, p. 49; "Burger Boat Completes One Year without Lost-Time Injury," *Herald Times (Manitowic, WI)*, May 8, 2011.

55. J.A. Bargh and M.J. Ferguson, "Beyond Behaviorism: On the Automaticity of Higher Mental Processes," *Psychological Bulletin* 126, no. 6 (2000), pp. 925–45. Some writers argue that behaviorists long ago accepted the relevance of cognitive processes in behavior modification. See I. Kirsch et al., "The Role of Cognition in Classical and Operant Conditioning," *Journal of Clinical Psychology* 60, no. 4 (April 2004), pp. 369–92.

56. A. Bandura, *Social Foundations of Thought and Action: A Social Cognitive Theory* (Englewood Cliffs, NJ: Prentice Hall, 1986); A. Bandura, "Social Cognitive Theory of Self-Regulation," *Organizational Behavior and Human Decision Processes* 50, no. 2 (1991), pp. 248–87; A. Bandura, "Social Cognitive Theory: An Agentic Perspective," *Annual Review of Psychology* 52 (2001), pp. 1–26.

57. M.E. Schnake, "Vicarious Punishment in a Work Setting," *Journal of Applied Psychology* 71 (1986), pp. 343–45; Trevino, "The Social Effects of Punishment in Organizations"; J. Malouff et al., "Effects of Vicarious Punishment: A Meta-Analysis," *Journal of General Psychology* 136, no. 3 (2009), pp. 271–86.

58. A. Pescuric and W.C. Byham, "The New Look of Behavior Modeling," *Training & Development* 50 (July 1996), pp. 24–30.

59. A. Bandura, "Self-Reinforcement: Theoretical and Methodological Considerations," *Behaviorism* 4 (1976), pp. 135–55; C.A. Frayne and J.M. Geringer, "Self-Management Training for Improving Job Performance: A Field Experiment Involving Salespeople," *Journal of Applied Psychology* 85, no. 3 (June 2000), pp. 361–72; J.B. Vancouver and D.V. Day, "Industrial and Organisation Research on Self-Regulation: From Constructs to Applications," *Applied Psychology: An International Journal* 54, no. 2 (April 2005), pp. 155–85.

60. S. Zeller, "Good Calls," *Government Executive*, May 15, 2005; C. Bailor, "Checking the Pulse of the Contact Center," *Customer Relationship Management*, November 2007, pp. 24–29.

61. A. Shin, "What Customers Say and How They Say It," *Washington Post*, October 18, 2006, p. D01; D. Ververidis and C. Kotropoulos, "Emotional Speech Recognition: Resources, Features, and Methods," *Speech Communication* 48, no. 9 (2006), pp. 1162–81.

62. G.P. Latham, "Goal Setting: A Five-Step Approach to Behavior Change," *Organizational Dynamics* 32, no. 3 (2003), pp. 309–18; E.A. Locke and G.P. Latham, *A Theory of Goal Setting and Task Performance* (Englewood Cliffs, NJ: Prentice Hall, 1990).

63. There are several variations of the SMARTER goal setting model; "achievable" is sometimes "acceptable," "reviewed" is sometimes "recorded," and "exciting" is sometimes "ethical." Based on an earlier SMART model, the SMARTER goal setting model seems to have originated in British sports psychology writing around the mid-1990s. For early examples, see P. Butler, *Performance Profiling* (Leeds, UK: The National Coaching Foundation, 1996), p. 36; R.C. Thelwell and I.A. Greenlees, "The Effects of a Mental Skills Training Program Package on Gymnasium Triathlon Performance," *The Sports Psychologist* 15, no. 2 (2001), pp. 127–41.

64. J. Romeo, "The Fine Art of Goal-Setting," *Alaska Business Monthly*, February 2011, p. 92.

65. This adage apparently was a sign that hung in Einstein's study. For further debate on the value and limitations of measurement, see J.M. Henshaw, *Does Measurement Measure Up? How Numbers Reveal and Conceal the Truth* (Baltimore, MD: Johns Hopkins Press, 2006).

66. A. Li and A.B. Butler, "The Effects of Participation in Goal Setting and Goal Rationales on Goal Commitment: An Exploration of Justice Mediators," *Journal of Business and Psychology* 19, no. 1 (Fall 2004), pp. 37–51.

67. Locke and Latham, *A Theory of Goal Setting and Task Performance*, Ch. 6–7; J. Wegge, "Participation in Group Goal Setting: Some Novel Findings and a Comprehensive Model as a New Ending to an Old Story," *Applied Psychology: An International Review* 49 (2000), pp. 498–516.

68. M. London, E.M. Mone, and J.C. Scott, "Performance Management and Assessment: Methods for Improved Rater Accuracy and Employee Goal Setting," *Human Resource Management* 43, no. 4 (Winter 2004), pp. 319–36; G.P. Latham and C.C. Pinder, "Work Motivation Theory and Research at the Dawn of the Twenty-First Century," *Annual Review of Psychology* 56 (2005), pp. 485–516.

69. "Multifaceted Leader Brings Unique Vision to Urban District," 2007, http://www.beyond-the-book.com/leadership/leadership_030707. html; Richmond Pubic Schools, *Balanced Scorecard—Strategic Objectives, Measures and Projects* (Richmond, VA: Richmond Pubic Schools, September 30, 2010).

70. R. Mostray, "The RCMP's Experience with the Balanced Scorecard: 8 Years+," paper presented at Centre of Excellence on Performance Management & Accountability, Ottawa, March 10, 2010.

71. S.P. Brown, S. Ganesan, and G. Challagalla, "Self-Efficacy as a Moderator of Information-Seeking Effectiveness," *Journal of Applied Psychology* 86, no. 5 (2001), pp. 1043–51; P.A. Heslin and G.P. Latham, "The Effect of Upward Feedback on Managerial Behaviour," *Applied Psychology: An International Review* 53, no. 1 (2004), pp. 23–37; D. Van-Dijk and A.N. Kluger, "Feedback Sign Effect on Motivation: Is It Moderated by Regulatory Focus?" *Applied Psychology: An International Review* 53, no. 1 (2004), pp. 113–35; J.E. Bono and A.E. Colbert, "Understanding Responses to Multi-Source Feedback: The Role of Core Self-Evaluations," *Personnel Psychology* 58, no. 1 (Spring 2005), pp. 171–203.

72. P. Drucker, *The Effective Executive* (Oxford, UK: Butterworth-Heinemann, 2007), p. 22. Drucker's emphasis on strengths was also noted by D.K. Whitney and A. Trosten-Bloom, *The Power of Appreciative Inquiry: A Practical Guide to Positive Change*, 2nd ed. (San Francisco: Berrett-Koehler Publishers, 2010), p. xii.

73. M. Buckingham, *Go Put Your Strengths to Work* (New York: The Free Press, 2007); S.L. Orem, J. Binkert, and A.L. Clancy, *Appreciative Coaching: A Positive Process for Change* (San Francisco: Jossey-Bass, 2007); S. Gordon, "Appreciative Inquiry Coaching," *International Coaching Psychology Review* 3, no. 2 (March 2008), pp. 19–31.

74. R. White, "Building on Employee Strengths at Sony Europe," *Strategic HR Review* 5, no. 5 (2006), pp. 28–31.

75. A. Terracciano, P.T. Costa, and R.R. McCrae, "Personality Plasticity after Age 30," *Personality and Social Psychology Bulletin* 32, no. 8 (August 2006), pp. 999–1009; Leary, "Motivational and Emotional Aspects of the Self."

76. D. Hendry, "Game-Playing: The Latest Business Tool," *Globe & Mail*, November 17, 2006, p. C11.

77. L. Hollman, "Seeing the Writing on the Wall," *Call Center*, August 2002, p. 37; S.E. Ante, "Giving the Boss the Big Picture," *Business-Week*, February 13, 2006, p. 48.

78. F.P. Morgeson, T.V. Mumford, and M.A. Campion, "Coming Full Circle: Using Research and Practice to Address 27 Questions about 360-Degree Feedback Programs," *Consulting Psychology Journal* 57, no. 3 (2005), pp. 196–209; J.W. Smither, M. London, and R.R. Reilly, "Does Performance Improve Following Multisource Feedback? A Theoretical Model, Meta-Analysis, and Review of Empirical Findings," *Personnel Psychology* 58, no. 1 (2005), pp. 33–66; L.E. Atwater, J.F. Brett, and A.C. Charles, "Multisource Feedback: Lessons Learned and Implications for Practice," *Human Resource Management* 46, no. 2 (Summer 2007), pp. 285–307.

79. A.S. DeNisi and A.N. Kluger, "Feedback Effectiveness: Can 360-Degree Appraisals Be Improved?" *Academy of Management Executive* 14 (February 2000), pp. 129–39; M.A. Peiperl, "Getting 360 Degree Feedback Right," *Harvard Business Review* 79 (January 2001), pp. 142–47; M.-G. Seo, L.F. Barrett, and J.M. Bartunek, "The Role of Affective Experience in Work Motivation," *Academy of Management Review* 29 (2004), pp. 423–49.

80. S.J. Ashford and G.B. Northcraft, "Conveying More (or Less) Than We Realize: The Role of Impression Management in Feedback Seeking," *Organizational Behavior and Human Decision Processes* 53 (1992), pp. 310–34; J.R. Williams et al., "Increasing Feedback Seeking in Public Contexts: It Takes Two (or More) to Tango," *Journal of Applied Psychology* 84 (December 1999), pp. 969–76.

81. J.B. Miner, "The Rated Importance, Scientific Validity, and Practical Usefulness of Organizational Behavior Theories: A Quantitative Review," *Academy of Management Learning and Education* 2, no. 3 (2003), pp. 250–68. Also see Pinder, *Work Motivation in Organizational Behavior,* p. 384.

82. P.M. Wright, "Goal Setting and Monetary Incentives: Motivational Tools That Can Work Too Well," *Compensation and Benefits Review* 26 (May–June 1994), pp. 41–49; E.A. Locke and G.P. Latham, "Building a Practically Useful Theory of Goal Setting and Task Motivation: A 35-Year Odyssey," *American Psychologist* 57, no. 9 (2002), pp. 705–17.

83. Latham, *Work Motivation,* p. 188.

84. R. Colman, "Packing the Perfect HR Punch," *CMA Management,* March 2007, pp. 40–43.

85. J. Greenberg and E.A. Lind, "The Pursuit of Organizational Justice: From Conceptualization to Implication to Application," in *Industrial and Organizational Psychology: Linking Theory with Practice,* ed. C.L. Cooper and E.A. Locke (London: Blackwell, 2000), pp. 72–108; R. Cropanzano and M. Schminke, "Using Social Justice to Build Effective Work Groups," in *Groups at Work: Theory and Research,* ed. M.E. Turner (Mahwah, NJ: Lawrence Erlbaum Associates, 2001), pp. 143–71; D.T. Miller, "Disrespect and the Experience of Injustice," *Annual Review of Psychology* 52 (2001), pp. 527–53.

86. M. Bloom, "The Performance Effects of Pay Dispersion on Individuals and Organizations," *Academy of Management Journal* 42, no. 1 (1999), pp. 25–40; P.A. Siegel and D.C. Hambrick, "Pay Disparities within Top Management Groups: Evidence of Harmful Effects on Performance of High-Technology Firms," *Organization Science* 16, no. 3 (May 2005), pp. 259–74; C. Grund and N. Westergaard-Nielsen, "The Dispersion of Employees' Wage Increases and Firm Performance," *Industrial & Labor Relations Review* 61, no. 4 (July 2008), pp. 485–501; M. Mondello and J. Maxcy, "The Impact of Salary Dispersion and Performance Bonuses in NFL Organizations," *Management Decision* 47, no. 1 (2009), pp. 110–23; H. Katayama and H. Nuch, "A Game-Level Analysis of Salary Dispersion and Team Performance in the National Basketball Association," *Applied Economics* 43, no. 10 (2011), pp. 1193–1207.

87. J.S. Adams, "Toward an Understanding of Inequity," *Journal of Abnormal and Social Psychology* 67 (1963), pp. 422–36; R.T. Mowday, "Equity Theory Predictions of Behavior in Organizations," in *Motivation and Work Behavior,* ed. L.W. Porter and R.M. Steers, 5th ed. (New York: McGraw-Hill, 1991), pp. 111–31; R.G. Cropanzano, "Progress in Organizational Justice: Tunneling through the Maze," in *International Review of Industrial and Organizational Psychology,* ed. C.L. Cooper and I.T. Robertson (New York: Wiley, 1997), pp. 317–72; L.A. Powell, "Justice Judgments as Complex Psychocultural Constructions: An Equity-Based Heuristic for Mapping Two- and Three-Dimensional Fairness Representations in Perceptual Space," *Journal of Cross-Cultural Psychology* 36, no. 1 (January 2005), pp. 48–73.

88. C.T. Kulik and M.L. Ambrose, "Personal and Situational Determinants of Referent Choice," *Academy of Management Review* 17 (1992), pp. 212–37; G. Blau, "Testing the Effect of Level and Importance of Pay Referents on Pay Level Satisfaction," *Human Relations* 47 (1994), pp. 1251–68.

89. T.P. Summers and A.S. DeNisi, "In Search of Adams' Other: Reexamination of Referents Used in the Evaluation of Pay," *Human Relations* 43 (1990), pp. 497–511.

90. Y. Cohen-Charash and P.E. Spector, "The Role of Justice in Organizations: A Meta-Analysis," *Organizational Behavior and Human Decision Processes* 86 (November 2001), pp. 278–321.

91. "Pierre Berton, Canadian Cultural Icon, Enjoyed Long and Colourful Career," *Times Colonist (Victoria, B.C.)*, November 30, 2004.

92. K.S. Sauleya and A.G. Bedeian, "Equity Sensitivity: Construction of a Measure and Examination of Its Psychometric Properties," *Journal of Management* 26 (September 2000), pp. 885–910; G. Blakely, M. Andrews, and R. Moorman, "The Moderating Effects of Equity Sensitivity on the Relationship between Organizational Justice and Organizational Citizenship Behaviors," *Journal of Business and Psychology* 20, no. 2 (2005), pp. 259–73.

93. M. Ezzamel and R. Watson, "Pay Comparability across and within UK Boards: An Empirical Analysis of the Cash Pay Awards to CEOs and Other Board Members," *Journal of Management Studies* 39, no. 2 (March 2002), pp. 207–32; J. Fizel, A.C. Krautman, and L. Hadley, "Equity and Arbitration in Major League Baseball," *Managerial and Decision Economics* 23, no. 7 (October–November 2002), pp. 427–35.

94. Greenberg and Lind, "The Pursuit of Organizational Justice"; K. Roberts and K.S. Markel, "Claiming in the Name of Fairness: Organizational Justice and the Decision to File for Workplace Injury Compensation," *Journal of Occupational Health Psychology* 6 (October 2001), pp. 332–47; J.B. Olson-Buchanan and W.R. Boswell, "The Role of Employee Loyalty and Formality in Voicing Discontent," *Journal of Applied Psychology* 87, no. 6 (2002), pp. 1167–74.

95. R. Hagey et al., "Immigrant Nurses' Experience of Racism," *Journal of Nursing Scholarship* 33 (Fourth Quarter 2001), pp. 389–95; Roberts and Markel, "Claiming in the Name of Fairness"; D.A. Jones and D.P. Skarlicki, "The Effects of Overhearing Peers Discuss an Authority's Fairness Reputation on Reactions to Subsequent Treatment," *Journal of Applied Psychology* 90, no. 2 (2005), pp. 363–72.

96. Miller, "Disrespect and the Experience of Injustice."

97. M.L. Ambrose, M.A. Seabright, and M. Schminke, "Sabotage in the Workplace: The Role of Organizational Injustice," *Organizational Behavior and Human Decision Processes* 89, no. 1 (2002), pp. 947–65.

CHAPTER 6

1. E. Clark, "The Cost of Fun," *The Telegraph (London),* March 26, 2007; D. Eimer, "China's Toy Makers Face Bleak Christmas as Factories Shut Down," *The Telegraph (London),* November 2, 2008, p. 31; A. Harney, *The China Price: The True Cost of Chinese Competitive Advantage* (London: Penguin, 2008), pp. 154–55; G. Chamberlain, "Apple Factories Accused of Exploiting Chinese Workers," *The Observer (London),* April 20, 2011; J. Johnson, "My Gadget Guilt," *Wired,* March 2011, pp. 96–102.

2. M.C. Bloom and G.T. Milkovich, "Issues in Managerial Compensation Research," in *Trends in Organizational Behavior,* ed. C.L. Cooper and D.M. Rousseau (Chichester, UK: John Wiley & Sons, 1996), pp. 23–47. For an excellent review of the history of money, see N. Ferguson, *The Ascent of Money: A Financial History of the World* (New York: Penguin, 2008).

3. S.E.G. Lea and P. Webley, "Money as Tool, Money as Drug: The Biological Psychology of a Strong Incentive," *Behavioral and Brain Sciences* 29 (2006), pp. 161–209; D. Valenze, *The Social Life of Money in the English Past* (New York: Cambridge University Press, 2006); G.M. Rose and L.M. Orr, "Measuring and Exploring Symbolic Money Meanings," *Psychology and Marketing* 24, no. 9 (2007), pp. 743–61.

4. D.W. Krueger, "Money, Success, and Success Phobia," in *The Last Taboo: Money as Symbol and Reality in Psychotherapy and Psychoanalysis,* ed. D.W. Krueger (New York: Brunner/Mazel, 1986), pp. 3–16.

5. P.F. Wernimont and S. Fitzpatrick, "The Meaning of Money," *Journal of Applied Psychology* 56, no. 3 (1972), pp. 218–26; T.R. Mitchell and A.E. Mickel, "The Meaning of Money: An Individual-Difference Perspective," *Academy of Management Review* (July 1999), pp. 568–78; R. Trachtman, "The Money Taboo: Its Effects in Everyday Life and in the Practice of Psychotherapy," *Clinical Social Work Journal* 27, no. 3 (1999), pp. 275–88; S. Lea, "Money: Motivation, Metaphors, and Mores," *Behavioral and Brain Sciences* 29, no. 2 (2006), pp. 196–209; Lea and Webley, "Money as Tool, Money as Drug"; T.L.-P. Tang et al., "The Love of Money and Pay Level Satisfaction: Measurement and Functional Equivalence in 29 Geopolitical Entities around the World," *Management and Organization Review* 2, no. 3 (2006), pp. 423–52.

6. A. Furnham and R. Okamura, "Your Money or Your Life: Behavioral and Emotional Predictors of Money Pathology," *Human Relations* 52 (September 1999), pp. 1157–77.

7. Tang et al., "The Love of Money and Pay Level Satisfaction"; T. Tang et al., "To Help or Not to Help? The Good Samaritan Effect and the Love of Money on Helping Behavior," *Journal of Business Ethics* (2007); T. Tang and Y.-J. Chen, "Intelligence vs. Wisdom: The Love of Money, Machiavellianism, and Unethical Behavior across College Major and Gender," *Journal of Business Ethics* 82, no. 1 (2008), pp. 1–26.

8. R. Lynn, *The Secret of the Miracle Economy* (London: SAE, 1991), cited in Furnham and Okamura, "Your Money or Your Life."

9. A. Furnham, B.D. Kirkcaldy, and R. Lynn, "National Attitudes to Competitiveness, Money, and Work among Young People: First, Second, and Third World Differences," *Human Relations* 47 (January 1994), pp. 119–32; G. Dell'Orto and K.O. Doyle, "Poveri Ma Belli: Meanings of Money in Italy and in Switzerland," *American Behavioral Scientist* 45, no. 2 (October 1, 2001), pp. 257–71; K.O. Doyle, "Introduction: Ethnicity and Money," *American Behavioral Scientist* 45, no. 2 (October 1, 2001), pp. 181–90; V.K.G. Lim, "Money Matters: An Empirical Investigation of Money, Face and Confucian Work Ethic," *Personality and Individual Differences* 35 (2003), pp. 953–70; T. L.-P. Tang, A. Furnham, and G.M.-T. Davis, "A Cross-Cultural Comparison of the Money Ethic, the Protestant Work Ethic, and Job Satisfaction: Taiwan, the USA, and the UK," *International Journal of Organization Theory and Behavior* 6, no. 2 (Summer 2003), pp. 175–94; R. Tung and C. Baumann, "Comparing the Attitudes toward Money, Material Possessions and Savings of Overseas Chinese vis-á-vis Chinese in China: Convergence, Divergence or Cross-Vergence, vis-á-vis 'One Size Fits All' Human Resource Management Policies and Practices," *International Journal of Human Resource Management* 20, no. 11 (2009), pp. 2382–401.

10. D. Gardner, V.D. Linn, and J.L. Pierce, "The Effects of Pay Level on Organization-Based Self-Esteem and Performance: A Field Study," *Journal of Occupational and Organizational Psychology* 77 (2004), pp. 307–22; S.L. Rynes, B. Gerhart, and K.A. Minette, "The Importance of Pay in Employee Motivation: Discrepancies between What People Say and What They Do," *Human Resource Management* 43, no. 4 (Winter 2004), pp. 381–94; B.S. Frey, "Awards as Compensation," *European Management Journal* 4 (2007), pp. 6–14.

11. J.S. Mill, *Utilitarianism,* 7th ed. (London: Longmans, Green, and Co., 1879; Project Gutenberg EBook), Ch. 4.

12. "'Shunto' Wage Talks Effectively Kicked Off in Japan," *Jiji Press English News Service,* January 19, 2010; "Japan Auto Workers Unions Not to Seek Base Pay Hike," *Jiji Press English News Service*, December 15, 2010; *Conditions of Employment* (Villigen, Switzerland: Paul Sherrer Institut, 2011).

13. D.M. Figart, "Equal Pay for Equal Work: The Role of Job Evaluation in an Evolving Social Norm," *Journal of Economic Issues* 34 (March 2000), pp. 1–19.

14. E.E. Lawler III, *Rewarding Excellence: Pay Strategies for the New Economy* (San Francisco: Jossey-Bass, 2000), see pp. 30–35, 109–19; R. McNabb and K. Whitfield, "Job Evaluation and High Performance Work Practices: Compatible or Conflictual?" *Journal of Management Studies* 38 (March 2001), pp. 293–312.

15. P.K. Zingheim and J.R. Schuster, "Competencies and Rewards: Substance or Just Style?" *Compensation Benefits Review* 35, no. 5 (2003), pp. 40–44.

16. The City of Flagstaff, Arizona, skill-based pay information is derived from the job advertisement "108-08–Multi Skilled Worker–Plant Operator–Plant Technician" (August 8, 2008) and "2008–2009 City of Flagstaff Pay Plan: Skill Based Pay."

17. R.J. Long, "Paying for Knowledge: Does It Pay?" *Canadian HR Reporter,* March 28, 2005, pp. 12–13; J.D. Shaw et al., "Success and Survival of Skill-Based Pay Plans," *Journal of Management* 31, no. 1 (February 2005), pp. 28–49; E.C. Dierdorff and E.A. Surface, "If You Pay for Skills, Will They Learn? Skill Change and Maintenance under a Skill-Based Pay System," *Journal of Management* 34, no. 4 (August 2008), pp. 721–43.

18. Zingheim and Schuster, "Competencies and Rewards"; F. Giancola, "Skill-Based Pay—Issues for Consideration," *Benefits & Compensation Digest* 44, no. 5 (2007), pp. 1–15.

19. L. Buchanan, "The Un-Factory," *Inc.* 32, no. 5 (June 2010), pp. 62–67; R.W. Hall, "Portionpac Chemical—Compression Pioneer," Hondo, TX, January 13, 2011, http://www.compression.org/portionpac-chemical-compression-pioneer/.

20. "Using Incentive Plans Wisely," *Receivables Report for America's Health Care Financial Managers* 23, no. 6 (2008), pp. 9–11.

21. N. Byrnes and M. Arndt, "The Art of Motivation," *BusinessWeek,* May 1, 2006, p. 56; M. Bolch, "Rewarding the Team," *HRMagazine,* February 2007, pp. 91–93.

22. G. Hamel, *The Future of Management* (Boston: Harvard Business School Press, 2007), pp. 73–75.

23. J.D. Ketcham and M.F. Furukawa, "Hospital-Physician Gainsharing in Cardiology," *Health Affairs* 27, no. 3 (2008), pp. 803–12; J. Ferenc, "Gainsharing Poised for a Comeback," *Hospitals & Health Networks,* June 2010, pp. 12–14, http://search.ebscohost.com/login.aspx?direct=true&db=heh&AN=51746178&site=ehost-live; I.M. Leitman et al., "Quality and Financial Outcomes from Gainsharing for Inpatient Admissions: A Three-Year Experience," *Journal of Hospital Medicine* 5, no. 9 (2010), pp. 501–07.

24. L.R. Gomez-Mejia, T.M. Welbourne, and R.M. Wiseman, "The Role of Risk Sharing and Risk Taking under Gainsharing," *Academy of Management Review* 25 (July 2000), pp. 492–507; K.M. Bartol and A. Srivastava, "Encouraging Knowledge Sharing: The Role of Organizational Reward System," *Journal of Leadership & Organizational Studies* 9 (Summer 2002), pp. 64–76.

25. D. Finlayson, "Top Employers—Premium Perks," *Edmonton Journal,* October 22, 2005, p. I1; L. Young, "Spruceland Millworks Benefits from Generosity," *Canadian HR Reporter,* October 22, 2007, p. 12.

26. C. Rosen, J. Case, and M. Staubus, "Every Employee an Owner [Really]," *Harvard Business Review* 83, no. 6 (June 2005), pp. 122–30; R.A. Wirtz, "Employee Ownership: Economic Miracle or ESOPs Fable?" *The Region (Magazine of the Federal Reserve Bank of Minneapolis),* June 2007, pp. 22–41.

27. M. Albright, "Could Publix Super Markets Go Public?" *St. Petersburg Times (Florida),* March 16, 2011.

28. O. Hammarström, *Handelsbanken, Sweden: Make Work Pay—Make Work Attractive,* company cases (Dublin, Ireland: Eurofound, October 2007).

29. J. Chelius and R.S. Smith, "Profit Sharing and Employment Stability," *Industrial and Labor Relations Review* 43 (1990), pp. 256s–73s; S.H. Wagner, C.P. Parkers, and N.D. Christiansen, "Employees That Think and Act Like Owners: Effects of Ownership Beliefs and Behaviors on Organizational Effectiveness," *Personnel Psychology* 56, no. 4 (Winter 2003), pp. 847–71; G. Ledford, M. Lucy, and P. Leblanc, "The Effects of Stock Ownership on Employee Attitudes and Behavior: Evidence from the Rewards at Work Studies," *Perspectives (Sibson),* January

2004; Rosen, Case, and Staubus, "Every Employee an Owner [Really]."

30. A.J. Maggs, "Enron, Esops, and Fiduciary Duty," *Benefits Law Journal* 16, no. 3 (Autumn 2003), pp. 42–52; C. Brodzinski, "ESOP's Fables Can Make Coverage Risky," *National Underwriter P&C,* June 13, 2005, pp. 16–17.

31. D. Ariely et al., "Large Stakes and Big Mistakes," *Review of Economic Studies* 76, no. 2 (2009), pp. 451–69.

32. J. Pfeffer, *The Human Equation* (Boston: Harvard Business School Press, 1998); B.N. Pfau and I.T. Kay, *The Human Capital Edge* (New York: McGraw-Hill, 2002); D. Guest, N. Conway, and P. Dewe, "Using Sequential Tree Analysis to Search for 'Bundles' of HR Practices," *Human Resource Management Journal* 14, no. 1 (2004), pp. 79–96. The problems with performance-based pay are discussed in W.C. Hammer, "How to Ruin Motivation with Pay," *Compensation Review* 7, no. 3 (1975), pp. 17–27; A. Kohn, *Punished by Rewards* (Boston: Houghton Mifflin, 1993); M. O'Donnell and J. O'Brian, "Performance-Based Pay in the Australian Public Service," *Review of Public Personnel Administration* 20 (Spring 2000), pp. 20–34; M. Beer and M.D. Cannon, "Promise and Peril of Implementing Pay-for-Performance," *Human Resource Management* 43, no. 1 (Spring 2004), pp. 3–48.

33. Watson Wyatt, *WorkCanada 2004/2005—Pursuing Productive Engagement* (Toronto: Watson Wyatt, January 2005); Kelly Services, "Majority of Canada's Workers Happy, Bosses among Best in World," news release, November 28, 2006); Hudson, *Rising above the Average: 2007 Compensation & Benefits Report,* June 2007.

34. S. Kerr, "Organization Rewards: Practical, Cost-Neutral Alternatives That You May Know, but Don't Practice," *Organizational Dynamics* 28 (Summer 1999), pp. 61–70.

35. S.A. Culbert and L. Rout, *Get Rid of the Performance Review!* (New York: Business Plus, 2010); "Should Performance Reviews Be Fired?" *Knowledge@Wharton,* April 27, 2011; R. Pyrillis, "The Reviews Are In," *Workforce Management,* May 2011, p. 20. Along with expert critiques, surveys indicate that most employees view performance reviews as more harmful than helpful.

36. C. Atchison, "How to Build a Super Staff," *Profit,* May 2010, pp. 30–34.

37. M. Buckingham and D.O. Clifton, *Now, Discover Your Strengths* (New York: The Free Press, 2001), p. 226; M. Rotundo and P. Sackett, "The Relative Importance of Task, Citizenship, and Counterproductive Performance to Global Ratings of Job Performance: A Policy-Capturing Approach," *Journal of Applied Psychology* 87 (February 2002), pp. 66–80.

38. M. Goldsmith, "Try Feedforward Instead of Feedback," *Leader to Leader,* Summer 2002, pp. 11–14; Culbert and Rout, *Get Rid of the Performance Review!* Ch. 7.

39. J.S. DeMatteo, L.T. Eby, and E. Sundstrom, "Team-Based Rewards: Current Empirical Evidence and Directions for Future Research," *Research in Organizational Behavior* 20 (1998), pp. 141–83; S. Rynes, B. Gerhart, and L. Parks, "Personnel Psychology: Performance Evaluation and Pay for Performance," *Annual Review of Psychology* 56 (2005), pp. 571–600.

40. R.M. Johnson, D. Lucking-Reiley, and J.C. Munos, '*The War for the Fare': How Driver Compensation Affects Bus System Performance* (SSRN, 2005); M. Munger, "Planning Order, Causing Chaos: Transantiago," *Library of Economics and Liberty,* September 1, 2008; R. Banick, *Bus Rapid Transit and the Latin American City: Successes to Date, but Miles to Go* (Washington, DC: Council on Hemispheric Affairs, December 2009).

41. "There's Only One Lesson to Learn from UBS," *Euromoney,* May 2008, p. 9; *Shareholder Report on UBS's Write-Downs* (Zurich, Switzerland: UBS, April 18, 2008); U. Harnischfeger, "UBS Says Excess of Ambition Led to Its Miscues on Subprime Loans," *The New*

York Times, April 22, 2008, p. C3; S. Reed, "Behind the Mess at UBS," *BusinessWeek,* no. 4073 (March 3, 2008), pp. 30–31.

42. A. Holecek, "Griffith, Ind., Native Takes Over as Steel Plant Manager," *Northwest Indiana Times (Munster, Ind.),* May 25, 2003.

43. B. Moses, "Time to Get Serious about Rewarding Employees," *Globe & Mail,* April 28, 2010, p. B16.

44. "Dream Teams," *Human Resources Professional* (November 1994), pp. 17–19.

45. D.R. Spitzer, "Power Rewards: Rewards That Really Motivate," *Management Review* (May 1996), pp. 45–50. For a classic discussion on the unintended consequences of pay, see S. Kerr, "On the Folly of Rewarding A, While Hoping for B," *Academy of Management Journal* 18 (1975), pp. 769–83.

46. "Strong Leaders Make Great Workplaces," *CityBusiness,* August 28, 2000; Kelly Services, *Generational Crossovers in the Workforce— Opinions Revealed* (Troy, NY: Kelly Services, 2009).

47. J.R. Edwards, J.A. Scully, and M.D. Brtek, "The Nature and Outcomes of Work: A Replication and Extension of Interdisciplinary Work-Design Research," *Journal of Applied Psychology* 85, no. 6 (2000), pp. 860–68; F.P. Morgeson and M.A. Campion, "Minimizing Tradeoffs When Redesigning Work: Evidence from a Longitudinal Quasi-Experiment," *Personnel Psychology* 55, no. 3 (Autumn 2002), pp. 589–612.

48. "Grads Find Job-Hopping Is Not a Career-Stopper," *Shanghai Daily,* June 23, 2008.

49. S. Leroy, "Why Is It So Hard to Do My Work? The Challenge of Attention Residue When Switching between Work Tasks," *Organizational Behavior and Human Decision Processes* 109, no. 2 (2009), pp. 168–81.

50. H. Fayol, *General and Industrial Management,* trans. C. Storrs (London: Pitman, 1949); E.E. Lawler III, *Motivation in Work Organizations* (Monterey, CA: Brooks/Cole, 1973), Ch. 7; M.A. Campion, "Ability Requirement Implications of Job Design: An Interdisciplinary Perspective," *Personnel Psychology* 42 (1989), pp. 1–24.

51. F.C. Lane, *Venice: A Maritime Republic* (Baltimore, MD: Johns Hopkins University Press, 1973), pp. 361–64; R.C. Davis, "*Arsenal* and *Arsenalotti*: Workplace and Community in Seventeenth-Century Venice," in *The Workplace before the Factory,* ed. T.M. Safley and L.N. Rosenband (Ithaca, NY: Cornell University Press, 1993), pp. 180–203.

52. A. Smith, *An Inquiry into the Nature and Causes of the Wealth of Nations,* 5th ed. (London: Methuen and Co., 1904), pp. 8–9.

53. F.W. Taylor, *The Principles of Scientific Management* (New York: Harper & Row, 1911); R. Kanigel, *The One Best Way: Frederick Winslow Taylor and the Enigma of Efficiency* (New York: Viking, 1997).

54. C.R. Walker and R.H. Guest, *The Man on the Assembly Line* (Cambridge, MA: Harvard University Press, 1952); W.F. Dowling, "Job Redesign on the Assembly Line: Farewell to Blue-Collar Blues?" *Organizational Dynamics* (Autumn 1973), pp. 51–67; E.E. Lawler III, *High-Involvement Management* (San Francisco: Jossey-Bass, 1986).

55. M. Keller, *Rude Awakening* (New York: Harper Perennial, 1989), p. 128.

56. F. Herzberg, B. Mausner, and B.B. Snyderman, *The Motivation to Work* (New York: Wiley, 1959).

57. S.K. Parker, T.D. Wall, and J.L. Cordery, "Future Work Design Research and Practice: Towards an Elaborated Model of Work Design," *Journal of Occupational and Organizational Psychology* 74 (November 2001), pp. 413–40. For a decisive critique of motivator-hygiene theory, see N. King, "Clarification and Evaluation of the Two Factor Theory of Job Satisfaction," *Psychological Bulletin* 74 (1970), pp. 18–31.

58. J.R. Hackman and G. Oldham, *Work Redesign* (Reading, MA: Addison-Wesley, 1980).

59. E. Ailworth, "Rodolfo 'Rudy' Magararu," Boston.com, 2010, http://www.boston.com/bostonworks/topworkplaces/2010/irunthisplace?pg=4.

60. C. Hosford, "Flying High," *Incentive* 181, no. 12 (December 2007), pp. 14–20; C. Hosford, "Training Programs Benefit Rolls-Royce," *B-to-B,* July 16, 2007, p. 14.

61. J.E. Champoux, "A Multivariate Test of the Job Characteristics Theory of Work Motivation," *Journal of Organizational Behavior* 12, no. 5 (September 1991), pp. 431–46; R.B. Tiegs, L.E. Tetrick, and Y. Fried, "Growth Need Strength and Context Satisfactions as Moderators of the Relations of the Job Characteristics Model," *Journal of Management* 18, no. 3 (September 1992), pp. 575–93.

62. These data were provided in several country-specific news releases from Kelly Services. For a white paper summary of the survey, see Kelly Services, *Employee Loyalty Rises during Global Economic Recession, Kelly International Workforce Survey Finds* (Troy, MI: Kelly Services, March 8, 2010). The percentages of employees in India choosing higher salary/benefits and employees in China choosing meaningful responsibility are inferred (i.e., they were not stated in available sources but received a lower percentage than the other two identified categories).

63. "Region Positioned among DCX Leaders in Advanced Manufacturing," *Toledo Business Journal,* August 2004, p. 1; M. Connelly, "Chrysler Boosts Belvidere Flexibility," *Automotive News,* February 13, 2006, p. 44.

64. Bang & Olufsen, "Manufacturing Environment," 2011, http://www.bang-olufsen.com/occupational-health-and-safety.

65. M.A. Campion and C.L. McClelland, "Follow-Up and Extension of the Interdisciplinary Costs and Benefits of Enlarged Jobs," *Journal of Applied Psychology* 78 (1993), pp. 339–51; N.G. Dodd and D.C. Ganster, "The Interactive Effects of Variety, Autonomy, and Feedback on Attitudes and Performance," *Journal of Organizational Behavior* 17 (1996), pp. 329–47.

66. J.R. Hackman et al., "A New Strategy for Job Enrichment," *California Management Review* 17, no. 4 (1975), pp. 57–71; R.W. Griffin, *Task Design: An Integrative Approach* (Glenview, IL: Scott Foresman, 1982).

67. E. Frauenheim, "Making the Call for Themselves," *Workforce Management,* August 2010, p. 16.

68. P.E. Spector and S.M. Jex, "Relations of Job Characteristics from Multiple Data Sources with Employee Affect, Absence, Turnover Intentions, and Health," *Journal of Applied Psychology* 76 (1991), pp. 46–53; P. Osterman, "How Common Is Workplace Transformation and Who Adopts It?" *Industrial and Labor Relations Review* 47 (1994), pp. 173–88; R. Saavedra and S.K. Kwun, "Affective States in Job Characteristics Theory," *Journal of Organizational Behavior* 21 (2000), pp. 131–46.

69. Hackman and Oldham, *Work Redesign,* pp. 137–38.

70. S. Wong, "Open Communication Gives Better Connection," *South China Morning Post (Hong Kong),* January 19, 2008, p. 4.

71. "Running a Business: Managing a Handelsbanken Branch," *A View from the Top (Handelsbanken Maidstone Newsletter),* Winter 2007, p. 1; Hammarström, *Handelsbanken, Sweden;* R.M. Lindsay and T. Libby, "Svenska Handelsbanken: Controlling a Radically Decentralized Organization without Budgets," *Issues in Accounting Education* 22, no. 4 (November 2007), pp. 625–40; "The *Sunday Times* 100 Best Companies to Work For 2008," March 10, 2008, http://www.handelsbanken.co.uk.

72. This definition is based mostly on G.M. Spreitzer and R.E. Quinn, *A Company of Leaders: Five Disciplines for Unleashing the Power in Your Workforce* (San Francisco: Jossey-Bass, 2001). However, most elements of this definition appear in other discussions of empowerment. See, for example, R. Forrester, "Empowerment: Rejuvenating a Potent Idea," *Academy of Management Executive* 14 (August 2000),

pp. 67–80; W.A. Randolph, "Re-Thinking Empowerment: Why Is It So Hard to Achieve?" *Organizational Dynamics* 29 (November 2000), pp. 94–107; S.T. Menon, "Employee Empowerment: An Integrative Psychological Approach," *Applied Psychology: An International Review* 50 (2001), pp. 153–80.

73. The positive relationship between these structural empowerment conditions and psychological empowerment is reported in H.K.S. Laschinger et al., "A Longitudinal Analysis of the Impact of Work-place Empowerment on Work Satisfaction," *Journal of Organizational Behavior* 25, no. 4 (June 2004), pp. 527–45.

74. C.S. Koberg et al., "Antecedents and Outcomes of Empowerment," *Group and Organization Management* 24 (1999), pp. 71–91; Y. Melhem, "The Antecedents of Customer-Contact Employees' Empowerment," *Employee Relations* 26, no. 1/2 (2004), pp. 72–93.

75. B.J. Niehoff et al., "The Influence of Empowerment and Job Enrichment on Employee Loyalty in a Downsizing Environment," *Group and Organization Management* 26 (March 2001), pp. 93–113; J. Yoon, "The Role of Structure and Motivation for Workplace Empowerment: The Case of Korean Employees," *Social Psychology Quarterly* 64 (June 2001), pp. 195–206; T.D. Wall, J.L. Cordery, and C.W. Clegg, "Empowerment, Performance, and Operational Uncertainty: A Theoretical Integration," *Applied Psychology: An International Review* 51 (2002), pp. 146–69.

76. G.M. Spreitzer, "Social Structural Characteristics of Psychological Empowerment," *Academy of Management Journal* 39 (April 1996), pp. 483–504; J. Godard, "High Performance and the Transformation of Work? The Implications of Alternative Work Practices for the Experience and Outcomes of Work," *Industrial & Labor Relations Review* 54 (July 2001), pp. 776–805; P.A. Miller, P. Goddard, and H.K. Spence Laschinger, "Evaluating Physical Therapists' Perception of Empowerment Using Kanter's Theory of Structural Power in Organizations," *Physical Therapy* 81 (December 2001), pp. 1880–88.

77. J.-C. Chebat and P. Kollias, "The Impact of Empowerment on Customer Contact Employees' Role in Service Organizations," *Journal of Service Research* 3 (August 2000), pp. 66–81; H.K.S. Laschinger, J. Finegan, and J. Shamian, "The Impact of Workplace Empowerment, Organizational Trust on Staff Nurses' Work Satisfaction and Organizational Commitment," *Health Care Management Review* 26 (Summer 2001), pp. 7–23.

78. A. Kravcova, "The Man behind the Curtain," *Baltic Times (Riga, Latvia),* August 4, 2010.

79. C.P. Neck and C.C. Manz, "Thought Self-Leadership: The Impact of Mental Strategies Training on Employee Cognition, Behavior, and Affect," *Journal of Organizational Behavior* 17 (1996), pp. 445–67.

80. C.C. Manz, "Self-Leadership: Toward an Expanded Theory of Self-Influence Processes in Organizations," *Academy of Management Review* 11 (1986), pp. 585–600; C.C. Manz and C. Neck, *Mastering Self-Leadership,* 3rd ed. (Upper Saddle River, NJ: Prentice Hall, 2004); C.P. Neck and J.D. Houghton, "Two Decades of Self-Leadership Theory and Research," *Journal of Managerial Psychology* 21, no. 4 (2006), pp. 270–95.

81. O.J. Strickland and M. Galimba, "Managing Time: The Effects of Personal Goal Setting on Resource Allocation Strategy and Task Performance," *Journal of Psychology* 135 (July 2001), pp. 357–67.

82. R.M. Duncan and J.A. Cheyne, "Incidence and Functions of Self-Reported Private Speech in Young Adults: A Self-Verbalization Questionnaire," *Canadian Journal of Behavioral Science* 31 (April 1999), pp. 133–36.

83. G. Hohmann, "Bayer to Add 24 Jobs at Institute," *Charleston Gazette,* August 6, 2008, p. 1A.

84. A. Hatzigeorgiadis et al., "Mechanisms Underlying the Self-Talk–Performance Relationship: The Effects of Motivational Self-Talk on Self-Confidence and Anxiety," *Psychology of Sport and Exercise* 10 (2009), pp. 186–92.

85. J.E. Driscoll, C. Copper, and A. Moran, "Does Mental Practice Enhance Performance?" *Journal of Applied Psychology* 79 (1994), pp. 481–92; C.P. Neck, G.L. Stewart, and C.C. Manz, "Thought Self-Leadership as a Framework for Enhancing the Performance of Performance Appraisers," *Journal of Applied Behavioral Science* 31 (September 1995), pp. 278–302. Some research separates mental imagery from mental practice, whereas most studies combine both into one concept.

86. A. Joyce, "Office Parks: Re-Energize to Get through the Blahs," *Washington Post,* August 28, 2005, p. F05.

87. A. Wrzesniewski and J.E. Dutton, "Crafting a Job: Revisioning Employees as Active Crafters of Their Work," *Academy of Management Review* 26 (April 2001), pp. 179–201.

88. "Steve Collier Profile," *CCMA Case Study,* 1st Quarter 2008.

89. M.I. Bopp, S.J. Glynn, and R.A. Henning, *Self-Management of Performance Feedback during Computer-Based Work by Individuals and Two-Person Work Teams,* paper presented at the APA-NIOSH conference (March 1999).

90. A.W. Logue, *Self-Control: Waiting until Tomorrow for What You Want Today* (Englewood Cliffs, NJ: Prentice-Hall, 1995).

91. Neck and Manz, "Thought Self-Leadership"; A.M. Saks and B.E. Ashforth, "Proactive Socialization and Behavioral Self-Management," *Journal of Vocational Behavior* 48 (1996), pp. 301–23; L. Morin and G. Latham, "The Effect of Mental Practice and Goal Setting as a Transfer of Training Intervention on Supervisors' Self-Efficacy and Communication Skills: An Exploratory Study," *Applied Psychology: An International Review* 49 (July 2000), pp. 566–78; J.S. Hickman and E.S. Geller, "A Safety Self-Management Intervention for Mining Operations," *Journal of Safety Research* 34 (2003), pp. 299–308.

92. S. Ming and G.L. Martin, "Single-Subject Evaluation of a Self-Talk Package for Improving Figure Skating Performance," *Sport Psychologist* 10 (1996), pp. 227–38; J. Bauman, "The Gold Medal Mind," *Psychology Today* 33 (May 2000), pp. 62–69; L.J. Rogerson and D.W. Hrycaiko, "Enhancing Competitive Performance of Ice Hockey Goaltenders Using Centering and Self-Talk," *Journal of Applied Sport Psychology* 14, no. 1 (2002), pp. 14–26; A. Papaioannou et al., "Combined Effect of Goal Setting and Self-Talk in Performance of a Soccer-Shooting Task," *Perceptual and Motor Skills* 98, no. 1 (February 2004), pp. 89–99; R.A. Hamilton, D. Scott, and M.P. MacDougall, "Assessing the Effectiveness of Self-Talk Interventions on Endurance Performance," *Journal of Applied Sport Psychology* 19, no. 2 (2007), pp. 226–39. For a review of self-talk research, including the limitations of this self-leadership strategy, see J. Hardy, "Speaking Clearly: A Critical Review of the Self-Talk Literature," *Psychology of Sport and Exercise* 7 (2006), pp. 81–97.

93. S. Williams, "Personality and Self-Leadership," *Human Resource Management Review* 7, no. 2 (1997), pp. 139–55; J. Houghton et al., "The Relationship between Self-Leadership and Personality: A Comparison of Hierarchical Factor Structures," *Journal of Managerial Psychology* 19, no. 4 (2004), pp. 427–41; R.W. Renn et al., "The Roles of Personality and Self-Defeating Behaviors in Self-Management Failure," *Journal of Management* 31, no. 5 (2005), pp. 659–79.

94. J.D. Houghton and S.K. Yoho, "Toward a Contingency Model of Leadership and Psychological Empowerment: When Should Self-Leadership Be Encouraged?" *Journal of Leadership & Organizational Studies* 11, no. 4 (2005), pp. 65–83; J.D. Houghton and D.L. Jinkerson, "Constructive Thought Strategies and Job Satisfaction: A Preliminary Examination," *Journal of Business and Psychology* 22 (2007), pp. 45–53.

CHAPTER 7

1. S. Marchionne, "Fiat's Extreme Makeover," *Harvard Business Review* (December 2008), pp. 45–48; "Marchionne's Weekend Warriors," *Automotive News,* June 22, 2009; D. Welch, D. Kiley, and C. Matlack, "Tough Love at Chrysler," *BusinessWeek,* August 24, 2009; B. Wernie

and L. Ciferri, "Life under Marchionne: New Stars, Hasty Exits," *Automotive News,* October 12, 2009, pp. 1, 42; "Marchionne Faces Tough Challenge to Match Ghosn's Success," *Automotive News,* April 28, 2010; J. Reed, "High Stakes for Fiat's Sergio Marchionne," *Financial Times (London),* February 19, 2010; D. Kiley, "Imported from France," *Advertising Age,* February 21, 2011, p. 1; E. Mayne, "Chrysler-Fiat Merger under Consideration, Says CEO Marchionne," *Ward's Dealer Business,* March 2011, p. 12.

2. F.A. Shull Jr., A.L. Delbecq, and L.L. Cummings, *Organizational Decision Making* (New York: McGraw-Hill, 1970), p. 31.

3. M.V. White, "Jevons in Australia: A Reassessment," *The Economic Record* 58 (1982), pp. 32–45; R.E. Nisbett, *The Geography of Thought: How Asians and Westerners Think Differently—and Why* (New York: The Free Press, 2003); R. Hanna, "Kant's Theory of Judgment" (Stanford Encyclopedia of Philosophy, 2004), http://plato.stanford.edu/entries/kant-judgment/; D. Baltzly, "Stoicism" (Stanford Encyclopedia of Philosophy, 2008), http://plato.stanford.edu/entries/stoicism/.

4. J.G. March and H.A. Simon, *Organizations* (New York: John Wiley & Sons, 1958).

5. This model is adapted from several sources, including H.A. Simon, *The New Science of Management Decision* (New York: Harper & Row, 1960); H. Mintzberg, D. Raisinghani, and A. Théorét, "The Structure of 'Unstructured' Decision Processes," *Administrative Science Quarterly* 21 (1976), pp. 246–75; W.C. Wedley and R.H.G. Field, "A Predecision Support System," *Academy of Management Review* 9 (1984), pp. 696–703.

6. P.F. Drucker, *The Practice of Management* (New York: Harper & Brothers, 1954), pp. 353–57; B.M. Bass, *Organizational Decision Making* (Homewood, IL: Irwin, 1983), Ch. 3.

7. L.R. Beach and T.R. Mitchell, "A Contingency Model for the Selection of Decision Strategies," *Academy of Management Review* 3 (1978), pp. 439–49; I.L. Janis, *Crucial Decisions* (New York: The Free Press, 1989), pp. 35–37; W. Zhongtuo, "Meta-Decision Making: Concepts and Paradigm," *Systematic Practice and Action Research* 13, no. 1 (February 2000), pp. 111–15.

8. N. Schwarz, "Social Judgment and Attitudes: Warmer, More Social, and Less Conscious," *European Journal of Social Psychology* 30 (2000), pp. 149–76; N.M. Ashkanasy and C.E.J. Hartel, "Managing Emotions in Decision-Making," in *Managing Emotions in the Workplace,* ed. N.M. Ashkanasy, W.J. Zerbe, and C.E.J. Hartel (Armonk, NY: M.E. Sharpe, 2002); S. Maitlis and H. Ozcelik, "Toxic Decision Processes: A Study of Emotion and Organizational Decision Making," *Organization Science* 15, no. 4 (July-August 2004), pp. 375–93.

9. A. Howard, "Opinion," *Computing* (July 8, 1999), p. 18.

10. For a recent discussion on problem finding in organizations, see M.A. Roberto, *Know What You Don't Know: How Great Leaders Prevent Problems before They Happen* (Saddle River, NJ: Wharton School Publishing, 2009).

11. T.K. Das and B.S. Teng, "Cognitive Biases and Strategic Decision Processes: An Integrative Perspective," *Journal of Management Studies* 36, no. 6 (November 1999), pp. 757–78; P. Bijttebier, H. Vertommen, and G.V. Steene, "Assessment of Cognitive Coping Styles: A Closer Look at Situation-Response Inventories," *Clinical Psychology Review* 21, no. 1 (2001), pp. 85–104; P.C. Nutt, "Expanding the Search for Alternatives during Strategic Decision-Making," *Academy of Management Executive* 18, no. 4 (November 2004), pp. 13–28.

12. W. Ocasio, "Toward an Attention-Based View of the Firm," *Strategic Management Journal* 18, no. S1 (1997), pp. 187–206; S. Kaplan, "Framing Contests: Strategy Making under Uncertainty," *Organization Science* 19, no. 5 (September 2008), pp. 729–52; J.S. McMullen, D.A. Shepherd, and H. Patzelt, "Managerial (in)Attention to Competitive Threats," *Journal of Management Studies* 46, no. 2 (2009), pp. 157–81.

13. R. Collison, "How Bata Rules Its World," *Canadian Business,* September 1990, p. 28; J. Portman, "Harry Potter Was Almost a Yankee," *Vancouver Sun,* July 5, 2007.

14. M. McCarthy, "Top 20 in 20 Years: Apple Computer—1984," 2003, www.adweek.com/adweek/creative/top20_20years/index.jsp; O.W. Linzmayer, *Apple Confidential 2.0: The Definitive Story of the World's Most Colorful Company* (San Francisco: No Starch Press, 2004), pp. 109–14.

15. T. Jones, *Innovating at the Edge* (San Francisco: Butterworth-Heinemann, 2002), pp. 59–62; R.K. Sawyer, *Explaining Creativity: The Science of Human Innovation* (New York: Oxford University Press, 2006), Ch. 15.

16. P.C. Nutt, *Why Decisions Fail* (San Francisco, CA: Berrett-Koehler, 2002); S. Finkelstein, *Why Smart Executives Fail* (New York: Viking, 2003).

17. E. Witte, "Field Research on Complex Decision-Making Processes—the Phase Theorum," *International Studies of Management and Organization,* no. 56 (1972), pp. 156–82; J.A. Bargh and T.L. Chartrand, "The Unbearable Automaticity of Being," *American Psychologist* 54, no. 7 (July 1999), pp. 462–79.

18. A.H. Maslow, *The Psychology of Science: A Reconnaissance* (Chapel Hill, NC: Maurice Bassett Publishing, 2002).

19. J. Brandtstadter, A. Voss, and K. Rothermund, "Perception of Danger Signals: The Role of Control," *Experimental Psychology* 51, no. 1 (2004), pp. 24–32; M. Hock and H.W. Krohne, "Coping with Threat and Memory for Ambiguous Information: Testing the Repressive Discontinuity Hypothesis," *Emotion* 4, no. 1 (2004), pp. 65–86.

20. "NASA Managers Differed over Shuttle Strike," *Reuters* (July 22, 2003); Columbia Accident Investigation Board, *Report, Volume 1* (Washington, DC: Government Printing Office, August 2003); C. Gibson, "Columbia: The Final Mission," *NineMSN* (July 13, 2003); S. Jefferson, "NASA Let Arrogance on Board," *Palm Beach Post,* August 30, 2003; R.J. Smith, "NASA Culture, Columbia Probers Still Miles Apart," *Washington Post,* August 22, 2003, p. A3.

21. R. Rothenberg, "Ram Charan: The Thought Leader Interview," *strategy + business,* Fall 2004.

22. H.A. Simon, *Administrative Behavior,* 2nd ed. (New York: The Free Press, 1957); H.A. Simon, "Rational Decision Making in Business Organizations," *American Economic Review* 69, no. 4 (September 1979), pp. 493–513.

23. Simon, *Administrative Behavior,* pp. xxv, 80–84.

24. S. Sacchi and M. Burigo, "Strategies in the Information Search Process: Interaction among Task Structure, Knowledge, and Source," *Journal of General Psychology* 135, no. 3 (2008), pp. 252–70.

25. P.O. Soelberg, "Unprogrammed Decision Making," *Industrial Management Review* 8 (1967), pp. 19–29; J.E. Russo, V.H. Medvec, and M.G. Meloy, "The Distortion of Information during Decisions," *Organizational Behavior & Human Decision Processes* 66 (1996), pp. 102–10; K.H. Ehrhart and J.C. Ziegert, "Why Are Individuals Attracted to Organizations?" *Journal of Management* 31, no. 6 (December 2005), pp. 901–19. This is consistent with the observations by Milton Rokeach, who famously stated, "Life is ipsative, because decisions in everyday life are inherently and phenomenologically ipsative decisions." M. Rokeach, "Inducing Changes and Stability in Belief Systems and Personality Structures," *Journal of Social Issues* 41, no. 1 (1985), pp. 153–71.

26. A.L. Brownstein, "Biased Predecision Processing," *Psychological Bulletin* 129, no. 4 (2003), pp. 545–68.

27. T. Gilovich, D. Griffin, and D. Kahneman, *Heuristics and Biases: The Psychology of Intuitive Judgment* (Cambridge: Cambridge University Press, 2002); D. Kahneman, "Maps of Bounded Rationality: Psychology for Behavioral Economics," *American Economic Review* 93, no. 5 (December 2003), pp. 1449–75; F. L. Smith et al.,

"Decision-Making Biases and Affective States: Their Potential Impact on Best Practice Innovations," *Canadian Journal of Administrative Sciences/Revue Canadienne des Sciences de l'Administration* 27, no. 4 (2010), pp. 277–91.

28. A. Tversky and D. Kahneman, "Judgment under Uncertainty: Heuristics and Biases," *Science* 185, no. 4157 (September 27, 1974), pp. 1124–31; I. Ritov, "Anchoring in Simulated Competitive Market Negotiation," *Organizational Behavior and Human Decision Processes* 67, no. 1 (1996), p. 16; D. Ariely, G. Loewenstein, and A. Prelec, "'Coherent Arbitrariness': Stable Demand Curves without Stable Preferences," *Quarterly Journal of Economics* 118 (2003), p. 73; N. Epley and T. Gilovich, "Are Adjustments Insufficient?" *Personality and Social Psychology Bulletin* 30, no. 4 (April 2004), pp. 447–60; J.D. Jasper and S.D. Christman, "A Neuropsychological Dimension for Anchoring Effects," *Journal of Behavioral Decision Making* 18 (2005), pp. 343–69; S.D. Bond et al., "Information Distortion in the Evaluation of a Single Option," *Organizational Behavior & Human Decision Processes* 102 (2007), pp. 240–54.

29. A. Tversky and D. Kahneman, "Availability: A Heuristic for Judging Frequency and Probability," *Cognitive Psychology* 5 (1973), pp. 207–32.

30. D. Kahneman and A. Tversky, "Subjective Probability: A Judgment of Representativeness," *Cognitive Psychology* 3, no. 3 (1972), p. 430; T. Gilovich, *How We Know What Isn't So: The Fallibility of Human Reason in Everyday Life* (New York: The Free Press, 1991); B.D. Burns, "Heuristics as Beliefs and as Behaviors: The Adaptiveness of the 'Hot Hand,'" *Cognitive Psychology* 48 (2004), pp. 295–331; E.M. Altmann and B.D. Burns, "Streak Biases in Decision Making: Data and a Memory Model," *Cognitive Systems Research* 6, no. 1 (2005), p. 5.

31. H.A. Simon, "Rational Choice and the Structure of Environments," *Psychological Review* 63 (1956), pp. 129–38.

32. S. Botti and S.S. Iyengar, "The Dark Side of Choice: When Choice Impairs Social Welfare," *Journal of Public Policy & Marketing* 25, no. 1 (2006), pp. 24–38; K.D. Vohs et al., "Making Choices Impairs Subsequent Self-Control: A Limited-Resource Account of Decision Making, Self-Regulation, and Active Initiative," *Journal of Personality and Social Psychology* 94, no. 5 (2008), pp. 883–98.

33. J. Beshears et al., "Simplification and Saving," 2006, http://ssrn.com/paper=1086462; J. Choi, D. Laibson, and B. Madrian, *Reducing the Complexity Costs of 401(K) Participation through Quick Enrollment^(tm)*, National Bureau of Economic Research, Inc., January 2006; S. Iyengar, *The Art of Choosing* (New York: Hachette, 2010), pp. 194–200.

34. S.S. Iyengar and M.R. Lepper, "When Choice Is Demotivating: Can One Desire Too Much of a Good Thing?" *Journal of Personality and Social Psychology* 79, no. 6 (2000), pp. 995–1006; Iyengar, *The Art of Choosing*, pp. 177–95.

35. A. Tofler, *Future Shock* (New York: Random House, 1970), p. 264.

36. P.C. Nutt, "Search during Decision Making," *European Journal of Operational Research* 160 (2005), pp. 851–76.

37. P. Winkielman et al., "Affective Influence on Judgments and Decisions: Moving Towards Core Mechanisms," *Review of General Psychology* 11, no. 2 (2007), pp. 179–92.

38. A.R. Damasio, *Descartes' Error: Emotion, Reason, and the Human Brain* (New York: Putnam Sons, 1994); P. Winkielman and K.C. Berridge, "Unconscious Emotion," *Current Directions in Psychological Science* 13, no. 3 (2004), pp. 120–23; A. Bechara and A.R. Damasio, "The Somatic Marker Hypothesis: A Neural Theory of Economic Decision," *Games and Economic Behavior* 52, no. 2 (2005), pp. 336–72.

39. J.P. Forgas and J.M. George, "Affective Influences on Judgments and Behavior in Organizations: An Information Processing Perspective," *Organizational Behavior and Human Decision Processes* 86

(September 2001), pp. 3–34; G. Loewenstein and J.S. Lerner, "The Role of Affect in Decision Making," in *Handbook of Affective Sciences,* ed. R.J. Davidson, K.R. Scherer, and H.H. Goldsmith (New York: Oxford University Press, 2003), pp. 619–42; M.T. Pham, "Emotion and Rationality: A Critical Review and Interpretation of Empirical Evidence," *Review of General Psychology* 11, no. 2 (2007), pp. 155–78; J.P. Forgas, L. Goldenberg, and C. Unkelbach, "Can Bad Weather Improve Your Memory? An Unobtrusive Field Study of Natural Mood Effects on Real-Life Memory," *Journal of Experimental Social Psychology* 45 (2009), pp. 254–57; H.J.M. Kooij-de Bode, D. Van Knippenberg, and W.P. Van Ginkel, "Good Effects of Bad Feelings: Negative Affectivity and Group Decision-Making," *British Journal of Management* 21, no. 2 (2010), pp. 375–92.

40. D. Miller, *The Icarus Paradox* (New York: HarperBusiness, 1990); D. Miller, "What Happens after Success: The Perils of Excellence," *Journal of Management Studies* 31, no. 3 (1994), pp. 325–68; A.C. Amason and A.C. Mooney, "The Icarus Paradox Revisited: How Strong Performance Sows the Seeds of Dysfunction in Future Strategic Decision-Making," *Strategic Organization* 6, no. 4 (November 2008), pp. 407–34.

41. M.T. Pham, "The Logic of Feeling," *Journal of Consumer Psychology* 14 (September 2004), pp. 360–69; N. Schwarz, "Metacognitive Experiences in Consumer Judgment and Decision Making," *Journal of Consumer Psychology* 14 (September 2004), pp. 332–49.

42. L. Sjöberg, "Intuitive vs. Analytical Decision Making: Which Is Preferred?" *Scandinavian Journal of Management* 19 (2003), pp. 17–29.

43. M. Lyons, "Cave-in Too Close for Comfort, Miner Says," *Saskatoon StarPhoenix,* May 6, 2002.

44. W.H. Agor, "The Logic of Intuition," *Organizational Dynamics,* Winter 1986, pp. 5–18; H.A. Simon, "Making Management Decisions: The Role of Intuition and Emotion," *Academy of Management Executive,* February 1987, pp. 57–64; O. Behling and N.L. Eckel, "Making Sense Out of Intuition," *Academy of Management Executive* 5 (February 1991), pp. 46–54. This process is also known as naturalistic decision making. For a discussion of research on naturalistic decision making, see the special issue in *Organization Studies,* especially R. Lipshitz, G. Klein, and J.S. Carroll, "Introduction to the Special Issue: Naturalistic Decision Making and Organizational Decision Making: Exploring the Intersections," *Organization Studies* 27, no. 7 (2006), pp. 917–23.

45. M.D. Lieberman, "Intuition: A Social Cognitive Neuroscience Approach," *Psychological Bulletin* 126 (2000), pp. 109–37; G. Klein, *Intuition at Work* (New York: Currency/Doubleday, 2003); E. Dane and M.G. Pratt, "Exploring Intuition and Its Role in Managerial Decision Making," *Academy of Management Review* 32, no. 1 (2007), pp. 33–54.

46. Klein, *Intuition at Work,* pp. 12–13, 16–17.

47. Y. Ganzach, A.H. Kluger, and N. Klayman, "Making Decisions from an Interview: Expert Measurement and Mechanical Combination," *Personnel Psychology* 53 (Spring 2000), pp. 1–20; A.M. Hayashi, "When to Trust Your Gut," *Harvard Business Review* 79 (February 2001), pp. 59–65. Evidence of high failure rates from quick decisions is reported in Nutt, *Why Decisions Fail;* Nutt, "Search during Decision Making"; P.C. Nutt, "Investigating the Success of Decision Making Processes," *Journal of Management Studies* 45, no. 2 (March 2008), pp. 425–55.

48. P. Goodwin and G. Wright, "Enhancing Strategy Evaluation in Scenario Planning: A Role for Decision Analysis," *Journal of Management Studies* 38 (January 2001), pp. 1–16; R. Bradfield et al., "The Origins and Evolution of Scenario Techniques in Long Range Business Planning," *Futures* 37, no. 8 (2005), pp. 795–812; G. Wright, G. Cairns, and P. Goodwin, "Teaching Scenario Planning: Lessons from Practice in Academe and Business," *European Journal of Operational Research* 194, no. 1 (April 2009), pp. 323–35.

49. *What if . . . Edition: Shipping* (Harstad, Norway: Dreyer Kompetense, July 16, 2009); Z.A. Wahab, "Norwegian Firm Offers Board Game as Training Tool," *Bernama Daily Malaysian News (Kuala Lumpur),* March 25, 2010.

50. J. Pfeffer and R.I. Sutton, "Knowing 'What' to Do Is Not Enough: Turning Knowledge into Action," *California Management Review* 42, no. 1 (Fall 1999), pp. 83–108; R. Charan, C. Burke, and L. Bossidy, *Execution: The Discipline of Getting Things Done* (New York: Crown Business, 2002).

51. R.S. Nickerson, "Confirmation Bias: A Ubiquitous Phenomenon in Many Guises," *Review of General Psychology* 2, no. 2 (1998), pp. 175–220; O. Svenson, I. Salo, and T. Lindholm, "Post-Decision Consolidation and Distortion of Facts," *Judgment and Decision Making* 4, no. 5 (2009), pp. 397–407.

52. G. Whyte, "Escalating Commitment to a Course of Action: A Reinterpretation," *Academy of Management Review* 11 (1986), pp. 311–21; J. Brockner, "The Escalation of Commitment to a Failing Course of Action: Toward Theoretical Progress," *Academy of Management Review* 17, no. 1 (January 1992), pp. 39–61.

53. D. Collins, "Senior Officials Tried to Stop Spending," *Irish Examiner,* October 5, 2005; M. Sheehan, "Throwing Good Money after Bad," *Sunday Independent* (Dublin), October 9, 2005; "Computer System Was Budgeted at Eur9m . . . Its Cost Eur170m . . . Now Health Chiefs Want a New One," *Irish Mirror,* July 7, 2007, p. 16; E. Kennedy, "Health Boss Refuses to Ditch Ill-Fated PPARS System," *Irish Independent,* February 5, 2007.

54. F.D. Schoorman and P.J. Holahan, "Psychological Antecedents of Escalation Behavior: Effects of Choice, Responsibility, and Decision Consequences," *Journal of Applied Psychology* 81 (1996), pp. 786–93; N. Sivanathan et al., "The Promise and Peril of Self-Affirmation in De-Escalation of Commitment," *Organizational Behavior and Human Decision Processes* 107, no. 1 (2008), pp. 1–14.

55. G. Whyte, "Escalating Commitment in Individual and Group Decision Making: A Prospect Theory Approach," *Organizational Behavior and Human Decision Processes* 54 (1993), pp. 430–55; D. Kahneman and J. Renshon, "Hawkish Biases," in *American Foreign Policy and the Politics of Fear: Threat Inflation since 9/11,* ed. T. Thrall and J. Cramer (New York: Routledge, 2009), pp. 79–96.

56. M. Keil, G. Depledge, and A. Rai, "Escalation: The Role of Problem Recognition and Cognitive Bias," *Decision Sciences* 38, no. 3 (August 2007), pp. 391–421.

57. J.D. Bragger et al., "When Success Breeds Failure: History, Hysteresis, and Delayed Exit Decisions," *Journal of Applied Psychology* 88, no. 1 (2003), pp. 6–14. A second logical reason for escalation, called the Martingale strategy, is described in J.A. Aloysius, "Rational Escalation of Costs by Playing a Sequence of Unfavorable Gambles: The Martingale," *Journal of Economic Behavior & Organization* 51 (2003), pp. 111–29.

58. I. Simonson and B.M. Staw, "De-Escalation Strategies: A Comparison of Techniques for Reducing Commitment to Losing Courses of Action," *Journal of Applied Psychology* 77 (1992), pp. 419–26; W. Boulding, R. Morgan, and R. Staelin, "Pulling the Plug to Stop the New Product Drain," *Journal of Marketing Research,* no. 34 (1997), pp. 164–76; B.M. Staw, K.W. Koput, and S.G. Barsade, "Escalation at the Credit Window: A Longitudinal Study of Bank Executives' Recognition and Write-Off of Problem Loans," *Journal of Applied Psychology,* no. 82 (1997), pp. 130–42; M. Keil and D. Robey, "Turning Around Troubled Software Projects: An Exploratory Study of the Deescalation of Commitment to Failing Courses of Action," *Journal of Management Information Systems* 15 (Spring 1999), pp. 63–87; B.C. Gunia, N. Sivanathan, and A.D. Galinsky, "Vicarious Entrapment: Your Sunk Costs, My Escalation of Commitment," *Journal of Experimental Social Psychology* 45, no. 6 (2009), pp. 1238–44.

59. D. Ghosh, "De-Escalation Strategies: Some Experimental Evidence," *Behavioral Research in Accounting,* no. 9 (1997), pp. 88–112.

60. J. Zhou and C.E. Shalley, "Research on Employee Creativity: A Critical Review and Directions for Future Research," *Research in Personnel and Human Resources Management* 22 (2003), pp. 165–217; M.A. Runco, "Creativity," *Annual Review of Psychology* 55 (2004), pp. 657–87.

61. V. Khanna, "The Voice of Google," *Business Times (Singapore),* January 12, 2008.

62. G. Wallas, *The Art of Thought* (London: Jonathan Cape, 1926). For recent applications of Wallas's classic model, see T. Kristensen, "The Physical Context of Creativity," *Creativity and Innovation Management* 13, no. 2 (June 2004), pp. 89–96; U.-E. Haner, "Spaces for Creativity and Innovation in Two Established Organizations," *Creativity and Innovation Management* 14, no. 3 (2005), pp. 288–98.

63. R.S. Nickerson, "Enhancing Creativity," in *Handbook of Creativity,* ed. R.J. Sternberg (New York: Cambridge University Press, 1999), pp. 392–430.

64. E. Oakes, *Notable Scientists: A to Z of STS Scientists* (New York: Facts on File, 2002), pp. 207–209.

65. For a thorough discussion of illumination or insight, see R.J. Sternberg and J.E. Davidson, *The Nature of Insight* (Cambridge, MA: MIT Press, 1995).

66. R.J. Sternberg and L.A. O' Hara, "Creativity and Intelligence," in *Handbook of Creativity,* ed. R.J. Sternberg (New York: Cambridge University Press, 1999), pp. 251–72; S. Taggar, "Individual Creativity and Group Ability to Utilize Individual Creative Resources: A Multilevel Model," *Academy of Management Journal* 45 (April 2002), pp. 315–30.

67. G.J. Feist, "The Influence of Personality on Artistic and Scientific Creativity," in *Handbook of Creativity,* ed. R.J. Sternberg (New York: Cambridge University Press, 1999), pp. 273–96; R.I. Sutton, *Weird Ideas That Work* (New York: The Free Press, 2002), pp. 8–9, Ch. 10; T. Åsterbro, S.A. Jeffrey, and G.K. Adomdza, "Inventor Perseverance after Being Told to Quit: The Role of Cognitive Biases," *Journal of Behavioral Decision Making* 20 (2007), pp. 253–72.

68. R.W. Weisberg, "Creativity and Knowledge: A Challenge to Theories," in *Handbook of Creativity,* ed. R.J. Sternberg (New York: Cambridge University Press, 1999), pp. 226–50.

69. Sutton, *Weird Ideas That Work,* pp. 121, 153–54; E. Dane, "Reconsidering the Trade-Off between Expertise and Flexibility: A Cognitive Entrenchment Perspective," *Academy of Management Review* 35, no. 4 (2010), pp. 579–603.

70. T. Koppell, *Powering the Future* (New York: Wiley, 1999), p. 15.

71. R.J. Sternberg and T.I. Lubart, *Defying the Crowd: Cultivating Creativity in a Culture of Conformity* (New York: Free Press, 1995); Feist, "The Influence of Personality on Artistic and Scientific Creativity"; S.J. Dollinger, K.K. Urban, and T.A. James, "Creativity and Openness to Experience: Validation of Two Creative Product Measures," *Creativity Research Journal* 16, no. 1 (2004), pp. 35–47; C.E. Shalley, J. Zhou, and G.R. Oldham, "The Effects of Personal and Contextual Characteristics on Creativity: Where Should We Go from Here?" *Journal of Management* 30, no. 6 (2004), pp. 933–58; T.S. Schweizer, "The Psychology of Novelty-Seeking, Creativity and Innovation: Neurocognitive Aspects within a Work-Psychological Perspective," *Creativity and Innovation Management* 15, no. 2 (2006), pp. 164–72.

72. J. Ross, "Interactive Design," *North Shore Outlook (North Vancouver),* December 1, 2010; L. Sin, "Ideas, Passion Drive Inspired Designer," *Vancouver Province,* October 19, 2010.

73. T.M. Amabile et al., "Leader Behaviors and the Work Environment for Creativity: Perceived Leader Support," *The Leadership Quarterly* 15, no. 1 (2004), pp. 5–32; Shalley, Zhou, and Oldham, "The Effects of Personal and Contextual Characteristics on Creativity";

S.T. Hunter, K.E. Bedell, and M.D. Mumford, "Climate for Creativity: A Quantitative Review," *Creativity Research Journal* 19, no. 1 (2007), pp. 69–90; T.C. DiLiello and J.D. Houghton, "Creative Potential and Practised Creativity: Identifying Untapped Creativity in Organizations," *Creativity and Innovation Management* 17, no. 1 (2008), pp. 37–46.

74. R. Westwood and D.R. Low, "The Multicultural Muse: Culture, Creativity and Innovation," *International Journal of Cross Cultural Management* 3, no. 2 (2003), pp. 235–59.

75. "Samsung CEO Yun Picks Google as New Role Model," *Korea Times*, October 1, 2007.

76. T.M. Amabile, "Motivating Creativity in Organizations: On Doing What You Love and Loving What You Do," *California Management Review* 40 (Fall 1997), pp. 39–58; A. Cummings and G.R. Oldham, "Enhancing Creativity: Managing Work Contexts for the High Potential Employee," *California Management Review*, no. 40 (Fall 1997), pp. 22–38; F. Coelho and M. Augusto, "Job Characteristics and the Creativity of Frontline Service Employees," *Journal of Service Research* 13, no. 4 (November 2010), pp. 426–38.

77. T.M. Amabile, "Changes in the Work Environment for Creativity during Downsizing," *Academy of Management Journal* 42 (December 1999), pp. 630–40.

78. J. Moultrie et al., "Innovation Spaces: Towards a Framework for Understanding the Role of the Physical Environment in Innovation," *Creativity & Innovation Management* 16, no. 1 (2007), pp. 53–65.

79. J.M. Howell and K. Boies, "Champions of Technological Innovation: The Influence of Contextual Knowledge, Role Orientation, Idea Generation, and Idea Promotion on Champion Emergence," *The Leadership Quarterly* 15, no. 1 (2004), pp. 123–43; Shalley, Zhou, and Oldham, "The Effects of Personal and Contextual Characteristics on Creativity"; S. Powell, "The Management and Consumption of Organisational Creativity," *Journal of Consumer Marketing* 25, no. 3 (2008), pp. 158–66.

80. A. Bryant, "I'm Prepared for Adversity. I Waited Tables," *The New York Times*, June 5, 2010.

81. A. Hiam, "Obstacles to Creativity—and How You Can Remove Them," *Futurist* 32 (October 1998), pp. 30–34.

82. M.A. West, *Developing Creativity in Organizations* (Leicester, UK: BPS Books, 1997), pp. 33–35.

83. C. Frey, *2009 Creativity Survey,* Innovation Tools, August 5, 2009; J. Burch and T.S. Axworthy, *Closing the Implementation Gap: Improving Capacity, Accountability, Performance and Human Resource Quality in the Canadian and Ontario Public Service,* (Kingston, ON: Queen's University, Centre for the Study of Democracy, January 2010); IBM, *Capitalizing on Complexity: Insights from the Global Chief Executive Officer Study* (Somers, NY: IBM Global Business Services, 2010); U.S. Office of Personnel Management, *Federal Employee Viewpoint Survey* (Washington, DC: U.S. Office of Personnel Management, 2010); "Wanted: Canadian Business Leaders Who Innovate," news release, Microsoft Canada, March 31, 2011.

84. S. Hemsley, "Seeking the Source of Innovation," *Media Week*, August 16, 2005, p. 22.

85. A. Hargadon and R.I. Sutton, "Building an Innovation Factory," *Harvard Business Review* 78 (May–June 2000), pp. 157–66; T. Kelley, *The Art of Innovation* (New York: Currency Doubleday, 2001), pp. 158–62; P.F. Skilton and K.J. Dooley, "The Effects of Repeat Collaboration on Creative Abrasion," *Academy of Management Review* 35, no. 1 (2010), pp. 118–34.

86. M. Burton, "Open Plan, Open Mind," *Director*, March 2005, pp. 68–72; A. Benady, "Mothers of Invention," *The Independent (London)*, November 27, 2006; B. Murray, "Agency Profile: Mother London," *Ihaveanidea*, January 28, 2007, www.ihaveanidea.org.

87. "John Collee—Biography," Internet Movie Database, 2009, http://www.imdb.com/name/nm0171722/bio.

88. N. Desai, "Management by Trust in a Democratic Enterprise: A Law Firm Shapes Organizational Behavior to Create Competitive Advantage," *Global Business and Organizational Excellence* 28, no. 6 (2009), pp. 7–21.

89. M. Fenton-O'Creevy, "Employee Involvement and the Middle Manager: Saboteur or Scapegoat?" *Human Resource Management Journal,* no. 11 (2001), pp. 24–40. Also see V.H. Vroom and A.G. Jago, *The New Leadership: Managing Participation in Organizations* (Englewood Cliffs, NJ: Prentice Hall, 1988).

90. Vroom and Jago, *The New Leadership.*

91. J.R. Foley and M. Polanyi, "Workplace Democracy: Why Bother?" *Economic and Industrial Democracy* 27, no. 1 (February 1, 2006 2006), pp. 173–91; P.A. Woods and P. Gronn, "Nurturing Democracy," *Educational Management Administration & Leadership* 37, no. 4 (July 1, 2009), pp. 430–51.

92. R. Semler, *The Seven-Day Weekend* (London: Century, 2003); G. de Jong and A. van Witteloostuijn, "Successful Corporate Democracy: Sustainable Cooperation of Capital and Labor in the Dutch Breman Group," *Academy of Management Executive* 18, no. 3 (2004), pp. 54–66.

93. K. Cloke and J. Goldsmith, *The End of Management and the Rise of Organizational Democracy* (San Francisco: Jossey-Bass, 2003); L. Gratton, *The Democratic Enterprise: Liberating Your Enterprise with Freedom, Flexibility, and Commitment* (London: FT Prentice-Hall, 2004).

94. P.E. Slater and W.G. Bennis, "Democracy Is Inevitable," *Harvard Business Review* (March–April 1964), pp. 51–59; D. Collins, "The Ethical Superiority and Inevitability of Participatory Management as an Organizational System," *Organization Science* 8, no. 5 (1997), pp. 489–507; W.G. Weber, C. Unterrainer, and B.E. Schmid, "The Influence of Organizational Democracy on Employees' Socio-Moral Climate and Prosocial Behavioral Orientations," *Journal of Organizational Behavior* 30, no. 8 (2009), pp. 1127–49.

95. R. Bussel, "'Business without a Boss': The Columbia Conserve Company and Workers' Control, 1917–1943," *Business History Review* 71, no. 3 (1997), pp. 417–43; Collins, "The Ethical Superiority and Inevitability of Participatory Management as an Organizational System"; J.D. Russell, M. Dirsmith, and S. Samuel, "Stained Steel: ESOPs, Meta-Power, and the Ironies of Corporate Democracy," *Symbolic Interaction* 27, no. 3 (2004), pp. 383–403.

96. T. Raggatt, "How Yabulu Rose from the Dust," *Townesville Bulletin (Australia)*, December 12, 2009; P. Michael, "Cliver Palmer Refines Fortunes at Yabulu Nickel Refinery," *Courier Mail (Brisbane, Australia),* January 21, 2010; E. Schwarten, "Palmer Gives Mercs as Xmas Bonus to Staff," *Sydney Morning Herald,* November 19, 2010.

97. Some of the early OB writing on employee involvement includes C. Argyris, *Personality and Organization* (New York: Harper & Row, 1957); D. McGregor, *The Human Side of Enterprise* (New York: McGraw-Hill, 1960); R. Likert, *New Patterns of Management* (New York: McGraw-Hill, 1961).

98. A.G. Robinson and D.M. Schroeder, *Ideas Are Free* (San Francisco: Berrett-Koehler, 2004).

99. R.J. Ely and D.A. Thomas, "Cultural Diversity at Work: The Effects of Diversity Perspectives on Work Group Processes and Outcomes," *Administrative Science Quarterly* 46 (June 2001), pp. 229–73; E. Mannix and M.A. Neale, "What Differences Make a Difference?: The Promise and Reality of Diverse Teams in Organizations," *Psychological Science in the Public Interest* 6, no. 2 (2005), pp. 31–55.

100. D. Berend and J. Paroush, "When Is Condorcet's Jury Theorem Valid?" *Social Choice and Welfare* 15, no. 4 (1998), pp. 481–88.

101. K.T. Dirks, L.L. Cummings, and J.L. Pierce, "Psychological Ownership in Organizations: Conditions under Which Individuals Promote

and Resist Change," *Research in Organizational Change and Development,* no. 9 (1996), pp. 1–23; J.P. Walsh and S.-F. Tseng, "The Effects of Job Characteristics on Active Effort at Work," *Work & Occupations* 25 (February 1998), pp. 74–96; B. Scott-Ladd and V. Marshall, "Participation in Decision Making: A Matter of Context?" *Leadership & Organization Development Journal* 25, no. 8 (2004), pp. 646–62.

102. Vroom and Jago, *The New Leadership.*

103. S. Litt, "Church's Transformation into Business Offers Answer to Many People's Prayers," *Plain Dealer (Cleveland),* September 12, 2003, p. E1; K. Palmer, "Design of the Times," *Smart Business Cleveland,* September 2003, p. 37; M. Smith, "A New Class: They're Creative, Driven and They're Here," *Inside Business,* April 2003, p. 48; D. Trattner, "Old Church Provides Inspiration for Designers," *Plain Dealer (Cleveland),* January 2, 2006, p. E3; A. Fisher, "Ideas Made Here," *Fortune,* June 11, 2007, p. 35; M.R. Kropko, "Designing Men," *Charleston Gazette,* November 5, 2007, p. P2C; J. Morgan, Lewis, "Wizards of Wal-Mart," *Inside Business,* March 2007, p. 34; L. Taxel, "It Takes Two," *Continental In-Flight Magazine,* April 2007.

CHAPTER 8

1. "Medical Marvel," *Works Management (Best Factory Awards Supplement),* October 2007, pp. 21–22; "A Clean Fight," *Works Management,* October 2010, p. 18; V. Clawson, "Why 'One Team, One Heart' = Our Core Values," Reckitt Benckiser, November 10, 2010, http://www.myrbopportunity.com; Gaonan, "What Makes a Global Team Work?" Reckitt Benckiser, June 30, 2010, http://www.myrbopportunity.com; "Day 1—Global Challenge 2011—RB Employees Come Together to Save the Children," Reckitt Benckiser, June 7, 2011, http://www.myrbopportunity.com.

2. "Trends: Are Many Meetings a Waste of Time? Study Says So," MeetingsNet news release, November 1, 1998; "Teamwork and Collaboration Major Workplace Trends," *Ottawa Business Journal,* April 18, 2006; "Go Teams! Firms Can't Do without Them," American Management Association, 2008, http://amalearning.com.

3. S. Wuchty, B.F. Jones, and B. Uzzi, "The Increasing Dominance of Teams in Production of Knowledge," *Science* 316 (May 2007), pp. 1036–39.

4. M.E. Shaw, *Group Dynamics,* 3rd ed. (New York: McGraw-Hill, 1981), p. 8; S.A. Mohrman, S.G. Cohen, and A.M. Mohrman Jr., *Designing Team-Based Organizations: New Forms for Knowledge Work* (San Francisco, CA: Jossey-Bass, 1995), pp. 39–40; E. Sundstrom, "The Challenges of Supporting Work Team Effectiveness," in *Supporting Work Team Effectiveness,* ed. E. Sundstrom et al. (San Francisco, CA: Jossey-Bass, 1999), pp. 6–9.

5. R.A. Guzzo and M.W. Dickson, "Teams in Organizations: Recent Research on Performance and Effectiveness," *Annual Review of Psychology* 47 (1996), pp. 307–38; D.A. Nadler, "From Ritual to Real Work: The Board as a Team," *Directors and Boards* 22 (Summer 1998), pp. 28–31; L.R. Offerman and R.K. Spiros, "The Science and Practice of Team Development: Improving the Link," *Academy of Management Journal* 44 (April 2001), pp. 376–92.

6. B.D. Pierce and R. White, "The Evolution of Social Structure: Why Biology Matters," *Academy of Management Review* 24 (October 1999), pp. 843–53; P.R. Lawrence and N. Nohria, *Driven: How Human Nature Shapes Our Choices* (San Francisco, CA: Jossey-Bass, 2002); J.R. Spoor and J.R. Kelly, "The Evolutionary Significance of Affect in Groups: Communication and Group Bonding," *Group Processes & Intergroup Relations* 7, no. 4 (2004), pp. 398–412. For a critique of this view, see G. Sewell, "What Goes Around, Comes Around," *Journal of Applied Behavioural Science* 37, no. 1 (March 2001), pp. 70–91.

7. M.A. Hogg et al., "The Social Identity Perspective: Intergroup Relations, Self-Conception, and Small Groups," *Small Group Research* 35, no. 3 (June 2004), pp. 246–76; N. Michinov, E. Michinov, and

M.-C. Toczek-Capelle, "Social Identity, Group Processes, and Performance in Synchronous Computer-Mediated Communication," *Group Dynamics: Theory, Research, and Practice* 8, no. 1 (2004), pp. 27–39; M. Van Vugt and C.M. Hart, "Social Identity as Social Glue: The Origins of Group Loyalty," *Journal of Personality and Social Psychology* 86, no. 4 (2004), pp. 585–98.

8. S. Schacter, *The Psychology of Affiliation* (Stanford, CA: Stanford University Press, 1959), pp. 12–19; R. Eisler and D.S. Levine, "Nurture, Nature, and Caring: We Are Not Prisoners of Our Genes," *Brain and Mind* 3 (2002), pp. 9–52; A.C. DeVries, E.R. Glasper, and C.E. Detillion, "Social Modulation of Stress Responses," *Physiology & Behavior* 79, no. 3 (August 2003), pp. 399–407; S. Cohen, "The Pittsburgh Common Cold Studies: Psychosocial Predictors of Susceptibility to Respiratory Infectious Illness," *International Journal of Behavioral Medicine* 12, no. 3 (2005), pp. 123–31.

9. Cohen, "The Pittsburgh Common Cold Studies"; M.T. Hansen, M.L. Mors, and B. Løvås, "Knowledge Sharing in Organizations: Multiple Networks, Multiple Phases," *Academy of Management Journal* 48, no. 5 (2005), pp. 776–93; R. Cross et al., "Using Social Network Analysis to Improve Communities of Practice," *California Management Review* 49, no. 1 (2006), pp. 32–60; P. Balkundi et al., "Demographic Antecedents and Performance Consequences of Structural Holes in Work Teams," *Journal of Organizational Behavior* 28, no. 2 (2007), pp. 241–60; W. Verbeke and S. Wuyts, "Moving in Social Circles: Social Circle Membership and Performance Implications," *Journal of Organizational Behavior* 28, no. 4 (2007), pp. 357–79.

10. L. Buchanan, "2011 Top Small Company Workplaces: Core Values," *Inc.,* June 2011, pp. 60–74.

11. "Safe Hands a Boost for Blue Care," *Northern Miner (Charters Towers, Queensland),* July 11, 2008, p. 5; "Powerhouse Team Switched on by Pride," *The Australian,* August 23, 2008, p. 4; C. Walker, "Call Answered with Vigour," *Fraser Coast Chronicle (Queensland),* November 20, 2008, p. 7.

12. M. Moldaschl and W. Weber, "The 'Three Waves' of Industrial Group Work: Historical Reflections on Current Research on Group Work," *Human Relations* 51 (March 1998), pp. 347–88. Several popular books in the 1980s encouraged teamwork, based on the Japanese economic miracle. These books include W. Ouchi, *Theory Z: How American Management Can Meet the Japanese Challenge* (Reading, MA: Addison-Wesley, 1981); R.T. Pascale and A.G. Athos, *Art of Japanese Management* (New York: Simon and Schuster, 1982).

13. C.R. Emery and L.D. Fredenhall, "The Effect of Teams on Firm Profitability and Customer Satisfaction," *Journal of Service Research* 4 (February 2002), pp. 217–29; G.S. Van der Vegt and O. Janssen, "Joint Impact of Interdependence and Group Diversity on Innovation," *Journal of Management* 29 (2003), pp. 729–51.

14. R.E. Baumeister and M.R. Leary, "The Need to Belong: Desire for Interpersonal Attachments as a Fundamental Human Motivation," *Psychological Bulletin* 117 (1995), pp. 497–529; S. Chen, H.C. Boucher, and M.P. Tapias, "The Relational Self Revealed: Integrative Conceptualization and Implications for Interpersonal Life," *Psychological Bulletin* 132, no. 2 (2006), pp. 151–79; J.M. Feinberg and J.R. Aiello, "Social Facilitation: A Test of Competing Theories," *Journal of Applied Social Psychology* 36, no. 5 (2006), pp. 1087–109; A.M. Grant, "Relational Job Design and the Motivation to Make a Prosocial Difference," *Academy of Management Review* 32, no. 2 (2007), pp. 393–417; N.L. Kerr et al., "Psychological Mechanisms Underlying the Kohler Motivation Gain," *Personality & Social Psychology Bulletin* 33, no. 6 (2007), pp. 828–41.

15. E.A. Locke et al., "The Importance of the Individual in an Age of Groupism," in *Groups at Work: Theory and Research,* ed. M.E. Turner (Mahwah, NJ: Lawrence Erbaum Associates, 2001),

pp. 501–28; N.J. Allen and T.D. Hecht, "The 'Romance of Teams': Toward an Understanding of Its Psychological Underpinnings and Implications," *Journal of Occupational and Organizational Psychology* 77 (2004), pp. 439–61.

16. I.D. Steiner, *Group Process and Productivity* (New York: Academic Press, 1972); N.L. Kerr and S.R. Tindale, "Group Performance and Decision Making," *Annual Review of Psychology* 55 (2004), pp. 623–55.

17. D. Dunphy and B. Bryant, "Teams: Panaceas or Prescriptions for Improved Performance?" *Human Relations* 49 (1996), pp. 677–99. For a discussion of Brooks's Law, see F.P. Brooks, ed., *The Mythical Man-Month: Essays on Software Engineering,* 2nd ed. (Reading, MA: Addison-Wesley, 1995).

18. J. Gruber, "Aperture Dirt," Daring Fireball, April 28, 2006, http://daringfireball.net/2006/04/aperture_dirt; J. Gruber, "More Aperture Dirt," Daring Fireball, May 4, 2006, http://daringfireball. net/2006/05/more_aperture_dirt.

19. S.J. Karau and K.D. Williams, "Social Loafing: A Meta-Analytic Review and Theoretical Integration," *Journal of Personality and Social Psychology* 65 (1993), pp. 681–706; R.C. Liden et al., "Social Loafing: A Field Investigation," *Journal of Management* 30 (2004), pp. 285–304; L.L. Chidambaram, "Is Out of Sight, Out of Mind? An Empirical Study of Social Loafing in Technology-Supported Groups," *Information Systems Research* 16, no. 2 (2005), pp. 149–68; U.-C. Klehe and N. Anderson, "The Moderating Influence of Personality and Culture on Social Loafing in Typical versus Maximum Performance Situations," *International Journal of Selection and Assessment* 15, no. 2 (2007), pp. 250–62.

20. J.R. Engen, "Tough as Nails," *Bank Director,* July 2009, p. 24.

21. M. Erez and A. Somech, "Is Group Productivity Loss the Rule or the Exception? Effects of Culture and Group-Based Motivation," *Academy of Management Journal* 39 (1996), pp. 1513–37; Kerr and Tindale, "Group Performance and Decision Making"; A. Jassawalla, H. Sashittal, and A. Malshe, "Students' Perceptions of Social Loafing: Its Antecedents and Consequences in Undergraduate Business Classroom Teams," *Academy of Management Learning and Education* 8, no. 1 (March 2009), pp. 42–54.

22. G.P. Shea and R.A. Guzzo, "Group Effectiveness: What Really Matters?" *Sloan Management Review* 27 (1987), pp. 33–46; J.R. Hackman et al., "Team Effectiveness in Theory and in Practice," in *Industrial and Organizational Psychology: Linking Theory with Practice,* ed. C.L. Cooper and E.A. Locke (Oxford, UK: Blackwell, 2000), pp. 109–29.

23. M.A. West, C.S. Borrill, and K.L. Unsworth, "Team Effectiveness in Organizations," *International Review of Industrial and Organizational Psychology* 13 (1998), pp. 1–48; R. Forrester and A.B. Drexler, "A Model for Team-Based Organization Performance," *Academy of Management Executive* 13 (August 1999), pp. 36–49; J.E. McGrath, H. Arrow, and J.L. Berdahl, "The Study of Groups: Past, Present, and Future," *Personality & Social Psychology Review* 4, no. 1 (2000), pp. 95–105; M.A. Marks, J.E. Mathieu, and S.J. Zaccaro, "A Temporally Based Framework and Taxonomy of Team Processes," *Academy of Management Review* 26, no. 3 (July 2001), pp. 356–76.

24. J.S. DeMatteo, L.T. Eby, and E. Sundstrom, "Team-Based Rewards: Current Empirical Evidence and Directions for Future Research," *Research in Organizational Behavior* 20 (1998), pp. 141–83; E.E. Lawler III, *Rewarding Excellence: Pay Strategies for the New Economy* (San Francisco, CA: Jossey-Bass, 2000), pp. 207–14; G. Hertel, S. Geister, and U. Konradt, "Managing Virtual Teams: A Review of Current Empirical Research," *Human Resource Management Review* 15 (2005), pp. 69–95.

25. These and other environmental conditions for effective teams are discussed in R. Wageman, "Case Study: Critical Success Factors for Creating Superb Self-Managing Teams at Xerox," *Compensation*

and Benefits Review 29 (September–October 1997), pp. 31–41; Sundstrom, "The Challenges of Supporting Work Team Effectiveness"; T.L. Doolen, M.E. Hacker, and E.M. Van Aken, "The Impact of Organizational Context on Work Team Effectiveness: A Study of Production Team," *IEEE Transactions on Engineering Management* 50, no. 3 (August 2003), pp. 285–96; G.L. Stewart, "A Meta-Analytic Review of Relationships between Team Design Features and Team Performance," *Journal of Management* 32, no. 1 (February 2006), pp. 29–54.

26. M.-P. Gröndahl, "Le Plan RéUssite Du Patron De Psa," *Paris Match,* September 27, 2010; M. Assayas, "Les Médias Sont Ennuyés," *Enjeux Les Echos,* February 1, 2011, p. 46; PSA Peugeot Citroën, *2010 Sustainable Development and Annual Report,* Paris, 2011.

27. M.A. Campion, E.M. Papper, and G.J. Medsker, "Relations between Work Team Characteristics and Effectiveness: A Replication and Extension," *Personnel Psychology* 49 (1996), pp. 429–52; D.C. Man and S.S.K. Lam, "The Effects of Job Complexity and Autonomy on Cohesiveness in Collectivistic and Individualistic Work Groups: A Cross-Cultural Analysis," *Journal of Organizational Behavior* 24 (2003), pp. 979–1001.

28. R. Wageman, "The Meaning of Interdependence," in *Groups at Work: Theory and Research* ed. M.E. Turner (Mahwah, NJ: Lawrence Erlbaum Associates, 2001), pp. 197–217; S.M. Gully et al., "A Meta-Analysis of Team-Efficacy, Potency, and Performance: Interdependence and Level of Analysis as Moderators of Observed Relationships," *Journal of Applied Psychology* 87, no. 5 (October 2002), pp. 819–32; M.R. Barrick et al., "The Moderating Role of Top Management Team Interdependence: Implications for Real Teams and Working Groups," *Academy of Management Journal* 50, no. 3 (2007), pp. 544–57.

29. A. Deutschman, "Inside the Mind of Jeff Bezos," *Fast Company,* August 2004, pp. 52–58; L. Gratton and T.J. Erickson, "Ways to Build Collaborative Teams," *Harvard Business Review* (November 2007), pp. 100–109.

30. G. Stasser, "Pooling of Unshared Information during Group Discussion," in *Group Process and Productivity,* ed. S. Worchel, W. Wood, and J.A. Simpson (Newbury Park, CA: Sage Publications, 1992); J.R. Katzenbach and D.K. Smith, *The Wisdom of Teams: Creating the High-Performance Organization* (Boston: Harvard University Press, 1993), pp. 45–47.

31. J. O'Toole, "The Power of Many: Building a High-Performance Management Team," http://www.ceoforum.com.au (March 2003).

32. C. Fishman, "The Anarchist's Cookbook," *Fast Company,* July 2004, p. 70.

33. P. Wise, "How Shell Finds Student World's Brightest Sparks," *Financial Times (London),* January 8, 2004, p. 12; S. Ganesan, "Talent Quest," *Malaysia Star,* January 28, 2007.

34. A.W. Woolley et al., "Evidence for a Collective Intelligence Factor in the Performance of Human Groups," *Science* 330, no. 6004 (October 2010), pp. 686–88.

35. F.P. Morgeson, M.H. Reider, and M.A. Campion, "Selecting Individuals in Team Setting: The Importance of Social Skills, Personality Characteristics, and Teamwork Knowledge," *Personnel Psychology* 58, no. 3 (2005), pp. 583–611; V. Rousseau, C. Aubé, and A. Savoie, "Teamwork Behaviors: A Review and an Integration of Frameworks," *Small Group Research* 37, no. 5 (2006), pp. 540–70. For a detailed examination of the characteristics of effective team members, see M.L. Loughry, M.W. Ohland, and D.D. Moore, "Development of a Theory-Based Assessment of Team Member Effectiveness," *Educational and Psychological Measurement* 67, no. 3 (June 2007), pp. 505–24.

36. C.E. Hârtel and D. Panipucci, "How 'Bad Apples' Spoil the Bunch: Faultlines, Emotional Levers, and Exclusion in the Workplace," *Research on Emotion in Organizations* 3 (2007), pp. 287–310.

The bad apple phenomenon is also identified in executive team "derailers." See R. Wageman et al., *Senior Leadership Teams* (Boston: Harvard Business School Press, 2008), pp. 97–102.

37. D. van Knippenberg, C.K.W. De Dreu, and A.C. Homan, "Work Group Diversity and Group Performance: An Integrative Model and Research Agenda," *Journal of Applied Psychology* 89, no. 6 (2004), pp. 1008–22; E. Mannix and M.A. Neale, "What Differences Make a Difference?: The Promise and Reality of Diverse Teams in Organizations," *Psychological Science in the Public Interest* 6, no. 2 (2005), pp. 31–55. For a positive view of team diversity, see G.K. Stahl et al., "A Look at the Bright Side of Multicultural Team Diversity," *Scandinavian Journal of Management* 26, no. 4 (2010), pp. 439–47.

38. D.C. Lau and J.K. Murnighan, "Interactions within Groups and Subgroups: The Effects of Demographic Faultlines," *Academy of Management Journal* 48, no. 4 (August 2005), pp. 645–59; R. Rico et al., "The Effects of Diversity Faultlines and Team Task Autonomy on Decision Quality and Social Integration," *Journal of Management* 33, no. 1 (February 2007), pp. 111–32.

39. J.P. Croxon, "Footsteps of the Ghostwalkers," *Airman Magazine*, March/April 2010, pp. 25–29.

40. B.W. Tuckman and M.A.C. Jensen, "Stages of Small-Group Development Revisited," *Group and Organization Studies* 2 (1977), pp. 419–42; B.W. Tuckman, "Developmental Sequence in Small Groups," *Group Facilitation* (Spring 2001), pp. 66–81.

41. G.R. Bushe and G.H. Coetzer, "Group Development and Team Effectiveness: Using Cognitive Representations to Measure Group Development and Predict Task Performance and Group Viability," *Journal of Applied Behavioral Science* 43, no. 2 (June 2007), pp. 184–212.

42. J.E. Mathieu and G.F. Goodwin, "The Influence of Shared Mental Models on Team Process and Performance," *Journal of Applied Psychology* 85 (April 2000), pp. 273–84; J. Langan-Fox and J. Anglim, "Mental Models, Team Mental Models, and Performance: Process, Development, and Future Directions," *Human Factors and Ergonomics in Manufacturing* 14, no. 4 (2004), pp. 331–52; B.-C. Lim and K.J. Klein, "Team Mental Models and Team Performance: A Field Study of the Effects of Team Mental Model Similarity and Accuracy," *Journal of Organizational Behavior* 27 (2006), pp. 403–18; R. Rico, M. Sánchez-Manzanares, and C. Gibson, "Team Implicit Coordination Processes: A Team Knowledge-Based Approach," *Academy of Management Review* 33, no. 1 (2008), pp. 163–84.

43. L.A. DeChurch and J.R. Mesmer-Magnus, "The Cognitive Underpinnings of Effective Teamwork: A Meta-Analysis," *Journal of Applied Psychology* 95, no. 1 (2010), pp. 32–53.

44. A.P. Hare, "Types of Roles in Small Groups: A Bit of History and a Current Perspective," *Small Group Research* 25 (1994), pp. 443–48; A. Aritzeta, S. Swailes, and B. Senior, "Belbin's Team Role Model: Development, Validity and Applications for Team Building," *Journal of Management Studies* 44, no. 1 (January 2007), pp. 96–118.

45. S.H.N. Leung, J.W.K. Chan, and W.B. Lee, "The Dynamic Team Role Behavior: The Approaches of Investigation," *Team Performance Management* 9 (2003), pp. 84–90; G.L. Stewart, I.S. Fulmer, and M.R. Barrick, "An Exploration of Member Roles as a Multilevel Linking Mechanism for Individual Traits and Team Outcomes," *Personnel Psychology* 58, no. 2 (2005), pp. 343–65.

46. W.G. Dyer, *Team Building: Current Issues and New Alternatives*, 3rd ed. (Reading, MA: Addison-Wesley, 1995); C.A. Beatty and B.A. Barker, *Building Smart Teams: Roadmap to High Performance* (Thousand Oaks, CA: Sage Publications, 2004).

47. Langan-Fox and Anglim, "Mental Models, Team Mental Models, and Performance"; J.E. Mathieu et al., "Scaling the Quality of Teammates' Mental Models: Equifinality and Normative Comparisons," *Journal of Organizational Behavior* 26 (2005), pp. 37–56.

48. A. Zayas, "A Search for Teamwork," *St. Petersburg Times (Florida)*, June 29, 2008, p. 1F; "Team Nestlé Stride Out in GCC Walking Challenge," Nestlé UK, 2009, http://www.nestle.co.uk; S.W. Leow, "Firms Whip Up a Dash of Team Spirit," *Straits Times (Singapore)*, December 4, 2009; D. Moss, "The Value of Giving," *HRMagainze*, December 2009, p. 22.

49. "German Businesswoman Demands End to Fun at Work," *Reuters*, July 9, 2003.

50. R.W. Woodman and J.J. Sherwood, "The Role of Team Development in Organizational Effectiveness: A Critical Review," *Psychological Bulletin* 88 (1980), pp. 166–86.

51. L. Mealiea and R. Baltazar, "A Strategic Guide for Building Effective Teams," *Personnel Management* 34, no. 2 (Summer 2005), pp. 141–60.

52. G.E. Huszczo, "Training for Team Building," *Training and Development Journal* 44 (February 1990), pp. 37–43; P. McGraw, "Back from the Mountain: Outdoor Management Development Programs and How to Ensure the Transfer of Skills to the Workplace," *Asia Pacific Journal of Human Resources* 31 (Spring 1993), pp. 52–61.

53. D.C. Feldman, "The Development and Enforcement of Group Norms," *Academy of Management Review* 9 (1984), pp. 47–53; E. Fehr and U. Fischbacher, "Social Norms and Human Cooperation," *Trends in Cognitive Sciences* 8, no. 4 (2004), pp. 185–90.

54. N. Ellemers and F. Rink, "Identity in Work Groups: The Beneficial and Detrimental Consequences of Multiple Identities and Group Norms for Collaboration and Group Performance," *Advances in Group Processes* 22 (2005), pp. 1–41.

55. J.J. Dose and R.J. Klimoski, "The Diversity of Diversity: Work Values Effects on Formative Team Processes," *Human Resource Management Review* 9, no. 1 (Spring 1999), pp. 83–108.

56. S. Taggar and R. Ellis, "The Role of Leaders in Shaping Formal Team Norms," *Leadership Quarterly* 18, no. 2 (2007), pp. 105–20.

57. D.J. Beal et al., "Cohesion and Performance in Groups: A Meta-Analytic Clarification of Construct Relations," *Journal of Applied Psychology* 88, no. 6 (2003), pp. 989–1004; S.W.J. Kozlowski and D.R. Ilgen, "Enhancing the Effectiveness of Work Groups and Teams," *Psychological Science in the Public Interest* 7, no. 3 (2006), pp. 77–124.

58. R.M. Montoya, R.S. Horton, and J. Kirchner, "Is Actual Similarity Necessary for Attraction? A Meta-Analysis of Actual and Perceived Similarity," *Journal of Social and Personal Relationships* 25, no. 6 (December 1, 2008), pp. 889–922; M.T. Rivera, S.B. Soderstrom, and B. Uzzi, "Dynamics of Dyads in Social Networks: Assortative, Relational, and Proximity Mechanisms," *Annual Review of Sociology* 36 (2010), pp. 91–115.

59. K.A. Jehn, G.B. Northcraft, and M.A. Neale, "Why Differences Make a Difference: A Field Study of Diversity, Conflict, and Performance in Workgroups," *Administrative Science Quarterly* 44, no. 4 (1999), pp. 741–63; van Knippenberg, De Dreu, and Homan, "Work Group Diversity and Group Performance." For evidence that diversity/similarity does not always influence cohesion, see S.S. Webber and L.M. Donahue, "Impact of Highly and Less Job-Related Diversity on Work Group Cohesion and Performance: A Meta-Analysis," *Journal of Management* 27, no. 2 (2001), pp. 141–62.

60. E. Aronson and J. Mills, "The Effects of Severity of Initiation on Liking for a Group," *Journal of Abnormal and Social Psychology* 59 (1959), pp. 177–81; J.E. Hautaluoma and R.S. Enge, "Early Socialization into a Work Group: Severity of Initiations Revisited," *Journal of Social Behavior & Personality* 6 (1991), pp. 725–48.

61. B. Mullen and C. Copper, "The Relation between Group Cohesiveness and Performance: An Integration," *Psychological Bulletin* 115 (1994), pp. 210–27; C.J. Fullagar and D.O. Egleston, "Norming and Performing: Using Microworlds to Understand the Relationship

between Team Cohesiveness and Performance," *Journal of Applied Social Psychology* 38, no. 10 (October 2008), pp. 2574–93.

62. Wageman et al., *Senior Leadership Teams*, pp. 69–70.

63. L. Hirsh, "Manufacturing in Action," *Press-Enterprise (Riverside, CA),* June 21, 2008, p. E01; J. Ford, "Snow: La-Z-Boy 'Here for the Long Haul," *Neosho Daily News (Missouri),* May 16, 2009.

64. M. Rempel and R.J. Fisher, "Perceived Threat, Cohesion, and Group Problem Solving in Intergroup Conflict," *International Journal of Conflict Management* 8 (1997), pp. 216–34; M.E. Turner and T. Horvitz, "The Dilemma of Threat: Group Effectiveness and Ineffectiveness under Adversity," in *Groups at Work: Theory and Research,* ed. M.E. Turner (Mahwah, NJ: Lawrence Erlbaum Associates, 2001), pp. 445–70.

65. W. Piper et al., "Cohesion as a Basic Bond in Groups," *Human Relations* 36 (1983), pp. 93–108; C.A. O'Reilly, D.E. Caldwell, and W.P. Barnett, "Work Group Demography, Social Integration, and Turnover," *Administrative Science Quarterly* 34 (1989), pp. 21–37.

66. Mullen and Copper, "The Relation between Group Cohesiveness and Performance"; A.V. Carron et al. , "Cohesion and Performance in Sport: A Meta-Analysis," *Journal of Sport and Exercise Psychology* 24 (2002), pp. 168–88; Beal et al., "Cohesion and Performance in Groups"; Fullagar and Egleston, "Norming and Performing"; DeChurch and Mesmer-Magnus, "The Cognitive Underpinnings of Effective Teamwork."

67. Fullagar and Egleston, "Norming and Performing."

68. C. Langfred, "Is Group Cohesiveness a Double-Edged Sword? An Investigation of the Effects of Cohesiveness on Performance," *Small Group Research* 29 (1998), pp. 124–43; K.L. Gammage, A.V. Carron, and P.A. Estabrooks, "Team Cohesion and Individual Productivity: The Influence of the Norm for Productivity and the Identifiability of Individual Effort," *Small Group Research* 32 (February 2001), pp. 3–18; N.L. Jimmieson, M. Peach, and K.M. White, "Utilizing the Theory of Planned Behavior to Inform Change Management," *Journal of Applied Behavioral Science* 44, no. 2 (June 2008), pp. 237–62. Concerns about existing research on cohesion–performance links are discussed by M. Casey-Campbell and M.L. Martens, "Sticking It All Together: A Critical Assessment of the Group Cohesion–Performance Literature," *International Journal of Management Reviews* 11, no. 2 (2009), pp. 223–46.

69. S.L. Robinson, "Trust and Breach of the Psychological Contract," *Administrative Science Quarterly* 41 (1996), pp. 574–99; D.M. Rousseau et al., "Not So Different after All: A Cross-Discipline View of Trust," *Academy of Management Review* 23 (1998), pp. 393–404; D.L. Duarte and N.T. Snyder, *Mastering Virtual Teams: Strategies, Tools, and Techniques That Succeed,* 2nd ed. (San Francisco, CA: Jossey-Bass, 2000), pp. 139–55. For the importance of trust in virtual teams, see L.M. Peters and C.C. Manz, "Getting Virtual Teams Right the First Time," in *The Handbook of High-Performance Virtual Teams: A Toolkit for Collaborating across Boundaries,* ed. J. Nemiro and M.M. Beyerlein (San Francisco, CA: Jossey-Bass, 2008), pp. 105–30.

70. Rousseau et al., "Not So Different after All."

71. D.J. McAllister, "Affect- and Cognition-Based Trust as Foundations for Interpersonal Cooperation in Organizations," *Academy of Management Journal* 38, no. 1 (February 1995), pp. 24–59; M. Williams, "In Whom We Trust: Group Membership as an Affective Context for Trust Development," *Academy of Management Review* 26, no. 3 (July 2001), pp. 377–96.

72. O.E. Williamson, "Calculativeness, Trust, and Economic Organization," *Journal of Law and Economics* 36, no. 1 (1993), pp. 453–86.

73. E.M. Whitener et al., "Managers as Initiators of Trust: An Exchange Relationship Framework for Understanding Managerial Trustworthy Behavior," *Academy of Management Review* 23 (July 1998), pp. 513–30; J.M. Kouzes and B.Z. Posner, *The Leadership Challenge,* 3rd ed. (San Francisco: Jossey-Bass, 2002), Ch. 2; T. Simons, "Behavioral Integrity: The Perceived Alignment between Managers' Words and Deeds as a Research Focus," *Organization Science* 13, no. 1 (January–February 2002), pp. 18–35.

74. S.L. Jarvenpaa and D.E. Leidner, "Communication and Trust in Global Virtual Teams," *Organization Science* 10 (1999), pp. 791–815; M.M. Pillutla, D. Malhotra, and J. Keith Murnighan, "Attributions of Trust and the Calculus of Reciprocity," *Journal of Experimental Social Psychology* 39, no. 5 (2003), pp. 448–55.

75. K.T. Dirks and D.L. Ferrin, "The Role of Trust in Organizations," *Organization Science* 12, no. 4 (July–August 2004), pp. 450–67.

76. Mohrman et al., *Designing Team-Based Organizations;* D.E. Yeatts and C. Hyten, *High-Performing Self-Managed Work Teams: A Comparison of Theory and Practice* (Thousand Oaks, CA: Sage Publications, 1998); E.E. Lawler, *Organizing for High Performance* (San Francisco, CA: Jossey-Bass, 2001); R.J. Torraco, "Work Design Theory: A Review and Critique with Implications for Human Resource Development," *Human Resource Development Quarterly* 16, no. 1 (Spring 2005), pp. 85–109.

77. Fishman, "The Anarchist's Cookbook"; J. Mackey, "Open Book Company," *Newsweek,* 28 November 2005, p. 42; K. Zimbalist, "Green Giant," *Time,* April 24, 2006, p. 24.

78. P. Panchak, "Production Workers Can Be Your Competitive Edge," *Industry Week,* October 2004, p. 11; S.K. Muthusamy, J.V. Wheeler, and B.L. Simmons, "Self-Managing Work Teams: Enhancing Organizational Innovativeness," *Organization Development Journal* 23, no. 3 (Fall 2005), pp. 53–66.

79. Emery and Fredenhall, "The Effect of Teams on Firm Profitability and Customer Satisfaction"; A. Krause and H. Dunckel, "Work Design and Customer Satisfaction: Effects of the Implementation of Semi-Autonomous Group Work on Customer Satisfaction Considering Employee Satisfaction and Group Performance [translated abstract]," *Zeitschrift Fur Arbeits-Und Organisationspsychologie* 47, no. 4 (2003), pp. 182–93; H. van Mierlo et al., "Self-Managing Teamwork and Psychological Well-Being: Review of a Multilevel Research Domain," *Group & Organization Management* 30, no. 2 (April 2005), pp. 211–35.

80. Moldaschl and Weber, "The 'Three Waves' of Industrial Group Work"; W. Niepce and E. Molleman, "Work Design Issues in Lean Production from Sociotechnical System Perspective: Neo-Taylorism or the Next Step in Sociotechnical Design?" *Human Relations* 51, no. 3 (March 1998), pp. 259–87; J.L. Cordery et al., "The Impact of Autonomy and Task Uncertainty on Team Performance: A Longitudinal Field Study," *Journal of Organizational Behavior* 31 (2010), pp. 240–58.

81. E. Ulich and W.G. Weber, "Dimensions, Criteria, and Evaluation of Work Group Autonomy," in *Handbook of Work Group Psychology,* ed. M.A. West (Chichester, UK: John Wiley & Sons, 1996), pp. 247–82.

82. K.P. Carson and G.L. Stewart, "Job Analysis and the Sociotechnical Approach to Quality: A Critical Examination," *Journal of Quality Management* 1 (1996), pp. 49–65; C.C. Manz and G.L. Stewart, "Attaining Flexible Stability by Integrating Total Quality Management and Socio-Technical Systems Theory," *Organization Science* 8 (1997), pp. 59–70.

83. J. Lipnack and J. Stamps, *Virtual Teams: People Working across Boundaries with Technology* (New York: John Wiley & Sons, 2001); Hertel et al., "Managing Virtual Teams"; L. Schweitzer and L. Duxbury, "Conceptualizing and Measuring the Virtuality of Teams," *Information Systems Journal* 20, no. 3 (2010), pp. 267–95.

84. "Virtual Teams Now a Reality," Institute for Corporate Productivity, news release, September 4, 2008.

85. G. Gilder, *Telecosm: How Infinite Bandwidth Will Revolutionize Our World* (New York: The Free Press, 2001); L.L. Martins, L.L. Gilson, and M.T. Maynard, "Virtual Teams: What Do We Know and Where

Do We Go From Here?" *Journal of Management* 30, no. 6 (2004), pp. 805–35.

86. N. Weil, "Global Team Management: Continental Divides," *CIO*, January 23, 2008.

87. S. Kiesler and J.N. Cummings, "What Do We Know about Proximity and Distance in Work Groups? A Legacy of Research," in *Distributed Work*, ed. P. Hinds and S. Kiesler (Cambridge, MA: MIT Press, 2002), pp. 57–80; Rivera et al., "Dynamics of Dyads in Social Networks."

88. L. Berlin, "Location, Location: It Still Pays to Be Near," *The New York Times*, June 14, 2009, p. 3.

89. M. O'Brien, "Long-Distance Relationship Troubles," *Human Resource Executive Online*, July 7, 2009.

90. VitalSmarts, *Long-Distance Loathing (Summary and Data)* (Provo, UT: VitalSmarts, 2009).

91. Martins et al., "Virtual Teams"; G. Hertel, U. Konradt, and K. Voss, "Competencies for Virtual Teamwork: Development and Validation of a Web-Based Selection Tool for Members of Distributed Teams," *European Journal of Work and Organizational Psychology* 15, no. 4 (2006), pp. 477–504; J.M. Wilson et al., "Perceived Proximity in Virtual Work: Explaining the Paradox of Far-but-Close," *Organization Studies* 29, no. 7 (July 1, 2008), pp. 979–1002.

92. G.G. Harwood, "Design Principles for Successful Virtual Teams," in *The Handbook of High-Performance Virtual Teams: A Toolkit for Collaborating across Boundaries*, ed. J. Nemiro and M.M. Beyerlein (San Francisco, CA: Jossey-Bass, 2008), pp. 59–84. Also see H. Duckworth, "How TRW Automotive Helps Global Virtual Teams Perform at the Top of Their Game," *Global Business and Organizational Excellence* 28, no. 1 (2008), pp. 6–16; L. Dubé and D. Robey, "Surviving the Paradoxes of Virtual Teamwork," *Information Systems Journal* 19, no. 1 (2009), pp. 3–30.

93. Dubé and Robey, "Surviving the Paradoxes of Virtual Teamwork."

94. V. H. Vroom and A.G. Jago, *The New Leadership* (Englewood Cliffs, NJ: Prentice Hall, 1988), pp. 28–29.

95. M. Diehl and W. Stroebe, "Productivity Loss in Idea-Generating Groups: Tracking Down the Blocking Effects," *Journal of Personality and Social Psychology* 61 (1991), pp. 392–403; R.B. Gallupe et al., "Blocking Electronic Brainstorms," *Journal of Applied Psychology* 79 (1994), pp. 77–86; B.A. Nijstad, W. Stroebe, and H.F.M. Lodewijkx, "Production Blocking and Idea Generation: Does Blocking Interfere with Cognitive Processes?" *Journal of Experimental Social Psychology* 39, no. 6 (November 2003), pp. 531–48; B.A. Nijstad and W. Stroebe, "How the Group Affects the Mind: A Cognitive Model of Idea Generation in Groups," *Personality & Social Psychology Review* 10, no. 3 (2006), pp. 186–213.

96. B.E. Irmer, P. Bordia, and D. Abusah, "Evaluation Apprehension and Perceived Benefits in Interpersonal and Database Knowledge Sharing," *Academy of Management Proceedings* (2002), pp. B1–B6.

97. I.L. Janis, *Groupthink: Psychological Studies of Policy Decisions and Fiascoes*, 2nd ed. (Boston: Houghton Mifflin, 1982); J.K. Esser, "Alive and Well after 25 Years: A Review of Groupthink Research," *Organizational Behavior and Human Decision Processes* 73, no. 2–3 (1998), pp. 116–41.

98. J.N. Choi and M.U. Kim, "The Organizational Application of Groupthink and Its Limitations in Organizations," *Journal of Applied Psychology* 84, no. 2 (April 1999), pp. 297–306; W.-W. Park, "A Comprehensive Empirical Investigation of the Relationships among Variables of the Groupthink Model," *Journal of Organizational Behavior* 21, no. 8 (December 2000), pp. 873–87; D.D. Henningsen et al., "Examining the Symptoms of Groupthink and Retrospective Sensemaking," *Small Group Research* 37, no. 1 (February 2006), pp. 36–64.

99. D. Miller, *The Icarus Paradox: How Exceptional Companies Bring About Their Own Downfall* (New York: HarperBusiness, 1990);

S. Finkelstein, *Why Smart Executives Fail* (New York: Viking, 2003); K. Tasa and G. Whyte, "Collective Efficacy and Vigilant Problem Solving in Group Decision Making: A Non-Linear Model," *Organizational Behavior and Human Decision Processes* 96, no. 2 (March 2005), pp. 119–29.

100. H. Collingwood, "Best-Kept Secrets of the World's Best Companies: Outside-In R&D," *Business 2.0*, April 2006, p. 82.

101. K.M. Eisenhardt, J.L. Kahwajy, and L.J. Bourgeois III, "Conflict and Strategic Choice: How Top Management Teams Disagree," *California Management Review* 39 (1997), pp. 42–62; R. Sutton, *Weird Ideas That Work* (New York: The Free Press, 2002); C.J. Nemeth et al., "The Liberating Role of Conflict in Group Creativity: A Study in Two Countries," *European Journal of Social Psychology* 34, no. 4 (2004), pp. 365–74. For a discussion on how all conflict is potentially detrimental to teams, see C.K.W. De Dreu and L.R. Weingart, "Task versus Relationship Conflict, Team Performance, and Team Member Satisfaction: A Meta-Analysis," *Journal of Applied Psychology* 88 (August 2003), pp. 587–604; P. Hinds and D.E. Bailey, "Out of Sight, Out of Sync: Understanding Conflict in Distributed Teams," *Organization Science* 14, no. 6 (2003), pp. 615–32.

102. Advertising executive Alex Osborn (the "O" in BBDO, the world's second largest creative agency) first described brainstorming in the little-known 1942 booklet *How to Think Up*. He originally called them "brain-storm suppers" (p. 29) because the company initially held these events in the evening, after a meal in the company dining room. Osborn gave a fuller description of the brainstorming process in his popular 1948 and 1953 books. See A.F. Osborn, *How to Think Up* (New York: McGraw-Hill, 1942), Ch. 4; A.F. Osborn, *Your Creative Power* (New York: Charles Scribner's Sons, 1948); A.F. Osborn, *Applied Imagination* (New York: Charles Scribner's Sons, 1953).

103. B.S. Benson, "Let's Toss This Idea Up," *Fortune*, October 1957, pp. 145–46.

104. B. Mullen, C. Johnson, and E. Salas, "Productivity Loss in Brainstorming Groups: A Meta-Analytic Integration," *Basic and Applied Psychology* 12 (1991), pp. 2–23.

105. R.I. Sutton and A. Hargadon, "Brainstorming Groups in Context: Effectiveness in a Product Design Firm," *Administrative Science Quarterly* 41 (1996), pp. 685–718; T. Kelley, *The Art of Innovation* (New York: Currency Doubleday, 2001); V.R. Brown and P.B. Paulus, "Making Group Brainstorming More Effective: Recommendations from an Associative Memory Perspective," *Current Directions in Psychological Science* 11, no. 6 (2002), pp. 208–12; K. Leggett Dugosh and P.B. Paulus, "Cognitive and Social Comparison Processes in Brainstorming," *Journal of Experimental Social Psychology* 41, no. 3 (2005), pp. 313–20.

106. N.W. Kohn, P.B. Paulus, and Y. Choi, "Building on the Ideas of Others: An Examination of the Idea Combination Process," *Journal of Experimental Social Psychology* 47 (2011), pp. 554–61.

107. R.B. Gallupe, L.M. Bastianutti, and W.H. Cooper, "Unblocking Brainstorms," *Journal of Applied Psychology* 76 (1991), pp. 137–42; W.H. Cooper et al., "Some Liberating Effects of Anonymous Electronic Brainstorming," *Small Group Research* 29, no. 2 (April 1998), pp. 147–78; A.R. Dennis, B.H. Wixom, and R.J. Vandenberg, "Understanding Fit and Appropriation Effects in Group Support Systems via Meta-Analysis," *MIS Quarterly* 25, no. 2 (June 2001), pp. 167–93; D.M. DeRosa, C.L. Smith, and D.A. Hantula, "The Medium Matters: Mining the Long-Promised Merit of Group Interaction in Creative Idea Generation Tasks in a Meta-Analysis of the Electronic Group Brainstorming Literature," *Computers in Human Behavior* 23, no. 3 (2007), pp. 1549–81.

108. 3M South Africa, "3M 'Innovation Live' Conference Aimed at Improving Brand Innovation in SA," BizCommunity.com, June 17, 2011, http://www.bizcommunity.com/Article/196/82/60722.html;

B. Schneider and K.B. Paul, "In the Company We Trust," *HRMagazine,* January 2011, pp. 40–43.

109. A.L. Delbecq, A.H. Van de Ven, and D.H. Gustafson, *Group Techniques for Program Planning: A Guide to Nominal Group and Delphi Processes* (Middleton, WI: Green Briar Press, 1986).

110. D.M. Spencer, "Facilitating Public Participation in Tourism Planning on American Indian Reservations: A Case Study Involving the Nominal Group Technique," *Tourism Management* 31, no. 5 (2011), pp. 684–90.

111. S. Frankel, "NGT + MDS: An Adaptation of the Nominal Group Technique for Ill-Structured Problems," *Journal of Applied Behavioral Science* 23 (1987), pp. 543–51; H. Barki and A. Pinsonneault, "Small Group Brainstorming and Idea Quality: Is Electronic Brainstorming the Most Effective Approach?" *Small Group Research* 32, no. 2 (April 2001), pp. 158–205.

112. P.P. Lago et al., "Structuring Group Decision Making in a Web-Based Environment by Using the Nominal Group Technique," *Computers & Industrial Engineering* 52, no. 2 (2007), pp. 277–95.

CHAPTER 9

1. T. Hsieh, "How Twitter Can Make You a Better (and Happier) Person," 2009, http://blogs.zappos.com/blogs/ceo-and-coo-blog; J. Vijayan, "Staying on Message," *Computerworld,* October 19, 2009; "Social Media Training Programs: Different Approaches, Common Goals," *PR News,* January 4, 2010; A. Bryant, "On a Scale of 1 to 10, How Weird Are You?" *The New York Times,* January 10, 2010; E. Ridgeway, "Zappos CEO on Getting Employees to 'Live the Brand,'" *CNN,* March 23, 2011.

2. A.H. Van de Ven, A.L. Delbecq, and R. Koenig Jr., "Determinants of Coordination Modes within Organizations," *American Sociological Review* 41, no. 2 (1976), pp. 322–38; R. Foy et al., "Meta-Analysis: Effect of Interactive Communication between Collaborating Primary Care Physicians and Specialists," *Annals of Internal Medicine* 152, no. 4 (February 2010), pp. 247–58; J.H. Gittell, R. Seidner, and J. Wimbush, "A Relational Model of How High-Performance Work Systems Work," *Organization Science* 21, no. 2 (March 2010), pp. 490–506.

3. C. Barnard, *The Functions of the Executive* (Cambridge, MA: Harvard University Press, 1938), p. 82. Barnard's entire statement also refers to the other features of organizations that we describe in Chapter 1: (a) people are willing to contribute their effort to the organization and (b) they have a common purpose.

4. M.T. Hansen, M.L. Mors, and B. Løvås, "Knowledge Sharing in Organizations: Multiple Networks, Multiple Phases," *Academy of Management Journal* 48, no. 5 (2005), pp. 776–93; S.R. Murray and J. Peyrefitte, "Knowledge Type and Communication Media Choice in the Knowledge Transfer Process," *Journal of Managerial Issues* 19, no. 1 (Spring 2007), pp. 111–33; S.L. Hoe and S.L. McShane, "Structural and Informal Knowledge Acquisition and Dissemination in Organizational Learning: An Exploratory Analysis," *Learning Organization* 17, no. 4 (2010), pp. 364–86.

5. M. DiGiovanni, "CUs View Best Workplace Recognition as a Starting Point," *Credit Union Times,* December 1, 2010.

6. J. O'Toole and W. Bennis, "What's Needed Next: A Culture of Candor," *Harvard Business Review* 87, no. 6 (2009), pp. 54–61.

7. N. Ellemers, R. Spears, and B. Doosje, "Self and Social Identity," *Annual Review of Psychology* 53 (2002), pp. 161–86; S.A. Haslam and S. Reicher, "Stressing the Group: Social Identity and the Unfolding Dynamics of Responses to Stress," *Journal of Applied Psychology* 91, no. 5 (2006), pp. 1037–52; M.T. Gailliot and R.F. Baumeister, "Self-Esteem, Belongingness, and Worldview Validation: Does Belongingness Exert a Unique Influence upon Self-Esteem?" *Journal of Research in Personality* 41, no. 2 (2007), pp. 327–45.

8. A.M. Saks, K.L. Uggerslev, and N.E. Fassina, "Socialization Tactics and Newcomer Adjustment: A Meta-Analytic Review and Test of a Model," *Journal of Vocational Behavior* 70, no. 3 (2007), pp. 413–46.

9. S. Cohen, "The Pittsburgh Common Cold Studies: Psychosocial Predictors of Susceptibility to Respiratory Infectious Illness," *International Journal of Behavioral Medicine* 12, no. 3 (2005), pp. 123–31; B.N. Uchino, "Social Support and Health: A Review of Physiological Processes Potentially Underlying Links to Disease Outcomes," *Journal of Behavioral Medicine* 29, no. 4 (2006), pp. 377–87.

10. C.E. Shannon and W. Weaver, *The Mathematical Theory of Communication* (Urbana, IL: University of Illinois Press, 1949); R.M. Krauss and S.R. Fussell, "Social Psychological Models of Interpersonal Communication," in *Social Psychology: Handbook of Basic Principles,* ed. E.T. Higgins and A. Kruglanski (New York: Guilford Press, 1996), pp. 655–701.

11. J.R. Carlson and R.W. Zmud, "Channel Expansion Theory and the Experiential Nature of Media Richness Perceptions," *Academy of Management Journal* 42 (April 1999), pp. 153–70.

12. P. Shachaf and N. Hara, "Behavioral Complexity Theory of Media Selection: A Proposed Theory for Global Virtual Teams," *Journal of Information Science* 33 (2007), pp. 63–75.

13. M. Hauben and R. Hauben, "Netizens: On the History and Impact of Usenet and the Internet," *First Monday* 3, no. 8 (August 1998); J. Abbate, (Cambridge, MA: MIT Press, 1999).

14. N.B. Ducheneaut and L.A. Watts, "In Search of Coherence: A Review of E-Mail Research," *Human-Computer Interaction* 20, no. 1-2 (2005), pp. 11–48.

15. W. Lucas, "Effects of E-Mail on the Organization," *European Management Journal* 16, no. 1 (February 1998), pp. 18–30; D.A. Owens, M.A. Neale, and R.I. Sutton, "Technologies of Status Management: Status Dynamics in E-Mail Communications," *Research on Managing Groups and Teams* 3 (2000), pp. 205–30; N.B. Ducheneaut, "Ceci N'est Pas Un Objet? Talking about Objects in E-Mail," *Human-Computer Interaction* 18, no. 1-2 (2003), pp. 85–110.

16. N.B. Ducheneaut, "The Social Impacts of Electronic Mail in Organizations: A Case Study of Electronic Power Games Using Communication Genres," *Information, Communication, & Society* 5, no. 2 (2002), pp. 153–88; N. Panteli, "Richness, Power Cues and Email Text," *Information & Management* 40, no. 2 (2002), pp. 75–86.

17. N. Epley and J. Kruger, "When What You Type Isn't What They Read: The Perseverance of Stereotypes and Expectancies over E-Mail," *Journal of Experimental Social Psychology* 41, no. 4 (2005), pp. 414–22.

18. J. Kruger et al., "Egocentrism over E-Mail: Can We Communicate as Well as We Think?" *Journal of Personality and Social Psychology* 89, no. 6 (2005), pp. 925–36.

19. J.B. Walther, "Language and Communication Technology: Introduction to the Special Issue," *Journal of Language and Social Psychology* 23, no. 4 (December 2004), pp. 384–96; J.B. Walther, T. Loh, and L. Granka, "Let Me Count the Ways: The Interchange of Verbal and Nonverbal Cues in Computer-Mediated and Face-to-Face Affinity," *Journal of Language and Social Psychology* 24, no. 1 (March 2005), pp. 36–65; K. Byron, "Carrying Too Heavy a Load? The Communication and Miscommunication of Emotion by Email," *Academy of Management Review* 33, no. 2 (2008), pp. 309–27; J.M. Whalen, P.M. Pexman, and A.J. Gill, "'Should Be Fun—Not!': Incidence and Marking of Nonliteral Language in E-Mail," *Journal of Language and Social Psychology* 28, no. 3 (September 2009), pp. 263–80.

20. Byron, "Carrying Too Heavy a Load?"

21. G. Hertel, S. Geister, and U. Konradt, "Managing Virtual Teams: A Review of Current Empirical Research," *Human Resource Management Review* 15 (2005), pp. 69–95; H. Lee, "Behavioral Strategies for Dealing with Flaming in an Online Forum," *Sociological Quarterly* 46, no. 2 (2005), pp. 385–403.

22. D.D. Dawley and W.P. Anthony, "User Perceptions of E-Mail at Work," *Journal of Business and Technical Communication* 17, no. 2 (April 2003), pp. 170–200; G.F. Thomas and C.L. King, "Reconceptualizing E-Mail Overload," *Journal of Business and Technical Communication* 20, no. 3 (July 2006), pp. 252–87; S. Carr, "Email Overload Menace Growing," *Silicon.com*, July 12, 2007.

23. R.D. Waters et al., "Engaging Stakeholders through Social Networking: How Nonprofit Organizations Are Using Facebook," *Public Relations Review* 35, no. 2 (2009), pp. 102–06; J. Cunningham, "New Workers, New Workplace? Getting the Balance Right," *Strategic Direction* 26, no. 1 (2010), p. 5; A.M. Kaplan and M. Haenlein, "Users of the World, Unite! The Challenges and Opportunities of Social Media," *Business Horizons* 53, no. 1 (2010), pp. 59–68.

24. "Atos Origin Abandoning Email," *Computerworld UK*, February 9, 2011; G. Nairn, "The Trouble with Office Email," *Financial Times (London)*, February 17, 2011.

25. J.H. Kietzmann et al., "Social Media? Get Serious! Understanding the Functional Building Blocks of Social Media," *Business Horizons* (in press).

26. "Cemex Wins Prestigious Social Media Award," news release, November 1, 2010; S.J.E. Serna, *The Collaboration Revolution* (Monterrey, Mexico: CEMEX, 2010).

27. S. Holtz, "Open the Door," *Communication World*, September 2010, p. 26.

28. Towers Watson, *Capitalizing on Effective Communication* (New York: Towers Watson, 2010).

29. S. Humphries, "Companies Warm Up to Social Networks," *Christian Science Monitor*, September 8, 2008, p. 13; R. Weston, "Facebook: Your Company's Intranet?" *Forbes*, March, 20 2009.

30. L.Z. Tiedens and A.R. Fragale, "Power Moves: Complementarity in Dominant and Submissive Nonverbal Behavior," *Journal of Personality and Social Psychology* 84, no. 3 (2003), pp. 558–68.

31. P. Ekman and E. Rosenberg, *What the Face Reveals: Basic and Applied Studies of Spontaneous Expression Using the Facial Action Coding System* (Oxford: Oxford University Press, 1997); P. Winkielman and K.C. Berridge, "Unconscious Emotion," *Current Directions in Psychological Science* 13, no. 3 (2004), pp. 120–23.

32. W.J. Becker and R. Cropanzano, "Organizational Neuroscience: The Promise and Prospects of an Emerging Discipline," *Journal of Organizational Behavior* 31, no. 7 (2010), pp. 1055–59.

33. E. Hatfield, J.T. Cacioppo, and R.L. Rapson, *Emotional Contagion* (Cambridge: Cambridge University Press, 1993); S.G. Barsade, "The Ripple Effect: Emotional Contagion and Its Influence on Group Behavior," *Administrative Science Quarterly* 47 (December 2002), pp. 644–75; M. Sonnby-Borgstrom, P. Jonsson, and O. Svensson, "Emotional Empathy as Related to Mimicry Reactions at Different Levels of Information Processing," *Journal of Nonverbal Behavior* 27 (Spring 2003), pp. 3–23; S.G. Barsade and D.E. Gibson, "Why Does Affect Matter in Organizations?" *Academy of Management Perspectives* (February 2007), pp. 36–59; S.K. Johnson, "I Second That Emotion: Effects of Emotional Contagion and Affect at Work on Leader and Follower Outcomes," *Leadership Quarterly* 19, no. 1 (2008), pp. 1–19.

34. J.R. Kelly and S.G. Barsade, "Mood and Emotions in Small Groups and Work Teams," *Organizational Behavior and Human Decision Processes* 86 (September 2001), pp. 99–130.

35. J. Fulk, "Social Construction of Communication Technology," *Academy of Management Journal* 36, no. 5 (1993), pp. 921–50; L.K. Treviño, J. Webster, and E.W. Stein, "Making Connections: Complementary Influences on Communication Media Choices, Attitudes, and Use," *Organization Science* 11, no. 2 (2000), pp. 163–82; B. van den Hooff, J. Groot, and S. de Jonge, "Situational Influences on the Use of Communication Technologies," *Journal of Business Communication* 42, no. 1 (January 1, 2005), pp. 4–27; J.W. Turner et al., "Exploring the Dominant Media: How Does Media Use Reflect Organizational Norms and Affect Performance?" *Journal of Business Communication* 43, no. 3 (July 2006), pp. 220–50; M.B. Watson-Manheim and F. Bélanger, "Communication Media Repertoires: Dealing with the Multiplicity of Media Choices," *MIS Quarterly* 31, no. 2 (2007), pp. 267–93.

36. Z. Lee and Y. Lee, "Emailing the Boss: Cultural Implications of Media Choice," *IEEE Transactions on Professional Communication* 52, no. 1 (March 2009), pp. 61–74.

37. R.C. King, "Media Appropriateness: Effects of Experience on Communication Media Choice," *Decision Sciences* 28, no. 4 (1997), pp. 877–910.

38. M. Madden and S. Jones, *Networked Workers*, Pew Internet & American Life Project (Washington, DC: Pew Research Center, 2008).

39. Madden and Jones, *Networked Workers*.

40. K. Griffiths, "KPMG Sacks 670 Employees by E-Mail," *The Independent (London)*, November 5, 2002, p. 19; "Shop Worker Sacked by Text Message," *The Post (Claremont/Nedlands, Western Australia)*, July 28, 2007, pp. 1, 78.

41. R.L. Daft and R.H. Lengel, "Information Richness: A New Approach to Managerial Behavior and Organization Design," *Research in Organizational Behavior* 6 (1984), pp. 191–233; R.H. Lengel and R.L. Daft, "The Selection of Communication Media as an Executive Skill," *Academy of Management Executive* 2 (1988), pp. 225–32.

42. R.E. Rice, "Task Analyzability, Use of New Media, and Effectiveness: A Multi-Site Exploration of Media Richness," *Organization Science* 3 (1992), pp. 475–500.

43. "Employer Snapshots: 2008," *Toronto Star*, October 13, 2007; H. Schachter, "Strange but True: Some Staff Meetings Are Actually Efficient," *Globe & Mail*, July 23, 2007.

44. J.W. Turner and N.L. Reinsch Jr., "The Business Communicator as Presence Allocator," *Journal of Business Communication* 44, no. 1 (2007), pp. 36–58; N.L. Reinsch Jr., J.W. Turner, and C.H. Tinsley, "Multicommunicating: A Practice Whose Time Has Come?" *Academy of Management Review* 33, no. 2 (2008), pp. 391–403.

45. Carlson and Zmud, "Channel Expansion Theory"; N. Kock, "Media Richness or Media Naturalness? The Evolution of Our Biological Communication Apparatus and Its Influence on Our Behavior toward E-Communication Tools," *IEEE Transactions on Professional Communication* 48, no. 2 (June 2005), pp. 117–30.

46. V.W. Kupritz and E. Cowell, "Productive Management Communication: Online and Face-to-Face," *Journal of Business Communication* 48, no. 1 (January 2011), pp. 54–82.

47. D. Muller, T. Atzeni, and F. Butera, "Coaction and Upward Social Comparison Reduce the Illusory Conjunction Effect: Support for Distraction-Conflict Theory," *Journal of Experimental Social Psychology* 40, no. 5 (2004), pp. 659–65; L.P. Robert and A.R. Dennis, "Paradox of Richness: A Cognitive Model of Media Choice," *IEEE Transactions on Professional Communication* 48, no. 1 (2005), pp. 10–21.

48. E.V. Wilson, "Perceived Effectiveness of Interpersonal Persuasion Strategies in Computer-Mediated Communication," *Computers in Human Behavior* 19, no. 5 (2003), pp. 537–52; K. Sassenberg, M. Boos, and S. Rabung, "Attitude Change in Face-to-Face and Computer-Mediated Communication: Private Self-Awareness Ad Mediator and Moderator," *European Journal of Social Psychology* 35 (2005), pp. 361–74; P. Di Blasio and L. Milani, "Computer-Mediated Communication and Persuasion: Peripheral vs. Central Route to Opinion Shift," *Computers in Human Behavior* 24, no. 3 (2008), pp. 798–815.

49. Kruger et al., "Egocentrism over E-Mail."

50. R.M. Krauss, "The Psychology of Verbal Communication," in *International Encyclopedia of the Social and Behavioral Sciences*, ed. N. Smelser and P. Baltes (London: Elsevier, 2002), pp. 16161–65.

51. H. Tsoukas, "The Missing Link: A Transformational View of Metaphors in Organizational Science," *Academy of Management Review* 16, no. 3 (1991), pp. 566–85; G. Morgan, *Images of Organization,* 2nd ed. (Thousand Oaks, CA: Sage Publications, 1997); J. Amernic, R. Craig, and D. Tourish, "The Transformational Leader as Pedagogue, Physician, Architect, Commander, and Saint: Five Root Metaphors in Jack Welch's Letters to Stockholders of General Electric," *Human Relations* 60, no. 12 (December 2007), pp. 1839–72.

52. M. Rubini and H. Sigall, "Taking the Edge Off of Disagreement: Linguistic Abstractness and Self-Presentation to a Heterogeneous Audience," *European Journal of Social Psychology* 32 (2002), pp. 343–51.

53. T. Walsh, "Nardelli Brags on VIP Recruits, Game Plan," *Detroit Free Press,* September 8, 2007.

54. D. Goleman, R. Boyatzis, and A. McKee, *Primal Leaders* (Boston: Harvard Business School Press, 2002), pp. 92–95.

55. O'Toole and Bennis, "What's Needed Next."

56. T. Koski, "Reflections on Information Glut and Other Issues in Knowledge Productivity," *Futures* 33 (August 2001), pp. 483–95.

57. A.G. Schick, L.A. Gordon, and S. Haka, "Information Overload: A Temporal Approach," *Accounting, Organizations & Society* 15 (1990), pp. 199–220; A. Edmunds and A. Morris, "The Problem of Information Overload in Business Organisations: A Review of the Literature," *International Journal of Information Management* 20 (2000), pp. 17–28; R. Pennington, "The Effects of Information Overload on Software Project Risk Assessment," *Decision Sciences* 38, no. 3 (August 2007), pp. 489–526.

58. D.C. Thomas and K. Inkson, *Cultural Intelligence: People Skills for Global Business* (San Francisco, CA: Berrett-Koehler, 2004), Ch. 6; D. Welch, L. Welch, and R. Piekkari, "Speaking in Tongues," *International Studies of Management & Organization* 35, no. 1 (Spring 2005), pp. 10–27.

59. D. Woodruff, "Crossing Culture Divide Early Clears Merger Paths," *Asian Wall Street Journal,* May 28, 2001, p. 9; "Differentstrokes," *Personnel Today,* November 25, 2008, p. 190.

60. S. Ohtaki, T. Ohtaki, and M.D. Fetters, "Doctor-Patient Communication: A Comparison of the USA and Japan," *Family Practice* 20 (June 2003), pp. 276–82; M. Fujio, "Silence during Intercultural Communication: A Case Study," *Corporate Communications* 9, no. 4 (2004), pp. 331–39.

61. T. Hasegawa and W.B. Gudykunst, "Silence in Japan and the United States," *Journal of Cross-Cultural Psychology* 29, no. 5 (September 1998), pp. 668–84.

62. D.C. Barnlund, *Communication Styles of Japanese and Americans: Images and Realities* (Belmont, CA: Wadsworth, 1988); H. Yamada, *American and Japanese Business Discourse: A Comparison of Interaction Styles* (Norwood, NJ: Ablex, 1992), Ch. 2.

63. P. Harris and R. Moran, *Managing Cultural Differences* (Houston, TX: Gulf, 1987); H. Blagg, "A Just Measure of Shame?" *British Journal of Criminology* 37 (Autumn 1997), pp. 481–501; R.E. Axtell, *Gestures: The Do's and Taboos of Body Language around the World,* revised ed. (New York: John Wiley & Sons, 1998).

64. D. Tannen, *You Just Don't Understand: Men and Women in Conversation* (New York: Ballentine Books, 1990); D. Tannen, *Talking from 9 to 5* (New York: Avon, 1994); M. Crawford, *Talking Difference: On Gender and Language* (Thousand Oaks, CA: Sage Publications, 1995), pp. 41–44; L.L. Namy, L.C. Nygaard, and D. Sauerteig, "Gender Differences in Vocal Accommodation: The Role of Perception," *Journal of Language and Social Psychology* 21, no. 4 (December 2002), pp. 422–32; H. Itakura and A.B.M. Tsui, "Gender and Conversational Dominance in Japanese Conversation," *Language in Society* 33, no. 2 (2004), pp. 223–48.

65. A. Mulac et al., "Uh-Huh. What's That All About? Differing Interpretations of Conversational Backchannels and Questions as Sources of Miscommunication across Gender Boundaries," *Communication Research* 25 (December 1998), pp. 641–68; N.M. Sussman and D.H. Tyson, "Sex and Power: Gender Differences in Computer-Mediated Interactions," *Computers in Human Behavior* 16 (2000), pp. 381–94; D.R. Caruso and P. Salovey, *The Emotionally Intelligent Manager* (San Francisco, CA: Jossey-Bass, 2004), p. 23; D. Fallows, *How Women and Men Use the Internet* (Washington, DC: Pew Internet and American Life Project, 2005).

66. Amernic et al., "The Transformational Leader as Pedagogue, Physician, Architect, Commander, and Saint."

67. This quotation is varied slightly from the original translations by E. Carter, *All the Works of Epictetus, Which Are Now Extant,* 3rd ed., 2 vols., Vol. 2 (London: J. and F. Rivington, 1768), p. 333; T.W. Higginson, *The Works of Epictetus* (Boston: Little, Brown, and Company, 1866), p. 428.

68. The three components of listening discussed here are based on several recent studies in the field of marketing, including S.B. Castleberry, C.D. Shepherd, and R. Ridnour, "Effective Interpersonal Listening in the Personal Selling Environment: Conceptualization, Measurement, and Nomological Validity," *Journal of Marketing Theory and Practice* 7 (Winter 1999), pp. 30–38; L.B. Comer and T. Drollinger, "Active Empathetic Listening and Selling Success: A Conceptual Framework," *Journal of Personal Selling & Sales Management* 19 (Winter 1999), pp. 15–29; K. de Ruyter and M.G.M. Wetzels, "The Impact of Perceived Listening Behavior in Voice-to-Voice Service Encounters," *Journal of Service Research* 2 (February 2000), pp. 276–84.

69. A. Hoak, "Say Goodbye to the Office Cubicle," *MarketWatch,* June 2, 2011.

70. A. Leaman and B. Bordass, "Productivity in Buildings: The Killer Variables," *Building Research & Information* 27, no. 1 (1999), pp. 4–19; T.J. Allen, "Architecture and Communication among Product Development Engineers," *California Management Review* 49, no. 2 (Winter 2007), pp. 23–41; F. Becker, "Organizational Ecology and Knowledge Networks," *California Management Review* 49, no. 2 (Winter 2007), pp. 42–61.

71. "The Shrinking Cubicle," *Chicago Tribune,* February 9, 2011; K. Shevory, "Office Work Space Is Shrinking, but That's Not All Bad," *The New York Times,* January 19, 2011, p. 8.

72. G. Evans and D. Johnson, "Stress and Open-Office Noise," *Journal of Applied Psychology* 85 (2000), pp. 779–83; F. Russo, "My Kingdom for a Door," *Time Magazine,* October 23, 2000, p. B1.

73. D. Bracken, "Open Office Plans Make 'Mine' a Thing of the Past," *News & Observer (Raleigh, NC),* March 13, 2011.

74. D. Waisberg, "Quiet Please! . . . We're Working," *National Post,* May 30, 2007.

75. S.P. Means, "Playing at Pixar," *Salt Lake Tribune (Utah),* May 30, 2003, p. D1; G. Whipp, "Swimming against the Tide," *Daily News of Los Angeles,* May 30, 2003, p. U6.

76. C. Wagner and A. Majchrzak, "Enabling Customer-Centricity Using Wikis and the Wiki Way," *Journal of Management Information Systems* 23, no. 3 (2006), pp. 17–43; R.B. Ferguson, "Build a Web 2.0 Platform and Employees Will Use It," *eWeek,* June 20, 2007; C. Karena, "Working the Wiki Way," *Sydney Morning Herald,* March 6, 2007.

77. T. Fenton, "Inside the Worldblu List: 1-800-Got-Junk?'s CEO on Why 'Being Democratic Is Extremely Important to Maintaining Our Competitive Advantage,'" Worldblu, January 3, 2008. The original term, "management by *wandering* around," has been replaced with "walking around" over the years. See W. Ouchi, *Theory Z* (New York: Avon Books, 1981), pp. 176–77; T. Peters and R. Waterman, *In Search of Excellence* (New York: Harper and Row, 1982), p. 122.

78. R. LaHood, "DOT Employees Give Department a Thumbs-Up," *Welcome to the Fastlane: The Official Blog of the U.S. Secretary of*

Transportation, July 12, 2010, http://fastlane.dot.gov/2010/07/dot-employees-give-department-a-thumbsup.html.

79. R. Rousos, "Trust in Leaders Lacking at Utility," *The Ledger (Lakeland, FL),* July 29, 2003, p. B1; B. Whitworth and B. Riccomini, "Management Communication: Unlocking Higher Employee Performance," *Communication World,* March-April 2005, pp. 18–21.

80. K. Davis, "Management Communication and the Grapevine," *Harvard Business Review* 31 (September-October 1953), pp. 43–49; W.L. Davis and J.R. O'Connor, "Serial Transmission of Information: A Study of the Grapevine," *Journal of Applied Communication Research* 5 (1977), pp. 61–72.

81. A. De Bruyn and G.L. Lilien, "A Multi-Stage Model of Word-of-Mouth Influence through Viral Marketing," *International Journal of Research in Marketing* 25, no. 3 (2008), pp. 151–63; J.Y.C. Ho and M. Dempsey, "Viral Marketing: Motivations to Forward Online Content," *Journal of Business Research* 63, no. 9-10 (2010), pp. 1000–06; M. Williams and F. Buttle, "The Eight Pillars of WOM Management: Lessons from a Multiple Case Study," *Australasian Marketing Journal* 19, no. 2 (2011), pp. 85–92.

82. K. Dyer, "Changing Perceptions Virally at Novo Nordisk," *Strategic Communication Management* 13, no. 2 (2009), pp. 24–27.

83. H. Mintzberg, *The Structuring of Organizations* (Englewood Cliffs, NJ: Prentice Hall, 1979), pp. 46–53; D. Krackhardt and J.R. Hanson, "Informal Networks: The Company behind the Chart," *Harvard Business Review* 71 (July-August 1993), pp. 104–11.

84. C.J. Walker and C.A. Beckerle, "The Effect of State Anxiety on Rumor Transmission," *Journal of Social Behaviour & Personality* 2 (August 1987), pp. 353–60; R.L. Rosnow, "Inside Rumor: A Personal Journey," *American Psychologist* 46 (May 1991), pp. 484–96; M. Noon and R. Delbridge, "News from Behind My Hand: Gossip in Organizations," *Organization Studies* 14 (1993), pp. 23–36.

85. N. Nicholson, "Evolutionary Psychology: Toward a New View of Human Nature and Organizational Society," *Human Relations* 50 (September 1997), pp. 1053–78; R.F. Baumeister, L. Zhang, and K.D. Vohs, "Gossip as Cultural Learning," *Review of General Psychology* 8, no. 2 (2004), pp. 111–21; E.K. Foster, "Research on Gossip: Taxonomy, Methods, and Future Directions," *Review of General Psychology* 8, no. 2 (2004), pp. 78–99.

CHAPTER 10

1. C. Chynoweth, "Subtle Art of Managing the Boss," *Sunday Times (London),* May 17, 2009, p. 1; J. Shetcliffe, "Questions Brokers Ask—How to Manage the Boss," *Insurance Brokers Monthly & Insurance Advisor,* February 4, 2009, p. 32; J. Espinoza, "Culture Change Is the Final Frontier," *The Wall Street Journal,* February 23, 2010; R.C. Matuson, *Suddenly in Charge: Managing Up, Managing Down, Succeeding All Around* (Boston: Nicholas Brealey, 2011).

2. J.R.P. French and B. Raven, "The Bases of Social Power," in *Studies in Social Power,* ed. D. Cartwright (Ann Arbor, MI: University of Michigan Press, 1959), pp. 150–67; A.D. Galinsky et al., "Power and Perspectives Not Taken," *Psychological Science* 17, no. 12 (2006), pp. 1068–74. Also see H. Mintzberg, *Power in and around Organizations* (Englewood Cliffs, NJ: Prentice Hall, 1983), Ch. 1; J. Pfeffer, *Managing with Power* (Boston: Harvard Business University Press, 1992), pp. 17, 30; A. Guinote and T.K. Vescio, "Introduction: Power in Social Psychology," in *The Social Psychology of Power,* ed. A. Guinote and T.K. Vescio (New York: Guilford Press, 2010), pp. 1–18.

3. R.A. Dahl, "The Concept of Power," *Behavioral Science* 2 (1957), pp. 201–18; R.M. Emerson, "Power-Dependence Relations," *American Sociological Review* 27 (1962), pp. 31–41; A.M. Pettigrew, *The Politics of Organizational Decision-Making* (London: Tavistock, 1973).

4. G.A. Van Kleef et al., "Breaking the Rules to Rise to Power: How Norm Violators Gain Power in the Eyes of Others," *Social Psychological and Personality Science* (2011), in press.

5. J. Pfeffer and G.R. Salancik, *The External Control of Organizations* (New York: Harper & Row, 1978), pp. 52–54; R. Gulati and M. Sytch, "Dependence Asymmetry and Joint Dependence in Interorganizational Relationships: Effects of Embeddedness on a Manufacturer's Performance in Procurement Relationships," *Administrative Science Quarterly* 52, no. 1 (2007), pp. 32–69.

6. French and Raven, "The Bases of Social Power"; P. Podsakoff and C. Schreisheim, "Field Studies of French and Raven's Bases of Power: Critique, Analysis, and Suggestions for Future Research," *Psychological Bulletin* 97 (1985), pp. 387–411; P.P. Carson and K.D. Carson, "Social Power Bases: A Meta-Analytic Examination of Interrelationships and Outcomes," *Journal of Applied Social Psychology* 23 (1993), pp. 1150–69. The alternative models of power bases are reviewed in a recent dissertation by Heinemann, who points out that most of them parallel French and Raven's list. See P. Heinemann, *Power Bases and Informational Influence Strategies: A Behavioral Study on the Use of Management Accounting Information* (Wiesbaden, Germany: Deutscher Universitäts-Verlag, 2008). Raven subsequently proposed information power as a sixth source of power. We present this concept as a derivation of the five sources of power rather than as a distinct sixth power base.

7. C. Barnard, *The Function of the Executive* (Cambridge, MA: Harvard University Press, 1938), pp. 167–70; C. Hardy and S.R. Clegg, "Some Dare Call It Power," in *Handbook of Organization Studies,* ed. S.R. Clegg, C. Hardy, and W. R. Nord (London: Sage, 1996), pp. 622–41.

8. A.I. Shahin and P.L. Wright, "Leadership in the Context of Culture: An Egyptian Perspective," *Leadership & Organization Development Journal* 25, no. 5/6 (2004), pp. 499–511; Y.J. Huo et al., "Leadership and the Management of Conflicts in Diverse Groups: Why Acknowledging versus Neglecting Subgroup Identity Matters," *European Journal of Social Psychology* 35, no. 2 (2005), pp. 237–54.

9. B.H. Raven, "Kurt Lewin Address: Influence, Power, Religion, and the Mechanisms of Social Control," *Journal of Social Issues* 55 (Spring 1999), pp. 161–86.

10. A.W. Gouldner, "The Norm of Reciprocity: A Preliminary Statement," *American Sociological Review* 25 (1960), pp. 161–78.

11. B. Crumley, "Game of Death: France's Shocking TV Experiment," *Time,* March 17, 2010; R.L. Parry, "Contestants Turn Torturers in French TV Experiment," *Yahoo! News,* March 16, 2010.

12. G. Yukl and C.M. Falbe, "Importance of Different Power Sources in Downward and Lateral Relations," *Journal of Applied Psychology* 76 (1991), pp. 416–23; Raven, "Kurt Lewin Address."

13. P.L. Dawes, D.Y. Lee, and G.R. Dowling, "Information Control and Influence in Emergent Buying Centers," *Journal of Marketing* 62, no. 3 (July 1998), pp. 55–68; D. Willer, "Power-at-a-Distance," *Social Forces* 81, no. 4 (2003), pp. 1295–334; D.J. Brass et al., "Taking Stock of Networks and Organizations: A Multilevel Perspective," *Academy of Management Journal* 47, no. 6 (December 2004), pp. 795–817.

14. L.S. Sya, "Flying to Greater Heights," *New Sunday Times (Kuala Lumpur),* July 31, 2005, p. 14; M. Bolch, "Rewarding the Team," *HRMagazine,* February 2007, pp. 91–93.

15. J.M. Peiro and J.L. Melia, "Formal and Informal Interpersonal Power in Organisations: Testing a Bifactorial Model of Power in Role-Sets," *Applied Psychology* 52, no. 1 (2003), pp. 14–35.

16. C.R. Hinings et al., "Structural Conditions of Intraorganizational Power," *Administrative Science Quarterly* 19 (1974), pp. 22–44. Also see C.S. Saunders, "The Strategic Contingency Theory of Power: Multiple Perspectives," *Journal of Management Studies* 27 (1990), pp. 1–21.

17. "The Judges," *Advertising Age's Creativity,* May 2008, p. 100; "Havas Worldwide Takes Majority Stake in Social Technology Startup," news release, January 25, 2011.

18. R.B. Cialdini and N.J. Goldstein, "Social Influence: Compliance and Conformity," *Annual Review of Psychology* 55 (2004), pp. 591–621.

19. C.K. Hofling et al., "An Experimental Study in Nurse-Physician Relationships," *Journal of Nervous and Mental Disease* 143, no. 2 (1966), pp. 171–77.

20. C. Perkel, "It's Not CSI," *Canadian Press,* November 10, 2007; "Dr. Charles Smith: The Man behind the Public Inquiry," *CBC News (Toronto),* August 10, 2010. Evidence-based management writers also warn against blindly following the advice of management gurus. See J. Pfeffer and R.I. Sutton, *Hard Facts, Dangerous Half-Truths, and Total Nonsense* (Boston: Harvard Business School Press, 2006), pp. 45–46.

21. K. Miyahara, "Charisma: From Weber to Contemporary Sociology," *Sociological Inquiry* 53, no. 4 (Fall 1983), pp. 368–88; J.D. Kudisch and M.L. Poteet, "Expert Power, Referent Power, and Charisma: Toward the Resolution of a Theoretical Debate," *Journal of Business & Psychology* 10 (Winter 1995), pp. 177–95; D. Ladkin, "The Enchantment of the Charismatic Leader: Charisma Reconsidered as Aesthetic Encounter," *Leadership* 2, no. 2 (May 2006), pp. 165–79.

22. D. J. Hickson et al., "A Strategic Contingencies Theory of Intraorganizational Power," *Administrative Science Quarterly* 16 (1971), pp. 216–27; Hinings et al., "Structural Conditions of Intraorganizational Power" ; R.M. Kanter, "Power Failure in Management Circuits," *Harvard Business Review* (July-August 1979), pp. 65–75.

23. A. Bryant, "The Right Job? It's Much Like the Right Spouse," *The New York Times,* May 22, 2011, p. 2. The "DNA" acronym is from M.D. Johnson, *Brand Me. Make Your Mark: Turn Passion into Profit* (Blacklick, OH: Ambassador Press, 2008).

24. Hickson et al., "A Strategic Contingencies Theory of Intraorganizational Power"; J.D. Hackman, "Power and Centrality in the Allocation of Resources in Colleges and Universities," *Administrative Science Quarterly* 30 (1985), pp. 61–77; D.J. Brass and M.E. Burkhardt, "Potential Power and Power Use: An Investigation of Structure and Behavior," *Academy of Management Journal* 36 (1993), pp. 441–70.

25. S.D. Harrington and B. Ivry, "For Commuters, a Day to Adapt," *The Record (Bergen, NJ),* December 21, 2005, p. A1; S. McCarthy, "Transit Strike Cripples New York," *Globe & Mail (Toronto),* December 21, 2005, p. A17.

26. M. Kennett, "Remote Control," *Management Today,* March 1, 2011, p. 46.

27. A. Chatterjee and D.C. Hambrick, "It's All about Me: Narcissistic Chief Executive Officers and Their Effects on Company Strategy and Performance," *Administrative Science Quarterly* 52, no. 3 (2007), pp. 351–86.

28. M.E. Porter, J.W. Lorsch, and N. Nohria, "Seven Surprises for New CEOs," *Harvard Business Review* 82, no. 10 (October 2004), pp. 62–72.

29. G. Owen and T. Kirchmaier, "The Changing Role of the Chairman: Impact of Corporate Governance Reform in the United Kingdom 1995–2005," *European Business Organization Law Review* 9, no. 2 (2008), pp. 187–213; M.A. Bliss, "Does CEO Duality Constrain Board Independence? Some Evidence from Audit Pricing," *Accounting & Finance* 51, no. 2 (2011), pp. 361–80.

30. J.G. Combs et al., "The Moderating Effect of CEO Power on the Board Composition–Firm Performance Relationship*," *Journal of Management Studies* 44, no. 8 (2007), pp. 1299–323.

31. C. Crossland and D.C. Hambrick, "Differences in Managerial Discretion across Countries: How Nation-Level Institutions Affect the Degree to Which CEOs Matter," *Strategic Management Journal* 32, no. 8 (2011), pp. 797–819.

32. D. Pressey, "Urbana, Ill.-Area Hospitals Chief Extends Personal Touch," *News-Gazette (Champaign-Urbana, IL),* April 18, 2011.

33. R. Madell, "Ground Floor," *Pharmaceutical Executive (Women in Pharma Supplement),* June 2000, pp. 24–31.

34. Kanter, "Power Failure in Management Circuits"; B.E. Ashforth, "The Experience of Powerlessness in Organizations," *Organizational Behavior and Human Decision Processes* 43 (1989), pp. 207–42; L. Holden, "European Managers: HRM and an Evolving Role," *European Business Review* 12 (2000).

35. D.C. Hambrick and E. Abrahamson, "Assessing Managerial Discretion across Industries: A Multimethod Approach," *Academy of Management Journal* 38, no. 5 (1995), pp. 1427–41; M.A. Carpenter and B.R. Golden, "Perceived Managerial Discretion: A Study of Cause and Effect," *Strategic Management Journal* 18, no. 3 (1997), pp. 187–206.

36. S. Wasserman and K. Faust, *Social Network Analysis: Methods and Applications, Structural Analysis in the Social Sciences* (Cambridge, UK: Cambridge University Press, 1994), Ch. 1; Brass et al., "Taking Stock of Networks and Organizations."

37. M. Grossetti, "Where Do Social Relations Come From?: A Study of Personal Networks in the Toulouse Area of France," *Social Networks* 27, no. 4 (2005), pp. 289–300.

38. Y. Fan, "Questioning Guanxi: Definition, Classification, and Implications," *International Business Review* 11 (2002), pp. 543–61; W.R. Vanhonacker, "When Good Guanxi Turns Bad," *Harvard Business Review* 82, no. 4 (April 2004), pp. 18–19; R.J. Taormina and J.H. Gao, "A Research Model for Guanxi Behavior: Antecedents, Measures, and Outcomes of Chinese Social Networking," *Social Science Research* 39, no. 6 (November 2010), pp. 1195–212.

39. D. Krackhardt and J.R. Hanson, "Informal Networks: The Company behind the Chart," *Harvard Business Review* 71 (July-August 1993), pp. 104–11; A. Portes, "Social Capital: Its Origins and Applications in Modern Society," *Annual Review of Sociology* 24 (1998), pp. 1–24.

40. P.S. Adler and S.-W. Kwon, "Social Capital: Prospects for a New Concept," *Academy of Management Review* 27, no. 1 (2002), pp. 17–40.

41. R.F. Chisholm, *Developing Network Organizations: Learning from Practice and Theory* (Reading, MA: Addison Wesley Longman, 1998); W.S. Chow and L.S. Chan, "Social Network, Social Trust and Shared Goals in Organizational Knowledge Sharing," *Information & Management* 45, no. 7 (2008), pp. 458–65.

42. R.S. Burt, *Structural Holes: The Social Structure of Competition* (Cambridge, MA: Harvard University Press, 1992).

43. D. Bushey and M. Joll, "Social Network Analysis Comes to Raytheon," *The Monitor (Raytheon news magazine),* 2006; J. McGregor, "The Office Chart That Really Counts," *BusinessWeek,* February 27, 2006, p. 48; J. Reingold, "What's Your OQ?" *Fortune,* July 23, 2007, pp. 98–106; T. Cox, "Map Quest," *Quality Progress,* May 2008, p. 44.

44. M.T. Rivera, S.B. Soderstrom, and B.I. Uzzi, "Dynamics of Dyads in Social Networks: Assortative, Relational, and Proximity Mechanisms," *Annual Review of Sociology* 36 (2010), pp. 91–115.

45. R. Cross and R.J. Thomas, *Driving Results through Social Networks: How Top Organizations Leverage Networks for Performance and Growth* (San Francisco, CA: Jossey-Bass, 2009); R. McDermott and D. Archibald, "Harnessing Your Staff's Informal Networks," *Harvard Business Review* 88, no. 3 (2010), pp. 82–89.

46. M. Kilduff and D. Krackhardt, *Interpersonal Networks in Organizations: Cognition, Personality, Dynamics, and Culture* (New York: Cambridge University Press, 2008).

47. N.B. Ellison, C. Steinfield, and C. Lampe, "The Benefits of Facebook 'Friends': Social Capital and College Students' Use of Online Social Network Sites," *Journal of Computer-Mediated Communication* 12, no. 4 (2007), pp. 1143–68.

48. M.S. Granovetter, "The Strength of Weak Ties," *American Journal of Sociology* 78 (1973), pp. 1360–80; B. Erickson, "Social Networks," in *The Blackwell Companion to Sociology,* ed. J.R. Blau (Malden, MA: Blackwell Publishing, 2004), pp. 314–26.

49. B. Uzzi and S. Dunlap, "How to Build Your Network," *Harvard Business Review* 83, no. 12 (2005), pp. 53–60.

50. S.C. de Janasz and M.L. Forret, "Learning the Art of Networking: A Critical Skill for Enhancing Social Capital and Career Success," *Journal of Management Education* 32, no. 5 (October 1, 2008), pp. 629–50.

51. A. Mehra, M. Kilduff, and D.J. Brass, "The Social Networks of High and Low Self-Monitors: Implications for Workplace Performance," *Administrative Science Quarterly* 46 (March 2001), pp. 121–46.

52. Burt, *Structural Holes.*

53. B.R. Ragins and E. Sundstrom, "Gender and Power in Organizations: A Longitudinal Perspective," *Psychological Bulletin* 105 (1989), pp. 51–88; M. Linehan, "Barriers to Women's Participation in International Management," *European Business Review* 13 (2001).

54. A. DeFelice, "Climbing to the Top," *Accounting Technology* 24, no. 1 (2008), pp. 12–18.

55. D.M. McCracken, "Winning the Talent War for Women: Sometimes It Takes a Revolution," *Harvard Business Review* (November-December 2000), pp. 159–67.

56. J. Lammers, J.I. Stoker, and D.A. Stapel, "Differentiating Social and Personal Power: Opposite Effects on Stereotyping, but Parallel Effects on Behavioral Approach Tendencies," *Psychological Science* 20, no. 12 (2009), pp. 1543–49.

57. D. Keltner, D.H. Gruenfeld, and C. Anderson, "Power, Approach, and Inhibition," *Psychological Review* 110, no. 2 (2003), pp. 265–84; B. Simpson and C. Borch, "Does Power Affect Perception in Social Networks? Two Arguments and an Experimental Test," *Social Psychology Quarterly* 68, no. 3 (2005), pp. 278–87; Galinsky et al., "Power and Perspectives Not Taken."

58. K. Atuahene-Gima and H. Li, "Marketing's Influence Tactics in New Product Development: A Study of High Technology Firms in China," *Journal of Product Innovation Management* 17 (2000), pp. 451–70; A. Somech and A. Drach-Zahavy, "Relative Power and Influence Strategy: The Effects of Agent/Target Organizational Power on Superiors' Choices of Influence Strategies," *Journal of Organizational Behavior* 23 (2002), pp. 167–79.

59. D. Kipnis, S.M. Schmidt, and I. Wilkinson, "Intraorganizational Influence Tactics: Explorations in Getting One's Way," *Journal of Applied Psychology* 65 (1980), pp. 440–52; A. Rao and K. Hashimoto, "Universal and Culturally Specific Aspects of Managerial Influence: A Study of Japanese Managers," *Leadership Quarterly* 8 (1997), pp. 295–312; L.A. McFarland, A.M. Ryan, and S.D. Kriska, "Field Study Investigation of Applicant Use of Influence Tactics in a Selection Interview," *Journal of Psychology* 136 (July 2002), pp. 383–398.

60. J. Crichton, *Between Sandra Mccullough and Otago Sheetmetal and Engineering Limited,* CA 153/08 (Dunedin, NZ: Employment Relations Authority Christchurch, October 14, 2008); "One-in-Four Workers Have Felt Bullied in the Workplace, Careerbuilder Study Finds," news release, CareerBuilder, April 20, 2011.

61. Cialdini and Goldstein, "Social Influence: Compliance and Conformity."

62. Rao and Hashimoto, "Universal and Culturally Specific Aspects of Managerial Influence." Silent authority as an influence tactic in non-Western cultures is also discussed in S.F. Pasa, "Leadership Influence in a High Power Distance and Collectivist Culture," *Leadership & Organization Development Journal* 21 (2000), pp. 414–26.

63. "Be Part of the Team If You Want to Catch the Eye," *Birmingham Post (UK),* August 31, 2000, p. 14; S. Maitlis, "Taking It from the Top: How CEOs Influence (and Fail to Influence) Their Boards," *Organization Studies* 25, no. 8 (2004), pp. 1275–311.

64. A.T. Cobb, "Toward the Study of Organizational Coalitions: Participant Concerns and Activities in a Simulated Organizational Setting," *Human Relations* 44 (1991), pp. 1057–79; E.A. Mannix, "Organizations as Resource Dilemmas: The Effects of Power Balance on Coalition Formation in Small Groups," *Organizational Behavior and Human Decision Processes* 55 (1993), pp. 1–22; D.J. Terry, M.A. Hogg, and K.M. White, "The Theory of Planned Behavior: Self-Identity, Social Identity and Group Norms," *British Journal of Social Psychology* 38 (September 1999), pp. 225–44.

65. A.P. Brief, *Attitudes in and around Organizations* (Thousand Oaks, CA: Sage Publications, 1998), pp. 69–84; D.J. O'Keefe, *Persuasion: Theory and Research* (Thousand Oaks, CA: Sage Publications, 2002).

66. These and other features of message content in persuasion are detailed by R. Petty and J. Cacioppo, *Attitudes and Persuasion: Classic and Contemporary Approaches* (Dubuque, IA: W.C. Brown, 1981); M. Pfau, E.A. Szabo, and J. Anderson, "The Role and Impact of Affect in the Process of Resistance to Persuasion," *Human Communication Research* 27 (April 2001), pp. 216–52; O'Keefe, *Persuasion,* Ch. 9; R. Buck et al., "Emotion and Reason in Persuasion: Applying the ARI Model and the CASC Scale," *Journal of Business Research* 57, no. 6 (2004), pp. 647–56; W.D. Crano and R. Prislin, "Attitudes and Persuasion," *Annual Review of Psychology* 57 (2006), pp. 345–74.

67. N. Rhodes and W. Wood, "Self-Esteem and Intelligence Affect Influenceability: The Mediating Role of Message Reception," *Psychological Bulletin* 111, no. 1 (1992), pp. 156–71.

68. D. Strutton and L.E. Pelton, "Effects of Ingratiation on Lateral Relationship Quality within Sales Team Settings," *Journal of Business Research* 43 (1998), pp. 1–12; R. Vonk, "Self-Serving Interpretations of Flattery: Why Ingratiation Works," *Journal of Personality and Social Psychology* 82 (2002), pp. 515–26.

69. C.A. Higgins, T.A. Judge, and G.R. Ferris, "Influence Tactics and Work Outcomes: A Meta-Analysis," *Journal of Organizational Behavior* 24 (2003), pp. 90–106.

70. D. Strutton, L.E. Pelton, and J.F. Tanner, "Shall We Gather in the Garden: The Effect of Ingratiatory Behaviors on Buyer Trust in Salespeople," *Industrial Marketing Management* 25 (1996), pp. 151–62; J. O' Neil, "An Investigation of the Sources of Influence of Corporate Public Relations Practitioners," *Public Relations Review* 29 (June 2003), pp. 159–69.

71. M.C. Bolino and W.H. Tunley, "More Than One Way to Make an Impression: Exploring Profiles of Impression Management," *Journal of Management* 29 (2003), pp. 141–60.

72. T. Peters, "The Brand Called You," *Fast Company,* August 1997, http://www.fastcompany.com/magazine/10/brandyou.html; J. Sills, "Becoming Your Own Brand," *Psychology Today* 41, no. 1 (February 2008), pp. 62–63.

73. J.S. Wilson, "Personal Branding in Today's Economy," *Atlanta Journal-Constitution,* May 29, 2011, p. D1.

74. S.L. McShane, "Applicant Misrepresentations in Résumés and Interviews in Canada," *Labor Law Journal,* January 1994, pp. 15–24; S. Romero and M. Richtel, "Second Chance," *The New York Times,* March 5, 2001, p. C1; P. Sabatini, "Fibs on Résumés Commonplace," *Pittsburgh Post-Gazette,* February 24, 2006.

75. J. Laucius, "Internet Guru's Credentials a True Work of Fiction," *Ottawa Citizen,* June 12, 2001.

76. C.M. Falbe and G. Yukl, "Consequences for Managers of Using Single Influence Tactics and Combinations of Tactics," *Academy of Management Journal* 35 (1992), pp. 638–52.

77. R.C. Ringer and R.W. Boss, "Hospital Professionals' Use of Upward Influence Tactics," *Journal of Managerial Issues* 12 (2000), pp. 92–108.

78. G. Blickle, "Do Work Values Predict the Use of Intraorganizational Influence Strategies?" *Journal of Applied Social Psychology* 30, no. 1 (January 2000), pp. 196–205; P.P. Fu et al., "The Impact of Societal Cultural Values and Individual Social Beliefs on the Perceived Effectiveness of Managerial Influence Strategies: A Meso Approach," *Journal of International Business Studies* 35, no. 4 (July 2004), pp. 284–305.

79. "The 2008 Wasting Time at Work Survey Reveals a Record Number of People Waste Time at Work," Salary.com, 2008; "When It Comes to Red Tape, Many Canadian Employers Might Just Need to Cut It: RBC Study," news release, January 23, 2008; "Survey: More than One-Quarter of Employees Have Had Ideas Stolen at Work," news release for OfficeTeam, October 8, 2009; "Survey: Majority of Employees Have Had Ideas Stolen at Work," news release for OfficeTeam, November 10, 2009; J. Gifford et al., *The Management Agenda 2009* (Horsham, UK: Roffey Park Institute, 2009).

80. This has become the dominant definition of organizational politics over the past 15 years. See G.R. Ferris and K.M. Kacmar, "Perceptions of Organizational Politics," *Journal of Management* 18 (1992), pp. 93–116; R. Cropanzano et al., "The Relationship of Organizational Politics and Support to Work Behaviors, Attitudes, and Stress," *Journal of Organizational Behavior* 18 (1997), pp. 159–80; E. Vigoda, "Stress-Related Aftermaths to Workplace Politics: The Relationships among Politics, Job Distress, and Aggressive Behavior in Organizations," *Journal of Organizational Behavior* 23 (2002), pp. 571–91. However, organizational politics was previously viewed as influence tactics outside the formal role that could be either selfish or altruistic. This older definition is less common today, possibly because it is incongruent with popular views of politics and because it overlaps too much with the concept of influence. For the older perspective of organizational politics, see J. Pfeffer, *Power in Organizations* (Boston, MA: Pitman, 1981); Mintzberg, *Power in and around Organizations.*

81. K.M. Kacmar and R.A. Baron, "Organizational Politics: The State of the Field, Links to Related Processes, and an Agenda for Future Research," in *Research in Personnel and Human Resources Management,* ed. G.R. Ferris (Greenwich, CT: JAI Press, 1999), pp. 1–39; Vigoda, "Stress-Related Aftermaths to Workplace Politics"; C.-H. Chang, C.C. Rosen, and P.E. Levy, "The Relationship between Perceptions of Organizational Politics and Employee Attitudes, Strain, and Behavior: A Meta-Analytic Examination," *Academy of Management Journal* 52, no. 4 (2009), pp. 779–801.

82. "Dark Theory of Alycia E-Mail," *New York Post,* June 5, 2008, p. 12; M. Klein, "Lane Suit Details Mendte Gossip," *Philadelphia Inquirer,* September 24, 2008, p. B01; M. Klein, "Alycia Lane Sues CBS3," *Philadelphia Inquirer,* June 20, 2008, p. B01; M. Klein, "Mendte Could Push Either Way," *Philadelphia Inquirer,* July 13, 2008, p. A01; P. Walters, "Fired Philly TV Anchor Charged in E-Mail Scandal," *Associated Press Newswires,* July 22, 2008.

83. C. Hardy, *Strategies for Retrenchment and Turnaround: The Politics of Survival* (Berlin: Walter de Gruyter, 1990), Ch. 14; M.C. Andrews and K.M. Kacmar, "Discriminating among Organizational Politics, Justice, and Support," *Journal of Organizational Behavior* 22 (2001), pp. 347–66.

84. S. Blazejewski and W. Dorow, "Managing Organizational Politics for Radical Change: The Case of Beiersdorf-Lechia S.A., Poznan," *Journal of World Business* 38 (August 2003), pp. 204–23.

85. L.W. Porter, R.W. Allen, and H.L. Angle, "The Politics of Upward Influence in Organizations," *Research in Organizational Behavior* 3 (1981), pp. 120–22; R.J. House, "Power and Personality in Complex Organizations," *Research in Organizational Behavior* 10 (1988), pp. 305–57.

86. R. Christie and F. Geis, *Studies in Machiavellianism* (New York: Academic Press, 1970); S.M. Farmer et al., "Putting Upward Influence Strategies in Context," *Journal of Organizational Behavior* 18 (1997), pp. 17–42; K.S. Sauleya and A.G. Bedeian, "Equity Sensitivity: Construction of a Measure and Examination of Its Psychometric Properties," *Journal of Management* 26 (September 2000), pp. 885–910.

87. G. R. Ferris et al., "Perceptions of Organizational Politics: Prediction, Stress-Related Implications, and Outcomes," *Human Relations* 49 (1996), pp. 233–63.

CHAPTER 11

1. D. Nebenzahl, "Managing the Generation Gap," *Montreal Gazette,* February 28, 2009, p. G1; D. Deveau, "L'oréal Canada Discovers the Beauty of Motivation," *Postmedia News (Toronto),* January 24, 2011.

2. D. Tjosvold, *Working Together to Get Things Done* (Lexington, MA: Lexington, 1986), pp. 114–15; J.A. Wall and R.R. Callister, "Conflict and Its Management," *Journal of Management* 21 (1995), pp. 515–58; D. Tjosvold, "Defining Conflict and Making Choices about Its Management," *International Journal of Conflict Management* 17, no. 2 (2006), pp. 87–95; M.A. Rahim, *Managing Conflict in Organizations,* 4th ed. (New Brunswick, NJ: Transaction Publishers, 2011), pp. 15–17.

3. For example, see L. Urwick, *The Elements of Administration,* 2nd ed. (London: Pitman, 1947); C. Argyris, "The Individual and Organization: Some Problems of Mutual Adjustment," *Administrative Science Quarterly* 2, no. 1 (1957), pp. 1–24; K.E. Boulding, "Organization and Conflict," *Conflict Resolution* 1, no. 2 (June 1957), pp. 122–34; R.R. Blake, H.A. Shepard, and J.S. Mouton, *Managing Intergroup Conflict in Industry* (Houston, TX: Gulf Publishing, 1964).

4. Rahim, *Managing Conflict in Organizations* .

5. C.K.W. De Dreu and L.R. Weingart, "A Contingency Theory of Task Conflict and Performance in Groups and Organizational Teams," in *International Handbook of Organizational Teamwork and Cooperative Working,* ed. M.A. West, D. Tjosvold, and K.G. Smith (Chichester, UK: John Wiley & Sons, 2003), pp. 151–66; K.A. Jehn and C. Bendersky, "Intragroup Conflict in Organizations: A Contingency Perspective on the Conflict-Outcome Relationship," *Research in Organizational Behavior* 25 (2003), pp. 187–242.

6. *Workplace Conflict and How Businesses Can Harness It to Thrive,* CPP Global Human Capital Report (Mountain View, CA: CPP, Inc., 2008).

7. Rahim, *Managing Conflict in Organizations,* pp. 6–7.

8. J. Dewey, *Human Nature and Conduct: An Introduction to Social Psychology* (New York: Holt, 1922), p. 300.

9. M.P. Follett, "Constructive Conflict," in *Dynamic Administration: The Collected Papers of Mary Parker Follett,* ed. H.C. Metcalf and L. Urwick (Bath, UK: Management Publications Trust, 1941), pp. 30–49.

10. M.A. Rahim, "Toward a Theory of Managing Organizational Conflict," *International Journal of Conflict Management* 13, no. 3 (2002), pp. 206–35; M. Duarte and G. Davies, "Testing the Conflict–Performance Assumption in Business-to-Business Relationships," *Industrial Marketing Management* 32 (2003), pp. 91–99. Although the 1970s marked a point when the benefits of conflict became more widely acknowledged, this view was expressed earlier by some writers. See L.A. Coser, *The Functions of Social Conflict* (New York: The Free Press, 1956); J.A. Litterer, "Conflict in Organization: A Re-Examination," *Academy of Management Journal* 9 (1966), pp. 178–86; H. Assael, "Constructive Role of Interorganizational Conflict," *Administrative Science Quarterly* 14, no. 4 (1969), pp. 573–82.

11. P.J. Carnevale, "Creativity in the Outcomes of Conflict," in *The Handbook of Conflict Resolution: Theory and Practice,* ed. M. Deutsch, P.T. Coleman, and E.C. Marcus, 2nd ed. (San Francisco, CA: Jossey-Bass, 2006), pp. 414–35.

12. K.M. Eisenhardt, J.L. Kahwajy, and L.J. Bourgeois III, "How Management Teams Can Have a Good Fight," *Harvard Business Review* (July-August 1997), pp. 77–85; K.M. Eisenhardt, J.L. Kahwajy, and L.J. Bourgeois III, "Conflict and Strategic Choice: How Top Management Teams Disagree," *California Management Review* 39 (Winter 1997), pp. 42–62; T. Greitemeyer et al., "Information Sampling and Group Decision Making: The Effects of an Advocacy Decision Procedure and Task Experience," *Journal of Experimental Psychology: Applied* 12,

no. 1 (March 2006), pp. 31–42; U. Klocke, "How to Improve Decision Making in Small Groups: Effects of Dissent and Training Interventions," *Small Group Research* 38, no. 3 (June 2007), pp. 437–68.

13. H. Guetzkow and J. Gyr, "An Analysis of Conflict in Decision-Making Groups," *Human Relations* 7, no. 3 (August 1954), pp. 367–82; L.H. Pelled, K.M. Eisenhardt, and K.R. Xin, "Exploring the Black Box: An Analysis of Work Group Diversity, Conflict, and Performance," *Administrative Science Quarterly* 44 (March 1999), pp. 1–28; Jehn and Bendersky, "Intragroup Conflict in Organizations." The notion of two types of conflict dates back to Georg Simmel, who described conflict with a personal and subjective goal, as well as conflict with an impersonal and objective quality. See Coser, *The Functions of Social Conflict,* p. 112. Contemporary scholars use various labels for constructive and relationship conflict. We avoid the "cognitive" and "affective" conflict labels, because cognitions and emotions are interconnected processes in all human activity.

14. C.K.W. De Dreu, "When Too Little or Too Much Hurts: Evidence for a Curvilinear Relationship between Task Conflict and Innovation in Teams," *Journal of Management* 32, no. 1 (February 2006), pp. 83–107.

15. R.S. Lau and A.T. Cobb, "Understanding the Connections between Relationship Conflict and Performance: The Intervening Roles of Trust and Exchange," *Journal of Organizational Behavior* 31, no. 6 (2010), pp. 898–917.

16. C.K.W. De Dreu and L.R. Weingart, "Task versus Relationship Conflict, Team Performance, and Team Member Satisfaction: A Meta-Analysis," *Journal of Applied Psychology* 88 (August 2003), pp. 587–604; A.C. Mooney, P.J. Holahan, and A.C. Amason, "Don't Take It Personally: Exploring Cognitive Conflict as a Mediator of Affective Conflict," *Journal of Management Studies* 44, no. 5 (2007), pp. 733–58.

17. J. Yang and K.W. Mossholder, "Decoupling Task and Relationship Conflict: The Role of Intergroup Emotional Processing," *Journal of Organizational Behavior* 25 (2004), pp. 589–605.

18. A.C. Amason and H.J. Sapienza, "The Effects of Top Management Team Size and Interaction Norms on Cognitive and Affective Conflict," *Journal of Management* 23, no. 4 (1997), pp. 495–516.

19. A. Grove, "How to Make Confrontation Work for You," in *The Book of Management Wisdom,* ed. P. Krass (New York: John Wiley & Sons, 2000), pp. 83–89; B. Schlender, "Inside Andy Grove's Latest Crusade," *Fortune,* August 23, 2004, p. 68; J. Detar, "Andy Grove, Intel's Inside Man," *Investor's Business Daily,* July 24, 2007; D. Senor and S. Singer, *Start-Up Nation: The Story of Israel's Economic Miracle* (New York: Hachette Book Group, 2009); "The Real Big Chip @ Intel," *Financial Express (India),* December 13, 2010.

20. L. Pondy, "Organizational Conflict: Concepts and Models," *Administrative Science Quarterly* 2 (1967), pp. 296–320; K.W. Thomas, "Conflict and Negotiation Processes in Organizations," in *Handbook of Industrial and Organizational Psychology,* ed. M.D. Dunnette and L.M. Hough, 2nd ed. (Palo Alto, CA: Consulting Psychologists Press, 1992), pp. 651–718.

21. H. Barki and J. Hartwick, "Conceptualizing the Construct of Interpersonal Conflict," *International Journal of Conflict Management* 15, no. 3 (2004), pp. 216–44.

22. M.A. Von Glinow, D.L. Shapiro, and J.M. Brett, "Can We Talk, and Should We? Managing Emotional Conflict in Multicultural Teams," *Academy of Management Review* 29, no. 4 (2004), pp. 578–92.

23. G.E. Martin and T.J. Bergman, "The Dynamics of Behavioral Response to Conflict in the Workplace," *Journal of Occupational & Organizational Psychology* 69 (December 1996), pp. 377–87; J.M. Brett, D.L. Shapiro, and A.L. Lytle, "Breaking the Bonds of Reciprocity in Negotiations," *Academy of Management Journal* 41 (August 1998), pp. 410–24.

24. R.E. Walton and J.M. Dutton, "The Management of Conflict: A Model and Review," *Administrative Science Quarterly* 14 (1969), pp. 73–84; S.M. Schmidt and T.A. Kochan, "Conflict: Toward Conceptual Clarity," *Administrative Science Quarterly* 17, no. 3 (September 1972), pp. 359–70.

25. V. Murphy, "Microsoft's Midlife Crisis," *Forbes,* October 3, 2005, p. 88; D. Brass, "Microsoft's Creative Destruction," *The New York Times,* February 4, 2010.

26. J.A. McMullin, T. Duerden Comeau, and E. Jovic, "Generational Affinities and Discourses of Difference: A Case Study of Highly Skilled Information Technology Workers," *British Journal of Sociology* 58, no. 2 (2007), pp. 297–316.

27. Data are from the 2009 Kelly Global Workforce Index, based on information published in news releases in each country by Kelly Services in September 2009.

28. S. McNulty, "XTO Bid Answers Questions on Exxon Strategy," *Financial Times (London),* December 15, 2009, p. 19; "Exxon Culture May Be Tough Fit for XTO Workers," *Reuters (Houston),* March 4, 2010.

29. R. Wageman and G. Baker, "Incentives and Cooperation: The Joint Effects of Task and Reward Interdependence on Group Performance," *Journal of Organizational Behavior* 18, no. 2 (1997), pp. 139–58; G.S. van der Vegt, B.J.M. Emans, and E. van der Vliert, "Patterns of Interdependence in Work Teams: A Two-Level Investigation of the Relations with Job and Team Satisfaction," *Personnel Psychology* 54, no. 1 (2001), pp. 51–69.

30. P.C. Earley and G.B. Northcraft, "Goal Setting, Resource Interdependence, and Conflict Management," in *Managing Conflict: An Interdisciplinary Approach,* ed. M.A. Rahim (New York: Praeger, 1989), pp. 161–70; K. Jehn, "A Multimethod Examination of the Benefits and Detriments of Intragroup Conflict," *Administrative Science Quarterly* 40 (1995), pp. 245–82.

31. A. Risberg, "Employee Experiences of Acquisition Processes," *Journal of World Business* 36 (March 2001), pp. 58–84.

32. Jehn and Bendersky, "Intragroup Conflict in Organizations."

33. M. Hewstone, M. Rubin, and H. Willis, "Intergroup Bias," *Annual Review of Psychology* 53 (2002), pp. 575–604; J. Jetten, R. Spears, and T. Postmes, "Intergroup Distinctiveness and Differentiation: A Meta-Analytic Integration," *Journal of Personality and Social Psychology* 86, no. 6 (2004), pp. 862–79.

34. Follett, "Constructive Conflict"; Blake, Shepard, and Mouton, *Managing Intergroup Conflict in Industry;* T. Ruble and K. Thomas, "Support for a Two-Dimensional Model of Conflict Behavior," *Organizational Behavior and Human Performance* 16 (1976), pp. 143–55; C.K.W. De Dreu et al., "A Theory-Based Measure of Conflict Management Strategies in the Workplace," *Journal of Organizational Behavior* 22 (2001), pp. 645–68; Rahim, "Toward a Theory of Managing Organizational Conflict."

35. Jehn, "A Multimethod Examination."

36. *Workplace Conflict and How Businesses Can Harness It to Thrive.*

37. A. Bryant, "We're Family, So We Can Disagree," *The New York Times,* February 21, 2010, p. 1.

38. D.W. Johnson et al., "Effects of Cooperative, Competitive, and Individualistic Goal Structures on Achievement: A Meta-Analysis," *Psychological Bulletin* 89 (1981), pp. 47–62; Rahim, "Toward a Theory of Managing Organizational Conflict"; G.A. Callanan, C.D. Benzing, and D.F. Perri, "Choice of Conflict-Handling Strategy: A Matter of Context," *Journal of Psychology* 140, no. 3 (2006), pp. 269–88.

39. R. A. Friedman et al., "What Goes Around Comes Around: The Impact of Personal Conflict Style on Work Conflict and Stress," *International Journal of Conflict Management* 11, no. 1 (2000), pp. 32–55; X.M. Song, J. Xile, and B. Dyer, "Antecedents and Consequences of Marketing Managers' Conflict-Handling Behaviors," *Journal of*

Marketing 64 (January 2000), pp. 50–66; M. Song, B. Dyer, and R.J. Thieme, "Conflict Management and Innovation Performance: An Integrated Contingency Perspective," *Academy of Marketing Science* 34, no. 3 (2006), pp. 341–56; L.A. DeChurch, K.L. Hamilton, and C. Haas, "Effects of Conflict Management Strategies on Perceptions of Intragroup Conflict," *Group Dynamics* 11, no. 1 (2007), pp. 66–78.

40. G.A. Chung-Yan and C. Moeller, "The Psychosocial Costs of Conflict Management Styles," *International Journal of Conflict Management* 21, no. 4 (2010), pp. 382–99.

41. C.K.W. De Dreu and A.E.M. Van Vianen, "Managing Relationship Conflict and the Effectiveness of Organizational Teams," *Journal of Organizational Behavior* 22 (2001), pp. 309–28; R.J. Lewicki et al., *Negotiation*, 4th ed. (New York: McGraw-Hill/Irwin, 2003), pp. 35–36.

42. J. Simms, "Blood in the Boardroom," *Director,* 2009, p. 48.

43. M.W. Morris and H.-Y. Fu, "How Does Culture Influence Conflict Resolution? Dynamic Constructivist Analysis," *Social Cognition* 19 (June 2001), pp. 324–49; C.H. Tinsley, "How Negotiators Get to Yes: Predicting the Constellation of Strategies Used across Cultures to Negotiate Conflict," *Journal of Applied Psychology* 86, no. 4 (2001), pp. 583–93; J.L. Holt and C.J. DeVore, "Culture, Gender, Organizational Role, and Styles of Conflict Resolution: A Meta-Analysis," *International Journal of Intercultural Relations* 29, no. 2 (2005), pp. 165–96.

44. D.A. Cai and E.L. Fink, "Conflict Style Differences between Individualists and Collectivists," *Communication Monographs* 69 (March 2002), pp. 67–87; C.H. Tinsley and E. Weldon, "Responses to a Normative Conflict among American and Chinese Managers," *International Journal of Conflict Management* 3, no. 2 (2003), pp. 183–94; F.P. Brew and D.R. Cairns, "Styles of Managing Interpersonal Workplace Conflict in Relation to Status and Face Concern: A Study with Anglos and Chinese," *International Journal of Conflict Management* 15, no. 1 (2004), pp. 27–57.

45. Holt and DeVore, "Culture, Gender, Organizational Role"; M. Davis, S. Capobianco, and L. Kraus, "Gender Differences in Responding to Conflict in the Workplace: Evidence from a Large Sample of Working Adults," *Sex Roles* 63, no. 7 (2010), pp. 500–14.

46. K. Lewin, *Resolving Social Conflicts* (New York: Harper, 1948).

47. J.D. Hunger and L.W. Stern, "An Assessment of the Functionality of the Superordinate Goal in Reducing Conflict," *Academy of Management Journal* 19, no. 4 (1976), pp. 591–605; M. Sherif, "Superordinate Goals in the Reduction of Intergroup Conflict," *American Journal of Sociology* 63, no. 4 (1958), pp. 349–56.

48. Sherif, "Superordinate Goals in the Reduction of Intergroup Conflict"; Eisenhardt, Kahwajy, and Bourgeois, "How Management Teams Can Have a Good Fight"; Song, Xile, and Dyer, "Antecedents and Consequences of Marketing Managers' Conflict-Handling Behaviors"; O. Doucet, J. Poitras, and D. Chenevert, "The Impacts of Leadership on Workplace Conflicts," *International Journal of Conflict Management* 20, no. 4 (2009), pp. 340–54.

49. Lau and Cobb, "Understanding the Connections between Relationship Conflict and Performance."

50. H.C. Triandis, "The Future of Workforce Diversity in International Organisations: A Commentary," *Applied Psychology: An International Journal* 52, no. 3 (2003), pp. 486–95.

51. "Can the New CEO End a Culture Clash after a Merger?" *Financial Times*, September 10, 2008, p. 16.

52. T.F. Pettigrew, "Intergroup Contact Theory," *Annual Review of Psychology* 49 (1998), pp. 65–85; S. Brickson, "The Impact of Identity Orientation on Individual and Organizational Outcomes in Demographically Diverse Settings," *Academy of Management Review* 25 (January 2000), pp. 82–101; J. Dixon and K. Durrheim, "Contact and the Ecology of Racial Division: Some Varieties of Informal Segregation," *British Journal of Social Psychology* 42 (March 2003), pp. 1–23.

53. Variations of this action plan are described in several sources, including: A. Jay, P. Smith, and H. Barlcay, "From 'No' to 'Yes': The Constructive Route to Agreement" (London, Video Arts, 1988); D. Stone, B. Patton, and S. Heen, *Difficult Conversations: How to Discuss What Matters Most* (New York: Penguin, 1999); K. Patterson et al., *Crucial Conversations: Tools for Talking When Stakes Are High* (New York: McGraw-Hill, 2002).

54. Triandis, "The Future of Workforce Diversity in International Organisations."

55. Von Glinow, Shapiro, and Brett, "Can We Talk, and Should We?"

56. "M-Tel with the Best Internal Communications," *ENP Newswire,* October 19, 2009; "Mobiltel with an Award for Consistent Policy in the Mane of the Employees," *ENP Newswire,* November 18, 2010; Mobiltel Bulgaria, *Don't Be Apart, Be a Part!* (Sophia: Mobiltel Bulgaria, 2010).

57. E. Horwitt, "Knowledge, Knowledge, Who's Got the Knowledge," *Computerworld,* April 8, 1996, pp. 80, 81, 84.

58. L.L. Putnam, "Beyond Third Party Role: Disputes and Managerial Intervention," *Employee Responsibilities and Rights Journal* 7 (1994), pp. 23–36; A.R. Elangovan, "The Manager as the Third Party: Deciding How to Intervene in Employee Disputes," in *Negotiation: Readings, Exercises, and Cases,* ed. R.J. Lewicki, J.A. Litterer, and D. Saunders, 3rd. ed. (New York: McGraw-Hill, 1999), pp. 458–69. For a somewhat different taxonomy of managerial conflict intervention, see P.G. Irving and J.P. Meyer, "A Multidimensional Scaling Analysis of Managerial Third-Party Conflict Intervention Strategies," *Canadian Journal of Behavioural Science* 29, no. 1 (January 1997), pp. 7–18. A recent review describes 10 species of third-party intervention, but these consist of variations of the three types described here. See D.E. Conlon et al., "Third Party Interventions across Cultures: No 'One Best Choice,'" in *Research in Personnel and Human Resources Management* (Greenwich, CT: JAI Press, 2007), pp. 309–49.

59. L.B. Bingham et al., "Mediating Employment Disputes at the United States Postal Service: A Comparison of in-House and Outside Neutral Mediator Models," *Review of Public Personnel Administration* 20, no. 1 (January 2000), pp. 5–19; T. Nabatchi, L.B. Bingham, and D.H. Good, "Organizational Justice and Workplace Mediation: A Six Factor Model," *International Journal of Conflict Management* 18, no. 2 (2007), pp. 148–74. Information also came from the USPS website: http://www.usps.com/redress/.

60. B.H. Sheppard, "Managers as Inquisitors: Lessons from the Law," in *Bargaining inside Organizations,* ed. M. H. Bazerman and R. J. Lewicki (Beverly Hills, CA: Sage Publications, 1983); N.H. Kim, D.W. Sohn, and J.A. Wall, "Korean Leaders' (and Subordinates') Conflict Management," *International Journal of Conflict Management* 10, no. 2 (April 1999), pp. 130–53; D.J. Moberg, "Managers as Judges in Employee Disputes: An Occasion for Moral Imagination," *Business Ethics Quarterly* 13, no. 4 (2003), pp. 453–77.

61. R. Karambayya and J.M. Brett, "Managers Handling Disputes: Third Party Roles and Perceptions of Fairness," *Academy of Management Journal* 32 (1989), pp. 687–704; R. Cropanzano et al., "Disputant Reactions to Managerial Conflict Resolution Tactics," *Group & Organization Management* 24 (June 1999), pp. 124–53.

62. A.R. Elangovan, "Managerial Intervention in Organizational Disputes: Testing a Prescriptive Model of Strategy Selection," *International Journal of Conflict Management* 4 (1998), pp. 301–35; P.S. Nugent, "Managing Conflict: Third-Party Interventions for Managers," *Academy of Management Executive* 16, no. 1 (February 2002), pp. 139–54.

63. J.P. Meyer, J.M. Gemmell, and P.G. Irving, "Evaluating the Management of Interpersonal Conflict in Organizations: A Factor-Analytic

Study of Outcome Criteria," *Canadian Journal of Administrative Sciences* 14 (1997), pp. 1–13; L.B. Bingham, "Employment Dispute Resolution: The Case for Mediation," *Conflict Resolution Quarterly* 22, no. 1-2 (2004), pp. 145–74; M. Hyde et al., "Workplace Conflict Resolution and the Health of Employees in the Swedish and Finnish Units of an Industrial Company," *Social Science & Medicine* 63, no. 8 (2006), pp. 2218–27.

64. W.H. Ross and D.E. Conlon, "Hybrid Forms of Third-Party Dispute Resolution: Theoretical Implications of Combining Mediation and Arbitration," *Academy of Management Review* 25, no. 2 (2000), pp. 416–27; W.H. Ross, C. Brantmeier, and T. Ciriacks, "The Impact of Hybrid Dispute-Resolution Procedures on Constituent Fairness Judgments," *Journal of Applied Social Psychology* 32, no. 6 (June 2002), pp. 1151–88.

65. R. Stagner and H. Rosen, *Psychology of Union–Management Relations* (Belmont, CA: Wadsworth, 1965), pp. 95–96, 108–110; R.E. Walton and R.B. McKersie, *A Behavioral Theory of Labor Negotiations: An Analysis of a Social Interaction System* (New York: McGraw-Hill, 1965), pp. 41–46; L. Thompson, *The Mind and Heart of the Negotiator* (Upper Saddle River, NJ: Prentice-Hall, 1998), Ch. 2.

66. B.J. Dietmeyer, *Strategic Negotiation* (Chicago: Dearborn Trade Publishing, 2004).

67. J.M. Brett, "Managing Organizational Conflict," *Professional Psychology: Research and Practice* 15 (1984), pp. 664–78.

68. K.G. Allred, "Distinguishing Best and Strategic Practices: A Framework for Managing the Dilemma between Creating and Claiming Value," *Negotiation Journal* 16 (2000), pp. 287–97.

69. S. Doctoroff, "Reengineering Negotiations," *Sloan Management Review* 39 (March 1998), pp. 63–71; D.C. Zetik and A.F. Stuhlmacher, "Goal Setting and Negotiation Performance: A Meta-Analysis," *Group Processes & Intergroup Relations* 5 (January 2002), pp. 35–52.

70. B. McRae, *The Seven Strategies of Master Negotiators* (Toronto: McGraw-Hill Ryerson, 2002), pp. 7–11.

71. A.F. Stuhlmacher, T.L. Gillespie, and M.V. Champagne, "The Impact of Time Pressure in Negotiation: A Meta-Analysis," *International Journal of Conflict Management* 9, no. 2 (April 1998), pp. 97–116; C.K.W. De Dreu, "Time Pressure and Closing of the Mind in Negotiation," *Organizational Behavior and Human Decision Processes* 91 (July 2003), pp. 280–95. However, one recent study reported that speeding up these concessions leads to better negotiated outcomes. See D.A. Moore, "Myopic Prediction, Self-Destructive Secrecy, and the Unexpected Benefits of Revealing Final Deadlines in Negotiation," *Organizational Behavior and Human Decision Processes* 94, no. 2 (2004), pp. 125–39.

72. R.J. Robertson, "Defusing the Exploding Offer: The Farpoint Gambit," *Negotiation Journal* 11, no. 3 (1995), pp. 277–85.

73. A. Tversky and D. Kahneman, "Judgment under Uncertainty: Heuristics and Biases," *Science* 185, no. 4157 (September 27, 1974), pp. 1124–31; J.D. Jasper and S.D. Christman, "A Neuropsychological Dimension for Anchoring Effects," *Journal of Behavioral Decision Making* 18 (2005), pp. 343–69.

74. Lewicki et al., *Negotiation*, pp. 90–96; S. Kwon and L. R. Weingart, "Unilateral Concessions from the Other Party: Concession Behavior, Attributions, and Negotiation Judgments," *Journal of Applied Psychology* 89, no. 2 (2004), pp. 263–78.

75. D. Malhotra, "The Fine Art of Making Concessions," *Negotiation* (January 2006), pp. 3–5.

76. J.Z. Rubin and B.R. Brown, *The Social Psychology of Bargaining and Negotiation* (New York: Academic Press, 1976), Ch. 9

77. For a critical view of the problem solving style in negotiation, see Brett, "Managing Organizational Conflict."

78. L.L. Thompson, "Information Exchange in Negotiation," *Journal of Experimental Social Psychology* 27 (1991), pp. 161–79.

79. S.R. Covey, *The 7 Habits of Highly Effective People* (New York: The Free Press, 1989), pp. 235–60.

80. Lewicki et al., *Negotiation*, p. 95; M. Olekalns and P. L. Smith, "Testing the Relationships among Negotiators' Motivational Orientations, Strategy Choices, and Outcomes," *Journal of Experimental Social Psychology* 39, no. 2 (March 2003), pp. 101–17.

81. M. Olekalns and P.L. Smith, "Moments in Time: Metacognition, Trust, and Outcomes in Dyadic Negotiations," *Personality and Social Psychology Bulletin* 31, no. 12 (December 2005), pp. 1696–707.

82. D.W. Choi, "Shared Metacognition in Integrative Negotiation," *International Journal of Conflict Management* 21, no. 3 (2010), pp. 309–33.

83. J.M. Brett et al., "Sticks and Stones: Language, Face, and Online Dispute Resolution," *Academy of Management Journal* 50, no. 1 (February 2007), pp. 85–99; D. Druckman and M. Olekalns, "Emotions in Negotiation," *Group Decision and Negotiation* 17, no. 1 (2008), pp. 1–11; D. Pietroni et al., "Emotions as Strategic Information: Effects of Other's Emotional Expressions on Fixed-Pie Perception, Demands, and Integrative Behavior in Negotiation," *Journal of Experimental Social Psychology* 44, no. 6 (2008), pp. 1444–54; M.J. Boland and W.H. Ross, "Emotional Intelligence and Dispute Mediation in Escalating and De-Escalating Situations," *Journal of Applied Social Psychology* 40, no. 12 (2010), pp. 3059–105.

84. P.J. Carnevale and A.M. Isen, "The Influence of Positive Affect and Visual Access on the Discovery of Integrative Solutions in Bilateral Negotiation," *Organizational Behavior and Human Decision Processes* 37 (1986), pp. 1–13; Thompson, *The Mind and Heart of the Negotiator.*

85. J.W. Salacuse and J.Z. Rubin, "Your Place or Mine? Site Location and Negotiation," *Negotiation Journal* 6 (January 1990), pp. 5–10; J. Mayfield et al., "How Location Impacts International Business Negotiations," *Review of Business* 19 (December 1998), pp. 21–24.

86. J. Margo, "The Persuaders," *Boss Magazine,* December 29, 2000, p. 38. For a full discussion of the advantages and disadvantages of face-to-face and alternative negotiations situations, see M.H. Bazerman et al., "Negotiation," *Annual Review of Psychology* 51 (2000), pp. 279–314.

87. Lewicki et al., *Negotiation*, pp. 298–322.

CHAPTER 12

1. M. Hiltzik, "Apple CEO's Visions Don't Guarantee Sustained Gains," *Los Angeles Times,* April 14, 2003, p. C1; P. Elkind and D. Burke, "The Trouble with Steve," *Fortune,* March 17, 2008, pp. 88ff; R. Siklos, "8 Stars Speak Out on Steve Jobs: Bob Iger," *Fortune,* September 11, 2009; K. Brinkbaumer and T. Schulz, "Irule," *Advertiser (Adelaide, Australia),* June 12, 2010; F. Manjoo and J. Caplan, "Apple Nation," *Fast Company,* July–August 2010, pp. 69–76; S. Goodley, "Apple: One-Man Brands," *Guardian (London),* January 19, 2011, p. 26; S. Lohr, "Imagining Apple without Its Visionary," *International Herald Tribune,* January 20, 2011, p. 18; J. Sonnenfeld, "The Genius Dilemma," *Newsweek,* January 31, 2011, p. 12. The origin of "reality distortion field" is described at www.folklore.org.

2. Many of these perspectives are summarized by R.N. Kanungo, "Leadership in Organizations: Looking Ahead to the 21st Century," *Canadian Psychology* 39 (Spring 1998), pp. 71–82; G.A. Yukl, *Leadership in Organizations,* 6th ed. (Upper Saddle River, NJ: Pearson Education, 2006).

3. R. House, M. Javidan, and P. Dorfman, "Project GLOBE: An Introduction," *Applied Psychology: An International Review* 50 (2001), pp. 489–505; R. House et al., "Understanding Cultures and Implicit Leadership Theories across the Globe: An Introduction to Project GLOBE," *Journal of World Business* 37 (2002), pp. 3–10.

4. *Testimony of Randall K. Edington on Behalf of the Arizona Public Service Company* (Phoenix: Arizona Public Service Company,

June 1, 2011); M. Fallon, "Every Employee Is a Leader," *Nuclear Plant Journal* 29, no. 2 (March-April 2011), pp. 48–50.

5. "Powered by Frontline People," *Employee Engagement Today,* September 2007; C. Hosford, "Flying High," *Incentive* 181, no. 12 (December 2007), pp. 14–20.

6. J.A. Raelin, "We the Leaders: In Order to Form a Leaderful Organization," *Journal of Leadership & Organizational Studies* 12, no. 2 (2005), pp. 18–30; C.L. Pearce, J.A. Conger, and E.A. Locke, "Shared Leadership Theory," *Leadership Quarterly* 19, no. 5 (2008), pp. 622–28; E. Engel Small and J.R. Rentsch, "Shared Leadership in Teams: A Matter of Distribution," *Journal of Personnel Psychology* 9, no. 4 (2010), pp. 203–11.

7. J.A. Raelin, *Creating Leaderful Organizations: How to Bring Out Leadership in Everyone* (San Francisco, CA: Berret-Koehler, 2003).

8. J.W. Gardner, *On Leadership* (New York: The Free Press, 1990), pp. 138–55.

9. C.A. Beatty, "Implementing Advanced Manufacturing Technologies: Rules of the Road," *Sloan Management Review* (Summer 1992), pp. 49–60; J.M. Howell, "The Right Stuff: Identifying and Developing Effective Champions of Innovation," *Academy of Management Executive* 19, no. 2 (2005), pp. 108–19; J.M. Howell and C.M. Shea, "Effects of Champion Behavior, Team Potency, and External Communication Activities on Predicting Team Performance," *Group & Organization Management* 31, no. 2 (April 2006), pp. 180–211.

10. Many of these perspectives are summarized by Kanungo, "Leadership in Organizations"; Yukl, *Leadership in Organizations.*

11. The history of the trait perspective of leadership, as well as current research on this topic, is nicely summarized by S.J. Zaccaro, C. Kemp, and P. Bader, "Leader Traits and Attributes," in *The Nature of Leadership,* ed. J. Antonakis, A.T. Cianciolo, and R.J. Sternberg (Thousand Oaks, CA: Sage, 2004), pp. 101–24.

12. R.M. Stogdill, *Handbook of Leadership* (New York: The Free Press, 1974), Ch. 5.

13. J. Intagliata, D. Ulrich, and N. Smallwood, "Leveraging Leadership Competencies to Produce Leadership Brand: Creating Distinctiveness by Focusing on Strategy and Results," *Human Resources Planning* 23, no. 4 (2000), pp. 12–23; J.A. Conger and D.A. Ready, "Rethinking Leadership Competencies," *Leader to Leader* (Spring 2004), pp. 41–47; Zaccaro, Kemp, and Bader, "Leader Traits and Attributes." For a recent discussion on leadership traits and evolutionary psychology, see T.A. Judge, R.F. Piccolo, and T. Kosalka, "The Bright and Dark Sides of Leader Traits: A Review and Theoretical Extension of the Leader Trait Paradigm," *Leadership Quarterly* 20 (2009), pp. 855–75.

14. This list is based on S.A. Kirkpatrick and E.A. Locke, "Leadership: Do Traits Matter?" *Academy of Management Executive* 5 (May 1991), pp. 48–60; R.M. Aditya, R.J. House, and S. Kerr, "Theory and Practice of Leadership: Into the New Millennium," in *Industrial and Organizational Psychology: Linking Theory with Practice,* ed. C.L. Cooper and E.A. Locke (Oxford, UK: Blackwell, 2000), pp. 130–65; D. Goleman, R. Boyatzis, and A. McKee, *Primal Leaders* (Boston: Harvard Business School Press, 2002); T.A. Judge et al., "Personality and Leadership: A Qualitative and Quantitative Review," *Journal of Applied Psychology* 87, no. 4 (August 2002), pp. 765–80; T.A. Judge, A.E. Colbert, and R. Ilies, "Intelligence and Leadership: A Quantitative Review and Test of Theoretical Propositions," *Journal of Applied Psychology* 89, no. 3 (June 2004), pp. 542–52; Zaccaro, Kemp, and Bader, "Leader Traits and Attributes."

15. M. Popper et al., "The Capacity to Lead: Major Psychological Differences between Leaders and Nonleaders," *Military Psychology* 16, no. 4 (2004), pp. 245–63; R.G. Lord and R.J. Hall, "Identity, Deep Structure and the Development of Leadership Skill," *Leadership Quarterly* 16, no. 4 (August 2005), pp. 591–615; D.V. Day, M.M. Harrison, and S.M. Halpin, *An Integrative Approach to*

Leader Development: Connecting Adult Development, Identity, and Expertise (New York: Routledge, 2009); D.S. DeRue and S.J. Ashford, "Who Will Lead and Who Will Follow? A Social Process of Leadership Identity Construction in Organizations," *Academy of Management Review* 35, no. 4 (2010), pp. 627–47.

16. The large-scale studies are reported in C. Savoye, "Workers Say Honesty Is Best Company Policy," *Christian Science Monitor,* June 15, 2000; J.M. Kouzes and B.Z. Posner, *The Leadership Challenge,* 3rd ed. (San Francisco, CA: Jossey-Bass, 2002), Ch. 2; J. Schettler, "Leadership in Corporate America," *Training & Development,* September 2002, pp. 66–73.

17. BlessingWhite, *The State of Employee Engagement 2008: Asia Pacific Overview* (Princeton, NJ: BlessingWhite, March 2008); M. Dolliver, "Deflating a Myth," *Brandweek,* May 12, 2008, pp. 30–32. For other surveys on low perceived integrity of business leaders, see Watson Wyatt Worldwide, "Asia-Pacific Workers Satisfied with Jobs Despite Some Misgivings with Management and Pay," news release, November 16, 2004; J. Cremer, "Asian Workers Give Low Marks to Leaders," *South China Morning Post (Hong Kong),* July 30, 2005, p. 8; D. Jones, "Optimism Puts Rose-Colored Tint in Glasses of Top Execs," *USA Today,* December 16, 2005, p. B1; E. Pondel, "Friends & Bosses?" *Seattle Post-Intelligencer,* April 10, 2006, p. C1.

18. R. Davidovitz et al., "Leaders as Attachment Figures: Leaders' Attachment Orientations Predict Leadership-Related Mental Representations and Followers' Performance and Mental Health," *Journal of Personality and Social Psychology* 93, no. 4 (2007), pp. 632–50.

19. J.B. Miner, "Twenty Years of Research on Role Motivation Theory of Managerial Effectiveness," *Personnel Psychology* 31 (1978), pp. 739–60; R.J. House and R.N. Aditya, "The Social Scientific Study of Leadership: Quo Vadis?" *Journal of Management* 23 (1997), pp. 409–73.

20. J. Hedlund et al., "Identifying and Assessing Tacit Knowledge: Understanding the Practical Intelligence of Military Leaders," *Leadership Quarterly* 14, no. 2 (2003), pp. 117–40; R.J. Sternberg, "A Systems Model of Leadership: WICS," *American Psychologist* 62, no. 1 (2007), pp. 34–42.

21. J. George, "Emotions and Leadership: The Role of Emotional Intelligence," *Human Relations* 53 (August 2000), pp. 1027–55; Goleman, Boyatzis, and McKee, *Primal Leaders;* Lord and Hall, "Identity, Deep Structure and the Development of Leadership Skill"; C. Skinner and P. Spurgeon, "Valuing Empathy and Emotional Intelligence in Health Leadership: A Study of Empathy, Leadership Behaviour and Outcome Effectiveness," *Health Services Management Research* 18, no. 1 (February 2005), pp. 1–12.

22. A. Bryant, "I'm Prepared for Adversity: I Waited Tables," *The New York Times,* June 6, 2010, p. BU2.

23. B. George, *Authentic Leadership* (San Francisco, CA: Jossey-Bass, 2004); W.L. Gardner et al., "'Can You See the Real Me?' A Self-Based Model of Authentic Leader and Follower Development," *Leadership Quarterly* 16 (2005), pp. 343–72; B. George, *True North* (San Francisco, CA: Jossey-Bass, 2007), Ch. 4; M.E. Palanski and F.J. Yammarino, "Integrity and Leadership: Clearing the Conceptual Confusion," *European Management Journal* 25, no. 3 (2007), pp. 171–84; F.O. Walumbwa et al., "Authentic Leadership: Development and Validation of a Theory-Based Measure," *Journal of Management* 34, no. 1 (February 2008), pp. 89–126.

24. G. Kohlrieser, "Herna Verhagen, Managing Director TNT Group HR: 'Live Your Dream; Success Is Built on Passion,'" *States News Service,* April 13, 2010.

25. Lisa Minnelli makes this statement to explain why she doesn't perform the songs made famous by her mother, Judy Garland. The earliest versions of this quotation are found in *New Woman* magazine, Vol. 8 (1978) and in Vincente Minnelli's 1975 autobiography. The version cited here is from E. Santosuosso, "Minnelli Brings a Real-Life Concert to Town," *Boston Globe,* September 24, 1992, p. 61.

26. B.J. Avolio et al., "Unlocking the Mask: A Look at the Process by Which Authentic Leaders Impact Follower Attitudes and Behaviors," *Leadership Quarterly* 15 (2004), pp. 801–23.

27. R.J. Ellis, "Self-Monitoring and Leadership Emergence in Groups," *Personality and Social Psychology Bulletin* 14, no. 4 (December 1988), pp. 681–93; D.V. Day et al., "Self-Monitoring Personality at Work: A Meta-Analytic Investigation of Construct Validity," *Journal of Applied Psychology* 87, no. 2 (April 2002), pp. 390–401; I.O. Tueretgen, P. Unsal, and I. Erdem, "The Effects of Sex, Gender Role, and Personality Traits on Leader Emergence—Does Culture Make a Difference?" *Small Group Research* 39, no. 5 (October 2008), pp. 588–615; D.U. Bryant et al., "The Interaction of Self-Monitoring and Organizational Position on Perceived Effort," *Journal of Managerial Psychology* 26, no. 2 (2011), pp. 138–54.

28. A.G. Bedeian and D.V. Day, "Can Chameleons Lead?" *Leadership Quarterly* 15, no. 5 (2004), pp. 687–718.

29. W. Bennis, "We Need Leaders," *Executive Excellence* 27, no. 12 (December 2010), p. 4.

30. Bedeian and Day, "Can Chameleons Lead?"

31. D. Gruenfeld and L. Zander, "Authentic Leadership Can Be Bad Leadership," *Harvard Business Review Blog*, 2011, http://blogs.hbr.org.

32. R. Jacobs, "Using Human Resource Functions to Enhance Emotional Intelligence," in *The Emotionally Intelligent Workplace*, ed. C. Cherniss and D. Goleman (San Francisco, CA: Jossey-Bass, 2001), pp. 161–63; Conger and Ready, "Rethinking Leadership Competencies."

33. R.G. Lord and D.J. Brown, *Leadership Processes and Self-Identity: A Follower-Centered Approach to Leadership* (Mahwah, NJ: Lawrence Erlbaum Associates, 2004); R. Bolden and J. Gosling, "Leadership Competencies: Time to Change the Tune?" *Leadership* 2, no. 2 (May 2006), pp. 147–63.

34. E.A. Fleishman, "The Description of Supervisory Behavior," *Journal of Applied Psychology* 37, no. 1 (1953), pp. 1–6. For discussion on methodological problems with the development of these people-versus task-oriented leadership constructs, see C.A. Schriesheim, R.J. House, and S. Kerr, "Leader Initiating Structure: A Reconciliation of Discrepant Research Results and Some Empirical Tests," *Organizational Behavior and Human Performance* 15, no. 2 (1976), pp. 297–321; L. Tracy, "Consideration and Initiating Structure: Are They Basic Dimensions of Leader Behavior?" *Social Behavior and Personality* 15, no. 1 (1987), pp. 21–33.

35. A.K. Korman, "Consideration, Initiating Structure, and Organizational Criteria—A Review," *Personnel Psychology* 19 (1966), pp. 349–62; E.A. Fleishman, "Twenty Years of Consideration and Structure," in *Current Developments in the Study of Leadership*, ed. E.A. Fleishman and J.C. Hunt (Carbondale, IL: Southern Illinois University Press, 1973), pp. 1–40; T.A. Judge, R.F. Piccolo, and R. Ilies, "The Forgotten Ones?: The Validity of Consideration and Initiating Structure in Leadership Research," *Journal of Applied Psychology* 89, no. 1 (2004), pp. 36–51; Yukl, *Leadership in Organizations*, pp. 62–75; D.S. Derue et al., "Trait and Behavioral Theories of Leadership: An Integration and Meta-Analytic Test of Their Relative Validity," *Personnel Psychology* 64, no. 1 (2011), pp. 7–52.

36. V.V. Baba, "Serendipity in Leadership: Initiating Structure and Consideration in the Classroom," *Human Relations* 42 (1989), pp. 509–25.

37. B.A. Scott et al., "A Daily Investigation of the Role of Manager Empathy on Employee Well-Being," *Organizational Behavior and Human Decision Processes* 113, no. 2 (2010), pp. 127–40.

38. S. Kerr et al., "Towards a Contingency Theory of Leadership Based upon the Consideration and Initiating Structure Literature," *Organizational Behavior and Human Performance* 12 (1974), pp. 62–82; L.L. Larson, J.G. Hunt, and R.N. Osbom, "The Great Hi–Hi Leader Behavior Myth: A Lesson from Occam's Razor," *Academy of Management Journal* 19 (1976), pp. 628–41.

39. R.K. Greenleaf, *Servant Leadership: A Journey into the Nature of Lergitimate Power & Greatness* (Mahwah, NJ: Paulist Press, 1977, 2002); D. van Dierendonck and K. Patterson, "Servant Leadership: An Introduction," in *Servant Leadership: Developments in Theory and Research*, ed. D. van Dierendonck and K. Patterson (Houndmills, UK: Palgrave Macmillan, 2010), pp. 3–11.

40. Greenleaf, *Servant Leadership*, p. 27.

41. J.E. Barbuto, Jr., and D.W. Wheeler, "Scale Development and Construct Clarification of Servant Leadership," *Group & Organization Management* 31, no. 3 (June 2006), pp. 300–26; R.C. Liden et al., "Servant Leadership: Development of a Multidimensional Measure and Multi-Level Assessment," *Leadership Quarterly* 19, no. 2 (2008), pp. 161–77; S. Sendjaya, J.C. Sarros, and J.C. Santora, "Defining and Measuring Servant Leadership Behaviour in Organizations," *Journal of Management Studies* 45, no. 2 (2008), pp. 402–24; K.-Y. Ng and C.S.-K. Koh, "Motivation to Serve: Understanding the Heart of the Servant-Leader and Servant Leadership Behaviours," in *Servant Leadership: Developments in Theory and Research*, ed. D. van Dierendonck and K. Patterson (Houndmills, UK: Palgrave Macmillan, 2010), pp. 90–104.

42. R. Tannenbaum and W.H. Schmidt, "How to Choose a Leadership Pattern," *Harvard Business Review* (May–June 1973), pp. 162–80.

43. R.P. Vecchio, J.E. Justin, and C.L. Pearce, "The Utility of Transactional and Transformational Leadership for Predicting Performance and Satisfaction within a Path-Goal Theory Framework," *Journal of Occupational and Organizational Psychology* 81 (2008), pp. 71–82.

44. For a thorough study of how the expectancy theory of motivation relates to leadership, see R.G. Isaac, W.J. Zerbe, and D.C. Pitt, "Leadership and Motivation: The Effective Application of Expectancy Theory," *Journal of Managerial Issues* 13 (Summer 2001), pp. 212–26.

45. R.J. House, "A Path-Goal Theory of Leader Effectiveness," *Administrative Science Quarterly* 16 (1971), pp. 321–38; M.G. Evans, "Extensions of a Path-Goal Theory of Motivation," *Journal of Applied Psychology* 59 (1974), pp. 172–78; R.J. House and T.R. Mitchell, "Path-Goal Theory of Leadership," *Journal of Contemporary Business* (Autumn 1974), pp. 81–97; M.G. Evans, "Path Goal Theory of Leadership," in *Leadership*, ed. L.L. Neider and C.A. Schriesheim (Greenwich, CT: Information Age Publishing, 2002), pp. 115–38.

46. R.J. House, "Path-Goal Theory of Leadership: Lessons, Legacy, and a Reformulated Theory," *Leadership Quarterly* 7 (1996), pp. 323–52.

47. "Driving the Engine," *Broadcasting & Cable* 133, no. 16 (April 21, 2003), p. 6A; S. Pappu, "The Queen of Tween," *Atlantic Monthly*, November 2004, pp. 118–25; A. Becker, "The Wonderful World of Sweeney," *Broadcasting & Cable*, February 25, 2008, p. 19; J.R. Littlejohn, "Distinguished Vanguard Award for Leadership," *Multichannel News*, May 19, 2008.

48. J. Indvik, "Path-Goal Theory of Leadership: A Meta-Analysis," *Academy of Management Proceedings* (1986), pp. 189–92; J.C. Wofford and L.Z. Liska, "Path-Goal Theories of Leadership: A Meta-Analysis," *Journal of Management* 19 (1993), pp. 857–76.

49. J.D. Houghton and S.K. Yoho, "Toward a Contingency Model of Leadership and Psychological Empowerment: When Should Self-Leadership Be Encouraged?" *Journal of Leadership & Organizational Studies* 11, no. 4 (2005), pp. 65–83.

50. R.T. Keller, "A Test of the Path-Goal Theory of Leadership with Need for Clarity as a Moderator in Research and Development Organizations," *Journal of Applied Psychology* 74 (1989), pp. 208–12.

51. C.A. Schriesheim and L.L. Neider, "Path-Goal Leadership Theory: The Long and Winding Road," *Leadership Quarterly* 7 (1996), pp. 317–21.

52. P. Hersey and K.H. Blanchard, *Management of Organizational Behavior: Utilizing Human Resources*, 5th ed. (Englewood Cliffs, NJ: Prentice Hall, 1988).

53. R.P. Vecchio, "Situational Leadership Theory: An Examination of a Prescriptive Theory," *Journal of Applied Psychology* 72 (1987), pp. 444–51; W. Blank, J.R. Weitzel, and S.G. Green, "A Test of the Situational Leadership Theory," *Personnel Psychology* 43 (1990), pp. 579–97; C.L. Graeff, "Evolution of Situational Leadership Theory: A Critical Review," *Leadership Quarterly* 8 (1997), pp. 153–70; G. Thompson and R.P. Vecchio, "Situational Leadership Theory: A Test of Three Versions," *Leadership Quarterly* 20, no. 5 (2009), pp. 837–48.

54. F.E. Fiedler, *A Theory of Leadership Effectiveness* (New York: McGraw-Hill, 1967); F.E. Fiedler and M.M. Chemers, *Leadership and Effective Management* (Glenview, IL: Scott, Foresman, 1974).

55. F.E. Fiedler, "Engineer the Job to Fit the Manager," *Harvard Business Review* 43, no. 5 (1965), pp. 115–22.

56. For a summary of criticisms, see Yukl, *Leadership in Organizations,* pp. 217–18.

57. Judge, Piccolo, and Ilies, "The Forgotten Ones?"; Judge, Piccolo, and Kosalka, "The Bright and Dark Sides of Leader Traits."

58. N. Nicholson, *Executive Instinct* (New York: Crown, 2000).

59. This observation has also been made by C.A. Schriesheim, "Substitutes-for-Leadership Theory: Development and Basic Concepts," *Leadership Quarterly* 8 (1997), pp. 103–08.

60. D.F. Elloy and A. Randolph, "The Effect of Superleader Behavior on Autonomous Work Groups in a Government Operated Railway Service," *Public Personnel Management* 26 (Summer 1997), pp. 257–72; C.C. Manz and H. Sims Jr., *The New SuperLeadership: Leading Others to Lead Themselves* (San Francisco, CA: Berrett-Koehler, 2001).

61. M.L. Loughry, "Coworkers Are Watching: Performance Implications of Peer Monitoring," *Academy of Management Proceedings* (2002), pp. O1–O6.

62. C.C. Manz and C. Neck, *Mastering Self-Leadership,* 3rd ed. (Upper Saddle River, NJ: Prentice Hall, 2004).

63. P.M. Podsakoff and S.B. MacKenzie, "Kerr and Jermier's Substitutes for Leadership Model: Background, Empirical Assessment, and Suggestions for Future Research," *Leadership Quarterly* 8 (1997), pp. 117–32; S.D. Dionne et al., "Neutralizing Substitutes for Leadership Theory: Leadership Effects and Common-Source Bias," *Journal of Applied Psychology* 87, no. 3 (June 2002), pp. 454–64; J.R. Villa et al., "Problems with Detecting Moderators in Leadership Research Using Moderated Multiple Regression," *Leadership Quarterly* 14, no. 1 (February 2003), pp. 3–23; S.D. Dionne et al., "Substitutes for Leadership, or Not," *Leadership Quarterly* 16, no. 1 (2005), pp. 169–93.

64. J.M. Burns, *Leadership* (New York: Harper & Row, 1978); B.J. Avolio and F.J. Yammarino, eds., *Transformational and Charismatic Leadership: The Road Ahead* (Greenwich, CT: JAI Press, 2002); B.M. Bass and R.E. Riggio, *Transformational Leadership,* 2nd ed. (Mahwah, NJ: Lawrence Erlbaum Associates, 2006).

65. V.L. Goodwin, J.C. Wofford, and J.L. Whittington "A Theoretical and Empirical Extension to the Transformational Leadership Construct," *Journal of Organisational Behavior* 22 (November 2001), pp. 759–74.

66. Burns, *Leadership,* pp. 19–20. Burns also describes transactional and "transforming leadership" in his more recent book: J.M. Burns, *Transforming Leadership* (New York: Grove Press, 2004). In both books, Burns describes both leadership concepts in complex and occasionally confounding ways.

67. For Burns's discussion of the ethics of transactional leadership, see Burns, *Transforming Leadership,* p. 28. Regarding transactional leadership and appealing to needs, justice, and morality, see Burns, *Leadership,* p. 258.

68. A. Zaleznik, "Managers and Leaders: Are They Different?" *Harvard Business Review* 55, no. 5 (1977), pp. 67–78; W. Bennis and B. Nanus, *Leaders: The Strategies for Taking Charge* (New York: Harper & Row, 1985). For a recent discussion regarding managing versus leading, see G. Yukl and R. Lepsinger, "Why Integrating the Leading and Managing Roles Is Essential for Organizational Effectiveness," *Organizational Dynamics* 34, no. 4 (2005), pp. 361–75.

69. Bennis and Nanus, *Leaders,* p. 20. Peter Drucker is also widely cited as the source of this quotation. The closest passage we could find, however, is in the first two pages of *The Effective Executive* (1966), where Drucker states that effective executives "get the right things done." On the next page, he states that manual workers only need efficiency, "that is, the ability to do things right rather than the ability to get the right things done." See P.F. Drucker, *The Effective Executive* (New York: Harper Business, 1966), pp. 1–2.

70. B.M. Bass et al., "Predicting Unit Performance by Assessing Transformational and Transactional Leadership," *Journal of Applied Psychology* 88 (April 2003), pp. 207–18; Yukl and Lepsinger, "Why Integrating the Leading and Managing Roles Is Essential for Organizational Effectiveness."

71. For a discussion on the tendency to slide from transformational to transactional leadership, see W. Bennis, *An Invented Life: Reflections on Leadership and Change* (Reading, MA: Addison-Wesley, 1993).

72. R.J. House, "A 1976 Theory of Charismatic Leadership," in *Leadership: The Cutting Edge,* ed. J.G. Hunt and L.L. Larson (Carbondale, IL: Southern Illinois University Press, 1977), pp. 189–207; J.A. Conger, "Charismatic Leadership," in *The Sage Handbook of Leadership,* ed. A. Bryman et al. (London: Sage, 2011), pp. 86–102.

73. J.E. Barbuto Jr., "Taking the Charisma out of Transformational Leadership," *Journal of Social Behavior & Personality* 12 (September 1997), pp. 689–97; Y.A. Nur, "Charisma and Managerial Leadership: The Gift That Never Was," *Business Horizons* 41 (July 1998), pp. 19–26; M.D. Mumford and J.R. Van Doorn, "The Leadership of Pragmatism—Reconsidering Franklin in the Age of Charisma," *Leadership Quarterly* 12, no. 3 (Fall 2001), pp. 279–309; A. Fanelli, "Bringing Out Charisma: CEO Charisma and External Stakeholders," *Academy of Management Review* 31, no. 4 (2006), pp. 1049–61; M.J. Platow et al., "A Special Gift We Bestow on You for Being Representative of Us: Considering Leader Charisma from a Self-Categorization Perspective," *British Journal of Social Psychology* 45, no. 2 (2006), pp. 303–20.

74. L. Greenfeld, "Reflections on Two Charismas," *British Journal of Sociology* 36, no. 1 (1985), pp. 117–32.

75. B. Shamir et al., "Correlates of Charismatic Leader Behavior in Military Units: Subordinates' Attitudes, Unit Characteristics, and Superiors' Appraisals of Leader Performance," *Academy of Management Journal* 41, no. 4 (1998), pp. 387–409; R.E. De Vries, R.A. Roe, and T.C.B. Taillieu, "On Charisma and Need for Leadership," *European Journal of Work and Organizational Psychology* 8 (1999), pp. 109–33; R. Khurana, *Searching for a Corporate Savior: The Irrational Quest for Charismatic CEOs* (Princeton, NJ: Princeton University Press, 2002). The effect of charismatic leadership on follower dependence was also noted earlier by noted U.S. government leader John Gardner: Gardner, *On Leadership,* pp. 34–36.

76. J. Lipman-Blumen, "A Pox on Charisma: Why Connective Leadership and Character Count," in *The Drucker Difference: What the World's Greatest Management Thinker Means to Today's Business Leaders,* ed. C.L. Pearce, J.A. Maciariello, and H. Yamawaki (New York: McGraw-Hill, 2010), pp. 149–74.

77. D. Olive, "The 7 Deadly Chief Executive Sins," *Toronto Star,* February 17, 2004, p. D01.

78. Y. Berson et al., "The Relationship between Vision Strength, Leadership Style, and Context," *Leadership Quarterly* 12, no. 1 (2001), pp. 53–73. Strategic collective vision has been identified as a key

factor in leadership since Chester Barnard's seminal book in organizational behavior: C. Barnard, *The Functions of the Executive* (Cambridge, MA: Harvard University Press, 1938), pp. 86–89.

79. Bennis and Nanus, *Leaders*, pp. 27–33, 89; I.M. Levin, "Vision Revisited," *Journal of Applied Behavioral Science* 36 (March 2000), pp. 91–107; R.E. Quinn, *Building the Bridge as You Walk on It: A Guide for Leading Change* (San Francisco, CA: Jossey-Bass, 2004), Ch. 11; J.M. Strange and M.D. Mumford, "The Origins of Vision: Effects of Reflection, Models, and Analysis," *Leadership Quarterly* 16, no. 1 (2005), pp. 121–48; D. Ulrich and W. Ulrich, *The Why of Work: How Great Leaders Build Abundant Organizations That Win* (New York: McGraw-Hill, 2010), Ch. 1.

80. J.R. Baum, E.A. Locke, and S.A. Kirkpatrick, "A Longitudinal Study of the Relation of Vision and Vision Communication to Venture Growth in Entrepreneurial Firms," *Journal of Applied Psychology* 83 (1998), pp. 43–54; S.L. Hoe and S.L. McShane, "Leadership Antecedents of Informal Knowledge Acquisition and Dissemination," *International Journal of Organisational Behaviour* 5 (2002), pp. 282–91.

81. C. LaWell, "The Game Plan," *Smart Business Pittsburgh*, November 2010, p. 10.

82. "Canadian CEOs Give Themselves Top Marks for Leadership!" *Canada NewsWire*, September 9, 1999; L. Manfield, "Creating a Safety Culture from Top to Bottom," *WorkSafe Magazine*, February 2005, pp. 8–9.

83. J.A. Conger, "Inspiring Others: The Language of Leadership," *Academy of Management Executive* 5 (February 1991), pp. 31–45; G.T. Fairhurst and R.A. Sarr, *The Art of Framing: Managing the Language of Leadership* (San Francisco, CA: Jossey-Bass, 1996); A.E. Rafferty and M.A. Griffin, "Dimensions of Transformational Leadership: Conceptual and Empirical Extensions," *Leadership Quarterly* 15, no. 3 (2004), pp. 329–54; D.A. Waldman, P.A. Balthazard, and S.J. Peterson, "Leadership and Neuroscience: Can We Revolutionize the Way That Inspirational Leaders Are Identified and Developed?" *Academy of Management Perspectives* 25, no. 1 (2011), pp. 60–74.

84. D.E. Berlew, "Leadership and Organizational Excitement," *California Management Review* 17, no. 2 (Winter 1974), pp. 21–30; Bennis and Nanus, *Leaders*, pp. 43–55; T. Simons, "Behavioral Integrity: The Perceived Alignment between Managers' Words and Deeds as a Research Focus," *Organization Science* 13, no. 1 (January–February 2002), pp. 18–35.

85. K. Tyler, "Evaluating Values," *HRMagazine*, April 2011, p. 57.

86. M. Webb, "Executive Profile: Peter C. Farrell," *San Diego Business Journal*, March 24, 2003, p. 32; P. Benesh, "He Likes Them Breathing Easy," *Investor's Business Daily*, September 13, 2005, p. A04. For a discussion of trust in leadership, see C.S. Burke et al., "Trust in Leadership: A Multi-Level Review and Integration," *Leadership Quarterly* 18, no. 6 (2007), pp. 606–32. The survey on leading by example is reported in J.C. Maxwell, "People Do What People See," *BusinessWeek*, November 19, 2007, p. 32.

87. C. Hymowitz, "Today's Bosses Find Mentoring Isn't Worth the Time and Risks," *The Wall Street Journal*, March 13, 2006, p. B1.

88. A. Mackey, "The Effect of CEOs on Firm Performance," *Strategic Management Journal* 29, no. 12 (2008), pp. 1357–67.

89. J. Barling, T. Weber, and E.K. Kelloway, "Effects of Transformational Leadership Training on Attitudinal and Financial Outcomes: A Field Experiment," *Journal of Applied Psychology* 81 (1996), pp. 827–32.

90. A. Bryman, "Leadership in Organizations," in *Handbook of Organization Studies*, ed. S.R. Clegg, C. Hardy, and W.R. Nord (Thousand Oaks, CA: Sage, 1996), pp. 276–92.

91. B.S. Pawar and K.K. Eastman, "The Nature and Implications of Contextual Influences on Transformational Leadership: A Conceptual Examination," *Academy of Management Review* 22 (1997), pp. 80–109; C.P. Egri and S. Herman, "Leadership in the North American Environmental Sector: Values, Leadership Styles, and Contexts of Environmental Leaders and Their Organizations," *Academy of Management Journal* 43, no. 4 (2000), pp. 571–604.

92. J.R. Meindl, "On Leadership: An Alternative to the Conventional Wisdom," *Research in Organizational Behavior* 12 (1990), pp. 159–203; L.R. Offermann, J.J.K. Kennedy, and P.W. Wirtz, "Implicit Leadership Theories: Content, Structure, and Generalizability," *Leadership Quarterly* 5, no. 1 (1994), pp. 43–58; R.J. Hall and R.G. Lord, "Multi-Level Information Processing Explanations of Followers' Leadership Perceptions," *Leadership Quarterly* 6 (1995), pp. 265–87; O. Epitropaki and R. Martin, "Implicit Leadership Theories in Applied Settings: Factor Structure, Generalizability, and Stability over Time," *Journal of Applied Psychology* 89, no. 2 (2004), pp. 293–310. For a broader discussion of the social construction of leadership, see G.T. Fairhurst and D. Grant, "The Social Construction of Leadership: A Sailing Guide," *Management Communication Quarterly* 24, no. 2 (May 2010), pp. 171–210.

93. R.G. Lord et al., "Contextual Constraints on Prototype Generation and Their Multilevel Consequences for Leadership Perceptions," *Leadership Quarterly* 12, no. 3 (2001), pp. 311–38; K.A. Scott and D.J. Brown, "Female First, Leader Second? Gender Bias in the Encoding of Leadership Behavior," *Organizational Behavior and Human Decision Processes* 101 (2006), pp. 230–42; S.J. Shondrick, J.E. Dinh, and R.G. Lord, "Developments in Implicit Leadership Theory and Cognitive Science: Applications to Improving Measurement and Understanding Alternatives to Hierarchical Leadership," *Leadership Quarterly* 21, no. 6 (2010), pp. 959–78.

94. R. Ilies, M.W. Gerhardt, and H. Le, "Individual Differences in Leadership Emergence: Integrating Meta-Analytic Findings and Behavioral Genetics Estimates," *International Journal of Selection and Assessment* 12, no. 3 (September 2004), pp. 207–19.

95. S.F. Cronshaw and R.G. Lord, "Effects of Categorization, Attribution, and Encoding Processes on Leadership Perceptions," *Journal of Applied Psychology* 72 (1987), pp. 97–106; J.L. Nye and D.R. Forsyth, "The Effects of Prototype-Based Biases on Leadership Appraisals: A Test of Leadership Categorization Theory," *Small Group Research* 22 (1991), pp. 360–79.

96. L.M. Fisher, "Ricardo Semler Won't Take Control," *strategy + business*, no. 41 (Winter 2005), pp. 1–11.

97. Meindl, "On Leadership"; J. Felfe and L.-E. Petersen, "Romance of Leadership and Management Decision Making," *European Journal of Work and Organizational Psychology* 16, no. 1 (2007), pp. 1–24; B. Schyns, J.R. Meindl, and M.A. Croon, "The Romance of Leadership Scale: Cross-Cultural Testing and Refinement," *Leadership* 3, no. 1 (February 2007), pp. 29–46.

98. J. Pfeffer, "The Ambiguity of Leadership," *Academy of Management Review* 2 (1977), pp. 102–12.

99. R. Weber et al., "The Illusion of Leadership: Misattribution of Cause in Coordination Games," *Organization Science* 12, no. 5 (2001), pp. 582–98; N. Ensari and S.E. Murphy, "Cross-Cultural Variations in Leadership Perceptions and Attribution of Charisma to the Leader," *Organizational Behavior and Human Decision Processes* 92 (2003), pp. 52–66; M.L.A. Hayward, V.P. Rindova, and T.G. Pollock, "Believing One's Own Press: The Causes and Consequences of CEO Celebrity," *Strategic Management Journal* 25, no. 7 (July 2004), pp. 637–53.

100. Six of the Project GLOBE clusters are described in a special issue of the *Journal of World Business*, 37 (2000). For an overview of Project GLOBE, see House, Javidan, and Dorfman, "Project GLOBE: An Introduction"; House et al., "Understanding Cultures and Implicit Leadership Theories across the Globe."

101. M.P. Mangaliso, "Building Competitive Advantage from Ubuntu: Management Lessons from South Africa," *Academy of Management Executive* 15 (August 2001), pp. 23–43; L.L. Karsten and H. Illa, "Ubuntu as a Key African Management Concept: Contextual Background and Practical Insights for Knowledge Application," *Journal*

of Managerial Psychology 20, no. 7 (July 2005), pp. 607–20; S. Botha and M. Claassens, "Leadership Competencies: The Contribution of the Bachelor in Management and Leadership (BML) to the Development of Leaders at First National Bank, South Africa," *International Business & Economics Research Journal* 9, no. 10 (October 2010), pp. 77–87; S.G. Marshall, "Vital Signs: Leading with a Spirit of Ubuntu," *Business Days (South Africa),* February 17, 2010; D. Mogadime et al., "Constructing Self as Leader: Case Studies of Women Who Are Change Agents in South Africa," *Urban Education* 45, no. 6 (2010), pp. 797–821; F.W. Ngunjiri, "Lessons in Spiritual Leadership from Kenyan Women," *Journal of Educational Administration* 48, no. 6 (2010), pp. 755–68; I. Wanasika et al., "Managerial Leadership and Culture in Sub-Saharan Africa," *Journal of World Business* 46, no. 2 (2011), pp. 234–41.

102. J.C. Jesiuno, "Latin Europe Cluster: From South to North," *Journal of World Business* 37 (2002), p. 88. Another GLOBE study, of Iranian managers, also reported that "charismatic visionary" stands out as a primary leadership dimension. See A. Dastmalchian, M. Javidan, and K. Alam, "Effective Leadership and Culture in Iran: An Empirical Study," *Applied Psychology: An International Review* 50 (2001), pp. 532–58.

103. D.N. Den Hartog et al., "Culture Specific and Cross-Cultural Generalizable Implicit Leadership Theories: Are Attributes of Charismatic/Transformational Leadership Universally Endorsed?" *Leadership Quarterly* 10 (1999), pp. 219–56; F.C. Brodbeck et al., "Cultural Variation of Leadership Prototypes across 22 European Countries," *Journal of Occupational and Organizational Psychology* 73 (2000), pp. 1–29; E. Szabo et al., "The Europe Cluster: Where Employees Have a Voice," *Journal of World Business* 37 (2002), pp. 55–68. The Mexican study is reported in C.E. Nicholls, H.W. Lane, and M.B. Brechu, "Taking Self-Managed Teams to Mexico," *Academy of Management Executive* 13 (August 1999), pp. 15–25.

104. G.N. Powell, "One More Time: Do Female and Male Managers Differ?" *Academy of Management Executive* 4 (1990), pp. 68–75; M.L. van Engen and T.M. Willemsen, "Sex and Leadership Styles: A Meta-Analysis of Research Published in the 1990s," *Psychological Reports* 94, no. 1 (February 2004), pp. 3–18.

105. R. Sharpe, "As Leaders, Women Rule," *BusinessWeek,* November 20, 2000, p. 74; M. Sappenfield, "Women, It Seems, Are Better Bosses," *Christian Science Monitor,* January 16, 2001; A.H. Eagly and L.L. Carli, "The Female Leadership Advantage: An Evaluation of the Evidence," *Leadership Quarterly* 14, no. 6 (December 2003), pp. 807–34; A.H. Eagly, M.C. Johannesen-Schmidt, and M.L. van Engen, "Transformational, Transactional, and Laissez-Faire Leadership Styles: A Meta-Analysis Comparing Women and Men," *Psychological Bulletin* 129 (July 2003), pp. 569–91.

106. A.H. Eagly, S.J. Karau, and M.G. Makhijani, "Gender and the Effectiveness of Leaders: A Meta-Analysis," *Psychological Bulletin* 117 (1995), pp. 125–45; J.G. Oakley, "Gender-Based Barriers to Senior Management Positions: Understanding the Scarcity of Female CEOs," *Journal of Business Ethics* 27 (2000), pp. 821–34; N.Z. Stelter, "Gender Differences in Leadership: Current Social Issues and Future Organizational Implications," *Journal of Leadership Studies* 8 (2002), pp. 88–99; M.E. Heilman et al., "Penalties for Success: Reactions to Women Who Succeed at Male Gender-Typed Tasks," *Journal of Applied Psychology* 89, no. 3 (2004), pp. 416–27; A.H. Eagly, "Achieving Relational Authenticity in Leadership: Does Gender Matter?" *Leadership Quarterly* 16, no. 3 (June 2005), pp. 459–74.

CHAPTER 13

1. S. Cherry, "Not without Its Merritt's," *Tulsa World,* April 13, 2001, p. 19; D. Blossom, "Bakery Has Recipe for Success," *Tulsa World,* October 28, 2002, p. A7; M. Reynolds, "A Difficult Choice Pays Off for Merritt's Bakery," *Modern Baking,* March 2010, p. 39; S. Cherry, "Bakery Adds Breakfast Items for Its Entourage," *Tulsa World,* February 10, 2011.

2. S. Ranson, R. Hinings, and R. Greenwood, "The Structuring of Organizational Structure," *Administrative Science Quarterly* 25 (1980), pp. 1–14; J.-E. Johanson, "Intraorganizational Influence," *Management Communication Quarterly* 13 (February 2000), pp. 393–435; K. Walsh, "Interpreting the Impact of Culture on Structure," *Journal of Applied Behavioral Science* 40, no. 3 (September 2004), pp. 302–22.

3. H. Mintzberg, *The Structuring of Organizations* (Englewood Cliffs, NJ: Prentice Hall, 1979), pp. 2–3.

4. E.E. Lawler III, *Motivation in Work Organizations* (Monterey, CA: Brooks/Cole, 1973); M.A. Campion, "Ability Requirement Implications of Job Design: An Interdisciplinary Perspective," *Personnel Psychology* 42 (1989), pp. 1–24.

5. G.S. Becker and K.M. Murphy, "The Division-of-Labor, Coordination Costs and Knowledge," *Quarterly Journal of Economics* 107, no. 4 (November 1992), pp. 1137–60; L. Borghans and B. Weel, "The Division of Labour, Worker Organisation, and Technological Change," *Economic Journal* 116, no. 509 (2006), pp. F45–72.

6. Mintzberg, *The Structuring of Organizations,* Ch. 1; D.A. Nadler and M.L. Tushman, *Competing by Design: The Power of Organizational Architecture* (New York: Oxford University Press, 1997), Ch. 6; J.R. Galbraith, *Designing Organizations: An Executive Guide to Strategy, Structure, and Process* (San Francisco, CA: Jossey-Bass, 2002), Ch. 4.

7. J. Stephenson Jr., "Making Humanitarian Relief Networks More Effective: Operational Coordination, Trust and Sense Making," *Disasters* 29, no. 4 (2005), p. 337.

8. Willem, M. Buelens, and H. Scarbrough, "The Role of Inter-Unit Coordination Mechanisms in Knowledge Sharing: A Case Study of a British MNC," *Journal of Information Science* 32, no. 6 (2006), pp. 539–61; R.R. Gulati, "Silo Busting," *Harvard Business Review* 85, no. 5 (2007), pp. 98–108.

9. Borghans and Weel, "The Division of Labour."

10. T. Van Alphen, "Magna in Overdrive," *Toronto Star,* July 24, 2006.

11. For a discussion of the role of brand manager at Procter & Gamble, see C. Peale, "Branded for Success," *Cincinnati Enquirer,* May 20, 2001, p. A1. Details about how to design integrator roles in organizational structures are presented in Galbraith, *Designing Organizations,* pp. 66–72.

12. M. Hoque, M. Akter, and Y. Monden, "Concurrent Engineering: A Compromise Approach to Develop a Feasible and Customer-Pleasing Product," *International Journal of Production Research* 43, no. 8 (2005), pp. 1607–24; S.M. Sapuan, M.R. Osman, and Y. Nukman, "State of the Art of the Concurrent Engineering Technique in the Automotive Industry," *Journal of Engineering Design* 17, no. 2 (2006), pp. 143–57; D.H. Kincade, C. Regan, and F.Y. Gibson, "Concurrent Engineering for Product Development in Mass Customization for the Apparel Industry," *International Journal of Operations & Production Management* 27, no. 6 (2007), pp. 627–49.

13. A.H. Van De Ven, A.L. Delbecq, and R.J. Koenig Jr., "Determinants of Coordination Modes within Organizations," *American Sociological Review* 41, no. 2 (1976), pp. 322–38.

14. M. Villano, "The Control Freak in the Corner Office," *The New York Times,* May 28, 2006, p. 10; "One-Third of Employees Feel Micromanaged by Boss," BlessingWhite news release, October 27, 2008; "Lack of Communication with Staff Most Damaging to Morale, Survey Finds," Accountemps news release, November 20, 2008; "SHRM Poll: Intergenerational Conflict in the Workplace," *HRMagazine,* May 2011; T. Gould, "How Employees Really Feel about Their Bosses," *HR Morning,* July 7, 2011.

15. Y.-M. Hsieh and A. Tien-Hsieh, "Enhancement of Service Quality with Job Standardisation," *Service Industries Journal* 21 (July 2001), pp. 147–66.

16. For recent discussion of span of control, see N.A. Theobald and S. Nicholson-Crotty, "The Many Faces of Span of Control: Organizational Structure across Multiple Goals," *Administration Society* 36, no. 6 (January 2005), pp. 648–60; R.M. Meyer, "Span of Management: Concept Analysis," *Journal of Advanced Nursing* 63, no. 1 (2008), pp. 104–12.

17. H. Fayol, *General and Industrial Management*, trans. C. Storrs (London: Pitman, 1949); D.D. Van Fleet and A.G. Bedeian, "A History of the Span of Management," *Academy of Management Review* 2 (1977), pp. 356–72; D.A. Wren, A.G. Bedeian, and J.D. Breeze, "The Foundations of Henri Fayol's Administrative Theory," *Management Decision* 40, no. 9 (2002), pp. 906–18.

18. D. Drickhamer, "Lessons from the Leading Edge," *Industry Week,* February 21, 2000, pp. 23–26.

19. G. Anders, "Overseeing More Employees—with Fewer Managers— Consultants Are Urging Companies to Loosen Their Supervising Views," *The Wall Street Journal,* March 24, 2008, p. B6.

20. D.D. Van Fleet and A.G. Bedeian, "A History of the Span of Management," *Academy of Management Review* 2 (July 1977), pp. 356–72; B. Davison, "Management Span of Control: How Wide Is Too Wide?" *Journal of Business Strategy* 24, no. 4 (2003), pp. 22–29; S. Nix et al., *Span of Control in City Government Increases Overall* (Seattle, WA: Office of City Auditor, City of Seattle, September 2005); "Fedex 2008 Shareowners Meeting," September 29, 2008; State of Iowa, "Results Iowa: Operational Scan," February 1, 2008; J. McLellan, *Administrative Review: An Agenda for Business Improvement* (Portland, OR: Multnomah County, May 2009); D. Thompson, "More on the Span of Control Issue," *Statesman Journal Blog (Oregon),* May 16, 2011.

21. J. Greenwald, "Ward Compares the Best with the Rest," *Business Insurance,* August 26, 2002, p. 16.

22. J.H. Gittell, "Supervisory Span, Relational Coordination and Flight Departure Performance: A Reassessment of Postbureaucracy Theory," *Organization Science* 12, no. 4 (July–August 2001), pp. 468–83.

23. T.D. Wall, J.L. Cordery, and C.W. Clegg, "Empowerment, Performance, and Operational Uncertainty: A Theoretical Integration," *Applied Psychology: An International Review* 51 (2002), pp. 146–69.

24. J. Denby, "Leaders in African Electricity," *African Business Review,* May 11, 2010.

25. Q.N. Huy, "In Praise of Middle Managers," *Harvard Business Review* 79 (September 2001), pp. 72–79; C.R. Littler, R. Wiesner, and R. Dunford, "The Dynamics of Delayering: Changing Management Structures in Three Countries," *Journal of Management Studies* 40, no. 2 (2003), pp. 225–56; H.J. Leavitt, *Top Down: Why Hierarchies Are Here to Stay and How to Manage Them More Effectively* (Cambridge: Harvard Business School Press, 2005); L. McCann, J. Morris, and J. Hassard, "Normalized Intensity: The New Labour Process of Middle Management," *Journal of Management Studies* 45, no. 2 (2008), pp. 343–71; "Why Middle Managers May Be the Most Important People in Your Company," *Knowledge @ Wharton,* May 25, 2011.

26. K. Tyler, "The Strongest Link," *HRMagazine,* 2011, pp. 51–53.

27. Littler, Wiesner, and Dunford, "The Dynamics of Delayering."

28. J. Morris, J. Hassard, and L. McCann, "New Organizational Forms, Human Resource Management and Structural Convergence? A Study of Japanese Organizations," *Organization Studies* 27, no. 10 (2006), pp. 1485–511.

29. "BASF Culling Saves (GBP) 4m," *Personnel Today,* February 19, 2002, p. 3; S. Marchionne, "Navigating the New Automotive Epoch," *Vital Speeches of the Day* (March 2010), pp. 134–37.

30. J. Kersnar, "Forget What You Think You Know," *CFO Magazine,* January/February 2011, pp. 29–33.

31. W. Stueck, "Revamped Barrick Keeps Eyes on the Hunt for the Golden Prize," *Globe & Mail,* September 17, 2005, p. B4; Barrick Gold Corporation, *Annual Report 2007* (Toronto: Barrick Gold Corporation, April 2008).

32. S. Wetlaufer, "The Business Case against Revolution: An Interview with Nestle's Peter Brabeck," *Harvard Business Review* 79, no. 2 (February 2001), pp. 112–19; H.A. Richardson et al., "Does Decentralization Make a Difference for the Organization? An Examination of the Boundary Conditions Circumscribing Decentralized Decision-Making and Organizational Financial Performance," *Journal of Management* 28, no. 2 (2002), pp. 217–44; G. Masada, "To Centralize or Decentralize?" *Optimize,* May 2005, pp. 58–61.

33. J.G. Kelley, "Slurpees and Sausages: 7-Eleven Holds School," *Richmond (Va.) Times-Dispatch,* March 12, 2004, p. C1; S. Marling, "The 24-Hour Supply Chain," *InformationWeek,* January 26, 2004, p. 43.

34. Mintzberg, *The Structuring of Organizations,* Ch. 5.

35. W. Dessein and T. Santos, "Adaptive Organizations," *Journal of Political Economy* 114, no. 5 (2006), pp. 956–95; A.A.M. Nasurdin et al., "Organizational Structure and Organizational Climate as Potential Predictors of Job Stress: Evidence from Malaysia," *International Journal of Commerce and Management* 16, no. 2 (2006), pp. 116–29; C.-J. Chen and J.-W. Huang, "How Organizational Climate and Structure Affect Knowledge Management—the Social Interaction Perspective," *International Journal of Information Management* 27, no. 2 (2007), pp. 104–18.

36. T. Burns and G. Stalker, *The Management of Innovation* (London: Tavistock, 1961).

37. J. Tata, S. Prasad, and R. Thom, "The Influence of Organizational Structure on the Effectiveness of TQM Programs," *Journal of Managerial Issues* 11, no. 4 (Winter 1999), pp. 440–53; A. Lam, "Tacit Knowledge, Organizational Learning and Societal Institutions: An Integrated Framework," *Organization Studies* 21 (May 2000), pp. 487–513.

38. P. Lavoie, "TAXI," *Campaign,* October 12, 2007, p. 15; L. Sylvain, "Taxi Deconstructed," *Strategy,* June 2007, p. 50; S. Vranica, "For Small Agency, a Battle to Shed 'Boutique Stigma,'" *The Wall Street Journal,* August 8, 2007, p. B2D; E. Wexler, "There's No Stopping TAXI," *Strategy,* January 2011, pp. 40–42. Information was also collected from the company's website: www.taxi.ca. Although it was recently acquired by WPP, the world's largest creative holding company, TAXI apparently will remain an autonomous business and use WPP's resources for European and further international expansion.

39. W.D. Sine, H. Mitsuhashi, and D.A. Kirsch, "Revisiting Burns and Stalker: Formal Structure and New Venture Performance in Emerging Economic Sectors," *Academy of Management Journal* 49, no. 1 (2006), pp. 121–32.

40. Mintzberg, *The Structuring of Organizations,* p. 106.

41. Ibid., Ch. 17.

42. Galbraith, *Designing Organizations,* pp. 23–25.

43. E.E. Lawler III, *Rewarding Excellence: Pay Strategies for the New Economy* (San Francisco, CA: Jossey-Bass, 2000), pp. 31–34.

44. These structures were identified from corporate websites and annual reports. These organizations typically rely on a mixture of other structures, so the charts shown have been adapted for learning purposes.

45. Toyota North American Quality Advisory Panel, *A Road Forward: The Report of the Toyota North American Quality Advisory Panel* (Washington, DC: Toyota North American Quality Advisory Panel, May 2011).

46. M. Goold and A. Campbell, "Do You Have a Well-Designed Organization," *Harvard Business Review* 80 (March 2002), pp. 117–24.

47. J.R. Galbraith, "Structuring Global Organizations," in *Tomorrow's Organization,* ed. S. A. Mohrman et al. (San Francisco, CA: Jossey-Bass, 1998), pp. 103–29; C. Homburg, J.P. Workman Jr., and O. Jensen,

"Fundamental Changes in Marketing Organization: The Movement toward a Corganizational Structure," *Academy of Marketing Science Journal* 28 (Fall 2000), pp. 459–78; T.H. Davenport, J.G. Harris, and A.K. Kohli, "How Do They Know Their Customers So Well?" *Sloan Management Review* 42 (Winter 2001), pp. 63–73; J.R. Galbraith, "Organizing to Deliver Solutions," *Organizational Dynamics* 31 (2002), pp. 194–207.

48. S.J. Palmisano, "The Globally Integrated Enterprise," *Foreign Affairs* 85, no. 3 (May/June 2006), pp. 127–36; S. Palmisano, "The Globally Integrated Enterprise," *Vital Speeches of the Day* 73, no. 10 (2007), pp. 449–53.

49. "IBM Moves Engineering VP to China as Part of Global Focus," *Manufacturing Business Technology,* September 2007, p. 13; J. Bonasia, "Globalization: Learning to Close the Continental Divide," *Investor's Business Daily,* September 7, 2007.

50. A. Deutschman, "The Fabric of Creativity," *Fast Company,* December 2004, pp. 54ff; P.J. Kiger, "Power to the Individual," *Workforce Management,* February 27, 2006, pp. 1–7; G. Hamel, *The Future of Management* (Boston: Harvard Business School Press, 2007), Ch. 5.

51. J.R. Galbraith, E.E. Lawler III, and associates, *Organizing for the Future: The New Logic for Managing Complex Organizations* (San Francisco, CA: Jossey-Bass, 1993); R. Bettis and M. Hitt, "The New Competitive Landscape," *Strategic Management Journal* 16 (1995), pp. 7–19.

52. P.C. Ensign, "Interdependence, Coordination, and Structure in Complex Organizations: Implications for Organization Design," *Mid-Atlantic Journal of Business* 34 (March 1998), pp. 5–22.

53. M.M. Fanning, "A Circular Organization Chart Promotes a Hospital-Wide Focus on Teams," *Hospital & Health Services Administration* 42 (June 1997), pp. 243–54; L.Y. Chan and B.E. Lynn, "Operating in Turbulent Times: How Ontario's Hospitals Are Meeting the Current Funding Crisis," *Health Care Management Review* 23 (June 1998), pp. 7–18.

54. R. Cross, "Looking before You Leap: Assessing the Jump to Teams in Knowledge-Based Work," *Business Horizons* (September 2000); M. Fenton-O'Creevy, "Employee Involvement and the Middle Manager: Saboteur or Scapegoat?" *Human Resource Management Journal* 11 (2001), pp. 24–40; G. Garda, K. Lindstrom, and M. Dallnera, "Towards a Learning Organization: The Introduction of a Client-Centered Team-Based Organization in Administrative Surveying Work," *Applied Ergonomics* 34 (2003), pp. 97–105; C. Douglas and W.L. Gardner, "Transition to Self-Directed Work Teams: Implications of Transition Time and Self-Monitoring for Managers' Use of Influence Tactics," *Journal of Organizational Behavior* 25 (2004), pp. 47–65.

55. R. Muzyka and G. Zeschuk, "Managing Multiple Projects," *Game Developer,* March 2003, pp. 34–42; M. Saltzman, "The Ex-Doctors Are In," *National Post,* March 24, 2004, p. AL4; R. McConnell, "For Edmonton's Bioware, Today's the Big Day," *Edmonton Journal,* April 14, 2005, p. C1; D. Gladstone and S. Molloy, "Doctors & Dragons," *Computer Gaming World,* December 2006.

56. R.C. Ford and W.A. Randolph, "Cross-Functional Structures: A Review and Integration of Matrix Organization and Project Management," *Journal of Management* 18 (1992), pp. 267–94.

57. Nestlé's geographic and product structure is somewhat more complex than described here, and its matrix is not quite as balanced. For discussion of these variations, see J.R. Galbraith, *Designing Matrix Organizations That Actually Work* (San Francisco, CA: Jossey-Bass, 2009).

58. G. Calabrese, "Communication and Co-Operation in Product Development: A Case Study of a European Car Producer," *R&D Management* 27 (July 1997), pp. 239–52; T. Sy and L.S. D'Annunzio, "Challenges and Strategies of Matrix Organizations: Top-Level and Mid-Level Managers' Perspectives," *Human Resource Planning* 28, no. 1 (2005), pp. 39–48.

59. D. Enrich, "Citigroup Will Revamp Capital-Markets Group," *The Wall Street Journal,* August 23, 2008, p. B7.

60. K. Poynter, *Data Security at HMRC,* Progress Report to Chancellor of the Exchequer and HM Treasury, December 14, 2007; V. Houlder, "The Merger That Exposed a Taxing Problem for Managers," *Financial Times,* July 11, 2008, p. 12; K. Poynter, *Review of Information Security at HM Revenue and Customs* (London: HM Treasury, Government of the United Kingdom, June 2008).

61. Nadler and Tushman, *Competing by Design,* Ch. 6; M. Goold and A. Campbell, "Structured Networks: Towards the Well-Designed Matrix," *Long Range Planning* 36, no. 5 (October 2003), pp. 427–39.

62. D. Ciampa and M. Watkins, "Rx for New CEOs," *Chief Executive,* January 2008.

63. P. Siekman, "This Is Not a BMW Plant," *Fortune,* April 18, 2005, p. 208; "Magna's Austria Plant to Lose Production of BMW X3," *Reuters,* May 16, 2007.

64. R.F. Miles and C.C. Snow, "The New Network Firm: A Spherical Structure Built on a Human Investment Philosophy," *Organizational Dynamics* 23, no. 4 (1995), pp. 5–18; C. Baldwin and K. Clark, "Managing in an Age of Modularity," *Harvard Business Review* 75 (September–October 1997), pp. 84–93.

65. J. Hagel III and M. Singer, "Unbundling the Corporation," *Harvard Business Review* 77 (March–April 1999), pp. 133–41; R. Hacki and J. Lighton, "The Future of the Networked Company," *McKinsey Quarterly* 3 (2001), pp. 26–39.

66. J. Dwyer, "Mind How You Go," *Facilities Management,* May 2008, pp. 22–25.

67. M.A. Schilling and H.K. Steensma, "The Use of Modular Organizational Forms: An Industry-Level Analysis," *Academy of Management Journal* 44 (December 2001), pp. 1149–68.

68. G. Morgan, *Images of Organization,* 2nd ed. (Newbury Park, CA: Sage, 1996); G. Morgan, *Imagin-I-Zation: New Mindsets for Seeing, Organizing and Managing* (Thousand Oaks, CA: Sage, 1997).

69. H. Chesbrough and D.J. Teece, "When Is Virtual Virtuous? Organizing for Innovation," *Harvard Business Review* (January–February 1996), pp. 65–73; P.M.J. Christie and R. Levary, "Virtual Corporations: Recipe for Success," *Industrial Management* 40 (July 1998), pp. 7–11.

70. L. Donaldson, *The Contingency Theory of Organizations* (Thousand Oaks, CA: Sage, 2001); J. Birkinshaw, R. Nobel, and J. Ridderstråle, "Knowledge as a Contingency Variable: Do the Characteristics of Knowledge Predict Organizational Structure?" *Organization Science* 13, no. 3 (May–June 2002), pp. 274–89.

71. P.R. Lawrence and J.W. Lorsch, *Organization and Environment* (Homewood, IL: Irwin, 1967); Mintzberg, *The Structuring of Organizations,* Ch. 15.

72. Burns and Stalker, *The Management of Innovation;* Lawrence and Lorsch, *Organization and Environment.*

73. Mintzberg, *The Structuring of Organizations,* p. 282.

74. C. Perrow, "A Framework for the Comparative Analysis of Organizations," *American Sociological Review* 32 (1967), pp. 194–208; D. Gerwin, "The Comparative Analysis of Structure and Technology: A Critical Appraisal," *Academy of Management Review* 4, no. 1 (1979), pp. 41–51; C.C. Miller et al., "Understanding Technology-Structure Relationships: Theory Development and Meta-Analytic Theory Testing," *Academy of Management Journal* 34, no. 2 (1991), pp. 370–99.

75. D.S. Pugh and C.R. Hinings, *Organizational Structure: Extensions and Replications* (Farnborough, England: Lexington Books, 1976); Mintzberg, *The Structuring of Organizations,* Ch. 13.

76. Galbraith, *Designing Organizations,* pp. 52–55; G. Hertel, S. Geister, and U. Konradt, "Managing Virtual Teams: A Review of Current

Empirical Research," *Human Resource Management Review* 15 (2005), pp. 69–95.

77. P. Glader, "It's Not Easy Being Lean," *The Wall Street Journal,* June 19, 2006, p. B1; Nucor Corporation, "About Us," 2008, http://www.nucor.com/indexinner.aspx?finpage=aboutus.

78. R.H. Kilmann, *Beyond the Quick Fix* (San Francisco, CA: Jossey-Bass, 1984), p. 38.

79. A.D. Chandler, *Strategy and Structure* (Cambridge, MA.: MIT Press, 1962).

80. D. Miller, "Configurations of Strategy and Structure," *Strategic Management Journal* 7 (1986), pp. 233–49.

CHAPTER 14

1. H. Blodget, "Mark Zuckerberg, Moving Fast and Breaking Things," *Business Insider,* October 14, 2010; K. Ladendorf, "For Facebook Workers, It's Not Just a Job," *Austin American-Statesman,* May 1, 2011, p. E1; K. Raghav, "'We Paint the Walls,'" *LiveMint,* June 10, 2011; M. Swift, "Facebook Landing Team Transports Company Culture," *San Jose Mercury News (Calif.),* March 25, 2011.

2. A. Williams, P. Dobson, and M. Walters, *Changing Culture: New Organizational Approaches* (London: Institute of Personnel Management, 1989); E.H. Schein, "What Is Culture?" in *Reframing Organizational Culture,* ed. P. J. Frost et al. (Newbury Park, CA: Sage, 1991), 243–53.

3. B.M. Meglino and E.C. Ravlin, "Individual Values in Organizations: Concepts, Controversies, and Research," *Journal of Management* 24, no. 3 (1998), pp. 351–89; B.R. Agle and C.B. Caldwell, "Understanding Research on Values in Business," *Business and Society* 38, no. 3 (September 1999), pp. 326–87; S. Hitlin and J.A. Pilavin, "Values: Reviving a Dormant Concept," *Annual Review of Sociology* 30 (2004), pp. 359–93.

4. N.M. Ashkanasy, "The Case for Culture," in *Debating Organization,* ed. R. Westwood and S. Clegg (Malden, MA: Blackwell, 2003), pp. 300–10.

5. Information about the corporate values of Zappos and Gap Adventures came from their company websites: http://about.zappos.com/our-unique-culture/zappos-core-values and http://www.gapadventures.com/about-us/gap-adventures/.

6. B. Kabanoff and J. Daly, "Espoused Values in Organisations," *Australian Journal of Management* 27, Special issue (2002), pp. 89–104.

7. *Netflix Culture: Freedom & Responsibility* (Los Gatos, CA: Netflix, 2011).

8. "Norway Criticizes BP, Smedvig over Safety," *Energy Compass,* January 3, 2003; J.A. Lozano, "BP Refinery Had History of Dangerous Releases, Report Finds," *Associated Press,* October 28, 2005; S. McNulty, "A Corroded Culture?" *Financial Times (London),* December 18, 2006, p. 17; U.S. Chemical Safety and Hazard Investigation Board, *Investigation Report: Refinery Explosion and Fire (BP, Texas City, Texas, March 23, 2005)* (Washington, DC: U.S. Chemical Safety Board, March 2007); S. Greenhouse, "BP Faces Record Fine for '05 Refinery Explosion," *The New York Times,* October 30, 2009; L.C. Steffy, *Drowning in Oil: BP and the Reckless Pursuit of Profit* (New York: McGraw-Hill, 2011).

9. C.A. O'Reilly III, J. Chatman, and D.F. Caldwell, "People and Organizational Culture: A Profile Comparison Approach to Assessing Person–Organization Fit," *Academy of Management Journal* 34 (1991), pp. 487–516; J.J. van Muijen, "Organizational Culture," in *A Handbook of Work and Organizational Psychology: Organizational Psychology,* ed. P.J.D. Drenth, H. Thierry, and C.J. de Wolff, 2nd ed. (East Sussex, UK: Psychology Press, 1998), pp. 113–32; P.A. Balthazard, R.A. Cooke, and R.E. Potter, "Dysfunctional Culture, Dysfunctional Organization: Capturing the Behavioral Norms That Form Organizational Culture and Drive Performance," *Journal of Managerial Psychology* 21, no. 8 (2006), pp. 709–32; C. Helfrich et al., "Assessing an Organizational Culture Instrument Based on the Competing Values

Framework: Exploratory and Confirmatory Factor Analyses," *Implementation Science* 2, no. 1 (2007), p. 13. For recent reviews of organizational culture survey instruments, see T. Scott et al., "The Quantitative Measurement of Organizational Culture in Health Care: A Review of the Available Instruments," *Health Services Research* 38, no. 3 (2003), pp. 923–45; D.E. Leidner and T. Kayworth, "A Review of Culture in Information Systems Research: Toward a Theory of Information Technology Culture Conflict," *MIS Quarterly* 30, no. 2 (2006), pp. 357–99; S. Scott-Findlay and C.A. Estabrooks, "Mapping the Organizational Culture Research in Nursing: A Literature Review," *Journal of Advanced Nursing* 56, no. 5 (2006), pp. 498–513.

10. J. Martin, P.J. Frost, and O.A. O'Neill, "Organizational Culture: Beyond Struggles for Intellectual Dominance," in *Handbook of Organization Studies,* ed. S. Clegg et al., 2nd ed. (London: Sage, 2006), pp. 725–53; N.E. Fenton and S. Inglis, "A Critical Perspective on Organizational Values," *Nonprofit Management and Leadership* 17, no. 3 (2007), pp. 335–47; K. Haukelid, "Theories of (Safety) Culture Revisited—An Anthropological Approach," *Safety Science* 46, no. 3 (2008), pp. 413–26.

11. J.A. Baker III et al., *The Report of the BP U.S. Refineries Independent Safety Review Panel* (Houston: The BP U.S. Refineries Independent Safety Review Panel, February 2007).

12. J. Martin and C. Siehl, "Organizational Culture and Counterculture: An Uneasy Symbiosis," *Organizational Dynamics* (Autumn 1983), pp. 52–64; G. Hofstede, "Identifying Organizational Subcultures: An Empirical Approach," *Journal of Management Studies* 35, no. 1 (1990), pp. 1–12; E. Ogbonna and L.C. Harris, "Organisational Culture in the Age of the Internet: An Exploratory Study," *New Technology, Work and Employment* 21, no. 2 (2006), pp. 162–75.

13. H. Silver, "Does a University Have a Culture?" *Studies in Higher Education* 28, no. 2 (2003), pp. 157–69.

14. A. Sinclair, "Approaches to Organizational Culture and Ethics," *Journal of Business Ethics* 12 (1993); T.E. Deal and A.A. Kennedy, *The New Corporate Cultures* (Cambridge, MA: Perseus Books, 1999), Ch. 10; A. Boisnier and J. Chatman, "The Role of Subcultures in Agile Organizations," in *Leading and Managing People in Dynamic Organizations,* ed. R. Petersen and E. Mannix (Mahwah, NJ: Lawrence Erlbaum Associates, 2003), pp. 87–112; C. Morrill, M.N. Zald, and H. Rao, "Covert Political Conflict in Organizations: Challenges from Below," *Annual Review of Sociology* 29 (2003), pp. 391–415.

15. J.S. Ott, *The Organizational Culture Perspective* (Pacific Grove, CA: Brooks/Cole, 1989), Ch. 2; J.S. Pederson and J.S. Sorensen, *Organizational Cultures in Theory and Practice* (Aldershot, England: Gower, 1989), pp. 27–29; M.O. Jones, *Studying Organizational Symbolism: What, How, Why?* (Thousand Oaks, CA: Sage, 1996).

16. E.H. Schein, "Organizational Culture," *American Psychologist* (February 1990), pp. 109–19; A. Furnham and B. Gunter, "Corporate Culture: Definition, Diagnosis, and Change," *International Review of Industrial and Organizational Psychology* 8 (1993), pp. 233–61; E.H. Schein, *The Corporate Culture Survival Guide* (San Francisco, CA: Jossey-Bass, 1999), Ch. 4.

17. M. Doehrman, "Anthropologists—Deep in the Corporate Bush," *Daily Record (Kansas City, Missouri),* July 19, 2005, p. 1.

18. K. Roman, "The House That Ogilvy Built," *strategy + business,* April 29, 2009, pp. 1–5.

19. T.E. Deal and A.A. Kennedy, *Corporate Cultures* (Reading, MA: Addison-Wesley, 1982), Ch. 5; C.J. Boudens, "The Story of Work: A Narrative Analysis of Workplace Emotion," *Organization Studies* 26, no. 9 (2005), pp. 1285–306; S. Denning, *The Leader's Guide to Storytelling* (San Francisco, CA: Jossey-Bass, 2005).

20. A.L. Wilkins, "Organizational Stories as Symbols Which Control the Organization," in *Organizational Symbolism,* ed. L. R. Pondy et al. (Greenwich, CT: JAI Press, 1984), pp. 81–92; R. Zemke, "Storytelling: Back to a Basic," *Training* 27 (March 1990), pp. 44–50; J.C. Meyer,

"Tell Me a Story: Eliciting Organizational Values from Narratives," *Communication Quarterly* 43 (1995), pp. 210–24; W. Swap et al., "Using Mentoring and Storytelling to Transfer Knowledge in the Workplace," *Journal of Management Information Systems* 18 (Summer 2001), pp. 95–114.

21. A.C.T. Smith and B. Stewart, "Organizational Rituals: Features, Functions and Mechanisms," *International Journal of Management Reviews* (2011), in press.

22. "The Ultimate Chairman," *Business Times Singapore,* September 3, 2005.

23. A. Gostick and C. Elton, *The Orange Revolution* (New York: The Free Press, 2010), pp. 214–16; A. Powers, "Zappos Tours Showcase Company's Quirks," *Los Angeles Times,* April 29, 2011.

24. D. Roth, "My Job at the Container Store," *Fortune,* January 10, 2000, pp. 74–78.

25. R.E. Quinn and N.T. Snyder, "Advance Change Theory: Culture Change at Whirlpool Corporation," in *The Leader's Change Handbook,* ed. J.A. Conger, G.M. Spreitzer, and E.E. Lawler III (San Francisco, CA: Jossey-Bass, 1999), pp. 162–93.

26. Churchill apparently made this statement on October 28, 1943, in the British House of Commons, when London, damaged by bombings in World War II, was about to be rebuilt.

27. G. Turner and J. Myerson, *New Workspace, New Culture: Office Design as a Catalyst for Change* (Aldershot, UK: Gower, 1998).

28. P. Roberts, "The Empire Strikes Back," *Fast Company,* no. 22 (February–March 1999), pp. 122–31; H. Nguyen, "Oakley Shades for Her Eyes Only," *Orange County Register (Santa Ana, California),* May 11, 2006. Details and photos also can be found at http://www.oakley.com; http://americahurrah.com/Oakley/Entry.htm.

29. K.D. Elsbach and B.A. Bechky, "It's More Than a Desk: Working Smarter through Leveraged Office Design," *California Management Review* 49, no. 2 (Winter 2007), pp. 80–101.

30. M. Burton, "Open Plan, Open Mind," *Director* (March 2005), pp. 68–72; B. Murray, "Agency Profile: Mother London," *Ihaveanidea,* January 28, 2007, http://www.ihaveanidea.org.

31. K. Frieberg and J. Frieberg, *Nuts!* (New York: Bantam Doubleday Dell, 1998), p. 144; P. Stafford, "Keeping Culture Intact as You Grow," *SmartCompany,* June 29, 2011, http://SmartCompany.com.au.

32. J.C. Collins and J.I. Porras, *Built to Last: Successful Habits of Visionary Companies* (London: Century, 1994); Deal and Kennedy, *The New Corporate Cultures;* R. Barrett, *Building a Values-Driven Organization: A Whole System Approach to Cultural Transformation* (Burlington, MA: Butterworth-Heinemann, 2006); J.M. Kouzes and B.Z. Posner, *The Leadership Challenge,* 4th ed. (San Francisco, CA: Jossey-Bass, 2007), Ch. 3.

33. C. Siehl and J. Martin, "Organizational Culture: A Key to Financial Performance?" in *Organizational Climate and Culture,* ed. B. Schneider (San Francisco, CA: Jossey-Bass, 1990), pp. 241–81; G.G. Gordon and N. DiTomasco, "Predicting Corporate Performance from Organizational Culture," *Journal of Management Studies* 29 (1992), pp. 783–98; J.P. Kotter and J.L. Heskett, *Corporate Culture and Performance* (New York: The Free Press, 1992); C.P.M. Wilderom, U. Glunk, and R. Maslowski, "Organizational Culture as a Predictor of Organizational Performance," in *Handbook of Organizational Culture and Climate,* ed. N.M. Ashkanasy, C.P.M. Wilderom, and M.F. Peterson (Thousand Oaks, CA: Sage, 2000), pp. 193–210; A. Carmeli and A. Tishler, "The Relationships between Intangible Organizational Elements and Organizational Performance," *Strategic Management Journal* 25 (2004), pp. 1257–78; S. Teerikangas and P. Very, "The Culture-Performance Relationship in M&A: From Yes/No to How," *British Journal of Management* 17, no. S1 (2006), pp. S31–48.

34. J.C. Helms Mills and A.J. Mills, "Rules, Sensemaking, Formative Contexts, and Discourse in the Gendering of Organizational

Culture," in *International Handbook of Organizational Climate and Culture,* ed. N. Ashkanasy, C. Wilderom, and M. Peterson (Thousand Oaks, CA: Sage, 2000), pp. 55–70; J.A. Chatman and S.E. Cha, "Leading by Leveraging Culture," *California Management Review* 45 (Summer 2003), pp. 20–34.

35. B. Ashforth and F. Mael, "Social Identity Theory and the Organization," *Academy of Management Review* 14 (1989), pp. 20–39.

36. Heidrick & Struggles, *Leadership Challenges Emerge as Asia Pacific Companies Go Global* (Melbourne: Heidrick & Struggles, 2008).

37. M.R. Louis, "Surprise and Sensemaking: What Newcomers Experience in Entering Unfamiliar Organizational Settings," *Administrative Science Quarterly* 25 (1980), pp. 226–51; S.G. Harris, "Organizational Culture and Individual Sensemaking: A Schema-Based Perspective," *Organization Science* 5 (1994), pp. 309–21.

38. J.W. Barnes et al., "The Role of Culture Strength in Shaping Sales Force Outcomes," *Journal of Personal Selling & Sales Management* 26, no. 3 (Summer 2006), pp. 255–70.

39. A. Krishnan, "CEOs from the Best Provide Insights Gained from Hewitt Best Employers Study," *The Edge (Malaysia),* July 21, 2008.

40. N. Byrnes, P. Burrows, and L. Lee, "Dark Days at Dell," *BusinessWeek,* September 4, 2006, p. 26; S. Lohr, "Can Michael Dell Refocus His Namesake?" *The New York Times,* September 9, 2007, p. 1.

41. C.A. O'Reilly III and J.A. Chatman, "Culture as Social Control: Corporations, Cults, and Commitment," *Research in Organizational Behavior* 18 (1996), pp. 157–200; B. Spector and H. Lane, "Exploring the Distinctions between a High Performance Culture and a Cult," *Strategy & Leadership* 35, no. 3 (2007), pp. 18–24.

42. The terms "organizational culture" and "corporate culture" were popularized in 1982 in Deal and Kennedy, *Corporate Cultures;* T.J. Peters and R.H. Waterman, *In Search of Excellence: Lessons from America's Best-Run Companies* (New York: Warner, 1982). However, there are several early references to an organization's culture, including N. Margulies, "Organizational Culture and Psychological Growth," *Journal of Applied Behavioral Science* 5, no. 4 (December 1, 1969), pp. 491–508; S. Silverzweig and R.F. Allen, "Changing the Corporate Culture," *Sloan Management Review* 17, no. 3 (1976), p. 33.

43. P.F. Hewlin, "And the Award for Best Actor Goes To . . . : Facades of Conformity in Organizational Settings," *Academy of Management Review* 28, no. 4 (2003), pp. 633–42.

44. G.R. Maio and J.M. Olson, "Values as Truisms: Evidence and Implications," *Journal of Personality and Social Psychology* 74, no. 2 (1998), pp. 294–311; G.R. Maio et al., "Addressing Discrepancies between Values and Behavior: The Motivating Effect of Reasons," *Journal of Experimental Social Psychology* 37, no. 2 (2001), pp. 104–17.

45. Kotter and Heskett, *Corporate Culture and Performance;* J.P. Kotter, "Cultures and Coalitions," *Executive Excellence* 15 (March 1998), pp. 14–15; B.M. Bass and R.E. Riggio, *Transformational Leadership,* 2nd ed. (New York: Routledge, 2006), Ch. 7. The term *adaptive culture* has a different meaning in organizational behavior than in cultural anthropology, where it refers to nonmaterial cultural conditions (such as ways of thinking) that lag the material culture (physical artifacts). For the anthropological perspective, see W. Griswold, *Cultures and Societies in a Changing World,* 3rd ed. (Thousand Oaks, CA: Pine Forge Press, Sage, 2008), p. 66.

46. W.E. Baker and J.M. Sinkula, "The Synergistic Effect of Market Orientation and Learning Orientation on Organizational Performance," *Academy of Marketing Science Journal* 27, no. 4 (Fall 1999), pp. 411–27; Z. Emden, A. Yaprak, and S.T. Cavusgil, "Learning from Experience in International Alliances: Antecedents and Firm Performance Implications," *Journal of Business Research* 58, no. 7 (2005), pp. 883–92.

47. "Get Me Rewrite: What's Next for Murdoch's Media Empire?" *Knowledge@Wharton,* July 20, 2011; D. Carr, "Troubles That Money Can't Dispel," *The New York Times,* July 17, 2011; I. Chandrasekhar,

M. Wardrop, and A. Trotman, "Phone Hacking: Timeline of the Scandal," *The Telegraph (London),* August 4, 2011; M. Pascoe, "Worst Is Yet to Come for Murdoch," *Sydney Morning Herald,* July 18, 2011.

48. M.L. Sirower, *The Synergy Trap: How Companies Lose the Acquisition Game* (New York: The Free Press, 1997); C. Cook and D. Spitzer, *World Class Transactions* (London: KPMG, 2001); J.P. Daly et al., "The Effects of Initial Differences in Firms' Espoused Values on Their Postmerger Performance," *Journal of Applied Behavioral Science* 40, no. 3 (2004), pp. 323–43; J. Krug, *Mergers and Acquisitions: Turmoil in Top Management Teams* (Williston, VT: Business Expert Press, 2009).

49. M.L. Marks, "Adding Cultural Fit to Your Diligence Checklist," *Mergers & Acquisitions* 34, no. 3 (November–December 1999), pp. 14–20; Schein, *The Corporate Culture Survival Guide,* Ch. 8; M.L. Marks, "Mixed Signals," *Across the Board* (May 2000), pp. 21–26.

50. Teerikangas and Very, "The Culture-Performance Relationship in M&A"; G.K. Stahl and A. Voigt, "Do Cultural Differences Matter in Mergers and Acquisitions? A Tentative Model and Examination," *Organization Science* 19, no. 1 (January 2008), pp. 160–76.

51. R. Smith and D. Fitzpatrick, "Cultures Clash as Merrill Herd Meets 'Wal-Mart of Banking,'" *The Wall Street Journal,* November 14, 2008, p. C1; "Bank of America–Merrill Lynch: A $50 Billion Deal from Hell," *Deal Journal (Wall Street Journal Blog),* January 22, 2009; M. Read, "Wall Street's Entitlement Culture Hard to Shake," *Associated Press,* January 23, 2009; D. Sarch, "Merrill Lynch: Culture Change or Just the Latest Innovation?" *Investment News,* May 27, 2010.

52. C.A. Schorg, C.A. Raiborn, and M.F. Massoud, "Using a 'Cultural Audit' to Pick M&A Winners," *Journal of Corporate Accounting & Finance* (May/June 2004), pp. 47–55; W. Locke, "Higher Education Mergers: Integrating Organisational Cultures and Developing Appropriate Management Styles," *Higher Education Quarterly* 61, no. 1 (2007), pp. 83–102.

53. T. Cody, "The Culture Club," *Mergers & Acquisitions Report* 23, no. 49 (December 6, 2010), p. 10.

54. A.R. Malekazedeh and A. Nahavandi, "Making Mergers Work by Managing Cultures," *Journal of Business Strategy* (May–June 1990), pp. 55–57; K.W. Smith, "A Brand-New Culture for the Merged Firm," *Mergers and Acquisitions* 35 (June 2000), pp. 45–50.

55. T. Hamilton, "RIM on a Roll," *Toronto Star,* February 22, 2004, p. C01.

56. M. Joyce, "Airtran Employees Getting New Culture," *Dallas Business Journal,* July 8, 2011.

57. E. Frauenheim, "Jungle Survival," *Workforce Management,* September 14, 2009, p. 19; B. Lennox and W. Nie, "The Case Study: Creating a Distinct Corporate Culture," *Financial Times (London),* February 17, 2011, p. 14.

58. Hewitt Associates, "Mergers and Acquisitions May Be Driven by Business Strategy—But Often Stumble over People and Culture Issues," PR Newswire news release, August 3, 1998.

59. J. Martin, "Can Organizational Culture Be Managed?" in *Organizational Culture,* ed. P.J. Frost et al. (Beverly Hills, CA: Sage, 1985), pp. 95–98.

60. I. Sharp, *Four Seasons: The Story of a Business Philosophy* (New York: Portfolio, 2009), Ch. 10–11.

61. E.H. Schein, "The Role of the Founder in Creating Organizational Culture," *Organizational Dynamics* 12, no. 1 (Summer 1983), pp. 13–28; R. House, M. Javidan, and P. Dorfman, "Project GLOBE: An Introduction," *Applied Psychology: An International Review* 50 (2001), pp. 489–505; R. House et al., "Understanding Cultures and Implicit Leadership Theories across the Globe: An Introduction to Project GLOBE," *Journal of World Business* 37 (2002), pp. 3–10.

62. A. S. Tsui et al., "Unpacking the Relationship between CEO Leadership Behavior and Organizational Culture," *Leadership Quarterly* 17 (2006), pp. 113–37; Y. Berson, S. Oreg, and T. Dvir, "CEO Values, Organizational Culture and Firm Outcomes," *Journal of Organizational Behavior* 29, no. 5 (July 2008), pp. 615–33.

63. M. De Pree, *Leadership Is an Art* (East Lansing, MI: Michigan State University Press, 1987).

64. J. Kerr and J.W. Slocum Jr., "Managing Corporate Culture through Reward Systems," *Academy of Management Executive* 1 (May 1987), pp. 99–107; J.M. Higgins et al., "Using Cultural Artifacts to Change and Perpetuate Strategy," *Journal of Change Management* 6, no. 4 (2006), pp. 397–415.

65. R. Charan, "Home Depot's Blueprint for Culture Change," *Harvard Business Review* (April 2006), pp. 61–70.

66. K. Tyler, "Evaluating Values," *HRMagazine,* April 2011, p. 57.

67. B. Schneider, "The People Make the Place," *Personnel Psychology* 40, no. 3 (1987), pp. 437–53; B. Schneider et al., "Personality and Organizations: A Test of the Homogeneity of Personality Hypothesis," *Journal of Applied Psychology* 83, no. 3 (June 1998), pp. 462–70; T.R. Giberson, C.J. Resick, and M.W. Dickson, "Embedding Leader Characteristics: An Examination of Homogeneity of Personality and Values in Organizations," *Journal of Applied Psychology* 90, no. 5 (2005), pp. 1002–10.

68. T.A. Judge and D.M. Cable, "Applicant Personality, Organizational Culture, and Organization Attraction," *Personnel Psychology* 50, no. 2 (1997), pp. 359–94; D.S. Chapman et al., "Applicant Attraction to Organizations and Job Choice: A Meta-Analytic Review of the Correlates of Recruiting Outcomes," *Journal of Applied Psychology* 90, no. 5 (2005), pp. 928–44; A.L. Kristof-Brown, R.D. Zimmerman, and E.C. Johnson, "Consequences of Individuals' Fit at Work: A Meta-Analysis of Person-Job, Person-Organization, Person-Group, and Person-Supervisor Fit," *Personnel Psychology* 58, no. 2 (2005), pp. 281–342; C. Hu, H.-C. Su, and C.-I. B. Chen, "The Effect of Person-Organization Fit Feedback via Recruitment Web Sites on Applicant Attraction," *Computers in Human Behavior* 23, no. 5 (2007), pp. 2509–23.

69. P. Nunes and T. Breene, "Reinvent Your Business before It's Too Late," *Harvard Business Review* 89, no. 1/2 (2011), pp. 80–87.

70. A. Kristof-Brown, "Perceived Applicant Fit: Distinguishing between Recruiters' Perceptions of Person-Job and Person-Organization Fit," *Personnel Psychology* 53, no. 3 (Autumn 2000), pp. 643–71; A.E.M. Van Vianen, "Person-Organization Fit: The Match between Newcomers' and Recruiters' Preferences for Organizational Cultures," *Personnel Psychology* 53 (Spring 2000), pp. 113–49.

71. S. Cruz, "Park Place Lexus Mission Viejo Seeing Improvements," *Orange County Business Journal,* May 12, 2008, p. 15; C. Hall, "'Emotional Intelligence' Counts in Job Hires," *Dallas Morning News,* August 20, 2008.

72. D.M. Cable and J.R. Edwards, "Complementary and Supplementary Fit: A Theoretical and Empirical Integration," *Journal of Applied Psychology* 89, no. 5 (2004), pp. 822–34.

73. "WestJet, Tim Hortons and RBC Financial Group," CNW news release, Waterstone Human Capital and National Post, October 13, 2005; Y. Lermusi, "The No. 1 Frustration of Your Job Candidates," August 15, 2006, http://www.ere.net; S. Singleton, "Starbucks, Goodlife Fitness among Most Admired Companies," *Money.Canoe.ca (Toronto),* November 12, 2009; Taleo Research, "Talent Management Processes," 2010, http://www.taleo.com.

74. J. Van Maanen, "Breaking In: Socialization to Work," in *Handbook of Work, Organization, and Society,* ed. R. Dubin (Chicago: Rand McNally, 1976).

75. S.L. McShane, G. O'Neill, and T. Travaglione, "Managing Employee Values in Values-Driven Organizations: Contradiction, Façade, and Illusions," in *21st Annual ANZAM Conference,* Sydney, Australia (December 2007); S.L. McShane, G. O'Neill, and T. Travaglione, "Rethinking the Values-Driven Organization Process: From Values

Engineering to Behavioral Domain Training," paper presented at Academy of Management 2008 Annual Meeting, Anaheim, CA (August 2008).

76. D.G. Allen, "Do Organizational Socialization Tactics Influence Newcomer Embeddedness and Turnover?" *Journal of Management* 32, no. 2 (April 2006), pp. 237–56; A.M. Saks, K.L. Uggerslev, and N.E. Fassina, "Socialization Tactics and Newcomer Adjustment: A Meta-Analytic Review and Test of a Model," *Journal of Vocational Behavior* 70, no. 3 (2007), pp. 413–46.

77. G. T. Chao et al., "Organizational Socialization: Its Content and Consequences," *Journal of Applied Psychology* 79 (1994), pp. 450–63; H.D. Cooper-Thomas and N. Anderson, "Organizational Socialization: A Field Study into Socialization Success and Rate," *International Journal of Selection and Assessment* 13, no. 2 (2005), pp. 116–28.

78. N. Nicholson, "A Theory of Work Role Transitions," *Administrative Science Quarterly* 29 (1984), pp. 172–91; B.E. Ashforth, D.M. Sluss, and A.M. Saks, "Socialization Tactics, Proactive Behavior, and Newcomer Learning: Integrating Socialization Models," *Journal of Vocational Behavior* 70, no. 3 (2007), pp. 447–62; T.N. Bauer, "Newcomer Adjustment during Organizational Socialization: A Meta-Analytic Review of Antecedents, Outcomes, and Methods," *Journal of Applied Psychology* 92, no. 3 (2007), pp. 707–21; A. Elfering et al., "First Years in Job: A Three-Wave Analysis of Work Experiences," *Journal of Vocational Behavior* 70, no. 1 (2007), pp. 97–115.

79. J.M. Beyer and D.R. Hannah, "Building on the Past: Enacting Established Personal Identities in a New Work Setting," *Organization Science* 13 (November/December 2002), pp. 636–52; H.D.C. Thomas and N. Anderson, "Newcomer Adjustment: The Relationship between Organizational Socialization Tactics, Information Acquisition and Attitudes," *Journal of Occupational and Organizational Psychology* 75 (December 2002), pp. 423–37.

80. M. Johne, "Workplace Loyalty a Two-Way Street," *Globe & Mail,* August 5, 2009, p. B13.

81. S.L. Robinson and E. Wolfe Morrison, "The Development of Psychological Contract Breach and Violation: A Longitudinal Study," *Journal of Organizational Behavior* 21, no. 5 (2000), pp. 525–46; K.J. McInnis, J.P. Meyer, and S. Feldman, "Psychological Contracts and Their Implications for Commitment: A Feature-Based Approach," *Journal of Vocational Behavior* 74, no. 2 (2009), pp. 165–80; M.-È. Lapalme, G. Simard, and M. Tremblay, "The Influence of Psychological Contract Breach on Temporary Workers' Commitment and Behaviors: A Multiple Agency Perspective," *Journal of Business and Psychology* (2011), in press.

82. S.L. Robinson and D.M. Rousseau, "Violating the Psychological Contract: Not the Exception but the Norm," *Journal of Organizational Behavior* 15 (1994), pp. 245–59; E.W. Morrison and S.L. Robinson, "When Employees Feel Betrayed: A Model of How Psychological Contract Violation Develops," *Academy of Management Review* 22 (1997), pp. 226–56; S.D. Montes and P.G. Irving, "Disentangling the Effects of Promised and Delivered Inducements: Relational and Transactional Contract Elements and the Mediating Role of Trust," *Journal of Applied Psychology* 93, no. 6 (2008), pp. 1367–81.

83. L.W. Porter, E.E. Lawler III, and J.R. Hackman, *Behavior in Organizations* (New York: McGraw-Hill, 1975), pp. 163–67; Van Maanen, "Breaking In: Socialization to Work"; D.C. Feldman, "The Multiple Socialization of Organization Members," *Academy of Management Review* 6 (1981), pp. 309–18.

84. B.E. Ashforth and A.M. Saks, "Socialization Tactics: Longitudinal Effects on Newcomer Adjustment," *Academy of Management Journal* 39 (1996), pp. 149–78; J.D. Kammeyer-Mueller and C.R. Wanberg, "Unwrapping the Organizational Entry Process: Disentangling Multiple Antecedents and Their Pathways to Adjustment," *Journal of Applied Psychology* 88, no. 5 (2003), pp. 779–94.

85. Porter, Lawler, and Hackman, *Behavior in Organizations,* Ch. 5.

86. Louis, "Surprise and Sensemaking."

87. Robinson and Rousseau, "Violating the Psychological Contract."

88. D.L. Nelson, "Organizational Socialization: A Stress Perspective," *Journal of Occupational Behavior* 8 (1987), pp. 311–24; Elfering et al., "First Years in Job."

89. J.P. Wanous, *Organizational Entry* (Reading, MA: Addison-Wesley, 1992); J.A. Breaugh and M. Starke, "Research on Employee Recruitment: So Many Studies, So Many Remaining Questions," *Journal of Management* 26, no. 3 (2000), pp. 405–34.

90. E. Simon, "Employers Study Applicants' Personalities," *Associated Press,* November 5, 2007. Also see the Lindblad RJP video at http://www.expeditions.com/Theater17.asp?Media=475.

91. J.M. Phillips, "Effects of Realistic Job Previews on Multiple Organizational Outcomes: A Meta-Analysis," *Academy of Management Journal* 41 (December 1998), pp. 673–90.

92. Y. Ganzach et al., "Social Exchange and Organizational Commitment: Decision-Making Training for Job Choice as an Alternative to the Realistic Job Preview," *Personnel Psychology* 55 (Autumn 2002), pp. 613–37.

93. C. Ostroff and S.W.J. Koslowski, "Organizational Socialization as a Learning Process: The Role of Information Acquisition," *Personnel Psychology* 45 (1992), pp. 849–74; Cooper-Thomas and Anderson, "Organizational Socialization: A Field Study into Socialization Success and Rate"; A. Baber and L. Waymon, "Uncovering the Unconnected Employee," *T&D,* May 2008, pp. 60–66.

94. L. Buchanan et al., "That's Chief Entertainment Officer," *Inc.* 29, no. 8 (August 2007), pp. 86–94; P. Burkes Erickson, "Welcoming Employees: Making That First Day a Great Experience," *Daily Oklahoman,* July 15, 2007.

CHAPTER 15

1. D. Kiley, "The New Heat on Ford," *BusinessWeek,* June 4, 2007, pp. 32–38; J. Cable, "Fighting through the Worst of Times," *Industry Week,* June 1, 2010, p. 24; P. Ingrassia, "Ford's Renaissance Man," *The Wall Street Journal,* February 28, 2010; C. Tierney, "Ford Sets Ambitious Global Plan for Growth," *Detroit News,* June 8, 2011, p. A1.

2. D. Howes, "Future Hinges on Global Teams," *Detroit News,* December 21, 1998.

3. J. Welch, *Jack: Straight from the Heart* (New York: Warner Business Books, 2001), p. 432.

4. K. Lewin, *Field Theory in Social Science* (New York: Harper & Row, 1951).

5. D. Coghlan and T. Brannick, "Kurt Lewin: The 'Practical Theorist' for the 21st Century," *Irish Journal of Management* 24, no. 2 (2003), pp. 31–37; B. Burnes, "Kurt Lewin and the Planned Approach to Change: A Re-Appraisal," *Journal of Management Studies* 41, no. 6 (September 2004), pp. 977–1002.

6. "Ogilvy & Mather Corporate Culture," http://www.ogilvy.com/About/Our-History/Corporate-Culture.aspx.

7. D. Howell, "Nardelli Nears Five-Year Mark with Riveting Record," *DSN Retailing Today,* May 9, 2005, pp. 1, 38; R. Charan, "Home Depot's Blueprint for Culture Change," *Harvard Business Review* (April 2006), pp. 61–70; R. DeGross, "Five Years of Change: Home Depot's Results Mixed under Nardelli," *Atlanta Journal-Constitution,* January 1, 2006, p. F1; B. Grow, D. Brady, and M. Arndt, "Renovating Home Depot," *BusinessWeek,* March 6, 2006, pp. 50–57.

8. M. Haid et al., *Ready, Get Set . . . Change!: The Impact of Change on Workforce Productivity and Engagement* (Philadelphia, PA: Right Management, 2009).

9. D. Miller, "Building Commitment to Major Change —What 1700 Change Agents Told Us Really Works," *Developing HR Strategy,*

no. 22 (September 2008), pp. 5–8; Towers Watson, *Capitalizing on Effective Communication,* New York, February 4, 2010.

10. Some experts suggest that resistance to change should be restated in a more positive way by its opposite frame: readiness for change. See M. Choi and W.E.A. Ruona, "Individual Readiness for Organizational Change and Its Implications for Human Resource and Organization Development," *Human Resource Development Review* 10, no. 1 (March 2011), pp. 46–73.

11. S. Chreim, "Postscript to Change: Survivors' Retrospective Views of Organizational Changes," *Personnel Review* 35, no. 3 (2006), pp. 315–35.

12. M. Johnson-Cramer, S. Parise, and R. Cross, "Managing Change through Networks and Values," *California Management Review* 49, no. 3 (Spring 2007), pp. 85–109.

13. J.K. Galbraith, *Economics, Peace, and Laughter* (Boston: Houghton Mifflin, 1971), p. 50.

14. B.J. Tepper et al., "Subordinates' Resistance and Managers' Evaluations of Subordinates' Performance," *Journal of Management* 32, no. 2 (April 2006), pp. 185–209; J.D. Ford, L.W. Ford, and A. D'Amelio, "Resistance to Change: The Rest of the Story," *Academy of Management Review* 33, no. 2 (2008), pp. 362–77.

15. K. Shimizu, "Hoppy Enjoying Comeback after Radical Shift in Management," *Japan Times,* August 15, 2007; S.K.S. Kotaka, "Hoppy Beverage's Heir Is Bubbling with Enthusiasm," *Kyodo News (Tokyo),* 2009.

16. E.B. Dent and S.G. Goldberg, "Challenging 'Resistance to Change,'" *Journal of Applied Behavioral Science* 35 (March 1999), pp. 25–41; D.B. Fedor, S. Caldwell, and D.M. Herold, "The Effects of Organizational Changes on Employee Commitment: A Multilevel Investigation," *Personnel Psychology* 59, no. 1 (2006), pp. 1–29.

17. S. Oreg et al., "Dispositional Resistance to Change: Measurement Equivalence and the Link to Personal Values across 17 Nations," *Journal of Applied Psychology* 93, no. 4 (2008), pp. 935–44

18. R.R. Sharma, *Change Management: Concepts and Applications* (New Delhi: Tata McGraw-Hill, 2007), Ch. 4; A.A. Armenakis and S.G. Harris, "Reflections: Our Journey in Organizational Change Research and Practice," *Journal of Change Management* 9, no. 2 (2009), pp. 127–42; I. Cinite, L.E. Duxbury, and C. Higgins, "Measurement of Perceived Organizational Readiness for Change in the Public Sector," *British Journal of Management* 20, no. 2 (2009), pp. 265–77; S. Jaros, "Commitment to Organizational Change: A Critical Review," *Journal of Change Management* 10, no. 1 (March 2010), pp. 79–108.

19. D.A. Nadler, "The Effective Management of Organizational Change," in *Handbook of Organizational Behavior,* ed. J.W. Lorsch (Englewood Cliffs, NJ: Prentice Hall, 1987), pp. 358–69; R. Maurer, *Beyond the Wall of Resistance: Unconventional Strategies to Build Support for Change* (Austin, TX: Bard Books, 1996); P. Strebel, "Why Do Employees Resist Change?" *Harvard Business Review* (May–June 1996), pp. 86–92; D.A. Nadler, *Champions of Change* (San Francisco, CA: Jossey-Bass, 1998).

20. L. Brody and D. Raffa, *Everything I Need to Know about Business . . . I Learned from a Canadian,* 2nd ed. (Mississauga, Ontario: John Wiley & Sons Canada, 2009), pp. 201–02.

21. V. Newman, "The Psychology of Managing for Innovation," *KM Review* 9, no. 6 (2007), pp. 10–15.

22. *Bosses Want Change but Workers Want More of the Same!* (Sydney: Talent2, June 29, 2005).

23. R. Davis, *Leading for Growth: How Umpqua Bank Got Cool and Created a Culture of Greatness* (San Francisco, CA: Jossey-Bass, 2007), p. 40.

24. C. Ressler and J. Thompson, *Why Work Sucks and How to Fix It* (New York: Portfolio, 2008), Ch. 2.

25. T.G. Cummings, "The Role and Limits of Change Leadership," in *The Leader's Change Handbook,* ed. J.A. Conger, G.M. Spreitzer, and E.E. Lawler III (San Francisco, CA: Jossey-Bass, 1999), pp. 301–20; J.P. Kotter and D.S. Cohen, *The Heart of Change* (Boston: Harvard Business School Press, 2002), pp. 15–36; J.P. Kotter, *A Sense of Urgency* (Boston: Harvard Business School Press, 2008).

26. S. Simpson, "White Spot Restaurants Keep Iconic Brand Sizzling," *Vancouver Sun,* March 24, 2011, p. C3.

27. C. Lawton and J. Lublin, "Nokia Names Microsoft's Stephen Elop as New CEO, Kallasvuo Ousted," *The Wall Street Journal,* September 11, 2010; C. Ziegler, "Nokia CEO Stephen Elop Rallies Troops in Brutally Honest 'Burning Platform' Memo? (Update: It's Real!)," *Engadget,* February 8, 2011.

28. L.D. Goodstein and H.R. Butz, "Customer Value: The Linchpin of Organizational Change," *Organizational Dynamics* 27 (June 1998), pp. 21–35.

29. I.J. Bozon and P.N. Child, "Refining Shell's Position in Europe," *McKinsey Quarterly,* no. 2 (2003), pp. 42–51.

30. D. Darlin, "Growing Tomorrow," *Business 2.0,* May 2005, p. 126.

31. L. Grossman and S. Song, "Stevie's Little Wonder," *Time,* September 19, 2005, p. 63; S. Levy, "Honey, I Shrunk the iPod. A Lot," *Newsweek,* September 19, 2005, p. 58.

32. T.F. Cawsey and G. Deszca, *Toolkit for Organizational Change* (Los Angeles: Sage Publications, 2007), p. 104.

33. J.P. Kotter and L.A. Schlesinger, "Choosing Strategies for Change," *Harvard Business Review* (March–April 1979), pp. 106–14.

34. M. Meaney and C. Pung, "Creating Organizational Transformations: McKinsey Global Survey Results," *McKinsey Quarterly,* July 2008, pp. 1–7.

35. B. Nanus and S.M. Dobbs, *Leaders Who Make a Difference* (San Francisco, CA: Jossey-Bass, 1999); Kotter and Cohen, *The Heart of Change,* pp. 83–98; J. Allen et al., "Uncertainty during Organizational Change: Managing Perceptions through Communication," *Journal of Change Management* 7, no. 2 (2007), pp. 187–210; T.L. Russ, "Communicating Change: A Review and Critical Analysis of Programmatic and Participatory Implementation Approaches," *Journal of Change Management* 8, no. 3 (2008), pp. 199–211.

36. G. Jones, "Chemical Reaction," *Smart Business Pittsburgh,* February 2011, p. 10.

37. "A Cornerstone for Learning," *T&D,* October 2008, pp. 66–89.

38. K.T. Dirks, L.L. Cummings, and J.L. Pierce, "Psychological Ownership in Organizations: Conditions under Which Individuals Promote and Resist Change," *Research in Organizational Change and Development* 9 (1996), pp. 1–23; A. Cox, S. Zagelmeyer, and M. Marchington, "Embedding Employee Involvement and Participation at Work," *Human Resource Management Journal* 16, no. 3 (2006), pp. 250–67; E.A. Lofquist, "Doomed to Fail: A Case Study of Change Implementation Collapse in the Norwegian Civil Aviation Industry," *Journal of Change Management* 11, no. 2 (July 8, 2011), pp. 223–43.

39. N.T. Tan, "Maximising Human Resource Potential in the Midst of Organisational Change," *Singapore Management Review* 27, no. 2 (2005), pp. 25–35.

40. M. McHugh, "The Stress Factor: Another Item for the Change Management Agenda?" *Journal of Organizational Change Management* 10 (1997), pp. 345–62; D. Buchanan, T. Claydon, and M. Doyle, "Organisation Development and Change: The Legacy of the Nineties," *Human Resource Management Journal* 9 (1999), pp. 20–37.

41. D. Blossom, "Lopez Foods Looks to Beef Up Profits, Take Bite into International Breakfasts," *The Daily Oklahoman,* April 9, 2008; A. Hanacek, "Star Power," *National Provisioner* 222, no. 2 (February 2008), pp. 22–29.

42. T. Wakefield, "No Pain, No Gain," *Canadian Business,* January 1993, pp. 50–54; M. Cash, "Standardaero Back on the Sale Block," *Winnipeg Free Press,* December 14, 2010.

43. D. Nicolini and M.B. Meznar, "The Social Construction of Organizational Learning: Conceptual and Practical Issues in the Field," *Human Relations* 48 (1995), pp. 727–46.

44. E.E. Lawler III, "Pay Can Be a Change Agent," *Compensation & Benefits Management* 16 (Summer 2000), pp. 23–26; Kotter and Cohen, *The Heart of Change,* pp. 161–77; M.A. Roberto and L.C. Levesque, "The Art of Making Change Initiatives Stick," *MIT Sloan Management Review* 46, no. 4 (Summer 2005), pp. 53–60.

45. Lawler, "Pay Can Be a Change Agent."

46. Goodstein and Butz, "Customer Value"; R.H. Miles, "Leading Corporate Transformation: Are You Up to the Task?" in *The Leader's Change Handbook,* ed. J.A. Conger, G.M. Spreitzer, and E.E. Lawler III (San Francisco, CA: Jossey-Bass, 1999), pp. 221–67.

47. E.G. Brown and J. Lubahn, "We Need 'to Talk,'" *Bank Marketing* 39, no. 7 (2007), pp. 32–36.

48. R.E. Quinn, *Building the Bridge As You Walk on It: A Guide for Leading Change* (San Francisco, CA: Jossey-Bass, 2004), Ch. 11; D.M. Herold et al., "The Effects of Transformational and Change Leadership on Employees' Commitment to a Change: A Multilevel Study," *Journal of Applied Psychology* 93, no. 2 (2008), pp. 346–57.

49. M.S. Cole, S.G. Harris, and J.B. Bernerth, "Exploring the Implications of Vision, Appropriateness, and Execution of Organizational Change," *Leadership & Organization Development Journal* 27, no. 5 (2006), pp. 352–67.

50. Kotter and Cohen, *The Heart of Change,* pp. 61–82; D.S. Cohen and J.P. Kotter, *The Heart of Change Field Guide* (Boston: Harvard Business School Press, 2005).

51. J.P. Kotter, "Leading Change: Why Transformation Efforts Fail," *Harvard Business Review* (March–April 1995), pp. 59–67.

52. J.B. Cunningham and S.K. James, "Implementing Change in Public Sector Organizations," *Management Decision* 47, no. 2 (2009), p. 330.

53. S. Keller and C. Aiken, *The Inconvenient Truth about Change: Why It Isn't Working and What to Do About It* (New York: McKinsey & Company, 2008).

54. A. De Bruyn and G.L. Lilien, "A Multi-Stage Model of Word-of-Mouth Influence through Viral Marketing," *International Journal of Research in Marketing* 25, no. 3 (2008), pp. 151–63; J.Y.C. Ho and M. Dempsey, "Viral Marketing: Motivations to Forward Online Content," *Journal of Business Research* 63, no. 9–10 (2010), pp. 1000–06; M. Williams and F. Buttle, "The Eight Pillars of WOM Management: Lessons from a Multiple Case Study," *Australasian Marketing Journal* 19, no. 2 (2011), pp. 85–92.

55. L. Herrero, *Homo Imitans* (Beaconsfield Bucks, UK: meetingminds, 2011).

56. N. Edwards, *Using a Viral Communication Approach for Engaging Pfizer's Field Workforce in Realising Its Vision,* May 19, 2008; K. Dyer, "Changing Perceptions Virally at Novo Nordisk," *Strategic Communication Management* 13, no. 2 (2009), pp. 24–27; Herrero, *Homo Imitans.*

57. J. Thottam, "Reworking Work," *Time,* July 25, 2005, p. 50; Ressler and Thompson, *Why Work Sucks and How to Fix It,* pp. 20, 45–48.

58. M. Beer, R.A. Eisenstat, and B. Spector, *The Critical Path to Corporate Renewal* (Boston, MA: Harvard Business School Press, 1990).

59. R.E. Walton, "Successful Strategies for Diffusing Work Innovations," *Journal of Contemporary Business,* Spring 1977, pp. 1–22; R.E. Walton, *Innovating to Compete: Lessons for Diffusing and Managing Change in the Workplace* (San Francisco, CA: Jossey-Bass, 1987); Beer, Eisenstat, and Spector, *The Critical Path to Corporate Renewal,* Ch. 5.

60. E.M. Rogers, *Diffusion of Innovations,* 4th ed. (New York: The Free Pree, 1995).

61. P. Reason and H. Bradbury, *Handbook of Action Research* (London: Sage Publications, 2001); Coghlan and Brannick, "Kurt Lewin";

C. Huxham and S. Vangen, "Researching Organizational Practice through Action Research: Case Studies and Design Choices," *Organizational Research Methods* 6 (July 2003), pp. 383–403.

62. V.J. Marsick and M.A. Gephart, "Action Research: Building the Capacity for Learning and Change," *Human Resource Planning* 26 (2003), pp. 14–18.

63. L. Dickens and K. Watkins, "Action Research: Rethinking Lewin," *Management Learning* 30 (June 1999), pp. 127–40; J. Heron and P. Reason, "The Practice of Co-Operative Inquiry: Research 'with' Rather Than 'on' People," in *Handbook of Action Research,* ed. P. Reason and H. Bradbury (Thousand Oaks, CA: Sage Publications, 2001), pp. 179–88.

64. D.A. Nadler, "Organizational Frame Bending: Types of Change in the Complex Organization," in *Corporate Transformation: Revitalizing Organizations for a Competitive World,* ed. R.H. Kilmann, T.J. Covin, and Associates (San Francisco, CA: Jossey-Bass, 1988), pp. 66–83; K.E. Weick and R.E. Quinn, "Organizational Change and Development," *Annual Review of Psychology* 50 (1999), pp. 361–86.

65. T.M. Egan and C.M. Lancaster, "Comparing Appreciative Inquiry to Action Research: OD Practitioner Perspectives," *Organization Development Journal* 23, no. 2 (Summer 2005), pp. 29–49.

66. P.K. Sweeney, "Corporate Compliance without Burdening the End User: Change Management Lessons from Ergon Energy," *iQ,* November 2006, pp. 24–26.

67. D. Miller and P.H. Friesen, "Momentum and Revolution in Organizational Adaptation," *Academy of Management Journal* 23, no. 4 (1980), pp. 591–614; D. Miller and M.-J. Chen, "Sources and Consequences of Competitive Inertia: A Study of the U.S. Airline Industry," *Administrative Science Quarterly* 39, no. 1 (1994), pp. 1–23.

68. J. Isern and C. Pung, "Driving Radical Change," *McKinsey Quarterly,* no. 4 (2007), pp. 24–35.

69. F.F. Luthans, "Positive Organizational Behavior: Developing and Managing Psychological Strengths," *Academy of Management Executive* 16, no. 1 (2002), pp. 57–72; N. Turner, J. Barling, and A. Zacharatos, "Positive Psychology at Work," in *Handbook of Positive Psychology,* ed. C.R. Snyder and S. Lopez (Oxford, UK: Oxford University Press, 2002), pp. 715–30; K. Cameron, J.E. Dutton, and R.E. Quinn, eds., *Positive Organizational Scholarship: Foundation of a New Discipline* (San Francisco, CA: Berrett Koehler Publishers, 2003); J.I. Krueger and D.C. Funder, "Towards a Balanced Social Psychology: Causes, Consequences, and Cures for the Problem-Seeking Approach to Social Behavior and Cognition," *Behavioral and Brain Sciences* 27, no. 3 (June 2004), pp. 313–27; S.L. Gable and J. Haidt, "What (and Why) Is Positive Psychology?" *Review of General Psychology* 9, no. 2 (2005), pp. 103–10; M.E.P. Seligman et al., "Positive Psychology Progress: Empirical Validation of Interventions," *American Psychologist* 60, no. 5 (2005), pp. 410–21.

70. D.K. Whitney and D.L. Cooperrider, "The Appreciative Inquiry Summit: Overview and Applications," *Employment Relations Today* 25 (Summer 1998), pp. 17–28; J.M. Watkins and B.J. Mohr, *Appreciative Inquiry: Change at the Speed of Imagination* (San Francisco, CA: Jossey-Bass, 2001).

71. "How I Spy Marketing Used the Strengths Approach to Embed a Culture of Success," 2011, http://www.thestrengthsfoundation.org.

72. S. Berrisford, "Using Appreciative Inquiry to Drive Change at the BBC," *Strategic Communication Management* 9, no. 3 (2005), pp. 22–25; M.-Y. Cheung-Judge and E.H. Powley, "Innovation at the BBC," in *The Handbook of Large Group Methods,* ed. B.B. Bunker and B.T. Alban (New York: John Wiley & Sons, 2006), pp. 45–61.

73. D.L. Cooperrider and D.K. Whitney, *Appreciative Inquiry: A Positive Revolution in Change* (San Francisco, CA: Berrett-Koehler, 2005). Recent writing has extended this list to eight principles. See D.K. Whitney and A. Trosten-Bloom, *The Power of Appreciative*

Inquiry: A Practical Guide to Positive Change, 2nd ed. (San Francisco, CA: Berrett-Koehler Publishers, 2010).

74. F.J. Barrett and D.L. Cooperrider, "Generative Metaphor Intervention: A New Approach for Working with Systems Divided by Conflict and Caught in Defensive Perception," *Journal of Applied Behavioral Science* 26 (1990), pp. 219–39; Whitney and Cooperrider, "The Appreciative Inquiry Summit"; Watkins and Mohr, *Appreciative Inquiry,* pp. 15–21.

75. M. Schiller, "Case Study: Avon Mexico," in *Appreciative Inquiry: Change at the Speed of Imagination,* ed. J.M. Watkins and B.J. Mohr (San Francisco, CA: Jossey-Bass, 2001), pp. 123–26; P. Babcock, "Seeing a Brighter Future," *HRMagazine* 50, no. 9 (September 2005), p. 48; D.S. Bright, D.L. Cooperrider, and W.B. Galloway, "Appreciative Inquiry in the Office of Research and Development: Improving the Collaborative Capacity of Organization," *Public Performance & Management Review* 29, no. 3 (2006), p. 285; D. Gilmour and A. Radford, "Using OD to Enhance Shareholder Value: Delivering Business Results in BP Castrol Marine," *Organization Development Journal* 25, no. 3 (2007), pp. P97–102; Whitney and Trosten-Bloom, *The Power of Appreciative Inquiry.*

76. T.F. Yaeger, P.F. Sorensen, and U. Bengtsson, "Assessment of the State of Appreciative Inquiry: Past, Present, and Future," *Research in Organizational Change and Development* 15 (2004), pp. 297–319; G.R. Bushe and A.F. Kassam, "When Is Appreciative Inquiry Transformational? A Meta-Case Analysis," *Journal of Applied Behavioral Science* 41, no. 2 (June 2005), pp. 161–81.

77. G.R. Bushe, "Five Theories of Change Embedded in Appreciative Inquiry," in *18th Annual World Congress of Organization Development,* Dublin, Ireland, July 14–18, 1998.

78. M. Weisbord and S. Janoff, *Future Search: An Action Guide to Finding Common Ground in Organizations and Communities* (San Francisco, CA: Berrett-Koehler, 2000); R.M. Lent, M.T. McCormick, and D.S. Pearce, "Combining Future Search and Open Space to Address Special Situations," *Journal of Applied Behavioral Science* 41, no. 1 (March 2005), pp. 61–69; S. Janoff and M. Weisbord, "Future Search as 'Real-Time' Action Research," *Futures* 38, no. 6 (2006), pp. 716–22.

79. J. Pratt, "Naturalists Deserve More Credit," *St. John's Telegram,* June 22, 2002, p. B3; C. Chowaniec, R. Gordezky, and J. Grieve, "Supporting the Merger of Two School Boards in Ottawa, Ontario, Canada: The Ottawa-Carleton Community and Public Education to 2015," in *Future Search in School District Change,* ed. R. Schweitz, K. Martens, and N. Aronson (Lanham, MD: ScarecrowEducation, 2005), pp. 56–70; P. Deans, K. Martens, and R. Gordezky, "Success and System Readiness: Lester B. Pearson School Board and Its Commitment to Educational Excellence, Montreal, Quebec," in *Future Search in School District Change,* ed. R. Schweitz, K. Martens, and N. Aronson (Lanham, MD: ScarecrowEducation, 2005), pp. 192–208; R. Lent, J. Van Patten, and T. Phair, "Creating a World-Class Manufacturer in Record Time," in *The Handbook of Large Group Methods,*

ed. B.B. Bunker and B.T. Alban (New York: John Wiley & Sons, 2006), pp. 112–24.

80. For a critique of future search conferences and similar whole system events, see A. Oels, "Investigating the Emotional Roller-Coaster Ride: A Case Study-Based Assessment of the Future Search Conference Design," *Systems Research and Behavioral Science* 19 (July–August 2002), pp. 347–55; M.F.D. Polanyi, "Communicative Action in Practice: Future Search and the Pursuit of an Open, Critical and Non-Coercive Large-Group Process," *Systems Research and Behavioral Science* 19 (July 2002), pp. 357–66; A. De Grassi, "Envisioning Futures of African Agriculture: Representation, Power, and Socially Constituted Time," *Progress in Development Studies* 7, no. 2 (2007), pp. 79–98.

81. G.R. Bushe and A.B. Shani, *Parallel Learning Structures* (Reading, MA: Addison-Wesley, 1991); E.M. Van Aken, D.J. Monetta, and D.S. Sink, "Affinity Groups: The Missing Link in Employee Involvement," *Organization Dynamics* 22 (Spring 1994), pp. 38–54.

82. D.J. Knight, "Strategy in Practice: Making It Happen," *Strategy & Leadership* 26 (July–August 1998), pp. 29–33; R.T. Pascale, "Grassroots Leadership—Royal Dutch/Shell," *Fast Company,* no. 14 (April–May 1998), pp. 110–20; R.T. Pascale, "Leading from a Different Place," in *The Leader's Change Handbook,* ed. J.A. Conger, G.M. Spreitzer, and E.E. Lawler III (San Francisco, CA: Jossey-Bass, 1999), pp. 301–20; R. Pascale, M. Millemann, and L. Gioja, *Surfing on the Edge of Chaos* (London: Texere, 2000).

83. T.C. Head and P.F. Sorenson, "Cultural Values and Organizational Development: A Seven-Country Study," *Leadership and Organization Development Journal* 14 (1993), pp. 3–7; R.J. Marshak, "Lewin Meets Confucius: A Review of the OD Model of Change," *Journal of Applied Behavioral Science* 29 (1993), pp. 395–415; C.-M. Lau, "A Culture-Based Perspective of Organization Development Implementation," *Research in Organizational Change and Development* 9 (1996), pp. 49–79; C.M. Lau and H.Y. Ngo, "Organization Development and Firm Performance: A Comparison of Multinational and Local Firms," *Journal of International Business Studies* 32, no. 1 (2001), pp. 95–114.

84. M. McKendall, "The Tyranny of Change: Organizational Development Revisited," *Journal of Business Ethics* 12 (February 1993), pp. 93–104; C.M.D. Deaner, "A Model of Organization Development Ethics," *Public Administration Quarterly* 17 (1994), pp. 435–46.

85. G.A. Walter, "Organization Development and Individual Rights," *Journal of Applied Behavioral Science* 20 (1984), pp. 423–39.

86. The source of this often-cited quotation has not been found. It does not appear, even in rough form, in the books that Andrew Carnegie wrote (e.g., *Gospel of Wealth,* 1900; *Empire of Business,* 1902; *Autobiography,* 1920). However, Carnegie may have stated these words (or similar ones) in other places. He gave a multitude of speeches and wrote many articles, and his words are reported by numerous other authors.

photo credits

organization name index

Note: Page numbers followed by *n* indicate material in source notes or endnotes.

name index

Note: Page numbers followed by *n* indicate material in endnotes and source notes.

A

Abdoulah, Colleen, 46–47
Abel, M. H., 516*n*
Abrahamson, E., 537*n*
Abusah, D., 532*n*
Ackerman, F., 497*n*
Adams, J. S., 519*n*
Adams, M., 504*n*
Adams, S., 517*n*
Adams, Scott, 83*n*
Aditya, R. M., 543*n*
Adler, P. S., 496*n*, 537*n*
Adomdza, G. K., 526*n*
Agle, B. R., 497*n*, 502*n*, 517*n*, 550*n*
Agor, W. H., 525*n*
Aiello, J. R., 528*n*
Aiken, C., 555*n*
Ailworth, E., 522*n*
Aizicovici, F., 514*n*
Ajzen, I., 509*n*
Akgün, A. E., 496*n*
Aksoy, L., 504*n*
Akter, M., 547*n*
Alam, K. F., 503*n*, 547*n*
Alarcon, G., 515*n*
Albarracin, D., 509*n*
Albi, Frank, 283
Albright, M., 521*n*
Alicke, M. D., 505*n*
Allen, D. G., 553*n*
Allen, I. A., 514*n*
Allen, J., 554*n*
Allen, Lori, 282
Allen, N. J., 500*n*, 529*n*
Allen, R. F., 551*n*
Allen, R. W., 539*n*
Allen, T. J., 535*n*
Alliger, G. M., 94*n*
Allport, G. W., 506*n*, 508*n*
Allred, K. G., 542*n*
Aloysius, J. A., 526*n*
Altman, D., 498*n*
Altmann, E. M., 506*n*, 525*n*
Álvares, A. C. T., 495*n*
Amabile, T. M., 526*n*, 527*n*
Amason, A. C., 525*n*, 540*n*
Ambady, N., 506*n*, 511*n*
Ambrose, M. L., 519*n*, 520*n*
Amernic, J., 535*n*
Amir, O., 503*n*
Anders, G., 548*n*
Anderson, B., 124*n*
Anderson, C., 538*n*
Anderson, Dave, 365
Anderson, J., 538*n*

Anderson, M., 499*n*
Anderson, N., 499*n*, 514*n*, 529*n*, 553*n*
Anderson, Trish, 282
Andrew, S., 514*n*
Andrews, M., 520*n*
Andrews, M. C., 502*n*, 539*n*
Andrews, Tracey, 289
Ang, S., 512*n*
Angle, H. L., 539*n*
Anglim, J., 530*n*
Anhalt, R. L., 508*n*
Anseel, F., 505*n*
Anthony, W. P., 534*n*
Antonakis, J., 512*n*
Appelbaum, E., 497*n*
Applebaum, S. H., 498*n*
Archibald, D., 537*n*
Argyris, C., 527*n*, 539*n*
Ariely, D., 503*n*, 521*n*, 525*n*
Aritzeta, A., 530*n*
Arledge, Roone, 349
Armenakis, A. A., 554*n*
Armour, S., 516*n*
Arndt, M., 521*n*, 553*n*
Aronson, E., 503*n*, 530*n*
Arrow, H., 529*n*
Arunski, Karl J., 299, 299*n*
Ashford, S. J., 519*n*, 543*n*
Ashforth, B. E., 505*n*, 510*n*, 523*n*, 537*n*, 551*n*, 553*n*
Ashkanasy, N. M., 506*n*, 509*n*, 511*n*, 512*n*, 524*n*, 550*n*
Ashmos, D. P., 496*n*
Ashton, M. C., 65*n*, 160*n*
Assael, H., 539*n*
Assanand, S., 504*n*
Assayas, M., 529*n*
Åsterbro, T., 526*n*
Atchison, C., 521*n*
Athos, A. G., 528*n*
Atuahene-Gima, K., 538*n*
Atwater, L. E., 518*n*, 519*n*
Atzeni, T., 534*n*
Au, K., 512*n*
Aubé, C., 234*n*, 529*n*
Auerbach, D. I., 500*n*
Augusto, M., 527*n*
Auh, S., 513*n*
Austin, E., 501*n*
Avolio, B. J., 505*n*, 506*n*, 515*n*, 544*n*, 545*n*
Axtell, C. M., 508*n*
Axtell, R. E., 535*n*
Axworthy, T. S., 527*n*
Aycan, Z., 503*n*
Ayers, S., 514*n*

B

Baba, V. V., 514*n*, 544*n*
Babcock, P., 556*n*
Baber, A., 553*n*
Bacharach, S. B., 500*n*
Back, M. D., 501*n*
Bacon, N., 507*n*
Bader, P., 543*n*
Bagozzi, R. P., 518*n*
Bailey, D. E., 499*n*, 532*n*
Bailey, Kate, 68
Bailor, C., 518*n*
Baiocco, Maja, 18
Baker, G., 540*n*
Baker, J. A., III, 550*n*
Baker, V., 502*n*
Baker, W. E., 551*n*
Bakker, A. B., 516*n*
Baldwin, C., 549*n*
Balkundi, P., 528*n*
Ballard, Geoffrey, 210
Ballmer, Steve, 148
Balsillie, Jim, 416
Baltazar, R., 530*n*
Balthazard, P. A., 546*n*, 550*n*
Baltzley, D., 509*n*
Baltzly, D., 524*n*
Bamberger, P., 500*n*
Banaji, M. R., 506*n*
Bandura, Albert, 144, 505*n*, 518*n*
Banick, R., 521*n*
Banister, C., 498*n*
Bansal, P., 496*n*
Barak, Eran, 299
Barber, Chris, 289
Barber, K., 507*n*
Barbieri, J. C., 495*n*
Barbuto, J. E., Jr., 511*n*, 544*n*, 545*n*
Barclay, H., 541*n*
Bardi, A., 497*n*, 503*n*
Barger, P. B., 513*n*
Bargh, J. A., 506*n*, 507*n*, 510*n*, 518*n*, 524*n*
Barjas, E., 504*n*
Barker, B. A., 530*n*
Barki, H., 533*n*, 540*n*
Barley, S. R., 495*n*
Barling, J., 497*n*, 514*n*, 546*n*, 555*n*
Barnard, Chester, 5–6, 260, 496*n*, 533*n*, 536*n*, 546*n*
Barnes, B., 499*n*
Barnes, J. W., 551*n*
Barnes, V. A., 516*n*
Barnett, M. L., 497*n*
Barnett, W. P., 531*n*
Barney, J., 496*n*